Probability Theory and Statistical Inference

This major new textbook from a distinguished econometrician is intended for students taking introductory courses in probability theory and statistical inference. No prior knowledge other than a basic familiarity with descriptive statistics is assumed.

The primary objective of this book is to establish the framework for the empirical modeling of observational (non-experimental) data. This framework is formulated with a view to accommodating the peculiarities of observational (as opposed to experimental) data in a unifying and logically coherent way. *Probability Theory and Statistical Inference* differs from traditional textbooks in so far as it emphasizes concepts, ideas, notions, and procedures which are appropriate for modeling observational data. Special emphasis is placed on relating probabilistic concepts to chance regularity patterns exhibited by observed data.

Aimed primarily at students at second-year undergraduate level and above studying econometrics and economics, this textbook will also be useful for students in other disciplines which make extensive use of observational data, including finance, biology, sociology, education, psychology, and climatology.

ARIS SPANOS is a leading researcher and teacher in econometrics. He is currently based at the University of Cyprus and Virginia Polytechnic Institute and State University and has taught previously at institutions including, Birkbeck College, the University of Cambridge, and the University of California. His previous books include *Statistical Foundations of Econometric Modelling*, published by Cambridge University Press in 1986.

Probability Theory and Statistical Inference

Econometric Modeling with Observational Data

Aris Spanos

CAMBRIDGE UNIVERSITY PRESS

PUBLISHED BY THE PRESS SYNDICATE OF THE UNIVERSITY OF CAMBRIDGE
The Pitt Building, Trumpington Street, Cambridge CB2 1RP, United Kingdom

CAMBRIDGE UNIVERSITY PRESS
The Edinburgh Building, Cambridge CB2 2RU, UK http://www.cup.cam.ac.uk
40 West 20th Street, New York, NY 10011-4211, USA http://www.cup.org
10 Stamford Road, Oakleigh, Melbourne 3166, Australia

First published 1999

Printed in the United Kingdom at the University Press, Cambridge

Typeset in MT Times NR 9½/12½ [SE]

A catalogue record for this book is available from the British Library

Library of Congress Cataloguing in Publication data

Spanos, Aris, 1952–
Probability Theory and Statistical Inference: econometric
modeling with observational data / Aris Spanos
     p.   cm.
Includes bibliographical references (p.   ) and index.
ISBN 0 521 41354 0
1. Econometrics. 2. Probabilities. I. Title.
HB139.S62   1998
330′.01′5195–dc21

ISBN 0 521 41354 0 hardback
ISBN 0 521 42408 9 paperback

Contents

v

Preface

1   Intended audience and distinguishing features

This is a textbook intended for an introductory course in *probability theory* and *statistical inference*, written for students who have had at least a semester course in calculus. The additional mathematics needed are coalesced into the discussion to make it self-contained, paying particular attention to the intuitive understanding of the mathematical concepts. *No prerequisites in probability and statistical inference are required but some familiarity with descriptive statistics will be of value.*

The primary objective of this book is to lay the foundations and assemble the overarching framework for the empirical modeling of **observational** (non-experimental) data. This framework, known as *probabilistic reduction*, is formulated with a view to accommodating the peculiarities of observational (as opposed to **experimental**) data in a unifying and logically coherent way. It differs from traditional textbooks in so far as it emphasizes concepts, ideas, notions, and procedures which are appropriate for modeling observational data.

The primary intended audience of this book includes interested undergraduate and graduate students of econometrics as well as practicing econometricians who have been trained in the traditional textbook approach. Special consideration has been given to the needs of those using the textbook for self-study. This text can also be used by students of other disciplines, such as biology, sociology, education, psychology, and climatology, where the analysis of observational data is of interest.

The traditional statistical literature over the last 50 years or so, has focused, almost exclusively, on procedures and methods appropriate for the analysis of **experimental-type** (experimental and sample survey) **data**. The traditional modeling framework has been that of the *experimental design* tradition, as molded by Fisher (1935) (and formulated by the sample survey literature of the 1940s and 1950s), and the "curve fitting" perspective of the *least-squares* tradition. Both of these traditions presume a modeling framework in the context of which the observed data are interpreted as a realization of an observable phenomenon which can be realistically viewed as a *nearly isolated* (by divine or human intervention) system; see Spanos (1995b). This book purports to redress (somewhat) the balance by expounding a modeling framework appropriate for observational data. This modeling framework can be viewed in the spirit of the *conditioning* perspective of the Biometric school (Galton, Karl Pearson, Yule) formulated in the late 19th and early 20th century. How conditioning can be used as the cornerstone of a framework for modeling observational data, will be elaborated upon in what follows. The alternative framework is deemed necessary because observational data constitute the rule and not the exception in fields such as econometrics. Indeed, *econometrics* will largely provide both the motivation as well as the empirical examples throughout the discussion that follows.

The most important **distinguishing features** of this text are the following:

(1)   The discussion revolves around the central pivot of *empirical modeling* and the order of introduction of the various concepts, ideas, and notions is largely determined by the logical coherence and completeness of the unfolding story. Probability theory and statistical inference are interweaved into empirical modeling by emphasizing the view of the former as a modeling framework; this is in contrast to probability theory as part of mathematics proper or as a rational decision making framework under uncertainty.

(2)   Special emphasis is placed on the notion of *conditioning* and related concepts because they provide the key to a modeling framework for observational data. The notion of *regression* arises naturally out of the modeler's attempt to capture *dependence* and *heterogeneity*, when modeling observational data. The discussion does not neglect the importance of the historical development of these ideas and concepts.

(3)   The interplay between abstract concepts of probability theory and the corresponding chance regularity patterns exhibited by the data is extensively utilized using a variety of graphical techniques. Special emphasis is placed on mastering the creative skill of "reading" data plots and discerning a number of different chance regularity patterns as well as relating the latter to the corresponding mathematical concepts.

(4)   A clear separating line is drawn between *statistical* and (economic) *theory information*, with a statistical model being specified exclusively in terms of statistical information (probabilistic assumptions relating to observable random variables); in contrast to specifying statistical models by attaching autonomous *error terms* (carrying the probabilistic structure) to theoretical relationships.

(5)   The discussion emphasizes certain neglected aspects of empirical modeling which are crucially important in the case of observational data. These facets include: *specification* (the choice of a statistical model), *misspecification testing* (assessing the validity of its assumptions), and *respecification;* the discussion puts the accent on the *empirical adequacy* of a statistical model.

(6)   A statistical model is viewed not as a set of probabilistic assumptions in the middle of nowhere, but contemplated in the context of the all-embracing perspective of the totality of possible statistical models. This view is adopted in an attempt to systematize the neglected facets of modeling by charting the territory beyond the postulated statistical model in broad terms using an assemblage of restrictions (*reduction assumptions*) on the set of all possible statistical models; hence the term probabilistic reduction.

REMARK: in view of the proposed bridge between probabilistic assumptions and observed data patterns, the neglected facets of modeling are thus transformed into informed procedures and not *hit-or-miss* attempts in connection with the probabilistic structure of some *unobservable* error term(s).

(7) The traditional textbook hypothesis testing is reinterpreted in an attempt to bring out the distinct nature of *misspecification testing*. The proposed interpretation calls into question the traditional view that the Neyman–Pearson approach to testing has (largely) superseded that of Fisher. It is argued that they constitute two distinct (although related) approaches to testing with very different objectives which can be used as complements to one another, not as substitutes.

2   Origins and pedigree*[1]

The present textbook has its roots in the author's book *Statistical Foundations of Econometric Modelling*, published in 1986 by CUP, and has been growing in the form of lecture notes ever since. The *Statistical Foundations* book was my first attempt to put forward an alternative comprehensive methodology to the traditional textbook approach to econometric modeling. This was motivated by the state of econometrics after its failure to fulfill the expectations fomented in the 1960s and 1970s; a failure which led to a re-examination of its foundations and elicited a number of different diagnoses from the critics of the traditional textbook approach in the early 1980s (Hendry, Sims, and Leamer; see Granger (1990)). Naturally, the seeds of the proposed methodology can be traced back to my graduate studies at the London School of Economics (LSE) in the late 1970s; see Hendry (1993).

The primary objective of the *Statistical Foundations* book was to put forward a **logically coherent methodological framework** by *entwining* probability theory and statistical inference into empirical modeling. The *modus operandi* of this modeling approach was the distinction between statistical and theory information and the related recasting of statistical models exclusively in terms of statistical information: probabilistic assumptions relating to the observable random variables underlying the data; the error was reinterpreted as the residuum (unmodeled part). In the context of this framework:

(a) not only the theory, but the nature and the (probabilistic) structure of the observed data is thoughtfully taken into consideration, and
(b) not only estimation and hypothesis testing, but also specification, misspecification testing and respecification, are explicitly recognized as both legitimate and necessary facets of modeling.

The ultimate objective of that book was to propose a framework in the context of which some of the problems that have troubled the traditional textbook approach since

[1] All sections marked with an asterisk (*) can be skipped at first reading without any serious interruption in the flow of the discussion.

the 1920s, including the problems raised by some critics in the 1970s and 1980s, can be resolved. These problems include general methodological issues in modeling such as the nature and structure of theories and the role of observed data, as well as statistical issues such as misspecification testing and respecification, the omitted variables bias, pre-test bias, identification, and exogeneity.

Looking back, the *Statistical Foundations* book was a bold, and some would say audacious, attempt to influence the way econometrics is taught and practiced. Despite its controversial nature and its mathematical level, its success was a pleasant surprise. A purely subjective assessment of its success has been based on:

(a) Its favorable reception in the market place.

(b) Its likely influence on several textbooks in econometrics published after 1986, which took several forms, the most important being:

    (i) A more substantive treatment of probability theory (not an appendage of definitions).

    (ii) A shift of emphasis from unobservable error terms to observable random variables.

    (iii) A historically more accurate interpretation of the regression model (as opposed to the Gauss linear model), proposed as being better suited for the analysis of observational (non-experimental) data.

    (iv) The introduction of the notion of a *statistical generating mechanism* (GM) as an orthogonal decomposition of a random variable (or vector), given an information set; as opposed to a functional relationship among theoretical variables with an error attached.

    (v) A more systematic treatment of misspecification testing and respecification.

In addition to some explicitly acknowledged influences (see *inter alia* Cuthbertson *et al.* (1992), Mills (1993), Davidson and MacKinnon (1993), Hendry (1995), Poirier (1995)), I would like to think that there has also been some indirect influence in relation to:

    (vi) Heightening the level and broadening the role of probability theory in econometrics (see Dhrymes (1989), Goldberger (1991), Amemiya (1994), Davidson (1994)).

    (vii) Helping to focus attention on the issue of misspecification testing (see Godfrey (1988)).

(c) Its influence on current practice in empirical modeling with regard to misspecification testing. Both, textbooks as well as econometric computer packages, nowadays, take a more serious view of misspecification testing; regrettably misspecification testing for systems of equations (see Spanos (1986) chapter 24) is yet to be implemented.[2] This should be contrasted with the pre-1980s treatment of misspecification testing and respecification, which amounted to little more than looking at the

---

[2] PcGive (see Doornik and Hendry (1997)) is the exception.

Durbin-Watson statistic and when the null was rejected, palliating the problem by modeling the error.

The *Statistical Foundations* book, however, was a work in progress with a number of crucial limitations arising from externally imposed restrictions (mainly the prohibitive cost of typesetting graphs at the time) as well as some initial hesitation on my behalf to focus my research exclusively on such a long term project. The advances in personal computing technology and the success of the *Statistical Foundations* book provided the spur to take the story a step further, unimpeded by the initial constraints.

This textbook represents a more ripened elucidation of the approach proposed in the *Statistical Foundations* book with particular attention paid to the exposition of concepts and ideas, and the logical coherence, consistency and completeness of the approach. The primary objective of the *Statistical Foundations* book is pursued further in a number of different ways:

(1)   Ameliorating the interweaving of probability theory and statistical inference into empirical modeling by presenting statistical models as constructs based on three basic forms of (statistical) information:

(D) Distribution,   (M) Dependence,   (H) Heterogeneity.

This information can be related to observed data (chance regularity) patterns using a variety of graphical techniques, rendering modeling an informed procedure.

(2)   Strengthening the logical coherence of the proposed methodology by stressing the distinction between theoretical and statistical information in terms of which the respective *theory* and *statistical models* are defined. *Statistical information* is codified exclusively in terms of probabilistic concepts and *theory information* in terms of economic agents' behavior.

(3)   Enhancing the probabilistic reduction framework by viewing statistical models in the context of a broader framework where the neglected facets of empirical modeling (specification, misspecification, respecification), can be implemented in a more systematic and informed fashion, in conjunction with a variety of graphical techniques.

(4)   Enriching the probabilistic reduction framework by extending empirical modeling beyond the Normal/linear/homoskedastic territory in all three dimensions of statistical information; the emphasis in the *Statistical Foundations* book was placed on modeling *dependence*, with only brief remarks in relation to exploring the other two dimensions of modeling; *distribution* (beyond Normality) and *heterogeneity*.

The ultimate objective of this textbook remains the same as that of the *Statistical Foundations*. In the context of the proposed methodology the nature and structure of theories as well as the role of the data in the assessment of theories is addressed without shying away from any difficult methodological issues as they arise naturally during the discussion. In the context of the proposed framework a purely statistical viewing angle (as opposed to the traditional theory viewing angle) is put forward, in an attempt to elucidate some statistical issues, such as the *omitted variables, pre-test bias, multicollinearity,* and *exogeneity*, which are often (misleadingly) viewed from the theoretical viewing angle creating confusion; see Spanos (1997a).

3   As a teaching and learning device

Empirical modeling is a difficult subject to master primarily because it inherits the sum (and then some) of the inherent difficulties in learning probability theory and statistical inference. Some of these inherent difficulties are:

(a)   The requirement to master too many concepts, ideas, and notions, too quickly.
(b)   The abstract nature of these concepts without any apparent connection to tangible counterparts.
(c)   The problem of terminology in so far as the (historically) established terminology is often inept as well as misleading because the same term is often used to denote several different notions.
(d)   The extensive utilization of mathematical symbols.

In a purposeful attempt to deal with (a), the most troublesome difficulty, the discussion that follows utilizes several *learning techniques* such as:

(i)   *repetition* of crucial concepts and notions,
(ii)   *story so far* abridgements,
(iii)   *bird's eye view of the chapter* outlines,
(iv)   *looking ahead* summaries, and
(v)   recurrent references to *what is important*.

In addition, the discussion utilizes *short historical excursions* in order to dilute the high concentration of concepts, ideas and notions.

The extensive utilization of graphical techniques enables the reader to build direct connections between abstract probability concepts, such as Normality, Independence and Identical Distribution, and the corresponding chance regularity patterns, rendering the task of mastering these concepts easier.

The problem of inept terminology is brought out at the appropriate places during the discussion and the reader is warned about possible confusions. For example, the term *mean* is used in the traditional literature to denote at least four different (but historically related) notions:

A   Probability theory
   (i)   the mean of a random variable X: $E(X) = \int_{x \in \mathbb{R}_X} x f(x) dx$,

B   Statistical inference
   (ii)   the sample mean: $\overline{X} = \frac{1}{n} \sum_{k=1}^{n} X_k$,

   (iii)   the value of the sample mean: $\overline{x} = \frac{1}{n} \sum_{k=1}^{n} x_k$,

C   Descriptive statistics
   (iv)   the arithmetic average of a data set $(x_1, x_2, \ldots, x_n)$: $\overline{x} = \frac{1}{n} \sum_{k=1}^{n} x_k$.

The teacher is obliged to spend a sizeable part of his/her limited time explaining to the students firstly, the (often subtle) differences between the different notions represented by the same term and secondly, how these different notions constitute relics of the historical development of the subject. In the case of the mean, up until the 1920s (see Fisher (1922)), the whole literature on statistics conflated probabilities and relative frequencies, leading to numerous befuddlements including that between $E(X)$, $\overline{X}$ and $\overline{x}$. What is more, very few statisticians of the 1920s and 1930s noticed the transition from descriptive statistics to statistical inference proper; Karl Pearson died in 1936 without realizing that Fisher had turned the tables on him; see chapters 11–13. In an attempt to ameliorate the inept terminology problem, new terms are introduced whenever possible. This is often impossible, however, because the terminology has been entrenched over several decades.

Students with a somewhat weaker background in mathematics are often intimidated by *mathematical terminology* and *symbolism*. On the issue of mathematical symbols every effort has been made to use uniform symbolism throughout this book. The student should know, however, that systematic thinking is made more accessible by the utilization of heedful symbolism. Symbols are essential for systematic thinking because they economize on unnecessary and nebulous descriptions! Hence, the proper utilization of symbols is considered a blessing not a hindrance. Unfortunately, undergraduates often confuse symbolism and haughty-sounding terminology with mathematical sophistication and develop a phobia to any hint of the Greek alphabet; fraternity parties not withstanding. The only known cure for such phobias is the reverse cold turkey treatment: face your phobia head on until it becomes a friend not a foe.

Another important feature of the book is that a lot of emphasis is placed on providing the reader with an opportunity to learn things properly, as opposed to pretend learning, so eloquently articulated by Binmore (1992, p. xxvi):

Much of what passes for an undergraduate education, both in the United States and in Europe, seems to me little more than an unwitting conspiracy between the teacher and the student to defraud whoever is paying the fees. The teacher pretends to teach, and the student pretends to learn, material that both know in their hearts is so emasculated that it cannot be properly understood in the form in which it is presented. Even the weaker students grow tired of such a diet of predigested pap. They understand perfectly well that 'appreciating the concepts' is getting them nowhere except nearer to a piece of paper that entitles them to write letters after their names. But most students want more than this. They want to learn things properly so that they are in a position to feel that they can defend what they have been taught without having to resort to the authority of their teachers or the textbook. Of course, learning things properly can be hard work. But my experience is that students seldom protest at being worked hard provided that their program of study is organized so that they quickly see that their efforts are producing tangible dividends.

I have instinctively subscribed to the creed of *learning things properly or don't even bother* since I can remember. As a student I refused to learn things by heart because I knew *in my heart* that it was (largely) a waste of time and intellectual energy; I even caught myself refusing to answer exam questions which were designed to test my ability to memorize in a parrot-like fashion. As a teacher of econometrics for over 18 years both in Europe and the United States, I have tried very hard to implement the creed of learning things properly and **think, things, through, systematically** with encouraging success.

After a few years of teaching in the United States, however, I found myself on the slippery declivity of unconsciously emasculating probability theory and statistical inference down to maize-porridge. After the first two years, I reluctantly reached the conclusion that fighting the system would be tantamount to jousting with windmills but at the same time I could not indulge in pretend teaching. The only strategy with a fighting chance to circumvent this problem seemed to be to *start* with a diet of predigested pap and gradually work my way up to something more solid. The reality was that the digestive system of the majority of students, after years on such a diet, would not accept anything but predigested pap. It goes without saying, that I consider the students as being the *real victims* of the "pretend teaching conspiracy" and in no circumstance share in the blame for this state of affairs. The educational system itself puts the overwhelming majority of the students on this diet from a very early age, encouraging them to think that the ultimate objective of learning is the exam which leads to the piece of paper and what that entitles them to; learning for exams fosters pretend learning. In view of this situation, I resigned myself to the idea of trying to reach everybody along the lines of learning things properly, but also to satisfy myself with galvanizing a minority of students who would be prepared to think along during the lectures. Inevitably, the predigested pap component of the course tended to expand slowly but surely. Fortunately, I stumbled across the above passage from Binmore just in time to salvage myself from sliding down this slippery declivity even further. The undergraduates of a different educational system, at the University of Cyprus, helped restore my faith in learning things properly and the somewhat emasculated lecture notes of the period 1989–1992 have been transformed into the current textbook after five years of teaching undergraduate econometrics.

I sympathize with the teachers of econometrics who find themselves in a situation where they have to teach something their students do not *really* want to learn and are forced to indulge in pretend teaching, but I offer no apologies for the level of difficulty and the choice of material in the current textbook. I know very well that this book could never qualify to be included in any of the popular series with titles such as "Econometrics for dummies," "An idiot's guide to econometrics" and "A *complete* idiot's guide to econometrics". Personally, I could not water-down the material any further without emasculating it; I leave that to better teachers.

This is a textbook designed for interested students who want to learn things properly and are willing to put in the necessary effort to master *a systematic way of thinking*. With that in mind, no effort has been spared in trying to explain the crucial concepts and ideas at both an intuitive as well as a more formal level. Special attention is given to Binmore's advice that "the program of study is organized so that they [the students] quickly see that their efforts are producing tangible dividends." Early in the discussion of probability theory, the book introduces a variety of graphical techniques (see chapters 5–6) in an attempt to enable the reader to relate the abstract probability concepts to discernible observed data patterns and thus develop an intuitive understanding of these concepts. Moreover, *the story so far* abridgements and *looking ahead* summaries in almost every chapter are designed to give the student a bird's eye view of the forest and encourage learning by presenting the material as an unfolding story with a single unifying plot. At the same time these abridgements and summaries can be used by the readers to assess their understanding of the crucial steps and the important concepts in the discussion.

Another dimension of learning things properly is related to the way the material is presented. I consider university teaching not as an attempt to force some predigested pap down students' throats but as an attempt to initiate the students into thinking, things, through, systematically in the context of a coherent framework; the teacher offers both the systematic thinking and the coherent framework. In class I try to induce the students to think along with me in a conscious attempt to coach them in a particular way of thinking. Needless to say that the present book largely reflects this attitude to teaching and learning and I have no delusions with regard to its suitability for students who prefer the force-feeding and pretend teaching and learning methods. The book does not subscribe to pretend teaching even when discussing some of the most difficult concepts and ideas in probability theory and statistical inference, such as *σ-fields, stochastic conditioning, limit theorems, the functional limit theorem, stochastic processes, maximum likelihood,* and *testing*. Instead, when the material is deemed necessary for a coherent and proper understanding of empirical modeling, every effort is made to **demystify** the concepts and ideas involved by ensuring that the discussion is both comprehensive and systematic. Special emphasis is placed on motivating the need for these concepts and on the intuitive understanding of their essence.

To those teachers who are not convinced that this material can be taught to interested undergraduates, I can only offer my experience at the University of Cyprus for a period of five years. The overwhelming majority of undergraduates in economics could assimilate the bulk of the material in a two semester course and over a third of these students, having toiled through this textbook, would then *choose* to specialize in econometrics and proceed to struggle through Spanos (1986, forthcoming). Moreover, when I returned to the United States for a semester, I was able to use the book in undergraduate courses by utilizing a number of shortcuts which affect only the depth of the discussion but not its coherence.

The creed of learning things properly entails a logically coherent, complete (as far as possible) and in depth discussion which goes beyond skimming the surface of the subject. Compromising the logical coherence and the completeness of the discussion will often be counterproductive. The book, however, is written in such a way so as to provide the teacher and student with options to decide the depth of the analysis by taking shortcuts when the going gets tough. As a general rule, all sections marked with an asterisk (*) can be skipped at first reading without any serious interruption in the flow of the discussion. This textbook includes enough material for two semester courses, but with some judicious choices the material can be shortened to design several one semester courses. Using my experience as a guide, I make several suggestions for one semester courses at different levels of difficulty.

1   **One semester undergraduate course in probability theory and statistical inference:**
    Chapter 1(1.1–1.5), chapter 2(2.1–2.2), chapter 3(3.4.2–3.7.1, 3.7.4), chapter 4(4.1–4.2.3, 4.3–4.4.4, 4.5.7, 4.7.1, 4.7.4), chapter 5(5.1–5.6), chapter 6(6.1–6.2, 6.4.1–6.4.2, 6.7.2), chapter 7(7.1–7.2), chapter 8(8.1–8.3, 8.10.1–8.10.3), chapter 9(9.1–9.2, 9.3.1–9.3.3, 9.4.1, 9.5.1, 9.9), chapter 11(11.1–11.2, 11.5–11.7.1), chapter 12(12.1–12.4), chapter 13(13.1–13.3), chapter 14(14.1–14.3).

2   **One semester undergraduate (intermediate) course in probability theory:**
    Chapter 1(1.1–1.6), chapter 2(2.1–2.9), chapter 3(3.1–3.7), chapter 4(4.1–4.7), chapter 5(5.1–5.6), chapter 6(6.1–6.7), chapter 7(7.1–7.2,), chapter 8(8.1–8.5, 8.9–10), chapter 9(9.1–9.5).

3   **One semester undergraduate (intermediate) course in statistical inference:**
    Chapter 1(1.1–1.6), chapter 5(5.1–5.6), chapter 7(7.1–7.6), chapter 9(9.1–9.5), chapter 11(11.1–11.6), chapter 12(12.1–12.5), chapter 13(13.1–13.5), chapter 14(14.1–14.6), chapter 15(15.1–15.5).

4   **One semester graduate course in probability theory and statistical inference:**
    Chapter 1(1.1–1.6), chapter 2(2.1–2.9), chapter 3(3.1–3.7), chapter 4(4.1–4.7), chapter 5(5.1–5.6), chapter 6(6.1–6.7), chapter 7(7.1–7.2), chapter 8(8.1–8.5, 8.9–8.10), chapter 9(9.1–9.5), chapter 11(11.1–11.6), chapter 12(12.1–12.5), chapter 13(13.1–13.4), chapter 14(14.1–14.6), chapter 15(15.1–15.5).

5   **One semester graduate course in probability theory:**
    Chapters 1–9; all sections marked with an asterisk (*) are optional.

6   **One semester graduate course in statistical inference:**
    Chapters 1, 5, 7, 9, 10–15; all sections marked with an asterisk (*) are optional.

In view of the fact that the book is written with a variety of audiences in mind, it should be apparent that another learning attitude that I do not subscribe to is that textbooks should include only the material everybody is supposed to toil through and any additional material can only confuse the helpless student. It is true that when a student wants to learn things by heart, additional material can only blur the part to be memorized, rendering such a task more difficult, but when the aim is to learn things properly, no such danger exists; seeing more of the jigsaw puzzle can only illuminate the part the student is trying to master. Indeed, some care has been taken to cater for the inquisitive student who wants to learn things properly and pursue certain lines of thought further.

4   Looking ahead: a bird's eye view

The text begins with an introductory chapter which demarcates the intended scope of empirical modeling and sets the scene for what is to follow by elaborating on the distinguishing features of modeling with observational data and summarizing the main methodological *prejudices* of the present author. The primary objective of the chapters that follow is to transform these prejudices into *theses*: contentions supported by coherent (and hopefully persuasive) arguments.

Probability theory

The journey through the probability theory forest, which commences in chapter 2 and stretches all the way to chapter 10, will take the reader along a specific pathway we call the **modeling trail**. This pathway has been designed so that the hiker reaches the other side (statistical inference) in the most direct way possible, avoiding, wherever possible, treacherous terrain and muddy valleys (however interesting) where the visibility is limited and the traveler is likely to get bogged down. The construction of the modeling trail sometimes led the author into uncharted territory which has been cleared of the undergrowth for that purpose. The pathway has been drawn mostly along mountain ridges in order to enable the hiker to:

(a) have a broader view of the forest and
(b) to catch periodic glimpses of the other side (data analysis), not to get disheartened along the trail.

The choice of concepts and ideas and the order in which they are introduced at different points of the trail are determined by the requirement to provide a coherent account of the modeling aspect of the problem, and might seem unorthodox when compared with the traditional treatment of these topics. Concepts and ideas are not introduced as required by strict adherence to the mathematical principles of consistency and completeness, but in the order needed for modeling purposes with emphasis placed not on mathematical rigor and sleekness, but on the intuitive understanding and the *coherence* of the discussion along this modeling trail.

The key to reaching the other side in a creative mood (mastering the material) is to keep one eye on the forest (the unfolding story along the modeling trail) and avoid getting distracted by the beauty (or ugliness!) of the trees along the chosen path or venturing into dense areas of the forest where visibility is limited. Moreover, any attempt to apply superficial memorization of the concepts and ideas along the pathway is doomed to failure. Anybody inclined to use learning by heart (as opposed to proper learning) is cautioned that the sheer number of different notions, concepts and ideas renders this a hopeless task.

In an attempt to help the reader make it to the other side, the discussion, as mentioned above, utilizes several *learning techniques* including:

(a) regular stops along the way at key points with exceptional visibility, and
(b) short historical excursions.

The regular stops are designed to give the hiker:

(i)   an opportunity to take a breather,
(ii) a break to reflect and take stock of what has been encountered along the way and
(iii) a chance to look back and master concepts missed during the first passing.

Such stops are signposted from afar and the reader is advised to take advantage of them; sometimes even retrace his/her steps in order to have a more coherent picture of the view from the modeling trail. The trail is also interspersed with short historical excursions designed to:

(1) offer a better perspective for certain crucial concepts and ideas,
(2) provide some initial coherence to the view from certain vantage points and, most importantly,
(3) present the forest as a living organism which grows and changes ceaselessly and not as an artificially-put-together amusement (or torture!) park.

The discussion in chapters 2–4 has one primary objective: to motivate probability theory as a modeling framework by introducing the idea of *a simple statistical model* as the mathematization of the simplest form of a stochastic phenomenon we call a random experiment. In chapter 5, we relate the basic probabilistic concepts defining a simple statistical model with observed data patterns using a variety of graphical techniques. This builds a bridge linking certain key abstract probability concepts with the reality we call observational data. In chapters 6–7, the discussion purports to show that more realistic statistical models, which can account for both dependence and heterogeneity, can be viewed as natural extensions of the simple statistical model. The key concept in this extension is that of *conditioning* which leads naturally to regression models viewed as models based on conditional distributions and the associated moments. The formal concept which is needed to make the transition from a simple statistical to a regression-type model is that of a stochastic process which is discussed in some detail in chapter 8. In anticipation of several important results in statistical inference, chapter 9 discusses limit theorems. Chapter 10 constitutes the bridge between probability theory and statistical inference and purports to solidify the notion of chance regularity introduced in chapters 1–2.

Statistical inference

Having made it to the other side (chapter 10) the hiker will soon realize that the worst is over! After an introductory chapter (see chapter 10), which purports to provide a more solid bridge between probability theory and statistical inference (and can be avoided at first reading), we proceed to provide an elementary overview of statistical inference in chapter 11. The discussion on estimation commences with the optimal properties of estimators which revolve around the notion of the *ideal estimator* (see chapter 12). In chapter 13 we proceed to discuss several estimation methods: the moment matching principle, the method of moments (Pearson's and the parametric versions), the least-squares and the maximum likelihood methods. A notable departure from the traditional treatment is the calling into question of the conventional wisdom on comparing the method of moments and the maximum likelihood method in terms of the efficiency of the resulting estimators. In a nutshell the argument is that the former method has little (if anything) to do with what Karl Pearson had in mind and any comparison constitutes an anachronism. This is because the nature of statistics has been changed drastically by Fisher but Pearson died before he had a chance to realize that a change has taken place. Using a crude analogy, Pearson was playing checkers but Fisher changed the game to chess and demonstrated that the former's strategies [designed for checkers] do not work as well [when playing chess] as his own strategies [designed for playing chess], leaving out the details in square brackets! The discussion on testing (see chapter 13) differs greatly from traditional treatments in several important respects, the most important of which is the comparison and the contrasting of two alternative paradigms, Fisher's pure significance testing and Neyman–Pearson's optimal testing. We call into question the conventional wisdom that the Fisher approach has been largely superseded by the Neyman–Pearson approach. In chapter 14, it is argued that the two approaches have very different objectives and are largely complementary. Fisher's approach is better suited for *testing without* and the Neyman–Pearson approach is more appropriate for *testing within* the boundaries of the postulated statistical model. In chapter 15 we discuss the problem of misspecification testing and argue that the Fisher approach is the procedure of choice with the Neyman–Pearson approach requiring certain crucial modifications to be used for such a purpose. When testing theoretical restrictions within a statistically adequate model, however, the Neyman–Pearson approach becomes the procedure of choice.

Enjoy the journey!

Acknowledgments

In a long-term project such as the one on which this textbook is based, it is only natural that one accumulates a huge debt to numerous colleagues and students. Foremost on this list is the intellectual debt I owe to my teachers at the London School of Economics in the late 1970s; grateful thanks go to David Hendry, Denis Sargan, Alan Stuart, Jim Durbin, Grayham Mizon, and Ken Binmore. In the same group I should include Jean-François Richard who brought a crucial dimension to the LSE tradition during my graduate studies (see Hendry (1993)). Indeed, thinking back, his (1980) paper was instrumental in setting me off in this great adventure!

I'm also greatly indebted to several colleagues, graduate students and research assistants who actively participated in the exploring of this uncharted territory. Special thanks go to my colleagues Anya McGuirk and John Robertson whose help in writing most of the computer programs behind the empirical analysis and the graphical techniques in this book, and their insightful comments during our long coffee sessions in my office at Virginia Tech, I gratefully acknowledge. Proof-reading, the most tedious stage in writing a book, became tolerable thanks to the invaluable help from Anya McGuirk. Many thanks also go to Elena Andreou and Christina Christou for their help in increasing my productivity over the last few years.

Several colleagues and students contributed significantly to the improvement of the discussion in this book by making detailed comments and suggestions on several chapters and sometimes several versions of the same chapter. I take pleasure in thanking my colleagues Louis Christofides, Yannis Ioannides, Julio Lopez, Nikitas Pittis, Djavad Salehi-Isfahani, and my students Elena Andreou, Andros Kourtellos, Maria Loizou, and Mohammad Arzaghi. I would like to single out Thanasis Stengos for a special thanks because his insightful comments and encouragement helped to shape several chapters of this text.

Over the years, many colleagues and students have been enthusiastic sounding-boards, helpful critics and discussion partners . They are of course too numerous to list, but certain ones truly deserve special mention. In particular, I would like to thank Rick Ashley, Paul Driscoll, Anna Hardman, Essie Maasoumi, Michalis Magdalinos, and Panos Pashardes.

I would also like to thank several generations of students who toiled through earlier versions of this text during the period 1989–1997, both at Virginia Tech and the University of Cyprus and whose questions helped to clarify several aspects of the approach.

It is inevitable that when one embarks on a long-term project whose primary objective is to put forward an alternative to the traditional approach, the road would often be arduous and the going would get very toilsome and solitary at times. During periods of forlorn hope a pat on the back or a vote of confidence from colleagues whose views one values, is of paramount importance in keeping one's enthusiasm going. It gives me great pleasure to thank David Hendry and Yannis Ioannides whose encouragement kept me going during times that I felt like throwing in the towel. I would also like to record my thanks to Peter Phillips and Essie Maasoumi whose open-minded editorship of *Econometric Theory* and *Econometric Reviews*, respectively, gives dissenting views a chance to be heard.

My sincerest apologies to any colleagues and students whose help I have inadvertently failed to acknowledge. I hope to have an opportunity to correct the omission in a second edition.

Finally, I owe a great debt to my wife Evie and daughters Stella, Marina and Alexia for their patience and support during the long period spent on writing this book.

Symbols

$\mathbb{T}$	index set; often $\mathbb{T} = \{1, 2, ..., \mathbb{T}, ..\}$
$\mathbb{Z}$	set of integers
$\mathbb{N}$	set of natural numbers
$\mathbb{Q}$	set of rational numbers
$\mathbb{R}$	the set of real numbers; real line $(-\infty, \infty)$
$\mathbb{R}^n$	$\overbrace{\mathbb{R} \times \mathbb{R} \times \cdots \times \mathbb{R}}^{n \text{ times}}$
$\mathbb{R}_+$	the set of positive real numbers; real line $(0, \infty)$
$\mathcal{B}(\mathbb{R})$	Borel $\sigma-$ field generated by $\mathbb{R}$
α_3	skewness coefficient
α_4	kurtosis coefficient
$f(x; \boldsymbol{\theta})$	density function of X with parameters $\boldsymbol{\theta}$
$F(x; \boldsymbol{\theta})$	cumulative distribution function
μ_r	central moment of order r
μ_r'	raw moment of order r
$\mathsf{N}(\mu, \sigma^2)$	Normal distribution with mean μ and variance σ^2
$\mathsf{U}(a, b)$	Uniform distribution over the interval $[a, b]$
$\mathsf{F}(m, n)$	F distribution with parameters m and n
$\chi^2(n)$	chi-square distribution with n degrees of freedom
$\mathsf{St}(\nu)$	Student's t distribution with ν degrees of freedom
S	outcomes set
$\widetilde{\mathscr{F}}$	event space (a σ-field)
$\mathbb{P}(.)$	probability set function
ε	random experiment
$\sigma(X)$	minimal sigma-field generated by X
$\sim\mathsf{D}(.)$	distributed as $\mathsf{D}(.)$
$\underset{\sim}{H}$	distributed under H
$\sim\mathsf{D}(.)$	asymptotically distributed as $\mathsf{D}(.)$
$\underset{\propto}{\alpha}$	proportional to

$E(.)$	expected value
$Var(X)$	variance of X
$Corr(X, Y)$	correlation between X and Y
$Cov(X, Y)$	covariance between X and Y
$\xrightarrow{a.s}$	almost sure convergence
$\xrightarrow{c}$	complete convergence
$\xrightarrow{\mathcal{D}}$	convergence in distribution
$\xrightarrow{\mathbb{P}}$	convergence in probability
$\xrightarrow{r}$	convergence in rth moment
$\mathbf{I}_T(\boldsymbol{\theta})$	Fisher's information matrix for T observations
$\mathbf{I}(\boldsymbol{\theta})$	Fisher's information matrix for 1 observation
$\mathbf{I}_\infty(\boldsymbol{\theta})$	Fisher's asymptotic information matrix
$\xi_n(\boldsymbol{\theta}; X)$	conditional information process

Acronyms

AR(p)	Autoregressive model of order p
ARMA(p,q)	Autoregressive-Moving Average model of order p,q
CAN	Consistent, Asymptotically Normal
cdf	cumulative distribution function
CLT	Central Limit Theorem
DGP	Data Generating Process
ecdf	empirical cumulative distribution function
FCLT	Functional Central Limit Theorem
GM	Generating Mechanism
ID	Identically Distributed
IID	Independent and Identically Distributed
LIL	Law of Iterated Logarithm
LS	Least-Squares
mgf	moment generating function
MLE	Maximum Likelihood Estimator
MSE	Mean Square Error
NIID	Normal, Independent and Identically Distributed
PMM	Parametric Method of Moments
PR	Probabilistic Reduction
SLLN	Strong Law Large Numbers
UMP	Uniformly Most Powerful
WLLN	Weak Law Large Numbers

1 An introduction to empirical modeling

1.1 Introduction

In an attempt to give some idea of what empirical modeling is all about, we begin the discussion with an epigrammatic demarcation of its intended scope:

> **Empirical modeling** is concerned with the parsimonious description of observable stochastic phenomena using statistical models.

The above demarcation is hardly illuminating because it involves the unknown terms *stochastic phenomenon* and *statistical model* which will be explained in what follows. At this stage, however, it suffices to note the following distinguishing features of empirical (as opposed to other forms of) modeling:

(a)   the *stochastic* nature of the phenomena amenable to such modeling,
(b)   the indispensability of the *observed data*, and
(c)   the nature of the description in the form of a *statistical model*.

The primary objective of empirical modeling is to provide an *adequate description* of certain types of observable phenomena of interest in the form of stochastic mechanisms we call *statistical models*. A statistical model purports to capture the *statistical systematic information* (see sections 2–3), which is different from the theory information (see section 4). In contrast to a *theory model*, a statistical model is codified exclusively in terms of probabilistic concepts and it is descriptive and anti-realistic in nature (see chapter 10 for further discussion). The *adequacy* of the description is assessed by how well the postulated statistical model accounts for all the statistical systematic information in the data (see section 5). In section 6 we provide a preliminary discussion of certain important dimensions of the constituent element of empirical modeling, the observed data.

Empirical modeling in this book is considered to involve a wide spectrum of inter-related procedures including:

(i)   *specification* (the choice of a statistical model),
(ii)   *estimation* (estimation of the parameters of the postulated statistical model),

(iii) *misspecification testing* (assessing the validity of the probabilistic assumptions of the postulated statistical model), and

(iv) *respecification* (an alternative choice of a statistical model).

As argued below, these facets of modeling are particularly involved in the case of **observational data**. In the case of **experimental data** the primary focus is on estimation because facets (i) and (iv) constitute the other side of the *design* coin and (iii) plays a subsidiary role.

A quintessential example of empirical modeling using observational data is considered to be *econometrics*. An important thesis adopted in this book is that econometrics differs from mainstream statistics (dominated by the experimental design and the least-squares traditions), not so much because of the economic theory dimension of modeling, but primarily because of the particular modeling issues that arise due to the *observational nature* of the overwhelming majority of economic data. Hence, we interpret the traditional definition of econometrics "the estimation of relationships as suggested by economic theory" (see Harvey (1990), p. 1), as placing the field within the experimental design modeling framework. In a nutshell, the basic argument is that the traditional econometric textbook approach utilizes the experimental design modeling framework for the analysis of non-experimental data (see Spanos (1995b) for further details).

1.1.1   A bird's eye view of the chapter

The rest of this chapter elaborates on the distinguishing features of empirical modeling (a)–(c). In section 2 we discuss the meaning of **stochastic observable phenomena** and why such phenomena are amenable to empirical modeling. In section 3, we discuss the relationship between stochastic phenomena and **statistical models**. This relationship comes in the form of *statistical systematic information* which is nothing more than the formalization of the chance regularity patterns exhibited by the observed data emanating from stochastic phenomena. In section 4 we discuss the important notion of statistical adequacy: whether the postulated statistical model "captures" all the statistical systematic information in the data. In section 5 we contrast the statistical and theory information. In a nutshell, the theoretical model is formulated in terms of the behavior of economic agents and the statistical model is formulated exclusively in terms of probabilistic concepts; a sizeable part of the book is concerned with the question of: What constitutes statistical systematic information? In section 6 we raise three important issues in relation to **observed data**, their different *measurement scales*, their *nature*, and their *accuracy*, as they relate to the statistical methods used for their modeling.

The main message of this chapter is that, in assessing the validity of a theory, the modeler is required to ensure that the observed data constitute an unprejudiced witness whose testimony can be used to assess the validity of the theory in question. A statistical model purports to provide an adequate summarization of the statistical systematic information in the data in the form of a stochastic mechanism that conceivably gave rise to the observed data in question.

1.2   Stochastic phenomena, a preliminary view

As stated above, the intended scope of empirical modeling is demarcated by the stochastic nature of observable phenomena. In this section we explain intuitively the idea of a stochastic phenomenon and relate it to the notion of a statistical model in the next section.

1.2.1   Stochastic phenomena and chance regularity

A **stochastic phenomenon** is one whose observed data exhibit what we call *chance regularity patterns*. These patterns are usually revealed using a variety of graphical techniques.

The essence of *chance regularity,* as suggested by the term itself, comes in the form of two entwined characteristics:

> *chance*: an inherent uncertainty relating to the occurence of particular outcomes,
> *regularity*: an abiding regularity in relation to the occurence of many such outcomes.

TERMINOLOGY: the term chance regularity is introduced in order to avoid possible confusion and befuddlement which might be caused by the adoption of the more commonly used term known as **randomness**; see chapter 10 for further discussion.

At first sight these two attributes might appear to be contradictory in the sense that *chance* refers to the *absence* of order and "regularity" denotes the *presence* of order. However, there is no contradiction because the disorder exists at the level of individual outcomes and the order at the aggregate level. Indeed, the essence of chance regularity stems from the fact that the disorder at the individual level creates (somehow) order at the aggregate level. The two attributes should be viewed as inseparable for the notion of chance regularity to make sense. When only one of them is present we cannot talk of chance regularity.

Any attempt to define formally what we mean by the term *chance regularity* at this stage will be rather pointless because one needs several mathematical concepts that will be developed in what follows. Instead, we will attempt to give some intuition behind the notion of chance regularity using a simple example and postpone the formal discussion until chapter 10.

Example

Consider the situation of casting two dice and adding the dots on the sides facing up. The *first* crucial feature of this situation is that at each trial (cast of the two dice) the outcome (the sum of the dots of the sides) cannot be guessed with any certainty. The only thing one can say with certainty is that the outcome will be one of the numbers:

$$\{2,3,4,5,6,7,8,9,10,11,12\},$$

we exclude the case where the dice end up standing on one of the edges! All 36 possible combinations behind the outcomes are shown in table 1.1. The *second* crucial feature of the situation is that under certain conditions, such as the dice are symmetric, we know that certain outcomes are more likely to occur than others. For instance, we know that the number 2 can arise as the sum of only one set of faces: {1,1} – each die comes up with 1; the same applies to the number 12 with faces: {6,6}. On the other hand, the number 3 can arise as the sum of two sets of faces: {(1,2), (2,1)}; the same applies to the number 11 with faces: {(6,5),(5,6)}. In the next subsection we will see that this line of combinatorial reasoning will give rise to a *probability distribution* as shown in table 1.3.

Table 1.1. *Outcomes in casting two dice*

	1	2	3	4	5	6
1	(1,1)	(1,2)	(1,3)	(1,4)	(1,5)	(1,6)
2	(2,1)	(2,2)	(2,3)	(2,4)	(2,5)	(2,6)
3	(3,1)	(3,2)	(3,3)	(3,4)	(3,5)	(3,6)
4	(4,1)	(4,2)	(4,3)	(4,4)	(4,5)	(4,6)
5	(5,1)	(5,2)	(5,3)	(5,4)	(5,5)	(5,6)
6	(6,1)	(6,2)	(6,3)	(6,4)	(6,5)	(6,6)

At this stage it is interesting to pause and consider the notions of chance regularity as first developed in the context of such games of chance. This is, indeed, the way probabilities made their first appearance. Historically, probabilities were introduced as a way to understand the differences noticed empirically between the likely occurrence of different betting outcomes, as in table 1.1. Thousands of soldiers during the medieval times could attest to the differences in the empirical relative frequencies of occurrence of different events related to the outcomes in table 1.1. While waiting to attack a certain town, the soldiers had thousands of hours with nothing to do and our historical records suggest that they indulged mainly in games of chance like casting dice. After thousands of trials they knew intuitively that the number 7 occurs more often than any other number and that 6 occurs less often than 7 but more often than 5. Let us see how this intuition was developed into something more systematic that eventually led to probability theory.

Table 1.2 reports 100 actual trials of the random experiment of casting two dice and adding the number of dots turning up on the uppermost faces of the dice. A look at the table confirms only that the numbers range from 2 to 12 but no real patterns are apparent, at least at first sight.

Table 1.2. *Observed data on dice casting*

3	10	11	5	6	7	10	8	5	11	2	9	9	6	8	4	7	6	5	12
7	8	5	4	6	11	7	10	5	8	7	5	9	8	10	2	7	3	8	10
11	8	9	5	7	3	4	9	10	4	7	4	6	9	7	6	12	8	11	9
10	3	6	9	7	5	8	6	2	9	6	4	7	8	10	5	8	7	9	6
5	7	7	6	12	9	10	4	8	6	5	4	7	8	6	7	11	7	8	3

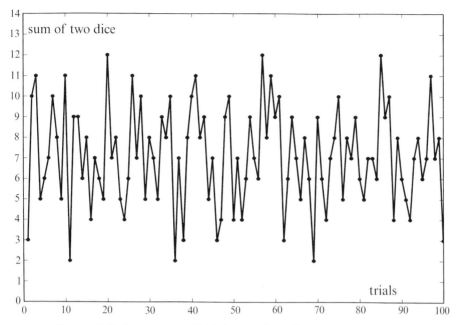

Figure 1.1 A sequence of 100 throws of two dice

In figure 1.1 the data are plotted over the index of the number of the trial. At the first casting of the dice the sum was 3, at the second the sum was 10, at the third the sum of 11 etc. Joining up these outcomes (observations) gives the viewer a better perspective with regard to the sequential nature of the observations. NOTE that the ordering of the observations constitutes an important dimension when discussing the notion of chance regularity.

Historically, the first chance regularity pattern discerned intuitively by the medieval soldiers was that of *a stable law of relative frequencies* as suggested by the histogram in figure 1.2 of the data in table 1.2; without of course the utilization of graphical techniques but after numerous casts of the dice. The question that naturally arises at this stage is:

How is the histogram in figure 1.2 related to the data in figure 1.1?

Today, *chance regularity* patterns become discernible by performing a number of thought experiments.

Thought experiment 1 Think of the observations as little squares with equal area and rotate the figure 1.1 clockwise by 90° and let the squares representing the observations fall vertically creating a pile on the *x*-axis. The pile represents the well-known histogram as shown in figure 1.2. This histogram exhibits a clear triangular shape that will be related to a probability distribution derived by using arguments based on combinations and permutations in the next sub-section. For reference purposes we summarize this regularity in the form of the following intuitive notion:

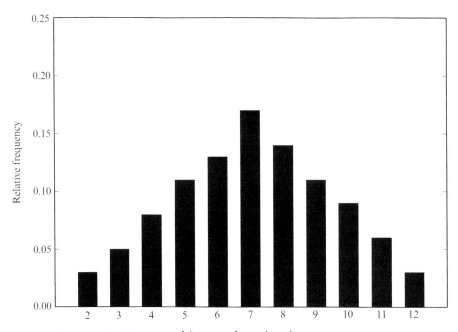

Figure 1.2 Histogram of the sum of two dice data

[1]   *Distribution*:   after several trials the outcomes form a (seemingly) stable law.

Thought experiment 2 Hide the observations following a certain value of the index, say $t = 40$, and try to guess the next outcome. Repeat this along the observation index axis and if it turns out that it is impossible to use the previous observations to guess the value of the next observation, excluding the extreme cases 2 and 12, then the chance regularity pattern we call *independence* is present. It is important to note that in the case of the extreme outcomes 2 and 12 one is almost sure that after 2 the likelihood of getting a number greater than that is much higher, and after 12 the likelihood of getting a smaller number is close to one. As argued below, this type of predictability is related to the regularity component of chance known as a stable relative frequencies law. Excluding these extreme cases, when looking at the previous observations, one cannot discern a pattern in figure 1.1 which helps narrow down the possible alternative outcomes, enabling the modeler to guess the next observation (within narrow bounds) with any certainty. Intuitively, we can summarize this notion in the form of:

[2]   *Independence*:   in any sequence of trials the outcome of any one trial does not influence and is not influenced by that of any other.

Thought experiment 3 Take a wide frame (to cover the spread of the fluctuations in a t-plot such as figure 1.1) that is also long enough (roughly less than half the length of the horizontal axis) and let it slide from left to right along the horizontal axis looking at the picture inside the frame as it slides along. In the case where the picture does not change significantly, the data exhibit *homogeneity*, otherwise *heterogeneity* is present; see chapter 5. Another way to view this pattern is in terms of the average and the *variation* around this average of the numbers as we move from left to right. It appears as though this *sequential average* and its *variation* are relatively constant around 7. The *variation* around this constant average value appears to be within constant bands. This chance regularity can be intuitively summarized by the following notion:

[3]   *Homogeneity*: the probabilities associated with the various outcomes remain identical for all trials.

NOTE that in the case where the pattern in a *t*-plot is such so as to enable the modeler to guess the next observation *exactly*, the data do not exhibit any chance pattern, they exhibit what is known as *deterministic* regularity. The easiest way to think about deterministic regularity is to visualize the graphs of mathematical functions from elementary (polynomial, algebraic, transcendental) to more complicated functions such as Bessel functions, differential and integral equations. If we glance at figure 1.1 and try to think of a function that can describe the zig-zag line observed, we will realize that no such mathematical function exists; unless we use a polynomial of order 99 which is the same as listing the actual numbers. The patterns we discern in figure 1.1 are chance regularity patterns.

1.2.2   Chance regularity and probabilistic structure

The step from the observed regularities to their formalization (mathematization) was prompted by the distribution regularity pattern as exemplified in figure 1.2. The formalization itself was initially very slow, taking centuries to materialize, and took the form of simple combinatorial arguments. We can capture the essence of this early formalization if we return to the dice casting example.

Example
In the case of the experiment of casting two dice, we can continue the line of thought that suggested differences in the likelihood of occurrences of the various outcomes in {2,3,4,5,6,7,8,9,10,11,12} as follows. We already know that 3 occurs twice as often as 2 or 11. Using the same common sense logic we can argue that since 4 occurs when any one of {(1,3), (2,2), (3,1)} occurs, its likelihood of occurrence is three times that of 2. Continuing this line of thought and assuming that the 36 combinations can occur with the same probability, we discover a distribution that relates each outcome with a certain likelihood of occurrence shown below in figure 1.3; first derived by Coordano in the 1550s. As we can see, the outcome most likely to occur is the number 7; it is no coincidence that several games of chance played with two dice involve the number 7. We think of the likelihoods of occurrence as *probabilities* and the overall pattern of such probabilities associated with each outcome as a *probability distribution*; see chapter 3.

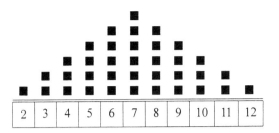

| 2 | 3 | 4 | 5 | 6 | 7 | 8 | 9 | 10 | 11 | 12 |

Figure 1.3 Regularity at the aggregate

Table 1.3. *The sum of two dice: a probability distribution*

outcomes	2	3	4	5	6	7	8	9	10	11	12
probabilities	$\frac{1}{36}$	$\frac{2}{36}$	$\frac{3}{36}$	$\frac{4}{36}$	$\frac{5}{36}$	$\frac{6}{36}$	$\frac{5}{36}$	$\frac{4}{36}$	$\frac{3}{36}$	$\frac{2}{36}$	$\frac{1}{36}$

The probability distribution in table 1.3 represents a probabilistic concept formulated by mathematicians in order to capture the chance regularity in figure 1.1. A direct comparison between figures 1.2 and 1.3 confirms the soldiers' intuition. The empirical relative frequencies in figure 1.2 are close to the theoretical probabilities shown in figure 1.3. Moreover, if we were to repeat the experiment 1000 times, the relative frequencies would have been even closer to the theoretical probabilities; see chapter 10. In this sense we can think of the histogram in figure 1.2 as an empirical realization of the probability distribution in figure 1.3 (see chapter 5 for further discussion).

Example
In the case of the experiment of casting two dice, the medieval soldiers used to gamble on whether the outcome is an odd or an even number (the Greeks introduced these concepts at around 300 BC). That is, soldier A would bet on the outcome being $A = \{3,5,7,9,11\}$ and soldier B on being $B = \{2,4,6,8,10,12\}$. At first sight it looks as though soldier B will be a definite winner because there are more even than odd numbers. The medieval soldiers, however, knew by empirical observation that this was not true! Indeed, if we return to table 1.3 and evaluate the probability of event A occurring, we discover that the soldiers were indeed correct: the probability of both events is $\frac{1}{2}$; the probability distribution is given in table 1.4.

Table 1.4. *The sum of two dice: odd and even*

outcomes	$A = \{3,5,7,9,11\}$	$B = \{2,4,6,8,10,12\}$
probabilities	$\frac{1}{2}$	$\frac{1}{2}$

We conclude this subsection by reiterating that the stochastic phenomenon of casting two dice gave rise to the observed data depicted in figure 1.1, which exhibit the three different forms' chance regularity patterns:

[1]   Distribution (triangular), [2] Independence, and [3] Homogeneity.

For reference purposes, it is important to note that the above discernible patterns, constitute particular cases of chance regularity patterns related to three different broad categories of probabilistic assumptions we call **Distribution**, **Dependence**, and **Heterogeneity**,
respectively; see chapter 5. The concepts underlying these categories of probabilistic
assumptions will be defined formally in chapters 3–4.

A digression – Chevalier de Mere's paradox

Historically, the connection between a stable law of relative frequencies and probabilities
was forged in the middle of the 17th century in an exchange of letters between Pascal and
Fermat. In order to get a taste of this early formulation, let us consider the following historical example.

   The Chevalier de Mere's paradox was raised in a letter from Pascal to Fermat on July
29, 1654 as one of the problems posed to him by de Mere (a French nobleman and a
studious gambler). De Mere observed the following empirical regularity:

>   the probability of getting at least one 6 in 4 casts of a die is greater than $\frac{1}{2}$, but

>   the probability of getting a double 6 in 24 casts with *two* dice is less than $\frac{1}{2}$.

De Mere established this empirical regularity and had no doubts about its validity
because of the enormous number of times he repeated the game. He was so sure of its
empirical validity that he went as far as to question the most fundamental part of
mathematics, arithmetic itself. Reasoning by analogy, de Mere argued that the two
probabilities should be identical because one 6 in 4 casts of one die is the same as a
double 6 in 24 casts of two dice since, according to his way of thinking: 4 is to 6 as 24 is
to 36.

   The statistical distribution in table 1.4 can be used to explain the empirical regularity
observed by de Mere. Being a bit more careful than de Mere, one can argue as follows
(the manipulations of probabilities are not important at this stage):

>   Probability of one double six $= \frac{1}{36}$,

>   Probability of one double six in n throws $= \left(\frac{1}{36}\right)^n$,

>   Probability of no double six in n throws $= \left(\frac{35}{36}\right)^n$,

>   Probability of at least one double six in n throws $= 1 - \left(\frac{35}{36}\right)^n = p$,

>   For $n = 24, p = 1 - \left(\frac{35}{36}\right)^{24} = 0.4914039$.

It is interesting to note that in the above argument going from the probability of one
double six in one trial to that of n trials we use the notion of *independence* to be defined
later.

   Using a statistical distribution for the case of *one* die, whose probability distribution is
given in table 1.5, one can argue analogously as follows:

Table 1.5. *One die probability distribution*

outcomes	1	2	3	4	5	6
probabilities	$\frac{1}{6}$	$\frac{1}{6}$	$\frac{1}{6}$	$\frac{1}{6}$	$\frac{1}{6}$	$\frac{1}{6}$

Probability of one six $= \left(\frac{1}{6}\right)$,

Probability of one six in n throws $= \left(\frac{1}{6}\right)^n$,

Probability of no six in n throws $= \left(\frac{5}{6}\right)^n$,

Probability of at least one six in n throws $= 1 - \left(\frac{5}{6}\right)^n = q$,

For $n = 4$, $q = 1 - \left(\frac{5}{6}\right)^4 = 0.5177469$.

The two probabilities $p = 0.4914039$ and $q = 0.5177469$ confirm de Mere's empirical regularity and there is no paradox of any kind! This clearly shows that de Mere's empirical frequencies were correct but his reasoning by analogy was faulty.

The chance regularity patterns of *unpredictability*, which we related to the probability concept of [2] *Independence* and that of sameness we related to [3] *homogeneity* using figure 1.1, are implicitly used throughout the exchange between Pascal and Fermat. It is interesting to note that these notions were not formalized explicitly until well into the 20th century. The probabilistic assumptions of Independence and homogeneity (Identical Distribution) underlay most forms of statistical analysis before the 1920s.

At this stage it is important to emphasize that the notion of probability underlying the probability distributions in tables 1.3–1.5, is one of *relative frequency* as used by de Mere to establish his regularity after a huge number of trials. There is nothing controversial about this notion of probability and the use of statistical models to discuss questions relating to games of chance, where the chance mechanism is explicitly an integral part of the phenomenon being modeled. It is not, however, obvious that such a notion of probability can be utilized in modeling other observable phenomena where the chance mechanism is not explicit.

1.2.3 Chance regularity in economic phenomena

In the case of the experiment of casting dice, the chance mechanism is explicit and most people will be willing to accept on faith that if this experiment is actually performed, the chance regularity patterns [1]–[3] noted above, will be present. The question which naturally arises is:

> Is this chance regularity conceivable in stochastic phenomena beyond games of chance?

In the case of stochastic phenomena where the chance mechanism is not explicit, we often:

(a)   cannot derive a probability distribution a priori using some physical symmetry argument as in the case of dice or coins, and

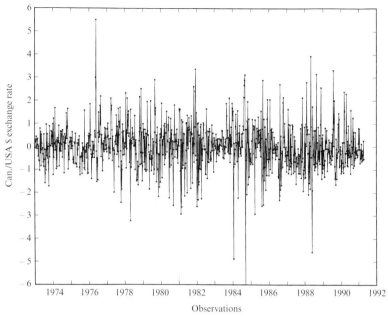

Figure 1.4 Changes in exchange rates data

(b)   cannot claim the presence of any explicit chance mechanisms giving rise to the observations.

Using these observations our first task is to decide whether the underlying phenomenon can be profitably viewed as *stochastic* and our second task is to utilize the chance regularity patterns discerned in such data so as to choose an appropriate statistical model. Hence, discerning chance regularity patterns from data plots and relating them to the corresponding probability theory concepts will be a crucial dimension of the discussion that follows.

A number of observable phenomena in econometrics can be profitability viewed as stochastic phenomena and thus amenable to statistical modeling. In an attempt to provide some support for this proposition, consider the time-plot of X-log changes of the Canadian/USA dollar exchange rate, for the period 1973–1992 (weekly observations) shown in figure 1.4. What is interesting about the data is the fact that they do exhibit a number of *chance regularity* patterns very similar to those exhibited by the dice observations in figure 1.1, but some additional patterns are also discernible. The regularity patterns exhibited by both sets of observations are:

(a)   the arithmetic average *over the ordering* (*time*) appears to be constant,
(b)   the band of variation around the average appears to be relatively constant.

The regularity pattern in relation to a (possibly) stable relative frequencies law exhibited by the exchange rate data, do not suggest a triangular stable law as in figure 1.2. Instead:

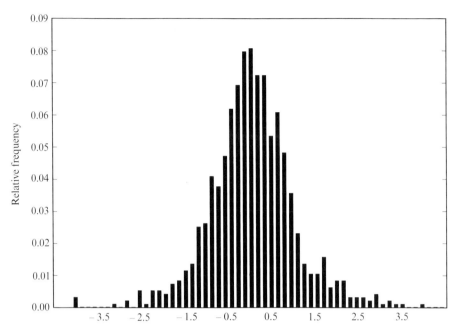

Figure 1.5 Histogram of exchange rates

(c)   the data in figure 1.4 exhibit a certain bell-shaped symmetry (there seems to be as many points above the average as there are below but the relative frequencies die out as the value of X moves away from the center to the tails). This regularity can be seen in the graph of the relative frequencies given in figure 1.5.

How the graphs in figures 1.4 and 1.5 are related will be discussed extensively in chapter 5, together with a more detailed account of how one can recognize the patterns (a)–(c) mentioned above.

In addition to the regularity patterns encountered in figure 1.1, it is worth noting that the data in figure 1.4 exhibit the following regularity pattern:

(d)   there seems to be a sequence of clusters of small changes and big changes succeeding each other.

At this stage the reader is unlikely to have been convinced that the features noted above are easily discernible from t-plots. However, an important dimension of modeling in this book is indeed how to *read* systematic information in data plots, which will begin in chapter 5.

In conclusion, the view adopted in this book is that **stochastic phenomena** (those exhibiting *chance regularity*) are susceptible to empirical modeling, irrespective of whether the built-in chance mechanism is apparent or not. Indeed, an important task for the modeler is to identify the observable phenomena which can be profitably viewed as stochastic phenomena. The question of whether there exists such a mechanism or not is only of metaphysical interest.

1.3   Chance regularity and statistical models

The discussion so far has identified the presence of chance regularity patterns in stochastic phenomena. Motivated by the desire to utilize the information conveyed by chance regularity patterns, probability theory proceeded to formalize them by developing (inventing) related (mathematical) probabilistic concepts; in the next few chapters we will introduce a number of probability theory concepts. In particular, the stable relative frequencies law regularity pattern will be formally related to the concept of a probability distribution; see tables 1.3–1.5. In the case of the exchange rate data the apparent stable relative frequencies law in figure 1.5 will be related to distributions such as the Normal and the Student's t, which exhibit the *bell-shaped symmetry* (see chapter 5). The unpredictability pattern will be formally related to the concept of Independence ([1]) and the sameness pattern to the Identical Distribution concept ([2]). The regularity patterns (a)–(b), exhibited by the exchange rate data, will be formally related to the concept of *stationarity* (see chapters 5 and 8), and (d) will be related to non-linear *dependence* (see chapter 6). It is important to emphasize that chance regularity patterns, such as those noted above, comprise the lifeblood of statistical modeling because their proper utilization constitutes the essence of empirical modeling.

The bridge between chance regularity patterns and probabilistic concepts, transforms the intuitive cognitive pattern recognition into **statistical (systematic) information**. In an attempt to render the utilization of the statistical systematic information easier for modeling purposes, the probabilistic concepts purporting to formalize the chance regularity patterns are placed into three broad categories:

   (D) Distribution, (M) Dependence, and (H) Heterogeneity.

This basic taxonomy is designed to provide a logically coherent way to view and utilize statistical information for modeling purposes. These broad categories can be seen as defining the basic components of a statistical model in the sense that every statistical model can be seen as a smooth blend of ingredients from all three categories. The smoothness of the blend in this context refers to the internal consistency of the assumptions making up a statistical model. The *first* recommendation to keep in mind in empirical modeling is

1   A statistical model is just a set of (internally) compatible probabilistic assumptions from the three broad categories: (D), (M), and (H).

REMARK: to those knowledgeable readers who are not convinced that this is indeed the case, we mention in passing that distribution assumptions are sometimes indirect in the form of smoothness and existence of moments conditions; see chapter 10.

The statistical model chosen represents a description of a tentative chance mechanism with which the modeler attempts to capture the systematic information in the data (the chance regularity patterns). A statistical model differs from other types of models in so far as it specifies a situation, a mechanism or a process in terms of a certain **probabilistic**

structure, which will be formally defined in chapters 2–4. Mathematical concepts such as *a probability distribution, independence,* and *identical distribution* constitute forms of probabilistic structure. Indeed, the main objective of the first part of the book is to introduce many additional concepts which enable the modeler to specify a variety of forms of probabilistic structure, rich enough to capture, hopefully all, chance regularity patterns. The statistical model is specified exclusively in terms of such probabilistic assumptions designed to capture the systematic information in observed data.

The examples of casting dice, discussed above, are important not because of their intrinsic interest in empirical modeling but because they represent examples of a simple stochastic phenomenon which will play an important role in the next few chapters. The stochastic phenomenon represented by the above examples is referred to generically as a *random experiment* and will be used in the next three chapters (2–4) to motivate the basic structure of probability theory. The observable phenomenon underlying the exchange rate data plotted in figure 1.4 cannot be considered as a random experiment and thus we need to extend the probabilistic framework in order to be able to model such phenomena as well; this is the subject matter of chapters 6–8.

In view of the above discussion, successful empirical modeling has two important dimensions:

(a)   recognize the chance regularity patterns as exhibited by the observed data, and
(b)   capture these patterns by postulating appropriate statistical models.

The first requires a skill on behalf of the modeler to detect such patterns using a variety of graphical techniques. Indeed, it will be impossible to overestimate the importance of graphical techniques in empirical modeling. This brings us conveniently to the *second* recommendation in empirical modeling:

2   Graphical techniques constitute an indispensable tool in empirical modeling!

If we return momentarily to the data in table 1.2, there is no doubt that the reader will have a hard time recognizing any chance regularity patterns in the data set. A glance at data plots in figures 1.1 and 1.4 provide an overall picture of the structure of both data sets that would require more than a thousand words to describe. This merely confirms the natural perceptual and cognitive capacities of the human brain; humans are able to recognize, classify, and remember visual patterns much more efficiently than numbers or words. Chapter 5 brings out the interplay between chance regularity patterns and probabilistic concepts using a variety of graphical displays.

Capturing the statistical systematic information in the data presupposes a mathematical framework rich enough to model whatever patterns are detected. It is through probability theory that chance regularity has been charmed into compliance. In this sense the interplay between modeling and probability theory is not a one way street. For example, as late as the early 20th century the pattern of *dependence* was rather nebulous and as a consequence the corresponding mathematical concept was not as yet formalized. In view of this, there are no good reasons to believe that there are no chance regularity patterns which we cannot recognize at present but will be recognized in the future. As more patterns are detected, additional probabilistic assumptions will be devised in order to

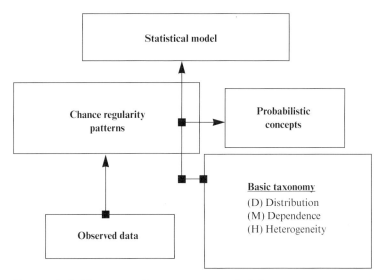

Figure 1.6 Chance regularity patterns, probabilistic assumptions, and a statistical model

formalize them and thus enrich probability theory as a modeling framework. Because of the importance of the interplay between observable patterns and formal probabilistic concepts, in figure 1.6 we present this relationship in a schematic way: chance regularity patterns are formalized in the form of probabilist concepts, these in turn are categorized into the basic taxonomy, and then utilized to postulate statistical models which (hopefully) capture the statistical systematic information; no effort will be spared in relating chance regularity patterns to the corresponding probabilistic concepts throughout this book.

The variety and intended scope of statistical models are constrained only by the scope of probability theory (as a modeling framework) and the training and the imagination of the modeler. There is no such thing as a complete list of statistical models which the modeler tries out in some sequence and chooses the one that looks the least objectionable. Moreover, empirical modeling is not about choosing optimal estimators (from some pre-specified menu), it is about choosing adequate statistical models; models which are *devised* by the modeler in an attempt to capture the systematic information in the data. In the discussion of statistical models in chapters 2–8 particular attention is paid to the relationship between observed data and the choice of statistical models. Some of the issues addressed in the next few chapters are:

(a)   What do we mean by a statistical model?
(b)   Why should statistical information be coded in a theory-neutral language?
(c)   What information do we utilize when choosing a statistical model?
(d)   What is the relationship between the statistical model and the features of the data?
(e)   How do we recognize the statistical systematic information in the observed data?

We conclude this section by emphasizing the fact that the *statistical systematic information* in the observed data has to be coded in a language which is free from any economic theory concepts. Probability theory offers such a theory-neutral language which will be utilized exclusively in the specification of statistical models. As shown in chapters 6–7, statistical models as specified in this book, do not rely on any theory-based *functional forms* among variables of interest; instead they are specified exclusively in terms of statistical relationships based on purely statistical information. The codification of statistical models exclusively in terms of statistical information is of paramount importance because one of the primary objectives of empirical modeling is to assess the empirical validity of economic theories. This assessment can be thought of as a trial for the theory under appraisal, with the theoretical model as the main witness for the defence and the observed data as the main witness for the prosecution. For the data to be an unprejudiced witness, no judge (modeler) should allow coaching of the main prosecution witness by the defence, before the trial! Statistical information has to be defined exclusively in terms of concepts which are free from any economic-theoretical connotations; only then can observed data be viewed as an independent (and fair) witness for the prosecution. The *third* recommendation in empirical model is:

3   Do not allow the observed data to be coached a priori by the theory to be appraised.

The statistical model is viewed initially as a convenient summarization of the systematic information in the data which exists irrespective of any theory. The *fourth* recommendation in empirical modeling is:

4   Statistical model specification is guided primarily by the nature and structure of the observed data.

1.4   Statistical adequacy

As argued above, the success of empirical modeling is judged by how adequately the postulated statistical model captures the statistical systematic information contained in the data. A central theme of this book is that of **statistical adequacy** and how it can be achieved in practice, by utilizing several methods including graphical displays (see chapters 5–6) and misspecification testing (see chapter 15). Without a statistically adequate model which captures the systematic information in the data, no valid statistical inference is possible, irrespective of the sophistication and/or the potential validity of the theory!

Statistical inference is often viewed as the quintessential *inductive* procedure: using a set of data (specific) to derive conclusions about the stochastic phenomenon (general) that gave rise to the data (see figure 1.7). However, it is often insufficiently recognized that this inductive procedure is embedded in a fundamentally deductive premise. The procedure from the postulated model (the premise) to the inference results (estimation, testing, prediction, simulation) is *deductive*; no data are used to derive results on the optimality of estimators, tests, etc.; estimators and tests are pronounced *optimal* based

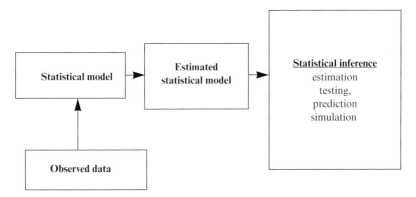

Figure 1.7 Statistical inference

on a purely deductive reasoning. The deductive component of the statistical inference reasoning amounts to:

if certain premises are assumed, certain conclusions necessarily follow.

More formally, if we denote the premises by p and the conclusions by q, then the above form of deductive reasoning takes the form of *modus ponens* (affirming the antecedent):

if p then q.

In this sense, statistical inference depends crucially on the validity of the premises: postulating a statistical model in the context of which the observed data are interpreted as a realization of the postulated stochastic mechanism. On the basis of this premise we proceed to derive statistical inference results using mathematical deduction. Correct deductive arguments show that if their premises are valid, their conclusions are valid. Using the observed data in question, the modeler relies on the validity of this deductive argument in order to draw general inference conclusions from specific data. However, if the premises are invalid the conclusions are generally unwarranted. In view of this, we consider the problem of assessing the validity of the postulated statistical model (misspecification testing) of paramount importance, especially in the case of observational data. The *fifth* recommendation in empirical modeling is:

5 No statistical inference result should be used to draw any conclusions unless the statistical adequacy of the postulated model has been established first.

The first and most crucial step in ensuring statistical adequacy is for the modeler to specify explicitly all the probabilistic assumptions making up the postulated model; without a complete set of probabilistic assumptions the notion of statistical adequacy makes no operational sense. For this reason the next several chapters pay particular attention to the problem of statistical model specification (probability and sampling models) to an extent that might seem unnecessary to a traditional textbook econometrician. It is emphasized at this stage that the notation, the terminology, and the various taxonomies introduced in the next four chapters play an important role in ensuring that

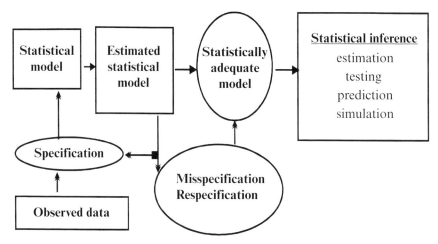

Figure 1.8 Statistical inference with statistical adequacy

the nature and structure of the probabilistic assumptions underlying the postulated model is made explicit and transparent to the modeler.

In the context of the probabilistic reduction approach, departures from the postulated statistical model are viewed as systematic information in the data that the postulated model does not account for. The statistical model needs to be respecified in order to account for the systematic information overlooked by the model postulated initially. Hence, the procedure in figure 1.7 is supplemented with the additional stages of misspecification testing and respecification. Figure 1.8 shows the modified procedure with the notion of a statistically adequate model coming between the estimated model and statistical inference. As shown in figure 1.8, reaching a statistically adequate model involves misspecification testing and respecification.

The notion of statistical adequacy is particularly crucial for empirical modeling because it can provide the basis for establishing *stylized facts* which economic theory will be required to account for. A cursory look at the empirical econometric modeling of the last 50 years or so will convince, even the most avid supporter of the traditional econometric approach, that it does not constitute a progressive research program because it has not led to any real accumulation of empirical evidence. Separating the statistical and theoretical models and ensuring the statistical adequacy of the former, will provide a good starting point for a progressive research strategy where empirical regularities are established by statistically adequate models (proper stylized facts) and theories are required to account for them. It is worth reiterating that in this book statistical and theoretical information are clearly distinguished in order to avoid any charges of circularity in implementing this research strategy.

1.5   Statistical versus theory information*

In an attempt to provide a more balanced view of empirical modeling and avoid any hasty indictments on behalf of traditional econometricians that "the approach adopted in this book ignores economic theory," this section will discuss briefly the role of economic theory in empirical modeling (see also Spanos (1986,1995b)).

Economic data are growing at an exponential rate but at the same time when a modeler attempts to give answers to specific questions he/she often finds that the particular data needed for the analysis do not exist in the form required. This is symptomatic of the absence of an adequate econometric methodology which would have played a coordinating role between economic theory and the appropriate observed data. More often than not, there exists a huge gap between theory-concepts and the data series that are usually available; the available data often measure something very different. As argued above this gap arises primarily because of the differences between the experimental-design circumstances assumed by economic theory, via the *ceteris paribus* clause, and the observational nature of the available data; the result of an on-going process with numerous influencing factors beyond the potential control of the modeler. The *sixth* recommendation in empirical modeling that one should keep in mind is:

6   Never assume that the available data measure the theory concept the modeler has in mind just because the names are very similar (or even coincide)!

A striking example is the theoretical concept *demand* versus the often available data in the form of *quantities transacted*; see Spanos (1995b). As a result of this gap, empirical modeling often attempts to answer theoretical questions of interest by utilizing data which contain no such information.

As argued in the previous three sections, the statistical systematic information is:

(a)   related to the chance regularity patterns exhibited by the observed data,
(b)   defined exclusively in terms of probabilistic concepts, and
(c)   devoid (initially) of any economic theory connotations.

The clear distinction between statistical and theoretical systematic information constitutes one of the basic pillars of the empirical modeling methodology expounded in this book; see also Spanos (1986, 1995b, forthcoming). Theory and statistical models constitute distinct entities built on different information, the behavior of economic agents, and statistical systematic information, respectively. This constitutes a necessary condition for the statistical model to be used as an unprejudiced witness on the basis of whose testimony the empirical adequacy of the theory model can be assessed.

The theory influences the choice of an appropriate statistical model in two ways. First, the theory determines the choice of the observed data of interest. Although the choice of the observed data is theory laden, once chosen, the data acquire an objective existence which is theory free. The only further influence the theory has on the specification of the statistical model is that the latter should be general enough to allow the modeler to pose theoretical questions of interest in its context. Hence, the misspecification testing and respecification facets of empirical modeling have nothing to do with the theory model; they are purely statistical procedures determined by the notion of statistical information. The *seventh* recommendation in empirical modeling is:

7   No theory, however sophisticated, can salvage a misspecified statistical model.

As argued in chapter 7, the statistical and theory viewpoints provide very different viewing angles for modeling purposes. These viewing angles are complementary but they are often used as substitutes with dire consequences; see Spanos (1997a).

A statistically adequate model provides a good summary (description) of the statistical systematic information in the data but does not constitute the ultimate objective of empirical modeling. Ultimately, the modeler wants to assess the theory in terms of a statistically adequate model, as well as to synthesize the statistical and theory models in an attempt to bestow economic-theoretic meaning and explanatory capability to the statistical model. Hence, the *eighth* recommendation to keep in mind in empirical modeling is:

8   The success of empirical modeling is assessed by how skillfully the modeler can synthesize the statistical and theory models, without short-changing either the theoretical or the statistical information!

In order to distinguish between a statistical model, built exclusively in terms of statistical systematic information, and the synthesis of the theory and statistical models we call the latter an **econometric model** (see Spanos (1986)).

1.6   Observed data

In this section we will attempt a preliminary discussion of the constituent element of empirical modeling, the observed data. Certain aspects of the observed data play an important role in the choice of statistical models.

1.6.1   Early data

Numerical data have been collected for one reason or another since the dawn of history. Early data collections, however, were non-systematic and the collected information was not generally available. The systematic collection of economic data can be dated to the 17th century as a by-product of government activities such as tax and customs collection, spending and regulating, as well as the desire to quantify certain aspects of government activity (see Porter (1995)). For instance, earlier data on income distribution were simply a by-product of tax data. Towards the end of the 19th century special censuses were undertaken by (in particular the US) governments in the agricultural and manufacturing sectors in order to consider specific questions of interest (see Christ (1985)) Thus, it should come as no surprise to find out that the data used in the early empirical work in economics (early 20th century) were mostly data on exports, imports, production and price (see Stigler (1954, 1962)). Gradually, however, governments began to appreciate the use of such data in assessing economic performance as well as providing guideposts for economic policy, a realization which led to the establishment of data collection agencies such as the Statistical Department of the Board of Trade in England. In addition, the formation of several statistical societies in Europe in the mid 19th century, such as the Statistical Societies of London and Manchester and the International Statistical Congress, created an impetus for more systematic efforts to collect and publish data which were also comparable between countries.

1.6.2 Economic data

In relation to economic data, it is worth noting the crucial role played by three pioneers in providing some additional impetus for more and better economic data in the 20th century, **Mitchell** in measuring the business cycles, **Kuznets** in setting up National Accounts and **Leontief** in operationalizing the input–output tables. These earlier efforts have given rise to billions of economic data series in the second half of the 20th century, which are currently collected on a daily basis by governments and other agencies, all over the world. The European Union alone is producing mountains of volumes containing economic data which apparently (based on hearsay evidence) no one has the time to utilize, as yet!

In most sciences, such as physics, chemistry, geology and biology, the observed data are usually generated by the modelers themselves in well-designed experiments. In econometrics the modeler is often faced with **observational** as opposed to **experimental** data. This has two important implications for empirical modeling in econometrics. First, the modeler is required to master very different skills than those needed for analyzing experimental data; the subject matter of this book. Second, the separation of the data collector and the data analyst requires the modeler to familiarize himself/herself thoroughly with the nature and structure of the data in question.

Alongside the above mentioned explosion of observational data collection grew the demand to analyze these data series with a view to a better understanding of economic phenomena such as inflation, unemployment, exchange rate fluctuations and the business cycle, as well improving our ability to forecast economic activity. A first step towards attaining these objectives is to get acquainted with the available data by ensuring that the modeler is well versed in the answers to questions such as:

(i)   How were the data collected?
(ii)   What is the subject of measurement?
(iii) What are the measurement units and scale?
(iv)   What is the measurement period?
(v)   What exactly do the numbers measure?
(vi)   What is the connection between the data and the corresponding theoretical concepts?

Hence, the *ninth* recommendation to keep in mind in empirical modeling is:

9   Get to know the important dimensions of your data thoroughly!

1.6.3 Observed data and the nature of a statistical model

A data set comprising n observations will be denoted by $\{x_1, x_2, \ldots, x_n\}$ or more compactly:

$$\{x_k, k = 1,2,3, \ldots, n\}.$$

REMARK: it is crucial to emphasize the value of mathematical symbolism in what follows. It is impossible to overemphasize the power and importance of mathematical symbolism when one is discussing probability theory. The clarity and concision this symbolism introduces to the discussion is indispensable.

It is customary to classify economic data according to the dimension (index) of observation into two primary categories:

(i) **Cross-section:** $\{x_k, k = 1,2, \ldots, n\}$, k denotes individuals (firms, states, etc.),
(iii) **Time series:** $\{x_t, t = 1,2, \ldots, T\}$, t denotes time (weeks, months, years, etc.).

For example, observed data on consumption might refer to consumption of different households at the same point in time or aggregate consumption (consumers' expenditure) over time. The first will constitute cross-section, the second, time series data. By combining these two, e.g. observing the consumption of the same households over time, we can define a third category:

(iii) **Panel (longitudinal):** $\{x_k, \mathbf{k} := (k,t), k = 1,2, \ldots, n, t = 1,2, \ldots, T\}$,
where k and t denote individuals and time, respectively.

NOTE that in this category the index $\mathbf{k}$ is two dimensional but x_k is one dimensional.

At first sight the two primary categories do not seem to differ substantively because the index sets appear identical; the index sets are subsets of the set of natural numbers. A moment's reflection, however, reveals that there is more to an index set than meets the eye. In the case where the index set $Z := \{1,2, \ldots, n\}$ refers to particular households, the index stands for the names of the households, say:

$$\{\text{Jones, Brown, Smith, Richard, } \ldots\}. \tag{1.1}$$

In the case of time series the index $T := \{1,2, \ldots, T\}$ refers to particular dates, say:

$$\{1952,1953, \ldots, 1997\}. \tag{1.2}$$

Comparing the two index sets we note immediately that they have very different mathematical structures. The most apparent difference is that the set (1.1) does not have a natural ordering, whether we put Brown before Smith is immaterial, but in the case of the index set (1.2) the ordering is a crucial property of the set.

In the above example the two index sets appear identical but they turn out to be very different. This difference renders the two data sets qualitatively dissimilar to the extent that the statistical analysis of one set of data will be distinctively different from that of the other. The reason for this will become apparent in later chapters. At this stage it is sufficient to note that a number of concepts such as *dependence* and *heterogeneity* (noted above) are inextricably bound up with the ordering of the index set.

The mathematical structure of the index set (e.g., the presence or absence of an ordering) is not the only criterion for classifying dissimilar data sets. The mathematical structure of the range of values of observations themselves constitutes another even more important criterion. For example data series on the "number of children" in different households can take values in a set of the form: $\{0,1,2, \ldots, 100\}$. We assume that there is an upper bound which we choose to be 100. This is a set of discrete values which has a very different mathematical structure from the set of values of the variable consumption which takes values over the positive real line:

$$\mathbb{R}_+ = (0,\infty).$$

Another variable which is different than both consumption and number of children in terms of its range of values is *religion* (Christian, Muslim, Buddhist) which cannot be treated in the same way as data on consumption or number of children because there is no natural way to measure religion in numerical terms. Even if we agree on a measurement scale for religion, say $\{-1,0,1\}$, the ordering is irrelevant and the difference between these numbers is meaningless. In contrast, both of these dimensions are meaningful in the case of the *consumption* and the *number of children* data.

The above discussion raised important issues in relation to the measurement of observed data. The first is whether the numerical values can be thought of as being values from a certain interval on the real line, say $[0,1]$ or they represent a set of discrete values, say $\{0,1,2,3,4,5,6,7,8,9\}$. The second is whether these values have a natural ordering or not.

Collecting these comments together we can see that the taxonomy which classifies the data into cross-section and time series is inadequate because there are several additional classifications which are ignored. These classifications are important from the modeling viewpoint because they make a difference in so far as the applicable statistical techniques are concerned. In its abstract formulation a data set takes the form:

$$\{x_k, k \in \mathbb{N}, x_k \in \mathbb{R}_X\},$$

where $\mathbb{N}$ denotes the index set and $\mathbb{R}_X$ denotes the range of values of x; NOTE that both sets $\mathbb{N}$ and $\mathbb{R}_X$ are subsets of the real line, denoted by $\mathbb{R}: = (-\infty,\infty)$. Depending on the mathematical structure of these two sets different classifications arise. Indeed, the mathematical structure of the sets $\mathbb{N}$ and $\mathbb{R}_X$ plays a very important role in the choice of the statistical model (see sections 3–5).

In terms of the range of values of the data, $\mathbb{R}_X$ can be a **discrete subset** of $\mathbb{R}$, such as $\mathbb{R}_X = \{0,1,2, \ldots\}$, or a **continuous subset** of $\mathbb{R}$, such as $\mathbb{R}_X = [0,\infty)$. In cases where the variable X can be thought of as taking only a countable number of values, $\mathbb{R}_X$ is considered as discrete, otherwise the variable X is considered continuous. In econometrics, variables such as consumption, investment, savings and inflation are considered continuous, but variables such as number of children, marital status and a number of choice variables, are viewed as discrete. The same *discrete-continuous* classification can also be applied to the index set $\mathbb{N}$ leading to a four way classification of variables and the corresponding data. As shown in chapters 3–4, the nature of both sets $\mathbb{N}$ (the index set) and $\mathbb{R}_X$ (the range of values of the numerical values of the data) plays an important role in determining the form and structure of the statistical model postulated to describe the observable phenomenon of interest.

1.6.4 Measurement scales

A very important dimension of any observed data is the **measurement scale** of the individual data series. In this subsection we discuss this important dimension and raise some of the issues related to the modeling of data measured on different scales.

The number of classifications introduced above increases substantially by realizing that the discrete-continuous dichotomy can be classified further according to the measurement scale bestowed on the set in question.

The measurement scales are traditionally classified into four broad categories.

Ratio scale Variables. in this category enjoy the richest mathematical structure in their range of values, where for any two values along the scale, say x_1 and x_2:

(a)   the ratio (x_1/x_2) is a meaningful quantity (there exists a natural origin for the measurement system),
(b)   the distance $(x_2 - x_1)$ is a meaningful quantity, and
(c)   there exists a natural ordering (ascending or descending order) of the values along the scale; the comparison $x_2 \gtreqless x_1$ makes sense.

Economic variables such as consumption and inflation belong to this category. For any two values x_1 and x_2 of a variable in this category, it is meaningful to ask the question:

How many times is x_1 bigger than x_2?

Interval scale A variable is said to be an *interval variable* if its measurement system is bestowed with (b)–(c) but not (a), e.g., temperature, systolic blood pressure. For any two values x_1 and x_2 of a variable in this category it is meaningful to ask the question:

How much do x_1 and x_2 differ?

Example
The index set (1.2) is measured on this scale because the distance (1970–1965) is a meaningful magnitude but the ratio $\left(\frac{1965}{1970}\right)$ is not.

Ordinal scale A variable belongs to this category if it is bestowed with (c) only, e.g. grading (excellent, very good, good, failed), income class (upper, middle, lower). For such variables the ordering exists but the distance between categories is not meaningfully quantifiable. For any two values x_1 and x_2 of a variable in this category it is meaningful to ask the question:

Is x_1 bigger or smaller than x_2?

Nominal scale A variable is said to be nominal if its measurement system is blessed with none of the above. The variable denotes categories which do not even have a natural ordering, e.g. marital status (married, unmarried, divorced, separated), gender (male, female, other), employment status (employed, unemployed, other). Due to the nature of such variables the modeler should be careful in attributing numerical values to avoid misleading inferences. For any two values x_1 and x_2 of a variable in this category the only meaningful question to ask is:

Is x_1 different from x_2?

The above measurement scales have been considered in a descending hierarchy from the highest (ratio, the richest in mathematical structure) to the lowest (nominal). It is important to note that statistical concepts and methods designed for one category of variables do not necessarily apply to variables of other categories (see chapter 6). For instance, the *mean*, *variance*, and *covariance* (the building blocks of regression analysis) make no sense in the case of ordinal and nominal variables, the *median* makes sense in the case of ordinal but not in the case of nominal variables. In the latter case the only measure of location that has a meaning is the *mode*. The only general rule for the methods of analysis of different measurement-scale variables one can state at this stage is that a method appropriate for a certain measurement-scale in the hierarchy is also appropriate for the scales above but not below. There are several books which discuss the methods of analysis of the so-called **categorical data**: data measured on the *nominal* or *ordinal* scale (see Bishop, Fienberg and Holland (1975), Agresti (1990) inter alia).

TERMINOLOGY. It is important to note that in the statistical literature there is widespread confusion between the measurement scales and three different categorizations: *discrete/continuous, qualitative/quantitative* and *categorical/non-categorical* variables. Discrete variables can be measured on all four scales and continuous variables can sometimes be grouped into a small number of categories. Categorical variables are only variables that can be measured on either the ordinal or the nominal scales but the qualitative variables category is fuzzy. In some books qualitative variables are only those measured on the nominal scale but in some others it also includes ordinal variables.

Measurement scales and the index set The examples of measurement scales used in the above discussion referred exclusively to the set $\mathbb{R}_X$: the range of values of a variable X. However, the discussion is also relevant for the index set $\mathbb{N}$. In the case of the variable *household consumption* discussed above, the index set (1.1) is measured on a nominal scale. On the other hand in the case of consumers' expenditure the index set (1.2) is measured on the interval scale. This is because the time dimension does not have a natural origin (zero is by convention) and in statistical analysis the index set (1.2) is often replaced by a set of the form $\mathbb{T} := \{1, 2, \ldots, T\}$. We note that the time series/cross-section categorization is exclusively based on measurement scale of the index set. The index set of time series is of interval scale and that of cross-section of nominal scale. There are also cases where the index set can be of a ratio or an ordinal scale. For example, there are data produced by a seismograph with a continuous index set $\mathbb{T} \subset \mathbb{R}_+$.

The nature of the index set plays an important role in empirical modeling as will be seen in the sequel. In view of the fact that in addition to the discrete/continuous dichotomy we have four different measurement scales for the range of values of the variable itself and another four for the index set, a bewildering variety of data types can be

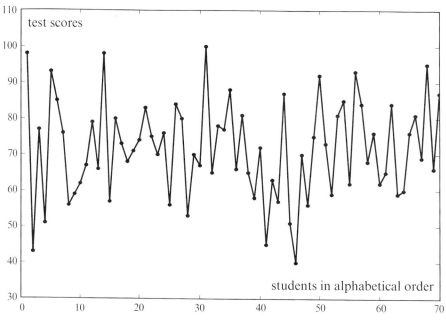

Figure 1.9 Exam scores data (alphabetical)

defined. Our concern is with those types which affect the kind of statistical methods that can be applied to the data in question. A cursory look at the applied econometrics litera-ture reveals that variables from very different measurement scales are involved in the same regression equation (see chapter 7), rendering some of these results suspect. As argued in chapter 3, the concepts of mean, variance and covariance (the raw materials of regression) make no sense for nominal or even ordinal variables.

1.6.5   Cross-section versus time series, is that the question?

In conclusion it is important to return to the traditional cross-section/time series taxon-omy to warn the reader against adopting aphorisms of the form *dependence or/and het-erogeneity are irrelevant for cross-section data*. What is important for considering dependence or/and heterogeneity is not whether the data are cross-section or time series but whether the data are ordered or not. It is true that for time series data there is a natural ordering (time) but that does not mean that cross-section data do not have natural orderings such as spatial or some other dimension of interest. Once an ordering is adopted both notions of dependence and heterogeneity become as relevant in cross-section as they are for time series.

Example
Consider the case of the data given in the table 1.6. The data refer to the test scores of a class taking a multiple choice exam on Principles of Economics in 1992 and are reported according to the alphabetical order of the students' names. The data are plotted in figure 1.9 with the *scores* measured on the vertical axis and the students in alphabetical order

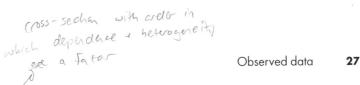
cross-section with order in
which dependence + heterogeneity
are a factor

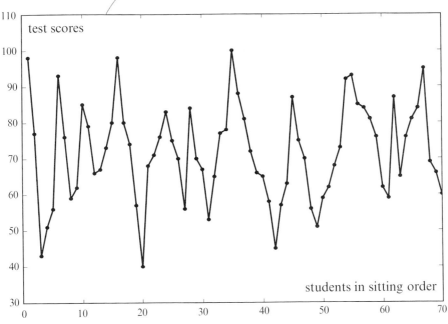

Figure 1.10 Exam scores data (sitting order)

on the horizontal axis. This ordering does not seem very interesting because there are no reasons to believe that there is a connection between scores and the *alphabetical order* of the students' names; just to be on the safe side one could assess this conjecture by comparing this *t*-plot with that shown in figure 1.1. On the other hand, ordering the observations according to the *sitting arrangement* during the exam, as shown in figure 1.10, seems to be more interesting in the sense that it might yield some interesting information. Indeed, looking at figure 1.10, we can see a rather different graphical display. The ups and downs of the latter graph are a bit more orderly than those of figure 1.9; they exhibit some sort of cyclical behavior. As explained in chapter 5, this pattern of non-identical cycles reveals that the data exhibit some form of positive dependence over the exam-sitting ordering. In plain English this means that there was a lot of *cheating* taking place in the exam room during the examination! As a result of the statistical analysis of the data as ordered in figure 1.10 (see chapters 5 and 15) that was the last multiple choice exam the author has administered.

Table 1.6. *Data on Principles of Economics exam scores*

98.0	43.0	77.0	51.0	93.0	85.0	76.0	56.0	59.0	62.0
67.0	79.0	66.0	98.0	57.0	80.0	73.0	68.0	71.0	74.0
83.0	75.0	70.0	76.0	56.0	84.0	80.0	53.0	70.0	67.0
100.0	78.0	65.0	77.0	88.0	81.0	66.0	72.0	65.0	58.0
45.0	63.0	57.0	87.0	51.0	40.0	70.0	56.0	75.0	92.0
73.0	59.0	81.0	85.0	62.0	93.0	84.0	68.0	76.0	62.0
65.0	84.0	59.0	60.0	76.0	81.0	69.0	95.0	66.0	87.0

The moral of the story is that although there is no natural ordering for cross-section data, there can be many interesting dimensions with respect to which they can be ordered. The tenth recommendation in empirical modeling is:

10   Classifications of data, by themselves, do not determine the form and probabilistic structure of the appropriate statistical model.

As argued below, statistical models take into consideration a variety of different dimensions and features of the data. Classifying models according to the classification of data based on only one such dimension is myopic.

1.6.6   Limitations of economic data

In relation with the limitations of economic data we will consider two important issues:

(i)   their accuracy and
(ii)   their nature.

An important milestone in using economic data for studying economic phenomena was the publication of a book by Morgenstern (1963) entitled *On the accuracy of economic observations*, first published in 1950. In this book the author disputed the accuracy of published economic data and questioned the appropriateness of such data for the purposes used. This book was influential in forming the practitioners' attitude toward economic data as described below by Griliches (1984, both quotes at p. 1466):

Econometricians have an ambivalent attitude towards economic data. At one level, the "data" are the world that we want to explain, the basic facts that economists purport to elucidate. At the other level, they are the source of all our trouble. Their imperfection makes our job difficult and often impossible. Many a question remains unresolved because of "multi-collinearity" or other sins of the data…

Griliches' view of the situation is that econometricians should not complain about the quality of their data because it is exactly this so-and-so quality that justifies their legitimacy:

If the data were perfect, collected from well designed randomized experiments, there would be hardly room for a separate field of econometrics …

Although this is clearly an extreme viewpoint there is some truth in it in so far as the available data in econometrics are rarely collected from well designed randomized experiments. Hence, the need for different statistical techniques and procedures arises because of the *nature* of the available data rather than their bad quality. The primary limitation of the available economic data arises from the fact that there is a sizeable gap between theory models and the available data. Economic theory, via the *ceteris paribus* clause, assumes a *nearly isolated* system but the observed data are the result of an on-going multidimensional process with numerous influencing factors beyond the control of the modeler (see Spanos, 1956).

The accuracy of economic data has improved substantially since Morgenstern (1963) and in some sectors, such as the financial, the data are often very accurate. Time series on *"bad" data often indicates a poor theory.*

exchange rates and stock prices are as accurate as economic data can get. In this book we do not subscribe to the view that when the data analysis does not give rise to the expected results (based on a certain preconceived idea), the quality of the data is to blame. This is the same as a bad carpenter blaming his tools.

In cases where the accuracy of the data is indeed problematical, the modeler should keep in mind that no statistical procedure can extract information from observed data when it is not there in the first place. The *eleventh* recommendation in empirical modeling is:

11 No statistical argument, however sophisticated, can salvage bad quality observed data.

In what follows we assume that the modeler has checked the observed data and deemed them accurate enough to be considered reliable for statistical inference purposes. As a rule, we do not consider bad inference results (judged against some a priori conceived prejudice) as symptomatic of bad quality data. Many a time the quality of the data is used as an excuse for the modeler's ascetic knowledge of the nature of the observed data and the shallow-mindedness often displayed in relating a theoretical model to the observed data in question (see Spanos (1995b)). Hence, the *last* recommendation in empirical modeling is:

12 Familiarize yourself thoroughly with the nature and the accuracy of your data.

This will make the modeler aware of what questions can and cannot be posed to a particular data set.

In conclusion, the author has no delusions with regard to the acceptability of the above recommendations. At this stage, the only status claimed for these recommendations is as the author's *prejudices* in empirical modeling. As mentioned in the Preface, the discussion in the rest of this book purports to transform these prejudices into *theses* supported by convincing arguments.

1.7   Looking ahead

The main objective of the next three chapters (2–4) is to motivate and build the quintessential form of a statistical model which we call a *simple statistical model*. The motivation is provided by presenting the latter as a formalization of a simple stochastic phenomenon we generically call a *random experiment*. The formalization introduces the necessary probabilistic concepts which are then blended together in order to build the generic form of a simple statistical model. The interplay between chance regularity patterns and the probabilistic concepts defining a simple statistical model is brought out in chapter 5 using a variety of graphical techniques. The primary objective of chapter 6 is to extend the simple statistical model in directions which enable the modeler to capture several forms of dependence, including the ones exhibited in the exchange rate data in figure 1.4. Chapter 7 continues the theme of chapter 6 with a view to showing that the key to modeling dependence in observational data is the notion of conditioning. This

stochastic data + probability concepts = statistical model leads naturally to regression and related models. Extending the simple statistical model in directions which enable the modeler to capture several forms of dependence and heterogeneity is completed in chapter 8. In a nutshell, the basic objective of chapters 2–8 is to introduce the necessary probability theory framework in the context of which such probabilistic concepts can be defined and related to observable patterns exhibited by observations from stochastic phenomena.

1.8   Exercises

1   How do we decide which economic phenomena of interest are amenable to empirical modeling?

2   Explain intuitively the notion of chance regularity.

3   Explain briefly the connection between chance regularity patterns and probability theory concepts.

4   Explain briefly the connection between chance regularity patterns and statistical models.

5   Explain the connection between a histogram and a probability distribution using de Mere's paradox.

6   Explain why it is important that the statistical information is summarized exclusively in terms of probabilistic concepts.

7   Under what circumstances can the modeler claim that the observed data constitute unprejudiced evidence in assessing the empirical adequacy of a theory?

8   Explain the notion of statistical adequacy and discuss its importance for statistical inference.

9   "Statistical inference is a hybrid of a deductive and an inductive procedure." Discuss.

10   Compare and contrast the different measurement scales for observed data.

11   Give four examples of variables measured on each of the different scales, beyond the ones given in the discussion above.

12   Why do we care about measurement scales in empirical modeling?

13   Beyond the measurement scales what features of the observed data are of interest from the empirical modeling viewpoint?

14   Compare and contrast time-series, cross-section, and panel data.

15   Explain how the different features of observed data can be formalized in the context of expressing a data series in the form of:

$$\{x_k, \, x_k \in \mathbb{R}_X, \, k \in \mathbb{N}\}.$$

Hint: explain the role and significance of the mathematical structure of the sets $(\mathbb{R}_X, \mathbb{N})$.

16   "In modeling cross-section data one cannot talk about dependence." Discuss.

2 Probability theory: a modeling framework

2.1 Introduction

2.1.1 Primary aim

The primary objective of this and the next several chapters is to introduce *probability theory* not as part of pure mathematics but as a mathematical framework for modeling certain **observable phenomena** which we call **stochastic**: phenomena that exhibit *chance regularity* (see chapter 1). Center stage in this modeling framework is given to the notion of a **statistical model**. This concept is particularly crucial in modeling observational (non-experimental) data. The approach adopted in this book is that the mathematical concepts underlying the notion of a statistical model are motivated by formalizing a generic simple stochastic phenomenon we call a *random experiment*. An example of such a phenomenon is that of "counting the number of calls arriving in a telephone exchange, over a certain period of time." The formalization (mathematization) of this generic stochastic phenomenon will motivate the basic constituent elements that underlie the notion of a statistical model and provide the foundation for a broader framework in the context of which empirical modeling takes place.

2.1.2 Why do we care?

The first question we need to consider before we set out on the long journey to explore the theory of probability as a modeling framework is:

> Why do we care about probability theory?

The answer in a nutshell is that it provides both the foundation and the frame of reference for data modeling and statistical inference. Indeed, what distinguishes statistical inference proper from descriptive statistics is the fact that the former takes place in the context of the mathematical framework we call probability theory.

In the context of **descriptive statistics** the modeler summarizes and exhibits the important features of a particular data set in a readily comprehensible form. This usually involves the presentation of data in tables, graphs, charts, and histograms, as well as the computation of summary numerical values, such as measures of central tendency and dispersion. Descriptive statistics, however, has one very crucial limitation:

> The conclusions of the analysis cannot be extended beyond the data in hand.

Any conclusions beyond these data are without any formal justification. In contrast, **statistical inference** proper has a built in *inductive argument* which enables the modeler to draw inferences and establish generalizations and claims about future observations (observations beyond the observed data set) on the basis of the observed data in hand. The *modus operandi* of this built-in inductive argument is the notion of a **statistical model** itself. To be more precise, in *statistical inference*:

> the observed data are viewed as a *particular realization* of a stochastic mechanism as specified by the *statistical model* postulated a priori.

In other words, the modeler's objective is to model the *stochastic mechanism* that gave rise to the data and not the data themselves; in contrast, the objective of descriptive statistics is to describe the data themselves. The observed data are viewed in a broader framework defined by the statistical model and this in turn enables the modeler to draw inferences about the *mechanism* underlying the observed data, not just the data in hand. The concept of a statistical model and its adornments are formulated within the mathematical framework of probability theory.

2.1.3 A bird's eye view of the chapter

In section 2 we introduce the notion of a simple statistical model at an informal and intuitive level, as a prelude to the more formal treatment undertaken in the rest of this and the next chapter. In many ways we jump ahead to chapter 4 where the formal discussion will culminate with the formulation of the notion of a simple statistical model. This is to help the less mathematically inclined students to come to grips with the main ideas at the outset and make the discussion that follows more focused for those who prefer a more formal and complete discussion. In section 3 we introduce the reader to probability theory from the viewpoint of statistical modeling. Instead of commencing the discussion with the primitive notions and the relevant axioms, we proceed, in section 4, to motivate both by formalizing a simple generic stochastic phenomenon we call a *random experiment* defined in terms of three conditions. The viewing angle is not that of a mathematician but that of a modeler. In section 5 we proceed to formalize the first of these conditions in the form of *the outcomes set*. In section 6, the formalization of the second condition gives rise to two mathematical concepts: *the event space* and *the probability set function*. The formalization of the third condition defining a generic random experiment, takes place in section 7 giving rise to *a simple sampling space* of random trials. In section 8 the various concepts introduced in sections 5–7 are collected together to define the concept of a statistical space.

2.2   Simple statistical model: a preliminary view

2.2.1   Main objective

As mentioned above, the notion of a statistical model takes center stage in the mathematical framework for modeling stochastic phenomena. In this section we attempt an informal discussion of the concept of a simple statistical model at an intuitive level with a healthy dose of handwaving. The main objective of this preliminary discussion is twofold. Firstly, for the mathematically weak students, the discussion, although incomplete, will provide an adequate description of the primary concept of statistical modeling. Secondly, this preliminary discussion will help the reader keep an eye on the forest, and not get distracted by the trees, as the formal argument of the next few sections unfolds. We note at the outset that when this formal argument unfolds completely in chapter 4, it will be shown that a simple statistical model can be viewed as a mathematization of the notion of a generic random experiment.

2.2.2   The basic structure of a simple statistical model

The **simple statistical model**, first aluded to by Fisher (1922), has two interrelated components:

[i]   Probability model: $\Phi = \{f(x;\theta),\ \theta \in \Theta,\ x \in \mathbb{R}_X\}$,
[ii]   Sampling model: $\mathbf{X} := (X_1, X_2, ..., X_n)$ is a random sample.

The *probability model* specifies a family of *densities* $(f(x;\theta),\ \theta \in \Theta)$, defined over the range of values $(\mathbb{R}_X)$ of the random variable X; one density function for each value of the *parameter* θ, as the latter varies over its range of values Θ: *the parameter space.* As we can see, when defining the concept of a probability model we need to introduce several other concepts, each one of which will require several pages of formal discussion to be explained. Indeed, the remaining sections in this and the next chapter deal with all these concepts. The purpose of the present section is to provide a less formal but intuitive explanation for some of these concepts as a prelude to the discussion that follows.

TERMINOLOGY. The simple statistical model as specified above is often called *parametric* because it is defined in terms of the parameter θ.

The most effective way to visualize the notion of a probability model is in terms of the diagram in figure 2.1.

This diagram represents several members of a particular family of densities known as the one parameter *Gamma* family and takes the explicit form:

$$\Phi = \left\{ f(x;\theta) = \frac{x^{\theta-1}}{\Gamma[\theta]} \exp\{-x\},\ \theta \in \mathbb{R}_+,\ x \in \mathbb{R}_+ \right\}. \tag{2.1}$$

NOTE that the particular formula is of no intrinsic interest at this stage. What is important for the discussion in this section is to use this example in order to get some idea as to

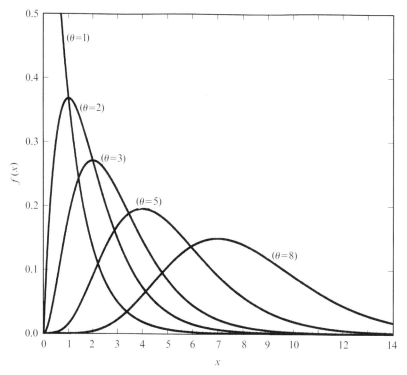

Figure 2.1 A Gamma probability model

what types of things lie behind the various symbols used in the generic case. For instance, the parameter space Θ and the range of values $\mathbb{R}_X$ of the random variable X, are the positive real line $\mathbb{R}_+ := (0, \infty)$, i.e., $\Theta := \mathbb{R}_+$ and $\mathbb{R}_X := \mathbb{R}_+$. Each curve in figure 2.1 represents the graph of one density function (varying over a subset of the range of values of the random variable X: $(0,14] \subset \mathbb{R}_+$) for a specific value of the parameter θ. In figure 2.1 we can see five such curves for the values: $\theta = 1,2,3,5,8$; the latter being a small subset of the parameter space $\mathbb{R}_+$. In other words, the graphs of the density functions shown in figure 2.1 represent a small subset of the set of densities in (2.1). This is, however, a minor detail. Figure 2.1 illustrates the notion of a probability model by helping us visualize several densities indexed by the parameter θ.

Let us now briefly discuss the various concepts invoked in the above illustration, beginning with the notion of a random variable.

2.2.3   The notion of a random variable: a simplistic view

The notion of a random variable constitutes one of the most important concepts in the theory of probability. For a proper understanding of the concept the reader is required to read through to chapter 3. In order to come to grips with the notion at an intuitive level, however, let us consider the simplistic view of the notion of a random variable, first introduced by Chebyshev (1821–1884) in the middle of the 19th century. He defined a random variable as:

a real variable which can assume different values with different probabilities.

This definition comes close to the spirit of the modern concept but it leaves a lot to be desired from the mathematical viewpoint.

As shown in chapter 3, a random variable is a *function* from a set of outcomes to the real line; attaching numbers to outcomes! The need to define such a function arises because the outcomes of certain stochastic phenomena do not always come in the form of numbers but the data do. The simplistic view of a random variable, in an attempt to simplify the concept, suppresses the set of outcomes and identifies the notion of a random variable with its range of values $\mathbb{R}_X$; hence the term *variable*:

Example
In the case of the experiment of casting two dice and looking at the uppermost faces, discussed in chapter 1, the outcomes come in the form of combinations of die faces (not numbers!), all 36 such combinations, denoted by, say, $\{s_1, s_2, \ldots, s_{36}\}$. We bypassed the many faces problem by proceeding directly to counting the total number of dots appearing on the two faces. This, in a sense, amounts to defining a random variable:

X: a function from the set of outcomes to the subset of the real line $\mathbb{R}_X := \{2, 3, \ldots, 12\}$:

$$X(.): \{s_1, s_2, \ldots, s_{36}\} \rightarrow \{2, 3, \ldots, 12\}.$$

However, this is not the only random variable we could have defined. Another such function might be to map the odd sums to 0 and the even sums to 1, i.e.

$$Y(.): \{s_1, s_2, \ldots, s_{36}\} \rightarrow \{0,1\}.$$

This example suggests that suppressing the outcomes set and identifying the random variable with its range of values can sometimes be misleading. Be that as it may, let us take this interpretation at face value and proceed to consider the other important dimension of the simplistic view of a random variable: its randomness. In an attempt to distinguish a random variable X from an ordinary mathematical variable, the simplistic view proceeds to associate probabilities with the range of its values $\mathbb{R}_X$. The simplest way to explain this dimension is to return to the above example.

Example
In the case of the experiment of casting two dice and counting the dots at the uppermost faces, we defined two random variables, which the simplistic view identifies with their respective range of values:

$$X \text{ with } \{2, 3, \ldots, 12\} \text{ and } Y \text{ with } \{0,1\}.$$

In the case of the random variable X the association of its values and the probabilities, as shown in chapter 1, takes the form:

x	2	3	4	5	6	7	8	9	10	11	12	
$f(x)$	$\frac{1}{36}$	$\frac{2}{36}$	$\frac{3}{36}$	$\frac{4}{36}$	$\frac{5}{36}$	$\frac{6}{36}$	$\frac{5}{36}$	$\frac{4}{36}$	$\frac{3}{36}$	$\frac{2}{36}$	$\frac{1}{36}$	(2.2)

After some thought, the relation between the values of the random variable Y and the associated probabilities takes the form:

y	0	1	
$f(y)$	$\frac{1}{2}$	$\frac{1}{2}$	(2.3)

It is important to note that the density function is defined by:

$$\mathbb{P}(X=x)=f(x), \text{ for all } x \in \mathbb{R}_X, \tag{2.4}$$

and satisfies the properties:

$$\textbf{(a)}\, f_x(x) \geq 0, \text{ for all } x \in \mathbb{R}_X, \quad \textbf{(b)}\, \sum_{x_i \in \mathbb{R}_X} f_x(x_i) = 1.$$

The last property just says that adding up the probabilities for all values of the random variable will give us one; verify this in the case of the above examples. The density function can be visualized as distributing a unit of mass (probability) over the range of values of X.

Continuous random variables

The above example involves two random variables which comply perfectly with Chebyshev's simplistic definition. With each value of the random variable we associate a probability. This is because both random variables are discrete: their range of values is *countable*. On the other hand, when a random variable takes values over an interval, i.e., its range of values is *uncountable*, things are not as simple. Attaching probabilities to particular values does not work (see chapter 3) and instead, we associate probabilities with intervals which belong to this range of values. Instead of (2.4), the density function for continuous random variables is defined over intervals as follows:

$$\mathbb{P}(x \leq X < x + dx) = f(x) \cdot dx, \text{ for all } x \in \mathbb{R}_X,$$

and satisfies the properties:

$$\textbf{(a)}\, f_x(x) \geq 0, \text{ for all } x \in \mathbb{R}_X, \quad \textbf{(b)} \int_{x \in \mathbb{R}_X} f_x(x) \cdot dx = 1.$$

It is important to note that the density function for continuous random variables takes values in the interval $[0, \infty)$ and thus cannot be interpreted as probabilities. In contrast, the density function for discrete random variables takes values in the interval $[0,1]$.

2.2.4 Parametric density functions

The densities of the random variables X and Y associated with the casting of the two dice experiment, introduced above, involve no unknown parameters because the probabilities are known. This has been the result of implicitly assuming that the dice are symmetric and each side arises with the same probability. In the case where it is known that the dice are loaded, the above densities will change in the sense that they will now involve some unknown parameters. For example, assuming that $\mathbb{P}(Y=1) = \theta$ (an unknown parameter), $0 \leq \theta \leq 1$, the density function of Y now takes the form:

y	0	1
$f(y;\theta)$	$1-\theta$	θ

(2.5)

This can be expressed in the more compact form of the formula:

$$f(y;\theta) = \theta^y (1-\theta)^{1-y}, \ \theta \in [0,1], \ y=0,1,$$

known as the **Bernoulli** density, with $\Theta := [0,1]$ and $\mathbb{R}_Y = \{0,1\}$.

The notion of a parametric distribution (density) goes back to the 18th century with Bernoulli proposing the **Binomial** distribution with density function:

$$f(x;\theta) = \binom{n}{x} \theta^x (1-\theta)^{n-x}, \ \theta \in [0,1], \ x=0,1, \ n=1,2, \ldots,$$

where $\binom{n}{x} = \frac{n!}{(n-x)!x!}$, $n! = n \cdot (n-1) \cdot (n-2) \cdots (3) \cdot (2) \cdot (1)$. In the early 19th century de Moivre and Laplace introduced the **Normal** distribution whose density takes the form:

$$f(x;\theta) = \frac{1}{\sigma\sqrt{2\pi}} \exp\left\{ -\frac{1}{2\sigma^2}(x-\mu)^2 \right\}, \ \theta := (\mu,\sigma^2) \in \mathbb{R} \times \mathbb{R}_+, \ x \in \mathbb{R}.$$

The real interest in parametric densities, however, began with Pearson (1895) who proposed a family of distributions known today as the Pearson family. This family is generated as a solution of a differential equation:

$$\frac{df(x)}{dx} = f(x)\left[\frac{(x-\theta_0)}{\theta_1 + \theta_2 x + \theta_3 x^2} \right], \ x \in \mathbb{R}_X.$$

(2.6)

Depending on the values taken by the parameters $(\theta_0, \theta_1, \theta_2, \theta_3)$, this equation can generate several well-known density functions such as the Student's t, the Laplace, the Pareto, the Gamma, and the Beta (see appendix A), in addition to the Normal. A discrete version of the above differential equation can be used to generate several well-known distributions such as the binomial, the Negative Binomial, the Hypergeometric and the Poisson (see appendix A). For a more extensive discussion of the Pearson family see chapter 4.

The parameter(s) θ

As can be seen in figure 2.1, the parameters θ are related to features of the density function such as the shape and the location. As the values of the parameters θ change over their range of values Θ, the parameter space, a whole collection of such densities is created. As shown in the next chapter, in order to understand and use these parameters more effectively we relate them to the so-called moments of the distribution. At this stage it is sufficient to remember that the parameters θ play a very important role in the context of empirical modeling and statistical inference.

The notion of a simple statistical model and its first component, a parametric family of densities, will be discussed at length in chapter 3 and thus no further discussion will be given in this section; see appendix A for a more complete list of parametric densities.

2.2.5 A random sample: a preliminary view

What makes the generic statistical model specified in section 2.2.2, *simple* is the form of the sampling model, the *random sample* assumption. This assumption involves two inter-related notions known as **Independence** and **Identical Distribution**. In order to explain these notions adequately we will need some of the concepts to be introduced in the next few sections. However, these notions can be explained intuitively as a prelude to the more formal discussion that follows:

> **Independence** The random variables $(X_1, X_2, \ldots, X_n)$ are said to be *independent* if the occurrence of any one, say X_i, does not influence and is not influenced by the occurrence of any other random variable in the set, say X_j, for $i \neq j$, $i,j = 1, 2, \ldots, n$.
>
> **Identical Distribution** The independent random variables $(X_1, X_2, \ldots, X_n)$ are said to be *identically distributed* if their density functions are identical in the sense:
>
> $$f(x_1;\theta) = f(x_2;\theta) = \cdots = f(x_n;\theta).$$

For observational data the validity of the IID assumptions can often be assessed using a battery of graphical techniques discussed in chapters 5–6. In these chapters we will discuss the connection between the probabilistic notions making a simple statistical model (such as Independence and Identical Distribution) and several graphical displays of real data. This discussion is particularly relevant for modeling observational data.

   For a better understanding of the notion of a random sample, it is worth considering the question of ensuring the appropriateness of IID assumptions in the case of sample survey data using a simple Bernoulli model. Before considering this question, it is important to emphasize that the appropriateness of the IID assumptions in experimental data, in contrast to observational data, is a matter of *good design*.

Example

Consider the problem of designing a sample survey in order to evaluate the voting intentions of the US electorate in the next presidential election. Assuming that there are only two candidates, the Democratic and Republican nominees, we can define the random variable:

$$X(\text{Democratic nominee}) = 1, \quad X(\text{Republican nominee}) = 0,$$

with the associated probabilities:

$$\mathbb{P}(X = 1) = \theta, \ \mathbb{P}(X = 0) = 1 - \theta.$$

This enables us to use the Bernoulli distribution and the question which arises is how to design a sample survey, of size $n = 1000$, so as to ensure that the random sample of the Bernoulli model as specified above is appropriate. In order to develop some intuition in relation to the notion of a random sample, let us consider a number of ways to collect sample surveys which *do not* constitute a random sample:

(a) Picking "at random" 1000 subscribers from the local telephone directory and ask them to register their voting intentions.

(b) Sending a team of students to the local shopping center to ask the first 1000 people entering the mall.

(c) Driving through all 51 states, stop at the largest shopping mall of the state capital and ask as many voters as the ratio of the voters of that state, to the total voting population allows.

In all three cases our action will not give rise to a random sample because:

(i) it does not give every potential voter the same likelihood of being asked; not everybody has a phone or goes to the mall, and

(ii) the local nature of the selection in cases (a) and (b) excludes the majority of the voting population; this induces some *heterogeneity* into the sample. The last feature might even induce some *dependence* in the sample if there is some local issue that renders the local population pro-Democrat or pro-Republican.

Why example a, b, c are not random samples

Theoretically, a way to design a random sample in this case is to allocate a number to every voter, irrespective of location, and then let a computer draw at random 1000 numbers. Then proceed to ask the voters corresponding to these numbers for their voting intentions. This is often impossible to achieve for a number of reasons beyond the scope of the present discussion; for further discussion see chapter 11.

In concluding this section it is interesting to NOTE that historically the assumption of a random sample has been implicitly used in empirical modeling throughout the 18th, 19th and the early 20th centuries. The territory of Dependence and/or non-Identical Distributions was largely uncharted until the first quarter of the 20th century.

2.2.6 Jumping ahead?

At this stage, the mathematically fainthearted readers are advised to proceed to section 3.4.2 where the discussion relating to the notion of a parametric family of densities continues. The brave are strongly advised to toil through the next several sections in order to get a more complete and coherent picture of the probabilistic foundations.

2.3   Probability theory: an introduction

2.3.1 Outlining the early milestones of probability theory

In an attempt to give the reader some idea as to the origins and the development of probability theory, we put forward an outline map, charting the historical development of probability in an attempt to semaphore the most important milestones over the last four centuries; for a more detailed account see Stigler (1986), Porter (1986), Hacking (1975), Hald (1990) and Maistrov (1974).

Glimpses of probabilistic ideas relating to odds in dice and card games can be traced back to the middle of the 16th century to **Gerlamo Cardano** (1501–1576) in his book *The book on dice games*, published posthumously in 1663. Cardano calculated the odds in dice and card games of chance in the context of discussing fair bets and introduced the idea of the *number of equally possible outcomes* and the proportion relating to an event. Apart from certain isolated instances of combinatorial calculations, nothing very significant happened for the next century or so until the well-known series of letters between **Pierre de Fermat** (1601–1665) and **Blaise Pascal** (1623–1662) in relation to probabilities associated with games of chance. The origins of probability theory as providing systematic ways for solving problems in games of chance appeared in these letters. Pascal and Fermat are credited with the first correct answer to an old problem of *dividing the stakes when a fair game is stopped before either player wins*. The next important milestone was the book *How to reason in dice games* by **Christiaan Huyghens** (1629–1695) which proved to be the first widely read textbook on probability for games of chance. Huyghens introduced the fundamental notion of *mathematical expectation* and the basic rules of addition and multiplication of probabilities. The next influential book on probability entitled *The art of conjecturing* was written by **James Bernoulli** (1654–1705) but published posthumously in 1713 by his nephew Nicolas. This was a turning point for probability theory because it went beyond the probabilities associated with games of chance and proved the first of the so-called *limit theorems* known today as the Law of Large Numbers as a justification for using observed frequencies as probabilities. This thread was taken up by **Abraham de Moivre** (1667–1754) who proved the second limit theorem, known today as the Central Limit theorem, in his book *The doctrine of chances* published in 1718. Important notions such as *independence* and *conditional probabilities* are formalized for the first time by de Moivre.

Pierre Simon Laplace (1749–1827) in his book *The analytical theory of probability*, published in 1812, drew together and extended the previous results on probabilities associated with games of chance and the limit theorems and related these results to the development of methods for reconciling observations. Laplace and **Carl Frederic Gauss** (1777–1855) founded the tradition known as the *theory of errors* which linked probability theory to the modeling of observed data by operationalizing the Central Limit theorem effect and introducing the method of *least squares*. This was achieved by viewing errors of observations as the cumulative effect of numerous independent errors. The reign of the Normal distribution began with Laplace and Gauss (hence Gaussian distribution) and continues unabated to this day. Laplace's synthesis of probability theory and the reconciliation of observations provided the foundation of mathematical statistics: analysis of data by fitting models to observations.

During the 19th century probability theory was identified with limit theorems and the dividing line between the probability of an event and its frequency of realization in a sequence of trials was nebulous. As a result of this, probability theory was introduced in diverse fields such as jurisprudence and social physics as well as in the analysis of real life data on population, mortality, and insurance risks.

The foundations of probability provided by games of chance proved wholly inadequate for the new applications of probability and the search for new foundations began with **Lvovich Pafnufty Chebyshev** (1821–1884) and was extended by his students **Andrei Andreiwich Markov** (1856–1922) and **Alexander Michailovich Lyapunov** (1857–1918). Chebyshev introduced the notion of a random variable and opened several new research paths with just four publications. His students Markov and Lyapunov met the challenge admirably and all three had a profound effect on probability theory. Their lasting effect is better seen in the limit theorems where they developed revolutionary new methods for studying the asymptotic behavior of sums of independent random variables. The modern mathematical foundations of probability theory were provided by **Andrei Nikolaevich Kolmogorov** (1903–1989) in his book *Foundations of probability theory* first published in 1933. This book established probability theory as part of mathematics proper and provided the understructure for modern statistical inference which had been founded a decade earlier by **Ronald A. Fisher** (1890–1963).

It is interesting to note that statistical inference and probability theory developed largely independently of each other during the first half of the 20th century; there is not a single reference to Kolmogorov's work in Fisher's three books (1925,1935,1956)! The first serious attempt to fuse the two lines of thought should be credited to Harald Cramer (1946); see also Cramer (1976). He begins his preface by stating:

During the last 25 years, statistical science has made great progress, thanks to the brilliant schools of British and American statisticians, among whom the name Professor R. A. Fisher should be mentioned in the foremost place. During the same time, largely owing to the work of French and Russian mathematicians, the classical calculus of probability has developed into a purely mathematical theory satisfying modern standards with respect to rigor. The purpose of the present work is to join these two lines of development in an exposition of the mathematical theory of modern statistical methods, in so far as these are based on the concept of probability...   (Cramer (1946), p. vii)

Since then, very few books in statistical inference make a purposeful attempt to bridge the gap between probability theory and data analysis using inference procedures. The present book attempts to follow in Cramer's footsteps by making a concerted effort to propose a bridge between the theoretical construct of a statistical model and the observed data.

2.3.2   A pragmatic approach to probability theory

Intuitively we can think of probability as an attempt to tame *chance regularity*. The failure to provide a satisfactory intrinsic definition of probability is mainly due to our failure to come to grips with the notion of chance regularity in a generally acceptable way. However, for most purposes the axiomatic (mathematical) definition, as given in section 5 below, is adequate. This definition amounts to saying that probability is what we define it to be via the chosen properties (axioms)!

The well-known axiomatic approach to a branch of mathematics, going back to Euclid, specifies the basic axioms and primitive objects and then develops the theory (theorems, lemmas, etc.) using deductive logic. The approach adopted in this chapter (see also Spanos (1986)) is somewhat more pragmatic in the sense that the axioms and basic concepts will be motivated by striving to formalize the regularity patterns exhibited by observable chance mechanisms of the type we seek to model in the context of probability theory. In particular, the basic concepts will be introduced initially as a formalization of a simple chance mechanism we call a *random experiment*. This approach has certain advantages for non-mathematicians over the usual axiomatic approach.

First, it enables the reader to keep an eye on the forest and not get distracted by the beauty or the ugliness (beauty is in the eye of the beholder) of the trees. It is imperative for the student not to lose sight of the main objective of probability theory, which is to provide a framework in the context of which stochastic phenomena can be modeled.

Second, motivating the mathematical concepts using a particular chance mechanism enables us to provide a manifest direct link between observable phenomena and abstract mathematical concepts throughout. This enhances the intuition for the mathematical concepts and gives an idea why we need these concepts.

Third, historically the development of many branches of mathematics follows the pragmatic approach and the axiomatization follows after the branch in question has reached a certain maturity. Probability theory existed for many centuries before it was axiomatized in 1933.

Fourth, it enables us to begin with a somewhat simplified mathematical structure, by formalizing a simple enough chance mechanism. We can then proceed to extend the mathematical apparatus to broaden its intended scope and encompass more realistic chance mechanisms of the type we encounter in econometrics.

2.3.3   A word of caution

Due to the simplicity of the random experiment, its formalization gives rise to a statistical model which is not adequate for modeling a number of stochastic phenomena in econometrics. The main objective of chapters 6–8 is to extend the domain of applicability in order to enable us to model more realistic observable phenomena of interest, such as the behavior of inflation, interest rates, and stock returns. The probability concepts introduced in these chapters will allow us to enrich the structure of a simple statistical model in order to accommodate features of observational as opposed to experimental data, rendering them suitable for modeling economic phenomena such as the ones mentioned above. Our eagerness to extend the intended scope of a simple statistical model, in a certain sense, constitutes the main difference between the present book and other books intended to provide the probabilistic foundations for statistical inference.

2.4   **Random experiments**

We remind the reader again that the purpose of introducing the notion of a random experiment is twofold. First, to give immediately an idea as to the nature of the stochastic phenomena we have in mind using a particularly simple example. Second, to bring out the essential features of such simple phenomena and then formalize them in a precise mathematical form. This will enable us to motivate the concepts of probability theory using intuitive notions as they relate to simple observable chance mechanisms. The notion of a random experiment is given a mathematical formulation in the form of a *statistical model* in the next two chapters. In the present chapter we present the first more abstract form of the formalization, known as the *statistical space*. The discussion that follows reverses the order followed by Kolmogorov (1933) in the sense that we begin with the phenomena of interest and proceed to formulate the axioms. The abstract notion of a statistical space provides the mathematical foundations of probability theory, and its less abstract form, that of a statistical model, provides an operational form useful for modeling purposes. The concept of a statistical space is formulated in this chapter and that of the statistical model in the next two chapters.

2.4.1 The notion of a random experiment

We note that the notion of a random experiment can be traced back to Kolmogorov's monograph entitled *Foundations of the theory of probability*, first published in 1933 in German and generally acknowledged as the book that founded modern probability theory (see pages 3–4).

A **random experiment** $\mathcal{E}$, is defined as a chance mechanism which satisfies the following conditions:

[a]   all possible distinct outcomes are known a priori,
[b]   in any particular trial the outcome is not known a priori but there exists a perceptible regularity of occurrence associated with these outcomes, and
[c]   it can be repeated under identical conditions.

Examples
[1]   Toss a coin and note the outcome. Assuming that we can repeat the experiment under identical conditions, this is a random experiment because the above conditions are satisfied. The possible distinct outcomes are: $\{H,T\}$, where (H) and (T) stand for "Heads" and "Tails," respectively.

[2]   Toss a coin twice and note the outcome. The possible distinct outcomes are:

$$\{(HH),(HT),(TH),(TT)\}.$$

[3]   Toss a coin three times and note the outcome. The possible distinct outcomes are:

$$\{(THH),(HHH),(HHT),(HTH),(TTT),(HTT),(THT),(TTH)\}.$$

[4]   Tossing a coin until the first "Heads" shows up. The possible distinct outcomes are:

$$\{(H),(TH),(TTH),(TTTH),(TTTTH),(TTTTTH),\ldots\}.$$

[5]   A document is transmitted repeatedly over a noisy channel until an error-free copy arrives. Count the number of transmissions needed. This represents a more realistic case of stochastic phenomena but it can be viewed as a random experiment since the above conditions can be ensured in practice. The possible distinct outcomes include all natural numbers:

$$\mathbb{N} := \{1,2,3,\ldots\}$$

[6] Count the number of calls arriving in a telephone exchange over a period of time. The possible distinct outcomes include all integers from 0 to infinity:

$$\mathbb{N}_0 := \{0, 1, 2, 3, ...\}.$$

[7] Measure the lifetime of a light bulb in a typical home environment. In theory the possible distinct outcomes include any real number from zero to infinity: $[0, \infty)$.

Let us also mention an observable stochastic phenomenon which does not constitute a random experiment.

[8] Observe the closing daily price of IBM shares on the New York stock exchange. The conditions [a]–[b] of a random experiment are easily applicable. [a] The possible distinct outcomes are real numbers between zero and infinity: $[0, \infty)$. [b] The closing IBM share price on a particular day is not known a priori. Condition [c], however, is inappropriate because the circumstances from one day to the next change and today's share prices are related to yesterday's. Millions of people use this information in an effort to "buy low" and "sell high" to make money.

2.4.2 A bird's eye view of the argument

The formalization of the notion of a random experiment will occupy us for the next two chapters. In the process of formalization several new concepts and ideas will be introduced. The ultimate aim is to set up a mathematical framework for modeling economic data which exhibit chance regularity. However, we begin with a simple case. In the discussion that follows, we will often find ourselves digressing from the main story line in an effort to do justice to the concepts introduced. Hence, it is of paramount importance for the reader to keep one eye firmly on the forest and not get distracted by the trees. With that in mind let us summarize the proposed formalization.

The *first step* will be to formalize condition [a], by defining the set of all possible distinct outcomes (S) (see section 3). In section 4 we take the *second step* which is concerned with the formalization of condition [b], relating to the uncertainty of the particular outcome in each trial. Even though at each trial the particular outcome is not known a priori, we often have information as to which outcomes are more probable (they are likely to occur more often) than others. This information will be formalized by attaching *probabilities* to the set of outcomes defined in the first step. In these two steps we construct what we call a *probability space*. It's worth summarizing the construction of a probability space to help the reader keep his/her eyes on the forest. We begin with a collection (a set) S of what we call *elementary events* and then proceed to define another collection $\mathfrak{F}$, made up of subsets of S we call *events*, so that $\mathfrak{F}$ is closed under set union, intersection and complementation. Probability is then defined as a non-negative function $\mathbb{P}(.)$ from $\mathfrak{F}$ to the subset of the real line $[0,1]$; assumed to satisfy $\mathbb{P}(S) = 1$ and the additivity property:

for $A \in \mathfrak{F}$, $B \in \mathfrak{F}$ and $A \cap B = \emptyset$, then $\mathbb{P}(A \cup B) = \mathbb{P}(A) + \mathbb{P}(B)$.

In the *third step*, taken in section 5, we will formalize condition [c]. The notion of repeating the experiment under identical conditions will be formalized in the form of *random trials*: a set of independent and identical trials.

The forest: the formalization of a random experiment into a simple statistical model is the main objective of this and the next two chapters.

The trees: the introduction of numerous concepts which enable us to supplement the simple statistical model with a view to setting up a mathematical framework for empirical modeling purposes.

2.5   Formalizing condition [a]: the outcomes set

2.5.1   The notion of a set

The first step in constructing a mathematical model for a random experiment is to formalize the notion of all distinct outcomes. We do this by collecting them together and defining a set. The notion of *a set* in the present context is used informally as *a collection of distinct objects* which we call its *elements*.

Example

$S = \{\clubsuit, \diamondsuit, \heartsuit, +\}$ is a set with elements the card suits and the plus sign:

$\clubsuit \in S$: reads "$\clubsuit$ belongs to S."

REMARKS:

(i)   This is clearly not a mathematically satisfactory definition of the notion of a set, because, in a certain sense, we replaced the term *set* with that of a *collection*. This is why it is often called *naive*. It provides, however, some intuition as to what a set is.

(ii)   The notion of membership is one of the fundamental primitive concepts of set theory and we use the notation $\in$ for the notion of being an element of a set and $\notin$ for its negation. The relation $a \in A$ means that a is one of the objects that make up the set A.

(iii)   It is important to note that the nature of the objects making up a set does not enter the notion of set. Hence, naive definitions which require the elements of a set to be of the same nature are simply non-sensical.

2.5.2   The outcomes set

A set S which includes *all possible distinct outcomes* of the experiment in question is called an **outcomes set**.

TERMINOLOGY: another more widely used name for the outcomes set is the term *sample space*. We avoid this term because it is clearly a misnomer, it has nothing to do with the notion of a sample as used later.

The notion of an outcomes set formalizes condition [a] of a random experiment $\mathcal{E}$ using the idea of *a set*. This might seem like a trivial step but in fact it is the key to the whole formalization because it renders the power of *set theory* available for the formalization of the rest of the conditions defining $\mathcal{E}$. In particular, set theory will be instrumental in formalizing condition [b]. In set theoretic language the outcomes set S is the so-called *universal set:* the set to which all objects we want to consider belong.

Examples
The *outcomes sets* for the random experiments [1]–[4] are:

$$S_1 = \{H, T\},$$
$$S_2 = \{(HH), (HT), (TH), (TT)\},$$
$$S_3 = \{(THH), (HHH), (HHT), (HTH), (TTT), (HTT), (THT), (TTH)\},$$
$$S_4 = \{(H), (TH), (TTH), (TTTH), (TTTTH), (TTTTTH), \ldots\}$$

In order to utilize the notion of *the outcomes set* effectively, we need to introduce some set theoretic notation which will be used extensively in this book. The way we defined *a set* in the above examples was by listing its elements.

An alternative way to define a set is to use a *property* shared by all the elements of the set. For example, the outcomes set for experiment [5] can be written as:

$$S_5 = \{x: x \in \mathbb{N} := \{1, 2, 3, \ldots\}\},$$

which reads "S_5 is the set of all xs such that x belongs to $\mathbb{N}$," i.e., x is a *natural number.* Similarly, the set of all *real numbers* can be written as:

$$\mathbb{R} = \{x: x \text{ a real number}, -\infty < x < \infty\}.$$

Using this set we can write the outcomes set for experiment [7] as:

$$S_7 = \{x: x \in \mathbb{R}, 0 \le x < \infty\}.$$

NOTE: a shorter notation for this set is $[0, \infty)$. It is important to note that when a square bracket is used, the adjacent element is included in the set, but when an ordinary bracket is used it is excluded:

(i)   the closed interval: $[a,b] = \{x: x \in \mathbb{R}, a \le x \le b\}$,
(ii)   the open interval: $(a,b) = \{x: x \in \mathbb{R}, a < x < b\}$,
(iii)   the half-closed interval: $(-\infty, a] = \{x: x \in \mathbb{R}, -\infty < x \le a\}$.

2.5.3 Special types of sets

In relation to the above examples, it is useful to make two distinctions. The first is the distinction between finite and infinite sets and the second is the further division of infinite sets into countable and uncountable. A set A is said to be **finite** if it can be expressed in the following form:

$$A = \{a_1, a_2, \ldots, a_n\} \text{ for some integer } n.$$

A set that is not finite is said to be **infinite**.

Examples

(1)   The set $C = \{\clubsuit, \diamond, \heartsuit\}$ is finite.

(2)   The intervals $[a,b]$, (a,b), $(-\infty,x]$ define infinite sets of numbers.

(3)   The most important infinite set in mathematics is the *real line*, defined by:
$$\mathbb{R} = \{x: x \text{ a real number}, -\infty < x < \infty\}.$$

(4)   The following sets are some of the most important infinite sets of *numbers*:
   (i)   natural numbers: $\mathbb{N} = \{1, 2, 3, \ldots\}$,
   (ii)   integers: $\mathbb{Z} = \{0, \pm 1, \pm 2, \pm 3, \ldots\}$,
   (iii)   rational numbers: $\mathbb{Q} = \left\{\frac{n}{m}: m \in \mathbb{Z} \text{ and } n \in \mathbb{N}\right\}$,
   (iv)   positive real numbers: $\mathbb{R}_+ = \{x: x \in \mathbb{R}, 0 < x < \infty\}$.

Among the infinite sets we need to distinguish between the ones whose elements we can arrange in a sequence and those whose elements are so many and so close together that no such ordering is possible. For obvious reasons we call the former countable and the latter uncountable. More formally, a set A is said to be **countable** if it is either finite or infinite and each element of A can be matched with a distinct natural number, i.e., there is a one-to-one matching of the elements of A with the elements of $\mathbb{N}$.

Examples

(1)   The set of *even* natural numbers is countable because we can define the following one-to-one correspondence between $\mathbb{N}_{even}$ and $\mathbb{N}$:

$$\mathbb{N}_{even} := \{2 \quad 4 \quad 6 \quad 8 \quad 10 \cdots 2n \cdots\}$$
$$\updownarrow \quad \updownarrow \quad \updownarrow \quad \updownarrow \quad \updownarrow \qquad \updownarrow$$
$$\mathbb{N} := \{1 \quad 2 \quad 3 \quad 4 \quad 5 \cdots n \cdots\}.$$

(2)   The set of *integers* is a countable set because we can define the following one-to-one correspondence:

$$\mathbb{Z} := \{\cdots -3 \quad -2 \quad -1 \quad 0 \quad 1 \quad 2 \quad 3 \cdots\}$$
$$\updownarrow \quad \updownarrow \quad \updownarrow \quad \updownarrow \quad \updownarrow \quad \updownarrow \quad \updownarrow$$
$$\mathbb{N} := \{\cdots 7 \quad 5 \quad 3 \quad 1 \quad 2 \quad 4 \quad 6 \cdots\}.$$

(3)   The set $\mathbb{Q}$ of *rational numbers* is a countable set. The one-to-one correspondence is more complicated in this case and beyond the scope of this book (see Binmore (1980)).

In view of the fact that between any two natural numbers, say $[1,2]$, there is an infinity of both rational and real numbers, intuition might suggest that the two sets $\mathbb{Q}$ and $\mathbb{R}$ have roughly speaking the same number of elements. In this case intuition is wrong! The set of real numbers is more numerous than the set of rational numbers (see Binmore (1980)):

$$\aleph_1 := [\text{number of elements of } \mathbb{R}] > \aleph_0 := [\text{number of elements } \mathbb{Q}]$$

An infinite set whose number of elements (coordinality) is of the same magnitude as that of $\mathbb{R}$, is called **uncountable**.

Example
The sets $\mathbb{R}$, $[a,b]$, (a,b), $(-\infty,x]$ are *uncountable*.

REMARK: giving examples of real numbers which are not rational numbers (irrational numbers) is not as straightforward as it might seem because we often use decimal approximations of irrational numbers. The most famous irrational number is the well-known ratio of the circumference to the diameter of a circle: $\pi = 3.1415926535897\ldots$; the three dots at the end of the last digit signify that the sequence would go on to infinity. What distinguishes rational and irrational numbers, when expressed in decimal form, is that in the case of rational numbers, when they have infinite decimal expansions, the sequence of digits will eventually repeat itself but for an irrational number no discernible pattern in the sequence exists; see chapter 10.

2.6   Formalizing condition [b]: events and probabilities

Having formalized condition [a] of **random experiment** ($\mathscr{E}$) in the form of an outcomes set, we can proceed to formalize the second condition:

[b] in any particular trial the outcome is not known a priori but there exists a percept-
      ible regularity of occurrence associated with these outcomes.

This condition entails two dimensions which appear contradictory at first sight. The first dimension is that individual outcomes are largely unpredictable but the second is that there exists some knowledge about their occurrence. In tossing a coin twice we have no idea which of the four outcomes will occur but we know that there exists some regularity associated with these outcomes. The way we deal with both of these dimensions is to formalize the perceptible regularity at the aggregate level. This formalization will proceed in two steps. The first involves the formalization of the notion of *events of interest* and the second takes the form of *attaching probabilities* to these events.

In this introduction we used a number of new notions which will be made more precise in what follows. One of these notions is that of an *event*. Intuitively, an event is a statement in relation to a random experiment for which the only thing that matters is its *occurrence value,* i.e., whether in a particular trial it has occurred or not. So far the only such statements we encountered are the *elementary outcomes.* For modeling purposes, however, we need to broaden this set of statements to include not just elementary outcomes but also combinations of them.

How do such events differ from elementary outcomes?

Example
In the context of the random experiment **[2]**: tossing a coin twice with the outcomes set $S_2 := \{(HH),(HT),(TH),(TT)\}$ we might be interested in the following events:

(a) $A-$ at least one H: $A = \{(HH),(HT),(TH)\}$.
(b) $B-$ two of the same: $B = \{(HH),(TT)\}$.
(c) $C-$ at least one T: $C = \{(HT),(TH),(TT)\}$.

In general, events are formed by *combining elementary outcomes* using set theoretic operations and we say that an event A has occurred when any one of its elementary outcomes occurs. In order to make this more precise we need to take a detour into set theoretic terrain.

2.6.1   A digression: set theoretic operations

Subsets
The concept of an event is formally defined using the notion of a subset. If A and S are sets, we say that A is a *subset* of S and denote it by $A \subset S$ if every element of A is also an element of S. More formally,

$$A \subset S \text{ if for each } a \in A \text{ implies } a \in S.$$

Examples
(1)   The set $D_1 = \{\clubsuit, \heartsuit\}$ is said to be a *subset* of $D = \{\clubsuit, \diamondsuit, \heartsuit\}$, and denoted by $D_1 \subset D$, because every element of D_1 is also an element of D.

(2)   The sets $\mathbb{N}, \mathbb{Z}, \mathbb{Q}, \mathbb{R}_+$ introduced above are all subsets of $\mathbb{R}$.

(3)   In the case of the outcomes set $S_2 := \{(HH),(HT),(TH),(TT)\}$ there are four elementary outcomes. By combining these we can form events such as:

$$A = \{(HH),(HT),(TH)\}, B = \{(HH),(TT)\}, C = \{(HH)\}, D = \{(HT),(TH)\}.$$

More formally events are subsets of S formed by applying the following set theoretic operations: *union* ($\cup$), *intersection* ($\cap$), and *complementation* ($^-$) to elements of S.

Union
The *union* of A and B, denoted by $A \cup B$, is defined as follows:

$A \cup B$: the set of outcomes that are either in A or B (or both).

More formally:

$$A \cup B := \{x : x \in A \text{ or } x \in B\}.$$

Example
For the sets $A = \{(HH),(TT)\}$ and $B = \{(TT),(TH)\}$:

$$A \cup B = \{(HH),(TH),(TT)\}.$$

Intersection

The *intersection* of A and B, denoted by $A \cap B$, is defined as follows:

$A \cap B$: the set of outcomes that are in both A and B.

More formally:

$$A \cap B := \{x : x \in A \text{ and } x \in B\}.$$

Example

In the case of events A and B defined above:

$$A \cap B = \{(TT)\}.$$

Complementation

The *complement* of an event A, relative to the universal set S, denoted by $\overline{A}$, is defined as follows:

$\overline{A}$: the set of outcomes in the universal set S which are not in A.

More formally:

$$\overline{A} := \{x : x \in S \text{ and } x \notin A\}.$$

The above three operations are illustrated in figure 2.2 using Venn diagrams. Note that the rectangle in the Venn diagrams represents the outcomes set S.

Examples

(i)   In the case of events A and B defined above: $\overline{A} = \{(TT)\}$, $\overline{B} = \{(TH),(HT)\}$. The union of A and $\overline{A}$ gives S i.e., $A \cup \overline{A} = S$ and their intersection yields the **empty set**, i.e., $A \cap \overline{A} = \{\} := \emptyset$. Also, $\overline{S} = \emptyset$ and $\overline{\emptyset} = S$.

(ii)   For the sets $A = \{(HH),(HT),(TH)\}$, $B = \{(HH),(TT)\}$, $C = \{(HH)\}$, $D = \{(HT),(TH)\}$:

$$A \cap B = \{(HH)\} = C \quad \text{and} \quad B \cap D = \emptyset.$$

(iii)   The complement of the set of rational numbers $\mathbb{Q}$ with respect to the set of real numbers $\mathbb{R}$:

$$\overline{\mathbb{Q}} := \{x : x \in \mathbb{R} \text{ and } x \notin \mathbb{Q}\}$$

is known as the infinite set of *irrational numbers*.

Using complementation we can define a duality result between unions and intersections:

[1] $\overline{(A \cup B)} = \overline{A} \cap \overline{B}.$

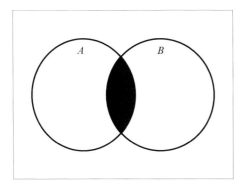

Figure 2.2 (a) Venn diagram of $A \cap B$

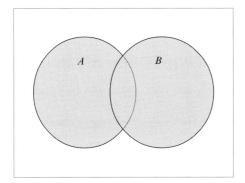

Figure 2.2 (b) Venn diagram of $A \cup B$

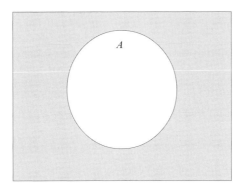

Figure 2.2 (c) Venn diagram of $\overline{A} = S - A$

Example

In the case of the sets $A = \{(HH),(HT)\}$ and $C = \{(HH)\}$ defined above, $(A \cup C) = A$ and thus: $\overline{(A \cup C)} = \overline{A} = \{(TT)\}$. On the other hand, $\overline{C} = \{(HT),(TH),(TT)\}$. Hence, $\overline{A} \cap \overline{C} = \{(TT)\} = \overline{(A \cup C)}$.

$$[2]\ \overline{(A \cap B)} = \overline{A} \cup \overline{B}.$$

Example

In the case of the sets A and C defined above, $(A \cap C) = C$ and thus $\overline{(A \cap C)} = \overline{C}$. On the other hand, $\overline{A} \cup \overline{C} = \{(HT),(TH),(TT)\} = \overline{C}$.

For completeness we note that by combining the above basic operations with sets we define two other operations often encountered in books on probability.

By combining the set operations of intersection and complementation we define the **difference** between two sets as follows:

$$A - B = A \cap \overline{B} := \{x : x \in A \text{ and } x \notin B\}.$$

By combining all three set operations we can define the *symmetric difference* between two sets as follows:

$$A \triangle B = (A \cap \overline{B}) \cup (\overline{A} \cap B) := \{x : x \in A \text{ or } x \in B \text{ and } x \notin (A \cap B)\}.$$

Equality of sets

Two sets are equal if they have the same elements. We can make this more precise by using the notion of a subset to define equality between two sets. In the case of two sets A and B if:

$$A \subset B \text{ and } B \subset A \text{ then } A = B.$$

Example

For the sets $A = \{\diamond, \heartsuit\}$ and $B = \{\heartsuit, \diamond\}$, we can state that $A = B$; NOTE that the order of the elements in a set is unimportant.

In concluding this subsection it is worth noting that all the above operations were defined in terms of the primitive notion of membership ($\in$) of a set.

2.6.2 Events

In set-theoretic language, an **event** is a *subset* of the outcomes set S; i.e.,

If $A \subset S$, A is an *event*.

In contrast, an **elementary outcome** s is an element of S, i.e.:

If $s \in S$, s is an *elementary outcome*.

That is, an outcome is also an event but the converse is not necessarily true. In order to distinguish between a subset and an element of a set consider the following example.

Example
Consider the sets $D = \{\clubsuit, \diamondsuit, \heartsuit\}$ and $C = \{\clubsuit, \heartsuit\}$. It is obviously true that:

$$C \subset D \text{ but } C \nsubseteq D.$$

On the other hand, in the case of the set: $E = \{(\clubsuit, \heartsuit), \diamondsuit\}$ which has two elements $(\clubsuit, \heartsuit)$ and $\diamondsuit$ C is an element of E:

$$C \in E.$$

The crucial property of an event is whether or not it has occurred in a trial. We say that $A = \{s_1, s_2, \ldots, s_k\}$ has *occurred* if one of its elements (outcomes) $s_1, s_2, \ldots, s_k$ has occurred.

Special events
In the present context there are two important events we need to introduce. The first is S itself (the universal set), referred to as the **sure event**: whatever the outcome, S occurs. In view of the fact that S is always a subset of itself ($S \subset S$), we can proceed to consider the empty set:

$$\emptyset = S - S,$$

called the **impossible event**: whatever the outcome, $\emptyset$ does not occur. NOTE that $\emptyset$ is always a subset of every S.

Using the impossible event we can define an important relation between two sets. Any two events A and B are said to be **mutually exclusive** if:

$$A \cap B = \emptyset.$$

Using the notion of mutually exclusive events in conjunction with S we define an important family of events. The events $A_1, A_2, \ldots, A_m$ are said to constitute a **partition** of S if they are:

(i)   mutually exclusive, i.e., $A_i \cap A_j = \emptyset$, for all $i \neq j$, $i, j = 1, 2, \ldots, m$, and
(ii) exhaustive, i.e., $\bigcup_{i=1}^{m} A_i = S$.

2.6.3   Event space

As argued at the beginning of this section the way we handle uncertainty relating to the outcome of a particular trial is first to structure it and then to articulate it in terms of probabilities attached to different events of interest. Having formalized the notion of an event as a subset of the outcomes set, we can proceed to make more precise the notion of *events of interest*.

An **event space** $\Im$ is a set whose elements are the events of interest as well as the related events; those we get by combining the events of interest using set theoretic operations. It is necessary to include such events because if we are interested in events A and B, we are also interested (indirectly) in $\overline{A}, \overline{B}, A \cup B, A \cap B, (\overline{A_1} \cap \overline{A_2})$, etc.:

$\overline{A}$: denotes the non-occurrence of A.

$(A \cup B)$: denotes the event that at least one of the events A or B occurs.

$(A \cap B)$: denotes the event that both A and B occur simultaneously.

In set theoretic language, an event space $\Im$ is *a set of subsets of S* which is *closed under the set theoretic operations* of union, intersection and complementation; when these operations are applied to any elements of $\Im$, the result is also an element of $\Im$. For any outcomes set S we can consider two extreme event spaces:

(a) $\Im_0 = \{S, \emptyset\}$: the *trivial* event space,
(b) $\mathcal{P}(S) = \{A : A \subset S\}$, i.e., the *power set*: the set of all subsets of S.

Neither of these extreme cases is very interesting for several reasons.

(a) The **trivial** event space $\Im_0$ is not very interesting because it contains no information; S and $\emptyset$ are known a priori.
(b) The **power set**. At first sight the set of all subsets of S seems to be an obvious choice for the event space, since it must include all the relevant events and be closed under the set theoretic operations of union, intersection, and complementation.

Example

In the case of the random experiment of tossing a coin twice the outcomes and the power sets are given as follows:

$$S_2 = \{(HH),(HT),(TH),(TT)\},$$
$$\mathcal{P}(S_2) = \{S_2,[(HH)(HT)(TH)],[(HH)(HT)(TT)],[(HH)(TH)(TT)],$$
$$[(TT)(HT)(TH)],[(HH)(HT)],[(HH)(TH)],[(HH)(TT)],[(HT)(TH)],$$
$$[(HT)(TT)],[(TH)(TT)],[(HH)],[(HT)],[(TH)],[(TT)],\emptyset\}.$$

The question that comes to mind is *whether we can always use the power set of S as the appropriate event space*. The short answer is **no** for two reasons, a practical and a mathematical one. First, in view of the fact that if S is countable and has N elements $\mathcal{P}(S)$ has 2^N elements, it often contains too many elements to be practical from the modeling viewpoint.

Example

To see this, consider the case of tossing a coin three times. The outcomes set S_3 has eight elements which implies that its power set has $2^8 = 256$ elements; too many to enumerate.

Things become more complicated in the case where S is countable but infinite, as in the case of the random experiment of "counting the number of calls coming into a telephone exchange over a period of time" where $S = \{0, 1, 2, 3, \ldots\}$. The power set of S in this case is not just infinite, it has the same order of infinity as the real numbers! Second, the mathematical reason why the power set is not always appropriate as an event space is that when the outcomes set is uncountable, such as:

$$S = \{x : 0 \leq x \leq 1, x \in \mathbb{R}\},$$

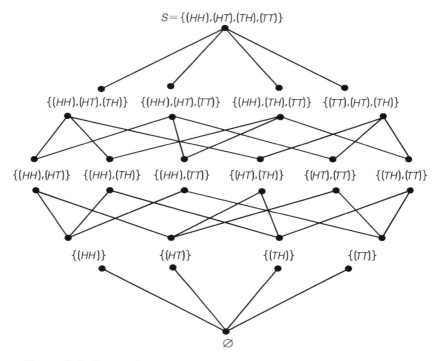

$$S = \{(HH),(HT),(TH),(TT)\}$$

$\{(HH),(HT),(TH)\}$　$\{(HH),(HT),(TT)\}$　$\{(HH),(TH),(TT)\}$　$\{(TT),(HT),(TH)\}$

$\{(HH),(HT)\}$　$\{(HH),(TH)\}$　$\{(HH),(TT)\}$　$\{(HT),(TH)\}$　$\{(HT),(TT)\}$　$\{(TH),(TT)\}$

$\{(HH)\}$　　$\{(HT)\}$　　$\{(TH)\}$　　$\{(TT)\}$

$\emptyset$

Figure 2.3 Constructing a power set

the power set includes subsets which cannot be considered as events and thus cannot be assigned probabilities. Putting it differently, if we proceed to assign probabilities to all these subsets as if they were events, we will run into technical (mathematical) difficulties (see Billingsley (1986)).

As shown below, the way to circumvent these difficulties is to avoid the power set by bestowing to the event space a specific mathematical structure (a field or a σ-field) which ensures that if A and B are events then any other events which arise when we combine these with set theoretic operations are also elements of the same event space.

Example

If we return to the random experiment of tossing a coin three times, and assume that the events of interest are only, say $A_1 = \{(HHH)\}$ and $A_2 = \{(TTT)\}$, there is no need to use the power set as the event space. Instead, we can define:

$$\Im_3 = \{S,\emptyset,A_1,A_2,(A_1 \cup A_2),\overline{A}_1,\overline{A}_2,(\overline{A}_1 \cap \overline{A}_2)\},$$

which has only 8 elements; in contrast to 256 elements in the power set. We can verify that $\Im_3$ is closed under the set theoretic operations:

$$(S_3 \cup \emptyset) = S_3 \in \Im_3, \; (S_3 \cap \emptyset) = \emptyset \in \Im_3, \quad \overline{S}_3 = \emptyset \in \Im_3, \overline{\emptyset} = S_3 \in \Im_3,$$

$$(\overline{A_1 \cup A_2}) = (\overline{A}_1 \cap \overline{A}_2) \in \Im_3, \text{ etc.}$$

The concept of an event space plays an important role in the formalization of condition [b] defining a random experiment by providing the necessary mathematical structure for a coherent assignment of probabilities to events. This is crucial for our purposes because if A and B are events of interest, the related events are also of interest because their occurrence or not is informative for the occurrence of A and B and thus we cannot ignore them when attaching probabilities.

Field   A collection $\Im$ of subsets of S, is said to be a *field* if it satisfies the conditions:

(i) $S \in \Im$,
(ii)   if $A \in \Im$ then $\overline{A}$ also belong to $\Im$,
(iii)   if $A, B \in \Im$, then $(A \cup B) \in \Im$.

This means that $\Im$ is non-empty (due to (i)) and it is closed under complementation (due to (ii)), finite unions (due to (iii)) and finite intersections (due to (ii)–(iii)).

Examples
(1)   The power set of any finite outcomes set, such as $\mathcal{P}(S_2)$, is a field.

(2) $\Im_0 = \{S, \emptyset\}$ is the trivial field for any outcomes set S. $\Im_0$ is a field because:

$$S \in \Im_0, \; S \cup \emptyset = S \in \Im_0, \; S \cap \emptyset = \emptyset \in \Im_0 \text{ and } S - \emptyset = S \in \Im_0.$$

(3) $\Im(A) = \{S, \emptyset, A, \overline{A}\}$ is the field generated by event A. $\Im(A)$ is a field because:

$$
\begin{array}{llll}
S \in \Im(A), & S \cup \emptyset = S \in \Im(A), & S \cap \emptyset = \emptyset \in \Im(A), & S - \emptyset = S \in \Im(A), \\
\overline{A} \in \Im(A), & A \cup \overline{A} = S \in \Im(A), & A \cap \overline{A} = \emptyset \in \Im(A), & A \cup S = S \in \Im(A), \\
A \cap S = A \in \Im(A), & \overline{A} \cup S = S \in \Im(A), & \overline{A} \cap S = \overline{A} \in \Im(A).
\end{array}
$$

Counter-examples
(4) $\{S, \emptyset, A, B\}$ cannot be a field because the event $(A \cup B)$ is not an element of this set, unless $B = \overline{A}$.

(5) $\{S, \emptyset, A, B, (A \cup B)\}$ cannot be a field because the event $(A \cap B)$ is not an element of this set, unless $A \cap B = \emptyset$.

(6) $\{S, A, \overline{A}\}$ cannot be a field because it does not contain $\emptyset$.

Generating a field   To illustrate how a field is generated from a set of events of interest, let us consider the case where the set is $D_1 = \{A, B\}$ and consider generating the corresponding field. In an effort to avoid getting lost in abstractions we will discuss the generation of a field in relation to our favorite example of "tossing a coin twice", where $S := \{(HH), (HT), (TH), (TT)\}$, $A = \{(HH), (HT)\}$, $B = \{(HT), (TH)\}$ and the field is the power set $\mathcal{P}(S_2)$ as defined above.

Step 1   Form the set $D_2 = \{S, \emptyset, A, B, \overline{A}, \overline{B}\}$ which includes the complements of events A and B.
        In relation to the example:

$$\overline{A} = \{(TH), (TT)\}, \; \overline{B} = \{(HH), (TT)\}.$$

Step 2 Form the set which also includes all intersections of the elements of D_2:

$$D_3 = \{S,\emptyset,A,B,\overline{A},\overline{B},(A \cap B),(\overline{A} \cap B),(A \cap \overline{B}),(\overline{A} \cap \overline{B})\}.$$

In relation to our example:

$$A \cap B = \{(HT)\}, (A \cap \overline{B}) = \{(HH)\}, (\overline{A} \cap B) = \{(TH)\}, (\overline{A} \cap \overline{B}) = \{(TT)\}.$$

Notice that these intersections generate all the events with one outcome.

Step 3 Form the set which also includes all unions of the elements of D_3:

$$\mathcal{D} = \{D_3, (A \cup B), (A \cup \overline{B}), (\overline{A} \cup B), (\overline{A} \cup \overline{B}), \text{etc.}\}.$$

In relation to our example:

$$[A \cup B] = \{(HH),(HT),(TH)\}, [A \cup \overline{B}] = \{(HH),(HT),(TT)\},$$

$$[\overline{A} \cup B] = \{(HT),(TH),(TT)\}, [\overline{A} \cup \overline{B}] = \{(HH),(TH),(TT)\},$$

$$[(A \cap \overline{B}) \cup (\overline{A} \cap B)] = \{(HH),(TH)\}, [(A \cap B) \cup (\overline{A} \cap \overline{B})] = \{(HT),(TT)\}.$$

The reader is encouraged to check that the power set of S has indeed been generated!

NOTE that $D_1 \subset D_2 \subset D_3 \subset \mathcal{D}$ and $\mathcal{D}$ is a field. Indeed, $\mathcal{D}$ is the smallest field containing D_1, referred to as *the field generated by* D_1, and denoted by $\Im(D_1) = \mathcal{D}$.

Example
In the case of tossing a coin three times:

$$S_3 = \{(HHH),(HHT),(HTT),(HTH),(TTT),(TTH),(THT),(THH)\}.$$

If the events of interest are, say $A_1 = \{(HHH)\}$ and $A_2 = \{(TTT)\}$, the set $\{A_1,A_2\}$ is clearly not a field but we can always generate such a field starting from this set. In this case the field of events of interest is:

$$\Im_3 = \{S_3,\emptyset,A_1,A_2,(A_1 \cup A_2),\overline{A}_1,\overline{A}_2,(\overline{A}_1 \cap \overline{A}_2)\}.$$

It should be clear from the above examples that generating a field using set theoretic operations, starting from a set of events of interest, is a non-trivial exercise in cases where the number of initial events of interest is greater than 2. The exception to this is the case where the initial events form a *partition* of S.

Consider the events $\{A_1, A_2, ..., A_m\}$ that constitute a *partition* of S, then the set of all possible unions of the elements of $\mathcal{A}:= \{\emptyset,A_1, A_2, ..., A_m\}$ forms a field:

$$\Im(\mathcal{A}) = \left\{\mathcal{B}: \mathcal{B} = \bigcup_{i \in I} A_i, I \subseteq \{1, 2, ..., n\}\right\}.$$

Example
In the case of tossing a coin three times:

$$S_3 = \{(HHH),(HHT),(HTT),(HTH),(TTT),(TTH),(THT),(THH)\},$$

consider the events $A_1 = \{(HHH),(HHT),(HTT)\}$, $A_2 = \{(HTH),(TTT),(TTH)\}$ and $A_3 = \{(THT),(THH)\}$; the set $\{A_1,A_2,A_3\}$ is clearly a partition of S_3. The field generated by this partition takes the form:

$$\mathfrak{I}_3 = \{S_3,\emptyset,A_1,A_2,A_3,(A_1 \cup A_2),(A_1 \cup A_3),(A_2 \cup A_3)\}.$$

This event space has the mathematical structure of being closed under the set theoretic operations ($\cup, \cap$ and $^-$), i.e., if we perform any of these operations on any elements of $\mathfrak{I}_3$ the derived events will be elements of $\mathfrak{I}_3$ (verify).

The above method can be extended to the case where S is infinite by defining a *countable partition* of it, say $\{A_1, A_2, ..., A_n, ...\} = \{A_i, i \in \mathbb{N}\}$. The set of subsets generated by $\mathcal{A} := \{\emptyset, A_1, A_2, ..., A_n, ...\}$ takes the form:

$$\mathfrak{I}(\mathcal{A}) = \left\{\mathcal{B}: \mathcal{B} = \bigcup_{i \in I} A_i, I \subseteq \mathbb{N}\right\},$$

and constitutes an extension of the notion of a field, known as a σ-field. The extension amounts to the σ-field being closed under countable unions and interesections of events.

TERMINOLOGY: the terms *algebra* and *σ-algebra* are often used instead of *field* and *σ-field,* respectively, in the literature. Although the former terms might be more appropriate (see Williams (1991)), we prefer the latter terminology for historical reasons (Kolmogorov (1933) used the term field).

σ-field A collection $\mathfrak{I}$ of subsets of S, is said to be a σ-field (pronounced sigma-field) if it satisfies the conditions:

(i) $S \in \mathfrak{I}$,
(ii)   if $A \in \mathfrak{I}$, then $\overline{A} \in \mathfrak{I}$,
(iii)   if $A_i \in \mathfrak{I}$ for $i = 1, 2, ..., n, ...$ the set $\bigcup_{i=1}^{\infty} A_i \in \mathfrak{I}$.

In view of (ii), from (iii) and De Morgan's law we can deduce that:

$$\bigcap_{i=1}^{\infty} A_i \in \mathfrak{I}, \quad \text{since } \overline{\bigcup_{i=1}^{\infty} A_i} = \bigcap_{i=1}^{\infty} \overline{A}_i.$$

That is, a σ-field is non-empty and closed under countable unions and intersections, providing the most general mathematical structure needed to formalize the notion of an event space. It goes without saying that a field is always a special case of a σ-field.

Borel σ-field The most important σ-field in probability theory is the one defined on the real line $\mathbb{R}$, known as a Borel σ-field, or *Borel-field* for short, and denoted by $\mathcal{B}(\mathbb{R})$. So far we considered σ-fields generated by arbitrary sets of outcomes S which were endowed with no other mathematical structure than the set theoretic. The real line $\mathbb{R}$ is obviously not just a set in the same sense of the set of outcomes of the experiment of tossing a coin twice. It enjoys a rich mathematical structure which enables us to define order among its elements, define distance between any two elements, define convergence in relation to a sequence of its elements, etc. The structure that is of particular interest in the present context is the one that enables us to define convergence, known to the mathematical connoisseurs as *topological structure.* Naturally, the Borel-field $\mathcal{B}(\mathbb{R})$ enjoys a certain additional mathematical structure inherited by that of the real line; in particular it enjoys some additional topological structure.

Given that the real line $\mathbb{R}$, has an infinite number of elements (with its infinity of higher order than that of the natural numbers), the question which naturally arises is: How do we define the Borel-field $\mathcal{B}(\mathbb{R})$? As shown above, the most effective way to define a σ-field over an infinite set is to define it via the elements that can generate this set. In the case of the real line a number of different intervals such as (a,∞), $(a,b]$ (a,b), $(-\infty,b)$, can be used to generate the Borel-field. However, it turns out that the half-infinite interval $(-\infty,x]$ is particularly convenient for this purpose. Let us consider how such intervals can generate the Borel-field $\mathcal{B}(\mathbb{R})$.

We begin with a set of subsets of the real line of the form:

$$B_x = \{(-\infty,x]: x \in \mathbb{R}\},$$

which is *closed under finite intersections,* i.e., for any two real numbers x and y:

$$(-\infty,x] \cap (-\infty,y] = (-\infty,z] \in B_x, \quad \text{where } z = \min(x,y).$$

We then proceed to define the σ-field generated by B_x, denoted by $\mathcal{B}(\mathbb{R}) = \sigma(B_x)$, using the set theoretical operations of union, intersection, and complementation; see Galambos (1995) for futher details.

This Borel-field $\mathcal{B}(\mathbb{R})$ includes just about all subsets of the real line $\mathbb{R}$, but not quite all! That is, there are subsets of $\mathbb{R}$ which belong to the power set but not to $\mathcal{B}(\mathbb{R})$, i.e.

$$\mathcal{B}(\mathbb{R}) \subset \mathcal{P}(\mathbb{R}), \text{ and } \mathcal{B}(\mathbb{R}) \neq \mathcal{P}(\mathbb{R}).$$

The Borel-field, however, includes all the subsets we usually encounter in practice, such as:

$$(a,\infty), (a,b], \{a\}, (a,b), \text{ for any real numbers } a < b,$$

in the sense that they can all be created using the set theoretic operations of union, intersection and complementation in conjunction with intervals of the form $(-\infty,x]$. This can be seen by noting that:

$$
\begin{aligned}
(a,\infty) &= \overline{(-\infty,a]}, & &\Rightarrow (a,\infty) \in \mathcal{B}(\mathbb{R}),\\
(a,b] &= (-\infty,b] \cap (a,\infty), & &\Rightarrow (a,b] \in \mathcal{B}(\mathbb{R}),\\
\{a\} &= \cap_{n=1}^{\infty} (a-\tfrac{1}{n},a], & &\Rightarrow \in \mathcal{B}(\mathbb{R}), \text{ etc.}
\end{aligned}
$$

The formalization so far In an attempt to help the reader keep track of the formalization as it unfolds, we summarize the argument so far below:

$$
\mathcal{E} \rightsquigarrow \begin{cases} [a] & \Rightarrow S \\ [b] & \Rightarrow (\Im,?), \\ [c] & \Rightarrow ? \end{cases}
$$

In concluding this subsection we collect the terminology introduced so far in table 2.1. The discerning reader would have noted that we used a pair of terms for most of the notions introduced above, one term is set theoretic and the other probabilistic. It is important for the reader to see the correspondence between the two different but related terminologies.

Table 2.1. *Contrasting the terminology*

Set theoretic	Probabilistic
universal set S	sure event S
empty set $\emptyset$	impossible event $\emptyset$
B is a subset of; $A : B \subset A$	when event B occurs event A occurs
set $A \cap B$	events A and B occur simultaneously
set $A \cup B$	events A or B occur
set $\bar{A} := S - A$	event A does not occur
disjoint sets: $A \cap B = \emptyset$	mutually exclusive events A, B
subset of S	event
element of S	elementary outcome
field	event space
σ-field	event space

In the next section we formalize the notion of probability and proceed to show how we attach probabilities to elements of an event space $\Im$.

2.6.4   A digression: what is a function?

Before we proceed to complete the second component in formalizing condition [b] defining a random experiment, we need to make a digression in order to define the concept of a *function* because the type of functions we will need in this and the next chapter go beyond the usual point-to-point numerical functions. The naive notion of a function as a *formula* enabling $f(x)$ to be calculated in terms of x, is embarrassingly inadequate for our purposes.

It is no exaggeration to claim that the notion of a function is perhaps the most important concept in mathematics. However, the lack of precision of the notion of a function has caused many problems in several areas of mathematics from the time of Euclid to the early 20th century. The problems caused by the absence of a precise notion of a function were particularly acute during the rigorization of calculus (analysis). The definitions adopted at different times during the 18th and 19th centuries ranged from "a closed (finite analytical) expression" to "every quantity whose value depends on one or several others" (see Klein (1972) for a fascinating discussion). One can go as far as to claim that the requirements of analysis forced mathematicians to invent more and more general categories of functions which were instrumental in the development of many areas of modern mathematics such as set theory, the modern theory of integration, and the theory of topological spaces. In turn, the axiomatization of set theory provided the first general and precise definition of a function in the early 20th century. Intuitively, as defined below, a function is a special type of "marriage" between two sets.

A **function** $f(.) : A \rightarrow B$ is a *relation* between the sets A and B satisfying the restriction that for each $x \in A$, there exists a *unique* element $y \in B$ such that $(x, y) \in f$. The sets A and B are said to be the *domain* and the *co-domain* of the function $f(.)$, respectively. The set:

$$G := \{(x,y) \in f : x \in A, y \in B\}$$

is called the *graph* of the function.

Unfortunately, this definition contains the term *relation* which has not been mathematically defined. In order to define the notion of a relation we need to go a step further back to define the notion of the *Cartesian product* of two sets, denoted by $A \times B$:

$A \times B$ is the set of all *ordered pairs* (x,y) where $x \in A$ and $y \in B$.

An ordered pair refers to a set with two elements whose order is important and cannot be changed; to indicate the order we use the set theoretic notation: $(x,y) := \{x, \{x,y\}\}$.

A **relation** R between the sets A and B is any *subset* of the Cartesian product $A \times B$. If $(x,y) \in R$, we say that the relation R holds between x and y and denote it by xRy.

In figure 2.4 we can see the Cartesian product $A \times B$ and the relation R (an elliptical disc) in grey.

Hence, a function is a special kind of a relation f (see figure 2.5) which ensures that:

(i)   every element x of the domain A is paired,
(ii)   for each $x \in A$, there exists a *unique* element $y \in B$ such that $(x,y) \in f$.

Looking at figure 2.6 brings out two important features of a function.

(i)   The nature of the two sets and their elements is arbitrary. In this sense the naive notion of a function as a formula relating numbers to numbers is much too narrow.
(ii)   The uniqueness restriction concerns the elements of the co-domain which are paired with elements of the domain ($B_A := f(A) \subset B$, and B_A is called the *range* of f) and intuitively means that only one arrow emanates from each element $x \in A$, but more than one arrow can end up with any one element $y \in B_A$.

NOTE that we distinguish between the co-domain and the *range* of f; in figure 2.6 the element Φ belongs to the co-domain but does not belong to the range of f. In the case where $B_A := f(A) = B$ the function is called *surjective* (onto). Also, in the case where for each $y \in B_A$ there corresponds a unique $x \in A$, the function is said to be *injective* (one-to-one). If the function is both one-to-one and onto it is called a *bijection*.

2.6.5 The mathematical notion of probability

The next step in our formalization of condition [b], defining a random experiment, is to find a way to attach probabilities to the events of interest as specified by the event space.

Example
In the case of tossing a coin three times, with the event space defined by $\Im_3$, common sense suggests that the following probabilities seem reasonable:

$$\mathbb{P}(S_3) = 1, \ \mathbb{P}(\emptyset) = 0, \ \mathbb{P}(A_2) = \tfrac{1}{8}, \ \mathbb{P}(\overline{A}_1) = \tfrac{7}{8},$$
$$\mathbb{P}(\overline{A}_2) = \tfrac{7}{8}, \ \mathbb{P}(A_1 \cup A_2) = \tfrac{1}{4}, \ \mathbb{P}(\overline{A}_1 \cap \overline{A}_2) = \tfrac{3}{4}.$$

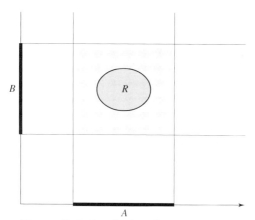

Figure 2.4 Graph of a relation

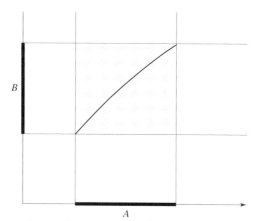

Figure 2.5 Graph of a function

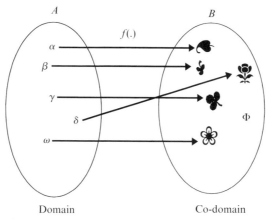

Figure 2.6 Defining a function

In calculating the above probabilities we assumed that the coin is fair and used common sense to argue that for an event such as $A_1 \cup A_2$ we find its probability by adding that of A_1 and A_2 together since the two are mutually exclusive. In mathematics, however, we cannot rely exclusively on such things as common sense when setting up a mathematical structure. We need to formalize the common sense arguments by giving a mathematical definition for $\mathbb{P}(.)$ as a function from an event space $\Im$ to real numbers between 0 and 1. The major breakthrough that led to the axiomatization of probability theory in 1933 by Kolmogorov was the realization that $\mathbb{P}(.)$ can be thought of as a *measure* in the newly developed advanced integration theory called *measure theory*. This realization enabled Kolmogorov to develop probability theory as a special chapter of measure theory:

This task would have been a rather hopeless one before the introduction of Lebesgue's theories of measure and integration. However, after Lebesgue's publication of his investigations, the analogies between measure of a set and probability of an event, ..., became apparent...

(Kolmogorov (1933), p. v)

Probability set function
$\mathbb{P}(.)$ is defined as a *function* from an event space $\Im$ to the real numbers between 0 and 1 which satisfies certain axioms. That is, the domain of the function $\mathbb{P}(.)$ is a set of subsets of S. To be more precise:

$$\mathbb{P}(.):\Im \to [0,1],$$

is said to be *a probability set function* if it satisfies the following axioms:

[1] $\mathbb{P}(S)=1$, for any outcomes set S,
[2] $\mathbb{P}(A)\geq 0$, for any event $A \in \Im$,
[3] *Countable additivity*. For a countable sequence of mutually exclusive events, i.e., $A_i \in \Im$, $i=1, 2, ..., n, ...$ such that $A_i \cap A_j = \emptyset$, for all $i \neq j$, $i,j=1, 2, ..., n, ...$, then

$$\mathbb{P}(\bigcup_{i=1}^{\infty} A_i)=\sum_{i=1}^{\infty} \mathbb{P}(A_i).$$

Axioms **[1]** and **[2]** are self-evident but **[3]** requires some explanation because it is not self-evident and it largely determines the mathematical structure of the probability set function. The countable additivity axiom provides a way to attach probabilities to events by utilizing mutually exclusive events. In an attempt to understand the role of this axiom let us consider a number of different types of outcomes sets in an ascending order of difficulty.

(a) Finite outcomes set: $S=\{s_1, s_2, ..., s_n\}$
In this case the elementary outcomes $s_1, s_2, ..., s_n$ are indeed mutually exclusive by definition and moreover, $\bigcup_{i=1}^{n} s_i = S$, i.e., the events $s_1, s_2, ..., s_n$ constitute a *partition* of S. Axiom **[3]** implies that

$$\mathbb{P}(\bigcup_{i=1}^{n} s_i)=\sum_{i=1}^{n} \mathbb{P}(s_i)=1,$$

(by axiom **[1]**) and suggests that by assigning probabilities to the outcomes yields the **simple probability distribution** on S:

$[p(s_1), p(s_2), \dots, p(s_n)]$, such that $\sum_{i=1}^{n} p(s_i) = 1$.

The probability of event A in $\Im$ is then defined as follows. First we express event A in terms of the elementary outcomes, say $A = \{s_1, s_2, \dots, s_k\}$. Then we derive its probability by adding the probabilities of the outcomes $s_1, s_2, \dots, s_k$, since they are mutually exclusive, i.e.,

$$\mathbb{P}(A) = p(s_1) + p(s_2) + \dots + p(s_k) = \sum_{i=1}^{k} p(s_i).$$

Examples

(1)   Consider the case of the random experiment of "tossing a coin three times," and the event space is the power set of:

$$S_3 = \{(HHH),(HHT),(HTT),(HTH),(TTT),(TTH),(THT),(THH)\}.$$

Let $A_1 = \{(HHH)\}$ and $A_2 = \{(TTT)\}$, and derive the probabilities of the events $A_3 := (A_1 \cup A_2)$, $A_4 := \overline{A}_1$, $A_5 := \overline{A}_2$ and $A_6 := (\overline{A}_1 \cap \overline{A}_2)$.

$$\mathbb{P}(A_3) = \mathbb{P}(A_1) + \mathbb{P}(A_2) = \tfrac{1}{8} + \tfrac{1}{8} = \tfrac{1}{4},$$

$$\mathbb{P}(A_4) = \mathbb{P}(S_3) - \mathbb{P}(A_1) = 1 - \tfrac{1}{8} = \tfrac{7}{8},$$

$$\mathbb{P}(A_5) = \mathbb{P}(S_3) - \mathbb{P}(A_2) = 1 - \tfrac{7}{8} = \tfrac{1}{8},$$

$$\mathbb{P}(A_6) = \mathbb{P}(\overline{A}_1 \cap \overline{A}_2) = 1 - \mathbb{P}(A_1 \cup A_2) = \tfrac{3}{4}.$$

If we go back to the previous section we can see that these are the probabilities we attached using common sense.

(2)   Consider the assignment of probability to the event:

$$A = \{(HH),(HT),(TH)\},$$

in the case of the random experiment of "tossing a fair coin twice." The probability distribution in this case takes the form:

$$\left[\mathbb{P}(HH) = \tfrac{1}{4},\ \mathbb{P}(HT) = \tfrac{1}{4},\ \mathbb{P}(TH) = \tfrac{1}{4},\ \mathbb{P}(TT) = \tfrac{1}{4}\right].$$

This suggests that $\mathbb{P}(A) = \mathbb{P}(HH) + \mathbb{P}(HT) + \mathbb{P}(TH) = \tfrac{3}{4}$.

In the case where the number of distinct outcomes is infinite, this way of assigning probabilities is inappropriate. A more efficient way to do that is provided by the concept of a density function, defined in the next section.

(b) Countable outcomes set: $S = \{s_1, s_2, \dots, s_n, \dots\}$

This case is a simple extension of the finite case where the elementary outcomes $s_1, s_2, \dots, s_n, \dots$ are again mutually exclusive and they constitute a partition of S, i.e., $\bigcup_{i=1}^{\infty} s_i = S$. Axiom [3] implies that:

$$\mathbb{P}(\textstyle\bigcup_{i=1}^{\infty} s_i) = \sum_{i=1}^{\infty} \mathbb{P}(s_i) = 1.$$

(by axiom [**1**]) and suggests that by assigning probabilities to the outcomes yields the **probability distribution** on S:

$$\wp = [p(s_1), p(s_2), ..., p(s_n), ...], \text{ such that } \sum_{i=1}^{\infty} p(s_i) = 1.$$

In direct analogy to case (a) the probability of event A in $\Im$ (which might coincide with the power set of S) is defined by:

$$\mathbb{P}(A) = \sum_{[i:s_i \in A]} p(s_i). \tag{2.7}$$

In contrast to the finite S case, the probabilities $\{p(s_1), p(s_2), ..., p(s_n), ...,\}$ cannot be equal because for any positive constant $p > 0$, however small, where $p(s_n) = p$, for all $n = 1, 2, 3, ...,$ i.e. for any $p > 0$,

$$\sum_{i=1}^{\infty} p = \infty.$$

NOTE that the only way to render this summation bounded is to make p a function of n. For example, for $p_n = \frac{1}{n^k}$:

$$\sum_{n=1}^{\infty} \frac{1}{n^k} < \infty, \text{ for } k > 1.$$

Example

Consider the case of the random experiment of "tossing a coin until the first H appears" and the event space is the power set of:

$$S_4 = \{(H), (TH), (TTH), (TTTH), (TTTTH), ...\}.$$

Assuming that $\mathbb{P}(H) = \theta$, and $\mathbb{P}(T) = 1 - \theta$, we can proceed to evaluate the probabilities of the outcomes as follows:

$$\mathbb{P}(TH) = (1-\theta)\theta, \qquad \mathbb{P}(TTH) = (1-\theta)^2\theta,$$
$$\mathbb{P}(TTTH) = (1-\theta)^3\theta, \qquad \mathbb{P}(TTTTH) = (1-\theta)^4\theta,$$
$$\mathbb{P}(\underbrace{TT...TH}_{n \text{ times}}) = (1-\theta)^{n-1}\theta, \quad \text{etc.}$$

(c) Uncountable outcomes set S

Without any loss of generality let us consider the case where the outcomes set is the interval $[0,1]$:

$$S = \{x: 0 \le x \le 1, x \in \mathbb{R}\}.$$

We can utilize axiom [**3**] if we can express the interval $[0,1]$ as a countable union of disjoint sets A_i, $i = 1, 2, 3, ...$ It turns out that with the use of some sophisticated mathematical arguments (axiom of choice, etc.) we can express this interval in the form of:

$$[0,1] = \bigcup_{i=1}^{\infty} A_i,$$

where $A_i \cap A_j = \varnothing$, $i \ne j$, $i, j = 1, 2, ...,$ and $\mathbb{P}(A_i)$ is the *same for all* A_i, $i = 1, 2, 3, ...$ This, however, leads to inconsistencies because by axiom [**3**]:

$$\mathbb{P}([0,1]) = \mathbb{P}(\bigcup_{i=1}^{\infty} A_i) = \sum_{i=1}^{\infty} \mathbb{P}(A_i),$$

and thus $\mathbb{P}([0,1]) = 0$, if $\mathbb{P}(A_i) = 0$, or $\mathbb{P}([0,1]) = \infty$, if $\mathbb{P}(A_i) > 0$.

The reason why the above attempt failed lies with the nature of the disjoint sets A_i, $i = 1, 2, 3, \ldots$ They are members of the power set $\mathcal{P}([0,1])$ but they are not necessarily members of a σ-field associated with this interval. As argued above, the mathematical structure necessary for a consistent assignment of probabilities is that of a σ-field.

How do we deal with the assignment of probabilities in the case of an uncountable outcomes set?

The question that comes to mind is whether we can start with an arbitrary class of subsets of S, say $\mathcal{D}$, with $\mathbb{P}(.)$ defined for every element of $\mathcal{D}$, and then proceed to extend it to a σ-field generated by $\mathcal{D}$. The answer is in the affirmative only if $\mathcal{D}$ is a *field*. This is because axiom [**3**] restricts the assignment of probabilities to countable unions of disjoint sets and given an arbitrary union of elements of $\mathcal{D}$, it can be expressed as a countable union of disjoint sets only if $\mathcal{D}$ is a field.

In formal mathematical terms the extension of the assignment of probabilities from a set of events to the event space is achieved by starting with a field $\mathcal{D}$ and expressing it as a countable union of disjoint sets on which $\mathbb{P}(.)$ is defined. We then extend $\mathcal{D}$ to the σ-field $\Im$ generated by $\mathcal{D}$, denoted by $\Im = \sigma(\mathcal{D})$ obtained by complementation, countable unions and intersections on the elements of $\mathcal{D}$. Having defined the probability set function $\mathbb{P}(.)$ on $\mathcal{D}$ we can then proceed to extend it to all the elements of $\Im$, using Caratheodory's extension theorem (see Williams (1991)).

Example

This procedure is best illustrated in the case where the outcomes set is the real line $\mathbb{R}$ and the appropriate σ-field is the Borel-field $\mathcal{B}(\mathbb{R})$ which is generated by subsets of the form:

$$B_x = \{(-\infty, x] : x \in \mathbb{R}\}.$$

We can define $\mathbb{P}(.)$ on B_x first and then proceed to extend it to all subsets of the form:

$$(a, \infty), (a, b], \{a\}, (a, b), \text{ for any real numbers } a < b.$$

using Caratheodory's extension theorem.

Let us return to the focus of the discussion which was the role of the axiom of countable additivity. In addition to its above-mentioned assignment role, the countability property is also needed to ensure the *continuity* of the probability set function discussed in the next subsection.

2.6.6 Probability space $(S, \Im, P(.))$

From the mathematical viewpoint this completes the formalization of the first two conditions defining a random experiment ($\mathcal{E}$). Condition [a] has become a set S called an outcomes set (with elements the elementary outcomes) and condition [b] has taken the form of $(\Im, \mathbb{P}(.))$ where $\Im$ is a σ-field of subsets of S called an event space and $\mathbb{P}(.)$ is a set function which satisfies axioms [1]–[3] called a probability set function. Collecting all these components together we can define what we call a probability space.

The trinity $(S, \mathfrak{I}, \mathbb{P}(.))$ where S is an outcomes set, $\mathfrak{I}$ is an *event space* associated with S, and $\mathbb{P}(.)$ a *probability function* that satisfies axioms [1]–[3] above, is referred to as a **probability space**; see Pfeiffer (1978) and Khazanie (1976) for further details. The probability space has the necessary mathematical structure to be used as the foundation on which one can build the whole edifice we call probability theory.

The next step in the mathematical approach is to use the above mathematical set up, in conjunction with mathematical logic, in order to derive a number of conclusions we call probability theory. The approach adopted in this book does not follow this procedure. For modeling purposes it is preferable to develop the theory of probability after we transform the probability space into something mathematically easier to handle. It is instructive, however, to get a taste of what the mathematical approach entails before we proceed to metamorphose the probability space into a probability model.

2.6.7 Mathematical deduction*

As a deductive science, mathematics begins with a set of fundamental statements we call axioms (the premises) and ends with other fundamental statements we call theorems which are derived from the axioms using deductive logical inference. To get a taste of what this is all about let us derive a few such theorems in the case of the probability space as specified above.

Accepting the axioms [1]–[3] as "true" we can proceed to derive certain corollaries which provide a more complete picture of the mathematical framework.

Theorem 1 $\mathbb{P}(\overline{A}) = 1 - \mathbb{P}(A)$.
Let us see how this follows from axioms [1]–[3]. In view of the fact that $\overline{A} \cup A = S$, and $\overline{A} \cap A = \emptyset$ we can use axioms [1] and [3] to deduce that:

$$\mathbb{P}(S) = 1 = \mathbb{P}(\overline{A} \cup A) = \mathbb{P}(\overline{A}) + \mathbb{P}(A), \Rightarrow \mathbb{P}(\overline{A}) = 1 - \mathbb{P}(A).$$

The first equality is axiom [1], the second follows from the fact that $\overline{A} \cup A = S$, and the third from the fact that $\overline{A} \cap A = \emptyset$ and axiom [3].

Example
In the case of tossing a coin twice let $A = \{(HH), (HT), (TH)\}$. Given that $\overline{A} = \{(TT)\}$, using theorem 1 we can deduce that $\mathbb{P}(\overline{A}) = \frac{1}{4}$.

The next result is almost self-evident but in mathematics we need to ensure that it follows from the axioms. Using theorem 1 in the case where $A = S$ (and hence $\overline{A} = \emptyset$), we deduce:

Theorem 2 $P(\emptyset) = 0$.
The next theorem extends axiom [3] to the case where the events are not mutually exclusive.

Theorem 3 $\mathbb{P}(A \cup B) = \mathbb{P}(A) + \mathbb{P}(B) - \mathbb{P}(A \cap B)$.

The way to prove this is to define $A \cup B$ in terms of mutually exclusive events and then use [3]. It is not difficult to see that the events $C = \{A - (A \cap B)\}$ and B are mutually exclusive and $C \cup B = A \cup B$. Hence, by axiom [3]:

$$\mathbb{P}(A \cup B) = \mathbb{P}(C \cup B) = \mathbb{P}\{A - (A \cap B) + \mathbb{P}(B) = \mathbb{P}(A) + \mathbb{P}(B) - \mathbb{P}(A \cap B)\}.$$

Example

For A as defined above and $B = \{(HH),(TT)\}$, theorem 3 implies that:

$$\mathbb{P}(A \cup B) = \tfrac{3}{4} + \tfrac{1}{2} - \tfrac{1}{4} = 1.$$

The next theorem is of considerable mathematical interest but its proof is much more involved than the ones encountered above. For this reason we will consider only a partial proof; see Karr (1993) for a complete proof.

Theorem 4 For $\{A_n\}_{n=1}^{\infty} \in \mathfrak{I}$, if $\lim_{n \to \infty} A_n = A \in \mathfrak{I}$, then $\lim_{n \to \infty} \mathbb{P}(A_n) = \mathbb{P}(A)$.

This theorem says that for a sequence of events $\{A_n\}_{n=1}^{\infty}$ in the event space of interest which converges to another event A, the limit of the sequence of probabilities coincides with the probability of A. Theorem 4 is known as the **continuity property** of the probability set function. This theorem raises the obvious question: What meaning can one attach to the statement: the limit of a sequence of events which is also supposed to be an event? A partial answer to this question is provided by noting that for two special types of sequences, the limit is defined in terms of countable unions and intersections.

Non-decreasing sequence A sequence of events $\{A_n\}_{n=1}^{\infty}$ is called *non-decreasing* if

$$A_1 \subset A_2 \subset \cdots \subset A_n \subset A_{n+1} \subset A_{n+2} \subset \cdots$$

For such a sequence:

$$\lim_{n \to \infty} A_n = \bigcup_{n=1}^{\infty} A_n. \tag{2.8}$$

Non-increasing sequence A sequence of events $\{A_n\}_{n=1}^{\infty}$ is called *non-increasing* if:

$$A_1 \supset A_2 \supset \cdots \supset A_n \supset A_{n+1} \supset A_{n+2} \supset \cdots$$

For such a sequence the following relationship holds:

$$\lim_{n \to \infty} A_n = \bigcap_{n=1}^{\infty} A_n. \tag{2.9}$$

Consider a partial proof of the above theorem concerned only with non-decreasing sequences. Assuming that the sequence $\{A_n\}_{n=1}^{\infty}$ is *non-decreasing*, we know that we can express the limit of the sequence as in (2.8). This limit can then be expressed in the form of mutually exclusive events of the form $(A_{k+1} - A_k)$ and $(A_{j+1} - A_j)$ for $k \neq j$, which have the properties:

$$(A_{k+1} - A_k) \cap (A_{j+1} - A_j) = \emptyset, \quad \mathbb{P}(A_{k+1} - A_k) = \mathbb{P}(A_{k+1}) - \mathbb{P}(A_k).$$

Using such events, and setting $A_0 = \emptyset$, we can define A_n via:

$$\lim_{n\to\infty} A_n = \bigcup_{n=1}^{\infty} A_n = A_1 + (A_2 - A_1) + (A_3 - A_2) + \cdots.$$

For $A = \lim_{n\to\infty} A_n$, we can use the above relationship in conjunction with axiom [3] to argue:

$$\mathbb{P}(\lim_{n\to\infty} A_n) = \mathbb{P}(A_1) + \mathbb{P}(A_2 - A_1) + \cdots + \mathbb{P}(A_{k+1} - A_k) + \cdots =$$
$$= \mathbb{P}(A_1) + \mathbb{P}(A_2) - \mathbb{P}(A_1) + \cdots + \mathbb{P}(A_{k+1}) - \mathbb{P}(A_k) + \cdots = \lim_{n\to\infty} \mathbb{P}(A_n).$$

The last equality follows from the fact that the partial sums on the right-hand side take the form $\sum_{k=1}^{n} [\mathbb{P}(A_k) - \mathbb{P}(A_{k-1})] = \mathbb{P}(A_n)$, and thus the limit is just the limit of $\mathbb{P}(A_n)$, giving rise to the result $\mathbb{P}(A) = \lim_{n\to\infty} \mathbb{P}(A_n)$. This amounts to proving that the probability set function $\mathbb{P}(.)$ is continuous from below. In order to prove theorem 4 in its full generality we need to prove it for non-increasing sequences (continuity from above) as well as for null sequences, i.e., for sequences of the form $\lim_{n\to\infty} A_n = \emptyset$ (continuity at $\emptyset$); for the details see Shiryayev (1984).

In conclusion, let us state a related theorem known as the **Bonferroni inequality** without proof; see Chung (1974), Feller (1968).

Theorem 5 $\mathbb{P}(\bigcap_{k=1}^{n} A_k) \geq 1 - \sum_{k=1}^{n} \mathbb{P}(\overline{A_k})$, $A_k \in \mathfrak{I}$, $k = 1, 2, \ldots, n$.

2.7   Formalizing condition [c]: random trials

The last condition defining the notion of a *random experiment* is:

[c]   the experiment can be repeated under identical conditions.

This is interpreted to mean that the circumstances and the state of affairs from one trial to the next remain unchanged, and thus it entails two interrelated but fundamentally different components:

(i)   the set up of the experiment remains the same for all trials and
(ii)   the outcome in one trial does not affect that of another.

How do we formalize these conditions?

The first notion we need to formalize is that of a finite sequence of trials. Let us denote the n trials by $\{\mathcal{A}_1, \mathcal{A}_2, \mathcal{A}_3, \ldots, \mathcal{A}_n\}$ and associate each trial with a probability space $(S_i, \mathfrak{I}_i, \mathbb{P}_i(.))$, $i = 1, 2, \cdots, n$, respectively. In order to be able to discuss any relationship between trials we need to encompass them in an overall probability space; without it we cannot formalize condition (ii) above. The overall probability space that suggests itself is the *product probability space*:

$$(S_1, \mathfrak{I}_1, \mathbb{P}_1(.)) \times (S_2, \mathfrak{I}_2, \mathbb{P}_2()) \times \ldots \times (S_n, \mathfrak{I}_n, \mathbb{P}_n(.)),$$

which can be thought of as a triple of the form:

$$([S_1 \times S_2 \times \cdots \times S_n], [\mathfrak{I}_1 \times \mathfrak{I}_2 \times \cdots \times \mathfrak{I}_n], [\mathbb{P}_1 \times \mathbb{P}_2 \times \cdots \times \mathbb{P}_n]) := (\mathbf{S}_{(n)}, \mathfrak{I}_{(n)}, \mathbb{P}_{(n)}),$$

in an obvious notation. The technical question that arises is whether $(\mathbf{S}_{(n)}, \Im_{(n)}, \mathbb{P}_{(n)})$ is a proper probability space. To be more precise, the problem is whether $\mathbf{S}_{(n)}$ is a proper outcomes set, $\Im_{(n)}$ has the needed structure of a σ-field, and $\mathbb{P}_{(n)}$ defines a set function which satisfies the three axioms. The answer to the first scale of the question is in the affirmative since the outcomes set can be defined by:

$$\mathbf{S}_{(n)} = \{\mathbf{s}_{(n)} : \mathbf{s}_{(n)} := (s_1, s_2, ..., s_n), s_i \in S_i, i = 1, 2, ..., n\}.$$

It turns out that indeed $\Im_{(n)}$ has the needed structure of a σ-field (for a finite n) and $\mathbb{P}_{(n)}$ defines a set function which satisfies the three axioms; the technical arguments needed to prove these claims are beyond the scope of the present book (see Parthasarathy (1977)).

Having established that the product probability space is a proper probability space, we can proceed to view the sequence of trials $\{\mathcal{A}_1, \mathcal{A}_2, \mathcal{A}_3, ..., \mathcal{A}_n\}$ as an *event* in $(\mathbf{S}_{(n)}, \Im_{(n)}, \mathbb{P}_{(n)})$; an event to which we can attach probabilities.

The **first component** of condition [c] can be easily formalized by ensuring that the probability space $(S, \Im, \mathbb{P}(.))$ remains the same from trial to trial in the sense:

$$\text{[i]} \quad (S_i, \Im_i, \mathbb{P}_i(.)) = (S, \Im, \mathbb{P}(.)), \text{ for all } i = 1, 2, ..., n, \qquad (2.10)$$

and we refer to this as the **Identical Distribution** (ID) condition.

Example
Consider the case where $S = \{s_1, s_2, ..., s_k\}$ is the outcomes set and:

$$\wp = [p(s_1), p(s_2), ..., p(s_k)] \text{ such that } \sum_{i=1}^{k} p(s_i) = 1$$

is the associated probability distribution. Then condition [i] amounts to saying that:

$$\text{[i]} \; \wp \text{ is the same for all n trials } \mathcal{A}_1, \mathcal{A}_2, \mathcal{A}_3, ..., \mathcal{A}_n.$$

More formally, the ID condition reduces the **product probability space** $(\mathbf{S}_{(n)}, \Im_{(n)}, \mathbb{P}_{(n)})$ to:

$$(S, \Im, \mathbb{P}(.)) \times (S, \Im, \mathbb{P}(.)) \times ... \times (S, \Im, \mathbb{P}(.)) = [(S, \Im, \mathbb{P}(.))]^n,$$

with the same probability space $(S, \Im, \mathbb{P}(.))$ associated with each trial.

The second component is more difficult to formalize because it involves ensuring that the outcome in the *i*th trial does not affect and is not affected by the outcome in the *j*th trial for $i \neq j$, $i, j = 1, 2, ..., n$. Viewing the n trials $\{\mathcal{A}_1, \mathcal{A}_2, \mathcal{A}_3, ..., \mathcal{A}_n\}$ as an event in the context of the product probability space $\{\mathbf{S}_{(n)}, \Im_{(n)}, \mathbb{P}_{(n)})$, we can formalize this in the form of *independence* among the trials. Intuitively, trial *i*, does not affect and is not affected by the outcome of trial *j*. That is, given the outcome in trial *j* the probabilities associated with the various outcomes in trial *i* are unchanged and vice versa. The idea that "given the outcome of trial *j* the outcome of trial *i* is unaffected" can be formalized using the notion of *conditioning*, discussed next.

2.7.1 A digression: conditional probability and independence

The notion of conditioning arises when we have certain additional information relating to the experiment in question.

Example

In the case of tossing a coin twice, if we (somehow) know that the actual outcome has at least one tails (T), this information will affect the probabilities of certain events. In view of such information we can deduce that the outcome (HH) is no longer possible and thus the outcomes (HT),(TH), and (TT) now have probabilities equal to $\frac{1}{3}$, not $\frac{1}{4}$ as before. Let us formalize this argument in a more systematic fashion by defining the event B "at least one T":

$$B = \{(HT),(TH),(TT)\}.$$

Without knowing B the outcomes set and the probability distribution are:

$$S_2 = \{(HH),(HT),(TH),(TT)\},$$
$$\wp = \{\mathbb{P}(HH) = \tfrac{1}{4}, \mathbb{P}(HT) = \tfrac{1}{4}, \mathbb{P}(TH) = \tfrac{1}{4}, \mathbb{P}(TT) = \tfrac{1}{4}\}$$

With the knowledge provided by B these become:

$$S_B = \{(HT),(TH),(TT)\}, \wp_B = \left\{ P_B(HT) = \tfrac{1}{3}, P_B(TH) = \tfrac{1}{3}, P_B(TT) = \tfrac{1}{3} \right\}.$$

In a sense the event B has, become the new outcomes set and the probabilities are now conditional on B in the sense that:

$$P_B(HT) = \mathbb{P}((HT)|B) = \tfrac{1}{3}, \ P_B(TH) = \mathbb{P}((TII)|B) = \tfrac{1}{3}, \ P_B(TT) = \mathbb{P}((TT)|B) = \tfrac{1}{3}.$$

A general way to derive these conditional probabilities, without having to derive S_B first, is the following formula:

$$\mathbb{P}(A|B) = \frac{\mathbb{P}(A \cap B)}{\mathbb{P}(B)}, \text{ for } \mathbb{P}(B) > 0, \tag{2.11}$$

for any event $A \in \Im$, where $\mathbb{P}(.)$ is the original probability set function defined on $\Im$.

Example

Let us verify this with $A = \{(TH)\}$. Given that $A \cap B = \{(TH)\}$ we can deduce that:

$$\mathbb{P}(A|B) = \frac{\tfrac{1}{4}}{\tfrac{3}{4}} = \tfrac{1}{3}.$$

Using the conditional probability formula (2.11) we can deduce the product probability rule:

$$\mathbb{P}(A \cap B) = \mathbb{P}(A|B) \cdot \mathbb{P}(B) = \mathbb{P}(B|A) \cdot \mathbb{P}(A).$$

Combining these two formulae we can derive **Bayes' formula**:

$$\mathbb{P}(A|B) = \frac{\mathbb{P}(A) \cdot \mathbb{P}(B|A)}{\mathbb{P}(B)}, \text{ for } \mathbb{P}(B) > 0. \tag{2.12}$$

Independence

The notion of conditioning can be used to determine whether two events A and B are related in the sense that information about the occurrence of one, say B, alters the probability of occurrence of A. If knowledge of the occurrence of B does not alter the probability of event A it is natural to say that A and B are independent. More formally A and B are **independent** if:

$$\mathbb{P}(A|B) = \mathbb{P}(A). \tag{2.13}$$

Using the conditional probability formula (2.11), we can deduce that two events A and B are **independent** if:

$$\mathbb{P}(A \cap B) = \mathbb{P}(A) \cdot \mathbb{P}(B). \tag{2.14}$$

NOTE. This notion of independence can be traced back to Cardano in the 1550s.

Example
For $A = \{(HH),(TT)\}$ and $B = \{(TT),(HT)\}$, $A \cap B = \{(TT)\}$ and thus:

$$\mathbb{P}(A \cap B) = \tfrac{1}{4} = \mathbb{P}(A) \cdot \mathbb{P}(B),$$

implying that A and B are independent.

It is very important to distinguish between *independent* and *mutually exclusive* events; the crucial difference being that the definition of the latter does not involve probability, but there is more to it than that. Two independent events with positive probability cannot be mutually exclusive. This is because if $\mathbb{P}(A) > 0$ and $\mathbb{P}(B) > 0$ and they are independent then $\mathbb{P}(A \cap B) = \mathbb{P}(A) \cdot \mathbb{P}(B) > 0$, but mutual exclusiveness implies that $\mathbb{P}(A \cap B) = 0$ since $A \cap B = \emptyset$. The intuition behind this result is that mutually exclusive events are informative about each other because the occurrence of one precludes the occurrence of the other.

Example
For $A = \{(HH),(TT)\}$ and $B = \{(HT),(TH)\}$, $A \cap B = \emptyset$ but:

$$\mathbb{P}(A \cap B) = 0 \neq \tfrac{1}{4} = \mathbb{P}(A) \cdot \mathbb{P}(B).$$

Joint independence   Independence can be generalized to more than two events but in the latter case we need to distinguish between pairwise, joint, and mutual independence. For example in the case of three events A, B, and C; we say that they are *jointly independent* if:

$$\mathbb{P}(A \cap B \cap C) = \mathbb{P}(A) \cdot \mathbb{P}(B) \cdot \mathbb{P}(C).$$

Pairwise independence   The notion of joint independence, however, is not equivalent to *pairwise independence* defined by the conditions:

$$\mathbb{P}(A \cap B) = \mathbb{P}(A) \cdot \mathbb{P}(B), \ \mathbb{P}(A \cap C) = \mathbb{P}(A) \cdot \mathbb{P}(C), \ \mathbb{P}(B \cap C) = \mathbb{P}(B) \cdot \mathbb{P}(C).$$

Example
Let the outcomes set be $S = \{(HH),(HT),(TH),(TT)\}$ and consider the events: $A = \{(TT),(TH)\}$, $B = \{(TT),(HT)\}$, and $C = \{(TH),(HT)\}$. Given that $A \cap B = \{(TT)\}$, $A \cap C = \{(TH)\}$, $B \cap C = \{(HT)\}$, and $A \cap B \cap C = \emptyset$, we can deduce:

$$\mathbb{P}(A \cap B) = \mathbb{P}(A) \cdot \mathbb{P}(B) = \tfrac{1}{4}, \qquad \mathbb{P}(B \cap C) = \mathbb{P}(B) \cdot \mathbb{P}(C) = \tfrac{1}{4},$$

$$\mathbb{P}(A \cap C) = \mathbb{P}(A) \cdot \mathbb{P}(C) = \tfrac{1}{4}, \text{ but } \quad \mathbb{P}(A \cap B \cap C) = 0 \neq \mathbb{P}(A) \cdot \mathbb{P}(B) \cdot \mathbb{P}(C) = \tfrac{1}{8}.$$

Similarly, joint independence does not imply pairwise independence. Moreover, both of these forms of independence are weaker than independence which involves joint independence for all subcollections of the events in question.

Independence The events $A_1, A_2, \ldots, A_n$ are said to be *independent* if and only if:

$$\mathbb{P}(A_1 \cap A_2 \cap \ldots \cap A_k) = \mathbb{P}(A_1) \cdot \mathbb{P}(A_2) \cdots \mathbb{P}(A_k), \text{ for each } k = 2, 3, \ldots, n.$$

That is, this holds for *any subcollection* $A_1, A_2, \ldots, A_k \ (k \leq n)$ of $A_1, A_2, \ldots, A_n$.

In the case of three events A, B, and C, pairwise and joint independence together imply independence and the converse.

2.8   Statistical space

Returning to the formalization of the notion of a random experiment ($\mathscr{E}$) we can now proceed to formalize the second component of condition [c]:

[ii] *the outcome in one trial does not affect that of another.*

Sampling space A sequence of n trials, denoted by $G_n = \{\mathcal{A}_1, \mathcal{A}_2, \mathcal{A}_3, \ldots, \mathcal{A}_n\}$ where $\mathcal{A}_i$, represents the ith trial of the experiment, associated with the product probability space $(\mathbf{S}_{(n)}, \mathfrak{I}_{(n)}, \mathbb{P}_{(n)})$, is said to be *a sampling space*.

As argued above, we view the n trials $G_n := \{\mathcal{A}_1, \mathcal{A}_2, \mathcal{A}_3, \ldots, \mathcal{A}_n\}$ as an event in the context of the product probability space $(\mathbf{S}_{(n)}, \mathfrak{I}_{(n)}, \mathbb{P}_{(n)})$. As such we can attach a probability to this event using the set function $\mathbb{P}_{(n)}$. Hence, we formalize [c][ii] by postulating that the trials are **independent** if:

[ii] $\mathbb{P}_{(n)}(\mathcal{A}_1 \cap \mathcal{A}_2 \cap \ldots \cap \mathcal{A}_k) = \mathbb{P}_1(\mathcal{A}_1) \cdot \mathbb{P}_2(\mathcal{A}_2) \cdots \mathbb{P}_k(\mathcal{A}_k),$ (2.15)
for each $k = 2, 3, \ldots, n,$

or

[ii]* $\mathbb{P}_{(n)}(\mathcal{A}_k | \mathcal{A}_1, \mathcal{A}_2, \ldots, \mathcal{A}_{k-1}, \mathcal{A}_{k+1}, \ldots, \mathcal{A}_n) = \mathbb{P}_k(\mathcal{A}_k),$
for each $k = 1, 2, \ldots, n.$

NOTE that $\mathbb{P}_{(n)}(.)$ and $\mathbb{P}_k(.)$ are different probability set functions which belong to the probability spaces $(\mathbf{S}_{(n)}, \mathfrak{I}_{(n)}, \mathbb{P}_{(n)})$ and $(\mathbf{S}_k, \mathfrak{I}_k, \mathbb{P}_k)$, respectively; see Pfeiffer (1978).

Taking the conditions of *Independence* (2.15) and *Identical Distribution* (2.10) we define what we call *a sequence of random trials*.

Random trials A sequence of trials $G_n^{\text{IID}} := \{\mathcal{A}_1, \mathcal{A}_2, \mathcal{A}_3, \ldots, \mathcal{A}_n\}$, which is both *independent* and *identically distributed* i.e.

$$\mathbb{P}_{(n)}(\mathcal{A}_1 \cap \mathcal{A}_2 \cap \ldots \cap \mathcal{A}_k) = \mathbb{P}(\mathcal{A}_1) \cdot \mathbb{P}(\mathcal{A}_2) \cdots \mathbb{P}(\mathcal{A}_k), \text{ for each } k = 2, 3, \ldots, n,$$

is referred to as a sequence of *Random trials*.

REMARK: G_n^{IID} is a particular form of a sampling space G_n associated with $(\mathbf{S}_{(n)}, \mathfrak{I}_{(n)}, \mathbb{P}_{(n)})$, defined above, in the sense that G_n^{IID} is associated with $(S, \mathfrak{I}, \mathbb{P}(.))^n$. NOTE that the notion of a sampling space is not inextricably bound up with the sequence of Random trials. The components of $(\mathbf{S}_{(n)}, \mathfrak{I}_{(n)}, \mathbb{P}_{(n)})$ can be both *non-Identically Distributed* (their set up differs from one trial to the next) and *non-Independent*.

Combining a simple product probability space and a sequence of Random trials we define a **simple statistical space**, denoted by:

$$[(S, \mathfrak{I}, \mathbb{P}(.))^n, G_n^{\text{IID}}].$$

The term simple stems from the fact that this represents a particular case of the more general formulation of a **statistical space**:

$$[(\mathbf{S}_{(n)}, \mathfrak{I}_{(n)}, \mathbb{P}_{(n)}), G_n],$$

where each trial, say $\mathcal{A}_i$, is associated with a different probability space $\{(S_i, \mathfrak{I}_i, \mathbb{P}_i(.))$ (i.e., non-ID) and the trials are not necessarily independent. As argued in chapters 5–8 in some fields such as econometrics we need to utilize the more general formulation. We will do it, however, in stages. Initially, (see chapters 3–4) we will deal with the simple case and then proceed to consider the more complicated one.

A simple statistical space $[(S, \mathfrak{I}, \mathbb{P}(.))^n, G_n^{\text{IID}}]$ represents our first complete formalization of the notion of a random experiment $\mathcal{E}$. This formulation, however, is rather abstract because it involves arbitrary sets and set functions, not numbers and numerical functions we are familiar with in calculus courses. The main aim of the next chapter is to reduce it to a more manageable form by mapping this mathematical structure onto the real line.

The story so far in symbols:

$$\mathcal{E} := \begin{bmatrix} [a] \\ [b] \\ [c] \end{bmatrix} \begin{matrix} \Rightarrow \\ \Rightarrow \\ \Rightarrow \end{matrix} \begin{pmatrix} S \\ (\mathfrak{I}, \mathbb{P}(.)) \\ G_n \end{pmatrix} \quad \Rightarrow \quad [(S, \mathfrak{I}, \mathbb{P}(.))^n, G_n^{\text{IID}}].$$

2.9   A look forward

The purpose of this chapter has been to provide an introduction to probability theory using the formalization of a simple chance mechanism we called a random experiment. The formalization of the three conditions, written in simple terms, to a formidable array of mathematical concepts had a purpose: to motivate some of the most important concepts of probability theory and define them in a precise mathematical way. The notion of a statistical space provides the mathematical foundation for the theory of probability. In the next two chapters we transform the simple statistical space into a simple statistical model with a view to operationalize the abstract formulation $[(S, \mathfrak{I}, \mathbb{P}(.))^n, G_n]$. In chapter 3 the probability space $(S, \mathfrak{I}, \mathbb{P}(.))$ is metamorphosed into a probability model defined on the real line and takes the form:

$$\Phi = \{f(\mathrm{x}; \theta), \ \theta \in \Theta, \ x \in \mathbb{R}\}.$$

In chapter 4 the sampling space is transformed into a special type of sampling model which we call a random sample: a set of random variables $\mathbf{X}:=(X_1, X_2, ..., X_n)$ which are both Independent and Identically Distributed. In chapter 5 an attempt is made to relate the various probabilistic notions associated with a simple statistical model to real data using graphical displays. In chapters 6–8 we extend the notion of a simple statistical model to a more general formulation which is appropriate for modeling economic phenomena that exhibit chance regularities beyond the random sample such as business cycles, growth, and exchange rate fluctuations.

2.10 Exercises

1   Why is descriptive statistics inadequate for modeling purposes in econometrics?

2   Explain intuitively the notion of *chance regularity*.

3   What is the main objective of probability theory in the context of modeling observable stochastic phenomena of interest.

4   Explain how we define the probability of an event A in the case where the outcomes set has a finite number of elements, i.e., $S = \{s_1, s_2, ..., s_n\}$.

5   Which of the following observable phenomena can be considered as random experiments:
(i)   A die is tossed and the number of dots facing up is counted.
(ii)   Select a ball from an urn containing balls numbered 1 to 20 and note the number.
(iii)   Observe the monthly changes of the consumer loan rate of interest.
(iv)   Select a ball from an urn containing balls numbered 1 to 3. Suppose balls 1 and 2 are black and ball 3 is red. Note the number and color of the ball drawn.
(v)   Toss a coin until Heads turns up and note the outcome.
Explain your answer.

6   For the experiments (i)–(v) in question **5,** specify the set of all distinct outcomes.

7   For the sets $A = \{2,4,6\}$ and $B = \{4,8,12\}$ derive the following:
(a) $A \cup B$, (b) $A \cap B$, (c) $\overline{A \cup B}$ relative to $S = \{2,4,6,8,10,12\}$.
Illustrate your answers using Venn diagrams.

8   Explain the difference between outcomes and events. Give examples from experiment (ii) in exercise **5.**

9   Explain the notions of mutually exclusive events and a partition of an outcomes set S. How is the partition useful in generating event spaces?

10   Define the concept of a σ-field and explain why we need such a concept for the set of all events of interest. Explain why we cannot use the power set as the event space in all cases.

11   Consider the outcomes set $S=\{2,4,6,8\}$ and let $A=\{2,4\}$ and $B=\{4,6\}$ be the events of interest. Show that the field generated by these two events coincides with the power set of S.

12   Explain how intervals of the form $(-\infty,x]$ can be used to define intervals such as $\{a\}, (a,b), [a,b), (a,b], [a,\infty)$, using set theoretic operations.

13   Explain the difference between a relation and a function.

14   Explain whether the probability functions defined below are proper ones:
   (i) $\mathbb{P}(A)=\frac{2}{3}, \mathbb{P}(\overline{A})=\frac{1}{3}, \mathbb{P}(S)=1, \mathbb{P}(\emptyset)=0,$

   (ii) $\mathbb{P}(A)=\frac{1}{3}, \mathbb{P}(\overline{A})=\frac{1}{3}, \mathbb{P}(S)=1, \mathbb{P}(\emptyset)=0,$

   (iii) $\mathbb{P}(A)=\frac{1}{4}, \mathbb{P}(\overline{A})=\frac{3}{4}, \mathbb{P}(S)=0, \mathbb{P}(\emptyset)=1,$

   (iv) $\mathbb{P}(A)=-\frac{1}{4}, \mathbb{P}(\overline{A})=\frac{5}{4}, \mathbb{P}(S)=1, \mathbb{P}(\emptyset)=0.$

15   Explain how we can define a simple probability distribution in the case where the outcomes set is finite.

16   How do we deal with the assignment of probabilities in the case of an uncountable outcomes set?

17   Describe briefly the formalization of conditions [a] and [b] of a random experiment into a probability space $(S,\Im,\mathbb{P}(.))$.

18   Describe briefly the formalization of condition [c] of a random experiment into a simple sampling space G_n^{IID}.

19   Explain the notions of Independent events and Identically Distributed trials.

20   Explain how conditioning can be used to define independence. Give examples if it helps.

21   Explain the difference between a sampling space in general and the simple sampling space G_n^{IID} in particular.

22   In the context of a random experiment of tossing a coin twice, derive the probability of event $A=\{(HT),(TH)\}$ given event $B=\{(HH),(HT)\}$. Are the two events independent?

3 The notion of a probability model

3.1 Introduction

3.1.1 The story so far

In the previous chapter we commenced the long journey to explore the theory of probability as it relates to fashioning a theoretical (mathematical) framework for modeling stochastic phenomena: observable phenomena that exhibit *chance regularity*. The particular path we followed began with the formalization of the notion of a **random experiment** $\mathcal{E}$, defined by the following conditions:

[a]   All possible distinct outcomes are known a priori,

[b]   in any particular trial the outcome is not known a priori but there exists a perceptible regularity of occurrence associated with these outcomes, and

[c]   it can be repeated under identical conditions.

The mathematization took the form of a **statistical space** $[(S,\Im,\mathbb{P}(.))^n, \mathcal{G}_n^{\mathrm{IID}}]$ where $(S,\Im,\mathbb{P}(.))$ is a *probability space* and $\mathcal{G}_n^{\mathrm{IID}}$ is a *simple sampling space*.

   The main purpose of this chapter is to metamorphose the abstract probability space $(S,\Im,\mathbb{P}(.))$ into something appropriate for empirical modeling using numerical data; something defined on the real line. The final target of this chapter is the formulation of what we call a **probability model**, one of the two pillars of a statistical model; the other being the sampling model which will be the subject matter of the next chapter where we consider the metamorphosis of $\mathcal{G}_n^{\mathrm{IID}}$.

3.1.2 Why do we care?

The statistical space, although adequate for mathematical purposes, does not lend itself naturally to the modeling of stochastic phenomena. Stochastic phenomena, such as the growth and inflation rate of the economy, are often observed in the form of numerical data and not in terms of abstract events. Hence, for modeling purposes we need to metamorphose the abstract statistical space, defined in terms of events and set functions, into something less abstract, defined in terms of numbers and numerical functions.

3.1.3   A bird's eye view of the chapter

The *modus operandi* of this metamorphosis is the notion of a *random variable*, one of the foremost concepts of probability theory. Its primary role is to enable us to map the statistical space $[(S,\Im,\mathbb{P}(.)),G_n^{\text{IID}}]$ on to the real line ($\mathbb{R}$). In an attempt to elucidate the role of this important concept we discuss the transformation of the abstract probability space $(S,\Im,\mathbb{P}(.))$ into a much simpler probability model, with the minimal mathematical machinery, in section 2 for the case where the outcomes set is countable. In section 3 we consider the concept of a random variable in a general setting. In section 4 we complete the metamorphosis chain by discussing the last link: the cumulative distribution and density functions which constitute the basic element of a probability model. In section 5 we bring together the results of the previous sections and we complete the transformation of the probability space into a probability model (we trade a space for a model!). In sections 6 and 7 we take an important digression in an attempt to relate the unknown parameters (the focus of *parametric* statistical inference) to the numerical characteristics of the distributions. We introduce numerous valuable concepts, such as the *moments* of a distribution, which will prove indispensable in the context of modeling as well as statistical inference. It suffices to say that modeling is often done via the moments of a distribution. In section 8 we state several probabilistic inequalities which relate probabilistic statements for a random variable X and certain moments.

3.2   The notion of a simple random variable

In order to help the reader keep one eye on the forest we state at the outset that the mapping of the probability space $(S,\Im,\mathbb{P}(.))$ on to the real line ($\mathbb{R}$) will be done in three steps. The **first step** is to map S into the real line $\mathbb{R}$, in such as way so as to preserve the event structure of interest $\Im$; the concept of a random variable X. Armed with the concept of a random variable we proceed to take the **second step**, which amounts to trading the probability set function:

$$\mathbb{P}(.): \Im \to [0,1],$$

with a much simpler point-to-point numerical function, the *cumulative distribution function* (cdf), defined in terms of X:

$$F_X(.): \mathbb{R} \to [0,1].$$

The **third step** is to simplify the cdf by transforming it into the *density function*:

$$f_x(.): \mathbb{R} \to [0,\infty).$$

The notion of a probability model is often defined in terms of the density function.

   From the mathematical viewpoint it is always more satisfying to define a concept in its full generality and then proceed to discuss the special cases. From the pedagogical viewpoint, however, it is often better to begin the discussion with the simplest case and then proceed to the more general formulation in order to help the reader understand the concept without undue mathematical machinery. In the case of the notion of a random variable what renders the definition easy or not so easy, from the mathematical viewpoint, is whether the outcomes set is countable or not. In the case of a countable outcomes set, the random variable is said to be simple (or discrete) because it takes a countable number of values. To help the reader understand the modern notion of a random variable and how it transforms the abstract statistical space into something much easier to handle, the discussion begins with the simplest case and proceeds to discuss the more complicated ones:

(i)   the outcomes set is finite,
(ii)   the outcomes set is countable but infinite,
(iii) the outcomes set is uncountable.

3.2.1   Finite outcomes set: $S = \{s_1, s_2, \ldots, s_n\}$

A simple random variable with respect to the event space $\Im$, is defined to be a function:

$$X(.): S \to \mathbb{R}_X, \text{ such that } A_x := \{s: X(s) = x\} \in \Im \text{ for each } x \in \mathbb{R}. \tag{3.1}$$

Heuristically, a random variable is a function which attaches numbers to all the elements of S in a way which preserves the event structure of $\Im$.

Example
The function $X(.): S \to \mathbb{R}_X := \{1,2\}$, where $S = \{\clubsuit, \spadesuit, \diamond, \heartsuit\}$ defined by:

$$X(\clubsuit) = X(\spadesuit) = 1, \; X(\diamond) = X(\heartsuit) = 2,$$

is a random variable with respect to the event space: $\Im = \{S, \emptyset, \{\clubsuit, \spadesuit\}, \{\diamond, \heartsuit\}\}$. This is because the events associated with $\mathbb{R}_X := \{1,2\}$: $A_1 = \{s: X(s) = 1\} = \{\clubsuit, \spadesuit\} \in \Im$, and $A_2 = \{s: X(s) = 2\} = \{\diamond, \heartsuit\} \in \Im$, are events which belong to $\Im$.

Counter-example
The function $Y(.): S \to \mathbb{R}_Y := \{0,1\}$ defined by:

$$Y(\heartsuit) = 0, \; Y(\clubsuit) = Y(\spadesuit) = Y(\diamond) = 1, \tag{3.2}$$

is not a random variable with respect to $\Im$ because the event $\{s: Y(s) = 0\} = \{\heartsuit\} \notin \Im$.

There are several things to NOTE about the above definition:

First, the name random variable is something of a misnomer. The definition of a random variable (3.1) has nothing to do with probabilities and thus it is neither random nor a variable; it is just a real-valued function.

Second, the notion of a random variable is always defined *relative* to an event space $\Im$; whether or not $X(.)$ satisfies condition (3.1) depends on $\Im$, not on $\mathbb{P}(.)$. The fact that a certain real-valued function is not a random variable with respect to a particular $\Im$ does

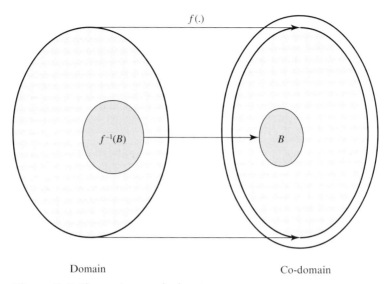

Figure 3.1 The pre-image of a function

not mean that it cannot be a random variable with respect to some other event space. Indeed, for any function $Y(.): S \rightarrow \mathbb{R}_Y$ we can always define a field $\mathfrak{I}_Y$ with respect to which $Y(.)$ is a random variable; we call $\mathfrak{I}_Y$ the *field generated by* $Y(.)$; see Bhat (1985).

Example

In the case of $Y(.)$ as defined by (3.2) we can generate an event space $\mathfrak{I}_Y$ with respect to which it is a simple random variable, as follows:

(i) define all the events associated with $Y(.)$:
$$\{s: Y(s) = 1\} = \{\clubsuit, \spadesuit, \diamondsuit\}, \quad \{s: Y(s) = 0\} = \{\heartsuit\}.$$

(ii) generate a field using the events derived in (i):
$$\mathfrak{I}_Y := \sigma(Y) = \{S, \emptyset, \{\clubsuit, \spadesuit, \diamondsuit\}, \{\heartsuit\}\}.$$

$\mathfrak{I}_Y := \sigma(Y)$ is known as *the minimal field generated by the random variable* Y.

Third, the set A_x is not a set on the real line, it is the pre-image of X at $X = x$, which can also be denoted by:

$$A_x := \{s: X(s) = x\} = X^{-1}(x), x \in \mathbb{R}.$$

NOTE that the pre-image of X is *not* the usual inverse function. The notion of a pre-image of an element of the co-domain is illustrated in figure 3.1.

Fourth, the values of $\mathbb{R}$ which do not belong to $\mathbb{R}_X$ have the empty set $\emptyset$ as their pre-image. The empty set, however, always belongs to all $\mathfrak{I}$:

$$X^{-1}(x) := \{s: X(s) = x\} = \emptyset \in \mathfrak{I}, \text{ for all } x \in \overline{\mathbb{R}}_X := (\mathbb{R} - \mathbb{R}_X).$$

In a certain sense the notion of a random variable preserves the event structure of a particular event space $\Im$, by ensuring that the pre-image of the function $X(.) : S \to \mathbb{R}_X$, defines a mapping:

$$X^{-1}(.) : \mathbb{R} \to \Im, \tag{3.3}$$

where for each $x \in \mathbb{R}_X$, $X^{-1}(x) \in \Im$, and for each $x \notin \mathbb{R}_X$, $X^{-1}(x) = \emptyset \in \Im$. This divides the real line into two sub-sets, $\mathbb{R}_X$ and $\overline{\mathbb{R}}_X$, with the former associated with the event structure of interest and the latter with everything of no interest.

Fifth, the nature of the random variable depends crucially on the size of the field in question. If $\Im$ is small, being a random variable relative to $\Im$ is very restrictive. For example in the case $\Im_0 = \{S, \emptyset\}$ the only $X(.) : S \to \mathbb{R}$ which is a random variable relative to $\Im_0$ is $X(s) = c$, for all $s \in S$; c being a constant X is a *degenerate* random variable. On the other hand, if $\Im$ is large, say the power set, then it takes a lot of weird imagination to define a function $X(.) : S \to \mathbb{R}$ which is not a random variable with respect to it.

After these comments on the definition of a random variable let us return to the notion itself to consider some examples.

Example

An important example of a simple random variable is the indicator function defined relative to a set A in $\Im$ as follows:

$$\mathbb{I}_A(s) = \begin{cases} 1, s \in A, \\ 0, s \notin A. \end{cases}$$

Let us show that $\mathbb{I}_A(s)$ is indeed a random variable. Taking its pre-image we get:

$$\mathbb{I}_A^{-1}(0) = \overline{A} \in \Im \text{ and } \mathbb{I}_A^{-1}(1) = A \in \Im.$$

We know this is true because if $A \in \Im$ then $\overline{A} \in \Im$. This shows that $\mathbb{I}_A(.)$ is a random variable with respect to $\Im$. Moreover, $\Im_A = \{A, \overline{A}, S, \emptyset\}$ is the minimal event space *generated* by the indicator function $\mathbb{I}_A(s)$.

Assigning probabilities

Using the concept of a random variable we mapped S (an arbitrary set) to a subset of the real line (a set of numbers) $\mathbb{R}_X$. Because we do not want to change the original probability structure of $(S, \Im, \mathbb{P}(.))$ we imposed condition (3.1) to ensure that all events defined in terms of the random variable X belong to the original event space $\Im$. We also want to ensure that the same events in the original probability space $(S, \Im, \mathbb{P}(.))$ and the new formulation, such as $A_x = \{s : X(s) = x\}$, get assigned the same probabilities. In order to ensure this, we define the point function $f_x(.)$, which we call a **density function** as follows:

$$f_x(x) := \mathbb{P}(X = x) \text{ for all } x \in \mathbb{R}_X. \tag{3.4}$$

NOTE that $(X = x)$ is a shorthand notation for $A :_x = \{s : X(s) = x\}$. Clearly, for $x \notin \mathbb{R}_X$, $X^{-1}(x) = \emptyset$, and thus $f_x(x) = 0$, for all $x \notin \mathbb{R}_X$.

Example. In the case of the indicator function, if we let $X(s) := I_A(s)$ we can define the probability density as follows:

$$f_x(1) := \mathbb{P}(X=1) = \theta \text{ and } f_x(0) := \mathbb{P}(X=0) = (1-\theta),$$

where $0 \leq \theta \leq 1$. This is known as the **Bernoulli density**:

x	0	1
$f_x(x)$	$(1-\theta)$	θ

(3.5)

What have we gained?

In the context of the original probability space $(S, \Im, \mathbb{P}(.))$, where $S = \{s_1, s_2, \ldots, s_n\}$, the probabilistic structure of the random experiment was specified in terms of:

$$\{p(s_1), p(s_2), \ldots, p(s_n)\}, \text{ such that } \sum_{i=1}^{n} p(s_i) = 1.$$

Armed with this we could assign a probability of any event $A \in \Im$ as follows. We know that all events $A \in \Im$ are just unions of certain outcomes. Given that outcomes are also mutually exclusive elementary events, we proceed to use axiom [3] (see chapter 2) to define the probability of A as equal to the sum of the probabilities assigned to each of the outcomes making up the event A, i.e., if $A = \{s_1, s_2, \ldots, s_k\}$, then:

$$\mathbb{P}(A) = \sum_{i=1}^{k} p(s_i).$$

Example

In the case of the random experiment of "tossing a coin twice":

$$S = \{(HH), (HT), (TH), (TT)\}, \Im = \mathcal{P}(S),$$

where $\mathcal{P}(S)$ denotes the *power set* of S: the set of all subsets of S (see chapter 2). The random variable of interest is defined by: X – the number of "Heads". This suggest that the events of interest are:

$$A_0 = \{s : X = 0\} = \{(TT)\},$$
$$A_1 = \{s : X = 1\} = \{(HT), (TH)\},$$
$$A_2 = \{s : X = 2\} = \{(HH)\}.$$

In the case of a fair coin, all four outcomes are given the same probability and thus:

$$\mathbb{P}(A_0) = \mathbb{P}\{s : X = 0\} = \mathbb{P}\{(TT)\} = \tfrac{1}{4},$$
$$\mathbb{P}(A_1) = \mathbb{P}\{s : X = 1\} = \mathbb{P}\{(HT), (TH)\} = \mathbb{P}(HT) + \mathbb{P}(TH) = \tfrac{1}{2},$$
$$\mathbb{P}(A_2) = \mathbb{P}\{s : X = 2\} = \mathbb{P}\{(HH)\} = \tfrac{1}{4}.$$

Returning to the main focus of this chapter, we can claim that using the concept of a random variable we achieved the following metamorphosis:

$$(S, \Im, \mathbb{P}(.)) \overset{X(.)}{\Rightarrow} (\mathbb{R}_X, f_x(.)),$$

where the original probabilistic structure has now been transformed into:

$$\{f_x(x_1), f_x(x_2), \ldots, f_x(x_m)\}, \text{ such that } \sum_{i=1}^{m} f_x(x_i) = 1, m \leq n;$$

this is referred to as **the probability distribution** of a random variable X.

The question which arises at this point is to what extent the latter description of the probabilistic structure is preferable to the former. At first sight it looks as though no mileage has been gained by this transformation. However, it turns out that this is misleading and a lot of mileage has been gained for two reasons.

(a) Instead of having to specify $\{f_x(x_1), f_x(x_2), \ldots, f_x(x_m)\}$ by listing them, we can use simple real valued functions in the form of formulae such as:

$$f_x(x;\theta) = \theta^x(1-\theta)^{1-x}, \; x=0,1, \text{ and } 0 \leq \theta \leq 1, \tag{3.6}$$

which specify the distribution implicitly. For each value of X the function $f_x(x)$ specifies its probability. This formula constitutes a more compact way of specifying the distribution given above.

(b) Using such formulae there is no need to know the probabilities associated with the events of interest a priori. In the case of the above formula, θ could be unknown and the set of such density functions is referred to as *a family of density functions* indexed by θ. This is particularly important for modeling purposes where such a collection of density functions provides the basis of probability models. In a sense, the uncertainty relating to the outcome of a particular trial (condition [b] defining a random experiment) has become the uncertainty concerning the "true" value of the unknown parameter θ.

The distribution defined by (3.6) is known as the **Bernoulli distribution**. This distribution can be used to describe random experiments with only two outcomes.

Example
Consider the random experiment of "tossing a coin twice":

$$S = \{(HH),(HT),(TH),(TT)\}, \Im = \{S, \emptyset, A, \overline{A}\},$$

where the event of interest is, say $A = \{(HH),(HT),(TH)\}$, with $\mathbb{P}(A) = \theta$, $\mathbb{P}(\overline{A}) = (1-\theta)$. By defining the random variable $X(A) = 1$ and $X(\overline{A}) = 0$, the probabilistic structure of the experiment is described by the Bernoulli density (3.6).

This type of random experiment can be easily extended to n repetitions of the same two-outcomes experiment, giving rise to the so-called *Binomial* distribution discussed next.

Example
Consider the random experiment of "tossing a coin n times and counting the number of Heads." The outcomes set for this experiment is defined by $S = \{H,T\}^n$ (the product of $\{H,T\}$ n times) with $\mathbb{P}(H) = \theta$ and $\mathbb{P}(T) = 1-\theta$. Define the random variable:

X: the total number of Hs in n trials.

NOTE that the range of values of this new random variable is $\mathbb{R}_X = \{0,1,2,3,\ldots,n\}$. The random variable X is **Binomially distributed** and its density function for $0 \leq x \leq n$ is:

$$f_x(x;\theta) = \binom{n}{x} \theta^x(1-\theta)^{n-x}, \; 0 \leq x \leq n, \; n=1,2,\ldots, \; 0 \leq \theta \leq 1, \tag{3.7}$$

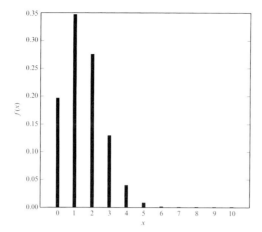

Figure 3.2 Binomial ($n = 10$, $\theta = 0.15$)

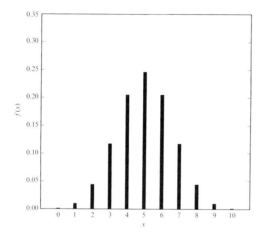

Figure 3.3 Binomial ($n = 10$, $\theta = 0.5$)

where $\binom{n}{k} = \frac{n!}{(n-k)!k!}$, where $n! = n \cdot (n-1) \cdot (n-2) \cdots (3) \cdot (2) \cdot 1$.

This formula can be graphed for specific values of θ. In figures 3.2 and 3.3 we can see the graph of the Binomial density function (3.7) with $n = 10$ and two different values of the unknown parameter, $\theta = 0.15$ and $\theta = 0.5$, respectively. The horizontal axis depicts the values of the random variable X ($\mathbb{R}_X = \{0,1,2,3, \ldots, n\}$) and the vertical axis depicts the values of the corresponding probabilities as shown below.

x	0	1	2	3	4	5	6	7	8	9	10
$f(x;0.15)$	0.197	0.347	0.276	0.130	0.040	0.009	0.001	0.000	0.000	0.000	0.000
$f(x;0.5)$	0.001	0.010	0.044	0.117	0.205	0.246	0.205	0.117	0.044	0.010	0.001

In concluding this subsection, it is worth mentioning that the gains from using density functions are even more apparent in the case where the outcomes set S is infinite but countable. As shown next, in such a case listing the probabilities for each $s \in S$ in a table is impossible. The assignment of probabilities using a density function, however, renders it trivial.

3.2.2 Countable outcomes set: $S = \{s_1, s_2, ..., s_n, ...\}$

Consider the case of the countable outcomes set $S = \{s_1, s_2, ..., s_n, ...\}$. This is a simple extension of the finite outcome set case where the probabilistic structure of the experiment is specified in terms of:

$$\{p(s_1), p(s_2), ..., p(s_n), ...\}, \text{ such that } \sum_{i=1}^{\infty} p(s_i) = 1.$$

The probability of an event $A \in \Im$, is equal to the sum of the probabilities assigned to each of the outcomes making up the event A:

$$\mathbb{P}(A) = \sum_{\{i:s_i \in A\}} p(s_i).$$

Example
Consider the random experiment of "tossing a coin until the first H turns up." The outcomes set is:

$$S = \{(H), (TH), (TTH), (TTTH), (TTTTH), (TTTTTH), ...\}$$

and let the event space be the power set of S. If we define the random variable $X(.)$ – the number of trials needed to get one H, i.e.

$$X(H) = 1, X(TH) = 2, X(TTH) = 3, \text{ etc.}$$

and $\mathbb{P}(H) = \theta$, then the density function for this experiment is:

$$f_x(x;\theta) = (1-\theta)^{x-1}\theta, \, 0 \leq \theta \leq 1, \, x \in \mathbb{R}_X = \{1, 2, 3, ...\}.$$

This is the density function of the **Geometric distribution**. This density function is graphed in figures 3.4–3.5 for $n = 20$ and two different values of the unknown parameter $\theta = 0.20$ and $\theta = 0.35$, respectively. Looking at these graphs we can see why it is called Geometric: the probabilities decline geometrically as the values of X increase.

3.3   The general notion of a random variable

Having introduced the basic concepts needed for the transformation of the abstract probability space $(S, \Im, \mathbb{P}(.))$ into something more appropriate (and manageable) for modeling purposes, using the simplest case of countable outcomes set, we will now proceed to explain these concepts in their full generality.

3.3.1 Uncountable outcomes set S

As a prelude to the discussion that follows, let us see why the previous strategy of assigning probabilities to each and every outcome in the case of an uncountable set, say $S = \mathbb{R}$,

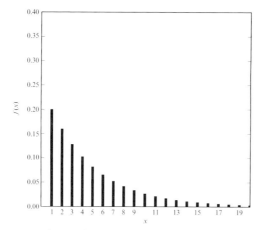

Figure 3.4 Geometric ($n = 20$, $\theta = 0.2$)

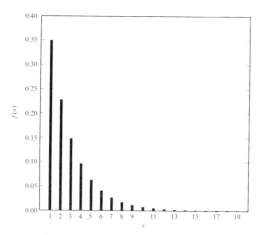

Figure 3.5 Geometric ($n = 20$, $\theta = 0.35$)

will not work. The reason is very simple: the outcomes set has so many elements that it is impossible to arrange them in a sequence and thus count them. Hence, any attempt to follow the procedure used in the countable outcomes set case will lead to insurmountable difficulties. Intuitively we know that we cannot cover the real line point by point. The only way to overlay $\mathbb{R}$, or any of its uncountable subsets, is to use a sequence of intervals of any one of the following forms:

$$(a,b),\ [a,b],\ [a,b),\ (-\infty,a],\ \text{where } a < b,\ a \text{ and } b \text{ are real numbers.}$$

We will see in the sequel that the most convenient form for such intervals is:

$$\{(-\infty, x]\} \text{ for each } x \in \mathbb{R}. \tag{3.8}$$

Random variable

In view of the above discussion any attempt to define a random variable using the definition of a simple random variable:

$$X(.): S \to \mathbb{R}_X, \text{ such that } \{s: X(s) = x\} := X^{-1}(x) \in \Im \text{ for each } x \in \mathbb{R}. \tag{3.9}$$

is doomed to failure. We have just agreed that the only way we can overlay $\mathbb{R}$ is by using *intervals* not *points*. The half-infinite intervals (3.8) suggest modifying the events $\{s: X(s) = x\}$ of (3.9) into events of the form $\{s: X(s) \le x\}$.

A random variable relative to $\Im$ is a function $X(.): S \to \mathbb{R}$, that satisfies the restriction:

$$\{s: X(s) \le x\} := X^{-1}((-\infty, x]) \in \Im \text{ for all } x \in \mathbb{R}. \tag{3.10}$$

NOTE that the only difference between this definition and that of a simple random variable comes in the form of the events used. Moreover, in view of the fact that:

$$\{s: X(s) = x\} \subset \{s: X(s) \le x\}$$

the latter definition includes the former as a special case, hence the term simple random variable. In principle we could have begun the discussion with the general definition of a random variable (3.10) and then applied it to the various different types of outcomes sets.

From this definition we can see that the pre-image of the random variable $X(.)$ takes us from intervals $(-\infty, x]$, $x \in \mathbb{R}$ back to the event space $\Im$. The set of all such intervals generates a σ-field on the real line we called the **Borel-field** $\mathcal{B}(\mathbb{R})$:

$$\mathcal{B}(\mathbb{R}) = \sigma((-\infty, x], x \in \mathbb{R}).$$

Hence, in a formal sense, the pre-image of the random variable $X(.)$ constitutes a mapping from the Borel-field $\mathcal{B}(\mathbb{R})$ to the event space $\Im$ and takes the form:

$$X^{-1}(.): \mathcal{B}(\mathbb{R}) \to \Im. \tag{3.11}$$

This ensures that the random variable $X(.)$ preserves the event structure of $\Im$ because the pre-image preserves the set theoretic operations (see Karr (1973)):

(i)   Union: $X^{-1}(\bigcup_{i=1}^{\infty} B_i) = \bigcup_{i=1}^{\infty} X^{-1}(B_i),$

(ii) Intersection: $X^{-1}(\bigcap_{i=1}^{\infty} B_i) = \bigcap_{i=1}^{\infty} X^{-1}(B_i),$

(iii) Complementation: $X^{-1}(\overline{B}) = (\overline{X^{-1}(B)}).$

The probability space induced by a random variable*

Let us take stock of what we have achieved so far. The metamorphosis of the probability space $(S, \Im, \mathbb{P}(.))$ into something more appropriate for modeling purposes has so far traded the outcomes set S with a subset of the real line $\mathbb{R}_X$ and the event space $\Im$ with the Borel-field $\mathcal{B}(\mathbb{R})$. The *modus operandi* of this transformation has been the concept of a random variable.

The next step will transform $\mathbb{P}(.): \Im \to [0,1]$ into a set function on the real line or more precisely on $\mathcal{B}(\mathbb{R})$. This metamorphosis of the probability set function takes the form:

$$\mathbb{P}(X \le x) = \mathbb{P} X^{-1}((-\infty, x]) = P_X((-\infty, x]).$$

It is very important to NOTE at this stage that the events in the first and second terms are elements of the event space $\Im$ but that of the last equality is an element of $\mathcal{B}(\mathbb{R})$. We are now in a position to assign probabilities to intervals of the form $\{(-\infty,x]:x\in\mathbb{R}\}$ whose pre-image belongs to $\Im$. For other intervals of the form (a,b), $[a,b]$, $[a,b)$, $(-\infty,a)$, etc. we can use Caratheodory's extension theorem to extend the probability set function $P_X(.)$ in order to assign probabilities to every element B_x of $\mathcal{B}(\mathbb{R})$:

$$\mathbb{P}X^{-1}(B_x)=P_X(B_x) \text{ for each } B_x\in\mathcal{B}(\mathbb{R}).$$

This defines a new probability set function as a composite function $\mathbb{P}X^{-1}(.)$ where $\mathbb{P}(.): \Im\to[0,1]$, $X^{-1}(.): \mathcal{B}(\mathbb{R})\to\Im$, and thus:

$$P_X(.):=\mathbb{P}X^{-1}(.): \mathcal{B}(\mathbb{R})\to[0,1].$$

Collecting the above elements together we can see that in effect a random variable X induces a new probability space $(\mathbb{R},\mathcal{B}(\mathbb{R}),P_X(.))$ with which we can replace the abstract probability space $(S,\Im,\mathbb{P}(.))$. The main advantage of the former over the latter is that everything takes place on the real line and not in some abstract space. In direct analogy to the countable outcomes set case, the general concept of a random variable induces the following mapping:

$$(S,\Im,\mathbb{P}(.))\overset{X(.)}{\Rightarrow}(\mathbb{R},\mathcal{B}(\mathbb{R}),P_X(.)).$$

That is, with the help of $X(.)$ we traded S for $\mathbb{R}$, $\Im$ for $\mathcal{B}(\mathbb{R})$ and $\mathbb{P}(.)$ for $P_X(.)$. For reference purposes we call $(\mathbb{R},\mathcal{B}(\mathbb{R}),P_X(.))$ the probability space *induced* by a random variable X; see Galambos (1995).

Borel (measurable) functions In probability theory we are interested not just in random variables but in well-behaved functions of such random variables as well. By well-behaved functions, in calculus, we usually mean continuous or differentiable functions. In probability theory by well-behaved functions we mean functions which preserve the event structure of their argument random variable. A function defined by:

$$h(.): \mathbb{R}\to\mathbb{R} \text{ such that } \{h(X)\leq x\}:=h^{-1}((-\infty,x])\in\mathcal{B}(\mathbb{R}), \text{ for any } x\in\mathbb{R},$$

is called a *Borel (measurable) function*. That is, a *Borel function* is a function which is a random variable relative to $\mathcal{B}(\mathbb{R})$. NOTE that indicator functions, monotone functions, continuous functions, as well as functions, with a finite number of discontinuities, are Borel functions; see Khazanie (1976), Bierens (1994).

Equality of random variables Random variables are unlike mathematical functions in so far as their probabilistic structure is of paramount importance. Hence, the notion of equality for random variables involves this probabilistic structure. Two random variables X and Y, defined on the same probability space $(S,\Im,\mathbb{P}(.))$, are said to be equal *with probability one* (or *almost surely*) if (see Karr (1993)):

$$\mathbb{P}(s:X(s)\neq Y(s))=0, \text{ for all } s\in S;$$

i.e., if the set $(s:X(s)\neq Y(s))$ is an event with zero probability.

3.4   The cumulative distribution and density functions

3.4.1 The cumulative distribution function

Using the concept of a random variable $X(.)$, so far we transformed the abstract probability space $(S,\Im,\mathbb{P}(.))$ into a less abstract space $(\mathbb{R},\mathcal{B}(\mathbb{R}),P_X(.))$. However, we have not reached our target yet because $P_X(.):=\mathbb{P}X^{-1}(.)$ is still a set function. Admittedly it is a much easier set function because it is defined on the real line, but a set function all the same. What we prefer is a numerical point-to-point function with which we are familiar.

The way we transform the set function $P_X(.)$ into a numerical point-to-point function is by a clever stratagem. By viewing $P_X(.)$ as only a function of the end point of the interval $(-\infty,x]$ we define the **cumulative distribution function** (cdf):

$$F_X(.):\mathbb{R}\to[0,1],\text{ where }F_X(x)=\mathbb{P}\{s:X(s)\le x\}=P_X((-\infty,x]). \qquad (3.12)$$

The ploy leading to this definition began a few pages ago when we argued that even though we could use any one of the following intervals (see Galambos (1995)):

$$(a,b),[a,b],[a,b),(-\infty,a],\text{ where }a<b,a\in\mathbb{R}\text{ and }b\in\mathbb{R},$$

to generate the Borel-field $\mathcal{B}(\mathbb{R})$, we chose the intervals of the form: $(-\infty,x]$, $x\in\mathbb{R}$.
In view of this, we can think of the cdf as being defined via:

$$\mathbb{P}\{s:a<X(s)\le b\}=\mathbb{P}\{s:X(s)\le b\}-\mathbb{P}\{s:X(s)\le a\}=P_X((a,b])=F_X(b)-F_X(a),$$

and then assume that $F_X(-\infty)=0$.

The properties of the cdf $F_X(x)$ of the random variable X are determined by those of $(S,\Im,\mathbb{P}(.))$. In particular, from axioms [1]–[3] of $\mathbb{P}(.)$ and the mathematical structure of the σ-fields $\Im$ and $\mathcal{B}(\mathbb{R})$. We summarize the **properties of the cumulative distribution function** (see Karr (1993)):

F1. $F_X(x)\le F_X(y)$, for $x\le y$, x,y real numbers,

F2. $\lim_{x\to x_0^+}F_X(x)=F_X(x_0)$, for any real number x_0,

F3. $\lim_{x\to\infty}F_X(x):=F_X(\infty)=1$, $\lim_{x\to-\infty}F_X(x):=F_X(-\infty)=0$.

where $x\to x_0^+$ reads "as x tends to x_0 through values greater than x_0." That is, $F_X(x)$ is a non-decreasing, right-continuous function such that $F_X(-\infty)=0$, and $F_X(\infty)=1$. Properties **F1** and **F3** need no further explanation but **F2** is not obvious. The right-continuity property of the cdf follows from the axiom of countable additivity [3] of the probability set function $\mathbb{P}(.)$ and its value lies with the fact that at every point of discontinuity x_0 property **F2** holds.

The cumulative distribution function (cdf) provides the last link in the chain of the metamorphosis of $(S,\Im,\mathbb{P}(.))$ into something more amenable to modeling. Before we proceed to enhance our intuitive understanding of the concept we need to relate it to the notion of a density function introduced in the context of simple (discrete) random variables.

The discerning reader would have noticed that in the context of simple (discrete) random variables the metamorphosis of the abstract probability space took the form:

$$(S,\Im,\mathbb{P}(.)) \overset{X(.)}{\Rightarrow} (\mathbb{R}_X, f_x(.)),$$

where $\mathbb{R}_X = \{x_1, x_2, \dots, x_n, \dots\}$. The original probabilistic structure has been transformed into:

$$\{f_x(x_1), f_x(x_2), \dots, f_x(x_m), \dots\} \text{ such that } \sum_{x_i \in \mathbb{R}_X} f_x(x_i) = 1.$$

The last link in the metamorphosis chain was the notion of a density function:

$$f_x(.): \mathbb{R}_X \to [0,1], f_x(x) := \mathbb{P}(X = x) \text{ for all } x \in \mathbb{R}_X.$$

On the other hand, in the context of a continuous random variable (uncountable outcomes set) the metamorphosis took the form:

$$(S,\Im,\mathbb{P}(.)) \overset{X(.)}{\Rightarrow} (\mathbb{R}_X, F_X(.)),$$

with the cdf being the last link in the chain. The reason why the density function could not be defined directly in this case has been discussed extensively in the previous chapter. The gist of the argument is that in the case of an uncountable outcomes set we cannot define probability at a point but only over an interval.

3.4.2   The density function

At this stage two questions arise naturally. The first is whether we can define a density function in the case of a continuous random variable. The second is whether we can define a cdf in the case of a discrete random variable. Both questions will be answered in the affirmative beginning with the first.

Having defined the cumulative distribution function over intervals of the form $((-\infty, x])$ we can proceed to recover the *density function* $f_x(.)$ (when it exists). Assuming that there exists a function of the form:

$$f_x(.): \mathbb{R} \to [0, \infty), \tag{3.13}$$

such that it is related to the cdf via:

$$F_X(x) = \int_{-\infty}^{x} f_x(u)\, du, \text{ where } f_x(u) \geq 0, \tag{3.14}$$

$f_x(.)$ is said to be a **density function** which corresponds to $F_X(.)$.

This recovery presupposes the existence of a non-negative function whose form one has to guess a priori. In cases where $f_x(.)$ is assumed to be *continuous*, one can recover it from $F_X(.)$ using the *fundamental theorem of calculus* (see Strang (1991), Binmore (1993)). Suppose that $f_x(x)$ is a *continuous* function of x:

(a)   if $F_X(x) = \int_{-\infty}^{x} f_x(u)\, du,$ then $\frac{dF_X(x)}{dx} = f_x(x),$

(b)   if $\frac{dF_X(x)}{dx} = f_x(x),$ then $\int_{a}^{b} f_x(u)\, du = F_X(b) - F_X(a).$

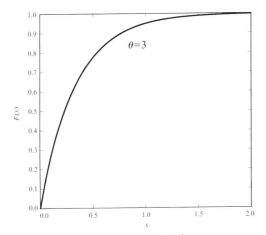

Figure 3.6 Exponential cdf

Using the fundamental theorem of calculus we can recover the density function much easier by differentiation using the fact that:

$$\frac{dF_X(x)}{dx} = f_x(x), \text{ at all continuity points } x \in \mathbb{R} \text{ of } f_x(x).$$

Example

Consider the random experiment of "measuring the lifetime of a light bulb in a typical home environment." The cumulative distribution function often used to model this experiment is that of the **exponential distribution**:

$$F_X(x;\theta) = 1 - e^{-\theta x}, \theta > 0, x \in \mathbb{R}_+ := [0,\infty).$$

The graph of the cdf for $\theta = 3$ is shown in figure 3.6. In view of the fact that $F_X(x;\theta)$ is continuous for all $x \in \mathbb{R}_+$, we can deduce that the density function is just the derivative of this function and takes the form (see figure 3.7):

$$f_x(x;\theta) = \theta e^{-\theta x}, \theta > 0, x \in \mathbb{R}_+.$$

The **density function,** for *continuous random variables*, defined by (3.14), satisfies the following **properties**:

f1. $f_x(x) \geq 0$, for all $x \in \mathbb{R}_X$,

f2. $\int_{-\infty}^{\infty} f_x(x)dx = 1$,

f3. $F_X(b) - F_X(a) = \int_a^b f_x(x)dx, a < b, a \in \mathbb{R}, b \in \mathbb{R}.$

We now turn our attention to the question whether we can define a cdf in the case of simple (discrete) random variables. The definition of the cumulative distribution function given in (3.12) is also applicable to the case where $X(.)$ takes values in a *countable* subset of $\mathbb{R}$. For $\mathbb{R}_X = \{x_1, x_2, \ldots, x_n\}$, where $x_1 < x_2 < \ldots < x_n$, the cdf function of a random variable $X(.)$ is defined in terms of the density function by:

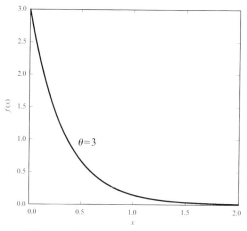

Figure 3.7 Exponential density

$$F_X(x_k) = \mathbb{P}(\{s : X(s) \leq x_k\}) = \sum_{i=1}^{k} f_x(x_i), \text{ for } k = 1, 2, \ldots, n. \tag{3.15}$$

That is, the cdf for a simple (*discrete*) random variable is a *step function* with the jumps defined by $f_x(.)$. The term *cumulative* stems from the fact that the cdf in both cases (3.12) and (3.15) accumulates the probabilities given by the density functions. This becomes apparent by ordering the values of X in ascending order $x_1 \leq x_2 \leq \ldots \leq x_n$ and assuming that $F_X(x_0) = 0$, then $F_X(.)$ and $f_x(.)$ are related via:

$$f_x(x_i) = F_X(x_i) - F_X(x_{i-1}), \ i = 1, 2, \ldots n.$$

The **density function**, in the case of a *discrete random variable*, has **properties** similar to those above with the integral replaced by a summation:

f1. $f_x(x) \geq 0$, for all $x \in \mathbb{R}_X$,

f2. $\sum_{x_i \in \mathbb{R}_X} f_x(x_i) = 1$,

f3. $F_X(b) - F_X(a) = \sum_{a < x_i \leq b} f_x(x_i), \ a < b, \ a \in \mathbb{R}, \ b \in \mathbb{R}.$

Example
In the case of the **Bernoulli** random variable the density function is:

$$f_x(1) = \theta \text{ and } f_x(0) = (1 - \theta),$$

where $0 \leq \theta \leq 1$ (see 3.5). This is shown in figure 3.8 for a known value of θ, denoted by $\theta = 0.6$. The corresponding cdf takes the form $F_X(0) = \theta$, $F_X(1) = 1$:

$$F_X(x) = \begin{cases} 0, & x < 0, \\ \theta, & 0 \leq x < 1, \\ 1, & 1 \leq x. \end{cases}$$

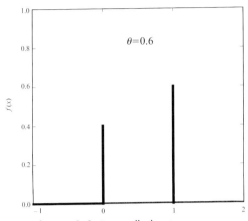

Figure 3.8 Bernoulli density

As can be seen from figure 3.9 the cdf is a step function with jumps at $x=0$ of height $(1 - \theta) = 0.4$ and $x = 1$ of height $\theta = 0.6$. The dots at points $(0,0.4)$ and $(1,1)$ symbolize the right continuity of the cdf; these points belong to the upper line not the lower.

Although the cdf appears to be the natural choice for assigning probabilities in cases where the random variable $X(.)$ takes values in an uncountable subset of $\mathbb{R}$, the density function offers itself more conveniently for modeling purposes. For this reason we conclude this section by mentioning some more distributions for both continuous and discrete random variables.

Continuous random variable A random variable $X(.)$ is said to be *continuous* if its range of values is any uncountable subset of $\mathbb{R}$. A glance at the definition (3.13)–(3.14) suggests that one should not interpret the density function of a continuous random variable as a function assigning probabilities, because the latter might take values greater than one!

Examples

(i)   The most widely used distribution in probability theory and statistical inference is without a doubt the **Normal** (or **Gaussian**) distribution whose density function is:

$$f_x(x;\theta) = \frac{1}{\sigma\sqrt{2\pi}}\exp\left\{-\frac{(x-\mu)^2}{2\sigma^2}\right\}, \ \theta:=(\mu,\sigma^2)\in\mathbb{R}\times\mathbb{R}_+, x\in\mathbb{R}. \tag{3.16}$$

The graph of this density function, shown in figure 3.10 with $\mu=0$ and $\sigma^2=1$, exhibits the well-known bell shape with which the Normal distribution is easily recognizable. The cdf for the Normal distribution is:

$$F_X(x;\theta) = \int_{-\infty}^{x}\frac{1}{\sigma\sqrt{2\pi}}\exp\left\{-\frac{(\mu-\mu)^2}{2\sigma^2}\right\}du, \ \theta:=(\mu,\sigma^2)\in\mathbb{R}\times\mathbb{R}_+, x\in\mathbb{R}. \tag{3.17}$$

The graph of this cdf, shown in figure 3.11, exhibits the distinct elongated S associated with the Normal distribution.

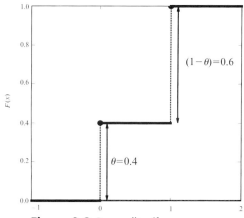

Figure 3.9 Bernoulli cdf

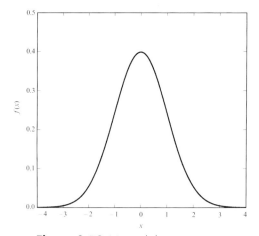

Figure 3.10 Normal density

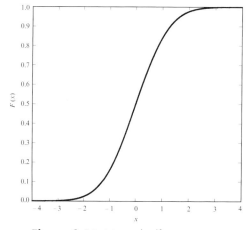

Figure 3.11 Normal cdf

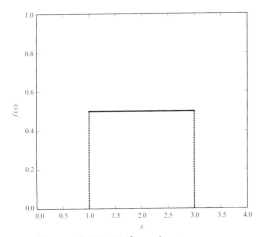

Figure 3.12 Uniform density

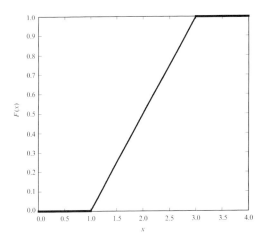

Figure 3.13 Uniform cdf

(ii)   Another widely used distribution is the **Uniform** (continuous) whose density function is of the form:

$$f_x(x;\boldsymbol{\theta}) = \frac{1}{b-a}, \ \boldsymbol{\theta} := (a,b) \in \mathbb{R}^2, \ a \le x \le b. \tag{3.18}$$

The graph of this density function, shown in figure 3.12 for a = 1 and b = 3, exhibits a rectangular shape. The cdf for the Uniform (continuous) distribution is:

$$F_X(x;\boldsymbol{\theta}) = \frac{x-a}{b-a}, \ \boldsymbol{\theta} := (a,b) \in \mathbb{R}^2, \ a \le x \le b. \tag{3.19}$$

The graph of this cdf is shown in figure 3.13.

Discrete random variable A random variable $X(.)$ is said to be *discrete* if its range $\mathbb{R}_X$ is a countable (it can be counted) subset of the real line $\mathbb{R}$; its density function is of the form:

$$f_x(.) : \mathbb{R} \to [0,1].$$

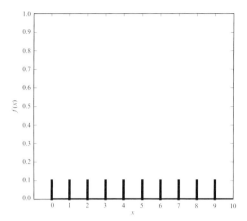

Figure 3.14 Uniform (discrete) density

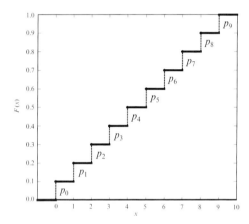

Figure 3.15 Uniform (discrete) cdf

In contrast to the continuous random variable case, this definition suggests that one could interpret the density function of a discrete random variable as a function assigning probabilities.

Examples

(i)   The **Uniform** distribution also has a **discrete** form, with a density function:

$$f_x(x;\theta) = \tfrac{1}{\theta+1}, \; \theta \text{ is an integer, } x = 0,1,2, \dots, \theta. \tag{3.20}$$

The graph of this density function, shown in figure 3.14 for $\theta = 9$, exhibits the well-known uniform spike shape. The cdf for the Uniform (discrete) distribution is:

$$F_X(x;\theta) = \tfrac{x+1}{\theta+1}, \; \theta \text{ is an integer, } x = 0,1,2, \dots, \theta. \tag{3.21}$$

Its graph is shown in figure 3.15 where the jumps are all of the form:

$$p_k = \tfrac{1}{\theta+1}, \text{ for } \theta = 9, k = 1,2, \dots, 9.$$

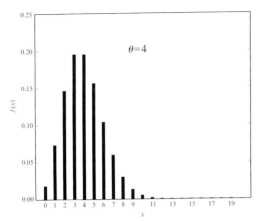

Figure 3.16 Poisson density

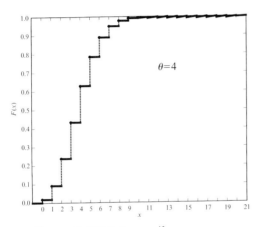

Figure 3.17 Poisson cdf

(ii) Another widely used discrete distribution is the **Poisson** whose density function is:

$$f_x(x;\theta) = \frac{e^{-\theta}\theta^x}{x!}, \ \theta > 0, \ x = 0,1,2,3, \ldots \tag{3.22}$$

The graph of this density function, shown in figure 3.16 for $\theta = 4$, where the asymmetry in the shape of the density is obvious. The cdf for the Poisson distribution is:

$$F_X(x;\theta) = \sum_{k=0}^{x} \frac{e^{-\theta}\theta^x}{k!}, \ \theta > 0, \ x = 0,1,2,3, \ldots \tag{3.23}$$

The graph of the cdf is shown in figure 3.17.

3.5   From a probability space to a probability model

Let us collect the various threads together. We began the discussion in this chapter with one primary target: to transform the abstract probability $(S,\Im,\mathbb{P}(.))$ built in the previous chapter into something more amenable to modeling with numerical data. The first stage

of the transformation amounted to introducing the notion of a real-valued function
from the outcomes space S to the real line $\mathbb{R}$, constrained to preserve the event structure
of the original event space $\Im$; the concept of a random variable. At the second stage we
used the concept of a random variable to map $(S,\Im,\mathbb{P}(.))$ into $(\mathbb{R},\mathcal{B}(\mathbb{R}),P_X(.))$; the latter
being an edifice on the real line. At the third stage we transformed the set function $P_X(.)$
into a numerical point-to-point function, the cumulative distribution function, by:

$$F_X(x) = P_X(-\infty,x].$$

At the last stage we simplified $F_X(.)$ even further by introducing the density function via:

$$F_X(x) = \int_{-\infty}^{x} f_X(u)\,du, \; f_X(x) \geq 0, \text{ for all } x \in \mathbb{R}.$$

We then extended the formulation to the case where the probabilities are known functions of certain **unknown parameter(s)** $\boldsymbol{\theta}$. This was done by introducing these parameters in the formulae for the cdf and density functions: $F(x;\boldsymbol{\theta})$, $f(x;\boldsymbol{\theta})$. The details of this
extension will be discussed in chapter 10. Symbolically the transformation has taken the
form:

$$(S,\Im,\mathbb{P}(.)) \overset{X(.)}{\Rightarrow} (\mathbb{R},\mathcal{B}(\mathbb{R}),P_X(.)) \Rightarrow \{f(x;\boldsymbol{\theta}), \boldsymbol{\theta} \in \Theta, x \in \mathbb{R}_X\}.$$

Ignoring the intermediate step, we can view the mapping at the level of the individual
components as:

$$S \Rightarrow \mathbb{R}_X, \text{ and } [\Im,\mathbb{P}(.)] \Rightarrow \{f(x;\boldsymbol{\theta}), \boldsymbol{\theta} \in \Theta\}.$$

The end result of this metamorphosis is that the original probability space $(S,\Im,\mathbb{P}(.))$
has been metamorphosed into a **probability model** defined by:

$$\Phi = \{f(x;\boldsymbol{\theta}), \boldsymbol{\theta} \in \Theta, x \in \mathbb{R}_X\}. \tag{3.24}$$

Φ is *a collection of density functions indexed by a set of unknown parameters* $\boldsymbol{\theta}$; one density
for each possible value of $\boldsymbol{\theta}$ in the **parameter space** Θ.

It is important to NOTE that we could use the cdf instead of the density function as the
basis of the probability model, in the sense that:

$$\Phi_F = \{F(x;\boldsymbol{\theta}), \boldsymbol{\theta} \in \Theta, x \in \mathbb{R}_X\},$$

is even more general than (3.24). As can be seen from the above graphs of the various
cdf and density functions, however, the shape of the density functions is easier to judge
than that of the cdf. For mathematical reasons we often prefer the cdf but for modeling
purposes we usually prefer the density function. The notion of a probability model, as
defined in terms of density functions, is convenient for modeling purposes because, as
shown in chapter 5, there is a helpful link between this theoretical concept and the
observed data. We will see how the notion of a density function constitutes the probability theory counterpart of the notion of a histogram in descriptive statistics and how
that relates to a t-plot of a set of data. In summary, we can build a direct link between
the probability model and real data in order to help in the choice of appropriate
models.

There are several things worth emphasizing about the probability model as defined in (3.24). *First,* the probability model represents a whole collection of densities, often an infinite number, depending on the nature of the parameter space Θ. In a certain sense the parameter(s) $\boldsymbol{\theta}$ encapsulate the initial uncertainty in relation to the outcome of a particular trial (condition [b]). *Second,* the probability model has three important components: (i) the density function of a random variable X, (ii) the parameter space Θ, and (iii) the range of values of the random variable in question $\mathbb{R}_X$. To signify the importance of component (iii) we give it a special name.

The **support** of the density $f_x(.)$ is the range of values of the random variable X for which the density function is positive, i.e.

$$\mathbb{R}_X := \{x \in \mathbb{R}_X : f_x(x) > 0\}.$$

Because of the paramount importance of the concept of a probability model we will consider several examples in order to enable the reader to understand the basic concepts.

Examples

(i)   Consider the probability model of a **Binomial distribution** specified by:

$$\Phi = \{f(x;\theta) = \binom{n}{x}\theta^x(1-\theta)^{n-x}, \, 0 < \theta < 1, \, 0 \le x \le n, \, n = 1,2, \dots\}. \tag{3.25}$$

In figures 3.18–3.21 we can see several members of this probability model for $n = 20$. Each graph represents a density for a specific value of the unknown parameter: $\theta = 0.15, \theta = 0.3, \theta = 0.5, \theta = 0.8$. In theory Φ includes an infinity of such densities (to wit a double infinity) because the parameter space $\Theta := [0,1]$ has an uncountable number of elements! For the densities shown in figures 3.18–3.21 the support is $\mathbb{R}_X^* := \{0,1,2, \dots, 20\}$.

(ii)   Another interesting example of a probability model is the **Beta:**

$$\Phi = \left\{f(x;\theta) = \frac{x^{\alpha-1}(1-x)^{\beta-1}}{B[\alpha,\beta]}, \, \boldsymbol{\theta} := (\alpha,\beta) \in \mathbb{R}_+^2, \, 0 < x < 1\right\}.$$

In figure 3.22 several members of this family of densities (one for each combination of values of $\boldsymbol{\theta}$) are shown. This probability model has two unknown parameters $\alpha > 0$ and $\beta > 0$; the parameter space is the product of the positive real line: $\Theta := \mathbb{R}_+^2$. This suggests that the set Φ has an infinity of elements, one for each combination of elements from two infinite sets. Its support is $\mathbb{R}_X := (0,1)$. As can be seen, this probability model involves density functions with very different shapes depending on the values of the two unknown parameters.

(iii)   Another important example of a probability model is the **Gamma:**

$$\Phi = \left\{f(x;\boldsymbol{\theta}) = \frac{\beta^{-1}}{\Gamma[\alpha]}\left(\frac{x}{\beta}\right)^{\alpha-1}\exp\left\{-\left(\frac{x}{\beta}\right)\right\}, \, \boldsymbol{\theta} := (\alpha,\beta) \in \mathbb{R}_+^2, x \in \mathbb{R}_+\right\}.$$

In figure 3.23 several members of this family of densities (one for each combination of values of $\boldsymbol{\theta}$) are shown. Again, the probability model has two unknown parameters $\alpha > 0$ and $\beta > 0$; the parameter space is the product of the positive real line: $\Theta := \mathbb{R}_+^2$. Its support is $\mathbb{R}_X := (0,\infty)$.

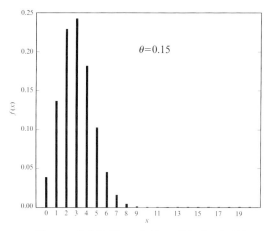

Figure 3.18 Binomial ($n = 20$, $\theta = 0.15$)

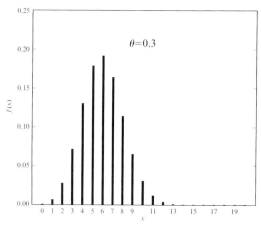

Figure 3.19 Binomial ($n = 20$, $\theta = 0.3$)

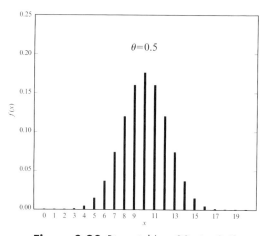

Figure 3.20 Binomial ($n = 20$, $\theta = 0.5$)

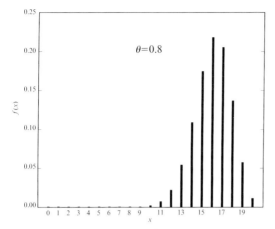

Figure 3.21 Binomial $(n = 20, \theta = 0.8)$

(iv)   The last example of a probability model is the **Weibull**:

$$\Phi = \left\{ f(x;\boldsymbol{\theta}) = \tfrac{\beta x^{\beta-1}}{\alpha^{\beta}} \exp\left\{ -\left(\tfrac{x}{\alpha}\right)^{\beta} \right\}, \; \boldsymbol{\theta} := (\alpha,\beta) \in \mathbb{R}^2_+, \; x > 0 \right\}.$$

Several members of this family of densities (one for each combination of values of $\boldsymbol{\theta}$) are shown in figure 3.24. Again, the model has two unknown parameters $\alpha > 0$ and $\beta > 0$; the parameter space is the product of the positive real line: $\Theta := \mathbb{R}^2_+$. Its support is $\mathbb{R}_X := (0,\infty)$.

The probability model constitutes one of the two pillars on which we are going to erect the notion of a statistical model, the cornerstone of statistical inference (and empirical modeling); the other pillar being the sampling model to be discussed in the next chapter.

For empirical modeling purposes we utilize the notion of a probability model as follows. We postulate a priori one such family of densities as underlying the stochastic mechanism that gave rise to the observed data in question: our task as modelers is to chose the most appropriate family for the data in question. A priori we do not commit ourselves to a particular density, say $f(x;\boldsymbol{\theta}_0)$, where $\boldsymbol{\theta}_0$ is a specific value of the unknown parameters θ, as providing *the* appropriate summary of the data in question. Instead, we assume that such a density is a member of the postulated family for some $\boldsymbol{\theta} \in \Theta$. In empirical modeling we define the probability model in terms of unknown parameter(s) $\boldsymbol{\theta}$ and let the data, using statistical inference, choose its appropriate value from Θ. The question that naturally arises at this stage is: How do we make the original decision regarding which probability model (see **appendix A** for several such models) is appropriate? An oversimplified answer is that the modeler considers how all three components (i)–(iii) of the probability model relate to the data in question.

The first component is the density function. The most convenient way to assess the appropriateness of the density function is to compare the distributional *shapes* (as presented in the above graphs) to the histogram of the observed data. These shapes will prove to be one of the guiding lights in choosing an appropriate statistical model for the

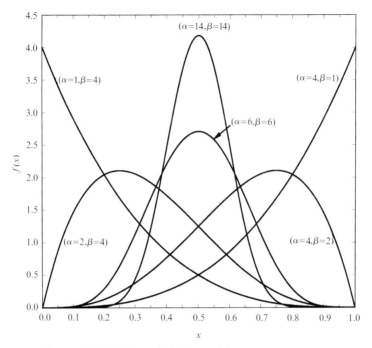

Figure 3.22 Beta probability model

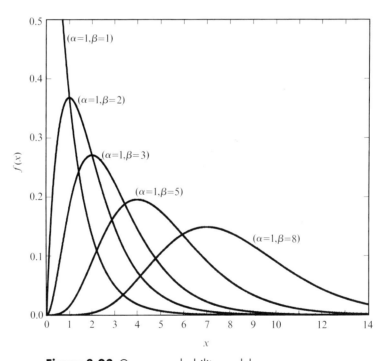

Figure 3.23 Gamma probability model

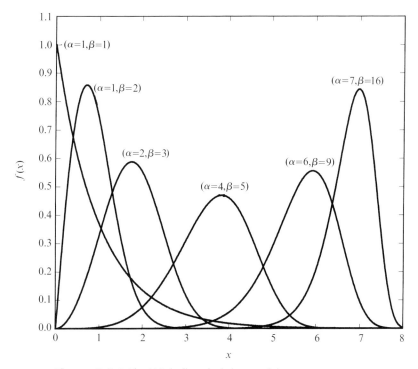

Figure 3.24 The Weibull probability model

stochastic phenomenon in question. In chapter 5 we will demonstrate how the histogram can be used to make informed decisions with regard to the appropriate density. Taking the Beta probability model as an example, we can see that it exhibits almost unlimited flexibility with regard to different distributional shapes; the shapes shown in figure 3.22 indicate this flexibility. However, the other two continuous probability models, the Gamma and Weibull also show enough flexibility in terms of shapes suggesting that they cannot by themselves provide answers to the question of choosing the appropriate probability model. Those readers who are not convinced of that should take a look at figure 3.25 where two very different densities are contrasted to show that it will be impossible to choose between them when faced with real data. In the dotted line we have the standard Normal density and in the solid line we have a Weibull density of the form:

$$f(x;\boldsymbol{\theta}) = \frac{\beta x^{\beta-1}}{\alpha^{\beta}} \exp\left\{-\left(\frac{x-\mu}{\alpha}\right)^{\beta}\right\}, \; \boldsymbol{\theta} := (\alpha,\beta) \in \mathbb{R}_{+}^{2}, \, x > \mu \in \mathbb{R},$$

with parameters $(\alpha = 3.34, \beta = 3.45, \mu = -3)$. The best way to distinguish between these very similar distributional shapes is via index measures based on moments (see next section) which are invariant to scale and location parameter changes; see the skewness and kurtosis coefficients below.

In addition to the distributional shapes and the related parameters of the densities one should consider the support of the density in making decisions about the appropriateness

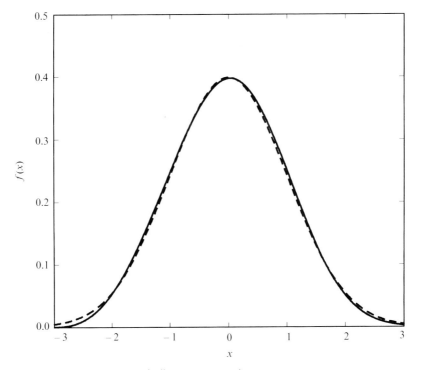

Figure 3.25 Weibull versus Normal

of probability models. For example, in the case of the Beta model the support limits its usefulness to cases where the data are percentages or can be expressed as such. For example in the case of modeling data referring to exam scores it is often more realistic to use the Beta and not the Normal distribution because all scores can be easily expressed in the interval [0,1]; the Normal distribution has support $(-\infty,\infty)$. On the other hand, if the data can take only positive values without an obvious upper bound the modeler should consider the other two probability models.

Finally, an important consideration in making a decision regarding the appropriate model is the richness of the choice menu; the more families of densities we have to choose from the higher is the likelihood that one of them will turn out to be appropriate in a given situation. This is why in **appendix A** we collected some of the most important probability models for reference purposes.

3.6   Parameters and moments

3.6.1   Why do we care?

In the previous section we introduced the concept of a *probability model*:

$$\Phi = \{f_x(x;\boldsymbol{\theta}),\ \boldsymbol{\theta}\in\Theta,\ x\in\mathbb{R}_X\},$$

as a formalization of conditions [a]–[b] of a *random experiment*. Before we proceed to formalize condition [c] (see next chapter), we make an **important digression** to introduce a most convenient way to handle the unknown parameter(s) $\boldsymbol{\theta}$ of the probability model. In the context of statistical inference and modeling in general, the most efficient way to deal with the unknown parameters $\boldsymbol{\theta}$ is to relate them to the *moments* of the distribution. As mentioned in the previous section one of the important considerations in choosing a probability model is the shapes different families of densities can give rise to. These shapes are obviously related to the unknown parameters but that is no comfort for the modeler who has to choose such a model a priori because they are unknown! Hence, we would like to use other information which is available a priori in making that choice. Along with the histogram of the data we often have a number of numerical values, such as arithmetic averages, from descriptive statistics. These numerical values are related to what we call *moments* of the distribution and can be used to make educated guesses regarding the unknown parameters and thus for the different distribution shapes.

The moments of a distribution are defined in terms of the mathematical expectation of certain functions of the random variable X, generically denoted by $h(X)$, as follows:

$$E[h(X)] = \int_{-\infty}^{\infty} h(x) \cdot f(x;\boldsymbol{\theta})dx. \tag{3.26}$$

In view of the fact that the integral is defined in terms of the density functions $f(x;\boldsymbol{\theta})$, in general $E[h(X)]$ is some function of $\boldsymbol{\theta}$, i.e.

$$E[h(X)] = g(\boldsymbol{\theta}). \tag{3.27}$$

By choosing specific forms of the function $h(X)$, such as:

$$h(X) = X^r, h(X) = |X|^r, r = 1, 2, \ldots, h(X) = e^{tx}, h(X) = e^{itx}, \tag{3.28}$$

we obtain several functions of the form $g(\boldsymbol{\theta})$ which involve what we call **moments** of $f(x;\boldsymbol{\theta})$.

In statistical modeling as well as statistical inference, it will be shown that the best way to handle probability models (postulate a statistical model, estimate $\boldsymbol{\theta}$, test hypotheses about these parameters $\boldsymbol{\theta}$, etc.) is often via the moments of the postulated probability distribution.

3.6.2 Numerical characteristics

In what follows we will consider several special cases of (3.26) in order to discuss their role in both modeling and inference.

Mean

For $h(X) := X$, where X takes values in $\mathbb{R}_X$, the above integral gives rise to the *mean* of the distribution:

$$E(X) = \int_{-\infty}^{\infty} x \cdot f_X(x;\boldsymbol{\theta})dx, \text{ for continuous random variables,} \tag{3.29}$$

$$E(X) = \sum_{x_i \in \mathbb{R}_X} x_i \cdot f_x(x_i; \boldsymbol{\theta}), \text{ for discrete random variables.} \qquad (3.30)$$

NOTE that the only difference in the definition between continuous and discrete random variables is the replacement of the integral by a summation. The mean is a *measure of location* in the sense that knowing what the mean of X is, we have some idea on where $f_x(x; \boldsymbol{\theta})$ is located. Intuitively, the mean represents a weighted average of the values of X, with the corresponding probabilities providing the weights. Denoting the mean by:

$$\mu := E(X),$$

the above definition suggests that μ is a function of the unknown parameters $\boldsymbol{\theta}$, i.e. $\mu(\boldsymbol{\theta})$.

Examples

(i)   For the *Bernoulli* distribution: $\mu(\theta) := E(X) = 0 \cdot (1-\theta) + 1 \cdot \theta = \theta$, and thus the mean coincides with the unknown parameter.

(ii) In the case of the *Poisson* distribution:

$$f(x; \theta) = \left(\frac{e^{-\theta} \theta^x}{x!} \right), \ \theta \in \Theta := (0, \infty), \ x = 0, 1, 2, 3, \ldots,$$

$$\mu(\theta) := E(X) = \sum_{k=0}^{\infty} k \left(\frac{e^{-\theta} \theta^k}{k!} \right) = \theta\, e^{-\theta} \sum_{k=0}^{\infty} \frac{\theta^{k-1}}{(k-1)!} = \theta, \text{ since } \sum_{k=0}^{\infty} \frac{\theta^{k-1}}{(k-1)!} = e^{\theta}.$$

(iii) For the *Uniform* distribution (a continuous distribution):

$$f(x; \boldsymbol{\theta}) = \frac{1}{(\theta_2 - \theta_1)}, \ x \in [\theta_1, \theta_2], \ \boldsymbol{\theta} := (\theta_1, \theta_2), \ -\infty < \theta_1 < \theta_2 < \infty,$$

$$\mu(\boldsymbol{\theta}) := E[X] = \int_{\theta_1}^{\theta_2} \frac{x}{(\theta_2 - \theta_1)} dx = \frac{1}{2} \frac{1}{(\theta_2 - \theta_1)} x^2 \Big|_{\theta_2}^{\theta_1} = \frac{\theta_1 + \theta_2}{2}.$$

(iv) For the *Normal* distribution:

$$f(x; \boldsymbol{\theta}) = \frac{1}{\sigma\sqrt{2\pi}} \exp\left[-\frac{(x-\mu)^2}{2\sigma^2} \right], \ \boldsymbol{\theta} := (\mu, \sigma^2) \in \mathbb{R} \times \mathbb{R}_+, \ x \in \mathbb{R}, \qquad (3.31)$$

the parameter μ is actually the *mean* of the distribution (hence the notation).

$$E(X) = \int_{-\infty}^{\infty} x \cdot \left(\frac{1}{\sigma\sqrt{2\pi}} \right) \exp\left[-\frac{(x-\mu)^2}{2\sigma^2} \right] dx = \int_{-\infty}^{\infty} \left(\frac{\sigma z + \mu}{\sigma\sqrt{2\pi}} \right) \exp\left[-\frac{z^2}{2} \right] (\sigma)\, dz =$$

$$= \left(\frac{\sigma}{\sqrt{2\pi}} \right) \int_{-\infty}^{\infty} z \exp\left[-\frac{z^2}{2} \right] dz + \mu \int_{-\infty}^{\infty} \left(\frac{1}{\sqrt{2\pi}} \right) \exp\left[-\frac{z^2}{2} \right] dz = 0 + \mu \cdot 1 = \mu.$$

The second equality follows using the substitution $z = \left(\frac{x-\mu}{\sigma} \right)$ or $x = \sigma z + \mu$, with $\frac{dx}{dz} = \sigma$.

For random variables X_1 and X_2 and the constants a, b and c, $E(.)$ satisfies the following **properties**:

E1. $E(c) = c$,

E2. $E(aX_1 + bX_2) = aE(X_1) + bE(X_2)$.

These properties designate $E(.)$ a *linear mapping*.

Example

Let $X_1, X_2, \ldots, X_n$ be Bernoulli distributed random variables with mean θ. Find $E(Y)$ for $Y = \sum_{i=1}^{n} X_i$. Using **[E2]** we can deduce that: $E(Y) = \sum_{i=1}^{n} E(X_i) = \sum_{i=1}^{n} \theta = n\theta$.

Variance

For $h(X) := [X - E(X)]^2$ the integral (3.26) yields *the variance*:

$$Var(X) := E[(X - E(X))^2] = \int_{-\infty}^{\infty} [x - \mu]^2 f_x(x; \boldsymbol{\theta}) dx,$$

where in the case of discrete random variables the integral is replaced by the usual summation (see (3.29) and (3.30)). In our context the variance represents a *measure of dispersion* (variation) around the mean.

Examples

(i)   In the case of the *Bernoulli* model:

$$Var(X) = E(X - E[X])^2 = (0 - \theta)^2 \cdot (1 - \theta) + (1 - \theta)^2 \cdot \theta = \theta(1 - \theta).$$

(ii) In the case where X has a Normal distribution (see (3.31)), using the same substitution, $x = \sigma z + \mu$, we can show that the variance coincides with the unknown parameter σ^2, i.e. $Var(X) = E(X^2) - (E(X))^2 = \sigma^2$, since:

$$E(X^2) = \int_{-\infty}^{\infty} x^2 \cdot \left(\frac{1}{\sigma\sqrt{2\pi}}\right) \exp\left[-\frac{(x-\mu)^2}{2\sigma^2}\right] dx = \int_{-\infty}^{\infty} \frac{(\sigma z + \mu)^2}{\sigma\sqrt{2\pi}} \exp\left[-\frac{z^2}{2}\right] (\sigma)\, dz =$$

$$= \sigma^2 \int_{-\infty}^{\infty} \frac{z^2}{\sqrt{2\pi}} \exp\left(-\frac{z^2}{2}\right) dz + \frac{2\sigma\mu}{\sqrt{2\pi}} \int_{-\infty}^{\infty} \frac{z}{\sqrt{2\pi}} \exp\left(-\frac{z^2}{2}\right) dz + \mu^2 \int_{-\infty}^{\infty} \frac{1}{\sqrt{2\pi}} \exp\left(-\frac{z^2}{2}\right) dz$$

$$= \sigma^2 + 0 + \mu^2 = \sigma^2 + \mu^2,$$

hence the notation $X \sim N(\mu, \sigma^2)$. In figure 3.26 we can see the Normal density (with $\mu = 0$) and different values of σ^2; the greater the value of σ^2 the greater the dispersion.

For *independent* random variables X_1 and X_2 and the constants a, b and c, $Var(.)$ satisfies the following **properties:**

V1. $Var(c) = 0$,

V2. $Var(aX_1 + bX_2) = a^2 Var(X_1) + b^2 Var(X_2)$.

Bienayme's lemma If $X_1, X_2, \ldots, X_n$ are Independently Distributed random variables:

$$Var\left(\sum_{i=1}^{n} a_i X_i\right) = \sum_{i=1}^{n} a_i^2 Var(X_i).$$

This lemma constitutes a direct extension of property **V2**.

Example

Let $X_1, X_2, \ldots, X_n$ be independent Bernoulli distributed random variables with mean θ. What is the variance of $Y = a + \sum_{i=1}^{n} X_i$?

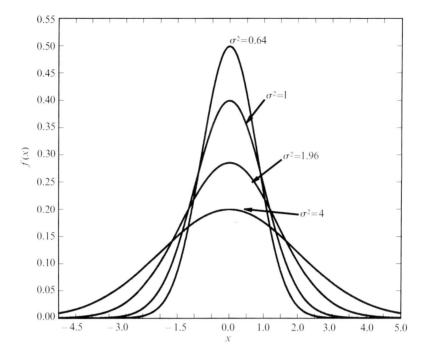

Figure 3.26 Normal: different σ^2

Using **V1** and Bienayme's lemma, we can deduce that:

$$Var(Y) = \sum_{i=1}^{n} Var(X_i) = \sum_{i=1}^{n} \theta(1-\theta) = n\theta(1-\theta).$$

A particularly useful inequality which testifies that the variance provides a measure of dispersion is that of Chebyshev.

Chebyshev's inequality   Let X be a random variable with bounded variance:

$$\mathbb{P}(|X - E(X)| > \varepsilon) \le \frac{Var(X)}{\varepsilon^2}, \text{ for any } \varepsilon > 0.$$

Standard deviation

The square root of the variance, referred to as the *standard deviation*, is also used as a measure of dispersion:

$$SD(X) = [Var(X)]^{\frac{1}{2}}.$$

The term standard deviation was first proposed by Pearson (1894) who used the notation $\sigma = [Var(X)]^{\frac{1}{2}}$. This measure is particularly useful in statistical inference because it provides us with the best way to standardize any random variable X whose variance exists. One of the most useful practical rules in statistical inference is the following:

A random variable is as "big" as its standard deviation (provided it exists!).

Hence, when we need to render a random variable free of its units of measurement we divide it by its standard deviation, i.e., we define the **standardized variable**:

$$X^* := \frac{X}{[Var(X)]^{\frac{1}{2}}}, \text{ where } Var(X^*) = 1.$$

which by definition is unitless. The term *standard error* is often used in place of standard deviation. The *standard error* terminology can be traced back to the 18th century tradition of the theory of errors. Galton (1877) was the first to replace the term error with deviation.

Although the mean and the variance are the most widely used moments, they do not suffice to determine the main characteristics of a distribution. That is, although we know the mean and the variance we know very little about the main features of the density function. We can easily think of very different density functions which have the same mean and variance. In order to be able to distinguish between such distributions we need to consider higher moments.

3.7   Moments

In this section we consider two types of moments, the higher raw and central moments, which constitute direct generalizations of the mean and variance, respectively. The notion of *moments* in general was borrowed from classical mechanics where the mean, $E(X)$, is the abscissa of the center of gravity of the mass of the distribution and the variance, $Var(X)$, represents the moment of inertia of the mass of the distribution with respect to a perpendicular axis through the point $x = E(X)$. The first six moments of the Normal distribution were used by a number of analysts throughout the 18th century including Gauss and Quetelet. The first to coin the term moments was Pearson (1893).

3.7.1   Higher raw moments

A direct generalization of the mean yields the so-called raw moments. For $h(X) := X^r, r = 2,3,4, \ldots$ the integral in (3.26) yields **the raw moments** defined by:

$$\mu'_r(\boldsymbol{\theta}) := E(X^r) = \int_{-\infty}^{\infty} x^r f_x(x; \boldsymbol{\theta}) dx, \ r = 1,2,3, \ldots$$

Examples

(i)   In the case of the Bernoulli distribution:

$$\mu'_r(\theta) = E(X^r) = 0^r \cdot [1 - \theta] + 1^r \cdot \theta = \theta, \text{ for all } r = 1,2,3,4, \ldots$$

That is, all the raw moments are the same. The second raw moment is often useful in deriving the variance using the equality:

$$Var(X) = E[(X - E(X))^2] = E(X^2) - [E(X)]^2.$$

We can verify this in the Bernoulli case where $E(X^2) = \theta$:

$$Var(X) = \theta - \theta^2 = \theta(1 - \theta).$$

(ii)   In the case where X is Normally distributed with density (3.31):

$$E(X^r) = \begin{cases} 0, & \text{for } r = 3,5,7,\ldots \\ (1 \cdot 3 \cdots (r-1))\sigma^r, & \text{for } r = 2,4,6,\ldots \end{cases}$$

(iii)   Consider the exponential random variable X with a density function:

$$f_x(x;\theta) = \theta\, e^{-\theta x}, \; x > 0, \; \theta > 0,$$
$$\mu_r'(\theta) := E(X^r) = \int_0^\infty x^r \theta e^{-\theta x} dx.$$

Using the change of variables $u = \theta x,\, dx = \frac{1}{\theta} du$:

$$\mu_r'(\theta) = \int_{-\infty}^\infty \frac{u^r}{\theta^r} e^{-u} du = \frac{1}{\theta^r} \int_{-\infty}^\infty u^{(r+1)-1} e^{-u} du = \frac{r!}{\theta^r!}.$$

IMPORTANT. In connection with the raw moments, it is interesting to note that when the fourth moment exists so do the first, second and third. The general result is given in the following lemma.

Lower moments lemma If $\mu_k' := E(X^k)$ exists for some positive integer k, then all the raw moments of order less than k also exist, i.e.:

$$E(X^i) < \infty, \text{ for all } i = 1,2,\ldots,k-1.$$

3.7.2 Moment generating function

A particularly convenient way to compute the raw moments is by way of the **moment generating function** (mgf) defined using the integral in (3.26) with $h(X) = e^{tX}$, i.e.

$$m_X(t) := E(e^{tX}) = \int_{-\infty}^\infty e^{tX} f(x) dx, \text{ for } t \in (-h,h), \; h > 0,$$

provided $E(e^{tX})$ exists for all t in some interval $(-h,h)$; for discrete random variables the aforementioned change of integrals and summations holds (see Gnedenko (1969)).

   The idea behind this mathematical device is to pack the moments into capsule form which would be immediately accessible. As shown below the mgf can be used to *generate these moments* by simple differentiation instead of integration.

Examples

(i)   Let X be a *Poisson* distributed random variable. Then:

$$m_X(t) = \sum_{r=0}^\infty e^{tX}\left(\frac{e^{-\theta}\theta^r}{r!}\right) = e^{-\theta}\sum_{r=0}^\infty \frac{(e^t\theta)^r}{r!} = e^{-\theta}e^{\theta e^t} = e^{\theta(e^t-1)}, \text{ since } \sum_{r=0}^\infty \left(\frac{\theta^r}{r!}\right) = e^\theta.$$

(ii)   Let X be a random variable which is *Uniformly* distributed over the interval $[a,b]$:

$$m_X(t) := \int_a^b e^{tX}\left(\frac{1}{b-a}\right) dx = \frac{e^{bt} - e^{at}}{(b-a)t}, \text{ for } t \neq 0. \tag{3.32}$$

The *intuition* behind the definition of $m_X(t)$ is as follows. In view of the fact that Maclaurin's series expansion of e^{tX} takes the form:

$$e^{tX} = 1 + Xt + \frac{(Xt)^2}{2!} + \frac{(Xt)^3}{3!} + \dots = \sum_{r=0}^{\infty} \frac{(Xt)^r}{r!}, \tag{3.33}$$

we can conclude that if $m_X(t)$ exists for $t \in (-h, h)$, and some $h > 0$, then we can write:

$$m_X(t) := E(e^{tX}) = E\left(\sum_{r=0}^{\infty} \frac{(Xt)^r}{r!}\right),$$

and interchanging the order of expectation and summation (we use some hand waving here), yields:

$$m_X(t) := E(e^{tX}) = \sum_{r=0}^{\infty} E(X^r) \frac{t^r}{r!}, \text{ for } t \in (-h, h), h > 0.$$

This suggests that, assuming that $m_X(t)$ exists, we can recover the raw moment $\mu_r' := E(X^r)$ as the $(r+1)$th term in the above expansion, either directly when the mgf can be expanded as a power series in powers of t, or indirectly using differentiation (there is some hand waving here as well) via:

$$E(X^r) = \frac{d^r}{dt^r} m_X(t)\bigg|_{t=0} := m_X^{(r)}(0), r = 1,2,3, \dots$$

$$\mu_1' := E(X) = \frac{dm_X(t)}{dt}\bigg|_{t=0}, \mu_2' := E(X^2) = \frac{d^2 m_X(t)}{dt^2}\bigg|_{t=0}, \dots, \mu_r' := E(X^r) = \frac{d^r m_X(t)}{dt^r}\bigg|_{t=0}.$$

The intuition behind this result is the following: looking at (3.33) we can see that by differentiating $m_X(t)$ r times, the terms up to $\left[E(X^r)\left(\frac{t^r}{r!}\right)\right]$ disappear and the latter becomes:

$$E(X^r)\left(\frac{[r \cdot (r-1) \cdot (r-2) \cdots 1] \cdot t^0}{r!}\right) = E(X^r).$$

The terms with power higher than r involve t, which means that when we substitute $t = 0$ they disappear, leaving us with just $E(X^r)$.

Example
For a Poisson distributed random variable X, $m_X(t) = e^{\theta}(e^{t-1})$, and thus:

$$E(X) = \frac{d}{dt} m_X(t)\bigg|_{t=0} = e^{\theta(e^t-1)}\theta e^t\bigg|_{t=0} = \theta,$$

$$E(X^2) = \frac{d^2}{dt} m_X(t)\bigg|_{t=0} = e^{\theta(e^t-1)}\theta\,e^t + e^{\theta(e^t-1)}\theta^2 e^{2t}\bigg|_{t=0} = \theta^2 + \theta.$$

Uniqueness lemma An important fact about the mgf is that when it exists (and it does not always), it is unique in the sense that two random variables X and Y that have the same mgf must have the same distribution, and conversely.

Using this lemma we can prove a very useful result which provides the basis for simulating random variables with specific distributional features. It enables us to use random numbers generated from a Uniform distribution as the basis for generating random numbers for several continuous distributions (see chapter 5).

Probability integral transformation lemma For any continuous random variable X, with cdf $F_X(x)$ (irrespective of its form), the random variable defined by $Y = F_X(X)$ has a *uniform distribution* over the range $(0,1)$, i.e.

$$Y = F_X(X) \sim \mathsf{U}(0,1). \tag{3.34}$$

Proof The mgf of Y takes the form:

$$m_Y(t) := E(e^{tY}) = E(e^{tF(X)}) = \int_{-\infty}^{\infty} e^{tF(x)} f(x) dx \left. \frac{e^{tF(x)}}{t} \right|_{-\infty}^{\infty} = \frac{e^t - 1}{t},$$

since $F(\infty) = 1$ and $F(-\infty) = 0$. Looking at the form of the mgf, and comparing it with (3.32), we can see that the random variable Y is uniformly distributed over the interval $(0,1)$.

There are two functions related to the moment generating functions, the cumulant generating and characteristic functions, considered next.

Cumulants*
A generating function related to $m_X(t)$ is the **cumulant generating function,** defined by:

$$\psi_X(t) = \ln(m_X(t)) = \sum_{r=1}^{\infty} \kappa_r \frac{t^r}{r!}, \text{ for } t \in (-h, h), h > 0,$$

where κ_r, $r = 1,2,3,\dots$ are referred to as **cumulants** (or semi-invariants). It is interesting to note that:

$$\kappa_1 = E(X) = \left. \frac{d\psi_X(t)}{dt} \right|_{t=0}, \ \kappa_2 = Var(X) = \left. \frac{d^2\psi_X(t)}{dt^2} \right|_{t=0},$$

and the cumulants are directly related to the raw moments. The first few cumulants are related to the raw moments as follows:

$$\kappa_1 = \mu_1',$$
$$\kappa_2 = \mu_2' - (\mu_1')^2,$$
$$\kappa_3 = \mu_3' - 3\mu_2'\mu_1' + 2(\mu_1')^3,$$
$$\kappa_4 = \mu_4' - 4\mu_3'\mu_1' - 3(\mu_2')^2 + 12\mu_2'(\mu_1')^2 - 6(\mu_1')^4,$$
$$\kappa_5 = \mu_5' - 5\mu_4'\mu_1' - 10\mu_2'\mu_3' + 20\mu_3'(\mu_1')^2 + 30(\mu_2')^2\mu_1' - 60\mu_2'(\mu_1')^3 + 24(\mu_1')^5.$$

From this we can see that the first two cumulants are the mean and the variance.

The cumulants are often preferable to the moments for several reasons including the following:

(i)   In the case of the Normal distribution: $\kappa_r = 0$, $r = 3,4,\dots$
(ii)   The rth cumulant is rth-order homogeneous: $\kappa_r(\alpha X) = \alpha^r \kappa_r(X)$, $r = 1,2,\dots$
(iii)   The rth cumulant is a function of the moments of order up to r,
(iv)   For independent random variables, the cumulant of the sum is the sum of the cumulants:

$$\kappa_r(\textstyle\sum_{k=1}^{n} X_k) = \sum_{k=1}^{n} \kappa_r(X_k), r = 1,2,\dots$$

Characteristic function*

The existence of the mgf depends crucially on $m_X(t)$ being finite on the interval $(-h, h)$. In such a case all the moments $E(X^r)$ are finite for all r. In cases where $E(X^r)$ is not finite for some r, $m_X(t)$ is not finite on any interval $(-h, h)$. To be able to deal with such cases we define the so-called **characteristic function** (see Cramer (1946)):

$$\varphi_X(t) := E(e^{itX}) = \int_{-\infty}^{\infty} e^{itX} f(x) dx = m_X(it), \text{ for } i = \sqrt{-1}.$$

which, in contrast to $m_X(t)$, always exists since for all t, $\varphi_X(t)$ is bounded:

$$|\varphi_X(t)| \leq E(|e^{itX}|) = 1,$$

and thus, for many random variables, we can find the characteristic function using the moment generating function.

The characteristic function is related to the moments (when they exist!) via the series:

$$\varphi_X(t) = \sum_{r=0}^{\infty} \frac{(it)^r}{r!} \mu_r', \text{ for } t \in (-h, h), h > 0. \tag{3.35}$$

There is also a direct relationship between the characteristic function on one side and the cumulative distribution (cdf) and density functions on the other, first noted by Lyapunov in the context of limit theorems.

Inversion theorem Let $F_X(x)$, $f(x)$, and $\varphi_X(t)$ denote the cdf, the density, and characteristic functions of a random variable X, respectively.

(a) Assuming that (a, b) are two real numbers $(a < b)$ at which $F(x)$ is continuous:

$$F_X(b) - F_X(a) = \lim_{n \to \infty} \frac{1}{2\pi} \int_{-n}^{n} \left(\frac{e^{-ita} - e^{-itb}}{it} \right) \varphi_X(t) dt.$$

(b) If $\int_{-\infty}^{\infty} |\varphi_X(t)| < \infty$, then, $F_X(x) = \int_{-\infty}^{x} f(u) \, du$ and $f(x) = \int_{-\infty}^{\infty} e^{-itx} \varphi_X(t) dt$.

(c) $\varphi_X(t)$ determines $F_X(x)$ uniquely in the sense that (see Karr (1993)):

$$F_X(x) = \lim_{z \to -\infty} \left(\lim_{n \to \infty} \frac{1}{2\pi} \int_{-n}^{n} \left(\frac{e^{-itz} - e^{-itb}}{it} \right) \varphi_X(t) dt \right).$$

3.7.3 The problem of moments*

As argued above, the primary usefulness of moments is that they enable us to handle distributions with unknown parameters for both modeling and inference purposes. The question that comes to mind at this stage is when do the moments $\{\mu_k' := E(X^k), k = 1, 2, \ldots\}$, assuming they exist, determine the distribution uniquely? This question is of paramount importance because if the moments do not determine the distribution uniquely, then the usefulness of the moments is reduced. Hence, the questions which arise are the following: given the set of moments:

$$\{\mu_k' := E(X^k) < \infty, k = 1, 2, \ldots\},$$

(i)   existence: Is there a function $f(x) \geq 0$, such that: $\mu_k' = \int_{-\infty}^{\infty} x^r f(x) dx$?

(ii)   uniqueness: Is the function $f(x)$ unique?

$$\text{i.e., does} \int_{-\infty}^{\infty} x^r f(x) dx = \int_{-\infty}^{\infty} x^r g(x) dx \Rightarrow f(x) = g(x)?$$

In general, the answer to both questions is no! Under certain conditions, however, the answer is yes. Let us see how these conditions are related to the convergence of the series in (3.35).

Lemma 1 A useful result on the *existence* of the moments is the following. A sufficient (but certainly not necessary) condition for the existence of moments is that the support of the random variable X is a bounded interval, i.e., $\mathbb{R}_X := [a,b]$, where $-\infty < a < b < \infty$. In this case all moments exist:

$$\mu_k' = \int_a^b x^r f(x) dx < \infty, \text{ for all } k = 1, 2, \ldots$$

In cases where the range of values of the random variable in question is unbounded we need to check the existence or otherwise of the moments.

A sufficient condition for the uniqueness problem is provided by lemma 2.

Lemma 2 The moments $\{\mu_k', k = 1, 2, \ldots\}$ (assuming they exist) determine the distribution function *uniquely* if:

$$\lim_{n \to \infty} \left(\sup \left[(2n)^{-1} (\mu_{2n}')^{\frac{1}{2n}} \right] \right) < \infty.$$

NOTE that on many occasions we will use the abbreviations sup and inf which stand for **supremum** and **infimum**, respectively. These are essentially the well-known max and min which stand for **maximum** and **minimum** with one qualification. Sometimes the maximum or/and the minimum of a set of numbers might not exist, e.g., the set $(0,1)$ does not have either a minimum or a maximum. In such cases we use inf and sup, which denote the largest lower and the smallest upper bounds, respectively, both of which always exist! The less mathematically inclined can interpret them as min and max, without worrying too much.

A useful check for a unique determination of the distribution function via the moments is provided by the *Carleman condition*:

$$\sum_{n=1}^{\infty} \left([\mu_{2n}']^{-\frac{1}{2n}} \right) = \infty.$$

A necessary and sufficient condition for the uniqueness problem in the case of continuous random variables is provided by lemma 3.

Lemma 3 The moments $\{\mu_k', k = 1, 2, \ldots\}$ of the continuous random variable X (assuming they exist) with density function $f(x)$ determine its distribution function *uniquely* if and only if:

$$\int_{-\infty}^{\infty} \frac{\ln f(x)}{(1 + x^2)} dx = -\infty.$$

This is known as the *Krein condition*; see Stoyanov (1987).

Example

Consider the case where the random variable X has a *log-Normal* distribution with density:

$$f(x) = \frac{1}{x\sqrt{2\pi}} \exp\left\{-\frac{1}{2}(\ln x)^2\right\}, \; x \in \mathbb{R}_+.$$

It can be shown that:

$$\mu_k' = e^{\frac{k^2}{2}}, \; k = 1, 2, \dots,$$

and thus:

$$\sum_{k=1}^{\infty}\left(\left[e^{k^2}\right]^{-\frac{1}{2k}}\right) = \sum_{k=1}^{\infty}\left(e^{-\frac{k}{2}}\right) < \infty,$$

i.e., the Carleman condition does not hold. However, in view of the fact that the Carleman condition is only sufficient we cannot conclude that the moments do not determine the distribution uniquely. On the other hand, since the Krein condition does not hold, i.e.

$$\int_0^{\infty} \frac{1}{(1+x^2)}\left[-\ln x - \frac{1}{2}(\ln x)^2\right] dx < \infty,$$

we can conclude that the log-Normal distribution is not determined by its moments because the Krein condition is both necessary and sufficient; see Heyde (1963).

The bottom line

The above lemmas suggest that, in general, moments do not determine distributions uniquely even if we use an *infinite* number of them. In addition, we know that, in general, no distribution is determined by a finite number of moments. In view of the fact that for modeling and statistical inference purposes we can only deal with a small number of moments (and certainly finite), the problem of moments appears insurmountable. However, if we are prepared to limit ourselves to a specific class of distributions the problem becomes tractable.

Example

Within the Pearson family we require at most four moments to determine the particular distribution (see chapter 12).

A CAUTIONARY NOTE: **moment matching can be very misleading!**

Consider the distribution as specified below (see Romano and Siegel (1986)).

x	$\sqrt{3}$	$-\sqrt{3}$	0
$f(x)$	$\frac{1}{6}$	$\frac{1}{6}$	$\frac{4}{6}$

(3.36)

We can show that the random variable whose distribution is defined by (3.36) has moments which match the first five moments of $Z \sim N(0, 1)$, since:

$$E(X) = \sqrt{3}\left(\frac{1}{6}\right) - \sqrt{3}\left(\frac{1}{6}\right) = 0, \qquad E(X^2) = 3\left(\frac{1}{6}\right) + 3\left(\frac{1}{6}\right) = 1,$$

$$E(X^3) = \left(\sqrt{3}\right)^3\left(\frac{1}{6}\right) - \left(\sqrt{3}\right)^3\left(\frac{1}{6}\right) = 0, \quad E(X^4) = 9\left(\frac{1}{6}\right) + 9\left(\frac{1}{6}\right) = 3,$$

This example might seem a bit extreme but it should serve as a cautionary note.

3.7.4 Higher central moments

The notion of the variance can be extended to define the **central moments** using the sequence of functions $h(X) := (X - E(X))^r, r = 3,4,\dots$ in (3.26):

$$\mu_r(\boldsymbol{\theta}) := E(X^r) = \int_{-\infty}^{\infty} (x - \mu)^r f(x;\boldsymbol{\theta})dx, \quad r = 2,3,\dots$$

Instead of deriving these moments directly, it is often more convenient to derive the central moments μ_r using their relationship with the raw moments and the cumulants (see Stuart and Ord (1994)):

$$
\begin{aligned}
\mu_2 &= \mu_2' - (\mu_1')^2, & \kappa_2 &= \mu_2, \\
\mu_3 &= \mu_3' - 3\mu_2'\mu_1' + 2(\mu_1')^3, & \kappa_3 &= \mu_3, \\
\mu_4 &= \mu_4' - 4\mu_3'\mu_1' + 6\mu_2'(\mu_1')^2 - 3(\mu_1')^4, & \kappa_4 &= \mu_4 - 3\mu_2^2.
\end{aligned}
$$

Examples

(i) For the *Poisson* density: $f(x;\theta) = \left(\frac{e^{-\theta}\theta^x}{x!}\right)$, $\theta \in (0,\infty)$, $x = 0,1,2,\dots$

we already know that $\mu = \theta$. From a previous example above, we know that:

$$\psi_X(t) = \ln(m_X(t)) = \theta(e^t - 1) = \theta\left(1 + t + \frac{t^2}{2!} + \frac{t^3}{3!} + \cdots\right).$$

Hence, we can deduce that:

$$\kappa_r = \left.\frac{d^r\psi_X(t)}{dt^r}\right|_{t=0} = \theta, r = 1,2,\dots$$

$$\kappa_1 = \theta, \kappa_2 = \theta, \kappa_3 = \theta, \kappa_4 = \theta, \Rightarrow \mu_2 = \theta, \mu_3 = \theta, \mu_4 = 3\theta^2 + \theta.$$

(ii) In the case where the random variable X is *Normal* with density (3.31):

$$\mu_1' = \mu, \ \mu_2 = \sigma^2, \ \mu_3 = 0, \ \mu_4 = 3\sigma^4, \ \mu_r = \begin{cases} 0, & r \text{ odd}, \\ \frac{r!\sigma^r}{(\cdot 5r)!2^{(\cdot 5r)}}, & r \text{ even}, \end{cases}$$

$$\kappa_1 = \mu, \kappa_2 = \sigma^2, \kappa_3 = 0, \kappa_4 = 0, \kappa_r = 0, r = 5,6,\dots$$

In direct analogy to the moment generating function (mgf) the *central mgf* is defined by:

$$M_X(t) := E[e^{(X-\mu)t}] = e_X^{-\mu t}m_X(t) = 1 + \sum_{r=1}^{\infty}\mu_r\frac{t^r}{r!}, \text{ for } t \in (-h,h), \ h > 0,$$

provided it exists.

One of the main uses of the central moments is that they can be used to give us a more complete picture of *the distribution's shape*. By standardizing the above central moments we define a number of useful measures which enable us to get a more complete idea of the possible shape of a density function. The first important feature of a distribution's shape is that of symmetry around a given point a; often $a = E(X)$.

Symmetry A random variable X with density $f(x)$ is said to be symmetric about a point a if the following condition holds:

$$f(a - x) = f(a + x), \text{ for all } x \in \mathbb{R}_X,$$

or more generally in terms of the cdf $F_X(x)$:

$$F_X(a-x) + F_X(a+x) = 1, \text{ for all } x \in \mathbb{R}.$$

The skewness coefficient

The first index of shape, designed to give us some idea about the possible asymmetry of a density function around the mean, is the *skewness* coefficient defined as the standardized third central moment, introduced by Pearson (1895):

$$\textbf{Skewness: } \alpha_3(X) = \frac{\mu_3}{(\sqrt{\mu_2})^3}.$$

NOTE that $\sqrt{\mu_2} = [Var(X)]^{\frac{1}{2}}$ denotes the standard deviation. If the distribution is *symmetric* around the mean then, $\alpha_3 = 0$; the converse does not hold!

Example

Looking at figure 3.10 we can see that the Normal density (3.10) is symmetric and thus $\alpha_3 = 0$; the same is true for the Uniform density as shown in figure 3.12. In figure 3.27, however, we can see two positively skewed density functions ($\alpha_3 > 0$). They both represent the same density, the Beta density:

$$f(x;\boldsymbol{\theta}) = \frac{x^{\alpha-1}(1-x)^{\beta-1}}{B[\alpha,\beta]}, \quad \boldsymbol{\theta} = (\alpha,\beta) \in \mathbb{R}_+^2, \ 0 < x < 1,$$

for different values of the parameters (α,β); $(\alpha=1,\beta=4)$ and $(\alpha=2,\beta=4)$. As shown in **appendix A** the skewness coefficient of the Beta distribution is:

$$\alpha_3 = \frac{2(\alpha-\beta)\sqrt{(\alpha+\beta+1)}}{(\alpha+\beta+2)\sqrt{\alpha\beta}}.$$

In figure 3.28 we can see two negatively skewed density functions ($\alpha_3 < 0$), representing the same Beta density with parameters: $(\alpha=4,\beta=1)$ and $(\alpha=4,\beta=2)$. It is instructive to compare figures 3.27–3.28 with 3.22.

A CAUTIONARY NOTE: $\alpha_3 = 0$ *does not imply* that the distribution is symmetric!

x	-2	1	3
$f(x)$	0.4	0.5	0.1

(3.37)

$$E(X) = (-2)(0.4) + 1(0.5) + 3(0.1) = 0, \ E(X^3) = (-2)^3(0.4) + 1(0.5) + 3^3(0.1) = 0.$$

Hence, $\alpha_3 = 0$ despite the fact that the above distribution is clearly non-symmetric (see Romano and Siegel (1986)). This example brings out the importance of looking at the graphs of the distributions and not just at some summary measures; the latter are no substitutes for the graphs themselves!

Kurtosis

The skewness coefficient enables the modeler to distinguish between a symmetric and a non-symmetric distribution but that still leaves us with the problem of distinguishing

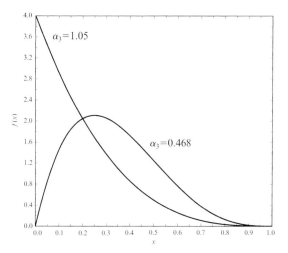

Figure 3.27 Positively skewed densities

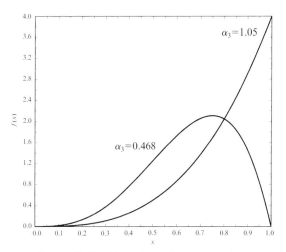

Figure 3.28 Negatively skewed densities

between two symmetric distributions with different shapes, such as the Normal and the Uniform densities shown in figures 3.10 and 3.12. Looking at these two graphs we can see that these two densities differ with respect to their peaks and their tails. The Normal has a bell-shaped peak but the Uniform has a flat peak (no peak!). The Normal has longish tails extending to infinity on both sides but the Uniform has no tails. Intuition suggests that one way to distinguish between them is to devise a measure which measures *peakedness* in relation to tails. The *kurtosis* coefficient is such a measure, originally introduced in Pearson (1895).

The kurtosis is a standardized version of the fourth central moment:

Kurtosis: $\alpha_4(X) = \dfrac{\mu_4}{(\mu_2)^2}.$

The term comes from the Greek word $\kappa \acute{\upsilon} \rho \tau \omega \sigma \eta$ which means *curvature of the spine* and purports to be a measure of *peakedness* in relation to the *shape of the tails*. NOTE that in some books the measure used is $(\alpha_4 - 3)$ referred to as *excess kurtosis* (the standardized fourth cumulant). In the case of the Normal distribution (3.31) $\alpha_4 = 3$, and it is referred to as a **mesokurtic distribution**; *meso* comes from the Greek word $\mu \acute{\epsilon} \sigma o \varsigma$ which means *middle*. In the case where the distribution in question has a flatter *peak* than the Normal ($\alpha_4 < 3$), we call it **platykurtic**, and in the case where it has a more pointed peak than the Normal ($\alpha_4 > 3$), we call it **leptokurtic**; *platy* and *lepto* come from the Greek words $\pi \lambda \alpha \tau \acute{\upsilon} \varsigma$ and $\lambda \epsilon \pi \tau \acute{o} \varsigma$ which mean *wide* and *slim*, respectively; these terms were introduced by Pearson (1906).

Intuitively, we can think of the kurtosis coefficient as a measure which indicates whether a symmetric distribution when compared with the Normal has thicker tails and more pointed peaks or not. Viewing the Normal density as a bell-shaped pile made of plaster the sculptor shaves off part of the shoulders and adds it to the tails and the peak to produce a leptokurtic distribution.

Examples

(i) **Leptokurtic** In figure 3.29 we compare the standard Normal density (dotted line) and a leptokurtic density, the standard **Student's** t density with $\nu = 5$:

$$f(x) = \frac{\Gamma\left[\frac{1}{2}(\nu+1)\right](\nu\pi)^{-\frac{1}{2}}}{\Gamma\left[\frac{1}{2}\nu\right]} \left(1 + \frac{x^2}{\nu}\right)^{-\frac{1}{2}(\nu+1)}, \; \nu > 2, \; x \in \mathbb{R}.$$

The Normal density differs from the Student's t in two respects:

(a)   The tails of the Student's t are thicker,
(b)   The curvature of the Student's t is more pointed.

REMARK: Figure 3.29 is a bit misleading because, although both densities are standard-ized, the Normal has unit standard deviation but the Student's t is equal to $\sqrt{\frac{\nu}{\nu-2}}$. In figure 3.30 the same curves are shown with unit standard deviations. This graph is better suited when looking at real data plots (see chapter 5).

(ii) **Leptokurtic** In figures 3.31–3.32 we compare the Normal density (dotted line) with another leptokurtic density, the **Logistic** density:

$$f(x; \boldsymbol{\theta}) = \frac{\exp\left\{-\left(\frac{x-\alpha}{\beta}\right)\right\}}{\beta \cdot \left(1 + \exp\left\{-\left(\frac{x-\alpha}{\beta}\right)\right\}\right)^2}, \; \boldsymbol{\theta} := (\alpha, \beta) \in \mathbb{R} \times \mathbb{R}_+, \; x \in \mathbb{R}$$

with parameters ($\alpha = 0, \beta = 0.56$) and ($\alpha = 0, \beta = 0.628$), respectively.

As shown in appendix A the kurtosis coefficient of the Logistic distribution is $\alpha_4 = 4.2$. Figure 3.32 shows how difficult it can be to distinguish the two distributions in empirical studies by just eye-balling them.

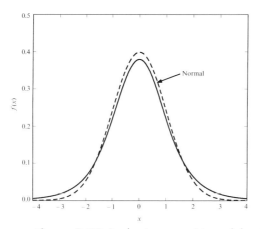

Figure 3.29 Student's t versus Normal densities normalized by σ_x

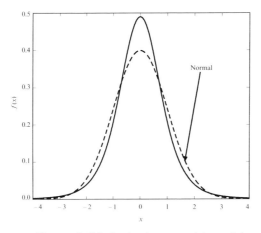

Figure 3.30 Student's t versus Normal densities normalized so that $Var(X) = 1$

(iii) **Platykurtic** In figure 3.33 we compare the Normal density (in dotted line) with a platykurtic density, the **Pearson type II** with $\nu = 3$:

$$f(x) = \frac{\Gamma\left[\frac{1}{2}\right] \cdot \Gamma[\nu + 1] \pi^{-\frac{1}{2}}}{\Gamma\left[\frac{1}{2} + \nu + 1\right] \cdot c} \left(1 + \frac{x^2}{\nu c^2}\right)^{-\frac{1}{2}(\nu + 1)}, \ -c \leq x \leq c, \ c^2 := 2(\nu + 2).$$

The Normal density differs from the Pearson type II in exactly the opposite way than it differs from the Student's t. In particular

(a) the tails of the Pearson II are slimmer,
(b) the curvature of the Pearson II is less pointed.

(iv) In figure 3.34 we can see the graph of a symmetric Beta density with parameters $(\alpha = 4, \beta = 4)$:

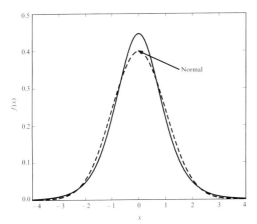

Figure 3.31 Logistic ($\alpha=0$, $\beta=0.56$) versus Normal $(0,1)$ densities

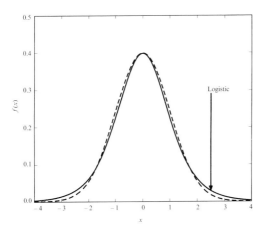

Figure 3.32 Logistic ($\alpha=0$, $\beta=0.628$) versus Normal $(0,1)$ densities

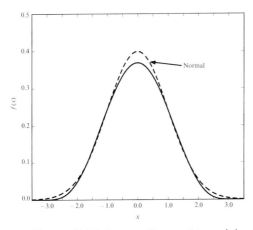

Figure 3.33 Pearson II versus Normal densities

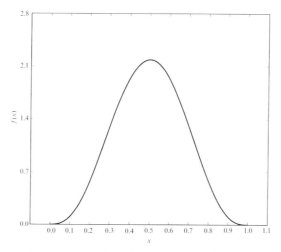

Figure 3.34 Beta $(\alpha=4,\ \beta=0.4)$ density

$$f(x;\boldsymbol{\theta})=\frac{x^{\alpha-1}(1-x)^{\beta-1}}{B[\alpha,\beta]},\ \boldsymbol{\theta}:=(\alpha,\beta)\in\mathbb{R}_+^2,\ 0<x<1.$$

Again we can see the same bell shape as in the case of the Normal, the Student's t, and the Pearson type II densities but in contrast to the Student's t it is platykurtic since:

$$\alpha_4=\frac{3(\alpha+\beta+1)[2(\alpha+\beta)^2+\alpha\beta(\alpha+\beta-6]}{\alpha\beta(\alpha+\beta-2)(\alpha+\beta-3)},$$

and thus for any $\alpha=\beta$, $\alpha_4\leq3$.

(v) **Polykurtic** Consider the **power Exponential** (or *error*) distribution whose density is:

$$f(x;\boldsymbol{\theta})=\frac{\beta-12-\left(\frac{\delta}{2}+1\right)}{\Gamma\left[1+\frac{\delta}{2}\right]}e^{\left(-\frac{1}{2}\left|\frac{x-\mu}{\beta}\right|^{\frac{2}{\delta}}\right)},\ \boldsymbol{\theta}:=(\mu,\beta,\delta)\in\mathbb{R}\times\mathbb{R}_+^2,\ x\in\mathbb{R}. \tag{3.38}$$

This is a symmetric distribution with $\alpha_3=0$ which includes the Normal $(\delta=1)$ and Laplace $(\delta=2)$ distributions (see appendix A). Moreover, it provides a convenient parameterization of the kurtosis coefficient because it nests all three forms of kurtosis via the parameter δ. In view of the fact that:

$$\alpha_4=\frac{\Gamma[5\delta/2]\cdot\Gamma[\delta/2]}{\Gamma[3\delta/2]^2},$$

(a)   for $\delta=1, f(x;\boldsymbol{\theta})$ is mesokurtic,
(b)   for $\delta<1, f(x;\boldsymbol{\theta})$ is platykurtic,
(c)   for $\delta>1, f(x;\boldsymbol{\theta})$ is leptokurtic (see figure 3.35).

(vi) **Platykurtic** It is instructive to return to figure 3.25 where we compared a Weibull density with parameters $(\alpha=3.345,\beta=3.45,\mu=-3)$ and a standard Normal density. Looking at the graphs of the two densities it is obvious that distinguishing between them is rather difficult. However, using the kurtosis coefficient we discover that the Weibull is platykurtic $(\alpha_4=2.71)$ as opposed to the Normal $(\alpha_4=3)$.

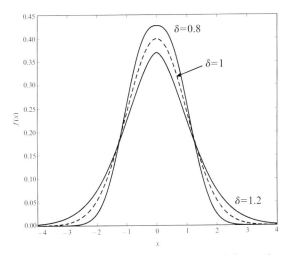

Figure 3.35 Power exponential: polykurtic density

In conclusion, it must be said that the usefulness of the kurtosis coefficient is reduced in the case of non-symmetric distributions because it does not have the same interpretation as in the symmetric cases above (see Balanda and MacGillivray (1988)).

Before we proceed to consider other numerical characteristics of distributions, it is instructive to discuss the derivation of the moments in cases where the distribution involves no unknown parameters.

Examples

(i)   Consider the discrete random variable X with a density given below:

x	0	1	2
$f(x)$	0.3	0.3	0.4

(3.39)

$E(X) = 0(0.3) + 1(0.3) + 2(0.4) = 1.1$, $E(X^2) = 0^2(0.3) + 1^2(0.3) + 2^2(0.4) = 1.9$,

$E(X^3) = 0^3(0.3) + 1^3(0.3) + 2^3(0.4) = 3.5$, $E(X^4) = 0^4(0.3) + 1^4(0.3) + 2^4(0.4) = 6.7$.

$Var(X) = [0 - 1.1]^2(0.3) + [1 - 1.1]^2(0.3) + [2 - 1.1]^2(0.4) = 0.69$,

$Var(X) = E(X^2) - [E(X)]^2 = 1.90 - 1.21 = 0.69$,

$E\{(X - E(X))^3\} = [0 - 1.1]^3(0.3) + [1 - 1.1]^3(0.3) + [2 - 1.1]^3(0.4) = 0.108$,

$E\{(X - E(X))^4\} = [0 - 1.1]^4(0.3) + [1 - 1.1]^4(0.3) + [2 - 1.1]^4(0.4) = 0.7017$,

$\alpha_3 = \left(\frac{0.108}{(0.83)^3}\right) = 0.18843$, $\alpha_4 = \left(\frac{0.7017}{(0.83)^4}\right) = 1.4785$.

(ii)   Consider the continuous random variable X with density function:

$f(x) = 2x, 0 < x < 1$.

$E(X) = \int_0^1 2x^2 dx = \frac{2}{3}x^3\big|_0^1 = \frac{2}{3}$, $E(X^3) = \int_0^1 2x^4 dx = \frac{2}{5}x^5\big|_0^1 = \frac{2}{5}$,

$E(X^2) = \int_0^1 2x^3 dx = \frac{2}{4}x^4\big|_0^1 = \frac{1}{2}$, $Var(X) = E(X^2) - [E(X)]^2 = \frac{1}{2} - \frac{4}{9} = \frac{1}{18}$.

Invariance of skewness and kurtosis We conclude the discussion of the skewness and kurtosis coefficients by reiterating that their usefulness stems from the fact that they are *invariant* to *location* and *scale* changes. That is, for any random variable X whose first four moments exist:

$$\alpha_3(X) = \alpha_3(a+bX) \text{ and } \alpha_4(X) = \alpha_4(a+bX).$$

3.7.5 Other numerical characteristics

It is sometimes the case that for certain random variables, the moments discussed above do not make sense. For example, in the case where the random variable X denotes religion of a person: $1 =$ Christian, $2 =$ Muslim, $3 =$ Jewish, $4 =$ Buddhist, the mean and variance do not make much sense. In addition, sometimes the mean and variance do not exist, as in the case of the Cauchy distribution (see next section). In such cases we need to consider other numerical characteristics.

Measures of location

(1) **The mode**, or modal value m_0, is that particular value of the random variable which corresponds to the maximum of the density function; proposed by Pearson (1894).

Examples

(i)   For the density function given in (3.39) the mode is equal to 2.
     In the case where $f(x)$ is differentiable the mode can be derived as the solution of:

$$\left(\frac{df(x)}{dx}\right) = 0, \text{ subject to } \left(\frac{df^2(x)}{dx^2}\right)\Big|_{x=m_0} < 0. \tag{3.40}$$

(ii)   For a log-Normal random variable X with density function:

$$f(x;\boldsymbol{\theta}) = \frac{(x\sigma)^{-1}}{\sqrt{2\pi}} \exp\left\{-\frac{1}{2}\frac{(\ln x - \mu)^2}{\sigma^2}\right\}, \; \boldsymbol{\theta} := (\mu,\sigma^2) \in \mathbb{R} \times \mathbb{R}_+, \; x \in \mathbb{R}_+, \tag{3.41}$$

the mode can be obtained using (3.40):

$$\left(\frac{df(x)}{dx}\right) = \left[-\frac{1}{x}\frac{(x\sigma)^{-1}}{\sqrt{2\pi}}\exp\left(-\frac{(\ln x - \mu)^2}{2\sigma^2}\right) - \frac{1}{x}\frac{(x\sigma)^{-1}}{\sqrt{2\pi}}\left(\frac{(\ln x - \mu)}{\sigma^2}\right)\exp\left(-\frac{(\ln x - \mu)^2}{2\sigma^2}\right)\right] = 0,$$

$$\Rightarrow \left(1 + \left(\frac{\ln x - \mu}{\sigma^2}\right)\right) = 0 \Rightarrow \left(\frac{\mu - \ln x}{\sigma^2}\right) = 1, \text{ or } (\mu - \sigma^2) = \ln x.$$

In view of the fact that $\left(\frac{df^2(x)}{dx^2}\right)\Big|_{x=m_0} < 0$, the mode of the density is: $m_0 = \exp(\mu - \sigma^2)$.
In figure 3.36 we can see the mode of the log-Normal density LN $(\mu = 1, \sigma = 0.7)$.
In figure 3.37 we can see the mode of the Cauchy density C$(\alpha = 0, \beta = 1)$.

(2) **The median** of a random variable X is that particular value which divides the probability into two equal halves, i.e., it corresponds to $x_{\frac{1}{2}}$ (assuming it is unique) such that:

$$\mathbb{P}(x < x_{\frac{1}{2}}) \leq 0.5 \text{ and } \mathbb{P}(x \leq x_{\frac{1}{2}}) \geq 0.5.$$

In the case where the cdf is continuous and strictly increasing, $x_{\frac{1}{2}}$ is defined by:

$$F(x_{\frac{1}{2}}) = 0.5 \text{ and } x_{\frac{1}{2}} \text{ is unique.}$$

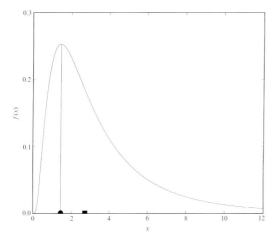

Figure 3.36 Mode of log-Normal density

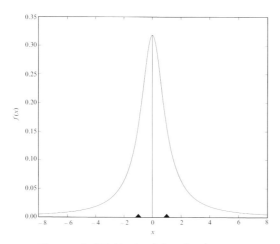

Figure 3.37 Mode of Cauchy density

Examples

(i) For a *Normal* random variable the median coincides with the other two measures of location:

   mean = median = mode.

NOTE that for *symmetric* distributions in general, the only equality holding is:

   mean = median.

(ii) For a log-Normal random variable the median is given by the value m such that:

$$\int_0^m \frac{1}{x\sigma\sqrt{2\pi}}\exp\left\{-\frac{1}{2}\left(\frac{\ln x - \mu}{\sigma}\right)^2\right\}dx = \tfrac{1}{2}, \text{ substituting } y = \ln x,$$

$$\frac{1}{\sigma\sqrt{2\pi}}\int_{-\infty}^{\ln m}\exp\left\{-\frac{1}{2}\left(\frac{y-\mu}{\sigma}\right)^2\right\}dx = \tfrac{1}{2}, \text{ this holds for } \ln m = \mu.$$

Hence, the median is:

$$x_{\frac{1}{2}} = e^{\mu}.$$

The median of the log-Normal density is shown in figure 3.36 as the spot in the middle of the black rectangle ($\mu = 1, \sigma = 0.7$ and thus $x_{\frac{1}{2}} = 2.71828$).

The median is an important measure of location because sometimes the mean does not exist (see the Cauchy distribution below) but the median always does. Extending the notion of a median to other values in the interval [0,1], not just $\left(\frac{1}{2}\right)$, we define what is know as a *quantile*.

(3) **Quantiles** The *p*th quantile, denoted by x_p, is defined as the smallest number satisfying the relationship:

$$F_X(x_p) \geq p, \text{ for } p \in [0,1].$$

More formally, the *p*th quantile is defined by:

$$x_p = F_X^-(p) := \inf_{x \in \mathbb{R}_X} \{x : F_X(x) \geq p\}, \text{ for } p \in (0,1). \tag{3.42}$$

As argued above, $\inf_{x \in \mathbb{R}_X}$; is just a glorified minimum. This definition suggests that in the case where the cumulative distribution function (cdf) is continuous and strictly increasing, x_p is unique and is defined by:

$$F(x_p) = p.$$

The value p is known as the *p*th *percentile* and the value x_p the corresponding *quantile*.

It is interesting to NOTE that the notion of a *quartile* was introduced by McAlister (1879), the notion of a *median* by Galton (1883), and that of a *percentile* by Galton (1885).

Beyond the median there are another two quantiles of particular interest. The **lower quartile** (NOTE the difference in the name) and the **upper quartile** are defined by:

$$x_{\frac{1}{4}} = F^-(0.25), \ x_{\frac{3}{4}} = F^-(0.75).$$

Examples

(i)   In the case of the standard Normal distribution (N(0,1)):

$$x_{\frac{1}{4}} = -0.6745, \ x_{\frac{3}{4}} = 0.6745.$$

Hence, for an arbitrary Normal distribution (N(μ, σ^2)):

$$x_{\frac{1}{4}} = \mu - 0.6745\sigma, \ x_{\frac{3}{4}} = \mu + 0.6745\sigma.$$

(ii)   It is well known that the Cauchy distribution (C(α, β)) has no moments. Consider the Cauchy distribution with cdf, quantile, and density functions:

$$F(x; \alpha, \beta) = \frac{1}{2} + \left(\frac{1}{\pi} \tan^{-1}\left(\frac{x - \alpha}{\beta}\right)\right), \quad F^{-1}(x; \alpha, \beta) = \alpha + \beta\left[\tan\left(\pi\left(x - \frac{1}{2}\right)\right)\right],$$

$$f(x; \alpha, \beta) = \frac{1}{\beta\left(1 + \left(\frac{x - \alpha}{\beta}\right)^2\right)}, \qquad \alpha \in \mathbb{R}, \beta \in \mathbb{R}_+, x \in \mathbb{R}.$$

The function defined by (3.42) is interesting in its own right and thus we will take a short digression to discuss its properties in some detail; see Karr (1993).

Quantile function The function defined by (3.42) in the form of:

$$F_X^-(.) : (0,1) \to \mathbb{R}_X,$$

is known as the *quantile function*. Looking at the definition it is not very difficult to see that the $F_X^-(.)$ is not the same as the ordinary inverse function of the cdf $F_X(.)$ since the inverse exists only in cases where $F_X(.)$ is one-to-one and onto, i.e., when $F_X(.)$ is continuous and strictly increasing. It does constitute, however, a kind of generalized inverse which exists even in cases where the ordinary inverse function does not exist. When the ordinary inverse function exists the two coincide in the sense that:

$$F_X^-(.) = F_X^{-1}(.).$$

As implied above, $F^-(.)$ exists even in cases where $F(.)$ is neither continuous nor strictly increasing. Intuitively, $F^-(.)$ jumps where $F(.)$ is flat and $F^-(.)$ is flat at the points where $F(.)$ jumps. Because of its importance we note several useful **properties** of the **quantile function**:

Q1. $F_X^-(p) \le x$ if and only if $p \le F_X(x)$ for all $x \in \mathbb{R}_X$ and $p \in (0,1)$,
Q2. $F_X^-(.)$ is increasing and left continuous,
Q3. If $F_X(.)$ is continuous, $F_X(F_X^-(p)) = p$.

Example
In figures 3.38–3.39 we can see the Cauchy cdf $F(x;0,1)$ and the corresponding quantile function:

$$G(x;0,1) := F^{-1}(x;0,1).(\alpha = 0, \beta = 1).$$

We can show that:

$$\int_{-\infty}^{\alpha} \frac{1}{\beta\left(1+\left(\frac{x-\alpha}{\beta}\right)^2\right)} dx = \frac{1}{2}, \quad \int_{-\infty}^{\alpha-\beta} \frac{1}{\beta\left(1+\left(\frac{x-\alpha}{\beta}\right)^2\right)} dx = \frac{1}{4}, \quad \int_{-\infty}^{\alpha+\beta} \frac{1}{\beta\left(1+\left(\frac{x-\alpha}{\beta}\right)^2\right)} dx = \frac{3}{4}.$$

That is, the median is equal to α, the lower quartile is equal to $(\alpha - \beta)$, and the upper quartile is equal to $(\alpha + \beta)$. These quantiles can often be used instead of the moments when using the Cauchy distribution. In figure 3.37 we can see the two quartiles shown with the little triangles on either side of the mean.

In relation to the quantile function we note a very useful result which can be viewed as the converse of the probability integral transformation mentioned above.

The inverse probability integral transformation For any continuous random variable X, with a cdf $F_X(x)$ such that $u = F_X(x)$ is invertible and $x = F_X^{-1}(u)$.

(a) For the random variable $U = F_X(X)$:

$$U = F_X(X) \sim \mathsf{U}(0,1). \tag{3.43}$$

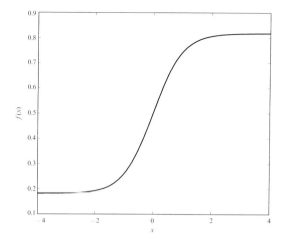

Figure 3.38 Cauchy cdf ($\alpha = 0$, $\beta = 1$)

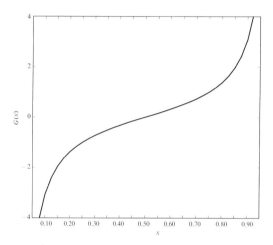

Figure 3.39 Cauchy quantile function

(b)   Let $U \sim \mathsf{U}(0,1)$ and define $X = F_X^{-1}(U)$. Then X has a distribution with cdf $F_X(.)$.

NOTE that, in contrast to the probability integral transformation, the inverse transformation result does not assume that $F(.)$ is continuous.

The above result provides a most remarkable way to generate random variables with a given distribution. Its usefulness can be easily seen in cases where $F(x)$ is invertible (see chapter 5).

Example
Consider the case where $U \sim \mathsf{U}(0,1)$ and we want to transform it into an exponentially distributed random variable X with:

$$F_X(x) = 1 - e^{-\theta x}, \; x > 0.$$

Using (3.43) together with the specific form of $F(x)$, we can deduce that $u = 1 - e^{-\theta x}$, $e^{-\theta x} = 1 - u$, $x = -\frac{1}{\theta} \ln (1 - u)$, and thus:

$$X = F_X^{-1}(u) = -\frac{1}{\theta} \ln (1 - u), u \in (0,1).$$

This result can be used to *simulate* exponentially distributed random variables using uniformly distributed random variables; see chapter 5.

Measures of dispersion

(1) **The Range**, is defined to be the difference between the largest and the smallest value taken by the random variable in question, i.e.

$$R(X) := X_{max} - X_{min}.$$

Example
In the case of the Uniform distribution ($U(a,b)$):

$$R(X) = X_{max} - X_{min} = b - a$$

(2) **The Interquartile Range**, is defined to be the difference between the lower and upper quartiles:

$$IQR(X) := (x_{3/4} - x_{1/4}).$$

Examples
(i)   In the case of the Normal distribution ($N(\mu, \sigma^2)$):

$$IQR(X) := (x_{3/4} - x_{1/4}) = \mu + 0.6745\sigma - \mu + 0.6745\sigma = 2(0.6745)\sigma.$$

In figure 3.40 we can see the Normal cdf for $N(0,1)$ with the following quantiles

q	x	$F(x)$	$f(x)$
$x_{0.05}$	-1.645	0.05	0.103
$x_{0.25}$	-0.6745	0.25	0.318
$x_{0.75}$	0.6745	0.75	0.318
$x_{0.95}$	1.645	0.95	0.103

In figure 3.41 we can see these quantiles in relation to the density function. NOTE that the maximum of the density function is just $\frac{1}{\sigma\sqrt{2\pi}} = 0.39894$.

(ii)   In the case of the Cauchy distribution considered above, we can easily see that:

$$IQR(X) = (\alpha + \beta) - (\alpha - \beta) = 2\beta.$$

This can be used as a measure of dispersion since the variance does not exist.

(3) **The quartile deviation** is defined as half of the interquartile range i.e.:

$$q(X) := \left(\frac{1}{2}\right)(x_{3/4} - x_{1/4}).$$

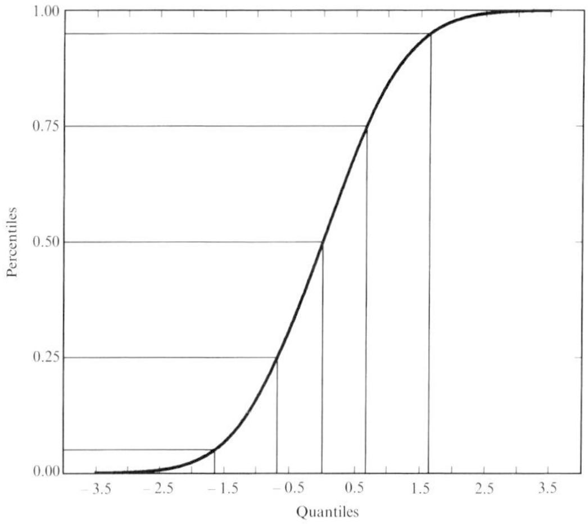

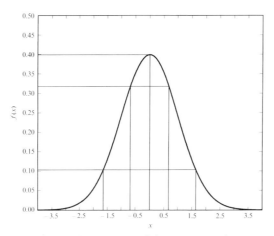

Figure 3.40 Normal cdf: quantiles

Figure 3.41 Normal density: quantiles

Examples

(i) For the Normal distribution ($N(\mu, \sigma^2)$): $q(X): = \left(\frac{1}{2}\right)(x_{3/4} - x_{1/4}) = (0.6745)\sigma.$

(ii) For the Cauchy distribution ($C(\alpha, \beta)$): $q(X): = \left(\frac{1}{2}\right)(x_{3/4} - x_{1/4}) = \beta.$

(4) The coefficient of variation, proposed by Pearson (1896), is defined to be the ratio of the standard deviation to the mean of the random variable in question, i.e.

$$cv(X): = \frac{\{Var(X)\}^{\frac{1}{2}}}{E(X)}.$$

Example

In the case of the Normal distribution ($N(\mu, \sigma^2)$):

$$cv(X): = \frac{\sigma}{\mu}.$$

3.8   Inequalities

A very important chapter of probability theory is that of probabilistic inequalities. The primary role of these inequalities is to provide upper and lower bounds for the evaluation of probabilities associated with random variables by utilizing their moments. In a way these inequalities provide ways for us to sidestep the distribution of certain random variables but still be in a position to make probabilistic statements relating to these random variables; see Shiryayev (1984), Karr (1993) and Loeve (1963).

General Chebyshev's inequality Let $X(.): S \to \mathbb{R}_X := (0,\infty)$ be a positive random variable and let $g(.): (0,\infty) \to (0,\infty)$ be a positive and increasing function. Then, for each $\varepsilon > 0$:

$$\mathbb{P}(g(X) \geq \varepsilon) \leq \frac{E(g(X))}{g(\varepsilon)}. \tag{3.44}$$

We note that the Chebyshev inequality encountered above is a special case of (3.44). Other such special cases are stated below. NOTE at the outset that the there is no standard terminology for these inequalities.

Markov's inequality Let X be a random variable such that $E(|X|^p) < \infty$, for $p > 0$:

$$\mathbb{P}(|X| \geq \varepsilon) \leq \frac{E(|X|^p)}{\varepsilon^p}.$$

The well-known saying that "there is no free lunch" can be illustrated by using this inequality to show that by postulating the existence of higher moments we can improve the upper bound.

Example
Let $\{X_n\}_{n=1}^{\infty} := \{X_1, X_2, \ldots, X_n \ldots\}$ be a sequence of Independent and Identically Bernoulli distributed (IID) random variables. It can be shown that:

$$S_n := \textstyle\sum_{k=1}^{n} X_k \sim \mathsf{Bi}(n\theta, n\theta(1-\theta)).$$

Using Chebyshev's inequality yields:

$$\mathbb{P}(|n^{-1}S_n - \theta| > \varepsilon) \leq \frac{\theta(1-\theta)}{n\varepsilon^2}.$$

On the other hand, using Markov's inequality for the fourth moment:

$$\mathbb{P}(|Y - E(Y)|^4 > \varepsilon) \leq \frac{E(|Y - E(Y)|^4}{\varepsilon^4},$$

noting that $E(|n^{-1}S_n - \theta|^4) = n\theta[1 + 3\theta(1-\theta)(n-2)]$ yields:

$$\mathbb{P}(|n^{-1}S_n - \theta| > \varepsilon) \leq \frac{3}{(16)n^2\varepsilon^4}.$$

As can be seen, the estimate of the upper bound given by Markov's inequality is less crude because it utilizes more information in relation to the existence of moments.

Bernstein's inequality Let $X(.): S \to \mathbb{R}_X := (0,\infty)$ be a positive random variable such that $E(e^{tX}) < \infty$ for some $t \in [0,c]$, $c > 0$:

$$\mathbb{P}(X \geq \varepsilon) \leq \frac{E(e^{tX})}{e^{tX}} \leq \inf_{0 \leq t \leq c} \{e^{-tX}E(e^{tX})\}.$$

Jensen's inequality Let $\varphi(.):\mathbb{R} \to \mathbb{R}$ be a convex function, i.e.:

$$\lambda\varphi(x) + (1-\lambda)\varphi(y) \geq \varphi(\lambda x + (1-\lambda)y), \ \lambda \in (0,1), \ x,y \in \mathbb{R}.$$

Assuming that $E(|X|) < \infty$, then:

$$\varphi(E(X)) \leq E(\varphi(X))$$

This inequality can be used to derive a whole series of inequalities.

Lyapunov's inequality Let X be a random variable such that $E(|X|^p) < \infty$, for $0 < q < p$:

$$E(|X|^q)^{\frac{1}{q}} \leq E(|X|^p)^{\frac{1}{p}}.$$

As a consequence of this inequality is the following sequence of inequalities:

$$E(|X|) \leq E(|X|^2)^{\frac{1}{2}} \leq E(|X|^3)^{\frac{1}{3}} \leq \cdots \leq E(|X|^n)^{\frac{1}{n}}.$$

Holder's inequality Let X and Y be random variables such that $E(|X|^p) < \infty$ and $E(|Y|^q) < \infty$, where $1 < q < \infty$, $1 < p < \infty$, $\frac{1}{p} + \frac{1}{q} = 1$, then:

$$E(X \cdot Y) \leq E(|X|^p)^{\frac{1}{p}} \cdot E(|Y|^q)^{\frac{1}{q}}.$$

Minkowski's inequality Let X and Y be random variables such that $E(|X|^p) < \infty$ and $E(|Y|^p) < \infty$, where $1 \leq p < \infty$, then:

$$E(|X+Y|^p)^{\frac{1}{p}} \leq [E(|X|^p)^{\frac{1}{p}} + E(|Y|^p)^{\frac{1}{p}}.$$

The above inequalities will be used extensively in the context of the limit theorems considered in chapter 9.

3.9   Summary

The basic aim of this chapter has been the metamorphosis of the abstract *probability space* $(S, \Im, \mathbb{P}(.))$ into an operational *probability model.* The end result is a family of densities indexed by a small number of unknown parameters:

$$\Phi = \{f(x;\boldsymbol{\theta}), \ \boldsymbol{\theta} \in \Theta, \ x \in \mathbb{R}_X\}.$$

This forms the foundation of the mathematical framework upon which the modeling and statistical inference will be built. The basic elements of the probability model being (i) the density function whose shapes will prove important in modeling, (ii) the parameter space which also plays an important role in statistical inference, and (iii) the support of the density. All three elements play important roles in choosing an appropriate probability model. In view of the fact that the distributional shapes depend crucially on the unknown parameters, we would like some way to assess the shapes suggested by the observed data before we choose the appropriate probability model without having to know the parameters. At the outset we can use descriptive statistics techniques, such as the histogram, as well as calculate features of the observed data such as the arithmetic average. As shown in chapter 5 these are directly related to the distributional shapes taken by density functions and the so-called moments of the distribution. That is the reason we digressed to discuss the moments of a distribution and how they relate to the unknown parameters.

The relationship between the unknown *parameters* $\boldsymbol{\theta}$ of the probability model and the *moments* of the distribution in question is given by:

$$E(X^r) := \int_{-\infty}^{\infty} x^r \cdot f(x;\boldsymbol{\theta})dx = g_r(\boldsymbol{\theta}), \ r = 1,2,\ldots$$

The concepts introduced during this digression will prove indispensable for modeling purposes because they represent crucial parts of the foundation.

In the next chapter we consider the metamorphosis of the abstract sampling space G_n^{IID} into an operational sampling model in terms of random variables: a set of random variables $\mathbf{X} := (X_1, X_2, \ldots, X_n)$ with a specific probabilistic structure.

3.10 Exercises

1 Explain why the abstract probability space is not convenient for modeling purposes.

2 (a) "A *random variable* is neither random nor a variable." Discuss.
   (b) "The concept of a random variable is a relative concept." Discuss.
   (c) Explain the difference between the inverse and the pre-image of a function.

3 Consider the random experiment of casting two dice and counting the total number of dots appearing on the uppermost faces. The random variable X takes the value 0 when the total number of dots is odd and 1 when the total number of dots is even.
   (a) Derive the density function of the random variable X assuming that the two dice are symmetric.
   (b) Derive the density function of the random variable X assuming that the two dice are non-symmetric.

4 Discuss the difference between the following probability set functions in terms of their domain:

$$\mathbb{P}(X \leq x) = \mathbb{P}X^{-1}((-\infty, x]) = P_x((-\infty, x]).$$

5 In the case of the random experiment of "tossing a coin twice":

$$S = \{(HH),(HT),(TH),(TT)\}, \Im = \{S, \emptyset, A, \overline{A}\},$$

where $A = \{(HH),(HT),(TH)\}$.
Consider the following functions:
     (i) $X(HH) = 1, \ X(HT) = 2, \ X(TH) = 2, \ X(TT) = 1,$
     (ii) $Y(HH) = 1, \ Y(HT) = 0, \ Y(TH) = 0, \ Y(TT) = 0,$
     (iii) $Z(HH) = 1, \ Z(HT) = 1, \ Z(TH) = 1, \ Z(TT) = 7405926.$
   (a) Which of the functions (i)–(iii) constitute random variables with respect to $\Im$?

(b) For the functions which are not random variables with respect to $\Im$, define the event space generated by them.

6 Compare and contrast the concepts of a simple random variable and a general random variable

7 Describe briefly the metamorphosis of the probability space $(S, \Im, \mathbb{P}(.))$ into a *probability model* of the form:

$$\Phi = \{f(x; \boldsymbol{\theta}), \boldsymbol{\theta} \in \Theta, x \in \mathbb{R}_X\}.$$

Explain the relationship between the components of the probability space and the probability model.

8 Explain the main components of a generic *probability model* of the form:

$$\Phi = \{f(x; \boldsymbol{\theta}), \boldsymbol{\theta} \in \Theta, x \in \mathbb{R}_X\}.$$

9 Why do we care about the moments of a distribution? How do the moments provide a way to interpret the unknown parameters?

10 The density function of the Exponential distribution is:

$$f(x; \theta) = \theta e^{-\theta x}, \theta > 0, x > 0.$$

(a) Derive its mean and variance.
(b) Derive its mode.

11 Consider the function:

$$f(x) = 140[x^3(1-x)^3], 0 < x < 1.$$

(a) Show that this is indeed a proper density function for a random variable X.
(b) Derive the mean, mode, variance, and kurtosis of X.

12 Consider the discrete random variable X whose distribution is given below:

x	-1	0	1
$f(x)$	0.2	0.4	0.4

(a) Derive its mean, variance, skewness, and kurtosis coefficients.
(b) Derive its mode and coefficient of variation.

13 (a) State the properties of a density function.
(b) Contrast the properties of the expected value and variance operators.
(c) Let X_1 and X_2 be two Independent random variables with the same mean μ and variance σ^2. Derive the mean and variance of the function: $Y = \frac{1}{3}X_1 + \frac{2}{3}X_2$.

14 Explain how the properties of the variance are actually determined by those of the mean operator.

15 Explain how the moment generating function can be used to derive the moments.

16 Explain the notion of skewness and discuss why $\alpha_3 = 0$ does not imply that the distribution in question is symmetric.

17 Explain the notion of kurtosis and discuss why it is of limited value when the distribution is non-symmetric.

18 For a Weibull distribution with parameters ($\alpha = 3.345, \beta = 3.45$) derive the kurtosis coefficient using the formulae in appendix A.

19 Explain why matching moments between two distributions can lead to misleading conclusions.

20 Compare and contrast the cumulative distribution function (cdf) and the quantile function. Explain why the quantile function is not always the inverse of the cdf.

21 Explain the notions of a percentile and a quantile and how they are related.

22 Why do we care about probabilistic inequalities?

23 "Moments do not characterize distributions in general and when they do we often need an infinite number of moments for the characterization". Discuss.

24 Explain the probability integral and the inverse probability integral transformations. How useful can they be in simulating non-uniform random variables?

Appendix A Univariate probability models

The purpose of this appendix is to summarize the most useful probability models and their parameterizations, their moments, and other numerical characteristics for reference purposes.

Notation

α_3 – skewness, α_4 – kurtosis, $m(t)$ – moment generating function.
IID – Independent and Identically Distributed.
$\Gamma[\alpha]$ is called the Gamma function and defined by:

$$\Gamma[\alpha] = \int_0^\infty \exp(-u) \cdot u^{\alpha-1} du.$$

$B[\alpha, \beta]$ is called the Beta function:

$$B[\alpha, \beta] = \int_0^1 u^{\alpha-1}(1-u)^{\beta-1} du$$

where there is a direct relationship between beta and gamma functions.

$$B[\alpha, \beta] = \frac{\Gamma[\alpha] \cdot \Gamma[\beta]}{\Gamma[\alpha + \beta]}.$$

$\mathbb{R}$: the real line, $\mathbb{R}_+$: the positive real line.

The following is a partial list of important probability models; Johnson, Kotz and Kemp (1992), Johnson, Kotz and Balakrishnan (1994, 1995) and Evans *et al.* (1993) for more details.

A.1   Discrete univariate distributions

Bernoulli: $B(\theta, \theta(1-\theta);1)$

$$\Phi = \{f(x;\theta) = \theta^x (1-\theta)^{1-x}, \ 0 < \theta < 1, \ x = 0,1\}.$$

Numerical characteristics

$$E(X) = \theta, \ Var(X) = \theta(1-\theta),$$

$$\alpha_3 = \left[(1-2\theta)[\theta(1-\theta)]^{-\frac{1}{2}}\right] (\alpha_4 - 3) = \left(\frac{1 - 6\theta(1-\theta)}{\theta(1-\theta)}\right),$$

$$\mu'_r = \theta \text{ for all } r = 3,4, \ldots, m(t) = (1 - \theta + \theta e^t).$$

Relationships with other distributions

(a)   Bernoulli–Binomial:

If $X_1, X_2, \ldots, X_m$ are IID Bernoulli distributed random variables, i.e. if $X_i \sim B(\theta, \theta(1-\theta);1), i = 1,2, \ldots, m$, then $Y = \sum_{i=1}^{m} X_i \sim Bi(\theta, \theta(1-\theta);m)$.

Binomial: $Bi(\theta, \theta(1-\theta);n)$

$$\Phi = \{f(x;\theta) = \binom{n}{x} \theta^x (1-\theta)^{n-x}, \ 0 < \theta < 1, \ x = 0,1, \ n = 1,2, \ldots\}.$$

Numerical characteristics

$$E(X) = n\theta, \ Var(X) = n\theta(1-\theta),$$

$$\alpha_3 = \frac{(1-2\theta)}{(n\theta\phi)^{\frac{1}{2}}}, \ \phi = 1 - \theta, \ \alpha_4 = 3 - \frac{6}{n} + \frac{1}{n\theta\phi},$$

$$m(t) = (1 - \theta + \theta e^t)^n.$$

Relationships with other distributions

(a)   Binomial–Bernoulli: see Bernoulli.

(b)   Binomial–Normal: (see Central Limit Theorem, chapter 9).

Geometric: $Geom(\theta)$

$$\Phi = \{f(x;\theta) = \theta(1-\theta)^{x-1}, \ 0 \le \theta \le 1, \ x = 1,2,3, \ldots\}.$$

Numerical characteristics

$$E(X) = \frac{1}{\theta}, \ Var(X) = \frac{(1-\theta)}{\theta^2}, \ \alpha_3 = \frac{2-\theta}{\sqrt{\theta}}, \ \alpha_4 = 9 + \frac{\theta^2}{\phi},$$

where $\phi := 1-\theta$, $m(t) = \frac{\theta e^t}{(1 - [1 - \theta] e^t)}$, for $[1 - \theta] e^t < 1$.

Hypergeometric: $HyG(K,M)$

$$\Phi = \left\{ f(x;\theta) = \frac{\binom{K}{x}\binom{M-K}{n-x}}{\binom{M}{n}}, \ 0 \le x \le \min(K,n) \right\}.$$

Numerical characteristics

$$E(X) = n\left(\frac{K}{M}\right), \; Var(X) = n\left(\frac{K}{M}\right)\left(\frac{M-K}{M}\right)\left(\frac{M-n}{M-1}\right)$$

Logarithmic series: LogS(θ)

$$\Phi = \{f(x;\theta) = \alpha\left(\frac{\theta^x}{x}\right), \; \alpha = -[\ln(1-\theta)]^{-1}, \; 0 < \theta < 1, \; x = 1,2,\dots\}.$$

Numerical characteristics

$$E(X) = \frac{\alpha\theta}{(1-\theta)}, \; Var(X) = \frac{\alpha\theta(1-\alpha\theta)}{(1-\theta)^2},$$

$$\alpha_3 = \frac{(1+\theta-3\alpha\theta+2\alpha^2\theta^2)}{(\alpha\theta)^{\frac{1}{2}}(1-\alpha\theta)^{\frac{3}{2}}}, \; \alpha_4 = \frac{1+4\theta+\theta^2-4\alpha\theta(1+\theta)+6\alpha^2\theta^2-3\alpha^3\theta^3}{\alpha\theta(1-\alpha\theta)^2},$$

$$\mu_r = \theta\frac{\partial\mu_r}{\partial\theta} + r\mu_2\mu_{r-1} \text{ for } r = 3,4,\dots, \; m(t) = \frac{\ln(1-\theta e^t)}{\ln(1-\theta)}.$$

Negative Binomial: NBi(θ,k)

$$\Phi = \{f(x;\theta,k) = \binom{k+x-1}{k-1}\theta^k(1-\theta)^x, \; 0 < \theta < 1, \; k = 1,2,\dots, \; x = 0,1,2,\dots\}$$

Numerical characteristics

$$E(X) = \frac{k(1-\theta)}{\theta}, \; Var(X) = \frac{k(1-\theta)}{\theta^2},$$

$$\alpha_3 = (2-\theta)(k(1-\theta))^{-\frac{1}{2}}, \; \alpha_4 - 3 = \frac{6}{k} + \left(\frac{\theta^2}{k(1-\theta)}\right),$$

$$m(t) = \left(\frac{\theta e^t}{(1-[1-\theta]e^t)}\right), \text{ for } [1-\theta]e^t < 1.$$

Poisson: Poisson(θ)

$$\Phi = \left\{f(x;\theta) = \frac{e^{-\theta}\theta^x}{x!}, \; \theta > 0, \; x = 0,1,2,3,\dots\right\}.$$

Numerical characteristics

$$E(X) = \theta, \; Var(X) = \theta, \; \alpha_3 = \frac{1}{\sqrt{\theta}}, \; \alpha_4 = 3 + \frac{1}{\theta},$$

$$m(t) = \exp(\theta[e^t - 1]).$$

Relationships with other distributions

(a) Poisson–Binomial: $\lim_{m\to\infty, [m\theta]\to\lambda}\{\binom{n}{x}\theta^x(1-\theta)^{1-x}\} = \frac{e^{-\lambda}\lambda^x}{x!}$.

(b) Poisson–Gamma: For $Y \sim \Gamma(\alpha,\beta)$, α an integer, then for any y,

$$\mathbb{P}(Y \le y) = \mathbb{P}(X \ge \alpha), \text{ where } X \text{ is Poisson}\left(\frac{y}{\beta}\right).$$

Uniform (discrete): Un(θ) (discrete)

$$\Phi = \left\{f(x;\theta) = \frac{1}{\theta+1}, \; \theta \text{ is a non-negative integer}, \; x = 0,1,2,3,\dots\right\}.$$

Numerical characteristics

$$E(X) = \left(\frac{\theta}{2}\right), \text{ no mode, } Var(X) = \left(\frac{\theta(\theta+2)}{12}\right),$$

$$\alpha_3 = 0, \ \alpha_4 = 3 - \left(\frac{6}{5}\right)\left(1 + \frac{2}{\theta(\theta+2)}\right).$$

A.2   Continuous univariate distributions

Beta: Beta(α, β)

$$\Phi = \left\{ f(x;\boldsymbol{\theta}) = \frac{x^{\alpha-1}(1-x)^{\beta-1}}{B[\alpha,\beta]}, \ \boldsymbol{\theta}:=(\alpha,\beta)\in\mathbb{R}_+^2, \ 0\le x\le 1 \right\}.$$

Numerical characteristics

$$E(X) = \frac{\alpha}{\alpha+\beta}, \ Var(X) = \frac{\alpha\beta}{(\alpha+\beta+1)(\alpha+\beta)^2},$$

$$\alpha_3 = \frac{2(\beta-\alpha)(\alpha+\beta+1)^{\frac{1}{2}}}{(\alpha+\beta+2)(\alpha\beta)^{\frac{1}{2}}}, \ \alpha_4 = \frac{3(\alpha+\beta+1)[2(\alpha+\beta)^2+\alpha\beta(\alpha+\beta-6)]}{\alpha\beta(\alpha+\beta-2)(\alpha+\beta-3)},$$

$$\mu_r' = \frac{B[r+\alpha,\beta]}{B[\alpha,\beta]}, \ r=2,3,\ \dots,\ m(t)=1+\sum_{k=1}^{\infty}\left(\prod_{r=0}^{k-1}\frac{\alpha+r}{\alpha+\beta+r}\right).$$

Relationships with other distributions

(a)   Beta–F: If $Y \sim \mathsf{F}(m_1, m_2)$ then $X = \left(\frac{m_1 Y}{m_2 + m_1 Y}\right) \sim \mathsf{Beta}(.,.)$.

(b)   Beta–Gamma: see Gamma.

Cauchy: C(α, β)

$$\Phi = \left\{ f(x;\boldsymbol{\theta}) = \frac{1}{\pi\beta[1+\{(x-\alpha)^2/\beta\}]}, \ \boldsymbol{\theta}:=(\alpha,\beta)\in\mathbb{R}\times\mathbb{R}_+, \ x\in\mathbb{R} \right\}.$$

Numerical characteristics
No moments exist, Mode = median = α.

Relationships with other distributions
(a)   Cauchy–Student's t: $\mathsf{St}(1):=\mathsf{C}(0,1)$.
(b)   Cauchy–Normal: see Normal.

Chi-square: $\chi^2(\nu)$

$$\Phi = \left\{ f(x;\nu) = \frac{2^{-\left(\frac{\nu}{2}\right)}}{\Gamma\left[\frac{\nu}{2}\right]} x^{\left(\frac{\nu-2}{2}\right)} \exp\left\{-\left(\frac{x}{2}\right)\right\}, \ \nu\in\mathbb{N}=\{1,2,\dots\}, \ x\in\mathbb{R}_+ \right\}.$$

Numerical characteristics
$E(X)=\nu$, mode $=\nu-2$, for $\nu>2$, $Var(X)=2\nu$,

$$\alpha_3 = 2^{\frac{3}{2}}\nu^{-\frac{1}{2}}, \ \alpha_4 = 3+\frac{12}{\nu}, \ \mu_r' = \frac{2^r\Gamma\left(\frac{\nu}{2}+r\right)}{\Gamma\left(\frac{\nu}{2}\right)}, \ r=2,3,\ \dots,$$

$$m(t) = (1-2t)^{-\frac{\nu}{2}}, \text{ for } t<\frac{1}{2}.$$

Relationships with other distributions

(a) Chi-square–Normal: If $X_1, X_2, \ldots, X_n$ are NIID (standard Normal)
$$Y = \textstyle\sum_{i=1}^{n} X_i^2 \sim \chi^2(n).$$

(b) Chi-square–F:

(i) If $X_1 \sim \chi^2(\nu_1)$, $X_2 \sim \chi^2(\nu_2)$ are independent,
$$Y = \left(\frac{(X_1/\nu_1)}{(X_2/\nu_2)}\right) \sim \mathsf{F}(\nu_1, \nu_2).$$

(ii) If $X \sim \chi^2(\nu)$ and $Y \sim \mathsf{F}(\nu, \infty)$ then $X = \nu Y$.

Exponential: $\mathsf{Ex}(\theta)$

$$\Phi = \left\{ f(x;\theta) = \frac{1}{\theta} e^{-\left(\frac{x}{\theta}\right)}, \ \theta \in \mathbb{R}_+, \ x \in \mathbb{R}_+ \right\}.$$

Numerical characteristics

$E(X) = \theta$, mode $= 0$, median $= \theta \ln 2$, $Var(X) = \theta^2$, $\alpha_3 = 2$,

$\alpha_4 = 9$, $\mu'_r = \Gamma[r+1]\theta^r$, $m(t) = \frac{1}{(1-\theta t)}$, for $t > \frac{1}{\theta}$.

Relationships with other distributions

(a) Exponential–Gamma: A special case of the Gamma with $\alpha = 1$.

(b) Exponential–Weibull: If $X \sim \mathsf{Ex}(\theta)$, $Y = X^{\frac{1}{\beta}} \sim \mathsf{W}(\theta, \beta)$.

(c) Exponential–Uniform: If $Y \sim \mathsf{U}(0,\theta)$ then $X = -\left(\frac{1}{\theta}\right) \ln\left(\frac{Y}{\theta}\right) \sim \mathsf{Ex}(\theta)$.

(d) Exponential–Pareto: If $X \sim \mathsf{Ex}(\theta)$ with $X \geq X_0 \geq \theta \geq 0$, then
$$Y = x_0 e^{X-\theta} \sim \mathsf{Par}(\theta; x_0).$$

Extreme value (Gumbel): $\mathsf{EV}(\alpha, \beta)$

$$\Phi = \left\{ f(x;\boldsymbol{\theta}) = \frac{1}{\beta} e^{-\frac{(x-\alpha)}{\beta}} \exp\left(-e^{-\frac{(x-\alpha)}{\beta}}\right), \ \boldsymbol{\theta} := (\alpha, \beta) \in \mathbb{R} \times \mathbb{R}_+, \ x \in \mathbb{R}_+ \right\}.$$

Numerical characteristics

$E(X) = \alpha + 0.5772\beta$, mode $= \alpha$, median $= \alpha + \beta \ln(\ln 2)$,

$Var(X) = \frac{\beta^2 \pi^2}{6}$, $\alpha_3 = 1.29857$, $\alpha_4 = 5.4$, $m(t) = e^{\frac{\alpha t}{\beta}} \Gamma[1 + t]$.

Relationships with other distributions

(a) Extreme–Logistic: If X_1 and X_2 are independent Extreme value,
$$Y = (X_1 - X_2) \sim \mathsf{Lg}(0, \pi^2/3).$$

(b) Extreme–Weibull: see Weibull.

Fisher's F: $\mathsf{F}(\nu, \eta)$

$$\Phi = \left\{ f(x;\boldsymbol{\theta}) = \frac{\left(\frac{\nu}{\eta}\right)^{\frac{1}{2}\nu}}{B\left[\frac{\nu}{2}, \frac{\eta}{2}\right]} \left(x^{\frac{1}{2}(\nu-2)}\right)\left(1 + \left(\frac{\nu}{\eta}\right)x\right)^{-\frac{1}{2}(\nu+\eta)}, \ \nu > 0, \ \eta > 0, \ x > 0 \right\}.$$

Numerical characteristics

$$E(X) = \frac{\eta}{\eta - 2}, \ \eta > 2, \ Var(X) = 2\left(\frac{\eta}{\eta - 2}\right)^2 \frac{(\nu + \eta - 2)}{\nu(\eta - 4)}, \ \eta > 4,$$

$$\alpha_3 = \frac{(2\nu + \eta - 2)\{8(\eta - 4)\}^{\frac{1}{2}}}{\nu^{\frac{1}{2}}(\eta - 6)(\nu + \eta - 2)^{\frac{1}{2}}}, \ \eta > 6, \ \alpha_4 = \frac{12\{(\eta - 2)^2(\eta - 4) + \nu(\nu + \eta - 2)(5\eta - 22)\}}{\nu(\eta - 6)(\eta - 8)(\nu + \eta - 2)}, \ \eta > 8,$$

$$\mu'_r = \frac{\Gamma\left(\frac{\nu + 2r}{2}\right)\Gamma\left(\frac{\eta - 2r}{2}\right)}{\Gamma\left(\frac{\nu}{2}\right)\Gamma\left(\frac{\eta}{2}\right)}\left(\frac{\eta}{\nu}\right)^r, \ r < \frac{\eta}{2}.$$

Relationships with other distributions
   (a)   F–Chi-square: see Chi-square.
   (b)   F–Student's t: see Student's t.
   (c)   F–Beta: see Beta.
   (d)   F–F: If $X \sim \mathsf{F}(\nu, \eta)$ then $Y = \left(\frac{1}{X}\right) \sim \mathsf{F}(\eta, \nu)$.

Gamma: $\mathsf{Gamma}(\alpha, \beta)$

$$\Phi = \left\{f(x;\boldsymbol{\theta}) = \frac{\beta^{-1}}{\Gamma[\alpha]}\left(\frac{x}{\beta}\right)^{\alpha - 1}\exp\left\{-\left(\frac{x}{\beta}\right)\right\}, \ \boldsymbol{\theta} := (\alpha, \beta) \in \mathbb{R}^2_+, x \in \mathbb{R}_+\right\}.$$

Numerical characteristics

$E(X) = \alpha\beta$, mode $= \beta(\alpha - 1)$, $\beta \geq 1$, $Var(X) = \alpha\beta^2$,

$$\alpha_3 = 2\alpha^{-\frac{1}{2}}, \ \alpha_4 = 3 + \left(\frac{6}{\alpha}\right), \ \mu'_r = \left(\frac{\Gamma[\alpha + r]\beta^{-r}}{\Gamma[\alpha]}\right), r = 2, 3, \ldots,$$

$m(t) = (1 - \beta t)^{-\alpha}$, for $t < \frac{1}{\beta}$.

Relationships with other distributions
   (a)   Gamma–Chi-square: see Chi-square.
   (b)   Gamma–Beta: $X_1 \sim \mathsf{Gamma}(1, m_1)$, $X_2 \sim \mathsf{Gamma}(1, m_2)$,

$$Y = \left(\frac{1}{X_1 + X_2}\right) \sim \mathsf{Beta}(m_1, m_2), \text{ if } (X_1, X_2) \text{ are independent.}$$

   (c)   Gamma–Erlang: $\mathsf{Gamma}(\alpha, \beta)$ with β an integer, is the Erlang.
   (d)   Gamma–Exponential: $\Gamma(1, \beta)$ is known as the Exponential.

Generalized Gamma: $\mathsf{G\Gamma}\,(\alpha, \beta, \delta)$

$$\Phi = \left\{f(x;\boldsymbol{\theta}) = \frac{\alpha^{-1}}{\Gamma[\beta]}\left(\frac{x}{\alpha}\right)^{\delta\beta - 1}\exp\left\{-\left(\frac{x}{\alpha}\right)^\delta\right\}, \ \boldsymbol{\theta} := (\alpha, \beta, \delta) \in \mathbb{R}^3_+, x \in \mathbb{R}_+\right\}.$$

Numerical characteristics

$E(X) = \alpha g_1$, mode $= \alpha(\delta\beta - 1)^{(1/\delta)}$, $\alpha \geq 1$, $Var(X) = \alpha^2(g_2 - g_1^2)$,

$$\alpha_3 = \frac{([g_3 - 3g_2g_1 + 2g_1^3])}{(\sqrt{[g_2 - g_1^2]})^3}, \ \alpha_4 = \frac{([g_4 - 4g_3g_1 + 6g_2^2g_2 - 3g_1^4])}{([g_2 - g_1^2])^2},$$

$$\mu'_r = \alpha^r g_r, \text{ where } g_r = \left(\frac{\Gamma\left[\beta + \left(\frac{\gamma}{\delta}\right)\right]}{\Gamma[\beta]}\right), r = 1, 2, 3.$$

Laplace (double exponential): $\mathsf{Lp}(\alpha,\beta)$

$$\Phi = \left\{ f(x;\boldsymbol{\theta}) = \tfrac{1}{2\beta} e^{-\left(\frac{|x-\alpha|}{\beta}\right)}, \ \boldsymbol{\theta} := (\alpha,\beta) \in \mathbb{R} \times \mathbb{R}_+, \ x \in \mathbb{R}. \right\}$$

Numerical characteristics

$E(X) = \alpha$, mode = median = α, $Var(X) = 2\beta^2$, $\alpha_3 = 0$, $\alpha_4 = 6$,

$\mu_r = 0$ for r odd, $\mu_r = r!\beta^r$ for r even,

$m(t) = \frac{e^{\alpha t}}{(1-\beta^2 t^2)}$, for $|t| < \frac{1}{\beta}$.

Logistic: $\mathsf{Lg}(\alpha,\beta)$

$$\Phi = \left\{ f(x;\boldsymbol{\theta}) = \frac{\exp\left\{-\left(\frac{x-\alpha}{\beta}\right)\right\}}{\beta\left(1 + \exp\left\{-\left(\frac{x-\alpha}{\beta}\right)\right\}\right)^2}, \ \boldsymbol{\theta} := (\alpha,\beta) \in \mathbb{R} \times \mathbb{R}_+, \ x \in \mathbb{R} \right\}.$$

Numerical characteristics

$E(X) = \alpha$, $Var(X) = \frac{\beta^2 \pi^2}{3}$, $\alpha_3 = 0$, $\alpha_4 = 4.2$,

$m(t) = \exp(\alpha t)\mathsf{B}[(1-\beta t),(1+\beta t)].$

Relationships with other distributions
  (a)   Logistic–Extreme value: see Extreme value.

Log-Normal: $\mathsf{LN}(\mu,\sigma^2)$

$$\Phi = \left\{ f(x;\boldsymbol{\theta}) = \frac{1}{x}\frac{1}{\sigma\sqrt{2\pi}} \exp\left\{-\frac{(\ln x - \mu)^2}{2\sigma^2}\right\}, \ \boldsymbol{\theta} := (\mu,\sigma^2) \in \mathbb{R} \times \mathbb{R}_+, \ x \in \mathbb{R}_+ \right\}.$$

Numerical characteristics

$E(X) = \exp\left\{\mu + \tfrac{1}{2}\sigma^2\right\}$, mode = $\exp\{\mu - \sigma^2\}$, median = e^μ,

$Var(X) = \gamma(\gamma-1)e^{2\mu}$, $\gamma = e^{\sigma^2}$, $\alpha_3 = (\gamma+2)(\gamma-1)^{\frac{1}{2}}$,

$\alpha_4 = (\gamma^4 + 2\gamma^3 + 3\gamma^2 - 3)$, $\mu_r' = \exp\left[r\mu + \tfrac{1}{2}r^2\sigma^2\right]$, $r = 3,4,\ldots$

Relationships with other distributions
  (a)   Log-Normal–Normal: If $X \sim \mathsf{LN}(\mu,\sigma^2)$, $Y = (\ln X) \sim \mathsf{N}(\mu,\sigma^2)$.

Non-central chi-square: $\chi^2(\nu,\delta)$

$$\Phi = \left\{ f(x;\boldsymbol{\theta}) = \frac{\exp\left\{-\left(\frac{x+\delta}{2}\right)\right\}}{2^{\left(\frac{\nu}{2}\right)}} \sum_{k=0}^{\infty} \frac{x^{\left(\frac{\nu}{2}\right)+k-1}\delta^k}{2^{2k}k!\Gamma\left[\frac{\nu}{2}+k\right]}, \ \boldsymbol{\theta} := (\nu,\delta) \in \mathbb{N} \times \mathbb{R}_+, \ x \in \mathbb{R}_+ \right\}.$$

Numerical characteristics
  $E(X) = \nu + \delta$, $Var(X) = 2(\nu + 2\delta)$, $\alpha_3 = \frac{\sqrt{8}(\nu + 3\delta)}{(\nu + 2\delta)^{\frac{3}{2}}}$,

$$\alpha_4 = 3 + \frac{12(\nu + 4\delta)}{(\nu + 2\delta)^2}, \ \mu_r' = 2^r \Gamma\left(\frac{\nu}{2} + r\right) \sum_{k=0}^{\infty} \binom{r}{k} \frac{\left(\frac{\delta}{2}\right)^k}{\Gamma\left(k + \frac{\nu}{2}\right)}, \ r = 2, 3, \ldots,$$

$$m(t) = (1 - 2t)^{-\frac{\nu}{2}} \exp\left(\frac{\delta t}{1 - 2t}\right), \text{ for } t < \frac{1}{2}.$$

Relationships with other distributions

(a) Non-central Chi-square–Normal: If $X_1, X_2, \ldots, X_n$ are NIID (standard Normal)

$$Y = \sum_{i=1}^{n} (X_i + a_i)^2 \sim \chi^2(n; \delta), \ \delta = \sum_{i=1}^{n} a_i^2.$$

(b) Non-central Chi-square–Non-central F: (i) If $X_1 \sim \chi^2(\nu_1; \delta)$, $X_2 \sim \chi^2(\nu_2)$,

$$Y = \left(\frac{(X_1/\nu_1)}{(X_2/\nu_2)}\right) \sim F(\nu_1, \nu_2; \delta) \text{ if } X_1 \text{ and } X_2 \text{ are independent.}$$

Non-central Student's t: St$(\nu; \delta)$

$$\Phi = \left\{ f(x; \nu, \delta) = \frac{\nu^{\frac{\nu}{2}}}{\Gamma\left[\frac{\nu}{2}\right]} \frac{e^{-\frac{\delta}{2}}}{\sqrt{\pi}(\nu + x^2)^{\frac{(\nu+1)}{2}}} \sum_{k=0}^{\infty} \Gamma\left[\frac{(\nu + k + 1)}{2}\right] \left(\frac{\delta^k}{k!}\right) \left(\frac{2x^2}{\nu + x^2}\right)^{\frac{k}{2}}, \ \boldsymbol{\theta} = (\nu, \delta) \in \mathbb{R}_+^2, \ x \in \mathbb{R} \right\}.$$

Numerical characteristics

$$\mu_r' = c_r \frac{\Gamma\left[\frac{(\nu - r)}{2}\right] \nu^{\frac{r}{2}}}{2^{\frac{r}{2}} \Gamma\left[\frac{\nu}{2}\right]} \text{ for } \nu > r,$$

$$c_{2r-1} = \sum_{k=1}^{r} \frac{(2r - 1)! \delta^{2r-1}}{(2k - 1)!(r - k)! 2^{r-k}}, \ c_{2r} - \sum_{k=1}^{r} \frac{(2r)! \delta^{2r}}{(2k)!(r - k)! 2^{r-k}}, \ r = 1, 2, \ldots$$

Relationships with other distributions

(a) Student's t–Chi-square–Normal: $X \sim N(\mu, \sigma^2)$, $\frac{Z}{\sigma} \sim \chi^2(\nu)$

$$Y = \frac{X}{\sqrt{\frac{Z}{\nu}}} \sim St(0, 1; \nu) \text{ if } X \text{ and } Z \text{ are independent.}$$

Normal (Gaussian): N(μ, σ^2)

$$\Phi = \left\{ f(x; \boldsymbol{\theta}) = \frac{1}{\sigma\sqrt{2\pi}} \exp\left\{-\frac{(x - \mu)^2}{2\sigma^2}\right\}, \ \boldsymbol{\theta} := (\mu, \sigma^2) \in \mathbb{R} \times \mathbb{R}_+, \ x \in \mathbb{R} \right\}.$$

Numerical characteristics

$E(X) = \mu$, mode = median = μ, $Var(X) = \sigma^2$, $\alpha_3 = 0$, $\alpha_4 = 3$,

$\mu_r = 0$ for r odd, $\mu_r = \frac{r! \sigma^r}{\left(\frac{1}{2}r\right)! 2^{\frac{1}{2}r}}$, for r even, $m(t) = e^{\mu t + \frac{1}{2}\sigma^2 t^2}$.

Relationships with other distributions

(a) Normal–standard Normal: If $X \sim N(\mu, \sigma^2)$ then

$$Y = \left(\frac{X - \mu}{\sigma}\right) \sim N(0, 1).$$

(b)   Normal–log-Normal: If $X \sim \mathsf{N}(\mu,\sigma^2)$ then $Y = e^X \sim \mathsf{LN}(\mu,\sigma^2)$.
(c)   Normal–Chi-square: If $X \sim \mathsf{N}(0,1)$ then $Y = X^2 \sim \chi^2(1)$.
(d)   Normal–Cauchy: If $X_1 \sim \mathsf{N}(0,1)$, $X_2 \sim \mathsf{N}(0,1)$ independent,

$$Y = \frac{X_1}{X_2} \sim \mathsf{C}(0,1).$$

(e)   Normal–F: If $X_1 \sim \mathsf{N}(0,1)$, $X_2 \sim \mathsf{N}(0,1)$ independent,

$$Y = \left(\frac{X_1}{X_2}\right)^2 \sim \mathsf{F}(1,1).$$

(f)   Normal–Student's t: If $X \sim \mathsf{N}(0,1)$, $Y \sim \chi^2(\nu)$ independent,

$$Z = \left(\frac{X}{\sqrt{\frac{Y}{\nu}}}\right) \sim \mathsf{St}(\nu).$$

Pareto: $\mathsf{Par}(\theta,x_0)$

$$\Phi = \{f(x;\theta) = (\theta\, x_0^\theta)x^{-(\theta+1)},\ \theta \in \mathbb{R}_+,\ x_0 > 0,\ x \geq x_0\}.$$

Numerical characteristics

$$E(X) = \frac{\theta x_0}{(\theta - 1)},\ \text{median} = 2^{\frac{1}{\theta}}x_0,\ \text{mode} = x_0,$$

$$Var(X) = \frac{\theta x_0^2}{(\theta - 2)(\theta - 1)^2},\ \mu'_r = \frac{\theta x_0^r}{(\theta - r)},\ \text{for } \theta > r.$$

Relationships with other distributions
(a)   Pareto–Exponential: see Exponential.
(b)   Pareto–Chi-square: If $X_1, X_2, \ldots, X_n$ are IID Pareto random variables,

$$Y = 2\theta \ln\left\{\prod_{i=1}^n \left(\frac{X_i}{x_0^n}\right)\right\} \sim \chi^2(2n).$$

Power exponential (or error): $\mathsf{PE}(\mu,\beta,\delta)$

$$\Phi = \left\{f(x;\boldsymbol{\theta}) = \frac{(\beta)^{-1}}{2^{\frac{\delta}{2}+1}\Gamma\left[1 + \frac{\delta}{2}\right]}e^{\left\{-\frac{1}{2}\left|\frac{x - \mu}{\beta}\right|^{\frac{2}{\delta}}\right\}},\ \boldsymbol{\theta} := (\mu,\beta,\delta) \in \mathbb{R} \times \mathbb{R}_+^2,\ x \in \mathbb{R}\right\}.$$

Numerical characteristics

$$E(X) = \mu,\ \text{mode} = \text{median} = \mu,\ Var(X) = \frac{2^\delta \beta^2 \Gamma[3\delta/2]}{\Gamma[\delta/2]},\ \alpha_3 = 0,$$

$$\alpha_4 = \frac{\Gamma[5\delta/2]\cdot\Gamma[\delta/2]}{\Gamma[3\delta/2]^2},\ \mu_r = 0,\ r\ \text{odd},\ \mu_r = \frac{2^{\delta r}\beta^r\Gamma[(r+1)\delta/2]}{\Gamma[\delta/2]},\ r\ \text{even}.$$

Relationships with other distributions
(a)   Power Exponential–Normal: $\mathsf{PE}(\mu,1,1) := \mathsf{N}(\mu,1)$.
(b)   Power Exponential–Laplace: $\mathsf{PE}(\mu,0.5,2) := \mathsf{L}(\mu,1)$.
(c)   Power Exponential–Uniform: As $\delta \to 0$, then

$$\mathsf{PE}(\mu,\beta,\delta) \Rightarrow \mathsf{U}(\mu - \beta,\mu + \beta).$$

Student's t: $\mathsf{St}(\nu)$

$$\Phi = \left\{ f(x;\boldsymbol{\theta}) = \frac{\Gamma\left[\frac{1}{2}(\nu+1)\right](\sigma^2\nu\pi)^{-\frac{1}{2}}}{\Gamma\left[\frac{1}{2}\nu\right]} \left(1 + \frac{(x-\mu)^2}{\nu\sigma^2}\right)^{-\frac{1}{2}(\nu+1)}, \; \boldsymbol{\theta} := (\mu,\sigma^2) \in \mathbb{R} \times \mathbb{R}_+, \; x \in \mathbb{R} \right\}.$$

Numerical characteristics

$$E(X) = \theta, \; Var(X) = \frac{\nu}{(\nu-2)}, \; \nu > 2, \; \alpha_3 = 0, \; (\alpha_4 - 3) = \frac{6}{(\nu-4)}, \; \nu > 4,$$

$$\mu_r = 0 \text{ for } r \text{ odd}, \; \mu_r = \nu^{\left(\frac{r}{2}\right)}\left(\frac{1\cdot 3\cdot 5\cdot 7\cdots(r-1)}{(\nu-2)(\nu-4)\cdots(\nu-r)}\right) \text{ for } \nu > r = 2,4,\ldots$$

Relationships with other distributions
   (a)   Student's t–Normal: as $\nu \to \infty$, $\mathsf{St}(\nu) \Rightarrow \mathsf{N}(0,1)$.
   (b)   Student's t–F: If $X \sim \mathsf{St}(\nu)$ then for $Y = X^2 \sim \mathsf{F}(1,\nu)$.

Uniform: $\mathsf{U}(\alpha,\beta)$ (continuous)

$$\Phi = \left\{ f(x;\boldsymbol{\theta}) = \frac{1}{(b-a)}, \; \boldsymbol{\theta} := (a,b), \; a \leq x \leq b \right\}.$$

Numerical characteristics

$$E(X) = \frac{(a+b)}{2}, \text{ no mode, median} = \frac{(a+b)}{2}, \; Var(X) = \frac{(b-a)^2}{12},$$

$$\alpha_3 = 0, \; \alpha_4 = 1.8, \; \mu_r = 0 \text{ for } r \text{ odd},$$

$$\mu_r = \left(\frac{(b-a)^r}{2^r(r+1)}\right), \text{ for } r \text{ even}, \; m(t) = \frac{e^{\beta t} - e^{\alpha t}}{(\beta-\alpha)t}.$$

Relationships with other distributions
   (a)   Uniform–Beta: If $X \sim \mathsf{U}(0,1)$, then $X \sim \mathsf{Beta}(1,1)$.
   (b)   Uniform–all other distributions: If $X \sim \mathsf{U}(0,1)$, then for any random variable Y with cdf $F(y)$, $Y = F^{-1}(x)$.

Weibull: $\mathsf{W}(\alpha,\beta)$

$$\Phi = \left\{ f(x;\boldsymbol{\theta}) = \frac{\beta x^{\beta-1}}{\alpha^\beta}\exp\left\{-\left(\frac{x}{\alpha}\right)^\beta\right\}, \; \boldsymbol{\theta} := (\alpha,\beta) \in \mathbb{R}_+^2, \; x > 0 \right\}.$$

Numerical characteristics

$$E(X) = \alpha^{\frac{1}{\beta}}\Gamma\left[\frac{1+\beta}{\beta}\right], \text{ mode} = \alpha(\beta-1), \; \alpha \geq 1,$$

$$Var(X) = \alpha^{\frac{2}{\beta}}\left(\Gamma\left[\frac{\beta+2}{\beta}\right]\right) - \left(\Gamma\left[\frac{\beta+1}{\beta}\right]^2\right), \; \mu_r' = \alpha^{\frac{r}{\beta}}\Gamma\left[\frac{r+\beta}{\beta}\right], \; r = 3,4,\ldots$$

Relationships with other distributions
   (a)   Weibull–Exponential: see Exponential.
   (b)   Weibull–Extreme value: If $X \sim \mathsf{W}(\alpha,\beta)$, then

$$Y = -\ln(\alpha X^\beta) \sim \mathsf{EV}(\alpha,\beta).$$

   (c)   Weibull–Rayleigh: $\mathsf{W}(\alpha,2)$ is the Rayleigh distribution.

4 The notion of a random sample

4.1 Introduction

4.1.1 Primary aim of this chapter

The primary objective of this chapter is to complete the metamorphosis of the *simple statistical space* to a **simple statistical model** which began in the previous chapter. In chapter 3 we converted the first component, the probability space, into a probability model. In this chapter we proceed to convert the second component, the *sampling space*, into a **sampling model**. The metamorphosis involves two of the most important notions of probability theory: *Independence* and *Identical Distribution*. Upon completion of the metamorphosis we reach one of our primary intermediate targets, the formulation of a *simple statistical model*, which constitutes the simplest form of a statistical model. The latter provides the cornerstone on which we will build both empirical modeling as well as statistical inference. As mentioned in chapter 1 what differentiates empirical modeling from other forms of modeling is the use of observed data in conjunction with statistical models. It will be very difficult to exaggerate the importance of the notion of a statistical model in the context of modeling with non-experimental data. This is because choosing a statistical model when modeling non-experimental data is the most difficult aspect of the problem and thus one needs a thorough and in-depth understanding of the concepts involved. This understanding concerns both the probabilistic (mathematical) aspects, as well as the intuitive dimension as it relates to the observed data.

4.1.2 The story so far

In chapter 2 we commenced the formalization of a *simple chance mechanism* generically known as a *random experiment* $\mathcal{E}$ specified by the following conditions:

[a]   all possible distinct outcomes are known a priori,
[b]   in any particular trial the outcome is not known a priori but there exists a perceptible regularity of occurrence associated with these outcomes, and
[c]   it can be repeated under identical conditions.

The first formalization in chapter 2 took the form of a *simple statistical space*:

[i]   simple probability space: $(S, \Im, \mathbb{P}(.))^n$,
[ii] simple sampling space: $G_n^{\text{IID}} = \{\mathcal{A}_1, \mathcal{A}_2, \mathcal{A}_3, \ldots, \mathcal{A}_n\}$.

This formalization, although adequate for mathematical purposes, is much too abstract for modeling purposes. In an attempt to transform it into something more suitable for analyzing numerical data, we used the concept of a random variable to metamorphose the probability space into a probability model:

$$
\begin{array}{cc}
\text{Probability space} & \text{Probability model} \\
(S, \Im, \mathbb{P}(.)) & \rightsquigarrow \quad \Phi = \{f(x; \boldsymbol{\theta}), \boldsymbol{\theta} \in \Theta, x \in \mathbb{R}_X\},
\end{array}
$$

where Φ denotes a collection of density functions $f(x; \boldsymbol{\theta})$, indexed by some unknown parameter(s) $\boldsymbol{\theta}$; the latter taking values in Θ (see chapter 3).

4.1.3   From random trials to a random sample: a first view

As argued in chapter 2 a simple sampling space $G_n^{\text{IID}} := \{\mathcal{A}_1, \mathcal{A}_2, \ldots, \mathcal{A}_n\}$ is a set of *random trials*, which satisfies the following conditions:

$$
\textit{Independent (I):} \ \mathbb{P}_{(n)}(\mathcal{A}_1 \cap \mathcal{A}_2 \cap \ldots \cap \mathcal{A}_k) = \prod_{i=1}^{k} \mathbb{P}_i(\mathcal{A}_i), \text{ for each } k = 2, 3, \ldots, n,
$$
$$(4.1)$$

$$
\textit{Identically Distributed (ID):} \ \mathbb{P}_1(.) = \mathbb{P}_2(.) = \cdots = \mathbb{P}_n(.) = \mathbb{P}(.).
$$
$$(4.2)$$

Independence is related to the condition that "the outcome of one trial does not affect and is not affected by the outcome of any other trial," or equivalently:

$$
\mathbb{P}_{(n)}(\mathcal{A}_k \mid \mathcal{A}_1, \mathcal{A}_2, \ldots \mathcal{A}_{k-1}, \mathcal{A}_{k+1}, \ldots, \mathcal{A}_n) = \mathbb{P}_k(\mathcal{A}_k), \text{ for each } k = 1, 2, \ldots, n. \quad (4.3)
$$

The ID condition has to do with "keeping the same probabilistic structure from one trial to the next"; the probabilities associated with the different outcomes remain the same for all trials.

   Armed with the notion of a *random variable*, let us now consider the metamorphosis of the abstract notion of a simple sampling space to something related to random variables. Looking at the definition of random trials (4.1)–(4.2), we can see that the independence condition is defined in terms of the probability set functions $\mathbb{P}_{(n)}(.)$ and $\mathbb{P}_k(.)$ which belong to the probability spaces $(\mathbf{S}_{(n)}, \Im_{(n)}, \mathbb{P}_{(n)})$ and $(S_k, \Im_k, \mathbb{P}_k)$, respectively. The difficulties one has to face in transforming the trials $\{\mathcal{A}_1, \mathcal{A}_2, \ldots, \mathcal{A}_n\}$ into a set of random variables $\mathbf{X}_{(n)} := (X_1, X_2, \ldots, X_n)$, have to do with defining the equivalent concepts to $\mathbb{P}_{(n)}(.)$ and $\mathbb{P}_k(.)$ in terms of random variables. The concept corresponding to the set function $\mathbb{P}_{(n)}(.)$, is the so-called *joint distribution function* and that corresponding to $\mathbb{P}_k(.)$, the *marginal distribution function*. Using these two notions we can define the concept of a *random sample*: a set of Independent and Identically Distributed (IID) random variables. The basic new concept needed for the formalization of both notions is that of a *joint distribution function*.

4.1.4   A bird's eye view of the chapter

In section 2 we introduce the notion of a joint distribution using the bivariate case for expositional purposes. In section 3 we relate the notion of the joint distribution to that of the marginal distribution introduced in the previous chapter, emphasizing the fact that the former often involves more information than the marginal distributions associated with it. In section 4 we introduce the notion of a conditional distribution and relate it to both the joint and marginal distributions. The notion of conditioning and conditional moments will play a very important role in the discussions that follow. In section 5 we define the notion of independence using the relationship between the joint, marginal and conditional distributions. In section 6 we define the notion of identically distributed in terms of the marginal distributions. Armed with the notions of independence and identical distribution we proceed to define the notion of a random sample in section 7. Before we complete the metamorphosis of a simple statistical space into a simple statistical model in section 10 we take an important digression. In section 8 we introduce the concept of a function of random variables and its distribution as a prelude to discussing the concept of an ordered random sample in section 8. The notion of a function of random variables is crucial in the context of statistical inference; the overwhelming majority of quantities of interest in statistical inference (estimators, test statistics, predictors) are such functions. The concept of an ordered sample is important in the present context because a simple re-ordering of a random sample yields a non-random sample! The concept of an ordered sample also plays an important role in statistical inference.

4.2   Joint distributions

The concept of a joint distribution is without a doubt one of the most important notions in both probability theory and statistical inference. As in the case of a single random variable, the discussion will proceed to introduce the concept from the simple to the more general case. In this context simple refers to the case of *countable* outcomes sets which give rise to *discrete* random variables. After we introduce the basic ideas in this simplified context we proceed to discuss them in their full generality.

4.2.1   Discrete random variables

In order to understand the notion of a set of random variables (a random vector) we consider first the two random variable cases since the extension to a larger number of random variables is simple in principle, but complicated in terms of notation.

Random vector   Consider the two *simple random variables* $X(.)$ and $Y(.)$ defined on the same probability space $(S, \Im, \mathbb{P}(.))$, i.e.

$$X(.): S \to \mathbb{R}, \text{ such that } X^{-1}(x) \in \Im, \text{ for all } x \in \mathbb{R},$$

$$Y(.): S \to \mathbb{R}, \text{ such that } Y^{-1}(y) \in \Im, \text{ for all } y \in \mathbb{R}.$$

REMARK: we remind the reader that $Y^{-1}(y) = \{s: Y(s) = y, s \in S\}$ denotes the *pre-image* of the function $Y(.)$ and not its inverse. Viewing them separately we can define their individual density functions, as explained in the previous chapter, as follows:

$$\mathbb{P}(s: X(s) = x) = f_x(x) > 0, \, x \in \mathbb{R}_X, \quad \mathbb{P}(s: Y(s) = y) = f_y(y) > 0, \, y \in \mathbb{R}_Y,$$

where $\mathbb{R}_X$ and $\mathbb{R}_Y$ denote the *support* of the density functions of X and Y. Viewing them together we can think of each pair $(x,y) \in \mathbb{R}_X \times \mathbb{R}_Y$ as events of the form:

$$\{s: X(s) = x, \, Y(s) = y\} := \{s: X(s) = x\} \cap \{s: Y(s) = y\}, \, (x,y) \in \mathbb{R}_X \times \mathbb{R}_Y.$$

In view of the fact that the event space $\Im$ is a σ-field, and thus closed under intersections, the mapping:

$$\mathbf{Z}(.,.) := (X(.), Y(.)): S \rightarrow \mathbb{R}^2,$$

is a **random vector** since the pre-image of $\mathbf{Z}(.)$ belongs to the event space $\Im$:

$$\mathbf{Z}^{-1}(x,y) = [(X^{-1}(x)) \cap (Y^{-1}(y))] \in \Im,$$

since $X^{-1}(x) \in \Im$ and $Y^{-1}(y) \in \Im$ by definition (see Spanos (1986)).

Joint density The joint density function is defined by:

$$f(.,.): \mathbb{R}_X \times \mathbb{R}_Y \rightarrow [0,1],$$

$$f(x,y) = \mathbb{P}\{s: X(s) = x, \, Y(s) = y\}, \, (x,y) \in \mathbb{R}_X \times \mathbb{R}_Y.$$

Example

Consider the case of the random experiment of tossing a fair coin twice, giving rise to the set of outcomes: $S = \{(HH),(HT),(TH),(TT)\}$.

Let us define the random variables $X(.)$ and $Y(.)$ on S as follows:

$$X(HH) = X(HT) = X(TH) = 1, X(TT) = 0,$$
$$Y(HT) = Y(TH) = Y(TT) = 1, Y(HH) = 0.$$

We can construct the individual density functions as follows:

x	0	1	y	0	1
$f(x)$	0.25	0.75	$f(y)$	0.25	0.75

(4.4)

To define the joint density function we need to specify all the events of the form:

$$(X = x, Y = y), x \in \mathbb{R}_X, y \in \mathbb{R}_Y,$$

and then attach probabilities to these events. In view of the fact that:

$$
\begin{aligned}
(X = 0, Y = 0) &= \{\} = \emptyset, & f(x = 0, y = 0) &= 0.00, \\
(X = 0, Y = 1) &= \{(TT)\}, & f(x = 0, y = 1) &= 0.25, \\
(X = 1, Y = 0) &= \{(HH)\}, & f(x = 1, x = 0) &= 0.25, \\
(X = 1, Y = 1) &= \{(HT),(TH)\}, & f(x = 1, y = 1) &= 0.50.
\end{aligned}
$$

That is, the joint density takes the form:

$y \backslash x$	0	1
0	0.00	0.25
1	0.25	0.50

$\qquad\qquad$ (4.5)

If we compare this joint density (4.5) with the univariate densities (4.4), there is no obvious relationship, but as shown below, this is misleading. As argued in the next chapter, the difference between the joint probabilities $f(x,y), x \in \mathbb{R}_X,\ y \in \mathbb{R}_Y$, and the product of the individual probabilities $(f(x) \cdot f(y))$ for $x \in \mathbb{R}_X, y \in \mathbb{R}_Y$, reflects the dependence between the random variables X and Y. At this stage it is crucial to note that a most important feature of the joint density function $f(x,y)$, is that it provides a general description of the dependence between X and Y.

Before we proceed to consider the continuous random variables case it is instructive to consider a particularly simple case of a bivariate discrete density function.

Example

The previous example is a particular case of a well-known discrete joint distribution, the *Bernoulli* distribution given below:

$y \backslash x$	0	1
0	$p(0,0)$	$p(1,0)$
1	$p(0,1)$	$p(1,1)$

$\qquad\qquad$ (4.6)

where $p(i,j)$ denotes the joint probability for $X = i$ and $Y = j$, $i,j = 0,1$. The Bernoulli joint density takes the form:

$$f(x,y) = p(0,0)^{(1-y)(1-x)} p(0,1)^{(1-y)x} p(1,0)^{y(1-x)} p(1,1)^{xy},\ x = 0,1 \text{ and } y = 0,1.$$

4.2.2 Continuous random variables

In the case where the outcomes set S is *uncountable* the random variables defined on it are said to be **continuous**, because their range of values is an interval on the real line $\mathbb{R}$.

Random vector Consider the two continuous random variables $X(.)$ and $Y(.)$ defined on the same probability space $(S, \Im, \mathbb{P}(.))$, i.e.

$$X(.): S \to \mathbb{R}, \text{ such that } X^{-1}((-\infty, x]) \in \Im, \text{ for all } x \in \mathbb{R},$$
$$Y(.): S \to \mathbb{R}, \text{ such that } Y^{-1}((-\infty, y]) \in \Im, \text{ for all } y \in \mathbb{R}.$$

Viewing them separately we can define their individual cumulative distribution functions (cdf) (see chapter 3), as follows:

$$\mathbb{P}(s: X(s) \leq x) = \mathbb{P}(X^{-1}(-\infty, x]) = P_X((-\infty, x]) = F_X(x),\ x \in \mathbb{R},$$
$$\mathbb{P}(s: Y(s) \leq y) = \mathbb{P}(Y^{-1}(-\infty, y]) = P_Y((-\infty, y]) = F_Y(y),\ y \in \mathbb{R}.$$

Viewing them together we can associate with each pair $(x,y) \in \mathbb{R} \times \mathbb{R}$ events of the form:

$$\{s : X(s) \leq x, \ Y(s) \leq y\} := \{s : X(s) \leq x\} \cap \{s : Y(s) \leq y\}, \ (x,y) \in \mathbb{R} \times \mathbb{R}.$$

As in the discrete random variable case, since $\Im$ is a σ-field (close under intersections) the mapping:

$$\mathbf{Z}(.,.) := (X(.), Y(.)) : S \to \mathbb{R}^2,$$

constitutes a **random vector**; the pre-image of $\mathbf{Z}(.)$:

$$\mathbf{Z}^{-1}((-\infty, x] \times (-\infty, y]) = [(X^{-1}((-\infty, x])) \cap (Y^{-1}((-\infty, y]))] \in \Im,$$

since $X^{-1}((-\infty, x]) \in \Im$ and $Y^{-1}((-\infty, y]) \in \Im$ by definition.

The **joint cumulative distribution function** (cdf) is defined by:

$$F_{XY}(.,.) : \mathbb{R}^2 \to [0,1],$$

$$F_{XY}(x,y) = \mathbb{P}\{s : X(s) \leq x, \ Y(s) \leq y\} = P_{XY}((-\infty, x] \times (-\infty, y]), \ (x,y) \in \mathbb{R}^2.$$

The joint cdf can also be defined on intervals of the form $(a,b]$:

$$\mathbb{P}\{s : x_1 < X(s) \leq x_2, y_1 < Y(s) \leq y_2\} = F(x_2, y_2) - F(x_1, y_2) - F(x_2, y_1) + F(x_1, y_1).$$

The **joint density function**, assuming that $f(x,y) \geq 0$ exists, is defined via:

$$F(x,y) = \int_{-\infty}^{x} \int_{-\infty}^{y} f(u,v) \, du \, dv.$$

NOTE that the subscripts will often be omitted when there is no possibility of confusion. In the case where $F(x,y)$ is differentiable at (x,y) we can derive the joint density by partial differentiation:

$$f(x,y) = \left(\frac{\partial^2 F(x,y)}{\partial x \partial y} \right), \text{ at all continuity points of } f(x,y).$$

Example
Let the joint cdf be that of the bivariate Exponential distribution:

$$F(x,y) = 1 - e^{-x} - e^{-y} + e^{-x-y}, \Rightarrow f(x,y) = \left(\frac{\partial^2 F(x,y)}{\partial x \partial y} \right) = e^{-x-y}, \ x \geq 0, \ y \geq 0.$$

In the case of *continuous* random variables we can think of the joint density as being defined over an interval of the form $(x < X \leq x + dx, y < Y \leq y + dy)$ as follows:

$$\mathbb{P}(x < X \leq x + dx, y < Y \leq y + dy) = f(x,y) \, dx \, dy.$$

Hence, as in the univariate case (see chapter 3), the joint density function takes values greater than one, i.e.

$$f(.,.) : \mathbb{R} \times \mathbb{R} \to [0,\infty).$$

In direct analogy to the univariate case, the **joint density function** has to satisfy certain **properties:**

[bf1] $f(x,y) \geq 0$, for all $(x,y) \in \mathbb{R}_X \times \mathbb{R}_Y$,

[bf2] $\int_{-\infty}^{\infty}\int_{-\infty}^{\infty} f(x,y)dx \cdot dy = 1,$

[bf3] $F_{XY}(a,b) = \int_{-\infty}^{a}\int_{-\infty}^{b} f(x,y)\, dx\, dy,$

[bf4] $f(x,y) = \left(\frac{\partial^2 F(x,y)}{\partial x \partial y}\right)$, at all continuity points of $f(x,y)$.

NOTE: in the discrete case the above integrals become summations over all values of X and Y, i.e., for $x_1 < x_2 < \cdots < x_n < \cdots$ and $y_1 < y_2 < \cdots < y_n < \cdots$

[bf2]′ $\sum_{i=1}^{\infty}\sum_{j=1}^{\infty} f(x_i,y_j) = 1$, **[bf3]′** $F(x_k,y_m) = \sum_{i=1}^{k}\sum_{i=1}^{m} f(x_i,y_j).$

Examples

(i)   An important *discrete* bivariate distribution, is the *Binomial* whose density takes the form:

$$f(x,y;\boldsymbol{\theta}) = \left(\frac{n!}{x!y!(n-x-y)!}\right)\theta_1^x\theta_2^y(1-\theta_1-\theta_2)^{n-x-y},\ \theta_i \in [0,1],\ i=1,2,$$

$\boldsymbol{\theta} := (\theta_1,\theta_2)$, n is an integer such that $x+y \leq n$, $x,y = 0,1,2,\ldots,n$.

(ii)   The most important *continuous* bivariate distribution is the *Normal*, whose density takes the form:

$$f(x,y;\boldsymbol{\theta}) = \frac{(1-\rho^2)^{-\frac{1}{2}}}{2\pi\sqrt{\sigma_{11}\sigma_{22}}}\exp\left\{-\frac{1}{2(1-\rho^2)}\left(\left(\frac{y-\mu_1}{\sqrt{\sigma_{11}}}\right)^2 - 2\rho\left(\frac{y-\mu_1}{\sqrt{\sigma_{11}}}\right)\left(\frac{x-\mu_2}{\sqrt{\sigma_{22}}}\right) + \left(\frac{x-\mu_2}{\sqrt{\sigma_{22}}}\right)^2\right)\right\} \quad (4.7)$$

where $\boldsymbol{\theta} := (\mu_1,\mu_2,\sigma_{11},\sigma_{22},\rho) \in \mathbb{R}^2 \times \mathbb{R}_+^2 \times [-1,1]$, $x \in \mathbb{R}$, $y \in \mathbb{R}$. In view of its apparent complexity, the bivariate density given in (4.7), is often denoted by:

$$\begin{pmatrix} Y \\ X \end{pmatrix} \sim N\left(\begin{pmatrix} \mu_1 \\ \mu_2 \end{pmatrix}, \begin{pmatrix} \sigma_{11} & \sigma_{12} \\ \sigma_{12} & \sigma_{22} \end{pmatrix}\right) \quad (4.8)$$

where $\sigma_{12} := \rho\sqrt{\sigma_{11}\sigma_{22}}$. A special case of this distribution, known as the **standard bivariate Normal**, is defined when the parameters take the values:

$$\mu_1 = \mu_2 = 0,\ \sigma_{11} = \sigma_{22} = 1.$$

Its density function takes the simplified form:

$$f(x,y;\boldsymbol{\theta}) = \frac{1}{2\pi\sqrt{(1-\rho^2)}}\exp\left\{-\frac{1}{2(1-\rho^2)}[x^2 - 2\rho xy + y^2]\right\}. \quad (4.9)$$

This density with $\boldsymbol{\theta} := (0,0,1,1,0.2)$ is shown in figure 4.1. The details of the bell shape of the surface can be seen from the inserted contours which can be viewed intuitively as the lines we get by slicing the surface at different heights.

Several additional bivariate distributions are listed in appendix B.

4.2.3 Joint moments

As in the case of univariate distributions the best way to interpret the unknown parameters is via the moments. In direct analogy to the univariate case, we define **the joint product moments** of order (k,m) by:

$$\mu'_{km} = E\{X^k Y^m\},\ k,m = 0,1,2,\ldots,$$

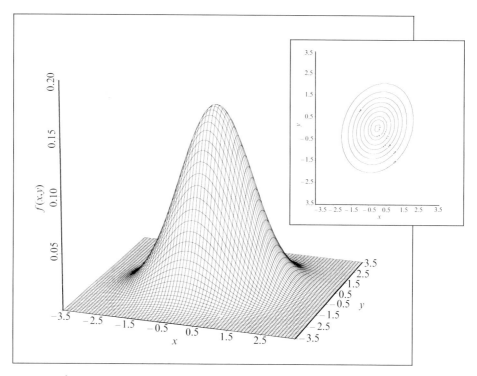

Figure 4.1 Bivariate Normal density surface with contours inserted

and the **joint central moments of order** (k,m) are defined by:

$$\mu_{km} = E\{(X - E(X))^k(Y - E(Y))^m\}, \; k,m = 0,1,2,\ldots$$

The first two joint product and central moments are:

$$
\begin{aligned}
\mu_{10}' &= E(X), & \mu_{10} &= 0, \\
\mu_{01}' &= E(Y), & \mu_{01} &= 0, \\
\mu_{20}' &= E(X)^2 + Var(X), & \mu_{20} &= Var(X), \\
\mu_{02}' &= E(Y)^2 + Var(Y), & \mu_{02} &= Var(Y), \\
\mu_{11}' &= E(XY). & \mu_{11} &= E[(X - E(X))(Y - E(Y))].
\end{aligned}
$$

The most important and widely used joint moment is the **covariance**, defined by:

$$\mu_{11} := Cov(X,Y) = E\{[X - E(X)][Y - E(Y)]\}. \tag{4.10}$$

Examples

(i) Consider the joint Normal distribution whose density is given in (4.7). We know from chapter 3 that the parameters $(\mu_1, \mu_2, \sigma_{11}, \sigma_{22})$ correspond to the moments:

$$\mu_1 = E(Y), \; \mu_2 = E(X), \; \sigma_{11} = Var(Y), \; \sigma_{22} = Var(X).$$

The additional parameter σ_{12} turns out to be the covariance between the two random variables, i.e.:

$$\sigma_{12} := Cov(X, Y).$$

(ii) Let us derive the covariance of X and Y, using the joint density given below:

$y\backslash x$	0	1	2	$f_y(y)$
0	0.2	0.2	0.2	0.6
2	0.1	0.1	0.2	0.4
$f_x(x)$	0.3	0.3	0.4	1

(4.11)

First, we need to derive the *moments* of the univariate distributions:

$$E(X) = (0)(0.3) + (1)(0.3) + (2)(0.4) = 1.1, \ E(Y) = (0)(0.6) + (2)(0.4) = 0.8,$$
$$Var(X) = [0–1.1]^2(0.3) + [1 - 1.1]^2(0.3) + [2 - 1.1]^2(0.4) = 0.69,$$
$$Var(Y) = [0 - 0.8]^2(0.6) + [2 - 0.8]^2(0.4) = 0.96.$$

Using these moments we proceed to derive the covariance:

$$Cov(X, Y) = E\{[X - E(X)][Y - E(Y)] = [0 - 1.1][0 - 0.8](0.2) +$$
$$+ [0 - 1.1][2 - 0.8](0.1) + [1 - 1.1][0 - 0.8](0.2) +$$
$$+ [1 - 1.1][2 - 0.8](0.1) + [2 - 1.1][0 - 0.8](0.2) +$$
$$[2 - 1.1][2 - 0.8](0.2) = 0.12.$$

Properties of the covariance

c1. $Cov(X, Y) = E(XY) - E(X) \cdot E(Y)$,
c2. $Cov(X, Y) = Cov(Y, X)$,
c3. $Cov(aX + bY, Z) = aCov(X, Y) + bCov(Y, Z)$, for $(a,b) \in \mathbb{R}^2$.

The first property shows the relationship between the raw and central joint moments for $k = m = 1$. The covariance is equal to the first **joint product moment** $E(XY)$ minus the product of the two means. The second property refers to the symmetry of the covariance with respect to the two random variables involved. The third property follows directly from the linearity of the expectation operator $E(.)$.

Let us verify **c1** using the above example. In view of the fact that:

$$E(XY) = (0)(0)(0.2) + (0)(2)(0.1) + (1)(0)(0.2) + (1)(2)(0.1) + (2)(0)(0.2) +$$
$$+ (2)(2)(0.2) = 1.0,$$

we can conclude that: $Cov(X, Y) = 1.0 - (1.1)(0.8) = 0.12$, which confirms the above value of $Cov(X, Y)$.

A digression It is interesting to note that using the covariance, we can extend property **V2** of the variance (see chapter 3), to the case where the two variables are *not independent*. In the case of two arbitrary random variables X and Y:

V2′ $Var(aX + bY) = a^2 Var(X) + b^2 Var(Y) + 2abCov(X, Y)$.

In the case where the random variables X and Y are independent, $Cov(X,Y)=0$ (but the converse is generally untrue) and the above relationship reduces to the one we saw in chapter 3: $Var(aX+bY)=a^2 Var(X)+b^2 Var(Y)$.

The third and fourth joint moments are also of interest because, as in the univariate case, they can be used to assess the symmetry and shape of the joint distribution. The formulae, however, become too complicated too quickly. For reference purposes let us consider the skewness and kurtosis coefficients for a bivariate distribution in the case where (X,Y) are uncorrelated, i.e.

$$\mu_{11}=0,\ \mu_{20}=Var(X),\ \mu_{02}=Var(Y),$$

skewness: $\alpha_3(X,Y)=\dfrac{\mu_{30}^2}{\mu_{20}^2}+\dfrac{\mu_{03}^2}{\mu_{02}^2}+3\dfrac{\mu_{21}^2}{\mu_{20}^2\mu_{02}}+3\dfrac{\mu_{21}^2}{\mu_{20}\mu_{02}^2},$

kurtosis: $\alpha_4(X,Y)=\dfrac{\mu_{40}}{\mu_{40}^2}+\dfrac{\mu_{04}}{\mu_{02}^2}+\dfrac{2\mu_{22}}{\mu_{20}\mu_{02}}.$

4.2.4 The *n*-random variables case

So far we have discussed the extension of the concept of a random variable to that of a two-dimensional random vector. It turns out that no additional difficulties arise in extending the notion of a random variable to the n-variable case $\mathbf{X}(.):=(X_1(.),X_2(.),\ \dots,\ X_n(.))$:

$$\mathbf{X}(.):S\rightarrow\mathbb{R}^n,$$

where $\mathbb{R}^n:=\mathbb{R}\times\mathbb{R}\times\cdots\times\mathbb{R}$ denotes the Cartesian product of the real line (see chapter 2).

The n-variable function $\mathbf{X}(.)$ is said to be a *random vector* relative to $\Im$ if:

$$\mathbf{X}(.):S\rightarrow\mathbb{R}^n,\ \text{such that } \mathbf{X}^{-1}((-\infty,\mathbf{x}])\in\Im,\ \text{for all } \mathbf{x}\in\mathbb{R}^n,$$

where $\mathbf{x}:=(x_1,x_2,\ \dots,\ x_n)$ and $(-\infty,\mathbf{x}]:=(-\infty,x_1]\times(-\infty,x_2]\times\cdots\times(-\infty,x_n]$.

NOTE that all random variables $(X_1(.),X_2(.),\ \dots,\ X_n(.))$ are defined on the same outcomes set S and relative to the same event space $\Im$.

In view of the fact that $\Im$ is a σ-field we know that $\mathbf{X}(.)$ is a random vector relative to $\Im$ if and only if the random variables $X_1(.),X_2(.),\ \dots,\ X_n(.)$ are random variables relative to $\Im$. This is because $X_k^{-1}((-\infty,x_k])\in\Im$ for all $k=1,2,\ \dots,\ n$, and thus:

$$\bigcap_{i=1}^n X_k^{-1}((-\infty,x_k])\in\Im.$$

The various concepts introduced above for the two random variable case can be easily extended to the n-random variable case. In direct analogy to the bivariate case, the **joint density function** satisfies the **properties:**

[mf1] $f(x_1,x_2,\ \dots,\ x_n)\geq0$, for all $(x_1,x_2,\ \dots,\ x_n)\in\mathbb{R}_X^n$,

[mf2] $\int_{-\infty}^{x_1}\int_{-\infty}^{x_2}\cdots\int_{-\infty}^{x_n}f(x_1,x_2,\ \dots,\ x_n)dx_1dx_2\cdots dx_n=1$,

[mf3] $F(x_1,x_2,\ \dots,\ x_n)=\int_{-\infty}^{x_1}\int_{-\infty}^{x_2}\cdots\int_{-\infty}^{x_n}f(u_1,u_2,\ \dots,\ u_n)du_1du_2\cdots du_n.$

Using the same line of reasoning we can easily extend the n-dimensions of the random vector $\mathbf{X}(.)$ to an infinity of dimensions, i.e., define $\mathbf{X}_\infty(.) := (X_1(.), X_2(.), ..., X_n(.), ...)$:

$$\mathbf{X}_\infty(.): S \to \mathbb{R}^\infty,$$

which is a random vector relative to some $\mathfrak{I}$ if and only if each element in the sequence $\mathbf{X}_\infty(.)$ is a random variable relative to $\mathfrak{I}$. This establishes the existence of an infinite random vector and prepares the way for chapter 8 where we will discuss the notion of a stochastic process $\{X_n(s)\}_{n=1}^\infty := \mathbf{X}_\infty(s)$, $s \in S$. The reader can now appreciate why σ-fields (countable additivity) were required and not just fields of events in order to define the notion of an event space. This becomes even more apparent when we proceed to utilize the mathematical (topological) structure of the Borel field $\mathcal{B}(\mathbb{R})$. This structure, enables us to discuss the convergence of such sequences of random variables:

$$\lim_{n\to\infty} X_n(s) = X(s), \text{ for all } s \in S.$$

This notion will be of paramount importance in chapter 9 where we discuss limit theorems; the topological structure of the Borel-field $\mathcal{B}(\mathbb{R})$ enables us to discuss notions of probabilistic convergence.

4.3   Marginal distributions

The second component of condition [c], relating to the independence of the trials is defined in terms of a simple relationship between the joint density function $f(x_1, x_2, ..., x_n; \phi)$ and the density functions of the individual random variables $X_1, X_2, ..., X_n$, referred to as the *marginal distributions*. Let us see how the marginal is related to the joint distribution.

It should come as no surprise to learn that from the joint distribution one can always recover the **marginal** (univariate) **distributions** of the individual random variables involved. In terms of the joint cdf, the marginal distribution is derived via a limiting process:

$$F_X(x) = \lim_{y\to\infty} F(x,y) \text{ and } F_Y(y) = \lim_{x\to\infty} F(x,y).$$

Example

Let us consider the case of the bivariate exponential cdf:

$$F(x,y) = (1 - e^{-\alpha x})(1 - e^{-\beta y}), \ \alpha > 0, \ \beta > 0, \ x > 0, \ y > 0.$$

Given that $\lim_{n\to\infty} (e^{-n}) = e^{-\infty} = 0$, we can deduce that:

$$F_X(x) = \lim_{y\to\infty} F(x,y) = 1 - e^{-\alpha x}, \ x > 0, \ F_Y(y) = \lim_{x\to\infty} F(x,y) = 1 - e^{-\beta y}, \ y > 0.$$

Let us see how the marginalization is defined in terms of the density functions. In view of the fact that:

$$F_X(x) = \lim_{y \to \infty} F(x,y) = \lim_{y \to \infty} \int_{-\infty}^{x} \int_{-\infty}^{y} f(x,y) dy dx = \int_{-\infty}^{x} \left[\int_{-\infty}^{\infty} f(x,y) dy \right] dx,$$

and the relationship between $F_X(x)$ and $f_x(x)$, we can deduce that:

$$f_x(x) = \int_{-\infty}^{\infty} f(x,y) \, dy, \; x \in \mathbb{R}_X. \tag{4.12}$$

Similarly, in terms of the joint density function, the marginal density function of Y is derived via:

$$f_y(y) = \int_{-\infty}^{\infty} f(x,y) dx, \; y \in \mathbb{R}_Y. \tag{4.13}$$

These suggest that *marginalization* amounts to integrating out the other random variable.

Examples

(i)   Let us consider the case of the bivariate exponential density:

$$f(x,y) = e^{-x-y}, \; x > 0, \, y > 0,$$

where the random variables X and Y are continuous. The formula in (4.12) suggests that to derive the marginal distribution of X, one needs to integrate out the random variable Y from $f(x,y)$:

$$f_x(x) = \int_0^{\infty} e^{-x-y} dy = e^{-x}.$$

(ii)   Consider the bivariate standard Normal density (4.9). In order to derive the marginal density of X, we need to integrate out Y, and vice versa. The manipulations for such a derivation are rather involved (and thus omitted) but the result is particularly useful. It turns out that:

$$f_x(x) = \int_{-\infty}^{\infty} f(x,y) dy = \tfrac{1}{\sqrt{2\pi}} \exp\left\{ -\tfrac{1}{2} x^2 \right\}, \; f_y(y) = \int_{-\infty}^{\infty} f(x,y) dx = \tfrac{1}{\sqrt{2\pi}} \exp\left\{ -\tfrac{1}{2} y^2 \right\}.$$

That is, both marginal distributions are (standard) Normal, denoted by:

$$X \sim N(0,1) \text{ and } Y \sim N(0,1).$$

Marginalization and intuition We can visualize the derivation of the marginal distribution of X, from the bivariate distribution $f(x,y)$, as *projecting* the bivariate surface into the $[x, f(x,y)]$ plane. As shown in figure 4.2, projecting a bell-shaped surface onto a plane opposite yields a bell-shape for both marginal distributions. Intuitively, going from the joint to the marginal density amounts to ignoring the information relating to the particular dimension represented by the random variable integrated out.

In the **discrete random variable case,** we can derive the marginal distribution of one random variable, from the joint density $f(x,y)$, by *summing out* the other random variable For example, the derivation of the marginal density of X takes the form of summing over all the values of Y, say $y_1 < y_2 < y_3 < \cdots < y_n < \cdots$, as follows:

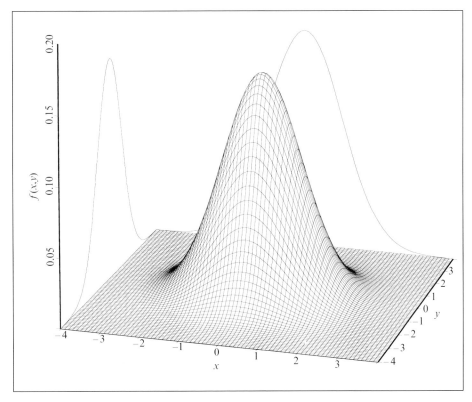

Figure 4.2 Bivariate Normal density with projected marginal densities

$$f_x(x) = \sum_{i=1}^{\infty} f(x,y_i), \ x \in \mathbb{R}_X. \tag{4.14}$$

Similarly, the marginal density of Y takes the form of summing over all the values of X, say $x_1 < x_2 < x_3 < \cdots < x_n < \cdots$:

$$f_y(y) = \sum_{i=1}^{\infty} f(x_i,y), \ y \in \mathbb{R}_Y. \tag{4.15}$$

Examples

(i) The joint density of the Bernoulli distribution is well defined, if the probabilities $p(i,j)$ for $i,j = 0,1$, in addition to being non-negative, also satisfy certain additional restrictions as required by the marginal distributions. The marginal distributions of X and Y are given below:

x	0	1
$f_x(x)$	$p_{\cdot 1}$	$p_{\cdot 2}$

y	0	1
$f_y(y)$	$p_{1\cdot}$	$p_{2\cdot}$

$$\tag{4.16}$$

$$p_{\cdot 1} = p(0,0) + p(0,1), \quad p_{1\cdot} = p(0,0) + p(1,0),$$

$$p_{\cdot 2} = p(1,0) + p(1,1). \quad p_{2\cdot} = p(0,1) + p(1,1).$$

For these marginal distributions to make sense they need to satisfy the properties of univariate density functions **f1**–**f3** (see chapter 3). This suggests that their probabilities must add up to one, i.e., $p_{.1} + p_{.2} = 1$ and $p_{1.} + p_{2.} = 1$.

(ii)   An important *discrete* distribution, is the bivariate *Binomial* (or trinomial as it is often called) whose density takes the form:

$$f(x,y;\boldsymbol{\theta}) = \left(\frac{n!}{x!y!(n-x-y)!}\right)\theta_1^x \theta_2^y (1-\theta_1-\theta_2)^{n-x-y}, \; \theta_i \in [0,1], \; i=1,2,$$

where $\boldsymbol{\theta} := (\theta_1, \theta_2)$ and n is an integer $x+y \le n$, $x,y = 0,1,2,\ldots,n$.

$$f_x(x;\boldsymbol{\theta}) = \sum_{k=1}^{n-x} \frac{n!(\theta_1^x \theta_2^k)}{x!k!(n-x-k)!}(1-\theta_1-\theta_2)^{n-x-k} = \frac{n!\theta_1^x}{x!}\sum_{k=1}^{n-x}\frac{\theta_2^k}{k!(n-x-k)!}(1-\theta_1-\theta_2)^{n-x-k} =$$

$$= \frac{n!\theta_1^x}{x!(n-x)!}\sum_{k=1}^{n-x}\frac{(n-x)!}{k!(n-x-k)!}\theta_2^k(1-\theta_1-\theta_2)^{n-x-k} = \binom{n}{x}\theta_1^x(1-\theta_1)^{n-x}.$$

(iii)   Let us derive the marginal distribution of X from the joint density given below:

$y\backslash x$	0	1	2
0	0.2	0.2	0.2
2	0.1	0.1	0.2

(4.17)

The formula in (4.12) suggests that by summing down the columns we derive the marginal density of X and summing over rows we derive the marginal density of Y:

x	0	1	2		y	0	2
$f_x(x)$	0.3	0.3	0.4		$f_y(y)$	0.6	0.4

(4.18)

These are clearly proper density functions, given that:

$$f_x(x) \ge 0, \; f_x(0) + f_x(1) + f_x(2) = 1, \text{ and } f_y(x) \ge 0, \; f_y(0) + f_y(2) = 1.$$

The two marginal densities are shown with the joint density below:

$y\backslash x$	0	1	2	$f_y(y)$
0	0.2	0.2	0.2	0.6
2	0.1	0.1	0.2	0.4
$f_x(x)$	0.3	0.3	0.4	1

(4.19)

Looking at the last column we can see that the probabilities associated with the values of Y contain no information relating to X.

4.4   Conditional distributions

4.4.1   Conditional probability

Let us return to chapter 2 and remind ourselves of the notion of conditional probability using our favorite example.

Example
Consider again the random experiment of "tossing a fair coin twice," with:

$$S = \{(HH),(HT),(TH),(TT)\}.$$

Assuming that $A = \{(HH),(HT),(TH)\}$ is an event of interest, without any additional information, common sense suggests that $\mathbb{P}(A) = \frac{3}{4}$. However, in the case where there exists some additional information, say somebody announces that in a particular trial "the first coin is a T," the situation changes. The available information defines the event $B = \{(TH),(TT)\}$ and knowing that B has occurred invalidates the probability $\mathbb{P}(A) = \frac{3}{4}$. This is because the information implies that, in this particular trial, the outcomes (HH) and (HT) cannot occur. That is, instead of S, the set of all possible distinct outcomes, given that B has occurred, is just B. This suggests that the new probability of A, given that B has occurred, denoted by $\mathbb{P}(A|B)$, is different. Common sense suggests that $\mathbb{P}(A|B) = \frac{1}{2}$, because A includes one of the two possible distinct outcomes. How can we formalize this argument?

The formula for the conditional probability of event A given event B, takes the form:

$$\mathbb{P}(A|B) = \frac{\mathbb{P}(A \cap B)}{\mathbb{P}(B)}, \text{ for } \mathbb{P}(B) > 0. \tag{4.20}$$

In the above example, $\mathbb{P}(A \cap B) = \mathbb{P}(TH) = \frac{1}{4}$, $\mathbb{P}(B) = \frac{1}{2}$, and thus $\mathbb{P}(A \cap B) = \frac{\frac{1}{4}}{\frac{1}{2}} = \frac{1}{2}$, which confirms the common sense answer.

4.4.2 Conditional density functions

As in the case of the joint and marginal distributions, we will consider the simple discrete random variable case first and then proceed to discuss the general random variable case.

Discrete random variables.
In the case of two discrete random variables X and Y, if we define the events:

$$A = \{Y = y\} \text{ and } B = \{X = x\},$$

then the translation of the above formulae in terms of density functions takes the form:

$$\mathbb{P}(X = x) = f(x),$$
$$\mathbb{P}(Y = y, X = x) = f(x,y),$$
$$\mathbb{P}(Y = y | X = x) = f(y|x),$$

giving rise to the conditional density formula:

$$f(y|x) = \frac{f(x,y)}{f_x(x)}, \text{ for } f(x) > 0, y \in \mathbb{R}_Y, \tag{4.21}$$

where $f(y|x)$ denotes the conditional density of Y given that $X = x$.

Example
Consider the joint density function for the discrete random variables X and Y given in

(4.19). From the above formula we can see that the conditional density of Y given $X=0$ takes the form:

$$f(y|x=0) = \frac{f(x=0,y)}{f_x(x=0)}, \; y \in \mathbb{R}_Y := \{0,2\}.$$

This suggests that the conditional probabilities $f(y|x=0)$, for $y \in \mathbb{R}_Y$, are scaled joint probabilities $f(x=0,y)$, for $y \in \mathbb{R}_Y$, with the marginal probability $f_x(x=0)$ providing the weight. In particular:

$$f(y|x=0) = \begin{cases} \frac{f(x=0,y=0)}{f_x(x=0)} = \frac{0.2}{0.3} = \frac{2}{3}, \; y=0, \\[2mm] \frac{f(x=0,y=2)}{f_x(x=0)} = \frac{0.1}{0.3} = \frac{1}{3}, \; y=2. \end{cases}$$

The conditional density is shown below:

y	0	2
$f(y|x=0)$	$\frac{2}{3}$	$\frac{1}{3}$

(4.22)

Continuous random variables

In the case of two continuous random variables X and Y we cannot use the events $A=\{Y=y\}$ and $B=\{X=x\}$ in order to transform (4.20) in terms of density functions, because as we know in such a case $P(X=x)=0$ and $P(Y=y)=0$ for all $x \in \mathbb{R}$, $y \in \mathbb{R}$. As in the case of the definition of the joint and marginal density functions we need to consider events of the form:

$$A=\{X \leq x\} \text{ and } B=\{Y \leq y\}.$$

However, even in the case of continuous random variables we would like to be able to refer to the conditional distribution of Y given $X=x$. The way we get around the mathematical difficulties is by way of the conditional cumulative distribution function defined as follows:

$$F_{Y|X}(y|X=x) = \lim_{h \to 0^+} \frac{\mathbb{P}(Y \leq y, \, x \leq X \leq x+h)}{\mathbb{P}(x \leq X \leq x+h)},$$

where $h \to 0^+$ reads "*as h tends to 0 through values greater than 0.*" After some mathematical manipulations we can show that:

$$F_{Y|X}(y|X=x) = \lim_{h \to 0^+} \frac{\mathbb{P}(Y \leq y, \, x \leq X \leq x+h)}{\mathbb{P}(x \leq X \leq x+h)} = \int_{-\infty}^{y} \frac{f(x,u)}{f_x(x)} du.$$

This suggests that in the case of two continuous random variables X and Y we could indeed define the conditional density function as in (4.21) but we should not interpret it as assigning probabilities because:

$$f(.|x): \mathbb{R}_Y \to [0,\infty).$$

As we can see, the **conditional density** is a proper density function, in so far as, in the case of continuous random variables, it satisfies the **properties**:

[cf1] $f(y|x) \geq 0$, for all $y \in \mathbb{R}_Y$,

[cf2] $\int_{-\infty}^{\infty} f(y|x)dy = 1$,

[cf3] $F(y|x) = \int_{-\infty}^{y} f(u|x) \, du$.

In the case of discrete random variables the integrals are replaced with summations.

Examples
(i) Consider the case where the joint density function takes the form:

$$f(x,y) = 8xy, \ 0 < x < y, \ 0 < y < 1.$$

The marginal densities of x and y can be derived from the joint density by integrating out y and X, respectively:

$$f_x(x) = \int_x^1 (8xy)dy = 4xy^2 \big|_{y=x}^{y=1} = 4x(1 - x^2), \ 0 < x < 1.$$
$$f_y(y) = \int_0^y (8xy)dx = 4x^2 y \big|_{x=0}^{x=y} = 4y^3, \qquad 0 < y < 1.$$

REMARK: The only difficulty in the above derivations is to notice that the range of X is constrained by Y and vice versa. Using these results we can deduce that:

$$f(y|x) = \frac{8xy}{4x(1-x^2)} = \frac{2y}{(1-x^2)}, \ x < y < 1, \ 0 < x < 1,$$

$$f(x|y) = \frac{8xy}{4y^3} = \frac{2x}{y^2}, \qquad 0 < x < y, \ 0 < y < 1.$$

(ii) Consider the bivariate standard *Normal distribution*. As seen in the previous section, in the case where $f(x,y)$ is Normal, the marginal distributions $f_x(x)$ and $f_y(y)$ are also Normal. Hence, the conditional density of Y given $X = x$ can be derived as follows:[1]

$$f(y|x) = \frac{2\pi(1 - \rho^2)^{-\frac{1}{2}} \exp\{-[2(1 - \rho^2)]^{-1}(x^2 - 2\rho xy + y^2)\}}{(\sqrt{2\pi}) \exp\left\{-\frac{1}{2}x^2\right\}},$$

$$f(y|x) = [2\pi(1 - \rho^2)]^{-\frac{1}{2}} \exp\left\{-[2(1-\rho^2)]^{-1}(x^2 - 2\rho xy + y^2) + \frac{1}{2}x^2\right\}.$$

Using the equality:

$$[2(1 - \rho^2)]^{-1}(x^2 - 2\rho xy + y^2) + \frac{1}{2}x^2 = [2(1-\rho^2)]^{-1}(y - \rho x)^2,$$

the conditional density takes the form:

$$f(y|x) = \frac{(1 - \rho^2)^{-\frac{1}{2}}}{\sqrt{2\pi}} \exp\left\{-\frac{1}{2(1-\rho^2)}[y - \rho x]^2\right\}.$$

Hence $f(y|x)$ is also Normal with mean ρx and variance $(1-\rho^2)$, denoted by:

$$(Y|X = x) \sim N(\rho x, (1 - \rho^2)).$$

---

[1] The mathematical manipulations are unimportant at this stage.

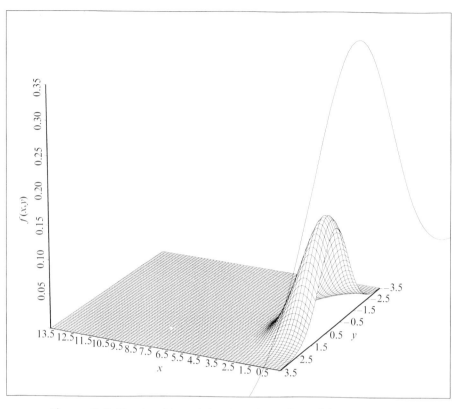

Figure 4.3 Bivariate Normal density with conditional density at $x = -0.5$)

The conditional density $f(y|x = -0.5)$ can be visualized as the one dimensional density we get by *slicing* the joint density using a perpendicular plane, parallel to the y-axis and passing through the point $x = -0.5$. In figure 4.3 we can see how the slicing of the bivariate surface at $x = -0.5$ scaled by $[1/f_x(-0.5)]$ yields a Normal univariate density.

4.4.3   Continuous/discrete random variables

In empirical modeling there are occasions when the modeler is required to model the relationship between continuous and discrete random variables. Naturally such discussions will involve the joint distribution of the random variables involved, and the question arises as to how to specify such distributions. It turns out that a most convenient way to specify such a joint distribution is via the conditional density.

Consider the case where $F(x,y)$ is the joint cdf of the random variables (X, Y) where X is discrete and Y is continuous. Let $\mathbb{R}_X = \{x_1, x_2, \ldots\}$ be the range of values of the random variable X. The joint cdf is completely determined by the sequence of pairs of a marginal probability and the associated conditional density:

$$(f_x(x_k), f(y|x_k), \text{ for all } y_k \in \mathbb{R}_X).$$

This can be visualized as a sequence of probability poles along the x-axis at the points $\{x_1,x_2,\ldots\}$ which are smudged along the y-axis in such a way that the density at any point x_k is $[f_x(x_k) \cdot f(y|x_k)]$.

The only technical difficulty in this result is how to specify the conditional density. It is defined by:

$$f(y|x_k) = \frac{1}{f_x(x_k)} \frac{d[F(x_k,y) - F(x_k - 0,y)]}{dy},$$

where the notation $(x_k - 0)$ indicates taking the derivative from the left, such that:

$$F(x,y) = \sum_{x_k \leq x} f_x(x_k) \int_{-\infty}^{y} f(u|x_k)du.$$

Similarly, the marginal distribution of the random variable Y is defined by:

$$F_Y(y) = \sum_{x_k \in \mathbb{R}_X} f_x(x_k) \int_{-\infty}^{y} f(u|x_k)du.$$

Example
Consider the case where the random variables (X,Y), X is Bernoulli and Y is Normally distributed and the joint density takes the form:

$$f(x,y;\boldsymbol{\phi}) = f(y|x_k;\boldsymbol{\theta}) \cdot f_x(x_k;p), \ x_k \in \mathbb{R}_X,$$

$$f(y|x_k;\boldsymbol{\theta}) = \frac{1}{\sigma\sqrt{2\pi}}\exp\left\{-\frac{1}{2\sigma^2}(y - \beta_0 - \beta_1 x_k)^2\right\}, f_x(1) = p, f_x(0) = 1 - p.$$

4.4.4 Conditional moments

The conditional density, being a proper density function, also enjoys numerical characteristics analogous to marginal density functions. In particular, for continuous random variables we can define the **conditional moments:**

raw: $\quad E(Y^r|X=x) = \int_{-\infty}^{\infty} y^r f(y|x)dy, r = 1,2, \ldots,$

central: $\ E\{(Y - E[Y|X=x])^r|X=x\} = \int_{-\infty}^{\infty} [y - E(y|x)]^r f(y|x)dy, r = 2,3,\ldots$

NOTE that the only difference between the marginal and conditional moments is that the relevant distribution with respect to which $E(.)$ is defined is now the conditional.

In the case of *discrete* random variables we replace the integrals with summations as exemplified in the case of the first of these conditional moments:

conditional mean: $\quad E(Y|X=x) = \sum_{y \in \mathbb{R}_Y} y \cdot f(y|x),$

conditional variance: $\ Var(Y|X=x) = \sum_{y \in \mathbb{R}_Y} [y - E(y|x)]^2 \cdot f(y|x).$

Examples
(i) *Discrete distribution, no unknown parameters.* For the conditional density (4.22):

$$E(Y|X=0) = 0 \cdot \left(\tfrac{2}{3}\right) + 2 \cdot \left(\tfrac{1}{3}\right) = \left(\tfrac{2}{3}\right),$$

$$Var(Y|X=0) = \left[0 - \left(\tfrac{2}{3}\right)\right]^2\left(\tfrac{2}{3}\right) + \left[2 - \left(\tfrac{2}{3}\right)\right]^2\left(\tfrac{1}{3}\right) = \left(\tfrac{24}{27}\right).$$

(ii)   *Continuous distribution, no unknown parameters.* Consider the case where the joint density function takes the form:

$$f(x,y) = 8xy, \ 0<x<y, 0<y<1.$$

As shown above, the marginal densities of x and y are:

$$f(x) = 4x(1-x^2), \ 0<x<1 \text{ and } f(y) = 4y^3, \ 0<y<1.$$

$$f(y|x) = \frac{8xy}{4x(1-x^2)} = \frac{2y}{(1-x^2)}, \ x<y<1, \ 0<x<1,$$

$$f(x|y) = \frac{8xy}{4y^3} = \frac{2x}{y^2}, \ 0<x<y, \ 0<y<1.$$

$$E(Y|X=x) = \int_x^1 y\left(\frac{2y}{(1-x^2)}\right) dy = \frac{2}{(1-x^2)}\int_x^1 y^2 dy = \frac{2}{(1-x^2)}\left(\frac{1}{3}y^3\Big|_{y=x}^{y=1}\right) = \frac{2}{3}\left(\frac{1-x^3}{1-x^2}\right),$$

$$E(X|Y=y) = \int_0^y x\left(\frac{2x}{y^2}\right) dx = \frac{2}{y^2}\left(\frac{1}{3}x^3\Big|_{x=0}^{x=y}\right) = \frac{2}{y^2}\left(\frac{1}{3}y^3\right) = \frac{2}{3}y,$$

$$Var(X|Y=y) = \int_0^y \left[x - \frac{2}{3}y\right]^2\left(\frac{2x}{y^2}\right) dx = \int_0^y \left[x^2 + \frac{4}{9}y^2 - \frac{4}{3}xy\right]\left(\frac{2x}{y^2}\right) dx =$$

$$\int_0^y \left[\left(\frac{2x^3}{y^2}\right) + \frac{8}{9}x - \frac{8}{3}\left(\frac{x^2}{y}\right)\right] dx = \left(\frac{x^4}{2y^2}\right) + \frac{4}{9}x^2 - \frac{8}{9}\left(\frac{x^3}{y}\right)\Big|_{x=0}^{x=y} = \frac{1}{18}y^2.$$

(iii)   *Continuous distribution, with unknown parameters.* Consider the case of the bivariate (standard) Normal distribution discussed in the previous subsection. It was shown that the conditional distribution of Y given $X=x$ takes the form:

$$(Y|X=x) \sim N(\rho x, (1-\rho^2)).$$

This suggests that:

$$E(Y|X=x) = \rho x, \text{ and } Var(Y|X=x) = (1-\rho^2).$$

The conditional moments are of interest in modeling dependence, because they often provide the most flexible way to capture the important aspects of probabilistic dependence (see chapter 6).

4.4.5 A digression: other forms of conditioning

Truncation
In addition to conditioning on events of the form $\{X=x\}$, it is often of interest to condition on events such as:

$$\{X>a\}, \{X<b\} \text{ or } \{a<X\leq b\}.$$

Example
In the case of the random experiment of "measuring the life of a light bulb" we might be interested in the probability that it will last n hours given that it has lasted at least m hours already $(n>m)$.

Consider the most general case of conditioning on the event $\{a<x\leq b\}$, referred to as *double truncation*; from the left at the point a and from the right at the point b. Intuition suggests that in the case of a discrete random variable X with a range of values $\mathbb{R}_X := \{x_1, x_2, \ldots\}$, the conditional probability function of X given $\{a<x\leq b\}$ should be given by:

$$f(x_i|a<X\leq b) = \frac{f(x_i)}{\sum_{a<x_j\leq b} f(x_j)}, \text{ for } a<x_i\leq b.$$

That is, the probability of $X=x_i$ given $\{a<x\leq b\}$ is just a weighted probability. Similarly, in the case of a continuous random variable X the above formula takes the form:

$$f(x|a<x\leq b) = \frac{f(x)}{\int_a^b f(x)dx} = \frac{f(x)}{F(b)-F(a)}, \text{ for } a<x\leq b. \tag{4.23}$$

Example
In the case of the Normal distribution the doubly truncated density takes the form:

$$f(x;\theta) = \frac{(\sigma\sqrt{2\pi})^{-1}}{(F(b)-F(a))}\exp\left\{-\frac{1}{2}\left(\frac{x-\mu}{\sigma}\right)^2\right\}, \; a<x\leq b.$$

Viewing the events $\{X>a\}$ and $\{X<b\}$ as special cases of $\{a<x\leq b\}$ we can modify the above formulae accordingly. For the cases $\{X>a\} = (a,\infty)$ and $\{X<b\} = (-\infty,b)$, using the result $F(\infty) = \lim_{x\to\infty} F(x) = 1$ we deduce that:

$$f(x|X>a) = \frac{f(x)}{1-F(a)}, \; x>a, \; f(x|X<b) = \frac{f(x)}{F(b)}, \; x<b. \tag{4.24}$$

The functions $f(x|a<x\leq b), f(x|X>a)$, and $f(x|X<b)$ are often referred to as **truncated density functions** and they enjoy the usual **properties**:

  [tf1] $f(x|a<x\leq b) \geq 0$, for all $x\in\mathbb{R}_X$,
  [tf2] $\int_a^b f(x|a<x\leq b)dx = 1$.

Example
Let X be an exponentially distributed random variable with:

$$f(x) = \theta e^{-\theta x}, \text{ and } F(x) = 1-e^{-\theta x}, \; y>0.$$

From (4.24) it follows that:

$$f(x|X>t) = \frac{\theta e^{-\theta x}}{e^{-\theta t}} = \theta e^{-\theta(x-t)}.$$

Hazard function
As can be seen from the above example, $f(x|X>t)$ is a function of both x and t. Viewing it as a function of t only, we define what is known as:

Hazard function: $h(t) = \frac{f(t)}{1-F(t)}, \; x>t.$

Intuitively, this can be thought of as the instantaneous rate of mortality for an individual who is alive up to time t.

Example

For X, an Exponentially distributed random variable, the hazard function takes the form:

$$h(t) = \frac{\theta e^{-\theta t}}{e^{-\theta t}} = \theta.$$

Intuitively, this means that the instantaneous rate of mortality is constant. This suggests that the Exponential distribution is not appropriate for modeling the life of the light bulb because it implicitly assumes that the probability of failing does not depend on the age of the bulb!

4.4.6 Marginalization versus conditioning

Marginal and conditional densities, viewed in relation to the joint density function:

Joint-	$f(.,.)$: $(\mathbb{R} \times \mathbb{R}) \rightarrow [0,\infty)$,
Marginal-	$f_y(.)$: $\mathbb{R} \rightarrow [0,\infty)$,
Conditional-	$f(.\,|x)$: $\mathbb{R} \rightarrow [0,\infty)$,

have one thing in common: they are both univariate densities. That is, they both reduce the dimensionality of the bivariate density function but the reduction takes different forms. In the case of the marginal density $f_y(.)$ the information relating to the other random variable X is ignored (integrated out). On the other hand, in the case of the conditional density $f(.\,|x)$ not all information relating to X is ignored. The conditional density retains part of the information relating to X; the information $X = x$.

The formula (4.21), defining the conditional density can be rearranged to yield:

$$f(x,y) = f(y\,|x) \cdot f_x(x), \text{ for each } (x,y) \in \mathbb{R}_X \times \mathbb{R}_Y. \qquad (4.25)$$

This decomposes the bivariate density $f(x,y)$, into a product of two univariate densities, $f(y\,|x)$ and $f_x(x)$; or so it appears. The importance of this decomposition will become apparent in the next section in relation to the notion of independence. Before we consider that, however, there are good reasons to elaborate on the intuition underlying marginalization and conditioning.

Example

Consider the joint density function represented below:

$y\backslash x$	1	2	3	$f_y(y)$
0	0.20	0.10	0.15	0.45
1	0.10	0.25	0.05	0.40
2	0.01	0.06	0.08	0.15
$f_x(x)$	0.31	0.41	0.28	1

$$(4.26)$$

Contemplate the following scenario. You wake up in a Cypriot hospital covered in plaster from head to toe with only the eyes and mouth showing and suffering from complete amnesia. A nurse, who just came on duty, walks in and informs you that, based on the report he had just read: you have been involved in a car accident, you are in bad shape (but out of danger) and you are likely to remain in hospital for a while. The first question that comes to mind is: Who am I? but the second thought that creeps in is: Can I afford the bills? The nurse seems to be reading your mind but he is unable to help. The only thing he could offer was the above table where X denotes *age* group and Y *income* group:

$$X=1: (18\text{--}35), \qquad X=2: (36\text{--}55), \qquad X=3: (56\text{--}70),$$
$$Y=0: \text{poor}, \qquad Y=1: \text{middle income}, \qquad Y=2: \text{rich}.$$

A glance at the joint probabilities brings some more confusion because the highest probability is attached to the event $(X=2, Y=1)$ (middle aged and middle income) and the lowest probability is attached to the event $(X=1, Y=2)$ (young but rich!). In an attempt to re-assure yourself you ignore income (as of secondary importance) for a moment and look at the marginal density of X. The probability of being in the age bracket of seniors (irrespective of income) is lower than the probabilities of being either young or middle-aged; a sigh of relief but not much comfort because the probability of being young is not very much higher! During this syllogism the nurse remembers that according to the report you were driving a Porsche! This additional piece of information suddenly changes the situation. Unless you were a thief speeding away when the accident happened (an unlikely event in a crime-free country like Cyprus!), you know that $Y=2$ has happened. How does this change the joint probabilities? The relevant probabilities now are given by the conditional density of X given $Y=2$:

$$f(x|y=2) = \begin{cases} \frac{f(x=1, y=2)}{f_y(y=2)} = \frac{0.01}{0.15} = 0.067, & x=1, \\[2ex] \frac{f(x=2, y=2)}{f_y(y=2)} = \frac{0.06}{0.15} = 0.400, & x=2, \\[2ex] \frac{f(x=3, y=2)}{f_y(y=2)} = \frac{0.08}{0.15} = 0.533, & x=3. \end{cases}$$

A glance at these conditional probabilities and you are begging the nurse to take the plaster off to check how old you are; there is more than 50 percent chance you are a senior!

Having discussed the concepts of marginal and conditional distributions we can proceed to formalize the notions of independence and identical distributions.

4.5   Independence

4.5.1 The 2–random variable case

As seen in chapter 2, two events A and B which belong to the same event space $\Im$, are said to be **independent** if:

$$\mathbb{P}(A \cap B) = \mathbb{P}(A) \cdot \mathbb{P}(B).$$

By translating the arbitrary events A and B into events of the form: $A := (s: X(s) \le x)$ and $B := (s: Y(s) \le y)$, $s \in S$, the above condition becomes:

$$\mathbb{P}(X\leq x, Y\leq y)=\mathbb{P}(X\leq x)\cdot\mathbb{P}(Y\leq y), \text{ for each } (x,y)\in\mathbb{R}^2.$$

$$F_{XY}(x,y)=F_X(x)\cdot F_Y(y), \text{ for each } (x,y)\in\mathbb{R}^2, \tag{4.27}$$

where $F_{XY}(.,.)$ denotes the joint cumulative distribution function (cdf). In terms of the density functions, X and Y are said to be **independent** if:

$$f(x,y)=f_x(x)\cdot f_y(y), \text{ for each } (x,y)\in\mathbb{R}^2. \tag{4.28}$$

That is, the joint density is equal to the product of the two marginal density functions. In other words the only case where the joint density contains no additional information from that contained in the marginal density functions is the case where the random variables are independent.

It is important to NOTE that in view of (4.25), when X and Y are *independent*:

$$f(y|x)=f_y(y) \text{ for all } y\in\mathbb{R}_Y. \tag{4.29}$$

Similarly, $f(x|y)=f_x(x)$, for all $x\in\mathbb{R}_X$. That is, when Y and X are independent, conditioning on X does not affect the marginal density of Y and vice versa. This provides a more intuitive way to understand the notion of independence.

Examples

(i) Consider the bivariate density (4.26). The random variables X and Y, are *not independent* since for the first value $(X, Y)=(1,0)$:

$$f(1,0)=(0.20)\neq f_x(1)\cdot f_y(0)=(0.31)(0.45)=(0.1395).$$

(ii) Consider the bivariate density given below:

$y\backslash x$	0	1	$f_y(y)$
0	0.3	0.3	0.6
2	0.2	0.2	0.4
$f_x(x)$	0.5	0.5	1

$$\tag{4.30}$$

To check whether X and Y are independent, we need to verify that the equality in (4.28) holds, for *all* values of X and Y:

$$(X,Y)=(0,0), f(0,0)=f_x(0)\cdot f_y(0)=(0.3)=(0.5)(0.6),$$
$$(X,Y)=(0,2), f(0,2)=f_x(0)\cdot f_y(2)=(0.2)=(0.5)(0.4),$$
$$(X,Y)=(1,0), f(1,0)=f_x(1)\cdot f_y(0)=(0.3)=(0.5)(0.6),$$
$$(X,Y)=(1,2), f(1,2)=f_x(1)\cdot f_y(2)=(0.2)=(0.5)(0.4).$$

These results suggest that X and Y are indeed independent.

(iii) In the case where (X, Y) are jointly Normally distributed, with density as defined in (4.9), we can deduce that when $\rho=0$, X and Y are independent. This follows by a simple substitution of the restriction $\rho=0$ in the joint density:

$$f(x,y) = \left(\frac{(1-\rho^2)^{-\frac{1}{2}}}{2\pi}\right)\exp\left\{-\frac{1}{2(1-\rho^2)}[x^2 - 2\rho xy + y^2]\right\}\bigg|_{\rho=0} = \frac{1}{2\pi}\exp\left\{-\frac{1}{2}[x^2 + y^2]\right\} =$$

$$= \left(\left(\frac{1}{\sqrt{2\pi}}\right)\exp\left\{-\frac{1}{2}x^2\right\}\right)\left(\left(\frac{1}{\sqrt{2\pi}}\right)\exp\left\{-\frac{1}{2}y^2\right\}\right) = f_x(x)\cdot f_y(y),$$

where $f_x(x)$ and $f_y(y)$ are standard Normal densities.

REMARK: The last example provides an important clue to the notion of independence by suggesting that when the joint density $f(x,y)$ can be factored into a product of two non-negative functions $u(x)$ and $v(y)$ i.e.

$$f(x,y) = u(x)\cdot v(y),$$

where $u(.)\geq 0$ depends only on x and $v(.)\geq 0$ depends only on y, then X and Y are independent.

(iv)   In the case where (X,Y) are jointly exponentially distributed, with density:

$$f(x,y;\theta) = [(1 + \theta x)(1 + \theta y) - \theta]\exp\{-x - y - \theta xy\}, x>0, y>0, \theta>0.$$

It is obvious that X and Y are independent only when $\theta = 0$, since the above factorization can be achieved only in that case:

$$f(x,y;0) = [(1 + \theta x)(1 + \theta y) - \theta]\exp\{-x - y - \theta xy\}|_{\theta=0} = (e^{-x})(e^{-y}).$$

4.5.2 Independence in the *n*-variable case

The extension of the above definitions of independence from the two to the *n*-variable case is not just a simple matter of notation. As argued in the previous chapter, the events $A_1, A_2, \ldots, A_n$ are *independent* if the following condition holds:

$$\mathbb{P}(A_1 \cap A_2 \cap \ldots \cap A_k) = \mathbb{P}(A_1)\cdot\mathbb{P}(A_2)\cdots\mathbb{P}(A_k), \text{ for each } k = 2,3, \ldots, n. \qquad (4.31)$$

That is, this must hold for all subsets of $\{A_1, A_2, \ldots, A_n\}$. For example, in the case $n=3$, the following conditions must hold for A_1, A_2, A_3 to be independent:

(a) $\mathbb{P}(A_1 \cap A_2 \cap A_3) = \mathbb{P}(A_1)\cdot\mathbb{P}(A_2)\cdot\mathbb{P}(A_3),$
(b) $\mathbb{P}(A_1 \cap A_2) = \mathbb{P}(A_1)\cdot\mathbb{P}(A_2),$
(c) $\mathbb{P}(A_1 \cap A_3) = \mathbb{P}(A_1)\cdot\mathbb{P}(A_3),$
(d) $\mathbb{P}(A_2 \cap A_3) = \mathbb{P}(A_2)\cdot\mathbb{P}(A_3).$

In the case where only conditions (b)–(d) hold, the events A_1, A_2, A_3 are said to be *pairwise independent*. For (complete) independence, however, we need all four conditions. The same holds for random variables as can be seen be replacing the arbitrary events A_1, A_2, A_3 with the special events $A_i = (X_i \leq x_i), i = 1,2,3.$

Independence The random variables $X_1, X_2, \ldots, X_n$ are said to be *independent* if the following condition holds:

$$F(x_1, x_2, \ldots, x_n) = F_1(x_1)\cdot F_2(x_2)\cdots F_n(x_n), \text{ for all } (x_1, \ldots, x_n)\in\mathbb{R}^n. \qquad (4.32)$$

In terms of the density functions, *independence* can be written in the form:

$$f(x_1,x_2, ..., x_n)=f_1(x_1)\cdot f_2(x_2)\cdots f_n(x_n), \text{ for all } (x_1, ..., x_n)\in\mathbb{R}^n. \tag{4.33}$$

From (4.33) we can see that the qualification *for all subsets of* $\{A_1,A_2, ..., A_n\}$ in the case of events has been replaced with the qualification *for all* $(x_1, ..., x_n)\in\mathbb{R}^n$. In other words, in the case of random variables we do not need to check (4.33) for any subsets of the set $X_1,X_2, ..., X_n$, but we need to check it for all values $(x_1, ..., x_n)\in\mathbb{R}^n$. It is also important to note that when (4.33) holds for all $(x_1, ..., x_n)\in\mathbb{R}^n$, it implies that it should hold for any subsets of the set $X_1,X_2, ..., X_n$, but not the reverse.

Example
Let us return to our favorite example of "tossing a fair coin twice" and noting the outcome: $S=\{(HH),(HT),(TH),(TT)\}$, $\Im$ being the power set. Define the following random variables:

$$X(HT)=X(HH)=0, X(TH)=X(TT)=1,$$
$$Y(TH)=Y(HH)=0, Y(TT)=Y(HT)=1,$$
$$Z(TH)=Z(HT)=0, Z(TT)=Z(HH)=1.$$

$$\mathbb{P}_{XYZ}(1,1,1)=\tfrac{1}{4}, \ \mathbb{P}_{XYZ}(1,1,0)=0,$$
$$\mathbb{P}_{XYZ}(1,0,0)=\tfrac{1}{4}, \ \mathbb{P}_{XYZ}(1,0,1)=0,$$
$$\mathbb{P}_{XYZ}(0,1,0)=\tfrac{1}{4}, \ \mathbb{P}_{XYZ}(0,1,1)=0,$$
$$\mathbb{P}_{XYZ}(0,0,1)=\tfrac{1}{4}, \ \mathbb{P}_{XYZ}(0,0,0)=0.$$

$$\mathbb{P}_X(0)=\sum_z\sum_y\mathbb{P}(0,y,z)=\mathbb{P}(0,1,0)+\mathbb{P}(0,0,1)+\mathbb{P}(0,1,1)+\mathbb{P}(0,0,0) \ =\tfrac{1}{2},$$
$$\mathbb{P}_X(1)=\sum_z\sum_y\mathbb{P}(1,y,z)=\mathbb{P}(1,1,1)+\mathbb{P}(1,0,0)+\mathbb{P}(1,1,0)+\mathbb{P}(1,0,1) \ =\tfrac{1}{2},$$

$$\mathbb{P}_Y(0)=\sum_z\sum_x\mathbb{P}(x,0,z)=\mathbb{P}(1,0,0)+\mathbb{P}(0,0,1)+\mathbb{P}(1,0,1)+\mathbb{P}(0,0,0) \ =\tfrac{1}{2},$$
$$\mathbb{P}_Y(1)=\sum_z\sum_x\mathbb{P}(x,1,z)=\mathbb{P}(1,1,1)+\mathbb{P}(0,1,1)+\mathbb{P}(1,1,0)+\mathbb{P}(0,1,0) \ =\tfrac{1}{2},$$

$$\mathbb{P}_Z(0)=\sum_y\sum_x\mathbb{P}(x,y,0)=\mathbb{P}(1,0,0)+\mathbb{P}(1,1,0)+\mathbb{P}(0,1,0)+\mathbb{P}(0,0,0) \ =\tfrac{1}{2},$$
$$\mathbb{P}_Z(1)=\sum_y\sum_x\mathbb{P}(x,y,1)=\mathbb{P}(1,1,1)+\mathbb{P}(0,0,1)+\mathbb{P}(1,0,1)+\mathbb{P}(0,1,1) \ =\tfrac{1}{2}.$$

In view of these results we can deduce that (X,Y), (X,Z) and (Y,Z) are independent in pairs since:

$$\mathbb{P}_{XY}(0,0)=\mathbb{P}_X(0)\cdot\mathbb{P}_Y(0)=\tfrac{1}{4}, \qquad \mathbb{P}_{XZ}(0,0)=\mathbb{P}_X(0)\cdot\mathbb{P}_Z(0)=\tfrac{1}{4},$$
$$\mathbb{P}_{XY}(1,0)=\mathbb{P}_X(1)\cdot\mathbb{P}_Y(0)=\tfrac{1}{4}, \qquad \mathbb{P}_{XZ}(1,0)=\mathbb{P}_X(1)\cdot\mathbb{P}_Z(0)=\tfrac{1}{4},$$
$$\mathbb{P}_{XY}(0,1)=\mathbb{P}_X(0)\cdot\mathbb{P}_Y(1)=\tfrac{1}{4}, \qquad \mathbb{P}_{XZ}(0,1)=\mathbb{P}_X(0)\cdot\mathbb{P}_Z(1)=\tfrac{1}{4},$$

$$\mathbb{P}_{YZ}(0,0) = \mathbb{P}_Y(0) \cdot \mathbb{P}_Z(0) = \tfrac{1}{4},$$

$$\mathbb{P}_{YZ}(1,0) = \mathbb{P}_Y(1) \cdot \mathbb{P}_Z(0) = \tfrac{1}{4},$$

$$\mathbb{P}_{YZ}(0,1) = \mathbb{P}_Y(0) \cdot \mathbb{P}_Z(1) = \tfrac{1}{4}.$$

On the other hand, all three random variables (X, Y, Z) are not independent, since:

$$\mathbb{P}_{XYZ}(1,1,1) = \frac{1}{4} \neq \mathbb{P}_X(1) \cdot \mathbb{P}_Y(1) \cdot \mathbb{P}_Z(1) = \frac{1}{8}.$$

The above definition completes the first stage of our quest for transforming the notion of random trials. The independence given in the introduction in terms of trials (see (4.1)) has now been recast in terms of random variables as given in (4.33). We consider the second scale of our quest for a random sample in the next section.

4.6　Identical distributions

As mentioned in the introduction, the notion of random trials has two components: independence and identical distributions. Let us consider the recasting of the Identically Distributed component in terms of random variables.

Example
Consider the Bernoulli density function:

$$f(x;\theta) = \theta^x(1-\theta)^{1-x}, \; x = 0,1,$$

where $\theta = P(X=1)$. Having a sample of n independent trials, say $(X_1, X_2, \ldots, X_n)$, amounts to assuming that the random variables $X_1, X_2, \ldots, X_n$ are *independent*, with each X_i having a density function of the form:

$$f(x_i;\theta_i) = \theta_i^{x_i}(1-\theta_i)^{1-x_i}, \; x_i = 0,1, \; i = 1,2, \ldots, n,$$

where $\theta_i = P(X_i = 1)$, $i = 1,2, \ldots, n$. Independence in this case ensures that:

$$f(x_1, x_2, \ldots, x_n; \boldsymbol{\phi}) = \prod_{i=1}^{n} f_i(x_i;\theta_i) = \prod_{i=1}^{n} \theta_i^{x_i}(1-\theta_i)^{1-x_i}, \; x_i = 0,1,$$

where $\boldsymbol{\phi} := (\theta_1, \theta_2, \ldots, \theta_n)$. Obviously, this does not satisfy the Identically Distributed component. For that to be the case we need to impose the restriction that for all trials the probabilistic structure remains the same, i.e., the random variables $X_1, X_2, \ldots, X_n$ are also *Identically Distributed* in the sense:

$$f(x_i;\theta_i) = \theta^{x_i}(1-\theta)^{1-x_i}, \; x_i = 0,1, \; i = 1,2, \ldots, n.$$

Let us formalize the concept of Identically Distributed random variables in the case of arbitrary but Independent random variables, beginning with the two-variable case. In general, the joint density involves the unknown parameters $\boldsymbol{\phi}$, and the equality in (4.28) takes the form:

$$f(x,y;\boldsymbol{\theta})=f_x(x;\boldsymbol{\theta}_1)\cdot f_y(y;\boldsymbol{\theta}_2),\ \text{for all}\ (x,y)\in\mathbb{R}_X\times\mathbb{R}_Y,$$

where the marginal distributions $f_x(x;\boldsymbol{\theta}_1)$ and $f_y(y;\boldsymbol{\theta}_2)$ can be very different.

Two independent random variables are said to be *Identically Distributed* if $f_x(x;\boldsymbol{\theta}_1)$ and $f_y(y;\boldsymbol{\theta}_2)$ are the same density functions, denoted by:

$$f_x(x;\boldsymbol{\theta}_1)\equiv f_y(y;\boldsymbol{\theta}_2),\ \text{for all}\ (x,y)\in\mathbb{R}_X\times\mathbb{R}_Y,$$

in the sense that they have the same functional form and the same unknown parameters:

$$f_x(.)=f_y(.)\ \text{and}\ \boldsymbol{\theta}_1=\boldsymbol{\theta}_2.$$

Examples
(i)   Consider the case where the joint density takes the form:

$$f(x,y;\boldsymbol{\theta})=\left(\frac{\theta_1}{\theta_2}\right)\frac{e^{-\frac{y}{\theta_2}}}{x^2},\ x\geq 1, y>0.$$

It is clear that the random variables X and Y are independent (the joint density factors into a product) with marginal densities:

$$f_x(x;\theta_1)=\frac{\theta_1}{x^2},\ x\geq 1,\ f_y(y;\theta_2)=\frac{1}{\theta_2}e^{-\frac{y}{\theta_2}},\ y>0.$$

However, the random variables X and Y are not Identically Distributed because neither of the above conditions for ID is satisfied. In particular, the two marginal densities belong to different families of densities ($f_x(x;\theta_1)$ belongs to the Pareto and $f_y(y;\theta_2)$ belongs to the Exponential family), they also depend on different parameters ($\theta_1\neq\theta_2$) and the two random variables X and Y have different ranges of values.

(ii)   Consider the three bivariate distributions given below:

y\x	1	2	$f_y(y)$
0	0.18	0.42	0.6
2	0.12	0.28	0.4
$f_x(x)$	0.3	0.7	1

(a)

y\x	0	1	$f_y(y)$
0	0.18	0.42	0.6
1	0.12	0.28	0.4
$f_x(x)$	0.3	0.7	1

(b)

y\x	0	1	$f_y(y)$
0	0.36	0.24	0.6
1	0.24	0.16	0.4
$f_x(x)$	0.6	0.4	1

(c)

The random variables (X,Y) are independent in all three cases (verify!). The random variables in (a) are not Identically Distributed because $\mathbb{R}_X\neq\mathbb{R}_Y$, and $f_x(x)\neq f_y(y)$ for some $(x,y)\in\mathbb{R}_X\times\mathbb{R}_Y$. The random variables in (b) are not Identically Distributed because even though $\mathbb{R}_X=\mathbb{R}_Y$, $f_x(x)\neq f_y(y)$ for some $(x,y)\in\mathbb{R}_X\times\mathbb{R}_Y$. Finally, the random variables in (c) are Identically Distributed because $\mathbb{R}_X=\mathbb{R}_Y$, and $f_x(x)=f_y(y)$ for all $(x,y)\in\mathbb{R}_X\times\mathbb{R}_Y$.

(iii)   In the case where $f(x,y;\boldsymbol{\theta})$ is *bivariate Normal*, as specified in (4.7), the two marginal density functions have the same functional form but $\boldsymbol{\theta}:=(\mu_1,\mu_2,\sigma_{11},\sigma_{22})$, $\boldsymbol{\theta}_1:=(\mu_1,\sigma_{11})$ and $\boldsymbol{\theta}_2:=(\mu_2,\sigma_{22})$, are usually different. Hence, for the random variables X and Y to be Identically Distributed, the two means and two variances should coincide: $\mu_1 = \mu_2$ and $\sigma_{11} = \sigma_{22}$:

$$f(x;\boldsymbol{\theta}_1) = \frac{1}{\sqrt{2\pi}\sigma_{11}} e^{-\frac{1}{2\sigma_{11}}[x-\mu_1]^2}, \; f(y;\boldsymbol{\theta}_2) = \frac{1}{\sqrt{2\pi}\sigma_{11}} e^{-\frac{1}{2\sigma_{11}}[y-\mu_1]^2}.$$

The concept of Identically Distributed random variables can be easily extended to the n-variable case in a straight forward manner.

Identical Distributions The random variables $(X_1, X_2, \ldots, X_n)$ are said to be *Identically Distributed* if:

$$f_k(x_k;\boldsymbol{\theta}_k) \equiv f(x_k;\boldsymbol{\theta}), \text{ for all } k = 1,2, \ldots, n.$$

This has two dimensions:

(i) $f_1(.) \equiv f_2(.) \equiv f_3(.) \equiv \cdots \equiv f_n(.) \equiv f(.),$
(ii) $\boldsymbol{\theta}_1 = \boldsymbol{\theta}_2 = \boldsymbol{\theta}_3 = \ldots = \boldsymbol{\theta}_n = \boldsymbol{\theta}.$

The equality sign $\equiv$ is used to indicate that all the marginal distributions have the same functional form.

4.6.1   A random sample

Our first formalization of condition [c] of a *random experiment* $\mathcal{E}$, where:

[c]   it can be repeated under identical conditions,

took the form of a set of *random trials* $\{\mathcal{A}_1, \mathcal{A}_2, \mathcal{A}_3, \ldots, \mathcal{A}_n\}$ which are both *Independent* and *Identically Distributed* (IID):

$$\mathbb{P}_{(n)}(\mathcal{A}_1 \cap \mathcal{A}_2 \cap \ldots \cap \mathcal{A}_k) = \mathbb{P}(\mathcal{A}_1) \cdot \mathbb{P}(\mathcal{A}_2) \cdots \mathbb{P}(\mathcal{A}_k), \text{ for each } k = 2,3, \ldots, n. \tag{4.34}$$

Using the concept of a *sample* $\mathbf{X} := (X_1, X_2, \ldots, X_n)$, where X_i denotes the ith trial, we can proceed to formalize condition [c] in the form of a sample where the random variables $X_1, X_2, \ldots, X_n$ are both *Independent* (I) and *Identically Distributed* (ID).

Random sample The sample $\mathbf{X}_{(n)}^{\text{IID}} := (X_1, X_2, \ldots, X_n)$ is called a *random sample* if the random variables $(X_1, X_2, \ldots, X_n)$ are:

(a)   Independent:

$$f(x_1, x_2, \ldots, x_n; \boldsymbol{\phi}) \overset{\text{I}}{=} \prod_{k=1}^{n} f_k(x_k;\boldsymbol{\theta}_k) \text{ for all } (x_1, \ldots, x_n) \in \mathbb{R}^n,$$

(b)   Identically Distributed:

$$f_k(x_k;\boldsymbol{\theta}_k) = f(x_k;\boldsymbol{\theta}), \text{ for all } k = 1,2, \ldots, n.$$

Putting the two together the joint density for $\mathbf{X}_{(n)}^{\text{IID}} := (X_1, X_2, \ldots, X_n)$ takes the form:

$$f(x_1, x_2, \ldots, x_n; \boldsymbol{\phi}) \overset{\text{I}}{=} \prod_{k=1}^{n} f_k(x_k;\boldsymbol{\theta}_k) \overset{\text{IID}}{=} \prod_{k=1}^{n} f(x_k;\boldsymbol{\theta}), \text{ for all } (x_1, \ldots, x_n) \in \mathbb{R}^n. \tag{4.35}$$

The first equality follows from the independence condition and the second from the Identical Distribution condition. NOTE that $f_k(x_k;\boldsymbol{\theta}_k)$ denotes the marginal distribution of $X_k(.)$, derived by integrating out all the other random variables apart from $X_k(.)$, i.e.

$$f_k(x_k;\boldsymbol{\theta}_k) = \int\limits_{-\infty}^{\infty} \int\limits_{-\infty}^{\infty} \cdots \int\limits_{-\infty}^{\infty} f(x_1, \ldots, x_{k-1},x_k,x_{k+1}, \ldots, x_n;\boldsymbol{\phi})dx_1\ldots dx_{k-1}dx_{k+1}\ldots dx_n.$$

As argued in chapter 2, the formalization of a random experiment was chosen to motivate several concepts because it was simple enough to avoid unnecessary complications. It was also stated, however, that simple stochastic phenomena within the intended scope of a simple statistical model are rarely encountered in economics. One of our first tasks, once the transformation is completed, is to extend it. In preparation for that extension we note at this stage that the notion of a random sample is a very special form of what we call a sampling model.

Sampling model A *sampling model* is a set of random variables $(X_1,X_2, \ldots, X_n)$ (a *sample*) with a certain *probabilistic structure*. The primary objective of the sampling model is to relate the observed data to the probability model.

4.6.2 A simple statistical model: concluding the metamorphosis

We are now in a position to complete the quest which began with the formalization of the notion of a random experiment $\mathscr{E}$, defined by the conditions:

[a]   All possible distinct outcomes are known a priori,
[b]   in any particular trial the outcome is not known a priori but there exists a perceptible regularity of occurrence associated with these outcomes, and
[c]   it can be repeated under identical conditions.

The initial abstract formalization took the form of a simple statistical space:
$[(S,\mathfrak{I},\mathbb{P}(.))^n, G_n^{\text{IID}}]$. The main aim of the previous chapter was to metamorphose the simple probability space $(S,\mathfrak{I},\mathbb{P}(.))^n$ into something defined on the real line. The key to the transformation was the notion of a random variable $X(.)$:

$$(S,\mathfrak{I},\mathbb{P}(.)) \overset{X(.)}{\Rightarrow} (\mathbb{R},\mathcal{B}(\mathbb{R}),P_X(.)) \Rightarrow \{f(x;\boldsymbol{\theta}), \boldsymbol{\theta}\in\Theta, x\in\mathbb{R}_X\}.$$

In this chapter we transformed the simple sampling space into a random sample:

$$G_n^{\text{IID}} = \{\mathcal{A}_1,\mathcal{A}_2,\mathcal{A}_3, \ldots, \mathcal{A}_n\} \overset{X(.)}{\Rightarrow} \mathbf{X}_{(n)}^{\text{IID}} := (X_1,X_2, \ldots, X_n).$$

Collecting the main results of the last two chapters together we define *a* **generic simple statistical model:**

[i]   Probability model: $\Phi = \{f(x;\boldsymbol{\theta}), \boldsymbol{\theta}\in\Theta, x\in\mathbb{R}_X\}$,
[ii]   Sampling model: $\mathbf{X}: = (X_1,X_2, \ldots, X_n)$ is a random sample.

The notion of the statistical model constitutes the basic contribution of probability theory to the theory of statistical inference. All forms of parametric statistical inference presume a particular statistical model, which, if invalid, renders any inference results fallacious. Hence, a sound understanding of the form and structure of a simple statistical model of the form given above is imperative. Particular examples of simple statistical models are given below:

Simple Bernoulli model

[i]   Probability model: $\Phi = \{f(x;\theta) = \theta^x(1-\theta)^{1-x}, 0 \le \theta \le 1, x = 0,1\}$,

[ii] Sampling model: $\mathbf{X} := (X_1, X_2, ..., X_n)$ is a random sample.

Simple Normal model

[i]   Probability model:

$$\Phi = \left\{ f(x;\boldsymbol{\theta}) = \frac{1}{\sigma\sqrt{2\pi}} \exp\left\{ -\frac{(x-\mu)^2}{2\sigma^2} \right\}, \boldsymbol{\theta} := (\mu,\sigma^2) \in \mathbb{R} \times \mathbb{R}_+, x \in \mathbb{R} \right\},$$

[ii] Sampling model: $\mathbf{X} := (X_1, X_2, ..., X_n)$ is a random sample.

Simple generalized Gamma model

[i]   Probability model:

$$\Phi = \left\{ f(x;\boldsymbol{\theta}) = \frac{1}{\Gamma(\beta)} \alpha^{-\beta\delta} x^{\beta\delta-1} \exp\left\{ -\left(\frac{x}{\alpha}\right)^\delta \right\}, \boldsymbol{\theta} \in \Theta, x \in \mathbb{R}_+ \right\},$$

[ii] Sampling model: $\mathbf{X} := (X_1, X_2, ..., X_n)$ is a random sample.

4.7   A simple statistical model in empirical modeling: a preliminary view

As mentioned above, every form of statistical inference presupposes the specification of a particular statistical model a priori. This specification amounts to choosing a set of probabilistic assumptions which the modeler deems appropriate for describing the stochastic mechanism that gave rise to the data set in question. The choice of an appropriate statistical model constitutes perhaps the most difficult and at the same time the most crucial decision a modeler has to make; in comparison the decision of choosing a good estimator for θ is trivial. In chapter 1 we argued that in the case of observational (non-experimental) data we need to establish a procedure which takes into consideration the structure of the observed data. After all, the statistical model chosen is considered appropriate only when it captures all the systematic information in the data in question.

What renders the above statistical model *simple* is the assumption of a *random sample*, that is, $(X_1, X_2, ..., X_n)$ are Independent and Identically Distributed random variables. Making an appropriate choice of a statistical model will require the modeler to develop both a formal and an intuitive understanding of such probabilistic assumptions. Similarly, postulating a parametric family of densities requires the modeler to appreciate what that decision entails.

4.7.1 Probability model

Looking at a probability model of a parametric family of densities:

$$\Phi = \{f(x;\boldsymbol{\theta}),\ \boldsymbol{\theta} \in \Theta,\ x \in \mathbb{R}_X\}, \tag{4.36}$$

from the modeling viewpoint, we discern two basic components:

(i)   the *parametric form* of the density function $f(x;\boldsymbol{\theta})$, $\boldsymbol{\theta} \in \Theta$,
(ii) the *support* of the density $\mathbb{R}_X := \{x \in \mathbb{R}: f(x;\boldsymbol{\theta}) > 0\}$.

In theory, empirical modeling commences from the "set of all possible probability models," say $\mathcal{P}$, and utilizing information relating to the form and structure of the data, the modeler narrows this set down to a subset $\mathcal{P}_0 \subset \mathcal{P}$, of admissible probability models, by choosing $f(x;\boldsymbol{\theta})$ and $\mathbb{R}_X$, felicitously.

The notion of a simple probability model was illustrated in chapter 3 with a number of density plots for different values of $\boldsymbol{\theta}$. As we will see in chapter 5, the choice of $f(x;.)$ and $\boldsymbol{\theta}$ does not have to be a hit or miss affair; it can be expedited by a number of data plots. The support of the density also plays an important role in the specification because the range of values of the observed data is a crucial dimension of modeling which is often neglected. In the case where the observed data refer to a data series measured in terms of *proportions* (i.e., the values taken by the data lie in the interval $[0,1]$), postulating a family of densities with support $(-\infty,\infty)$ is often inappropriate. Using the Beta family of densities might often be a better idea.

Example
In the case of the exam scores data in (see table 1.6), there are good reasons to believe that, based primarily on the support of the data, the Beta probability model might indeed be a better choice; see chapter 15.

A CAUTIONARY NOTE. In the context of statistical inference center stage will be given to the unknown parameter(s) $\boldsymbol{\theta}$; estimation and testing revolve around $\boldsymbol{\theta}$. However, the modeler should not lose sight of the fact that the estimation of $\boldsymbol{\theta}$ (using the observed data in order to choose a good estimator $\hat{\boldsymbol{\theta}}$) is a means to an end. The primary objective of empirical modeling is to describe adequately the stochastic phenomenon underlying the data in question. This model comes in the form of the estimated probability model:

$$\hat{\Phi} = \{f(x;\hat{\boldsymbol{\theta}}),\ y \in \mathbb{R}_X\}, \tag{4.37}$$

which provides the basis of any form of statistical inference, including prediction and simulation. It represents an idealized stochastic mechanism purporting to provide an adequate description of the stochastic phenomenon underlying the observed data in question. In this sense, undue focusing on the unknown parameters will result in losing sight of the forest for the trees.

4.7.2   Identifiability and parameterizations

It must be stressed at the outset that for modeling purposes the parameters $\boldsymbol{\theta} \in \Theta$, must be associated with unique probability distributions, otherwise our choice of a good estimator of $\boldsymbol{\theta}$, and thus a choice of stochastic mechanism as given in (4.37) is meaningless.

In other words, it is imperative that for different values of $\boldsymbol{\theta}$ in Θ there correspond different distributions. The condition which ensures this is specified below.

Identifiability: for all $\boldsymbol{\theta}_1 \neq \boldsymbol{\theta}_2$, where $\boldsymbol{\theta}_1 \in \Theta$, $\boldsymbol{\theta}_2 \in \Theta$, $f(x;\boldsymbol{\theta}_1) \neq f(x;\boldsymbol{\theta}_2)$, $x \in \mathbb{R}_X$.

IMPORTANT In what follows we will assume that all the probability models are identifiable in relation to the parameterization postulated.

In relation to the uniqueness of the parameterization it must be emphasized that it is defined up to one-to-one mappings. That is, when specifying the probability model (4.36) the modeler can choose a number of equivalent parameterizations if there exists a one-to-one mapping between the two parameter spaces. In particular, an equivalent parameterization of (4.36) is:

$$\Phi = \{f(x;\boldsymbol{\psi}), \boldsymbol{\psi} \in \Psi, x \in \mathbb{R}_X\}, \tag{4.38}$$

only in the case where there exists a one-to-one mapping $\boldsymbol{\psi} = \mathbf{g}(\boldsymbol{\theta})$:

$$\mathbf{g}(.): \Theta \to \Psi.$$

If we want to emphasize the reparameterization we can write (4.38) in the form:

$$\Phi = \{f(x;\boldsymbol{\psi}), \boldsymbol{\psi} = \mathbf{g}(\boldsymbol{\theta}), \boldsymbol{\theta} \in \Theta, x \in \mathbb{R}_X\}, \tag{4.39}$$

which parameterization will be used in a particular case depends on a number of factors including interpretability.

Example

Consider the case of the Exponential distribution where the $\theta \in \Theta$ parameterization takes the form:

$$\Phi = \{f(x;\theta) = \theta \exp[-\theta x], \; x > 0, \; \theta \in \Theta := (0, \infty)\}.$$

An equivalent parameterization is defined in terms of $\psi = \frac{1}{\theta}$:

$$\Phi = \left\{ f(x;\theta) = \frac{1}{\psi} \exp\left[-\frac{1}{\psi} x \right], \; x > 0, \; \psi \in \Psi := (0, \infty) \right\}.$$

Beyond statistical parameterizations an important role in econometric modeling is played by theoretical parameterizations. In a nutshell, a **statistical parameterization** has a clear interpretation in terms of distributional features of the family of densities in question, such as moments and quantiles. In contrast, a **theoretical parameterization** has a clear interpretation in terms of the economic theory (or theories) in question. So far we encountered only statistical parameterizations. In econometrics, however, we are ultimately interested in (economic) theoretical parameterizations $\boldsymbol{\alpha} \in \mathbf{A}$, which are often different from the postulated statistical parameterizations $\boldsymbol{\theta} \in \Theta$. More often than not we have fewer theoretical than statistical parameters of interest. In such a case we need to ensure that there exists a many-to-one mapping of the form:

$$\mathbf{h}(.): \Theta \to \mathbf{A},$$

which defines $\boldsymbol{\alpha}$ uniquely (up to one-to-one parameterizations). NOTE that a many-to-one mapping $\mathbf{h}(.)$ will *reparameterize* and *restrict* the statistical parameters. This is often necessary in order to reduce the data specificity of a statistical model as well as render the statistical parameters theoretically meaningful.

4.7.3   Important parametric families of distributions

The success of empirical modeling will depend crucially on the richness of the parametric families of distributions available to the modeler. In this section will consider briefly some of the most important families of distributions used in empirical modeling. The first important breakthrough in making parametric families of distributions available to the modeler was made by Karl Pearson (1895).

The Pearson family

The Pearson family of density functions was initially motivated by the desire to generate non-Normal distributions (especially non-symmetric) to be used for modeling biological data. Pearson noticed that the Normal density function $\phi(x)$ satisfies the simple differential equation:

$$\frac{d\phi(x)}{dx} = \phi(x)\left[\frac{(x-\theta_0)}{\theta_1}\right], \; x \in \mathbb{R}, \text{ where } \mu := \theta_0 \text{ and } \sigma^2 := -\theta_1.$$

He went on to generalize this differential equation to four unknown parameters $(\theta_0, \theta_1, \theta_2, \theta_3)$:

$$\frac{df(x)}{dx} = f(x)\left[\frac{(x-\theta_0)}{\theta_1 + \theta_2 x + \theta_3 x^2}\right], \; x \in \mathbb{R}_X.$$

Depending on the values taken by the unknown parameters, this equation, in addition to the Normal, can generate several well-known density functions such as:

$$\text{Student's t: } f(x;\boldsymbol{\theta}) = \frac{\Gamma\left[\frac{1}{2}(\nu+1)\right](\sigma^2\nu\pi)^{-\frac{1}{2}}}{\Gamma\left[\frac{1}{2}\nu\right]}\left(1 + \frac{(x-\mu)^2}{\nu\sigma^2}\right)^{-\frac{1}{2}(\nu+1)}, \; \boldsymbol{\theta} := (\mu, \sigma^2) \in \mathbb{R} \times \mathbb{R}_+, x \in \mathbb{R},$$

$$\text{Laplace: } f(x;\boldsymbol{\theta}) = \frac{1}{2\beta}e^{-\left(\frac{|x-\alpha|}{\beta}\right)}, \; \boldsymbol{\theta} := (\alpha, \beta) \in \mathbb{R} \times \mathbb{R}_+, x \in \mathbb{R},$$

$$\text{Pareto: } f(x;\theta) = (\theta\, x_0^\theta)x^{-(\theta+1)}, \; \theta \in \mathbb{R}_+, x_0 > 0, x \geq x_0,$$

$$\text{Gamma: } f(x;\boldsymbol{\theta}) = \frac{\beta^{-1}}{\Gamma[\alpha]}\left(\frac{x}{\beta}\right)^{\alpha-1}\exp\left\{-\left(\frac{x}{\beta}\right)\right\}, \; \boldsymbol{\theta} := (\alpha, \beta) \in \mathbb{R}_+^2, x \in \mathbb{R}_+,$$

$$\text{Beta: } f(x;\boldsymbol{\theta}) = \frac{x^{\alpha-1}(1-x)^{\beta-1}}{B[\alpha,\beta]}, \; \boldsymbol{\theta} := (\alpha, \beta) \in \mathbb{R}_+^2, 0 \leq x \leq 1.$$

In the case of *discrete random variables*, the corresponding difference equation is:

$$f_k - f_{k-1} = f_k\left[\frac{(k-\theta_0)}{\theta_1 + \theta_2 x + \theta_3 x(1-x)}\right], \; k = 1,2,3\ldots, x \in \mathbb{R}_X.$$

In addition to the binomial distribution, this equation can be used to generate several well-known discrete distributions such as:

$$\text{Hypergeometric: } f(x;\theta) = \frac{\binom{K}{x}\binom{M-K}{n-x}}{\binom{M}{n}}, \; 0 \leq x \leq \min{(K,n)},$$

Negative Binomial: $f(x;\theta,k) = \binom{k+x-1}{k-1}\theta^k(1-\theta)^x, 0<\theta<1, k=1,2, ..., y=0,1,2, ...,$

Poisson: $f(x;\theta) = \frac{e^{-\theta}\theta^x}{x!}, \theta>0, x=0,1,2,3,...$

Exponential family of distributions

This family of distributions was initially introduced into statistics by Fisher (1934) as a natural extension of the Normal distribution for inference purposes. As argued in chapter 12, this family retains some of the important properties of the Normal distribution in relation to inference. NOTE that the Exponential family is different from the exponential distribution encountered above. The density function of the Exponential family can expressed in the form:

$$f(x;\boldsymbol{\theta}) = c(\boldsymbol{\theta}) \cdot h(x)\exp\left(\sum_{i=1}^{k} g_i(\boldsymbol{\theta}) \cdot \tau_i(x)\right),$$

(a) $c(\boldsymbol{\theta}) \geq 0,$
(b) $h(x) \geq 0,$
(c) $g_i(\boldsymbol{\theta}), i=1,2, ..., k$: real-valued functions (free of x),
(d) $\tau_i(x), i=1,2, ..., k$: real-valued functions (free of $\boldsymbol{\theta}$).

Many well-known distributions such as the Normal, Gamma, Beta, Binomial, Poisson, and Negative Binomial belong to this family; see Barndorff-Nielsen and Cox (1989), Azallini (1996).

Examples

(i)   The Poisson distribution is a discrete member of the Exponential family with density function:

$$f(x;\theta) = \frac{e^{-\theta}\theta^x}{x!} = \left(\frac{e^{-\theta}}{x!}\right)\exp\left(x\ln(\theta)\right), x=0,1,2, ..., \theta>0.$$

Hence, for this density: $k=1, c(\boldsymbol{\theta}) = e^{-\theta}, h(x) = \frac{1}{x!}, g(\boldsymbol{\theta}) = \ln(\theta), \tau(x) = x.$

(ii)   The Normal distribution is a continuous member of the Exponential family with a density function:

$$f(x;\boldsymbol{\theta}) = \frac{1}{\sqrt{2\pi\sigma^2}}\exp\left(-\frac{(x-\mu)^2}{2\sigma^2}\right) = \frac{\exp\left(-\frac{\mu^2}{2\sigma^2}\right)}{\sqrt{2\pi\sigma^2}}\exp\left(-x^2\left(\frac{1}{2\sigma^2}\right) + x\left(\frac{\mu}{\sigma^2}\right)\right), x \in \mathbb{R},$$

$\boldsymbol{\theta} := (\mu,\sigma^2) \in \mathbb{R} \times \mathbb{R}_+$. Hence, for the Normal density: $k=2, c(\boldsymbol{\theta}) = \frac{1}{\sqrt{2\pi\sigma^2}}\exp\left(-\frac{\mu^2}{2\sigma^2}\right),$ $h(x)=1, g_1(\boldsymbol{\theta}) = \frac{\mu}{\sigma^2}, g_2(\boldsymbol{\theta}) = \frac{-1}{2\sigma^2}, \tau_1(x) = x, \tau_2(x) = x^2.$

The stable (Pareto-Levy) family

The stable family of distributions was initially motivated by the important property of *the domain of attraction*: the sum of independent random variables from a certain distribution, appropriately normalized, has the same distribution as the individual random variables. This family of distributions has been used extensively for modeling speculative prices (see Campbell *et al.* (1997)). A major drawback of this family is that most of its members do not have an explicit closed-form density function and thus modelers work directly with the cumulant (log of the characteristic) function (see chapter 3) which is given by:

$$\log \phi(t) = \begin{cases} i\mu t - \sigma |t|^{\alpha} \left\{ 1 - [\text{sign}(t)] \cdot i\beta \left[\tan \left(\frac{\pi\alpha}{2} \right) \right] \right\}, \text{ for } \alpha \neq 1 \\ i\mu t - \sigma |t| \left\{ 1 + [\text{sign}(t)] \cdot i\beta \left[\left(\frac{2}{\pi} \right) \ln (|t|) \right] \right\}, \text{ for } \alpha = 1. \end{cases}$$

This family is defined in terms of four parameters (see Galambos (1995)):

   α: the characteristic exponent, where $0 < \alpha \leq 2$,
   β: the skewness, where $-1 \leq \beta \leq 1$,
   μ: the location, where $\mu \in \mathbb{R}$,
   σ: the scale, where $\sigma \in \mathbb{R}_{+}$.

This is a continuous family of unimodal (one mode) densities. For $\alpha < 2$ the tails of the density function decay like a power function (hence the term Pareto), exhibiting more dispersion than the Normal; the smaller α, the thicker the tails. For $\beta = 0$ the density is symmetric around μ but $\beta > 0$ and $\beta < 0$ give rise to left- and right-skewed densities, respectively; the cases $|\beta| = 1$ give rise to the extreme stable distributions.

   The support of this family depends on the parameters (α, β):

$$\mathbb{R}_X^*(\alpha, \beta) = \begin{cases} \mathbb{R}, & \text{for } \alpha \geq 1, |\beta| \neq 1, \\ (-\infty, 0), & \text{for } \alpha < 1, \beta = 1, \\ (0, \infty), & \text{for } \alpha < 1, \beta = -1. \end{cases}$$

Examples
(i)   For $\alpha = 2$ and $\beta = 0$, the stable family reduces to the *Normal* distribution.

(ii)   For $\alpha = 1$ and $\beta = 0$, the stable family reduces to the *Cauchy* distribution with density:

$$f(x; \mu, \sigma) = \frac{\sigma}{\pi[\sigma^2 + (x - \mu)^2]}, \ x \in \mathbb{R}, \ \mu \in \mathbb{R}, \ \sigma \in \mathbb{R}_{+}.$$

   NOTE that for the case $0 < \alpha \leq 1$ no moments exist!

(iii) For $\alpha = \frac{1}{2}$ and $\beta = 1$, the stable family reduces to the *Levy* distribution with density:

$$f(x; \mu, \sigma) = \sqrt{\frac{\sigma}{2\pi(x - \mu)^3}} \exp \left(-\frac{1}{2(x - \mu)} \right), \ x > \mu, \ \mu \in \mathbb{R}, \ \sigma \in \mathbb{R}_{+}.$$

The Johnson transformation family
The Johnson transformation family of distributions was initially motivated by an attempt to introduce non-Normal distributions which can be viewed as monotone transformations of the Normal. Johnson (1949) proposed the transformation:

$$X = \gamma + \delta h(Y) = \gamma + \delta h \left(\frac{Z - \mu}{\sigma} \right), \ X \sim N(0,1), \ h(.) \text{ a monotone function.}$$

The most important members of this family are based on the following transformations:

(i) S_L, log Normal:

$$h(Y) = \ln(Y), \; \mu < Z < \infty.$$

(ii) S_B, bounded range:

$$h(Y) = \ln\left(\frac{Y}{1-Y}\right), \; \mu < Z < \mu + \sigma.$$

(iii) S_U, unbounded range:

$$h(Y) = \ln(Y + \sqrt{1+Y^2}), \; -\infty < Z < \infty.$$

4.7.4 Random sample

In so far as the sampling model is concerned we note that from the modeling viewpoint the basic components of a random sample: $\mathbf{X}_{(n)}^{\text{IID}} := (X_1, X_2, \ldots, X_n)$, are the assumptions:

(i)   Independence, and
(ii)   Identical Distribution.

For observational data the validity of these assumptions can often be assessed using a battery of graphical techniques discussed in chapters 5–6. In these chapters we will discuss the connection between the probabilistic notions making a simple statistical model (such as Independence and Identical Distribution) and various plots of real data. The discussion is particularly relevant to modeling observational data.

In an attempt to show how easy it is to end up with a non-random sample, it is shown in the next section that a simple rearrangement of the sample gives rise to a non-random sample.

4.8   Ordered random samples*

Consider the case where the original sampling model is a random sample $(X_1, X_2, \ldots, X_n)$ with cdf $F(x; \boldsymbol{\theta})$, i.e.

(i) $F(x_1, x_2, \ldots, x_n; \boldsymbol{\phi}) = \prod_{k=1}^{n} F_k(x_k; \boldsymbol{\theta}_k),$
(ii) $F_k(x_k; \boldsymbol{\theta}_k) = F(x; \boldsymbol{\theta})$, for $k = 1, 2, \ldots, n.$

For a number of reasons, which will be explored in the next few chapters, it is often interesting to consider the *ordered sample* where the random variables are arranged in ascending order, i.e.

$$(X_{[1]}, X_{[2]}, \ldots, X_{[n]}) \text{ where } X_{[1]} \leq X_{[2]} \leq \ldots \leq X_{[n]}.$$

NOTE: it is important to emphasize that the ordered sample constitutes a mental construct because before the sample is realized no such ordering is possible! Be that as it may, it might come as a surprise to the reader that even though the sample $(X_1, X_2, \ldots, X_n)$ is random (IID) the ordered sample $(X_{[1]}, X_{[2]}, \ldots, X_{[n]})$ is *non-random*; the random variables $X_{[1]}, X_{[2]}, \ldots, X_{[n]}$ are neither Independent nor Identically Distributed. Let us see this in some detail.

4.8.1 Marginal distributions

Consider first the distribution function of the random variable

$$X_{[1]} := \min (X_{[1]}, X_{[2]}, \ldots, X_{[n]})$$

and let its cdf be denoted by $F_{[1]}(x)$. Then, from first principles we know that:

$$F_{[1]}(x) = \mathbb{P}(X_{[1]} \leq x) = 1 - \mathbb{P}(X_{[1]} > x).$$

In view of the fact that the random variable $X_{[1]}$ is the smallest, the event $(X_{[1]} > x)$ occurs if and only if all the X_ks exceed x, i.e.

$$(X_{[1]} > x) = (X_1 > x, X_2 > x, \cdots, X_n > x).$$

From the randomness of the sample $(X_1, X_2, \ldots, X_n)$ we know that:

$$\mathbb{P}(X_1 > x, X_2 > x, \cdots, X_n > x) = [1 - F(x; \boldsymbol{\theta})]^n$$

and thus:

$$F_{[1]}(x) = \mathbb{P}(X_{[1]} \leq x) = 1 - [1 - F(x; \boldsymbol{\theta})]^n.$$

Consider next the distribution function of the random variable

$$X_{[n]} := \max (X_{[1]}, X_{[2]}, \ldots, X_{[n]})$$

and let its cdf be denoted by $F_{[n]}(x)$. Then, from first principles we know that:

$$F_{[n]}(x) = \mathbb{P}(X_{[n]} \leq x).$$

In view of the fact that the random variable $X_{[n]}$ is the largest, the event $(X_{[n]} \leq x)$ occurs if and only if all the X_ks do not exceed x, i.e.

$$(X_{[n]} \leq x) = (X_1 \leq x, X_2 \leq x, \cdots, X_n \leq x).$$

From the randomness of the sample $(X_1, X_2, \ldots, X_n)$ we know that:

$$\mathbb{P}(X_1 \leq x, X_2 \leq x, \cdots, X_n \leq x) = [F(x; \boldsymbol{\theta})]^n,$$

and thus:

$$F_{[n]}(x) = \mathbb{P}(X_{[n]} \leq x) = [F(x; \boldsymbol{\theta})]^n.$$

Noting that the event:

$$(X_{[k]} \leq x) = (\text{at least } k \text{ random variables from } X_1, X_2, \ldots, X_n \text{ do not exceed } x),$$

we can derive the cdf of any random variable $X_{[k]}$ as follows. From the Binomial distribution we know that:

$$\mathbb{P}(\text{exactly } k \text{ from } X_1, X_2, \ldots, X_n \text{ do not exceed } x) = \binom{n}{k}[F(x;\boldsymbol{\theta})]^k[1 - F(x;\boldsymbol{\theta})]^{n-k},$$

and thus (see David (1981)):

$$F_{[k]}(x) = \mathbb{P}(X_{[k]} \leq x) = \mathbb{P}(X_{[k]} \leq x) = \sum_{m=k}^{n}\binom{n}{k}[F(x;\boldsymbol{\theta})]^m[1 - F(x;\boldsymbol{\theta})]^{n-m}.$$

NOTE that the cdf for $X_{[1]}$ and $X_{[n]}$ constitute special cases of the above result.

Collecting the above results together we deduce that the ordered sample $(X_{[1]}, X_{[2]}, \ldots, X_{[n]})$ is clearly non-ID since the distribution of $X_{[k]}$ changes with k.

Example

Consider the case where $(X_1, X_2, \ldots, X_n)$ constitutes a random sample from a Uniform distribution:

$$X_k \sim \mathsf{U}(0,1), k = 1, 2, \ldots, n.$$

We can easily show that the first two moments of these variables (see appendix A) are:

$$E(X_k) = \tfrac{1}{2}, \ Var(X_k) = \tfrac{1}{12}, \ Cov(X_k, X_j) = 0, j \neq k, j,k = 1, \ldots, n.$$

On the other hand, the first two moments of the ordered sample $(X_{[1]}, X_{[2]}, \ldots, X_{[n]})$ are:

$$E(X_{[k]}) = \tfrac{k}{n+1}, \ Var(X_k) = \tfrac{k(n-k+1)}{(n+1)^2(n+2)}, \ Cov(X_k, X_j) = \tfrac{j(n-k+1)}{(n+1)^2(n+2)}, j < k, j,k = 1, \ldots, n.$$

The fact that the covariance is non-zero suggests that the ordered sample cannot be Independent (see chapter 6).

4.8.2 Joint distributions

The dependence among the ordered random variables $(X_{[1]}, X_{[2]}, \ldots, X_{[n]})$ can be best seen in the context of the bivariate joint distribution for any two of these random variables, say $X_{[i]}, X_{[j]}$ $(1 \leq i < j \leq n)$. By definition:

$$F_{[i,j]}(x_i, x_j) = \mathbb{P}(X_{[i]} \leq x_i, X_{[j]} \leq x_j) =$$
$$= \mathbb{P}(\text{at least } i \text{ random variables from } X_1, X_2, \ldots, X_n \text{ do not exceed } x_i \text{ and at}$$
$$\text{least } j \text{ random variables from } X_1, X_2, \ldots, X_n \text{ do not exceed } x_j) =$$
$$= \sum_{k=j}^{n}\sum_{\ell=i}^{k} \mathbb{P}(\text{exactly } i \text{ random variables from } X_1, X_2, \ldots, X_n \text{ do not exceed}$$
$$x_i \text{ and exactly } j \text{ random variables from } X_1, X_2, \ldots, X_n \text{ do not exceed } x_j).$$

Following the same common sense argument used above we can deduce that (see David (1981)):

$$F_{[i,j]}(x_i, x_j) = \sum_{k=j}^{n}\sum_{\ell=i}^{k} \frac{n!}{\ell!(k-\ell)!(n-k)!}[F(x_i)]^\ell[F(x_j) - F(x_i)]^{k-\ell}[1 - F(x_j)]^{n-k}.$$

As we can see, the above joint distribution cannot be expressed as a product of the two marginal distributions and thus the random variables $(X_{[i]}, X_{[j]})$ are not independent.

4.9   Summary

In this chapter we completed the transformation of the initial formalization of the notion of a random experiment in the form of the abstract statistical space $[(S,\Im,\mathbb{P}(.))^n, \mathcal{G}_n^{IID}]$ into a simple statistical model. The phenomena of interest that can be modeled in the context of this simple model are the ones that exhibit chance regularity patterns of:

(1) Independence and (2) Identical Distribution (homogeneity).

4.9.1   What comes next?

In order to enhance our understanding of the notion of a simple statistical model we will relate the probabilistic concepts making up this model to real data. The bridge between these probabilistic concepts and graphs of real data is built in the next chapter. The question of extending the formalization in order to model more realistic chance mechanisms encountered in economics will be undertaken in chapters 6–8.

4.10   Exercises

1 Explain why the joint distribution can be used to describe the heterogeneity and dependence among random variables.

2 "Marginalizing amounts to throwing away all the information relating to the random variable we are summing (integrating) out." Comment.

3 Consider the random experiment of tossing a coin twice and define the random variables: X – the number of Hs, and $Y = |$the number of Hs – the number of $Ts|$.
    Derive the joint distribution of (X, Y), assuming a fair coin, and check whether the two random variables are independent.

4 Let the joint density function of two random variables X and Y be:

$y \backslash x$	-1	0	1
-1	0.2	0.2	0.2
1	0.1	0.1	0.2

(a)   Derive the marginal distributions of X and Y.
(b)   Determine whether X and Y are independent.
(c)   Verify your answer in (b) using the conditional distribution(s).

5 Define the concept of independence for two random variables X and Y in terms of the joint, marginal and conditional density functions.

6 Explain the concept of a *random sample* and explain why it is often restrictive for most economic data series.

7 Describe briefly the formalization of the condition: [c] we can repeat the experiment under identical conditions, in the form of the concept of a random sample.

8 Explain intuitively why it makes sense that when the joint distribution $f(x,y)$ is Normal the marginal distributions $f_x(x)$ and $f_y(y)$ are also Normal.

9 Define the raw and central joint moments and prove that:

$$Cov(X,Y) = E(XY) - E(X)\cdot E(Y).$$

Why do we care about these moments?

10 Explain the notion of an ordered sample.

11 Explain intuitively why an ordered random sample is neither Independent nor Identically Distributed.

12 Explain the notions of identifiability and parameterization.

13 "In relating statistical models to (economic) theoretical models we often need to reparameterize/restrict the former in order to render the estimated parameters theoretically meaningful." Explain.

Appendix B   Bivariate distributions

B.1   Discrete bivariate distributions

Bivariate Binomial:

$$f(x,y;\boldsymbol{\theta}) = \left\{\left(\frac{n!}{x!y!(n-x-y)!}\right)\theta_1^x\theta_2^y(1-\theta_1-\theta_2)^{n-x-y}\right\}, \ x,y = 0,1,2,\ldots$$

$\boldsymbol{\theta} := (\theta_1,\theta_2) \in [0,1]\times[0,1]$, n integer, $x+y\leq n$,

Numerical characteristics

$E(X) = n\theta_1, \ Var(X) = n\theta_1(1-\theta_1), \ Cov(X,Y) = -n\theta_1\theta_2.$

Bivariate Poisson:

$$f(x,y;\boldsymbol{\theta}) = \exp\{-\theta_1 - \theta_2 + \theta_3\}\left(\frac{\alpha^x\beta^y}{x!y!}\right)\sum_{i=0}^{s}\left\{\left(\frac{x^{[i]}}{\alpha^{[i]}}\right)\left(\frac{y^{[i]}}{\beta^{[i]}}\right)\frac{\theta_3^i}{i!}\right\}$$

$\boldsymbol{\theta} := (\theta_1,\theta_2,\theta_3), \ \theta_1>\theta_3>0, \ \theta_2>\theta_3>0, \ s = \min(x,y),$

$\alpha = (\theta_1-\theta_3), \ \beta = (\theta_2-\theta_3), \ x^{[i]} = x\cdot(x-1)\cdots(x-i+1)$

Marginals and conditionals

$f(x;\theta_1)$ and $f(y;\theta_2)$ are Poisson but $f(y|x;\theta_1,\theta_3)$

and $f(x|y;\theta_2,\theta_3)$ are not Poisson distributed.

Numerical characteristics

$E(X) = \theta_1, \ Var(X) = \theta_1, \ Cov(X,Y) = \theta_3,$

$0 < Cov(X,Y) < \min(\theta_1,\theta_2).$

Bivariate Negative Binomial (see Pearson (1924)):

$$f(x,y;\boldsymbol{\theta}) = \left\{ \left(\tfrac{(x+y+k-1)!}{x!y!k!} \right) \theta_1^x \theta_2^y (1-\theta_1-\theta_2)^k \right\}, \; x, y = 0,1,\dots$$

$\boldsymbol{\theta} := (\theta_1, \theta_2), \; 0 < \theta_1, \theta_2 < 1, \; (\theta_1 + \theta_2) < 1, \; k > 0.$
Numerical characteristics
$E(X) = \tfrac{k\theta_1}{\alpha}, \; E(Y) = \tfrac{k\theta_2}{a}, \; Var(X) = \tfrac{k(1-\theta_2)\theta_1}{a^2},$
$Var(Y) = \tfrac{k(1-\theta_1)\theta_2}{a^2}, \; Cov(X,Y) = \tfrac{\theta_1\theta_2 k}{a^2}, \; a = 1 - \theta_1 - \theta_2.$

B.2 Continuous bivariate distributions

Bivariate Beta (**Filon-Isserlis**) (see Isserlis (1914) and Pearson (1923a)):

$$f(x,y;\boldsymbol{\theta}) = \left(\tfrac{\Gamma(\nu_1 + \nu_2 + \nu_3)}{\Gamma(\nu_1) \cdot \Gamma(\nu_2)\Gamma(\nu_3)} \right) \left\{ x^{\nu_1 - 1} y^{\nu_2 - 1} (1 - x - y)^{\nu_3 - 1} \right\},$$

$\boldsymbol{\theta} := (\nu_1, \nu_2, \nu_3) \in \mathbb{R}_+^3, \; x \geq 0, \; y \geq 0, \; x + y \leq 1.$
Numerical characteristics
$E(X) = \left(\tfrac{\nu_1}{\nu} \right), \; E(Y) = \left(\tfrac{\nu_2}{\nu} \right), \; Var(X) = \left(\tfrac{\nu_1(\nu_2 + \nu_3)}{\nu^2(\nu + 1)} \right), \nu = (\nu_1 + \nu_2 + \nu_3),$
$Var(Y) = \left(\tfrac{\nu_2(\nu_1 + \nu_3)}{\nu^2(\nu + 1)} \right), \; Corr(Y,X) = -\left(\tfrac{\nu_1\nu_2}{(\nu_1 + \nu_3)(\nu_2 + \nu_3)} \right)^{\frac{1}{2}}.$

Bivariate Cauchy (see Pearson (1923b)):

$$f(x,y;\boldsymbol{\theta}) = \left(\tfrac{(\nu\pi)^{-1}\Gamma\left[\frac{3}{2}\right]}{\Gamma\left[\frac{1}{2}\right]\sqrt{[(1-\rho^2)\sigma_{11}\sigma_{22}]}} \right) \left\{ 1 + \tfrac{1}{(1-\rho^2)} [\check{Y}^2 - 2\rho\check{Y}\check{X} + \check{X}^2] \right\}^{-\frac{3}{2}},$$

$\check{Y} := \tfrac{(y - \mu_1)}{\sqrt{\sigma_{11}}}, \check{X} := \tfrac{(x - \mu_2)}{\sqrt{\sigma_{22}}}, x \in \mathbb{R}, y \in \mathbb{R}.$

Marginals and conditionals
$f(x;\boldsymbol{\theta}_1)$ and $f(y;\boldsymbol{\theta}_2)$ are Cauchy but $f(y|x;\boldsymbol{\varphi})$ is Student's t with $\nu = 2$.
Numerical characteristics
No moments exist!

Bivariate Exponential (**Gumbel**) (see Gumbel (1960)):

$$f(x,y;\theta) = [(1 + \theta x)(1 + \theta y) - \theta] \exp\{-x - y - \theta xy\},$$

$\theta \in \mathbb{R}_+, x \in \mathbb{R}_+, y \in \mathbb{R}_+.$
Marginals and conditionals
$f(x;\theta), f(y;\theta)$ and $f(y|x;\theta)$ are all Exponential.
Numerical characteristics
$E(X) = \theta, \; Var(X) = \theta^2,$
$Corr(X,Y) = -1 + \int_0^\infty \{\exp(-y)/[1 + \theta y]\} \, dy.$

Bivariate Exponential (**Marshall–Olkin**) (see Marshall and Olkin (1967a,b)):

$$F(x,y;\boldsymbol{\theta}) = 1 - \exp\{-[\theta_1 + \theta_3]x\} - \exp\{-[\theta_2 + \theta_3]y\} +$$
$$+ \exp\{-\theta_1 x - \theta_2 y + \theta_3\} \max(xy)$$

$\boldsymbol{\theta} := (\theta_1, \theta_2, \theta_3) \in \mathbb{R}_+^3, \; x \in \mathbb{R}_+, y \in \mathbb{R}_+.$

Marginals and conditionals
$f(x;\theta), f(y;\theta)$ and $f(y|x;\theta)$ are all Exponential.
Numerical characteristics
$$E(X) = \frac{1}{(\theta_1 + \theta_3)},\ Var(X) = \frac{1}{(\theta_1 + \theta_3)^2},\ Corr(X,Y) = \frac{\theta_3}{(\theta_1 + \theta_2 + \theta_3)}.$$

Bivariate F:
$$f(x,y;\theta) = \left\{\prod_{i=1}^{2}\left[\frac{\nu_i^{\frac{1}{2}\nu_i}}{\Gamma(\frac{1}{2}\nu_i)}\right]\right\}\Gamma(\tfrac{1}{2}\nu)(\nu_0 + \nu_1 x + \nu_2 y)^{-\frac{1}{2}\nu}x^{\frac{1}{2}\nu_1 - 1}y^{\frac{1}{2}\nu_2 - 1},$$
$\theta := (\nu_0,\nu_1,\nu_2)\in\mathbb{R}^3_+,\ \nu = (\nu_0 + \nu_1 + \nu_2),\ x\in\mathbb{R}_+,\ y\in\mathbb{R}_+.$
Numerical characteristics
$$E(Y) = \left(\frac{\nu_0}{\nu_0 - 2}\right),\ E(X) = \left(\frac{\nu_0}{\nu_0 - 2}\right),\ \nu_0 > 2,\ Var(X) = \left(\frac{2\nu_0(\nu_0 + \nu_1 - 2)}{\nu_1(\nu_0 - 2)^2(\nu_0 - 4)}\right),$$
$$Var(Y) = \left(\frac{2\nu_0(\nu_0 + \nu_2 - 2)}{\nu_2(\nu_0 - 2)^2(\nu_0 - 4)}\right),\ Corr(Y,X) = \left(\frac{\nu_1\nu_2}{(\nu_0 + \nu_1 - 2)(\nu_0 + \nu_2 - 2)}\right)^{\frac{1}{2}},\ \nu_0 > 4.$$

Bivariate Gamma (Cherian) (see Cherian (1941)):
$$f(x,y;\theta) = \frac{e^{-(x+y)}}{\Gamma(\theta_0)\Gamma(\theta_1)\Gamma(\theta_2)}\int_0^{\min(x,y)} e^z z^{\theta_0 - 1}(x - z)^{\theta_1 - 1}(y - z)^{\theta_2 - 1}dz,$$
$\theta := (\theta_0,\theta_1,\theta_2)\in\mathbb{R}^3_+,\ x\geq 0,\ y\geq 0,$
Marginals and conditionals
$f(x;\theta), f(y;\theta)$ and $f(y|x;\theta)$ are also Gamma.
Numerical characteristics
$E(X) = \theta_1 + \theta_0,\ Var(X) = \theta_1 + \theta_0,\ Corr(X,Y) = \frac{\theta_0}{\sqrt{(\theta_1 + \theta_0)(\theta_2 + \theta_0)}}.$

Bivariate Gamma (Kibble) (see Kibble (1941)):
$$f(x,y;\theta) = \left(\frac{\alpha^{-\frac{1}{2}(\beta-1)}}{\Gamma(\beta)(1-\alpha)}\right)\exp\left(-\frac{(x+y)}{(1-\alpha)}\right)[xy]^{-\frac{1}{2}(\beta-1)}\cdot I_{\beta-1}\left(\frac{2(\alpha xy)^{\frac{1}{2}}}{(1-\alpha)}\right),$$
$\theta := (\alpha,\beta)\in[0,1]\times\mathbb{R}_+,\ y\geq 0, y\geq 0,$ and $I_n(z) = \sum_{k=0}^{\infty}\frac{(\frac{1}{2}z)^{n+2k}}{[k!\Gamma(n+k+1)]};$
$I_n(z)$ is modified Bessel function (see Muirhead (1982)).
Marginals and conditionals
$f(x;\beta), f(y;\beta)$ and $f(y|x;\beta,\alpha)$ are also Gamma.
Numerical characteristics
$E(X) = \beta,\ Var(X) = \beta,\ Corr(X,Y) = \alpha.$

Bivariate Gamma (McKay) (see McKay (1934)):
$$f(x,y;\theta) = \frac{a^{(\theta_1+\theta_2)}}{\Gamma(\theta_1)\Gamma(\theta_2)}e^{-ay}x^{\theta_1-1}(y-x)^{\theta_2-1},\ y > x \geq 0,$$
$\theta := (a,\theta_1,\theta_2)\in\mathbb{R}^3_+,$
Marginals and conditionals
$f(x;\theta), f(y;\theta)$ and $f(y|x;\theta)$ are Gamma but $f(x|y;\theta)$ is Beta.

Numerical characteristics

$$E(X) = \theta_1/a, \; Var(X) = \theta_1/a^2, \; Corr(X,Y) = \sqrt{\frac{\theta_1}{(\theta_1 + \theta_2)}}.$$

Bivariate Normal (see Galton (1886)):

$$f(x,y;\boldsymbol{\theta}) = \left(\frac{(1-\rho^2)^{-\frac{1}{2}}}{2\pi\sqrt{\sigma_{11}\sigma_{22}}}\right)\exp\left\{-\frac{1}{2(1-\rho^2)}[\breve{Y}^{-2} - 2\rho\breve{Y}\breve{X} + \breve{X}^2]\right\}$$

$$\breve{Y} := \frac{(y-\mu_1)}{\sqrt{\sigma_{11}}}, \; \breve{X} := \frac{(x-\mu_2)}{\sqrt{\sigma_{22}}}, \; x \in \mathbb{R}, \; y \in \mathbb{R},$$

$$\boldsymbol{\theta} := (\mu_1, \mu_2, \sigma_{11}, \sigma_{22}, \rho) \in \mathbb{R}^2 \times \mathbb{R}_+^2 \times [-1,1].$$

Marginals and conditionals

$f(x;\theta_2), f(y;\theta_1)$ and $f(y|x;\theta)$ are also Normal.

Numerical characteristics

$E(Y) = \mu_1, \; E(X) = \mu_2, \; Var(Y) = \sigma_{11},$

$Var(X) = \sigma_{22}, \; Corr(X,Y) = \rho.$

Bivariate Pareto (see Mardia (1962)):

$$f(x,y;\boldsymbol{\theta}) = \gamma(\gamma + 1)(\alpha\beta)^{\gamma+1}[\alpha x + \beta y - \alpha\beta]^{-(\gamma+2)},$$

$$\boldsymbol{\theta} := (\alpha, \beta, \gamma), \; x > \beta > 0, \; y > \alpha > 0, \; \gamma > 0.$$

Marginals and conditionals

$f(y;\alpha,\gamma), f(x;\beta,\gamma),$

$f(y|x;\theta) = \beta(\gamma + 1)(\alpha x)^{\gamma+1}[\alpha x + \beta y - \alpha\beta]^{-(\gamma+2)},$

all three densities are Pareto.

Numerical characteristics

$$E(Y) = \left(\frac{\alpha\gamma}{(\gamma-1)}\right), \; E(X) = \left(\frac{\beta\gamma}{(\gamma-1)}\right), \; Var(Y) = \left(\frac{\alpha^2\gamma}{(\gamma-1)^2(\gamma-2)}\right),$$

$$Var(X) = \left(\frac{\beta^2\gamma}{(\gamma-1)^2(\gamma-2)}\right), \; Corr(Y,X) = \frac{1}{\gamma}, \text{ for } \gamma > 2.$$

Bivariate Pearson type II (see Pearson (1923b)):

$$f(x,y;\boldsymbol{\theta}) = \left(\frac{[(1-\rho^2)\sigma_{11}\sigma_{22}]^{-\frac{1}{2}}}{2\pi}\right)\left(\frac{(\nu+1)}{(\nu+2)}\right)\left\{1 - \frac{(1-\rho^2)^{-1}}{2(\nu+2)}[\breve{Y}^2 - 2\rho\breve{Y}\breve{X} + \breve{X}^2]\right\}^\nu$$

$$\breve{Y} := \frac{(y-\mu_1)}{\sqrt{\sigma_{11}}}, \; \breve{X} := \frac{(x-\mu_2)}{\sqrt{\sigma_{22}}}, \; \boldsymbol{\theta} := (\mu_1, \mu_2, \sigma_{11}, \sigma_{22}, \rho) \in \mathbb{R}^2 \times \mathbb{R}_+^2 \times [-1,1].$$

$$\nu > 0, \; -\gamma\sqrt{\sigma_{11}} < y < \gamma\sqrt{\sigma_{11}}, \; -\gamma\sqrt{\sigma_{22}} < x < \gamma\sqrt{\sigma_{22}}, \; \gamma^2 = 2(\nu+2).$$

Marginals and conditionals

$f(x;\theta_2), f(y;\theta_1)$ and $f(y|x;\theta)$ are also type II.

Numerical characteristics

$E(Y) = \mu_1, \; E(X) = \mu_2, \; Var(Y) \propto \sigma_{11}, \; Var(X) \propto \sigma_{22}, \; Corr(X,Y) = \rho.$

Bivariate Student's t (see Pearson (1923b)):

$$f(x,y;\boldsymbol{\theta}) = \left(\frac{(\nu\pi)^{-1}\Gamma\left[\frac{1}{2}(\nu+2)\right]}{\Gamma\left[\frac{1}{2}\nu\right]\sqrt{[(1-\rho^2)\sigma_{11}\sigma_{22}]}}\right)\left\{1 + \frac{(1-\rho^2)^{-1}}{\nu}[\breve{Y}^{-2} - 2\rho\breve{Y}\breve{X} + \breve{X}^2]\right\}^{-\frac{1}{2}(\nu+2)},$$

$$\breve{Y} := \frac{(y-\mu_1)}{\sqrt{\sigma_{11}}}, \; \breve{X} := \frac{(x-\mu_2)}{\sqrt{\sigma_{22}}}, \; x \in \mathbb{R}, \; y \in \mathbb{R},$$

$$\boldsymbol{\theta} := (\mu_1, \mu_2, \sigma_{11}, \sigma_{22}, \rho) \in \mathbb{R}^2 \times \mathbb{R}_+^2 \times [-1,1].$$

Marginals and conditionals

$f(x;\theta_2)$, $f(y;\theta_1)$ and $f(y|x;\theta)$ are also Student's t.

Numerical characteristics

$E(Y)=\mu_1,\ E(X)=\mu_2,\ Var(Y)=\frac{\nu}{(\nu-2)}\sigma_{11},$

$Var(X)=\frac{\nu}{(\nu-2)}\sigma_{22},\ Corr(X,Y)=\rho.$

5 Probabilistic concepts and real data

5.1 Introduction

In completing the formalization of the notion of a *simple* statistical model in chapter 4 we have reached one of our primary intermediate targets. The qualifier simple is used to emphasize the fact that the model is restrictive in the sense that the notion of a random sample renders it appropriate only for observed data which can be viewed as a realization of a set of random variables which are both *Independent* and *Identically Distributed* (IID). In the next three chapters we will extend this simple model to more realistic forms of statistical models which can be used to model economic data exhibiting *non-IID* chance regularity patterns. Before we proceed in that direction, however, we need to solidify the ground charted so far by building a bridge between the theoretical concepts defining a simple statistical model (a family of densities, Independence and Identically Distributed random variables) and the corresponding chance regularity patterns exhibited by observed data. As argued in chapter 1, in the context of the development of probability theory, the probabilistic concepts are usually motivated by *chance regularity patterns* in observed data. In this chapter we consider the question of utilizing *graphical displays* of the observed data in order to establish their connection with the probabilistic assumptions underlying simple statistical models.

5.1.1 Why do we care?

As argued in the previous chapter, any form of statistical inference presupposes postulating a statistical model which provides the foundation of the empirical modeling. The statistical model is a consistent set of probabilistic assumptions which purports to provide a probabilistic description of the stochastic mechanism that gave rise to the data in question. The choice (*specification*) of a statistical model, given a particular data set, constitutes the most crucial and the most difficult decision facing the modeler. In general, an inappropriate choice of a statistical model will invalidate any statistical inference results built upon the premises of the postulated model. As argued in chapter 1, the specification problem is particularly difficult in the case of *non-experimental* (observational) data, because the theoretical model can only provide rough guidelines. The primary information that a modeler should use in making the choice of an appropriate statistical model, is the data itself. For the purposes of statistical model specification, any theoretical information relating to the behavior of the economic agents giving rise to the observed data, should be utilized once an adequate statistical model is established. As argued in chapter 1, the situation is very different in the case of *experimental* data because the design of the experiment itself is, in a certain sense, the other side of the coin of choosing the appropriate statistical model. Hence the specification of the statistical model is decided upon at the design stage and the resulting data should not be used to choose the model (see Spanos (1995b)). In the latter case the specification usually takes the form of attaching white error terms to the design. In addition, in most cases we can repeat experiments when the data are not adequate for answering the questions posed. This opportunity does not arise in the case of non-experimental (observational) data and thus we need to utilize the available observed data in our attempt to specify an *appropriate* statistical model; a statistical model which constitutes an adequate summary of the systematic information in the data.

Graphical techniques are also invaluable at the *misspecification* stage where the modeler assesses the empirical adequacy of the estimated statistical model; whether the assumptions making up the postulated model are data acceptable (see chapter 1). This often takes the form of exploring the features of the observed data in conjunction with the *residuals* of the estimated model in an attempt to detect departures from the underlying assumptions of the model. In cases where the original model is found to be misspecified the modeler will proceed to respecify the statistical model and that also involves the utilization of graphical techniques.

Consider an example of a simple statistical model we encountered in chapters 3 and 4, known as the **Gamma statistical model**:

[i]   Probability model:

$$\Phi = \left\{ f(x;\boldsymbol{\theta}) = \frac{\alpha^{-1}}{\Gamma[\beta]} \left(\frac{x}{\alpha}\right)^{\beta-1} \exp\left\{ -\left(\frac{x}{\alpha}\right) \right\}, \; \boldsymbol{\theta} := (\alpha,\beta) \in \mathbb{R}^2_+, \; x \in \mathbb{R}_+ \right\},$$

[ii]   Sampling model: $\mathbf{X} := (X_1, X_2, \ldots, X_n)$ is a random sample.

Figure 5.1 shows several members of this family of densities (one for each combination of values of $\boldsymbol{\theta}$). The probability model has two unknown parameters $\alpha > 0$ and $\beta > 0$; the parameter space is the product of the positive real line: $\Theta := \mathbb{R}^2_+$. Its support is $\mathbb{R}_X := (0, \infty)$. This pictorial representation of a probability model will prove very useful in relating this abstract notion to chance regularity patterns. So far we have seen no pictorial representation of the theoretical concepts defining a random sample. In the previous chapter, we provided only a mathematical definition of the notion of a random sample $\mathbf{X}^{\text{IID}}_{(n)} := (X_1, X_2, \ldots, X_n)$. To remind the reader, we defined a random sample as a set of random variables which satisfy two probabilistic assumptions:

(I) Independence: $f(x_1, x_2, \ldots, x_n; \boldsymbol{\phi}) \; \text{I} \; \prod_{k=1}^n f_k(x_k; \boldsymbol{\theta}_k)$ for all $(x_1, \ldots, x_n) \in \mathbb{R}_X$,

(ID) Identical Distribution: $f_k(x_k; \boldsymbol{\theta}_k) \overset{\text{ID}}{=} f(x_k; \boldsymbol{\theta})$, for all $k = 1, 2, \ldots, n$.

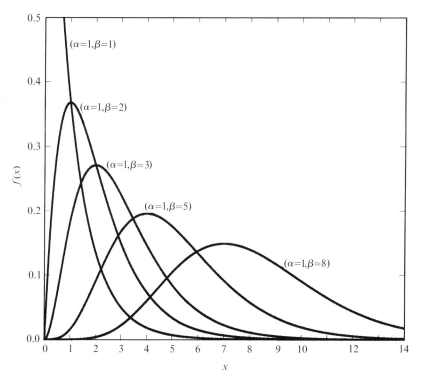

Figure 5.1 Gamma probability model

The question to be considered in this chapter is:

> How can one utilize graphical displays of the observed data to decide upon the most appropriate statistical model?

The discussion that follows will attempt to bring out the connection between concepts such as Independence and Identical Distribution and the corresponding chance regularity patterns discernible in a t-plot and related graphical representations of observed data.

5.1.2 A bird's eye view of the chapter

The primary purpose of this chapter is to provide an introduction to graphical methods for data analysis which have a direct connection with the theoretical concepts introduced in the context of a simple statistical model. The three concepts making up a simple statistical model are:

(D) Distribution (density function), (M) Independence, (H) Identical Distribution.

All three of these probabilistic concepts will be related to chance regularity patterns exhibited by observed data. It turns out that a t-plot can be used to access chance regularity patterns which correspond to all three of the above theoretical notions.

In section 2 we review early developments of graphical displays in statistics as a prelude to the discussion of the visual representation of data for statistical model specification purposes. Section 3 considers the question of using a particular graphical display, the *t*-**plot,** as a tool in assessing the chance regularity patterns that would be appropriately modeled in the context of simple statistical models. Our basic tool is the use of pseudo-random numbers (simulated data) which satisfy certain properties by design; we discuss the question of generating such pseudo-random numbers in section 8. In section 4 we consider the question of assessing the appropriateness of a distribution assumption by looking at the connection between *t*-plots and the histogram (or the smoothed histogram). In sections 5 and 6 we consider the question of assessing the appropriateness of the Independence and Identical Distribution assumptions, respectively, using the information conveyed by *t*-plots. In section 7 we return to graphical displays for assessing distribution assumptions. We consider several graphical displays associated with the empirical cumulative distribution function, such as the P-P and Q-Q plots, which can be used to assess the distribution assumption for IID data. In section 8 we discuss briefly the question of generating *ideal data* in the form of pseudo-random numbers.

5.2   Early developments

Looking at masses of observed data (dozens of numbers) is usually hopeless for discerning any chance regularity patterns. The visual representation of the data, in the form of graphs, is often the only way to utilize the data at the specification stage of modeling. Well-designed data graphs can help the modeler make educated (as opposed to wild) guesses about the nature of the statistical model that might be appropriate for a certain set of data. The way such graphs can help the specification of statistical models will be the subject matter of this chapter.

Although descriptive statistics can be traced back to John Graunt (1662) and William Petty (1690), the systematic use of graphical techniques in descriptive statistics dates back to William Playfair (1786,1801), who introduced *bar diagrams*, *pie charts*, and *line graphs*. A few years later Fourier introduced the *cumulative frequency polygon* and in the mid-19th century Quetelet (1849) introduced the widely used diagrams known as the *histogram* and its sister the *frequency polygon*.

Karl Pearson was a devotee to the graphical analysis of data and coined most of the terminology in use today, including that of the histogram utilizing mostly Greek words (see Pearson (1892)). *Histogram* is a compound of two Greek words $\iota\sigma\tau\grave{o}\varsigma$ (wooden pole) and $\gamma\rho\alpha\mu\mu\acute{\eta}$ (line). *Polygon* is also a compound Greek word made up of the words $\pi o\lambda\grave{\upsilon}$ (many) and $\gamma\omega\nu\acute{\iota}\alpha$ (angle).

In a certain sense the histogram provided the motivation for the probabilistic notion of a density function and for a long time the dividing line between the two was blurred. The blurring of the dividing line between relative frequencies and probabilities was the rule and not the exception until the 20th century. As a result of this, the notion of an unknown parameter and the corresponding *estimate* in terms of the observations was made indistinct.

The first to draw the line clearly and bring out the confusion between *unknown parameters* and their *estimates* was R. A. Fisher in his path breaking paper (Fisher 1922a), where he considered this confusion to be one of the two reasons for the neglect of statistics. He diagnosed the problem through its symptom: the use of the same terminology for both the theoretical unknown parameter and its estimate:

it has happened that in statistics a purely verbal confusion has hindered the distinct formulation of statistical problems; for it is customary to apply the same name, mean, standard deviation, correlation coefficient, etc., both to the true value which we should like to know, but can only estimate, and to the particular value at which we happen to arrive by our methods of estimation...   (p. 311)

During the rapid development of practical statistics in the past few decades, the theoretical foundations of the subject have been involved in great obscurity. Adequate distinction has seldom been drawn between the sample recorded and the hypothetical population from which it is regarded as drawn ...   (p. 333)

Unfortunately for statistics the problem of terminology diagnosed by Fisher three quarters of a century ago is still bedeviling the subject even though the distinction is clearly established. A lot of grey matter and effort is frittered away by the students (and teachers) of statistics because of the confusion created by the terminology.

Fisher went on to make the distinction between the *histogram* and the *density function* (called a frequency curve at the time) very clear:

No finite sample has a frequency curve: a finite sample may be represented by a histogram, or a frequency polygon, which to the eye more and more resembles a curve as the size of the sample is increased. To reach a true curve, not only would an infinite number of individuals have to be placed in each class, but the number of classes (arrays) into which the population is divided must be made infinite ...   (p. 312)

The confusion between unknown parameters and their estimates pervades the statistical literature of the early 20th century (Galton, Edgeworth, Pearson, Yule) because this literature had one leg in the descriptive statistics tradition of the previous century and the other in the statistical inference tradition which began with Gossett (1908) and was formulated by Fisher in the 1920s and 1930s.

R. A. Fisher, in his book *Statistical Methods for Research Workers* (the first textbook on statistical inference in its modern sense), published in 1925, begins the second chapter entitled "Diagrams" (devoted to the usefulness of graphical techniques in statistical inference), with the following paragraph:

The preliminary examination of most data is facilitated by the use of diagrams. Diagrams prove nothing, but bring outstanding features readily to the eye; they are therefore no substitute for such critical tests as may be applied to the data, but are valuable in suggesting such tests, and in explaining the conclusions founded upon them...   (Fisher (1925a), p. 24)

There is no doubt that graphical methods have always been an integral part of observed data analysis.

The modern era of graphical analysis in empirical modeling can be dated back to Tukey (1962) but the paper which revived interest in graphical techniques is arguably Anscombe (1973) who demonstrated the dangers of relying (exclusively) on the numerical results when modeling in the context of the linear regression model. A good summary of the graphical techniques as of the early 1980s is given in Tukey (1977) and Cleveland (1985).

5.3   Graphical displays: a *t*-plot

As stated in chapter 1 the primary aim of probability theory is to provide a framework in the context of which we can formalize *chance regularity patterns* with a view to modeling observable phenomena which exhibit such patterns. The purpose of this section is to set up a bridge between the various *theoretical concepts* introduced so far and the *observable phenomena* we aspire to model. An attempt will be made to establish such a relationship by utilizing a number of graphical techniques.

This bridge between theoretical concepts and observed data has two components. The *first* component establishes a connection between theoretical concepts, such as Independence, non-Correlation, Identical Distribution and Normality on the one hand and the ideal data on the other. The ideal data come in the form of *pseudo-random* numbers generated by computer algorithms so as to artificially satisfy the restrictions we impose upon them. Generating pseudo-random numbers enables the modeler to create a pictionary of ideal data plots which can be used as reference for assessing the features of real data.

The *second* component is concerned with comparing these ideal plots with real data plots, in an attempt to relate the purposefully generated patterns with those in real data. The pictionary of simulated *t*-plots will provide a reference framework for assessing the features of actual data plots. In this chapter we concentrate on the first component. The problem of generating pseudo-random numbers will be considered in section 8. In the meantime we take the generation of the pseudo-random numbers for granted and proceed to provide a pictionary of simulated series designed to teach the reader how to discern particular patterns of chance regularity.

A statistical graph constitutes a visual representation of observable data series. Such visual representations can take numerous forms (see Chambers *et al.* (1983)). In this section we consider one such graph known as the **t-plot**. A *t*-plot is drawn with the values of the variable Z measured on the y-axis and the index (dimension) t, with respect to which the data are ordered, such as time or geographical position, on the x-axis:

t-plot: $\{(t,Z_t), t = 1,2,\ldots, T\}$.

NOTE that the original term for a *t*-plot, introduced by Playfair, was *line graph*. In practice t could represent any dimension which is measured on an ordinal scale (see below). Our aim is to compile a pictionary of *t*-plots of simulated IID data from several well-known distributions and bring out the kind of probabilistic information such a graph can convey.

When reading *t*-plots the reader should keep a number of useful hints in mind.

First, it is important to know what exactly is measured on each axis, the units of measurement used and the so-called *aspect ratio*: the physical length of the vertical axis

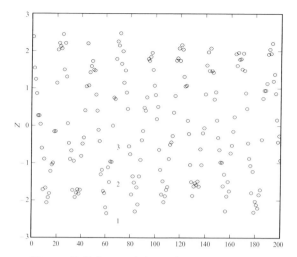

Figure 5.2 Data exhibiting heterogeneity

divided by that of the horizontal axis. A number of patterns associated with dependence and heterogeneity can be hidden by choosing the aspect ratio non-intelligently! In figures 5.2 and 5.3 we can see the same heterogeneous data series with different aspect ratios. The regularity patterns are more visible in figure 5.3. To enhance our ability to discern patterns over the t-index it is often advisable to use lines to connect the observations even in cases where the data are not observed continuously. In order to appreciate the value of connecting the observations we urge the reader to look at figure 5.35 where the same data are shown with a line connecting consecutive observations. In what follows we employ this as the default option.

Second, it must be noted at the outset that the t-plots which follow are only a small sample of the variety of patterns one could get by simulating data from different distributions. The reader should interpret the above plots as *representative* of t-plots from these distributions and not as providing *exact pictures* one expects to see in real data plots. Moreover, the discussion that follows separates the various features of the data into the three categories (D),(M),(H) and assesses them in isolation for expositional purposes. In practice, real data are not as helpful and the modeler needs to separate these features at a preliminary stage.

In the next two sections we consider the connection between a t-plot and the appropriateness of a probability model and the random sample, respectively. Our discussion focuses on the most widely used model: the simple **Normal statistical model**:

[i]   Probability model:

$$\Phi = \left\{ f(x;\boldsymbol{\theta}) = \frac{1}{\sigma\sqrt{2\pi}}\exp\left\{ -\frac{(x-\mu)^2}{2\sigma^2}\right\}, \; \boldsymbol{\theta}:=(\mu,\sigma^2)\in\mathbb{R}\times\mathbb{R}_+, \, x\in\mathbb{R}\right\},$$

[ii]   Sampling model: $\mathbf{X}:=(X_1,X_2,...,X_n)$ is a random sample

Our aim is to provide a visual guide on what the observed data would look like for this model to be appropriate. In order to help the reader keep an eye on the forest, we state at

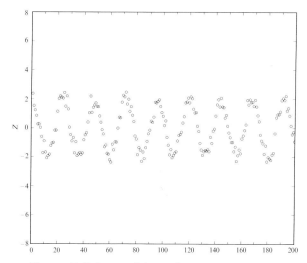

Figure 5.3 Data exhibiting heterogeneity

the outset that the *t*-plot of Normal IID data (see figure 5.4) exhibits three chance regularity patterns:

(1)   a bell-shaped symmetry,
(2)   an unpredictability, and
(3)   a certain uniformity.

The first one relates to the probability model and the other two to the sampling model of a random sample.

We have already discussed the notion of a probability model and how this notion can be represented graphically as a family of density functions. In figure 5.5 we can see such a family of Normal density functions indexed by the variance only, for simplicity.

Figure 5.4 represents a realization of a simulated data series which can be appropriately modeled in the context of the above simple Normal Statistical model.

5.4   Assessing distribution assumptions

5.4.1   Normal IID data

Looking at the pictorial representation of a Normal family of densities in figure 5.5 the issue that naturally arises is the connection between this theoretical construct and the data plot in figure 5.4. In particular, when looking at the *t*-plot in figure 5.4: Where is the bell-shaped symmetry exhibited by figure 5.5? The best way to discern the bell-shaped symmetry in figure 5.4 is through the following thought experiment:

> *Imagine that each observation has an area equal to that of the square around it and we turn the t-plot 90° clockwise so it sits on the opposite end of the y-axis. If*

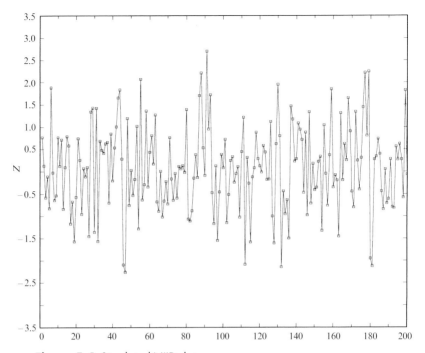

Figure 5.4 Simulated NIID data

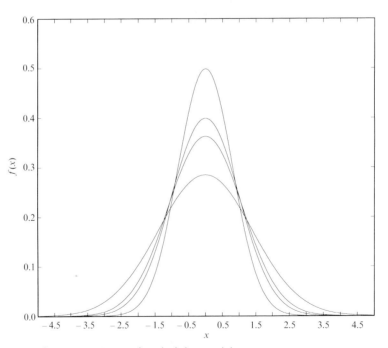

Figure 5.5 Normal probability model

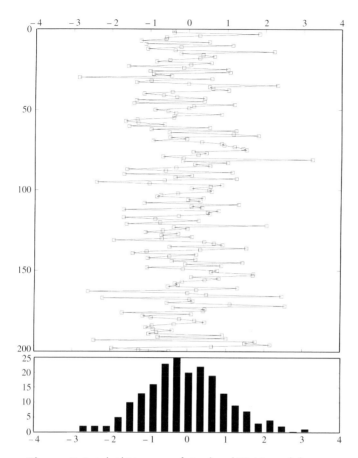

Figure 5.6 *t*-plot histogram of simulated IID Normal data

> *we then let the squares fall vertically on the y-axis they will form a pile (a pseudo-histogram) (see figure 5.6).*

The histogram in figure 5.6 reminds one of the bell shape of the Normal distribution. To be more precise, the *bell-shaped symmetry*, associated with the *Normal distribution*, amounts to the following:

(*a*)   *symmetry:* roughly the same number of observations above and below the imaginary mean axis at zero,

(*b*)   *middle humpback:* a concentration of observations around the imaginary mean axis,

(*c*)   *dying out tails:* a reduction in the number of observations as we go away from this mean axis with the overwhelming majority of observations being within 2.5 standard deviations around the data mean band.

Although the histogram created by the above thought experiment often suffices to narrow down the set of possible distributions, it is often advisable to reduce the *data*

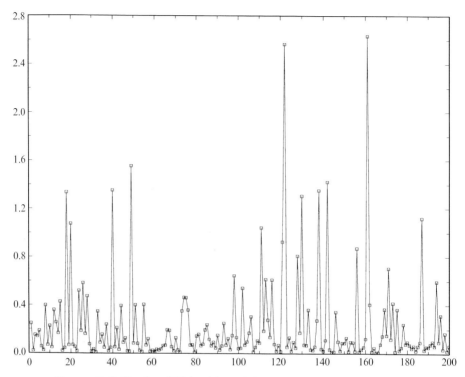

Figure 5.7 Simulated IID log-Normal data

specificity of the histogram by *smoothing* it. The histogram needs to be smoothed somewhat in order to go beyond the specific data in hand and bridge the gap between the actual data and the theoretical notion of a distribution (density function). The question of smoothing the histogram is discussed below.

The *t*-plot of Normal IID data constitutes the cornerstone upon which one can build a pictionary of *t*-plots. The choice of the Normal distribution is no coincidence but reflects the center stage given to this distribution in statistical inference. In an attempt to enhance our understanding of the peculiarities of Normality in *t*-plots of IID data, we will contrast it to several other distributions.

5.4.2 Non-Normal IID data

Log-Normal IID data

The above thought experiment, when used in conjunction with IID data, can be used as a guide in order to narrow down the possible probability models. Figure 5.7, depicting IID log-Normal data, exhibits none of the features associated with the bell-shaped symmetry of the Normal distribution. Instead, the *t*-plot exhibits the following chance regularity patterns:

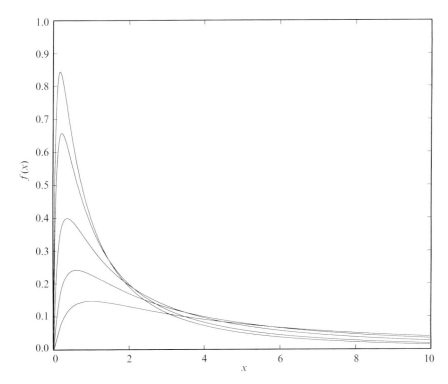

Figure 5.8 Log-Normal family of densities

(*a*) *asymmetry:* a lot more observations appear to be on one side of the distribution (the left side),

(*b*) *left humpback:* the highest concentration of observations seems to be on the left of the distribution,

(*c*) *long right-hand tail:* the number of observations on the right-hand side, as one moves away from the imaginary data mean, decreases smoothly but the left tail appears to cut off abruptly. This should be seen in conjunction with the log-Normal family of densities shown in figure 5.8.

These features appear most clearly in figure 5.9 where we performed the thought experiment of turning the *t*-plot 90° clockwise and letting the observations drop vertically into a pile. As we can see from figure 5.9, the majority of observations are piled up on the extreme left and the histogram has a long right tail. A smoothed version of the histogram reminds us of the family of densities in figure 5.8.

Exponential IID data
A glance at figure 5.10, depicting simulated IID Exponential data, reveals a similar form of asymmetry (skewed to the right) as the log-Normal distribution. The connection between the skewed pattern exhibited by the data and the theoretical family of densities becomes apparent when looking at figure 5.11.

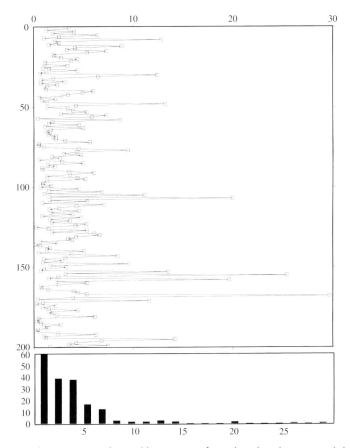

Figure 5.9 *t*-plot and histogram of simulated IID log-Normal data

Weibull IID data

The plot depicted in figure 5.12, which represents simulated IID data from the Weibull distribution, reveals a less extreme form of asymmetry than both of the previous two *t*-plots. The pseudo-histogram created by the thought experiment will be skewed to the right but in a less extreme form than the one in figure 5.9.

Beta IID data

The plot depicted in figure 5.13, which represents simulated IID data from the Beta distribution, reveals an even less extreme form of asymmetry than the previous three *t*-plots, with the longer tail on the left.

So far the comparison between Normal IID data and IID data from skewed distributions was designed to enable the reader to develop a pictionary where the symmetry is at center stage. Normality, however, does not mean just any symmetry. The next two *t*-plots come from symmetric but non-Normal distributions. The first is rectangularly shaped symmetric and hopefully easy to distinguish from Normality but the other is bell shaped and not as easy to distinguish from the Normal bell-shape.

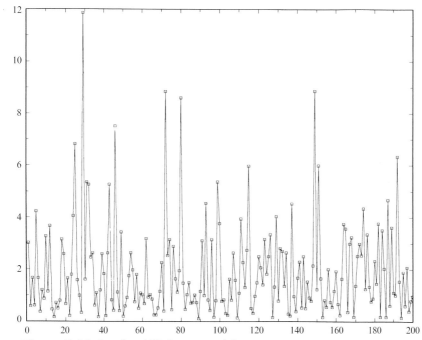

Figure 5.10 Simulated IID Exponential data

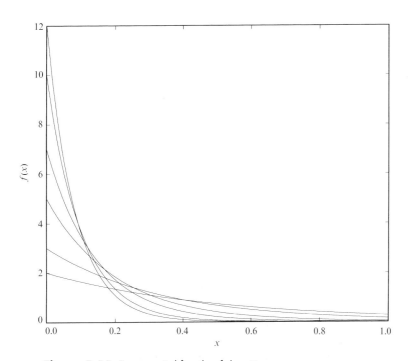

Figure 5.11 Exponential family of densities

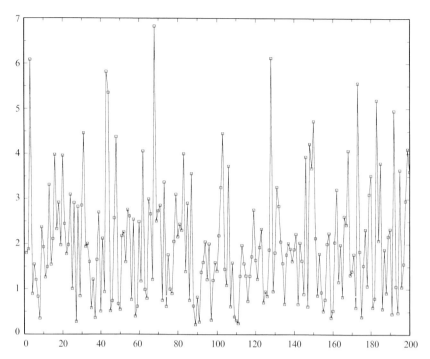

Figure 5.12 Simulated IID Weibull data

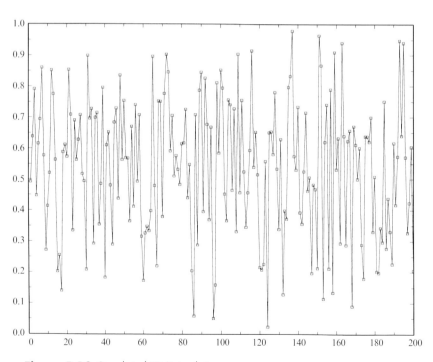

Figure 5.13 Simulated IID Beta data

Uniform IID data

A glance at figure 5.14, depicting simulated IID Uniform data, exhibits a different form of symmetry than the bell shape of the Normal distribution. The thought experiment of letting the observation squares drop vertically along the *t*-axis will form a pile that will appear more like a rectangle than a bell shape. This is the result of the uniformity of pattern created by the particular way these squares are scattered around the mean of the observed data. There does not appear to be any concentration of points in any section of the *t*-plot.

Student's t IID data

One will need more than a glance to discern the differences between the Normal IID data depicted in figure 5.4 and the IID Student's t data shown in figure 5.15. The latter *t*-plot exhibits the same bell-shaped symmetry the uninitiated often associate with the Normal distribution. A closer look, however, reveals two important differences that distinguish the leptokurtic Student's t from the Normal distribution (see figure 5.16):

(i)   the middle humpback appears more accentuated, and
(ii) the tails appear to be longer (notice the range of values on the *y*-axis).

5.4.3   The histogram and its connection to the density function

The histogram constitutes a graphical way to summarize the relative frequencies of occurrence of the values $(x_1, x_2, \ldots, x_n)$ of the variable X underlying this data. Let us first partition the range of values of the variable, say $a < x_i < b$, $i = 1, 2, \ldots, n$, into:

$$a = x_{[0]} < x_{[1]} < x_{[2]} < \cdots < x_{[m]} = b,$$

and then express the relative frequency of interval i as:

$$\varphi_i = \frac{\nu_i}{n(x_{[i]} - x_{[i-1]})}, \quad i = 1, 2, \ldots, m, \ (m < n),$$

where ν_i is the *number of observations falling* in the ith interval. The **histogram** can be viewed as the step function:

$$g(x) = \frac{\nu_i}{n(x_{[i]} - x_{[i-1]})}, \quad \text{for } x_{[i-1]} \le x < x_{[i]}, \ i = 1, 2, \ldots, m, \ x \in \mathbb{R}_X,$$

whose graph depicts the relative frequencies on the *y*-axis and the intervals on the *x*-axis. The histogram, as defined above, is a cumbersome step function with jumps at the points $(x_{[i]}, i = 1, 2, \ldots, m)$ (irrespective of whether the data represent realizations of discrete or continuous random variables), which also depend on the choice of the origin x_0 and the bandwidth. In this sense the histogram is unlike its theoretical counterpart: the *density function*.

In a very insightful paper, Rosenblatt (1956) proposed a variation on the histogram which opened the way to bridge the gap between this descriptive statistics device and its probability theoretic counterpart, the density function.

The *first* proposed change was in the form of equal length intervals (of width h), defining the so-called *bins*:

$$[x_{[0]} + kh, \ x_{[0]} + (k+1)h], \ k = 1, 2, \ldots, m.$$

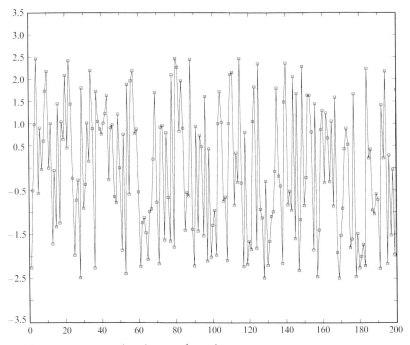

Figure 5.14 Simulated IID Uniform data

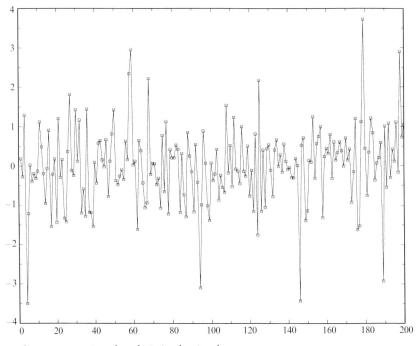

Figure 5.15 Simulated IID Student's t data

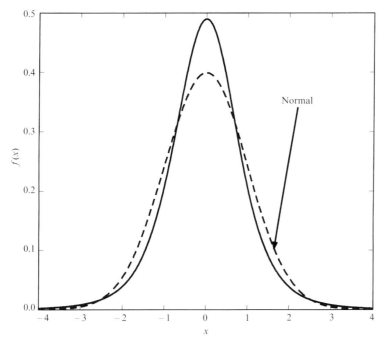

Figure 5.16 Student's t versus Normal

The *second* change was to unfix the origin and the intervals defined relative to that origin and render every point in the range $x \in \mathbb{R}_X$ a mid point of a bin. These changes enable us to avoid the cumbersome notation of the specific intervals by making every value $x \in \mathbb{R}_X$ the mid point of a mesh of intervals covering the range $\mathbb{R}_X$. In terms of these overlapping bins we can think of the *rolling histogram* as:

$$g_h(x) = \frac{1}{n}\left(\frac{\text{no. of } x_i's \text{ in the same bin as } x}{h}\right) = \frac{1}{nh}\left(\text{no. of } x_i's \text{ in } \left(x - \left(\frac{h}{2}\right), x + \left(\frac{h}{2}\right)\right)\right),$$

where $x \in \mathbb{R}_X$. This can be written equivalently as:

$$g_h(x) = \frac{1}{nh}\sum_{i=1}^{n}\mathbb{I}\left(\left(x + \frac{h}{2}\right) \le x_i \le \left(x - \frac{h}{2}\right)\right), \ x \in \mathbb{R}_X,$$

where $\mathbb{I}(.)$ is an indicator function of the form:

$$\mathbb{I}(x_i) = \begin{cases} 1, \text{ if } x_i \in [x \pm (h/2)], \\ 0, \text{ if } x_i \notin [x \pm (h/2)]. \end{cases}$$

Intuitively, the rolling histogram is constructed by placing a box of width h and height $(1/nh)$ on each observation and then summing the boxed observations. A more allusive notation for $g_h(x)$ is:

$$g_h(x) = \frac{1}{nh}\sum_{i=1}^{n}\mathbb{I}\left(-\frac{1}{2} \le \left(\frac{x_i - x}{h}\right) \le \frac{1}{2}\right),$$

$$\begin{cases} 1, \text{ if } \psi_i \in [-(1/2),(1/2)], \\ 0, \text{ if } \psi_i \notin [-(1/2),(1/2)], \end{cases} \text{ where } \psi_i := \left(\frac{x_i - x}{h}\right).$$

Viewed this way, the rolling histogram is still a step function with a lot more jumps whose graph is a step closer to the density function. The *third* and most crucial change to the histogram came in the form of the weighting. We can think of the above histogram as a function of the form:

$$g_h(x) = \frac{1}{nh}\sum_{i=1}^{n} \mathbb{K}\left(\frac{x_i - x}{h}\right) = \frac{1}{nh}\sum_{i=1}^{n} \mathbb{K}(\psi_i),$$

where $\mathbb{K}(z)$ is a weight function (see figure 5.20):

$$\mathbb{K}(z) := \begin{cases} \frac{1}{2}, & \text{if } |z| \leq 1 \\ 0, & \text{if } |z| > 1. \end{cases}$$

This function gives the same weight to all the observations in a certain bin irrespective of whether they are at the center of the bin or at the edges. It reminds us of the uniform density over the interval $\mathbb{R}_z := [-1,1]$, with the properties:

$$\text{(i) } \mathbb{K}(z) \geq 0, z \in \mathbb{R}, \text{ (ii) } \int_{z \in \mathbb{R}_z} \mathbb{K}(z)\, dz = 1. \tag{5.1}$$

This realization led to the most decisive step toward bridging the gap between the histogram and the density function: *smoothing* over the edges. The smoothing effect can be achieved by replacing the Uniform weight function with another weight function which gives more weight to the observations close to the value x and less to those at the edges of the bin. That is, make the weight a function of the distance from the point x. Such weight functions are called **kernels** and the most widely used are:

[1]   Normal kernel: $\mathbb{K}(z) = \frac{1}{\sqrt{2\pi}}\exp\left\{-\frac{1}{2}z^2\right\}$,

[2]   Epanechnikov kernel: $\mathbb{K}(z) = \frac{3}{4}(1 - z^2), |z| \leq 1$,

[3]   Biweight kernel: $\mathbb{K}(z) = \frac{15}{16}(1 - z^2)^2, |z| \leq 1$,

[4]   Uniform kernel: $\mathbb{K}(z) = \frac{1}{2}, |z| \leq 1$.

The smoothed histogram is defined by:

$$\hat{f}_h(x) = \frac{1}{nh}\sum_{i=1}^{n} \mathbb{K}\left(\frac{x_i - x}{h}\right),$$

where the kernel satisfies the conditions (5.1) above. As we can see from figures 5.17–5.19, the kernel functions give more weight to the values close to the designated value z. The exception to this rule is the uniform kernel shown in figure 5.20 which gives the same weight to all values of z. It turns out that the choice between the first three kernels above does not make much difference to the smoothing. What is crucially important for the smoothing, however, is the value of the width for the bins h; called the *bandwidth*.

In view of the fact that we can think of the histogram as a sum of boxes placed at the observations, we can think of the *smoothed histogram* as a sum of bell-shaped lumps. Hence, the smaller the value of h the more even the outline of the smoothed histogram. Ironically, the choice of the h depends both on the true underlying density as well as the

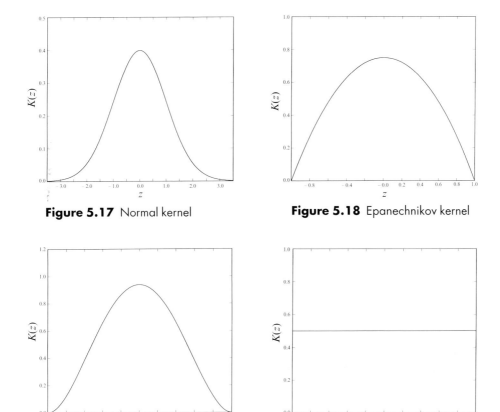

Figure 5.17 Normal kernel

Figure 5.18 Epanechnikov kernel

Figure 5.19 Biweight kernel

Figure 5.20 Uniform kernel

number of observations n. The rule of thumb often used in conjunction with the Normal kernel is (see Silverman (1986)):

$$h \simeq \sigma \cdot (1.06) \cdot n^{-\frac{1}{5}}.$$

Using the Normal kernel we can evaluate the smoothed histogram:

$$\hat{f}_h(x) = \frac{1}{nh} \sum_{k=1}^{n} \mathbb{K}\left(\frac{x_k - x}{h}\right) = \frac{1}{nh\sqrt{2\pi}} \sum_{k=1}^{n} \exp\left\{-\frac{1}{2}\left(\frac{x_k - x}{h}\right)^2\right\}, \; h = \sigma \cdot (1.06) \cdot n^{-\frac{1}{5}}.$$

The effect of Normal kernel smoothing on the histogram is shown in figures 5.21 and 5.22 in the case of IID data from a Normal and a log-Normal distribution, respectively.

In connection with our thought experiment of turning the t-plot 90° clockwise and letting the observations drop vertically into a pile, when we endow each observation with a rectangle the thought experiment yields a histogram but when we endow them with a bell-shaped lump the experiment yields a smoothed histogram. Intuitively, if we think of a histogram as a two-dimensional area under the step function defined above, smoothing amounts to nothing more than taking a trowel and literally smoothing the edges. In figure 5.23 we can see the rotation experiment together with the histogram and smoothed histogram in the case of NIID data.

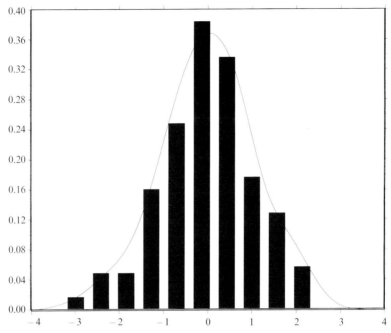

Figure 5.21 Smoothed histogram of simulated NIID data

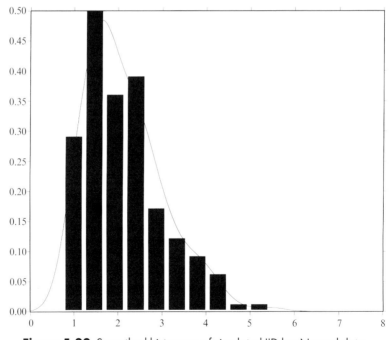

Figure 5.22 Smoothed histogram of simulated IID log-Normal data

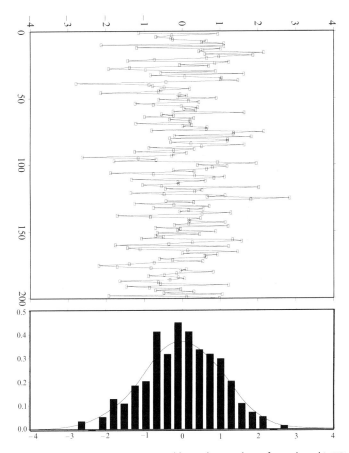

Figure 5.23 Histogram and kernel smoother of simulated NIID data

Smoothed histogram: parametric versus non-parametric

In the context of the above framework a smoothed histogram is nothing more than a useful device for exploratory data analysis. It is important to remind the reader that the histogram, as part of descriptive statistics, is data specific! As argued many times in this book, the major difference between descriptive statistics and statistical inference is that the former is data specific and thus the conclusions refer to the data in question. In order to reduce the data specificity of such descriptive measures we utilize a device called smoothing. In this sense we view smoothing as giving operational meaning to Fisher's statement:

… To reach a true curve, not only would an infinite number of individuals have to be placed in each class, but the number of classes (arrays) into which the population is divided must be made infinite …   (Fisher (1922b), p. 312).

A smoothed histogram constitutes the bridge between the observed data set $(x_1, x_2, \ldots, x_n)$ and the theoretical concept of a density function $f(x)$, the data viewed as a realization of an IID sample $(X_1, X_2, \ldots, X_n)$. As mentioned above, the smoothing is necessary in order to reduce the *data specificity* of the histogram.

In traditional statistical inference a smoothed histogram is commonly viewed as a *non-parametric* estimator of the unknown density function. This interpretation raises a number of interesting methodological issues which are beyond the scope of the present chapter. This issue will be discussed further in chapter 10.

5.5   Independence and the *t*-plot

The notion of a random sample has been historically confused with the notion of randomness. A careful reading of Von Mises' discussion of *randomness* (see Von Mises (1957)) reveals that the meaning attributed to this term is inextricably bound up with the concepts of IID. The restriction that the ordering of the observations leaves the relative frequencies invariant, has to do with both Independence and Identical Distribution. In addition, the Law of Large Numbers used to provide an empirical foundation for these relative frequencies was considered at the time in relation to IID sequences of random variables (see chapter 10). In this book we consider randomness as a notion which goes beyond IID sequences. Indeed, this notion underlies our notion of chance regularity which applies to non-IID sequences equally well.

As mentioned above, in the case of assessing the distributional nature of a data set using a *t*-plot the ordering of the observations is irrelevant and thus suppressed. In the case of assessing independence and identical distribution the ordering is the all-important dimension.

Apart from the bell-shaped symmetry, the **second** important feature exhibited by figure 5.4 (reproduced on opposite page for reference) comes in the form of the *unpredictability* of the ups and downs of the plot from one observation to the next. This unpredictability of the direction of change (ups and downs) corresponds to the probabilistic notion of *Independence*.

If we imagine ourselves standing at any one point on the observations axis *t* (hiding away the plot to our right) and try to predict the direction of the next few observations we will have great difficulty guessing correctly. In other words, there is no obvious pattern to be used to help narrow down the possibilities that will enable us to guess correctly the direction of the next observation. The only information we have is with regard to the likely values of the data series as they relate to the underlying distribution. If the underlying distribution is Normal as in figure 5.4, then we know that the values around the mean (zero in this case) are more likely to arise than observations in the tails. This information, however, is often of very little help when we seek to predict the direction of the next observation.

CAUTION: the one occasion when knowledge of the distribution might provide some assistance in our attempt to predict the direction of change is in the case of extreme observations. In the case of the plot in figure 5.4, an observation above 2.5 is likely to be succeeded by a smaller observation and one below -2.5 by an observation greater in value because the probability of getting too many such extreme observations is very low.

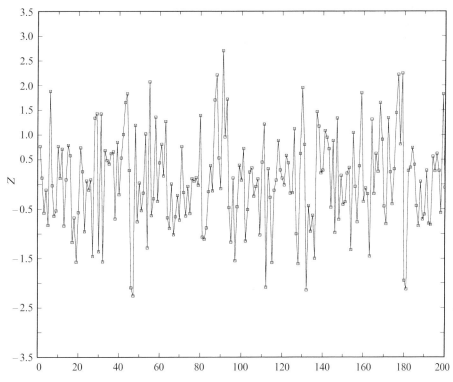

Figure 5.4 Simulated NIID data

Runs up and down Another way to look at this unpredictability of direction of change is to ignore the values taken by the data series altogether and concentrate just on the sign (direction) of the differences (changes):

$$d_1 = x_2 - x_1, d_2 = x_3 - x_2, \ldots, d_{n-1} = x_n - x_{n-1},$$

denoting an increase (a positive difference) by a plus ($+$) and a decrease by a minus ($-$). The observations 65–105 in figure 5.4 give rise to the following pattern of ups and downs:

$$+--+-+-+--+++-+--+-+--+-++-+-+++-+-++-+-$$

From this sequence of pluses and minuses we discern no regular pattern to be utilized to guess the next up or down. The patterns we have in mind come in the form of **runs**: a subsequence of one type (pluses only or minuses only) immediately proceeded and succeeded by an element of the other type. In the early time series literature (see Yule and Kendall (1950)) the beginning of each run is also known as a *turning point* because the direction changes at that point. In the above case the number of runs up and down are:

$$\{1,1,1,3,2,1,1,1,2,1,3,2,2,1\}^+, \{2,1,2,1,2,1,2,1,1,1,1,1,1,1\}^-$$

respectively. Looking at this we can see that at first sight these runs exhibit no discernible regularity.

By treating the sequence of pluses and minuses as Bernoulli trials we can use combinatorial arguments to evaluate the number of runs expected if the observations were independent. Defining the following random variables:

R: number of runs of any size,
R_k: number of runs of size k,
R'_k: number of runs of size k or greater,

combinatorial arguments can be used to show (see Levene (1952)) that:

$$E(R) = \left(\tfrac{2n-1}{3}\right),$$

$$E(R_k) = 2n\left(\tfrac{k^2+3k-1}{(k+3)!}\right) - 2\left(\tfrac{k^3+3k^2-k-4}{(k+3)!}\right), \ k \le (n-2),$$

$$E(R'_k) = 2n\left(\tfrac{k+1}{(k+2)!}\right) - 2\left(\tfrac{k^2+k-1}{(k+2)!}\right), \ k \le (n-2).$$

In the case of the above data for $n = 40$:

$$E(R) = 26.3, \ E(R_1) = 16.7, \ E(R_2) = 7.1, \ E(R'_3) = 2.5.$$

These numbers do not differ significantly from the actual numbers of various sized runs derived above; for more formal tests see chapter 15. The number of all size runs is 28, very close to the number expected under independence: 26. The number of size 1 runs is 18, very close to the number expected under independence: 17. The number of size 2 runs is 8, close to the number expected under independence: 7. Finally, the number of size 3 or greater runs is 2, very close to the number expected under independence: 2.5. NOTE that NID stands for Normal, Identical Distribution.

In order to come to grips with the patterns indicating independence and how to recognize it on a t-plot, contrast figure 5.4 with figure 5.24, where the assumption of independence does not hold. In the latter plot we can discern a pattern of **cycles** which enable the observer to make educated guesses regarding the next observation. This can be done by exploiting the pattern of the cycles. The observations 65–105 in figure 5.24 give rise to the following pattern of signs:

$$+++++-++++-++---+---+-++--+--++-+++--+++.$$

From this sequence of pluses and minuses we discern a regular pattern of runs up and down which can be utilized to guess the next up or down. In particular, the sequence of runs up and down are, respectively:

$$\{5,4,2,1,1,2,1,2,3,3\}^+, \ \{1,1,3,3,1,2,2,1,2\}^-.$$

Looking at these runs we can see that if we were trying to guess the next change and the previous was an increase (decrease) we would be correct in a sizeable proportion of our guesses to predict an increase (decrease). This pattern indicates the presence of *positive dependence*: an increase tends to be followed by an increase and a decrease by a decrease. The presence of dependence is confirmed by the various sizes of runs which differ significantly from the expected numbers derived above under independence. For instance, the number of all size runs is just 19, much smaller than the expected under independence: 26.

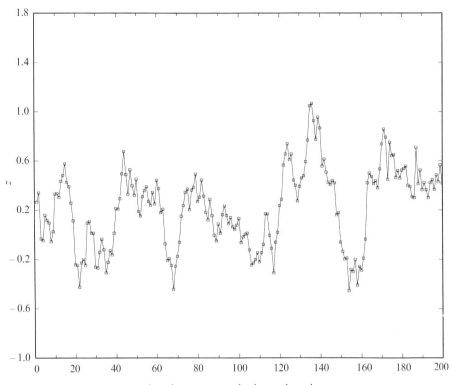

Figure 5.24 Simulated NID positively dependent data

A different pattern of dependence is exhibited in figure 5.25 where we can see **alternating ups and downs** which can help us predict the next observation in most of the cases along the *t*-axis! The observations 65–105 in figure 5.25 give rise to the following pattern of signs:

$$+-+-+-+-+-+-+-++++-+-+-+-+-++-+-+-+-+-+-.$$

From this sequence of pluses and minuses we discern a regular pattern of runs which can be utilized to guess the next up or down. In particular, the sequence of runs up and down are:

$$\{1,1,1,1,1,1,1,4,1,1,1,1,1,1,1,1,1,1\}^{+}, \{1,1,1,1,1,1,1,1,1,1,1,1,2,1,1,1,1,1,1\}^{-}.$$

Looking at these runs we can see that if we were trying to guess the next change and the previous was an increase (decrease) we would be correct in a sizeable proportion of our guesses to predict a decrease (increase). This pattern indicates the presence of *negative dependence*: an increase tends to be followed by a decrease and a decrease by an increase. The presence of dependence is confirmed by the various sizes of runs which differ significantly from the expected numbers derived above under independence. For instance, the number of all size runs is just 36, much larger than the expected under independence: 26.

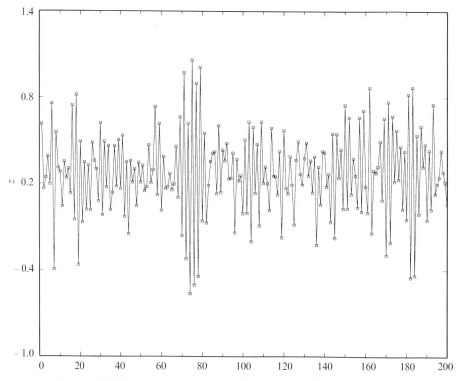

Figure 5.25 Simulated NID negatively dependent data

Example

Let us return to the exam scores data; see table 1.6 and figure 1.9 and figure 1.10, reproduced for convenience. In the case of the exam scores data arranged in alphabetical order
we observe the following runs:

$$\{1,1,4,1,1,3,1,1,1,1,2,1,1,1,1,1,1,2,2,1,1,2,3,1,1\}^+,$$

$$\{1,1,3,1,1,2,2,1,2,1,2,2,3,1,2,1,2,1,2,1,2,1,1,1,1\}^-.$$

From above, expected mean values of the various runs are:

$$E(R)=46.3,\ E(R_1)=29,\ E(R_2)=12.6,\ E(R_3')=4.5.$$

The number of all size runs is 50, the number of size 1 runs is 32, the number of size 2
runs is 13, the number of size 3 or greater runs is 5, and they are all very close to the
numbers expected under independence.

On the other hand, the marks data arranged according to the sitting arrangement
during the exam (see figure 1.2) exhibit very different runs up and down:

$$\{3,2,4,4,1,4,3,6,1,4\}^+,\ \{2,2,2,4,3,3,7,4,6,1,3\}^-,$$

which are nowhere near the numbers expected under independence. The number of all
size runs is 21 (expected 46), the number of size 1 runs is 3 (expected 29), the number of
size 2 runs is 4 (expected 13), the number of size 3 or greater runs is 13, (expected 5).

Table 1.6. *Data on Principles of economics exam scores*

98.0	43.0	77.0	51.0	93.0	85.0	76.0	56.0	59.0	62.0
67.0	79.0	66.0	98.0	57.0	80.0	73.0	68.0	71.0	74.0
83.0	75.0	70.0	76.0	56.0	84.0	80.0	53.0	70.0	67.0
100.0	78.0	65.0	77.0	88.0	81.0	66.0	72.0	65.0	58.0
45.0	63.0	57.0	87.0	51.0	40.0	70.0	56.0	75.0	92.0
73.0	59.0	81.0	85.0	62.0	93.0	84.0	68.0	76.0	62.0
65.0	84.0	59.0	60.0	76.0	81.0	69.0	95.0	66.0	87.0

In chapter 15 we will make the above informal checks more precise by specifying proper tests for departures from independence. For that we need to use not just the mean values of the various random variables referring to the runs up and down but also their second moments; the difference between the expected and the actual runs has to be considered relative to the standard deviation to decide whether it is large enough. Intuitively, the departure is measured in terms of the standard deviations of the random variable in question. For reference purposes we also note the second moments below:

$$Var(R) = \frac{16n - 29}{90},$$

$$Var(R_1) = \frac{305n - 347}{720}, \quad Var(R_2) = \frac{51106n - 73859}{453600}, \quad Cov(R_1, R_2) = -\frac{19n + 11}{210},$$

$$Var(R_1') = \frac{16n - 29}{90}, \quad Var(R_2') = \frac{57n - 43}{720}, \quad Cov(R_1', R_2') = -\frac{5n - 3}{60}.$$

For these as well as the general formulae (which are highly complicated) see Wolfowitz (1944), Levene and Wolfowitz (1944) and Levene (1952). As shown in chapter 15, the above conjectures relating to the various data plots are confirmed by formal testing. As will be apparent in the sequel, the above informal checks for detecting departures from independence will also be sensitive to departures from homogeneity.

We conclude this subsection by emphasizing once more that the various plots presented above are indicative in nature and should not be interpreted as unique visualizations of the corresponding probabilistic concepts. Indeed, a major characteristic of randomness is the lack of uniqueness. The reader who has access to computer software which allows for simulating pseudo-random numbers is strongly encouraged to generate his own *t*-plots and compare them with those given above.

5.6   Homogeneity and the *t*-plot

The **third** important feature exhibited by figure 5.4 comes in the form of a certain apparent homogeneity over *t* exhibited by the plot. With the mind's eye we can view *t*-homogeneity by imagining a density function cutting the *x*-axis at each observation point and standing vertically across the *t*-plot with its support parallel to the *y*-axis. Under complete homogeneity all such density functions are identical in shape and location and create a dome-like structure over the observations. That is, for each observation we have

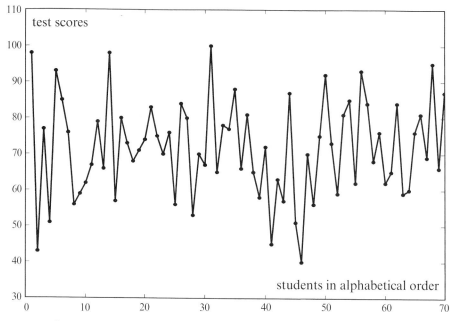

Figure 1.9 Exam scores data (alphabetical)

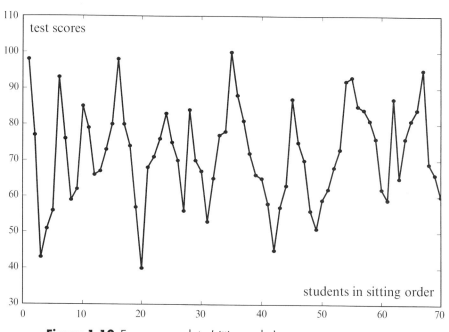

Figure 1.10 Exam scores data (sitting order)

a density over it and we view the observation as the one realized from the particular density hanging over it. Naturally, if the relevant distribution is Normal we expect more observations in the middle of the density but if the distribution is Uniform we expect the observations to be dispersed uniformly over the relevant area.

This *t*-homogeneity can be assessed in two different but equivalent ways. The first way to assess the *t*-homogeneity exhibited by the data in figure 5.4 is to use the first two data moments evaluated via a thought experiment. The mean of the data can be imagined by averaging the values of $\{Z_t, t = 1, 2, ..., T\}$ moving along the *t*-axis. As can be seen, such averaging will give rise to a constant mean close to zero. The variance of the data can be imagined using the virtual bands on either side of the mean of the data which will cover almost all observations. In the case where the bands appear to be parallel to the mean axis there appears to exist some sort of second-order homogeneity. In the case of the observed data in figure 5.4 it looks as though the data exhibit both mean and variance homogeneity.

The second way to assess *t*-homogeneity is in terms of the following thought experiment.

Thought experiment *Choose a frame high enough to cover the values on the y-axis but smaller than half of the x-axis and slide this frame along the latter axis keeping an eye on the picture inside the frame. If that picture does not change drastically, then the observed data exhibit homogeneity along the dimension t.*

In the case of the data in figure 5.26 we can see that this thought experiment suggests that the particular data do exhibit complete homogeneity because the picture in the three frames shown do not differ in any systematic way. The chance regularity pattern of homogeneity, as exhibited by the data in figure 5.26, corresponds to the probabilistic notion of *Identical Distribution*. Note that NI denotes Normal, Independent.

In contrast to figures 5.4 and 5.26, the mean of the data in figure 5.27 is no longer constant (it increases with *t*) and the thought experiment of sliding a frame along the *x*-axis (see figure 5.28 where the picture in each windows changes drastically) will easily detect such heterogeneity over *t*. When the change looks like a function of the index *t* we call it a **trend**.

Viewing the variance of the data as being related to the two the bands on either side of the mean which cover the large majority of the observations, we conclude that, because the variation around the data mean is relatively constant, the variance in figure 5.27 seems to be homogeneous.

To understand what this entails it should be contrasted with figure 5.29 where the variance changes with *t*. Again, the thought experiment of sliding the frame will easily detect such a variance heterogeneity (see figure 5.30); the first frame differs substantially from the second and the third, indicating the presence of heterogeneity. Heterogeneity, however, comes in numerous forms.

Figures 5.31 and 5.32 depict simulated data series which exhibit a different kind of heterogeneity in terms of the first two moments. In figure 5.31 the data exhibit **a shift** in the mean and in figure 5.32 the data exhibit a shift in the variance. These forms of moment heterogeneity can be combined to yield data *t*-plots which exhibit heterogeneity

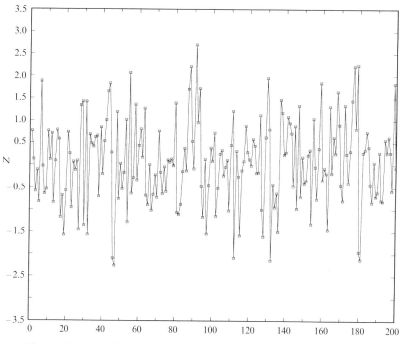

Figure 5.4 Simulated NIID data

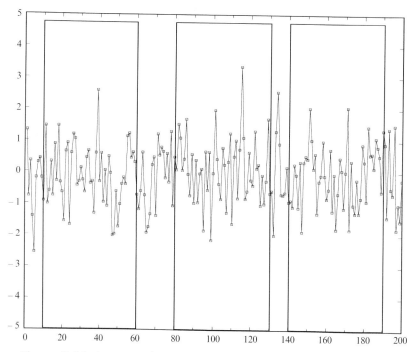

Figure 5.26 Assessing *t*-homogeneity using the window experiment

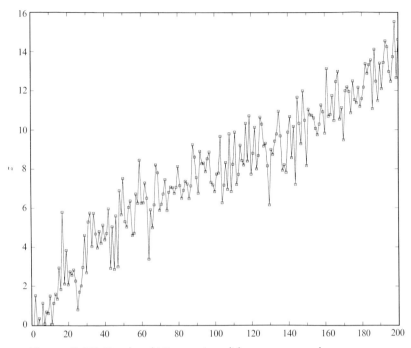

Figure 5.27 Simulated NI mean (trend) heterogeneous data

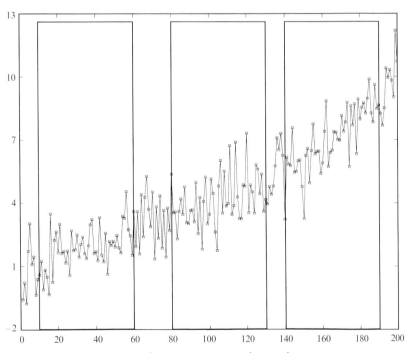

Figure 5.28 Assessing *t*-homogeneity using the window experiment

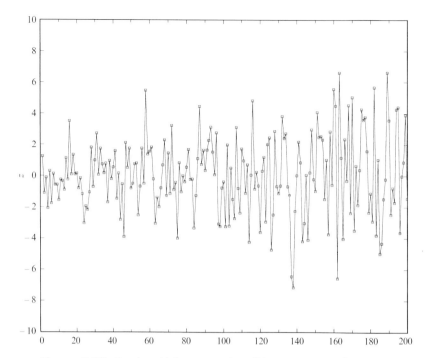

Figure 5.29 Simulated NI variance (trend) heterogeneous data

in both the mean and the variance. In figure 5.33 both the mean and variance are trending and in figure 5.34 both moments exhibit shifts at observation $t = 100$.

At this stage it is important to note that some forms of heterogeneity can be utilized to improve the modeler's ability to predict. In the case of the mean-heterogeneity exhibited by the data in figure 5.27, the modeler can utilize this heterogeneity in order to predict the general direction of the next few observations. However, the modeler is in no better position to predict the next observation than in the case of the data in figure 5.4. The heterogeneity in figure 5.27 establishes general trends but is unrelated to the dependence that might exist in the data.

Yet another important form of heterogeneity is related to the so-called *seasonal effects*. The term **seasonality** refers to a particular form of heterogeneity which repeats itself at regular intervals (we call seasons). In figure 5.35 we can see a regular pattern in the form of a sinusoidal function which repeats itself every 24 observations. In figure 5.36 the data exhibit both mean heterogeneity (a trend) and a seasonal pattern.

In cases where the observed data are dominated by the presence of strong seasonal effects as in the case of the data exhibited in figures 5.35 and 5.36, predicting the next observation is relatively easy because the patterns are almost non-stochastic. This should be contrasted with the cycles in connection with positive dependence discussed above.

It is very important to bring out the difference between the regular seasonal pattern and the positive dependence pattern exhibited in figure 5.37. In figures 5.37 and 5.38 the data exhibit positive dependence which is clearly not half as regular as the seasonal pattern exhibited in figures 5.35 and 5.36, respectively. In the case of the data in figure

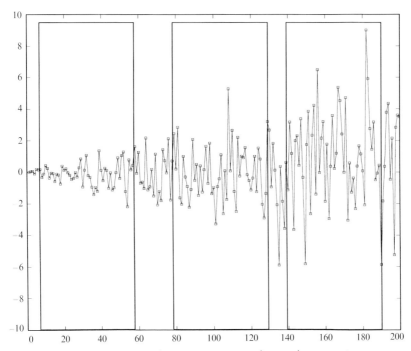

Figure 5.30 Assessing *t*-homogeneity using the window experiment

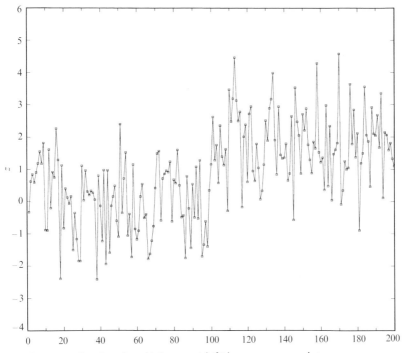

Figure 5.31 Simulated NI mean (shift) heterogeneous data

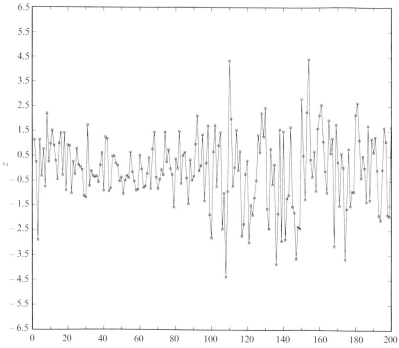

Figure 5.32 Simulated NI variance (shift) heterogeneous data

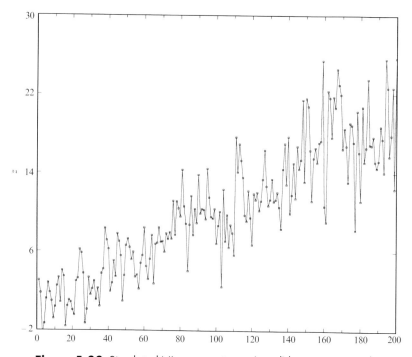

Figure 5.33 Simulated NI mean-variance (trend) heterogeneous data

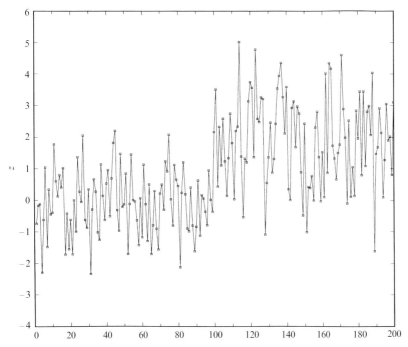

Figure 5.34 Simulated NI mean-variance (shift) heterogeneous data

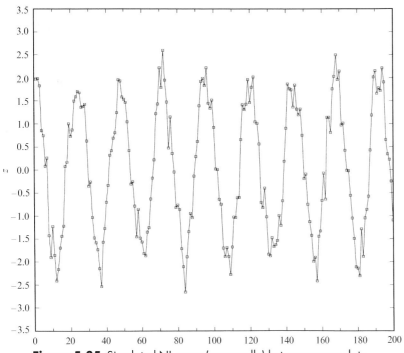

Figure 5.35 Simulated NI mean (seasonally) heterogeneous data

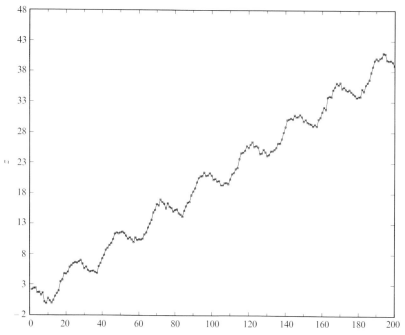

Figure 5.36 Simulated NI mean (seasonally, trend) heterogeneous data

5.38, in addition to the positive dependence we can also discern a strong mean heterogeneity. It must be said that most economic macro data series exhibit both of these features.

5.6.1 Assessing the distribution in non-random samples

As noted above, in cases where the sample is non-IID it not advisable to proceed to assess its distribution because the results will usually be very misleading. This can be easily confirmed using the thought experiment of turning the t-plot 90° clockwise and letting the observations drop vertically into a pile in the case of the figures 5.27–5.38. This statement appears convincing in the cases of heterogeneity but it might not be as clear in the case of dependence.

To convince the reader that it is a bad idea to proceed to assess the distribution assumption in cases of dependent data, consider the data in figure 5.37 exhibiting positive dependence but no heterogeneity. The histogram, the smoothed histogram (line with triangles) and the Normal density (line with circles) are shown in figure 5.39. As we can see, the histogram and smoothed histogram appear skewed to the left and close to bimodal; the Normal density is plotted on the same graph for comparison purposes. Any attempt to assess the distribution by looking at the histogram (or smoothed histogram) will lead the modeler astray.

The question which arises at this stage is: How does one proceed to assess the distribution assumption in cases where the data exhibit dependence and/or heterogeneity? The

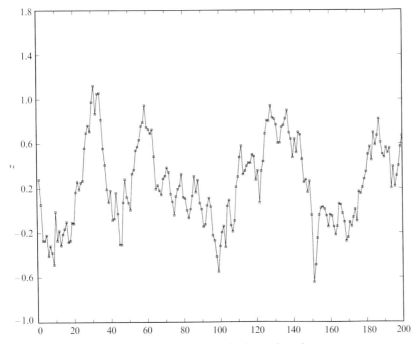

Figure 5.37 Simulated NID, positively dependent data

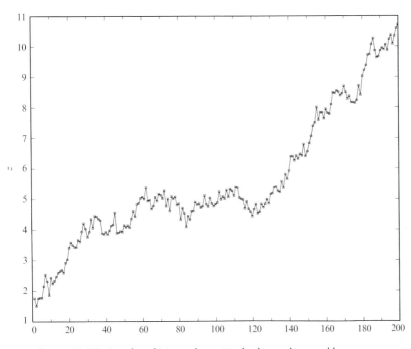

Figure 5.38 Simulated Normal, positively dependent and heterogeneous data

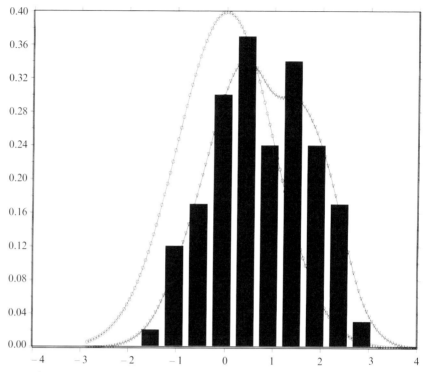

Figure 5.39 Smoothing the histogram of simulated Normal, dependent data

simple answer is to find a way to "remove" such features before the assessment of the distribution. The act of removing the dependence and heterogeneity will be referred to as *dememorizing* and *detrending*, respectively. It goes without saying that dememorizing and detrending are used to find a way to make a preliminary assessment of the nature of the distribution that might describe certain data and not to throw away such information!

In practice the success of dememorizing and/or detrending depends on how well we can describe the nature of dependence and heterogeneity exhibited by a certain data set. The discussion that follows is very brief because in order to be able to describe dependence and heterogeneity we need to use numerous concepts which will be introduced in the next few chapters. In the meantime, however, we will give some indication what dememorizing and detrending entails.

Although heterogeneity can come in many flavors, the three most widely used types are the ones used in the t-plots above. The first kind comes in the form of mean (or variance) heterogeneity as a polynomial in t:

$$E(Z_t) := \mu_t = \alpha_0 + \alpha_1 t + \alpha_2 t^2 + \ldots + \alpha_m t^m, \text{ for some } m \geq 1, t \in \mathbb{T}.$$

The second is also mean (or variance) heterogeneity in the form of a shift at t_m:

$$E(Z_t) := \mu_t = \alpha_0 + \alpha_m D_m, \text{ for some } m \geq 1, t \in \mathbb{T},$$

where D_m is a so-called dummy variable of the form:

$$D_m = \begin{cases} 1, \text{ for } t = t_m, \\ 0, \text{ for } t \neq t_m, \end{cases} t \in \mathbb{T},$$

$$\overset{t_m}{D_m} = \{0,0,0,\dots,0,1,0,\dots,0,\dots\}$$

This can be easily extended to any subset $\mathbb{T}_m \subset \mathbb{T}$, not just one observation. The third type of heterogeneity comes in the form of seasonality which is often captured in one of two ways: (a) dummy variables (one for each "season") or using the trigonometric polynomials. The *seasonal dummy variables*, say for quarterly data, take the form:

$$Q_{1t} := \{1,0,0,0,1,0,0,0,1,0,0,0,1,0,0,0,1,0,0,0,\dots\},$$
$$Q_{2t} := \{0,1,0,0,0,1,0,0,0,1,0,0,0,1,0,0,0,1,0,0,\dots\},$$
$$Q_{3t} := \{0,0,1,0,0,0,1,0,0,0,1,0,0,0,1,0,0,0,1,0,\dots\},$$
$$Q_{4t} := \{0,0,0,1,0,0,0,1,0,0,0,1,0,0,0,1,0,0,0,1,\dots\}.$$

The *trigonometric polynomials*, say for monthly data, take the form:

$$E(Z_t) := \mu_t = \sum_{k=0}^{m} \alpha_k \cos\left(\frac{2\pi kt}{12}\right) + \delta_k \sin\left(\frac{2\pi kt}{12}\right), t \in \mathbb{T}.$$

In the case of dependence the most widely used technique for describing it (and thus being able to remove it) comes in the form of the *autoregressive representation*, for $p \geq 1$:

$$E(Z_t|Z_{t-1},\dots,Z_1) = \alpha_0 + \alpha_1 Z_{t-1} + \alpha_2 Z_{t-2} + \dots + \alpha_p Z_{t-p}, t \in \mathbb{T}.$$

Dememorizing amounts to estimating such representations and then subtracting out the estimated effects (see chapters 8, 15, and Spanos (1986) for details).

The above representations can be easily combined in order to capture both the dependence and heterogeneity features, say for some $p \geq 1$:

$$E(Z_t|Z_{t-1},\dots,Z_1) = \alpha_0 + \alpha_1 t + \dots + \alpha_m t^m + \beta_1 Z_{t-1} + \dots + \beta_p Z_{t-p}, t \in \mathbb{T}.$$

We conclude this subsection emphasizing again that in real data modeling the issue of assessing the distribution, dependence, and heterogeneity features of the data will not be as straightforward as they seem from the above discussion. An exploratory data analysis is often needed in order to separate the various features at a preliminary stage and assess them properly. In terms of separation of features the distribution assumption should not be assessed before the dependence and heterogeneity features are removed.

5.7   The empirical cdf and related graphs*

5.7.1   The notion of the empirical cdf (ecdf)

The distribution assumption of a random variable X in the proceeding discussion was assessed in terms of the density function and its sample analogue. In this section we proceed to consider assessing the distribution assumption in terms of the cumulative

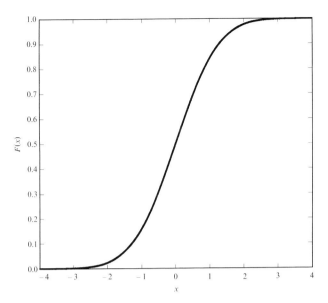

Figure 5.40 The cdf of the Normal distribution

distribution function (cdf) and its sample analogue. To remind the reader, the cdf of a random variable X is defined by (see chapter 3):

$$F_X(x) := \mathbb{P}(s : X(s) \le x) = \mathbb{P}X^{-1}(-\infty, x].$$

The cdf of the Normal distribution is shown in figure 5.40. For a given realization of the sample $\mathbf{X} := (X_1, X_2, \ldots, X_n)$, say $\mathbf{x} := (x_1, x_2, \ldots, x_n)$, the sample equivalent of the cdf is the *empirical cumulative distribution function* (ecdf):

$$\hat{F}_n(x) = \frac{[\text{no. of } (X_1, X_2, \ldots, X_n) \text{ whose realization do not exceed } x]}{n} = \frac{1}{n} \sum_{k=1}^{n} \mathbb{1}_{(-\infty, x]}(X_k),$$

where $\mathbb{1}_A(x)$ is the indicator function defined by:

$$\mathbb{1}_A(x_i) = \begin{cases} 1, & \text{if } x \in A, \\ 0, & \text{if } x \in A. \end{cases}$$

NOTE that the ecdf as defined above is a function of the form:

$$\hat{F}_n(.): \mathbb{R} \to U_n, \text{ where } U_n := \left\{ 0, \frac{1}{n}, \frac{2}{n}, \ldots, \frac{n-1}{n}, 1 \right\}.$$

In this sense $\hat{F}_n(x)$ refers to the *relative frequency* of the observations not exceeding the value x. In terms of the *ordered sample* $(X_{[1]} \le X_{[2]} \le \cdots \le X_{[n]})$ (see chapter 4) and its realization:

$$x_{[1]} \le x_{[2]} \le \cdots \le x_{[n]}, \tag{5.2}$$

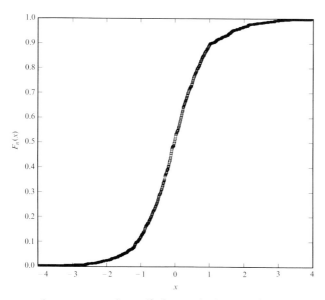

Figure 5.41 The ecdf of Canada/USA exchange rate data

the ecdf function $F_n(x)$ is defined by:

$$\hat{F}_n(x) := \begin{cases} 0 \text{ for } x < x_{[1]}, \\ \dfrac{k}{n} \text{ for } x_{[k]} \le x < x_{[k+1]}, \ k = 1,2,\ldots,n-1, \\ 1 \text{ for } x \ge x_{[n]}. \end{cases}$$

In the case where all the values in (5.2) are distinct then strict inequalities hold and at each point $x_{[k]}$ the function $\hat{F}_n(x)$ has a jump equal to $\frac{1}{n}$. In the case where some of the values are the same, say m of them have the same value, then at that point the function $\hat{F}_n(x)$ has a jump equal to $\frac{m}{n}$. That is, the ecdf assigns to each set $A_k := \{x_{k-1} < X_i \le x_k\}$, on the real line the proportion of the sample observations that lie in that set. When viewed as a function of the observations $(x_1, x_2, \ldots, x_n)$, $\hat{F}_n(x)$ has the following properties:

(a) uniquely defined,
(b) its range is $[0,1]$,
(c) non-decreasing and continuous on the right, and
(d) it is piecewise constant with jumps $\left(\text{multiples of } \frac{1}{n}\right)$ at the observed points,

i.e., it enjoys all the properties of its theoretical counterpart, the cdf.

In figure 5.41 we can see the ecdf of the exchange rate data shown in figure 5.63 (see also figure 1.4) which because of the number of observations involved ($n = 953$) looks very smooth. This is the result of the fact that the range of values of the ecdf is U_n: $= \left\{ 0, \frac{1}{n}, \frac{2}{n}, \ldots, \frac{(n-1)}{n}, 1 \right\}$, and as n increases the jumps become smaller and smaller, giving the impression of a continuous function such as the case of figure 5.41.

By comparing the cdf of the Normal (see figure 5.40) and the ecdf of the exchange rate data (see figure 5.41) it looks as though the Normal is not the most appropriate distribution for this data; see figure 5.42 which superimposes both plots.

The problem, however, is how to argue that the discrepancies shown in figure 5.42 are "large enough" to warrant rejecting the distribution assumption in question. In figure 5.42 we can see that around the median the ecdf appears to be close to the cdf of the Normal distribution but as we move towards the tails there is an apparent discrepancy. One thing, however, is obvious: that the ecdf points towards a symmetric distribution.

In figures 5.43 and 5.44 we can see the cdf of the discrete Uniform distribution and the ecdf of the data which refer to the first 1000 digits of the irrational number $\sqrt{2}$ (see chapter 10). A direct comparison between the two reveals that they are not very far apart but again the problem is to find a more convenient way to assess the discrepancy.

The problem of comparing two curves in the context of the above plots is illustrated in figure 5.45. The first problem facing the modeler is the difficulty in choosing the distance between the two curves. As we can see in figure 5.45 the distance can be measured in two different ways: horizontally in terms of the *quantiles* x_q or vertically in terms of the *percentiles* $p = F_X(x)$ (see chapter 3). The second problem is that assessing curved distances by eye is treacherous. The eye finds it much easier to assess discrepancies from straight lines rather than curves.

The plots considered next will transform the above discrepancies into departures from straight lines. The first type of plot called a P-P plot uses the percentile distance and the other called the Q-Q plot uses the quantile distance.

5.7.2   Probability plots

In this subsection we consider two important graphical displays known as the P-P and Q-Q plots which provide a simple but effective way to evaluate the appropriateness of a probability model through the visual assessment of the discrepancy between shapes created by the pattern of points on a plot and some reference straight line. Both of these plots are based on the ordered sample and are based on a very simple idea: we plot the *ordered sample* (or some transformation of it) against some theoretical reference sample. The latter is chosen so as to ensure that if the postulated distribution is valid the graph of the ordered sample against the reference sample will be a straight line.

From chapter 4 we know that the cdf for $X_{[k]}$ for any random variable from the ordered sample $(X_{[1]}, X_{[2]}, \ldots, X_{[n]})$ takes the form:

$$F_{[k]}(x) = \mathbb{P}(X_{[k]} \leq x) = \sum_{m=k}^{n} \binom{n}{k} [F(x; \boldsymbol{\theta})]^m [1 - F(x; \boldsymbol{\theta})]^{n-m}.$$

The corresponding density function takes the form:

$$f_k(x) = \frac{n!}{(k-1)!(n-k)!} [F(x)]^{k-1} [1 - F(x)]^{n-k}.$$

The probability plots discussed next revolve around a Uniformly distributed ordered random sample; see Wilk and Gnadadesikan (1968).

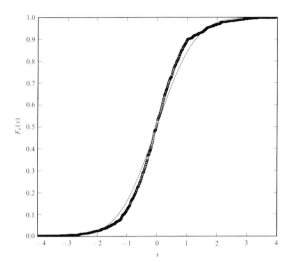

Figure 5.42 The ecdf of exchange rate data compared with the Normal cdf

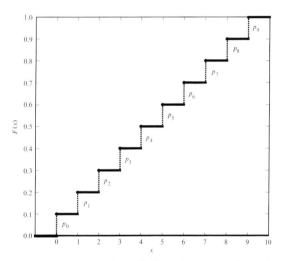

Figure 5.43 The cdf of the discrete Uniform distribution

P-P plots

Of particular interest is the case where X is *Uniformly distributed*:

$$X_k \sim \mathsf{U}(0,1),\ k = 1,2,\dots,n.$$

The density function of the ordered random variable $X_{[k]}$ takes the form:

$$f_k(x) = \frac{n!}{(k-1)!(n-k)!} x^{k-1}[1-x]^{n-k} f(x),\ x \in [0,1].$$

This is the density function of a *Beta* distribution with parameters $(k, n-k+1)$ (see appendix A) and thus:

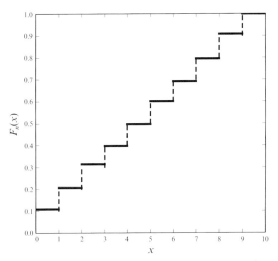

Figure 5.44 The ecdf of the data on the $\sqrt{2}$ expansion

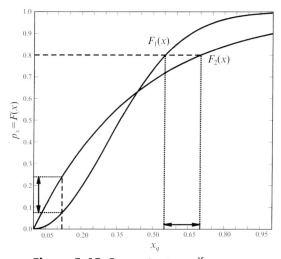

Figure 5.45 Comparing two cdfs

$$E(X_{[k]}) = \frac{k}{n+1}, \quad Var(X_{[k]}) = \frac{k(n-k+1)}{(n+1)^2(n+2)}, \quad Cov(X_{[k]}, X_{[j]}) = \frac{k(n-j+1)}{(n+1)^2(n+2)}, \quad k, j = 1, 2, \ldots, n.$$

In view of these results we can deduce that a plot of $x_{[k]}$ on $\frac{k}{n+1}$, $k = 1, 2, \ldots, n$ will give rise to a straight line given the proportionality and monotonicity between the two sets of values. This suggests an obvious graphical way to check the distribution assumption of a Uniform distribution using the *Uniform Probability-Plot* (*P-P*):

$$\left\{ \left(\frac{k}{n+1}, x_{[k]} \right), k = 1, 2, \ldots, n \right\}. \tag{5.3}$$

If the underlying distribution is indeed Uniform then this plot should look roughly like a straight line through the origin.

In figure 5.46 we can see a *t*-plot of simulated Uniform IID data whose P-P plot is given in figure 5.47. The P-P plot confirms our initial conjecture of a straight line. Caution should be exercised in checking linearity of plots because we are not talking about mathematical straight lines but empirical ones.

The above Uniform P-P plot can easily be extended to any other continuous distribution using the *probability integral transformation lemma* encountered in chapter 4. This lemma states that in the case where the random variable X is continuous and has cdf $F_X(.)$, then the transformation:

$$Y := F_X(X) \sim U(0,1). \tag{5.4}$$

This suggests that after we transform the ordered observations using their own cdf, $y_{[k]} := F_X(x_{[k]})$, $k = 1,2,\ldots,n$, we can assess the appropriateness of $F_X(.)$ by utilizing the $F_X(.)$ *distribution P-P plot*:

$$\left\{\left(\frac{k}{n+1}, F_X(x_{[k]})\right), k = 1,2,\ldots,n\right\}.$$

The distribution, which is almost always used as the comparison rod, is the Normal distribution with cdf:

$$\Phi(x) = \frac{1}{\sqrt{2\pi}} \int_{-\infty}^{x} \exp\left(-\tfrac{1}{2}z^2\right) dz.$$

The *Normal P-P plot* takes the form:

$$\left\{\left(\frac{k}{n+1}, \Phi(x_{[k]})\right), k = 1,2,\ldots,n\right\}. \tag{5.5}$$

In figure 5.49 we can see the Normal P-P plot for the Normal IID data shown in figure 5.48, which confirms the above theoretical result of a straight line.

In the same way, we can define many different P-P plots for a variety of distributions such as the Beta, the Gamma and the Weibull. What is more interesting, however, is to be able not only to assess whether the distribution underlying a certain set of IID observations belongs to a specific probability model but also to get some indications toward alternative probability models in cases where the original choice was inappropriate. For example we would like to know what the Normal P-P plot would look like if the observations came from alternative distributions such as the Uniform, the Exponential, the Cauchy, etc. This can be achieved using a particular form of the P-P plot we call standardized.

Standardized P-P plot

The probability integral transformation lemma says that in the case of a continuous random variable X, the transformation defined by its own cdf induces a Uniform distribution (see (5.4)) irrespective of the nature of the cdf $F_X(.)$. The reverse of this result, known as the *quantile transformation* (see chapter 3), says that the distribution of any continuous random variable X is determined via:

$$X = F_X^{-1}(y), \quad y \in [0,1] \tag{5.6}$$

This suggests that in cases where there exists an analytical expression for $F_X^{-1}(.)$ we can generate a theoretical sequence $(y_1, y_2, \ldots, y_n)$ of ordered, $F_X(.)$ distributed, random variables using:

$$y_{[k]} = F_X^{-1}(u_k), \quad u_k := \frac{k}{n+1}, \quad k = 1,2,\ldots,n. \tag{5.7}$$

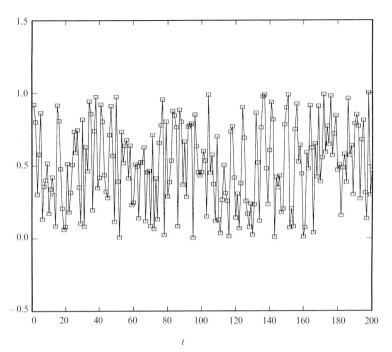

Figure 5.46 *t*-plot of simulated IID uniform data

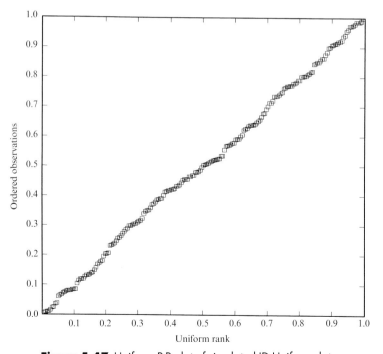

Figure 5.47 Uniform P-P plot of simulated ID Uniform data

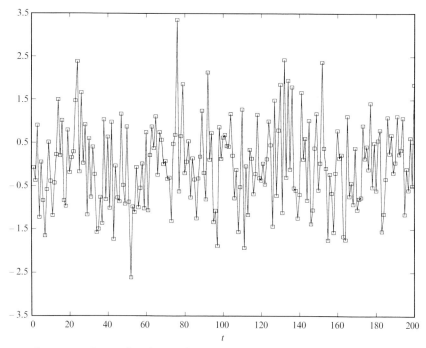

Figure 5.48 Simulated NIID data

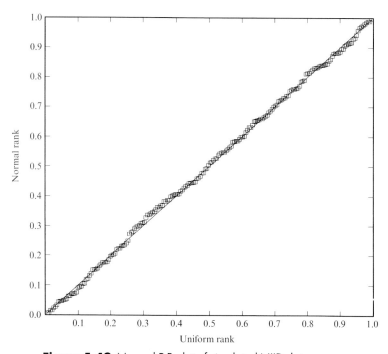

Figure 5.49 Normal P-P plot of simulated NIID data

Analytical expressions for the **inverse of cdf** in the case of three distributions are given below:

Cauchy $\qquad F^{-1}(u) = \tan\left[\pi\left(u - \tfrac{1}{2}\right)\right],$

Extreme value $\quad F^{-1}(u) = -\ln[-\ln(u)],$

Exponential $\quad F^{-1}(u) = [-\ln(1-u)].$ $\qquad\qquad$ (5.8)

Using this result we can proceed to generate distribution curves for any reference distribution by passing the artificially generated sequence $(y_{[1]}, y_{[2]}, \ldots, y_{[n]})$, after being standardized, through the cdf of the reference distribution using (5.4). The *standardization* of the theoretical sequence $(y_{[1]}, y_{[2]}, \ldots, y_{[n]})$ takes the form (see Gan *et al.* (1991)):

$$ y_k^* := \left(\frac{y_{[k]} - \bar{y}}{s_Y}\right),\ \bar{y} := \frac{1}{n}\sum_{i=1}^{n} y_{[i]},\ s_Y^2 := \frac{1}{n-1}\sum_{i=1}^{n}(y_{[i]} - \bar{y})^2. \qquad (5.9)$$

The *standardized P-P plot* for the reference distribution $F_R(.)$ takes the form:

$$\left\{(u_k, F_R(y_k^*)),\ \text{where}\ u_k = \frac{k}{n+1},\ k = 1,2,\ldots,n\right\}.$$

That is, beginning with the artificial sequence $\left\{u_k = \frac{k}{n+1},\ k = 1,2,\ldots,n\right\}$ we use (5.7) to artificially generate a sequence $(y_{[1]}, y_{[2]}, \ldots, y_{[n]})$ which traces a curve for a particular distribution $F_X(.)$. After standardizing the latter sequence we pass it through the *filter* of the reference cdf function $F_R(.)$ to trace a curve for $F_X(.)$ *viewed through the prism of the reference distribution*. This amounts to applying both the probability integral and the quantile transformations in the sense that, apart from the standardization, this amounts to:

$$F_R(F_X^{-1}(u_k)),\ k = 1,2,\ldots,n.$$

Having constructed the standardized P-P plot for the reference distribution $F_R(.)$ and introduced several distribution curves, we can proceed to assess a particular data set $(x_1, x_2, \ldots, x_n)$ using the line:

$$\left\{\left(\frac{k}{n+1}, F_R(x_k^*)\right),\ k = 1,2,\ldots,n\right\},$$

where $x_k^* := \left(\frac{x_{[k]} - \bar{x}}{s_X}\right)$ is the standardized data.

To illustrate this type of graph let us take the reference distribution to be the Normal and consider the question of generating distribution curves using the inverse cdfs given in (5.8). The *standardized Normal P-P plot* takes the form:

$$\left\{\left(\frac{k}{n+1}, \Phi(z_k^*)\right),\ k = 1,2,\ldots,n\right\}, \qquad\qquad (5.10)$$

where $\Phi(.)$ denotes the standard normal cdf and z_k^* denotes the *standardized form* of the ordered observations or the artificially generated sequences of distribution curves. In figure 5.50 we can see the simulated distribution curves of the Uniform (circle), the Exponential (square) and the Cauchy (inverted triangle) distributions.

The above reference distribution curves can be utilized to make informed guesses in cases where other plots indicate departures from Normality. In figure 5.51 we can see the standardized Normal P-P plot for the Uniform IID data together with the reference Uniform distribution curve. As we can see, the match between the two is remarkable.

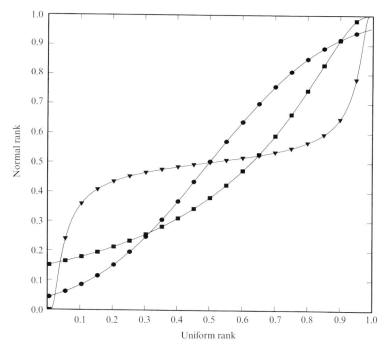

Figure 5.50 Normal S(P-P) plot and reference distribution

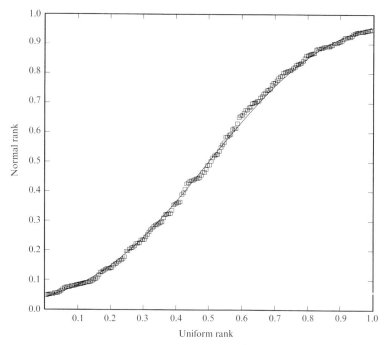

Figure 5.51 Normal S(P-P) plot of simulated ID Uniform data

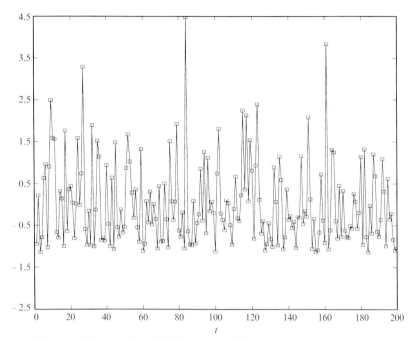

Figure 5.52 Simulated ID Exponential data

Less remarkable but still quite impressive is the match shown in figure 5.53, the standardized Normal P-P, between the reference Exponential distribution curve and the Exponential IID data whose t-plot is shown in figure 5.52. In figure 5.55 we can see the standardized Normal P-P plot of simulated Cauchy IID observations, whose t-plot is given in figure 5.54, matched against the reference Cauchy curve.

Q-Q plots

Let us return to the ordinary P-P plot. The Normal P-P plot (5.49) extends the Uniform P-P plot (5.47) in so far as it changes the ordered observations $(x_{[1]}, x_{[2]}, \ldots, x_{[n]})$ measured on the y-axis by replacing them with the normal *probability integral transformation* of the ordered observations denoted by $(y_{[1]}, y_{[2]}, \ldots, y_{[n]})$, where $(y_{[k]} := \Phi(x_{[k]}), k = 1, \ldots, n)$. In the case of any other continuous cdfs, say $F_X(.)$, $(y_{[k]} := F_X(x_{[k]}), k = 1, \ldots, n)$.

Another interesting graphical display arises if we keep the ordered observations on the y-axis but replace the sequence $\left\{u_k := \left(\frac{k}{n+1}\right), k = 1, 2, \ldots, n\right\}$, measured on the x-axis by the sequence $\{F_X^{-1}(u_k), k = 1, 2, \ldots, n\}$. Recall from chapter 3 that $\left\{F_X^{-1}\left(\frac{k}{n+1}\right)\right\}$ is the $\left(\frac{k}{n+1}\right)$-quantile of the distribution $F_X(.)$. Moreover, the ordered observations $(x_{[1]}, x_{[2]}, \ldots, x_{[n]})$ are related to the quantiles via:

$$\left\{F_X^{-1}(q) = x_{[k]}, \text{ for any } q \text{ such that } \left(\frac{k-1}{n}\right) < q < \left(\frac{k}{n}\right)\right\}.$$

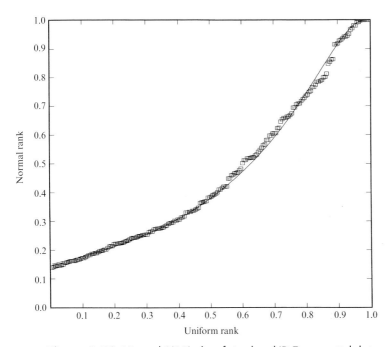

Figure 5.53 Normal S(P-P) plot of simulated ID Exponential data

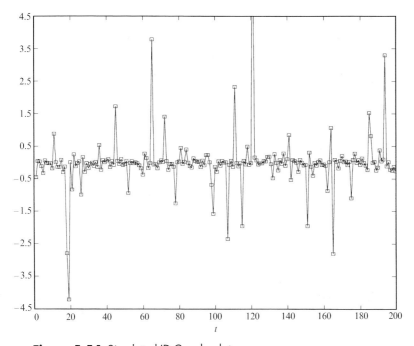

Figure 5.54 Simulated ID Cauchy data

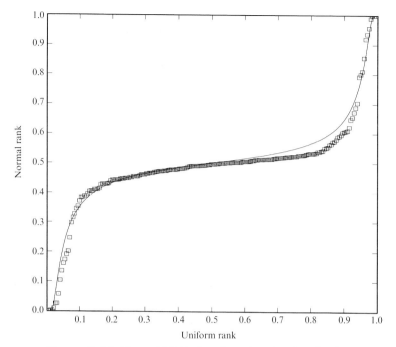

Figure 5.55 Normal S(P-P) plot of simulated ID Cauchy data

This suggests that instead of the uniform sequence $\left\{u_k := \left(\frac{k}{n+1}\right), k = 1,2,\ldots,n\right\}$ we could use a sequence $\{q_k, k = 1,2,\ldots,n\}$ which is chosen in a such way so as to ensure that:

$$F_X^{-1}(q_k) \simeq E(X_{[k]}).$$

We NOTE that the choice of the sequence $\{q_k, k = 1,2,\ldots,n\}$ is not a trivial matter because it depends on the nature of the distribution $F_X(.)$. However, in most cases the sequence takes the form:

$$q_k := \frac{(k-c)}{(n-2c+1)}, \text{ where } 0 \leq c \leq 1.$$

Putting the above pieces together will give rise to the so-called $F_X(.)$ *distribution Q-Q plot*:

$$\{(F_X^{-1}(q_k), X_{[k]}), k = 1,2,\ldots,n\}, \tag{5.11}$$

which, as in the case of the P-P plot, should yield roughly a straight line. The name derives from the fact that the variables measured on both axes can be thought of as *quantiles*; the ordered observations can be thought of as the sample (observation) quantiles and that of the y-axis as the theoretical quantiles of the distribution in question.

The most widely used Q-Q plot is that of the *Normal*, which is based on the sequence of approximate values: $q_k = \left(\frac{k-(0.375)}{n+0.25}\right), k = 1,2,\ldots,n$. Again, if the observations come from a Normal IID sample the Normal Q-Q plot should be roughly a straight line. Figure 5.56

shows the Normal Q-Q plot for simulated NIID observations. The Normal Q-Q plot is close to a straight line and very few observations are beyond the two standard deviations range.

As with the *t*-plots and smoothed histograms, the Normal is often used as a yardstick in comparisons with other distributions. The Normal rank Q-Q plot is used to indicate how other distributions differ from the Normal. For example, figure 5.57 shows the Normal Q-Q plot of the simulated data exhibited in figure 5.52. As we can see, the tails bend up on the left and down on the right indicating lighter tails than the Normal; what we called *platykurtosis* in chapter 3. It must be emphasized that the figures 5.47, 5.51 and 5.57 represent different plots for the same simulated Uniform IID data. The former is a Uniform P-P plot and measures the Uniform rank $\left(\frac{k}{n+1}, k=1,2,...,n\right)$ on the *x*-axis but the latter is a Normal Q-Q plot with the Normal rank $\left(\Phi^{-1}\left(\frac{k-(0.375)}{n+0.25}\right), k=1,2,...,n\right)$, on the *x*-axis. As a result, the Normal Q-Q plot should be interpreted as assessing the distribution features of the data through the viewing angle of the Normal distribution; see D'Agostino (1986).

The Normal Q-Q plot in figure 5.57 should be contrasted with the Normal Q-Q plot of simulated Student's t IID data with 5 degrees of freedom, shown in figure 5.59; the *t*-plot of the simulated data is given in figure 5.58. As we can see, the Normal Q-Q plot of the Student's t data bends down at the left and up at the right end, indicating more negative observations in the left tail and more positive observations in the right tail, i.e., heavier tails than the Normal (what we called *leptokurtosis* in chapter 3).

The Normal Q-Q plot is often the easiest way to check both platykurtosis and leptokurtosis. The Normal rank P-plot is also useful in assessing skewness. In figure 5.60 we can see the Normal Q-Q plot of simulated log-Normal IID.

In view of the above discussion in relation to the heavy and light tails we can see that the Normal Q-Q plot of the log-Normal IID data is bent up at the left (lighter left tail) and up on the right (heavier right tail); what we called *skewed* to the right in chapter 3. The opposite of course happens in the case of IID observations from a distribution *skewed* to the left. In figures 5.61 and 5.62 we can see the *t*-plot and Q-Q plot of simulated IID Beta (with parameters 7 and 1) data.

P-P versus Q-Q plots

The P-P plot amounts to plotting a set of uniformly distributed ordered observations against the theoretical values assuming that the random sample is uniformly distributed: the uniform rank sequence $\left\{u_k:=\frac{k}{n+1}, k=1,...,n\right\}$. Its theoretical basis is the probability integral transformation lemma. The Q-Q plot amounts to plotting a set of ordered observations against a set of theoretical values $\{F_X^{-1}(q_k), k=1,...,n\}$ chosen to ensure that $F_X^{-1}(q_k) \simeq E(X_{[k]})$. Its theoretical basis is the quantile transformation lemma.

P-P plot: $\left\{(u_k, F_X(X_{[k]})), k=1,2,...,n, \text{ where } u_k:=\frac{k}{n+1}\right\}$,

Q-Q plot: $\{(F_X^{-1}(q_k), X_{[k]}), k=1,2,...,n, \text{ where } F_X^{-1}(q_k) \simeq E(X_{[k]})\}$.

In view of the fact that the values $(u_k, k=1,2,...,n)$ are uniformly spaced but the values $(F_X^{-1}(q_k), k=1,2,...,n)$ are often more tightly bunched together in the region around the

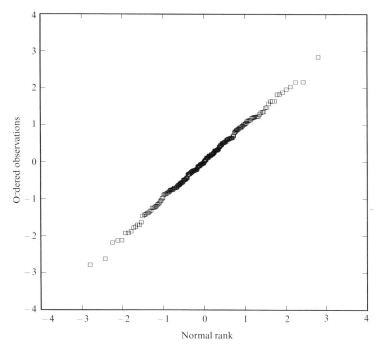

Figure 5.56 Normal Q-Q plot of simulated NIID data

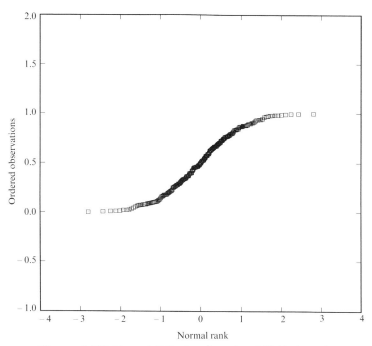

Figure 5.57 Normal Q-Q plot of simulated IID Uniform data

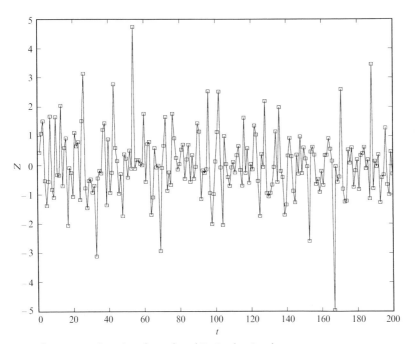

Figure 5.58 *t*-plot of simulated ID Student's *t* data

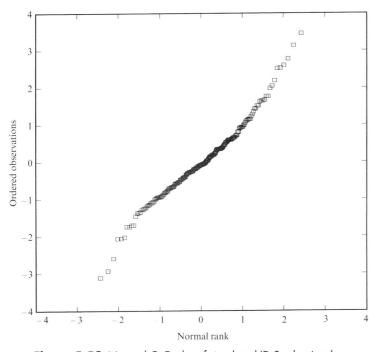

Figure 5.59 Normal Q-Q plot of simulated ID Student's *t* data

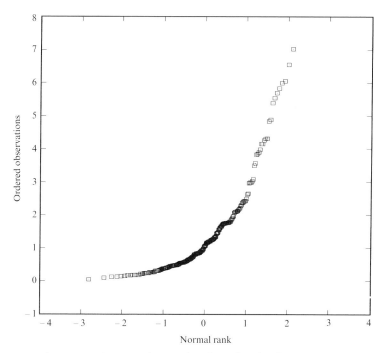

Figure 5.60 Normal Q-Q plot of simulated ID log-Normal data

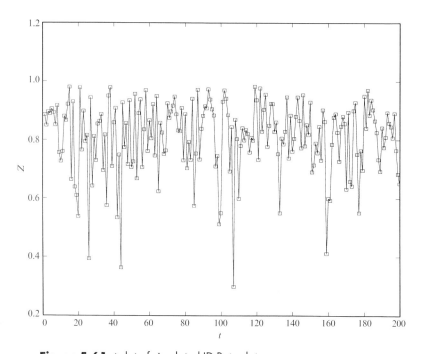

Figure 5.61 t-plot of simulated ID Beta data

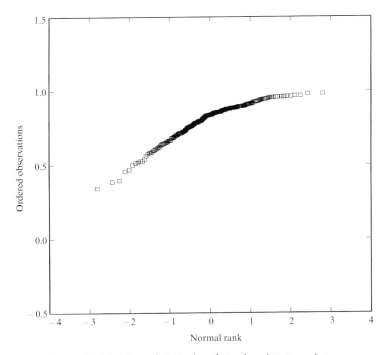

Figure 5.62 Normal Q-Q plot of simulated ID Beta data

mode on the x-axis, one would expect that the Q-Q plot will be more sensitive to discrepancies in the tail regions than a P-P plot. By the same token a P-P plot is likely to be
more sensitive to discrepancies in the modal region of the assumed distribution. This
suggests that these two plots can be used as complements not substitutes.

One disadvantage of the Q-Q plot is that the reference distribution curves are not
readily available as in the case of the P-P plot. In addition, the P-P plot is easier to work
with because the range of values on both axes is always the same: $[0,1]$. We conclude this
section by mentioning an advantage of the Q-Q plot in so far as it can be used to estimate
the location and scale parameters of the reference distribution as the intercept and slope
of the straight line the observations give rise to, since the graph:

$$\left(\left(\tfrac{X_{[k]}-\mu}{\sigma}\right), F_X^{-1}(q_k)\right), \text{ and } (X_{[k]}, \mu + \sigma\, G_X^{-1}(q_k)), k = 1,2,\ldots,n,$$

are equivalent for $G_X(x) = F_X\left(\left(\tfrac{x-\mu}{\sigma}\right)\right)$ (see D'Agostino and Stephens (1986)).

A cautionary note

We conclude this subsection by noting that in assessing the distributional nature of the
data using a t-plot we have suppressed the indexing dimension. That is, the ordering of
the observations plays no role in assessing its distributional features. This, however, presupposes that the plotted data are IID. In the case of non-IID data suppressing the
ordering can give rise to very misleading histograms as shown above. It is very important
to emphasize again that before one can assess the distributional nature of the data, it is

imperative to ensure that the data are IID. As argued above, in cases where the data exhibit some dependence and/or heterogeneity the modeler needs to filter out these features before assessing the distributional features of such data.

5.7.3 Empirical example: exchange rates data

In order to illustrate some of the graphical techniques discussed above let us consider the exchange rate data plotted in figure 1.4, also shown in figure 5.63. As mentioned in chapter 1, these data refer to log-changes ($\Delta \ln X_t$) of the Canadian/US exchange rate for the period 1973–1992 and refer to weekly observations ($T = 953$). The sample size was chosen to be very large in order to bypass problems of inadequate information which arise in cases of small sample size. Also, at this stage we assume that the data are close to a random sample.

At first sight the t-plot of the data exhibits the bell-shaped symmetry we associate with Normal and other elliptically symmetric distributions. In order to assess its distributional features we begin with a Normal Q-Q plot shown in figure 5.64. This plots shows most clearly that the data cannot be described by a Normal distribution because the graph is not a straight line; the shape reminds one of figure 5.65 representing simulated Student's t data with the reference distribution being the Cauchy.

This conjecture is explored further in figure 5.67 in a Normal P-P plot for the exchange rate data (the curve in squares) with the Cauchy as a reference distribution (the inverted S solid line). NOTE that we use the Cauchy as the reference distribution because the inverse cdf of the Student's t distribution does not have an analytic expression in general, but it has one in the case of one degree of freedom (d.f.); the Cauchy distribution. This plot leaves no doubts in the mind of the observer that the exchange rate data are clearly leptokurtic and exhibit some affinity with the Student's t distribution.

The smoothed histogram, shown in figure 5.66 (inverted triangles identify the curve), provides additional evidence that the Normal distribution (identified by the circles) is clearly inadequate for describing the data and some leptokurtic distribution, such as the Student's t, might provide a better description. The difficulty with deciding to adopt the Student's t distribution is the degrees of freedom parameter ν which determines the extent of its leptokurticity:

$$\alpha_4 := 3 + \frac{6}{\nu - 4}.$$

Figure 5.65 indicates that for the exchange rate data the degrees of freedom parameter ν lies somewhere between 1 and 12. One can justify this on the basis that $\nu > 1$ since the Cauchy is somewhat off and $\nu < 12$ because the Student's t with degrees of freedom higher than that is very close to the Normal. One way to proceed in order to narrow down the range of values of this parameter is to plot Student's t densities in figure 5.66 with different degrees of freedom and choose the one closest to the smoothed histogram. Although this procedure does not seem unreasonable, it can be misleading because, as mentioned above, the smoothed histogram depends crucially on the value of the bandwidth h chosen. In this case the problem of choosing h is particularly crucial because any

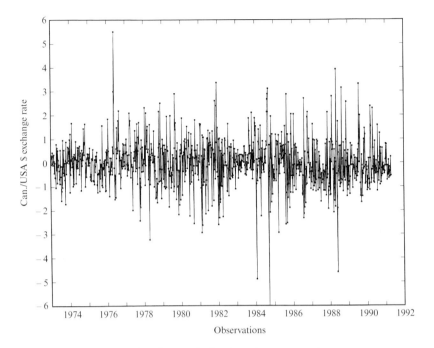

Figure 5.63 *t*-plot of Canada/USA exchange rate data

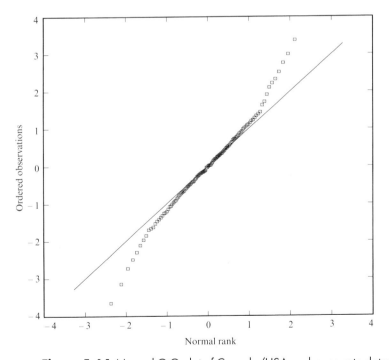

Figure 5.64 Normal Q-Q plot of Canada/USA exchange rate data

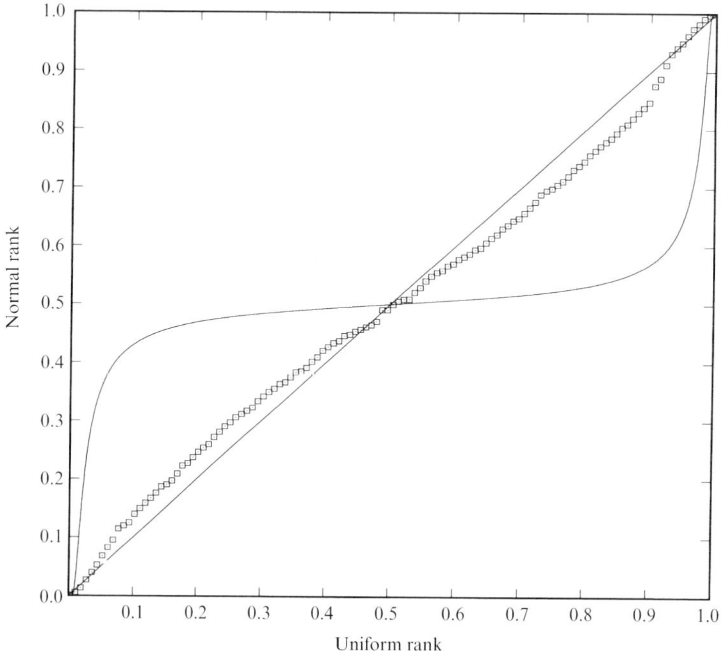

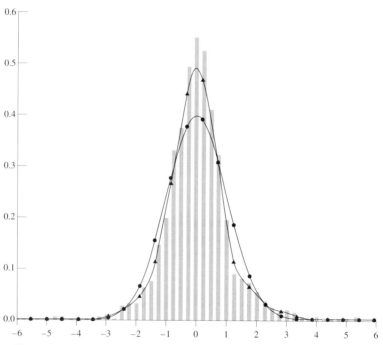

Figure 5.65 Normal S(P-P) plot of Canada/USA exchange rate data

Figure 5.66 Histogram and smoothed histogram of Canada/USA exchange rate data

oversmoothing (higher than the optimal value for the bandwidth) will suggest a higher value of the degrees of freedom parameter than its true value.

A much safer way to proceed will be to construct a standardized Student's t P-P plot of the form (see Spanos (1996d)):

Standardized Student's t P-P plot:

$$\left\{(u_k, F_{St}(y^*_{[k]}; \nu)), u_k = \tfrac{k}{n+1}, k = 1,2,\ldots,n\right\}.$$

where $F_{St}(.;\nu)$ denotes the cdf of the Student's t distribution with ν degrees of freedom (chosen a priori). It is very important to NOTE that the ordered observations $y^*_{[k]}, k = 1,2,\ldots,n$ should be *standardized* to have standard deviation not 1 but $\sqrt{\left(\frac{\nu}{\nu-2}\right)}$, i.e.

$$\tfrac{1}{n-1}\sum_{k=1}^{n}\left(\tfrac{y_{[k]}-\bar{y}}{s_y}\right) = \left(\tfrac{\nu}{\nu-2}\right).$$

In figure 5.67 we can see such a standardized Student's t P-P plot for the exchange rate data together with the reference Cauchy distribution. The reference distribution is the standard Student's t with 4 d.f., denoted by St(0,1;4). It is interesting to NOTE how the Cauchy distribution curve when viewed through the prism of the Student's t distribution has changed its shape when compared with that in the context of the standardized Normal P-P plot. Figure 5.67 suggests that the Student's t distribution with 4 degrees of freedom provides a remarkable fit to the exchange rate data. In order to provide support for this choice we present the standardized Student's t P-P plot for different degrees of freedom in figures 5.68–5.70.

Commencing with figure 5.68, where the reference distribution is St (0,1;5), we can see that the plot of the data is very close to the diagonal straight line but the lower half of the observations appears slightly above the diagonal and the higher half slightly below. It must be emphasized, however, that for real data the plot with 4 d.f. constitutes a remarkable fit and it is only the close fit that enables us to put a possible question mark on the fit of the 5 d.f. graph. Some people might prefer the case of 5 d.f. for theoretical reasons such as the existence of the kurtosis coefficient!

The discrepancy noted in figure 5.68 is more apparent in figure 5.69 where the degrees of freedom parameter was increased to 6; the reference distribution is St(0,1;6). The opposite discrepancy can be seen in figure 5.70 where the reference distribution is St(0,1;3). As we can see the lower half of the observations lie below the diagonal and the higher half lie above the diagonal.

The patterns exhibited in these standardized P-P plots in conjunction with the Cauchy distribution curve can be used as a guide in deciding whether to increase or decrease the degrees of freedom parameter to achieve a better fit. For example, in the case of the reference distribution St (0,1;3) it is clear that the discrepancy is towards the Cauchy distribution and to correct it we need to move in the opposite direction, i.e., increase the degrees of freedom.

In concluding this subsection we deduce that in the case of the exchange rate data the graphical techniques introduced above proved adequate to assess its distributional features. These data can best be described by the Student's t distribution with 4 degrees of freedom.

Finally, we note that the use of large samples in this section was designed to ensure that the created pictionary was reliable enough. This, however, does not mean that the

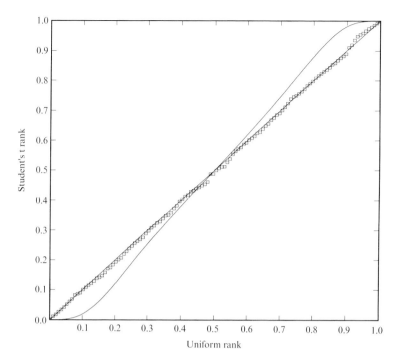

Figure 5.67 Student's t [St(0,1;4)] S(P-P) plot of exchange data

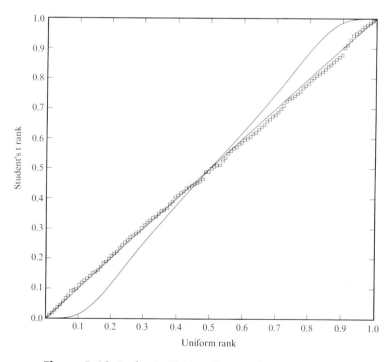

Figure 5.68 Student's t [St(0,1;5)] S(P-P) plot of exchange data

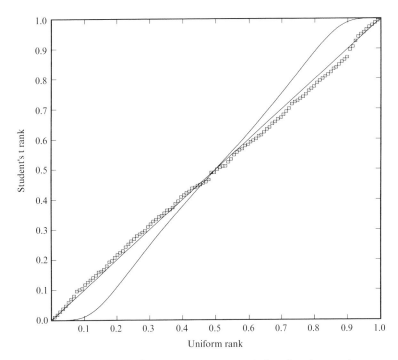

Figure 5.69 Student's t [St(0,1;6)] S(P-P) plot of exchange data

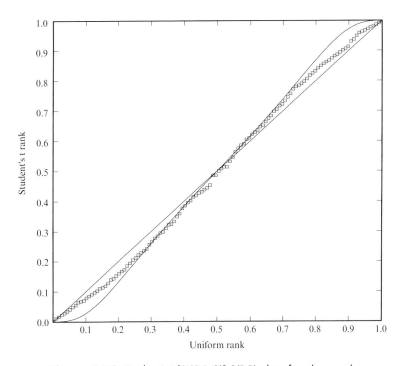

Figure 5.70 Student's t [St(0,1;3)] S(P-P) plot of exchange data

above graphical displays cannot be used for sample sizes smaller than $T = 200$. Any sample beyond $T = 20$ could be assessed using these plots but the modeler should be more careful in the case of small samples.

5.8   Generating pseudo-random numbers*

5.8.1   Uniform pseudo-random numbers: conguential methods

How do we generate the *ideal random numbers* used in the above t-plots? The most commonly used method has two stages: the first stage generates "ideal" Uniformly distributed random numbers and the second stage transforms these numbers into ideal pseudo-random numbers from other distributions. This is because the generation of ideal Uniformly distributed random numbers is mathematically an easier proposition.

The *pseudo-random numbers* $\{u_i, i = 1,2,\ldots\}$ are so called because they appear to be realizations of a sequence of Independent and Identically Distributed (IID) random variables $\{U_i, i = 1,2,\ldots\}$ that follow the Uniform distribution $\mathsf{U}(0,1)$. These are numbers such that for any finite collection $\{u_{i1}, u_{i2}, \ldots, u_{in}\}$ of size $n \geq 2$, the following relationship holds:

$$\mathbb{P}(U_{i1} \leq u_{i1}, U_{i2} \leq u_{i2}, \cdots, U_{in} \leq u_{in}) = \sum_{j=1}^{n} u_{ij}.$$

The appearance of IID is established via some computer-based algorithm which chooses rational numbers in ways that ensure the absence of any patterns associated with dependence and/or non-identical distribution.

The most widely used method for generating pseudo-random numbers is the so-called **multiplicative congruential method** which involves the following recursive formula (see Johnson (1987)):

$$u_k = a u_{k-1} \bmod m, k = 1,2,\ldots,$$

$u_k, k = 1,2,\ldots,$ denotes the output pseudo-random numbers,
u_0 is the initial value known as the *seed*,
a is a chosen constant (known as the *multiplier*) such that $a < m$, and
m is a prime number, known as the *modulus*.

Mod is shorthand for modulus. In words, u_k is generated by dividing the product au_{k-1} by m and letting u_k be the remainder of the division; (u_k/m) is a rational number in the interval $[0,1]$.

Example
Consider the case $m = 11, a = 7, u_0 = 1$,

$$u_1 = \text{remainder of } \left(\tfrac{7}{11}\right) = 7,$$
$$u_2 = \text{remainder of } \left(\tfrac{7 \times 7}{11}\right) = 5,$$

$u_3 = $ remainder of $\left(\frac{7 \times 5}{11}\right) = 2,$

$u_4 = $ remainder of $\left(\frac{7 \times 2}{11}\right) = 3,$

...   .

the first pseudo-random numbers: $((1/11),(7/11),(5/11),(2/11),(3/11),(10/11),\cdots)$.

The pseudo-random numbers generated using this algorithm will repeat themselves with the maximum period $m - 1$; the maximum period is achieved when a is a primitive root of m. For these numbers to exhibit no patterns of dependence and/or heterogeneity the numbers a and m should be chosen appropriately; the rule is to choose a to be a positive primitive root of m and the latter should be a large prime number. The experience of the last few decades has shown that there are good and bad choices. Some of the better choices for these numbers are:

$$m = (2^{31} - 1), \ a = 950706376, \ a = 742938285, \ a = 1226874159.$$

A simple extension of this algorithm, known as a **linear conguential method** for generating uniform pseudo-random numbers, takes the recursive form:

$$u_k = au_{k-1} + c, \text{mod } m, \ k = 1,2,\ldots,$$

where c is some constant (often an odd integer). This algorithm yields the sequence of pseudo-random numbers:

$$v_k = \left(\frac{u_k}{m}\right) \in [0,1), k = 1,2,\ldots$$

In the literature this linear congruential method has been extended in a number of directions such as the *non-linear* congruential method and the *inverse* congruential method in an attempt to improve the quality of the pseudo-random numbers generated (see Lewis and Orav (1989)).

Before the sequences of pseudo-random numbers generated by these algorithms are used one needs to check whether they enjoy the required properties, i.e., represent realizations of an IID sample of random variables. This question will be raised again in chapter 10.

5.8.2 Generating non-Uniform pseudo-random numbers

The inverse distribution function method

The pseudo-random numbers for the Uniform distribution can then be transformed into numbers from all the other distributions using two variants of the *probability integral transformation* introduced in the previous chapter.

(i) **The probability integral transformation.** Assuming that X has a cdf $F(x)$ so that $F^{-1}(u)$ exists for $0 < u < 1$, the random variable defined by $U = F(x)$, has a Uniform distribution over the range $(0,1)$, i.e.

$$U = F(X) \sim \mathsf{U}(0,1).$$

This is a remarkable result because in cases where $F^{-1}(u)$ is computable for $0 < u < 1$, it can be used to transform a Uniformly distributed random variable into another random variable with distribution $F(x)$ using the **quantile transformation**:

$$X = F^{-1}(u),\, u \in (0,1),\text{ where } F^{-1}(u) = \inf\, \{x : F(x) \geq u,\, 0 \leq u \leq 1\}.$$

Some examples of continuous distributions for which $F^{-1}(.)$ has an analytical expression are given below (see also Lewis and Orav (1989)):

Distribution	$F(x)$	$F^{-1}(u)$
Uniform:	$\frac{1}{\beta - \alpha}$	$\alpha + (\beta - \alpha)u$
Cauchy:	$\frac{\beta}{\pi \beta^2 + (x - \alpha)^2}$	$\alpha + \beta \tan\left(\pi\left(u - \frac{1}{2}\right)\right)$
Exponential:	$\frac{1}{\beta}e^{-\frac{1}{\beta}x}$	$-\beta \ln(1 - u)$
Logistic:	$\dfrac{\exp\left\{-\frac{(x-\alpha)}{\beta}\right\}}{\beta\left[1 + \exp\left\{-\frac{(x-\alpha)}{\beta}\right\}\right]^2}$	$\alpha + \beta \ln\left(\frac{u}{1-u}\right)$
Pareto:	$\alpha\beta^\alpha x^{-(\alpha+1)}$	$\frac{\beta}{(1-u)^{\frac{1}{\alpha}}}$
Weibull:	$\left(\frac{\alpha}{\beta^\alpha}\right)x^{\alpha-1}\exp\left\{-\left(\frac{x}{\beta}\right)^\alpha\right\}$	$\beta(-\ln(1-u))^{\frac{1}{\alpha}}$
Beta$(\alpha,1)$:	$\alpha x^{\alpha-1}$	$u^{\frac{1}{\alpha}}$
Beta$(1,\beta)$:	$\beta(1-x)^{\beta-1}$	$1 - (1-u)^{\frac{1}{\beta}}$

$$(5.12)$$

Example

Consider the case where $U \sim \mathsf{U}(0,1)$ and we want to use it to generate pseudo-random numbers from a logistically distributed random variable X with:

$$F(x) = \frac{e^x}{1 + e^x},\quad -\infty < x < \infty.$$

Setting $u = \frac{e^x}{1 + e^x}$, or $u = e^x(1 - u)$, we deduce that $x = F^{-1}(u) = \ln u - \ln(1 - u)$, and thus:

$$X = F^{-1}(u) = \ln u - \ln(1 - u),\, u \in (0,1),$$

can be used to simulate logistically distributed pseudo-random numbers.

(ii) **Simulation for a discrete random variable** X. Let $U \sim \mathsf{U}(0,1)$. Set $X = x_n$ whenever:

$$F(x_{n-1}) < U \leq F(x_n),\text{ for } n = 1,2,\ldots \text{ (set } F(x_{-1}) = 0\text{)},$$

$$P(X = x_n) = F(x_n) - F(x_{n-1}) = p_n,\, n = 1,2,\ldots,$$

by the definition of the distribution function of a Uniform random variable with range $(0,1)$.

Example

Consider the case where $U \sim U(0,1)$ and we want to use it to generate pseudo-random numbers from a Bernoulli distributed random variable X with density:

$$f(x;p) = p^x (1-p)^{1-x}, \, x = 1,0.$$

The algorithm suggested by the above procedure is:

1. If $U \le p$, set $X = 1$,   2. If $U > p$, set $X = 0$.

Normal pseudo-random numbers

The most popular distribution in probability and statistical inference is undoubtedly the Normal distribution for which the following method is often used to generate random numbers. Consider the case where $U_i \sim U(0,1)$, $i = 1,2$, and independent. These pseudo-random numbers can be used to generate the Normal pseudo-random numbers:

$$\begin{pmatrix} X_1 \\ X_2 \end{pmatrix} \sim N \left(\begin{bmatrix} 0 \\ 0 \end{bmatrix}, \begin{bmatrix} 1 & 0 \\ 0 & 1 \end{bmatrix} \right)$$

i.e., $X_i \sim N(0,1)$, $i = 1,2$, and independent, using the transformation:

$$X_1 = \sqrt{(-2 \ln U_1)} \cdot \cos(2\pi U_2), \, X_2 = \sqrt{(-2 \ln U_1)} \cdot \sin(2\pi U_2). \quad (5.13)$$

This is based on a change of variables result from two independently distributed random variables (r, θ) via the transformation:

$$X_1 = r \cos \theta, \, X_2 = r \sin \theta, \, 0 < r < \infty, \, 0 \le \theta \le 2\pi, \quad (5.14)$$

whose Jacobian (see Box and Muller (1958)) takes the form:

$$\frac{\partial(x_1, x_2)}{\partial(r, \theta)} = \det \begin{pmatrix} \cos \theta & \sin \theta \\ -r \sin \theta & r \cos \theta \end{pmatrix} = r.$$

The joint distribution of (r, θ) is (see chapter 11):

$$f(r, \theta) = f(x_1) f(x_2) \cdot r = \frac{r}{2\pi} \exp \left\{ -\frac{1}{2} (x_1^2 + x_2^2) \right\} = f(u_1) f(u_2),$$

where (U_1, U_2) are independent and Uniformly distributed random variables defined by:

$$U_1 = \exp \left(-\tfrac{1}{2} r^2 \right) \sim U(0,1], \, U_2 = \tfrac{\theta}{2\pi} \sim U(0,1].$$

The transformation (5.13) is derived by inverting (5.14).

5.8.3 The rejection method

Another commonly used method for generating pseudo-random numbers from distributions other than the Uniform is the rejection–acceptance method. The idea behind this method is to start from another distribution which is easy to simulate and is very similar in shape to the one we want to simulate, and cut and paste the simulated numbers from the first distribution by accepting the ones which agree with the second distribution.

This method presupposes (i) the existence of a density function, i.e., there exists a non-decreasing function $f(x)$ such that (see Devroye (1986)):

$$F(x) = \int_{-\infty}^{x} f(u)du \text{ for all } x \in \mathbb{R},$$

and (ii) the existence of a distribution $G(x)$ with density $g(x)$, for which pseudo-random numbers are readily available, such that:

$$f(x) \leq cg(x) \text{ for some constant } c \geq 1, x \in \mathbb{R}.$$

Armed with these two density functions one proceeds to generate two independent random samples, $\{u_k, k = 1,2,\ldots,n\}$ from the Uniform distribution and $\{z_k, k = 1,2,\ldots,n\}$ from the distribution $G(x)$. The decision rule for selecting an IID sample from $F(x)$ is as follows:

(i)   If $cu_k > \frac{f(z_k)}{g(z_k)}$ then reject z_k and try again with other u_k and z_k,

(ii)   If $cu_k \leq \frac{f(z_k)}{g(z_k)}$ then accept z_k, for $k = 1,2,\ldots,n$.

The output is the sequence $x_k = z_k$, $k = 1,2,\ldots,m$ ($m \leq n$). The theory underlying this method is encapsulated in the following relationship:

$$\Pr(Z \leq x \text{ and } z \text{ is accepted}) = \int_{-\infty}^{x_k} \frac{f(u)}{cg(u)} g(u)du = \frac{1}{c} \int_{-\infty}^{x_k} f(u)du = \frac{1}{c} F(x_k)$$

Hence, taking $x \to \infty \Rightarrow \Pr(z \text{ is accepted}) = \frac{1}{c}$, yielding

$$\Pr(Z \leq x | z \text{ is accepted}) = \frac{\frac{1}{c}F(x)}{\frac{1}{c}} = F(x).$$

That is, the random variable X has the cdf function $F(x)$.

There are many other methods for generating non-Uniform pseudo-random numbers such as the *composition* and the *ratio of uniforms* methods. The interested reader is referred to Devroye (1986) for an extensive discussion.

5.9   Summary

In this chapter we considered the question of bridging the gap between the observed data and the theoretical concepts defining a **simple statistical model**:

[i]   Probability model: $\Phi = \{f(x;\theta), \theta \in \Theta, x \in \mathbb{R}\}$,
[ii]   Sampling model: $\mathbf{X}_{(n)}^{\text{IID}} := (X_1, X_2, \ldots, X_n)$ is a random sample.

The tentative bridge between the two came in the form of the graphical displays of simulated data. In particular, it was shown that the graphical display known as a *t*-plot conveys information relating to the appropriateness of all three probabilistic assumptions making up any simple statistical model:

(D)   Distribution: arbitrary distribution,
(M)   Dependence: independence,
(H)   Heterogeneity: identical distribution.

In the case of assessing the distribution assumption we related the *t*-plot to other plots such as the histogram, the smoothed histogram, the Q-Q and P-P plots of the data. All these plots will be particularly useful at the specification stage of modeling where we need to make a preliminary assessment of the assumptions defining the statistical model chosen.

The tentative bridge will be reinforced in the next few chapters with additional graphical displays but there will be some loose ends which will be tied together in chapter 10.

5.10 Exercises

1   Explain the concept of a random sample and its restrictiveness in the case of most economic data series.

2   How do we assess the distributional features of a data series using a *t*-plot?

3   "A smoothed histogram is more appropriate in assessing the distributional features of a data series than the histogram itself because the former is less data specific." Explain.

4   Explain how one can distinguish between a *t*-plot of NIID and a *t*-plot of Student's t IID observations.

5   Explain the relationship between the abstract concept of independence and the corresponding chance regularity pattern in a *t*-plot of a data series.

6   Explain how any form of dependence will help the modeler in prediction.

7   Explain the relationship between the abstract concept of identical distribution and the corresponding chance regularity pattern in a *t*-plot of a data series.

8   "Without an ordering of the observations one cannot talk about dependence and heterogeneity." Discuss.

9   Explain the notion of a P-P plot and the Normal P-P plot in particular.

10   Compare and contrast a Normal P-P and a Normal Q-Q plot.

11   Explain how the standardized Student's t P-P plot can be used to evaluate the degrees of freedom parameter.

12   Explain the notion of a reference distribution in a P-P plot. Why does the Cauchy reference distribution take different shapes in the context of a standardized Normal and a Student's t P-P plot?

13   Explain the notion of a pseudo-random number.

14   Explain the linear conguential method for generating Uniform pseudo-random numbers.

15   Compare and contrast the P-P and standardized P-P plots.

6 The notion of a non-random sample

6.1 Introduction

In this chapter we take the first step toward extending the simple statistical model (formalized in chapters 2–4) in directions which allow for dependence and heterogeneity. Both of these dimensions are excluded in the context of the simple statistical model because the latter is built upon the notion of a random sample: a set of random variables which are both *Independent* and *Identically Distributed* (IID). In this chapter we concentrate on the notion of dependence, paving the way for more elaborate statistical models in the next few chapters. We also extend the bridge between theoretical concepts and real data introduced in chapter 5, by introducing some additional graphical techniques.

6.1.1 The story so far

In chapter 2 we commenced our quest for a mathematical framework in the context of which we can model stochastic phenomena: phenomena exhibiting *chance regularity*. We viewed probability theory as the appropriate mathematical set up which enables one to model the *systematic information* in such phenomena. In an attempt to motivate this mathematical framework, we introduced probability theory as a *formalization* (mathematization) of a simple *chance mechanism*, we called a *random experiment* $\mathcal{E}$, defined by the following three conditions:

[a] all possible distinct outcomes are known a priori,
[b] in any particular trial the outcome is not known a priori but there exists a perceptible regularity of occurrence associated with these outcomes,
[c] it can be repeated under identical conditions.

The idea behind this formalization was twofold. First, to bring out the fact that probability theory, like other branches of mathematics, is not just a sequence of slick theorems and lemmas! It is a branch of mathematics which grew out of the need to model certain phenomena of interest. Moreover, it changes continuously, broadening and extending its intended scope in order to provide a framework for modeling stochastic phenomena.

260

Second, to bring out the connection between chance regularity patterns and the corresponding abstract mathematical concepts; the former motivating the formalization of the latter. The chance mechanism represented by a random experiment was chosen to be simple enough (the chance regularity patterns are manageable) but not simpler (to paraphrase a statement by Einstein), with a view to motivating the main concepts underlying a statistical model.

The initial mathematical formalization of $\mathcal{E}$, given in chapter 2, came in the form of a **simple statistical space** $[(S,\Im,\mathbb{P}\,(.))^n, G_n^{\text{IID}}]$, which has two components:

(i)   Probability space: $(S,\Im,\mathbb{P}(.))^n := (S,\Im,\mathbb{P}(.)) \times (S,\Im,\mathbb{P}(.)) \times \cdots \times (S,\Im,\mathbb{P}(.))$,
(ii) Sampling space: $G_n^{\text{IID}} = \{\mathcal{A}_1,\mathcal{A}_2,\mathcal{A}_3,\ldots,\mathcal{A}_n\}$.

These two pillars provide the mathematical foundations upon which one can erect probability theory as a branch of mathematics. From the *modeling viewpoint*, however, this mathematical framework is more abstract than needed because our data are often numerical and thus, in chapters 3 and 4, we set out to metamorphose it into an equivalent formulation on the real line. It is important to NOTE that, even after the metamorphosis, this abstract formulation is still of interest because it constitutes the mathematical foundations of probability theory. Whenever we introduced a new concept in the context of the transformed formulation we need to return to the abstract formulation to check whether it makes sense or not. As shown below, in extending the simple statistical model we retain the notion of a probability space $(S,\Im,\mathbb{P}(.))$ but we define on it, random variables, which can be both dependent and heterogeneous (see chapter 8 for the details).

The metamorphosis of the abstract statistical space $[(S,\Im,\mathbb{P}(.))^n, G_n^{\text{IID}}]$ took the form of a **simple (generic) statistical model**.

[i]   Probability model: $\Phi = \{f(x;\boldsymbol{\theta}),\ \boldsymbol{\theta}\in\Theta,\ x\in\mathbb{R}\}$,
[ii] Sampling model: $\mathbf{X}_{(n)}^{\text{IID}} := (X_1,X_2,\ldots,X_n)$ is a random sample.

In the previous chapter a bridge has been erected between the probabilistic concepts of:

(i)   Distribution (a cumulative distribution or a density function),
(ii)   Independent, and
(iii) Identically Distributed random variables,

and the corresponding chance regularity patterns exhibited in a number of graphical displays of observed data. In extending the simple statistical model we also need to extend this bridge in order to introduce additional graphical techniques relevant for dependence and heterogeneity chance regularity patterns.

6.1.2 Extending a simple statistical model

The intended scope of the simple statistical model is limited by the concept of *a random sample*; it can only be used to model stochastic phenomena that exhibit *independence* and *complete homogeneity* over *t*. Unfortunately, this is rarely the case in economics. Economic data often exhibit *non-random sample* features: *dependence* and/or *heterogeneity*. A typical economic time series is shown in figure 6.1, where monthly data on the US

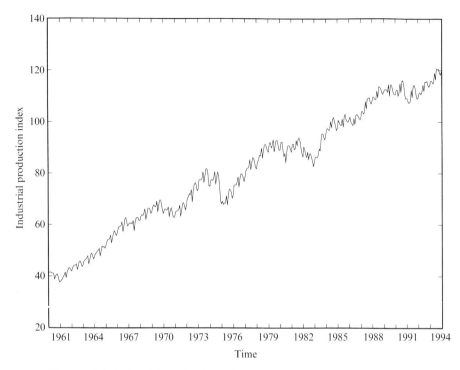

Figure 6.1 Industrial production index

Industrial Production Index (1985 = 100), for the period January 1960 to May 1994, are plotted over time.

Using the expertise acquired in the previous chapter, we can see that this t-plot exhibits positive dependence in the form of *business cycles* and distinct heterogeneity, in the form of an upward trend, and a possible seasonality pattern.

The **primary objective** of the next few chapters is to extend the simple statistical model with a view to modeling observable phenomena, such as the behavior of stock returns, exchange rates, inflation and GDP growth, which cannot be viewed as realizations of a random sample. The main objective of this chapter is to take the first step towards extending the simple statistical model in order to enhance its scope. This step takes the form of introducing several notions of dependence.

6.1.3   Introducing a fundamental taxonomy

One of the basic themes that underlays the discussion in this book is a fundamental classification of probabilistic assumptions into three broad categories:

    (D) Distribution,   (M) Dependence,   (H) Heterogeneity.

This taxonomy will be utilized extensively in the chapters that follow for both pedagogical as well as substantive reasons. It constitutes one of the unifying themes of the approach to statistical inference and modeling that runs through this book. The taxonomy is not supposed to provide a partition of the set of probabilistic assumptions; just a broad grouping. Some assumptions will straddle over the boundary between these categories but that does not reduce the usefulness of the taxonomy.

At this stage it is important to emphasize that, in terms of the above taxonomy, a simple statistical model can be viewed as imposing extreme assumptions in two of the three categories. From the (M) (for memory) category it imposes independence and from the (H) category complete homogeneity:

(D)   Distribution: arbitrary distribution,
(M)   Dependence: Independent random variables,
(H)   Heterogeneity: Identically Distributed random variables.

In the same way we can view statistical models with broader intended scope as built upon assumptions from the above three categories other than independence from the category (M) and identical distributions from the category (H). This suggests that a pre-requisite of this broadening of the intended scope is the availability of different notions of dependence and heterogeneity beyond the two extreme restricted cases.

The concept of a *statistical model* in general is of paramount importance in statistical inference. The main purpose of a statistical model is to provide an adequate summary of the systematic information in the data by capturing all statistical systematic information as it relates to the chance regularity patterns exhibited by the data.

6.2   Non-random sample: a preliminary view

What makes a random sample such a fundamentally important notion? The short answer is that the assumptions of Independence and Identical Distribution simplify both the modeling as well as the statistical inference concerning simple statistical models. This simplification is encapsulated by the form of the reduction of the joint distribution of the sample. To see this we remind the reader that:

Independence: $f(x_1, x_2, \ldots, x_n; \boldsymbol{\phi}) = \prod_{k=1}^{n} f_k(x_k; \boldsymbol{\theta}_k)$, for all $\mathbf{x} \in \mathbb{R}^n$,

Identical Distribution: $f_k(x_k; \boldsymbol{\theta}_k) = f(x_k; \boldsymbol{\theta})$, for all $k = 1, 2, \ldots, n$.

The end result of these assumptions is that the joint distribution is simplified immensely by its reduction to a product of univariate (identical) marginal distributions:

$$f(x_1, x_2, \ldots, x_n; \boldsymbol{\phi}) \overset{\text{I}}{=} \prod_{k=1}^{n} f_k(x_k; \boldsymbol{\theta}_k) \overset{\text{IID}}{=} \prod_{k=1}^{n} f(x_k; \boldsymbol{\theta}), \text{ for all } \mathbf{x} \in \mathbb{R}^n. \qquad (6.1)$$

Looking at this result we can see that the random sample assumption simplified the joint distribution (distribution of the sample) drastically in two important respects:

(i)   Dimensionality reduction:
      $f(x_1, x_2, \ldots, x_n; \boldsymbol{\phi})$ is n-dimensional and $f(x_k; \boldsymbol{\theta})$ is 1-dimensional, and
(ii) Parameter reduction:
      the number of unknown parameters in $\boldsymbol{\theta}$ is often considerably smaller than that of $\boldsymbol{\phi}$.

Example

Consider the case where the joint distribution of the random variables $(X_1, X_2, \ldots, X_n)$ is Normal, i.e., $f(x_1, x_2, \ldots, x_n; \boldsymbol{\phi})$ takes the form:

$$
\begin{pmatrix} X_1 \\ X_2 \\ X_3 \\ \vdots \\ X_n \end{pmatrix} \sim N \left(\begin{bmatrix} \mu_1 \\ \mu_2 \\ \mu_3 \\ \vdots \\ \mu_n \end{bmatrix}, \begin{bmatrix} \sigma_{11} & \sigma_{12} & \sigma_{13} & \cdots & \sigma_{1n} \\ \sigma_{21} & \sigma_{22} & \sigma_{23} & \cdots & \sigma_{2n} \\ \sigma_{31} & \sigma_{32} & \sigma_{33} & \cdots & \sigma_{3n} \\ \vdots & \vdots & \vdots & \ddots & \vdots \\ \sigma_{n1} & \sigma_{n2} & \sigma_{n3} & \cdots & \sigma_{nn} \end{bmatrix} \right).
\tag{6.2}
$$

As it stands, the joint distribution has at least $N = n + \frac{1}{2}[n(n+1)]$ unknown parameters:

$$\boldsymbol{\phi} := (\mu_i, \sigma_{ij}, \ i,j = 1,2, \ldots, n),$$

with n means: $(E(X_i) := \mu_i, i = 1, 2, \ldots, n)$ and $\frac{1}{2}[n(n+1)]$ covariances (due to symmetry):

$$Cov(X_i, X_j) = Cov(X_j, X_i) := \sigma_{ij}, \ i,j = 1, 2, \ldots, n.$$

If we impose the *Independence* assumption on the joint distribution the result will be that the covariances become zero:

$$
\sigma_{ij} = \begin{cases} \sigma_{ii}, \ \text{for } i = j, \\ 0, \ \text{for } i \neq j, \end{cases}, \ i,j = 1, 2, \ldots, n,
$$

the original joint distribution reduces to:

$$
\begin{pmatrix} X_1 \\ X_2 \\ X_3 \\ \vdots \\ X_n \end{pmatrix} \sim N \left(\begin{bmatrix} \mu_1 \\ \mu_2 \\ \mu_3 \\ \vdots \\ \mu_n \end{bmatrix}, \begin{bmatrix} \sigma_{11} & 0 & 0 & \cdots & 0 \\ 0 & \sigma_{22} & 0 & \cdots & 0 \\ 0 & 0 & \sigma_{33} & \cdots & 0 \\ \vdots & \vdots & \vdots & \ddots & \vdots \\ 0 & 0 & 0 & \cdots & \sigma_{nn} \end{bmatrix} \right).
\tag{6.3}
$$

In terms of the reduction (6.1), the first equality is the result of imposing Independence, with the univariate marginal densities $f_k(x_k; \boldsymbol{\theta}_k)$, $\boldsymbol{\theta}_k := (\mu_k, \sigma_{kk})$, $k = 1, 2, \ldots, n$ being:

$$X_k \sim N(\mu_k, \sigma_{kk}), \ k = 1, 2, \ldots, n.
\tag{6.4}$$

This reduction, although drastic, does not yield an operational model because there are still $2n$ unknown parameters:

$$\boldsymbol{\theta}_k := (\mu_k, \sigma_{kk}), \ k = 1, 2, \ldots, n,$$

which are increasing with the sample size! Imposing the *Identical Distribution* assumption at the second stage in (6.1) ensures that:

$$\boldsymbol{\theta}_1 = \boldsymbol{\theta}_2 = \cdots = \boldsymbol{\theta}_n = \boldsymbol{\theta} := (\mu, \sigma^2),$$

and thus the joint density is reduced to a product of univariate marginal densities $f(x_k; \boldsymbol{\theta})$, where $\boldsymbol{\theta} := (\mu, \sigma^2)$, of the form:

$$X_k \sim N(\mu, \sigma^2), \ k = 1, 2, \ldots, n.$$

NOTE the corresponding reduction in the unknown parameters in (6.1):

$$\boldsymbol{\phi} := (\mu_i, \sigma_{ij}, \ i,j = 1,2,\dots,n) \rightsquigarrow \boldsymbol{\theta}_k := \{(\mu_k, \sigma_{kk}), k = 1,2,\dots,n\}, \rightsquigarrow \boldsymbol{\theta} := (\mu, \sigma^2).$$

The above reduction yields the **simple Normal model**:

[i]   Probability model:

$$\Phi = \left\{ f(x;\boldsymbol{\theta}) = \frac{1}{\sigma\sqrt{2\pi}} \exp\left\{ -\frac{(x-\mu)^2}{2\sigma^2} \right\}, \ \boldsymbol{\theta} := (\mu, \sigma^2) \in \mathbb{R} \times \mathbb{R}_+, \ x \in \mathbb{R} \right\},$$

[ii]   Sampling model: $\mathbf{X} := (X_1, X_2, \dots, X_n)$ is a random sample.

This example illustrates most clearly the drastic reduction in both the dimensionality and the number of unknown parameters achieved by the random sample assumption. By the same token, the above example can also be used to indicate the kind of difficulties that will arise in the case of a non-random sample, where one or both of the assumptions do not hold.

Looking at (6.2) we realize that the above blessings in the case of a random sample become curses in the case of a non-random sample. If no restrictions are placed on the dependence and heterogeneity two difficult problems arise:

(a)   Dimensionality curse: $f(x_1, x_2, \dots, x_n; \boldsymbol{\phi})$ is n-dimensional,
(b)   Incidental parameters curse: the number of unknown parameters in $\boldsymbol{\phi}$, say N, increases with the sample size n.

6.2.1   Sequential conditioning

Let us consider the *dimensionality* curse first. For modeling and statistical inference purposes the high dimensionality of the joint distribution is a difficult problem. The key to dispelling the dimensionality curse was presented in the previous chapter in the form of a conditional distribution. It was shown that in the case of two arbitrary random variables X and Y (defined on the same probability space) the following relationship holds:

$$f(x,y;\boldsymbol{\phi}) = f(y \mid x; \boldsymbol{\varphi}_2) \cdot f_x(x; \boldsymbol{\varphi}_1), \text{ for all } (x,y) \in \mathbb{R}_X \times \mathbb{R}_Y. \tag{6.5}$$

NOTES:
(i)   The reduction is symmetric with respect to X and Y in the sense that:

$$f(x,y;\boldsymbol{\phi}) = f(x \mid y; \boldsymbol{\psi}_2) \cdot f_y(y; \boldsymbol{\psi}_1), \text{ for all } (x,y) \in \mathbb{R}_X \times \mathbb{R}_Y, \tag{6.6}$$

(ii) $f(y \mid x; \boldsymbol{\varphi}_2)$ and $f(x \mid y; \boldsymbol{\psi}_2)$ are both univariate distributions.
(iii)   The reduction in dimensionality is not accompanied by any corresponding reduction in the number of unknown parameters §. In order to avoid introducing cumbersome notation consider an example of the simple two-variable case.

Example
Consider the case where the random variables (X, Y) are Normally distributed, i.e. $f(x,y;\boldsymbol{\phi})$ takes the form:

$$\begin{pmatrix} Y \\ X \end{pmatrix} \sim \mathsf{N}\left(\begin{bmatrix} \mu_1 \\ \mu_2 \end{bmatrix}, \begin{bmatrix} \sigma_{11} & \sigma_{12} \\ \sigma_{12} & \sigma_{22} \end{bmatrix} \right). \tag{6.7}$$

The reduction in (6.6) takes the form (see chapter 4):

$$X \sim \mathsf{N}(\mu_2, \sigma_{22}), \ (Y|X=x) \sim \mathsf{N}(\beta_0 + \beta_1 x, \sigma^2), \ x \in \mathbb{R},$$

where $\beta_0 := \mu_1 - \beta_1 \mu_2$, $\beta_1 := \frac{\sigma_{12}}{\sigma_{22}}$, $\sigma^2 = \sigma_{11} - \frac{\sigma_{12}^2}{\sigma_{22}}$. These results show that:

$$\phi := (\mu_1, \mu_2, \sigma_{11}, \sigma_{12}, \sigma_{22}), \ \varphi_1 := (\mu_2, \sigma_{22}), \ \varphi_2 := (\beta_0, \beta_1, \sigma^2),$$

and thus the number of unknown parameters remains the same! This is true in the n-dimensional case but the notation gets a bit complicated.

Comparing (6.5) to the case where X and Y are *independent*:

$$f(x,y;\phi) = f_x(x;\theta_1) \cdot f_y(y;\theta_2), \text{ for all } (x,y) \in \mathbb{R}_X \times \mathbb{R}_Y, \tag{6.8}$$

we can see that in the non-independent case the conditional distribution $f(y|x;\phi)$ provides the key to a reduction of a bivariate to a product of two univariate distributions.

Example
Returning to the above case where the random variables (X_1, X_2) are Normally distributed, we can see that:

$$\sigma_{12} = 0 \Rightarrow \beta_1 = 0, \ \beta_0 = \mu_1 \text{ and } \sigma^2 = \sigma_{11}.$$

That is, under the restriction $\sigma_{12} = 0$, $f(y|x;\varphi_2)$ takes the form:

$$(Y|X=x)|_{\sigma_{12}=0} \sim \mathsf{N}(\mu_1, \sigma_{11}), \ x \in \mathbb{R},$$

which implies that $f(y|x;\varphi_2)|_{\sigma_{12}=0} = f_y(y;\theta_2)$. It turns out that the restriction $\sigma_{12} = 0$ is both necessary and sufficient for the conditional to reduce to the marginal distribution and thus under this restriction the joint distribution of (X,Y) satisfies the independence condition in (6.8).

The reduction in (6.5) can be easily extended to the n-variable case using *sequential conditioning*. Consider the case of three random variables (X_1, X_2, X_3):

$$\begin{aligned} f(x_1,x_2,x_3;\phi) &= f(x_3|x_2,x_1;\psi_3) \cdot f(x_2,x_1;\vartheta_1), \\ &= f(x_3|x_2,x_1;\psi_3) \cdot f(x_2|x_1;\psi_2) \cdot f(x_1;\psi_1), \quad (x_1,x_2,x_3) \in \mathbb{R}_X^3, \end{aligned}$$

where we conditioned X_3 on (X_1, X_2) first and then conditioned X_2 on X_1. In the general n-variable case, the sequential conditioning yields:

$$f(x_1,x_2,\dots,x_n;\phi) \overset{\text{non-IID}}{=} f_1(x_1;\psi_1) \prod_{k=2}^n f_k(x_k|x_{k-1},\dots,x_1;\psi_k), \text{ for all } \mathbf{x} \in \mathbb{R}_X^n. \tag{6.9}$$

This dispels the dimensionality curse because the right-hand side is a product of univariate densities but raises two different problems:

(c)   *The increasing conditioning set*: the number of conditioning variables changes with the index in the sense that $f_k(x_k|x_{k-1},\dots,x_1;\psi_k)$ has $(k-1)$ conditioning variables but the index changes $k = 2,3,\ldots,n$, rendering these densities different, e.g. for $n = 5$:

$$f(x_2|x_1;\psi_2),$$
$$f(x_3|x_2,x_1;\psi_3),$$
$$f(x_4|x_3,x_2,x_1;\psi_4),$$
$$f(x_5|x_4,x_3,x_2,x_1;\psi_5).$$

(d)   *The stochastic conditioning problem*: the right-hand side of (6.9) is the product of n univariate distributions ($n-1$ conditional and one marginal) for *each* value $\mathbf{x} \in \mathbb{R}^n_X$; i.e., one such n-tuple for every value of $\mathbf{x} \in \mathbb{R}^n_X$. In the reduction in (6.5) there exists one joint distribution $f(x,y;\phi)$ and one marginal density $f_x(x;\varphi_1)$, but several conditional densities $f(y|x;\varphi_2)$; one for each value $x \in \mathbb{R}_X$, since the notion of a conditional density is defined for a specific value of the conditioning variable.

These problems are symptomatic of the dependence among the random variables in the sequence because the random variables involved never *forget*. The fact of the matter is that the way to deal with both of these problems is to impose some *restrictions* on the *dependence* and *heterogeneity* of the set of random variables $(X_1, X_2, \ldots, X_n)$ (see chapter 8). In order to convince the reader that we need restrictions from both categories, let us return to the Normal example with independence imposed. The reduction in (6.10) simplifies to:

$$f(x_1,x_2,\ldots,x_n;\phi) \overset{\text{I}}{=} \prod_{k=1}^{n} f_k(x_k;\theta_k), \text{ for all } \mathbf{x} \in \mathbb{R}^n_X, \tag{6.10}$$

but the problem of over-parameterization remains: $\theta_k := (\mu_k, \sigma_{kk})$, $k = 1,2,\ldots,n$. This is symptomatic of the heterogeneity of the sequence.

Collecting the various threads of our reasoning above, we conclude that the dimensionality curse raised by the notion of a non-random sample can be theoretically removed using sequential conditioning but this raises two other problems (the increasing conditioning set and the stochastic conditioning). It also leaves the incidental parameters problem intact.

6.2.2 Keeping an eye on the forest!

Our objective in this and the next two chapters is to landscape the territory beyond Independent and Identically Distributed (IID) random variables by introducing alternative forms of dependence and heterogeneity which enable us to capture the chance regularity patterns exhibited by the time series data such as figure 6.1.

The preliminary discussion in connection with the difficulties arising in the case of non-random samples brought out the role of several useful concepts which relate to the joint and the conditional distributions. Two things have become apparent from the above discussion:

(i)   the key to taming non-IID sequences is the notion of *conditioning* and

(ii)   measuring dependence has to do with the relationship between *joint* and *marginal* distributions or equivalently between *conditional* and marginal distributions.

The primary objective of this chapter is to introduce several notions of dependence in connection with pairs of random variables, as a prelude to the discussion of the general case of a sequence of random variables in chapter 8. Special attention is given to qualitatively different random variables. Chapter 7 concentrates on the stochastic conditioning problem and discusses the way conditional distributions and their moments can be extended to deal with this problem. The concepts developed in these two chapters are then utilized in chapter 8 to provide a systematic discussion for *sequences* of random variables as they relate to dependence and heterogeneity. In other words, all these threads will be tied together in chapter 8 to show how the newly charted territory of the non-IID jungle can help model chance regularity patterns associated with dependence and/or heterogeneity.

6.2.3   Statistical models beyond the simple: a preliminary view

The above preliminary discussion set the scene for extending the simple statistical model to more general models which allow for some dependence and/or heterogeneity. We say some dependence and/or heterogeneity because statistical models with unrestricted dependence and/or heterogeneity are unattainable in the case of non-experimental (observational) data.

In an attempt to be more concrete let us return to the example of the case where the joint distribution of $(X_1, X_2, \ldots, X_n)$ is Normal, i.e. $f(x_1, x_2, \ldots, x_n; \boldsymbol{\phi})$ takes the form (6.2) where $\boldsymbol{\phi} := (\mu_i, \sigma_{ij}, i,j = 1,2, \ldots, n)$ includes $N = n + \frac{1}{2}n(n+1)$ unknown parameters. In the case of observational data we have just one realization of the sample $(X_1, X_2, \ldots, X_n)$, i.e. n numbers $(x_1, x_2, \ldots, x_n)$ and there is no way we can estimate N unknown parameters (see chapter 11).

In the case of *experimental data* we are often in a position to generate more than one realization of the sample, say $(x_{1i}, x_{2i}, \ldots, x_{ni})$, $i = 1,2, \ldots, M$. These additional realizations, under certain restrictions, will be sufficient to estimate all N unknown parameters. These methods, however, are beyond the scope of the present book which concentrates on the modeling and inference with observational data.

Returning to statistical models for *observational data*, we NOTE, as a prelude to the discussion that follows, that each one of these operational models is made up of three basic compatible components from the broad categories mentioned in the case of the **simple statistical model**:

(D)   Distribution: arbitrary univariate,
(M)   Dependence: Independence, Markov, martingale, non-correlation, …
(H)   Heterogeneity: Identical Distribution, weak and strict stationarity ….

Our main task in this and the next two chapters is to enrich the Dependence and Heterogeneity categories with a variety of notions between the two extremes of Independence and Identical Distribution at one end and unrestricted dependence and heterogeneity at the other end of the spectrum. In modeling the aim is to combine components from all three categories in a consistent way with a view to specifying operational statistical models for observational data. The secret of modeling lies with the utilization of all the systematic information in the data. What is systematic, however, depends on how effective the theoretical concepts we use are to capture the patterns we call chance regularity.

6.3   Dependence between two random variables: joint distributions

Intuitively, probabilistic dependence between two random variables X and Y refers to "how information about X helps one infer the value of Y." If X and Y are perfectly dependent, knowing X enables us to infer Y, *with probability one*. In this sense, perfect dependence provides a probabilistic counterpart to the notion of mathematical functional dependence, where $Y = h(X)$ for some function:

$$h(.): \mathbb{R}_X \rightarrow \mathbb{R}_Y.$$

In addition, independence provides a probabilistic counterpart to the notion of *no functional dependence* between two mathematical variables. The main difference is that probabilistic dependence, unlike functional dependence, makes sense for cases between these two extremes. The statement "the random variables X and Y are highly (but not perfectly) dependent" is a meaningful probabilistic statement. Measuring the degree of probabilistic dependence, however, is a difficult, multifaceted problem.

In chapter 2 we defined **independence** between two *events* A, B in $\Im$ $((S,\Im,\mathbb{P}(.))$ being the relevant probability space) as follows:

$$\mathbb{P}(A \cap B) = \mathbb{P}(A) \cdot \mathbb{P}(B), \text{ or } \mathbb{P}(A|B) = \mathbb{P}(A), \text{ for } \mathbb{P}(B) > 0.$$

We could easily extend this to independence between any two *event subspaces* (σ-fields) $\mathcal{A}$ and $\mathcal{B}$ of $\Im$:

$$\mathbb{P}(A \cap B) = \mathbb{P}(A) \cdot \mathbb{P}(B) \text{ for all events } A \in \mathcal{A} \text{ and } B \in \mathcal{B},$$

or

$$\mathbb{P}(A|B) = \mathbb{P}(A) \text{ for all events } A \in \mathcal{A} \text{ and } B \in \mathcal{B}, \mathbb{P}(B) > 0.$$

This definition can be easily adapted to the case of two *random variables* X and Y defined on $(S,\Im,\mathbb{P}(.))$ by choosing $\mathcal{A} := \sigma(X)$ and $\mathcal{B} := \sigma(Y)$, where $\sigma(X)$ denotes the minimal σ-field generated by X; see chapter 3.

In the case where the two *event subspaces* $\mathcal{A}$ and $\mathcal{B}$ are not independent (i.e. they are **dependent**), this is no longer true and the *difference* between the two sides:

$$\|\mathbb{P}(A \cap B) - \mathbb{P}(A) \cdot \mathbb{P}(B)\|, \text{ or } \|\mathbb{P}(A|B) - \mathbb{P}(A)\|,$$

where $\|\|$ denotes some meaningful measure of distance, can be used as *measures of dependence*.

Illustrations

Let $\mathcal{A} \subset \mathfrak{I}$ and $\mathcal{B} \subset \mathfrak{I}$, the following are measures of dependence between them:

(1) $\alpha(\mathcal{A}, \mathcal{B}) = \displaystyle\sup_{A \in \mathcal{A},\, B \in \mathcal{B}} |\mathbb{P}(A \cap B) - \mathbb{P}(A) \cdot \mathbb{P}(B)|,$

(2) $\phi(\mathcal{A}, \mathcal{B}) = \displaystyle\sup_{A \in \mathcal{A},\, B \in \mathcal{B}} |\mathbb{P}(A|B) - \mathbb{P}(A)|, \text{ for } \mathbb{P}(B) > 0,$

(3) $\psi(\mathcal{A}, \mathcal{B}) = \displaystyle\sup_{A \in \mathcal{A},\, B \in \mathcal{B}} \frac{|\mathbb{P}(A \cap B) - \mathbb{P}(A) \cdot \mathbb{P}(B)|}{\mathbb{P}(A) \cdot \mathbb{P}(B)}, \text{ for } \mathbb{P}(B) > 0,\ \mathbb{P}(A) > 0.$

Choosing $\mathcal{A} := \sigma(X)$ and $\mathcal{B} := \sigma(Y)$, the above quantities measure dependence between the random variables X and Y.

Example

Consider again our favorite random experiment of tossing a fair coin twice and noting the outcome with $S := \{(HH),(HT),(TH),(TT)\}$, the event space being the power set of S, i.e., $\mathfrak{I} := \mathcal{P}(S)$. Define the random variables:

$$X(HH) = X(TT) = 0,\ X(HT) = X(TH) = 1,$$

$$Y(HH) = Y(HT) = 0,\ Y(TT) = Y(TH) = 1,$$

$$Z(HH) = 0,\ Z(HT) = Z(TH) = 1,\ Z(TT) = 2.$$

$$\sigma(X) := \{S, \emptyset, A, \overline{A}\}, \text{ where } A := \{(HH),(TT)\},$$

$$\sigma(Y) := \{S, \emptyset, B, \overline{B}\}, \text{ where } B := \{(HH),(HT)\},$$

$$\sigma(Z) := \{S, \emptyset, C_1, C_2, C_3, \overline{C_1}, \overline{C_2}, \overline{C_3}\},\ C_1 := \{(HH)\},$$
$$C_2 := \{(HT),(TH)\},\ C_3 := \{(TT)\}.$$

From these results we can deduce that the random variables X and Y are independent:

$$\mathbb{P}(A \cap B) = \tfrac{1}{4} = \mathbb{P}(A) \cdot \mathbb{P}(B) \text{ for all } A \in \sigma(X) \text{ and } B \in \sigma(Y).$$

On the other hand, the random variables X and Z are not independent because for at least one of the intersection events:

$$\mathbb{P}(A \cap C_1) = \tfrac{1}{4} \neq \mathbb{P}(A) \cdot \mathbb{P}(C_1) = \tfrac{1}{8}.$$

In view of the fact that the random variables X and Z are dependent we can proceed to measure their dependence using any one of the measures **(1)**–**(3)** above.

$$\tfrac{1}{4} = \mathbb{P}(A \cap C_1) = \mathbb{P}(HH),\quad \mathbb{P}(A) \cdot \mathbb{P}(C_1) = \left(\tfrac{1}{2}\right)\tfrac{1}{4} = \tfrac{1}{8},$$

$$0 = \mathbb{P}(A \cap C_2) = \mathbb{P}(\emptyset),\qquad \mathbb{P}(A) \cdot \mathbb{P}(C_2) = \left(\tfrac{1}{2}\right)\tfrac{1}{2} = \tfrac{1}{4},$$

$$\tfrac{1}{4} = \mathbb{P}(A \cap C_3) = \mathbb{P}(TT),\quad \mathbb{P}(A) \cdot \mathbb{P}(C_3) = \left(\tfrac{1}{2}\right)\tfrac{1}{4} = \tfrac{1}{8},$$

$$\tfrac{1}{4} = \mathbb{P}(A \cap \overline{C_1}) = \mathbb{P}(TT),\quad \mathbb{P}(A) \cdot \mathbb{P}(\overline{C_1}) = \left(\tfrac{1}{2}\right)\tfrac{3}{4} = \tfrac{3}{8},$$

$$\tfrac{1}{2} = \mathbb{P}(A \cap \overline{C_2}) = \mathbb{P}(HH),\quad \mathbb{P}(A) \cdot \mathbb{P}(\overline{C_2}) = \left(\tfrac{1}{2}\right)\tfrac{1}{2} = \tfrac{1}{4},$$

$$\tfrac{1}{4} = \mathbb{P}(A \cap \overline{C_3}) = \mathbb{P}(HH), \quad \mathbb{P}(A) \cdot \mathbb{P}(\overline{C_3}) = \left(\tfrac{1}{2}\right)\tfrac{3}{4} = \tfrac{3}{8},$$

$$\alpha(\sigma(X), \sigma(Z)) = \sup_{A \in \sigma(X),\, B \in \sigma(Z)} |\mathbb{P}(A \cap B) - \mathbb{P}(A) \cdot \mathbb{P}(B)| = \tfrac{1}{4}.$$

The other measures of dependence such as $\phi(\mathcal{A}, \mathcal{B})$ and $\psi(\mathcal{A}, \mathcal{B})$ are evaluated similarly.

In chapter 4 we defined **independence** between two *random variables* X and Y using the joint density function as follows:

$$f(x,y) = f_x(x) \cdot f_y(y), \text{ for all } (x,y) \in \mathbb{R}_X \times \mathbb{R}_Y. \tag{6.11}$$

This equality suggests that in the case where the random variables X and Y are independent, the joint distribution contains the same information as the two marginal distributions.

Example
Consider joint distribution of the random variables X and Y above:

$y \backslash x$	0	1	$f_y(y)$
0	0.25	0.25	0.50
1	0.25	0.25	0.50
$f_x(x)$	0.50	0.50	1

$$\tag{6.12}$$

It can be easily verified that these two random variables are indeed independent.

In terms of the conditional density function we defined *independence* between two random variables X and Y via:

$$f(y|x) = f_y(y), \text{ for all } (x,y) \in \mathbb{R}_X \times \mathbb{R}_Y. \tag{6.13}$$

Because of the symmetry of the notion of independence, it can defined equivalently by:

$$f(x|y) = f_x(x), \text{ for all } (x,y) \in \mathbb{R}_X \times \mathbb{R}_Y.$$

In the case where the random variables X and Y are not independent, they are **dependent**, (6.11) is no longer true; the joint distribution contains more information than the two marginal distributions. The additional information is indeed the information relating to the dependence between the random variables X and Y. In this sense functions of the form:

$$\|f(x,y) - f_x(x) \cdot f_y(y)\|, \text{ or } \|f(y|x) - f_y(y)\| \tag{6.14}$$

can be used as *measures of dependence* based on density functions.

Examples
1 Hoeffding's Δ

$$\Delta(X,Y) = \left(\int_{-\infty}^{\infty} \int_{-\infty}^{\infty} [f(x,y) - f_x(x)f_y(y)]^2 f(x,y) dx dy \right).$$

2 The absolute value analogues to Δ

$$\delta_1(X,Y) = 12(\int_{-\infty}^{\infty}\int_{-\infty}^{\infty}|f(x,y) - f_x(x)f_y(y)|f(x,y)dxdy)$$

$$\delta_2(X,Y) = 12(\int_{-\infty}^{\infty}\int_{-\infty}^{\infty}|f(x,y) - f_x(x)f_y(y)|f_x(x)f_y(y)dxdy).$$

3 Informational distance

$$\mathcal{K}(X,Y) = \int_{-\infty}^{\infty}\int_{-\infty}^{\infty} \ln\left(\frac{f(x,y)}{f_x(x)\cdot f_y(y)}\right)f(x,y)dxdy,$$

where ln denotes the natural (base e) logarithm; this measure is based on the Kullback measure of divergence between two distributions.

4 Square contingency coefficient

$$\varphi^2(X,Y) = \left(\int_{-\infty}^{\infty}\int_{-\infty}^{\infty}\left[\frac{f(x,y)}{f_x(x)f_y(y)}\right]f(x,y)dxdy - 1\right).$$

5 Spearman's rank coefficient

$$S(X,Y) = 3\int_{-\infty}^{\infty}\int_{-\infty}^{\infty} [2F_X(x) - 1][2F_Y(y) - 1]f(x,y)dxdy,$$

where $[2F_X(x) - 1]$ is chosen instead of $F_X(x)$ to render the latter distribution symmetric around zero. In fact, it can be shown that for $u = F_X(x)$, whatever the nature of $F_X(x)$, the distribution of u is uniform with range $[0,1]$, i.e. $F_U(u) = u$, for $0 \leq u \leq 1$ (see chapter 3). Hence, the distribution of $u = [2F_X(x) - 1]$ is uniform around 0, i.e.

$$[2F_X(x) - 1] \sim U(-1,1).$$

The presence of multiple integrals in the above measures of dependence based on density functions, renders them cumbersome and close to unattainable in the case of more than two random variables. As argued in the previous section we need measures of dependence for a sequence of random variables $\{X_1, X_2, \ldots, X_n\}$. On the other hand the mixing condition measures **(1)**–**(3)**, based on subevent spaces, are easier to handle because they involve maximization over sets of subsets. As shown in chapter 8, the latter measures of dependence form the basis of the so-called *mixing conditions* on *temporal* dependence in a sequence of random variables.

6.4   Dependence between two random variables: moments

6.4.1 Joint moments and dependence

Measuring dependence using distances such as those mentioned above can be a very difficult task and thus in modeling we often resort to measures based on the moments. The connection between these two categories of dependence measures passes through the following lemma.

Independence lemma Two random variables X and Y are said to be **independent**, if for *any* well-behaved (Borel) functions $u = g(X)$ and $v = h(Y)$:

$$f(g(X),h(Y)) = f_u(g(X)) \cdot f_v(h(Y)), \text{ for each } (u,v) \in \mathbb{R}^2. \tag{6.15}$$

In simple terms, this result means that if X and Y are independent, then any functions of these random variables, say $u = X^2$ and $v = \ln Y$, are also independent random variables.

Clearly, this lemma cannot be used to establish independence because one needs to demonstrate that (6.15) holds *for all* possible Borel functions; an impossible task. It is, however, very useful for two reasons. First, it can be used to demonstrate non-independence by finding just one counter-example. Second, it is of theoretical interest because after establishing independence using, say (6.11), one can declare that any Borel functions of the original random variables are also necessarily independent.

A WORD OF CAUTION: it must be emphasized that in the case where X and Y are not independent (6.15) might be true for some functions $g(X)$ and $h(Y)$, as the following example demonstrates.

Example
Consider the joint distribution as specified below.

$y\backslash x$	-1	0	1
-1	0	0.25	0
0	0.25	0.25	0
1	0	0	0.25

(a)

$v\backslash u$	0	1	$f_v(v)$
0	0.25	0.25	0.50
1	0.25	0.25	0.50
$f_x(x)$	0.50	0.50	1

(b)

(6.16)

X and Y are not independent because:

$$f(-1,-1) = 0 \neq f_x(-1) \cdot f_y(-1) = 0.062.$$

However, the random variables $u = X^2$ and $v = Y^2$ turn out to be independent, as can be verified from (6.16)(b). The moral of the story being that even in cases where the random variables X and Y are not independent, there might exist some functions of them which turn out to be independent.

In view of the fact that the expectation $E(.)$ is always defined with respect to a specific distribution, it should come as no surprise to learn that the condition (6.15) can be written equivalently in the following form:

$$E(g(X),h(Y)) = E(g(X)) \cdot E(h(Y)), \tag{6.17}$$

assuming the expectations exist. It is important to NOTE that $E(.)$ on the left-hand side is defined in terms of $f(x,y)$ but the other two are defined in terms of $f_x(.)$ and $f_y(.)$:

$$E(h(X) \cdot g(Y)) = \int_{-\infty}^{\infty} \int_{-\infty}^{\infty} [h(X) \cdot g(Y)] \cdot f(x,y) dx dy,$$

$$E(h(X)) = \int_{-\infty}^{\infty} h(X) \cdot f_x(x)dx,$$

$$E(g(Y)) = \int_{-\infty}^{\infty} g(Y) \cdot f_y(y)dy.$$

Using this result in conjunction with simple functions of X and Y, which give rise to the moments of the joint distribution, we can define different forms of independence (and dependence) in terms of the joint product and central moments.

In the case where all the moments of the random variables X and Y exist ($E(X^k)$ $< \infty$ and $E(Y^k) < \infty$, for all $k = 1,2,...$), we can use the above independence lemma in conjunction with the joint product moments to deduce that X and Y are *independent* if and only if:

$$(a) \quad \mu'_{km} := E\{X^k Y^m\} = E(X^k) \cdot E(Y^m), \text{ for all } k,m = 0,1,2,... \quad (6.18)$$

This is, again, a non-operational result for demonstrating independence because we need to verify these equalities for an infinite number of joint moments. However, its negation can be used to charter the territory between the two extreme positions of *independence* and *complete dependence*, in the sense that if:

$$E(X^k \cdot Y^m) \neq E(X^k) \cdot E(Y^m), \text{ for any } k,m = 1,2,... \quad (6.19)$$

the random variables X and Y are (k,m)-**order dependent**. Unfortunately, the only special case of (6.19) explored thoroughly so far in the literature is the case $(1,1)$:

$$E(X \cdot Y) \neq E(X) \cdot E(Y),$$

known as **first-order (linear) dependence**. In the case where the equality holds:

$$E(X \cdot Y) = E(X) \cdot E(Y),$$

it is called **first-order independence**.

The notion of *independence* in terms of an infinite number of moments can be defined equivalently in terms of the *joint central moments*:

$$(b) \quad \mu_{km} := E\{[X - E(X)]^k [Y - E(Y)]^m\} = 0, \text{ for all } k,m = 0,1,2,... \quad (6.20)$$

Similarly, we can define the notion of (k,m)-**dependence** using its negation:

$$E\{[X - E(X)]^k [Y - E(Y)]^m\} \neq 0, \text{ for any } k,m = 0,1,2,...$$

The equivalence of the two definitions in terms of the joint product and joint central moments can be demonstrated easily in the case $k = 1, m = 1$. The notion of *first-order independence* is equivalent to saying that the first central moment, the **covariance** is zero:

$$\mu_{11} := Cov(X,Y) = E\{[X - E(X)][Y - E(Y)]\} = 0.$$

The equivalence of the two definitions follows from the fact that:

$$Cov(X,Y) = E(XY) - E[X \cdot E(Y)] - E[Y \cdot E(X)] + E[E(X) \cdot E(Y)] =$$

$$= E(XY) - 2[E(X) \cdot E(Y)] + [E(X) \cdot E(Y)] = E(XY) - [E(X) \cdot E(Y)],$$

$$Cov(X,Y) = 0 \Leftrightarrow E(XY) - E(X) \cdot E(Y) = 0.$$

It is interesting to NOTE that there is a direct relationship between the covariance and the dependence distances used in defining independence in the previous section:

$$Cov(X,Y) = \int_{-\infty}^{\infty} \int_{-\infty}^{\infty} [F_{XY}(x,y) - F_X(x)F_Y(y)] f(x,y) dxdy.$$

Correlation and dependence

An important weakness of the covariance, when used as a measure of the dependence between X and Y, is that it depends on their units of measurement. The standardized version of the covariance, known as the *correlation coefficient*, was first proposed by Galton (1880) as *co-relation*.

Correlation coefficient For any two random variables X and Y such that $Var(X) < \infty$, $Var(Y) < \infty$, defined on the same probability space $(S, \Im, \mathbb{P}(.))$, the *correlation coefficient* is defined by:

$$Corr(X,Y) = \frac{Cov(X,Y)}{\sqrt{Var(X) \cdot Var(Y)}}.$$

Example

Let us derive the correlation coefficient between X and Y, using the joint density 4.19 (see chapter 4):

$$E(X) = 1.1,\ E(Y) = 0.8,\ Var(X) = 0.69,\ Var(Y) = 0.96,\ Cov(X,Y) = 0.12.$$

Hence, the correlation coefficient is: $Corr(X,Y) = \frac{0.12}{\sqrt{(0.69) \cdot (0.96)}} = 0.147.$

Properties of the correlation coefficient

$\rho 1.$ $-1 \leq Corr(X,Y) \leq 1$,

$\rho 2.$ $Corr(aX + b, cY + d) = Corr(X,Y)$, for $(a,b,c,d) \in \mathbb{R}^4$, $(a \cdot c) > 0$,

$\rho 3.$ $Corr(X,Y) = \pm 1$, if and only if $Y = a_0 + a_1 X$, $(a_0, a_1) \in \mathbb{R}^2$.

The first property relating to the range of values for the correlation coefficient follows from the so-called *Schwarz inequality*:

$$|Cov(X,Y)| \leq [Var(X)]^{\frac{1}{2}} [Var(Y)]^{\frac{1}{2}}.$$

The second property follows from the definition of the correlation coefficient which renders it invariant to linear transformations. The third property is more involved but the proof of this result can throw some light on the relationship between dependence in general and correlation in particular.

Perfect correlation Two random variables X and Y are perfectly correlated, i.e., $Corr(X,Y) = \pm 1$, if and only if they are *linearly related*.

Proof (the proof can be omitted without any loss of continuity). The *if* part follows directly by assuming that the random variables X and Y are linearly related:

$$Y = a_0 + a_1 X,\ a_1 > 0. \tag{6.21}$$

By simple algebra and the properties of $E(.)$ (see chapter 3), it follows that:

$$Cov(X, Y) = E\{[a_0 + a_1 X - E(a_0 + a_1 X)][X - E(X)]\} =$$
$$= a_1 E\{[X - E(X)][X - E(X)]\} = a_1 \, Var(X).$$

In view of the fact that $Var(Y) = a_1^2 \, Var(X)$, substitution into the correlation coefficient formula yields:

$$Corr(X, Y) = \frac{a_1 \, Var(X)}{(\sqrt{a_1^2 \, Var(X) \cdot Var(X)})} = 1.$$

NOTE that in the case $a_1 < 0$, $Corr(X, Y) = -1$. The *only if* part of this result is a bit more complicated. Assume that $Corr(X, Y) = 1$ (the case $Corr(X, Y) = -1$ can be dealt with, similarly) and define the standardized variables:

$$X^* = \frac{X - E(X)}{\sqrt{Var(X)}}, \; Y^* = \frac{Y - E(Y)}{\sqrt{Var(Y)}}.$$

From this we can deduce that:

$$E\{(X^* - Y^*)^2\} = Var(X^*) + Var(Y^*) - 2E(X^* Y^*) = 2 - 2 = 0.$$

This implies that $\mathbb{P}(s: X^*(s) \neq Y^*(s)) = 0$, for all $s \in S$ (see chapter 3), which can be equivalently written in the form:

$$\mathbb{P}(s: X^*(s) = Y^*(s)) = 1, \; s \in S \text{ or } X^* = Y^*, \textit{with probability one}.$$

Substituting the original variables and rearranging the terms yields:

$$Y = E(Y) + \left(\frac{Var(Y)}{Var(X)}\right)^{\frac{1}{2}} (X - E(X)), \textit{with probability one},$$

which coincides with (6.21) for: $a_0 = E(Y) - a_1 E(X)$, $a_1 = \left(\frac{Var(Y)}{Var(X)}\right)^{\frac{1}{2}}$.

The above result suggests that *correlation* is a measure of *linear dependence*. This fact is brought out most emphatically by the following example.

Example

Let X be uniformly distributed between minus one and plus one, denoted by

$$X \sim U(-1, 1), \text{ and } Y := X^2.$$

As we can see, X and Y are perfectly dependent on each other (but non-linearly); knowledge of one determines the other completely. We can show, however, that the two are *uncorrelated*. In view of the fact that:

$$f_x(x) = \tfrac{1}{2}, \; E(X) = 0,$$

$$Cov(X, Y) = E(XY) - E(X) \cdot E(Y) = E(X^3) - E(X) \cdot E(X^2).$$

Hence, X and Y are uncorrelated if $E(X^3) = 0$. Indeed:

$$E(X^3) = \int_{-1}^{1} x^3 \left(\tfrac{1}{2}\right) dx = \tfrac{1}{2}\left[\left(\tfrac{1}{4}\right) x^4 \Big|_{-1}^{1}\right] = \tfrac{1}{2}\left[\left(\tfrac{1}{4}\right) - \left(\tfrac{1}{4}\right)\right] = 0 \cdot$$

At this stage, it is imperative to differentiate non-correlation from independence. We know from the above discussion that the correlation coefficient defines a measure of *linear dependence*, not dependence in general. Hence, the general conclusion we can draw about the relationship between non-correlation and independence is that:

independence $\Rightarrow$ non-correlation

but the converse is not true:

non-correlation $\nRightarrow$ independence

In concluding this subsection we NOTE a concept closely related to uncorrelatedness, the notion of *orthogonality.* Two random variables X and Y, whose second moments are finite, are said to be **orthogonal** if:

$$E(X \cdot Y) = 0.$$

NOTE that if two random variables are *uncorrelated*, their mean deviations,

$$X^* := [X - E(X)], \; Y^* := [Y - E(Y)],$$

are *orthogonal*:

$$E(X^* \cdot Y^*) = 0.$$

6.4.2 Conditional moments and dependence

Returning to the definition of **independence** of two random variables X and Y in terms of the conditional density:

$$f(y|x) = f_y(y), \text{ for all } (x,y) \in \mathbb{R}_X \times \mathbb{R}_Y, \tag{6.22}$$

we NOTE that the conditional moments condition analogous to (6.18) is:

$$E(Y^r | X = x) = E(Y^r), \text{ for all } x \in \mathbb{R}_X, r = 1,2,\ldots \tag{6.23}$$

It is interesting to see how these equalities arise in the case of independence.

Step 1 From the definition of independence we know that for any well-behaved functions $h(.)$ and $g(.)$ of the random variables X and Y:

$$E(h(X) \cdot g(Y)) = E(h(X)) \cdot E(g(Y)), \text{ for all } (x,y) \in \mathbb{R}_X \times \mathbb{R}_Y. \tag{6.24}$$

Step 2 Choosing the functions:

$h(X)$ arbitrarily but, $g_r(Y) := Y^r, r = 1,2,\ldots,$

(6.24) reduces to (assuming the moments exist):

$$E(h(X) \cdot Y^r) = E(h(X)) \cdot E(Y^r), \text{ for all } r = 1,2,\ldots, \tag{6.25}$$

Step 3 In general:

$$E(h(X) \cdot Y^r) = E[E(h(X) \cdot Y^r) | \sigma(X)] = E(h(X)) \cdot E(Y^r) | \sigma(X)), \tag{6.26}$$

where the first equality follows from the property CE2: $E(Y) = E[E(Y|\sigma(X))]$ and the second from the CE3 property of conditional expectations (see chapter 7); we remind the reader that $\sigma(X)$ denotes the set of all events generated by the random variable X (see chapter 3).

Step 4 Comparing (6.25) with (6.26) we deduce that the two random variables X and Y are independent when (6.23) holds.

As in the case of joint and marginal moments (6.18), (6.23) does not provide a way to verify independence because it involves an infinite number of moments. However, as with (6.19), their negation can be used to chart the territory beyond independence. Unlike (6.19) the conditional moments offer a more systematic taxonomy of dependence in the sense that we can talk about first, second, third, etc. orders of dependence. This measure of dependence is defined in terms of the distance function:

$$d_r^*(X,Y) := [E(Y^r|\sigma(X)) - E(Y^r)],\tag{6.27}$$

or equivalently (see chapter 7):

$$d_r(Y|x) := [E(Y^r|X=x) - E(Y^r)] \text{ for all } x\in\mathbb{R}_X.\tag{6.28}$$

rth-**order dependence**. Any two random variables X and Y, whose moments of rth-order exist and $d_k(Y|x)=0$ for all $k=1,2,\ldots,r-1$ are:

rth-*order dependent* if: $d_r(Y|x)\neq 0$, for all $x\in\mathbb{R}_X$, $r=1,2,3,\ldots$

On the other hand, the random variables X and Y are:

rth-*order independent* if: $d_r(Y|x)=0$, for all $x\in\mathbb{R}_X$, $r=1,2,3,\ldots$

This definition enables us to chart the territory of dependence using this hierarchical scheme of first, second, third, etc. order of dependence. For example any random variables X and Y whose first-order moments exist:

$$d_1(Y|x)\neq 0, \text{ for all } x\in\mathbb{R}_X \Rightarrow X \text{ and } Y \text{ are } \textit{first-order dependent}.$$

The above charting of dependence can be done equivalently in terms of the central moments distance function:

$$\eth_r^*(X,Y) := [E([Y-E(Y|\sigma(X))]^r|\sigma(X)) - E([Y-E(Y)]^r)],\tag{6.29}$$

or equivalently:

$$\eth_r(Y|x) := [E([Y-E(Y|X=x)]^r|X=x) - E([Y-E(Y)]^r)], \text{ for all } x\in\mathbb{R}_X.\tag{6.30}$$

For example second-order independence is defined by:

$$\eth_2(Y|x)=0 \Leftrightarrow Var(Y|X=x)= Var(Y), \text{ for all } x\in\mathbb{R}_X.$$

In this sense, two random variables X and Y can be first-order independent but second-order dependent, i.e., $E(Y|X)= E(Y)$ but $Var(Y|X)\neq Var(Y)$; see chapter 8.

It is important to NOTE that the conditional moments give rise to a much easier classification of dependence than the double index notions defined in terms of the joint moments in (6.19). However, the above derivation based on (6.26) suggests that the notions of independence defined in terms of the conditional moments are somewhat stronger. To see this consider the case of first-order dependence where (6.26) takes the form:

$$E(h(X)\cdot Y) = E[E(h(X)\cdot Y)|X] = E(h(X))\cdot E(Y|X). \tag{6.31}$$

This suggests that *first-order independence*, is stronger than *non-correlation* because in the case of the latter the function $h(.)$ cannot be arbitrary as in first-order independence but has to be of the form: $h(X) = X$. In turn, first-order independence is weaker than (complete) independence because for the latter to hold we need all conditional moments to coincide with the marginal moments. In summary:

Independence $\Rightarrow$ first-order independence $\Rightarrow$ non-correlation.

6.4.3 Conditional independence

An important form of dependence is what we call *conditional independence*. In the context of a probability space $(S,\Im,\mathbb{P}(.))$ two events $A\in\Im$ and $B\in\Im$, are *conditionally independent* given a third event $D\in\Im$, for which $\mathbb{P}(D)>0$, if:

$$\mathbb{P}(A\cap B|D) = \mathbb{P}(A|D)\cdot\mathbb{P}(B|D).$$

That is, knowing that D has occurred renders the events A and B independent.

The random variables X and Y are said to be **conditionally independent** given Z, if and only if:

$$f(x,y|z) = f(x|z)\cdot f(y|z), \text{ for all } (x,y,z)\in[\mathbb{R}_X\times\mathbb{R}_Y\times\mathbb{R}_Z], \tag{6.32}$$

$\mathbb{R}_Z := \{z\in\mathbb{R}: f_Z(z)>0\}$ is the support set of $f_Z(z)$. That is, the joint density of (X,Y,Z) factors into two conditional densities. Intuitively, X and Y are conditionally independent given Z, if X and Y are related only through Z.

Example
Consider the case where (X_1,X_2,X_3) are Normally distributed with joint distribution denoted by:

$$\begin{pmatrix}X_1\\X_2\\X_3\end{pmatrix}\sim N\left(\begin{bmatrix}\mu_1\\\mu_2\\\mu_3\end{bmatrix},\begin{bmatrix}\sigma_{11}&\sigma_{12}&\sigma_{13}\\\sigma_{12}&\sigma_{22}&\sigma_{23}\\\sigma_{13}&\sigma_{23}&\sigma_{33}\end{bmatrix}\right) \tag{6.33}$$

$$E(X_k) = \mu_k, Var(X_k) = \sigma_{kk}, k=1,2,3, Cov(X_i,X_j) = \sigma_{ij}, i\neq j, i,j = 1,2,3.$$

NOTE that the general formula for the joint Normal distribution of $\mathbf{X}$ (an $n\times 1$ vector) is:

$$f(\mathbf{x};\boldsymbol{\theta}) = \frac{(\det\boldsymbol{\Sigma})^{-\frac{1}{2}}}{(\sqrt{2\pi})^n}\exp\left\{-\frac{1}{2}(\mathbf{x}-\boldsymbol{\mu})^\top\boldsymbol{\Sigma}^{-1}(\mathbf{x}-\boldsymbol{\mu})\right\}, E(\mathbf{X}) = \boldsymbol{\mu}, Cov(\mathbf{X}) = \boldsymbol{\Sigma}. \tag{6.34}$$

As shown above, the Normal distribution allows only first-order dependence and thus for any $i\neq j$, $i,j = 1,2,3$:

$$\sigma_{ij} = 0 \Leftrightarrow X_i \text{ and } X_j \text{ are independent.}$$

It turns out that conditional independence is also easy to define in this context in terms of the inverse of the variance–covariance matrix:

$$\begin{bmatrix} \sigma_{11} & \sigma_{12} & \sigma_{13} \\ \sigma_{12} & \sigma_{22} & \sigma_{23} \\ \sigma_{13} & \sigma_{23} & \sigma_{33} \end{bmatrix}^{-1} = \begin{bmatrix} \omega_{11} & \omega_{12} & \omega_{13} \\ \omega_{12} & \omega_{22} & \omega_{23} \\ \omega_{13} & \omega_{23} & \omega_{33} \end{bmatrix}.$$

For any $i \neq j \neq k$, $i,j,k = 1,2,3$:

$$\omega_{ij} = 0 \Leftrightarrow X_i \text{ and } X_j \text{ are conditionally independent given } X_k.$$

Returning to the notion of *conditional independence* between the random variables X and Y given Z we NOTE that it can be defined equivalently by:

$$(M): f(y|x,z) = f(y|z), \text{ for all } (x,y,z) \in [\mathbb{R}_X \times \mathbb{R}_Y \times \mathbb{R}_Z]. \tag{6.35}$$

This form is directly related to the widely used notion of *Markov dependence*. In the context of (6.35), Y and X are conditionally independent given Z, but if we interpret Y as the "future," X as the "past," and Z as the "present," (M) says that, given the present the future is independent of the past; this is known as Markov dependence. Using the points $0 < t_1 < t_2 < t_3$ the **Markov dependence** can be written in the more heedful form:

$$(M): f(x_{t_3}|x_{t_2}, x_{t_1}) = f(x_{t_3}|x_{t_2}), \text{ for all } (x_{t_1}, x_{t_2}, x_{t_3}) \in \mathbb{R}_X^3.$$

A third useful way to define conditional independence, which involves no reference to conditional distributions, is:

$$f(x,y,z) = \frac{1}{f_z(z)} (f(x,z) \cdot f(y,z)), \text{ for all } (x,y,z) \in [\mathbb{R}_X \times \mathbb{R}_Y \times \mathbb{R}_Z].$$

NOTE. The conditional independence of X and Y given Z is often denoted by:

$$[X \perp Y]|(Z).$$

Using this notation we state several useful results in relation to conditional independence (see Whittaker (1990)):

(i) $([Y \perp (X_1, X_2)]|(Z)) \Rightarrow ([Y \perp X_1]|(Z))$,
(ii) $([Y \perp (X_1, X_2)]|(Z)) \Leftrightarrow ([Y \perp X_1]|(Z, X_2))$ and $([Y \perp X_2]|(Z, X_1))$,
(iii) $([Y \perp X]|(Z))$ and $U = h(X) \Rightarrow ([Y \perp U]|(Z))$,
(iv) $([Y \perp X]|(Z))$ and $U = h(X) \Rightarrow ([Y \perp X]|(Z, U))$,

where $h(.)$ is a Borel function. NOTE that these results hold unchanged in the case where X, Y, Z are random vectors.

A concept related to conditional independence but less general is defined in terms of the covariance of the conditional means. This is known as a **partial covariance** between the random variables X and Y given Z and defined by:

$$Cov(X, Y|Z) = E([X - E(X|Z)][Y - E(Y|Z)]).$$

In direct analogy to the simple covariance, the partial covariance measures conditional *linear* independence. Since, it shares with its sister the same dependence on the units of measurement, we proceed to standardize it to define the **partial correlation**:

$$Corr(X,Y|Z) = \frac{E([X - E(X|Z)][Y - E(Y|Z)])}{\sqrt{Var(X|Z) \cdot Var(Y|Z)}}.$$

This measures the linear dependence between two random variables X and Y after removing the effect of a third random variable Z. This was first introduced by Yule (1897), who called it the *nett* correlation coefficient.

NOTE that the partial correlation is related to the simple correlations via:

$$\rho_{ij.k} := Corr(X_i, X_j | X_k) = \frac{(\rho_{ij} - \rho_{ik}\rho_{jk})}{\sqrt{(1 - \rho_{ik}^2) \cdot (1 - \rho_{jk}^2)}}, \ \rho_{ij} := \frac{\sigma_{ij}}{\sqrt{\sigma_{ii}\sigma_{jj}}}, \ i \neq j \neq k, \ i,j,k = 1,2,3.$$

Example

In the case where (X_1, X_2, X_3) are Normally distributed, discussed above, one can show that the conditional covariances coincide with the elements of the inverse variance–covariance matrix, i.e.:

$$Cov(X_i, X_j | X_k) = \omega_{ij}, \ i \neq j \neq k, \ i,j,k = 1,2,3.$$

In view of the fact that for $i,j,k = 1,2,3$, $i \neq j \neq k$:

$$\rho_{ij.k} = 0 \Leftrightarrow \omega_{ij} = 0 \text{ we deduce that } [X_i \perp X_j] | X_k \Leftrightarrow \omega_{ij} = 0.$$

Motivated by the variety of dependence structures among several random variables that can be generated using different conditional independence restrictions, a literature called *graphical analysis* has been developed recently (see Whittaker (1990), Edwards (1995) and Pearl (1988)). The term derives from the fact that these models are represented as graphs connecting the various random variables involved. In order to provide a taste of graphical analysis let us consider the case of the Normally distributed random variables (X_1, X_2, X_3, X_4) with a joint distribution:

$$\begin{pmatrix} X_1 \\ X_2 \\ X_3 \\ X_4 \end{pmatrix} \sim N \left(\begin{bmatrix} \mu_1 \\ \mu_2 \\ \mu_3 \\ \mu_4 \end{bmatrix}, \begin{bmatrix} \sigma_{11} & \sigma_{12} & \sigma_{13} & \sigma_{14} \\ \sigma_{12} & \sigma_{22} & \sigma_{23} & \sigma_{24} \\ \sigma_{13} & \sigma_{23} & \sigma_{33} & \sigma_{34} \\ \sigma_{14} & \sigma_{24} & \sigma_{34} & \sigma_{44} \end{bmatrix} \right), \tag{6.36}$$

where, as above, we denote the inverse variance–covariance by:

$$\begin{bmatrix} \sigma_{11} & \sigma_{12} & \sigma_{13} & \sigma_{14} \\ \sigma_{12} & \sigma_{22} & \sigma_{23} & \sigma_{24} \\ \sigma_{13} & \sigma_{23} & \sigma_{33} & \sigma_{34} \\ \sigma_{14} & \sigma_{24} & \sigma_{34} & \sigma_{44} \end{bmatrix}^{-1} = \begin{bmatrix} \omega_{11} & \omega_{12} & \omega_{13} & \omega_{14} \\ \omega_{12} & \omega_{22} & \omega_{23} & \omega_{24} \\ \omega_{13} & \omega_{23} & \omega_{33} & \omega_{34} \\ \omega_{14} & \omega_{24} & \omega_{34} & \omega_{44} \end{bmatrix}.$$

(i) Model 1: $\omega_{ij} \neq 0$, for all $i,j = 1,2,3$; complete dependence.

(ii)   Model 2: $\omega_{13} = 0$, X_1 conditionally independent of X_3 given X_2, X_4,
$\omega_{12} \neq 0$, $\omega_{14} \neq 0$, $\omega_{23} \neq 0$, $\omega_{24} \neq 0$, $\omega_{34} \neq 0$.

(iii) Model 3: $\omega_{13} = 0$, $\omega_{12} \neq 0$, $\omega_{14} \neq 0$, $\omega_{23} \neq 0$, $\omega_{34} \neq 0$,
$\omega_{24} = 0$, X_2 conditionally independent of X_4 given X_1, X_3.

(iv) Model 4: $\omega_{13} = 0$, $\omega_{24} = 0$, $\omega_{12} \neq 0$, $\omega_{23} \neq 0$, $\omega_{34} \neq 0$,
$\omega_{14} = 0$, X_1 conditionally independent of X_4 given X_2, X_3.

(v)   Model 5: $\omega_{13} = 0$, $\omega_{24} = 0$, $\omega_{12} \neq 0$, $\omega_{14} \neq 0$, $\omega_{23} \neq 0$,
$\omega_{34} = 0$, X_3 conditionally independent of X_4 given X_1, X_2.

(vi) Model 6: $\omega_{13} = 0$, $\omega_{24} = 0$, $\omega_{14} = 0$, $\omega_{34} = 0$, $\omega_{12} \neq 0$, $\omega_{23} \neq 0$.

6.5   Dependence and the measurement system

6.5.1   Measurement scales and dependence

An important limitation of the correlation coefficient, as a measure of linear dependence, is that *linearity* makes sense only in cases where the random variable in question takes values in a measurement system such as the *interval* or *ratio* system. In the case of random variables of the *nominal* or the *ordinal* type (see chapter 1 and Spanos (1986), p. 409), linearity does not make much sense. In chapter 1 we discussed the following hierarchy of measurement scales:

(i) ratio,   (ii) interval,   (iii) ordinal,   (iv) nominal.

As argued there, the ratio variables have the richest mathematical structure and then followed by interval, ordinal, and nominal variables in that order. Statistical methods designed for one category of variables do not necessarily apply to variables of other categories. The only general rule we can use as a guide is that a statistical method designed for one category of variables applies also to variables which belong to a higher category but not necessarily to a lower category. For example, a statistical concept designed for an ordinal variable is meaningful for interval and ratio variables but not necessarily for nominal variables. For nominal variables the only measure of location that makes sense is the mode and for ordinal variables we can add the median. In terms of measures of dispersion the interquantile range makes sense only for ordinal variables. Anything that involves the mean or variance does not make much sense for nominal and ordinal variables.

Measuring dependence among the last two categories (nominal, ordinal) of random variables is somewhat problematical because it is not obvious what dependence means in their context. The problem is even more serious when measuring dependence among variables from different categories. These problems were recognized early in the 20th century and became an issue that led to acrimonious arguments between K. Pearson and Yule. Yule (1900, 1910, 1912) was in favor of designing specific measures of association between discrete variables by utilizing their discreteness. K. Pearson (1910, 1913a,b), on

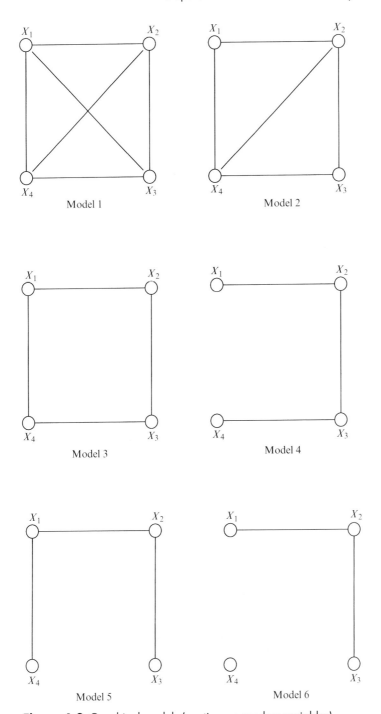

Figure 6.2 Graphical models (continuous random variables)

the other hand, favored the use of continuous distributions to approximate the bivariate discrete distribution for categorical variables and use them in order to measure association; see also Heron (1911). The arguments from both sides were heated and those who think that probability theory and statistical inference are unemotional mathematical subjects should read the following vilification from K. Pearson to his former, student, assistant and co-worker:

> We regret having to draw attention to the manner in which Mr Yule has gone astray at every stage in his treatment of association, but criticism of his methods has been thrust on us not only by Mr Yule's recent attack, but also by the unthinking praise which has been bestowed on a textbook (Yule's) which at many points can only lead statistical students hopelessly astray.
> (Pearson and Heron (1913), p. 310)

Karl Pearson was no stranger to controversy and later suffered greatly at the hands of R. A. Fisher; see chapters 7, 11, and 13.

6.5.2 Dependence for categorical variables

For categorical (*ordinal* and *nominal*) random variables the concept of *linearity* (and thus moments) does not make much sense and thus measuring linear dependence using correlation is inappropriate. The notion of *monotonicity*, however, in the sense that one variable tends to increase when the other increases (concordance) or tends to decrease when the other decreases (discordance), does make sense for ordinal variables. Defining dependence between nominal variables is not easy because neither linearity nor monotonicity makes sense.

One of the most widely used measures of association (dependence) between ordinal (and sometimes nominal) variables is the cross-product ratio.

Cross-product ratio
The *cross-product ratio* between two events A and B is defined as:

$$crp(A,B) = \frac{\mathbb{P}(A \cap B) \cdot \mathbb{P}(\bar{A} \cap \bar{B})}{\mathbb{P}(\bar{A} \cap B) \cdot \mathbb{P}(A \cap \bar{B})}.$$

In the case where the events A and B are **independent**: $crp = 1$, or $\ln(crp) = 0$.

$y \backslash x$	x_1	x_2	$f_y(y)$
y_1	π_{11}	π_{12}	$\pi_1.$
y_2	π_{22}	π_{22}	$\pi_2.$
$f_x(x)$	$\pi_{.1}$	$\pi_{.2}$	1

The above formula can be adapted to the case of a bivariate distribution $f(x,y)$ where the random variables X and Y are ordinal variables with only two values (x_1, x_2 and y_1, y_2, respectively) of the form given above. In this case the cross-product ratio is defined as the ratio of the products $\pi_{22} \pi_{11}$ and $\pi_{12} \pi_{21}$ of probabilities from diagonally opposite cells (hence the name), i.e.

$$crp(X, Y) = \frac{\pi_{22} \cdot \pi_{11}}{\pi_{12} \cdot \pi_{21}}.$$

Using this measure, we say that X and Y are **independent** if and only if:

$$\ln(crp(X, Y)) = 0.$$

Yule's Q (coefficient of association)

A closely related measure of *dependence* is that of Yule's Q (in honor of the Belgian statistician Quetelet) defined by (see Yule (1900)):

$$Q = \frac{\pi_{11}\pi_{22} - \pi_{12}\pi_{21}}{\pi_{11}\pi_{22} + \pi_{12}\pi_{21}}.$$

Examples

(i) Consider the case where $\pi_{11} = 0.3$, $\pi_{12} = 0.1$, $\pi_{21} = 0.2$ and $\pi_{22} = 0.4$.
$crp(X, Y) = \frac{(0.4)(0.3)}{(0.1)(0.2)} = 6$, and in view of the fact that $\ln(crp(X, Y)) = 1.792$, we can deduce that X and Y are not independent. This is confirmed by Yule's Q:

$$Q = \frac{(0.3)(0.4) - (0.1)(0.2)}{(0.3)(0.4) + (0.1)(0.2)} = 0.07.$$

(ii) Consider the case where $\pi_{11} = 0.2$, $\pi_{12} = 0.3$, $\pi_{21} = 0.2$ and $\pi_{22} = 0.3$. In view of the fact that:

$$crp(X, Y) = \frac{(0.3)(0.2)}{(0.3)(0.2)} = 1, \text{ and } \ln(crp(X, Y)) = 0,$$

we can conclude that the cross-product ratio coefficient confirms the independence shown in terms of the joint density function (see chapter 4). This is confirmed by Yule's Q:

$$Q = \frac{(0.3)(0.2) - (0.3)(0.2)}{(0.3)(0.2) + (0.3)(0.2)} = 0.$$

Gamma coefficient

Yule's Q can be extended to ordinal variables which take more than two values by noticing that $\Pi_c = \pi_{11}\pi_{22}$ can be thought of as a measure of concordance and $\Pi_d = \pi_{12}\pi_{21}$ as a measure of discordance. Two random variables X and Y are said to be *concordant* if the unit ranking higher with respect to X also ranks higher with respect to Y, and *discordant* if the unit ranking higher in X ranks lower in Y.

In the case where X takes m values and Y takes n values, we can use the following measures:

Concordance: $\Pi_c = 2\sum_{i=1}^{m}\sum_{j=1}^{n} \pi_{ij}(\sum_{h>i}\sum_{k>j}\pi_{hk})$,

Discordance: $\Pi_d = 2\sum_{i=1}^{m}\sum_{j=1}^{n} \pi_{ij}(\sum_{h>i}\sum_{k<j}\pi_{hk})$.

Using these measures we say that the association (dependence) between X and Y is positive if $(\Pi_c - \Pi_d) > 0$ and negative if $(\Pi_c - \Pi_d) < 0$. A scaled version of the distance $(\Pi_c - \Pi_d)$ is the so-called *Gamma coefficient*, introduced by Goodman and Kruskal (1954)), and defined by:

$$\gamma = \frac{\Pi_c - \Pi_d}{\Pi_c + \Pi_d}, \text{ where } -1 \leq \gamma \leq 1.$$

Like the correlation coefficient, if $|\gamma| = 1$ the two random variables are perfectly associated. Moreover, like the correlation coefficient, if $\gamma = 0$ the two random variables are not necessarily independent. Independence, however, implies that $\gamma = 0$.

Example

Consider the joint density function represented in (6.37), where X denotes *age* bracket and Y *income* bracket:

$$X = 1: (18\text{–}35), \qquad X = 2: (36\text{–}55), \qquad\qquad X = 3: (56\text{–}70),$$
$$Y = 0: \text{poor}, \qquad\quad Y = 1: \text{middle income}, \qquad Y = 2: \text{rich}.$$

$y\backslash x$	1	2	3	$f_y(y)$
0	0.20	0.10	0.15	0.45
1	0.10	0.25	0.05	0.40
2	0.01	0.06	0.08	0.15
$f_x(x)$	0.31	0.41	0.28	1

(6.37)

Consider evaluating the concordance coefficient:

$$i = 0, j = 1:\ \pi_{01}(\textstyle\sum_{h>0}\sum_{k>1}\pi_{hk}) = 0.20(0.25 + 0.05 + 0.06 + 0.08) = 0.088,$$
$$i = 0, j = 2:\ \pi_{02}(\textstyle\sum_{h>0}\sum_{k>2}\pi_{hk}) = 0.10(0.05 + 0.08) = 0.013,$$
$$i = 1, j = 1:\ \pi_{11}(\textstyle\sum_{h>1}\sum_{k>1}\pi_{hk}) = 0.10(0.06 + 0.08) = 0.014,$$
$$i = 1, j = 2:\ \pi_{12}(\textstyle\sum_{h>1}\sum_{k>2}\pi_{hk}) = 0.25(0.08) = 0.020.$$
$$\Pi_c = 2(0.088 + 0.013 + 0.014 + 0.020) = 0.270.$$

The discordance coefficient:

$$i = 0, j = 2:\ \pi_{02}(\textstyle\sum_{h>0}\sum_{k<2}\pi_{hk}) = 0.10(0.10 + 0.01) = 0.011,$$
$$i = 0, j = 3:\ \pi_{03}(\textstyle\sum_{h>0}\sum_{k<3}\pi_{hk}) = 0.15(0.10 + 0.25 + 0.01 + 0.06) = 0.063,$$
$$i = 1, j = 2:\ \pi_{12}(\textstyle\sum_{h>1}\sum_{k<2}\pi_{hk}) = 0.25(0.01) = 0.0025,$$
$$i = 1, j = 3:\ \pi_{13}(\textstyle\sum_{h>1}\sum_{k<3}\pi_{hk}) = 0.05(0.01 + 0.06) = 0.0035.$$
$$\Pi_d = 2(0.011 + 0.063 + 0.0025 + 0.0035) = 0.160.$$

Hence:

$$\gamma = \frac{\Pi_c - \Pi_d}{\Pi_c - \Pi_d} = \frac{0.270 - 0.160}{0.270 + 0.160} = 0.2558,$$

i.e., there is a low positive dependence between income and age.

6.5.3 Dependence between nominal variables

As mentioned above defining dependence between nominal variables is not easy because neither linearity nor monotonicity makes any sense. The only notion of dependence we can entertain in this context is in terms of:

how does knowledge of the classification on the random variable X can help us conjecture the classification on the random variable Y?

The uncertainty of conjecturing the classification of Y without any help from X is measured by the variance of Y: $Var(Y)$. This uncertainty changes to $Var(Y|X=x_1)$ for a specific value x_1 of the conditional variable. Given that the random variable X takes more than one value, we take the average of these conditional variance values, i.e., $E(Var(Y|X))$, leading to the standardized measure:

$$\frac{Var(Y)-E(Var(Y|X))}{Var(Y)}=1-\frac{E(Var(Y|X))}{Var(Y)}.$$

This ratio has been used by Goodman and Kruskal (1954) in conjunction with the contingency table (bivariate density) given below:

$y\backslash x$	x_1	x_2	x_3	$\cdots$	x_n	$f_y(y)$
y_1	π_{11}	π_{12}	π_{13}	$\cdots$	π_{1n}	$\pi_1.$
y_2	π_{21}	π_{22}	π_{23}	$\cdots$	π_{2n}	$\pi_2.$
y_3	π_{31}	π_{32}	π_{33}	$\cdots$	π_{3n}	$\pi_3.$
$\cdots$	$\cdots$			$\cdots$	$\cdots$	$\cdots$
y_m	π_{m1}	π_{m2}	π_{m3}	$\cdots$	π_{mn}	$\pi_m.$
$f_x(x)$	$\pi._1$	$\pi._2$	$\pi._3$	$\cdots$	$\pi._n$	1

where the variance of Y takes the form:

$$Var(Y)=\sum_{k=1}^{m}\pi_k.(1-\pi_k.)=1-\sum_{k=1}^{m}\pi_{k\cdot}^2,$$

and the conditional variance given $X=x_h$ is:

$$Var(Y|X=x_h)=1-\sum_{k=1}^{m}\pi_{k\cdot}^2|h,\ \pi_{k|h}=\frac{\pi_{hk}}{\pi._h},\ h=1,2,\ldots,n.$$

$$E(Var(Y|X))=\sum_{h=1}^{n}\pi._h\left(1-\sum_{k=1}^{m}\pi_{k|h}^2\right)=1-\sum_{h=1}^{n}\sum_{k=1}^{m}\frac{\pi_{hk}^2}{\pi._h},$$

to suggest the so-called *Goodman and Kruskal tau* (or *concentration coefficient*):

$$\tau=\frac{\sum_{h=1}^{n}\sum_{k=1}^{m}\frac{\pi_{hk}^2}{\pi._h}-\sum_{k=1}^{m}\pi_k^2}{1-\sum_{k=1}^{m}\pi_k^2}.$$

Theil (1950), using an alternative measure of dispersion based on *Entropy*:

$$V(Y)=\sum_{k=1}^{m}\pi_k.\ln\pi_k.,$$

proposed the *uncertainty coefficient*:

$$U=\frac{\sum_{h=1}^{n}\sum_{k=1}^{m}\pi_{kh}\ln(\pi_{kh}/\pi_k.\cdot\pi._h)}{\sum_{k=1}^{m}\pi_k.\ln\pi_k.}.$$

Both, the concentration and uncertainty coefficients are measures of dependence that take values between zero and one; $\tau = 0$, $U = 0$ both imply that the random variables X and Y are independent.

In order to formulate such measures we need the notion of conditioning introduced in the next chapter where a number of additional measures of dependence is discussed. The main argument of the next chapter is that the best way to handle dependence and joint density functions is via the notion of conditioning and conditional distributions.

6.5.4 The Bernoulli distribution

The Bernoulli distribution can be used to model both ordinal and nominal variables and the modeler should decide when to use which measures to assess dependence between such variables. The Bernoulli bivariate density function takes the form:

$$f(x,y) = p(0,0)^{(1-y)(1-x)}p(0,1)^{(1-y)x}p(1,0)^{y(1-x)}p(1,1)^{xy}, \ x=0,1 \text{ and } y=0,1,$$

with the marginal and conditional distributions being again Bernoulli:

$$f_x(x) = [p(0,0) + p(1,0)]^{(1-x)}[p(0,1) + p(1,1)]^x, \ x=0,1,$$

$$f_y(y) = [p(0,0) + p(0,1)]^{(1-y)}[p(1,0) + p(1,1)]^y, \ y=0,1.$$

Of particular interest is the log-linear form of the joint density which is:

$$\ln f(x,y) = \ln p(0,0) + y\ln \tfrac{p(1,0)}{p(0,0)} + x\ln \tfrac{p(0,1)}{p(0,0)} + xy\ln \tfrac{p(1,1)p(0,0)}{p(1,0)p(0,1)},$$

$$= u_0 + yu_1 + xu_2 + xyu_{12}, \ x=0,1, \ y=0,1,$$

in an obvious notation. The latter is known as the log-linear expansion and we note that the u_{12} term is simply the log of the cross-product ratio:

$$u_{12} := \ln(crp(X,Y)) = \ln \frac{p(1,1) \cdot p(0,0)}{p(1,0) \cdot p(0,1)}.$$

When $u_{12} = 0$ we say that the Bernoulli random variables X and Y are independent.

The above results can be extended to the trivariate Bernoulli distribution whose density function (in direct analogy to the bivariate) takes the form:

$$f(x,y,z) = p(0,0,0)^{(1-y)(1-x)(1-z)} \cdots p(1,1,1)^{xyz}, \ x=0,1 \text{ and } y=0,1, z=0,1.$$

Its log-linear form is:

$$\ln f(x,y) = u_0 + yu_1 + xu_2 + zu_3 + yxu_{12} + yzu_{13} + xzu_{23} + xyzu_{123},$$

where, as above, the us denote interaction terms:

$$u_{23} := \ln(cpr(X,Z|Y=0)), \ u_{123} := \ln\left(\tfrac{cpr(X,Z|Y=1)}{cpr(X,Z|Y=0)}\right),$$

$$crp(X,Z|Y=y_1) = \frac{p(y_1,1,1) \cdot p(y_1,0,0)}{p(y_1,1,0) \cdot p(y_1,0,1)}, \text{ for } y_1 = 0,1.$$

Using this representation we can define conditional independence in terms of the u-

terms. The random variables X and Z are conditionally independent given Y, denoted by $([X \perp Z]| Y)$, if and only if:

$$u_{23} = 0 \text{ and } u_{123} = 0,$$

or equivalently:

$$crp(X,Z| Y = y_1) = 1 \text{ for } y_1 = 0,1.$$

In concluding this section it is important to note that the numerical values of the interaction terms u_{ij}, $i,j = 1,2,3$ and u_{123} are not of intrinsic interest; the basic interest lies with what they imply in terms of the dependence structure among the random variables involved. Using the graphical models introduced in the previous section we can see how they identify this dependence structure.

(i)   Model 1: $u_{123} = 0$, $u_{ij} \neq 0$, for $i,j = 1,2,3$.
(ii) Model 2: $u_{123} = 0$, $u_{13} = 0$, $u_{23} \neq 0$, $u_{12} \neq 0$, $([X \perp Z]| Y)$.
(iii) Model 3: $u_{123} = 0$, $u_{13} = 0$, $u_{23} = 0$, $u_{12} \neq 0$, $([X \perp Z]| Y)$, $([Y \perp Z]| Y)$.

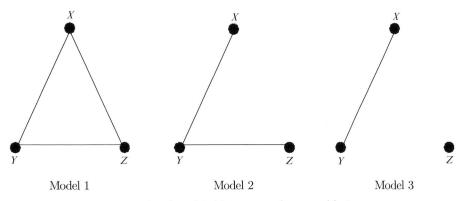

Model 1   Model 2   Model 3

Figure 6.3 Graphical models (discrete random variables)

NOTE that the nodes in the case of discrete random variables are no longer circles but discs; for more discussion on graphical models see Edwards (1995) and Lauritzen (1996).

6.5.5 Dependence in mixed (discrete/continuous) random variables

The discussion of dependence in this chapter has one focus point:

> *dependence is inextricably bound up with the joint distribution of the random variables involved.*

In cases where all the random variables involved are all discrete or all continuous no problems arise because we can use joint discrete or continuous distributions, respectively, to describe the dependence. Problems arise in the case where some of the random variables are discrete and the others are continuous and the modeler considers the question of the dependence among these random variables.

As argued in chapter 4, the joint density function of (X,Y,Z) where (X,Y) are continuous and Z is a discrete random variable can be best defined indirectly via the product:

$$f(x,y,z) = f(x,y\mid z) \cdot f_Z(z), \text{ for all } (x,y,z) \in \mathbb{R}_X \times \mathbb{R}_Y \times \mathbb{R}_Z.$$

Similarly, the joint cumulative distribution function is defined via:

$$F(x,y,z) = \sum_{z_k \leq z} f_z(z_k) \int_{-\infty}^{x} \int_{-\infty}^{y} f(x,y\mid z_k) du dv.$$

This suggests most clearly that in the case of a mixture of continuous and discrete random variables the dependence structure between them should be best accommodated in the context of the conditional moments of $f(x,y\mid z)$. Motivated by this observation Lauritzen and Wermuth (1989) introduced the so-called conditional Gaussian distribution which in the case of the random variables (X,Y,Z), the conditional density $f(x,y\mid z)$ takes the form:

$$\left(\binom{Y}{X} \middle| Z=z \right) \sim N\left(\begin{bmatrix} \mu_1(z) \\ \mu_2(z) \end{bmatrix}, \begin{bmatrix} \sigma_{11}(z) & \sigma_{12}(z) \\ \sigma_{12}(z) & \sigma_{22}(z) \end{bmatrix} \right), \ z \in \mathbb{R}_Z. \tag{6.38}$$

That is, the moments of the joint distribution of (X,Y) are assumed to be functions of the conditioning variable; in the spirit of conditional moment functions. The functional forms that should be postulated by a modeler for:

$$\mu_i(z), \ \sigma_{ij}(z), \ i,j = 1,2,$$

is not a trivial issue because it concerns the parameterization of dependence between variables from different measurement scales. Anybody who thinks this is child's play should reflect for a moment on the question of parameterizing the (possible) dependence between family income and religion!

6.6   Joint distributions and dependence

As suggested above, joint distributions constitute the quintessential way of modeling dependence. In this sense progress in modeling different types of dependence relies crucially on the development of such joint distributions. Unfortunately, the road from marginal to joint distributions is treacherous. There are infinitely many joint (multivariate) distributions with the same marginal distributions! In this sense there is no systematic (generally applicable) way to specify multivariate distributions. Some of the most notable attempts to specify bivariate and multivariate distributions will be summarized in this section.

The first attempts to generate non-Normal joint distributions were made by Karl Pearson in the late 1890s. His success in generating a very rich family of univariate distributions, we nowadays call the *Pearson family*, using a differential equation (see chapters 4, 13), encouraged him to try and extend the method to two differential equations:

$$\frac{\partial \ln f(x,y)}{\partial x} = \frac{h_3(x,y)}{h_4(x,y)}, \text{ where } h_3(x,y), h_4(x,y) \text{ are third and fourth degree polynomials,}$$

$$\frac{\partial \ln f(x,y)}{\partial y} = \frac{g_3(x,y)}{g_4(x,y)}, \text{ and } g_4(x,y) = h_4(x,y).$$

It turned out that without restrictions on the coefficients of the three polynomials no progress was possible. Important breakthroughs along these lines were made by Pretorius (1930) and then Van Uven (1947,1948) who simplified these equations to:

$$\frac{\partial \ln f(x,y)}{\partial x} = \frac{h_1(x,y)}{h_2(x,y)}, \text{ where } h_1(x,y), h_2(x,y) \text{ are first and second degree polynomials,}$$

$$\frac{\partial \ln f(x,y)}{\partial y} = \frac{g_1(x,y)}{g_2(x,y)}, \text{ subject to } \frac{\partial^2 \ln f(x,y)}{\partial x \partial y} = \frac{\partial}{\partial y}\left(\frac{h_1(x,y)}{h_2(x,y)}\right) = \frac{\partial}{\partial x}\left(\frac{g_1(x,y)}{g_2(x,y)}\right).$$

The following special cases turned out to be of particular interest (see Mardia (1970) for the details):

(1) $h_2(x,y)$ and $g_2(x,y)$ have no common factors (as polynomials),
(2) $h_2(x,y)$ and $g_2(x,y)$ have one common factor,
(3) $h_2(x,y)$ and $g_2(x,y)$ are identical, and
(4) $g_2(x,y)$ is a linear factor of $h_2(x,y)$.

Case 1 provides us with sufficient conditions for independence between X and Y; no common factors implies that:

$$f(x,y) = f_x(x) \cdot f_y(y).$$

Case 2 assuming that $h_2(x,y) = h_{12}(x,y) \cdot \ell(x,y)$ and $g_2(x,y) = g_{12}(x,y) \cdot \ell(x,y)$ where all the right-hand side polynomials are of degree one, yields a joint distribution of the general form:

$$f(x,y) = c_0(\alpha x + \beta)^{\theta_1}(\gamma y + \delta)^{\theta_2}(ax + by + c)^{\theta_3}.$$

This joint distribution includes the bivariate *Beta*, *Pareto* and *F*-distribution (see appendix B) as special cases.

Case 3 assuming that $h_2(x,y) = g_2(x,y)$, gives rise to a joint distribution of the form:

$$f(x,y) = c_0(ax^2 + by^2 + 2\theta_1 xy + 2\theta_2 x + 2\theta_3 y + c)^m.$$

This joint distribution includes the bivariate *Cauchy*, *Student's t*, and *Pearson type II* distribution (see appendix B) as special cases.

Case 4 assuming that $h_2(x,y) = h_{12}(x,y) \cdot \ell(x,y)$ and $g_2(x,y) = \ell(x,y)$, gives rise to a joint distribution of the general form:

$$f(x,y) = c_0(\alpha x + \beta)^{\theta_1} e^{-\theta_2 y}(ax + by + c)^{\theta_3}.$$

This joint distribution includes the bivariate (*McKay*) *Gamma* distribution (see appendix B) as a special case.

Several other methods to generate joint distributions, such as the bivariate Edgeworth expansion and the translation method, proved only of marginal value; see Mardia (1970) for an excellent discussion. The least effective way to create joint distributions is to take linear combinations of marginal distributions. The first to propose this method was Steffensen (1922). Assuming that the two independent random variables (Z_1, Z_2) have known marginal densities $f_1(z_1)$ and $f_2(z_2)$, he considered the joint distribution of the linear transformations:

$$X = a_1 Z_1 + b_1 Z_2 + c_1, \quad Y = a_2 Z_1 + b_2 Z_2 + c_2.$$

In view of the fact that the inverse transformation is:

$$Z_1 = X + aY, \quad Z_2 = Y + bX,$$

the joint density takes the general form (see chapter 11):

$$f(x,y) = |ab - 1| f_1(x + ay) \cdot f_2(y + bx).$$

This is the most ineffective way to generate joint distributions because by construction the only form of dependence built into the joint distribution is that of linear dependence (correlation). As argued above, however, linear dependence characterizes distribution-related dependence only in the case of the Normal distribution.

Several extensions of this restricted result have been suggested in the literature. For reference purposes we summarize the most important of these results. Let $F(x,y)$, $F_X(x)$ and $F_Y(y)$ denote the joint and marginal distributions of the random variables X and Y. The marginal distributions are given and the modeler combines them in a variety of ways to construct the joint distribution.

1   Frechet (1951):

$$F(x,y) = \beta \max (0, F_X(x) + F_Y(y) - 1) + (1 - \beta) \min (F_X(x), F_Y(y)), \ 0 \le \beta \le 1.$$

2   Morgenstern (1956):

$$F(x,y) = F_X(x) \cdot F_Y(y)[1 + a(1 - F_X(x))(1 - F_Y(y))], \ a \in [-1,1].$$

3   Gumbel (1960):

$$(-\ln F(x,y))^m = (-\ln F_X(x))^m + (-\ln F_Y(y))^m, \ m \ge 1.$$

4   Plackett (1965): $F(x,y)$ is the solution of the equation:

$$F(x,y)(1 - F_X(x) - F_Y(y) + F(x,y)) = \alpha (F_X(x) - F(x,y))(F_Y(y) - F(x,y)), \ \alpha > 0.$$

5   Ali, Mikhail and Haq (1978):

$$F(x,y) = \frac{F_X(x) \cdot F_Y(y)}{[1 - a(1 - F_X(x))(1 - F_Y(y))]}, \ a \in [-1,1].$$

As we can see, the bivariate distribution in all these cases is constructed using a parameter that connects the marginal distributions. This is clearly of limited scope because the dependence is now captured by this one parameter which is often related to the correlation coefficient.

The most effective method to formulate joint distributions is by direct generalization of univariate densities in cases where the functional form of the density function allows substituting a random variable with a random vector such as the case of the *elliptically symmetric family* of distributions discussed below. This is because all the features of the univariate distributions are naturally extended to the joint and the dependence is not artificially restricted.

The assessment of the current situation by the author is that we need to focus our attention on the development of additional parametric families of joint distributions with a view to extending the existing concepts of distribution-related dependence.

6.6.1 Dependence and the Normal distribution

The first attempt to develop a joint distribution with a view to capturing the dependence observed in a particular data set was made by Galton (1886) with the help of his mathematician friend Dickson. It is instructive to refer to the way Galton stumbled upon the bivariate Normal distribution because it constitutes an important early example of how patterns in the observed data can be utilized to construct mathematical concepts in an attempt to model them. While examining observed data on the height of mid-parents (x) and their offsprings (y), Galton mapped out a scatterplot (the data $(x_1, x_2, ..., x_n)$ are plotted against $(y_1, y_2, ..., y_n)$; see below) and noticed (by his own account):

that lines drawn through entries of the same value formed a series of concentric and similar ellipses...
(Galton (1885), p. 255).

That is, the scatterplot of the two data series exhibited a clear elliptical shape which on closer examination revealed that when collecting the data points with the same relative frequency they formed concentric elliptical shapes. This is a remarkable piece of detective work which exemplifies Galton's observation prowess. His first reaction was to use these concentric ellipses in order to construct the bivariate surface (joint frequency curve) that lies behind them. Knowing that his mathematical skills were inadequate for the task he called upon his friend Dickson (a mathematician at Cambridge University). The result, published as an appendix to Galton (1886), was the **bivariate Normal density**:

$$f(x,y;\boldsymbol{\theta}) = \frac{(1-\rho^2)^{-\frac{1}{2}}}{2\pi\sqrt{\sigma_{11}\sigma_{22}}} \exp\left\{-\frac{(1-\rho^2)^{-1}}{2}\left(\left(\frac{y-\mu_1}{\sqrt{\sigma_{11}}}\right)^2 - 2\rho\left(\frac{y-\mu_1}{\sqrt{\sigma_{11}}}\right)\left(\frac{x-\mu_2}{\sqrt{\sigma_{22}}}\right) + \left(\frac{x-\mu_2}{\sqrt{\sigma_{22}}}\right)^2\right)\right\}, \tag{6.39}$$

where the unknown parameters $\boldsymbol{\theta} := (\mu_1, \mu_2, \sigma_{11}, \sigma_{22}, \rho)$ are related to the moments via:

$$\mu_1 := E(Y), \qquad\qquad\qquad \mu_2 := E(X),$$
$$\sigma_{11} := Var(Y), \quad \rho := Corr(X, Y), \quad \sigma_{22} := Var(X).$$

Using this bivariate distribution Galton went on to develop the concepts of regression (see next chapter) and correlation. As shown in chapter 4, both the marginal and conditional densities are also Normal (but univariate of course). Using the notation for the bivariate Normal distribution, introduced in chapter 4:

$$\begin{pmatrix} Y \\ X \end{pmatrix} \sim N\left(\begin{bmatrix} \mu_1 \\ \mu_2 \end{bmatrix}, \begin{bmatrix} \sigma_{11} & \sigma_{12} \\ \sigma_{12} & \sigma_{22} \end{bmatrix}\right),$$

where the correlation coefficient can be expressed in the form $\rho = \frac{\sigma_{12}}{\sqrt{\sigma_{11}\sigma_{22}}}$, we deduced that:

(a) $Y \sim N(\mu_1, \sigma_{11})$, $(Y|X=x) \sim N(\beta_0 + \beta_1 x, \sigma_1^2)$,

(b) $X \sim N(\mu_2, \sigma_{22})$, $(X|Y=y) \sim N(\alpha_0 + \alpha_1 x, \sigma_2^2)$,

$$\beta_0 := \mu_1 - \beta_1\mu_2, \; \beta_1 := \frac{\sigma_{12}}{\sigma_{22}}, \; \sigma_1^2 := \sigma_{11} - \frac{\sigma_{12}^2}{\sigma_{22}},$$

$$\alpha_0 := \mu_2 - \alpha_1\mu_1, \; \alpha_1 := \frac{\sigma_{12}}{\sigma_{11}}, \; \sigma_2^2 := \sigma_{22} - \frac{\sigma_{12}^2}{\sigma_{11}}.$$

The multivariate Normal is by far the most widely used joint distribution in empirical modeling. Because of its dominating role in statistical inference it is important to examine the dependence structure of this distribution using the concepts developed in the previous sections. In so far as the order of dependence is concerned we argued that the most direct way to assess it is via the conditional moments. In the case of the bivariate Normal distribution we know that:

(a) $E(Y|X=x) = \beta_0 + \beta_1 x,$

(b) $E[(Y - E(Y|X=x))^r | X=x] = \begin{cases} 0 & \text{for } r \text{ odd}, \\ \frac{r!\sigma_1^r}{(0.5r)!2^{0.5r}} & \text{for } r \text{ even.} \end{cases}$

In particular, $Var(Y|X=x) = \sigma_1^2$. In view of the parameterizations involved we can see that in the case where $\rho=0$ ($\sigma_{12}=0$), all the conditional moments coincide with the marginal moments:

(a) $E(Y|X=x)|_{\rho=0} = \mu_1,$

(b) $E[(Y - E(Y|X=x))^r | X=x]|_{\rho=0} = \begin{cases} 0 & \text{for } r \text{ odd}, \\ \frac{r!\sigma_1^{0.5r}}{(0.5r)!2^{0.5r}} & \text{for } r \text{ even.} \end{cases}$

This suggests that when the correlation coefficient is zero the two random variables are independent, i.e.

for X and Y jointly Normal, $\rho=0 \Rightarrow Y$ and X are independent,

(see chapter 4). This is clearly an exception to the general rule stated in chapter 4 that non-correlation does not imply independence. The intuition behind this exception is that the only form of dependence one can describe using the Normal distribution is linear dependence. In other words, dependence in the context of the joint Normal distribution is encapsulated in the correlation coefficient parameter ρ (or equivalently σ_{12}).

From the modeling viewpoint it is important to NOTE the relationship between the correlation coefficient and the shape of the joint Normal density. In order to get some idea as to how the shape changes with the value of ρ, let us compare the joint density in figure 6.4 where $\rho=0$ with that given in figure 6.5 where $\rho=0.8$. The dependence takes the form of a "squashed" joint density. This effect can be easily seen on the inserted *equal probability contours* (a bivariate map of the density) which are circular in the case $\rho=0$ and ellipses in the case of $\rho \neq 0$. NOTE that the equal probability contours are the theoretical counterparts to Galton's notion in terms of relative frequency. From the above graphs it is obvious that the more squashed the density (and the ellipses) the higher the correlation.

The graph of the equal probability contours is of particular interest in connection with real data plots (see section 6) and worth having a closer look at. They are called equal probability (*equiprobability*) contours because every ellipse of the form:

$$\left(\left(\frac{y - \mu_1}{\sqrt{\sigma_{11}}} \right)^2 - 2\rho \left(\frac{y - \mu_1}{\sqrt{\sigma_{11}}} \right) \left(\frac{x - \mu_2}{\sqrt{\sigma_{22}}} \right) + \left(\frac{x - \mu_2}{\sqrt{\sigma_{22}}} \right)^2 \right) = c_i, \; i = 1, 2, \ldots, n, \tag{6.40}$$

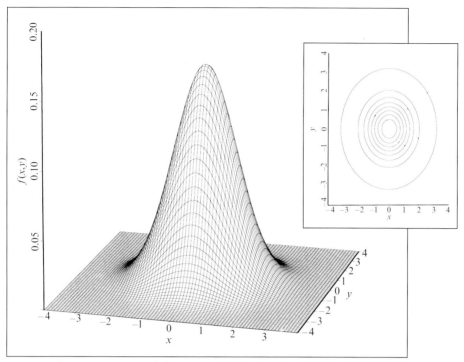

Figure 6.4 Normal density with $\rho = 0$

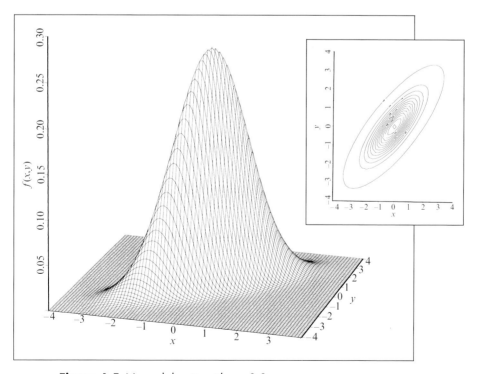

Figure 6.5 Normal density with $\rho = 0.8$

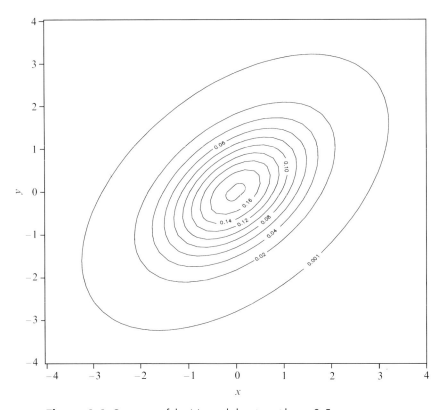

Figure 6.6 Contours of the Normal density with $\rho = 0.5$

represents a set of points with the same probability. Intuitively, they can be thought of as being created by slicing the three-dimensional surface of the density across, parallel to the x–y plane at equal distances, say (0.001), (0.02), (0.04),…,(0.18), and drawing the outside elliptical shape of the slices beginning with the lowest on the outside (0.001) and ending with the highest (0.18) representing the last slice which includes the peak. In this sense equal probability contour graphs have a lot in common with ordinary map contour lines representing a mountainous three dimensional surface in a two-dimensional map. In both cases the map arises by projecting the *equal elevation* slices of a three dimensional surface onto a two-dimensional diagram. As with the map contour lines, the closer the contours the sharper the elevation.

In figures 6.6 and 6.7 one can see the equal probability contours of a bivariate Normal density with correlation $\rho = 0.5$ and $\rho = -0.5$, respectively. Looking at the graph of the equal probability contours we should be able to visualize the three-dimensional surface. If we compare the contour plot in figure 6.6 with that of figure 6.7 we can see that they differ in terms of their orientation, the slope of the principal axis of the ellipses in figure 6.6 is positive but that of figure 6.7 is negative; this stems from the fact that the correlation in figure 6.6 is positive but that of figure 6.7 is negative.

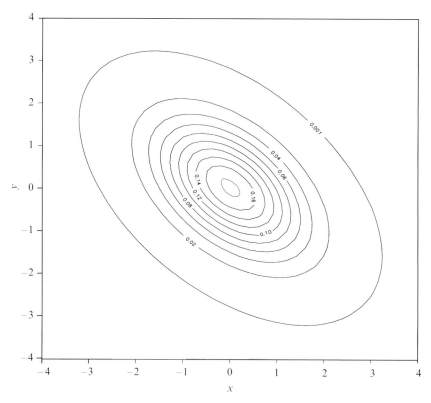

Figure 6.7 Contours of the Normal density with $\rho = -0.5$

6.6.2 Dependence and the elliptically symmetric family

Unknown to Galton the same equiprobability contours (6.40) can be used to generate a whole family of symmetric distributions, known as the *elliptically symmetric family* (see Kelker (1970)) which includes the Normal as a special case. The bivariate form of these distributions depends on (a) the quadratic form generating the concentric ellipses:

$$\ell(x,y) = \left(\frac{y-\mu_1}{\sqrt{\sigma_{11}}}\right)^2 - 2\rho\left(\frac{y-\mu_1}{\sqrt{\sigma_{11}}}\right)\left(\frac{x-\mu_2}{\sqrt{\sigma_{22}}}\right) + \left(\frac{x-\mu_2}{\sqrt{\sigma_{22}}}\right)^2,$$

and (b) the determinant of $\Sigma := \begin{bmatrix} \sigma_{11} & \sigma_{12} \\ \sigma_{12} & \sigma_{22} \end{bmatrix}$, where $\det(\Sigma) = \sigma_{11}\sigma_{22} - \sigma_{12}^2 = [(1-\rho^2)\sigma_{11}\sigma_{22}]$.

The generic form of this family can be generally written as:

$$f(x,y;\boldsymbol{\theta}) = c_0 \cdot \delta(\det(\Sigma)) \cdot h(\ell(x,y)),$$

where $\delta(.)$ *and* $h(.)$ are arbitrary positive functions over the range of values $\mathbb{R}_X \times \mathbb{R}_Y$ and c_0 a normalizing constant which ensures that $f(x,y;\boldsymbol{\theta})$ is a proper density, i.e.

$$\int\int_{\mathbb{R}_X \times \mathbb{R}_Y} f(x,y;\boldsymbol{\theta})dxdy = 1.$$

This family can be easily extended to the m-variable case ($m > 2$) by defining $\ell(.)$ as:

$$\ell(x_1,\ldots,x_m) := (\mathbf{x} - \boldsymbol{\mu})^\top \boldsymbol{\Sigma}^{-1}(\mathbf{x} - \boldsymbol{\mu}), \text{ and } \int \cdots \int_{\mathbb{R}_1 \times \mathbb{R}_2 \ldots \times \mathbb{R}_m} f(x_1,\ldots,x_m;\boldsymbol{\theta})dx_1 \cdots dx_m = 1,$$

$$\boldsymbol{\Sigma} := \begin{bmatrix} \sigma_{11} & \sigma_{12} & \cdots & \sigma_{1m} \\ \sigma_{21} & \sigma_{22} & \cdots & \vdots \\ \vdots & \vdots & \ddots & \vdots \\ \sigma_{m1} & \cdots & \cdots & \sigma_{mm} \end{bmatrix}, (\mathbf{x} - \boldsymbol{\mu}) := \begin{pmatrix} x_1 - \mu_1 \\ x_2 - \mu_2 \\ \vdots \\ x_m - \mu_m \end{pmatrix}.$$

In addition to the Normal, the elliptically symmetric family includes the Student's t, the Pearson type II, and a form of the Logistic distributions (see Fang *et al.* (1990)). For example, the bivariate density of the Student's t takes the form:

$$f(x,y;\boldsymbol{\theta}) = \frac{(\nu\pi)^{-1}\Gamma\left[\frac{1}{2}(\nu+2)\right]}{\Gamma\left[\frac{1}{2}\nu\right]\sqrt{\det(\boldsymbol{\Sigma})}}\left\{1 + \frac{(1-\rho^2)^{-1}}{\nu}[\ell(x,y)]\right\}^{-\frac{1}{2}(\nu+2)}, (x,y) \in \mathbb{R}^2.$$

The equal probability contours of this density for $\rho = 0.5$ and $\rho = -0.5$ are shown in figures 6.8 and 6.9, respectively. Comparing figures 6.6 and 6.8 we can see that the equal probability contours for the Student's t are closer together than those of the Normal and the peak of the former is higher than that of the latter. This is confirmed by comparison of figure 6.7 with 6.9.

The difference between the Student's t and Normal distributions becomes even more apparent when we compare figure 6.10 (Normal with $\rho = 0.2$) with figure 6.11 (Student's t with $\rho = 0.2$ and $\nu = 5$). As we can see the main difference between the two is that the Student's t distribution is *leptokurtic* (kurtosis > 3). We can detect the leptokurtosis by looking at the measurements on the z-axis (the Student's t peaks at 0.30 and the Normal at 0.18) and the contours (the Student's t are much closer together). For an extensive discussion of the multivariate Student's t distribution see Spanos (1994).

The comparison between the Normal and Student's t densities becomes more apparent when both of these distributions are compared with another member of the elliptic family, the so-called Pearson type II distribution whose density takes the form:

$$f(x,y;\boldsymbol{\theta}) = \left(\frac{(\det(\boldsymbol{\Sigma})^{-\frac{1}{2}}}{2\pi}\right)\left(\frac{(\nu+1)}{(\nu+2)}\right)\left\{1 - \frac{(1-\rho^2)^{-1}}{2(\nu+2)}[\ell(x,y)]\right\}^\nu.$$

In contrast to the Student's t distribution is the Pearson which is platykurtic (see chapter 3). The bivariate density of the Pearson type II, together with its equiprobability contours, is shown in figure 6.12.

The above comparison suggests that in the case of the elliptic family we can distinguish between the various members only by careful examination of how crammed the

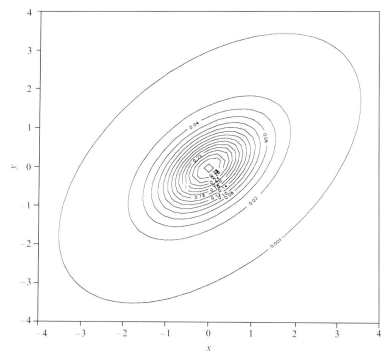

Figure 6.8 Contours of the Student's t density with $\rho = 0.5$

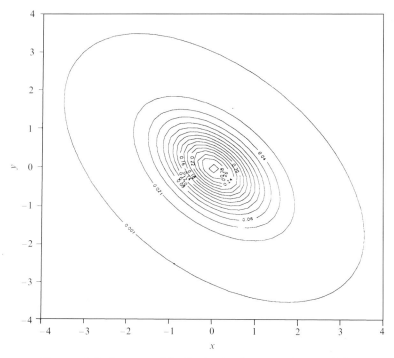

Figure 6.9 Contours of the Student's t density with $\rho = -0.5$

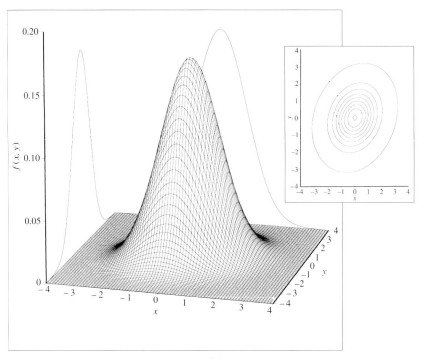

Figure 6.10 Bivariate Normal density

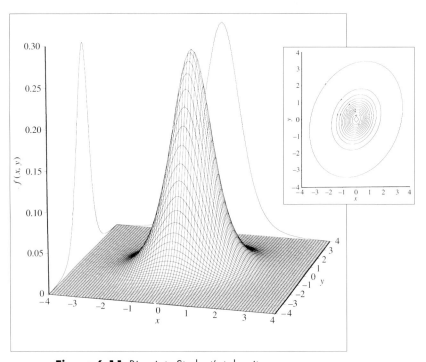

Figure 6.11 Bivariate Student's t density

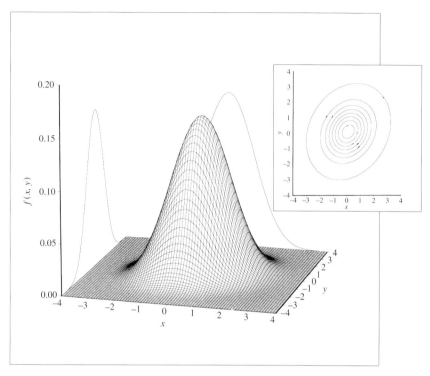

Figure 6.12 Bivariate Pearson type II density

equiprobability contours are. In all cases, however, the correlation can be assessed by how squashed the elliptical contours are. However, a word of caution is in order: zero correlation does not imply independence for the elliptic family, except in the case of the Normal distribution. Let us consider this in some more detail.

The question that naturally arises at this stage concerns the dependence structure of the elliptically symmetric family. The whole of the elliptic family has the same conditional mean, the conditional mean we encountered above in relation to the Normal distribution, but the higher conditional moments are in general functions of the conditioning variable, i.e.

(a) $E(Y|X=x) = \beta_0 + \beta_1 x$,

(b) $E[(Y - E(Y|X=x))^r | X=x] = \begin{cases} 0 \text{ for } r \text{ odd,} \\ q_r(x) \text{ for } r \text{ even.} \end{cases}$

For example, in the case of the Student's t and Pearson type II the conditional variances (see appendix B) take the form:

Student's t: $Var(Y|X=x) = \sigma_1^2 \left(\frac{\nu}{\nu-1}\right)\left(1 + \frac{1}{\nu}\frac{(x-\mu_2)^2}{\sigma_{22}}\right)$,

Pearson type II: $Var(Y|X=x) = \sigma_1^2 \left(\frac{1}{2\nu+3}\right)\left(1 - \frac{(x-\mu_2)^2}{\sigma_{22}}\right)$.

This result suggests that in the case where $\rho = 0$ all members of the elliptic family become first-order independent but the only distribution for which this is equivalent to complete independence is the Normal. For instance, in the case of the Student's t distribution:

$$Var(Y|X=x)|_{\rho=0} = \left(\frac{\nu\sigma_{11}}{\nu-1}\right)\left(1 + \frac{1}{\nu}\frac{(x-\mu_2)^2}{\sigma_{22}}\right),$$

which is clearly different from the marginal variance, $Var(Y) = \frac{\nu\sigma_{11}}{\nu-2}$. In this sense the Student's t distribution is *second-order dependent* even after we impose the zero correlation restriction.

6.6.3 Dependence and skewed distributions

It is important to consider several additional joint distributions which are not bell-shaped symmetric as is the elliptic family in order to provide the reader with a balanced view of bivariate distributions. Unfortunately, there is no systematic way to present the distributions and the reader should consider this section as just a collection of examples whose basic objective is to provide the reader with a less-distorted picture of the Normal dominated textbook literature.

Bivariate Logistic density

The bivariate Logistic density takes the form:

$$f(x,y;\boldsymbol{\theta}) = \frac{2\exp\left\{-\left(\frac{y-\mu_1}{\sqrt{\sigma_{11}}}\right)-\left(\frac{x-\mu_2}{\sqrt{\sigma_{22}}}\right)\right\}}{\sqrt{\sigma_{11}\sigma_{22}}\left[1+\exp\left\{-\left(\frac{y-\mu_1}{\sqrt{\sigma_{11}}}\right)\right\}+\exp\left\{-\left(\frac{x-\mu_2}{\sqrt{\sigma_{22}}}\right)\right\}\right]^3}, \quad \boldsymbol{\theta}\in\mathbb{R}^2\times\mathbb{R}^2_+, (x,y)\in\mathbb{R}^2,$$

where $\boldsymbol{\theta} := (\mu_1,\mu_2,\sigma_{11},\sigma_{22})$. In figure 6.13 we can see the standardized form of this bivariate density with $\boldsymbol{\theta} := (0,0,1,1)$. As we can see, this density is non-symmetric with contours which remind one of a Paleolithic axe. However, it is important to note that the marginal densities are symmetric (being logistic). Unfortunately, the dependence structure of this distribution is rather inflexible because it gives rise to a constant correlation coefficient $\rho := Corr(X,Y) = 0.5$, irrespective of the values of $\boldsymbol{\theta}$.

For a more flexible correlation structure this bivariate distribution has been generalized by introducing an additional parameter α to form:

$$F(x,y;\alpha) = \left\{1 + [\exp(-\alpha x)]^{\frac{1}{\alpha}} + [\exp(-\alpha y)]^{\frac{1}{\alpha}}\right\}^{-1},$$

yielding:

$$\rho := Corr(X,Y) = 1 - \frac{1}{2\alpha^2}, \text{ where } \rho \geq \frac{1}{2},$$

which includes the above case as a special case with $a = 1$. It is interesting to note that there is a form of the bivariate Logistic distribution which belongs to the elliptically symmetric family but it does not have a close form (see Fang *et al.* (1990)). Note that the multivariate extension of this distribution takes the form:

$$F(x_1,x_2,\ldots,x_m;\boldsymbol{\theta}) = \left[1 + \left(\sum_{k=1}^m \exp\left\{-\alpha\left(\frac{x_k-\mu_k}{\sqrt{\sigma_{kk}}}\right)\right\}\right)^{\frac{1}{\alpha}}\right]^{-1}, \quad \alpha \geq 1;$$

the ordinary Logistic being a special case with $a = 1$.

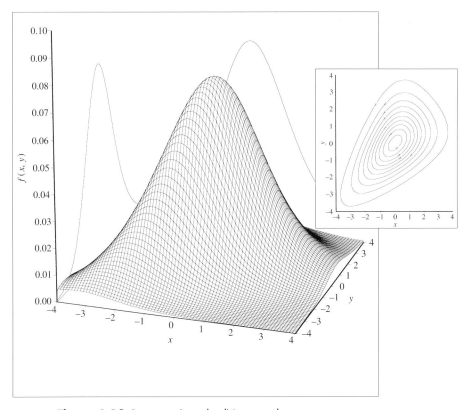

Figure 6.13 Bivariate (standard) Logistic density

Bivariate Gamma density

The bivariate Gamma distribution comes in a number of different forms (see appendix B for three of these forms), each one with its own dependence structure. In this section we will consider two of these forms.

The Cherian bivariate Gamma density takes the form:

$$f(x,y;\boldsymbol{\theta}) = \frac{e^{-(x+y)}}{\Gamma(\theta_0)\Gamma(\theta_1)\Gamma(\theta_2)} \int_0^{\min(x,y)} e^z z^{\theta_0-1}(x-z)^{\theta_1-1}(y-z)^{\theta_2-1}dz, \ (x,y)\in\mathbb{R}^2,$$

where $\boldsymbol{\theta} := (\theta_0,\theta_1,\theta_2) \in \mathbb{R}^3_+$. The correlation coefficient is:

$$\rho := Corr(X,Y) = \frac{\theta_0}{\sqrt{(\theta_0+\theta_1)(\theta_0+\theta_2)}}, \ 0<\rho\le 1.$$

In figures 6.14–6.15 we can see the bivariate density with the contours inserted for two sets of parameters $\boldsymbol{\theta} := (1,3,3)$ with $\rho=0.25$ and $\boldsymbol{\theta} := (8,3,3)$ with $\rho=0.727$, respectively.

The McKay form of the bivariate Gamma density is:

$$f(x,y;\boldsymbol{\theta}) = \frac{a^{(\theta_1+\theta_2)}}{\Gamma(\theta_1)\Gamma(\theta_2)} e^{-ay} x^{\theta_1-1}(y-x)^{\theta_2-1}, \ \boldsymbol{\theta} := (a,\theta_1,\theta_2)\in\mathbb{R}^3_+, \ (x,y)\in\mathbb{R}^2,$$

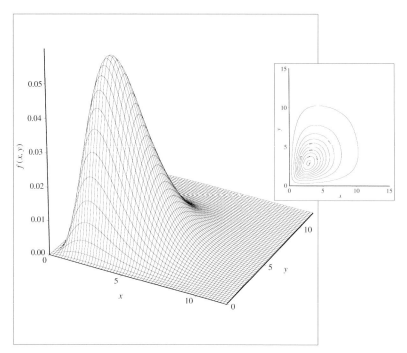

Figure 6.14 Bivariate (Cherian) Gamma (1,3,3) density

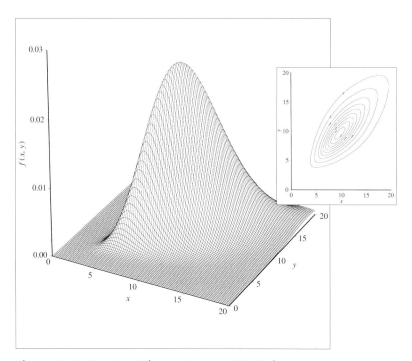

Figure 6.15 Bivariate (Cherian) Gamma (8,3,3) density

with correlation coefficient:

$$\rho := Corr(X,Y) = \sqrt{\frac{\theta_1}{(\theta_1 + \theta_2)}}.$$

In figures 6.16–6.17 we can see the bivariate Gamma (McKay) density with the contours inserted for two sets of parameters $\theta := (2,2,6)$ with $\rho = 0.5$ and $\theta := (2,6,4)$ with $\rho = 0.775$, respectively. In these figures the asymmetry is different from that in figures 6.14–6.15.

Bivariate Exponential density
As in the case of the bivariate Gamma distribution the bivariate Exponential has several forms. The **Gumbel** bivariate Exponential density takes the form:

$$f(x,y;\theta) = [(1 + \theta x)(1 + \theta y) - \theta]\exp\{-x - y - \theta xy\}, \theta \in \mathbb{R}_+, (x,y) \in \mathbb{R}_+^2.$$

This density, together with its equiprobability contours, for two different values of θ, is shown in figures 6.18 and 6.19. In the case of figure 6.18 $\theta = 0.2$ which implies a correlation coefficient $\rho = -0.148$. In the case of figure 6.19 $\theta = 1.0$ which is implies a correlation coefficient $\rho = -0.404$. NOTE that this bivariate density gives rise only to negative correlation. A direct comparison between the two surfaces and the equiprobability contours suggests that the higher correlation can be detected by a higher concentration of probability at the arms of the density.

Bivariate F density
The bivariate F density takes the form:

$$f(x,y;\theta) = \Gamma[0.5\nu]\prod_{i=0}^{2}\left(\frac{\nu_i^{0.5\nu_i}}{\Gamma[0.5\nu_i]}\right)(\nu_0 + \nu_1 x + \nu_2 y)^{-0.5\nu}x^{0.5\nu_1 - 1}y^{0.5\nu_2 - 1}, (x,y) \in \mathbb{R}_+^2,$$

where $(\nu_0,\nu_1,\nu_2) \in \mathbb{R}_+^3$, $\nu = (\nu_0 + \nu_1 + \nu_2)$. This density, together with its equiprobability contours, for two different values of θ, is shown in figures 6.20 and 6.21. In the case of figure 6.20 $\theta := (\nu_0 = 12, \nu_1 = 8, \nu_2 = 8)$, implying a correlation coefficient $\rho = 0.444$. In the case of figure 6.21 $\theta := (\nu_0 = 5, \nu_1 = 60, \nu_2 = 60)$, implying a correlation coefficient $\rho = 0.953$. Comparing the two surfaces and their equiprobability contours we can see that the higher the correlation the more squashed the density. However, this should be interpreted carefully because the correlation coefficient is insufficient to capture the dependence structure of the F distribution (see next section). In order to get a more complete picture consider two other shapes for the bivariate F distribution in figures 6.22 and 6.23 whose correlations are not very different but the parameters are $\theta := (\nu_0 = 80, \nu_1 = 4, \nu_2 = 2)$ with correlation $\rho = 0.035$ and $\theta := (\nu_0 = 200, \nu_1 = 20, \nu_2 = 20)$ with correlation $\rho = 0.092$.

NOTE that in the case where the correlation is zero the bivariate F looks similar to the bivariate Exponential without the inward curvature.

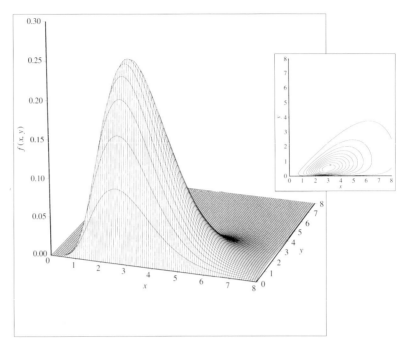

Figure 6.16 Bivariate (McKay) Gamma (2,2,6) density

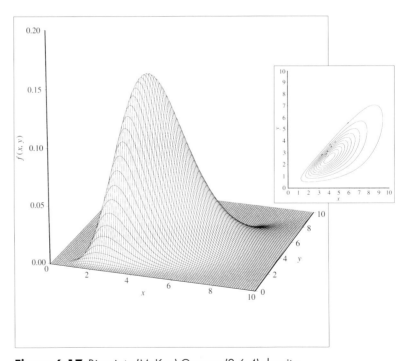

Figure 6.17 Bivariate (McKay) Gamma (2,6,4) density

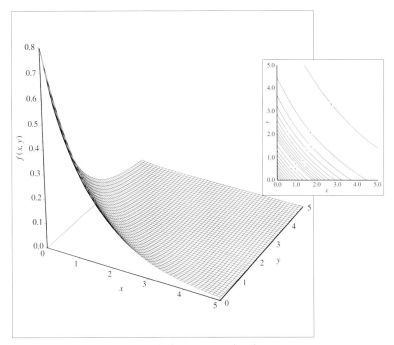

Figure 6.18 Bivariate Gumbel Exponential with $\theta = 0.2$

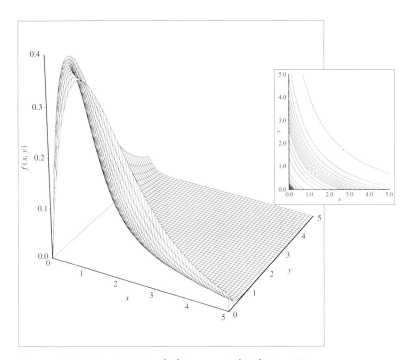

Figure 6.19 Bivariate Gumbel Exponential with $\theta = 1.0$

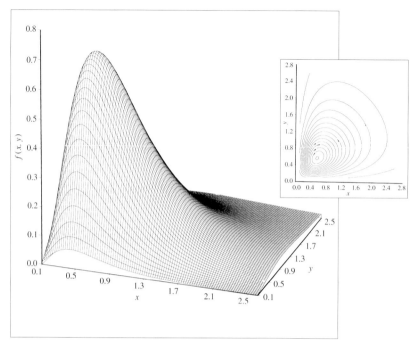

Figure 6.20 Bivariate F density with $\theta := (12,8,8)$

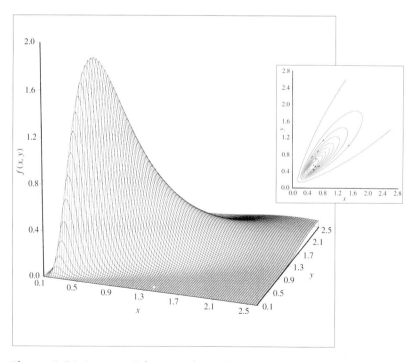

Figure 6.21 Bivariate F density with $\theta := (5,60,60)$

Bivariate Beta density

As in the case of the bivariate Exponential, there are several joint distributions which are called Beta. The **Filon–Isserlis** bivariate Beta density takes the form:

$$f(x,y;\boldsymbol{\theta}) = \left(\frac{\Gamma(\nu_1 + \nu_2 + \nu_3)}{\Gamma(\nu_1)\cdot\Gamma(\nu_2)\Gamma(\nu_3)}\right)\{y^{\nu_1 - 1}x^{\nu_2 - 1}(1 - x - y)^{\nu_3 - 1}\}, \; x \geq 0, y \geq 0, \; x + y \leq 1,$$

where $(\nu_1, \nu_2, \nu_3) \in \mathbb{R}^3_+$. This density, together with its equiprobability contours, for two different values of $\boldsymbol{\theta}$, is shown in figures 6.24 and 6.25. In the case of figure 6.24 the bivariate density has parameter values $\boldsymbol{\theta} := (\nu_1 = 3, \nu_2 = 3, \nu_3 = 6)$, implying a correlation coefficient $\rho = -0.333$. In the case of figure 6.25 the bivariate density has parameter values $\boldsymbol{\theta} := (\nu_1 = 6, \nu_2 = 6, \nu_3 = 8)$, implying a correlation coefficient $\rho = -0.429$. Comparing the two surfaces on the basis of the correlation coefficient is not such a good idea in this case because the distribution exhibits a lot of flexibility, and correlation by itself will not provide a reliable guide.

In the above discussion of dependence in the context of non-symmetric bivariate distributions we used the correlation coefficient in order to explore how these densities change when dependence changes. This is clearly unsatisfactory because we know that the correlation coefficient measures only first-order dependence. We clearly need a more general viewing angle in order to assess the dependence structure of different joint distributions. As an extension of the correlation coefficient we might consider utilizing the first few conditional moments, say up to order four, in order to get a more complete picture of the dependence structure. This will be discussed further in the next chapter in relation to the first few conditional moment functions.

6.7   From probabilistic concepts to observed data

6.7.1   Generating pseudo-random numbers*

The techniques for generating pseudo-random numbers introduced in chapter 5 can be extended to joint distributions. In the case of Independent and Identically Distributed random variables the extension is trivial because the relationship:

$$f(x_1, x_2, \ldots, x_n) \overset{\text{IID}}{=} \prod_{k=1}^{n} f(x_k), \text{ for all } \mathbf{x} \in \mathbb{R}^n,$$

suggests that generating pseudo-random numbers for the joint distribution of the random vector $\mathbf{X} := (X_1, X_2, \ldots, X_n)$ can be done for each random variable X_k separately. Things are not appreciably more complicated in the case where $(X_1, X_2, \ldots, X_n)$ are Independent but non-Identically Distributed since:

$$f(x_1, x_2, \ldots, x_n) \overset{\text{I, non-ID}}{=} \prod_{k=1}^{n} f_k(x_k), \text{ for all } \mathbf{x} \in \mathbb{R}^n.$$

This suggests that, at least theoretically, heterogeneity can be handled without insurmountable difficulties. Things become much more complicated in the case where $(X_1, X_2, \ldots, X_n)$ are *dependent* because the generating scheme has to handle the dependencies among these random variables. In this section we will consider several methods of generating pseudo-random numbers for a random vector $\mathbf{X} := (X_1, X_2, \ldots, X_n)$.

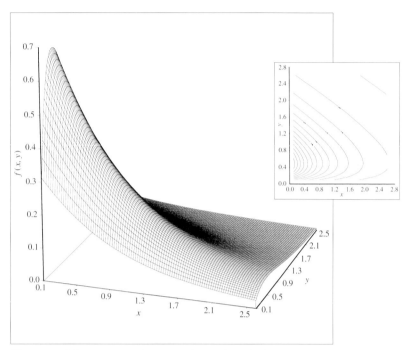

Figure 6.22 Bivariate F density with $\theta := (80,4,2)$

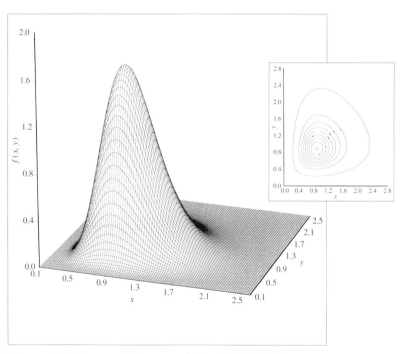

Figure 6.23 Bivariate F density with $\theta := (200,20,20)$

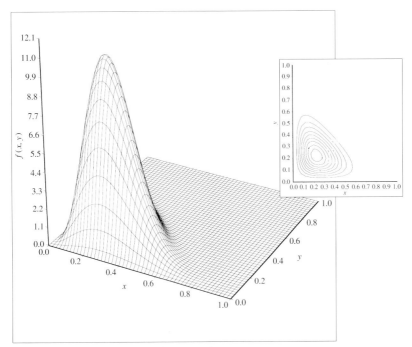

Figure 6.24 Bivariate Beta density with $\theta := (3,3,6)$

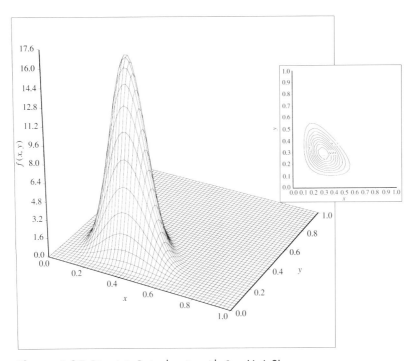

Figure 6.25 Bivariate Beta density with $\theta := (6,6,8)$

The conditional distribution approach

In section 2 above we argued that in the case where $(X_1, X_2, \ldots, X_n)$ are neither independent nor identically distributed the only reduction to a product of univariate distributions possible is that derived by sequential conditioning and takes the form (6.9) which, when simplified by ignoring the unknown parameters, is:

$$f(x_1, x_2, \ldots, x_n) \overset{\text{non-IID}}{=} f_1(x_1) \prod_{k=2}^{n} f_k(x_k | x_{k-1}, x_{k-2}, \ldots, x_1), \text{ for all } \mathbf{x} \in \mathbb{R}^n. \qquad (6.41)$$

This reduction suggests that generating pseudo-random numbers for the random vector $(X_1, X_2, \ldots, X_n)$ amounts to using univariate distributions sequentially.

1   Generate the observations for X_1 using the marginal distribution $f_1(x_1)$.
2   Generate the observations for X_2 using the conditional distribution $f_2(x_2 | x_1)$ given $X_1 = x_1$.
3   Generate the observations for X_3 using the conditional distribution $f_3(x_3 | x_2, x_1)$ given $X_2 = x_2$ and $X_1 = x_1$.
⋮
$n.$ Generate the observations for X_n using the conditional distribution
   $f_n(x_n | x_{n-1}, \ldots, x_1)$ given $X_{n-1} = x_{n-1}, X_{n-2} = x_{n-2}, \ldots, X_2 = x_2$ and $X_1 = x_1$.

The implementation of this result requires that the modeler specifies explicitly these conditional cdfs.

Example

Consider the case $n = 2$ where the joint density function takes the form:

$$f(x, y) = \exp\{c - ax - by + \gamma xy\}, \ a > 0, b > 0, \gamma \leq 0, (x, y) \in \mathbb{R}_+^2.$$

The corresponding marginal and conditional densities take the form (see Arnold *et al.* (1992)):

$$f_x(x) = h\left(\frac{-\gamma}{ab}\right)\left(\frac{abe^{-ax}}{b - \gamma x}\right), \ x > 0, \text{ where } h(u) = [\int_0^\infty e^{-z}(1 + uz)^{-1} dz]^{-1},$$

$$f(y|x) = (b - \gamma x) e^{-(b - \gamma x) y}, \ y > 0.$$

This suggests that the modeler can generate pseudo-random numbers for X using the rejection method (see chapter 5.7) and then proceed to use the simulated values of X to generate Y using the inverse distribution function method (see chapter 5.7) via the conditional density $f(y|x)$.

In terms of the cumulative distribution functions (cdfs) the reduction (6.41) takes the form:

$$F(x_1, x_2, \ldots, x_n) \overset{\text{non-IID}}{=} F_1(x_1) \prod_{k=2}^{n} F_k(x_k | x_{k-1}, x_{k-2}, \ldots, x_1), \text{ for all } \mathbf{x} \in \mathbb{R}^n.$$

Using this result Rosenblatt (1952) extended the probability integral transformation (see chapter 4) to the case of a random vector as follows.

Conditional probability integral transformation Let $(X_1, X_2, \ldots, X_n)$ be a continuous random vector with joint cdf $F(x_1, x_2, \ldots, x_n)$, then the n random variables defined by:

$$Z_1 := F_1(X_1),\ Z_2 := F_2(X_2 | X_1),\ Z_3 := F_3(X_3 | X_2, X_1),\ \cdots, Z_n := F_n(X_n | X_{n-1}, \ldots, X_1),$$

are IID Uniformly distributed random variables, i.e.:

$$Z_1 = F_1(X_1) \sim \mathsf{U}(0,1),\ Z_k = F_k(X_k | X_{k-1}, X_{k-2}, \ldots, X_1) \sim \mathsf{U}(0,1),\ k = 2,3,\ldots,n.$$

Rosenblatt suggested using pseudo-random numbers from a random vector of IID Uniform random variables and via the use of the inverse transformations:

$$X_k = F_k^{-1}(Z_k),\ k = 1,2,\ldots,n,$$

generate the pseudo-random numbers for the random vector $(X_1, X_2, \ldots, X_n)$.

Example
Consider the case $n = 2$ where the joint density function takes the form:

$$f(x,y) = \exp\{-y\},\ x < y,\ (x,y) \in \mathbb{R}_+^2.$$

The corresponding marginal and conditional cdfs take the form:

$$F_X(x) = 1 - \exp(-x),\ x > 0,\ F(y|x) = 1 - \exp(x - y),\ 0 < x < y < \infty.$$

The conditional probability integral transformation suggests that:

$$\left. \begin{aligned} Z_1 &:= F_X(X) = 1 - \exp(-X) \sim \mathsf{U}(0,1), \\ Z_2 &:= F(Y|X) = 1 - \exp(X - Y) \sim \mathsf{U}(0,1), \end{aligned} \right\} \ 0 < X < Y < \infty.$$

The inverse distribution function method can be easily used in the present case to generate pseudo-random numbers for the random vector (X, Y). This result can be verified directly using the following lemma (see Devroye (1986)).

Lemma Let (Z_1, Z_2) be bivariate uniform with joint density $g(z_1, z_2)$. Let f_1 and f_2 be two pre-specified marginal density functions with F_1 and F_2 the corresponding cdfs. Then the joint density of $(X, Y) := (F_1^{-1}(Z_1), F_2^{-1}(Z_2))$, takes the form:

$$f(x,y) = f_1(x) \cdot f_2(y) \cdot g(F_1(x), F_2(y)).$$

Conversely, if the random vector (X, Y) has joint density $f(x,y)$ as given above, then (f_1, f_2) are the marginal density functions of X and Y, respectively. Furthermore, $(Z_1, Z_2) := (F_1(X), F_2(Y))$ is a bivariate random vector with joint density:

$$g(z_1, z_2) = \frac{f(F_1^{-1}(z_1), F_2^{-1}(z_2))}{f_1(F_1^{-1}(z_1)) \cdot f_2(F_2^{-1}(z_2))},\ z_1 \in [0,1],\ z_2 \in [0,1].$$

Returning to the above example we can deduce that:

$$g(z_1, z_2) = e^{-y} \cdot e^x \cdot e^{(y-x)} = e^0 = 1,\ z_1 \in [0,1],\ z_2 \in [0,1],$$

which is a bivariate Uniform density.

The rejection method

The rejection method for generating pseudo-random numbers in the case of univariate distributions was encountered in chapter 5.7. Theoretically, this method can be extended to the case of a random vector $\mathbf{X}$ without any difficulties. In practice, however, several traps await the unaware; see Devroye (1986) and Johnson (1987). The basic result underlying this method is as follows.

Rejection method lemma Let $f(\mathbf{x})$ be the joint density function of the random vector $\mathbf{X}$. Assume that $f(\mathbf{x})$ can be represented in the form:

$$f(\mathbf{x}) = c \cdot h(\mathbf{x}) \cdot g(\mathbf{x}), \text{ where } c > 1, 0 < h(\mathbf{x}) < 1 \text{ and } g(\mathbf{x}) \geq 0, h(\mathbf{x}) \in \mathbb{R}_X^n.$$

Let $Z \sim U(0,1)$ and $\mathbf{Y}$ be a random vector with joint density $g(\mathbf{y})$; $\mathbf{Y}$ and Z independent. Then the conditional distribution of $\mathbf{Y}$ given $Z \leq g(\mathbf{y})$ coincides with the distribution of $\mathbf{X}$, i.e.

$$F(\mathbf{y} \mid Z \leq g(\mathbf{y})) = F(\mathbf{x}).$$

The dependence function method

A promising method for generating pseudo-random numbers, which is yet to be explored, could be based on the dependence function (see Castillo (1988)).

Dependence function Let $F(x,y)$ be the cdf of the random variables (x,y) with marginal cdfs $F_X(x)$ and $F_Y(y)$. The dependence function is defined as the transformation that maps marginal Uniform cdfs into a joint cdf:

$$d(F_X(x), F_Y(y)) = F(x,y), (x,y) \in \mathbb{R}_X \times \mathbb{R}_Y \text{ where } d(.,.): [0,1]^2 \to [0,1]. \tag{6.42}$$

In the case where $F(x,y)$ is a continuous cdf with univariate marginal cdfs $(F_X(.),F_Y(.))$, and quantile functions $(F_X^{-1}(.),F_Y^{-1}(.))$, then:

$$d(z_1,z_2) = F(F_X^{-1}(z_1),F_Y^{-1}(z_2)), (z_1,z_2) \in \mathbb{R}_1 \times \mathbb{R}_2. \tag{6.43}$$

The dependence function constitutes an important way to isolate the dependence structure of jointly distributed random variables.

We can use the latter form of the dependence function in order to gain some additional insight. In chapter 3 we encountered the integral probability transformation which states that for any continuous cdfs $F_X(.)$ $F_Y(.)$, the random variables $Z_1 = F_X(X)$ and $Z_2 = F_Y(Y)$ are uniformly distributed, i.e.:

$$Z_1 = F_X(X) \sim U(0,1), \ Z_2 = F_Y(Y) \sim U(0,1),$$

and the inverse integral probability transformation which ensures that:

$$F_X^{-1}(Z_1) \sim F_X(.), \ F_Y^{-1}(Z_2) \sim F_Y(.).$$

Hence, we can view the dependence function in (6.43) as a mixing mapping of (independent) uniformly distributed random variables giving rise to dependent random variables with joint cdf $F(x,y)$. Hence, given the dependence function the modeler can use uniform pseudo-random numbers to generate such numbers for the random vector (X,Y).

Examples (see Castillo (1988))

(i) Consider the Gumbel Exponential distribution whose cdf takes the form:

$$F(x,y) = \exp(-x - y + \theta xy) + 1 - \exp(-x) - \exp(-y).$$

In view of the fact that the inverse integral transformation of the cdf $F_X(x) = 1 - \exp(-x)$ is $F_X^{-1}(z_1) = -\ln(1-z_1)$ we can show that:

$$\begin{aligned}
d(z_1,z_2) &= F(-\ln(1-z_1), -\ln(1-z_2)) = \\
&= \exp[\ln(1-z_1) + \ln(1-z_2) + \theta\ln(1-z_1)\ln(1-z_2)] + 1 - (1-z_1) - (1-z_2) \\
&= (1-z_1)(1-z_2)\exp[\theta\ln(1-z_1)\ln(1-z_2)] - 1 + z_1 + z_2,
\end{aligned}$$

the dependence function is:

$$d(x,y) = (1-x)(1-y)\exp[\theta\ln(1-x)\ln(1-y)] - 1 + x + y.$$

(ii) Consider the Mardia Exponential distribution whose cdf takes the form:

$$F(x,y) = [\exp(x) + \exp(y) - 1]^{-1} + 1 - \exp(-x) - \exp(-y).$$

Again, using the same inverse integral probability transformation we can show that:

$$\begin{aligned}
d(z_1,z_2) &= F(-\ln(1-z_1), -\ln(1-z_2)) = \\
&= \left(\frac{1}{z_1-1} + \frac{1}{z_2-1} - 1\right)^{-1} + 1 - (1-z_1) - (1-z_2) = \\
&= \left(\frac{1}{z_1-1} + \frac{1}{z_2-1} - 1\right)^{-1} - 1 + z_1 + z_2.
\end{aligned}$$

Hence, the dependence function is:

$$d(x,y) = \left(\frac{1}{x-1} + \frac{1}{y-1} - 1\right)^{-1} - 1 + x + y.$$

6.7.2 A graphical display: the scatterplot

In the previous chapter we introduced the graphical display of a *t*-plot and other related graphical representations of observational data, such as the histogram and the smoothed histogram, to provide a link between theoretical concepts and real data. In this section we take the story one step further by introducing another important graphical display which can provide a link between the probabilistic notions of joint density and dependence and the observed data. This is known as the **scatterplot** (or *cross-plot*) and has its roots back in the mid-19th century.

A scatterplot is a two-dimensional graphical display of the form:

scatterplot: $\{(x_t,y_t),\ t = 1,2,\ldots,T\},$

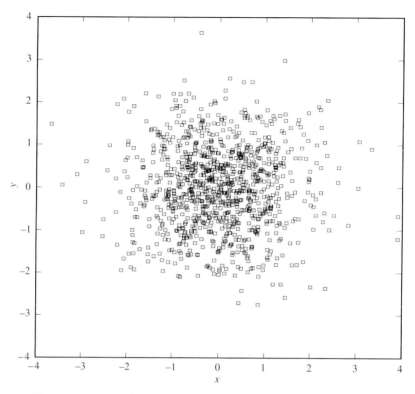

Figure 6.26 Simulated bivariate Normal data with $(\rho = 0)$

where the y-axis represents the range of values of the random variable Y_t and the x-axis represents the range of values of the random variable X_t. In figures 6.26 and 6.27 we can see two such scatter-plots of simulated bivariate Normal IID data. As we can see, figure 6.26 exhibits a certain circular shape with the number of observations increasing as one moves from the outskirts to the center of the circular shape. Figure 6.27 exhibits an elliptical shape with the same tendency for the number of observations to increase as one moves from the tails to the principal axis of the elliptical shape. It turns out that the only difference between the two plots is the correlation coefficient which is $\rho = 0$ for figure 6.26 and $\rho = 0.8$ for figure 6.27.

The key to relating these data plots to the theoretical concept of a joint density function was given to us by Galton (1886) who was able to join the equal-frequency points into elliptical contours and then derive the density itself. With today's graphical techniques we can formalize Galton's procedure and make the necessary distinctions between theoretical concepts and their empirical counterparts.

Smoothed stereogram As in the case of a single data series discussed in chapter 5, the **first step** in relating the scatterplot in figure 6.26 to a theoretical joint density function is to construct the *two-dimensional histogram*, coined **stereogram** by Pearson, and then

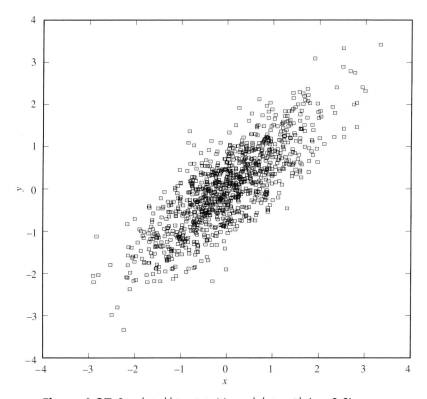

Figure 6.27 Simulated bivariate Normal data with $(\rho = 0.8)$

smooth it. The most widely used smoother is an extension of the one-dimensional kernel discussed in chapter 5. A kernel smoother of a histogram takes the form:

$$\hat{g}_h(x) = \tfrac{1}{nh} \Sigma_{k=1}^n \mathbb{K}\left(\tfrac{x_k - x}{h}\right), \; h > 0, \; \mathbb{K}(z) \geq 0, \; \int_{z \in \mathbb{R}_Z} \mathbb{K}(z) \, dz = 1,$$

where $\mathbb{K}(.)$ denotes the kernel; for several examples of such kernels see chapter 5. The most widely used kernel is that based on the Normal density yielding the smoothed histogram:

$$\hat{g}_h(x) = \tfrac{1}{nh\sqrt{2\pi}} \Sigma_{k=1}^n \exp\left\{-\tfrac{1}{2}\left(\tfrac{x_k - x}{h}\right)^2\right\}, \; h \simeq \sigma \cdot (1.06) \cdot n^{-\frac{1}{5}}.$$

The simplest form of the smoothed stereogram extends this to:

$$\hat{g}_h(x,y) = \tfrac{1}{nh} \Sigma_{j=1}^n \Sigma_{i=1}^n \mathbb{K}\left(\left[\tfrac{x_i - x}{h}\right]\left[\tfrac{y_i - y}{h}\right]\right), \; h > 0,$$

where the kernel takes the form (see Cacoullos (1966)):

$$\mathbb{K}(x,y) \geq 0, \quad \int\int_{x \in \mathbb{R}_X \, y \in \mathbb{R}_Y} \mathbb{K}(x,y) \, dy dx = 1.$$

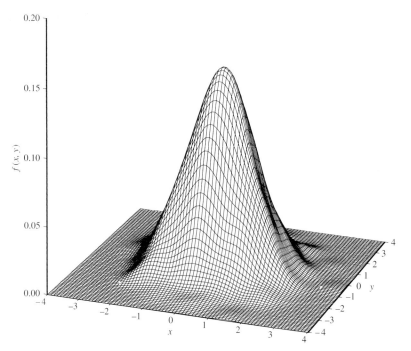

Figure 6.28 Smoothed stereogram of normal simulated data with $(\rho = 0)$

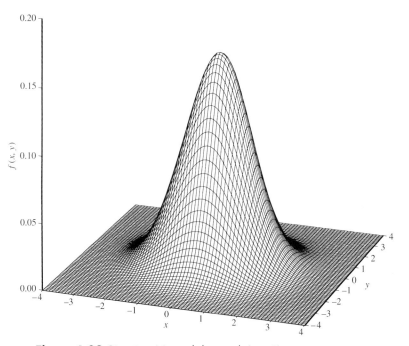

Figure 6.29 Bivariate Normal data with $(\rho = 0)$

More general forms of smoothing kernels allow for different bandwidths and/or correlation (see Silverman (1986)).

The smoothed stereogram for the data in figure 6.26 is shown in figure 6.28. This can be compared with the theoretical bivariate Normal density with $\rho=0$, shown in figure 6.29. As we can see, the smoothed stereogram is very similar to the theoretical surface.

Contours The **second step** is to assess how good an approximation the smoothed stereogram is to the bivariate density function. This assessment can be made in terms of the contours of these two surfaces. In figure 6.30 we can see the contours of the smoothed stereogram and in figure 6.31 the same contours are overlaid with those of the bivariate Normal density ($\rho=0$).

As we can see, this overlay provides a graphical display where the differences between the bivariate density and its empirical counterpart can easily be assessed at different heights. In this example it is obvious that the two are quite close for most heights except the very top where a certain difference can be detected. For the novice we note that such small (but insignificant) differences are the rule and not the exception in empirical modeling; so do not expect the two to coincide!

This exercise is repeated for the scatterplot in figure 6.27. In figures 6.32–6.33 we can see the smoothed stereogram and the bivariate Normal density with $\rho=0.8$, respectively. A glance at these plots suggests that the latter is a good approximation of the former. This conclusion is confirmed by the plot of the contours of the smoothed stereogram in figure 6.34 which are overlaid with those of the bivariate density with $\rho=0.8$, shown in figure 6.35.

A comparison between the figures 6.26 and 6.28–6.31 on the one side and the figures 6.27 and 6.32–6.35 on the other, can be used as a framework in the context of which the modeler can assess the dependence in Normal IID data (where I refers to temporal independence). Perhaps the best way to summarize the two groups of plots is to overlay the contours of the smoothed stereogram with the scatterplot. In figures 6.36 and 6.37 we can see these two plots for the simulated data from a bivariate Normal with different correlation.

The elliptical shape together with the increasing concentration of points of the scatterplot as the eye moves toward the intersection of the two principal axes, point toward the Normality assumption and the degree of eccentricity of the elliptical shape (how squashed it looks) indicates the level of correlation.

The discussion in the previous section, however, suggested that the elliptical shape of the scatterplot is not a feature of the Normal only but a feature of a whole family of joint distributions we called elliptically symmetric. In order to illustrate this point let us return to the Canadian/US exchange rate data introduced in chapter 1 and discussed in chapter 5 in relation to their distributional features. In chapter 1 we noted the chance regularity patterns exhibited by the t-plot of these data including the bell-shaped symmetry. The preliminary conclusion in chapter 5, based on standardized P-P plots, was that the data exhibit a bell shape symmetry closer to the Student's t distribution with 4 degrees of freedom rather than the Normal distribution. Moreover, at first sight the data did not seem to exhibit any significant first-order temporal dependence or any heterogeneity.

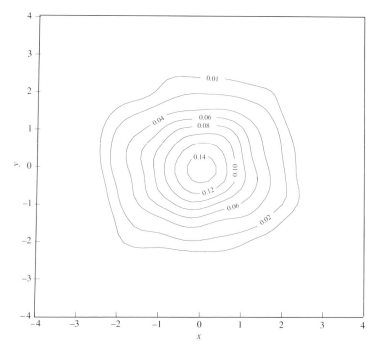

Figure 6.30 Smoothed stereogram contours of simulated Normal ($\rho = 0$) data

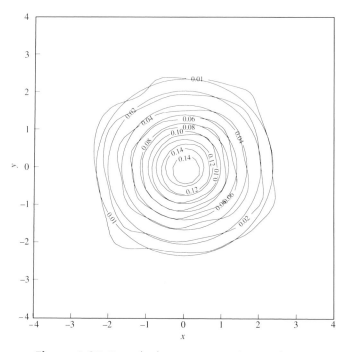

Figure 6.31 Smoothed stereogram and Normal ($\rho = 0$) contours

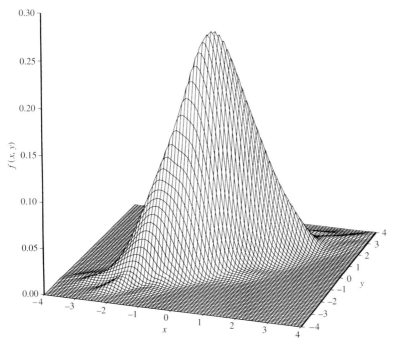

Figure 6.32 Smoothed stereogram of simulated Normal ($\rho = 0.8$) data

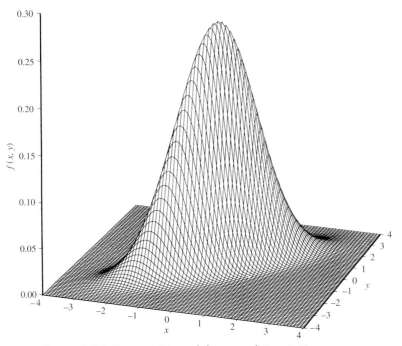

Figure 6.33 Bivariate Normal density with ($\rho = 0.8$)

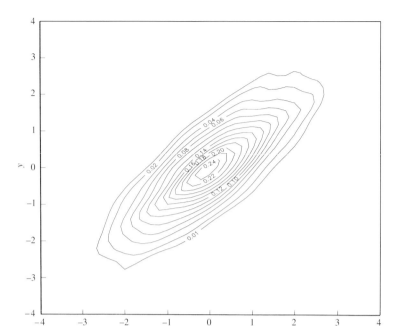

Figure 6.34 Smoothed stereogram contours of simulated Normal ($\rho = 0.8$) data

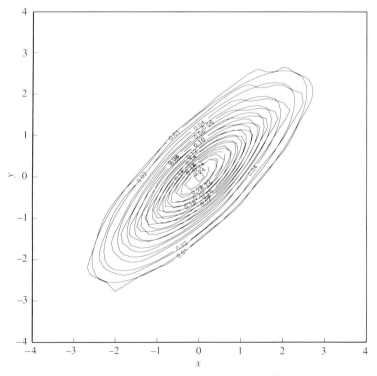

Figure 6.35 Smoothed stereogram and Normal ($\rho = 0.8$) contours

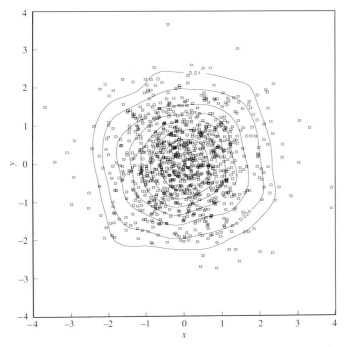

Figure 6.36 Smoothed stereogram contours and scatterplot of Normal $(\rho = 0)$ data

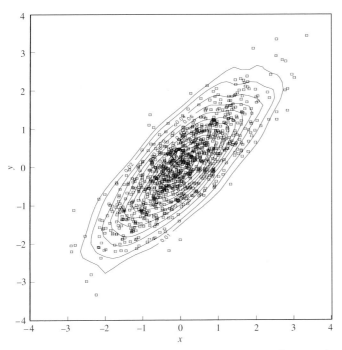

Figure 6.37 Smoothed stereogram contours and scatterplot of Normal $(\rho = 0.8)$ data

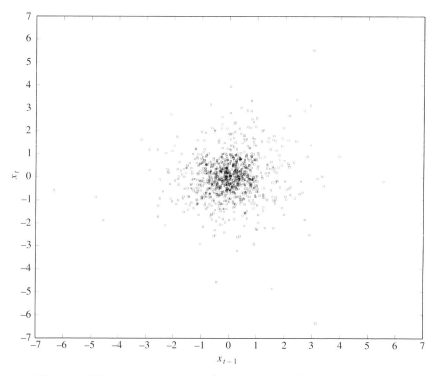

Figure 6.38 Scatterplot (x_t, x_{t-1}) of exchange rate data

In this chapter we proceed to consider the question of distribution-related temporal dependence. Despite the importance of the distinction between contemporaneous and temporal dependence in the context of modeling, in relation to assessing distribution-related dependence the distinction is just a matter of notation. Using the appropriate joint distribution we can discuss the dependence related to the distribution $f(x_t, y_t)$ as easily as that of $f(x_t, x_{t-1})$; the difference is just one of notation. In the present context we can use the scatterplot:

$$\{(x_t, x_{t-1}),\ t = 1, 2, \ldots, T\},$$

shown in figure 6.38, to assess the temporal dependence between successive elements of the stochastic process $\{X_t\}_{t=1}^{\infty}$. The scatterplot exhibits a clear elliptical (close to circular) shape with the concentration of observations increasing as we move toward the center of this elliptical shape. With the eye of our mind we can visualize the two-dimensional surface (stereogram) suggested by this plot. As the number of observations increases moving toward the center of the elliptical shape the corresponding stereogram increases in height. The smoothed stereogram is plotted in figure 6.39 and it represents the data analogue to the two-dimensional surface representing the density function. Looking at this plot we can say that it is surprisingly close to the theoretical bivariate density for the Student's t distribution.

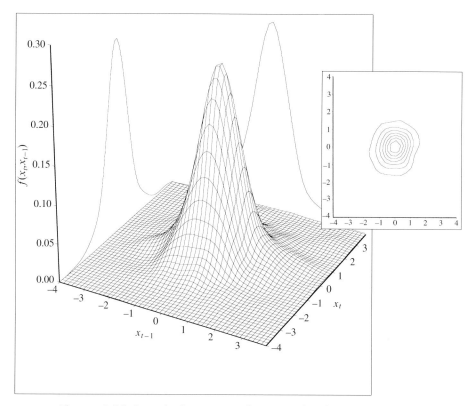

Figure 6.39 Smoothed stereogram/contours of exchange rate data

In figure 6.39 we can also see the corresponding marginal smoothed densities as well as the contours inserted on the right margin. Figure 6.39 confirms that the bivariate Student's t constitutes a much more appropriate distribution assumption than the Normal because a glance at figures 6.10 and 6.11, depicting these bivariate densities, suggest most clearly that the smoothed bivariate density for these data is closer to the density shown in figure 6.11 than that of figure 6.10; it is important to note the measurements on the vertical axis. This is confirmed in figure 6.40 where the contours of the smoothed stereogram in figure 6.39 are superimposed on those of the bivariate Student's t density with 4 degrees of freedom.

The correlation (first-order dependence) between X_t and X_{t-1} does not appear to be significant because the elliptical shapes are close to circles. It should be noted that zero correlation in this context does not mean that the stochastic process $\{X_t\}_{t=1}^{\infty}$ is temporally independent. As argued above, non-correlation does not imply independence in the case of the Student's t distribution. For a more accurate assessment, however, we need to apply proper testing procedures (see chapter 15).

In order to ensure that the conclusions about distribution-related dependence drawn

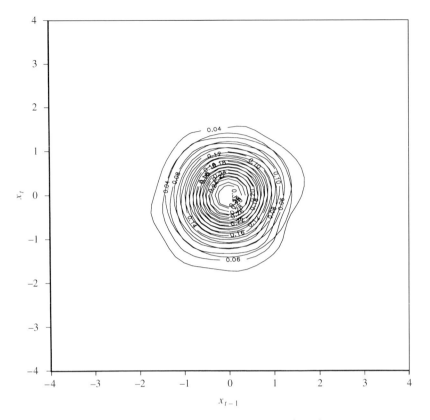

Figure 6.40 Smoothed stereogram (x_t, x_{t-1}) and Student's t $(\nu = 4)$ contours

on the basis of the scatterplot $\{(x_t, x_{t-1}), \; t = 1, 2, \ldots, T\}$, are indeed valid for the process $\{X_t\}_{t=1}^{\infty}$, we need to consider additional scatterplots of the form:

$$\{(x_t, x_{t-k}), \, k \geq 2, \, t = 1, 2, \ldots, T\}.$$

For illustration purposes we consider the scatterplot in the case $k = 2$ in figure 6.42 and the corresponding smoothed stereogram in figure 6.43; we can assure the reader that the additional plots for values $k > 2$ are very similar. As we can see, both of these graphical displays confirm the conclusions drawn on the basis of figures 6.38–6.40. This is reinforced by figure 6.41 where the contours of the smoothed stereogram in figure 6.43 are superimposed on those of a bivariate Student's t density with 4 degrees of freedom.

In the previous section we discussed the importance of overcoming the undue influence of the Normal distribution in empirical modeling. The above empirical example takes the modeler a step away from the Normal distribution and into the elliptic family. Further steps are required, however, in order to get away from Normality's spell. With that in mind let us consider some additional scatterplots of simulated data from asymmetric distributions in order to ensure that the reader does not complete

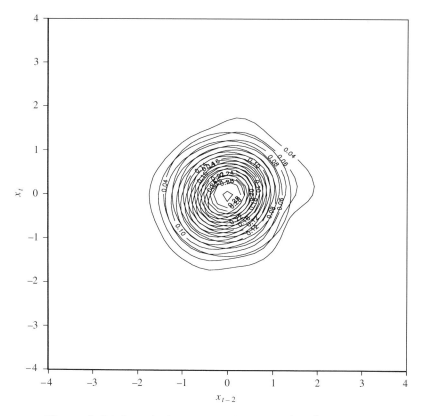

Figure 6.41 Smoothed stereogram (x_t, x_{t-2}) and Student's t $(v = 4)$ contours

this chapter with the erroneous impression that scatterplots appear as symmetric elliptical shapes.

The non-symmetric bivariate distribution we consider first is the Gamma (Cherian) distribution. We choose the parameters in such a way so as to yield a nearly symmetrical distribution in an attempt to illustrate some of the more subtle forms of asymmetry. In figure 6.44 we can see a scatterplot from a bivariate Gamma distribution with parameters ($\theta_0 = 2, \theta_1 = 16, \theta_2 = 16$) which imply a correlation coefficient $\rho = 0.111$; NOTE that the Cherian form of the bivariate Gamma distribution allows only for positive correlation. Figure 6.45 shows the contours of the corresponding theoretical density which exhibit an egg-shaped asymmetry with the yolk (the mode) closer to the more kurtic end pointing toward the origin.

The asymmetry of the scatterplot is not as apparent but a close examination of the data scatterplot in figure 6.44 in conjunction with the contours of the theoretical density shown in figure 6.45 reveals the asymmetry.

In relation to the scatterplot in figure 6.44 it is worth making the point that if the modeler decides to pronounce some of the observations in the tails as **outliers**, the exhibited asymmetry could very easily be lost; and with it the very information that

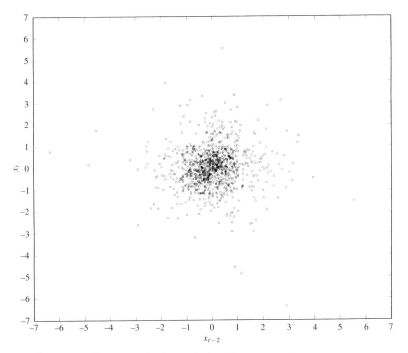

Figure 6.42 Scatterplot (x_t, x_{t-2}) of exchange rate data

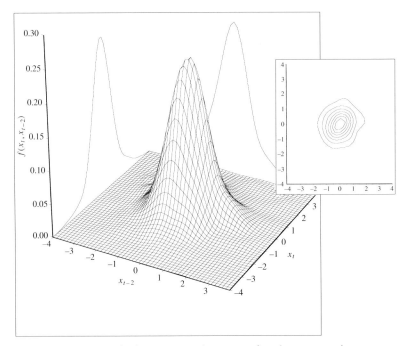

Figure 6.43 Smoothed stereogram/contours of exchange rate data

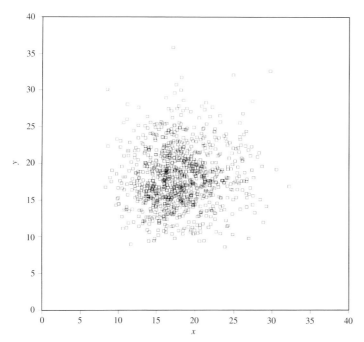

Figure 6.44 Simulated data: bivariate Gamma (Cherian) ($\theta_0 = 2$, $\theta_1 = 16$, $\theta_2 = 16$)

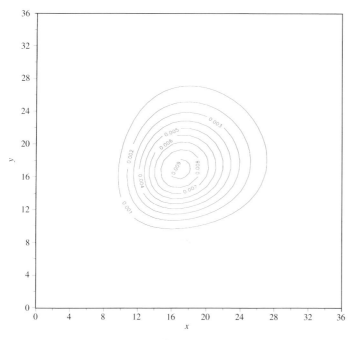

Figure 6.45 Contours of a Gamma (Cherian) ($\theta_0 = 2$, $\theta_1 = 16$, $\theta_2 = 16$) density

would direct the modeler towards the correct distribution.

The same egg-shaped asymmetry is exhibited in figures 6.46–6.47 where the correlation coefficient is $\rho = 0.5$. As in the case of the Normal distribution higher correlation is visualized as squashed contours.

In figures 6.48–6.49 the correlation is increased to $\rho = 0.8$ and the compression of the contours increases.

As an example of a highly skewed distribution we consider scatterplots of simulated data from the Exponential (Gumbel) distribution with correlation, $\rho = -0.01$ and $\rho = -0.36$, in figures 6.50–6.51, respectively. These scatterplots correspond roughly to the bivariate densities shown in figures 6.18–6.19, respectively. As we can see, the negative correlation in a Gumbel Exponential distribution is exhibited by the concentration of the observations along the axes in a fish-tail form.

Although the Gumbel bivariate Exponential does not allow for positive correlation, other forms allow for a complete range of correlations $-1 \le \rho \le 1$ (see Devroye (1986)). In figure 6.52 we can see a scatterplot of simulated data from a non-Gumbel Exponential with positive correlation $\rho = 0.36$. The positive dependence is visualized in figure 6.52 as closing up of the triangular shape in figure 6.50. This becomes more apparent in figure 6.53 where the correlation has been increased to $\rho = 0.9$ inducing a comet-like shape for the scatterplot.

We conclude this section by emphasizing once more that the above plots are only indicative in nature and constitute just the tip of the iceberg in terms of the variety of shapes and patterns one should expect in modeling with real data. The reader is strongly encouraged to generate such scatterplots and the corresponding smoothed densities in order to appreciate the wealth of information such graphical displays can furnish.

A CAUTIONARY NOTE. In this section we discussed the problem of relating the scatterplot of the data series $\{(x_t, y_t), t = 1, 2, \ldots, T\}$ to the distribution structure of the bivariate density $f(x,y), (x,y) \in \mathbb{R}_X \times \mathbb{R}_Y$. Going to three data series, the scatterplot becomes a scattercloud and certain problems arise in rotating the cloud to get a more reliable view. When the modeller attempts to relate the scattercloud to the joint distribution, he/she is required to think in four dimensions. In the above discussion we focused exclusively on two data series because human cognition is limited to three dimensions. Hence, it is often more practical to consider the m data series case by viewing two such series at a time and putting together a more complete picture using the three-dimensional snapshots.

6.8   What comes next?

After the above discussion of dependence, we proceed to discuss the problem raised by stochastic conditioning. Chapter 7 concentrates on conditional distributions and their moments as they relate to dependence and/or homogeneity concentrating again on the simple two-variable case:

$$f(x,y;\phi) = f(y \mid x;\varphi_2) \cdot f_x(x;\varphi_1), \text{ for all } (x,y) \in \mathbb{R}_X \times \mathbb{R}_Y.$$

Of particular interest in chapter 7 will be the concept of distribution-related dependence

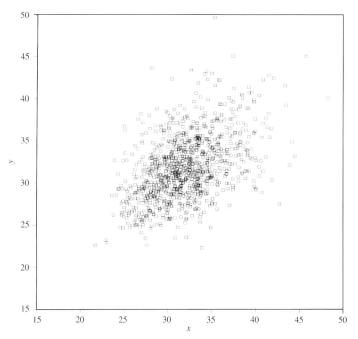

Figure 6.46 Simulated data: bivariate Gamma (Cherian)
$(\theta_0 = 16,\ \theta_1 = 16,\ \theta_2 = 16)$

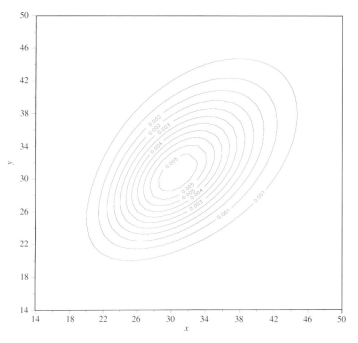

Figure 6.47 Contours of a Gamma (Cherian) $(\theta_0 = 16,\ \theta_1 = 16,\ \theta_2 = 16)$
density

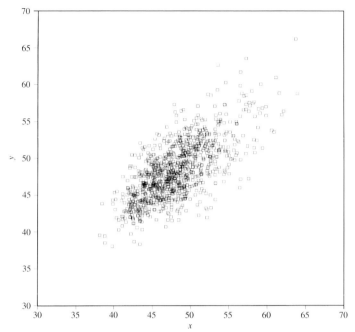

Figure 6.48 Simulated data: bivariate Gamma (Cherian)
$(\theta_0 = 32,\ \theta_1 = 16,\ \theta_2 = 16)$

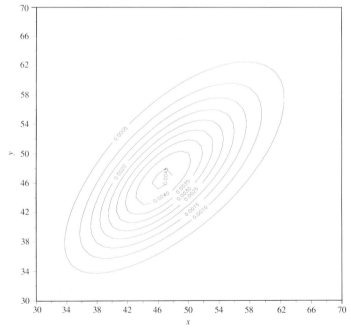

Figure 6.49 Contours of a Gamma (Cherian) $(\theta_0 = 32,\ \theta_1 = 16,\ \theta_2 = 16)$ density

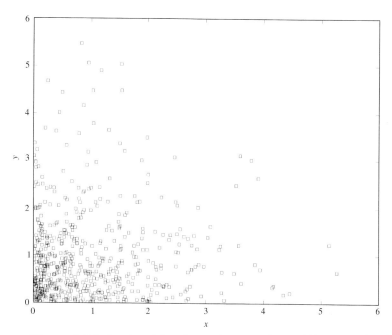

Figure 6.50 Simulated data from a bivariate Gumbel Exponential with $(\rho = -0.01)$

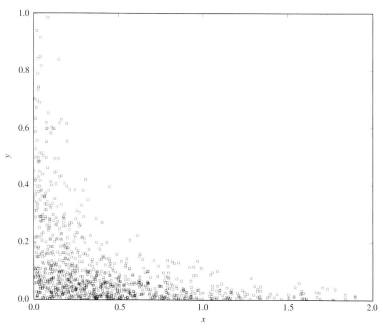

Figure 6.51 Simulated data from a bivariate Gumbel Exponential with $(\rho = -0.36)$

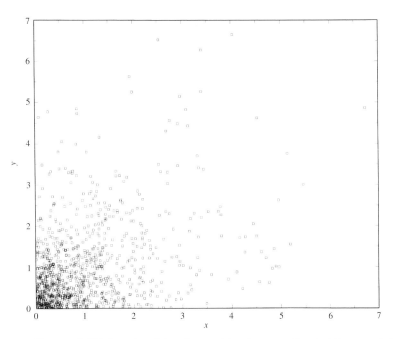

Figure 6.52 Simulated data from a bivariate non-Gumbel Exponential with $(\rho = 0.36)$

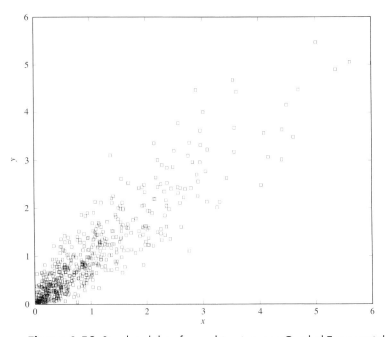

Figure 6.53 Simulated data from a bivariate non-Gumbel Exponential with $(\rho = 0.09)$

and how that relates to the conditional distributions $f(y|x;\varphi_2)$, for all $x \in \mathbb{R}_X$. It is argued that the most effective way to model such forms of dependence is via the concept of *conditional moment functions*:

$$E(Y^r|X=x)=h_r(x),\ x\in\mathbb{R}_X,\ r=1,2,\dots$$

The concepts developed in these two chapters are then extended in chapter 8 beyond the simple two-variable case in order to provide a general framework for modeling dependence and heterogeneity as they relate to *sequences* of random variables. That is, we return to the general case where the reduction of the joint distribution takes the form:

$$f(x_1,x_2,\dots,x_n;\boldsymbol{\phi})\overset{\text{non-IID}}{=}f_1(x_1;\boldsymbol{\psi}_1)\prod_{k=2}^{n}f_k(x_k|x_{k-1},\dots,x_1;\boldsymbol{\psi}_k),\ \text{for all }\mathbf{x}\in\mathbb{R}_X^n,$$

and proceed to consider the question of imposing dependence and heterogeneity restrictions in order for the above reduction to give rise to operational models.

6.9 Exercises

1 Why do we care about heterogeneity and dependence in statistical models?

2 Explain how the idea of sequential conditioning helps to deal with the problem of many dimensions of the joint distribution of a non-random sample.

3 Define the following concepts:
(a) joint moments, (b) conditional moments, (c) non-correlation, (d) orthogonality, (e) cross-product ratio, (e) Gamma coefficient.

4 Let the joint density function of two random variables X and Y be:

$x\backslash y$	0	1	2
0	0.1	0.2	0.2
1	0.2	0.1	0.2

(a) Derive the conditional distributions: $f(y|x),\ x=0,1$.
(b) Derive the following moments:
$E(X),\ E(Y),\ Var(X),\ Var(Y),\ Cov(X,Y),\ E(XY),\ Corr(X,Y),$
$E(Y|X=0),\ E(Y|X=1),\ Var(Y|X=0).$

5 Explain the difference between dependence, correlation and non-orthogonality.

6 Explain the notion of rth-order dependence and compare it with that of (m,k)th-order dependence.

7 Explain the notion of conditional independence and relate it to that of Markov dependence.

8 Explain why non-correlation implies independence in the case of a bivariate Normal distribution. How does one assess the correlation by looking at a scatterplot of observed data?

9 Explain how one can distinguish between the equiprobability contours of the Normal, Student's t and Pearson type II bivariate densities.

10 Explain why zero correlation does not imply independence in the case of the Student's t and Pearson type II bivariate distributions.

11 Explain how an increase in correlation will affect the bivariate Exponential density. What does that mean for the scatterplot?

12 Explain why the notion of correlation makes no sense in the case of random variables measured on the nominal scale.

13 Consider the random variable $X \sim N(0,1)$ and define the random variable $Y = X^2 - 1$. Prove that:

$$Cov(X, Y) = 0,$$

but the two random variables are not independent.

7 Regression and related notions

7.1 Introduction

In the previous chapter we took the first step into the *non-random* sample territory of probability theory. The reader would have realized by now that this territory can be both treacherous and exciting at the same time. It suffices to NOTE that this was a largely uncharted territory until the first quarter of the 20th century. The main target of the discussion that follows is to extend the concept of a simple statistical model, and in particular the notion of a random sample (*Independent* and *Identically Distributed* random variables), toward more realistic formulations. Such models will allow for random variables which are endowed with *dependence* and/or *heterogeneity*. In this chapter we continue this journey and discover that we have been holding the **key** to the non-random sample territory since chapter 4: *the concept of conditioning*.

The manageability of the simple statistical model stems from the fact that the joint distribution of the sample can be greatly simplified by its reduction to a product of univariate (identical) marginal distributions:

$$f(x_1, x_2, \ldots, x_n; \boldsymbol{\phi}) \stackrel{\text{I}}{=} \prod_{k=1}^{n} f_k(x_k; \boldsymbol{\theta}_k) \stackrel{\text{IID}}{=} \prod_{k=1}^{n} f(x_k; \boldsymbol{\theta}), \text{ for all } \mathbf{x}: = (x_1, x_2, \ldots, x_n) \in \mathbb{R}^n. \quad (7.1)$$

In the case of a non-random sample, if we view non-randomness negatively as the absence of independence and homogeneity (ID) the only result available is:

$$f(x_1, x_2, \ldots, x_n; \boldsymbol{\phi}) \stackrel{\text{non-IID}}{\neq} \prod_{k=1}^{n} f(x_k; \boldsymbol{\theta}), \text{ for all } \mathbf{x}: = (x_1, x_2, \ldots, x_n) \in \mathbb{R}^n. \quad (7.2)$$

In chapter 6 we viewed non-randomness positively as the presence of dependence and/or heterogeneity and it was argued that the key to dealing with the joint distribution of a non-random sample was the notion of *sequential conditioning* simplifying the joint distribution to:

$$f(x_1, x_2, \ldots, x_n; \boldsymbol{\phi}) \stackrel{\text{non-IID}}{=} f_1(x_1; \boldsymbol{\psi}_1) \prod_{k=2}^{n} f_k(x_k | x_{k-1}, \ldots, x_1; \boldsymbol{\psi}_k), \text{ for all } \mathbf{x} \in \mathbb{R}_X^n. \quad (7.3)$$

A direct comparison between (7.1) and (7.3) reveals that for non-random samples we trade marginal for conditional distributions. These conditional distributions will provide the means to model dependence and/or heterogeneity.

The first problem we need to address when modeling dependence in the context of the reduction (7.3) is that of *the stochastic conditioning problem*. This problem arises because the right-hand side of (7.3) is not just a product of one marginal density ($f_1(x_1; \boldsymbol{\psi}_1)$) and $(n-1)$ conditional densities ($f_k(x_k | x_{k-1}, ..., x_1; \boldsymbol{\psi}_k), k = 2, 3, ..., n$) as it might appear at first sight. In view of the fact that the concept of a conditional density function is defined for a specific value of the conditioning variables, for each k, the set of conditional densities:

$$\{f_k(x_k | x_{k-1}, ..., x_1; \boldsymbol{\psi}_k), \text{ for all } (x_{k-1}, ..., x_1) \in \mathbb{R}_X^{k-1} \tag{7.4}$$

represents a whole family of density functions; one for each value of $(x_{k-1}, ..., x_1)$ in $\mathbb{R}_X^{k-1}$, and that changes with k. Addressing these problems in their full generality in the context of (7.3) and (7.4), however, will prove very tangled. For this reason we simplify the problem by sidestepping the issues of dependence and heterogeneity associated with a general $k > 2$ and concentrate exclusively on the $k = 2$ case. In a sense we circumvent the problems of (a) the changing conditioning set (the number of conditioning variables changes with k) and (b) the heterogeneity of the conditional densities (they change with k). These two issues will be discussed in the next chapter.

7.1.1   A bird's eye view of the chapter

In section 2 we discuss the conditioning problem in the context of the simplest two random variable case:

$$f(x, y; \boldsymbol{\phi}) = f(y | x; \boldsymbol{\varphi}_2) \cdot f_x(x; \boldsymbol{\varphi}_1), \text{ for all } (x, y) \in \mathbb{R}_X \times \mathbb{R}_Y. \tag{7.5}$$

NOTE that, as in the previous chapter, in order to simplify the notation we use (x, y) instead of (x_1, x_2). In this simple case the increasing conditioning set and the heterogeneity problems do not arise. In this context the conditioning problem is effectively dealt with by extending the notion of conditional moments to *functions* of the values of the *conditioning variable*. In section 3 we extend the notion of conditional moment functions to take account of the presence of the marginal distribution $f_1(x_1; \boldsymbol{\varphi}_1)$. This gives rise to the concept of *stochastic conditional moment functions*. In section 4 we consider the question, Under what circumstances can the modeler ignore the marginal distribution? – the answer to which leads to the notion of *weak exogeneity*. In section 5 we introduce a new component to the notion of a statistical model in addition to the probability and sampling models. This new component is called a *statistical generating mechanism* (GM) and constitutes a bridge between statistical and theory models. In section 6 we take a short historical excursion to trace the roots of regression back to Francis Galton (1822–1911) and Karl Pearson (1857–1936) with a view to providing a brief overview of the *biometric tradition* in statistics. This tradition was later reformulated by R. A. Fisher (1890–1962) into modern statistical inference. We remind the reader that in chapter 1 we mentioned briefly two older traditions in statistics, the *theory of errors* and the *experimental design*, arguing that they are better suited for the statistical analysis of experimental data; or data that can be viewed as generated by a *nearly isolated* system. A particularly important line of argument that runs through this book is that the biometric tradition is better suited for modeling observational (non-experimental) data. Moreover, it is argued that Karl Pearson's approach using the conditional moment functions constitutes the procedure of choice for modeling dependence and/or heterogeneity.

7.2 Conditioning and regression

7.2.1 Reduction and conditional moment functions

As argued above, the equality in the reduction (7.5) does not represent a joint distribution on the left and a product of one conditional and one marginal distribution on the right! The notion of a conditional distribution discussed in chapter 6 is defined with respect to a specific value of the conditioning variable, but the qualifier for all $(x,y) \in \mathbb{R}_X \times \mathbb{R}_Y$ means that for each value of the conditioning variable, $x \in \mathbb{R}_X$, there exists a conditional distribution. From the modeling viewpoint, the conditioning problem has two dimensions. The first dimension is that:

$$f(y|x;\varphi_2), \ (x,y) \in \mathbb{R}_X \times \mathbb{R}_Y, \tag{7.6}$$

defines a (possibly infinite) *family of conditional densities* indexed by different values of the random variable X. The second dimension is that each conditional density in (7.5) is weighted by the marginal probability associated with the corresponding conditioning value of the random variable X. In this section we consider the problem of many (possibly an infinite number of) conditional distributions. The weighting dimension will be discussed in sections 3–4. In order to make the discussion less abstract let us consider this issue using some examples.

Examples
(i)   Consider the joint and marginal distribution as given below:

y\x	1	2	3	$f_y(y)$
0	0.20	0.10	0.15	0.45
1	0.10	0.25	0.05	0.40
2	0.01	0.06	0.08	0.15
$f_x(x)$	0.31	0.41	0.28	1

(7.7)

According to (7.6) this joint distribution gives rise to three different conditional distributions, $f(y|X=x)$ for $x=1,2$ and 3, given by (see chapter 4):

$$f(y|x=1)=\begin{cases} \frac{f(x=1,y=0)}{f_x(x=1)}=\frac{0.20}{0.31}, y=0, \\ \frac{f(x=1,y=1)}{f_x(x=1)}=\frac{0.10}{0.31}, y=1, \\ \frac{f(x=1,y=2)}{f_x(x=1)}=\frac{0.01}{0.31}, y=2, \end{cases}$$

y	0	1	2
$f(y|x=1)$	0.645	0.323	0.032

$$f(y|x=2) = \begin{cases} \frac{f(x=2,y=0)}{f_x(x=2)} = \frac{0.10}{0.41}, y=0, \\ \frac{f(x=2,y=1)}{f_x(x=2)} = \frac{0.25}{0.41}, y=1, \\ \frac{f(x=2,y=2)}{f_x(x=2)} = \frac{0.06}{0.41}, y=2, \end{cases}$$

y	0	1	2
$f(y|x=2)$	0.244	0.610	0.146

(7.8)

$$f(y|x=3) = \begin{cases} \frac{f(x=3,y=0)}{f_x(x=3)} = \frac{0.15}{0.28}, y=0, \\ \frac{f(x=2,y=1)}{f_x(x=3)} = \frac{0.05}{0.28}, y=1, \\ \frac{f(x=2,y=2)}{f_x(x=3)} = \frac{0.08}{0.28}, y=2. \end{cases}$$

y	0	1	2
$f(y|x=3)$	0.536	0.179	0.285

(ii) Consider the case where $f(x,y;\phi)$ is bivariate Normal of the form:

$$\begin{pmatrix} Y \\ X \end{pmatrix} \sim N\left(\begin{bmatrix} \mu_1 \\ \mu_2 \end{bmatrix}, \begin{bmatrix} \sigma_{11} & \sigma_{12} \\ \sigma_{12} & \sigma_{22} \end{bmatrix}\right).$$

(7.9)

NOTE that $\mu_1 = E(Y)$, $\mu_2 = E(X)$, $\sigma_{11} = Var(Y)$, $\sigma_{22} = Var(X)$, $\sigma_{12} = Cov(X,Y)$. The conditional and marginal distributions in (7.5) take the form:

$$(Y|X=x) \sim N(\beta_0 + \beta_1 x, \sigma^2), \ x \in \mathbb{R}, \ X \sim N(\mu_2, \sigma_{22}),$$

$$\beta_0 = \mu_1 - \beta_1 \mu_2, \ \beta_1 = \left(\frac{\sigma_{12}}{\sigma_{22}}\right), \ \sigma^2 = \sigma_{11} - \left(\frac{\sigma_{12}^2}{\sigma_{22}}\right).$$

(7.10)

This shows that the conditional distribution represents an infinite family of conditional densities, one each value $x \in \mathbb{R}$.

The above examples suggest that any attempt to deal with the modeling of the reduction (7.5) by concentrating on the moments of the distributions involved is doomed. This is because of the presence of a conditional density for each value of the conditioning variable. That is, even though the joint distribution on the left and the marginal distribution on the right can (possibly) be modeled via their moments, the conditional densities give rise to a possibly infinite number of conditional moments (one set for each value of the random variable X). That is, the use of conditional moments does not deal with the reduction effectively. This is because conditional moments are defined for each member of the family (7.6) separately and the modeler will be faced with the question: Which set of conditional moments does one use?

Example
In the case of the joint distribution given in (7.7), there correspond three different conditional distributions (see (7.8)), one for each value of X. Hence, there are three pairs of conditional means and variances:

$$f(y|x=1): E(Y|x=1)=0.387, \ Var(Y|x=1)=0.301,$$

$$f(y|x=2): E(Y|x=2)=0.902, \ Var(Y|x=2)=0.380,$$

$$f(y|x=3): E(Y|x=3)=0.749, \ Var(Y|x=3)=0.758.$$

The answer to the question of which set of conditional moments to use is, in a nut-shell, all of them combined by extending the conditional moments in a way analo-gous to the family (7.6). That is, by extending the notion of conditional moments to account for all values of the random variable X, we define the **conditional moment functions**:

Raw: $E(Y^r|X=x)=h_r(x)$, $x\in\mathbb{R}$, $r=1,2,\ldots$

Central: $E([Y-E(Y|X=x)]^r|X=x)=g_r(x)$, $x\in\mathbb{R}$, $r=2,3,\ldots$,   (7.11)

where for a specified value $X=\bar{x}$ these conditional moments are defined (see chapter 4) by:

$$E(Y^r|X=\bar{x})=\int_{y\in\mathbb{R}_Y}y^r\cdot f(y|\bar{x})dy, r=1,2,\ldots$$

$$E([Y-E(Y|X=\bar{x})]^r|X=\bar{x})=\int_{y\in\mathbb{R}_Y}[y-E(y|\bar{x})]^r\cdot f(y|\bar{x})dy, r=2,3,\ldots$$

Example
In the case of the joint distribution given in (7.7) and the conditional moments as given in the example above, the functions associated with the conditional mean and variance take the form:

x	$E(Y|X=x)=h_1(x)$	x	$Var(Y|X=x)=g_2(x)$
1	0.387	1	0.301
2	0.902	2	0.380
3	0.749	3	0.758

The utilization of the concept of functions deals directly with the problem of many different sets of conditional moments by rendering the moments functions of the values of the conditioning variable. In cases where these functions can be defined in terms of specific functional forms they provide easy ways to model dependence. As argued next, for most bivariate distributions we can derive these functions explicitly.

7.2.2 Regression and skedastic functions

In modeling dependence we often concentrate only on the first few of these functions related to the family of densities (7.6). In particular, the main objective of **regression models** is to model (7.6) via the first few conditional moment functions as defined in (7.11). The current literature on regression models concentrates almost exclusively on the first two of such conditional moment functions.

(i)   The **regression function** is defined to be the conditional mean of Y given $X=x$, *interpreted as a function of x*:

$$E(Y|X=x)=h(x), x\in\mathbb{R}_X.$$ (7.12)

NOTE that the term *Regression* was first coined by Galton (1885); see below.

(ii)   The **skedastic function** is defined to be the conditional variance *interpreted as a function of x*:

$$Var(Y|X=x)=g(x),\ x\in\mathbb{R}_X. \tag{7.13}$$

The term skedastic was coined by Pearson (1905) and it is based on the Greek words $\sigma\kappa\acute\epsilon\delta\alpha\sigma\eta$ = scattering, and $\sigma\kappa\epsilon\delta\alpha\sigma\tau\acute o\varsigma$ = scattered.

REMARK: the graphs $(h(x),x)$ and $(g(x),x)$ for all $x\in\mathbb{R}_X$, constitute what we call the **regression** and **skedastic curves**, respectively.

(1) Bivariate Normal As shown above, in the case of the bivariate Normal distribution (7.9) with $\boldsymbol{\phi}:=(\mu_1,\mu_2,\sigma_{11},\sigma_{12},\sigma_{22})$, the conditional density of Y given $X=x$ is also Normal of the form:

$$(y|X=x)\sim N\left(\left[\mu_1+\left(\tfrac{\sigma_{12}}{\sigma_{22}}\right)(x-\mu_2)\right],\left[\sigma_{11}-\left(\tfrac{\sigma_{12}^2}{\sigma_{22}}\right)\right]\right),\ x\in\mathbb{R}. \tag{7.14}$$

This shows that $\boldsymbol{\varphi}_1:=(\mu_2,\sigma_{22})$, $\boldsymbol{\varphi}_2:=(\beta_0,\beta_1,\sigma^2)$ and the regression and skedastic functions take the form given below:

$$E(Y|X=x)=\beta_0+\beta_1 x,\ Var(Y|X=x)=\sigma^2,\ x\in\mathbb{R},$$

$$\beta_0=(\mu_1-\beta_1\mu_2)\in\mathbb{R},\ \beta_1=\left(\tfrac{\sigma_{12}}{\sigma_{22}}\right)\in\mathbb{R},\ \sigma^2=\left(\sigma_{11}-\tfrac{\sigma_{12}^2}{\sigma_{22}}\right)\in\mathbb{R}_+. \tag{7.15}$$

As we can see, the regression function for the joint normal is *a linear function* of x and the skedastic function is *free of x*.

The regression and skedastic functions (7.15) are shown in figures 7.1 and 7.2, respectively, with parameter values $\mu_1=1.5$, $\mu_2=1$, $\sigma_{11}=1$, $\sigma_{22}=1$, and three different values of $\sigma_{12}=-0.8, 0.1, 0.9$. As we can see, the slope of the regression line depends on the sign of the covariance. In figure 7.2 we can see the corresponding skedastic curves which are parallel to the x-axis, as expected. The Normal regression model is one of the few such models where the marginal distribution of X can be ignored because, as shown in section 4 below, X is *weakly exogenous* with respect to the parameters $\boldsymbol{\varphi}_2$.

Linear regression In the case where the conditional mean takes the form given in (7.15), the regression function is said to be *linear* in x.

CAUTION. It is important to distinguish between linearity in x and linearity in the parameters. The second degree polynomial of the form:

$$h(x)=a_0+a_1 x+a_2 x^2, \tag{7.16}$$

is non-linear in x but linear in the parameters (a_1,a_2,a_3). On the other hand, the function:

$$h(x)=\gamma_1-\gamma_3(x-\gamma_2)^2,$$

is non-linear in both the parameters $(\gamma_1,\gamma_2,\gamma_3)$ and x. NOTE that there is a direct relationship between the two sets of parameters: $a_0=\gamma_1-\gamma_3\gamma_2^2$, $a_1=2\gamma_2\gamma_3$, $a_2=-\gamma_3$. This suggests that the particular parameterization of interest is often a matter of choice.

The regression function (7.15) is linear in both x and the parameters (β_0,β_1) but from (7.14) it is obvious that it is non-linear in the primary parameters $(\mu_1,\mu_2,\sigma_{11},\sigma_{22},\sigma_{12})$.

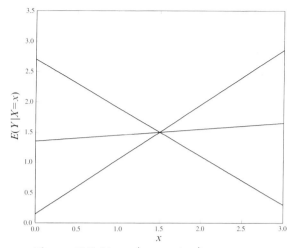

Figure 7.1 Normal regression lines

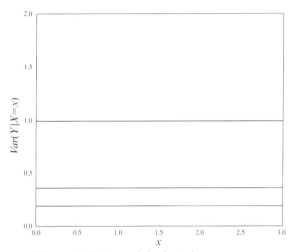

Figure 7.2 Normal skedastic lines

Homoskedasticity In the case where the conditional variance does not depend on the conditioning variable, i.e., for some constant $c_0 \in \mathbb{R}$:

$$Var(Y|X=x) = c_0, \ x \in \mathbb{R}_X,$$

it is said to be *homoskedastic* (see (7.15)).

Heteroskedasticity In the case where the skedastic function depends on the values of the conditioning variable, i.e.:

$$Var(Y|X=x) = g(x), \ x \in \mathbb{R}_X,$$

it is said to be *heteroskedastic*.

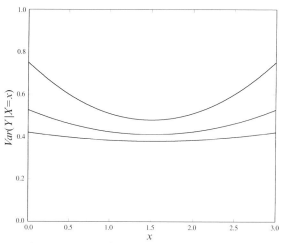

Figure 7.3 Student's t skedastic curves

It is interesting to NOTE that the notions (and the terminology) of *homoskedasticity/heteroskedasticity* were first introduced by Pearson (1905).

(2) **Bivariate Student's t** In the case of the bivariate Student's t distribution with $\nu > 2$ degrees of freedom, denoted by:

$$\begin{pmatrix} Y \\ X \end{pmatrix} \sim \mathsf{St}\left(\begin{bmatrix} \mu_1 \\ \mu_2 \end{bmatrix}, \begin{bmatrix} \sigma_{11} & \sigma_{12} \\ \sigma_{12} & \sigma_{22} \end{bmatrix}; \nu \right), \tag{7.17}$$

the conditional density of Y given $X = x$ and the marginal density of X are also Student's t (see Appendix B). The regression and skedastic functions take the form given below:

$$E(Y \mid X = x) = \beta_0 + \beta_1 x, \ Var(Y \mid X = x) = \frac{\nu \sigma^2}{\nu - 1}\left\{ 1 + \frac{1}{\nu \sigma_{22}}[x - \mu_2]^2 \right\}, \ x \in \mathbb{R},$$

$$\beta_0 = (\mu_1 - \beta_1 \mu_2) \in \mathbb{R}, \ \beta_1 = \left(\frac{\sigma_{12}}{\sigma_{22}} \right) \in \mathbb{R}, \ \sigma^2 = \left(\sigma_{11} - \frac{\sigma_{12}^2}{\sigma_{22}} \right) \in \mathbb{R}_+. \tag{7.18}$$

As we can see, the parameters β_0, β_1 and σ^2 coincide with those of the conditional Normal in (7.10). The skedastic function differs from that of the Normal in so far as (7.18) is *heteroskedastic*: a function of the conditioning variable. In figure 7.3 we can see three Student's t skedastic functions ($\nu = 4,8,20$) with parameters ($\mu_2 = 1$, $\sigma_{22} = 1$, $\sigma_{12} = -0.8$). The curvature of the skedastic curve is inversely related to the degrees of freedom parameter: the smaller the value of ν the greater the curvature of the skedastic function. It is interesting to NOTE that in the case where $\nu = 20$ the skedastic curve is very close to a straight line (a Normal skedastic line).

(3) **Bivariate Exponential** In contrast to the form of the regression and skedastic functions of the bivariate Normal, in the case of the bivariate Exponential distribution the regression and skedastic functions are highly non-linear in x (and thus heteroskedastic):

$$E(Y \mid X = x) = \frac{(1 + \theta + \theta x)}{(1 + \theta x)^2}, \ Var(Y \mid X = x) = \frac{[(1 + \theta + \theta x)^2 - 2\theta^2]}{[1 + \theta x]^4}, \ x \in \mathbb{R}_+, \theta > 0.$$

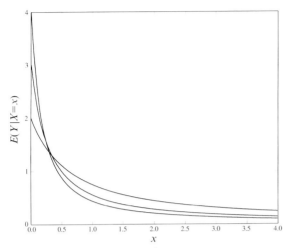

Figure 7.4 Exponential regression curves

The parameter θ is non-linearly related to the correlation coefficient via:

$$\rho := -1 + \int_0^\infty (e^{-x}/(1 + \theta x))) \, dx,$$

with some typical values given below:

$\theta =$	0.01	0.2	0.5	1	2	3	4	8	12	20	600
$-\rho =$	0.01	0.148	0.278	0.404	0.538	0.614	0.665	0.770	0.820	0.870	0.990

In figure 7.4 we can see three Exponential regression curves ($\theta = 1,2,3$) and the corresponding skedastic curves are shown in figure 7.5.

Regression: additional continuous distributions

Several additional examples of regression and skedastic functions associated with other joint distributions are shown below in an attempt to dispel the erroneous impression that the linearity of the regression function and the homoskedasticity of the skedastic function is the rule.

(4) Bivariate Pearson type II

$$E(Y|X=x) = \beta_0 + \beta_1 x, \quad \left[-2(\nu+2)\sqrt{\sigma_{22}}\right] < x < \left[2(\nu+2)\sqrt{\sigma_{22}}\right]$$

$$Var(Y|X=x) = \sigma^2 \left\{ \left(\frac{1}{(2\nu+3)}\right) \left(1 - \frac{(x-\mu_2)^2}{\sigma_{22}}\right) \right\}, \quad x \in \mathbb{R}$$

$$\beta_0 = (\mu_1 - \beta_1 \mu_2) \in \mathbb{R}, \quad \beta_1 = \left(\frac{\sigma_{12}}{\sigma_{22}}\right) \in \mathbb{R}, \quad \sigma^2 = \left(\sigma_{11} - \frac{\sigma_{12}^2}{\sigma_{22}}\right) \in \mathbb{R}_+.$$

The regression function of the Pearson type II distributions coincides with that of the Normal and Student's t distributions. Its skedastic function, shown in figure 7.6 for three different values for the degrees of freedom ($\nu = 1,2,3$) and ($\mu_2 = 1, \sigma_{22} = 1, \sigma_{12} = -0.8$), is

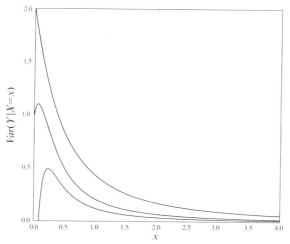

Figure 7.5 Exponential skedastic curves

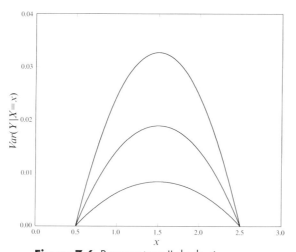

Figure 7.6 Pearson type II skedastic curves

heteroskedastic but unlike that of the Student's t, it has a finite range (compare figures 7.3 and 7.6).

Elliptically symmetric family The fact that the regression functions of the Normal, Student's t and Pearson type II distributions coincide is a special case of a general result. All three distributions belong to the elliptically symmetric family of distributions which share the same regression function (when the required moments exist). Moreover, the skedastic function for all distributions but the Normal are heteroskedastic (see Spanos (1994) for further discussion). The basic difference between these three elliptically symmetric distributions is in terms of their kurtosis: the Normal is mesokurtic (kurtosis =

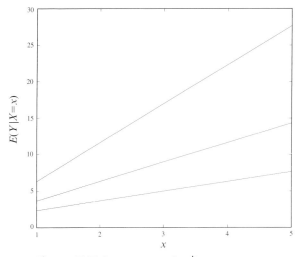

Figure 7.7 Pareto regression lines

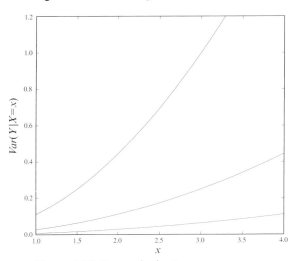

Figure 7.8 Pareto skedastic curves

3), the Student's t distribution is *leptokurtic* (kurtosis >3) and the Pearson type II is *platykurtic* (kurtosis <3).

(5) Bivariate Pareto

$$E(Y|X=x) = \theta_1 + \left(\frac{\theta_1 \theta_3}{\theta_2}\right)x, \; Var(Y|X=x) = \left(\frac{\theta_1}{\theta_2}\right)^2 \frac{(1+\theta_3)}{(1+\theta_3)\theta_3^2}x^2, \; x \in \mathbb{R}_+,$$

$$y > \theta_1 > 0, \; x > \theta_2 > 0, \; \theta_3 > 0.$$

In figures 7.7 and 7.8 we can see the Pareto regression and skedastic curves with parameters $(\theta_1 = 1, \theta_2 = 1.5)$ and three different values of $\theta_3 = 2,4,8$, respectively.

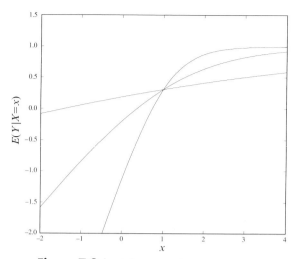

Figure 7.9 Logistic regression curves

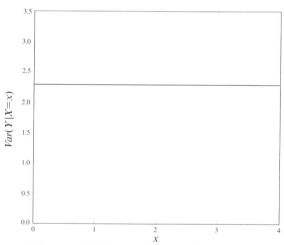

Figure 7.10 Logistic skedastic line

(6) **Bivariate Logistic**

$$E(Y|X=x)=1-\log_e\left[1+\exp\left(-\frac{(x-\mu)}{\sigma}\right)\right],\ x\in\mathbb{R},$$

$$Var(Y|X=x)=\tfrac{1}{3}\pi^2-1=2.29,\ \mu\in\mathbb{R},\ \sigma\in\mathbb{R}_+.$$

In figures 7.9 and 7.10 we can see regression and skedastic curves from the Logistic distribution with parameters ($\mu=1,\sigma=0.5,1.2,4.5$), respectively. As can be seen, the bivariate Logistic distribution yields a highly non-linear regression curve and a homoskedastic conditional variance function. It is worth noting that the bivariate Logistic is among very few distributions with a constant skedasticity function.

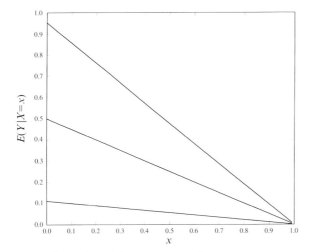

Figure 7.11 Beta regression lines

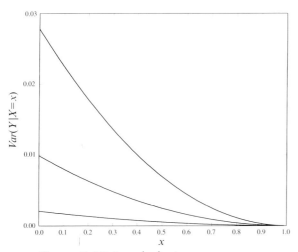

Figure 7.12 Beta skedastic curves

(7) Bivariate Beta

$$E(Y|X=x)=\frac{\theta_2}{[\theta_2+\theta_3]}(1-x), \ Var(Y|X=x)=\left[\frac{\theta_2\theta_3}{(\theta_2+\theta_3)^2(1+\theta_2+\theta_3)}\right](1-x)^2,$$

for $x \in [0,1]$, where $\theta_1>0, \theta_2>0, \theta_3>0$.

In figure 7.11 we can see skedastic curves from the Beta distribution with parameters $(\theta_1=20, \theta_2=20, \theta_3=1)$, $(\theta_1=4, \theta_2=4, \theta_3=4)$, $(\theta_1=1, \theta_2=1, \theta_3=8)$. In view of the fact that the correlation coefficient takes the form:

$$\rho=-\sqrt{\frac{\theta_1\theta_2}{(\theta_1+\theta_3)(\theta_2+\theta_3)}},$$

we can see that the slope of these lines is directly related to the correlation. In figure 7.12 we can see the corresponding skedastic curves.

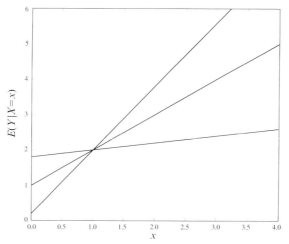

Figure 7.13 Gamma (Kibble) regressions

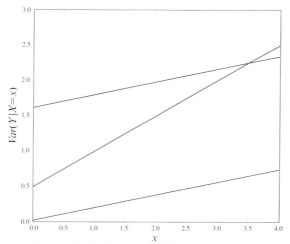

Figure 7.14 Gamma (Kibble) skedastic curves

(8) Bivariate Gamma (Kibble)

$$E(Y|X=x) = \theta_2(1-\theta_1) + \theta_1 x, \; x \in \mathbb{R}_+, \; \theta_1 \in (0,1), \; \theta_2 \in \mathbb{R}_+,$$

$$Var(Y|X=x) = (1-\theta_1)[\theta_2(1-\theta_1) + 2\theta_1 x], \; x \in \mathbb{R}_+.$$

In figures 7.13–14 we can see regression and skedastic curves from the Gamma (Kibble) distribution with parameters ($\theta_1 = 1.0, 1.5, 2.0$, $\theta_2 = 2.0$). NOTE that θ_1 is the correlation coefficient.

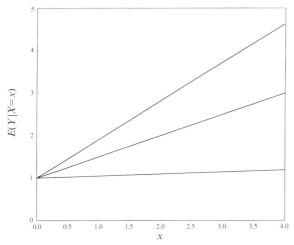

Figure 7.15 Gamma (Cherian) regressions

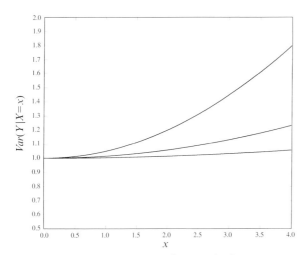

Figure 7.16 Gamma (Cherian) skedastic curves

(9) Bivariate Gamma (Cherian)

$$E(Y|X=x) = \theta_2 + \left[\frac{\theta_0}{(\theta_1 + \theta_0)}\right]x, \; x \in \mathbb{R}_+, \; (\theta_0, \theta_1, \theta_2) \in \mathbb{R}_+^3,$$

$$Var(Y|X=x) = \theta_2 + \left[\frac{\theta_0 \theta_1}{(\theta_1 + \theta_0)^2(1 + \theta_1 + \theta_0)}\right]x^2, \; x \in \mathbb{R}_+.$$

In figures 7.15–16 we can see regression and skedastic curves from the Gamma (Cherian) distribution with parameters ($\theta_0 = 0.1, 2.0, 20.0$, $\theta_1 = 2.0, \theta_2 = 1$). NOTE that the correlation coefficient takes the form $\rho = \frac{\theta_0}{\sqrt{(\theta_1 + \theta_0)(\theta_2 + \theta_0)}}$, and thus for the above three values of θ_0 the correlation takes the values: 0.066, 0.577, 0.930, respectively. The slope of the regression lines is higher the higher the correlation and the curvature of the skedastic curves being higher the higher the correlation.

(10) Bivariate Gamma (McKay)

$$E(Y|X=x)=\left[\frac{\theta_1}{a}\right]+x, \; x\in\mathbb{R}_+, \; (\theta_1,\theta_2,a)\in\mathbb{R}^3_+,$$

$$Var(Y|X=x)=\left[\frac{\theta_1}{a^2}\right], \; x\in\mathbb{R}_+,$$

$$E(X|Y=y)=\left[\frac{\theta_1}{(\theta_1+\theta_2)}\right]y, \; y>x\in\mathbb{R}_+, \; (\theta_1,\theta_2,a)\in\mathbb{R}^3_+,$$

$$Var(X|Y=y)=\left[\frac{\theta_1\theta_2}{(\theta_1+\theta_2)^2(1+\theta_1+\theta_2)}\right]y^2, \; y>x\in\mathbb{R}_+.$$

IMPORTANT NOTE. This bivariate Gamma distribution illustrates an important issue in relation to regression type models. Given the dominance of the bivariate Normal distribution, there is a misconception that all bivariate distributions are symmetric with respect to the random variables X and Y. In the above case of the McKay bivariate Gamma distribution the conditional distributions $f(y|x;\boldsymbol{\theta})$ and $f(x|y; \boldsymbol{\theta})$ are very different, leading to conditional moments which bear no resemblance to each other. For instance $f(y|x;\boldsymbol{\theta})$ gives rise to a homoskedastic function but $f(x|y;\boldsymbol{\theta})$ gives rise to a heteroskedastic function.

(11) Bivariate F

$$E(Y|X=x)=\frac{\theta_0}{(\theta_0+\theta_1-2)}+\left[\frac{\theta_1}{(\theta_0+\theta_1-2)}\right]x, \; x\in\mathbb{R}_+, \; (\theta_0,\theta_1,\theta_2)\in\mathbb{R}^3_+,$$

$$Var(Y|X=x)=\left[\frac{2(\theta_1+\theta_2+\theta_0-2)}{\theta_2(\theta_1+\theta_0-4)(\theta_1+\theta_0-2)^2}\right](\theta_0+\theta_1x)^2, \; x\in\mathbb{R}_+, \; (\theta_1+\theta_2)>4.$$

In figures 7.17–18 we can see three regression and skedastic curves from the F distribution with parameters $(\theta_0=80,\theta_1=4,\theta_2=2)$, $(\theta_0=12,\theta_1=8,\theta_2=8)$, $(\theta_0=5,\theta_1=60,\theta_2=60)$. NOTE that the correlation coefficient takes the form:

$$\rho=\sqrt{\frac{\theta_1\theta_2}{(\theta_1+\theta_0-2)(\theta_2+\theta_0-2)}},$$

and thus for the above three sets of values the correlation is 0.035, 0.444, and 0.952, respectively. The regression lines have a higher slope the higher the correlation and the skedastic curves exhibit higher curvature the higher the correlation.

(12) Bivariate log-Normal

$$E(Y|X=x)=\left(\frac{x}{\mu_2}\right)^\beta e^{\mu_1+\frac{1}{2}\sigma^2}, \; x\in\mathbb{R}_+, \; \sigma^2=\sigma_{11}-(\sigma_{12}^2/\sigma_{22})\in\mathbb{R}_+,$$

$$Var(Y|X=x)=\left(\frac{x}{\mu_2}\right)^{2\beta} e^{2\mu_1+\sigma^2}(e^{\sigma^2}-1), \; x\in\mathbb{R}_+, \; \beta=\left(\frac{\sigma_{12}}{\sigma_{22}}\right)\in\mathbb{R}.$$

Figure 7.19 shows three regression functions from a log-normal distribution with parameters $(\mu_1=1,\mu_2=1,\sigma^2=0.4)$ and three different values of $\beta=0.2, 0.4, 0.8$. NOTE that the main difference between these regression curves and the corresponding skedastic curves shown in figure 7.20 is the scaling factor $(e^{\sigma^2}-1)$.

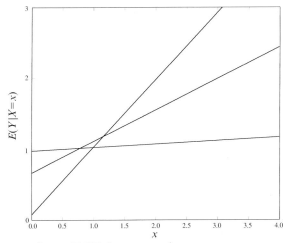

Figure 7.17 F regression lines

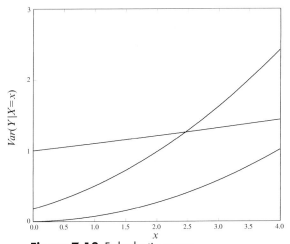

Figure 7.18 F skedastic curves

Regression: discrete distributions

(13) **Bivariate Binomial**

$$E(Y|X=x) = \theta_2(1-\theta_1)(n-x), \ Var(Y|X=x) = \frac{\theta_2(1-\theta_1-\theta_2)}{(1-\theta_1)}(n-x),$$

$$\theta_1 \in (0,1), \ \theta_2 \in (0,1), \ n = 1,2,\ldots, \ \theta_1 + \theta_2 < 1, \ x = 0,1,\ldots$$

(14) **Bivariate Poisson**

$$E(Y|X=x) = (\theta_2 - \theta_3) + \left(\frac{\theta_1}{\theta_3}\right)x, \ x = 0,1,2, \ \ldots, \ \theta_1 > 0, \ \theta_2 > 0, \ \theta_3 > 0,$$

$$Var(Y|X=x) = (\theta_2 - \theta_3) + \left([\theta_1 - \theta_3]\frac{\theta_3}{\theta_1^2}\right)x, \ x = 0,1, \ \ldots, \ \theta_3 < \min(\theta_1,\theta_2).$$

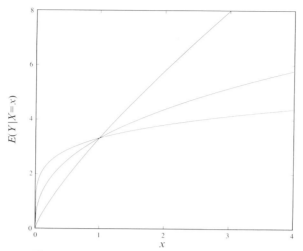

Figure 7.19 Log-Normal regression curves

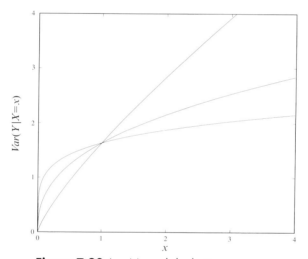

Figure 7.20 Log-Normal skedastic curves

(15) **Bivariate Negative Binomial**

$$E(Y|X=x) = \frac{\theta_2}{(1-\theta_2)}(\theta_1 + x), \quad x = 0,1,2, \ldots, \quad \theta_2 \in (0,1), \quad \theta_1 > 0,$$

$$Var(Y|X=x) = \frac{\theta_2}{(1-\theta_2)^2}(\theta_1 + x), \quad x = 0,1,2, \ldots$$

We conclude this subsection by NOTING that among the above examples, the Normal is the only joint distribution with a linear regression function and a homoskedastic conditional variance. The majority of the above distributions have heteroskedastic conditional variances and several have non-linear regression curves.

7.2.3   Clitic and kurtic functions

The question that naturally arises at this stage is: Why consider only the first two conditional moment functions (regression and skedastic) in modeling dependence? We know
that in general we need many (often and infinite number) of moments to characterize distributions (see chapter 3). The fact of the matter is that there is no convincing argument
why the modeler should consider only the first two conditional moment functions unless
the distribution is assumed to be Normal; see chapter 3. Once more this situation arose
because the Normal distribution has exercised its well-known undue influence. In econometric modeling there is an almost exclusive focus on the regression function with rare
excursions into the skedastic function territory. A cursory look at current traditional
econometric literature, however, reveals a kind of schizophrenia about the specification
of the linear model as it is traditionally called. On the one hand, traditional textbooks
extol the virtues of the Gauss Markov theorem, based on a linear regression and a homoskedastic function (see chapter 13), because of its non-reliance on the Normality
assumption. The question, however, arises: Why specify only the first two conditional
moments if one does not assume Normality? On the other hand, there is an unexplained
attachment to the Normal distribution even in cases where heteroskedasticity is explicitly modeled (see Spanos (1995a)). Moreover, the tendency in modeling heteroskedasticity is to use *ad hoc* functions instead of specific functional forms related to joint
distributions other than the Normal. The above examples suggest that there are several
other distributions that give rise to different forms of heteroskedasticity which remain
unexplored; see Spanos (1994) on results relating to the symmetrically elliptic family.

  Probability theory suggests that there are good reasons to believe that when dealing
with non-symmetrically elliptic joint distributions some additional conditional moment
functions will be needed to capture higher-order dependence. The next two central
conditional moment functions, first introduced by Pearson (1905), are:

(iii)   clitic function: $E([Y - E(Y|X=x)]^3|X=x) = g_3(x)$, $x \in \mathbb{R}_X$,
(iv)   kurtic function: $E([Y - E(Y|X=x)]^4|X=x) = g_4(x)$, $x \in \mathbb{R}_X$.

Examples
(i)   In the case of the **bivariate Beta distribution** these functions take the form:

$$E([Y - E(Y|X=x)]^3|X=x) = \left[\frac{2\theta_2\theta_3(\theta_3 - \theta_2)}{(\theta_2 + \theta_3)^3(1 + \theta_2 + \theta_3)(2 + \theta_2 + \theta_3)}\right](1-x)^3, \ x \in [0,1],$$

$$E([Y - E(Y|X=x)]^4|X=x) = \left[\frac{3\theta_2\theta_3(2\theta_2^2 - 2\theta_2\theta_3 + \theta_2^2\theta_3 + 2\theta_3^2 - \theta_2\theta_3^2)}{(\theta_2 + \theta_3)^4(1 + \theta_2 + \theta_3)(2 + \theta_2 + \theta_3)(3 + \theta_2 + \theta_3)}\right](1-x)^4.$$

As we can see, the bivariate Beta distribution yields *heteroclitic* and *heterokurtic* functions. The notions and the terminology *homoclitic/heteroclitic* were introduced by
Pearson (1905).
(ii)   In the case of the **bivariate Student's t distribution** these functions take the form:

$$E([Y - E(Y|X=x)]^3|X=x) = 0, \ x \in \mathbb{R},$$

$$E([Y - E(Y|X=x)]^4|X=x) = \frac{3(v-1)}{(v-3)}[Var(Y|X)]^2, \ x \in \mathbb{R}.$$

As we can see, the bivariate student's t distribution yields *homoclitic* and *heterokurtic* functions; the latter is of a special form being a function of the skedastic function. Both features are due to the elliptic nature of the distribution.

7.3   Reduction and stochastic conditioning

Having dealt with the problem of many conditional distributions by extending the notion of moments to conditional moment functions, let us return to the original reduction:

$$f(x,y;\phi) = f(y|x;\varphi_2) \cdot f_x(x;\varphi_1), \text{ for all } (x,y) \in \mathbb{R}_X \times \mathbb{R}_Y. \tag{7.19}$$

We observe that on the right-hand side there exists a family of conditional densities, where each one is weighted by the corresponding marginal probability. In defining the conditional moment functions:

$$h_r(x) = E(Y^r|X=x), x \in \mathbb{R}_X,$$

we ignored the marginal weights and concentrated exclusively on the family of conditional densities $\{f(y|X=x;\varphi_2), (x,y) \in \mathbb{R}_X \times \mathbb{R}_Y\}$. In some sense this amounts to assuming that the different values taken by the random variable X occur with probability one:

$$h_r(x) = E(Y^r|X=x), \text{ where } \mathbb{P}(X=x) = 1, \text{ for all } x \in \mathbb{R}_X. \tag{7.20}$$

However, as shown in (7.19) this is not quite correct. A more appropriate way to specify these functions is to take into consideration the marginal probabilities associated with the different values $x \in \mathbb{R}_X$. The problem is to specify these functions without ignoring the fact that different values of X occur with different probabilities as given by the marginal density $f(x;\varphi_1)$. NOTE again that in the case of continuous random variables, as mentioned in chapter 3, the weights are not proper probabilities.

The formal way to deal with this problem is to extend the concept of conditioning one step further: to account for all events associated with the random variable X; not just its range of values. That is, instead of concentrating exclusively on conditioning events of the form:

$$\{s:X(s)=x\}, \text{ for all } x \in \mathbb{R}_X,$$

in the context of the probability space $(S,\Im,\mathbb{P}(.))$, we consider the σ-field *generated by the random variable X* (for all possible events associated with X; see chapter 3):

$$\sigma(X) := \sigma(X^{-1}(-\infty,x] \in \Im, \text{ for all } x \in \mathbb{R}_X).$$

This enables us to define the stochastic conditional moment functions:

$$h_r(X) = E(Y^r|\sigma(X)), \text{ for } X \sim \mathsf{D}_X(.), \tag{7.21}$$

where $\mathsf{D}_X(.)$ denotes the marginal distribution of the random variable X. This conditioning is meaningful because $\sigma(X) \subset \Im$. The question, however, is: What meaning do we attach to such stochastic conditioning functions? It is obvious that the functions

$h_r(X) = E(Y^r | \sigma(X))$ are different from those in (7.20) because the former are random variables, being a function of the random variable X; hence a random variable itself! They look like conditional moments but they are stochastic in nature!

REMARK: without any loss of generality we concentrate on the simple case $r = 1$. This is because for any random variable Z and any function of the form Z^r we can define a new random variable $Y = Z^r$.

7.3.1 Meaning of $E(Y | \sigma(X))$

We first encountered conditioning in the context of the probability space $(S, \Im, \mathbb{P}(.))$ in relation to events $A, B \in \Im$. We remind the reader that the mathematical notion of probability $\mathbb{P}(.)$ requires the modeler to specify the set of all events of interest associated with S, say $\Im$, and the mathematical setup is defined by the probability space $(S, \Im, \mathbb{P}(.))$. In this context, the conditional probability of A given B takes the form:

$$\mathbb{P}(A|B) = \frac{\mathbb{P}(A \cap B)}{\mathbb{P}(B)}, \text{ for } \mathbb{P}(B) > 0,$$

and conditioning on B it can be intuitively understood that "it is known that event B has occurred." Conditioning in general is defined relative to knowing that certain *event(s)* have occurred. In this sense the conditional density:

$$f(y|\bar{x}) = \frac{f(\bar{x}, y)}{f_x(\bar{x})}, \, y \in \mathbb{R}_Y,$$

should be understood as the revised density of the random variable Y given that the event $\{s : X(s) = \bar{x}\}$ has occurred. At this point it is crucial to emphasize once more that a conditional distribution is defined *at a particular value* of the conditioning variable. Using the conditional density we can define the conditional expectation unambiguously as:

$$E(Y|X = \bar{x}) = \int_{y \in \mathbb{R}_Y} y f(y|\bar{x}) dy.$$

In view of the above discussion the expression:

$$E(Y|X), \tag{7.22}$$

makes no mathematical sense because the conditioning is not relative to an event; a random variable is not an event (a subset of the reference outcomes set S). Intuitively, however, we know that for each value $X = x$ this is well defined and so one can think of (7.22) as a function of X and hence a random variable itself. Our intuition is indeed correct but we need to formalize it. For a random variable X defined on S, the event $\{s : X(s) = \bar{x}\}$ constitutes an element of $\Im$, in the sense that $X^{-1}(\bar{x}) \in \Im$. Indeed, by definition (see chapter 3):

$$X^{-1}(x) \in \Im, \text{ for all values } x \in \mathbb{R}_X.$$

In view of this we can deduce that the only way (7.22) could make mathematical sense is to turn the conditioning random variable into a set of events. That is, define $\sigma(X)$: the

σ-field generated by the random variable X (see chapter 3). In this sense the conditional expectation:

$$E(Y|\sigma(X)), \tag{7.23}$$

should be meaningful because, at least intuitively, this represents the expectation given that "some event related to X has occurred." Common sense suggests that the ordinary expectation $E(Y)$ can be viewed from this angle as:

$E(Y|\mathcal{D}_0)$, where $\mathcal{D}_0 = \{S,\emptyset\}$, the trivial event space (non-informative).

Viewed in this light $\sigma(X)$ constitutes a restriction on $\Im$ (all-informative) in the sense that (see chapter 3):

$$\{S,\emptyset\} \subset \sigma(X) \subset \Im.$$

Having agreed that (7.23) does make intuitive sense we need to ensure that it also makes mathematical sense.

A simple case Before we consider the general case let us discuss first the case where both random variables Y and X are discrete and take only a finite number of values, i.e.:

$$\mathbb{R}_Y := \{y_1, y_2, \ldots, y_n\}, \ \mathbb{R}_X := \{x_1, x_2, \ldots, x_m\}.$$

In this case the conditional mean (7.23) can be thought of in terms of the events:

$$\mathcal{B} := \{B_k, k = 1, \ldots, m\}, \text{ where } B_k := \{s : X(s) = x_k\}, \tag{7.24}$$

which constitute a partition of S, in the sense that:

$$S = \bigcup_{k=1}^{m} B_k, \text{ and } B_k \cap B_i = \emptyset, \ i \neq k, \ i,k = 1,2, \ldots, m.$$

In terms of these events we can think of $\sigma(X)$ as defined by their 2^m unions; no intersections or complementations are needed because $\mathcal{B}$ constitutes a partition of S.

Example
Consider the example of tossing a coin twice, $S = \{(HH),(HT),(TH),(TT)\}$, $\Im$ is chosen to be the power set, and define the random variables:

$$X(TT) = 0, \ X(HT) = X(TH) = 1, \ X(HH) = 2,$$
$$Y(TT); = Y(HH) = 2, \ Y(HT) = Y(TH) = 1.$$

Taking the pre-image of the random variable X we can see that:

$$B_0 = X^{-1}(0) = \{(TT)\}, \ B_1 = X^{-1}(1) = \{(HT),(TH)\}, \ B_2 = X^{-1}(2) = \{(HH)\},$$

showing that this constitutes a partition of S, since:

$$B_0 \cap B_1 = \emptyset, \ B_1 \cap B_2 = \emptyset, \ B_0 \cap B_2 = \emptyset, \text{ and } S = B_0 \cup B_1 \cup B_2.$$

Hence, $\sigma(X) = \{S,\emptyset,B_0,B_1,B_2,B_0 \cup B_1,B_0 \cup B_2,B_1 \cup B_2\}$.

Returning the conditional mean (7.23), we can view it in terms of the events B_k:

$$E(Y|X_k=x_k)=\sum_{i=1}^n y_i \cdot \mathbb{P}(Y=y_i|X=x_k), \quad k=1,2,\ldots,m, \tag{7.25}$$

which defines a sequence of conditional means, one for each value of X, where:

$$\mathbb{P}(Y=y_i|X=x_k)=\frac{\mathbb{P}(Y=y_i,X=x_k)}{\mathbb{P}(X=x_k)}, \quad i=1,2,\ldots,n, \; k=1,2,\ldots,m. \tag{7.26}$$

In this sense the different conditional means in (7.25) can be interpreted in terms of the random variable:

$$Z(.):=E(Y(.)|\sigma(X(.))): S\to\mathbb{R}, \tag{7.27}$$

such that when $X(s)=x_k$ then $Z(s)=z_k$, $k=1,2,\ldots,m$. Moreover, substituting (7.26) into (7.25) and re-arranging the terms yields:

$$E(Y|X_k=x_k)\cdot\mathbb{P}(X=x_k)=\sum_{i=1}^n y_i\cdot\mathbb{P}(Y=y_i,X=x_k), \quad k=1,2,\ldots,m.$$

At this stage we should resist the temptation to interpret the conditional mean (7.23) as the summation:

$$\sum_{k=1}^m E(Y|X_k=x_k)\cdot\mathbb{P}(X=x_k)=\sum_{k=1}^m\sum_{i=1}^n y_i\cdot\mathbb{P}(Y=y_i,X=x_k), \tag{7.28}$$

because, as shown above, $\sigma(X)$ involves more events than just $\bigcup_{k=1}^m B_k$. A moment's reflection, however, suggests that this summation (7.28) defines the stochastic conditional mean:

$$E(Y(.)|\mathcal{B}): S\to\mathbb{R}.$$

Reminding ourselves that going from $\mathcal{B}$ as defined in (7.24) (not a σ-field) to $\sigma(X)$ we just add all unions of the events $B_k\in\mathcal{B}$, the random variable (7.27) can be thought of in terms of all events $B\in\sigma(X)$ as:

$$\sum_{B\in\sigma(X)} E(Y|\sigma(X))\cdot\mathbb{P}(B)=\sum_{B\in\sigma(X)}\sum_{i=1}^n y_i\cdot\mathbb{P}(Y=y_i,B) \text{ for all } B\in\sigma(X). \tag{7.29}$$

It is clear that $E(Y|\sigma(X))$ is a random variable relative to $\sigma(X)$.

Example
Consider the following joint distribution:

$x\backslash y$	-1	0	1	$f(x)$
-1	0.1	0.2	0.1	0.4
1	0.2	0.1	0.3	0.6
$f(y)$	0.3	0.3	0.4	1

$$\tag{7.30}$$

The conditional distribution(s) of $(Y|X=x)$ for $x=-1$ and $x=1$ is given below:

y	-1	0	1
$f(y|x=-1)$	$\frac{1}{4}$	$\frac{1}{2}$	$\frac{1}{4}$

y	-1	0	1
$f(y|x=1)$	$\frac{1}{3}$	$\frac{1}{6}$	$\frac{1}{2}$

$$\tag{7.31}$$

Moreover, the conditional means in these cases are:

$$E(Y|X=-1)=(-1)\tfrac{1}{4}+0\left(\tfrac{1}{2}\right)+1\left(\tfrac{1}{4}\right)=0,\ E(Y|X=1)=(-1)\left(\tfrac{1}{3}\right)+0\left(\tfrac{1}{6}\right)+1\left(\tfrac{1}{2}\right)=\tfrac{1}{6}.$$

$E(Y|\sigma(X))$ is a random variable relative to $\sigma(X)$ in the sense that it can take two values $\left(0,\tfrac{1}{6}\right)$ with probabilities $(0.4, 0.6)$, respectively:

x	-1	1
$\mathbb{P}(X=x)$	0.4	0.6
$E(Y|\sigma(X))$	0	$\tfrac{1}{6}$

(7.32)

The general case More mathematically inclined books express (7.29) in the general case, where (X, Y) are arbitrary random variables, using the rather unappetizing expression:

$$\int_B E(Y|\sigma(X))\cdot d\mathbb{P}=\int_B Y\cdot d\mathbb{P},\ \text{for all } B\in\sigma(X).$$

(7.33)

This says that the average of $E(Y|\sigma(X))$ over B is the same as the average of Y itself over the all subsets $B\subset\sigma(X)\subset\Im$.

NOTE that in general $Y\neq E(Y|\sigma(X))$ because Y is not necessarily a random variable relative to $\sigma(X)$. This result was first proved by Kolmogorov (1933a), but the mathematics needed to derive the above relationship rigorously are rather demanding (see Ash (1972) for a more rigorous derivation). However, an intuitive understanding of (7.33) can be gained by viewing the expectation as a smoothing operator.

The most convenient way to get rid of the unappetizing integrals (or summations) in (7.33) (and (7.29)) is to use the indicator function in conjunction with the expectation operator, i.e.:

$$\int_B Z\cdot d\mathbb{P}:=E[Z\cdot \mathbb{1}_B],$$

where $\mathbb{1}_B$ denotes the indicator function of the set B: $\mathbb{1}_B(s)=\begin{cases}1, \text{ if } s\in B,\\ 0, \text{ if } s\notin B.\end{cases}$

This enables us to express (7.33) in the less intimidating form:

$$E[E(Y|\sigma(X))\cdot \mathbb{1}_B]=E[Y\cdot \mathbb{1}_B],\ \text{for all } B\in\sigma(X).$$

(7.34)

REMARK: in view of the fact that $\sigma(X)$ includes all possible Borel functions of the random variable X, we can define $E(Y|\sigma(X))$ in terms of such functions via:

$$E[E(Y|\sigma(X))\cdot g(X)]=E[Y\cdot g(X)],\ \text{for any Borel function } g(X),$$

assuming that $E[Y\cdot g(X)]<\infty$; see Parzen (1962).

A further extension The above definition of conditional expectation (7.34) in the context of the probability space $(S,\Im,\mathbb{P}(.))$, can be extended further to:

$$E[E(Y|\mathcal{D})\cdot \mathbb{1}_D]=E[Y\cdot \mathbb{1}_D],\ \text{for any } D\in\mathcal{D}\subset\Im,$$

where the definition of the random variable $E(Y|\mathcal{D})$ revolves around the choice of $\mathcal{D}$. At the one extreme of the spectrum we can choose $\mathcal{D}$ to be the *non-informative* sub-field $\mathcal{D}_0 := \{S,\emptyset\}$ in which case:

$$E(Y|\mathcal{D}_0) = E(Y),$$

where $Y_0 := E(Y|\mathcal{D}_0)$ can be viewed as a degenerate random variable of the form:

$$Y_0(.): S \rightarrow E(Y), \text{ with probability one (w.p.1)}.$$

NOTE that this is a random variable with respect to any $\mathcal{D} \subset \mathfrak{I}$; all σ-fields include $\{S,\emptyset\}$. Viewed as a smoothing operation, the random variable Y is completely smoothed down to a constant. At the other extreme of the spectrum we can choose $\mathcal{D}$ to be the *all-informative* (for Y) sub-σ-field $\mathcal{D}_Y := \sigma(Y)$, in which case the conditioning gives rise to:

$$E(Y|\mathcal{D}_Y) = Y, \text{ where } Y(.): S \rightarrow \mathbb{R}_Y.$$

Viewing the conditional expectations as a smoothing operation, the random variable Y is left intact. NOTE that in general Y is not a random variable with respect to $\mathcal{D}_0$. Between these two extreme cases we can choose $\mathcal{D}$ to be any sub-σ-field such that:

$$\mathcal{D} \cap \mathcal{D}_Y = \mathcal{D}^* \neq \emptyset. \tag{7.35}$$

This enables us to think of $\mathcal{D}^*$ as the amount of information about Y that $\mathcal{D}$ contains and $E(Y|\mathcal{D})$ can be viewed as a smoothing operation whose effect is inversely related to how close $\mathcal{D}^*$ is to $\mathcal{D}_Y$. In particular, the choice $\mathcal{D}_0 := \{S,\emptyset\}$ contains no information about Y (yielding a degenerate random variable) and the choice $\mathcal{D}_Y$ contains all the relevant information about Y (yielding the random variable Y itself). The choice $\mathcal{D}_X := \sigma(X)$ for which (7.35) holds, will give rise to some smoothing of Y which lies between these two extremes.

Stochastic conditional expectation function Collecting the above threads together we define $E(Y|\sigma(X))$ as a random variable which satisfies the following properties:

(i) $E(Y|\sigma(X))$ is a random variable relative to $\sigma(X)$,
(ii) $E(Y|\sigma(X)) = h(X)$, for some $h(.): \mathbb{R} \rightarrow \mathbb{R}$,
(iii) $E[E(Y|\sigma(X)) \cdot \mathbb{1}_B] = E([Y \cdot \mathbb{1}_B]$ for all $B \in \sigma(X))$.

NOTE that we need to establish existence as well as uniqueness of $E(Y|\sigma(X))$. The existence is established by the mathematical derivation of (7.33) (using the so-called Radon-Nikodym derivative). The uniqueness of the conditional expectation $E(Y|\sigma(X)) = h(X)$ also stems from the same mathematical apparatus but it is an *almost sure* (a.s.) (see chapter 3) uniqueness which says that for any two conditional expectations $E(Y|\sigma(X)) = h_1(X)$ and $E(Y|\sigma(X)) = h_2(X)$, it must be true that:

$$\mathbb{P}(h_1(X) = h_2(X)) = 1 \text{ or } h_1(X) = h_2(X) \text{ a.s.}$$

This notion of conditional expectation can be extended to any sub-σ-field $\mathcal{D} \subset \mathfrak{I}$, since we can always find a random variable X such that $\sigma(X) = \mathcal{D}$, in the sense that all events $(X \leq x) \in \mathcal{D}$, for all $x \in \mathbb{R}$. This is another way of saying that the information $\mathcal{D}$ conveys to the modeler what the random variable X does. NOTE that X could easily be a random vector.

Example

It is interesting to note the two extreme cases of such a conditional expectation which are $\mathcal{D}_0 = \{S, \emptyset\}$ and $\mathcal{D} = \mathfrak{S}$:

$$E(Y|\{S, \emptyset\}) = E(Y), \ E(Y|\mathfrak{S}) = Y.$$

The first follows from the fact that $\mathcal{D}_0$ is non-informative and the second because $\mathfrak{S}$ includes all relevant information including $\sigma(Y)$.

7.3.2 Determining $h_r(X) = E(Y^r \mid \sigma(X))$

Having established the existence and the a.s. uniqueness of $E(Y^r|\sigma(X))$, we proceed to consider the question of determining the functional form of $h_r(X) = E(Y^r|\sigma(X))$. Common sense suggests that the similarity between (7.20) and (7.21) will carry over to the functional forms. That is, when the ordinary conditional moment functions takes the form:

$$E(Y^r|X = x) = h_r(x), \ x \in \mathbb{R}_X, r = 1, 2, \ldots,$$

we interpret the stochastic conditional moment functions as:

$$E(Y^r|\sigma(X)) = h_r(X), \text{ for } X \sim \mathsf{D}_X(.), r = 1, 2, \ldots \tag{7.36}$$

In this sense one can conjecture that:

$$E(Y^r|X = x_i) = h_r(x_i), \text{ for all } x_i \in \mathbb{R}_X \Rightarrow E(Y^r|\sigma(X)) = h_r(X). \tag{7.37}$$

This conjecture turns out to be valid. That is, the functional form of the ordinary and the corresponding stochastic conditional moment functions coincide. The only difference being that the stochastic conditional moment functions are random variables.

The question which naturally arises is how does one determine the function $h_r(x)$ in the first place. The answer from the modeling viewpoint is that both the conditional densities as well as the conditional moment functions are determined by the joint density as shown in (7.19). However, this answer is not always feasible and we need to consider alternative ways to determine these functions. Again, without any loss of generality we consider the simplest case $r = 1$.

Defining property Let X and Y be two random variables defined on the same probability space $(S, \mathfrak{S}, \mathbb{P}(.))$ such that $E(|Y|) < \infty$, then

$$E(Y|\sigma(X)) = h(X), \text{ defined via: } E[(Y - h(X)) \cdot g(X)] = 0, \text{ for all } g(.), \tag{7.38}$$

where $g(.): \mathbb{R}_X \rightarrow \mathbb{R}$ is any bounded Borel function.

7.3.3 Properties of stochastic conditional expectation

From the discussion above it is obvious that any attempt to operationalize the reduction of the joint distribution in (7.3) will require not just ordinary conditional distributions of the form encountered in chapter 6, but products of the form:

$$f(x,y;\phi)=f(y|x;\psi_2)\cdot f(x;\psi_1), \text{ for all } (x,y)\in\mathbb{R}_X\times\mathbb{R}_Y. \tag{7.39}$$

As argued above, the notion of the corresponding conditional moment functions changes to:

$$E(Y^r|\sigma(X))=h_r(X), r=1,2,\ldots$$

In order to be able to handle such random moments we proceed to state certain useful properties of the conditional expectation $E(Y|\sigma(X))$. We note at the outset that for the purposes of the discussion that follows $E(Y|X=x)$ can be profitably viewed as a special case of $E(Y|\sigma(X))$.

Consider the three random variables X, Y, and Z defined on the same probability space $(S,\Im,\mathbb{P}(.))$, whose moments, as required in each case, exist. The first important property is that the conditional expectation enjoys the same linear mathematical structure as the ordinary expectation (see chapter 3).

> **Linearity**
> **CE1** $E(aX+bY|\sigma(Z))=aE(X|\sigma(Z))+bE(Y|\sigma(Z))$, a and b constants.

This property can be easily adapted to the special case: $E(aX+bY|Z=z)$.

A second important property is that the conditional expectation is related to the ordinary expectation by taking another expectation with respect to the conditioning variable.

> **The law of iterated logarith (lie)**
> **CE2** $E(Y)=E[E(Y|\sigma(X))]$.

This property follows directly from the definition of the conditional expectation since:

$$E[E(Y|\sigma(X))\cdot\mathbb{I}_{\sigma(X)}]=E[Y\cdot\mathbb{I}_{\sigma(X)}]=E(Y).$$

NOTE: the double expectation is defined as follows:

$$E[E(Y|X)]=\int_{-\infty}^{\infty}\left[\int_{-\infty}^{\infty}y\cdot f(y|x)dy\right]\cdot f(x)dx.$$

In other words, to derive the (marginal) mean using the conditional mean, we take expectations of the conditional expectation, with respect to the marginal distribution of the random variable X.

Example
Consider the joint distribution (7.30) together with the conditional densities (7.31). Let

us derive $E(Y)$ via the conditional expectations. The property CE2 suggests taking expectations of $E(Y|X)$ over X i.e.

$$E(Y)=(0.4)E(Y|X=-1)+(0.6)E(Y|X=1)=0.1,$$

which coincides with the direct evaluation of the expectation:

$$E(Y)=(-1)(0.3)+0(0.3)+1(0.4)=0.1.$$

Similarly, the conditional distribution(s) of x given $y=-1,0,1$ are given below:

x	-1	1
$f(x|y=-1)$	$\frac{1}{3}$	$\frac{2}{3}$

x	-1	1
$f(x|y=0)$	$\frac{2}{3}$	$\frac{1}{3}$

x	-1	1
$f(x|y=1)$	$\frac{1}{4}$	$\frac{3}{4}$

$$E(X|Y=-1)=(-1)\tfrac{1}{3}+1\left(\tfrac{2}{3}\right)=\tfrac{1}{3},\ E(X|Y=0)=(-1)\tfrac{2}{3}+1\left(\tfrac{1}{3}\right)=-\tfrac{1}{3},$$

$$E(X|Y=1)=(-1)\left(\tfrac{1}{4}\right)+1\left(\tfrac{3}{4}\right)=\tfrac{1}{2}.$$

$$E(X)=(0.3)E(X|Y=-1)+(0.3)E(X|Y=0)+(0.4)E(X|Y=1)=0.2$$

which coincides with the direct evaluation: $E(X)=(-1)(0.4)+1(0.6)=0.2$.

A third property of the conditional expectation is that any Borel function of the random variable X (which is a random variable relative to $\sigma(X)$) passes through the conditioning unaltered.

Taking out what is known property
CE3 $E(h(Y)\cdot g(X)|\sigma(X))=g(X)\cdot E(h(Y)|\sigma(X)).$

This property implies that in the case where Y is a random variable relative to $\sigma(X)$:

$$E(Y|\sigma(X))=Y\ a.s.$$

The property CE3 can be easily adapted to the special case $E(h(Y)\cdot g(X)|X=x)$, and can be used to enhance our intuition. When a conditioning random variable is "nailed down" at some value $X=x$, this indirectly "nails down" any functions of X.

Example
Consider the functions $h(Y)=\sqrt{Y}$, $g(X)=X^2$:

$$E(h(Y)\cdot g(X)|X=-1)=(-1)^2E(\sqrt{Y}|X=-1)=E(\sqrt{Y}|X=-1).$$

The above properties are particularly useful in the context of regression models for numerous reasons which will be discussed in the next few sections. At this point it is instructive to use these properties in order to derive an important result in relation to linear regressions.

   Example. In the case of the bivariate Normal distribution the conditional mean takes the form:

$$E(Y|\sigma(X))=\beta_0+\beta_1X, \tag{7.40}$$

where the parameters (β_0,β_1) take the form given in (7.10). If we start from (7.40), the question that arises is: How are the parameters β_0 and β_1 related to the moments of $f(x,y)$? Using the **lie** (CE2) we can deduce that $E(Y) = \beta_0 + \beta_1 E(X)$ i.e.

$$\beta_0 = E(Y) - \beta_1 E(X). \tag{7.41}$$

Applying the **lie** (CE2) and the "taking out what is known" (CE3) properties we can deduce that:

$$E(X \cdot Y) = E[E(X \cdot Y | \sigma(X))] = E[X \cdot E(Y | \sigma(X))].$$

Substituting the form of the stochastic conditional mean we can deduce that:

$$
\begin{aligned}
E(XY) &= E[X \cdot (\beta_0 + \beta_1 X)] = E\{X \cdot [E(Y) - \beta_1 E(X) + \beta_1 X]\} = \\
&= E(X) \cdot E(Y) + \beta_1 E\{[X - E(X)] \cdot X\} = \\
&= E(X) \cdot E(Y) + \beta_1 \{E(X^2 - E(X) \cdot E(X)\} = \\
&= E(X) \cdot E(Y) + \beta_1 [E(X^2) - [E(X)]^2] = E(X) \cdot E(Y) + \beta_1 Var(X),
\end{aligned}
$$

$$\Rightarrow Cov(XY) = E(X \cdot Y) - E(X) \cdot E(Y) = \beta_1 Var(X),$$

$$\beta_1 = \frac{Cov(X,Y)}{Var(X)}. \tag{7.42}$$

This result implies that, irrespective of the nature of the joint density $f(x,y)$, if the regression function is linear, when expressed in the form $E(Y | \sigma (X)) = \beta_0 + \beta_1 X$, the parameters β_0 and β_1 are related to the moments of $f(x,y)$ via (7.41) and (7.42). Also note that in view of the relationship between the covariance and correlation coefficient $Corr(X,Y) = \frac{Cov(X,Y)}{\sqrt{Var(X) \cdot Var(Y)}}$, β_1 can also be expressed in the equivalent form:

$$\beta_1 = \left[\sqrt{\frac{Var(Y)}{Var(X)}}\right] Corr(X,Y).$$

This is the reason why in section 2 we related the linear regression functions to the correlation coefficient even in cases of non-symmetric distributions where the correlation is not an adequate measure of the distribution dependence. The bottom line is that when one postulates (7.40) the implicit parameterization coincides with the parameterization under the bivariate Normality assumption given in (7.10).

The best least-squares predictor property
CE4 $E[Y - E(Y | \sigma(X))]^2 \le E[Y - g(X)]^2$ for all $g(.)$.

This means that from among all possible functions $g(.)$ of $X,(E(Y - g(X))^2 < \infty)$ the distance, referred to as the *mean squared error* (MSE): $E(Y - g(X))^2$, is minimized by the function: $g(X) = E(Y | \sigma (X))$.

That is, the conditional mean provides a *best* mean squared error predictor. This is a particularly useful property because it renders conditional expectation the obvious choice for a predictor (forecasting rule).

The last property of stochastic conditional expectation is related to the size of the conditioning information set.

The corset property

CE5 $E\{E(Y|\sigma(X,Z))|\sigma(X)\} = E\{E(Y|\sigma(X))|\sigma(X,Z)\} = E(Y|\sigma(X))$.

The intuition underlying this property is that in sequential conditioning the smaller conditional information set (note that $\sigma(X) \subset \sigma(X,Z)$) dominates the conditioning. Like wearing two corsets; the smaller will dominate irrespective of the order you are wearing them!

7.4 Weak exogeneity*

In the previous two sections we discussed the question of dealing with the reduction:

$$f(x,y;\boldsymbol{\phi}) = f(y|x;\boldsymbol{\varphi}_2) \cdot f(x;\boldsymbol{\varphi}_1), \text{ for all } (x,y) \in \mathbb{R}_X \times \mathbb{R}_Y. \quad (7.43)$$

In section 2 we ignored the marginal distribution $f(x;\boldsymbol{\varphi}_1)$ and argued that we can deal with the many conditional distributions (one for each value of X) by extending the notion of conditional moments to functions. In section 3 we extended the concept of conditional moment functions to its stochastic version which takes account of the weights as defined by the marginal distribution.

The question which naturally arises at this stage is whether there exist any circumstances under which the modeler can actually ignore the marginal distribution and model in terms of the conditional moment functions. This would be useful because by ignoring the marginal distribution we reduce the number of unknown parameters and thus deal with the problem of overparameterization. As argued in the introduction, the reduction in (7.3) offers no relief from the problem of overparameterization. In order to make the discussions less abstract we will discuss this issue in relation to a specific example.

Example
As shown above, in the case where $f(x,y;\boldsymbol{\phi})$ is bivariate Normal as given in (7.9), the conditional and marginal densities are also Normal:

$$(Y|X=x) \sim \mathsf{N}(\beta_0 + \beta_1 x, \sigma^2), \ x \in \mathbb{R}, \ X \sim \mathsf{N}(\mu_2, \sigma_{22}),$$

$$\beta_0 = \mu_1 - \beta_1\mu_2, \ \beta_1 = \left(\frac{\sigma_{12}}{\sigma_{22}}\right), \ \sigma^2 = \sigma_{11} - \left(\frac{\sigma_{12}^2}{\sigma_{22}}\right). \quad (7.44)$$

The reduction has induced a re-parameterization of the form: $\boldsymbol{\phi} \rightarrow (\boldsymbol{\varphi}_1, \boldsymbol{\varphi}_2)$:

$$\boldsymbol{\phi} := (\mu_1, \mu_2, \sigma_{12}, \sigma_{11}, \sigma_{22}) \in \Phi := (\mathbb{R}^3 \times \mathbb{R}_+^2),$$
$$\boldsymbol{\varphi}_1 := (\mu_2, \sigma_{22}) \in \Phi_1 := (\mathbb{R} \times \mathbb{R}_+),$$
$$\boldsymbol{\varphi}_2 := (\beta_0, \beta_1, \sigma^2) \in \Phi_2 := (\mathbb{R}^2 \times \mathbb{R}_+),$$

but the number of unknown parameters has not changed.

This suggests that unless there is some way to ignore certain parameters, say the parameters $\boldsymbol{\varphi}_1$ of the marginal distribution, there is no real simplification of the modeling problem because, in a sense, we are still dealing with the joint distribution. The question which naturally arises at this stage is to what extent can we concentrate exclusively on the conditional distribution and its parameters in the case where the marginal distribution is of no intrinsic interest. The answer in a nutshell is it depends on how the two sets of parameters $\varphi_1 \in \Phi_1$, $\varphi_2 \in \Phi_2$ constrain each other. The answer is yes in the case where Φ_2 (the set of permissible values of φ_2) is not affected by any of the values taken by $\varphi_1 \in \Phi_1$ and vice versa, but no otherwise. The concept we need is the so-called variation freeness.

Variation freeness We say that φ_1 and φ_2 are *variation free* if for all values of $\varphi_1 \in \Phi_1$, the range of possible values of φ_2 remains in the original parameter space Φ_2 and not some proper subset of it.

Using the notion of variation freeness we can give a more formal answer to the above question on whether we can concentrate on the conditional distribution.

Weak exogeneity In the case where the parameters of interest are those of φ_2 (or some function of them) only and φ_1 and φ_2 are variation free, then X is said to be *weakly exogenous* with respect to φ_1 and $f(x;\varphi_1)$ can be ignored. In cases where X is not weakly exogenous with respect to φ_1 we need to construct the statistical model taking into consideration both the conditional and marginal distributions in (7.43); (see Engle, Hendry and Richard (1983)).

The notion of weak exogeneity will be illustrated below in the context of specific examples, beginning with the Normal bivariate case.

(i)   **Bivariate Normal.** In the case where $f(x,y;\phi)$ is bivariate Normal, as given in (7.9), we note that $\varphi_1 \in \Phi_1 := \mathbb{R} \times \mathbb{R}_+$ and $\varphi_2 := (\beta_0, \beta_1, \sigma^2) \in \Phi_2 := \mathbb{R}^2 \times \mathbb{R}_+$. Hence, one can argue that X is *weakly exogenous* with respect to φ_2 because, no matter what values of φ_1 in Φ_1 one chooses, the parameters φ_2 can take all their possible values in Φ_2.

(ii) **Bivariate Student's t.** In the case of the bivariate Student's t distribution with $\nu > 2$ degrees of freedom, denoted by:

$$\begin{pmatrix} Y \\ X \end{pmatrix} \sim \mathsf{St}\left(\begin{pmatrix} \mu_1 \\ \mu_2 \end{pmatrix}, \begin{pmatrix} \sigma_{11} & \sigma_{12} \\ \sigma_{12} & \sigma_{22} \end{pmatrix}; \nu \right), \tag{7.45}$$

the conditional density of Y given $X = x$ and the marginal density of X are also Student's t of the form:

$$(y|X=x) \sim \mathsf{St}\left(\beta_0 + \beta_1 x, \tfrac{\nu\sigma^2}{\nu - 1}\left\{ 1 + \tfrac{1}{\nu\sigma_{22}}[x - \mu_2]^2 \right\} \nu + 1 \right), \ x \in \mathbb{R}.$$

$$X \sim \mathsf{St}(\mu_2, \sigma_{22}; \nu), \tag{7.46}$$

where the parameters $(\beta_0, \beta_1, \sigma^2)$ coincide with those of the bivariate Normal (see (7.44)). The parameterizations involved take the form:

$$\phi := (\mu_1, \mu_2, \sigma_{12}, \sigma_{11}, \sigma_{22}) \in \Phi := \mathbb{R}^3 \times \mathbb{R}_+^2,$$
$$\varphi_1 := (\mu_2, \sigma_{22}) \in \Phi_1 := \mathbb{R} \times \mathbb{R}_+,$$
$$\varphi_2 := (\beta_0, \beta_1, \mu_2, \sigma_{22}, \sigma^2) \in \Phi_2 := \mathbb{R}^3 \times \mathbb{R}_+^2.$$

In view of these results one can argue that X is not *weakly exogenous* with respect to φ_2 because the parameter values taken by φ_2 in Φ_2 can be directly restricted via φ_1, because (μ_2, σ_{22}) appear in both sets of unknown parameters. As a result of this, the modeling cannot ignore the marginal distribution of X, even if the parameters of interest are those in φ_2. In this sense the above conditioning is rather misleading; we should have used conditioning on the σ-field $\sigma(X)$ instead, with the regression and skedastic curves being:

$$E(Y|\sigma(X)) = \beta_0 + \beta_1 X, \quad Var(Y|\sigma(X)) = \frac{v\sigma^2}{v-1}\left\{1 + \frac{1}{v\sigma_{22}}(X - \mu_2)^2\right\}. \tag{7.47}$$

We conclude this section by noting two important features of weak exogeneity.

(i)   The concept of weak exogeneity is inextricably bound up with the joint distribution and its parameterization in relation to that of the conditional and marginal distributions.

(ii)   In view of the results in the previous two sections, weak exogeneity is likely to be the exception and not the rule in practice.

7.5   The notion of a statistical generating mechanism (GM)

As argued in chapter 1, for observed data to provide unprejudiced evidence in assessing the validity of a certain theory it is imperative that we built the statistical model (a convenient summary of the data) in terms of non-theory concepts. In chapters 2–6 we introduced several probabilistic concepts purporting to provide the foundation and the scaffolding of the framework in the context of which such statistical models can be built. The concept of a statistical model defined so far has just two components, the *probability* and the *sampling models*. Although this is sufficient for simple statistical models, for modeling economic phenomena which exhibit dependence and heterogeneity we need to introduce a third component we call a **statistical generating mechanism** (GM). The primary objective of this component is to provide a bridge between the statistical model and the theoretical model, as suggested by economic theory. The ultimate objective of empirical modeling is not just the summarization of the systematic information in the data in the form of a parsimonious parametric model, but the use of such models to understand economic phenomena. In this sense relating such statistical models to economic theory models is of fundamental importance. In the present book relating an adequate statistical model to the economic theory models in question is called *identification* (see also Spanos (1986,1990)).

7.5.1   The theory viewing angle

The above thesis should be contrasted with the traditional textbook approach to econometric modeling (see *inter alia* Gujarati (1995)) which assumes at the outset that the statistical GM and the theoretical model coincide apart from some error term, *irrespective* of the nature and structure of the observed data. Let us consider the theory-model known as the absolute income hypothesis:

$$C = a + \beta Y^D, \text{ where } \alpha > 0, 0 < b < 1,$$

where C and Y^D denote the theoretical variables *consumption* and *income*, respectively. This model is metamorphosed into the Linear Regression model:

$$C_t = a + \beta Y_t^D + \varepsilon_t, \; \varepsilon_t \sim \text{NIID}(0,\sigma^2), \; t = 1,2, \ldots, T, \tag{7.48}$$

(i)   by pretending that these theory variables coincide with whatever the available observed data happens to measure, and

(ii) by attaching a (Normal) white-noise error term to the theory model.

It goes without saying that (i) is childlike naive and (ii) destroys at the outset any possibility that the data might provide unprejudiced evidence in assessing the validity of the theory in question. The modeler is simply forcing the theory on the data and then proceeds to play Procrustes; chop off the bits that seem to stick out! Moreover, this viewpoint gives the impression that a theory model in the form of a linear equation between two observable variables is a pre-requisite for the modeler to be able to specify a linear regression model. This constitutes the **theory viewing angle**: contemplating (7.48) from *right to left*, as a mechanism that generates C_t given (Y_t^D,ε_t). The argument is that this viewpoint assumes that:

(a)   the error term ε_t is an autonomous prosthesis to the theoretical model,

(b)   the theoretical parameters (α,β) enjoy a clear theory interpretation (α-subsistence income, β-the marginal propensity to consume), they are the invariants of the system and unrelated to the variables (C_t, Y_t^D).

This viewing angle is appropriate for analyzing the theoretical aspects of the theory model as a system but it can be shortsighted and misleading when used to analyze the statistical aspects of the model. For the latter we need to introduce an alternative viewpoint which contemplates (7.48) in purely probabilistic terms and is directly built upon the structure of the observed data. This viewpoint contemplates (7.48) as a statistical GM which, in a nutshell, constitutes an orthogonal decomposition of the random variable C_t given the information set associated with the value of the random variable Y_t^D. Let us consider this concept in some detail.

7.5.2   The notion of a conditioning information set

Let the probability space of interest be $(S,\Im,\mathbb{P}(.))$. In view of the fact that all events of interest are elements of $\Im$, we define *information* in terms of subsets of $\Im$, i.e., $\mathcal{D}$ constitutes *information* in the context of the probability space $(S,\Im,\mathbb{P}(.))$ if $\mathcal{D}\subset\Im$, where $\mathcal{D}$ ranges from the *non-informative* case $\mathcal{D}_0 = \{S,\varnothing\}$, we know this a priori, to the *fully informative* case $\mathcal{D}^* = \Im$, we know everything. In view of the fact that we can always define a random variable X such that the minimal σ-field generated by X coincides with $\mathcal{D}$, i.e., $\sigma(X) = \mathcal{D}_X$, we can think of information as a restriction on the event space $\Im$ relative to some observable aspect of the chance mechanism in question. This will enable us to operationalize expressions of the form $E(Y|\mathcal{D})$, which can be interpreted as the conditional expectation of the random variable Y given the subset $\mathcal{D}$: a set of events known to the modeler. In addition, we know that by transforming information there is no possibility to increase it but there is some possibility that the transformation might decrease it. More formally, for any well-behaved (Borel) function $g(.)$ of X:

$$\sigma(g(X)) \subset \sigma(X),$$

but the converse is also true only in the case where the function is one-to-one, i.e.

$$\sigma(g(X)) = \sigma(X), \text{ only if } g(.): \mathbb{R}_X \to \mathbb{R} \text{ is one-to-one}.$$

7.5.3   Orthogonal decompositions and the statistical GM

The **statistical GM** relating to the first stochastic conditional moment of a *response* random variable Y (assuming that $E(|Y|^2) < \infty$), relative to the information set $\mathcal{D}$ is specified to be the *orthogonal decomposition* of the form:

$$Y = E(Y|\mathcal{D}) + u, \tag{7.49}$$

$$E(Y|\mathcal{D}): \text{the systematic component,}$$

$$u = (Y - E(Y|\mathcal{D})): \text{the non-systematic component,}$$

relative to the *conditioning information set* $\mathcal{D}$. The *existence* of such an orthogonal decomposition is guaranteed by the existence of the second moment (*square integrability* for the mathematical connoisseurs) of the random variable Y. Its *uniqueness* is the *almost sure* (or with probability one) equivalence discussed above; see also chapter 9. By viewing the random variables with bounded variance as elements of a linear space, $E(Y|\mathcal{D})$ represents an orthogonal projection and the decomposition (7.49) is analogous to the orthogonal projection theorem (see Luenberger (1969)), with $E(Y|\mathcal{D})$ the best predictor in the sense defined by property CE4 above. The connection between orthogonal projections and conditional expectations can be traced back to Kolmogorov (1941a,b), extending the work of Wold (1938).

The non-systematic component is often called the *error* or the *disturbance term*. The two components satisfy the following properties:

(i) $E(u|\mathcal{D}) = 0,$
(ii) $E(u^2|\mathcal{D}) = Var(Y|\mathcal{D}) < \infty,$ (7.50)
(iii) $E(u \cdot [E(Y|\mathcal{D})]) = 0.$

The above orthogonal decomposition is made operational when the conditioning information set $\mathcal{D}$ is related to observable random variables as in the case where: $\mathcal{D} = \sigma$ **(X)**, **X** being a vector of random variables defined on the same probability space $(S, \Im, \mathbb{P}(.))$. NOTE that in this case (7.49) is a regression function decomposition.

The above orthogonal decomposition can be easily extended to **higher conditional moment functions** in the sense that (assuming the required moments exist):

$$u^r = E(u^r|\mathcal{D}) + v_r, \; r = 2,3, \ldots,$$

where $u = (Y - E(Y|\mathcal{D}))$. Of particular interest are the first few conditional central moments.

IMPORTANT: the above decompositions assume implicitly the existence of moments up to a certain order. In general, the orthogonal decomposition of the rth conditional moment exists when the moments up to order $2r$ are bounded, i.e. $E(|Y|^{2r})<\infty$.

In section 2 it was argued that the main objective of *regression models* is to model (7.6) via the first few conditional moment functions as defined in (7.11). Using the above orthogonal decompositions we can proceed to specify regression models in terms of the first four conditional moment functions as follows:

$$Y_t = E(Y_t|\sigma(\mathbf{X}_t)) + u_t,$$

$$u_t^r = E(u_t^r|\sigma(\mathbf{X}_t)) + v_{rt}, r=2,3,4.$$

Let us consider several examples of such decompositions.

Simple statistical GM

In order to understand the role of the conditioning information set $\mathcal{D}$, let us first consider the case where there is no dependence information. In this case we choose $\mathcal{D}$ to be the non-informative set $\mathcal{D}_0=\{S,\emptyset\}$. $\mathcal{D}_0$ is said to be uninformative because, as mentioned above, for any random variable Y defined on S, $E(Y|\mathcal{D}_0)=E(Y)$. In this case the decomposition in (7.49) takes the form:

$$Y_k = E(Y_k) + \varepsilon_k, k\in\mathbb{N},$$

and the conditions [i]–[iii] are trivially true.

Simple Normal model

[1] Statistical GM: $Y_k = E(Y_k) + \varepsilon_k, k\in\mathbb{N},$
[2] Probability model:

$$\Phi = \left\{ f(y;\boldsymbol{\theta}) = \frac{(\sigma_{11})^{-\frac{1}{2}}}{\sqrt{2\pi}}\exp\left\{-\frac{1}{2\sigma_{11}}(y-\mu_1)^2\right\}\right\}, \boldsymbol{\theta}\in\mathbb{R}\times\mathbb{R}_+, x\in\mathbb{R},$$

$$\boldsymbol{\theta}:=(\mu_1,\sigma_{11}), E(X)=\mu_1, Var(X)=\sigma_{11},$$

[3] Sampling model: $\mathbf{Y}:=(Y_1,Y_2,...,Y_n)$ is a random sample.

This is a particularly important example of a simple statistical model which will be widely used in chapters 11–15.

Hence, in the case of simple statistical models (a random sample is postulated), we can supplement the probability and sampling models with a statistical GM of the simple form given above.

Regression statistical GM

In the case where $\mathcal{D}$ includes some dependence information as in the case of the regression models where:

$$\mathcal{D}_t = (X_k = x_k),$$

the statistical GM takes the general form:

$$Y_k = E(Y_k|X_k = x_k) + u_k, \; k \in \mathbb{N}.$$

By design, the *systematic* and *non-systematic components*, defined by:

$$\mu(x_k) := E(Y_k|X_k = x_k), \; u_k = Y_k - E(Y_k|X_k = x_k), \; k \in \mathbb{N},$$

respectively, are *orthogonal*. This follows directly from the conditional expectation properties CE1–CE3 (see above):

[i] $E(u_k|X_k = x_k) = E\{[Y_k - E(Y_k|X_k = x_k)] | X_k = x_k\} =$
$$= E(Y_k|X_k = x_k) - E(Y_k|X_k = x_k) = 0, \; k \in \mathbb{N},$$

i.e., u_k conditional on $X_k = x_k$, has no systematic mean effects. Moreover:

[ii] $E\{u_k \cdot \mu(x_k)\} = E(E\{u_k \cdot [E(Y_k|X_k = x_k)]\} | X_k = x_k) =$
$$= E(Y_k|X_k = x_k) \cdot E\{(u_k|X_k = x_k)\} = 0, \; k \in \mathbb{N},$$

from CE2, CE3, and [i], i.e., u_k and $E(Y_k|X_k = x_k)$, conditional on $X_k = x_k$, are *mutually orthogonal*; denoted by:

$$u_k \perp E(Y_k|X_k = x_k), \; k \in \mathbb{N}.$$

In addition to properties [i]–[ii] we can show that u_k and Y_k have the same conditional variance:

[iii] $E(u_k^2|X_k = x_k) = Var(Y_k|X_k = x_k), \; k \in \mathbb{N},$

from CE1. Moreover, the unconditional mean of u_k is also zero:

[iv] $E(u_k) = E(E(u_k|X_k = x_k)) = 0, \; k \in \mathbb{N},$

from CE2 and from CE2 and CE3, i.e. u_k is **orthogonal** to X_k.

IMPORTANT: It is important to note that conditional zero mean for the non-systematic component implies unconditional zero mean:

$$E(u_k|X_k = x_k) = 0 \Rightarrow E(u_k) = 0,$$

but the converse is not true: $E(u_k) = 0 \nRightarrow E(u_k|X_k = x_k) = 0.$

In order to see this consider the following example.

Example
Returning to the joint distribution (7.7) and the related conditional distributions, we observe that neither of these conditional expectations is zero. On the other hand, the unconditional expectation of Y, evaluated using the law of iterated expectation is:

$$E(Y) = E\{E(Y|X = x)\} = (1/5)(0.5) - (1/5)(0.5) = 0.$$

Similarly, conditional orthogonality between X_k and u_k implies unconditional orthogonality:

$$E(X_k \cdot u_k|X_k = x_k) = 0 \Rightarrow E(X_k \cdot u_k) = 0,$$

but the converse is not true: $E(X_k \cdot u_k) = 0 \nRightarrow E(X_k \cdot u_k | X_k = x_k) = 0.$

REMARK: The intuition behind this result is that for the unconditional mean there is one more averaging (over the values of X), beyond the conditional mean.

Normal/linear regression The most widely used regression model is the *Normal/Linear regression*, whose statistical GM takes the form:

$$Y_t = \beta_0 + \beta_1 x_t + u_t, \ t \in \mathbb{T},$$

where the error term u_t, satisfies the properties [i]–[v] derived above. The complete specification of the **Normal/linear regression model** takes the form:

[1] Statistical GM: $Y_t = \beta_0 + \beta_1 x_t + u_t, \ t \in \mathbb{T},$

[2] Probability model:

$$\Phi = \left\{ f(y_t | x_t; \boldsymbol{\theta}) = \frac{1}{\sigma \sqrt{2\pi}} \exp\left\{ -\frac{(y_t - \beta_0 - \beta_1 x_t)^2}{2\sigma^2} \right\}, \ \boldsymbol{\theta} \in \Theta, \ y_t \in \mathbb{R} \right\},$$

$$\boldsymbol{\theta} := (\beta_0, \beta_1, \sigma^2), \ \Theta := \mathbb{R}^2 \times \mathbb{R}_+, \tag{7.51}$$

$$\beta_0 := E(Y_t) - \beta_1 E(X_t), \ \beta_1 := \frac{Cov(X_t, Y_t)}{Var(X_t)}, \ \sigma^2 := Var(Y_t) - \frac{[Cov(X_t, Y_t)]^2}{Var(X_t)}.$$

[3] Sampling model: $(Y_1, Y_2, \ldots, Y_n)$ is an independent sample, sequentially drawn from $f(y_t | x_t; \boldsymbol{\theta}), \ t = 1, 2, \ldots, T.$

A direct comparison between the simple Normal and Normal/linear regression models reveals some interesting differences. Comparing the two *probability models* we can see that the regression model is specified in terms of the conditional distribution $f(y_t | x_t; \boldsymbol{\theta})$ but the simple Normal model in terms of the marginal distribution $f(y_t; \boldsymbol{\theta})$. A comparison of the *sampling models* reveals that in the regression case the sample is no longer random (independent and identically distributed), it is just independent. This is the case because the conditional densities $f(y_t | x_t; \boldsymbol{\theta}), \ t \in \mathbb{T}$ are changing with t, because the conditional means are changing with x_t:

$$(Y_t | X_t = x_t) \sim \text{NI}(\beta_0 + \beta_1 x_t, \sigma^2), \ t \in \mathbb{T},$$

i.e., they are not identically distributed.

As argued above, using the conditional moment functions (often the regression and skedastic functions) introduced in the previous section, we can specify a different regression model for each bivariate distribution. The Normal/linear regression model can be very misleading as the basis of regression models in general because a number of important issues do not arise in its context. Beyond the Normal/linear regression model several new issues are raised. Some idea of the difficulties raised by other regression models can be gained by considering the Student's t/linear regression model.

Student's t linear regression

[1] Statistical GM: $Y_t = \beta_0 + \beta_1 X_t + u_t, \ t \in \mathbb{T},$

$$u_t^2 = \frac{v\sigma^2}{(v-1)} \left[1 + \frac{1}{v\sigma_{22}} [X_t - \mu_2]^2 \right] + v_{2t},$$

[2] Probability model:

$$\Phi = \{f(y_t|x_t;\boldsymbol{\theta}) \cdot f(x_t;\boldsymbol{\phi}_2), \ \boldsymbol{\theta} := (\beta_0,\beta_1,\mu_2,\sigma^2,\sigma_{22}) \in \mathbb{R}^3 \times \mathbb{R}^2_+, \ (x_t, y_t) \in \mathbb{R}^2\},$$

$$f(y_t|x_t;\boldsymbol{\theta}) = \left(\frac{\Gamma\left(\frac{1}{2}[\nu+2]\right)}{\Gamma\left(\frac{1}{2}[\nu+1]\right)}\right) \left((\nu-1)\pi\, h_t(x_t)\right)^{-\frac{1}{2}} \left\{1 + \frac{(y_t - \beta_0 - \beta_1 x_t)^2}{(\nu-1)h_t(x_t)}\right\}^{-\frac{1}{2}(\nu+2)},$$

$$f(x_t;\boldsymbol{\phi}_2) = \left(\frac{\Gamma\left(\frac{1}{2}[\nu+1]\right)}{\Gamma\left(\frac{1}{2}\nu\right)}\right) [\nu\pi\sigma_{22}]^{-\frac{1}{2}} \left\{1 + \frac{1}{\nu\sigma_{22}}[x_t - \mu_2]^2\right\}^{-\frac{1}{2}(\nu+1)}, \ \mu_2 = E(X_t),$$

$$\sigma_{22} = Var(X_t), \ \beta_0 = E(Y_t) - \beta_1\mu_2, \ \beta_1 = \tfrac{Cov(X_t,Y_t)}{Var(X_t)}, \ \sigma^2 = Var(Y_t) - \tfrac{[Cov(X_t,Y_t)]^2}{Var(X_t)}.$$

[3] Sampling model: $(Y_1, Y_2, \ldots, Y_n)$ is an independent sample, sequentially drawn from the distribution $f(y_t|x_t;\boldsymbol{\theta})$, $t = 1,2, \ldots, T$. 　　　　　　　　　(7.52)

This model differs from the Normal/linear regression in two important respects:

(i) X is not weakly exogenous with respect to the parameters of the conditional distribution, and thus we cannot ignore the marginal distribution $f(x;\boldsymbol{\theta}_2)$.

(ii) The conditional variance is heteroskedastic and thus we need to supplement the orthogonal decomposition of the regression function with that of the skedastic function.

In concluding this subsection we note that the traditional econometric literature until the 1980s confined itself to the regression function. Recently, however, there have been attempts to relate economic theory to the skedastic function, especially in connection with theoretical models in finance. The fact that higher conditional moments have not been considered is the result of viewing these moments from the theory viewing angle which requires economic theory to introduce relationships connected with these moments.

7.5.4 The statistical viewing angle

The statistical GM as defined in (7.49) with properties (7.50) defines the **statistical viewpoint** in contrast to the theoretical one discussed in the previous subsection. As we can see, the statistical GM is defined for all statistical models, not just regression models, and has a purely probabilistic interpretation. For example, in the case of the Normal/linear model the statistical viewing angle contemplates:

$$Y_t = \beta_0 + \beta_1 x_t + u_t, \ t \in \mathbb{T}, \tag{7.53}$$

from *left to right* as an orthogonal decomposition of the observable random variable (Y_t) into a systematic component $E(Y_t|X_t = x_t)$, and a non-systematic (unmodeled) component $u_t = Y_t - E(Y_t|X_t = x_t)$. In contrast to the implicit assumptions (a)–(b) of the theory viewing angle, the **statistical viewing angle** explicitly postulates that:

(a)* the error term u_t is derived and bound up with the probabilistic structure of (Y_t, X_t), (b)*   the statistical parameters $(\beta_0, \beta_1, \sigma^2)$ enjoy a clear probabilistic interpretation and they are inextricably bound up with the probabilistic structure of (Y_t, X_t).

A closer look at the other statistical models specified above reveals that all the parameters have a probabilistic interpretation in terms of the moments of the observable random variables involved and there is no part defined in terms of theory concepts. In the next few chapters these models will be extended in a number of directions but their basic structure will remain the same.

A stochastic generating mechanism

It turns out that for certain aspects of statistical analysis the statistical GM could profitably be viewed as a stochastic generating mechanism. That is, a viewpoint that contemplates (7.53) from *right to left*, as a mechanism that generates Y_t given (x_t, u_t). This alternative interpretation appears at first to have a certain affinity with the theory viewpoint but in fact the similitude turns out to be more apparent than real.

The statistical GM of the simple Normal model, when viewed as a stochastic generating mechanism, is expressed in the form:

$$Y_k = \mu_1 + (\sigma_{11})^{\frac{1}{2}} \epsilon_k, \; \epsilon_k \sim \text{NIID}\,(0,1), \, k \in \mathbb{N}. \tag{7.54}$$

The easiest way to interpret this is as the mechanism which when simulated using *pseudo-random numbers* (see chapter 5) will yield data with the same probabilistic structure as the postulated sample; Normal, Independent and Identically Distributed (NIID). Similarly, the statistical GM of the Normal and Student's t linear regression models, as stochastic generating mechanisms, take the form:

$$Y_t = \beta_0 + \beta_1 x_t + \sigma \epsilon_t, \; \epsilon_t \sim \text{NIID}(0,1),$$

$$t \in \mathbb{T}, \tag{7.55}$$

$$Y_t = \beta_0 + \beta_1 X_t + (h(X_t))^{\frac{1}{2}} \epsilon_t, \; \epsilon_t \sim \text{St}(0,1;\nu+1), \, X_t \sim \text{St}(\mu_2, \sigma_{22};\nu),$$

where $h(X_t) = \frac{\nu \sigma^2}{(\nu-1)} \left[1 + \frac{1}{\nu \sigma_{22}} [X_t - \mu_2]^2 \right]$, respectively.

There are several things to note about this interpretation.

First, this is a statistical interpretation because the primary aim is to simulate (using pseudo-random numbers) a probabilistic structure for the sample $(Y_1, Y_2, \ldots, Y_n)$ as defined by its joint distribution. *Second*, an integral part of the simulation viewpoint is the statistical interpretation of the parameters involved. As seen above, these parameters are defined in terms of the moments of the observable random variables involved and thus well-designed simulations should take this into consideration since they represent implicit restrictions. This is particularly crucial when designing Monte Carlo simulations to tackle difficult sampling distribution problems. A design which ignores any of the implicit constraints relating the parameters and the moments of the underlying distributions is likely to give rise to misleading results. *Third*, the stochastic generating mechanism interpretation is based on the statistical GM of the first conditional moment but it should be modified to involve the information contained in the higher conditional moments. In the case of the simple Normal and the Normal/linear regression models there is no additional information because the second moment is constant. In the case of the Student's t regression model, however, this is no longer true and the additional information should be integrated into the statistical **GM** as shown above.

7.5.5 Dependence ratio*

The notion of a statistical generating mechanism (GM), introduced above, suggests a natural way to measure the dependence between Y and the random variable(s) X, defining the conditioning information set. Corresponding to the orthogonal decomposition based on the conditional mean:

$$Y = E(Y|X) + u,$$

there exists a relationship between the variances of the three terms:

$$Var(Y) = Var[E(Y|X)] + Var(u). \tag{7.56}$$

This follows directly from the orthogonality of the systematic and non-systematic components and indirectly from the equality:

$$Var(Y) = E[Var(Y|X)] + Var[E(Y|X)],$$

and the fact that (CE2 property above):

$$E[Var(Y|X)] = E[E(u^2|X)] = E(u^2) = Var(u).$$

Given that u represents the non-systematic component (the unmodeled part) of the statistical GM, a measure of dependence which suggests itself is, the **dependence ratio**:

$$Dr(Y|X) = \frac{Var\{E(Y|X)\}}{Var(Y)} = 1 - \frac{E\{Var(Y|X)\}}{Var(Y)} = 1 - \frac{Var(u)}{Var(Y)}.$$

This was first introduced by Kolmogorov (1933a), who called it the **correlation ratio,** attributing the idea to Pearson (1903). As mentioned in chapter 6, this a measure of dependence which can be used whatever the measurement system of the random variables in question.

The dependence ratio, as a measure of dependence, satisfies certain *desirable properties:*

[1] $0 \leq Dr(Y|X) \leq 1$,
[2] $Dr(Y|X) = 0$ if X and Y are independent,
[3] $Dr(Y|X) = 1$ if and only if $Y = h(X)$ a.s.

The first property stems from (7.56) directly. The second property follows from the fact that when X and Y are independent:

$$E(Y|X) = E(Y) \Rightarrow Var[E(Y|X)] = 0.$$

The *if* part of the third property is trivial since $Dr(Y|X) = 1$ implies that:

$$E\{[Y - E(Y|X)]^2\} = 0 \Rightarrow Y = h(X) \text{ a.s.}$$

The *only if* part follows from the fact that if $Y = h(X)$ then the function $\sigma(h(X)) \subset \sigma(X)$, and thus $h(X) = E(Y|X)$ with probability one (a.s.).

In view of property [3], $Dr(Y|X)$ can be interpreted as a measure of probabilistic dependence analogous to the notion of mathematical *functional dependence* $Y = h(X)$, where the function $h(.)$ coincides with the regression function of Y given $X = x$. To take it a step further, this property can be used to characterize the regression function. That is, $Dr(Y|X)$ can be interpreted as the maximal correlation between Y and all possible functions $h(X)$, with the maximum achieved for the *regression function* $h_0(X) = E(Y|X)$:

$$Dr(Y|X) = \max_{h(\cdot)} Corr^2[Y, h(X)] = Corr^2[Y, h_0(X)]. \tag{7.57}$$

Renyi (1970) introduced such a characterization by adding the following conditions:

[1] $E[h_0(X)] = E(Y)$,
[2] $Var[h_0(X)] = Var(Y) \cdot Dr(Y|X)$,
[3] $E[h_0(X) \cdot Y] > 0$.

This follows from property CE4 which says that the conditional mean of Y given X provides the best predictor (in the mean square error sense) of Y.

REMARKS:
(i)   The dependence ratio is not a symmetric function of Y and X, as is the correlation coefficient. The intuitive reason for the asymmetry is the fact that the two regression functions, say $E(Y|X) = h(X)$ and $E(X|Y) = g(Y)$ do not necessarily have the same functional form.
(ii) In the case where the *regression function* is *linear* in X, $E(Y|X) = \beta_0 + \beta_1 X$, the dependence ratio coincides with the squared correlation coefficient:

$$Dr(Y|X) = [Corr(X, Y)]^2.$$

This follows from the fact in this case: $Var[E(Y|X)] = \frac{[Cov(X,Y)]^2}{Var(X)}$.

In concluding this section we note that an important advantage of the dependence ratio is that it can be easily extended to the case where $\mathbf{X}$ is a vector of random variables, say $\mathbf{X} := (X_1, X_2, \ldots, X_m)$:

$$Dr(Y|\mathbf{X}) = \frac{Var\{E(Y|\mathbf{X})\}}{Var(Y)} = 1 - \frac{E(Var\{Y|\mathbf{X}\})}{Var(Y)}.$$

In the case where the regression function $E(Y|\mathbf{X})$ is *linear* in $\mathbf{X}$, $Dr(Y|\mathbf{X})$ coincides with the multiple correlation coefficient $\mathcal{R}^2$, where: $\mathcal{R}^2 = \max_\alpha Corr^2(Y, \boldsymbol{\alpha}'\mathbf{X})$, $\boldsymbol{\alpha}'\mathbf{X} = \sum_{i=1}^m \alpha_i X_i$ and $Corr^2(.)$, the square correlation (see Spanos (1986), chapter 15).

7.6   The biometric tradition in statistics

As argued in Spanos (1995b), the traditional textbook approach can be viewed as a hybrid of two older traditions in statistics: the *theory of errors* and the *experimental design* traditions. It was also argued that both of these traditions are better suited for modeling experimental data as opposed to observational (non-experimental) data; the result of passively observing a system without the means to interfere with or control the data generating process. It was mentioned in chapter 1 that the *biometric tradition*, developed in the late 19th and early 20th centuries is better suited for modeling with observational data. In this section we digress shortly to trace the roots of the biometric tradition. For a more extensive discussion see *inter alia* Stigler (1986), Porter (1986), MacKenzie (1981) and Kevles (1985)).

7.6.1 Galton

The concept of regression is one of very few concepts in statistics whose roots are both clear and unquestionable. The concept was first proposed by Galton (1877), formalized in Galton (1885,1886), extended by Pearson (1894,1895,1896) and related to the least-squares tradition by Yule (1897). The father of modern statistical inference R. A. Fisher credits Galton and his pioneering studies in inheritance as providing the foundations of modern statistics. In the foreword of Fisher (1956) he praises the pioneering studies of Galton and continues:

Galton's great gift lay in his awareness, which grew during his life, of the vagueness of many of the phrases in which men tried to express themselves in describing natural phenomena. He was before his time in his recognition that such vagueness could be removed, and a certain precision of thought attempted by finding quantitative definitions of concepts fit to take the place of such phrases as "the average man", "variability", "the strength of inheritance", and so forth, through the assembly of objective data, and its systematic examination…

(Fisher (1956), p. 2)

Galton was greatly impressed by the variety of measured variables whose histogram Quetelet (1849) was able to describe using the Normal distribution (known at the time as the *law of error*), ranging from the number of suicides and rapes in Paris over a year, to several anthropomorphic measurements. Galton's interest was primarily in *eugenics*: improving the human stock of Britain using selective breeding (see Kevles (1985)). According to MacKenzie (1981, p. 11):

One specific set of social purposes was common to the work of Galton, Karl Pearson and R. A. Fisher. All were eugenists. They claimed that the most important human characteristic, such as mental ability, were inherited from one generation to the next. People's ancestry, rather than their environment, was crucial to determining their characteristics. The only secure long-term way to improve society, they argued, was to improve the characteristics of the individuals in it, and the best way to do this was to ensure that those in the present generation with good characteristics (the "fit") had more children than those with bad characteristics (the "unfit")…

In a terrible twist of fate, the appalling cause of eugenics was used by Hitler to provide pseudo-scientific justification for his racist policies, provided the primary impetus for the development of modern statistics. Let us retrace the first tentative steps of modern statistics that led to regression and correlation.

Quetelet applied extensively the earlier statistical tradition, the theory of errors (see Spanos (1995b)), first developed in astronomy and geodesy, to the statistical analysis of social measurements with the hope of developing *social physics*. In the theory of errors tradition, center stage was given to errors of measurement. The observed data were viewed as measurements of the same (true) variable but each observation had a measurement error which could be described as random. Moreover, when several observations were collected they tended to exhibit the chance regularity pattern associated with the bell-shaped Normal distribution. In this context the primary objective of modeling was to uncover the true variable by minimizing the errors of measurement. Gauss introduced the Normal distribution as that which, under certain restrictions, uncovers the true variable via the mean of the distribution. Quetelet adapted this procedure to give rise to social physics by associating the mean with *l'homme moyen* (the average man), representing some sort of an ideal, and viewing social behavior as deviations from the average man; see Stigler (1986), Porter (1986).

Galton, continuing the tradition associated with Quetelet, used the *frequency curve of the law of error* (Normal) to describe several data sets of anthropomorphic measurements, such as mental ability and physical characteristics of human populations, such as height and weight, and was amazed by how well the Normal curve described these data. The first problem Galton had to face was the interpretation of the deviations from the mean inherited from Quetelet. When describing mental ability using the Normal curve the obvious question is does a genius constitute an error of nature and the average mind the ideal? For a eugenist the answer was certainly not! Moreover, for Galton the variation around the mean was not an error to be minimized. In his memoirs Galton (1908, p. 305) explains how he had to break with the theory of errors tradition:

The primary objects of the Gaussian Law of Error were exactly opposed, in one sense, to those to which I applied them. They were to get rid of, or to provide a just allowance for errors. But these errors or deviations were the very things I wanted to preserve and know about…

In this sense Galton turned the tables on the theory of errors tradition by viewing randomness as inherent in nature and not introduced by our attempt to observe and measure. Moreover, the variability associated with this randomness was the very thing he was interested in. As a result of this change of attitude the observable random variables took center stage and the mean was just a characteristic of the distribution describing this variability. Indeed, Galton (1875a) went a step further and proposed replacing the notion of the mean and the *probable error* with the notions of the median and the interquartile range (see chapter 3) as more appropriate measures for anthropomorphic measurements. Galton's break with the theory of errors tradition can be easily discerned from his proposal to replace the term *standard error* (known at the time as probable error) with the term *standard deviation*; deviations from the mean were no longer viewed as errors.

The *second* major departure from the theory of errors initiated by Galton was motivated by his interest in discovering the dependence between variables which led naturally to joint and conditional distributions. The most influential concepts introduced by Galton were those of *regression* and *correlation*, which as shown in this and the last chapters are based on the conditional and joint distributions and can be used to model (and quantify) the dependence among random variables. The term *regression* was coined by Galton (1885) in the context of studying inheritance in human populations. In his attempt to discover a relationship between the height of the parents and the height of their children, he introduced the notion of a *regression curve* in the context of Normal populations. Interestingly enough, he formulated the concept of regression by studying the relationship between two data sets using scatterplots. Let us consider this in some detail.

The notion of regression was first proposed by Galton (1877) in studying the inherited characteristics between two generations of sweet peas and was initially called *reversion*. The paper that established regression in statistics was Galton (1885), studying the connection between the height of the parent and that of the offspring. Galton (1885), looking at the distribution of height from one generation of humans to the next, observed that the height distribution (histogram) of his sample population appeared to remain the same, as in the case of sweet peas (see Galton (1877)). To be more specific, in his study of inheritance, Galton noticed that the histogram of the measurements:

$$X_t - \text{the height of the mid-parent} \quad \text{and} \quad Y_t - \text{the height of the offspring,}$$

could be described with an almost identical Normal frequency curve. He defined the height of the mid-parent as:

$$X_t := \frac{X_{1t} + (1.08)X_{2t}}{2},$$

where X_{1t} is the height of the father, X_{2t} is the height of the mother. The scaling by 1.08 was based on the difference between the average height of men versus that of women.

The question that naturally arose in Galton's mind was the same as in the case of sweet peas:

How is it that although each individual does not as a rule leave his like behind him, yet successive generations resemble each other with great exactitude in all their general features?...

(Galton (1877), p. 492)

His ultimate explanation of this apparent puzzle relied primarily on the **regression line** defined by:

$$[E(Y_t|X_t = x_t) - E(Y_t)] = \left(\frac{Cov(Y_t, X_t)}{Var(X_t)}\right)[x_t - E(X_t)], \ x_t \in \mathbb{R}. \tag{7.58}$$

How he derived the regression line is a fascinating story that is worth telling in some detail.

Step 1 He plotted the scatterplot of the two data sets $\{(x_t, y_t), t = 1, ..., T\}$.

Step 2 He joined the data points with approximately the same frequency of occurrence and realized that these equal-frequency curves formed concentric elliptical contours.

Step 3 Using the argument that "as the number of observations increases the equal-frequency curves get smoother and smoother" he assumed that at the limit they form perfect ellipses.

Step 4 Realizing that his mathematical training was insufficient to take him from these concentric elliptical contours of the corresponding bivariate distribution, he requisitioned the help of his mathematician friend Dickson. With Dickson's help, he derived the bivariate Normal density (see appendix to Galton (1886)).

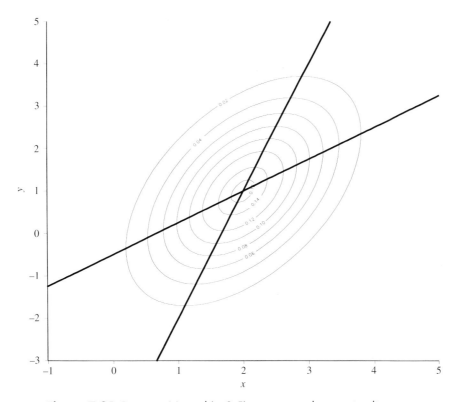

Figure 7.21 Bivariate Normal $(=0.5)$ contours and regression lines

Step 5 Using an ingenious argument, Galton suggested that the line which describes best the relationship between (X_t, Y_t) (what he called the regression line) is the one that passes through the center of the ellipses (the point at which the two principal axes meet) and cuts the ellipses at their point of tangency with the lines parallel to the y-axis. In figure 7.21 we can see the contours of a bivariate Normal density with parameters:

$E(Y_t) = 1.0$, $E(X_t) = 2.0$, $Var(Y_t) = 0.8$, $Var(X_t) = 1.8$, $Cov(X_t, Y_t) = 0.6$,

and both regression lines:

$E(Y_t | X_t = x_t) = 0.333 + 0.333x_t$,

$E(X_t | Y_t = y_t) = 1.25 + 0.75y_t$.

Note that the regression line:

$E(X_t | Y_t = y_t) = E(X_t) + \frac{Cov(Y_t, X_t)}{Var(Y_t)}[y_t - E(Y_t)]$, $y_t \in \mathbb{R}$,

also passes through the center of the ellipses but cuts them at the point of tangency with straight lines parallel to the x-axis; another Galton insight!

What is fascinating from our viewpoint is that Galton was able to proceed from the observed data, generate the theoretical bivariate density underlying these data using the scatter plot, and then proceed to define the regression line.

REMARKS:

(i)   Galton implicitly assumed that $E(Y_t) = E(X_t) := \mu$ and $Var(X_t) = Var(Y_t)$, in which case the above regression line reduces to the proportional relationship:

$$[E(Y_t|X_t = x_t) - \mu] = \rho(x_t - \mu),\, x_t \in \mathbb{R}, \tag{7.59}$$

$$\rho := Corr(X_t, Y_t),\, |\rho| \le 1. \tag{7.60}$$

From this Galton concluded that there is a tendency to *regress to the mean* (due to $|\rho| \le 1$) in the sense that very tall mid-parents produce offsprings who are not as tall and very short mid-parents produce offsprings who are not as short.

(ii)   Galton viewed (7.59) as the *law of heredity* which underlies the apparent stability of the population features in successive generations. Galton was clearly wrong in drawing **causality** implications based solely on the regression curve, because by the same token, from the statistical viewpoint, the reverse regression:

$$[E(X_t|Y_t = y_t) - \mu] = \rho(y_t - \mu),\, y_t \in \mathbb{R},$$

has as much justification as the original. The reverse regression cuts the ellipses at their point of tangency with the lines parallel to the x-axis (see figure 7.21).

(iii)   It is worth noting that Galton assumed implicitly joint and marginal *Normality* for both random variables X_t and Y_t.

To a modern student of statistics it looks very odd that the notion of *correlation* was introduced by Galton (1888) (initially as co-relation) via that of regression by utilizing the slopes of the regression and reverse-regression lines:

$$[E(Y_t|X_t = x_t) - \mu] = \left[\tfrac{Cov(X_t, Y_t)}{Var(X_t)}\right](x_t - \mu),\, x_t \in \mathbb{R},$$

$$[E(X_t|Y_t = y_t) - \mu] = \left[\tfrac{Cov(X_t, Y_t)}{Var(Y_t)}\right](y_t - \mu),\, y_t \in \mathbb{R}.$$

Multiplying the two slopes gives rise to the square of the correlation coefficient:

$$[Corr(X_t, Y_t)]^2 = \left[\tfrac{Cov(X_t, Y_t)}{Var(X_t)}\right]\left[\tfrac{Cov(X_t, Y_t)}{Var(Y_t)}\right].$$

For the details of this fascinating story see Stigler (1986).

7.6.2   Karl Pearson

Karl Pearson was the first to appreciate the importance of Galton's contributions in relation to regression and correlation and proceeded to formalize both and extend them in different directions.

The *first* crucial contribution by Pearson (1895,1896) was the formalization of the procedure for *fitting frequency curves* to observed data, by utilizing the first four moments (see chapter 3); the fitting of the Normal distribution before Pearson took the form of drawing the bell-shaped curve over the histogram of the observed data. It is interesting to NOTE that the notion of *moments* has been used during the 18th and 19th centuries but Pearson coined the term and introduced the concept into statistics; Chebyshev utilized the notion of moments in probability theory in relation to the Central Limit Theorem in the 1870s, but the two developments were largely separate until the mid-20th century. Pearson (1895) was also the first to introduce the notions of skewness and kurtosis.

Pearson began his statistical work on issues raised by Weldon's attempt to apply Galton's results on correlation to populations of crab; Weldon was a distinguished zoologist at University College where Pearson was a Professor of Applied Mathematics. It turned out that the histogram of the measurements for Naples crabs was both asymmetrical and bimodal and Pearson (1894), in his first statistical paper, attempted to show that the histogram might be described by the sum of two Normal curves with different means and variances; the first attempt to deal with the hetero-geneity problem. The asymmetry exhibited by biological data and Edgeworth's price data convinced Pearson that the Normal distribution was not of universal applicabil-ity, as previously believed by Quetelet and Galton. This realization led to Pearson's *second* crucial contribution to the biometric tradition which came in the form of what we call today the *Pearson family of distributions* which includes the Normal and most of the most widely used distributions, including several non-symmetric distributions, as special cases (see chapter 4).

Related to the modeling procedure of fitting Pearson family frequency curves to observed data is Pearson's *third* important contribution, the *chi-square test* for assessing the goodness of fit as part of his modeling strategy; see Pearson (1900). This test consti-tutes the first *misspecification test* (see chapter 15) which had a crucial impact on the development of statistical inference in the 20th century. Pearson is best known by social scientists with any interest in statistics for this test than for any of his other contribu-tions.

Pearson's *fourth* important contribution was the formalization and extension of regression and correlation from bivariate to multivariate distributions; see Pearson (1896,1901,1902,1903,1904). The modern formulae for correlation and regression coefficients are largely due to Pearson. In relation to these formulae we should also mention Yule (1895–96,1896) who was the first student of Pearson's and later his assist-ant; in his publications he gives full credit to this teacher. The extensions of correlation and regression include not only *multiple correlation* but also *partial correlation*. It is interesting to NOTE that Pearson was also the first to warn the modeler of the problem of *spurious* correlation in the case of variables measured as ratios with common denomina-tors or/and numerators (see Pearson (1897)).

The *fifth*, and arguably the least influential of his contributions, is his extension of regression and higher conditional moment functions to non-Normal joint distributions; see Pearson (1905,1906,1920,1923a–b,1924,1925). Pearson was the first to appreciate the generality of the concept of regression and proceeded to argue that the concept applies to all joint distributions whose first two moments exist. He conjectured that linearity and homoskedasticity were inextricably bound up with the joint Normality assumption and urged modelers to explore non-symmetric joint distributions. Pearson's joint research with Weldon on populations of crabs led him to non-symmetric distributions and he conjectured that the regression curve is unlikely to be linear and homoskedastic in such cases. However, Pearson could not offer tangible examples of other functional forms of regression curves because there were no other bivariate distributions at the time. Unfortunately, before such distributions became generally available his suggestion was overtaken by certain crucial developments.

In a seminal paper Yule (1897) went further than both Galton and Pearson and put forward a direct link between Galton's regression and the linear relationship between two variables as suggested by the theory of errors (least-squares) tradition:

$$y_t = \beta_0 + \beta_1 x_t + \varepsilon_t, \ \varepsilon_t \sim \text{IID}(0, \sigma^2), \ t = 1, 2, \ldots, T.$$

He went on to point out that:

(a)   (7.58) can be estimated using the least-squares method (see chapter 13), and
(b)   the Normality assumption plays no role in the estimation.
       He proceeded to argue in favor of using least-squares to approximate a regression line even in cases where the imaginary line through the cross-plot "is not quite a straight line" (Yule (1897), p. 817).

Karl Pearson objected immediately to Yule's apparent generality and argued in favor of retaining the Normality of the joint distribution for specification purposes:

Pearson wanted to start with a frequency surface and, if a regression line was sought, find that line appropriate to the surface. If the surface followed the normal law, then he could accept the route to straight lines fit by least squares. But, "why should not another law even symmetrical frequency lead to the pth powers of the residuals being minimum?"…

(Stigler (1986), p. 352)

Unfortunately for statistics Pearson was much less persuasive than Yule and as a result, the linear regression model is often confused with a number of different linear models, such as the Gauss linear model (see Spanos (1986,1999)). Pearson's conviction had no impact on statistics because his efforts to generate non-symmetric bivariate distributions via a pair of partial differential equations was largely unsuccessful until the 1930s (see chapter 6 and Mardia (1970). The major stumbling block was the availability of joint distributions whose conditional moment functions could be derived analytically and then used to specify regression models. The partially successful attempts by Pretorius (1930) and then Van Uven (1947a–b,1948a–b) had very little impact because by the 1930s Yule's success was complete. From the regression viewpoint Van Uven's results (see chapter 6) are interesting in so far as the conditional distributions implied by the restricted partial differential equations belong to the Pearson family in the sense that they satisfy the general relationship:

$$\frac{\partial \ln f(y|x)}{\partial y} = \frac{g_1(x,y)}{g_2(x,y)}.$$

The extent of Yule's success was such that even the earlier success by Narumi (1923a–b), who reversed the procedure by specifying the regression and skedastic functions and then proceeded to derive the joint distribution, went largely unnoticed. Narumi's results are of interest in the present context and are summarized for reference purposes; for more details see Mardia (1970). Yule's impact can be partly explained by the fact that he wrote the first widely used textbook in statistics (see Yule (1911)).

Motivated by the relationship:

$$f(x,y;\phi) = f(y|x;\varphi_2) \cdot f_x(x;\varphi_1), \text{ for all } (x,y) \in \mathbb{R}_X \times \mathbb{R}_Y,$$

Narumi's bivariate density function takes the restricted form:

$$f(x,y) = \psi_1(x) \cdot \varphi_1\left(\tfrac{y - h_1(x)}{g_1(x)}\right), f(x,y) = \psi_2(y) \cdot \varphi_2\left(\tfrac{x - h_2(y)}{g_2(y)}\right).$$

This bivariate distribution is restricted because it belongs to the location-scale family of distributions. The conditional densities take the form:

$$f(y|x) = c_1 \cdot \varphi_1\left(\tfrac{y - h_1(x)}{g_1(x)}\right), f(x|y) = c_2 \cdot \varphi_2\left(\tfrac{x - h_2(y)}{g_2(y)}\right),$$

where c_1 and c_2 denote two normalizing constants. Although Narumi explored several cases by specifying the functional form of the regression and skedastic functions, the most interesting from our viewpoint are the following.

1 Linear regression and homoskedastic conditional variance By postulating:

$$\mu(y|x) = \beta_0 + \beta_1 x, \ \mu(x|y) = \gamma_0 + \gamma_1 x,$$

$$\sigma^2(y|x) = \sigma_1^2, \ \sigma^2(x|y) = \sigma_2^2,$$

he derived conditional and marginal densities which turned out to be Normal, yielding a bivariate Normal distribution.

2 Linear regression and heteroskedastic conditional variance (linear) By postulating:

$$\mu(y|x) = \beta_0 + \beta_1 x, \ \mu(x|y) = \gamma_0 + \gamma_1 x,$$

$$\sigma^2(y|x) = a_1 + x, \ \sigma^2(x|y) = a_2 + y,$$

he derived a joint density of the general form:

$$f(x,y) = c_0(\alpha x + \beta)^{\theta_1}(\gamma y + \delta)^{\theta_2}(ax + by + c)^{\theta_3}.$$

This joint distribution includes the bivariate *Beta*, *Pareto* and *F* distributions (see appendix B) as special cases. By restricting the conditional variance of *Y* given *X* to be

$$\sigma^2(y|x) = a_1,$$

Narumi derived the bivariate density:

$$f(x,y) = c_0(\alpha x + \beta)^{\theta_1} e^{-\theta_2 y}(ax + by + c)^{\theta_3}.$$

which includes the (*McKay*) *Gamma* distribution (see appendix B) as a special case.

3 Linear regression and heteroskedastic conditional variance (parabolic). By postulating:

$$\mu\,(y|x) = \beta_0 + \beta_1 x, \;\; \mu\,(x|y) = \gamma_0 + \gamma_1 x,$$

$$\sigma^2(y|x) = \sqrt{a_1 + x^2}, \;\; \sigma^2(x|y) = \sqrt{a_2 + y^2},$$

he showed that the joint density takes the general form:

$$f(x,y) = c_0(ax^2 + by^2 + 2\theta_1 xy + 2\theta_2 x + 2\theta_3 y + c)^m.$$

This joint distribution includes the bivariate *Cauchy*, *Student's t* and *Pearson type II*-distribution (see appendix B) as special cases.

REMARK: the discerning reader would have noticed the connection between Narumi's and Van Uven's results (see chapter 6).

A century after Pearson's first unsuccessful attempt to generate joint distributions we can now argue that Pearson was right all along. Section 2 above can be interpreted as testament to Pearson's thesis presenting several regression models associated with different bivariate distributions. Indeed, if Yule's suggestion is followed when estimating regression models such as that associated with the bivariate Exponential distribution, the result is likely to be way off the target! In the next subsection we revisit Pearson's modeling strategy.

7.6.3   Revisiting Pearson's modeling strategy

From the point of view of empirical modeling Pearson's modeling strategy (see Pearson (1905, 1923a–b,1924,1925)) makes perfectly good sense and provides the foundation for the approach adopted in this book. Galton's approach to the Normal/linear regression can be easily extended to several other regression models as discussed in section 2. In chapter 6 we considered the question of using the scatterplots in order to get some idea of the nature of the bivariate density by *smoothing* the *stereogram* (bivariate histogram). This is simply a modern version of Galton's procedure as described above. The smoothed stereogram surface (see chapter 6) will give the modeler ideas as to the most befitting bivariate distribution, and this information can be used in order to postulate the appropriate regression model.

In order to illustrate the relationship between the bivariate density and the regression curves let us return to the bivariate distributions discussed in chapter 6.

In figures 7.22–7.23 we can see the bivariate F density with $\boldsymbol{\theta}$: $= (12,8,8)$ and the corresponding equiprobability contours which are clearly non-elliptic and asymmetric. The relationship between the joint distribution and the regression line can be seen in figure 7.23 which has a certain affinity with that of the joint Normal distribution in figure 7.21 but there is also an obvious difference. The Normal and F regression lines are similar in so far as the sign of the correlation coefficient determines their slope but differ in so far as the latter does not pass through the mode of the bivariate density.

Moreover, there is no apparent simple relationship between the slope of the contours at the points of intersection with the regression line as pointed out by Galton in the case of

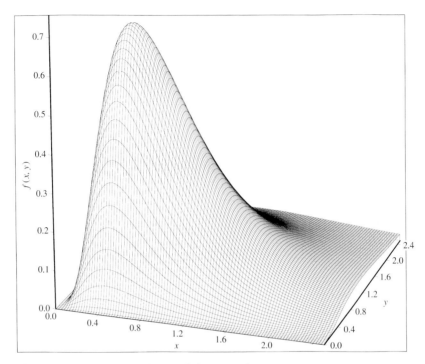

Figure 7.22 Bivariate F (23,8,8) density surface

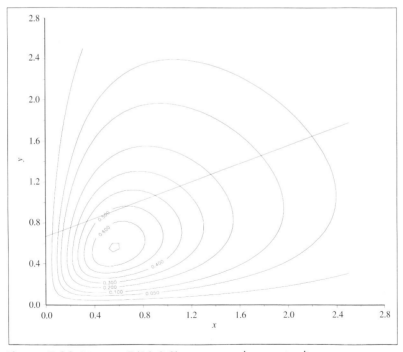

Figure 7.23 Bivariate F (12,8,8) contours and regression line

the bivariate Normal density. NOTE that the correlation coefficient in figures 7.22–7.23 is $\rho = 0.444$.

In figures 7.24–7.25 we can see the same graphs in the case where the correlation between the random variables (X, Y) is quite high ($\rho = 0.953$). As we can see the regression line is much closer to (but does not coincide with) the principal axis of the asymmetric near elliptic contours. As in the case of the Normal distribution, increasing the correlation coefficient has the effect of squashing the contours.

The connection between the correlation coefficient and the regression line becomes clearer in figures 7.26–7.27 where the correlation between the random variables (X, Y) is low ($\rho = 0.035$); confirming the direct connection between the correlation coefficient and the slope of the regression line.

In figures 7.28–7.29 we can see the bivariate Gamma (2,3,4) (Cherian) density and the corresponding contours with the regression line inserted, respectively. As we can see, the bivariate Gamma is very similar to the F distribution but with a different form of asymmetry. The regression line is similar to both the Normal and F regression lines in so far as they are directly related to the correlation coefficient. This is the general result derived in section 3 above which says that in the case of linear regressions, the line takes the form:

$$E(Y|\sigma(X)) = E(Y) - \tfrac{Cov(X,Y)}{Var(X)}[X - E(X)]. \qquad (7.61)$$

In figures 7.30–7.31 we can see the bivariate Beta (3,3,6) density and the corresponding contours with the regression line inserted, respectively. Again, the asymmetry exhibited by the contours is quite different from both the F and Gamma bivariate distributions. As shown in appendix B, this form of the bivariate Beta distribution allows only for negative correlation and thus the regression line, also of the general form (7.61), can only have negative slope.

In an attempt to avoid the misleading impression that "regression curves are usually straight lines" we present two bivariate distributions with non-linear regression functions.

In figures 7.32–7.33 we can see the bivariate Exponential density and the corresponding contours with the regression curve inserted, respectively. Again we note the apparent lack of any connection between the slope of the contours and the regression curve at the points of intersection. The form of the regression functions for this and the other distributions discussed above were given in section 2 above.

In figures 7.34 and 7.35 we can see the bivariate (standard) Logistic density and the corresponding contours with the regression curve inserted, respectively.

A comparison between figures 7.35 and 7.29 suggests that deciding whether the regression is linear or non-linear by just looking at the scatterplot can be risky! A better modeling strategy will be to evaluate the smoothed stereogram contours (see chapter 6) before any decisions relating to the nature of the regression function are made. Indeed, Pearson's modeling strategy might be the best choice: decide upon the joint distribution first (utilizing the smoothed stereogram contours) and then proceed to the regression and other conditional moment functions; see Pearson (1905,1920,1923a–b,1924,1925). This strategy can be supplemented by the non-parametric kernel smoothing regression

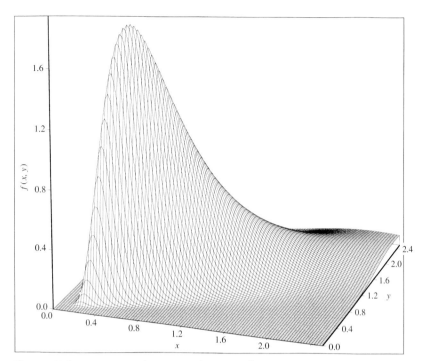

Figure 7.24 Bivariate F (5,60,60) density surface

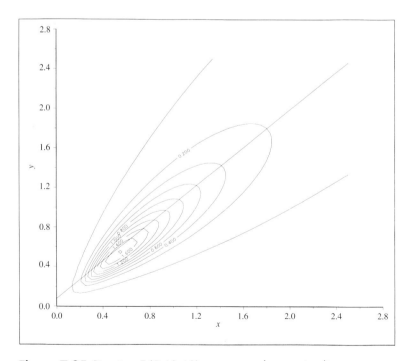

Figure 7.25 Bivariate F (5,60,60) contours and regression line

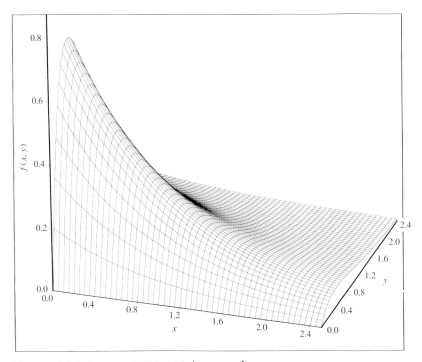

Figure 7.26 Bivariate F (80,4,1) density surface

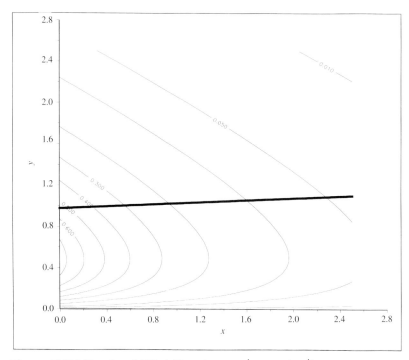

Figure 7.27 Bivariate F (80,4,1) contours and regression line

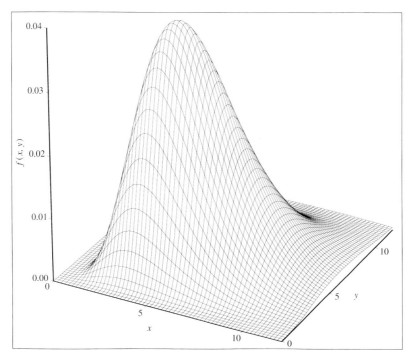

Figure 7.28 Bivariate Gamma (2,3,4) (Cherian) density surface

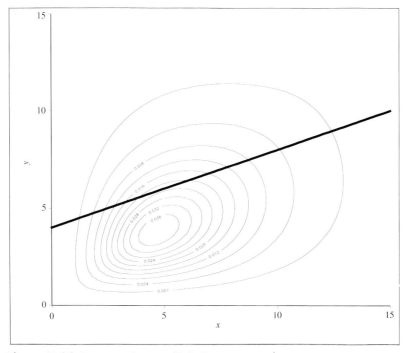

Figure 7.29 Bivariate Gamma (2,3,4) contours and regression curve

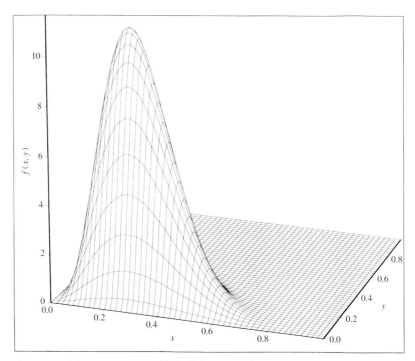

Figure 7.30 Bivariate Beta (3,3,6) density surface

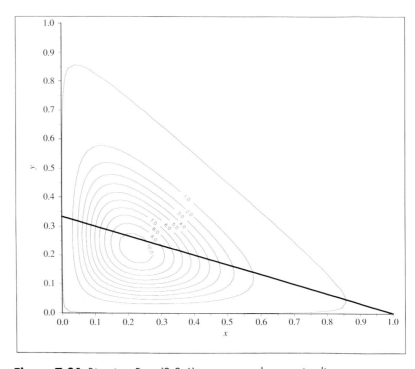

Figure 7.31 Bivariate Beta (3,3,6) contours and regression line

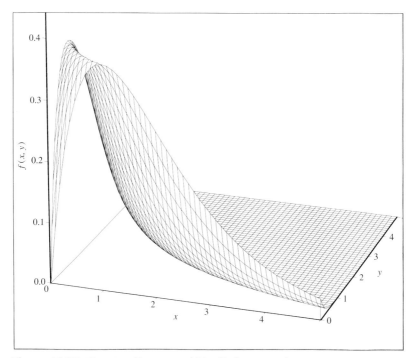

Figure 7.32 Bivariate Exponential $(\theta=1)$ density surface

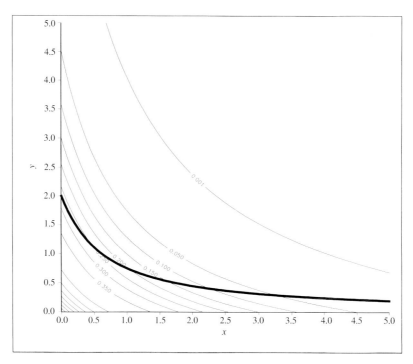

Figure 7.33 Bivariate Exponential $(\theta=1)$ contours and regression curve

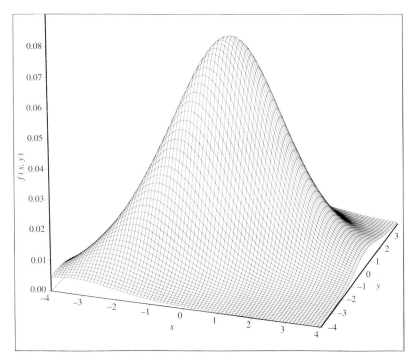

Figure 7.34 Bivariate Logistic density surface

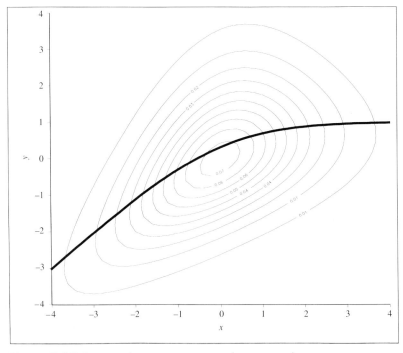

Figure 7.35 Bivariate Logistic contours and regression line

procedure discussed next so as to assess the appropriateness of the postulated joint distribution.

7.6.4 Kernel smoothing and regression

The kernel smoothing techniques introduced in chapters 5–6 can be utilized to provide the modeler with a further visual aid in deciding on the appropriateness of the postulated regression model. The basic idea is to use the information conveyed by the scatterplot in order to evaluate a non-parametric regression curve directly.

As argued above, the regression function is defined by:

$$E(Y|X=x) = \int_{y \in \mathbb{R}_Y} y \cdot f(y|x) dy = h(x), \ x \in \mathbb{R}_X.$$

Substituting $f(y|x) = \frac{f(x,y)}{f_x(x)}$ into this definition yields:

$$E(Y|X=x) = \int_{y \in \mathbb{R}_Y} y \cdot \left(\frac{f(x,y)}{f_x(x)}\right) dy = h(x), \ x \in \mathbb{R}_X.$$

From this relationship we can see that the modeler can get a non-parametric evaluation of the regression curve from the smoothed histogram (see chapter 5) and stereogram (see chapter 6), which represent the empirical equivalents to the densities $f_x(x)$ and $f(x,y)$, respectively:

$$\hat{f}_x(x) = \frac{1}{nh_x}\sum_{k=1}^n \mathbb{K}_X\left(\frac{x_k-x}{h_x}\right), \ h_x>0,$$

$$\hat{f}(x,y) = \frac{1}{nh_xh_y}\sum_{k=1}^n \mathbb{K}_X\left(\frac{x_k-x}{h_x}\right) \cdot \mathbb{K}_Y\left(\frac{y_k-y}{h_y}\right), \ h_x>0, h_y>0,$$

where both kernels satisfy the properties.

$$[a] \ \mathbb{K}(z) \geq 0, \ [b] \int_{z \in \mathbb{R}_Z} \mathbb{K}(z) dz = 1.$$

The regression function can be evaluated empirically via:

$$E(\widehat{Y|X}=x) = \int_{y \in \mathbb{R}_Y} y \cdot \left(\frac{\hat{f}(x,y)}{\hat{f}_x(x)}\right) dy = \frac{\sum_{k=1}^n \mathbb{K}_X\left(\frac{x_k-x}{h_x}\right) \cdot y_k}{\sum_{k=1}^n \mathbb{K}_X\left(\frac{x_k-x}{h_x}\right)} = \sum_{k=1}^n w_k \cdot y_k, \ x \in \mathbb{R}_X, \qquad (7.62)$$

where the weights take the form:

$$w_k = \frac{\mathbb{K}_X\left(\frac{x_k-x}{h_x}\right)}{\sum_{k=1}^n \mathbb{K}_X\left(\frac{x_k-x}{h_x}\right)}.$$

The right-hand side of (7.62) follows from the fact that:

$$\int_{y \in \mathbb{R}_Y} \mathbb{K}_Y(y) dy = 1 \text{ and } \int_{y \in \mathbb{R}_Y} y \cdot \mathbb{K}_Y(y) dy = 0.$$

The non-parametric evaluator of the regression function in (7.62) is known as the Nadaraya-Watson "estimator." For more sophisticated evaluators of the regression function based on kernel smoothing and other techniques see Härdle (1990).

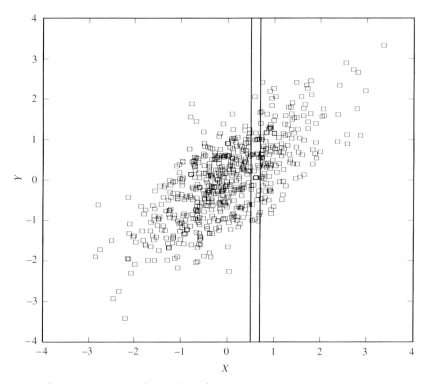

Figure 7.36 Kernel smoothing for evaluating the regression curve

Intuitively, the above regression curve smoother amounts to taking a *weighted average* (w_k, $k = 1,2, ..., n$ being the weights) of all points (x_k, y_i) within the interval ($x_k \pm h_x$) as k varies over all values of X. In figure 7.36 we can see one such interval (0.6 ± 0.1) within which several points will be averaged vertically to reduce them to a point.

In this book we consider the above non-parametric evaluator of the regression function not as a substitute of the modeling strategy expounded above but as a complement in evaluating the appropriateness of the postulated regression model. This is because the smoothed regression evaluator ignores the other conditional moment functions. In contrast, postulating a bivariate distribution enables the modeler to derive the higher conditional moment functions. As we have seen in section 2 above, most bivariate distributions give rise to heteroskedastic conditional variance functions. Hence, the best use of the smoothed regression is for the modeler to superimpose the theoretical regression curve (which corresponds to the postulated bivariate distribution) and the empirical non-parametric regression curve in a scatterplot in order to assess visually the appropriateness of the former. For alternative uses of such non-parametric evaluators see chapter 15.

7.7   Summary

The main objective of the previous three chapters has been the extension of the simple statistical model, built on the notion of a random sample, toward more realistic models which can accommodate some dependence and/or heterogeneity. Having argued that the best way to model dependence and heterogeneity is via the joint distributions, we proceeded to find ways to deal with the problems of multidimensionality and overparameterization arising from such distributions. In chapter 6, in addition to developing a number of dependence notions, it was shown that sequential conditioning provides a most efficient way to deal with the dimensionality problem raised by joint distributions. Any joint distribution can be reduced into a product of univariate conditional distributions. However, this product often represents an infinite family of densities whose information cannot be modeled using the ordinary conditional moments. The main purpose of the present chapter has been to develop the notion of the stochastic conditional moment function. These functions are defined in terms of the conditional moments but are viewed as functions of the conditioning variables. The best-known conditional moment functions are the regression and skedastic functions. Another objective of this chapter has been to show that the conditional moment functions (regression, skedastic, clitic and kurtic) can be integrated into the specification of statistical models by introducing an additional component, the statistical generating mechanism (GM). The statistical GM will play an important role at the estimation and the identification stage: relating a statistical model to a theoretical model.

The approach proposed in this chapter for modeling dependence/heterogeneity using general regression models can be traced back to the *biometric tradition* founded by Galton, formalized and extended by Karl Pearson (and to some extent Yule) and transformed into modern statistics by Fisher (see chapters 11–15). Our interest in the biometric tradition has been restricted to its empirical modeling dimension and no reference has been made to its connection to the subject of Biology; for that see MacKenzie (1981) and Kevles (1985). However, it is important to mention the crucial lesson that was learned from the failure of the biometric tradition to give rise to *statistical biology*, as originally envisioned by Karl Pearson. The lesson is that statistical models by themselves provide description and not *explanation*. For the latter we need to synthesize empirically adequate statistical models with theory models (see chapter 1). When Fisher (1930) synthesized the biometric statistical tradition with Mendel's theory of heredity, the hybrid turned out to be a major success! Fisher's claim to fame is not just as the father of modern statistics but also as a major figure in 20th century genetics; see MacKenzie (1981).

7.8   Exercises

1   Explain how the notion of conditioning enables us to deal with the dimensionality problem raised by joint distributions of samples.

2   Explain why in the reduction $f(x,y) = f(y|x) \cdot f_x(x)$, using conditional moments for modeling purposes raises a problem in relation to $x \in \mathbb{R}_X$.

3   Consider the joint distribution as given below:

$x\backslash y$	1	2	3	$f_x(x)$
-1	0.10	0.08	0.02	0.2
0	0.15	0.06	0.09	0.3
1	0.02	0.20	0.10	0.5
$f_y(y)$	0.45	0.34	0.21	1

(a)   Derive the conditional distributions of $(Y|X=x)$ for all values of the random variable X.

(b)   Derive the regression and skedastic functions for the distributions in (a).

4   Let the joint density function of two random variables X and Y be:

$x\backslash y$	0	1	2
0	0.1	0.2	0.2
1	0.2	0.1	0.2

(a)   Derive the following conditional moments:

$$E(Y|X=1), \ Var(Y|X=1), \ E\{[Y - E(Y|X=1)]^3|X=1\}.$$

(b)   Verify the equalities:

(i) $Var(Y|X=1) = E(Y^2|X=1) - \{E[Y|X=1]\}^2$.

(ii) $E(Y) = E\{E(Y|X)\}$.

(iii)* $Var(Y) = E\{Var(Y|X)\} + Var\{E(Y|X)\}$.

5   Compare and contrast the concepts $E[Y|X=x]$ and $E[Y|\sigma(X)]$.

6   Define and explain the following concepts:

(a)   Conditional moment functions,

(b)   Regression function,

(c)   Skedastic function,

(d)   Homoskedasticity,

(e)   Heteroskedasticity.

7   From the bivariate distributions of chapter 7 collect the regression functions which are linear and the skedastic functions which are homoskedastic.

8   Explain the notion of linear regression. Explain the difference between linearity in x and linearity in the parameters.

9   Consider the joint normal distribution denoted by:

$$\begin{pmatrix} Y \\ X \end{pmatrix} \sim N\left(\begin{pmatrix} \mu_1 \\ \mu_2 \end{pmatrix}, \begin{pmatrix} \sigma_{11} & \sigma_{12} \\ \sigma_{12} & \sigma_{22} \end{pmatrix} \right).$$

(a) For values $\mu_1 = 1$, $\mu_2 = 1.5$, $\sigma_{11} = 1$, $\sigma_{12} = -0.8$, $\sigma_{22} = 2$, plot the conditional expectation $E(Y|X=x)$ and conditional variance $Var(Y|X=x)$ for $x=0,1,2$.

(b) Plot $E(Y|X=x)$ and $Var(Y|X=x)$ for $x=0,1,2$ for a bivariate Student's t distribution whose moments take the same values as those given in (a) for $\nu = 3,5,7$.

(c) State the marginal distributions of Y and X.

10 Explain the notion of stochastic conditional moment functions. Why do we care?

11 Explain the notion of weak exogeneity. Why do we care?

12 Explain the notion of a statistical generating mechanism. Why do we need it?

13 Let Y be a random variable and define the error term by: $u = Y - E(Y|\sigma(X))$.

Show that by definition, this random variable satisfies the following properties:
[i] $E(u|\sigma(X)) = 0$,
[ii] $E(u \cdot X|\sigma(X)) = 0$,
[iii] $E(u) = 0$,
[iv] $E\{u \cdot [E(Y|\sigma(X))]|\sigma(X)\} = 0$.

14 Explain the difference between temporal and contemporaneous dependence.

15 Compare and contrast the statistical GMs of:
(a) the simple Normal model,
(b) the linear/Normal regression model, and
(c) the linear/Normal autoregressive model.

16 Compare and contrast the simple Normal and Normal/linear regression models in terms of their probability and sampling models.

17 Compare and contrast the Normal/linear and Student's t regression models in terms of their probability and sampling models.

18 Explain Karl Pearson's strategy in postulating regression models.

19 "The argument that, looking at graphical displays of bivariate distributions and the associated contour plot with the regression curve, is very misleading when one has $m > 2$ variables, is tantamount to telling the astronomers to abandon their telescopes because they can only see 2 percent of the universe at best." Discuss.

8 Stochastic processes

8.1 Introduction

In chapter 6 we set out to broaden the intended scope of the simple statistical model, based on the notion of a random sample (a set $(X_1, X_2, \ldots, X_n)$ of *Independent* and *Identically Distributed* (IID) random variables), to encompass stochastic phenomena which cannot be considered as realizations of random samples. In that chapter we discussed the concept of *dependence* in general. The question of *modeling dependence* was pursued in chapter 7 where we reached the conclusion that an effective way to deal with the modeling issues raised was through the conditional distributions and in particular via the *stochastic conditional moment functions*. The discussion in both chapters was confined to the two variables case in order to sidestep several additional issues raised by the general case. The main objective of the present chapter is to return to the general *n-variable* case and tie together all the loose ends. The basic concept required is that of *a stochastic process* which extends the notion of a random variable.

8.1.1 The story so far

As shown in chapters 6 and 7, the qualifier *simple* in a simple statistical model stems from the fact that the random sample assumption simplifies the analysis considerably; the joint distribution of the sample is reduced to a product of univariate (identical) marginal distributions:

$$f(x_1, \ldots, x_n; \boldsymbol{\phi}) \underset{\mathrm{I}}{=} \prod_{k=1}^{n} f_k(x_k; \boldsymbol{\theta}_k) \underset{\mathrm{III}}{=} \prod_{k=1}^{n} f(x_k; \boldsymbol{\theta}), \text{ for all } \mathbf{x} := (x_1, \ldots, x_n) \in \mathbb{R}_X^n. \quad (8.1)$$

As shown in chapter 6, in the case of a non-random sample the corresponding reduction based on *sequential conditioning* takes the form:

$$f(x_1, \ldots, x_n; \boldsymbol{\phi}) \overset{\text{non-IID}}{=} f_1(x_1; \boldsymbol{\psi}_1) \prod_{k=2}^{n} f_k(x_k | x_{k-1}, \ldots, x_1; \boldsymbol{\psi}_k), \text{ for all } \mathbf{x} \in \mathbb{R}_X^n. \quad (8.2)$$

By comparing the two reductions (8.1) and (8.2) we can see that the key to modeling the non-randomness comes in the form of conditional distributions. Indeed, from the

preliminary discussion of the problem of measuring dependence in chapter 6 we con-
cluded that the most promising way comes in the form of conditional moments. In
chapter 7, however, it became obvious that conditional moments could not do the job
because for each k:

$$\{f_k(x_k|x_{k-1}, \ldots, x_1; \psi_k), (x_{k-1}, \ldots, x_1) \in \mathbb{R}_X^{k-1}\}, \tag{8.3}$$

represents a whole collection of density functions; one for each possible value in $\mathbb{R}_X^{k-1}$,
each one with its own conditional moments. The solution to this problem comes in the
form of conditional moment functions, such as the regression and skedastic functions.
Even these functions, however, do not suffice to deal with the problem because they
ignore the probabilistic structure of the conditioning variable. In chapter 7 we extended
the conditional moment functions to take account of the probabilistic structure of the
conditioning variables in the form of *stochastic conditional moment functions*.

Throughout the discussion in both of the previous chapters we concentrated on the
simple two variable case:

$$f(x,y;\phi) = f(y|x;\varphi_2) \cdot f_x(x;\varphi_1), \text{ for all } (x,y) \in \mathbb{R}_X \times \mathbb{R}_Y, \tag{8.4}$$

for a very good reason: to sidestep two interrelated problems that arise in the context of
the sequential conditional distributions (8.3):

(i)   The *changing conditioning information set:* the number of conditioning variables
       changes with the index in the sense that the number of conditioning variables
       involved in $f_k(x_k|x_{k-1}, \ldots, x_1; \psi_k)$ changes with $k = 2,3, \ldots, n$, rendering these densi-
       ties different, e.g.. for $n = 5$:

$$f_2(x_2|x_1; \psi_2),$$
$$f_3(x_3|x_2,x_1; \psi_3),$$
$$f_4(x_4|x_3,x_2,x_1; \psi_4),$$
$$f_5(x_5|x_4,x_3,x_2,x_1; \psi_5).$$

(ii)   The *inherent heterogeneity:* in addition to the fact that the conditional densities can
       be different for each k ($f_k(.|.), k = 1,2, \ldots, n$), there is also the problem of the hetero-
       geneity introduced by the changing conditioning information set.

In order to motivate the discussion that follows, let us proceed to apply the solutions
proposed in chapter 7 to the general case (8.3). In particular, let us consider the concepts
of conditional moment functions in the case of the sequence of conditional densities
(8.3). The first thing that becomes apparent looking at these densities is that we cannot
use the ordinary conditional moment functions because the marginal densities are certainly relevant. With the exception of the last X_n random variables the others appear on
both sides of the conditioning. Hence, we need to consider the stochastic conditional
moment functions. The first two stochastic conditional moment functions, known as the
autoregressive and *autoskedastic functions*, take the general form:

$$E(X_k|\sigma(X_{k-1}, \ldots, X_1)) = h_k(X_{k-1}, \ldots, X_1), k = 2,3, \ldots, n,$$

$$Var(X_k|\sigma(X_{k-1}, \ldots, X_1)) = g_k(X_{k-1}, \ldots, X_1), k = 2,3, \ldots, n. \tag{8.5}$$

A glance at (8.5) reveals that these do not yield operational models because they are changing with the index k. This indicates that without some *restrictions* on the *dependence* and *heterogeneity* of the set of random variables $(X_1, X_2, \ldots, X_n)$ no operational models will arise via the stochastic conditional moments; the question of imposing such restrictions will be pursued in this chapter.

8.1.2   Random variables and ordering

In the case of a random sample $(X_1, X_2, \ldots, X_n)$, the *ordering* of the random variables involved, although specified, is immaterial because the random variables are replicas of each other and we cannot distinguish between, say X_1 and X_3 even if we wanted to, unless the realization of these values takes place at successive instances and their order is noted. This is apparent in (8.1) because any re-shuffling of the sequence will make no difference to the right-hand side. In contrast to this, in the case of a non-random sample the reduction in (8.2) makes it abundantly clear that the ordering is all important.

The notion of a random variable X (see chapter 3) defined on a probability space $(S, \Im, \mathbb{P}(.))$, (where S denotes the outcomes set, $\Im$ the appropriate set of events of interest and $\mathbb{P}(.)$ a probability set function), as a function of the form:

$$X(.): S \to \mathbb{R}, \text{ such that } X^{-1}(-\infty, x] \in \Im,$$

is basically *dimensionless* and cannot be endowed with dependence and heterogeneity. In our attempt to define the notion of a non-random sample we need to endow the notion of a random variable with *dependence* and *heterogeneity*. Both of these concepts are defined relative to some ordering of the random variables involved. This requires us to endow the notion of a random variable with a dimension (an index) that represents this ordering and often represents time, spatial position, etc. The indexed sequence of random variables $\{X_1, X_2, \ldots, X_n, \ldots\}$, called a **stochastic process**, is the required extension. The discerning reader would have noted that the notion of a stochastic process was implicitly used in the previous three chapters, when the sample was specified.

8.1.3   A bird's eye view of the chapter

The main objective of this chapter is to define and explain the notion of a stochastic process, and related restrictions of dependence and heterogeneity, needed to specify operational statistical models which can be used for modeling non-IID data.

The discussion of stochastic processes can end up being one of the most involved and confusing parts of probability theory mainly because of the numerous overlapping types of stochastic processes one encounters. The difficulties of mastering the material are alleviated when the discussion is structured in a way that makes it easier to compare and contrast the various stochastic processes. In an attempt to mitigate the confusion for the uninitiated we use the following learning aids:

(i)   We begin the discussion with a brief overview of the early developments in stochastic processes. This is to lessen the problem of introducing too many concepts too quickly and to establish some basic terminology.

(ii)   The probabilistic structure of stochastic processes is discussed in relation to the three basic categories of probabilistic assumptions:

(D) Distribution,   (M) Dependence,   (H) Homogeneity.   (8.6)

This renders the comparison between different processes much clearer and more intuitive.

(iii) We use several taxonomies of stochastic processes, commencing the discussion with the discrete/continuous distinction.

(iv)   In view of the fact that most stochastic processes are specified indirectly as functions of other (often simpler) stochastic processes, we emphasize the distinction between the distributional and constructionist viewpoints.

In section 2 we define the concept of a **stochastic process** and discuss its basic structure. In section 3 we consider briefly the early development of some of the most important stochastic processes and the associated dependence and heterogeneity restrictions. A more complete discussion of dependence and heterogeneity restrictions for stochastic processes is given in sections 4 and 5, respectively. Emphasis is placed on the distinction between the distributional and constructionist approaches to specifying stochastic processes; the former refers to the specification via the joint distribution of a finite number of elements of the process and the latter to specifying a stochastic process via a function of another (often simpler) process. Section 6 introduces some of the stochastic processes used as building blocks for constructing such processes. The major categories of stochastic processes, Markov processes, random walk processes, martingale processes, Gaussian processes, and Point processes, are discussed in sections 7–11. In relation to the specification of a stochastic process we wrap up the question of specifying operational statistical models by imposing dependence and heterogeneity restrictions in section 10.

8.2   The notion of a stochastic process

8.2.1   Defining a stochastic process

A **stochastic process** is simply an indexed collection $\{X_t, t \in \mathbb{T}\}$ of random variables defined on the same probability space $(S, \Im, \mathbb{P}(.))$, i.e., X_t is a random variable relative to $(S, \Im, \mathbb{P}(.))$, for each t in the *index set* $\mathbb{T}$.

Example
The number of telephone calls arriving in a telephone exchange over the interval $[0,t]$ can be modeled using such an indexed sequence of random variables where X_t measures the number of calls up to time t; its possible values are: $0,1,2,3,\ldots$

Reminding ourselves that a random variable $X(.)$ is a function from an outcomes set S to the real line $\mathbb{R}$, we observe that a stochastic process is a function with two arguments:

$$X(.,.): S \times \mathbb{T} \to \mathbb{R}.$$

A more heedful notation for a stochastic process is:

$$\{X(s,t),\, s \in S,\, t \in \mathbb{T}\}.$$

In view of the two arguments, we can look upon a stochastic process from two different but interrelated viewing angles.

(i)   *The random variable viewing angle.* For a given $t = \bar{t}$, $\{X(s,\bar{t}),\, s \in S\}$:

$$X(.,\bar{t}): S \to \mathbb{R},$$

is an ordinary random variable on $(S,\mathcal{F},\mathbb{P}(.))$ with its own distribution and density functions as before. For a given subset of $\mathbb{T}$, say $\{t_1,t_2,\ \dots,\ t_n\}$, $\{X(.,t_1),X(.,t_2),\ \dots,$ $X(.,t_n)\}$ is just a collection of random variables like the ones we used to define the notion of a sample in the previous chapters. The probabilistic structure of this collection is fully described by their joint cumulative distribution or their joint density function $f(x(t_1),x(t_2),x(t_3),\ \dots,\ x(t_n))$.

(ii) *The functional viewing angle.* For a given $s = \bar{s}$, $\{X(\bar{s},t),\, t \in \mathbb{T}\}$:

$$X(\bar{s},.): \mathbb{T} \to \mathbb{R},$$

is just an ordinary *function* from $\mathbb{T}$ to $\mathbb{R}$. The graph of this function is often called a *sample path* (or *sample realization*) because this is the feature of the stochastic process that we often associate with observed data. In figure 8.1 and 8.2 we can see the sample paths of a discrete and a continuous stochastic process, respectively.

Allowing s to change (always within S), and take the values, say $\{s_1,s_2,s_3,\ \dots,\ s_k\}$, the functions $\{X(s_1,.),X(s_2,.),X(s_3,.),\ \dots,\ X(s_k,.)\}$, $t \in \mathbb{T}$, define a collection of different *sample paths*, called an *assemble*. The mathematical structure of the assemble also plays an important role in the formalization of the notion of a stochastic process.

NOTES:

(a)   It is important to stress at this stage that it is common practice to connect the points of a sample path of a discrete process. This suggests some caution when looking at data plots to avoid confusing a discrete process with a continuous one because one observes a continuous sample path (see figure 8.2).

(b)   We often cannot resist the temptation to interpret t as time for convenience, but it could easily be some other dimension we are interested in, such as space and geographical position, as long as the index set for the particular dimension is ordered.

(c)   The index t can easily be multidimensional in the sense that the stochastic process $\{X_t,\ t \in \mathbb{R}^3\}$ could represent the velocity of a particle suspended in liquid with $\mathbf{t}$ being its position in the three-dimensional Euclidean space.

(d)   The stochastic process $\{X_t,\ t \in \mathbb{T}\}$ can be easily extended to the case where X_t is a $k \times 1$ vector of random variables: $\mathbf{X}_t := (X_{1t}, X_{2t},\ \dots,\ X_{kt})^\top$.

From the modeling viewpoint there is a very important difference between having a realization $\mathbf{x}_T := (x_1,x_2,x_3,\ \dots,\ x_T)$ from a random sample $(X_1,X_2,X_3,\ \dots,\ X_T)$ or from a

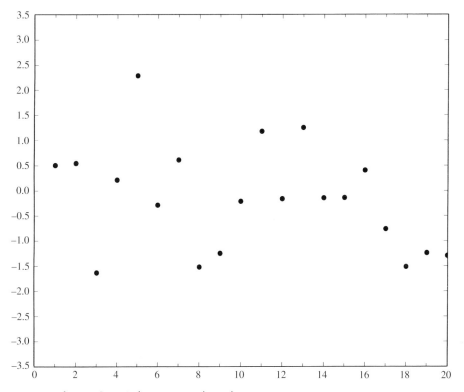

Figure 8.1 A discrete sample path

non-IID stochastic process $\{X_t, t \in \mathbb{T}\}$. In the random sample case, due to the fact that each value x_t comes from the same distribution $f(x;\boldsymbol{\theta})$, the date t is immaterial since the random variables are replicas of each other. As a result of this we can use the *t-averages* (sample moments) such as:

$$\frac{1}{T}\sum_{t=1}^{T}x_t^r, \; r = 1,2,\ldots \tag{8.7}$$

to estimate the corresponding distribution moments (*probability averages*):

$$E(X^r) = \int_{x \in \mathbb{R}_X} x^r f(x)dx, \; r = 1,2,\ldots \tag{8.8}$$

In a sense (8.7) is defined by averaging over $t \in \mathbb{T}$ and (8.8) by averaging over $s \in S$; remember the probability space $(S, \Im, P(.))$.

These two types of averaging can be visualized in the context of figure 8.3 which depicts 5 sample paths from a Normal IID stochastic process. The *t*-averaging takes place horizontally and the distribution averaging takes place vertically. When these sample paths constitute realizations of IID samples the *t*-averages (sample moments) will converge to the distribution averages (moments) because we know that the random variables involved have common moments and as shown in chapter 9 the *t*-averages

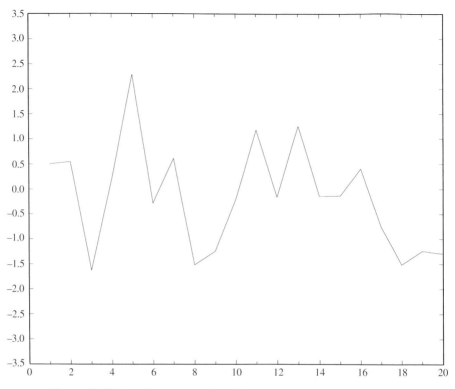

Figure 8.2 A continuous sample path

$\frac{1}{T}\sum_{t=1}^{T}x_t^r$ converge to these common moments. However, the situation in the context of a non-random sample is drastically different because, without any dependence and hetero-geneity restrictions, each value of X_t comes from a different distribution and thus there are no common moments to which the t-averages will converge!

Another way of looking at this problem is to note that for a non-IID stochastic process the unknown parameters $\boldsymbol{\theta}_t$ in $f_t(x_t;\boldsymbol{\theta}_t)$ are by definition functions of the moments which change with t:

$$E(X_t^r) = \mu_r(\boldsymbol{\theta}_t,t),\ r = 1,2,\ ...,\ t\in\mathbb{T}.$$

In a sense the problem is that we have just one observation for each set of unknown para-meters $\boldsymbol{\theta}_t$. The question that suggests itself at this stage is whether only in the case of IID random variables, the t-averages will converge to the distribution averages (moments). The answer is, not necessarily, but the random variables involved are required to have something in common for the convergence to take place. This something in common is defined in terms of restrictions on the probabilistic structure of the process in question so as to enable the modeler to use t-averages such as (8.7) as reliable estimates of the unknown parameters (moments). This calls for dependence/heterogeneity restrictions which will be the focus of the present chapter.

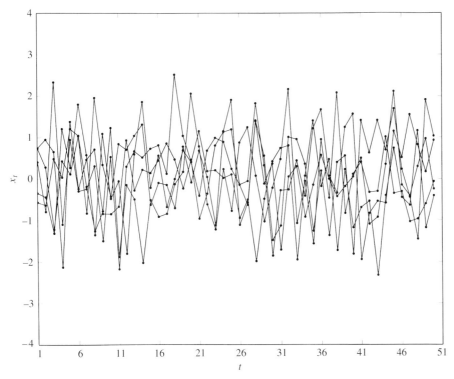

Figure 8.3 An assemble of five sample paths

8.2.2 Classifying stochastic processes

The structure of the stochastic process $\{X_t,\ t\in\mathbb{T}\}$ depends partly on the nature of two sets: the **index set** $\mathbb{T}$ and the **range** of the random variable X, say $\mathbb{R}_X$. In view of the fact that the range of the random variable X_t might change with t, we define the range of the stochastic process $\{X_t,\ t\in\mathbb{T}\}$ to be the union of the sets of values of $X(.,t)$ for each t, say $\mathbb{R}_{X(t)}$:

$$\mathcal{R}_x = \cup_{t\in\mathbb{T}}\mathbb{R}_{X(t)},$$

known as the **state space** of the stochastic process. What renders the stochastic processes mathematically different is whether the sets $(\mathbb{T},\mathcal{R}_x)$ are *countable* or *uncountable*; a distinction already encountered in chapter 2.

(a) In the case where $\mathbb{T}$ is a *countable* set, such as $\mathbb{T}=\{0,1,2,3,\ldots\}$, we call $\{X_t,\ t\in\mathbb{T}\}$ a **discrete index** stochastic process. On the other hand, when $\mathbb{T}$ is an *uncountable* set, such as $\mathbb{T}=[0,\infty)$, we call $\{X(t),\ t\in\mathbb{T}\}$ a **continuous index** stochastic process. When we need to emphasize the distinction between continuous and discrete index processes for expositional purposes, we will use the NOTATION: $\{X(t),\ t\in\mathbb{T}\}$ for a continuous index process.

(b)   Similarly, the state space $\mathcal{R}_x$ of the stochastic process $\{X_t, t \in \mathbb{T}\}$, can be countable or uncountable, introducing a four way *index set/state space* $(\mathbb{T}, \mathcal{R})$ classification of stochastic processes:

	Index set $\mathbb{T}$	State space $\mathcal{R}$	Example
D–D	countable	countable	Simple random walk
D–C	countable	uncountable	Normal process
C–D	uncountable	countable	Poisson process
C–C	uncountable	uncountable	Brownian motion process

This classification constitutes a schematic, mutually exclusive grouping of stochastic processes which is useful for organizing our thoughts at the initial stages of mastering the material, but it is not the only, or even the most useful classification because it ignores the probabilistic structure of a stochastic process. A number of other overlapping classifications of stochastic processes, such as stationary/non-stationary, Markov/non-Markov, Gaussian/non-Gaussian, ergodic/non-ergodic, are based on their probabilistic structure and provide useful groupings of stochastic processes. A bird's eye view of a categorization based on the probabilistic structure of stochastic process is given in figure 8.4 (see Srinivasan and Mehata (1988) for more details).

8.2.3   Specifying a stochastic process

In view of the fact that the probabilistic structure of a set of random variables is best described by their joint distribution, it is only natural to use the same device for specifying the probabilistic structure of a stochastic process. This, however, raises the question of specifying infinite dimensional distributions because a stochastic process $\{X_t, t \in \mathbb{T}\}$ often has an infinite index set. An effective solution to this problem was proposed by Kolmogorov in the same 1933 book that founded modern probability.

NOTATIONAL DEVICE. In many cases during the discussion that follows we are going to discuss concepts which are applicable to both discrete and continuous index stochastic processes. The notation for discrete index processes is of course more natural and less complicated than that of a continuous index process and more often than not the former will be used. However, in cases where we want to emphasize the general applicability of a concept we use a notational device which in a sense enables us to use the discrete notation to cover both cases. Instead of using the sequence $\{X_k\}_{k=1}^{\infty}$ which is clearly discrete we use $\{X_{t_k}\}_{k=1}^{\infty}$, such that:

$$0 < t_1 < t_2 < t_3 < \cdots < t_n < \cdots < \infty, \text{ where } t_k \in \mathbb{T}, \text{ for } k = 1,2,3, \ldots, n, \ldots$$

A stochastic process $\{X_t, t \in \mathbb{T}\}$ is said to be specified if its finite joint cumulative distribution function (cdf):

$$F(x_{t_1}, x_{t_2}, \ldots x_{t_n}),$$

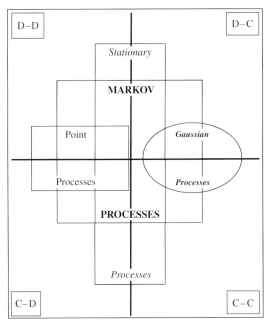

Figure 8.4 A taxonomy of stochastic processes

is defined for all finite subsets $\{t_1, t_2, \ldots, t_n\} \subset \mathbb{T}$. This result is very useful because its converse is also true (see Kolmogorov (1933a)).

Kolmogorov's extension theorem

For each n let $F_n(x_{t_1}, x_{t_2}, \ldots x_{t_n})$ be the joint cumulative distribution function. If the following consistency condition holds:

$$\lim_{(x_{t_{n+1}}) \to \infty} F_{n+1}(x_{t_1}, x_{t_2}, \ldots x_{t_n}, x_{t_{n+1}}) = F_n(x_{t_1}, x_{t_2}, \ldots x_{t_n}),$$

for each $(n+1) > 1$ and $(x_{t_1}, x_{t_2}, \ldots x_{t_n}) \in \mathbb{R}^n$, there exists a probability space $(S, \mathcal{F}, \mathbb{P}(.))$, and a stochastic process $\{X_t, t \in \mathbb{T}\}$ defined on it, such that $F_n(x_{t_1}, x_{t_2}, \ldots x_{t_n})$ is the joint cumulative distribution function of $(X_{t_1}, X_{t_2}, \ldots, X_{t_n})$ for each n (see Billingsley (1986)). In this sense we are safe to assume that the probabilistic structure of a stochastic process can be described completely using only finite dimensional joint distributions.

It is interesting to NOTE that the above extension theorem enables the modeler to proceed from the joint distribution $F_2(x_{t_1}, x_{t_2})$ to the marginal $\lim\limits_{(x_{t_2}) \to \infty} F_2(x_{t_1}, x_{t_2}) = F_1(x_{t_1})$ and then to the conditional $F_{2|1}(x_{t_2} | x_{t_1}) = \int_{-\infty}^{x_2} \frac{f(x_{t_1}, u)}{f_1(x_{t_1})} du$.

Viewing a stochastic process via the joint distribution of a finite subset of the components is called the *distributional viewpoint*. Historically, however, the notion of a stochastic process emerged in the early 20th century as functions of simple IID processes. This *constructionist viewpoint* amounts to specifying a stochastic process $\{Y_k, k \in \mathbb{N}\}$, by defining it as a function of a simpler stochastic process (often IID or just independent) $\{X_t, t \in \mathbb{T}\}$:

$$Y_k = g(X_{t_1}, X_{t_2}, \ldots, X_{t_k}), \ k \in \mathbb{N}. \tag{8.9}$$

This means that we can think of a lot of stochastic processes as systems built using simpler building blocks. The probabilistic structure of the constructed process $\{Y_k, k \in \mathbb{N}\}$ is determined from that of the simpler process $\{X_t, t \in \mathbb{T}\}$ via the mapping (8.9).

Examples

(i)   Consider the following function:

$$Y_k = X_1 \cos \omega k + X_2 \sin \omega k, \ X_i \sim \text{NIID}(0, \sigma^2), \ i = 1, 2, k \in \mathbb{N}.$$

This defines a stochastic process $\{Y_k, k \in \mathbb{N}\}$.

(ii) A very important mapping which plays a crucial role for the constructionist viewpoint is the mappings defining the partial sums of a process $\{X_k, k \in \mathbb{N}\}$:

$$Y_k = \sum_{i=1}^{k} X_i, \ k \in \mathbb{N}.$$

The stochastic process $\{Y_k, k \in \mathbb{N}\}$ has played an important role in the development of the notion of a stochastic process as argued below.

It must be emphasized, however, that even in the context of the constructionist approach the best way to understand the structure of a stochastic process is to derive the joint distribution of the constructed processes.

Returning to the joint distribution of a finite subset of elements of a stochastic process, as the most general description of a stochastic process, we note that for modeling purposes we need to tame the process by imposing some probabilistic structure on it. The reason is that as it stands (without any restrictions) the joint distribution does not yield operational models. Beginning with a general stochastic process $\{X_t, t \in \mathbb{T}\}$ we proceed to tame it by imposing certain distribution, heterogeneity, and dependence restrictions. These restrictions enable us to deal with both the problems of dimensionality and overparameterization raised in chapters 6–7.

In an attempt to explore some of the concepts concerning restrictions of dependence and heterogeneity, we provide a brief historical perspective for some of the earlier attempts to come to grips with the notion of a stochastic process.

8.3   Stochastic processes: a preliminary view

The mathematical concept of a stochastic process as given above was formulated in the early 1930s. Before that time the notion of a stochastic process existed only in the form of a model for specific stochastic phenomena. These models of stochastic phenomena were almost exclusively in physics. The notable exception to this is the attempt by Bachelier

(1900) to put forward a model for the behavior of prices in the Paris stock market. From the probabilistic viewpoint the concepts one needs to define a stochastic process were not developed until the 1920s. Indeed, from the time of Cardano (1501–1576), when the notion of independence between two events was first encountered and then formalized by de Moivre in the 1730s, until the late 19th century, dependence was viewed as a nuisance and interpreted negatively as non-independence. Beyond the well-charted land of independence there is situated an unexplored territory known as non-independence/heterogeneity. We begin with a short account of the early attempts to formulate a model for the physical phenomenon known as Brownian motion.

8.3.1 Brownian motion and the foundations of probability

The Brownian motion process was coined after the botanist Robert Brown (1773–1858) who noted the erratic movement of a particle of pollen suspended in fluid, as far back as 1827. It was erroneously believed at the time that the erratic behavior was the result of live molecules. It turned out that this movement was the result of the bombardment of the particle by millions of fluid molecules caused by thermal diffusion. The effect of the particle colliding with any one of the molecules is negligible but the cumulative effect of millions of such collisions produces the observable erratic behavior which exhibits certain chance regularity patterns.

The first systematic attempt to model the observable chance regularity patterns of the particles' erratic behavior was made by Einstein in 1905 using a stochastic differential equation of the form:

$$\frac{\partial f(x,t)}{\partial t} = \delta \left(\frac{\partial^2 f(x,t)}{\partial x^2} \right),$$

where $\delta := \lim_{\Delta t \to 0} \left(\frac{(\Delta x)^2}{2\Delta t} \right)$, is the coefficient of *diffusion* and $f(x,t)dx$ is the probability that $X(t)$ lies in the interval $(x, x + dx)$. Solving this differential equation subject to the initial condition $X(0) = 0$, it can be shown that the particle displacement distribution (after sufficiently long time t) takes the form:

$$f(x,t) = \frac{n}{\sqrt{4\pi\delta t}} \exp \left\{ -\frac{x^2}{4\delta t} \right\}.$$

This is the Normal density with moments:

$$E(X(t)) = 0, \ Var(X(t)) = 2\delta t.$$

Intuitively, this can be explained by the fact that the net displacement of the particle $X(\tau)$ during any time interval $(t, t + \tau)$ will be the sum of numerous small (largely independent) contributions of individual molecule impacts. The Central Limit Theorem (see chapter 9) suggests that under such conditions the erratic displacement of the particle can be approximated by a Normally distributed random variable $X(\tau)$.

The Brownian motion as a stochastic process can be viewed as the integral of an NIID process:

$$X(t) = \int_0^t Z(u)du, \ Z(t) \sim \mathsf{NIID}(0,1), \ t \in (0,\infty). \tag{8.10}$$

The first attempt to formulate this process as a model for the changes of stock exchange rates was made by Bachelier (1900). Unfortunately, his thesis was not appreciated by mathematicians such as Poincare (one of his two examiners) and his results, reported in his book *The Calculus of Probability* (published in 1912), went unnoticed until the early 1930s when Kolmogorov (1931) referred to them in unflattering terms for their mathematical rigor. Mathematical rigor aside Bachelier should be credited with the first formulation of the stochastic process known today as Brownian motion. It is interesting to note that Bachelier understood the problem of modeling much better than some of the mathematicians in the 1920s. He went as far as recognizing the necessity of dependence/heterogeneity restrictions and introducing what came to be known afterwards as Markov dependence and Markov homogeneity (see Von Plato (1994)). The first rigorous mathematical formulation of the Brownian motion stochastic process was given by Wiener in 1920s and elaborated further by Levy in the 1930s and 1940s.

The Brownian motion is by far the most important continuous index stochastic process whose study initially was based on its sample paths. However, the paths followed by the irregular movement of particles were found to be continuous but nowhere differentiable. That was a shock to the scientific community because that meant that particles travel with infinite speeds! Einstein's theory was confirmed in 1916 by Pierre Perrin who received the Nobel prize in 1926 for his efforts. The ball was squarely in the court of the probabilists who did not have a consistent theory of probability to cover Einstein's model. The classical theory of probability based on the model of a lottery was seriously inadequate for such a purpose. By the late 1920s Wiener proved the existence of probabilities for Einstein's model but a consistent theory of probability which covered this model had to wait until 1933 when Kolmogorov published his classic book on the foundations of probability theory (1933a).

Kolmogorov's extension theorem, roughly speaking, suggests that phenomena which exhibit chance regularity can be modeled within the mathematical framework demarcated by the probability space $(S, \Im, \mathbb{P}(.))$, endowed with the mathematical structure given in chapter 2, unless they contain inconsistencies of the form stated in the theorem. Kolmogorov's foundation became an instant success because it cleared up all the mess created with the study of Brownian motion and freed the subject from the straitjacket forced upon it by the lottery model of probability.

8.3.2   Partial sums and associated stochastic processes

A number of important stochastic processes, such as Markov, random walk, independent increments, and martingales and their associated dependence and heterogeneity restrictions, can be viewed in the context of the constructionist approach as partial sums of independent random variables. It is only natural that the first attempts to extend the IID stochastic processes $\{Z_t\}_{t \in \mathbb{T}}$ would be associated with simple functions of such processes such as the sum. Indeed, the Brownian motion process as defined by (8.10) is the integral (summation over a continuum) of a NIID process.

Consider a sequence of IID random variables $\{Z_t\}_{t\in\mathbb{T}}$ which for $0 < t_1 < \cdots < t_k < \cdots < \infty$, $t_k \in \mathbb{T}$, $k = 1,2, \ldots$, is partially summed to create a derived process $\{S_k\}_{k=1}^{\infty}$:

$$S_k = \sum_{i=1}^{k} Z_{t_i}, \ k = 1,2,3,\ldots \tag{8.11}$$

The first to venture into the uncharted territory of non-IID stochastic processes from the probabilistic viewpoint was Markov in 1908 who noticed that the derived process $\{S_k\}_{k=1}^{\infty}$ is no longer IID; it has both dependence and heterogeneity. To see this let us simplify the problem by considering the first two moments (assuming they exist) of the IID sequence:

(i) $E(Z_{t_k}) = \mu$, $k = 1,2,3, \ldots$,

(ii) $Var(Z_{t_k}) = \sigma^2$, $k = 1,2,3, \ldots$

Using the linearity of the expectation (see chapter 3) we can deduce that:

(a) $E(S_k) = k\mu$, $k = 1,2,3, \ldots$,

(b) $Var(S_k) = k\sigma^2$, $k = 1,2,3, \ldots$,

(c) $Cov(S_k, S_m) = \sigma^2 \min(k,m)$, $k,m = 1,2,3,\ldots$ \hfill (8.12)

The results (a) and (b) are trivial to derive but (c) can be demonstrated as follows:

$$Cov(S_k, S_m) = E\{(S_k - k\mu)(S_m - m\mu)\} = E\left\{\left(\sum_{i=1}^{k}(Z_{t_i} - \mu)\right)\left(\sum_{j=1}^{m}(Z_{t_j} - \mu)\right)\right\} =$$

$$= \sum_{i=1}^{k}\sum_{j=1}^{m} E[(Z_{t_i} - \mu)(Z_{t_j} - \mu)] = \sum_{i=1}^{\min(k,m)} E(Z_{t_i} - \mu)^2 = \sigma^2 \min(k,m),$$

since $Cov(Z_{t_i}, Z_{t_j}) = 0$, $i \neq j$. The sequence of the partial sums $\{S_k\}_{k=1}^{\infty}$ was later called a **random walk** process and provided the impetus for numerous developments in stochastic processes.

CAUTION. The reader is reminded again that the above structure is only indicative of the more general dependence structure of partial sums because we concentrated exclusively on the first two moments, which in general might not even exist!

Markov was working in the context of a discrete state space/discrete index set framework and concentrated mostly on the dependence structure of such processes. In particular, he realized two things:

(i)   all the elements of the process $\{S_k\}_{k=1}^{\infty}$ are mutually dependent irrespective of the distance between them, but

(ii)   the dependence becomes easier to model when viewed via the *conditional distribution*.

What is so special about this process?

The conditional distribution of S_k given its past $(S_{k-1}, S_{k-2}, \ldots, S_1)$ depends only on the most recent past, i.e.

$$f_k(s_k | s_{k-1}, \ldots, s_1; \psi_k) = f_k(s_k | s_{k-1}; \varphi_k), \text{ for all } \mathbf{s}_{(k)} \in \mathbf{R}^k, \ k = 2,3,\ldots \tag{8.13}$$

That is, the dependence structure between S_k and its past $(S_{k-1}, \ldots, S_1)$ is fully captured by its conditional distribution given its most recent past S_{k-1}; we call it *Markov dependence*. Processes which satisfy this dependence restriction are called *Markov processes*. Markov's result was formalized in its full generality by Kolmogorov (1928b,1931); see section 7.

It is very important to emphasize that Markovness does not involve any heterogeneity restrictions. An obvious way to deal with the problem of *heterogeneity* in this context is to assume homogeneity of the conditional distributions, i.e.

$$f_k(x_{t_k}|x_{t_{k-1}};\varphi_k)=f(x_{t_k}|x_{t_{k-1}};\varphi), \; k=2,3, \ldots, n,$$

which we could call *Markov homogeneity*. NOTE that this involves only the conditional densities; there is no homogeneity assumption for the marginal density $f_1(x_{t_1};\psi_1)$ which can still be a source of heterogeneity.

Another important stochastic process that arises by partially summing independent random variables is the random walk process.

The stochastic process $\{S_k\}_{k=1}^{\infty}$ is said to be a *random walk* if it can specified as the *partial sum* of IID random variables $\{Z_t\}_{t \in \mathbb{T}}$, i.e., for $0<t_1<t_2<t_3<\cdots<t_n<\cdots<\infty$, $t_k \in \mathbb{T}, k=1,2, \ldots$, i.e.:

$$S_k = \sum_{i=1}^{k} Z_{t_i}, \text{ where } Z_{t_i} \sim \text{IID}(.), i=1,2, \ldots, k=1,2,3,\ldots \qquad (8.14)$$

NOTE that this notation enables us to define the partial sum process (a discrete index process) in terms of an IID process $\{Z_{t_k}\}_{k=1}^{\infty}$ which can be either a discrete or continuous index process. For a continuous partial sum process we need to replace the summation with an integral as in (8.10).

In terms of our taxonomy of probabilistic assumptions, both a Markov and a random walk process are defined without any distribution assumptions and thus one should be careful when discussing their dependence and heterogeneity structure in terms of moments. The tendency to concentrate on the first two moments of the process can be very misleading because:

(a)   they might not exist ($Z_i \sim \text{Cauchy}(0,1)$, $i=1,2, \ldots$),
(b)   they capture only limited forms of dependence/heterogeneity.

In a certain sense the notion of a random walk process is an empty box which can be filled with numerous special cases by imposing some additional probabilistic structure. By choosing the distribution to be discrete (e.g., Poisson) or continuous (e.g., Normal) we can define several different kinds of stochastic processes which, nevertheless, share a certain common structure. It is instructive to discuss briefly this common structure.

The probabilistic structure imposed on the generic notion of a random walk is via its definition as a sequence of partial sums of IID random variables. The probabilistic structure of the IID process $\{Z_k\}_{k=1}^{\infty}$ (we use the discrete index notation for convenience) is transformed via the partial sums to determine indirectly the probabilistic structure of the random walk process $\{S_k\}_{k=1}^{\infty}$. Let us consider the problem of determining the probabilistic structure of $\{S_k\}_{k=1}^{\infty}$ from first principles.

First, let us consider the dependence structure of a random walk process. From (8.14) we can deduce that the partial sum process can be written in the form:

$$S_k = S_{k-1} + Z_k, \ k = 1, 2, 3, \dots, \text{ with } S_0 = 0. \tag{8.15}$$

As we can see, the random walk process has a Markov dependence structure because:

$$f(s_k | s_{k-1}, s_{k-2}, \dots, s_1) = f(s_k | s_{k-1}), \ k = 2, 3, \dots$$

It is important to note that the notion of a Markov process is considerably more general than that of a random walk. In the case of the latter the Markovness is induced by the transformation of the partial sums. The Markov dependence, however, does not depend on the partial sum transformation as exemplified by the following example.

Example
Let $\{Z_k\}_{k=1}^{\infty}$ be an IID process with zero mean $(E(Z_k) = 0, \ k = 1, 2, ..)$. Then the sequence defined by the recursion:

$$Y_k = h(Y_{k-1}) + Z_k, \ k = 2, 3, \dots,$$

for any well-behaved (Borel) function $h(.)$ is a Markov process.

This demonstrates most clearly that the Markov dependence structure does not depend on the linearity of the transformation but on its recursiveness.

Returning to the dependence structure of a random walk process we conclude that its form is restricted to that of Markov dependence. In view of the above discussion it should come as no surprise to discover that the heterogeneity structure of a random walk process is also of a special type. This also stems from the fact that, as shown above, the process $\{S_k\}_{k=1}^{\infty}$ has increments $\{S_k - S_{k-1}\}_{k=1}^{\infty}$ which are IID random variables. Hence, the joint distribution takes the form:

$$f(s_1, s_2, \dots, s_n; \boldsymbol{\phi}) = f_1(s_1; \boldsymbol{\theta}_1) \prod_{k=2}^{n} f_k(s_k - s_{k-1}; \boldsymbol{\theta}_k) = f_1(s_1; \boldsymbol{\theta}_1) \prod_{k=2}^{n} f(s_k - s_{k-1}; \boldsymbol{\theta}), \ \mathbf{s} \in \mathbb{R}^n. \tag{8.16}$$

where the first equality follows from the fact that the increments process $\{S_k - S_{k-1}\}_{k=1}^{\infty}$ is independent and the second from the ID assumption for the same process. This suggests that the heterogeneity structure of the random walk process $\{S_k\}_{k=1}^{\infty}$ will have a component which is common to all subsets of the process and a component which depends on the distance from the initial condition $S_0 = 0$; what we call *separable heterogeneity*.

This is best exemplified using the first two moments (assuming they exist!) derived above. Looking at (8.12) we can see that the first two moments are separable in the sense that they have an ID component (the corresponding moment of the IID process) and a heterogeneous component which is a function of the index of the random variables involved. A more general formulation of this type of heterogeneity, known as *second-order separable heterogeneity*, takes the form:

(a) $E(X_k) := \mu_k = h(k) \cdot \mu$, $k = 1, 2, \ldots$,

(b) $Cov(X_k, X_m) := v_{k,m} = q(k,m) \cdot \sigma^2$, $k, m = 1, 2, \ldots$ (8.17)

NOTE that in the case of a random walk process $\{S_k\}_{k=1}^{\infty}$:

$$h(k) = k, \; q(k,m) = \min(k,m).$$

Such forms of heterogeneity give rise to operational models in a number of interesting cases encountered in practice. This should be contrasted with arbitrary heterogeneity which means that the moments are functions of the index with the type of functional dependence unspecified (the first equality in (a) and (b)).

Historically, the notion of a Markov process was introduced in the early 1900s and by the early 1920s (see Kolmogorov (1928a, b)) several other forms of stochastic processes, often motivated by the partial sum formulation, made their appearance. We have already encountered the IID increments process associated with a random walk process. A natural extension of this is to relax the ID assumption and define a process $\{X_t\}_{t\in\mathbb{T}}$ which has *independent increments* for all $0 < t_0 < t_1 < t_2 < \cdots < t_n < \infty$, the increments $\{X_{t_k} - X_{t_{k-1}}\}_{k=1}^{n}$ are independent:

$$f(x_{t_1}, x_{t_2}, \ldots, x_{t_n}; \boldsymbol{\phi}) = f_1(x_{t_1}; \boldsymbol{\theta}_1) \prod_{k=2}^{n} f_k(x_{t_k} - x_{t_{k-1}}; \boldsymbol{\theta}_k), \; \mathbf{x} \in \mathbb{R}^n. \quad (8.18)$$

In terms of its dependence structure, we know from the above discussion that an independent increments process $\{X_t\}_{t\in\mathbb{T}}$ is Markov dependent:

$$f_k(x_{t_k} | x_{t_{k-1}}; \boldsymbol{\varphi}_k) = f_k(x_{t_k} - x_{t_{k-1}}; \boldsymbol{\theta}_k), \; k = 2, 3, \ldots \quad (8.19)$$

What an independent increments sequence has in addition, however, is a sort of *linearity* built into the structure of the sequence of random variables $\{X_t\}_{t\in\mathbb{T}}$, when taking the difference between adjacent random variables. This can be seen by defining the independent sequence $\{Y_{tk}\}_{k=1}^{\infty}$, where:

$$Y_{t_1} := X_{t_1}, \; Y_{t_k} := X_{t_k} - X_{t_{k-1}}, \; k = 2, 3, \ldots,$$

and observing that:

$$X_{t_k} = \sum_{i=1}^{k} Y_{t_i}, \; k = 1, 2, 3, \ldots, n.$$

From this we can deduce that X_{t_k} is *linearly* related to the previous increments:

$$X_{t_k} = X_{t_1} + \sum_{i=2}^{k} (X_{t_i} - X_{t_{i-1}}).$$

This partial sum linearity restricts the joint distribution $f(x_{t_1}, x_{t_2}, \ldots, x_{t_n}; \boldsymbol{\phi})$ in so far as the distribution of $X_{t_3} - X_{t_1}$ must be the same as the distribution of the sum $(X_{t_3} - X_{t_2}) + (X_{t_2} - X_{t_1})$. Conversely, if $\{Y_{t_k}\}_{k=1}^{\infty}$ is an Independent process, then for some arbitrary random variable X_{t_1}, the process $\{X_{t_k}\}_{k=1}^{\infty}$ defined by:

$$X_{t_n} - X_{t_1} = \sum_{i=1}^{n} Y_{t_i}, \; n \geq 1,$$

is a stochastic process with independent increments.

Returning to (8.18) we observe that the definition of a sequence with independent increments raises a problem of *homogeneity* beyond the Identical Distribution assumption, in so far as the definition involves the marginal as well as the distributions of the differences $f_k(x_{t_k} - x_{t_{k-1}}; \theta_k)$, $k = 2,3\ldots$ One obvious solution is to impose the ID assumption on the marginal distributions of both sequences $\{X_{t_k}\}_{k=1}^{\infty}$ and $\{X_{t_k} - X_{t_{k-1}}\}_{k=1}^{\infty}$:

(i) $f_k(x_{t_k}; \psi_k) = f(x_{t_k}; \psi)$, $k = 1,3, \ldots$,

(ii) $f_k(x_{t_k} - x_{t_{k-1}}; \theta_k) = f(x_{t_k} - x_{t_{k-1}}; \theta)$, $k = 2,3, \ldots$,

The homogeneity assumption (ii) might be called *Identically Distributed increments*. NOTE that in view of the relationship (8.19), this is equivalent to Markov homogeneity.

The homogeneity conditions introduced above led to the important notion of *Stationarity*. Khinchine (1934) noticed that the homogeneity condition (ii) amounted to the restriction that the joint distribution of two adjacent random variables depends only on the *difference* of the dates not the actual dates, i.e. for any two dates: $0 < t_1 < t_2 < \infty$:

$$f_{t_1, t_2}(x_{t_1}, x_{t_2}; \theta) = f_{t_2 - t_1}(x_{t_1}, x_{t_2}; \theta).$$

Continuing along the same line, this can be extended to the n-variable case $\{X_{t_1}, X_{t_2}, \ldots, X_{t_n}\}$, $0 < t_1 < t_2 < \cdots < t_n < \infty$, such that the joint density depends only on the $(n-1)$ differences $\{t_2 - t_1, t_3 - t_1, t_4 - t_1, \ldots, t_n - t_1\}$, i.e.

(iii) $f_{t_1, t_2, \ldots, t_n}(x_{t_1}, x_{t_2}, \ldots, x_{t_n}; \theta) = f_{t_2 - t_1, t_3 - t_1, t_4 - t_1, \ldots, t_n - t_1}(x_{t_1}, x_{t_2}, \ldots, x_{t_n}; \theta).$

Khinchine showed that these homogeneity conditions amounted to the restriction that the joint distribution of $\{X_{t_1}, X_{t_2}, \ldots, X_{t_n}\}$ is invariant to a shift τ of the dates, i.e.

$$f_{t_1, t_2, \ldots, t_n}(x_{t_1}, x_{t_2}, \ldots, x_{t_n}; \theta) = f_{t_1 + \tau, \ldots, t_n + \tau}(x_{t_1 + \tau}, x_{t_2 + \tau}, \ldots, x_{t_n + \tau}; \theta). \tag{8.20}$$

This is known as the *strict stationarity* condition which became the dominant homogeneity restriction in the development of such sequences of random variables.

Another important stochastic process motivated by the partial sums formulation is the *martingale process*. The importance of this process stems from the fact that it allows for sufficient dependence and heterogeneity for the partial sums process to behave asymptotically like a simple IID process. The notion of a martingale process was introduced in the late 1930s but its importance was not fully appreciated until the 1950s. The notion of a martingale process, in contrast to the Markov process, concentrates mostly on the first conditional moment instead of the distribution itself.

Consider the partial sums stochastic process $\{S_k\}_{k=1}^{\infty}$ where:

$$S_k = \sum_{i=1}^{k} Z_i, \text{ where } Z_i \sim D(0,.), \ i = 1,2, \ldots, k = 1,2,3, \ldots \tag{8.21}$$

are independent but non-ID distributed random variables with zero means $(E(Z_k) = 0,$ $k = 1,2, \ldots, n)$. As shown above the partial sums process can be written in the form:

$$S_k = S_{k-1} + Z_k, \ S_0 = 0, \ k = 1,2,3, \ldots$$

We can show that the conditional expectation of S_k given its past takes the form:

$$E(S_k | S_{k-1}, S_{k-2}, \ldots, S_1) = E((S_{k-1} + Z_k) | S_{k-1}, S_{k-2}, \ldots, S_1) = S_{k-1}, \ k = 2,3, \ldots, n. \tag{8.22}$$

This follows from the property CE4 "taking what is known out" (see chapter 7) and the fact that $\sigma(S_{k-1}, S_{k-2}, \ldots, S_1) = \sigma(Z_{k-1}, Z_{k-2}, \ldots, Z_1)$, i.e., the two event spaces coincide in view of the one-to-one mapping between them, and thus:

$$E(Z_k | S_{k-1}, S_{k-2}, \ldots, S_1) = E(Z_k | Z_{k-1}, Z_{k-2}, \ldots, Z_1) = E(Z_k) = 0.$$

The essential element of this argument is not the independence of the Z_ks but the combination of the conditional and unconditional zero means:

(a) $E(Z_k) = 0, k = 1, 2, \ldots$,

(b) $E(Z_k | Z_{k-1}, Z_{k-2}, \ldots, Z_1) = 0, k = 2, 3, \ldots$

neither of which requires independence but the existence of the first moment. In section 8 we will call the process $\{Z_k\}_{k=1}^{\infty}$ satisfying (a)–(b) a *martingale difference process*.

Collecting the above elements together, we say that the stochastic process $\{Y_k\}_{k=1}^{\infty}$ is a *martingale* if

(i) $E(|Y_k|) < \infty, k = 1, 2, \ldots, k = 1, 2, \ldots$,

(ii) $E(Y_k | \sigma(Y_{k-1}, Y_{k-2}, \ldots, Y_1)) = Y_{k-1}, k = 2, 3, \ldots, n.$ (8.23)

A martingale process is specified exclusively in terms of the first conditional moment on which it also implicitly imposes a heterogeneity restriction. This is because the martingale dependence condition (8.23) implies that if we use property CE1 "the law of iterated expectation" we get:

$$E[E(Y_k | \sigma(Y_{k-1}, Y_{k-2}, \ldots, Y_1))] = E(Y_k) = E(Y_{k-1}), k = 2, 3, \ldots, n,$$

which holds only in the case where the mean of the process is constant. This is a homogeneity restriction which is defined in terms of the first moment and called **first-order (or mean) homogeneity**.

In figure 8.5 we summarize the relationship between the stochastic processes discussed above for reference purposes. As we can see, the random walk and the independent increments processes are subsets of the Markov process category. On the other hand, martingale processes are not a proper subset of the Markov process category because the former impose the additional restriction of a bounded first moment which none of the other categories requires.

8.3.3 Gaussian process

As mentioned many times so far, the Normal (Gaussian) is by far the most important distribution in probability theory and statistical inference. When we apply the above notions of dependence (Markov, independent increments, martingale) to a Normal (Gaussian) stochastic process $\{X_k\}_{k=1}^{\infty}$ we find ourselves looking at bivariate Normal distributions of the form (see chapter 4):

$$f(x_1, x_2; \boldsymbol{\theta}_{12}) = \frac{(1-\rho^2)^{-\frac{1}{2}}}{2\pi\sqrt{\sigma_{11}\sigma_{22}}} \exp\left\{ -\frac{(1-\rho^2)^{-1}}{2} \left(\left(\frac{x_1-\mu_1}{\sqrt{\sigma_{11}}}\right)^2 - 2\rho\left(\frac{x_1-\mu_1}{\sqrt{\sigma_{11}}}\right)\left(\frac{x_2-\mu_2}{\sqrt{\sigma_{22}}}\right) + \left(\frac{x_2-\mu_2}{\sqrt{\sigma_{22}}}\right)^2 \right) \right\}$$ (8.24)

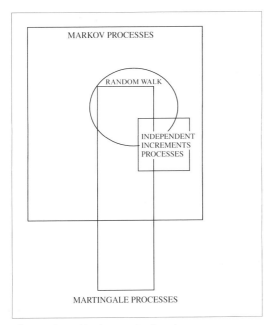

MARKOV PROCESSES

RANDOM WALK

INDEPENDENT
INCREMENTS
PROCESSES

MARTINGALE PROCESSES

Figure 8.5 Markov and related processes

where $\boldsymbol{\theta}_{12}:=(\mu_1,\mu_2,\sigma_{11},\sigma_{22},\rho)\in\mathbb{R}^2\times\mathbb{R}^2_+\times[-1,1],(x_1,x_2)\in\mathbb{R}^2$. This is because these forms of dependence can be captured by adjacent random variables. As argued in chapter 6, under Normality the only form of dependence possible is first-order dependence captured by the *correlation coefficient* ρ.

The above reasoning in relation to the Normal distribution gave rise to a form of dependence specified in terms of the first two moments of any two random variables X_k and X_m $(m>k)$; known as *linear dependence* defined by (see chapter 6):

$$\rho_{k,m}:= Corr(X_k,X_m)\neq 0. \tag{8.25}$$

As with the other notions of dependence, the notion of correlated random variables raises the problem of the homogeneity associated with it. In direct analogy to strict stationarity (8.20) we can specify the following conditions in terms of the first two moments:

(i) $E(X_k)= E(X_{k+\tau})$, for all $k,\tau= 1,2,\ldots$
(ii) $E(X_kX_m)= E(X_{k+\tau}X_{m+\tau})$, for all $k,m,\tau= 1,2,\ldots$

These conditions ensure that the correlation (8.25) will be free of the dates. A more transparent but equivalent way of expressing this is that the first two moments depend neither on k nor on m but on the difference $|m-k|$:

(a) $E(X_k)= \mu$, for all $k= 1,2,\ldots,$

(b) $E[X_k- E(X_k)]^2= \sigma^2$, for all $k= 1,2,\ldots,$

(c) $E\{[X_k - E(X_k)][X_m - E(X_m)]\} = h(|m - k|),\ k,m = 1,2,\dots$

The conditions (a)–(c) define what is known as **weak (or second-order) stationarity**.

8.4   Dependence restrictions

Having introduced a number of important notions using the historical development of stochastic processes, we proceed to define a number of dependence and heterogeneity restrictions. We limit ourselves to very few examples because the rest of this chapter will be devoted to the usefulness of the notions introduced in this section in the context of different stochastic processes. For notational convenience we use the discrete index notation but with minor modifications the following concepts can be written in the more general notation $0 < t_1 < t_2 < \cdots < t_n < \infty$.

8.4.1   Distribution-based notions

Historically, the earliest dependence restriction adopted was the extreme case of no dependence.

Independence   The stochastic process $\{Y_t,\ t \in \mathbb{T}\}$ is said to be *independent* if:

$$f(y_1, y_2, \dots, y_T; \phi) = \prod_{i=1}^{T} f_i(y_i; \psi_i),\ \text{for all } \mathbf{y} := (y_1, \dots, y_T) \in \mathcal{R}_Y.$$

This concept has been discussed extensively in the previous chapters. We proceed to define less restrictive assumptions relating to dependence.

Markov dependence   The stochastic process $\{Y_t,\ t \in \mathbb{T}\}$ is said to be *Markov dependent* if:

$$f_k(y_k | y_{k-1}, y_{k-2}, \dots, y_1; \varphi_k) = f_k(y_k | y_{k-1}; \psi_k),\ k = 2,3,\dots$$

This notion of dependence can be easily extended to higher-orders as follows.

Markov dependence of order m   The stochastic process $\{Y_t,\ t \in \mathbb{T}\}$ is said to be *Markov dependent of order m* if for $m \geq 1$:

$$f_k(y_k | y_{k-1}, y_{k-2}, \dots, y_1; \varphi_k) = f_k(y_k | y_{k-1}, \dots y_{k-m}; \psi_k),\ k = m+1, m+2, \dots.$$

The intuition behind this form of dependence is that the conditional information relevant for predicting y_n is only the recent past which goes back only m periods.

Martingale difference dependence   The stochastic process $\{Y_t,\ t \in \mathbb{T}\}$ is said to be *martingale difference dependent* if $E(Y_k) = 0,\ k = 1,2,\dots$, and:

$$E(Y_k | \sigma(Y_{k-1}, Y_{k-2}, \dots, Y_1)) = 0,\ k = 2,3,\dots$$

That is, the process is first-order conditionally independent of its past.

m-dependence   The stochastic process $\{Y_t,\ t \in \mathbb{T}\}$ is said to be *m-dependent* if for $\tau \geq m > 0$:

$$f(y_1, \ldots, y_n, y_{n+\tau}, y_{n+\tau+1}, \ldots, y_{2n+\tau}; \boldsymbol{\phi}_{n,\tau}) = f(y_1, \ldots, y_n; \boldsymbol{\psi}_n) \cdot f(y_{n+\tau}, \ldots, y_{2n+\tau}; \boldsymbol{\psi}_{n,\tau}).$$

The intuition behind this form of dependence is that when the elements of the stochastic process are m or more periods apart they are independent. This form of dependence arises naturally when the modeler considers an IID, mean zero sequence $\{X_t\}_{t=1}^{\infty}$ and defines:

$$Y_k = X_k \cdot X_{k+m}, \quad k = 1,2,\ldots$$

The stochastic process $\{Y_t\}_{k=1}^{\infty}$ is an m-dependent process.

Asymptotic independence The stochastic process $\{Y_t, t \in \mathbb{T}\}$ is said to be *asymptotically independent* if as $\tau \to \infty$:

$$f(y_{n+\tau}|y_n, y_{n-1}, \ldots, y_1; \boldsymbol{\phi}_{n,\tau}) \approx f(y_{n+\tau}; \boldsymbol{\psi}_{n+\tau}).$$

The intuition behind this form of dependence is that the elements of the stochastic process become independent as the distance between them increases to infinity.

8.4.2 Correlation-based notions

Historically, the earliest dependence restriction based on the first two moments was the extreme case of non-correlation.

Non-correlation The stochastic process $\{Y_t, t \in \mathbb{T}\}$ is said to be *uncorrelated* if $E(|Y_t^2|) < \infty$ for all $t \in \mathbb{T}$, and:

$$Corr(Y_t, Y_k) = 0, \text{ for } t \neq k, \ t,k \in \mathbb{T}.$$

This notion of no linear dependence can be extended to non-correlation m or more periods apart.

mth order non-correlation The stochastic process $\{Y_t, t \in \mathbb{T}\}$ is said to be *mth order uncorrelated* if $E(|Y_t^2|) < \infty$ for all $t \in \mathbb{T}$ and:

$$Corr(Y_t, Y_k) = \begin{cases} c_{tk} \neq 0, & \text{for } |t-k| \leq m > 0, \\ 0, & \text{for } |t-k| > m > 0, \end{cases} \quad t,k = 1,2,\ldots.$$

The intuition behind this form of dependence is that when the elements of the stochastic process are m or more periods apart they are uncorrelated.

Asymptotic non-correlation The stochastic process $\{Y_t, t \in \mathbb{T}\}$ is said to be *asymptotically uncorrelated* if $E(|Y_t^2|) < \infty$ for all $t \in \mathbb{T}$ and:

$$Corr(Y_t, Y_{t-\tau}) \to 0, \text{ as } \tau \to \infty.$$

The intuition behind this form of dependence is that the elements of the stochastic process become uncorrelated as the distance between them increases to infinity.

Asymptotic average non-correlation The stochastic process $\{Y_t, \ t \in \mathbb{T}\}$ is said to be *weakly asymptotically uncorrelated* if $E(|Y_t^2|) < \infty$ for all $t \in \mathbb{T}$ and:

$$\lim_{T \to \infty} \frac{1}{T} \sum_{i=1}^{T} Corr(Y_t, Y_{t-\tau}) = 0, \text{ for any } \tau \neq 0. \tag{8.26}$$

This is a weaker form of asymptotic non-correlation because it requires not the individual correlations but their average to go to zero as T goes to infinity. This condition is of interest because it is sufficient for ergodicity (see below).

8.4.3   Mixing conditions

Mixing conditions have recently replaced ergodicity (see below) as the most widely used restrictions of asymptotic independence for statistical inference purposes. These mixing conditions amount to certain forms of asymptotic independence.

In chapter 6 we introduced a number of measures of dependence based on σ-fields which can be adapted to provide measures of temporal dependence. Let $(S, \Im, \mathbb{P}(.))$ be the relevant probability space and consider two *event subspaces* $\mathcal{A}$ and $\mathcal{B}$ of $\Im$. As shown in chapter 6, several measures of *dependence* between these sub-σ-fields can be defined:

(1) $\qquad \alpha(\mathcal{A}, \mathcal{B}) = \sup_{A \in \mathcal{A}, B \in \mathcal{B}} |\mathbb{P}(A \cap B) - \mathbb{P}(A) \cdot \mathbb{P}(B)|,$

(2) $\qquad \phi(\mathcal{A}, \mathcal{B}) = \sup_{A \in \mathcal{A}, B \in \mathcal{B}} |\mathbb{P}(A|B) - \mathbb{P}(A)|, \text{ for } \mathbb{P}(B) > 0,$

(3) $\qquad \psi(\mathcal{A}, \mathcal{B}) = \sup_{A \in \mathcal{A}, B \in \mathcal{B}} \frac{|\mathbb{P}(A \cap B) - \mathbb{P}(A) \cdot \mathbb{P}(B)|}{\mathbb{P}(A) \cdot \mathbb{P}(B)}, \text{ for } \mathbb{P}(B) > 0, \mathbb{P}(A) > 0.$

In the present context of a stochastic process we can choose $\mathcal{A}$ and $\mathcal{B}$ to correspond to the future and the past (τ periods apart):

$$\mathcal{A} := \Im_{n+\tau}^{\infty} = \sigma(y_{n+\tau}, y_{n+1+\tau} \dots), \ \mathcal{B} := \Im_{-\infty}^{n} = \sigma(\dots, y_1, y_2, \dots, y_n), \tag{8.27}$$

where $\sigma(\dots, y_1, y_2, \dots, y_n)$ denotes the minimal σ-field generated by $(\dots, y_1, y_2, \dots, y_n)$. Using these measures we can define several notions of **asymptotic independence**, which take the general formulation:

$$\xi\text{-mixing: if } \xi(\tau) \to 0, \text{ as } \tau \to \infty, \text{ for } \xi(\tau) = \sup_n \xi(\Im_{n+\tau}^{\infty}, \Im_{-\infty}^{n}),$$

where ξ stands for any one of:

$$\alpha(\tau) = \sup_n \alpha(\Im_{n+\tau}^{\infty}, \Im_{-\infty}^{n}), \ \phi(\tau) = \sup_n \phi(\Im_{n+\tau}^{\infty}, \Im_{-\infty}^{n}), \ \psi(\tau) = \sup_n \psi(\Im_{n+\tau}^{\infty}, \Im_{-\infty}^{n}),$$

where $\alpha(\tau), \phi(\tau)$ and $\psi(\tau)$ were defined above.

A closely related notion is *asymptotic non-correlation*, defined in a more general way than in the previous subsection via:

$$\rho(\tau) = \sup_{X \in \Im_{n+\tau}^{\infty}, Y \in \Im_{-\infty}^{n}} |Corr(X_{n+\tau}, X_n)|, \text{ if } E(X_t^2) < \infty \text{ for all } t \in \mathbb{T}.$$

It can be shown that all the above measures of dependence are non-negative and satisfy the following inequalities (see Hall and Heyde (1980)):

$$\alpha(\tau)\leq\tfrac{1}{4},\ \phi(\tau)\leq 1,\ \psi(\tau)\leq 1,\ \rho(\tau)\leq 1.$$

Moreover, some of the above mixing conditions are weaker than others:

$$\psi(\tau)\to 0 \Rightarrow \phi(\tau)\to 0 \Rightarrow \rho(\tau)\to 0 \Rightarrow \alpha(\tau)\to 0,\ \text{as}\ \tau\to\infty,$$

assuming that the required second moments exist. This suggests that the weakest form of asymptotic independence (and the most widely used) is that of α-mixing. Another interesting result is that all the above mixing conditions are stronger than ergodicity (see next) in the sense that when we impose stationarity on a stochastic process $\{Y_t,\ t\in\mathbb{T}\}$, then any one of the above mixing conditions implies ergodicity.

Another widely used form of asymptotic independence, which combines the notions of martingale dependence and mixing, is that of a *mixingale* first introduced by McLeish (1975). In an attempt to motivate the notion of a mixingale consider a stochastic process $\{X_t,\ t\in\mathbb{T}\}$ with a bounded second moment $E(|X_t|^2<\infty)$. The variance of a partial sum of the process, without any restrictions, takes the form:

$$Var\left(\tfrac{1}{n}\sum_{k=1}^{n}X_k\right)=\left(\tfrac{1}{n}\right)^2\left[\sum_{k=1}^{n}Var(X_k)+2\sum_{k=1}^{n-1}\sum_{m=1}^{n-k}Cov(X_{k+m},X_k)\right].$$

NOTE: the reason we consider the asymptotic negligibility of the variance of a partial sum will become apparent in the context of limit theorems in chapter 9. The assumption of bounded variance ensures that the first term after the equality is asymptotically negligible. The left-hand side will converge to zero if we impose certain restrictions on the temporal covariances. Consider the instances $1\leq k\leq m<\infty$ and define the σ-field: $\mathfrak{I}_k^m=\sigma(X_k,X_{k+1},\cdots,X_{m-1},X_m)$. Then:

$$Cov(X_{k+m},X_k)=E([X_{k+m}-E(X_{k+m})]\,[X_k-E(X_k)])=$$

$$=E\{E([X_{k+m}-E(X_{k+m})]\,[X_k-E(X_k)])\,|\,\mathfrak{I}_{-\infty}^k\}=$$

$$=E([E(X_{k+m}|\mathfrak{I}_{-\infty}^k)-E(X_{k+m})]\,[X_k-E(X_k)]),$$

where the second equality follows from the property CE2 and the third from the CE4 property of conditional expectations (see chapter 7). Using the Cauchy–Swartz inequality we can deduce that:

$$|Cov(X_{k+m},X_k)|\leq\left(E\{[E(X_{k+m}|\mathfrak{I}_{-\infty}^k)-E(X_{k+m})]^2\}\right)^{\tfrac{1}{2}}[Var(X_k)^{\tfrac{1}{2}}].$$

In view of the fact that the last term is bounded, we concentrate on the other term which we require to converge to zero as $m\to\infty$.

Mixingale The stochastic process $\{X_t,\ t\in\mathbb{T}\}$ with bounded second moment $E(|X_t|^2)<\infty$, is said to be a *mixingale* if there exist constants c_k and ψ_m:

$$\left(E\{[E(X_{k+m}|\mathfrak{I}_{-\infty}^k)-E(X_{k+m})]^2\}\right)^{\tfrac{1}{2}}\leq c_{k+m}\psi_m,$$

such that: $c_{k+m}<\infty,\ \psi_m\to 0,\ \text{as}\ m\to\infty$.

Examples

(i)   Consider the independent process $\{X_t, t \in \mathbb{T}\}$ with bounded second moment $E(|X_t|^2 < \infty)$. Then,

$$E(X_{t+m} | \mathfrak{J}_{-\infty}^t) = E(X_{t+m}) \text{ for } m \geq 1,$$

and thus we may choose $\psi_0 = 1$, $\psi_m = 0$, for $m \geq 1$, $c_t = [Var(X_t)^{\frac{1}{2}}]$.

(ii) Consider the m-dependent process $\{X_t, t \in \mathbb{T}\}$ with bounded second moment $E(|X_t|^2 < \infty)$. Then,

$$E(X_{t+k} | \mathfrak{J}_{-\infty}^t) = E(X_{t+k}) \text{ for } k \geq m,$$

and thus we may choose $\psi_k = 1$, for $k < m$, and $\psi_k = 0$, for $k \geq m$,

$$c_t = \sup_{0 \leq k \leq m} \left(E\{[E(X_{t+k} | \mathfrak{J}_{-\infty}^t) - E(X_{t+k})]^2\} \right)^{\frac{1}{2}}.$$

8.4.4 Ergodicity

Historically, the most important early restriction on the dependence associated with stationary stochastic processes came in the form of *ergodicity*. Intuitively, ergodicity refers to the property of a stationary stochastic process which will enable us to use a single sample path (realization) in order to estimate reliably the moments of the distribution underlying the stochastic process in question (see figure 8.4).

To explain the notion of ergodicity we need to use the notation $X(s,t)$, introduced at the beginning of this chapter, where $s \in S$ (outcomes set), $t \in \mathbb{T}$. If for every well-behaved (Borel) function:

$$h(.): \mathbb{R} \rightarrow \mathbb{R} \text{ such that } E(|h(X_t)|) < \infty,$$

$$\lim_{T \to \infty} \frac{1}{T} \Sigma_{t=1}^T h(X(s,t)) = E(h(X(s,t))) := \int_{x \in \mathbb{R}_X} h(x(t,s)) f(x(s,t)) \, dx(s),$$

the stationary stochastic process $\{X_t, t \in \mathbb{T}\}$ is said to be **ergodic**. That is, if the limit as $T \to \infty$ of the *time averages* of such functions $(\frac{1}{T} \Sigma_{t=1}^T h(X(t)))$ converges to the *distribution averages* $E(h(X(t)))$, then the process is said to be ergodic. It is important to emphasize that the t-average is over a subset of the index set $\mathbb{T}$ but the distribution average is over $s \in S$.

REMARK: the notion of *limit* in this context is not the same as the mathematical limit because $h(X(t))$ are random variables (see chapter 9).

The above definition has two interrelated conditions. The *first* is whether the limit of the time-average exists, i.e., there exists a constant $\bar{h}_x < \infty$ and:

$$\bar{h}_x = \lim_{T \to \infty} \frac{1}{T} \Sigma_{t=1}^T h(X(s,t)).$$

The *second* condition is whether the constant $\bar{h}_x$ coincides with $\xi_h := E(h(X(t)))$. Let us illustrate these conditions in the simplest case possible.

Example

Consider the second-order stationary stochastic process $\{X_t, t \in \mathbb{T}\}$ with moments:

(i) $E(X_t) = \mu, \ t = 1,2,3,\ldots$
(ii) $Cov(X_t, X_{t-\tau}) = c(|\tau|), \ t,\tau = 1,2,3,\ldots$

For the simple function $h(X_t) = X_t$ its distribution average is μ. The question we are interested in is whether $\lim_{T \to \infty} \frac{1}{T} \sum_{t=1}^{T} X_t$ exists, and if it does whether it coincides with μ. Taking convergence in probability (see chapter 9) as our relevant mode of convergence, we can answer yes to both questions if:

$$Var\left(\frac{1}{T} \sum_{t=1}^{T} X_t\right) \xrightarrow[T \to \infty]{} 0.$$

In view of the fact that $Var\left(\frac{1}{T} \sum_{t=1}^{T} X_t\right) = \frac{1}{T^2}\left(\sum_{t=1}^{T} c(0) + 2\sum_{t>s}^{T} c(t-s)\right)$, we know $\frac{1}{T^2}\left(\sum_{t=1}^{T} c(0)\right) \xrightarrow[T \to \infty]{} 0$, but the second term in the above brackets goes to zero only under certain circumstances, such as:

$$c(\tau) \xrightarrow[\tau \to \infty]{} 0, \tag{8.28}$$

i.e., the dependence dies out as the distance between observations increases. We can say that $\{X_t, t \in \mathbb{T}\}$ is *mean-ergodic* if:

$$\lim_{T \to \infty} \frac{1}{T} \sum_{\tau=0}^{T-1} c(\tau) = 0. \tag{8.29}$$

NOTE that condition (8.28) implies (8.29). The latter is the so-called Cesaro sum which ensures that when the average of a sequence of partial sums converges its limit is the same as the original sequence.

The general result for mean ergodicity is as follows. Consider the stochastic process $\{X_t, t \in \mathbb{T}\}$ with moments:

(i) $E(X_t) = \mu, \ t = 1,2,3,\ldots$
(ii) $Cov(X_t, X_s) \le c_0, \ t,s = 1,2,3,\ldots$

Define the covariance between the sample means:

$$m_t = \frac{1}{t} \sum_{k=1}^{t} X_k, \ t = 2,3,\ldots$$

and the last element X_t:

$$v(t) = Cov(m_t, X_t) = \frac{1}{t} \sum_{k=1}^{t} E(X_k X_t).$$

A necessary and sufficient condition for ergodicity in the mean is that (see Parzen (1962)):

$$\lim_{t \to \infty} v(t) = 0,$$

i.e., the covariance between the sample mean and the last element of the process involved weakens as t increases.

This result can help us delineate certain important features of the notion of ergodicity.

First, to be able to talk about convergence to certain quantities such as moments we need to impose at least asymptotic stationarity on the process at the outset. The condition for a bounded covariance amounts to second-order asymptotic stationarity because $Cov(X_t, X_s) \leq c_0$ holds for all $t, s = 1, 2, 3, \dots$ if:

$$\lim_{t \to \infty} Var(X_t) = v_0 \leq c_0.$$

This is because the variance dominates the covariances and we know that a bounded sequence with positive terms converges. *Second*, stationarity and ergodicity, although related as we just stated, are very different concepts. Condition (8.28) which is sufficient for mean ergodicity has nothing to do with stationarity; it is a *dependence restriction*. Let us now return to the general notion of ergodicity.

Although the above definition of ergodicity is defined in terms of arbitrary well-behaved (Borel) functions $h(X(t))$, in practice we are interested in particular functions such as:

(i) $y(t) = \begin{cases} 1, \text{ if } (X(t) \leq x) \\ 0, \text{ if } (X(t) > x) \end{cases}$, (ii) $h_r(X(t)) = X(t)^r, r = 1, 2, \dots$

The random variable $y(t)$ takes values in $\mathbb{R}_Y := \{0, 1\}$ with probabilities $\mathbb{P}(X(t) \leq x)$ and $\mathbb{P}(X(t) > x)$, respectively. Hence:

$$E(y(t)) = \mathbb{P}(X(t) \leq x) := F(x),$$

where $F(x)$ is the cumulative distribution function, leading to the notion of *distribution ergodicity*. On the other hand, the expected value of $X(t)^r$ gives rise to the raw moments of the process. In the same way we can proceed to define other Borel functions whose expectations give rise to joint moments. Examples of such moments are the mean and covariance leading to *mean ergodicity* and *covariance ergodicity* respectively, based on the conditions:

$$\lim_{T \to \infty} \frac{1}{T} \sum_{t=1}^{T} X(t) dt = E(X(t)) := \int_{x \in \mathbb{R}_X} x(t) f(x(t)) dx,$$

$$\lim_{T \to \infty} \frac{1}{T} \sum_{t=1}^{T} X(t) X(t+\tau) dt = E(X(t) X(t+\tau)) := \int_{x \in \mathbb{R}_X} x(t) x(t+\tau) f(x(t)) dx.$$

Distribution ergodicity can be viewed as mean ergodicity for the stochastic process $\{y_t, t \in \mathbb{T}\}$. The latter process is mean ergodic if:

$$\lim_{T \to \infty} \frac{1}{T} \sum_{t=1}^{T} [F(x_1, x_2; \tau) - F(x_1) \cdot F(x_2)] = 0, \tag{8.30}$$

where $F(x_1, x_2; \tau) := \mathbb{P}(X(t+\tau) \leq x_1, X(t) \leq x_2)$. Sufficient condition for (8.28) is:

$$F(x_1, x_2; \tau) \underset{\tau \to \infty}{\longrightarrow} F(x_1) \cdot F(x_2).$$

That is, the dependence weakens as $\tau \to \infty$.

8.5   Homogeneity restrictions

The most restrictive form of homogeneity for an independent process $\{Y_t, t \in \mathbb{T}\}$ is that of *complete homogeneity*: identical distributions.

8.5.1   Identically distributed

An independent stochastic process $\{Y_t, t\in\mathbb{T}\}$ is said to be *Identically Distributed* if:

$$f_t(y_t;\boldsymbol{\theta}_t):=f(y_t;\boldsymbol{\theta}) \text{ for all } t\in\mathbb{T}, \tag{8.31}$$

where equality denotes the same formula as well as the same $\boldsymbol{\theta}$.

8.5.2   Strict stationarity

The stochastic process $\{Y_t, t\in\mathbb{T}\}$ is said to be *strictly stationary* if:

$$f(y_{t_1}, y_{t_2}, \ldots, y_{t_n}; \boldsymbol{\theta}) := f(y_{t_1+\tau}, y_{t_2+\tau}, \ldots, y_{t_n+\tau}; \boldsymbol{\theta}), \text{ for any } \tau, (t_i+\tau)\in\mathbb{T}, \tag{8.32}$$

i.e., the joint distribution remains unchanged if we shift each point 1,2, ..., T by a constant τ.

The main attraction of this notion of homogeneity is the following invariance property.

Lemma If the stochastic process $\{Y_{t_1}, Y_{t_2}, \ldots, Y_{t_n}, \ldots\}$ is strictly stationary, then the transformed sequence $\{X_{t_1}, X_{t_2}, \ldots, X_{t_n}, \ldots\}$, where:

$$X_{t_k}:=g(Y_{t_k}), \ k=1,2,\ldots,$$

and where $g(.)$ is a well-behaved (Borel) function, is also strictly stationary.

In the case where $n=1$, (8.32) implies that:

$$f_t(y_t;\boldsymbol{\theta}_t):=f(y_t;\boldsymbol{\theta}) \text{ for all } t\in\mathbb{T},$$

a condition which coincides with (8.31). That is, strict stationarity implies Identical Distribution (ID) for all the marginal distributions. In this sense we can think of strict stationarity as an extension of the ID homogeneity assumption to the case where there is some dependence. This can be easily seen in the case where $n=2$, where (8.32) implies that:

$$f(y_1, y_2; \boldsymbol{\theta}):=f(y_{1+\tau}, y_{2+\tau}; \boldsymbol{\theta}), \text{ for any } (t+\tau)\in\mathbb{T}, \tag{8.33}$$

which suggests that the unknown parameters $\boldsymbol{\theta}$ cannot depend on the actual dates but only on the difference between the dates, i.e.

$$f(y_t, y_s; \boldsymbol{\theta}(t,s)):=f(y_t, y_s; \boldsymbol{\theta}(|t-s|)), \text{ for all } t,s\in\mathbb{T}. \tag{8.34}$$

Examples

The Normal process as defined above is not stationary because its moments depend on t. However, if we assume that:

(a) $E(X_t)=\mu$, $t=1,2,3,\ldots$

(b) $Cov(X_t, X_s)=c(|t-s|),$ $t,s=1,2,3,\ldots$

then it becomes stationary.

Concepts which involve the distribution function are often difficult to handle in the context of empirical modeling. This has been ascertained many times before and the usual way out has been to introduce similar concepts which involve only certain moments of the distribution. With this in mind let us introduce several notions of stationarity which involve only moments.

8.5.3   First-order stationarity

The stochastic process $\{Y_t, t \in \mathbb{T}\}$ is said to be *first-order stationary* if:

$$E(Y_t) = E(Y_{t+\tau}) = \mu, \text{ for all } (t + \tau) \in \mathbb{T}.$$

Example
Consider the stochastic process $\{Y_t, t \in \mathbb{T}\}$, which is assumed to be a martingale, i.e.:

$$E(Y_t \mid \sigma(Y_{t-1}, Y_{t-2}, \dots, Y_0)) = Y_{t-1}.$$

As shown above, taking another expectation yields:

$$E\{E(Y_t \mid \sigma(Y_{t-1}, Y_{t-2}, \dots, Y_0)) = E(Y_t) = E(Y_{t-1}), \ t = 1,2, \dots,$$

which suggests that the last equality holds if and only if $E(Y_t) = \mu$, for all $t \in \mathbb{T}$, i.e., the martingale process is first-order stationary.

8.5.4   Second-order stationarity

The stochastic process $\{Y_t, t \in \mathbb{T}\}$ is said to be *second-order stationary* if:

(i) $E(Y_t) = E(Y_{t+\tau})$, for any $(t + \tau) \in \mathbb{T}$,

(ii) $E(Y_t Y_s) = E(Y_{t+\tau} Y_{s+\tau})$, for any $(t + \tau) \in \mathbb{T}, (s + \tau) \in \mathbb{T}$

or equivalently:

(a) $E(Y_t) = \mu,$ for any $t \in \mathbb{T}$,

(b) $Cov(Y_t, Y_{t+\tau}) = c(|\tau|)$,   for any $t, t + \tau \in \mathbb{T}$.

Examples
Consider the stochastic process $\{Y_t, t \in \mathbb{T}\}$ defined via:

$$Y_t = X_1 \cos \theta t + X_2 \sin \theta t,$$

where $X_i \sim IID(0, \sigma^2), i = 1,2$. The process $\{Y_t, t \in \mathbb{T}\}$ is *not strictly stationary* because some of the moments higher than the second depend on t:

$$E(Y_t^3) = h_3(t).$$

It is, however, *second-order* stationary since:

$$E(Y_t) = 0, \ Var(Y_t) = \sigma^2, \ Cov(Y_t, Y_s) = \sigma^2 \cos(t - s).$$

Hence, in the case where $X_i \sim \text{NIID}(0,\sigma^2), i=1,2$, the process is also strictly stationary. This follows from the fact that the odd moments of the Normal distribution are zero and the even ones are stationary functions of the variance.

NOTE: It is important to emphasize the fact that strict stationarity does not imply and is not implied by second-order stationarity. The reason is that the latter assumes the existence of the moment $E(|Y_t^2|) < \infty$. The two coincide, however, in the case of Normality.

The above definitions of first- and second-order stationarity are special cases of a more general notion of stationarity defined below.

8.5.5 Stationarity of order m

The stochastic process $\{Y_t, t \in \mathbb{T}\}$ is said to be *stationary of order m* if for all positive integers $m_1, m_2, \ldots, m_n$ such that $\sum_{i=1}^{n} m_i \leq m$:

$$E(Y_{t_1}^{m_1} \cdot Y_{t_2}^{m_2} \cdot Y_{t_3}^{m_3} \cdots Y_{t_n}^{m_n}) = E(Y_{t_1+\tau}^{m_1} \cdot Y_{t_2+\tau}^{m_2} \cdot Y_{t_3+\tau}^{m_3} \cdots Y_{t_n+\tau}^{m_n}) \text{ for any } (\tau + t_i) \in \mathbb{T}. \tag{8.35}$$

It is instructive to illustrate this notion using the special cases $m=1$ and $m=2$.

(i)   In the case $m=1$ the only combination of positive integers such that $\sum_{i=1}^{n} m_i \leq 1$ is to set any one of the m_is to one, say $m_1 = 1$ ($m_i = 0$ for $i=2,3,\ldots,n$), and (8.35) reduces to:

$$E(Y_{t_1}) = E(Y_{t_1+\tau}) \text{ for any } (\tau + t_1) \in \mathbb{T}.$$

This can only happen if $E(Y_t) = \mu$ for all $t \in \mathbb{T}$.

(ii) In the case $m=2$ there are five possibilities which involve two m_is (say m_1, m_2):

$$m = 1: (m_1 = 1, m_2 = 0), (m_1 = 0, m_2 = 1)$$
$$m = 2: (m_1 = 2, m_2 = 0), (m_1 = 0, m_2 = 2), (m_1 = 1, m_2 = 1).$$

Hence, for any $(\tau + t_i) \in \mathbb{T}, i=1,2$, (8.35) gives rise to:

$$m = 1: E(Y_{t_1}) = E(Y_{t_1+\tau}), E(Y_{t_2}) = E(Y_{t_2+\tau}),$$
$$m = 2: E(Y_{t_1}^2) = E(Y_{t_1+\tau}^2), E(Y_{t_2}^2) = E(Y_{t_2+\tau}^2), E(Y_{t_1} Y_{t_2}) = E(Y_{t_1+\tau} Y_{t_2+\tau}).$$

These conditions coincide with those given above for the second-order stationarity. To verify this all we need is to remind ourselves of the following formulae:

$$Var(X) = E(X^2) - (E(X))^2, \ Cov(X,Y) = E(X \cdot Y) - (E(X) \cdot E(Y)).$$

8.5.6 Exchangeability

The stochastic process $\{Y_t, t \in \mathbb{T}\}$ is said to be *exchangeable* if for every finite subsequence $(Y_1, Y_2, \ldots, Y_n)$, the joint distribution of each subset $(Y_1, Y_2, \ldots, Y_m), m=1,2,\ldots,$ n, is the same for any permutation of $(1,2,\ldots,m)$ or equivalently, any reordering of $(Y_1, Y_2, \ldots, Y_m)$; see Chow and Teicher (1978). That is,

$$f(y_k; \psi) = f(y; \psi) \text{ for all } k = 1,2,3, \dots,$$
$$f(y_k, y_h; \varphi) = f(y_i, y_j; \varphi) \text{ for all } k, h, i, j = 1,2,3, \dots,$$
$$f(y_k, y_h, y_\ell; \phi) = f(y_i, y_j, y_m; \phi) \text{ for all } k, h, \ell, i, j, m = 1,2,3, \dots,$$
$$\vdots \qquad\qquad \vdots$$
$$f(y_1, y_2, \dots, y_m; \vartheta) = f(y_{i1}, y_{i2}, \dots, y_{im}; \vartheta), (i_1, i_2, \dots, i_m) := \text{permutation}(1, 2, \dots, m).$$

This suggests that *exchangeability* is an extension of the notion of *Identical Distribution* which involves only the marginal distributions. Exchangeability involves all joint distributions (k random variables at a time, where $k = 1,2,3, \dots$) as well because it does not presuppose *Independence*.

Example

Consider the case where the stochastic process $\{Y_t, t \in \mathbb{T}\}$ is Gaussian (Normal) with parameters:

$$
\begin{aligned}
E(Y_k) &= 0, & k &= 1,2,3, \dots \\
Var(Y_k) &= 1 + \rho, & k &= 1,2,3, \dots \\
Cov(Y_k, Y_\ell) &= \rho & k, \ell &= 1,2,3, \dots
\end{aligned}
\tag{8.36}
$$

This process is exchangeable because (using the notation of chapter 4):

$$m = 1: Y_k \sim N(0, 1 + \rho), \ k = 1,2, \dots$$

$$m = 2: \begin{bmatrix} Y_k \\ Y_h \end{bmatrix} \sim N\left(\begin{bmatrix} 0 \\ 0 \end{bmatrix}, \begin{bmatrix} (1 + \rho) & \rho \\ \rho & (1 + \rho) \end{bmatrix} \right), \ k, h = 1,2, \dots$$

$$m = 3: \begin{bmatrix} Y_k \\ Y_h \\ Y_\ell \end{bmatrix} \sim N\left(\begin{bmatrix} 0 \\ 0 \\ 0 \end{bmatrix}, \begin{bmatrix} (1 + \rho) & \rho & \rho \\ \rho & (1 + \rho) & \rho \\ \rho & \rho & (1 + \rho) \end{bmatrix} \right), \ k, h, \ell = 1,2, \dots$$

$$\vdots \qquad \vdots \qquad\qquad\qquad \vdots$$

These joint distributions remain the same for all values of the index. In other words, the joint distribution of (Y_1, Y_{13}) is the same as that of (Y_{11}, Y_{102}), (Y_2, Y_{13}, Y_{111}) has the same distribution as (Y_{20}, Y_{11}, Y_1), and so on.

   This example shows most clearly that exchangeability does not presuppose independence but some kind of *distribution symmetry* among the random variables $(Y_1, Y_2, \dots, Y_n)$. The random variables are clearly dependent but the dependence is of a very special type: invariant with respect to the index, as in the case of stationarity, but unlike stationarity the dependence is not a function of the distance between the random variables, as can be seen from (8.36). In this sense the concept of exchangeability imposes not only almost complete homogeneity on the stochastic process but also a restricted form of dependence which is of limited value for modeling purposes. It turns out, however, that exchangeable processes are of great value in providing an intrinsic definition of probability itself (see chapters 2 and 10). Hence, an exchangeable stochastic process should be seen as the first step beyond IID processes, because the latter is always an exchangeable process but the converse is not true.

8.6 "Building block" stochastic processes

As mentioned above, it might be more appropriate to view a stochastic process via the joint distribution of a finite subset of the components (the *distributional viewpoint*), but for modeling purposes it is often advantageous to construct a process as a mapping of a much simpler process (the *constructionist viewpoint*). That is a stochastic process $\{Y_n, n \in \mathbb{N}\}$ is defined as a function of a simpler stochastic process $\{X_t, t \in \mathbb{T}\}$:

$$Y_n = g(X_1, X_2, \dots, X_n), n \in \mathbb{N}. \tag{8.37}$$

The probabilistic structure of the process $\{Y_n, n \in \mathbb{N}\}$ is determined from that of the simpler process $\{X_t, t \in \mathbb{T}\}$ via the functional form 8.37. In the next section we consider the simpler stochastic processes that are often used as building blocks.

8.6.1 IID stochastic processes

The simplest form of a building block stochastic process $\{X_t, t \in \mathbb{T}\}$ is the one where the X_ts constitute a sequence of Independent and Identically Distributed (IID) random variables. We encountered this family of random variables already in our discussions relating to random samples (see chapter 4). In terms of the index set/state space $(\mathbb{T}, \mathcal{R})$ taxonomy this stochastic process could belong to any one of the four categories. Its simplicity arises from the fact that its probabilistic structure is very restrictive:

(i)   Dependence: independence,
(ii) Heterogeneity: complete homogeneity.

The Bernoulli IID process

Let $\{X_n, n = 1,2,3,\dots\}$, be an IID Bernoulli process with density function:

$$f(x_n; p) = p^{x_n}(1-p)^{1-x_n}, \; x_n = 0,1, p \in [0,1], n = 1,2,\dots$$

$$\mathbb{P}(X_n = 1) = p, \; \mathbb{P}(X_n = 0) = 1 - p, n = 1,2,\dots$$

The first two moments take the form:

(i) $E(X_n) = p$, (ii) $Cov(X_n, X_m) = \begin{cases} p(1-p), & n = m, \\ 0, & n \neq m \end{cases}$, $n,m = 1,2,3,\dots$

NOTE that $Cov(X_n, X_m)$ for $n = m$ denotes the $Var(X_n)$. Moreover, because of independence:

$$P(X_n = 1, X_m = 1, X_k = 0) = P(X_n = 1) \cdot P(X_m = 1) \cdot P(X_k = 0) =$$
$$= p^2(1-p), n \neq m \neq k, n,m,k = 1,2,\dots$$

In terms of the index set/state space $(\mathbb{T}, \mathcal{R})$ taxonomy the IID Bernoulli process belongs to category D–D: $\mathbb{T} := \{1,2,3,\dots\}$ – countable, $\mathcal{R}_x := \{0,1\}$ – countable.

In the case where the Bernoulli process $\{X_n, n = 1,2,3,\dots\}$ is just independent (not ID) the first two moments take the form:

$$E(X_n) = p_n, \; Var(X_n) = p_n(1-p_n), \; Cov(X_n, X_m) = 0, n \neq m, n = 1,2, \dots$$

This shows that no operational model arises without additional information relating to the heterogeneity of the process.

An interesting variation on this process is the one defined by:

$$Y_n := 2X_n - 1, \ n = 1,2,3,\dots \tag{8.38}$$

The mean, variance, and covariance of the Bernoulli-type process, with $\mathcal{R} := \{-1,1\}$, take the form:

(i) $E(Y_n) = 2p - 1$, (ii) $Cov(Y_n, Y_m) = \begin{cases} 4p(1-p), & n=m, \\ 0, & n \neq m \end{cases}$, $n,m = 1,2,3,\dots$

The Exponential IID process

Let $\{X_n, n = 1,2,3,\dots\}$, be an IID Exponential process. Its density function takes the form:

$$f(x_n;\lambda) = \lambda e^{-\lambda x_n}, \ x_n \in [0,\infty), \ \lambda \in (0,\infty), \ n = 1,2,\dots$$

In terms of the index set/state space $(\mathbb{T}, \mathcal{R})$ taxonomy the IID Exponential process belongs to category D–C: $\mathbb{T} := \{1,2,3,\dots\}$ – countable, $\mathcal{R} := [0,\infty)$ – uncountable. As far as the probabilistic structure of the process is concerned, the mean, variance, and covariance of this process take the form:

(i) $E(X_n) = \frac{1}{\lambda}$,   (ii) $Cov(X_n, X_m) = \begin{cases} \frac{1}{\lambda^2}, & n=m, \\ 0, & n \neq m \end{cases}$, $n,m = 1,2,3,\dots$

The Normal IID process

Let $\{X_n, n = 1,2,3,\dots\}$, be an IID Normal process, denoted by:

$$X_n \sim N(\mu,\sigma^2), \ n = 1,2,\dots$$

Its density function takes the form:

$$f(x_n;\mu,\sigma^2) = \frac{1}{\sigma\sqrt{2\pi}} \exp\left\{-\frac{(x_n - \mu)^2}{2\sigma^2}\right\}, \ x_n \in \mathbb{R}, \ n = 1,2,\dots \tag{8.39}$$

In terms of the index set/state space $(\mathbb{T}, \mathcal{R})$ taxonomy the IID Normal process belongs to category D–C: $\mathbb{T} := \{1,2,3,\dots\}$ – countable, $\mathcal{R} := \mathbb{R}$ – uncountable. As far as the probabilistic structure of the process is concerned, the mean, variance, and covariance of this process take the form:

(i) $E(X_n) = \mu$, (ii) $Cov(X_n, X_m) = \begin{cases} \sigma^2, n=m, \\ 0, n \neq m \end{cases}$, $n,m = 1,2,3,\dots$

8.6.2   Uncorrelated, second-order homogeneous processes

If instead of independence we impose the less-restrictive assumption of *uncorrelatedness*, and instead of the identically distributed assumption, we assume the *homogeneity of the first two moments* we can define a number of widely used building block processes. It must be noted at the outset that, although non-correlation and second-order homogeneity seem less restrictive than IID, both concepts assume the existence of the first two moments; not presumed by the IID assumptions.

The white-noise process

The stochastic process $\{Z_t, t=1,2,3,\ldots\}$, where:

(i) $E(Z_t)=0$, (ii) $Cov(Z_t,Z_s) = \begin{cases} \sigma^2, & t=s, \\ 0, & t \neq s, t \end{cases}$, $t,s=1,2,3,\ldots$

is said to be a *white-noise process*. The definition of this process involves only the first two moments which are assumed homogeneous: constant for all the values of the index. Its simplicity arises from the fact that its probabilistic structure is:

(i) Dependence: non-correlation,
(ii) Heterogeneity: second-order homogeneity.

As argued in chapter 5, non-correlation amounts to *linear independence*, which is much less restrictive than independence.

The Normal white-noise process Consider the case where the white-noise process $\{Z_t, t=1,2,3,\ldots\}$, is assumed to be Normally distributed, i.e.:

$$Z_t \sim N(0,\sigma^2),\ t=1,2,3,\ldots$$

Its density function coincides with $f(x_t;\mu,\sigma^2)$ in (8.39) ($\mu=0$).

NOTICE that the Normal white-noise process coincides with an IID Normal process. The reason is that the Normal distribution is completely determined by the first two moments and the only form of dependence that can be modeled via the Normal distribution is linear dependence.

8.7 Markov processes

A stochastic process $\{X_t\}\in\mathbb{T}$, is said to be *Markov* if for:

$$0<t_1<t_2<t_3<\cdots<t_k<\cdots<\infty,\text{ where }t_k\in\mathbb{T}, k=1,2,3,\ldots,$$

$$f_k(x_{t_k}|x_{t_{k-1}},\ldots,x_{t_1};\varphi_k)=f_k(x_{t_k}|x_{t_{k-1}};\psi_k),\ \mathbf{x}_{(k)}:=(x_{t_1},\ldots,x_{t_k})\in\mathbb{R}^k, k=2,3,\ldots$$
$$(8.40)$$

There are several implications that follow from the above definition worth noting. First, a Markov process is also Markov relative to a reversal of the time dimension:

$$f_t(x_t|x_{t+1},x_{t+2},\ldots,x_{t+k};\psi_t)=f_t(x_t|x_{t+1};\phi_t),\text{ for all }t\in\mathbb{T}. \qquad (8.41)$$

Second, as mentioned in section 3 above, Markov dependence is a form of conditional independence (see chapter 6) in the sense that, for any three instances $m<k<n$:

$$f(x_n,x_m|x_k;\psi_{n,m})=f_n(x_n|x_k;\psi_n)\cdot f_m(x_m|x_k;\psi_n),\text{ for all }(x_n,x_m,x_k)\in\mathbb{R}^3. \qquad (8.42)$$

Related to this property is the following relationship among the conditional densities of the three instances $m<k<n$:

$$f_n(x_n|x_m;\psi_{n,m})=\int_{-\infty}^{\infty} f_n(x_n|x_k;\psi_{n,k})\cdot f_k(x_k|x_m;\psi_{k,m})dx_k,\text{ for all }(x_n,x_m,x_k)\in\mathbb{R}^3,$$
$$(8.43)$$

known as the *Chapman-Kolmogorov equation*. This equation is interesting because it enables one to bridge the big gap between n and m using two smaller bridges; see Chung (1982) for further details.

Third, in the case where the moments exist (and this might not be the case in general):

$$E(X_t^r \mid \sigma(X_{t-1}, X_{t-2}, \ldots, X_1)) = E(X_t^r \mid \sigma(X_{t-1})), \; r = 1,2,3, \ldots, t \in \mathbb{T}.$$

In terms of the basic taxonomy of probabilistic assumptions, a Markov process is composed of the following ingredients:

(D)   Distribution: arbitrary,
(M)   Dependence: Markov (conditional independence),
(H)   Heterogeneity: unrestricted.

Given this, we can see that in terms of the index set/state space $(\mathbb{T}, \mathcal{R})$ taxonomy a Markov process can belong to any one of the four categories (see figure 8.4). The distribution can be chosen to be either discrete or continuous and the same applies to the index set. Of particular interest is the case where the distribution is discrete giving rise to the so-called Markov chains introduced by Markov in the early 20th century; see Markov (1951).

In order to understand the implications of Markov dependence, let us return to the problem posed in the introduction and consider what would happen if we impose Markov dependence on the reduction (8.2):

$$f(x_1, x_2, \ldots, x_n; \boldsymbol{\phi}) \overset{\text{Markov}}{=} f_1(x_1; \boldsymbol{\psi}_1) \prod_{k=2}^{n} f_k(x_k \mid x_{k-1}; \boldsymbol{\psi}_k), \text{ for all } \mathbf{x} \in \mathbb{R}^n. \qquad (8.44)$$

Comparing (8.2) with (8.44) we can see that the assumption of Markov dependence has simplified the situation considerably. The problem of the increasing conditioning set has been dealt with in a most effective way and the Markov solution amounts to trading the marginal $f_k(x_k; \theta_k)$ with conditional densities $f_k(x_k \mid x_{k-1}; \varphi_k)$, $k = 1, 2, \ldots, n$. However, despite the simplification, (8.44) does not as yet yield operational models because we need to impose certain heterogeneity restrictions as well.

8.7.1 Markov chains

The most well-known stochastic process is the so-called Markov chain process. This is a special Markov process whose distribution (state space) is *discrete* (countable); their index set can be either discrete or continuous. For convenience we assume that the state space is a subset of the integers $\mathbb{Z} = \{0, \pm 1, \pm 2, \ldots\}$.

The stochastic process $\{X_{t_n}, t_n \in \mathbb{N}\}$ is said to be a *Markov chain* if for arbitrary times $0 \leq t_1 < t_2 < \cdots < t_{n-1} < t_n$:

$$\mathbb{P}(X_{t_n} = x_n \mid X_{t_{n-1}} = x_{n-1}, X_{t_{n-2}} = x_{n-2}, \ldots, X_{t_1} = x_1) = \mathbb{P}(X_{t_n} = x_n \mid X_{t_{n-1}} = x_{n-1}).$$

The joint distribution of the process takes the form:

$$\mathbb{P}(X_{t_n} = x_n, X_{t_{n-1}} = x_{n-1}, X_{t_{n-2}} = x_{n-2}, \ldots, X_{t_1} = x_1) =$$

$$= \mathbb{P}(X_{t_1} = x_1) \prod_{k=2}^{n} \mathbb{P}(X_{t_k} = x_k \mid X_{t_{k-1}} = x_{k-1}),$$

where $\mathbb{P}(X_{t1} = x_1)$ is called the **initial conditions** and:

$$p_{ij}^{(k)} := \mathbb{P}(X_{tk} = j \mid X_{tk-1} = i), \, k = 2,3, \ldots,$$

the *one-step* **transition probabilities**. A particularly important case is when the process is *homogeneous* in time:

$$p_{ij}^{(k)} = p_{ij}, \, \text{for all } k = 2,3, \ldots$$

In this case the *n-step* transition probabilities take the form:

$$p_{ij}(n) = \mathbb{P}(X_{tn+k} = j \mid X_{tk} = i), \, n \geq 1, \, k = 2,3, \ldots$$

An important property of such homogeneous Markov chain processes is that the initial conditions and the local behavior determine the global behavior as the following relationship, known as the *Chapman–Kolmogorov equation*, attests:

$$p_{ij}(n+m) = \sum_k p_{ik}(m) p_{kj}(n), \, n,m \geq 1.$$

Example

Consider the simple random walk process $\{S_n, \, n = 1,2,3, \ldots\}$, where the state space is $\mathcal{R} = \{0, \pm 1, \pm 2, \ldots\}$:

$$p_{ij} = \begin{cases} p & \text{if } j = i+1, \\ (1-p) & \text{if } j = i-1, \end{cases}$$

$$p_{ij}(n) = \begin{cases} \binom{n}{\frac{1}{2}(n+j-i)} p^{\frac{1}{2}(n+j-i)} (1-p)^{\frac{1}{2}(n+j-i)} & \text{if } n+j-i \text{ is even}, \\ 0, & \text{otherwise}. \end{cases}$$

Consider the Markov chain process $\{X(t), \, t \in \mathbb{T}\}$ whose transition probabilities take the form:

$$p_{ij}(t,\tau) := \Pr\left(X(t+\tau) = j \mid X(t) = i\right), \, \tau \geq 0.$$

If we assume that these depend only on the difference between the times, i.e.:

$$p_{ij}(\tau) := \Pr\left(X(t+\tau) = j \mid X(t) = i\right) = \\ = \Pr\left(X(\tau) = j \mid X(0) = i\right), \, \tau \geq 0, \, t \in \mathbb{T},$$

then the process is said to be stationary.

8.8   Random walk processes

As mentioned above, the generic notion of a random walk is defined as the *partial sum* process of IID random variables, i.e. the process $\{Y_t\}_{t=1}^{\infty}$ is said to be a random walk if it takes the form:

$$Y_t = \sum_{k=1}^{t} Z_k, \, t = 1,2,3, \ldots$$

where $\{Z_t, \, t = 1,2,3, \ldots\}$ is an IID process. A number of well-known stochastic processes can be classified under this category if we introduce some additional probabilistic structure. In order to avoid confusion, however, we reserve the term *random walk* only for the generic case. Moreover, processes which relax the assumptions of the generic case are not classified under this random walk category. For example the process $\{Z_t, t = 1,2,3,...\}$ cannot be a white noise process because it is uncorrelated, not independent. There are other forms of stochastic processes such as the martingale difference and innovation processes which can easily accommodate white noise processes (see below).

8.8.1 Second-order random walk

Consider the sequence of IID random variables $\{X_n, n = 1,2,3,...\}$, such that:

(a) $E(X_i) = \mu$, $i = 1,2,3,\ ...,\ n,\ ...,$
(b) $Var(X_i) = \sigma^2$, $i = 1,2,3,\ ...,\ n,\ ...,$
(c) $Cov(X_i, X_j) = 0$, $i \neq j,\ i,j = 1,2,3,\ ...,\ n, ...$ (8.45)

The stochastic process of partial sums $\{S_n = \sum_{i=1}^{n} X_i, n = 1,2,3,...\}$, specified by:

$$S_n = S_{n-1} + X_n, S_0 = 0, n = 1,2,3,\ ...,$$ (8.46)

is said to be a *second-order random walk*.

As shown in section 3, the partial sums stochastic process has the following moments:

(a) $E(S_n) = n\mu$, $n = 1,2,3,\ ...,$
(b) $Var(S_n) = n\sigma^2$, $n = 1,2,3,\ ...,$
(c) $Cov(S_n, S_m) = \sigma^2 \min(n,m)$, $n,m = 1,2,3, ...$ (8.47)

We can see that the summation of an IID process, in contrast to the latter, enjoys some degree of both dependence and heterogeneity.

	Dependence	Homogeneity
$\{X_n, n = 1,2,3,...\}$	independent	identical distribution
$\{S_n, n = 1,2,3,...\}$	dependent	non-homogeneous

In terms of the basic taxonomy of probabilistic assumptions, a random walk process is defined by:

(D) Distribution: arbitrary,
(M) Dependence: Markov (conditional independence),
(H) Heterogeneity: separable heterogeneity.

In terms of the index set/state space $(\mathbb{T}, \mathcal{R})$ taxonomy the random walk process $\{S_n, n = 1,2,3,...\}$ is **discrete,** on the basis of the index set $\mathbb{T} := \{0,1,2,\ ...,\}$, but its state space can be either discrete or continuous. As seen in the previous section the simple random walk process has a discrete (countable) state space but the Wiener process has a continuous (uncountable) state space.

8.8.2 Simple random walk

Consider the case where the sequence of IID random variables $\{X_n, n = 1,2,3,\ldots\}$, has a Bernoulli-type distribution with values 1 and -1 instead of the usual 1 and 0 (see (8.38)). That is, its range is $\mathbb{R}_X := \{1,-1\}$ and the distribution of X_n takes the form:

$$P(X_n = 1) = p, \; P(X_n = -1) = 1 - p, \; n = 1,2,\ldots$$

The stochastic process $\{S_n, n = 1,2,3,\ldots\}$ where:

$$S_n = \sum_{i=1}^{n} X_i, \; n = 1,2,3, \ldots, \tag{8.48}$$

is called a *simple random walk* process.

The term *random walk* is due to the fact that (8.48) can be written in the recursive form:

$$S_n = S_{n-1} + X_n, \; S_0 = 0, \; n = 1,2,3, \ldots, \tag{8.49}$$

which can be thought of as taking a random step X_n from the previous position S_{n-1}. If it helps, we can think of S_n as the position (in a two-dimensional Cartesian space) of a particle, starting at 0, which moves in steps of 1 and -1. The term *simple* stems from the fact that the distribution of the processes is Bernoulli type.

In this case the notion of homogeneity can be related to different dimensions of the process. It is trivial to show that this process is *spatially homogeneous*:

$$\mathbb{P}(S_n = k \,|\, S_0 = 0) = \mathbb{P}(S_n = k + b \,|\, S_0 = b),$$

$$\mathbb{P}(S_n = k \,|\, S_0 = 0) = \mathbb{P}(\sum_{i=1}^{n} X_i = k) = \mathbb{P}(S_n = k + b \,|\, S_0 = b).$$

This process is not just spatially but also *temporally homogeneous*:

$$\mathbb{P}(S_n = k \,|\, S_0 = 0) = \mathbb{P}(S_{n+m} = k \,|\, S_0 = 0),$$

$$\mathbb{P}(S_n = k \,|\, S_0 = 0) = \mathbb{P}(\sum_{i=1}^{n} X_i = k) = \mathbb{P}(\sum_{i=m+1}^{n+m} X_i = k) = \mathbb{P}(S_{n+m} = k \,|\, S_0 = 0).$$

The distribution of S_n, being the sum of Bernoulli distributed random variables, is Binomially distributed (see chapter 11), taking the form:

$$P(S_n = k) = \binom{n}{\frac{n+k}{2}} p^{\frac{1}{2}(n+k)} (1 - p)^{\frac{1}{2}(n-k)},$$

$$E(S_n) = n(2p - 1), \; Var(S_n) = 4np(1 - p).$$

This suggests separable heterogeneity in the first two moments; the homogeneous part being $(2p - 1)$ and $4p(1 - p)$, respectively, and the heterogeneous part n.

In terms of the basic taxonomy of probabilistic assumptions, a simple random walk process is defined by:

(D) Distribution: Bernoulli (Binomial),
(M) Dependence: Markov (conditional independence),
(H) Heterogeneity: temporally and spatially homogeneous, random walk heterogeneity.

In terms of the index set/state space $(\mathbb{T}, \mathcal{R})$ taxonomy this stochastic process belongs to category D–D: $\mathbb{T} := \{1,2,3,\ldots\}$ – countable, $\mathcal{R} := \{\pm 1, \pm 2, \pm 3, \ldots\}$ – countable.

8.9   **Martingale processes**

Martingale A stochastic process $\{Y_n, n \in \mathbb{N}\}$, is said to be a *martingale* if the following conditions hold:

(1) $E(|Y_n|) < \infty$, $n \in \mathbb{N}$,

(2) $E(Y_n | \sigma(Y_{n-1}, Y_{n-2}, \ldots, Y_0)) = Y_{n-1}$, $n \in \mathbb{N}$.   (8.50)

That is, the conditional expectation of Y_n given its past $\sigma(Y_{n-1}, Y_{n-2}, \ldots, Y_0)$ is equal to the immediate past.

Examples

(i)   Consider an IID process $\{X_t, t = 1,2,\ldots\}$ such that $E(X_t) = 0$, $t = 1,2,3,\ldots$ The random walk process defined by the partial sums:

$$\{S_t = \Sigma_{k=1}^t X_k, t = 1,2,\ldots\},$$

is a martingale because $S_t = S_{t-1} + X_t$, and $\sigma(S_{t-1}, \ldots, S_1) = \sigma(X_{t-1}, \ldots, X_1)$:

$$E(S_t | \sigma(S_{t-1}, S_{t-2}, \ldots, S_1)) = E(S_{t-1} + X_t | \sigma(S_{t-1}, S_{t-2}, \ldots, S_1)) = S_{t-1}.$$

NOTE that in the case where $E(X_t) = \mu \neq 0$, $t = 1,2,\ldots$, $\{S_t = \Sigma_{k=1}^t X_k, t = 1,2,\ldots\}$ is no longer a martingale but the process $\{Y_t = (S_t - \mu t), t = 1,2,\ldots\}$ with $S_0 = 0$ is a martingale.

(ii)   Consider the IID process $\{X_t, t = 1,2,3,\ldots\}$ such that $E(X_t) = 0$, $E(X_t^2) = \sigma^2 < \infty$, $t = 1,2,3,\ldots$ The process $\{V_t, t = 0,1,2,\ldots\}$ defined by

$$\{V_0 = 0, V_t = (S_t^2 - \sigma^2 t), t = 1,2,\ldots\},$$

where $S_t = \Sigma_{k=1}^t X_k$, is a martingale. This can be shown as follows:

$$E(V_t | \sigma(S_{t-1}, S_{t-2}, \ldots, S_1)) = E(S_t^2 | \sigma(S_{t-1}, S_{t-2}, \ldots, S_1)) - \sigma^2 t. \quad (8.51)$$

In view of the fact that $S_t = S_{t-1} + X_t$, and, S_{t-1} and X_t are independent, we can deduce that:

$$E(S_t^2 | \sigma(S_{t-1}, S_{t-2}, \ldots, S_1)) = E(S_{t-1}^2 + 2S_{t-1}X_t + X_t^2 | \sigma(S_{t-1}, S_{t-2}, \ldots, S_1)) =$$

$$= S_{t-1}^2 + 2S_{t-1}E(X_t) + E(X_t^2) = S_{t-1}^2 + \sigma^2. \quad (8.52)$$

Returning to (8.51) and noting that $\sigma(S_{t-1}, S_{t-2}, \ldots, S_1) = \sigma(V_{t-1}, V_{t-2}, \ldots, V_1, V_0)$:

$$E(V_t | \sigma(V_{t-1}, V_{t-2}, \ldots, V_1, V_0)) = S_{t-1}^2 + \sigma^2 - \sigma^2 t = S_{t-1}^2 - \sigma^2(t-1) = V_{t-1}.$$

(iii)   Consider the IID process $\{X_t, t = 1,2,3,\ldots\}$ such that $E(X_t) = 1$, $t = 1,2,3,\ldots$ The process $\{M_t, t = 1,2,3,\ldots\}$ defined by $M_t = \Pi_{k=1}^t X_k$, is a martingale because the process can be written in the form $M_t = M_{t-1} \cdot X_t$, and thus:

$$E(M_t | \sigma(M_{t-1}, M_{t-2}, \ldots, M_1)) = E(M_{t-1} \cdot X_t | \sigma(M_{t-1}, M_{t-2}, \ldots, M_1)) =$$

$$= M_{t-1}E(X_t | \sigma(M_{t-1}, M_{t-2}, \ldots, M_1)) = M_{t-1}. (8.53)$$

where the second equality follows from property CE3 ("take out what is known" see chapter 7). NOTE that in the case where $E(X_t) = \mu \neq 0$, $t = 1,2, \ldots$, for $\{M_t, t = 1,2,3,\ldots\}$ to be a martingale we need to define it as:

$$M_t = \left(\frac{1}{\mu}\right)^t \Pi_{k=1}^t X_k.$$

8.9.1 Probabilistic structure of a martingale

As shown in section 3, a martingale process involves both a dependence and a homogeneity restriction:

$$E(Y_n) = E(Y_1) = \mu \in \mathbb{R}, n = 1,2,\ldots$$

The dependence restriction of a martingale is related to that of a Markov process in so far as the only relevant information from its past for predicting Y_n is contained in Y_{n-1}. However, a Markov process does not assume the existence of any moments, while a martingale process assumes the existence of the mean. In addition a martingale process imposes first-order homogeneity in contrast to the Markov process which assumes none. If we assume that for a certain Markov process the mean exists, then (8.40) implies that:

$$E(Y_n | \sigma(Y_{n-1}, Y_{n-2}, \ldots, Y_1)) = E(Y_n | Y_{n-1}), n \in \mathbb{N}. \tag{8.54}$$

Comparing (8.50) with (8.54) we can see that a martingale imposes a certain form of linearity on the conditional mean in contrast to a Markov process which makes no assumptions on the functional form of the conditional mean (when it exists!).

In terms of the basic taxonomy of probabilistic assumptions, a martingale process is composed of the following ingredients:

(D) Distribution: arbitrary (existence of first moment),
(M) Dependence: martingale dependence,
(H) Heterogeneity: first-order stationarity.

In order to appreciate the power of the notion of a martingale in handling the dependence structure of an arbitrary process whose first moment is bounded consider the following examples.

Examples
(i)   **Taming a wild process.** Consider an arbitrary stochastic process $\{X_n, n \in \mathbb{N}\}$ whose only restriction is the existence of the mean: $E(|X_n|) < \infty, n \in \mathbb{N}$; no homogeneity or dependence restrictions. This wild stochastic process could be tamed in two steps:
Step 1: Take deviations from its conditional mean given its own past:

$$Z_n := X_n - E(X_n | \sigma(X_{n-1}, X_{n-2}, \ldots, X_1)), n \in \mathbb{N}.$$

Step 2: Take the partial sums of the new stochastic process $\{Z_n, n \in \mathbb{N}\}$:

$$Y_n := \sum_{k=1}^n Z_k = \sum_{k=1}^n X_n - E(X_k | \sigma(X_{k-1}, X_{k-2}, \ldots, X_1)), n \in \mathbb{N}. \tag{8.55}$$

The stochastic process $\{Y_n, n \in \mathbb{N}\}$ satisfies the restriction $E(|Y_n|) < \infty$, $n = 1, 2, \ldots$, and in view of the fact that (8.55) it is a martingale since:

$$Y_n = Y_{n-1} + Z_n, n \in \mathbb{N},$$

$$E(Y_n | \sigma(Y_{n-1}, Y_{n-2}, \ldots, Y_1)) = E(Y_{n-1} + Z_n | \sigma(Y_{n-1}, Y_{n-2}, \ldots, Y_1)) = Y_{n-1}.$$

This follows from property CE3 ("take out what is known"; see chapter 7):

(i) $E(Y_n | \sigma(Y_{n-1}, Y_{n-2}, \ldots, Y_1)) = Y_{n-1}$, (ii) $E(Z_n | \sigma(Y_{n-1}, Y_{n-2}, \ldots, Y_1)) = 0, n \in \mathbb{N}$.

This is a remarkable result which illustrates the usefulness of two different modeling notions which lead to the taming of an arbitrary process:

(i)   the idea of *centering* a process at its conditional mean and
(ii)   the notion of taking *partial sums*.

The above result, as it stands, although remarkable is *non-operational* because we do not know $E(X_k | \sigma(X_{k-1}, X_{k-2}, \ldots, X_1))$ to be used in the context of (8.55), without some additional restrictions on the probabilistic structure of the process.

IMPORTANT NOTE   Before we consider the next important example of a martingale it is important to note that the general notion of a martingale is more general than the definition given above in the following sense. A martingale can be defined relative to any increasing sequence of σ-fields, say $G_1 \subset G_2 \subset \cdots \subset G_{n-1} \subset G_n$, assuming that Y_n is a random variable relative to G_n for all $n = 1, 2, \ldots$ That is, $\{Y_n, n \in \mathbb{N}\}$ is a martingale relative to $\{G_n, n \in \mathbb{N}\}$ if:

(1) $E(|Y_n|) < \infty$, $n \in \mathbb{N}$,
(2) $E(Y_n | G_{n-1}) = Y_{n-1}$, $n \in \mathbb{N}$.   (8.56)

(ii)   **Doob martingale** Consider a random variable Y such that $E(|Y|) < \infty$, and a stochastic process $\{X_n, n \in \mathbb{N}\}$ defined on the same probability space $(S, \mathfrak{I}, \mathbb{P}(.))$. The stochastic process $\{Z_n, n \in \mathbb{N}\}$ defined by:

$$Z_n = E(Y | \sigma(X_n, X_{n-1}, \ldots, X_1)),$$

is a martingale relative to $\{\sigma(X_{n-1}, X_{n-2}, \ldots, X_1), n \in \mathbb{N}\}$ because:

$$E(Z_{n+1} | \sigma(X_n, X_{n-1}, \ldots, X_1)) = E[E(Y | \sigma(X_{n+1}, X_n, \ldots, X_1)) | \sigma(X_n, X_{n-1}, \ldots, X_1)] =$$

$$= E(Y | \sigma(X_n, X_{n-1}, \ldots, X_1)) = Z_n,$$ (8.57)

where the second equality follows from the "corset" property (see CE5 in chapter 7) which says that the smaller of the two σ-fields in the conditioning dominates. This particular example demonstrates the flexibility of the concept of a martingale and its significance in prediction.

The notion of a martingale process is of considerable value for statistical inference purposes because it has enough dependence and heterogeneity restrictions to allow the assumption of IID to be replaced by martingale dependence and heterogeneity in limit theorems (see chapter 9). However, for modeling purposes a martingale, as defined above, is of limited value because it involves only the first moment. For this reason we often supplement the notion of a martingale difference with additional assumptions relating to higher moments. For example, we often supplement the structure of a martingale with bounded moments assumptions such as:

$$E(|Y_n|^p) < \infty, \text{ for some } p > 1.$$

Of particular interest for statistical inference and modeling purposes is the case $p = 2$:

$$E(|Y_n|^2) < \infty,$$

the stochastic process $\{Y_n, n \in \mathbb{N}\}$, is called a *second-order martingale*.

8.9.2 Martingale difference process

Martingale difference A stochastic process $\{X_n, n \in \mathbb{N}\}$ is said to be a *martingale difference* if the following conditions hold:

(1) $E(|X_n|) < \infty, n \in \mathbb{N},$

(2) $E(X_n | \sigma(X_{n-1}, X_{n-2}, \ldots, X_0)) = 0, n \in \mathbb{N}.$ (8.58)

The crucial property is that the conditional mean with respect to its past is zero. Using the law of iterated expectations (lie) (see chapter 7) in conjunction with (2) we can deduce that the marginal mean is not just bounded but equals zero, i.e.:

$$E(X_n) = E(E(X_n | \sigma(X_{n-1}, X_{n-2}, \ldots, X_0))) = 0, n \in \mathbb{N}.$$

The term martingale difference stems from the fact that this process can always be generated as a difference of a martingale process $\{Y_n, n \in \mathbb{N}:\}$. That is, we can define the process $\{X_n, n \in \mathbb{N}\}$ as:

$$\{X_n := Y_n - Y_{n-1}, n \in \mathbb{N}\}.$$

Then by definition $\sigma(X_{n-1}, X_{n-2}, \ldots, X_0) = \sigma(Y_{n-1}, Y_{n-2}, \ldots, Y_0)$ and thus:

$$E(X_n | \sigma(X_{n-1}, X_{n-2}, \ldots, X_1)) = E(Y_n - Y_{n-1} | \sigma(X_{n-1}, X_{n-2}, \ldots, X_1)) =$$
$$= E(Y_n | \sigma(X_{n-1}, X_{n-2}, \ldots, X_1)) - Y_{n-1} = 0.   (8.59)$$

Reversing the argument, consider the martingale difference process $\{X_n, n \in \mathbb{N}\}$, such that (8.59) holds, then:

$$Y_n = \sum_{k=1}^n X_k, n \in \mathbb{N},$$

is a martingale. In this sense a martingale difference process can be thought of as a building block process for a martingale.

As in the case of a martingale we often need to supplement the probabilistic structure of a martingale difference with assumptions relating to the higher moments. This is done directly in terms of assumptions such as $E(|X_n|^p) < \infty$, for some $p > 1$, or indirectly by making distribution assumptions about the process $\{X_n, n \in \mathbb{N}\}$. Let us consider the case of assuming the existence of the second moment.

Consider the martingale difference process $\{X_n := Y_n - Y_{n-1}, n \in \mathbb{N}\}$, with a bounded second moment $E(|X_n|^2) < \infty$, and take $i < j$:

$$E(X_i X_j | X_{j-1}, X_{j-2}, \ldots, X_1) = X_i E(X_j | X_{j-1}, X_{j-2}, \ldots, X_1) = 0, \ i,j = 1,2,\ldots$$

This, however, implies that the elements of a second-order martingale difference process are uncorrelated:

$$Cov(X_i X_j) = E(X_i X_j) = 0, \ i < j, \ i,j = 1,2, \ldots,$$

and thus the variance of the summation is the summation of the individual variances:

$$Var(S_n) = \sum_{k=1}^{n} Var(X_k).$$

These two properties render this process an ideal replacement of the IID process in limit theorems (see chapter 9).

The importance of the notion of the second-order martingale difference can be best appreciated in the context of the following example. Consider the stochastic process $\{X_t, t \in \mathbb{N}\}$, which is assumed to be a white-noise process, i.e., zero-mean and uncorrelated. Supplementing these with the assumption that the process is Student's t with ν degrees of freedom, i.e., for the subset $(X_1, X_2, \ldots, X_n)$:

$$\begin{pmatrix} X_1 \\ X_2 \\ X_3 \\ \vdots \\ X_n \end{pmatrix} \sim \text{St} \left(\begin{bmatrix} 0 \\ 0 \\ 0 \\ \vdots \\ 0 \end{bmatrix}, \begin{bmatrix} \sigma_0^2 & 0 & 0 & \cdots & 0 \\ 0 & \sigma_0^2 & 0 & \cdots & 0 \\ 0 & 0 & \sigma_0^2 & \cdots & 0 \\ \vdots & \vdots & \vdots & \ddots & \vdots \\ 0 & 0 & 0 & \cdots & \sigma_0^2 \end{bmatrix}; \nu \right)$$

we can proceed to show that $\{X_t, t \in \mathbb{N}\}$, is a *martingale difference* process:

$$E(X_t | \sigma(X_{t-1}, X_{t-2}, \ldots, X_1)) = 0, \ t = 1,2,\ldots$$

The distribution assumption enables us to talk about higher moments and in particular the second conditional moment (see Spanos (1994)):

$$E(X_t^2 | \sigma(X_{t-1}, X_{t-2}, \ldots, X_1)) = \left(\frac{\nu \sigma_0^2}{\nu + t - 3} \right) \left(1 + \frac{1}{\nu \sigma_0^2} \sum_{k=1}^{t-1} X_{t-k}^2 \right), \ t = 1,2,\ldots$$

There are several things worth noting in relation to this example.

(i)   This is an example of a stochastic process for which non-correlation does not coincide with independence. Hence, a white-noise process does not mean that its past is irrelevant for forecasting its future.

(ii) The unconditional process is white-noise but its conditional formulation is a martingale difference with the past affecting all even moments, i.e.:

$$E(X_t^r | X_{t-1}, X_{t-2}, \ldots, X_1) = h_r \left(\sum_{k=1}^{t} = X_k^2 \right), \ r = 2,4,\ldots, \ t = 1,2,\ldots$$

NOTE that the odd moments are zero due to the symmetry of the Student's t distribution.

8.9.3 Martingale and innovation process

Another important stochastic process which is related to a second-order martingale is the innovation process.

Innovation process A stochastic process $\{Z_n, n \in \mathbb{N}\}$ is said to be an *innovation process* if it satisfies the following conditions:

(i) $E(Z_n | \sigma(Z_{n-1}, Z_{n-2}, \ldots, Z_1)) = 0,$ $n = 1,2,3, \ldots$

(ii) $Cov(Z_n, Z_m | \sigma(Z_{n-1}, Z_{n-2}, \ldots, Z_1)) = \begin{cases} \sigma^2, & n=m, \\ 0, & n \neq m \end{cases},$ $n,m = 1,2,3, \ldots$

This process can be defined in terms of a second-order martingale process $\{Y_n, n \in \mathbb{N}\}$:

(1) $E(|Y_n|^2) < \infty,\ n \in \mathbb{N},$
(2) $E(Y_{n-1} | \sigma(Y_{n-1}, Y_{n-2}, \ldots, Y_1)) = Y_{n-1},\ n \in \mathbb{N}.$

The process $\{Z_n := Y_n - Y_{n-1},\ n \in \mathbb{N}\}$, turns out to be an *innovation process*. Reversing the argument, we can claim that an innovation process $\{Z_n, n \in \mathbb{N}\}$ can be used to define a second-order martingale process $\{Y_n, n \in \mathbb{N}\}$ via:

$$Y_n = \sum_{k=1}^{n} X_k = Y_{n-1} + Z_n,\ n \in \mathbb{N}.$$

This follows from the fact that:

$$E(Y_n | \sigma(Z_{n-1}, Z_{n-2}, \ldots, Z_1)) = E([Y_{n-1} + Z_n] | \sigma(Z_{n-1}, Z_{n-2}, \ldots, Z_1)) = Y_{n-1},\ n \in \mathbb{N}.$$

in view of (2) above.

    The probabilistic structure of an innovation process involves no distribution assumption but it involves strict dependence and heterogeneity restrictions:

    (D)   Distribution: arbitrary (existence of first two moments),
    (M)   Dependence: martingale difference dependence,
    (H)   Heterogeneity: 2nd order stationarity.

      White-noise versus innovation process.
The innovation process is often confused with a white-noise process. In a nutshell an innovation process differs from the white-noise process mainly in terms of their dependence assumptions with the former being more restrictive since:

(i)   From the tower property of conditional expectation (see chapter 7):

$$E(Z_t) = E[E(Z_t | \sigma(Z_{t-1}, Z_{t-2}, \ldots, Z_1))] = 0,\ t = 1,2,3, \ldots$$

(ii)   Using the notation $\mathbf{Z}_{t-1}^0 := (Z_{t-1}, Z_{t-2}, \ldots, Z_1)$ we know that:

$$Cov(Z_t, Z_s) = E(Cov(Z_t, Z_s | \sigma(\mathbf{Z}_{t-1}^0))) + Cov(E(Z_t | \sigma(\mathbf{Z}_{t-1}^0))\, E(Z_s | \sigma(\mathbf{Z}_{t-1}^0))),$$

and thus:

$$Cov(E(Z_t | \sigma(\mathbf{Z}_{t-1}^0)) \cdot E(Z_s | \sigma(\mathbf{Z}_{t-1}^0))) = Cov(0 \cdot Z_s) = 0.$$

This implies that:

$$E(Z_s|\sigma(\mathbf{Z}_{t-1}^0)) = Z_s, \Rightarrow Cov(Z_t, Z_s) = \begin{cases} \sigma^2, & t = s, \\ 0, & t \neq s, \end{cases} \quad t > s = 1,2,3,\dots$$

This result suggests that the white-noise and the innovation are similar in so far as they are both defined in terms their first two moments, but differ in terms of their *dependence* structure. The IID process assumes that all its components are *independent*. The white-noise process assumes that its components are *pairwise uncorrelated*. The innovation process assumes that every component Z_t is *martingale difference independent* with respect to its past $\sigma(\mathbf{Z}_{t-1}^0)$.

An innovation process belongs to the category of simple stochastic processes which are used as basic *building blocks* for derived processes. The other three members of this category are the IID, the white-noise, and the martingale difference processes. An innovation process differs from a second-order martingale difference process in one important respect: the conditional variance of the former is constant. It is interesting to note how these four processes differ in terms of their *dependence* structure.

8.10 Gaussian processes

8.10.1 Normal processes: the distributional viewpoint

A stochastic process $\{X_t, t \in \mathbb{T}\}$ whose joint distribution $f(x_1, x_2, \dots, x_n; \boldsymbol{\phi})$ for any finite collection $(X_1, X_2, \dots, X_n)$ is Normal, i.e.

$$\begin{pmatrix} X_1 \\ X_2 \\ X_3 \\ \vdots \\ X_n \end{pmatrix} \sim \mathsf{N} \left(\begin{bmatrix} \mu_1 \\ \mu_2 \\ \mu_3 \\ \vdots \\ \mu_n \end{bmatrix}, \begin{bmatrix} \sigma_{11} & \sigma_{12} & \sigma_{13} & \cdots & \sigma_{n1} \\ \sigma_{21} & \sigma_{22} & \sigma_{23} & \cdots & \sigma_{n2} \\ \sigma_{31} & \sigma_{32} & \sigma_{33} & \cdots & \sigma_{n3} \\ \vdots & \vdots & \vdots & \ddots & \vdots \\ \sigma_{n1} & \sigma_{n2} & \sigma_{n3} & \cdots & \sigma_{nn} \end{bmatrix} \right), \tag{8.60}$$

is said to be a *Normal* (or *Gaussian*) *process*. That is, the only definitional characteristic is the distribution assumption of Normality. As argued in the previous chapters without restrictions on the dependence and heterogeneity of this process no operational model is possible. The only possible reduction of the joint distribution is the one based on *sequential conditioning*:

$$f(x_1, x_2, \dots, x_n; \boldsymbol{\phi}) \overset{\text{non-IID}}{=} f_1(x_1; \boldsymbol{\psi}_1) \prod_{k=2}^{n} f_k(x_k | x_{k-1}, \dots, x_1; \boldsymbol{\psi}_k), \text{ for all } \mathbf{x} \in \mathbb{R}^n. \tag{8.61}$$

with the conditional distributions in (8.61) being Normal. The *autoregressive* and *autoskedastic* functions (see the introduction above) take the form (see Spanos (1986)):

$$E(X_k | \sigma(X_{k-1}, \dots, X_1)) = \beta_0(k) + \sum_{i=1}^{k-1} \beta_i(k) X_{k-i}, \ k = 2,3,\dots,n,$$

$$Var(X_k | \sigma(X_{k-1}, \dots, X_1)) = \sigma_0^2(k), \ k = 2,3,\dots,n. \tag{8.62}$$

This, however, does not give rise to an operational model because the overparameterization problem remains: the number of unknown parameters in $\{\psi_1, \psi_2, \ldots, \psi_n\}$ is the same as those in ϕ (and increasing with n). This problem is demonstrated by the above example where:

$$\psi_k := (\beta_0(k), \beta_1(k), \ldots, \beta_{k-1}(k), \sigma_0^2(k)), \; k = 2, \ldots, n.$$

There are $(k+1)$ unknown parameters for each value of $k = 2, \ldots, n$. If we add all the unknown parameters in $(\psi_1, \psi_2, \ldots, \psi_n)$ we conclude that the original number of unknown parameters remains the same, i.e., the sequential conditioning has no effect on the number of unknown parameters.

As argued in the previous chapter, the way to deal with both problems, the increasing conditioning information set and the overparameterization, is to impose some *restrictions* on the *dependence* and *heterogeneity* of the set of random variables $(X_1, X_2, \ldots, X_n)$. Let us pursue that line of argument by imposing Markov dependence without any heterogeneity restrictions first in order to bring out the role of each set of restrictions and then proceed to impose Markovness and stationarity to derive the family of models known as autoregressive.

8.10.2 The probabilistic reduction approach: autoregressive models

Consider the case where in addition to Normality we also impose Markov dependence:

(D) Distribution: Normal,
(M) Dependence: Markov,
(H) Heterogeneity: unrestricted heterogeneity.

The Markov dependence assumption when applied to the reduction in (8.61) yields:

$$f(x_1, x_2, \ldots, x_n; \phi) \overset{\text{Markov}}{=} f_1(x_1; \psi_1) \prod_{k=2}^{n} f_k(x_k | x_{k-1}; \psi_k), \text{ for all } \mathbf{x} \in \mathbb{R}^n. \tag{8.63}$$

Moreover, under the Normality assumption the first two stochastic conditional moments take the form:

$$E(X_k | \sigma(X_{k-1}, \ldots, X_1)) = \alpha_0(k) + \alpha_1(k) X_{k-1}, \quad k = 2, 3, \ldots, n,$$

$$Var(X_k | \sigma(X_{k-1}, \ldots, X_1)) = \sigma_0^2(k), \quad\quad\quad k = 2, 3, \ldots, n.$$

If we compare these moments with the unrestricted ones in (8.62) we can see the Markov dependence assumption deals with the problem of the increasing conditioning information set but the parameters are still index dependent. In order to deal with the last problem we need to impose some restrictions on the heterogeneity of the process.

For argument's sake let us impose second-order stationarity as well, i.e., consider the following combination of assumptions:

(D) Distribution: Normal,
(M) Dependence: Markov,
(H) Heterogeneity: second-order stationarity.

Under both the Markov dependence and Stationarity assumptions, the reduction in (8.61) takes the simplified form:

$$f(x_1,x_2,\ldots,x_T;\boldsymbol{\phi}) \overset{\text{Markov}}{=} f_1(x_1;\boldsymbol{\psi}_1)\prod_{t=2}^{T}f_t(x_t|x_{t-1};\boldsymbol{\psi}_t)=$$

$$\overset{\text{Stationary}}{=} f(x_1;\boldsymbol{\psi}_1)\prod_{t=2}^{T}f(x_t|x_{t-1};\boldsymbol{\psi}). \tag{8.64}$$

The first equality follows after imposing Markovness and the second from the stationarity assumption. Roughly speaking, stationarity deals with the overparametrization problem and Markovness with the increasing conditioning information set. It is easy to see that by supplementing these assumptions with some distribution assumption, such as Normality, the above decomposition gives rise to operational models.

Assuming Normality and Markov dependence enables us to concentrate only on a bivariate joint distribution, i.e.

$$\begin{pmatrix}X_t\\X_{t-1}\end{pmatrix}\sim N\left(\begin{bmatrix}\mu(t)\\\mu(t-1)\end{bmatrix},\begin{bmatrix}\sigma(t,t) & \sigma(t,t-1)\\\sigma(t-1,t) & \sigma(t-1,t-1)\end{bmatrix}\right).$$

The conditional density takes the form:

$$(X_t|X_{t-1})\sim N(\alpha_0(t)+\alpha_1(t)X_{t-1},\sigma_0^2(t)),$$

where the unknown parameters are: $\boldsymbol{\psi}_t:=(\alpha_0(t),\alpha_1(t),\sigma_0^2(t))$, where:

$$\alpha_0(t):=\mu(t)-\alpha_1(t)\mu(t-1),\ \alpha_1(t):=\frac{\sigma(t,t-1)}{\sigma(t-1,t-1)},\ \sigma_0^2(t):=\sigma(t,t)-\frac{\sigma(t,t-1)^2}{\sigma(t-1,t-1)}.$$

In order to see what Markov dependence implies for a Normal (Gaussian) process consider the case where $\{X_t,t\in\mathbb{T}\}$, is zero mean ($E(X_t)=0$ for simplicity) and take three successive points: $t_1<t_2<t_3$. The covariance of such a Markov Gaussian process takes the form:

$$Cov(X_{t_1},X_{t_3})=\frac{Cov(X_{t_1},X_{t_2})\cdot Cov(X_{t_2},X_{t_3})}{Var(X_{t_2})}.$$

This can be demonstrated as follows:

$$Cov(X_{t_1},X_{t_3})=E(X_{t_1}X_{t_3})=E\{E(X_{t_1}X_{t_3})|X_{t_2}\}=E\{E(X_{t_1}|X_{t_2})E(X_{t_3}|X_{t_2})\}=$$

$$=E\left\{\left(\frac{Cov(X_{t_1},X_{t_2})}{Var(X_{t_2})}\right)X_{t2}\left(\frac{Cov(X_{t_3},X_{t_2})}{Var(X_{t_2})}\right)X_{t2}\right\}=\frac{Cov(X_{t_1},X_{t_2})\cdot Cov(X_{t_2}X_{t_3})\cdot E(X_{t_2}^2)}{[Var(X_{t_2})]^2}$$

$$=\frac{Cov(X_{t_1},X_{t_2})\cdot Cov(X_{t_2}X_{t_3})}{Var(X_{t_2})},$$

where the first equality follows from the iterated expectation property of conditional expectations (see CE3 in chapter 7), the second equality follows from the Markov dependence and the third from the Normality assumption. NOTE that in the case of non-zero mean the above holds for the mean deviations of the process.

If, in addition to the Markov and Gaussian assumptions, we impose *stationarity* then:

$$Cov(X_t,X_s)=\frac{Cov(X_s,X_0)\cdot Cov(X_0,X_t)}{Var(X_0)}=\frac{c(s)\cdot c(t)}{c(0)}=Cov(X_{t-s},X_0)=c(t-s).$$

The last equation can be written in the form:

$$c(0)\cdot c(t-s)=c(0)\cdot c(t+s)=c(t)\cdot c(s). \tag{8.65}$$

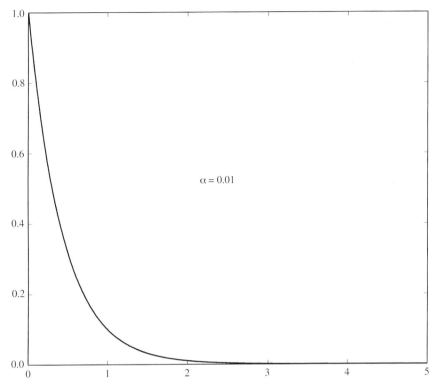

Figure 8.6 $\delta = 4.605 \Rightarrow \alpha = 0.01$

The solution to this functional equation depends on the range of values of t and s.

(i)   In the case where t and s take continuous values, say, $t,s \in \mathbb{R}_+$, (8.65) is the well-known Cauchy (Exponential form) functional equation (see Eichhorn (1978)) whose unique solution is:

$$c(\tau) = c(0)\exp\{-\delta\tau\}, \ \delta > 0 \text{ a real constant,} \tag{8.66}$$

implying that $c(\tau) \underset{\tau \to \infty}{\to} 0$ at an Exponential rate. In figures 8.6 and 8.7 we can see the exponential function with two different values of δ. As we can see, for bigger values of δ the rate of decrease is very rapid; it reaches zero just after $\tau > 2$. In contrast, for small values of δ the Exponential function decreases very slowly; for values of τ up to 1000 the rate of decrease looks linear.

(ii)   In the case where t and s take discrete values, say, $t,s = 0,1,2, \ldots,$ (8.65) implies the solution (see Doob (1953), p. 237):

$$c(\tau) = c(0)a^\tau, |a| \leq 1 \text{ a real constant.} \tag{8.67}$$

The two cases are clearly related via: $\delta = \ln\left(\frac{1}{\alpha}\right)$.

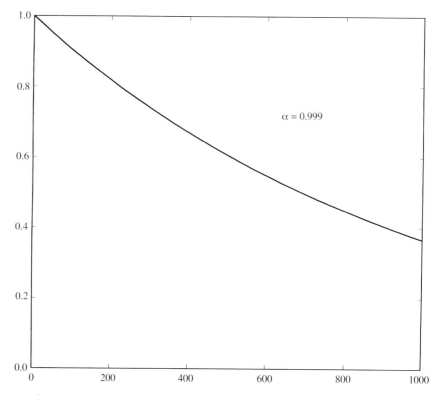

Figure 8.7 $\delta = 0.001 \Rightarrow \alpha = 0.999$

Taking the above results together we can conclude that assuming that the Normal stochastic process $\{X_t,\ t \in \mathbb{T}\}$, $\mathbb{T} := \{0,1,2,...\}$ is both Markov and Stationary, then its dependence decays at an Exponential rate (see (8.67)). The conditional density $f(x_t|x_{t-1};\psi)$ is Normal and takes the form:

$$(X_t|X_{t-1}) \sim N(\alpha_0 + \alpha_1 X_{t-1}, \sigma_0^2),\ t = 2,3,...$$

That is, stationarity gets rid of the index in both the density and the parameters, since:

$$E(X_t) = \mu,\ Var(X_t) = \sigma(0),\ Cov(X_t, X_{t-1}) = \sigma(1),\ t \in \mathbb{T},$$

$$\alpha_0 := (1-\alpha_1)\,\mu,\ \alpha_1 := \frac{\sigma(1)}{\sigma(0)},\ \sigma_0^2 := \sigma(0) - \frac{\sigma(1)^2}{\sigma(0)}.$$

It is interesting to NOTE that the coefficient α_1 coincides with α in (8.67) and the two values of δ in figures 8.6 and 8.7 correspond to the values $a = 0.01$ and $a = 0.999$, respectively.

These moments can be used to specify the so-called Normal/linear first-order **autoregressive model** (AR(1)), in terms of the statistical GM with $\mathcal{D}_t := \sigma(X_{t-1}, X_{t-2}, ..., X_1)$:

$$X_t = E(X_t | \mathcal{D}_t) + u_t = \alpha_0 + \alpha_1 X_{t-1} + u_t, \ t = 2,3, \ldots, \tag{8.68}$$

$$u_t = X_t - E(X_t | \mathcal{D}_t), \ t = 2,3, \ldots, \tag{8.69}$$

is an innovation process. As shown in chapter 7, the process $\{u_t, t \in \mathbb{T}\}$, enjoys the following properties:

(i) $\quad E(u_t | \mathcal{D}_t) = 0, \qquad\qquad t = 2,3,\ldots$

(ii) $\quad E(u_t \cdot u_s | \mathcal{D}_t) = \begin{cases} \sigma^2, & t = s, \\ 0, & t \neq s \end{cases}, \quad t > s, \ t,s = 2,3,\ldots$

(iii) $\quad E(u_t \cdot [E(X_t | \mathcal{D}_t)] | \mathcal{D}_t) = 0, \qquad t = 2,3,\ldots$

Normal autoregressive model

[1] Statistical GM: $X_t = \alpha_0 + \alpha_1 X_{t-1} + u_t, \ t \in \mathbb{T}$,

[2] Probability model:

$$\Phi = \left\{ f(x_1, x_2, \ldots, x_T; \boldsymbol{\theta}) = f(x_1; \boldsymbol{\theta}_1) \prod_{t=2}^{T} \frac{(\sigma_0)^{-1}}{\sqrt{2\pi}} \exp\left\{ -\frac{1}{2} \frac{(x_t - \alpha_0 - \alpha_1 x_{t-1})^2}{\sigma_0^2} \right\}, \ \boldsymbol{\theta} \in \Theta, \mathbf{x} \in \mathbb{R}^T \right\},$$

where $\boldsymbol{\theta} := (\alpha_0, \alpha_1, \sigma_0^2) \in \Theta := \mathbb{R}^2 \times \mathbb{R}_+, \ \mathbf{x} := (x_1, x_2, \ldots, x_T)$

[3] Sampling model: $(X_1, X_2, \ldots, X_T)$ is a stationary and Markov dependent sample, sequentially drawn from $f(x_t | x_{t-1}; \boldsymbol{\theta}), \ t \in \mathbb{T}$.

The results derived above can be easily extended to the case where we replace Markov dependence with pth order Markov dependence giving rise to the pth order **autoregressive model** (AR(p)), in terms of the statistical GM:

$$X_t = \alpha_0 + \sum_{k=1}^{p} \alpha_k X_{t-k} + u_t, \ t = p+1, p+2, \ldots, \tag{8.70}$$

$$u_t = X_t - E(X_t | \sigma(X_{t-1}, X_{t-2}, \ldots, X_1)), \ t = p+1, p+2, \ldots, \tag{8.71}$$

is an innovation process with the same properties as those of (8.69).

The autoregressive (AR(p)) model in the form (8.70) was first proposed by Yule (1927) as a stochastic difference equation. That is, it was originally viewed from the theoretical viewpoint (see chapter 7) and not from the statistical viewpoint as above. Looking at the last edition of Yule's textbook (see Yule (1911)), published jointly with Kendall in 1950, one can see that the relationship between the AR(p) and the linear regression model is not given explicitly. For the purposes of this book this relationship is *particularly important* because it unifies all models of dependence (contemporaneous or temporal) via conditioning, under the same umbrella: the adapted Pearson research strategy (see chapter 7).

The above Normal/linear AR(p) models constitute the most important members of the **Autoregressive family of models** which is based on the following assumptions:

(D) Distribution: arbitrary continuous distribution,
(M) Dependence: Markov,
(H) Heterogeneity: strict stationarity.

The results of chapter 7, relating to the regression and skedastic functions of bivariate distributions, can be easily modified to specify a number of AR(1) models such as the following (for the notation see chapter 7):

1   **Student's t:**

$$E(X_t|X_{t-1}) = \alpha_0 + \alpha_1 X_{t-1}, \ Var(X_t|X_{t-1}) = \frac{v\sigma^2}{v-1}\left\{1 + \frac{\alpha_2}{v}[X_{t-1}-\mu]^2\right\}.$$

2   **Pareto:**

$$E(X_t|X_{t-1}) = a_1 + \left[\frac{a_1 a_3}{a_2}\right] X_{t-1}, \ Var(X_t|X_{t-1}) = \left[\left(\frac{a_1}{a_2}\right)^2 \frac{(1+a_3)}{(1+a_3)a_3^2}\right] X_{t-1}^2.$$

3   **Exponential:**

$$E(X_t|X_{t-1}) = \frac{(1+\theta+\theta X_{t-1})}{(1+\theta X_{t-1})^2}, \ Var(X_t|X_{t-1}) = \frac{[(1+\theta+\theta X_{t-1})^2 - 2\theta^2]}{[1+\theta X_{t-1}]^4}.$$

4   **Log-Normal:**

$$E(X_t|X_{t-1}) = \left(\frac{X_{t-1}}{\mu}\right)^\beta e^{\mu + \frac{1}{2}\sigma^2}, \ Var(X_t|X_{t-1}) = \left(\frac{X_{t-1}}{\mu}\right)^{2\beta} e^{2\mu + \sigma^2} \cdot [e^{\sigma^2} - 1].$$

The autoregressive models which are based on the above conditional moment functionals can be viewed as a systematic way to specify non-linear and/or heteroskedastic time series models (see Spanos (1986, forthcoming)).

8.10.3 The constructionist approach: moving average processes

An important stochastic process can be constructed by taking a moving average of a Normal white-noise process. Consider the Normal white-noise stochastic process ε_t, $t = 1,2,3,...\}$, where:

$$\varepsilon_t \sim NIID(0,\sigma^2), \ t = 1,2,...$$

The stochastic process $\{Y_t, t = 1,2,3,...\}$, defined by:

$$Y_t = a_0 + \sum_{k=1}^{m} a_k \varepsilon_{t-k} + \varepsilon_t, \ t = 1,2,... \tag{8.72}$$

is said to be a *moving average process* of order m, denoted by MA(m). By construction the latter process is Normal with probabilistic structure of the form:

(i) $E(Y_t) = a_0,$ $t = 1,2,3,...$

(ii) $Cov(Y_t, Y_{t-\tau}) = \begin{cases} \sigma^2(1 + \sum_{k=1}^{m} a_k^2), & \tau = 0, \\ \sigma^2(a_\tau + a_1 a_\tau + 1 + \cdots + a_{m-\tau} a_m), & \tau = 1,2, ..., m, \\ 0, & \tau > m. \end{cases}$

In terms of the basic taxonomy of probabilistic assumptions, a MA(m) process consists of the following ingredients:

(D)   Distribution: Normal (or white noise),
(M)   Dependence: m-dependence,
(H)   Heterogeneity: second-order stationarity.

The derivation of the mean is trivial because all the white-noise terms have zero means. Let us derive the covariance for the simple case $m=2$, $\tau>0$:

$$Y_t = a_0 + a_1\varepsilon_{t-1} + a_2\varepsilon_{t-2} + \varepsilon_t. \tag{8.73}$$

$$\begin{aligned}
\text{Cov}(Y_t, Y_{t-\tau}) &= E([Y_t - a_0][Y_{t-\tau} - a_0]) = \\
&= E([a_1\varepsilon_{t-1} + a_2\varepsilon_{t-2} + \varepsilon_t][a_1\varepsilon_{t-1-\tau} + a_2\varepsilon_{t-2-\tau} + \varepsilon_{t-\tau}]) = \\
&= E(a_1^2\varepsilon_{t-1}\varepsilon_{t-1-\tau} + a_1\varepsilon_{t-1}\varepsilon_{t-\tau} + a_1a_2\varepsilon_{t-2}\varepsilon_{t-1-\tau} + a_2^2\varepsilon_{t-2}\varepsilon_{t-2-\tau} + a_2\varepsilon_{t-2}\varepsilon_{t-\tau} + \varepsilon_{t-\tau}\varepsilon_t),
\end{aligned}$$

where the cross-product terms with different indexes have already been put equal to zero. Taking expectations of the terms inside the brackets yields:

$$\text{Cov}(Y_t, Y_{t-\tau}) = \begin{cases} \sigma^2(1 + a_1^2 + a_2^2), & \tau=0, \\ \sigma^2(a_1 + a_1a_2), & \tau=1, \\ \sigma^2 a_2, & \tau=2, \\ 0, & \tau>2. \end{cases}$$

NOTE that the MA(m) process is often specified without the Normality assumption. The view taken in this book is that the generality claimed without the Normality is more apparent than real.

8.10.4 Autoregressive versus moving average processes*

The reader should note that in this section we will use a number of linear space concepts.

In the discussion above the autoregressive model (AR(p)) was introduced using the reduction from the joint distribution of the Normal process approach but the moving average model (MA(q)) was introduced via the constructionist approach. The aim of this section is to demonstrate that the two formulations are related.

In order to simplify the derivation consider a zero mean (to get rid of α_0) Normal process $\{X_t, t\in\mathbb{T}:=\{0, \pm 1, \pm 2, ...\}$. The AR(p) formulation is based on the statistical GM:

$$X_t = \sum_{k=1}^{p} \alpha_k X_{t-k} + u_t,\ t\in\mathbb{T}_p := \pm(p+1), \pm(p+2), ...,$$

where the error process with $\mathcal{D}_{t-1} := \sigma(X_{t-1}, X_{t-2}, ..., X_1, X_0, X_{-1}...)$:

$$u_t = X_t - E(X_t|\mathcal{D}_{t-1}),\ t\in\mathbb{T}_p, \tag{8.74}$$

is an innovation process $\{u_t,\ t\in\mathbb{T}\}$. By design the error process enjoys the following properties:

(a) $E(u_t|\mathcal{D}_{t-1}) = 0,$ $\qquad\qquad\qquad t\in\mathbb{T}_p,$

(b) $E(u_t \cdot u_s|\mathcal{D}_{t-1}) = \begin{cases} \sigma^2, t=s, \\ 0,\ \ t\neq s, \end{cases}$ $\qquad t>s, t, s\in\mathbb{T}_p,$

(c) $E(u_t \cdot [E(X_t|\mathcal{D}_{t-1})]|\mathcal{D}_{t-1}) = 0,$ $\qquad t\in\mathbb{T}_p.$

In view of the fact that this error process is a linear function of the process $\{X_t, t \in \mathbb{T} := \{0, \pm 1, \pm 2, \ldots\}$:

$$\sigma(X_{t-1}, X_{t-2}, \ldots, X_1, X_0, X_{-1} \ldots) = \sigma(u_{t-1}, u_{t-2}, \ldots, u_1, u_0, u_{-1} \ldots) := \mathcal{D}_{t-1}.$$

Viewing these random variables as elements of a Hilbert space (a sophisticated linear space), the fact that the error process is orthogonal enables us to use a Fourier series type expansions (see Luenberger (1969)) to express it in the following form:

$$X_t = \sum_{k=0}^{\infty} [\sigma^{-2} E(X_t u_{t-k})] u_{t-k}, \ t \in \mathbb{T},$$

which, for $a_k = [\sigma^{-2} E(X_t u_{t-k})]$, this can be expressed in the form of a MA(∞) representation:

$$X_t = \sum_{k=1}^{\infty} a_k u_{t-k} + u_t, \ t \in \mathbb{T}. \tag{8.75}$$

An alternative way to view this is to re-write the statistical GM of the AR(p) formulation as a polynomial in the lag operator $L^k X_t := X_{t-k}$:

$$\left(X_t - \sum_{k=1}^{p} \alpha_k X_{t-k} \right) := \left(1 - \sum_{k=1}^{p} \alpha_k L^k \right) X_t = u_t, \ t \in \mathbb{T}_p. \tag{8.76}$$

The fact that the inverse of the polynomial can (under certain restrictions) be expressed as an infinite polynomial enables us to express the AR(p) formulation in the MA(∞) form:

$$X_t = \left(1 - \sum_{k=1}^{p} \alpha_k L^k \right)^{-1} u_t = a_\infty(L) \cdot u_t := \sum_{k=1}^{\infty} a_k u_{t-k}, \ t \in \mathbb{T}_p, \tag{8.77}$$

where $a_\infty(L)$ is an infinite polynomial in the lag operator L:

$$a_\infty(L) := 1 + a_1 L + a_2 L^2 + \cdots + a_k L^k + \cdots$$

This relationship between the AR(p) and MA(∞) formulations is very interesting because in view of the fact that a MA(m) model has a dependence structure we called m-dependence (see above), this result suggests that any AR(p), $p \geq 1$ has infinite memory. As it stands the MA(∞) representation is only of theoretical interest because it involves an infinite number of unknown parameters. For modeling purposes the AR(p) representation is certainly more parsimonious but there is a modification of the above MA(∞) representation which yields very parsimonious formulations. The theoretical basis of such a modification is that under certain regularity conditions the infinite polynomial $a_\infty(L)$ can be approximated by a ratio of two finite polynomials (see Dhrymes (1971)):

$$a_\infty(L) = \frac{\gamma_q(L)}{\delta_p(L)} := \frac{(1 + \gamma_1 L + \gamma_2 L^2 + \cdots + \gamma_q L^q)}{(1 + \delta_1 L + \delta_2 L^2 + \cdots + \delta_p L^p)}, \ p \geq q \geq 0.$$

Using this approximation we can proceed to specify the autoregressive, moving average model ARMA(p,q) popularized by Box and Jenkins (1976)):

$$X_t = \sum_{k=1}^{p} \delta_k X_{t-k} = \sum_{k=1}^{q} \gamma_k u_{t-k} + u_t, \ t \in \mathbb{T}_p.$$

Such models proved very efficient in capturing the temporal dependence in time series data in a parsimonious way but failed to capture the imagination of economic modelers because they find it very difficult to relate such models to economic theory.

The AR(p) and other related models are discussed further in Spanos (1986).

8.10.5 The constructionist approach: the Wiener process

Consider the case where $\{X_t, t = 1,2,3,\ldots\}$ is an IID Normal process with moments:

(i) $E(X_t) = \mu$, (ii) $Cov(X_t, X_s) = \begin{cases} \sigma^2, & t = s, \\ 0, & t \neq s \end{cases}$, $t,s = 1,2,3,\ldots$

The stochastic process $\{W_t, t = 1,2,3,\ldots\}$, defined by:

$$W_t = \Sigma_{k=1}^{t} X_k, \tag{8.78}$$

is called a *Wiener process*. The joint density, based on the index subset $0 < t_1 < t_1, \ldots, < t_n$ is:

$$f(w_1, w_2, \ldots, w_n; \boldsymbol{\phi}) = f_1(w_1; \boldsymbol{\psi}_1) \prod_{k=2}^{n} f_{tk-tk-1}(w_{tk} - w_{tk-1}; \boldsymbol{\psi}_{tk-tk-1}) =$$

$$= \frac{\exp\left\{-\frac{1}{2\sigma^2}\left[\frac{(w_{t1})^2}{[t_1]} + \frac{(w_{t2}-w_{t1})^2}{[t_2-t_1]} + \frac{(w_{t3}-w_{t2})^2}{[t_3-t_2]} + \cdots + \frac{(w_{tn}-w_{tn-1})^2}{[t_n-t_{n-1}]}\right]\right\}}{\sqrt{(2\pi\sigma^2)^{n+1} t_1 [t_2-t_1][t_3-t_2]\cdots[t_n-t_{n-1}]}}, \tag{8.79}$$

$$f_{tk-tk-1}(w_{tk} - w_{tk-1}; \boldsymbol{\psi}_{tk-tk-1}) = \frac{1}{\sigma\sqrt{2\pi[t_k-t_{k-1}]}} \exp\left\{-\frac{(w_{tk}-w_{tk-1})^2}{2\sigma^2[t_k-t_{k-1}]}\right\}. \tag{8.80}$$

Due to the Normality assumption, the probabilistic structure of a Wiener process can be seen from any bivariate distribution of (W_t, W_s) for $t > s$ (see chapter 4 for the notation):

$$\begin{pmatrix} W_t \\ W_s \end{pmatrix} \sim \mathsf{N}\left(\begin{pmatrix} \mu t \\ \mu s \end{pmatrix}, \begin{pmatrix} \sigma^2 t, & \sigma^2 s \\ \sigma^2 s, & \sigma^2 s \end{pmatrix}\right), \quad t > s \in \mathbb{T},$$

(a) $E(W_t) = \mu t$, $t \in \mathbb{T}$,
(b) $Var(W_t) = \sigma^2 t$, $t \in \mathbb{T}$,
(c) $Cov(W_t, W_s) = \sigma^2 \min(t,s)$, $t,s \in \mathbb{T}$.

REMARK: in a number of publications it is noted that from (c) follows that for any $\tau > 0$ the autocorrelation is:

$$Corr(W_t, W_{t+\tau}) = \frac{t}{\sqrt{(t^2 + t\tau)}}, \text{ for all } (t + \tau) \in \mathbb{T}.$$

This is often interpreted as suggesting that for large values of t, and irrespective of the distance between observations τ:

$$Corr(W_t, W_{t+\tau}) \underset{t \to \infty}{\to} 1.$$

Notice first that the autocorrelation is a function of both t and τ, i.e., the process is index-heterogeneous. Second, this interpretation should be viewed with caution because the event $t \to \infty$ does not represent anything interesting; t is just an index, it has no connection to the sample size! This is better shown by the following alternative way to express the autocorrelation:

$$Corr(Y_t, Y_s) = \begin{cases} \sqrt{t/s}, & \text{if } t \leq s, \\ \sqrt{s/t}, & \text{if } t \geq s. \end{cases}$$

In terms of the basic elements of a statistical model, a Wiener process is composed of the following ingredients:

(D) Distribution: Normal,
(M) Dependence: martingale dependence,
(H) Heterogeneity: partial sum heterogeneity.

In view of the above moments the Wiener process is *not* stationary because its moments depend on t, but it has second-order separable (partial sum) heterogeneity. Let us ignore for a moment the fact that we constructed the Wiener process as a sequence of partial sums of IID Normal random variables and consider the properties of the *difference* process $\{\Delta W_t := W_t - W_{t-1}, t \in \mathbb{T}\}$:

$$E(\Delta W_t) = E(W_t - W_{t-1}) = \mu t - \mu(t-1) = \mu, \qquad t = 1,2,\dots$$

$$Var(\Delta W_t) = Var(W_t) + Var(W_{t-1}) - 2Cov(W_t, W_{t-1}) =$$
$$= \sigma^2 t + \sigma^2(t-1) - 2\sigma^2(t-1) = \sigma^2, \qquad t = 1,2,\dots$$

$$Cov(\Delta W_t, \Delta W_{t-\tau}) = 0, \ \tau \geq 1, \qquad t = 1,2,\dots$$

These results show that the process $\{\Delta W_t, t \in \mathbb{T}\}$ is both second-order and strictly stationary because for a *Gaussian* process second-order stationary implies strict stationarity.

In terms of the index set/state space $(\mathbb{T}, \mathcal{R})$ taxonomy the Wiener process $\{W_t, t = 1,2, \dots\}$ belongs to category D–C: $\mathbb{T} = \{1,2,\dots\}$ – countable, $\mathcal{R} = (-\infty,\infty)$ – uncountable. This process is closely related to the Brownian motion process $\{B(t), \sim t \in [0,\infty)\}$ (see below) but differs from it in one important respect; the latter has an uncountable index set: $\mathbb{T} = [0,\infty)$.

8.10.6 The Brownian motion process

The Brownian motion process $\{B(t), t \in [0,\infty)\}$ is of particular interest in the context of stochastic processes for several reasons. First, the process itself can be used to model the behavior of prices in financial markets (e.g., stock returns, exchange rates and interest rates). Second, it constitutes the principal element for a class of stochastic processes called *diffusions* which are based on the stochastic differentials:

$$dX(t) = \mu(X(t))\, dt + \sigma(X(t))\, dB(t),$$

so that the change in $X(t)$ is made up of two components: a drift of $\mu(X(t))$ and a Brownian increment with variance $\sigma^2(X(t))$. Third, it is useful for the description of the asymptotic behavior of a number of estimators and test statistics based on the partial sums discussed above; see Dhrymes (1998) for an extensive discussion.

TERMINOLOGY: there is a confusion in the literature in so far as the process first noticed by Brown is called a Brownian motion or a Wiener process. In the finance literature the confusion is even more pervasive because this process is often confused with the *random walk* process as well. To minimize the confusion and also give credit where it is due, it was decided in this book to call the original continuous process a *Brownian motion* but its discrete counterpart a *Wiener process*; this, however, is not standard terminology.

The stochastic process $\{B(t), t\in[0,\infty)\}$ is said to be a *standard Brownian motion process* if the following conditions hold:

(i) $B(t+h)-B(t)\sim N(0,|h|)$, for $(t+h)\in[0,\infty)$,
(ii) $B(t)$ has independent increments, i.e. for $0\le t_1<t_2<t_3<\infty$,

$$\begin{pmatrix}B(t_1)-B(t_2)\\B(t_2)-B(t_3)\end{pmatrix}\sim N\left(\begin{pmatrix}0\\0\end{pmatrix}\begin{pmatrix}t_2-t_1 & 0\\0, & t_3-t_2\end{pmatrix}\right).$$

The joint density, based on the index subset $0<t_0<t_1, ...,<t_n,$ takes the same form as (8.79) with:

$$f_{t_k-t_{k-1}}(b(t_k)-b(t_{k-1});\psi_{tk})=\frac{1}{\sqrt{2\pi(t_k-t_{k-1})}}\exp\left\{-\frac{[b(t_k)-b(t_{k-1})]^2}{2[t_k-t_{k-1}]}\right\},$$

(iii) $B(0)=0$.

REMARK: the condition (iii) is just a normalization in the sense that in the case where $B(0)\ne 0$ we can define the process $\{B(t)-B(0), t\in[0,\infty)\}$ which is now a Brownian motion.

In terms of the index set/state space $(\mathbb{T},\mathcal{R})$ taxonomy the Brownian motion process belongs to category C–C: $\mathbb{T}:=[0,\infty)$ – uncountable, $\mathcal{R}:=\mathbb{R}$ – uncountable.

In view of the above definition the only thing we need in order to determine the complete distribution of the Brownian motion process $\{B(t), t\in[0,\infty)\}$ is its covariance structure for $0\le t_1<t_2$:

$$E(B(t_1)\cdot B(t_2))=E\{B(t_1)[B(t_2)-B(t_1)]+B(t_1)^2\},=E(B(t_1)^2)=t_1.$$

In general, for any $t_1\in[0,\infty)$, $t_2\in[0,\infty)$: $Cov(B(t_1),B(t_2))=\min(t_1,t_2)$.

Using this result we can show that for $0\le t_1<t_2<t_3<t_4$:

$$\begin{aligned}E([B(t_2)-B(t_1)][B(t_4)-B(t_3)])&=[Cov(B(t_2),B(t_4))-Cov(B(t_2),B(t_3))]-\\&-[Cov(B(t_1),B(t_4))-Cov(B(t_1),B(t_3))]=\\&=(t_2-t_2)-(t_1-t_1)=0.\end{aligned}$$

which proves that $\{B(t),t\in[0,\infty)\}$ is indeed an independent increments process.

In terms of the basic taxonomy of probabilistic assumptions, a Brownian motion process is composed of the following ingredients:

(D) Distribution: Normal,
(M) Dependence: martingale dependence,
(H) Heterogeneity: partial sum heterogeneity.

Interesting properties of a Brownian motion process

(i)   The Brownian motion is a Markov process. This follows directly from the fact that if $\{B(t), t\in[0,\infty)\}$ is a Brownian motion then:

$$B(t_2+t_1)=B(t_1)+[B(t_1+t_2)-B(t_1)],$$

which suggests that the new state $B(t_2 + t_1)$ is the sum of the old state $B(t_1)$ and an independent Normal random variable $[B(t_2 + t_1) - B(t_1)]$. This property was first noted by Bachelier in 1900.

(ii)   The sample paths $\{B(\bar{s},t), t \in [0,\infty)\}$ ($\bar{s}$ is a given element of the outcomes set S) of a Brownian motion process are continuous but almost nowhere differentiable. If we can think of the zig-zag trace of a particle in a liquid we can understand why it is non-differentiable.

(iii)   The scaling property. The Brownian motion processes $\left\{\sqrt{c}B\!\left(\frac{t}{c}\right),\ t \in [0,\infty)\right\}$ and $\{B(t),\ t \in [0,\infty)\}$ have the same joint distribution.

(iv)   The Brownian motion is a Normal (Gaussian) process. This property follows directly from the definition but what is surprising is that the reverse is also true. That is, every stochastic process with independent increments is Gaussian if its sample paths are continuous with probability one (see Breiman (1968)).

Stochastic processes related to the Brownian motion

For reference purposes we mention three related stochastic processes.

1   The stochastic process $\{B^*(t), t \in [0,\infty)\}$ is said to be a *Brownian motion with a drift* and variance σ^2 if:

$$\{B^*(t) = \mu t + \sigma B(t), t \in [0,\infty)\}$$

where $\{B(t), t \in [0,\infty)\}$ is a standard Brownian motion.

2   The stochastic process $\{X(t), t \in [0,\infty)\}$ is said to be a *Brownian bridge* if:

$$\{X(t) = B(t) - tB(1), t \in [0,1]\}$$

where $\{B(t), t \in [0,\infty)\}$ is a standard Brownian motion. By definition the first two moments of a Brownian bridge process are:

$$E(X(t)) = E(B(t)) - tE(B(1)) = 0,$$

$$Cov(X(t),X(s)) = Cov([B(t) - tB(1)],[B(s) - sB(1)]), \text{ for } t \geq s, (t,s) \in [0,1] \times [0,1],$$
$$= Cov(B(t),B(s)) - sCov(B(t),B(1)) -$$
$$- tCov(B(s),B(1)) + stCov(B(1),B(1)) =$$
$$= s - st - ts + st = s(1 - t).$$

3   The stochastic process $\{X(t), t \in [0,\infty)\}$ defined by:

$$\{X(t) = \sqrt{\alpha}e^{-\beta t}B(e^{2\beta t}), t \in [0,\infty)\},$$

where $\{B(t), t \in [0,\infty)\}$ is a standard Brownian motion, is said to be an *Ornstein–Uhlenbeck process*. This process constitutes a more realistic model for the motion of small particles suspended in liquid because its sample paths are also differentiable, providing a measure for the velocity of the particle. It was first proposed by Ornstein and Uhlenbeck in 1930 and it was based on Newton's second law of motion as formulated by Langevin (see Breiman (1968), Bhattacharya and Waymire (1990)). The Ornstein–Uhlenbeck process can be viewed as stationary version of the Brownian motion process in the following sense. It was shown above that the standard Brownian motion $\{B(t), t \in [0,\infty)\}$ is not stationary because its first two moments are linear functions of t. However, consider the transformation of the index:

$\tau = \ln t$ or $t = e^\tau$,

which, in conjunction with the scaling property of the Brownian motion process defines the new process:

$X(t) = e^{-t} B(e^{2t}),\ t \in [0,\infty).$

This is a second-order stationary process because its first two moments are:

$E(X(t)) = E(e^{-t} B(e^{2t})) = e^{-t} E(B(e^{2t})) = 0,\ t \in [0,\infty),$

$E(X(t) \cdot X(\tau)) = e^{-(t+\tau)} E(B(e^{2t}) B(e^{2\tau})) = e^{-(t+\tau)} e^{2\min(t,\tau)} = e^{-|t-\tau|},\ t \in [0,\infty).$

This is an example of how a simple transformation of the index can lead to a temporally homogeneous process. The Ornstein–Uhlenbeck stochastic process is a scaled version of this process with moments:

$E(X(t)) = 0,\ E(X(t) \cdot X(\tau)) = \alpha e^{-\beta |t-\tau|},\ t \in \mathbb{T}, \tau \in \mathbb{T}.$

Both of the above processes are also strictly stationary because of Normality.

4 The stochastic process $\{X(t), t \in [0,\infty)\}$ is said to be an *Integrated Brownian motion process* if:

$$\left\{ X(t) = \int_0^t B(u)du,\ t \in [0,\infty) \right\}.$$

It can be shown that (see Parzen (1962)):

$E(X(t)) = \int_0^t E(B(u))\,du = 0,$

$E(X^2(t)) = \int_0^t \int_0^t E(B(u)B(v))\,dudv = \int_0^t [\int_0^u 2u\,du]\,dv = \left(\frac{t^3}{3}\right),$

$E(X(t)X(s)) = E(X^2(s)) + (t-s)E(X(s)B(s)) = s^2\left(\frac{t}{2} - \frac{s}{6}\right),\ t > s \geq 0.$

5 The stochastic process $\{X(t), t \in [0,\infty)\}$ is said to be a *Geometric Brownian motion process* if:

$\{X(t) = \exp(B(t)), t \in [0,\infty)\}.$

The name stems from the fact that this process can be viewed in relation to an IID process:

$$\left\{ Z(t) = \left(\frac{X(t)}{X(t-1)}\right), t \in [0,\infty) \right\}.$$

Taking $X(0) = 1$, we can deduce that $Z(t)$ is the geometric mean of the $X(t)$s, i.e.

$$Z(t) = \prod_{k=1}^t X(k),\ \text{or equivalently } \ln Z(t) = \sum_{k=1}^t \ln X(k).$$

In view of the fact that the $X(t)$s are IID, $\ln Z(t)$, would converge to the Geometric Brownian motion.

Brownian motion as a limit of a random walk

The Brownian motion process constitutes an important variation of the simple random walk. Consider the case where the sequence of IID random variables $\{X_n, n=1,2,3,...\}$, has a symmetric distribution $\left(p=\frac{1}{2}\right)$ and instead of steps of 1 and -1, takes steps of magnitude h every δ seconds. By defining $B_\delta(t)$ to be the accumulated sum up to time t, i.e.:

$$B_\delta(t)=h(X_1+X_2+X_3+...+X_n)=hS_n, \text{ where } n=\frac{t}{\delta},$$

and simultaneously shrinking both the size of the jumps ($h \to 0$) and the time between jumps ($\delta \to 0$), the resulting process $\{B(t),t\in[0,\infty)\}$, where $\mathbb{T}:=[0,\infty)$ is the non-negative part of the real line, is a continuous time process. Let us see this in some detail.

The mean and variance of the process $\{B_\delta(t),t\in[0,\infty)\}$ are:

$$E(B_\delta(t))=hE(S_n)=0, \;\; Var(B_\delta(t))=h^2n\,Var(X_n)=h^2n=h^2\left(\frac{t}{\delta}\right),$$

since $Var(X_n)=4p(1-p)=1$ for $p=\frac{1}{2}$. Defining $h=\sigma\sqrt{\delta}$ and letting both go to zero we define a continuous-time process $\{B(t),\,t\in[0,\infty)\}$ which begins at the origin and has mean and variance:

$$E(B(t))=0, \;\; Var(B(t))=\left(\sigma\sqrt{\delta}\right)^2\left(\frac{t}{\delta}\right)=\sigma^2 t.$$

Also, by noting that as $\delta \to 0, n=\left(\frac{t}{\delta}\right)\to\infty$, we can use the *Central Limit Theorem* (see chapter 9) to argue that the distribution of the stochastic process $\{B(t),t\in[0,\infty)\}$ approaches the Normal, i.e., $f(b(t);\sigma^2)=\frac{1}{\sigma\sqrt{2\pi t}}e^{-\frac{1}{2\sigma^2 t}b(t)^2}$; see Bhattacharya and Waymire (1990).

8.11 Point processes

8.11.1 The constructionist approach

Point processes can be thought of as generalizations of the Poisson process.

A stochastic process $\{N(t),\,t\in[0,\infty)\}$ is called a *point (or renewal) process* if:

$$N(t)=\max\{n:S_n\le t\},$$

where $S_n=\sum_{i=1}^n X_i$ for $n\ge 1$, $S_0=0$, and $\{X_n,\,n=1,2,...\}$ is a sequence of IID, non-negative random variables. In terms of the index set/state space $(\mathbb{T},\mathcal{R})$ taxonomy a point process $\{N(t),\,t\in\mathbb{T}\}$ has a *discrete state space* but the index set $\mathbb{T}$, can be either discrete or continuous.

From the process $\{N(t),\,t\in[0,\infty)\}$ we can proceed to construct the other two processes associated with it:

$$S_n=\min\{t:N(t)=n\}, \;\; X_n=S_n-S_{n-1}, n=1,2,...$$

where $\{S_n, n=1,2,...\}$ and $\{X_n, n=1,2,...\}$. The most important member of this class of processes is the Poisson process considered next.

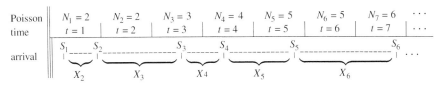

Figure 8.8 Stochastic processes associated with a Poisson process

8.11.2   The Poisson process

Consider the partial sums stochastic process $\{S_n, \; n=1,2,3,...\}$, where $S_n = \sum_{i=1}^{n} X_i$, $S_0 = 0$, and $\{X_n, n = 1,2,3,...\}$ is an *IID Exponential process*. If it helps, think of each S_n as the time at which the telephone rings for the nth time. NOTE that:

$$X_n = S_n - S_{n-1}, \; n = 1,2, \; ...,$$

denotes the time interval between telephone calls $n-1$ and n.

Consider the following function of the partial sum process:

$$N(t) = \max \; \{n : S_n \leq t\}, \; t \in [0,\infty)\},$$

which denotes the number of calls up to time t. $N(t)$ is constant until an event occurs, at which point it increases by 1. This function defines the so-called *Poisson process* $\{N(t), t \in [0,\infty)\}$. In terms of the index set/state space $(\mathbb{T}, \mathcal{R})$ taxonomy the stochastic process $\{N(t), t \in [0,\infty)\}$ belongs to category C–D: $\mathbb{T} := [0,\infty)$ – uncountable, $\mathcal{R} := \{0,1,2,...\}$ – countable.

In a more general set up we can define the three interrelated processes as follows:

(a) $N(t)$: the number of arrivals in the time interval $[0, t)$,
(b) S_n : the arrival times $0 = S_0 < S_1 < S_2 < \cdots < S_n < \cdots$ is related to $N(t)$ via:

$$S_n = \min \; \{t : N(t) = n\},$$

(c) X_n: the times between arrivals (see figure 8.8).

The joint density of a Poisson process, based on the index subset $0 < t_0 < t_1, \; ..., < t_n$, and the corresponding integers $k_0 \leq k_1 \leq k_2 \cdots \leq k_n$, takes the form:

$$\mathbb{P}(N(t_0) = k_0, N(t_1) = k_1, \; ..., \; N(t_n) = k_n) = \frac{e^{-\lambda t(\lambda t)^{k_0}}}{k_0!} \prod_{\ell=1}^{n} e^{-\lambda(t\ell - t\ell - 1)} \frac{[\lambda(t_\ell - t_{\ell-1})]^{k_\ell - k_{\ell-1}}}{(k_\ell - k_{\ell-1})!}.$$

This is because:

$$\mathbb{P}(N(t_0) = k_0, N(t_1) - N(t_0) = k_1 - k_0, \; ..., \; N(t_n) - N(t_{n-1}) = k_n - k_{n-1}) =$$
$$= \mathbb{P}(N(t_0) = k_0) \prod_{\ell=1}^{n} \mathbb{P}(N(t_\ell) - N(t_{\ell-1}) = k_\ell - k_{\ell-1}) =$$
$$= \mathbb{P}(N(t_0) = k_0) \prod_{\ell=1}^{n} \mathbb{P}(N(t_\ell - t_{\ell-1}) = k_\ell - k_{\ell-1}).$$

Noticing that the event $(N(t) \geq k)$ is equivalent to the event $(S_k \leq t)$, it follows that:

$$\mathbb{P}(N(t) \geq k) = \mathbb{P}(S_k \leq t).$$

In view of the fact that S_n is the sum of IID exponentially distributed random variables we can deduce that its distribution is Gamma (see chapter 3). Hence, the density function of $N(t)$ takes the form:

$$\mathbb{P}(N(t)=k):=f_N(k)=\mathbb{P}(S_k\leq t)-\mathbb{P}(S_{k+1}\leq t)=$$

$$=\int_0^1\left(\frac{\lambda^k v^{k-1}}{(k-1)!}-\frac{\lambda^{k+1}v^k}{k!}\right)e^{-\lambda v}dv=\frac{e^{-\lambda t}(\lambda t)^k}{k!},$$

i.e., $\{N(t),t\in[0,\infty)\}$ is a Poisson stochastic process with mean and variance:

$$E(N(t))=\lambda t,\ Var(N(t))=\lambda t.$$

That is, the Poisson process is *not* stationary because as we can see its first two moments depend on t, but it enjoys separable heterogeneity.

8.12 Exercises

1 Why do we need the notion of a stochastic process? How does it differ from the concept of a random variable?

2 Explain the notion of a sample path of a stochastic process.

3 Compare the notions of time and probability averages. When do the two coincide? What happens if they are unrelated?

4 Explain the classification of stochastic processes using the index set and the state space.

5 Explain intuitively the Kolmogorov extension theorem. What is its significance?

6 What is the difference between the distributional and constructive approaches to specifying stochastic processes?

7 Explain the notions of Markov dependence and homogeneity.

8 Explain the relationship between Markov and independent increments processes.

9 What is the relationship between identically distributed increment processes and stationarity?

10 Explain the notion of a partial sum stochastic process.

11 Compare and contrast a partial sum processes and a martingale processes.

12 Explain the probabilistic structure of a random walk process.

13 Explain the notion of separable heterogeneity.

14 Discuss briefly the role of a Brownian motion process in the formation of the foundations of probability theory.

15 Explain the following notions of dependence:
    (a) Independence,
    (b) Markov dependence,
    (c) Markov dependence of order m,
    (d) m-dependence,
    (e) asymptotic independence,
    (f) non-correlation,

    (g) α-mixing,

    (h) ϕ-mixing.

16 Explain the relationship between ψ-mixing and a mixingale.

17 Explain the notion of ergodicity.

18 Explain the following notions of heterogeneity:

    (a)   Identical Distribution,

    (b)   strict stationarity,

    (c)   first-order stationarity,

    (d)   second-order stationarity,

    (e) mth-order stationarity,

    (f)   exchangeability

19 Define the block stochastic processes:

    (a)   IID Bernoulli process,

    (b)   IID exponential process,

    (c)   white-noise process,

    (d)   innovation process,

    (e)   martingale difference process.

20 Compare and contrast the stochastic processes:

    (a)   white-noise process,

    (b)   innovation process,

    (c)   martingale difference process.

    Explain why a martingale difference process can accommodate dynamic heteroskedasticity but the innovation process cannot.

21 A Markov chain is a special Markov process. Explain.

22 Explain the notion of a Poisson process.

23 Explain the probabilistic structure of a martingale process.

24 Consider the IID process $\{X_t,\ t=1,2,3,\ldots\}$ such that $E(X_t)=\mu\neq 0,\ t=1,2,\ldots$ Show that the process $\{M_t,\ t=1,2,3,\ldots\}$ defined by $M_t=\left(\frac{1}{\mu}\right)^t\prod_{k=1}^{t}X_k$ is a martingale.

25 Explain the probabilistic structure of a Gaussian Markov process.

26 Explain how a Gaussian, Markov stationary process can give rise to an AR(1) model.

27 "An ARMA(p,q) representation constitutes a parsimonious version of a MA(∞)." Discuss.

28 Explain the probabilistic structure of a Wiener process.

29 Explain how a Brownian motion process can be changed into a second-order stationary process by a transformation of the index.

30 Compare and contrast the Normal autoregressive model and the Normal/linear regression model specified in chapter 7.

9 Limit theorems

9.1 Introduction to limit theorems

The main purpose of this chapter is to introduce the reader to one of the most fascinating and at the same time one of the most difficult areas of probability theory. The material is naturally technical and it is often served as a dreary catalogue of theorems. An attempt is made to deal with both problems using the following devices:

(i) The *historical development* of limit theorems is used as a backdrop for the discussion. A number of concepts are first introduced as part of the historical development in order to avoid the high concentration of concepts when stating or proving the theorems themselves. Moreover, the historical development enables us to bring out one of the most important dimensions of limit theorems: the *gradual weakening* of the conditions giving rise to the results.

(ii) This gradual weakening is considered in conjunction with the basic taxonomy of probabilistic assumptions into:

$$\text{(D) Distribution, \quad (M) Dependence, \quad (H) Homogeneity.} \tag{9.1}$$

This brings out another important aspect of limit theorems: the *trade off* between assumptions from different categories.

9.1.1 A bird's eye view of the chapter

After some important introductory remarks relating to (a) why we care, (b) terminology, and (c) certain misconceptions about limit theorems, we proceed to discuss briefly the historical development of the various limit theorems in section 2. In sections 3 and 4 we consider the *Law of Large Numbers* which comes in two flavors, the weak and the strong, respectively. In section 5 we discuss briefly the Law of Iterated Logarithm. Section 6 discusses the development of the *Central Limit Theorem*. Section 7 comments briefly on how the results of the limit theorems can be extended to arbitrary functions of a sequence of random variables. In section 8 we discuss the so-called *Functional Central Limit Theorem* which constitutes a recent refinement of the classical Central Limit

Theorem. Section 9 considers the various modes of convergence for random variables in some more detail. The chapter concludes with a general summary and discussion.

9.1.2 Why do we care?

Limit theorems constitute the mathematical backbone of probability theory. For modeling purposes limit theorems are useful mainly because they provide approximate answers to the question of determining the behavior of statistics (estimators, test statistics, and predictors) of interest in statistical inference.

The most important problem in statistical inference is the determination of the *distribution* of a *function of random variables*:

$$Y = g(X_1, X_2, \ldots, X_n),$$

when the distribution of $(X_1, X_2, \ldots, X_n)$ is known; the latter distribution is usually given by the postulated statistical model. Theoretically the distribution of Y is determined by:

$$F(Y \le y) = \mathbb{P}\{(X_1, X_2, \ldots, X_n) \in B_x\} = \underbrace{\int \int \cdots \int}_{B_X} f(x_1, x_2, \ldots, x_n) dx_1 dx_2 \cdots dx_n,$$

$$B_x = [g^{-1}(Y \le y)] := \{g(x_1, x_2, \ldots, x_n) \le y\}. \tag{9.2}$$

However, multiple integrals are difficult to solve at the best of times, and thus it should come as no surprise to learn that this is often a very difficult problem to solve even for simple functions $g(.)$. For this reason the results in this area are rather sparse and related mostly to simple functions of certain distributions such as the Normal and the Binomial. In statistical inference, however, we need to solve this problem somehow before we can derive results on estimation, testing, and prediction. In cases where the problem posed in (9.2) does not have a usable solution, we usually resort to approximate solutions, based on $n \to \infty$, utilizing the limit theorems that follow. This is the primary usefulness of limit theorems.

9.1.3 Terminology and taxonomy

The term **limit theorems** is used to refer to a group of results which relate to the behavior of well-behaved functions (Borel functions) of a set of random variables $(X_1, X_2, \ldots, X_n)$, as n goes to infinity, i.e.:

$$Y_n := g(X_1, X_2, \ldots, X_n), \text{ as } n \to \infty.$$

The most important sub-categories of these limit theorems are:

(i)   the *Weak Law of Large Numbers* (*WLLN*),
(ii) the *Strong Law of Large Numbers* (*SLLN*), and
(iii) the *Central Limit theorem* (*CLT*).

All these limit theorems have three things in common:

(a)   they all postulate a sequence of random variables $\{X_n\}_{n=1}^{\infty} := \{X_1, X_2, \ldots, X_n, \ldots\}$.

(b)   they all impose certain restrictions on the probabilistic structure of this sequence,

(c)   they are all concerned with the behavior of scaled versions of summations:

$$c_n^{-1}S_n := c_n^{-1}(\sum_{k=1}^{n}[X_k - E(X_k)]), \text{ as } n \to \infty, \tag{9.3}$$

where $\{c_n\}_{n=1}^{\infty}$ is a sequence of appropriately chosen real numbers.
They *differ* in two important respects:

(d)   the scaling sequences $\{c_n\}_{n=1}^{\infty}$, and

(e)   their conclusions:

$$\text{(i) WLLN}: a_n^{-1}S_n \xrightarrow{\mathbb{P}} 0, \quad \text{(ii) SLLN}: a_n^{-1}S_n \xrightarrow{a.s.} 0, \quad \text{(iii) CLT}: c_n^{-1}S_n \xrightarrow{\mathcal{D}} \Phi(x).$$

The details of these, including the symbolism, will be discussed at length in what follows.
   Limit theorems are useful in deriving approximate results for the behavior of the summation, irrespective of the distribution of $(X_1, X_2, \ldots, X_n)$. It must be emphasized at the outset that these limit theorems provide only *approximations* to the actual behavior of $(\sum_{k=1}^{n}[X_k - E(X_k)])$ for a given n, and can be misleading for a small n. Hence, such results should be used as a last resort; when the distribution of $(\sum_{k=1}^{n}[X_k - E(X_k)])$ cannot be derived by the methods discussed in chapter 11.

   It must be noted that these three generic names of limit theorems refer to three categories of limit results, which, however, do not exhaust all limit theorems.

9.1.4   Popular misconceptions

It is imperative to clear up at the outset certain misconceptions in connection with limit theorems and in particular the CLT.

(i)   The WLLN *does not* say that in a given run of n tosses of a fair coin the difference between the number of "Heads" and the number of "Tails" will be small. This misconception is discussed in the next section.

(ii)   The most popular misconception about the CLT is the well-known lame excuse for using Normality even in cases where it is clearly inappropriate. The excuse is that "all distributions converge to the Normal as the sample size increases." The CLT *does not say* that! No! No! The nature of a distribution *does not* usually change with the sample size. What does change is the nature of the distribution of certain *scaled summations of random variables*, but always under certain *restrictions*. These restrictions can be crudely summarized by saying that they are designed to ensure that *no one random variable in the sequence* $\{X_n\}_{n=1}^{\infty}$ *dominates the behavior of the summation* $(\sum_{k=1}^{n}[X_k - E(X_k)])$. The conditions that ensure the insignificance of the individual random variable when compared with the summation take numerous forms and this is why we have numerous versions such limit theorems.

(iii)   Another misconception is related to the *aggregation* of data by averaging and it concerns the so-called *CLT effect*. It is often mistakenly argued that in cases where daily data are aggregated to weekly or even monthly data by averaging, i.e., $x_w := \frac{1}{n}\sum_k^n x_k$, the CLT effect means that the weekly observations will have a distribution that tends to the Normal, irrespective of the distribution of the daily observations. The fallacy here is a bit more subtle than (i) but it is a fallacy all the same. In view of the fact that a week has only seven days and a month only four weeks, etc., no CLT effect can be called upon. In other words, n in the above averaging does not increase to infinity in any sense and thus the most important ingredient of the CLT is missing!

(iv)   The Normal distribution is not the only distribution scaled summations converge to. There is a Central Limit Theorem for every member of the so-called *Levy–Khintchine family* of distributions which includes not just the Normal, Poisson and Cauchy distributions but a whole group known as the *infinitely divisible distributions* (see Hoffmann-Jorgensen (1994)). Moreover, continuous functions of scaled summations of random variables converge to several well-known distributions including the Chi-square (in case of quadratic functions).

(v)   When we consider other functions (not scaled summations) of stochastic sequences, such as their maximum, the limit distributions are never Normal.

9.2   Tracing the roots of limit theorems

James Bernoulli in 1713 proved the first Law of Large Numbers. This thread was taken up by de Moivre who proved the first Central Limit Theorem in 1718. Laplace in 1812, drew together and extended the previous two limit theorems. Apart from some marginal weakening of the conditions underlying the LLN by Poisson in the 1830s, the next important milestone was the founding of the Russian school of probability by Chebyshev in the 1870s. Chebyshev was the first to recognize the generality of these limit theorems and provided the foundation upon which the other members of this school of thought, his students Markov and Lyapunov, extended the limit theorems to their modern form. The last member of that illustrious school, Kolmogorov, not only improved upon the work of his predecessors but, in 1933, provided probability theory with its modern mathematical foundations. Let us see how the story of limit theorems unfolds in some more detail.

The first limit theorem was proved by **James Bernoulli** (1654–1705) in his book *Ars Conjectandi*, published posthumously in 1713. Bernoulli revealed his views about the importance of the theorem by calling it *the golden theorem*; today it is known as the *Law of Large Numbers* (LLN), a term first introduced by Poisson in 1837. According to Bernoulli's LLN:

if we toss a fair coin n times and it falls k times heads (H's), then, by increasing the number of tosses the probability of the event $\left\{ \left| \left(\frac{k}{n} \right) - \frac{1}{2} \right| < \varepsilon \right\}$ goes to one.

In order to understand what this theorem says it is important to clear a misinterpretation of this law, known as *gambler's delusion:*

if a fair coin, when tossed 8 times, yields the sequence $\{T,H,T,H,H,H,H,H\}$ i.e., falls heads for the last 5 consecutive tosses, the probability of getting tails in the next toss is (somehow) greater than that of heads.

This is based on the misguided intuition that for Bernoulli's LLN to be true, after many tosses the number of heads ($\#H$) and tails ($\#T$) will be more or less equal. We know, however, that coins have no memory and the probabilities remain the same for all trials. The fact is that Bernoulli's LLN says nothing about the *difference* $[(\#H) - (\#T)]$; indeed conditions of the form $[(\#H) - (\#T)] < \varepsilon$, for some small $\varepsilon > 0$, would invalidate the independence of the sequence of tosses. What the law talks about is the probability associated with the difference of the *ratio* $\left(\frac{(\#H)}{n}\right)$ and $\frac{1}{2}$ or by implication with the difference of the ratio $\left(\frac{(\#H)}{\#T}\right)$ and 1.

Bernoulli's LLN is better understood when expressed in terms of Bernoulli distributed random variables:

$$\{X_k = 1\} = \{H\}, \{X_k = 0\} = \{T\}, \mathbb{P}(X_k = 1) = \mathbb{P}(X_k = 0) = \tfrac{1}{2}, k = 1,2, \ldots$$

In terms of the sequence of Bernoulli random variables $\{X_n\}_{n=1}^{\infty}$, we can express the ratio of heads to the total number of tosses in the form

$$\left(\frac{(\#H)}{n}\right) := \left(\frac{k}{n}\right) = \frac{1}{n}\sum_{i=1}^{n} X_i, \tag{9.4}$$

and Bernoulli's LLN can be written as:

$$\lim_{n\to\infty}\mathbb{P}(|\tfrac{1}{n}\sum_{i=1}^{n} X_i - \tfrac{1}{2}| < \varepsilon) = 1, \text{ for any } \varepsilon > 0. \tag{9.5}$$

The next important milestone in the history of limit theorems was provided by **Abraham de Moivre** (1667–1754) in his book *Doctrine of Chances*, first published in 1718. In the second edition of his book, published in 1734, de Moivre evaluated the probabilities associated with the event $\frac{1}{n}\sum_{i=1}^{n} X_i = \frac{1}{2}$, using the equivalent event of getting n heads in $2n$ tosses (with a fair coin) being:

$$\mathbb{P}\left(\sum_{i=1}^{2n} X_i = n\right) = \binom{2n}{n} 2^{-2n}.$$

Given that $\binom{n}{k} = \frac{n!}{k![n-k]!}$, where $n! = n \cdot (n-1) \cdot (n-2) \cdots (2) \cdot 1$, it is easy to see that for large n (and k) it was impossible to use this formula to evaluate the probabilities. Instead de Moivre used Stirling's formula (Stirling was a friend of his) to derive the approximation:

$$\mathbb{P}\left(\sum_{i=1}^{2n} X_i = n\right) \simeq \frac{1}{\sqrt{n\pi}}.$$

He noticed, however, that this probability goes to zero as n increases to infinity unless the event is pre-multiplied with the factor $\sqrt{n}$. By scaling these quantities he was able to derive a number of useful approximations. In terms of the sum in (9.4) the scaling takes the form:

$$Z_n := \sqrt{n}\left(\tfrac{1}{n}\sum_{i=1}^{n} X_i - \tfrac{1}{2}\right) = \frac{1}{\sqrt{n}}\left(\sum_{i=1}^{n} X_i - \tfrac{n}{2}\right).$$

Using this insight de Moivre went on to derive the general approximation:

$$\lim_{n\to\infty}\mathbb{P}(Z_n \leq z) = \frac{2}{\sqrt{2n}}\sum_{k=0}^{\infty}(-1)^k \frac{2^k \cdot z^{2k-1}}{k!(2k+1)}, \text{ for } z \in \mathbb{R}.$$

What he didn't know at the time was that the right-hand side is a series expansion of the Normal distribution with $E(Z) = 0$ and variance $Var(Z) = \frac{1}{4}$:

$$\tfrac{2}{\sqrt{2n}}\Sigma_{k=0}^{\infty}(-1)^k\tfrac{2^k \cdot z^{2k-1}}{k!(2k+1)}=\sqrt{\tfrac{2}{\pi}}\int_0^z e^{-2x^2}dx, \text{ for } z\in\mathbb{R}.$$

This was first recognized by **Pierre-Simon Laplace** (1749–1827) in the third edition of his book *Analytic Theory of Probability*, published in 1820. The Normal distribution was discovered a decade earlier by Legendre and Gauss and independently by Robert Adrain (1777–1855), a little known American surveyor. Laplace extended this result to the case of a general Bernoulli distribution with $\mathbb{P}(X=1)=p$ and $\mathbb{P}(X=0)=1-p$. For this reason the above result is known as the *De Moivre–Laplace central limit theorem*.

At this point it is interesting to note that the above Central Limit Theorem assumes that p is fixed and it can be used to provide reasonable approximations to Binomial probabilities when p is not close to either 0 or 1. For the case where p is close to zero it was found that the Normal provided a poor approximation. A much better approximation was provided by the Poisson distribution which turns out to be the limit distribution if we consider the asymptotic behavior of the partial sums assuming that as $n\to\infty, p\to 0$. The result is known as Poisson's limit theorem or the *Law of Small Numbers*.

Poisson's limit theorem Consider a sequence of independent Bernoulli trials such that the partial sum $S_n=\Sigma_{i=1}^n X_i$ has a Binomial distribution of the form:

$$S_n\sim\mathsf{Bi}(n,p_n), np_n\to\lambda \text{ as } n\to\infty \Rightarrow \lim_{n\to\infty}\mathbb{P}(S_n=k)=e^{-\lambda}\tfrac{\lambda^k}{k!}.$$

The next important development in relation to Bernoulli's LLN was provided by **Emile Borel** (1871–1956) who proved in 1909 a more profound result:

$$\mathbb{P}\left(s: \lim_{n\to\infty}\left[\tfrac{1}{n}\Sigma_{k=1}^n X_k(s)\right]=\tfrac{1}{2}\right)=1, \tag{9.6}$$

where we attach a probability to the set of elements $s\in S$ (the original probability space being $(S,\mathcal{F},\mathbb{P}(.))$) for which $\left|\tfrac{1}{n}\Sigma_{k=1}^n X_k(s)\right|$ converges to $\tfrac{1}{2}$ as $n\to\infty$. In Bernoulli's result (9.5) the convergence takes place in terms of the *probabilities*. The latter does not involve any convergence of $\tfrac{1}{n}\Sigma_{k=1}^n X_k$.

Example
Consider the random experiment of tossing a coin indefinitely and noting whether it turns up heads (H) or tails(T). The outcomes set S consists of all infinite sequences of Hs and Ts, i.e., the elementary events are of the form $\mathbf{s}:=\{s_1,s_2, ..., s_n,...\}$. Define the random variable:

$$X_k(\mathbf{s})=\begin{cases}1 \text{ if } s_k=H,\\0 \text{ if } s_k=T,\end{cases}$$

and $Y_n(\mathbf{s}):=\Sigma_{k=1}^n X_k(\mathbf{s})$. What we would like to say, but of course we *cannot*, is that:

$$\lim_{n\to\infty}\left[\tfrac{1}{n}\Sigma_{k=1}^n X_k(\mathbf{s})\right]=\tfrac{1}{2},$$

because firstly the limit might not exist, and secondly there might be infinite sequences such as $\mathbf{s}_T:=\{T,T, ..., T,...\}, \mathbf{s}_H:=\{H,H, ..., H,...\}$, whose limit is certainly *not* $\tfrac{1}{2}$.

What we can claim, however, is that (9.6) holds for *almost all* sequences in S. That is, for a large n, the probability of the subset $S_0 \subset S$ of the form:

$$S_0 = \left\{ s : \lim_{n \to \infty} \left[\frac{1}{n} \sum_{k=1}^{n} X_k(s) \right] \neq \frac{1}{2} \right\},$$

(e.g. S_0 includes sequences such as s_T and s_H) is negligible and as $n \to \infty$, the set S_0 involves fewer and fewer sequences such as s_T and s_H; in measure theoretic terminology S_0 is said to be a *set of measure zero*.

At this stage it is imperative to take stock of the various convergence results encountered so far before we proceed to discuss further the historical development of these results.

9.2.1 Convergence in limit theorems: a first view

We begin with the type of convergence involved in Bernoulli's LLN, known as *convergence in probability* to a constant, which can be expressed equivalently as:

$$\lim_{n \to \infty} \mathbb{P}\left(s \in S : \left| \frac{1}{n} \sum_{k=1}^{n} X_k(s) - \frac{1}{2} \right| \geq \varepsilon \right) = 0, \text{ for any } \varepsilon > 0. \tag{9.7}$$

This convergence has two components:

(i) the *events* associated with the distances: $\left\{ \left| \frac{1}{n} \sum_{k=1}^{n} X_k(s) - \frac{1}{2} \right| \geq \varepsilon \right\}$,

(ii) the *tail probabilities* associated with these events, say $\{p_n\}_{n=1}^{\infty}$, defined by: $p_n := \mathbb{P}\left(s \in S : \left| \frac{1}{n} \sum_{k=1}^{n} X_k(s) - \frac{1}{2} \right| \geq \varepsilon \right)$.

The convergence takes place at the level of the tail probabilities, always in conjunction with the events in (i), and amounts to:

$$\lim_{n \to \infty} p_n = 0.$$

The theorems along the lines drawn by Bernoulli, and associated with convergence in probability, are known as the *Weak Law of Large Numbers* (WLLN) in contrast to the *Strong Law of Large Numbers* (SLLN) associated with Borel's result (convergence almost surely), considered next.

The convergence mode associated with Borel's theorem is known as *converges almost surely* to a constant:

$$\mathbb{P}\left(s : \lim_{n \to \infty} \left[\frac{1}{n} \sum_{k=1}^{n} X_k(s) \right] = \frac{1}{2} \right) = 1. \tag{9.8}$$

Again the convergence has two components:

(i) the set of *events* associated with the distances: $\left\{ \left| \frac{1}{n} \sum_{k=1}^{n} X_k(s) - \frac{1}{2} \right| \geq \varepsilon \right\}$, defined by
$S_0 := \left\{ s : \left| \frac{1}{n} \sum_{k=1}^{n} X_k(s) - \frac{1}{2} \right| \geq \varepsilon \right\}$, a subset of S, and

(ii) the probability of this subset: $\mathbb{P}(s : s \in S_0) = 0$.

In contrast to convergence in probability, the convergence here takes place at the level of $\frac{1}{n} \sum_{k=1}^{n} X_k(s)$ in the sense that as $n \to \infty$ the set S_0 becomes a null event.

In terms of the indefinite tossing of a coin in the example discussed above, we can think of S_0 as the set of points of S which includes elements of the form

$s_T := \{T,T, ..., T,...\}$ and $s_H := \{H,H, ..., H,...\}$. As n increases such events become rarer and rarer (shrinking of the set S_0) rendering it a set of probability zero.

Intuitively, it feels as though convergence almost surely is a more powerful result then convergence in probability. Our intuition is indeed valid and we can prove (see section 8) that the former implies the latter, i.e., the conditions needed for the SLLN are more than adequate for the WLLN to hold.

As mentioned in section 2, the LLN says nothing about the *rate of convergence*. De Moivre was the first to notice that by multiplying the difference $|\frac{1}{n}\sum_{k=1}^{n} X_k(s) - \frac{1}{2}|$ with $\sqrt{n}$, the probability of the standardized quantity did not go to zero but converged to something non-degenerate. In this sense we can think of the CLT as providing information about the *rate of convergence* of the LLN.

The De Moivre–Laplace result entails a different mode of convergence known as *converges in distribution*:

$$\lim_{n\to\infty} F_n(x) = \Phi(x),$$

where $F_n(x)$ and $\Phi(x)$ denote the cdf of $\frac{1}{n}\sum_{k=1}^{n} X_k$ and that of the Normal distribution, respectively. The convergence here takes place only at the level of the cumulative distribution function as an ordinary convergence of bounded functions, NOTING that $\Phi(-\infty)=0$ and $\Phi(\infty)=1$, both being continuity points of $\Phi(.)$. The group of results developing the De Moivre–Laplace result is known generically as the *Central Limit Theorem*. As shown in section 8, convergence in distribution is the weakest of the three modes and convergence in probability implies convergence in distribution.

The next three sections can be viewed as a gradual weakening of the initial restrictions giving rise to the above three theorems.

9.3   The Weak Law of Large Numbers

As a prelude to the discussion that follows we make it clear at the outset that when we refer to a sequence of random variables $\{X_n\}_{n=1}^{\infty} := \{X_1, X_2, ..., X_n....\}$ we are in effect talking about a stochastic process as defined in chapter 8. The reader is strongly advised to refer back to chapter 8 for a number of concepts used in this chapter.

The WLLN, in its general form, can be stated crudely as saying that *under certain restrictions* on the sequence of random variables $\{X_n\}_{n=1}^{\infty}$:

$$\lim_{n\to\infty} \mathbb{P}\left(|\frac{1}{n}\sum_{k=1}^{n} X_k - \frac{1}{n}\sum_{k=1}^{n} E(X_k)| < \varepsilon\right) = 1, \text{ for any } \varepsilon > 0. \tag{9.9}$$

9.3.1   Bernoulli's WLLN

In an attempt to bring out the gradual weakening of the conditions giving rise to the WLLN let us begin with the general form of Bernoulli's WLLN; see Bernoulli (1713).

Bernoulli's WLLN Let $\{X_n\}_{n=1}^{\infty} := \{X_1, X_2, ..., X_n....\}$ be a sequence of random variables which satisfy the following conditions:

(D)   Bernoulli: $f(x_k;\theta_k) = \theta_k^{x_k}(1 - \theta_k)^{1-x_k}, x_k = 0,1, k = 1,2,...$

(M)   Independence: $f(x_1, x_2, \ldots, x_n; \varphi) = \prod_{k=1}^{n} f(x_k; \theta_k),$
(H)   Identical Distribution: $\theta_k = \theta$, for all $k = 1, 2, \ldots,$

$$\lim_{n \to \infty} \mathbb{P}\left(\left|\tfrac{1}{n}\sum_{k=1}^{n} X_k - \theta\right| < \varepsilon\right) = 1, \text{ for any } \varepsilon > 0, \tag{9.10}$$

and denoted by:

$$\tfrac{1}{n}\sum_{k=1}^{n} X_k \overset{\mathbb{P}}{\to} \theta.$$

That is, the probability of the event $\{|\tfrac{1}{n}\sum_{k=1}^{n} X_k - \theta| < \varepsilon\}$ approaches one, as n goes to infinity $(n \to \infty)$.

There are several things to NOTE about this result.

(i)   The function whose behavior the theorem is about is $\tfrac{1}{n}\sum_{k=1}^{n} X_k$.

(ii)   The event of interest is the difference between $\tfrac{1}{n}\sum_{k=1}^{n} X_k$ and its expected value $\left(E\left(\tfrac{1}{n}\sum_{k=1}^{n} X_k\right) = \theta\right)$.

(iii) What converges is the probability of this event, not $\tfrac{1}{n}\sum_{k=1}^{n} X_k$ itself.

(vi)   IMPORTANT. The basic assumptions underlying the result (9.10) can be viewed in the context of the fundamental taxonomy (9.1) used throughout the discussion in chapters 4–8. This is no coincidence; there is a direct connection between operational statistical models and limit theorems as shown in chapters 11–15.

Proof It is instructive to prove this result using *Chebyshev's inequality* (which, by the way, was not available to Bernoulli 1713):

$$\mathbb{P}(|X - E(X)| \epsilon) \leq \tfrac{Var(X)}{\epsilon^2}, \text{ for any } \epsilon > 0, \tag{9.11}$$

(see chapter 3), in order to bring out the role of the above conditions (1)–(3). Note that the above inequality pre-supposes that the random variable X has finite mean and variance ($E(X) < \infty$ and $Var(X) < \infty$). The proof amounts to a simple application of this inequality to the case of the random variable $\tfrac{1}{n}\sum_{k=1}^{n} X_k$ above.

Step 1 Derive the mean and variance of $\tfrac{1}{n}\sum_{k=1}^{n} X_k$:

(i) $E\left(\tfrac{1}{n}\sum_{k=1}^{n} X_k\right) = \tfrac{1}{n}\sum_{k=1}^{n} E(X_k) = \tfrac{1}{n}\sum_{k=1}^{n} \theta = \theta,$

(ii) $Var\left(\tfrac{1}{n}\sum_{k=1}^{n} X_k\right) = \tfrac{1}{n^2}\sum_{k=1}^{n} Var(X_k) = \tfrac{1}{n^2}\sum_{k=1}^{n}(\theta[1-\theta]) = \tfrac{1}{n}(\theta[1-\theta]),$

using $E(X_k) = \theta$ and $Var(X_k) = \theta(1-\theta)$ for all $k = 1, 2, \ldots, n$.

Step 2 Apply the Chebyshev inequality to deduce that:

$$\mathbb{P}\left(\left|\tfrac{1}{n}\sum_{k=1}^{n} X_k - \theta\right| \geq \varepsilon\right) \leq \tfrac{\theta(1-\theta)}{n\varepsilon^2}, \text{ or } \mathbb{P}\left(\left|\tfrac{1}{n}\sum_{k=1}^{n} X_k - \theta\right| < \varepsilon\right) \geq 1 - \tfrac{\theta(1-\theta)}{n\varepsilon^2}$$

Step 3 Consider the limit of this probability as $n \to \infty$:

$$\left(\tfrac{\theta[1-\theta]}{n\varepsilon^2}\right) \to 0, \Rightarrow \lim_{n \to \infty} \mathbb{P}\left(\left|\tfrac{1}{n}\sum_{k=1}^{n} X_k - \theta\right| < \varepsilon\right) = 1. \quad \blacksquare$$

If we take a closer look at this proof, we can see that some of the conditions assumed in the Bernoulli WLLN play only a minor role in establishing the result.

(i)   The distribution assumption of a *Bernoulli distribution* played no role beyond the boundedness of the first two moments:

   (a) $E(X_k) = \theta < \infty,$ (b) $Var(X_k) = \theta(1-\theta) < \infty$, for all $k = 1,2,\dots$

(ii)   The *Independence* assumption played a role in so far as at the last step it ensured that:

$$Var\left(\tfrac{1}{n}\Sigma_{k=1}^n X_k\right) \underset{n\to\infty}{\to} 0.$$

(iii) The *Identical Distribution* assumption played some role at step one in ensuring that the mean of the average equals the mean of any X_k:

$$E\left(\tfrac{1}{n}\Sigma_{k=1}^n X_k\right) = \theta.$$

   In a certain sense these remarks sketch out the progression of weaker and weaker conditions giving rise to the conclusion (9.10).

9.3.2 Poisson's WLLN

The first condition to be weakened was that of Identical Distribution (*complete homogeneity*) when **Simeon Denis Poisson** (1781–1840) proved in 1837 that (iii) could be relaxed without affecting the result.

Poisson's WLLN Let $\{X_n\}_{n=1}^\infty$ be a sequence of random variables which satisfy the following conditions:

   (D)   Bernoulli: $f(x_k;\theta_k) = \theta_k^{x_k}(1-\theta_k)^{1-x_k}, \; x_k = 0,1, \, k = 1,2,\dots$
   (M)   Independence: $f(x_1,x_2,\dots,x_n;\varphi) = \Pi_{k=1}^n f(x_k;\theta_k),$
   (H)   Heterogeneity: $\theta_i \neq \theta_j, \, i,j = 1,2,\dots$

$$\lim_{n\to\infty} \mathbb{P}\left(|\tfrac{1}{n}\Sigma_{k=1}^n X_k - \tfrac{1}{n}\Sigma_{i=1}^n \theta_k| < \varepsilon\right) = 1, \text{ for any } \varepsilon > 0. \tag{9.12}$$

At first sight this appears to suggest that Poisson was able to allow for *complete heterogeneity* for the sequence $\{X_n\}_{n=1}^\infty$, by allowing a different θ_n for each X_n:

$$E(X_n) = \theta_n, \; Var(X_n) = \theta_n(1-\theta_n), n = 1,2,\dots$$

This, however, is illusory because in conjunction with the Bernoulli assumption (D) we know that for each θ_n:

   (a) $0 < \theta_n < 1,$ (b) $\theta_n(1-\theta_n) \leq \tfrac{1}{4}, n = 1,2,\dots$

These indirect restrictions on the heterogeneity imply that

$$[1]\quad \lim_{n\to\infty}\left\{\tfrac{1}{n}\Sigma_{k=1}^n \theta_k\right\} = \vartheta < 1, \quad [2]\lim_{n\to\infty}\left\{\tfrac{1}{n}\Sigma_{k=1}^n \theta_k(1-\theta_k)\right\} = c \leq \tfrac{1}{4}.$$

This follows from the fact that in both cases we have sequences of partial sums with non-negative terms which are bounded (as shown in (a)–(b)); thus they converge (see Knopp (1947)). As we can see, the conditions [1]–[2] amount to *asymptotic homogeneity* and thus some form of homogeneity has been indirectly imposed. This is in accordance with the discussion throughout this book that for operational models one needs to impose certain restrictions from all three categories of probabilistic assumptions (see especially chapters 7–8).

9.3.3 Chebyshev's WLLN

The first general (in its modern form) WLLN was proved by Chebyshev (1821–1884), the founder of the Russian school of thought which included Markov (1856–1922), Lyapunov (1857–1918), and Kolmogorov (1903–1989). This school of thought had a profound effect on probability theory.

In addition to the complete homogeneity relaxed by Poisson, Chebyshev noticed that when using the inequality bearing his name to prove the WLLN:

(a) the Bernoulli distributed assumption seemed totally unnecessary; it is only role in the above proof was in deriving the mean and variance of $\frac{1}{n}\sum_{k=1}^{n} X_k$,

(b) the Independence assumption was unnecessarily restrictive; its only role is in ensuring that the variance of the sum is equal to the sum of the individual variances. In the case of dependence:

$$Var\left(\frac{1}{n}\sum_{i=1}^{n} X_i\right) = \frac{1}{n^2}\left[\sum_{i=1}^{n} Var(X_i) + \sum\sum_{i \neq j} Cov(X_i, X_j)\right]. \tag{9.13}$$

For the last term to be zero, however, one does not need to assume complete independence; non-correlation will suffice. Chebyshev in 1867 went on to impose the somewhat stronger dependence restriction of *pairwise independence*, because the difference between the latter condition and non-correlation was not very clear at the time.

Chebyshev's WLLN Let $\{X_n\}_{n=1}^{\infty}$ be a sequence of random variables which satisfy the following conditions:

(D) Bounded moments: $E(X_k) < \infty$, $Var(X_k) < c < \infty$, $k = 1,2,\ldots$
(M) Pairwise independence: $f(x_i, x_j; \varphi) = f_i(x_i; \theta_i) \cdot f_j(x_j; \theta_j)$, $i \neq j$, $i,j = 1,2,\ldots$
(H) Heterogeneity: $E(X_k) = \mu_k$, $Var(X_k) = \sigma_k^2$, $k = 1,2,\ldots$

$$\lim_{n \to \infty} \mathbb{P}\left(\left|\frac{1}{n}\sum_{k=1}^{n} X_k - \frac{1}{n}\sum_{k=1}^{n} E(X_k)\right| < \varepsilon\right) = 1, \text{ for any } \varepsilon > 0. \tag{9.14}$$

Proof The result follows directly from applying the *Chebyshev inequality* (see (9.11)) to the random variable $\frac{1}{n}\sum_{k=1}^{n} X_k$ and noting that:

$$Var\left(\frac{1}{n}\sum_{k=1}^{n} X_k\right) = \frac{1}{n^2}\sum_{k=1}^{n} Var(X_k) \leq \frac{c}{n} \underset{n \to \infty}{\to} 0. \blacksquare \tag{9.15}$$

There are several things to note about the above conditions.

(i) The boundedness of the first two moments assumed by Chebyshev's WLLN ensures that there is asymptotic homogeneity of the variance:

$$\lim_{n \to \infty}\left[\frac{1}{n}\sum_{k=1}^{n} \sigma_k^2\right] = \sigma^2 \leq c < \infty.$$

(ii) From chapter 3 we know that if μ'_r exists for some $r > 1$, then all moments of order lower than r also exist. In other words, in connection with the above theorem we could have left out the existence of the mean because if the variance exists so does the mean!

(iii) The most important departure from the previous results that Chebyshev's WLLN establishes, is the replacement of the distribution assumption by the existence of moments, and therein lies the value of such limit theorems.

The relationship between distribution and existence of moments assumptions has been discussed in chapter 3, where it was argued that existence of moments and smoothness conditions are in effect indirect *distribution assumptions*. This is because existence of moments and smoothness assumptions amount to a narrowing down of the set of possible distributions, in the sense that these conditions constitute indirect exclusion of certain distributions. In chapter 11 it is argued that for modeling purposes the use of direct distribution assumptions gives rise to more precise results. On the other hand, the use of indirect distribution assumptions, in the form of existence of moments, compels the modeler to use **inequalities**, such as that of Chebyshev and related inequalities, which are often *very crude* compared with what one can get when postulating a distribution assumption. In the context of limit theorems, however, this is no drawback because the very purpose of these theorems is the derivation of approximate results when exact results are not available. In such cases limit theorems are indispensable.

9.3.4 Markov's WLLN

Andrei Markov, a student of Chebyshev, was the first to exploit in full the opportunities offered by the proof of the WLLN using Chebyshev's inequality in order the relax the assumptions giving rise to the result. He saw that even the non-correlation was too restrictive.

Markov's LLN Let $\{X_n\}_{n=1}^{\infty}$ be a sequence of random variables which satisfy the following conditions:

(D)   Bounded moments: $\qquad\qquad E(X_k) < \infty, \; Var(X_k) < c < \infty, \; k = 1,2,\ldots$

(M)   Asymptotic non-correlation: $\left(\frac{1}{n^2}\right) Var\left(\sum_{k=1}^{n} X_k\right) \underset{n\to\infty}{\to} 0,$

(H)   Heterogeneity: $\qquad\qquad\qquad E(X_k) = \mu_k, \; Var(X_k) = \sigma_k^2, \; k = 1,2,\ldots$

Then (9.14) holds. Condition (M) is called asymptotic non-correlation because in view of (9.13), it holds only if:

$$\frac{1}{n^2}\left[\sum_{i\neq j}\sum Cov(X_i, X_j)\right] \underset{n\to\infty}{\to} 0.$$

Examples

(i)   Consider the sequence of discrete independent random variables $\{X_n\}_{n=1}^{\infty}$ with probability distribution:

$$\mathbb{P}(X_n=0)=1-2^{-2n}, \mathbb{P}(X_n=\pm 2^n)=2^{-(2n+1)}, n=1,2,\dots$$

(a) $E(X_n)=2^n(2^{-(2n+1)})-2^n(2^{-(2n+1)})=0,$

(b) $Var(X_n)=(2^n)^2(2^{-(2n+1)})+(-2^n)^2(2^{-(2n+1)})=1,$

$$Var\left(\tfrac{1}{n}\sum_{k=1}^n X_k\right)=\tfrac{1}{n^2}\sum_{k=1}^n 1=\tfrac{1}{n}\underset{n\to\infty}{\to}0.$$

Hence, the sequence of random variables $\{X_n\}_{n=1}^\infty$ obeys the Weak Law of Large Numbers.

(ii)   Consider the sequence of discrete independent random variables $\{X_n\}_{n=1}^\infty$ with probability distribution:

$$\mathbb{P}(X_n=\pm 1)=\tfrac{1}{2}(1-2^{-n}), \mathbb{P}(X_n=\pm 2^n)=2^{-(n+1)}, n=1,2,\dots$$

(a) $E(X_n)=0,$

(b) $Var(X_n)=(1)^2\left(\tfrac{1}{2}\right)(1-2^{-n})+(-1)^2\left(\tfrac{1}{2}\right)(1-2^{-n})+$
$$+(2^n)^2(2^{-(n+1)})+(-2^n)^2(2^{-(n+1)})=1-2^{-n}+2^n,$$

$$Var\left(\tfrac{1}{n}\sum_{k=1}^n X_k\right)=\tfrac{1}{n^2}\sum_{k=1}^n(1-2^{-k}+2^k)\underset{n\to\infty}{\to}\infty.$$

Does this mean that $\{X_n\}_{n=1}^\infty$ does not obey the Weak Law of Large Numbers? The answer is we do not know because the asymptotic non-correlation condition (M) is only sufficient, not necessary. It turns out that in this particular case the WLLN does hold despite the above result!

(iii)   Consider the sequence $\{X_n\}_{n=1}^\infty$ as specified above with the asymptotic non-correlation condition (M) replaced by the Markovness assumption:

$$f(x_1,x_2,\dots,x_n;\varphi)=\prod_{k=1}^n f_k(x_k|x_{k-1};\theta_k), (x_1,x_2,\dots,x_n)\in\mathbb{R}^n.$$

Does $\{X_n\}_{n=1}^\infty$ satisfy the Weak Law of Large Numbers?
Let $\rho_{k,k+1}:=Corr(X_k,X_{k+1})$:

$$Var\left(\tfrac{1}{n}\sum_{i=1}^n X_i\right)=\tfrac{1}{n^2}\left(\sum_{k=1}^n \sigma_k^2+2\sum_{k=1}^{n-1}\rho_{k,k+1}\sigma_k\sigma_{k+1}\right).$$

If we replace all variances with their upper bound c we can deduce that the sequence obeys the WLLN since:

$$Var\left(\tfrac{1}{n}\sum_{i=1}^n X_i\right)\le\left[\tfrac{c}{n}+\tfrac{2c}{n^2}\sum_{k=1}^{n-1}|\rho_{k,k+1}|\right]\underset{n\to\infty}{\to}0.$$

The result follows from the fact that $\rho_{k,k+1}$ constitutes a bounded sequence. Since the left-hand side cannot be negative its limit must be zero.

9.3.5   Bernstein's WLLN

Bernstein, building on the results of Chebyshev and Markov, was able to prove in 1918 the following theorem.

Bernstein's LLN Let $\{X_n\}_{n=1}^{\infty}$ be a sequence of random variables which satisfy the following conditions:

(D) Bounded moments: $\qquad\qquad$ $E(X_i) < \nu < \infty,\ Var(X_i) < c < \infty,\ i = 1, 2, \ldots$

(M) Asymptotic non-correlation: $\quad$ $Corr(X_i, X_j) \le \rho\,(|i - j|) \le 1,\ i, j = 1, 2, \ldots$
$$\rho(0) = 1 \text{ and } \lim_{n \to \infty} \rho(k) = 0,$$

(H) Heterogeneity: $\qquad\qquad\qquad$ $E(X_i) = \mu_i,\ Var(X_i) = \sigma_i^2,\ i = 1, 2, \ldots,$

$$\lim_{n \to \infty} \mathbb{P}\left(\left| \tfrac{1}{n}\textstyle\sum_{i=1}^{n} X_i - \tfrac{1}{n}\textstyle\sum_{i=1}^{n} \mu_i \right| < \varepsilon \right) = 1, \text{ for any } \varepsilon > 0. \tag{9.16}$$

There are three things to NOTE about this theorem.

(i) Condition (D) ensures that the heterogeneity does not persist asymptotically in the sense that:

$\qquad$ (a) $\displaystyle\lim_{n \to \infty} \left\{ \tfrac{1}{n}\textstyle\sum_{i=1}^{n} \mu_i \right\} = \mu < \nu < \infty,$ $\qquad$ (b) $\displaystyle\lim_{n \to \infty} \left\{ \tfrac{1}{n}\textstyle\sum_{i=1}^{n} \sigma_i^2 \right\} = \sigma^2 < c < \infty.$

(ii) The dependence condition ensures that the correlation between the X_i and X_j decreases as the distance between them $|i - j|$ increases. This ensures that the linear dependence dies out as the distance between random variables increases. Intuitively, we can think of the variance of the sum:

$$Var\left(\tfrac{1}{n}\textstyle\sum_{i=1}^{n} X_i \right) = \tfrac{1}{n^2}\left(\textstyle\sum_{i=1}^{n} \textstyle\sum_{j=1}^{n} \rho_{i,j}\sigma_i\sigma_j \right) \le \tfrac{c}{n^2}\left(\textstyle\sum_{i=1}^{n} \textstyle\sum_{j=1}^{n} |\rho\,(|i-j|)| \right).$$

In view of the fact that $\rho\,(|i - j|)$ is a bounded sequence (hence it converges) the right-hand side converges to zero and thus the asymptotic non-correlation condition holds.

(iii) Bernstein's theorem can be applied to **second-order stationary processes,** in which case:

$$Var\left(\tfrac{1}{n}\textstyle\sum_{i=1}^{n} X_i \right) = \tfrac{\sigma^2}{n^2}\left(\textstyle\sum_{i=1}^{n} \textstyle\sum_{j=1}^{n} \rho\,(i - j) \right) = \tfrac{\sigma^2}{n}\textstyle\sum_{k=0}^{n-1} \rho(k) - \tfrac{2\sigma^2}{n}\textstyle\sum_{k=1}^{n-1} \tfrac{k}{n}\rho(k),$$

using the fact that $\rho(k) = \rho(-k)$. Given that the sequence $\{\rho(k)\}_{k=0}^{\infty}$ is bounded, the condition $\lim_{k \to \infty} \rho(k) = 0$ implies asymptotic average non-correlation:

$$\lim_{n \to \infty} \tfrac{1}{n}\textstyle\sum_{k=0}^{n-1} \rho(k) = 0.$$

9.3.6 Kolmogorov's WLLN

The above theorems provide sufficient conditions for the WLLN to hold. Kolmogorov (1927,1928a,b) proposed a condition that is both necessary and sufficient for (9.14) to hold. For:

$$n^{-1}S_n := \tfrac{1}{n}\textstyle\sum_{i=1}^{n} (X_i - E(X_i)),$$

the WLLN (9.14) holds if and only if: $\displaystyle\lim_{n \to \infty} \left\{ E\left(\tfrac{S_n^2}{n^2 + S_n^2} \right) \right\} = 0.$

To understand this condition we need to note that the quantity involved in (9.14) is:

$$\left[\tfrac{1}{n}\textstyle\sum_{i=1}^{n} X_i - \tfrac{1}{n}\textstyle\sum_{i=1}^{n} E(X_i) \right] = \tfrac{1}{n}\textstyle\sum_{i=1}^{n} (X_i - E(X_i)) = n^{-1}S_n,$$

but even then this condition is of limited use because it refers to the behavior of the sum and not the individual random variables involved.

9.3.7 Khintchine's WLLN

The discerning reader would have noticed that, in addition to the gradual weakening of the initial conditions used by James Bernoulli, the above theorems also show a trade off between the restrictiveness of the three types of conditions. For instance Poisson, by retaining the Bernoulli assumption, was able to relax the complete homogeneity condition to asymptotic homogeneity. This trade off is made in Khintchine's WLLN, proved in 1928 by retaining the IID assumptions, we can relax the boundedness of the variance; we do not need to assume a finite variance.

Khintchine's WLLN

Let $\{X_n\}_{n=1}^{\infty}$ be a sequence of random variables which satisfy the following conditions:

 (D) Bounded mean: $E(X_k) = \mu < \infty$, $k = 1,2,\ldots$
 (M) Independence: $f(x_1,x_2,\ldots,x_n;\varphi) = \prod_{k=1}^{n} f_k(x_k;\boldsymbol{\theta}_k)$, $(x_1,x_2,\ldots,x_n) \in \mathbb{R}^n$,
 (H) Identical Distribution: $f_k(x_k;\boldsymbol{\theta}_k) = f(x_k;\boldsymbol{\theta})$, for all $k = 1,2,\ldots$

$$\lim_{n\to\infty}\mathbb{P}\left(\left|\frac{1}{n}\sum_{k=1}^{n}|X_k - \mu|<\varepsilon\right.\right) = 1, \text{ for any } \varepsilon > 0. \tag{9.17}$$

The progressive weakening and the trade off between the three types of restrictions can also be seen in relation to the Strong Law of Large Numbers (SLLN) which we consider next.

9.4 The Strong Law of Large Numbers

As argued above, the convergence involved in the SLLN is stronger than that of the WLLN and thus the conclusions are more powerful: the validity of the SLLN implies the validity of the WLLN. For this reason we did not continue with the weakening of the restrictions for the validity of the WLLN with sequences such as *martingales* and *stationary-mixing* stochastic processes. This weakening can be seen in the context of the SLLN results. It must be noted, however, that the more powerful conclusions of the SLLN are based on restrictions that are often more stringent than those for the validity of the WLLN.

 The SLLN, in its general form, can be stated crudely as saying that *under certain restrictions* on the sequence of random variables $\{X_n\}_{n=1}^{\infty}$:

$$\mathbb{P}\left(\lim_{n\to\infty}\left[\frac{1}{n}\sum_{k=1}^{n}X_k - \frac{1}{n}\sum_{i=1}^{n}E(X_k)\right] = 0\right) = 1. \tag{9.18}$$

 We begin the discussion with Borel's result that provided the spark for the SLLN results.

9.4.1 Borel's SLLN

Let $\{X_n\}_{n=1}^{\infty}$ be a sequence of random variables which satisfy the following conditions (see Borel (1909)):

(D) Bernoulli: $f(x_k;\theta_k)=\theta_k^{x_k}(1-\theta_k)^{1-x_k}$, $x_k=0,1,k=1,2,\dots$
(M) Independence: $f(x_1,x_2,\dots,x_n;\varphi)=\prod_{k=1}^n f(x_k;\theta_k)$, $(x_1,x_2,\dots,x_n)\in\mathbb{R}^n$
(H) Identical Distribution: $\theta_k=\theta$, for all $k=1,2,\dots,$

$$\mathbb{P}\left(\lim_{n\to\infty}\left[\frac{1}{n}\sum_{k=1}^n X_k\right]=\theta\right)=1. \tag{9.19}$$

This is the first and least general SLLN in the sense that it is tied up with the Bernoulli distribution. But as in the case of the WLLN this restriction, under closer examination, proved unnecessary. The progressive weakening of the restrictions runs parallel to the results of the WLLN.

9.4.2 Kolmogorov's SLLN

The result analogous to Chebyshev's WLLN but with a stronger convergence mode was proved by Kolmogorov (1930).

Kolmogorov's first SLLN Let $\{X_n\}_{n=1}^{\infty}$ be a sequence of random variables which satisfy the following conditions:

(D) Bounded moments: $E(X_k)<\infty$, $Var(X_k)<\infty$, $\sum_{k=1}^{\infty}\frac{Var(X_k)}{k^2}<\infty$,
(M) Independence: $f(x_1,x_2,\dots,x_n;\varphi)=\prod_{k=1}^n f_k(x_k;\theta_k)$, $x\in\mathbb{R}^n$,
(H) Heterogeneity: $E(X_k)=\mu_k$, $Var(X_k)=\sigma_k^2$, $k=1,2,\dots$

$$\mathbb{P}\left(\lim_{n\to\infty}\left[\frac{1}{n}\sum_{k=1}^n X_k-\frac{1}{n}\sum_{i=1}^n E(X_k)\right]=0\right)=1, \tag{9.20}$$

and denoted by: $\left(\frac{1}{n}\sum_{k=1}^n(X_k-E(X_k))\right)\overset{a.s.}{\underset{n\to\infty}{\to}}0$.

The proof of this result depends on an important result about convergence of series.

Kronecker's lemma Let $\{a_n\}_{n=1}^{\infty}:=\{a_1,a_2,\dots,a_n\dots\}$ be a sequence of real numbers such that:

$$\sum_{k=1}^{\infty}\frac{a_k}{k}<\infty, \text{ then } \lim_{n\to\infty}\frac{1}{n}\sum_{k=1}^n a_k=0.$$

A heuristic proof of Kolmogorov's SLLN goes as follows. Define the new random variables $Y_k:=\frac{1}{k}X_k$. Since:

$$Var\left(\sum_{k=1}^n Y_k\right)=\sum_{k=1}^n Var(Y_k)=\sum_{k=1}^n\frac{1}{k^2}Var(X_k)<\infty, \tag{9.21}$$

we can deduce that (this is a theorem we take for granted!):

$$\mathbb{P}\left(\lim_{n\to\infty}\left(\sum_{k=1}^n\frac{1}{k}[X_k-E(X_k)]\right)<\infty\right)=1.$$

Using Kronecker's lemma in relation to:

$$\frac{1}{n}\sum_{k=1}^{n}[X_k - E(X_k)] = \frac{1}{n}\sum_{i=1}^{n}k\left(\frac{[X_k - E(X_k)]}{k}\right),$$

the result follows; see Petrov (1995).

There are several things to NOTE about Kolmogorov's SLLN.

(i) The above theorem holds if we replace the condition

$$\sum_{k=1}^{\infty}\frac{Var(X_k)}{k^2} < \infty, \tag{9.22}$$

with (see Gnedenko and Kolmogorov (1954)):

$$\sum_{k=1}^{\infty}\frac{Var(X_k)}{b_k^2} < \infty, \tag{9.23}$$

$\{b_k\}_{n=1}^{\infty}$ being an increasing sequence of positive real numbers such that $b_k \to \infty$.

(ii) The main difference with Chebyshev's WLLN is that the restrictions:

$$E(X_k) < \infty, \ Var(X_k) < c < \infty, \ k = 1, 2, \ldots,$$

have been replaced with (9.22). In the context of Chebyshev's WLLN the boundedness of the variances enabled us to derive (9.15). It is not very difficult to show that (9.22) is a stronger condition than (9.15) because the latter follows from the former but not vice versa. That is, the stronger result follows by strengthening (9.15) to (9.22).

(iii) Condition (9.22) is satisfied in the case where the variances are bounded by the same constant in the sense that:

$$Var(X_k) < c < \infty, \ k = 1, 2, \ldots,$$

since $\sum_{k=1}^{\infty}\frac{Var(X_k)}{k^2} \le c\sum_{k=1}^{\infty}\frac{1}{k^2} = c\left(\frac{\pi^2}{6}\right) < \infty.$

(iv) Condition (9.22) is indeed a boundedness condition because the result follows that if we replace it by the moments condition (see Williams (1991)):

$(1)'$ $E(X_k) = \mu$, $E(X_k^4) < c < \infty$, $k = 1, 2, \ldots$

or by the conditions (see Revesz (1967)):

$(1)'$ $E(X_k) = 0$, $E(|X_k|^{2r}) < \infty$, and $\sum_{k=1}^{\infty}\frac{E(|X_k|^{2r})}{k^{r+1}} < \infty$, $r \ge 1$, $k = 1, 2, \ldots$

(v) If we weaken the Independence assumption to that of non-correlation then the moment restriction should be strengthened to (see Doob (1953), p. 158):

$$\sum_{k=1}^{\infty}\frac{(\ln k)^2 \cdot Var(X_k)}{k^2} < \infty.$$

The trade off between the restrictions from the three different categories of assumptions is further illustrated by the second theorem by Kolmogorov where the strengthening of the homogeneity restriction can be traded against the existence of only the first moment.

Kolmogorov's second SLLN Let $\{X_n\}_{n=1}^{\infty}$ be a sequence of random variables which satisfy the following conditions:

(D) Bounded mean: $E(|X_k|) = \mu < \infty, k = 1,2,\ldots$
(M) Independence: $f(x_1,x_2,\ldots,x_n;\varphi) = \prod_{k=1}^{n} f_k(x_k;\theta_k), x \in \mathbb{R}^n,$
(H) Identical Distribution: $f_k(x_k;\theta_k) = f(x_k;\theta), k = 1,2,\ldots$

These conditions are both necessary and sufficient for:

$$\mathbb{P}\left(\lim_{n\to\infty}\left[\frac{1}{n}\Sigma_{i=1}^{n} X_i - \mu\right] = 0\right) = 1. \tag{9.24}$$

9.4.3 SLLN for martingales

It is instructive to consider the SLLN in the case where $\{S_n, \mathcal{F}_n\}_{n=1}^{\infty}$ is a *martingale* (see chapter 8). As argued in chapter 8, a martingale $\{S_n, \mathcal{F}_n\}_{n=1}^{\infty}$ where $\mathcal{F}_n := \sigma(S_1, S_2, \ldots, S_n)$, has by construction certain restrictions built into its structure which we can summarize as follows:

(D) Bounded mean: $E(|S_k|) < \infty, k = 1,2,\ldots,$
(M) Martingale dependence: $E(S_k|\mathcal{F}_{k-1}); = S_{k-1}, k = 2,3,\ldots,$
(H) First-order homogeneity: $E(S_k) = \mu, k = 1,2,\ldots$

We also know that every martingale can be expressed as the partial sum of a *martingale difference* process, i.e.:

$$S_n := \Sigma_{k=1}^{n} X_k, \text{ or } X_k := (S_k - S_{k-1}), k = 2,3,\ldots,$$

$$E(X_k|\mathcal{F}_{k-1}) = 0, \text{ where } \mathcal{F}_{k-1} := \sigma(S_1, S_2, \ldots, S_k) = \sigma(X_1, X_2, \ldots, X_k).$$

As seen above, the key to both Laws of Large Numbers is the behavior of the variance of the summation. Hence, the simplest case of the SLLN is an adaptation of Kolmogorov's first theorem, by assuming the existence of its variance $Var(S_k) < \infty, k = 1,2,\ldots$, the so-called *square integrable* martingale case, denoted by $\mathcal{L}_2$. It turns out that a square integrable martingale difference process behaves like a sequence of uncorrelated random variables. To see this let us investigate the behavior of this variance, assuming $E(S_k) = 0, k = 1,2,\ldots$, for simplicity:

$$Var(S_k) = \Sigma_{k=1}^{n} E(X_k^2) + 2\Sigma_k^n\Sigma_{\ell=1}^{n} E(X_k \cdot X_\ell).$$
$$\scriptstyle k > \ell$$

Concentrating on the second summation we observe that since $E(X_k|\mathcal{F}_{k-1}) = 0$:

$$E(X_k \cdot X_\ell) = E\{E(X_k \cdot X_\ell|\mathcal{F}_{k-1})\} = E\{X_\ell \cdot E(X_k|\mathcal{F}_{k-1})\} = 0,$$

and thus: $Var(S_k) = \Sigma_{k=1}^{n} E(X_k^2)$.

That is, in terms of the variance, a square integrable martingale behaves like a sum of a sequence of uncorrelated random variables. Hence, it should come as no surprise to learn that the SLLN holds for such sequences.

SLLN for $\mathcal{L}_2$ martingales Let $\{S_n, \mathcal{F}_n\}_{n=1}^{\infty}$ be a *martingale* sequence with $\{X_n := (S_n - S_{n-1}), \mathcal{F}_n\}_{n=1}^{\infty}$ the corresponding *martingale difference* sequence which satisfies the following conditions (see Shiryayev (1984), pp. 471–2):

(D) Bounded moments: $E(X_k^2) < \infty, \ k = 1,2, \ldots, \sum_{k=1}^{n} \frac{E(X_k^2)}{k^2} < \infty,$

(M) Martingale dependence: $E(X_k | \mathcal{F}_{k-1}) = 0, \ k = 2,3, \ldots$

(H) Heterogeneity: $E(X_k) = 0, E(X_k^2) = \sigma_k^2, \ k = 1,2, \ldots$

$$\mathbb{P}\left(\lim_{n \to \infty} \left(\frac{1}{n} \sum_{i=1}^{n} X_i\right) = 0\right) = 1. \tag{9.25}$$

As argued in chapter 8, the usefulness of the martingale concept emanates from its power to tame arbitrary stochastic processes. Commencing with an arbitrary stochastic process $\{Y_n\}_{n=1}^{\infty}$, whose only initial restriction is the existence of the first moment, i.e., $E(|Y_n|) < \infty, \ n = 1,2, \ldots$, we can proceed to define the *martingale difference* process $\{X_n, \mathcal{F}_n := \sigma(Y_1, Y_2, \ldots, Y_n)\}_{n=1}^{\infty}$:

$$X_n := Y_n - E(Y_n | \sigma(Y_1, Y_2, \ldots, Y_n)),$$

with the restrictions (D)–(H) above built into this process.

If we are not prepared to impose the existence of the second moment, as in the previous theorem, we need to impose certain additional homogeneity restrictions in order for the process $\{X_n, \mathcal{F}_n\}_{n=1}^{\infty}$ to satisfy the LLN. For example, supplementing the built-in conditions (D)–(H) with the homogeneity restriction that this stochastic process is *bounded* by a random variable X:

$$\mathbb{P}(|X_n| > x) \le c\mathbb{P}(|X| > x) \text{ for all } x \ge 0, n \ge 1, \tag{9.26}$$

enables us to deduce the WLLN (for any $\varepsilon > 0$):

$$\lim_{n \to \infty} \mathbb{P}\left(\left|\frac{1}{n} \sum_{k=1}^{n} [Y_k - E(Y_k | \mathcal{F}_{k-1})]\right| < \varepsilon\right) = 1. \tag{9.27}$$

NOTE. The importance of the boundedness condition (9.26) stems from the fact that the process $\{X_n, \mathcal{F}_n\}_{n=1}^{\infty}$ will be nearly stationary given that the process $\{X_1, X_2, \ldots, X_n, \ldots\}$ is an IID process and thus trivially stationary.

For the Strong Law of Large Numbers to hold we need to replace the boundedness condition (9.26) with the strict stationarity of the stochastic processes in question.

SLLN for $\mathcal{L}_1$ martingale differences Let the martingale difference process $\{X_n := [Y_n - E(Y_n | \mathcal{F}_{n-1})], \mathcal{F}_n\}_{n=1}^{\infty}$ satisfy the following conditions:

(D) Bounded mean: $E(|X_k|) < \infty, \ k = 1,2, \ldots$

(M) Martingale dependence: $E(X_k | \mathcal{F}_{k-1}) = 0, \ k = 2,3, \ldots$

(H) Strict stationarity: $f(x_1, x_2, \ldots, x_n) = f(x_{1+\tau}, x_{2+\tau}, \ldots, x_{n+\tau})$, for any τ.

$$\mathbb{P}\left(\lim_{n \to \infty} \left[\frac{1}{n} \sum_{k=1}^{n} (Y_k - E(Y_k | \mathcal{F}_{k-1}))\right] = 0\right) = 1.$$

9.4.4   SLLN for stationary processes

SLLN for strictly stationary processes   Let $\{X_n\}_{n=1}^{\infty}$ be a sequence of random variables satisfying the following conditions:

(D)   Bounded moments: $E(|X_k|^{2+\delta})<\infty,\ \delta>0,\ k=1,2,\ldots,$

(M) α-mixing: $\alpha(k)\underset{k\to\infty}{\to}0,$ such that $\sum_{k=1}^{\infty}\alpha(k)^{\frac{\delta}{2+\delta}}<\infty,$

(H)   Strict stationarity: $f(x_1,x_2,\ldots,x_n)=f(x_{1+\tau},x_{2+\tau},\ldots,x_{n+\tau}),$ for any $\tau,$

$$\mathbb{P}\left(\lim_{n\to\infty}\left[\frac{1}{n}\sum_{i=1}^{n}X_i-\mu\right]=0\right)=1. \tag{9.28}$$

9.5   The Law of Iterated Logarithm*

The Law of Iterated Logarithm (LIL) provides fluctuation bounds for the sequence of partial sums $\{S_n\}_{n=1}^{\infty}$ in the SLLN. The SLLN states that the mean deviations of partial sums converge to zero with probability one, as $n\to\infty$, but provides no information about the speed of convergence: How fast does $\left|\frac{1}{n}\sum_{i=1}^{n}X_i-\mu\right|$ converge to zero?

It turns out that the speed of convergence depends crucially on the restrictions imposed on the distribution of the sequence $\{X_k\}_{k=1}^{\infty}$. For example, if the only thing the modeler is prepared to assume is the existence of the mean of the process, then nothing can be said about the speed of convergence. At the other extreme, if the modeler assumes that *all moments of the sequence* $\{X_k\}_{k=1}^{\infty}$ *exist and are bounded*, then one can show that for any $\varepsilon>0$:

Hausdorff: $\mathbb{P}\left(\lim_{n\to\infty}\left[\frac{|\sum_{k=1}^{n}X_k-\mu|}{n^{\frac{1}{2}+\varepsilon}}\right]\le M\right)=1,$ for some $0<M<\infty.$

Intuitively, this can be interpreted as saying that the paths of $\{[S_n:=\sum_{k=1}^{n}X_k-\mu]\}_{n=1}^{\infty}$ fluctuate within the Hausdorff (1914) bounds $\pm n^{\frac{1}{2}+\varepsilon}$, for any $\varepsilon>0$.

The LIL deals with the speed of convergence of the partial sums where the restrictions on the distribution of the sequence $\{X_k\}_{k=1}^{\infty}$ lie between the two extremes. From the outset it is apparent that this rate of convergence must be a sequence $\{\psi(n)\}_{n=1}^{\infty}$ such that:

$$n^{\frac{1}{2}}<\psi(n)<n.$$

The earliest result in relation to the speed of convergence of partial sums was derived by Hardy and Littlewood in 1914; see Hardy, Littlewood and Polya (1952). The result was in the context of number theory and assumed a simple random walk sequence $\{X_k\}_{k=1}^{\infty}$ (see chapter 8), proving that the rate of convergence is $\psi(n)=\sqrt{n\ln(n)}$, i.e.

Hardy and Littlewood: $\mathbb{P}\left(\lim_{n\to\infty}\left[\frac{|\sum_{k=1}^{n}X_k-\mu|}{\sqrt{n\ln(n)}}\right]\le M\right)=1.$

The first general result was derived by Khintchine (1924) who sharpened the bounds provided by Hardy and Littlewood.

Khintchine's LIL Let $\{X_n\}_{n=1}^{\infty}$ be a sequence of random variables which satisfy the following conditions:

(D)   Bounded mean and variance: $E(|X_k|) = \mu$, $Var(X_k) = \sigma^2 < \infty$, $k = 1,2,\dots$
(M)   Independence: $f(x_1, x_2, \dots, x_n; \varphi) = \prod_{k=1}^{n} f_k(x_k; \theta_k)$, $x \in \mathbb{R}^n$.
(H)   Identical Distribution: $f_k(x_k; \theta_k) = f(x_k; \theta)$, $k = 1,2,\dots$

Khintchine: $\mathbb{P}\left(\limsup_{n \to \infty} \left[\frac{|\Sigma_{k=1}^{n} X_k - \mu|}{\sqrt{n \ln(\ln(n))}} \right] = \sqrt{2\sigma^2} \right) = 1.$

NOTES:
(i)   The above form was first proved by Hartman and Wintner (1941).
(ii)   Intuitively, this result says that the paths of the stochastic sequence
       $\{[S_n := \Sigma_{k=1}^{n} X_k - \mu]\}_{n=1}^{\infty}$ fluctuate within the Khintchine bounds $\pm \sqrt{2\sigma^2 n \ln(\ln(n))}$.
(iii) The LIL is often written in the form:

$$\mathbb{P}\left(\limsup_{n \to \infty} \left[\frac{(\Sigma_{k=1}^{n} X_k - \mu)}{\sqrt{2n \ln(\ln(n))}} \right] = \sigma \right) = 1, \quad \mathbb{P}\left(\liminf_{n \to \infty} \left[\frac{(\Sigma_{k=1}^{n} X_k - \mu)}{\sqrt{2n \ln(\ln(n))}} \right] = -\sigma \right) = 1.$$

(iv)   Kolmogorov (1928a,1929a) was instrumental in the development of the Hartman and Wintner form of the LIL proving the result for sequences of bounded random variables; see Petrov (1995).
(v)   In order to get some idea on how the Khintchine bounds improve upon the result by Hardy and Littlewood, we plot the bounds for the fluctuations of $\{[S_n := \Sigma_{k=1}^{n} X_k - \mu]\}_{n=1}^{\infty}$ for $n \geq 100$ up to $n = 10000$, in figure 9.1.
(vi)   The relationship between the Khintchin and Hausdorff bounds exemplifies once more the principle of *more restrictions more precise results*, encountered many times in the discussion so far; it will be discussed further in the context of non-parametetric versus parametric inference in chapter 10.

9.6   The Central Limit Theorem

The LLN provides information about the probability of the event that a particular function of a sequence of random variables, their sum $\Sigma_{i=1}^{n} X_i$, differs from its expected value by some positive real number ϵ. This convergence result forms the basis of a number of related results which can help us in our quest for approximate distributions for well-behaved functions $g(X_1, X_2, \dots, X_n)$. For example, by standardizing the sum, subtracting its mean and dividing by its standard deviation, we can often derive its *asymptotic distribution*: its distribution as $n \to \infty$. This group of results are collectively referred to as the Central Limit Theorem. As mentioned in section 2, the Central Limit Theorem (CLT) can be viewed as convergence to a non-degenerate random variable after rescaling the distance used in the LLN.

The CLT, in its general form, can be stated crudely as saying that *under certain restrictions* on the sequence of random variables $\{X_n\}_{n=1}^{\infty}$, for $S_n = \Sigma_{i=1}^{n} X_i$:

$$\lim_{n \to \infty} \mathbb{P}\left(\frac{S_n - E(S_n)}{\sqrt{Var(S_n)}} \leq z \right) = \Phi(z) := \frac{1}{\sqrt{2\pi}} \int_{-\infty}^{z} e^{-\frac{1}{2}u^2} du, \text{ for all } z \in \mathbb{R}. \tag{9.29}$$

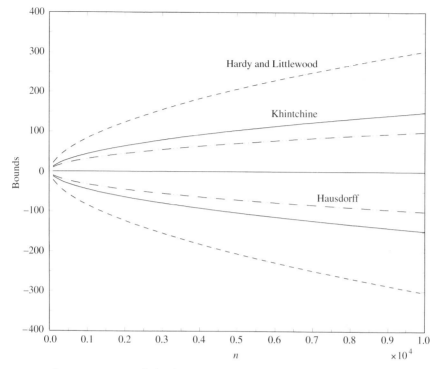

Figure 9.1 Bounds for the LIL

9.6.1 De Moivre–Laplace CLT

Let us begin with a formal statement of the first Central Limit Theorem.

De Moivre–Laplace CLT Let $\{X_n\}_{n=1}^{\infty} := \{X_1, X_2, \ldots, X_n \ldots\}$ be a sequence of random variables which satisfy the following conditions:

(D)   Bernoulli: $f(x_i; \theta_i) = \theta_i^{x_i}(1 - \theta_i)^{1-x_i}, \ x_i = 0,1, \ i = 1,2,\ldots$

(M)   Independence: $f(x_1, x_2, \ldots, x_n; \varphi) = \prod_{k=1}^{n} f(x_i; \theta_i), \ x \in \mathbb{R}^n.$

(H)   Identical Distribution: $\theta_i = \theta,$ for all $i = 1,2,\ldots,$

then for $S_n = \sum_{i=1}^{n} X_i,$ and $Z_n := \left(\frac{S_n - E(S_n)}{\sqrt{Var(S_n)}}\right),$ we can deduce that:

$$\lim_{n \to \infty} \mathbb{P}(Z_n \leq z) = \Phi(z) := \frac{1}{\sqrt{2\pi}} \int_{-\infty}^{z} e^{-\frac{1}{2}u^2} du, \text{ for all } z \in \mathbb{R}, \tag{9.30}$$

where $\Phi(z)$ is the cumulative distribution function of the *standard Normal distribution* denoted by:

$$\left(\frac{S_n - E(S_n)}{\sqrt{Var(S_n)}}\right) \xrightarrow{D} Z \sim N(0,1), \text{ or even } \left(\frac{S_n - E(S_n)}{\sqrt{Var(S_n)}}\right) \underset{a}{\sim} N(0,1).$$

It is important to NOTE that Z_n is a standardized version of S_n ($E(S_n)=n\theta$ and $Var(S_n)=n[\theta(1-\theta)]$), which is often expressed in a number of different forms:

$$Z_n := \left(\frac{S_n - E(S_n)}{\sqrt{Var(S_n)}}\right) = \left(\frac{\sum_{k=1}^n X_k - n\theta}{\sqrt{n\theta(1-\theta)}}\right) = \frac{\sqrt{n}\left(\frac{1}{n}\sum_{k=1}^n (X_k - \theta)\right)}{\sqrt{\theta(1-\theta)}}.$$

It is apparent from these forms that the CLT deals with the same distance $(S_n - E(S_n))$ as the Laws of Large Numbers but standardized; divided by its standard deviation.

As with the LLN, some of the conditions imposed on the sequence $\{X_n\}_{n=1}^\infty$ by the De Moivre–Laplace CLT do not contribute significantly to the result. Since the 19th century numerous extensions of this theorem, in the form of weaker conditions on the X_is, have been proposed in the literature. The first serious attempt to extend the De Moivre–Laplace CLT was made by Chebyshev in the 1870s who proposed the following theorem.

Chebyshev's "near" CLT Let $\{X_n\}_{n=1}^\infty$ be a sequence of independent random variables such that: $E(X_k)=0$, $Var(X_k)=\sigma_k^2$, $k=1,2,\ldots$ and $|X_k|\leq b>0$, $k\geq 1$. Then for:

$$s_n^2 := Var\left(\sum_{k=1}^n X_k\right) = \sum_{k=1}^n \sigma_k^2,$$

$$\lim_{n\to\infty} \mathbb{P}\left(\frac{1}{s_n}\sum_{k=1}^n X_k \leq z\right) = \frac{1}{\sqrt{2\pi}}\int_{-\infty}^z e^{-\frac{1}{2}u^2}du, \text{ for all } z\in\mathbb{R}. \tag{9.31}$$

Chebyshev's claim was *invalid*! His approach, however, was essentially valid. His students, Markov and Lyapunov, in their attempt to correct his mistakes and improve upon his result provided the foundation upon which numerous extensions of the CLT since the 1880s have been erected.

Firstly, Chebyshev's primary mistake was pointed out by Markov who proved that for the result (9.31) to go through one needs to impose the additional condition:

$$s_n^2 := Var\left(\sum_{k=1}^n X_k\right) \underset{n\to\infty}{\to} \infty.$$

This condition was the predecessor of the now famous *Lindeberg condition* discussed below.

Secondly, Chebyshev's "proof" amounted to demonstrating that the moments of the quantity $\frac{1}{s_n}\sum_{k=1}^n X_k$ converge to those of the standard Normal distribution, unaware of the moments problem (see chapter 3). Indeed, his presumption was instrumental in raising the question of whether the moments determine the distribution uniquely.

Thirdly, Chebyshev, in order to ensure the existence of all moments, required the *boundedness condition* $|X_k|\leq b>0$, $k\geq 1$; moments of all orders exist for random variables with bounded support (see chapter 3). This condition was rather restrictive because it included random variables with distributions such as the Beta and the Uniform but excluded most well-known distributions such as the Normal, Student's t, Exponential, Gamma, and Pareto. Markov circumvented this problem by introducing a technique widely used today known as the *truncation method* which amounts to the following:

Let X be a random variable whose range might be unbounded. We introduce the artificial random variable $\tilde{X}$:

$$\tilde{X}:=X\cdot\mathbb{1}_{\{|X|\le b\}}=\begin{cases}X\text{ for }|X|\le b,\\0\text{ for }|X|>b,\end{cases}$$

where $\mathbb{1}_A$ is the well-known indicator function. That is, $\tilde{X}$ is obtained by setting to zero the values of $|X|$ exceeds some $b>0$.

For the truncated random variable $\tilde{X}$ all moments exist and can be used in proving a number of results in probability theory, e.g., apply Chebyshev's inequality. To ensure that the same result holds for X, all we need to show is that the difference between the two random variables is asymptotically negligible for the purposes needed. Given that the feature of interest in a random variable is its probabilistic structure, we need to relate the truncation to that. This takes the form $\mathbb{P}(|X|\le b):=\mathbb{P}(X\cdot\mathbb{1}_{\{|X|\le b\}})=1$ or equivalently $\mathbb{P}(|X|>b):=\mathbb{P}(X\cdot\mathbb{1}_{\{|X|>b\}})=0$ for some $b>0$.

Using the truncation method for a sequence of random variables $\{X_n\}_{n=1}^{\infty}$ we can define an important condition known as the *Uniform integrability condition*:

$$\lim_{b\to\infty}\left(\sup_{1\le k\le n}E\{X_k\cdot\mathbb{1}_{\{|X|>b\}}\}\right)=0,$$

which is a useful result in the context of convergence of random variables.

Another important notion which can be defined by combining $\mathbb{P}(|X_k|>\varepsilon)=0$ for some $\varepsilon>0$, $k=1,2,\ldots$ with Markov's condition $s_n^2\underset{n\to\infty}{\to}\infty$, is known as the *uniformly asymptotic negligibility condition*:

$$\text{UAN: }\lim_{n\to\infty}\left(\max_{1\le k\le n}\mathbb{P}\left(\left|\tfrac{X_k-\mu_k}{s_n}\right|>\varepsilon\right)\right)=0.$$

i.e., each random variable X_k in the sequence $\{X_n\}_{n=1}^{\infty}$ is small compared with the summation $\sum_{k=1}^{n}X_k$. As argued below this condition forms the cornerstone on which modern versions of the CLT are built.

Fourthly, in his attempt to avoid Chebyshev's boundedness conditions, Lyapunov introduced a moments-boundedness condition appropriately known as *Lyapunov's condition* whose key aspect is the (*u.a.n.*) component (see below).

9.6.2 Lyapunov's CLT

The first modern Central Limit Theorem was proved by Lyapunov in 1901.

Lyapunov's CLT Let $\{X_n\}_{n=1}^{\infty}$ be a sequence of random variables satisfying the following conditions:

(D) Bounded moments: $E(|X_k|^{2+\delta})<\infty$, $\delta>0$, $k=1,2,\ldots$, such that:

$$\tfrac{1}{s_n^{2+\delta}}\sum_{k=1}^{n}|X_k-\mu_k|^{2+\delta}\underset{n\to\infty}{\to}0,$$

(M) Independence: $f(x_1,x_2,\ldots,x_n;\varphi)=\prod_{k=1}^{n}f_k(x_k;\theta_k),\ x\in\mathbb{R}^n$
(H) Heterogeneity: $E(X_k)=\mu_k,\ Var(X_k)=\sigma_k^2,\ k=1,2,\ldots$

$$\lim_{n\to\infty}\mathbb{P}\left(\left[\tfrac{1}{s_n}\sum_{k=1}^{n}(X_k-\mu_k)\right]\le z\right)=\Phi(z):=\tfrac{1}{\sqrt{2\pi}}\int_{-\infty}^{z}e^{-\frac{1}{2}u^2}du,\text{ for all }z\in\mathbb{R}.\qquad(9.32)$$

There are several things to NOTE about Lyapunov's CLT.

(i) Heuristically, this theorem suggests that for large n the distribution of the sum $\sum_{k=1}^{n} X_k$ is approximately $\mathsf{N}(\sum_{k=1}^{n}\mu_k, \sum_{k=1}^{n}\sigma_k^2)$.

(ii) The heart of the theorem is Lyapunov's condition:

$$\frac{1}{s_n^{2+\delta}}\sum_{k=1}^{n}|X_k - \mu_k|^{2+\delta} \underset{n\to\infty}{\to} 0,$$

which for $\delta = 1$ and $\nu_n^3 := \sum_{k=1}^{n}|X_k - \mu_k|^3$ amounts to: $\lim_{n\to\infty}\left(\frac{\nu_n}{s_n}\right) = 0$.

This condition ensures that no one random variable X_k dominates the summation.

(iii) The theorem allows for moment heterogeneity but imposes boundedness conditions for moments higher than the second.

(iv) We mentioned in section 3 above that the approximations based on inequalities are often very crude; see also chapter 10. The same can be said for the approximations provided by the CLT. In relation to this, we state the following result due to Berry (1941) and Esseen (1945).

Berry–Esseen theorem Let $\{X_n\}_{n=1}^{\infty}$ be a sequence of IID random variables with bounded moments of order 3, i.e., $E|X_n|^3 < \infty$, $n = 1, 2, \ldots$ There exists an absolute constant C (where $0.4097 \leq C \leq 0.7975$ and is unrelated to the nature of the distribution of X_n; see Beeck (1972)) such that:

$$\sup_{z\in\mathbb{R}}|\mathbb{P}\left(\left[\frac{1}{s_n}\sum_{k=1}^{n}(X_k - \mu)\right]\leq z\right) - \Phi(z)| \leq C\frac{E|X_1|^3}{\sqrt{n}}.$$

Roughly speaking, the Berry–Esseen upper bound estimate suggests that for accuracy up to two decimal places we need $n = 10000$! This should not come as a surprise because as demonstrated in chapter 10, without explicit distribution assumptions, probabilistic statements are often very crude.

(v) When the modeler is prepared to make assumptions about the existence of the fourth moment of the underlying (unknown) distribution, the Normal approximation might be improved upon using higher-order terms in the asymptotic expansion of the cdf (or the density or the characteristic functions); the Normal approximation provided by the CLT is viewed as the first term of this expansion. The most well-known expansion is known as the *Edgeworth expansion* which is based on terms with different powers of n and takes the form:

$$F_n(x) = \Phi(x) - \varphi(x)\left[\frac{\alpha_3(x^2 - 1)}{6\sqrt{n}}\right] + \varphi(x)\left[\frac{\alpha_4(x^3 - 3x)}{24n} + \frac{\alpha_3^2(x^5 - 10x^3 + 15x)}{72n}\right] + O(n^{-\frac{1}{2}}),$$

where (α_3, α_4) denote the skewness and kurtosis coefficients (see chapter 3) and $(\Phi(x), \varphi(x))$ denote the standard Normal cdf and density function, respectively. The term $O(n^{-\frac{1}{2}})$ denotes the remainder of this expansion which is to be understood in the sense that when multiplied by $n^{\frac{1}{2}+\varepsilon}$ for any $\varepsilon > 0$, it converges to zero; for further details see Cramer (1972), Spanos (1986) and Barndorff-Nielsen and Cox (1989, 1994).

9.6.3 Lindeberg–Feller's CLT

The most well known Central Limit Theorem is known as the Lindeberg–Feller theorem. This theorem assumes the existence of the second moment and provides both necessary (proposed by Feller in 1935) as well as sufficient conditions (Lindeberg (1922)).

Lindeberg's CLT Let $\{X_n\}_{n=1}^{\infty}$ be a sequence of random variables satisfying the following conditions:

(D) Bounded moments: $E(X_k)^2 < \infty, k = 1, 2, \ldots$, such that for any $\varepsilon > 0$:

$$(\mathbb{L}): \quad \lim_{n \to \infty} \left(\frac{1}{s_n^2} \sum_{k=1}^{n} E[(X_k - \mu_k)^2 \cdot \mathbf{1}_{\{|Xk - \mu k| > \varepsilon s n\}}] \right) = 0,$$

(M) Independence: $f(x_1, x_2, \ldots, x_n; \varphi) = \prod_{k=1}^{n} f_k(x_k; \theta_k), \ x \in \mathbb{R}^n,$

(H) Heterogeneity: $E(X_k) = \mu_k, \ Var(X_k) = \sigma_k^2, k = 1, 2, \ldots$

$$(\mathbb{CLT}): \lim_{n \to \infty} \mathbb{P}\left(\left[\frac{1}{s_n} \sum_{k=1}^{n} (X_k - \mu_k) \right] \leq z \right) = \frac{1}{\sqrt{2\pi}} \int_{-\infty}^{z} e^{-\frac{1}{2} u^2} du, \text{ for all } z \in \mathbb{R}.$$

(i) The heart of this theorem is the Lindeberg condition ($\mathbb{L}$) which intuitively says that no one random variable should dominate the summation. In an attempt to de-mystify this condition we note the following results:

(a) It can be shown that if $\{X_n\}_{n=1}^{\infty}$ satisfies condition ($\mathbb{L}$) then (see Shiryayev (1984)):

$$(\mathbb{UAN}): \lim_{n \to \infty} \left(\max_{1 \leq k \leq n} \mathbb{P}(|X_k - \mu_k| > \varepsilon s_n) \right) = 0,$$

$$(\mathbb{F}): \quad \lim_{n \to \infty} \left(\max_{1 \leq k \leq n} \left(\frac{\sigma_k^2}{s_n^2} \right) \right) = 0,$$

where condition ($\mathbb{F}$) is known as the *Feller condition* (see below). It is worth looking at the result ($\mathbb{L}$) $\Rightarrow$ ($\mathbb{F}$). Noting that:

$$\mathbb{R} = \{|X_k - \mu_k| > \varepsilon s_n\} \cup \{|X_k - \mu_k| \leq \varepsilon s_n\},$$

$$\sigma_k^2 = E[(X_k - \mu_k)^2 \cdot \mathbf{1}_{\{|Xk - \mu k| \leq \varepsilon s n\}}] + E[(X_k - \mu_k)^2 \cdot \mathbf{1}_{\{|Xk - \mu k| > \varepsilon s n\}}]$$
$$\leq \varepsilon^2 s_n^2 + E[(X_k - \mu_k)^2 \cdot \mathbf{1}_{\{|Xk - \mu k| > \varepsilon s n\}}].$$

Hence, we have:

$$\max_{1 \leq k \leq n} \left(\frac{\sigma_k^2}{s_n^2} \right) \leq \varepsilon^2 + \max_{1 \leq k \leq n} \frac{1}{s_n^2} E[(X_k - \mu_k)^2 \cdot \mathbf{1}_{\{|Xk - \mu k| > \varepsilon s n\}}] \leq$$

$$\leq \varepsilon^2 + \frac{1}{s_n^2} \sum_{k=1}^{n} E[(X_k - \mu_k)^2 \cdot \mathbf{1}_{\{|Xk - \mu k| > \varepsilon s n\}}].$$

In view of the fact that $\varepsilon > 0$ can be chosen arbitrarily small, the Lindeberg condition implies the Feller condition.

(b) The Lyapunov condition $\frac{1}{s_n^{2+\delta}} \sum_{k=1}^{n} |X_k - \mu_k|^{2+\delta} \xrightarrow[n \to \infty]{} 0$, implies the Lindeberg condition.

Lindeberg–Feller's CLT For a sequence of random variables $\{X_n\}_{n=1}^{\infty}$ satisfying the following conditions:

(D) Bounded moments: $\quad E(X_k) < \infty, \, E(X_k)^2 < \infty, \, k = 1, 2, \ldots,$

(M) Independence: $\quad f(x_1, x_2, \ldots, x_n; \varphi) = \prod_{k=1}^{n} f_k(x_k; \boldsymbol{\theta}_k), \, (x_1, x_2, \ldots, x_n) \in \mathbb{R}^n,$

(H) Heterogeneity: $\quad E(X_k) = \mu_k, \, Var(X_k) = \sigma_k^2, \, k = 1, 2, \ldots,$

$$(\mathbb{L}) \Leftrightarrow (\mathbb{CLT}) \text{ and } (\mathbb{F}). \tag{9.33}$$

That is, the Lindeberg condition implies that $\{X_n\}_{n=1}^{\infty}$ obeys the CLT and the Feller condition, and the latter two imply the former. It is also interesting to note that:

$$(\mathbb{L}) \Leftrightarrow (\mathbb{CLT}) \text{ and } (\mathbb{UAN}). \tag{9.34}$$

This equivalence brings out the role of the three conditions for the validity of the CLT. In order to consolidate this role consider the following example.

Example
Let $\{X_n\}_{n=1}^{\infty}$ be a sequence of random variables such that $X_k \sim N(0, \sigma_k^2)$ where $\sigma_1^2 = 1$, $\sigma_k^2 = 2^{k-2}$ for $k \geq 2$. Hence, $s_n^2 := Var(\sum_{k=1}^{n} X_k) = 2^{n-2}$, $\left(\frac{X_k}{s_n}\right) \sim N\left(0, \frac{1}{2}\right)$: $\left(\frac{1}{s_n} \sum_{k=1}^{n} X_k\right) \sim N(0,1)$.

Hence the CLT is satisfied trivially. However, the Feller and u.a.n. conditions:

$$\lim_{n \to \infty} \left(\max_{1 \leq k \leq n} \left(\frac{\sigma_k^2}{s_n^2} \right) = \frac{2^{n-2}}{2^{n-1}} = \frac{1}{2} \right) \neq 0,$$

$$\lim_{n \to \infty} \left(\max_{1 \leq k \leq n} \mathbb{P}\left(\left| \frac{X_k}{s_n} \right| > \varepsilon \right) \geq \mathbb{P}\left(\left| \frac{X_n}{s_n} \right| > \varepsilon \right) = 1 - \frac{1}{\sqrt{\pi}} \int_{-\varepsilon}^{\varepsilon} e^{-u^2} du \right) > 0,$$

are not satisfied. Thus, in view of fact that the Lindeberg condition is necessary and sufficient for both $(\mathbb{CLT})$ and $(\mathbb{F})$ (see (9.33)) and the latter does not hold, it means that the Lindeberg condition cannot be satisfied (see Stoyanov (1987)).

We are now in a position to return to Chebyshev's theorem to see it in the light of the Lindeberg–Feller theorem.

Chebyshev's CLT A sequence of random variables $\{X_n\}_{n=1}^{\infty}$ obeys the $\mathbb{CLT}$ if it satisfies the following conditions:

(D) Boundedness: $\quad E(X_k)^2 < \infty, \, k = 1, 2, \ldots,$ and

$\quad (\mathbb{UB})\text{: } P(|X_n| < b) \underset{n \to \infty}{\longrightarrow} 1, \text{ for } b > 0,$

$\quad (\mathbb{M})\text{: } s_n^2 := Var(\sum_{i=1}^{n} X_i) \underset{n \to \infty}{\longrightarrow} \infty,$

(M) Independence: $\quad f(x_1, x_2, \ldots, x_n; \varphi) = \prod_{k=1}^{n} f_k(x_k; \boldsymbol{\theta}_k), \, (x_1, x_2, \ldots, x_n) \in \mathbb{R}^n,$

(H) Heterogeneity: $\quad E(X_k) = \mu_k, \, Var(X_k) = \sigma_k^2, \, k = 1, 2, \ldots$

As we can see, by expressing Chebyshev's boundedness condition in probabilistic terms (known as the *uniform boundedness condition*) and adding Markov's condition, the CLT holds. The conditions $(\mathbb{UB})$ and $(\mathbb{M})$ imply the Lindeberg condition $(\mathbb{L})$ since $s_n^2 \underset{n \to \infty}{\longrightarrow} \infty$

implies that $\varepsilon s_n \xrightarrow[n\to\infty]{} \infty$ for any $\varepsilon>0$ and $\sum_{k=1}^{n}E[(X_k-\mu_k)^2\cdot\mathbb{1}_{\{|X_k-\mu_k|>\varepsilon s_n\}}]$ must grow less fast than s_n^2.

9.6.4 CLT for martingales

CLT for martingales For a martingale difference stochastic process $\{X_n,\mathcal{F}_n\}_{n=1}^{\infty}$, where $\mathcal{F}_n:=\sigma(X_1,X_2,...,X_n)$, the CLT holds if it satisfies the following conditions:

(D) Square integrability: $E(X_k)^2<\infty,\ k=1,2,...,$ such that for any $\varepsilon>0$:

$(\mathbb{L})$: $\lim_{n\to\infty}\left(\frac{1}{s_n^2}\sum_{k=1}^{n}E[X_k^2\cdot\mathbb{1}_{\{|X_k|>\varepsilon s_n\}}]\right)=0.$

(M) Martingale dependence: $E(X_k|\mathcal{F}_{k-1})=0,\ k=1,2,...$
(H) Heterogeneity: $E(E(X_k^2|\mathcal{F}_{k-1}))=\sigma_k^2,\ k=1,2,...$

$$\lim_{n\to\infty}\mathbb{P}\left(\left[\frac{1}{s_n}\sum_{k=1}^{n}X_k\right]\le z\right)=\frac{1}{\sqrt{2\pi}}\int_{-\infty}^{z}e^{-\frac{1}{2}u^2}du,\text{ for all }z\in\mathbb{R}. \tag{9.35}$$

9.6.5 CLT for stationary processes

Before proceeding to the next two CLT results, the reader is strongly advised to refer back to chapter 8, where the notions of stationarity and mixing are discussed. We remind the reader that the various mixing conditions denote different forms of asymptotic independence.

CLT for strictly stationary processes Let $\{X_n\}_{n=1}^{\infty}$ be a sequence of random variables satisfying the following conditions:

(D) Bounded moments: $E(|X_k|^{2+\delta})<\infty,\ \delta>0,\ k=1,2,...,$
(M) α-mixing: $\alpha(k)\xrightarrow[k\to\infty]{}0,$
(H) Strict Stationarity: $f(x_1,x_2,...,x_n)=f(x_{1+\tau},x_{2+\tau},...,x_{n+\tau})$, for any τ,

$$\lim_{n\to\infty}\mathbb{P}\left(\left[\frac{1}{s_n}\sum_{k=1}^{n}(X_k-\mu)\right]\le z\right)=\frac{1}{\sqrt{2\pi}}\int_{-\infty}^{z}e^{-\frac{1}{2}u^2}du,\text{ for all }z\in\mathbb{R}. \tag{9.36}$$

CLT for second-order stationary processes The sequence of random variables $\{X_n\}_{n=1}^{\infty}$ obeys the CLT (9.36) if it satisfies the following conditions:

(D) Bounded moments: $E(X_k)^2<\infty,\ k=1,2,...,$
(M) ρ-mixing: $s_n^2\xrightarrow[n\to\infty]{}\infty$, and $\lim_{n\to\infty}\sum_{k=1}^{n}\rho(2^k)<\infty,$
(H) 2nd order Stationarity: $E(X_k)=\mu,\ Var(X_k)=\sigma^2,\ k=1,2,...$

9.6.6 Stable and other limit distributions*

Up until the 1930s the study of limiting distributions concentrated exclusively on finding conditions for convergence to the Normal (and to a lesser extend the Poisson) distribution. In a series of papers in the 1920s and 1930s, Paul Levy showed that a whole family of distributions share with the Normal the property that renders them limit distributions for partial sums; see Levy (1937). For sequences of IID random variables this family became known as the *Stable family* which includes the Normal and the Cauchy distributions as a special cases. Even this family, however, was not large enough to include all limit distributions of partials sums. In the case of sequences of Independent but not necessarily Identical Distribution, the family of limit distributions is known as the *Infinitely Divisible family*; as expected the stable is a subset of this family. For a more balanced view of the limit theorems we need to consider these families of distributions briefly.

Stable family of distributions

The property that renders a distribution a possible candidate for a limit distribution is known as the self-reproducing property: in a sequence of IID random variables $\{X_n\}_{n=1}^{\infty}$, the individual components and the scaled partial sums have distributions of the same type. Two random variables X and Y, with cdfs $F_X(.)$ and $F_Y(.)$, are said to have distributions of the same type if for:

$$Y = aX + b, \ a \in \mathbb{R}_+, b \in \mathbb{R},$$

$$F_Y(z) = F_X\left(\frac{z-b}{a}\right), \text{ for all } z \in \mathbb{R}.$$

It is interesting to note that being of the same type is an equivalence relation (symmetric, reflexive, and transitive) which divides the set of all distributions into equivalent classes.

Stable family Let $\{X_n\}_{n=1}^{\infty}$ be a sequence of IID random variables with a non-degenerate cdf $F(x)$. The distribution $F(x)$ is said to be *stable* if the distribution of $S_n = \sum_{k=1}^{n} X_k$ is of the same type for every positive integer n. A random variable is called stable if its distribution satisfies this property. This amounts to the existence of constants $a_n > 0$ and b_n such that:

$$\mathbb{P}\left(\frac{S_n - b_n}{a_n} \leq z\right) = \mathbb{P}(X_1 \leq z), \text{ for all } n > 1.$$

Intuitively, this says that $F(x)$ is *stable* if the distribution of $S_n = \sum_{k=1}^{n} X_k$ is of the same type as $a_n X + b_n$ where $(X_1, X_2, \ldots, X_n)$ are IID random variables with the same distribution as X. It turns out that the members of this family have explicit formulae density functions only in special cases such as the Normal and the Cauchy distributions. For the other members of the stable family, the characteristic function is used to specify them (see Galambos (1995)).

Levy's theorem Let $\{X_n\}_{n=1}^{\infty}$ be a sequence of IID random variables with $S_n = \sum_{k=1}^{n} X_k$. Assume that there exist constants $a_n > 0$ and b_n such that:

$$\lim_{n \to \infty} \mathbb{P}\left(\frac{S_n - b_n}{a_n} \leq x\right) = F(x), \text{ where } F(x) \text{ is non-degenerate.}$$

Then $F(x)$ is a stable distribution.

Max-stable family of distributions

Using the equivalence relation "being of the same type" we can unify another category of limit distributions associated with the maximum (not the partial sum) of a sequence.

Max-stable family Let $\{X_n\}_{n=1}^{\infty}$ be a sequence of IID random variables with a non-degenerate cdf $F(x)$. The distribution $F(x)$ is said to be *max-stable* if the distribution of:

$$X_{max}(n) = \max(X_1, X_2, \ldots, X_n),$$

is of the same type for every positive integer n.

Gnedenko's theorem Let $\{X_n\}_{n=1}^{\infty}$ be a sequence of IID random variables with $X_{max}(n) = \max(X_1, X_2, \ldots, X_n)$. Assume that there exist constants $a_n > 0$ and b_n such that:

$$\lim_{n \to \infty} \mathbb{P}\left(\frac{X_{max}(n) - b_n}{a_n} \leq x\right) = F(x), \text{ where } F(x) \text{ is non-degenerate.}$$

Then $F(x)$ is a max-stable distribution. Fortunately, the members of the max-stable family can be categorized into **three types of distributions for** $X_{max}(n)$ (see Galambos (1995)):

(a) $G_{1,\alpha}(x) = \begin{cases} \exp(-x^{-\alpha}), & \text{for } x > 0, \\ \exp 0, & \text{for } x \leq 0. \end{cases}$

(b) $G_{2,\alpha}(x) = \begin{cases} \exp(-(-x)^{\alpha}), & \text{for } x < 0, \\ \exp 1, & \text{for } x > 0. \end{cases}$

(c) $G_{3,\alpha}(x) = \exp(-e^{-x}), \text{ for all } x \in \mathbb{R}.$

Infinitely divisible family of distributions

The infinitely divisible family of distributions constitutes a natural extension of the stable family in the case where the random variables in the sequence $\{X_n\}_{n=1}^{\infty}$ are Independent but non-ID. The basic result in relation to this family is that the limit distribution (assumed to be non-degenerate) of the partial sums of Independent but not necessarily ID random variables is infinitely divisible; for further details see Moran (1968) and Galambos (1995).

9.7 Extending the limit theorems*

The first obvious extension of the above limit theorems is to the case of a random vector $\mathbf{X} := (X_1, X_2, \ldots, X_m) \in \mathbb{R}_X^m$. In the case of the LLN this is trivially true because when the law holds for every element it holds for the random vector. For the CLT, however, it is different because the asymptotic distribution is defined in terms of the first two moments which involve the covariances among the elements of the random vector.

Multivariate CLT Let $\{X_k\}_{k=1}^{\infty}$ be a sequence of IID random vectors with $E(\mathbf{X}_k) = \boldsymbol{\mu}$ (an $m \times 1$ vector), and $Cov(\mathbf{X}_k) = \boldsymbol{\Sigma}$ (an $m \times m$ matrix), for all $k = 1, 2, \ldots, n, \ldots$, then under certain restrictions which ensure that no random vector dominates the summation:

$$\sqrt{n}\left(\overline{X}_n - \boldsymbol{\mu}\right) \underset{\alpha}{\sim} N(\mathbf{0}, \boldsymbol{\Sigma}), \text{ where } \overline{\mathbf{X}}_n = \frac{1}{n}\sum_{k=1}^n \mathbf{X}_k.$$

The question which naturally arises at this point is to what extent the above limit theorems can help our quest for approximate distribution results for arbitrary functions $g(X_1, X_2, \ldots, X_n)$. After all the above theorems are related to a very specific function:

$$c_n^{-1} S_n := c_n^{-1}\left(\sum_{k=1}^n [X_k - E(X_k)]\right), \quad n \to \infty. \tag{9.37}$$

The gap between asymptotic results of general functions and the results of the above limit theorems is bridged in several ways. The first is trivial in the sense that the scaled sum in (9.37) includes cases such as:

$$\sum_{i=1}^n X_i^r, \text{ for } r = 1, 2, 3, \ldots,$$

when the modeler can ensure that the new random variables $Z_i = X_i^r$ for $i = 1, 2, \ldots$, satisfy the conditions of the above limit theorems. As shown in chapters 11–15, numerous estimators and test statistics (the stuff that statistical inference is built upon) fall into this category of functions.

The second way we can bridge the gap between scaled sums as in (9.37) and arbitrary functions is the following theorem which ensures that not only sums but any *continuous functions* of them can be accommodated in a general limit theorem framework.

Mann and Wald theorem Assuming that $\{X_n\}_{n=1}^\infty$ is a sequence of random variables, X is another random variable on the same probability space $(S, \Im, \mathbb{P}(.))$, and $g(.): \mathbb{R} \to \mathbb{R}$ is a continuous function, then:

(a) $X_n \overset{a.s.}{\to} X, \Rightarrow g(X_n) \overset{a.s.}{\to} g(X),$

(b) $X_n \overset{\mathbb{P}}{\to} X, \Rightarrow g(X_n) \overset{\mathbb{P}}{\to} g(X),$

(c) $X_n \overset{\mathcal{D}}{\to} X, \Rightarrow g(X_n) \overset{\mathcal{D}}{\to} g(X).$

Examples

(i)   An interesting example of this theorem is the following:

$$\text{if } X_n \overset{\mathcal{D}}{\to} X \sim N(0,1), \text{ then } X_n^2 \overset{\mathcal{D}}{\to} X^2 \sim \chi^2(1).$$

(ii)   Let $X_n \overset{\mathcal{D}}{\to} X \sim N(0,1)$ and consider the function $Y_n = \frac{1}{X_n}$. It turns out that:

$$Y_n \overset{\mathcal{D}}{\to} Z, \text{ where } f(z) = \frac{1}{z^2\sqrt{2\pi}} \exp\left\{-\frac{1}{2z^2}\right\}, z \neq 0,$$

despite the fact that $g(x) = \frac{1}{x}$ is not continuous at $x = 0$, because the probability at this point is zero, $f(z)$ is known the inverse Gaussian distribution.

There are two things worth noting about the Mann-Wald theorem.

(i)   Mann and Wald (1943) proved a more general result where $g(.)$ is a Borel function with discontinuities on a set of probability zero; just being a Borel function will not work!

(ii)   This theorem is more general than we need in the sense that the SLLN and the

WLLN refer to convergence almost surely and in probability to a constant not a random variable. Moreover, the CLT entails the convergence to a very specific distribution: the Normal. The above theorem refers to any limit distribution.

Another useful result in our quest for asymptotic distribution results is the following theorem.

Cramer's theorem Let $g(.)\colon \mathbb{R} \to \mathbb{R}$ be a function such that $\frac{dg(\theta)}{d\theta} \neq 0$ is continuous in the neighborhood of $\theta \in \mathbb{R}$. Assuming that:

$$\sqrt{n}(X_n - \theta) \underset{\alpha}{\sim} N(0, \sigma^2),$$

then, $\sqrt{n}(g(X_n) - g(\theta)) \underset{\alpha}{\sim} N\left(0, \left[\frac{dg(\theta)}{d\theta}\right]^2 \sigma^2\right).$

The vector form of this theorem with:

$$\mathbf{g}(.)\colon \mathbb{R}^m \to \mathbb{R}^k, \text{ with rank}\left(\left[\frac{\partial \mathbf{g}(\boldsymbol{\theta})}{\partial \boldsymbol{\theta}}\right]\right) = k,$$

$$\sqrt{n}(\mathbf{X}_n - \boldsymbol{\theta}) \underset{\alpha}{\sim} N(\mathbf{0}, \boldsymbol{\Sigma}),$$

takes the form:

$$\sqrt{n}(\mathbf{g}(\mathbf{X}_n) - \mathbf{g}(\boldsymbol{\theta})) \underset{\alpha}{\sim} N\left(\mathbf{0}, \left[\frac{\partial \mathbf{g}(\boldsymbol{\theta})}{\partial \boldsymbol{\theta}}\right] \boldsymbol{\Sigma} \left[\frac{\partial \mathbf{g}(\boldsymbol{\theta})}{\partial \boldsymbol{\theta}}\right]'\right).$$

Example

Consider the case where:

$$\sqrt{n}(\overline{X}_n - \theta) \xrightarrow{\mathcal{D}} Z \sim N(0, \sigma^2),$$

and take $g(x) = x^2$. We know that $\frac{dg(\theta)}{d\theta} = 2\theta$ and thus:

$$\sqrt{n}(\overline{X}_n^2 - \theta^2) \xrightarrow{\mathcal{D}} Y \sim N(0, 4\theta^2 \sigma^2).$$

It is clear from the above approximate result, often known as the *delta method approximation*, that it is a first-order Taylor's approximation, which for linear functions $g(.)$ provides an exact result. For non-linear functions, however, it can provide a poor approximation. In such cases we can proceed to derive a second-order approximation as follows.

The second-order Taylor's approximation of a function $g(.)\colon \mathbb{R} \to \mathbb{R}$ at $x = \theta$ such that $\frac{d^2 g(\theta)}{d\theta^2} \neq 0$ takes the form:

$$g(x) - g(\theta) \simeq \left[\frac{dg(\theta)}{d\theta}\right](x - \theta) + \frac{\left[\frac{d^2 g(\theta)}{d\theta^2}\right]}{2}(x - \theta)^2 = \frac{\left[\frac{d^2 g(\theta)}{d\theta^2}\right]}{2}\left(\left(x - \theta + \frac{\left[\frac{dg(\theta)}{d\theta}\right]}{\left[\frac{d^2 g(\theta)}{d\theta^2}\right]}\right)^2 - \frac{\left[\frac{dg(\theta)}{d\theta}\right]^2}{\left[\frac{d^2 g(\theta)}{d\theta^2}\right]^2}\right).$$

NOTE that the second equality follows by completing the square. Hence, for:

$$\sqrt{n}(X_n - \theta) \underset{\alpha}{\sim} N(0, \sigma^2),$$

the second-order approximation takes the form:

$$n(g(X_n) - g(\theta)) \simeq \frac{\sigma^2 \left[\frac{d^2 g(\theta)}{d\theta^2}\right]}{2}\left(\left(\frac{\sqrt{n}(X_n - \theta)}{\sigma} + \delta_n\right)^2 - \delta_n^2\right), \; \delta_n := \frac{\sqrt{n}\left[\frac{dg(\theta)}{d\theta}\right]}{\sigma\left[\frac{d^2 g(\theta)}{d\theta^2}\right]}.$$

We know that the square of a standard Normally distributed random variable is chi-square distributed and thus:

$$\left(\frac{\sqrt{n}(X_n - \theta)}{\sigma} + \delta_n\right)^2 \underset{\alpha}{\sim} \chi^2(1;\delta_n^2),$$

where $\chi^2(\delta_n)$ denotes a chi-square with one degree of freedom and non-centrality parameter δ_n^2. Hence, the second-order approximation takes the form:

$$n(g(X_n) - g(\theta)) \simeq \frac{\sigma^2 \left[\frac{d^2 g(\theta)}{d\theta^2}\right]}{2}(\chi^2(1;\delta_n^2) - \delta_n^2), \; \delta_n := \frac{\sqrt{n}\left[\frac{dg(\theta)}{d\theta}\right]}{\sigma\left[\frac{d^2 g(\theta)}{d\theta^2}\right]}.$$

Example

Let us reconsider the above example where:

$$\sqrt{n}\left(\overline{X}_n - \theta\right) \overset{D}{\to} Z \sim \mathsf{N}(0,\sigma^2),$$

and take $g(x) = x^2$. We know that $\frac{dg(\theta)}{d\theta} = 2\theta$ and $\frac{d^2 g(\theta)}{d\theta^2} = 2$. Using the second-order approximation we deduce that:

$$n\left(\overline{X}_n^2 - \theta^2\right) \overset{D}{\to} Y \sim \sigma^2[\chi^2(1;\delta_n^2) - \delta_n^2], \; \delta_n^2 = \frac{n\theta^2}{4\sigma^2},$$

which is now an exact result.

We conclude this section on a positive note that the above results go a long way to help the modeler extend the CLT and derive asymptotic distribution results for arbitrary functions $Y_n = g(X_1, X_2, \ldots, X_n)$; for a more detailed discussion and further results see chapter 11 and Spanos (1986).

9.7.1 A uniform SLLN

In statistical inference the modeler often finds herself dealing with a function of the random variables $(X_1, X_2, \ldots, X_n)$ which includes some unknown parameter(s) θ, say:

$$\frac{1}{n}\sum_{k=1}^{n} h(X_k, \theta) \text{ where } E(h(X_k, \theta)) = \tau(\theta).$$

The modeler often assumes that if one replaces the unknown parameter with a good estimator $\hat{\theta}_n$ (see chapter 12), then, using the SLLN one can deduce that:

$$\frac{1}{n}\sum_{k=1}^{n} h(X_k, \theta) \overset{a.s.}{\to} \tau(\theta). \tag{9.38}$$

This, however, will be an erroneous conclusion because the SLLN by itself is not strong enough to yield (9.38).

It turns out that for (9.38) to hold we need to (a) restrict the parameter space Θ to be closed and bounded, (b) ensure that $h(.)$ is well behaved with respect to both arguments (such as continuous), and (c) strengthen the almost sure convergence to uniform convergence in θ:

$$\sup_{\theta \in \Theta} \left| \frac{1}{n} \sum_{k=1}^{n} h(X_k, \theta) - \tau(\theta) \right| \overset{a.s.}{\to} 0.$$

For further details see Bierens (1994).

9.8   Functional Central Limit Theorem*

The Functional Central Limit Theorem (FCLT) constitutes the latest important refinement of the classical CLT considered above. The initial form of this theorem, which is sometimes called the *Invariance Principle*, was first proved by Erdos and Kac (1946) and generalized by Donsker (1951). Its current form was given by Prokhorov (1956); a number of extensions have appeared since. The problem the FCLT purports to address is the following. For a number of reasons we are often interested not just in the sum $S_n = \sum_{i=1}^{n}(X_i - \mu)$, the focus of the CLT, but functions of the form $h(S_1, S_2, ..., S_n)$ which involve a set of such partial sums, such as:

$$\max_{1 \leq k \leq n} \sum_{i=1}^{k}(X_i - \mu) = \max (S_1, S_2, ..., S_n). \tag{9.39}$$

This function cannot be handled using a function of S_n, say $g(S_n)$, because as seen from (9.39) it cannot be expressed just as a function of S_n. In some sense the FCLT extends the classical CLT to such situations.

To simplify the discussion that follows let $\{X_n\}_{n=1}^{\infty}$ be an IID stochastic process with $E(X_k) = 0$ and $Var(X_k) = \sigma^2$. The classical CLT concerns the sequence of partial sums $\{S_n, n = 1, 2, ...\}$ where:

$$S_n = \sum_{i=1}^{n} X_i.$$

Define the function process $\{ Y_n(t), 0 \leq t \leq 1, n = 1, 2, ... \}$ by:

$$Y_n(0) = 0, \ Y_n\left(\frac{k}{n}\right) = \frac{1}{\sqrt{n}} S_k, \ 1 \leq k \leq n.$$

Looking at this *random function* we can see that it is a function of k via $\frac{k}{n}$; the latter being

a proportion with upper bound one. Hence, by using a proportionality factor $t \in [0,1]$ directly we can define $\frac{k}{n}$ in terms of $[nt]$, with the square brackets denoting the integer part of the number (nt). As a result, we can express the random function of partial sums as:

$$Y_n(t) = \begin{cases} S_0 := 0, & \text{for } 0 \leq t \leq \frac{1}{n}, \\ (\sqrt{n})^{-1} S_1 := X_1, & \text{for } \frac{1}{n} \leq t \leq \frac{2}{n}, \\ (\sqrt{n})^{-1} S_2 := X_1 + X_2, & \text{for } \frac{2}{n} \leq t \leq \frac{3}{n}, \\ (\sqrt{n})^{-1} S_3 := X_1 + X_2 + X_3, & \text{for } \frac{3}{n} \leq t \leq \frac{4}{n}, \\ \quad \vdots & \vdots \quad \vdots \quad \vdots \\ (\sqrt{n})^{-1} S_n := X_1 + X_2 + \cdots + X_n, & \text{for } t = 1. \end{cases}$$

$$Y_n(t) = \frac{1}{\sqrt{n}} \sum_{i=1}^{[nt]} X_i, \ t \in [0,1].$$

More explicitly:

Intuitively, what we are doing here is to speed up the process by forcing it to take an increasing number of steps in unit time while the size of the step gets smaller and smaller. The CLT implies that as $n \to \infty$, the distribution of the random variable $Y_n(t)$ for any $t > 0$ converges to $N(0,t)$; to the distribution of a Brownian motion process $Y(t)$. Moreover, for any finite set of values $0 < t_1 < t_2 < \cdots < t_k$ the joint distribution of $(Y_n(t_1), Y_n(t_2), \ldots, Y_n(t_k))$ will be Normal. More specifically, the stochastic process $\{Y_n(t),$ $t \in [0,1]\}_{n=1}^{\infty}$ maps the discrete process $\{S_n\}_{n=1}^{\infty}$ into a continuous scale process. The result is that over any interval $(t_1, t_2] \subset [0,1]$ the difference $(Y_n(t_2) - Y_n(t_1))$ is the *sum* of a large number (approximately $[nt_2] - [nt_1] \simeq n(t_2 - t_1)$ in number) and increasing with n IID random variables:

$$\frac{1}{\sqrt{n}} X_{[nt_1]+1}, \frac{1}{\sqrt{n}} X_{[nt_1]+2}, \ldots, \frac{1}{\sqrt{n}} X_{[nt_2]},$$

inducing a Central Limit Theorem effect (see section 6 above).

This is not a very easy random quantity to understand because it involves three different arguments and thus it can be interpreted in a number of different ways. The most general way to view $Y_n(t)$ is as a stochastic process with three arguments $Y(n,s,t)$:

$$Y(.,.,.) : (\mathbb{N} \times S \times [0,1]) \to \mathbb{R}.$$

In order to understand the structure of this random function, however, we need to reduce the dimensionality of its domain by fixing certain arguments, leading to alternative viewing angles.

A first interesting viewing angle is created by fixing $t \in [0,1]$. In this case we can think of $Y_n(t) := Y(n,s,\bar{t})$ as an ordinary stochastic process (a real-valued function from $(S \times \mathbb{N})$ into $\mathbb{R}$). In view of the fact that as $[nt] \underset{n \to \infty}{\to} \infty$, $\left(\frac{[nt]}{n}\right) \underset{n \to \infty}{\to} t$ we can deduce that for large n:

$$E(Y_n(t)) = 0, \ Var(Y_n(t)) = \sigma^2 \left(\frac{[nt]}{n}\right) \simeq \sigma^2 t, \ Cov(Y_n(t+\tau), Y_n(t)) = \sigma^2 \left(\frac{[n\tau]}{n}\right) \simeq \sigma^2 \tau.$$

Moreover, we can call upon the classical CLT to conclude:

$$Y_n(t) \overset{D}{\to} Z \sim N(0, \sigma^2 t), \text{ for each } t \in [0,1].$$

These results suggest that at the limit the process $\{Y_n(t), \ t \in [0,1]\}_{n=1}^{\infty}$ behaves like a Brownian motion (see chapter 8).

A second viewing angle becomes available by fixing $s \in S$. In this case we can think of $Y_n(t) := Y(n,\bar{s},t)$ as a function from $(\mathbb{N} \times [0,1])$ into $\mathbb{R}$, which defines an indexed sequence of real-valued functions defined over the closed interval $[0,1]$. In order to make things easier we proceed to consider a third narrow viewing angle created by fixing both $s \in S$ and $n \in \mathbb{N}$. In this highly simplified case we can think of $Y_n(t) := Y(\bar{n},\bar{s},t)$ as a function from $[0,1]$ into $\mathbb{R}$, which by allowing $t \in [0,1]$ to take all its values in that interval we define a set of real-valued functions $\{Y_n(t), 0 \le t \le 1\}$. The nature of this set of functions is of interest because the convergence we have in mind involves this set. As defined above the function $Y_n(t)$ is not continuous. For convergence purposes we prefer continuous func-

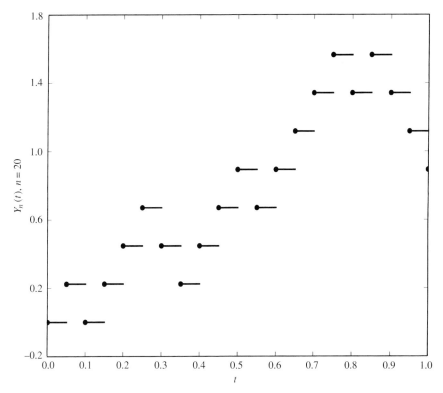

Figure 9.2 $\{Y_k(t),\ t\in[0,1]\}_{k=1}^{p},\ n=20$

tions and thus we smooth out its jumps by adding an interpolating term:

$$Y_n^*(t) = \tfrac{1}{\sqrt{n}}\left(\textstyle\sum_{k=1}^{[nt]} X_k + (nt - [nt])\,X_{[nt]+1}\right),\ t\in[0,1].\tag{9.40}$$

Example

In order to enhance our understanding of the difference between these two stochastic processes, consider the case where $\{X_n\}_{n=1}^{\infty}$ is an IID modified Bernoulli process with $\mathbb{P}(X_k = 1) = \tfrac{1}{2}$, $\mathbb{P}(X_k = -1) = \tfrac{1}{2}$, $E(X_k) = 0$ and $Var(X_k) = 1$ and $\mathcal{R} = \{-1,1\}$. As shown in chapter 8, the partial sum process in this case is a *simple random walk*. In figure 9.2 we can see the graph of the process $\{Y_k(t),\ t\in[0,1]\}_{k=1}^{n}$, for a realization of $\{X_k\}_{k=1}^{n}$ size $n=20$:

$$\{1,-1,1,1,1,-1,-1,1,1,1,1,-1,1,1,1,1,1,-1,1,-1,-1,-1,-1\},$$

which is clearly a step function (non-continuous). NOTE that on the vertical axis the units of measurement are $\left\{\tfrac{1}{\sqrt{n}}, \tfrac{2}{\sqrt{n}}, \dots, \tfrac{n}{\sqrt{n}}\right\}$ and on the horizontal axis are $\left[\tfrac{1}{n}, \tfrac{2}{n}, \dots, \tfrac{n}{n}\right]$, and thus the units are changing with n. In figure 9.3 we can see the graph of the process $\{Y_n^*(t),\ t\in[0,1]_k\}_{k=1}^{n}$, which is a continuous polygonal line.

The new functions are continuous and thus the set: $\{Y_n^*(t),\ 0\le t\le 1\}$, can be viewed as a subset of the set of all *continuous* real-valued functions defined over the closed interval

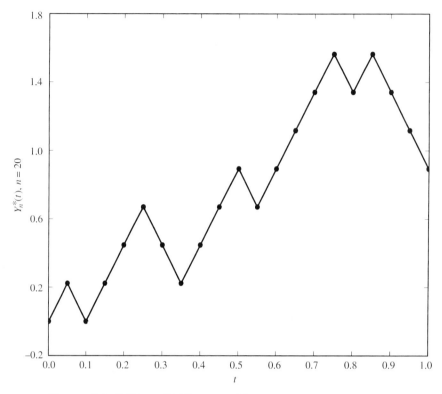

Figure 9.3 $\{Y_k^*(t),\, t \in [0,1]\}_{k=1}^9,\, n = 20$

[0,1], denoted by $C[0,1]$. Embedding these smoothed functions into the space $C[0,1]$ is very significant because we can discuss convergence in this space using well established results. For example we know that for two such continuous functions, say $f, g \in C[0,1]$, we can define convergence in terms of the distance function:

$$d_\infty(f,g) := \sup_{0 \le t \le 1} |f(t) - g(t)|, \tag{9.41}$$

known as a *uniform metric* to the mathematical connoisseurs; see Dhrymes (1998).

We can now return to the previous viewpoint $Y_n(t) := Y(n,\bar{s},t)$ which enables us to consider the convergence of such continuous functions within $C[0,1]$. The metric (9.41) assures us that when a sequence of such functions $\{f_n(t),\, 0 \le t \le 1,\, _n = 1\}_{n=1}^\infty$ converges, the limit function $f(t)$ exists and $f(t) \in C[0,1]$ (see Kolmogorov and Fomin (1970)). However, this discussion of convergence ignores the essence of stochastic processes, their probabilistic structure, since we kept $s \in S$ fixed.

To get the complete picture we need to return to $Y_n^*(t) := Y^*(n,s,t)$, and add to the discussion of convergence the probabilistic structure of $\{Y_n^*(s,t),\, s \in S,\, 0 \le t \le 1\}$. Before we do that, however, it is illuminating to consider a fourth viewing angle where we fix both $n \in \mathbb{N}$ and $t \in [0,1]$, viewing $Y_n^*(t) := Y^*(\bar{n},s,\bar{t})$ as just a random variable (a function from S to $\mathbb{R}$) with:

$$Var(Y_n^*(t)) = \frac{1}{n}\left(\sum_{k=1}^{[nt]}\sigma^2 + (nt - [nt])^2\sigma^2\right) \to t\sigma^2.$$

With the above discussion in mind let us return to the general viewpoint where $Y_n^*(t) := Y^*(n,s,t)$:

$$Y^*(.,.,.): (\mathbb{N} \times S \times [0,1]) \to \mathbb{R}.$$

In order to avoid thinking in four dimensions (!), it pays to fuse the sets $[0,1]$ and $\mathbb{R}$ into $C[0,1]$: the set of continuous real-valued functions, and interpret $Y^*(n,s,t)$ as:

$$Y_n^*(.): (\mathbb{N} \times S) \to C[0,1].$$

$Y_n^*(.)$ now represents a *random function:* a function from an outcomes set to a set of functions. This fusion resulted in trading $\mathbb{R}$ for $C[0,1]$, which obviously raises a few technical problems because every element in $\mathbb{R}$ is a number but every element in $C[0,1]$ is function. However, mathematicians have already tackled these problems with spectacular success. Indeed, the essence of a branch of mathematics known as Functional Analysis is the economy of thought gained by treating dissimilar sets such as $\mathbb{R}$ and $C[0,1]$ as sets with the same mathematical structure, irrespective of the nature of their elements. It turns out that if we attach a certain notion of distance to the two sets above then we can treat the pairs $(\mathbb{R}, |a - b|)$ and $(C[0,1], \sup_{0 \le t \le 1} |f(t) - g(t)|)$,as if they are the same for our purposes; as it happens they are both complete and separable metric spaces (see Kolmogorov and Fomin (1970)). All that is needed is to ensure that the sample paths of the relevant processes in $C[0,1]$ are well behaved. As far as our discussion is concerned, what matters is that the notion of a stochastic process and the relevant joint distribution can be defined on $C[0,1]$ in a way very similar to the one with respect to $\mathbb{R}$. The details, although fascinating from the mathematical viewpoint, will take us far away from our main path and thus we refer the interested reader to the excellent books: Billingsley (1968), Breiman (1968), and Dhrymes (1998).

Donsker's functional CLT Let $\{X_n\}_{n=1}^{\infty}$ be an IID stochastic process with $E(X_k) = 0$ and $Var(X_k) = \sigma^2$, for $Y_n^*(t)$ as defined by (9.40):

$$\left(\frac{Y_n^*(.)}{\sigma}\right) \overset{D}{\to} Z(.) \sim B(.), \tag{9.42}$$

where $B(.)$ is a *Brownian motion* process defined over the interval $[0,1]$, i.e., $\{B(t), t \in [0,1]\}$ is the process defined by:

(i) $B(t+h) - B(t) \sim N(0, |h|)$, for $(t+h) \in [0,1]$,

(ii) $B(t)$ has independent increments, i.e. for $0 \le t_1 < t_2 < t_3 \le 1$,

$$\begin{pmatrix} B(t_1) - B(t_2) \\ B(t_2) - B(t_3) \end{pmatrix} \sim N\left(\begin{pmatrix} 0 \\ 0 \end{pmatrix}, \begin{pmatrix} t_2 - t_1, & 0 \\ 0, & t_3 - t_2 \end{pmatrix}\right)$$

(iii) $B(0) = 0$ (see chapter 8).

It is important to NOTE that this theorem constitutes a refinement of the classical CLT because we can derive the latter as a special case. Choosing $t = 1$, the above theorem yields:

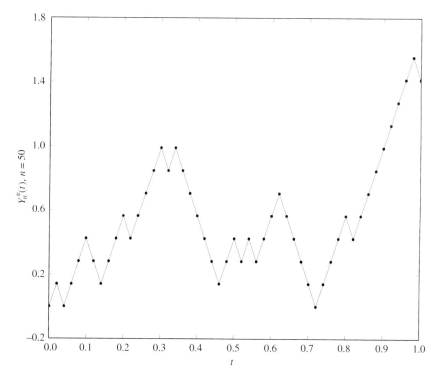

Figure 9.4 $\{Y_k^*(t),\ t\in[0,1]\}_{k=1}^p$, for $n=50$

$$\left(\tfrac{Y_n^*(1)}{\sigma}\right) \overset{\mathcal{D}}{\to} Z \sim B(1) = \mathsf{N}(0,1).$$

It extends the classical CLT in important directions, however, because it enables us to deduce other limit results on distributions which relate to *any continuous functions g(.)* (defined on $C[0,1]$) of $Y_n^*(t)$ in the sense given in the following theorem.

Continuous mapping theorem Let $Y_n(.) \overset{\mathcal{D}}{\to} Z(.) \sim B(.)$, then for a continuous function:

$$g(.):C[0,1] \to \mathbb{R} \Rightarrow g(Y_n(.)) \overset{\mathcal{D}}{\to} g(Z(.)) \sim g(B(.)).$$

Example

$$\left(\tfrac{Y_n^*(.)}{\sigma}\right)^2 \overset{\mathcal{D}}{\to} Z^2(.) \sim (B(.))^2.$$

It is interesting to NOTE that the above result is valid for any continuous function from the metric space $(C[0,1],\ \mathsf{d}_\infty\ (f,g))$, to any other separable and complete metric space, including itself or $(\mathbb{R}, |a-b|)$.

Example

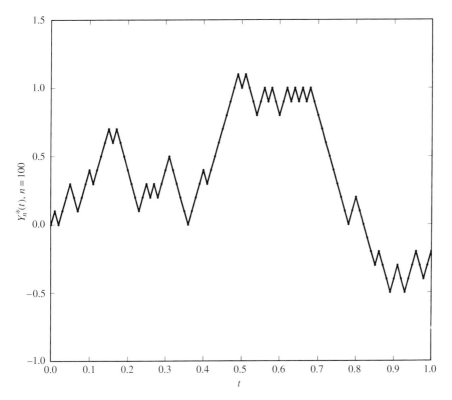

Figure 9.5 $\{Y_k^*(t), t \in [0,1]\}_{k=1}^n$, for $n = 100$

The figures 9.4–9.7 show how the FCLT can be seen pictorially in the case of the simple random walk process used in the example shown in figure 9.3. The effect of increasing the size of n is to render the graph increasingly more polygonous as we proceed from $n = 20$ to $n = 50$ to $n = 100$ to $n = 200$ to $n = 1000$ (see figures 9.4 to 9.7, respectively). The graph of $\{Y_k^*(t), t \in [0,1]\}_{k=1}^n$ for $n = 1000$ looks very much like the graph of a Brownian motion process.

As with the classical CLT several extensions of the FCLT have been proved since the early 1950s by adding minor additional restrictions on those giving rise to the result. In view of the extensive discussion of such variations on the basic theme of the LLN and CLT we will consider only one such extension in the present context; see Herrndorf (1984).

FCLT for second-order stationary processes Let the sequence of random variables $\{X_n\}_{n=1}^{\infty}$ satisfy the following conditions:

(D) Bounded moments: $E(X_k)^2 < \infty, k = 1, 2, \ldots,$

(M) ρ-mixing: $s_n^2 \underset{n \to \infty}{\to} \infty, \lim_{n \to \infty} \sum_{k=1}^{n} [\rho(2^k)]^r < \infty$ for $r = \tfrac{1}{2}, 1,$

(H) Second-order Stationarity: $E(X_k) = \mu, Var(X_k) = \sigma^2, k = 1, 2, \ldots$

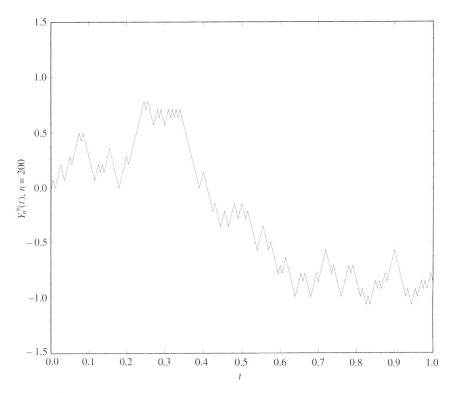

Figure 9.6 $\{Y_k^*(t),\ t \in [0,1]\}_{k=1}^{\rho}$, for $n = 200$

then for $Y_n(t) = \frac{1}{\sqrt{n}} \sum_{i=1}^{[nt]} (X_i - \mu),\ t \in [0,1]$:

$$\left(\frac{Y_n(.)}{\sigma}\right) \overset{\mathcal{D}}{\to} Z(.) \sim B(.). \tag{9.43}$$

NOTE that, in general, the smoothing term is not needed for the result to go through (see Billingsley (1968)).

If we compare this FCLT with the corresponding CLT we observe that for the former result to hold we require the additional restriction: $\lim_{n \to \infty} \sum_{k=1}^{n} [\rho\,(2^k)]^{\frac{1}{2}} < \infty$.

In unit root asymptotics (see Banerjee *et al.* (1993)) we are interested in quantities of the form:

$$\sum_{\frac{k-1}{n} \le t \le \frac{k}{n}} Y_n(t) = \frac{1}{\sqrt{n}} \sum_{\frac{k-1}{n} \le t \le \frac{k}{n}} \sum_{i=1}^{[nt]} (X_i - \mu) = \frac{1}{\sqrt{n}} (S_1 + S_2 + \cdots + S_n).$$

It should be NOTED that this constitutes an example of what is known in the divergent series literature as a *Cesaro sum* which with the appropriate scaling is summable. It should come as no surprise to discover that:

$$\sum_{\frac{k-1}{n} \le t \le \frac{k}{n}} (Y_n(t)) \overset{\mathcal{D}}{\to} Z(.) \sim \int_0^1 B(t)dt.$$

Such results can extend the above FCLT to unit-root, non-stationary stochastic processes; see Phillips (1987), Dhrymes (1998), Stock and Watson (1988).

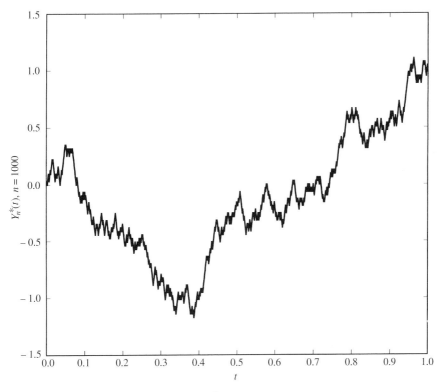

Figure 9.7 $\{Y_k^*(t),\ t\in[0,1]\}_{k=1}^{\rho}$, for $n = 1000$

We conclude this section by summarizing the main steps of the FCLT without the (possibly) intimidating notation. The first step is to transform the partial sums process $\{S_n\}_{n=1}^{\infty}$ to $\{Y_k^*(t),\ t\in[0,1]\}_{k=1}^{n}$ by forcing it to take an *increasing* number of steps within the confined interval $[0,1]$ and simultaneously *decreasing* the size of the steps to zero as $n\to\infty$. This induces a Central Limit Theorem effect with $Y_k^*(t)$ converging to a Brownian motion process. At the same time the state space of $\{S_n\}_{n=1}^{\infty}$ is mapped into $C[0,1]$ inducing a probability set function on its Borel sets, which (happily) converges to that of a Brownian motion, defined on the same space. With the help of the continuous mapping theorem this result can be extended to any continuous functions of $Y_k^*(t)$ converging to the same continuous functions of a Brownian motion process; see Davidson (1994) and Dhrymes (1998).

9.9   Modes of convergence

In section 2 above we considered briefly the three different types of convergence involved in the WLLN, the SLLN, and the CLT. In this section we take that discussion one step further by comparing these convergence notions in order to understand the differences between the results. We begin, however, with a review of some important notions of convergence in calculus and real analysis.

The basic object of interest in convergence of real analysis is that of a **sequence of real numbers** $\{a_n\}_{n=1}^\infty := \{a_1, a_2, \ldots, a_n, \ldots\}$ where a_n constitutes a function from the set of *natural numbers* $\mathbb{N} := \{1, 2, \ldots, n, \ldots\}$ to the *real line*:

$$a_n: \mathbb{N} \to \mathbb{R}.$$

We say that the sequence $\{a_n\}_{n=1}^\infty$ *converges* to a *limit* $a \in \mathbb{R}$, and we write $\lim_{n\to\infty} a_n = a$, if for every $\varepsilon > 0$ there is an integer N such that:

$$|a_n - a| < \varepsilon \text{ whenever } n \geq N(\varepsilon),$$

where $N(\varepsilon)$ indicates that the integer N depends on the value of the chosen ε. That is, far out in the sequence the terms can be made arbitrarily close to the limit.

This notion of convergence of sequences of real numbers can be easily extended to that of a sequence of real-valued **functions** $\{f_n\}_{n=1}^\infty$ of the form:

$$f_n(.): \mathbb{A} \to \mathbb{R},$$

where $\mathbb{A}$ is an arbitrary set and $\mathbb{R}$ denotes the real line. The difference between a real-valued sequence and a sequence of real-valued functions is the new element in the domain ($\mathbb{A}$) of a sequence of functions. A more formal way to think about this sequence of functions is in terms of two arguments:

$$f(.,.): (\mathbb{N} \times \mathbb{A}) \to \mathbb{R}.$$

The presence of the domain $\mathbb{A}$ of the function enables one to distinguish between two different modes of convergence.

Pointwise convergence A sequence of real-valued functions $\{f_n\}_{n=1}^\infty$ is said to *converge pointwise* to a function f, and we write $\lim_{n\to\infty} f_n(x) = f(x)$, if for each $\varepsilon > 0$:

$$|f_n(x) - f(x)| < \varepsilon, \text{ for each } x \in \mathbb{A}, \text{ whenever } n \geq N(\varepsilon, x).$$

Uniform convergence A sequence of real-valued functions $\{f_n\}_{n=1}^\infty$ is said to *converge uniformly* to a limit function f if for each $\varepsilon > 0$:

$$|f_n(x) - f(x)| < \varepsilon, \text{ for all } x \in \mathbb{A}, \text{ whenever } n \geq N(\varepsilon).$$

Intuitively, uniform convergence of $f_n(x)$ to $f(x)$ means that for $n \geq N(\varepsilon)$ the graphs of $f_n(x)$ and $f(x)$ become indistinguishable; see Binmore (1980).

NOTE that the integer N does not depend on the particular value $x \in \mathbb{A}$ and thus, uniform convergence implies pointwise convergence but not the converse.

These notions of convergence can be applied without any changes to a sequence of random variables $\{X_n\}_{n=1}^\infty := \{X_1, X_2, \ldots, X_n, \ldots\}$ because, as seen in chapter 8, this is just a sequence of indexed functions from an outcomes set S (part of the probability space $(S, \widehat{\mathfrak{F}}, \mathbb{P}(.))$ in the context of which all of these take place) to the real line:

$$X_n(.): S \to \mathbb{R}.$$

This is the reason why we left the domain of the functions ($\mathbb{A}$) above unspecified!

These notions of convergence for a sequence of random variables are *not very interesting*, however, because they ignore a fundamental feature of a random variable, its *probabilistic structure*.

The probabilistic convergence encountered in the context of the limit theorems (WLLN, SLLN, CLT) is directly related to the above notions of convergence of real-valued functions which in turn can be seen as an adaptation of pointwise convergence.

Convergence almost surely A sequence of random variables $\{X_n\}_{n=1}^{\infty}$ *converges almost surely* to a random variable X, denoted by:

$$X_n \overset{a.s.}{\to} X,$$

if for each $\varepsilon > 0$, the set $\mathbb{C} \subset S$, defined by:

$$\mathbb{C} := \{s \in S : |X_n(s) - X(s)| < \varepsilon, \text{ whenever } n \geq N(\varepsilon,s)\},$$

has probability one, i.e.

$$\mathbb{P}\left(s: \lim_{n \to \infty} X_n(s) = X(s)\right) = 1, \tag{9.44}$$

which is the same as $\mathbb{P}(s: s \in \mathbb{C}) = 1$, or equivalently $\mathbb{P}(\overline{\mathbb{C}}) = 0$.

If we compare this with pointwise convergence we NOTE that in pointwise convergence the requirement "for each $s \in S$" means that $\mathbb{C} = S$ and thus the adaptation is that we do not require that $\mathbb{C}$ be the whole of the outcomes set but we do require that its complement has probability zero.

In terms of the repeated tossing of a coin example discussed above we can think of $\overline{\mathbb{C}}$ as the set of points of S for which $\{|X_n(s) - X(s)| > \varepsilon\}$, for $n \geq N(\varepsilon,s)$, i.e. the set which includes elements of the form $\mathbf{s}_T := \{T,T, \ldots, T,\ldots\}$ and $\mathbf{s}_H := \{H,H, \ldots, H,\ldots\}$. Intuitively, we can think of almost sure convergence as a shrinking of the set $\overline{\mathbb{C}}$ to one of probability zero.

Proving convergence almost surely is not a trivial exercise and we can do with as many criteria as we can gather. The following theorem provides a simple but often useful criterion.

Borel–Cantelli lemma Let $\{X_n\}_{n=1}^{\infty}$ be a sequence of random variables. If for every $\varepsilon > 0$:

$$\sum_{n=1}^{\infty} \mathbb{P}(s \in S : |X_n(s) - X(s)| \geq \varepsilon) < \infty, \text{ then } X_n \overset{a.s.}{\to} X.$$

The convergence underlying the SLLN is a special case of the convergence almost surely because the limit is a degenerate (a constant) random variable.

Convergence in probability A sequence of random variables $\{X_n\}_{n=1}^{\infty}$ *converges in probability* to a random variable X, denoted by:

$$X_n \overset{\mathbb{P}}{\to} X,$$

if for each $\varepsilon > 0$:

$$\lim_{n \to \infty} \mathbb{P}(s \in S: |X_n(s) - X(s)| < \varepsilon) = 1. \tag{9.45}$$

We can think of this convergence as a convergence of a sequence of real numbers associated with the probability of a sequence of events. Consider the sequence of probabilities $\{p_n\}_{n=1}^{\infty}$:

$$p_n := \mathbb{P}(s \in S: |X_n(s) - X(s)| \geq \varepsilon),$$

which refer to the tail probabilities of the random variable $Y_n := |X_n(s) - X(s)|$, i.e.

$$p_n = \int_{\{Y_n \geq \varepsilon\}} f_n(y) dy,$$

where for expositional purposes we assume that $f_n(y)$ is the density function of Y_n. Convergence in probability amounts to:

$$\lim_{n \to \infty} p_n = 0.$$

The convergence underlying the WLLN is a special case of the above convergence probability because the limit is a degenerate (a constant) random variable

A comparison between (9.44) and (9.45) suggests that convergence almost surely is a stronger form of convergence. This becomes apparent when we use the following lemma.

Lemma 1 For the sequence of random variables $\{X_n\}_{n=1}^{\infty}$: $X_n \overset{a.s.}{\to} X$, if and only if for each $\varepsilon > 0$,

$$\lim_{n \to \infty} \mathbb{P}\left(s \in S: \bigcup_{k=n}^{\infty} |X_k(s) - X(s)| \geq \varepsilon\right) = 0. \tag{9.46}$$

This shows most clearly that in terms of the events $A_k(s) := \{s \in S: |X_k(s) - X(s)| \geq \varepsilon\}$:

$$X_n \overset{\mathbb{P}}{\to} X \Leftrightarrow \lim_{n \to \infty} \mathbb{P}(A_n(s)) = 0,$$

$$X_n \overset{a.s.}{\to} X \Leftrightarrow \lim_{n \to \infty} \mathbb{P}\left(\bigcup_{k=n}^{\infty} A_k(s)\right) = 0.$$

Hence, in view of the fact that $\mathbb{P}\left(\bigcup_{k=n}^{\infty} A_k(s)\right) = \mathbb{P}(\sup_{k \geq n} A_k(s)) \geq \mathbb{P}(A_n(s))$:

$$[X_n \overset{a.s.}{\to} X] \Rightarrow [X_n \overset{\mathbb{P}}{\to} X],$$

but the converse may not be true.

Example
Consider the sequence of discrete random variables $\{X_n\}_{n=1}^{\infty}$ with probability distribution:

$$\mathbb{P}(X_n = 1) = \frac{1}{n}, \ \mathbb{P}(X_n = 0) = 1 - \frac{1}{n}, \ n = 1, 2, \ldots$$

Noting that $E(X_n) = \left(\frac{1}{n}\right) \underset{n\to\infty}{\to} 0$, and for $0<\varepsilon<1$, $\mathbb{P}(|X_n - 0|>\varepsilon) = \frac{1}{n} \underset{n\to\infty}{\to} 0$, we can deduce that $X_n \overset{\mathbb{P}}{\to} 0$. On the other hand:

$$\mathbb{P}\left(\bigcup_{k=n}^{\infty} A_k(s)\right) = \left[1 - \prod_{k=m}^{\infty}\left(1 - \frac{1}{k}\right)\right] \underset{n\to\infty}{\to} 1,$$

since $\prod_{k=m}^{\infty}\left(1 - \frac{1}{k}\right) \underset{n\to\infty}{\to} 0$, and thus $X_n \overset{a.s.}{\nrightarrow} 0$.

Having gone the extra mile to define these two modes of convergence in terms of the sequence of probabilities associated with the events $A_n(s)$ we should take advantage of it and define another mode of convergence, known as *complete convergence*, which implies convergence almost surely.

Complete convergence A sequence of random variables $\{X_n\}_{n=1}^{\infty}$ *converges completely* to a random variable X, denoted by $X_n \overset{c}{\to} X$, if for each $\varepsilon>0$:

$$\lim_{n\to\infty} \sum_{k=1}^{n} \mathbb{P}(s\in S: |X_k(s) - X(s)|\varepsilon)<\infty. \tag{9.47}$$

From the Borel–Cantelli lemma stated above, it is obvious that:

$$[X_n \overset{c}{\to} X] \Rightarrow [X_n \overset{a.s.}{\to} X]. \tag{9.48}$$

Moreover, the condition (9.47) can be written equivalently as:

$$\lim_{n\to\infty} \sum_{k=n}^{\infty} \mathbb{P}(A_k(s)) = 0,$$

which, from axiom 3 of the probability set functions, implies that:

$$\lim_{n\to\infty} \mathbb{P}\left(\bigcup_{k=n}^{\infty} A_k(s)\right) \le \lim_{n\to\infty} \sum_{k=n}^{\infty} \mathbb{P}(A_k(s)).$$

This shows most clearly that (9.48) always holds but the converse holds for sure when the sequence $\{X_n\}_{n=1}^{\infty}$ is independent.

In view of these results we could think of $X_n \overset{\mathbb{P}}{\to} X$ as being valid when $\mathbb{P}(A_n(s)) \underset{n\to\infty}{\to} 0$, while $X_n \overset{a.s.}{\to} X$, if in addition, the convergence is *fast enough* (Borel–Cantelli fast) that their sum is finite.

Convergence in distribution A sequence of random variables $\{X_n\}_{n=1}^{\infty}$ *converges in distribution* to a random variable X, denoted by:

$$X_n \overset{D}{\to} X,$$

if for each $\varepsilon>0$, there exists a positive integer $N(\varepsilon,x)$ such that:

$$|F_n(x) - F(x)|<\varepsilon, \text{ for } n\ge N(\varepsilon,x), \text{ whenever } x \text{ is a point of continuity of } F(x),$$

where $F_n(x)$ denotes the cdf of X_n; this is often expressed by:

$$\lim_{n\to\infty} F_n(x) = F(x), \text{ whenever } x \text{ is a point of continuity of } F(.). \tag{9.49}$$

This is a convergence of a sequence of functions with the qualification that one considers only the continuity points of the limit function. The problem forcing us to use this qualification is that neither $F_n(x)$ nor $F(x)$ may be continuous everywhere (e.g., discrete distributions) and thus at the jump point $F_n(x)$ may not converge to $F(x)$.

The convergence underlying the CLT is a special case of the above convergence in distribution because the limit random variable has a Normal distribution ($\Phi(x)$). In view of the fact that the latter is continuous everywhere there was no need to refer to the qualification about the points of continuity of $\Phi(x)$.

Convergence in distribution is the weakest mode of convergence which is implied by all the previous modes. In summary, the implications which are valid are:

$$[X_n \xrightarrow{c} X] \Rightarrow [X_n \xrightarrow{a.s.} X] \Rightarrow [X_n \xrightarrow{P} X] \Rightarrow [X_n \xrightarrow{D} X].$$

Intuitively, convergence in distribution is weaker than convergence in probability because the former is defined exclusively in terms of the convergence of the distribution functions without any direct references to the underlying random variables. On the other hand, convergence in probability involves the random variables themselves via the events: $A_n(s) := \{s \in S : |X_k(s) - X(s)| \geqslant \varepsilon, \; n = 1, 2, \ldots\}$ As a consequence of this, convergence in distribution can be defined even in cases where the random variables involved are defined on different probability spaces; something impossible for the other modes of convergence.

The fact that convergence in distribution does not involve the random variables and their values directly is apparent from the following result.

Lemma 2 For the sequence of random variables $\{X_n\}_{n=1}^{\infty}$: $X_n \xrightarrow{D} X$, if and only if:

$$\lim_{n \to \infty} E(g(X_n)) = E(g(X)), \tag{9.50}$$

for every *bounded continuous* function $g(x)$.

Although in general $[X_n \xrightarrow{D} X] \nRightarrow [X_n \xrightarrow{P} X]$ there is one important special case for which this is true. The following result is directly related to the above comment that convergence in distribution does not entail the values of the random variables $\{X_n\}_{n=1}^{\infty}$ and X directly.

Lemma 3 For the sequence of random variables $\{X_n\}_{n=1}^{\infty}$ and c a constant:

$$[X_n \xrightarrow{D} c] \Rightarrow [X_n \xrightarrow{P} c],$$

Another form of convergence which can help establish convergence in probability is the so-called convergence in the rth mean.

Convergence in rth mean A sequence of random variables $\{X_n\}_{n=1}^{\infty}$ with bounded moments of order $r > 0$ (i.e., $E|X_k|^r < \infty$, $k = 1, 2, \ldots$), *converges in rth mean* to a random variable X, denoted by:

$$X_n \xrightarrow{r} X,$$

if for each $\varepsilon > 0$, there exists a positive integer $N(\varepsilon)$ such that:

$$E(|X_n - X|^r) < \varepsilon, \text{ for } n \geq N(\varepsilon).$$

This is often expressed by:

$$\lim_{n \to \infty} E(|X_n - X|^r) = 0, \text{ for } r > 0. \tag{9.51}$$

It is obvious that the higher the value of r the more stringent the condition since from Jensen's inequality we can deduce that:

$$[X_n \xrightarrow{r} X] \Rightarrow [X_n \xrightarrow{s} X] \text{ for } 0 < s < r.$$

Using the Markov inequality $\mathbb{P}(|X| \geq \varepsilon) \leq \frac{E(|X|^p)}{\varepsilon^p}$, we can deduce:

$$\mathbb{P}(|X_n - X \geq \varepsilon) \leq \frac{E(|X_n - X|^r)}{\varepsilon^r},$$

and in view of the fact that $\lim_{n \to \infty} E(|X_n - X|^r) = 0$, we conclude that:

$$[X_n \xrightarrow{r} X] \Rightarrow [X_n \xrightarrow{\mathbb{P}} X].$$

That is, convergence in rth mean implies convergence in probability but the converse is invalid in general. It is, however, true that for bounded random variables convergence in probability implies convergence in rth mean.

Lemma 4 For the sequence of random variables $\{X_n\}_{n=1}^{\infty}$, with $E|X_k|^r < \infty, k = 1, 2, \ldots,$

$$[X_n \xrightarrow{\mathbb{P}} X] \Rightarrow [X_n \xrightarrow{r} X],$$

if the sequence is *bounded*, i.e. $\mathbb{P}(|X_n - X| < c) = 1$, for some $0 < c < \infty$.

A special case of the above result is the case where $\{X_n\}_{n=1}^{\infty}$ is *uniformly integrable* (see section 6 above).

In general, convergence in the rth mean does not imply convergence almost surely. For the latter to be the case we need to impose certain restrictions on the rate of convergence of the former.

Lemma 5 For the sequence of random variables $\{X_n\}_{n=1}^{\infty}$, with $E|X_k|^r < \infty, k = 1, 2, \ldots:$

$$[X_n \xrightarrow{r} X] \Rightarrow [X_n \xrightarrow{a.s.} X],$$

if $\sum_{n=1}^{\infty} E(|X_n - X|^r) < \infty.$

$$\boxed{[X_n \xrightarrow{c} X]} \Rightarrow \boxed{[X_n \xrightarrow{a.s.} X]} \searrow$$
$$\Rightarrow \boxed{[X_n \xrightarrow{\mathbb{P}} X]} \Rightarrow \boxed{[X_n \xrightarrow{D} X]}.$$
$$\boxed{[X_n \xrightarrow{r} X]} \nearrow$$

We conclude this section by collecting together all the above implications that hold without additional restrictions (see also McGabe and Tremayne (1993)):

9.10 Summary and conclusion

The main aim of this chapter has been to provide a readable and (hopefully) understandable account of one of the most important but at the same time one of the most difficult chapters of probability theory: the limit theorems. Using the historical development as our main axis and the taxonomy of probabilistic assumptions (9.1) as the cornerstone of our discussion, we examined the WLLN, SLLN, CLT and FCLT trying to bring out two important aspects of such theorems:

(a) the gradual weakening of the restrictions giving rise to the results, and
(b) the trade off between the three categories of assumptions.

In conclusion we emphasize again that, although the limit theorems are indispensable for statistical inference purposes, it is a mistake, for modeling purposes, to trade in specific distribution assumptions for bounded moments assumptions. The latter give rise to very crude results (probabilistic statements).

9.11 Exercises

1 "Going from weekly to monthly observations by averaging ensures that the CLT effect induces Normality to the latter." Explain the fallacy in this argument.

2 "There is no point in using the Student's t distribution in modeling speculative prices. One should adopt the Normal distribution at the outset because as the number of observations increases (and in my case I have over 3000 observations) the Student's t converges to the Normal anyway." Explain the fallacy in this argument.

3 A gambler betting on Red and Black at a roulette wheel contemplates: "for the last 6 times in a row the ball stopped in a Red, if the WLLN is valid, it means that the probability that the next one will be Black must be greater than $\frac{1}{2}$." Discuss.

4 "The Law of Large Numbers and the Central Limit theorem hold for stochastic processes for which we need to postulate restrictions of three types: (a) Distribution, (b) Dependence, and (c) Homogeneity." Discuss.

5 "Poisson's WLLN postulates complete heterogeneity for the Bernoulli random variables involved but implicitly assumes asymptotic homogeneity." Discuss.

6 How is the Law of Large Numbers related to the Central Limit Theorem?

7 For the random variable X, where $E(X) = 0$ and $Var(X) = \frac{1}{3}$, derive an upper bound on the probability of the event $\{|X - 0.6| > 0.1\}$. How does this probability change if one knows that $X \sim U(-1, 1)$?

8 For the random variable X, where $E(X) = 0$ and $Var(X) = 1$, derive an upper bound on the probability of the event $\{|X - 0.6| > 0.1$. How does this probability change if one knows that $X \sim N(0,1)$? How accurate is the following inequality:

$$\mathbb{P}(|X| \geq \varepsilon) \leq \frac{1}{\sqrt{2\pi}} \int_\varepsilon^\infty \frac{x}{\varepsilon} e^{-\frac{x^2}{2}} dx = \frac{1}{\sqrt{2\pi}} \left(\frac{1}{\varepsilon}\right) e^{-\frac{\varepsilon^2}{2}}, \text{ for } x > \varepsilon?$$

9 Explain the conclusion of Bernstein's WLLN and discuss which assumptions are crucial for the validity of the conclusion.

10 Compare and contrast Bernoulli's WLLN with that of Bernstein.

11 Explain how the conditions underlying Lyapunov's CLT ensure that no one random variables in the sequence dominates the summation.

12 Discuss the relationship between the Lindeberg and Feller conditions and their connection with the CLT.

13 Discuss the relationship between the Lindeberg and uniform asymptotic negligibility conditions.

14 How do we explain the fact that convergence in probability implies convergence in distribution but we need more stringent conditions to prove the CLT than those for the LLN?

15 Explain how the CLT can be extended beyond the scaled summations.

16 Explain how the FCLT improves upon the classical CLT.

17 Compare and contrast the classical CLT and FCLT in the case of second-order stationary processes.

18 Explain intuitively why converge in probability is a stronger mode of convergence than convergence in distribution.

19 Explain intuitively why convergence almost surely is a stronger mode of convergence than convergence in probability.

20 Compare and contrast convergence almost surely and rth-order convergence.

21 "For modeling purposes specific distribution assumptions are indispensable if we need precise and sharp results. Results based on bounded moment conditions are naturally imprecise and blunt." Discuss.

22 "For modeling purposes specific distribution assumptions are indispensable as testified by the Berry–Esseen result." Discuss.

10 From probability theory to statistical inference*

10.1 Introduction

In chapter 2 we began a long journey into the part of mathematics known as *probability theory*, in our attempt to set up a mathematical framework for modeling *stochastic phenomena*: observable phenomena which exhibit, what we call, *chance regularity*. The main path along which our discussion of probability theory unfolded has been that of *empirical modeling*. Center stage in this discussion was given to the concept of a *statistical model*, which provides the foundation upon which the second part of this book, known as *statistical inference*, will be built. The primary aim of this chapter is to set up a tentative bridge between the mathematical framework we call probability theory and statistical inference.

10.1.1 The story so far in a nutshell

The mathematical set up for probability theory was motivated by formalizing a simple chance mechanism we called a *random experiment* $\mathcal{E}$. The basic mathematical structure arising from the formalization came in the form of a *simple statistical space* $[(S, \Im, \mathbb{P}(.))^n, G_n^{IID}]$, where S is the *outcomes set* (the set of all possible distinct outcomes), $\Im$ the *event space* (a set of subsets of S with the mathematical structure of a σ-field), $\mathbb{P}(.)$ the *probability set function* (an additive set function $\mathbb{P}(.): \Im \rightarrow [0,1]$ which satisfies three axioms) and G_n^{IID} a set of *random trials* (Independent and Identical trials). In chapters 3–4 the simple statistical space was then metamorphosed into a **simple statistical model**:

[i]   probability model: $\Phi = \{f(\mathbf{x}; \boldsymbol{\theta}), \boldsymbol{\theta} \in \Theta, \mathbf{x} \in \mathbb{R}_X\}$,
[ii]   sampling model: $\mathbf{X} := (X_1, X_2, \ldots, X_n)$ is a random sample.

    The primary reason behind the metamorphosis is that, more often than not, the phenomena which exhibit *chance regularity* are observed in the form of numerical data. As we can see, the above statistical model is specified exclusively in terms of a *random variable* $X(.)$ whose primary role is to map events into numbers:

$$X(.): S \rightarrow \mathbb{R}, \text{ such that } X^{-1}((-\infty, x]) \in \Im, \text{ for all } x \in \mathbb{R}.$$

The cardinal aim of chapters 6–9 has been to extend this simple statistical model in the direction of *non-random samples* in order to broaden its intended scope. The broadening is necessary in order to enable us to model observable phenomena which exhibit *dependence* and *heterogeneity* patterns. The mathematical framework for modeling dependence and heterogeneity has been instituted in these chapters. It was argued that the *modus operandi* of modeling dependence and/or heterogeneity is the notion of *conditioning* and related concepts: conditional distributions and conditional moment functions.

10.1.2 The missing bridge

The notion of a random experiment was used primarily in chapter 2 to motivate the mathematical concepts and was subsequently largely ignored because the proposed mathematical concepts and their structure acquired a life of their own. Apart from the occasional motivating example, the discussion in chapters 2–4 and 6–9 belongs to the realm of mathematics with one important difference: the emphasis was placed on ideas and concepts rather than on theorems and proofs. The formal theory developed in these chapters can be applied in any discipline where probability theory is used, in the same way as calculus (differential and integral) can be used in physics, biology and economics to model different dynamic deterministic phenomena.

Throughout the discussion in chapters 2–4 and 6–9, with the exception of a few examples, *probability* was just a set function of the form:

$$\mathbb{P}(.): \Im \to [0,1],$$

which satisfies the following axioms:

[1] $\mathbb{P}(S) = 1$,
[2] $\mathbb{P}(A) \geq 0$ for all events $A \in \Im$,
[3] If $\{A_n\}_{n=1}^{\infty}$ is a sequence of mutually exclusive events in $\Im$, for $A = \bigcup_{n=1}^{\infty} A_n$, $\mathbb{P}(A) = \sum_{n=1}^{\infty} \mathbb{P}(A_n)$.

In a nutshell, probability is any function that satisfies the above mathematical structure, irrespective of any intrinsic interpretations. In this sense probability is purely a mathematical concept in the same way the real line $\mathbb{R}$ is a mathematical concept. However, when using a number of examples to illustrate the mathematical concepts, such as the random experiment of tossing a coin twice, where:

$$S = \{(HH),(HT),(TH),(TT)\}, \quad \Im = \{A,\bar{A},S,\emptyset\}, A = \{(HH),(TT)\},$$

we often went beyond the mathematical definition. As given, the mathematical definition provides no way to evaluate $\mathbb{P}(A)$; all one can say is that since $A \cup \bar{A} = \emptyset$ and $A \cup \bar{A} = S$:

$$\mathbb{P}(A) = 1 - \mathbb{P}(\bar{A}).$$

In other words, the probability space $(S, \Im, \mathbb{P}(.))$ offers us the rules to manipulate the probabilities of the various events of interest, but does not provide ways to *evaluate* these probabilities. This is why the mathematical theory of probability is often called the *calculus of probabilities.* When utilizing such examples most books on probability theory go beyond the mathematical definition. In a certain sense they *beguile* the reader by invoking seemingly common sense arguments such as the physical symmetry of the chance devises (fair coins). A typical example of this is the following argument:

Given that the coin is fair $\mathbb{P}(HH)=\mathbb{P}(HT)=\mathbb{P}(TH)=\mathbb{P}(TT)=\frac{1}{4}$, since for the random experiment of tossing a coin twice there are four *equally likely outcomes.* Hence, $\mathbb{P}(A)=\frac{1}{2}$ because event A occurs when two out of the four outcomes occur.

As argued below, this argument implicitly uses the *lottery-based* interpretation of probability.

All of these common sense arguments have nothing to do with the mathematical theory but are designed to add something to the intuitive understanding of the mathematical concepts. This is pedagogically the correct way to proceed, assuming that the necessary cautionary notes are spelled out. Examples in probability theory are easier to comprehend when they refer to simple games of chance where the chance mechanism is explicit and with the help of *combinatorics* one can define the relevant probabilities as above. However, the intended scope of probability theory extends well beyond such games and in particular to phenomena where the chance mechanism is not explicit. As mentioned repeatedly, we aspire to include any observable phenomenon which exhibits chance regularity patterns within its intended scope. For this to be possible, however, we need to build a bridge between the mathematical concept of a statistical model and what we called chance regularity.

Some tentative steps toward building such a bridge were taken in chapters 5 and 6 using graphical displays but the emphasis there was placed on intuition. In this chapter we will tie together several loose ends and an attempt will be made to complete this bridge. Building such a bridge is of paramount importance because its traits will determine to a large extent the nature of the statistical inference to be erected on the other side. It turns out that the choice of a particular bridge between statistical models and chance regularity will determine to a large extent the approach to statistical inference one adopts; the main approaches being *Classical, Bayesian,* and *Decision theoretic.* Efforts to build such a bridge are inextricably bound up with one's interpretation of probability which we discuss next as a prelude to the discussion of previous attempts to build such bridges.

10.2 Interpretations of probability

It must be said at the outset that probability has a unique place in science in so far as it represents a notion with more interpretations than any other concept in the history of science. Any attempt to propose a taxonomy for all these interpretations is doomed because there are no clear cut boundaries between them. Commonly used categorizations such as objective/subjective, epistemic/physical are only schematically useful because a number of interpretations are hybrids of various components of these categorizations. Be that as it may, we focus on a small subset of such interpretations using the nature of statistical inference they are commonly associated with as the criterion. From the viewpoint of statistical inference we choose to consider the following three interpretations of probability:

(i)   the lottery-based,
(ii)   the observed relative frequencies,
(iii)   the degrees of belief.

TERMINOLOGY: it should be noted that the *lottery-based* definition of probability is often known as the *classical* definition. This, however, often leads to confusion with regard to the *classical* approach to statistical inference which is based on the *frequency* interpretation. For this reason we avoid the term classical interpretation of probability.

   We note at the outset that for a proper understanding of the various interpretations of probability one should discuss them in the context in which they were first developed (see Hacking (1975)). As early as the 18th century all three basic interpretations of probability were being used in different contexts without much thought of choosing one interpretation for all purposes. The *lottery-based* interpretation was used in the context of games of chance and was viewed as *equal probabilities based on some sort of physical symmetry*. The *relative frequency* interpretation originated from mortality and natality data gathered over long periods of time from the 16th century onwards. The *degrees of belief* originated from attempts to quantify the relationship between the evidence presented in courts and the degree of conviction in the mind of the judge.

10.2.1 The lottery (classical) interpretation of probability

It is generally accepted that, historically, the theory of probability was developed in the context of gambling based on games of chance such as casting dice or tossing coins. It was only natural then that the first interpretation of probability was inextricably bound up with the chance mechanism of such games. Although implicit in the calculations going back to Cardano in the 17th century, the first explicit definition of the lottery definition of probability is given by Laplace at the beginning of the 19th century.

The lottery definition Consider the random experiment $\mathcal{E}$ which has N *equally likely* outcomes and event A occurs when N_A of them occur, then according to *the lottery definition of probability*:

$$\mathbb{P}(A) = \left(\frac{N_A}{N}\right).$$

The first important feature of this definition is its reliance on the nature of an explicit chance mechanism such as casting dice or tossing coins. Its second crucial feature is that it utilizes the apparent physical symmetry of the device underlying the chance mechanism to define probability *by evaluating* it as "the ratio of the number of outcomes favorable to the event to the total number of possible outcomes, each assumed to be equally likely" (see Laplace (1814)).

   For the purposes of providing the missing link between the mathematical concept of a statistical model and the notion of chance regularity, this definition of probability is inadequate for a number of reasons including the fact that:

(i)   it is based on some explicit chance mechanism,
(ii)   the chance mechnism has a build-in physical symmetry that leads to equally likely outcomes, and
(iii) it assumes that one can partition the set of outcomes into a finite number of equally likely events.

This definition has been severely criticized in the literature but the critics tend to concentrate their arrows on the *equally likely* clause. What do we mean by equally likely, and how do we recognize equally likely outcomes? Laplace, in an attempt to avoid this problem, proposed a principle for finding equally likely cases. This rule was later named *the principle of insufficient reason* or *the principle of indifference* and amounts to the idea that *if we have no reason to favor one case over the another they are considered equally likely.* This principle has given rise to several paradoxes and has been widely discussed in the literature (see Hacking (1975)).

In addition to the objection to the equally likely clause, there is one crucial objection to the lottery definition that renders it a relic of a bygone age. It assumes that one can partition the set of outcomes into a finite number of equally likely events. What happens when the random experiment does not enjoy this symmetry, such as the case of a biased coin? What about axiom (1) of the mathematical definition (see chapter 2)? In the case of an infinite sample space the denominator of the above definition will get us into trouble (see Barnett (1982) for further discussion).

In view of these problems the lottery interpretation of probability could not be used as the cornerstone for the missing bridge between a statistical model and chance regularity patterns. Having said that, there is nothing wrong with using the lottery interpretation of probability as a means to evaluating certain probabilities in cases where the random experiment allows its use: there exists an explicit chance mechanism which necessarily enjoys a certain physical symmetry.

10.2.2 The frequency interpretation of probability

Our interest in the frequency interpretation of probability stems from the fact that it underlies the approach to statistical inference discussed in this book and it is invariably known as the *classical approach* (see Barnett (1982)).

The frequency interpretation of probability can be traced back to the *statistical regularities* established during the 18th and 19th centuries. After the initial impetus provided by Grant's Bills of Mortality in 1622, there was a concerted effort to collect more and more demographic, anthropomorphic, economic and social (crimes, violent deaths, etc.) data. The descriptive analysis of these data led to an amazing conclusion:

despite the unpredictability at the individual level (people, firms etc.) there was a remarkable stability of the relative frequencies at the aggregate level (groups) over long periods of time.

By the 1830s the main field of application became *social statistics*: numerical science of society. Its focus was the unpredictability of human action and behavior and the search for order (statistical regularity) in larger groups. The main conclusion arising from these studies was that: *regularity could emerge from disorder and irrationality!* Society could be characterized by relatively stable rates of height, weight, education, intelligence, fertility, marriage, crime, suicides, and deaths. This in turn led to the search for effects whose causes could be discerned in large numbers in an attempt to facilitate the discovery of *laws* analogous to those of *Newtonian mechanics* in the domain of society. The protagonist in this search was the Belgian polymath Quetelet who, by the 1870s, amassed an impressive collection of evidence of such large-scale statistical regularities (see Stigler (1986)). So much so that the idea of disorder at the individual level leading to order at the aggregate was brought into Physics. Maxwell and Boltzmann, in their attempt to justify their statistical interpretation of *gas laws*, invoked the idea of a model of numerous autonomous and unpredictable individuals (insignificant compared with the assemblage), where regularities associated with the assemblage and can be used to explain macroscopic behavior. This analogy was borrowed from Quetelet's *social physics* and founded an important pillar of modern physics known as statistical mechanics (see Von Plato (1994)).

In the context of the frequency interpretation, the probability of an event A is viewed as an empirical regularity associated with this event. The probability of event A represents the limit of the *relative frequency* with which A will be obtained if the experiment related to A is repeated a large number of times under identical conditions.

The frequency definition Consider the case where one is able to repeat an experiment under identical conditions, and denote the relative frequency of the event A after N trials by $\left(\frac{N_A}{N}\right)$, then the frequency definition of the probability of event A is defined as the limit of this ratio as the number of trials goes to infinity, i.e.

$$\mathbb{P}(A) = \lim_{N\to\infty}\left(\tfrac{N_A}{N}\right).$$

The frequency interpretation of probability was first worked out during the mid 19th century as the frequency of like events in the *long run* but its formal definition is credited to John Venn (1866) (of the Venn diagrams fame). In this sense the number of favorable outcomes N_A and the limit of the relative frequency are defined in terms of what happens *on average* if we were to imagine an infinite sequence of identical trials of the experiment.

In view of this it should come as no surprise to learn that initially the mathematical foundation of this definition was thought to be the (Weak) *Law of Large numbers* (*WLLN*). In the case where the probability of event A is the same, say $\mathbb{P}(A)$, for all trials, it was customary to invoke the WLLN proved by James Bernoulli (1713):

$$\lim_{N\to\infty}\Pr\left(\left|\tfrac{1}{N}\sum_{k=1}^{N}X_k - \mathbb{P}(A)\right| < \varepsilon\right) = 1, \text{ for any } \varepsilon > 0, \tag{10.1}$$

$$\tfrac{1}{N}\sum_{k=1}^{N}X_k = \left(\tfrac{N_A}{N}\right), \quad X_k = \begin{cases} 1 \text{ if } A \text{ occurs at the } k\text{th trial,} \\ 0 \text{ if } A \text{ does not occur at the } k\text{th trial.} \end{cases}$$

However, in cases where the probabilities of the event A are allowed to fluctuate from trial to trial, say the probability of A in trial k, is $p_k = \mathbb{P}_k(A)$, $k = 1,2,\ldots$, Poisson's WLLN:

$$\lim_{N\to\infty} \Pr\left(\left|\tfrac{1}{N}\Sigma_{k=1}^N X_k - \tfrac{1}{N}\Sigma_{k=1}^N p_k\right|<\varepsilon\right)=1, \text{ for any } \varepsilon>0,$$

was interpreted as a mathematical demonstration of the fact that the repetition of an experiment does necessarily lead to a constant mean value. As argued in chapter 9, however, the convergence of the average to some constant value:

$$\lim_{N\to\infty} \tfrac{1}{N}\Sigma_{k=1}^N p_k = p,$$

is not the result of some invisible hand forcing order upon the system but a consequence of the mathematical restrictions:

$$(a) \quad 0<p_k<1, \qquad (b) \quad (1-p_k)\cdot p_k \le \tfrac{1}{4}.$$

The secret is that (a)–(b) implicitly impose asymptotic homogeneity over the sequence of probabilities but it is not obvious that the asymptotically homogeneous value p will coincide with $\mathbb{P}(A)$.

   The issue often raised, when invoking the WLLN as a justification for the frequency definition of probability, is that the argument suffers from some sort of *circularity*:

we use convergence in *probability* to define *probability*!

This is denied by some notable mathematicians such as Borel and Renyi. Renyi argues that the concept of probability in *convergence in probability* is purely a mathematical concept and as such it does not lead to a circular argument:

The "definition" of the probability stating that the probability is the numerical value around which the relative frequency is fluctuating at random is not a mathematical definition: it is an intuitive description of the realistic background concept of probability. Bernoulli's law of large numbers, on the other hand, is a theorem deduced from the mathematical concept probability; there is no vicious circle...   (Renyi (1970), p. 159)

10.2.3 The degrees of belief interpretation of probability

Our interest in the degree of belief interpretation of probability stems from the fact that it leads to an approach to statistical inference known as the *Bayesian approach*.

   During the 17th, 18th and most of the 19th centuries, the objective and subjective interpretations of probability coexisted happily even in the writings of the same mathematician such as James Bernoulli. Poisson (1837) was the first to make explicit the distinction between the subjective and objective interpretations of probability and a decade later the battle lines between frequentists and subjectivists were forged. The degree of belief interpretation of probability covers both the subjective and objective interpretations of probability.

Degrees of subjective belief

The *subjective* interpretation considers the probability of an event A as based on the personal judgment of whoever is assigning the probability; the personal judgment being based on the individual's environmental experience. In this sense the probability of event A is based on the person's beliefs and information relating to the experiment giving rise to event A.

Example
In the case of tossing a fair coin a person is likely to assign the subjective probability $\mathbb{P}(H) = \frac{1}{2}$, because with no special information about the chance mechanism involved the two outcomes seem a priori equally likely. In the case where the person in question has additional information relating to the mechanism, such as the coin is bent, the subjective probability is likely to change.

In view of the fact that a person's assessment of probabilities is inextricably bound up with his environmental and psychological experiences, probabilities can only be *conditional* on an individual's experience.

A most convenient way to think of subjective probabilities is in terms of betting odds, even though historically risk in gambling and insurance did not have any appreciable effect on the development of this interpretation. Let us consider the case of betting on the occurrence of an event A and somebody offers odds 2 to 1, or in a ratio form $\frac{1}{2}$. If the person whose degrees of subjective belief we are trying to assess *thinks that these are fair odds*, then we can proceed to evaluate her subjective probability via: $\frac{\frac{1}{2}}{1+\frac{1}{2}} = \frac{1}{3}$. More generally, if the subjective probability for the occurrence of the event A is p (i.e. $\Pr(A) = p$), then the odds ratio $\ddot{o}$ and the corresponding subjective probability p take the form:

$$\ddot{o} = \frac{p}{(1-p)} \Rightarrow p = \frac{\ddot{o}}{1+\ddot{o}}.$$

As we can see, the subjective dimension of this probability arises from the fact that it is the decision of a particular individual whether the odds are fair or not. Another individual might consider as fair the odds ratio $\ddot{o}'$, which implies that her subjective probability is $p' = \frac{\ddot{o}'}{1+\ddot{o}'} \neq p$. This is not surprising because the personal experiences which influence judgment are often different between individuals.

The question which naturally arises at this stage is to whether such personal subjective probabilities will behave in accordance with the mathematical definition of probability. It turns out that this is the case as demonstrated by Ramsey (1926) and De Finetti (1937).

Degrees of objective belief
Another question with regard to the degree of belief interpretation of probability that comes to mind is whether one could find some way to establish that a particular odds ratio will be considered fair by any *rational person*; assuming a formal definition of *rational*. In such a case the personal dimension of the interpretation will change to a more objective one. The first to attempt such a recasting was Keynes (1921) and he was later followed by Carnap (1950). The interpretation of subjective probability based on odds ratios which will be considered fair by any rational person is often called *logical probability*, as opposed to the *personal* subjective probability championed by Ramsey (1926), De Finetti (1974), and Savage (1954); see Barnett (1982) and Fine (1973) for further discussion.

10.2.4 Which interpretation of probability?

We conclude this section by stating that on philosophical grounds both, the degrees of belief and frequency interpretations of probability, are equally relevant and the discussions about their relative merits are likely to continue for many years to come. On methodological grounds, however, the present book adopts the frequency interpretation of probability. For the empirical modeling of observational data (in a non-experimental set up) we consider that the frequentist constitutes the most appropriate interpretation. As argued in chapter 1, a statistical model is built upon the systematic information contained in the observed data in an attempt to provide an appropriate description of the stochastic mechanism that gave rise to the data. Given that in modeling with observational data the modeler has no control over the collection of the observations, the notion of degrees of belief interpretation is difficult to justify. Moreover, if the data contain systematic information, it must be possible to establish the model independently of the modeler's beliefs. Indeed, the bridge between probability and observed data proposed in chapters 5–6 took a pragmatic attitude toward the essence of stochastic phenomena. Chance regularity has to be assessed independently of the modeler's beliefs. A statistical model was contrasted to a theory model, arguing that the latter is built upon the behavior of economic agents and not on the structure of the observed data. In view of this, the degrees of belief interpretation of probability might be more appropriate for describing the behavior of economic agents facing uncertainty.

The interpretation of probability adopted in this book has important implications for the nature of statistical inference considered appropriate for observational data. As argued in the next chapter the observational nature of the data raises several modeling issues that are not as relevant in the context of modeling with experimental data.

10.3 Attempts to build a bridge between probability and observed data

In this section we discuss briefly the two most notable attempts to bridge the gap between a statistical model and the chance regularity pointed out in the above discussion: the attempts by Von Mises and De Finetti. Von Mises adopts the frequency interpretation and De Finetti the degrees of subjective belief interpretation of probability.

10.3.1 The frequency approach: Von Mises' collective

The first systematic attempt to build a bridge between probability and chance regularity using the *frequency interpretation* was made by Von Mises in the 1920s (see Von Mises (1957)). The backbone of the bridge comes in the form of a **collective**: an infinite sequence $\{\omega_k\}_{k=1}^{\infty}$ of outcomes drawn from a set Ω and characterized only by which attribute of Ω they manifest. This collective satisfies two conditions:

(1) convergence: $\lim_{N \to \infty} \left(\frac{N_\ell}{N} \right) = p_\ell, \; \ell = 1, 2, \dots, m,$

(2) randomness: $\lim_{\varphi(N \to \infty)} \left(\frac{\varphi(N_\ell)}{\varphi(N)} \right) = p_\ell, \; \ell = 1, 2, \dots, m,$

where N_ℓ denotes the number of occurrences of an outcome with attribute ℓ, and the function $\varphi(.)$ constitutes a mapping of *place-selection* chosen before the realization of the sequence $\{\omega_k\}_{k=1}^\infty$. The place selection mapping is designed in order to select sub-sequences from a collective which will converge to the same probabilities. The idea was that in the context of a collective the relative frequencies of occurrence of the attributes of interest converge to certain limits (interpreted as probabilities) and these limits are invariant to transformations of place-selection. Intuitively, one can think of a Von Mises' collective as a gambling machine that generates a sequence of integers and offers odds:

$$\{\ddot{o}_1, \ddot{o}_2, \ddot{o}_3, \ldots, \ddot{o}_m\} \text{ where } \ddot{o}_\ell = \left(\frac{p_\ell}{1-p_\ell}\right), \ell = 1, 2, \ldots, m,$$

for each different integer between 1 and m. NOTE that the probabilities are not sub-jective; the implicit probability distribution is given by:

$$\mathcal{P} := \{p_1(\boldsymbol{\theta}), p_2(\boldsymbol{\theta}), \ldots, p_m(\boldsymbol{\theta})\}. \tag{10.2}$$

The *randomness* condition is designed to ensure that in the long run the machine cannot be defeated by any gambling scheme (a place selection mapping). That is, the sequence of outcomes produced exhibit no patterns that can be utilized to predict systematically the next integer in an ongoing sequence of bets.

Von Mises' notion of a place-selection mapping was rather vague and was made more precise by Church (1940) using the idea of a *recursive* selection rule. The recursive nature of the place selection mapping is crucial for mathematical (the algorithmic computabil-ity) as well as modeling purposes (Independence and Identical Distribution are defined in terms of a pre-specified *ordering* of the random variables). The version as improved by Church amounts to saying that there is *no* recursive place-selection algorithm $\varphi(.)$ which selects an infinite sub-sequence $\{\varphi(\omega_k, k)\}_{k=1}^\infty$ whose relative frequencies of the attributes converge to a set of different limits than those of the whole sequence (see Stigum (1990)). It turned out that even the new version of a collective, as improved by Church, had major problems. Ville (1939) showed that there exist sequences which satisfy the conditions of a collective but a judicious choice of a gambling strategy can still make money for the gambler. Moreover, certain limit theorems relating to the fluctuations of the limits of sequences do not hold for the Von Mises–Church collectives; see the Law of Iterated Logarithm in chapter 9.

Von Mises' collective was an attempt to build a bridge between the concept of proba-bility and what we called chance regularity patterns in this book. The *convergence* condi-tion purports to bridge the gap between relative frequencies and the notion of a probability model such as (10.2) where the probabilities can be functions of some unknown parameter(s) $\boldsymbol{\theta}$. The *randomness* condition purports to bridge the gap between the sequence of observations and the notion of a random sample (a set of IID random variables). Von Mises' randomness purports to operationalize the notion of IID random variables by associating independence with the invariance to the *place-selection* in a sequence of realizations.

Von Mises' attempt has been criticized severely over the years by many philosophers and mathematicians on a number of grounds. The most crucial weaknesses of his formulation being the ones inherited from the frequency definition of probability: the convergence condition has zero empirical content because it cannot be verified or falsified. In his attempt to reply to this charge Von Mises invoked a number of arguments including the speed of convergence of such sequences and the Law of Large Numbers. As argued in the previous section, however, both of these arguments have been criticized as suffering from circularity because they employ probabilistic statements to define probability (see above for the case of the WLLN). For example invoking the Strong LLN:

$$\mathbb{P}\left(\lim_{N\to\infty}\left(\tfrac{N_\ell}{N}\right)=p_\ell\right)=1,$$

presupposes the notion of convergence *with probability one*! Renyi (1970) disagrees by saying that the latter convergence is a purely mathematical concept and there is no circularity in the argument (see above). Be that as it may, we conclude this subsection by stating that a Von Mises collective does have some empirical content because, as argued below, the IID assumptions are testable in practice (see also chapters 14–15 on testing).

10.3.2 The Bayesian approach: De Finetti's representation theorem

As mentioned above, the *degrees of belief* interpretation of probability has its roots in the attempt to quantify judges' degree of belief, in view of the evidence presented in a court. Utilizing a combination of intrinsic evidence (information based on the nature of things) and from the extrinsic evidence (testimonies), a studious judge forms a degree of subjective belief with regard to the guilt or innocence of the accused. Leibniz (1705) viewed the calculus of probabilities as a mathematical translation of legal reasoning that carefully proportioned degrees of belief to the kinds of evidence submitted.

The problem facing the mathematicians of that time, including the Bernoullis (James and Nicholas) and Poisson, was to find ways to combine the two sources of information so as to quantify this degree of belief into probabilities. There were endless discussions on the relative merits of intrinsic versus extrinsic evidence with Hume (1739) using the case of miracles to nullify the value of intrinsic evidence by arguing that "miracles are by definition violations of the laws of nature, and therefore their intrinsic probability is zero."

The first attempt to quantify this degree of belief was made by James Bernoulli using his WLLN (10.1). By interpreting the probabilities with respect to which the limit is taken as the quantification of degrees of belief, Bernoulli thought that (10.1) provided the way to utilize the evidence in the form of the relative frequencies to quantify them. As the number of observations (repetitions) increases the degree of belief increases but there was no clear answer to the question: How many observations warrant what degree of belief? The real problem with Bernoulli's argument was much deeper. What the WLLN could give an answer to is the question: Given the probability $\Pr(A)$, how likely is it that the sequence of relative frequencies would approximate it to any degree of precision? The question posed by the quantification attempt was the converse: Given the observed frequency how likely is it to approximate the unknown probability? This became the problem of inverse probabilities and solutions were given independently by both Bayes (1763) and Laplace (1774) in the form of the what is known today as **Bayes' theorem** (see chapter 2):

$$\Pr(A|e)=\tfrac{\Pr(A)\cdot\Pr(e|A)}{\Pr(e)},\ \text{for}\ \Pr(e)>0,$$

where $\Pr(A|e)$ denotes the conditional probability of event A given the *evidence e*, $\Pr(A)$ is the a priori probability of A, $\Pr(e)$ is the weight of the evidence, and $\Pr(e|A)$ the weight of the evidence given A. Bayes' theorem can be seen as a coherent way one can update one's degrees of belief relating to an event A in the light of evidence e.

This result, although intuitively appealing for quantifying degrees of belief, was largely ignored for the analysis of statistical observations because of the subjective interpretation of probability. Jeffreys (1939) should be credited with renewing interest in Bayes' theorem as a systematic way to revise one's degrees of belief in view of the evidence furnished by observations. This gave rise to what is known today as the Bayesian approach to statistical inference with Ramsey, De Finetti, and Savage as the main pioneers.

The first attempt to provide a bridge between observable phenomena exhibiting chance regularity and statistical models within the degrees of subjective belief paradigm was made by De Finetti (1937). Within this paradigm, probability distributions such as (10.2), reflect an *individual's beliefs* about a feature of the real world; they do not reflect a feature of the real world itself.

What distinguishes the degrees of belief approach to inference from that of other approaches is that any parameter θ constitutes part of the same system of an individual's beliefs and thus it is a *random quantity* defined on the same probability space $(S, \mathfrak{I}, \mathbb{P}(.))$, where S is the outcomes set, $\mathfrak{I}$ is the event space of interest (a σ-field), and $\mathbb{P}(.): \mathfrak{I} \to [0,1]$, i.e.

$$\theta(.): S \to \Theta, \text{ such that } \theta^{-1}(B_\theta) \in \mathfrak{I} \text{ for all } B_\theta \in B(\Theta),$$

where $B(\Theta)$ is a Borel-field associated with Θ. Moreover, as in the case of an ordinary random variable $X(.)$, $\theta(.)$ induces a probability set function, via $A_\theta = \theta^{-1}(B_\theta)$, of the form:

$$\mathbb{P}(A_\theta) = \mathbb{P}\theta^{-1}(B_\theta) = P_\theta(B_\theta).$$

In the case where $\Theta \subset R$ we can define the cdf and density functions of θ, say $F(\theta)$ and $f(\theta)$, respectively.

NOTATION: when we need to emphasize the random nature of θ within the Bayesian framework we will use the notation $\theta(s)$, $s \in S$.

De Finetti's *modus operandi* for operationalizing the notion of a simple statistical model was the concept of *exchangeability* encountered in chapter 8 and repeated here for convenience.

Exchangeability A stochastic process $\{X_t, t \in \mathbb{T}\}$ is said to be *exchangeable* if for every finite subsequence $(X_1, X_2, ..., X_n)$, the joint distribution of each subset $(X_1, ..., X_m)$, $m = 1, 2, ..., n$, is the same for any permutation of $(1, 2, ..., m)$ or, equivalently, any reordering of $(X_1, ..., X_m)$. That is, the joint distribution of any subset $(X_1, ..., X_m)$ of $(X_1, ..., X_n)$ depends only on m (for $m = 1, 2, ..., n$) but does not depend on which m random variables are involved.

This suggests that *exchangeability* is an extension of the notion of *Identical distribution* which involves only the marginal distributions. Exchangeability involves all joint distributions (k random variables at a time, where $k = 1,2,3,\ldots$) as well because it does not presuppose *Independence*.

Using the concept of an exchangeable sequence of random variables De Finetti was able to prove the following remarkable theorem for Bernoulli distributed random variables.

De Finetti's representation theorem (Bernoulli) The sequence of Bernoulli distributed random variables $\{X_k\}_{k=1}^{\infty}$ is *exchangeable* if and only if for any $n > 0$ the joint density function of the random variables involved takes the form:

$$f(x_1, x_2, \ldots, x_n) = \int_0^1 \prod_{k=1}^{n} \theta^{x_k} (1-\theta)^{1-x_k} dF(\theta) = \int_0^1 \theta^{\sum_{k=1}^{n} x_k} (1-\theta)^{\sum_{k=1}^{n}(1-x_k)} dF(\theta),$$

$$(10.3)$$

where $F(\theta)$ denotes a proper cdf over the interval $(0,1)$ and $dF(\theta)$ can be thought of as equivalent to $f(\theta)d\theta$ (in the sense of the Stieltjes integral) when $F(\theta)$ is continuous. Furthermore, exchangeability of $\{X_k\}_{k=1}^{\infty}$ implies that:

(ii) $\mathbb{P}\left(\lim_{n \to \infty} \left[\frac{1}{n} \sum_{k=1}^{n} X_k(s)\right] = \theta(s)\right) = 1,$

where (ii) is evaluated with respect to any mixing cdf $F(\theta)$, irrespective of its nature.

As it stands, the importance of this theorem is not apparent, and thus we need to add some explanatory comments. The result in (10.3) suggests that the random variables $(X_1, X_2, \ldots, X_n)$ are *conditionally IID* given $\theta(s) = \theta$. Using the notion of conditional independence introduced in chapter 6 in the case of a sequence of random variables $\{X_k\}_{k=1}^{\infty}$, we say that this process is *conditionally independent* of its past given $Y = y$, with conditional density $f(x|y)$ and marginal density $f(y)$, when the joint density of $(X_1, X_2, \ldots, X_n)$ takes the form:

$$f(x_1, x_2, \ldots, x_n) = \int_{y \in \mathbb{R}_Y} \prod_{k=1}^{n} f(x_k|y) \cdot f(y) dy.$$

Thus, conditional independence reduces to: $f(x_k|y, x_{k-1}, x_{k-2}, \ldots, x_1) = f(x_k|y)$.

The identically distributed property follows from the fact that in (10.3) all the conditional densities have the same parameter θ.

An equivalent but more expressive way to state the above representation theorem is in terms of the sum of the sequence: $S_n := \sum_{k=1}^{n} X_k$ which represents the number of successes in n exchangeable Bernoulli trials:

(i) $f(s_n = r) = \int_0^1 \binom{n}{r} \theta^r (1-\theta)^{(n-r)} dF(\theta),$

(ii) $F(\theta) = \lim_{n \to \infty} \mathbb{P}\left(\frac{1}{n} S_n \leq \theta\right).$ (10.4)

It turns out that this form of the representation theorem is somewhat misleading because it seems to suggest that the probability distribution $F(\theta)$ of θ arises naturally in this context. As shown in Spanos (1996b), this arises largely because of the restrictive nature of the Bernoulli distribution where the parameterization of the empirical cumulative distribution is unique. To see this let us consider a more general form of the representation theorem.

De Finetti's representation theorem (non-parametric) The sequence of random variables $\{X_k\}_{k=1}^{\infty}$ is exchangeable if and only if the random variables are IID *conditional* on the limit of their *empirical cumulative distribution function* (ecdf) $\hat{F}_n(x)$ defined by:

$$\hat{F}_n(x) = \frac{[\text{no. of } X_k\text{s} \leq x]}{n} := \frac{1}{n}\sum_{i=1}^{n} \mathbb{1}_{(-\infty,x]}X_i, \quad x \in \mathbb{R},$$

where $\mathbb{1}_{(-\infty,x]}(X_i)$ is the indicator function defined by:

$$\mathbb{1}_{(-\infty,x]}(X_i) = \begin{cases} 1 \text{ if } X_i \in (-\infty, x], \\ 0 \text{ if } X_i \notin (-\infty, x]. \end{cases}$$

The theorem takes the form of the *existence* of a probability set function $\mathbb{Q}(.)$ (see Bernardo and Smith (1994), p. 177):

$$\mathbb{P}(X_1 \leq x_1, X_2 \leq x_2, \ldots, X_n \leq x_n) = \int_{\mathcal{P}} \prod_{k=1}^{n} F(x_k) d\mathbb{Q}(F), \tag{10.5}$$

$\mathcal{P}$ is the space of all distribution functions in $\mathbb{R}$ and:

$$\mathbb{Q}(F) = \lim_{n \to \infty} \mathbb{P}(\hat{F}_n). \tag{10.6}$$

This is referred to as the non-parametric version of the representation theorem because the cdf $F(.)$ does not involve any parameters explicitly. This form of the representation theorem says that exchangeability of the sequence of random variables $\{X_k\}_{k=1}^{\infty}$ is equivalent to assuming that this sequence constitutes a random sample *conditional* on an unknown cdf $F(x)$. The latter is directly related to the limit of the empirical distribution function (ecdf) in the sense given in (10.5)–(10.6). In other words, conditional on the particular form of the cdf, $F(x)$, as suggested by the ecdf as the number of observations increases, exchangeability coincides with IID. The question that naturally arises at this stage is how do the unknown parameters $\boldsymbol{\theta}$ come into the picture? In the case of Bernoulli distributed random variables the parameter θ entered the result because the cdf has a unique parameterization. In general, however, this is rarely true. As it stands, the form of the representation theorem given by (10.5)–(10.6), suggests the existence of some $F(x)$ in $\mathcal{P}$, the space of all distribution functions in $\mathbb{R}$, whose nature is determined by the limit of the $\hat{F}_n(x)$. In view of the fact that:

$$\mathbb{Q}(F): \mathcal{B}(\mathbb{R}) \to \mathcal{P}, \text{ and, } \mathbb{P}(\hat{F}_n): \mathcal{B}(\mathbb{R}^n) \to \mathcal{P},$$

$F(x)$ can be interpreted as an infinite dimensional unknown element of $\mathcal{P}$. In a certain sense this poses the **problem of specification** in its most general form: choosing the distribution that describes the probabilistic structure of a sequence of observable random variables $\{X_k\}_{k=1}^{\infty}$. De Finetti's theorem says that in the case of exchangeable random variables the modeler should look no further than the limit $\mathbb{Q}(F)$ of the ecdf. If the latter assigns all its probability to the set of Normal distributions, then $F(x)$ is finitely parameterized in terms of certain parameters, say $\boldsymbol{\theta} := (\mu, \sigma^2) \in \mathbb{R} \times \mathbb{R}_+$. In this sense a parametric family of cdfs:

$$\Phi_F = \{F(x; \boldsymbol{\theta}), \boldsymbol{\theta} \in \Theta, x \in \mathbb{R}_X\}, \tag{10.7}$$

constitutes a mapping of the form:

$$\mathcal{P}_0 \to \Theta \subset \mathbb{R}^m, \ 0 < m < n, \ \mathcal{P}_0 \subset \mathcal{P}.$$

De Finetti's representation theorem (parametric) The sequence of random variables $\{X_k\}_{k=1}^{\infty}$ is exchangeable if and only if:

$$\mathbb{P}(X_1 \le x_1, X_2 \le x_2, \ldots, X_n \le x_n) = \int_{\theta \in \Theta} \prod_{k=1}^{n} F(x_k; \boldsymbol{\theta}) d\mathbb{Q}(\boldsymbol{\theta}), \tag{10.8}$$

where $\boldsymbol{\theta} \in \Theta$ defines the space of the relevant distribution functions in $\mathcal{P}_0$. According to Bernardo and Smith (1994, p. 179):

The general form of representation for real-valued exchangeable random quantities is therefore as if we have independent observations $x_1, x_2, \ldots, x_n$ conditional on F, an unknown (i.e. random) distribution function (which plays the role of an infinite dimensional parameter in this case), with a belief distribution Q for F, having the operational interpretation of what we believe the empirical distribution function would look like for a large sample...

NOTE:
(i)   The parameters $\boldsymbol{\theta}$ can also be viewed as finite parameterizations of $F(x)$ via its moments. This is exemplified by Feller (1971) in his proof of De Finetti's representation theorem by showing that the representation is inextricably bound up with the *moments* of the sequence $\{X_k\}_{k=1}^{\infty}$ (see also Diaconis and Freedman (1990)).
(ii)   In the case of a Bernoulli sequence the parameter θ was built into the probability set function directly and thus appeared as the limit of the first sample moment. In general, however, without prior information relating to the distribution of the sequence $\{X_k\}_{k=1}^{\infty}$, the unknown parameters do not arise naturally as functions related to $F(x)$.

The question that naturally arises at this stage is: What about the subjective (degrees of belief) interpretation of probability adopted by De Finetti? The fact of the matter is that the only subjective judgment involved is in going from $\mathbb{P}(\hat{F}_n)$ to $\mathbb{Q}(F)$; a judgment which has to be made by the modeler in view of the observations. This, however is not the same thing as choosing a prior distribution for $\boldsymbol{\theta}$, as it seems in the Bernoulli form of the representation theorem. The subjective belief acquires empirical content when it is tested against the observations. The judgment is subjective but *testable* against the observations at the misspecification stage of the modeling. The Bernoulli representation theory is somewhat misleading because it creates the impression that there is a direct relationship between $\mathbb{Q}(F)$ and a particular $\boldsymbol{\theta}$, which is certainly not true. In the general case the mixing distribution is the limit of the ecdf whose relationship to any parameters is neither direct nor obvious. Moreover, any distributions relating to unknown parameters will be induced distributions via the probability attached to the observables.

A direct comparison between (10.5) and (10.8) brings out the main difference between *parametric* from *non-parametric* statistical models. In a nutshell in the former case the modeler postulates a probability model of the form (10.7) and thus restricts the set of all possible models to a subset $\mathcal{P}_0$, but in the latter case the modeler works with $F(x) \in \mathcal{P}$ directly, where $\mathcal{P}$ is an infinite dimensional space. This will be discussed further in section 6 below.

10.3.3 Von Mises versus De Finetti

Having discussed Von Mises' and De Finetti's attempts to build a bridge between the mathematical concept of probability and the empirical notion of chance regularity let us take stock of their similarities and differences.

In contrast to Von Mises' randomness, which places the emphasis on imposing an extreme *dependence restriction* (the impossibility of devising a winning gambling strategy), De Finetti's exchangeability places the emphasis on an extreme *heterogeneity restriction*. Both concepts, however, implicitly involve a certain restriction from the other category. Randomness involves (asymptotic) homogeneity of the marginal distributions of $(X_1, X_2, \ldots, X_n)$ and exchangeability allows for a very restricted form of dependence; the form of dependence which arises from the *symmetry* of equidimensional joint distributions. The essence of De Finetti's theorem is: conditional on the limit of the ecdf, the exchangeable sequence becomes an IID sequence. The only apparent difference seems to be Von Mises' convergence condition which does not seem to play any role in De Finetti's result. A moment's reflection, however, reveals that the existence of the limit of the ecdf constitutes an implicit assumption whose only difference from Von Mises' is that it involves the ecdf and not the relative frequencies directly. In view of this, it should come as no surprise to learn that exchangeability of the sequence $\{X_k\}_{k=1}^{\infty}$ for all $k > 0$ implies that, with probability one, the underlying experiment will give rise to a Von Mises collective (see Spielman (1976)).

In the next section we proceed to discuss a tentative bridge between the mathematical concept of a statistical model and the empirical notion of chance regularity which borrows several elements from both of the above attempts. The Von Mises–Church collective is relied upon to provide an intuitive formalization of the *chance* component and the De Finetti representation theorem is used to build a bridge between the *regularity* component and the concept of a probability model. In a nutshell, the chance component is related to numerical sequences which when tested appear to satisfy the probabilistic assumptions postulated a priori. The quintessential form of a *chance sequence* is a sequence of Uniform, Independent, and Identically Distributed (UIID) random variables. Other forms of chance sequences can be viewed as transformations of this primary form. Hence, the emphasis will be placed on UIID chance sequences. The regularity component will be related to the empirical cumulative distribution function and its empirical content will be established using a number of limit theorems which do not suffer from the apparent circularity noted above in relation to the Law of Large

Numbers. The De Finetti representation theorem will also be reinterpreted to provide the foundation of an alternative approach to the specification of statistical models for observational data: the probabilistic reduction approach.

10.4 Toward a tentative bridge

It is no coincidence that, in chapter 2, we chose to motivate the mathematical theory of probability by formalizing the notion of a *random experiment* $\mathcal{E}$, defined by the conditions:

[a]   all possible distinct outcomes are known a priori,
[b]   in any particular trial the outcome is not known a priori but there exists a perceptible regularity of occurrence associated with these outcomes, and
[c]   it can be repeated under identical conditions.

The latter represents the simplest form of a *stochastic phenomenon*: a phenomenon which exhibits chance regularity. It must be said that condition [c] prejudices our discussion in favor of the frequency interpretation of probability. Other interpretations of probability such as the degrees of belief interpretation do not necessarily need such a condition. We will see, however, that De Finetti's attempt requires an infinite sequence of trials.

The final formalization of the conditions [a]–[c] defining a random experiment took the form of a *simple statistical model* as specified above. As mentioned many times in the previous chapters, the statistical model represents a chance mechanism that purports to model the stochastic mechanism that gave rise to the observed data by capturing the systematic information in the latter. The chance mechanism, however, is not fully defined before the values of the unknown parameters are determined. Hence, the unknown parameter(s) θ constitute the focus of the modeler's attention in statistical inference. In a certain sense the original uncertainty in relation to the particular outcomes of the stochastic phenomenon has been reduced to uncertainty in relation to these unknown parameters. Once the value of θ is (somehow) established utilizing the observed data, the statistical model can be used to draw conclusions beyond the observed data in hand. This is the built-in inductive argument we referred to throughout the discussion in the previous chapters.

It should be emphasized once more that a statistical model is a purely mathematical construct but throughout the discussion in chapters 2–9 we purposefully kept one eye on the connection between these mathematical concepts and their empirical counterparts by relating them to chance regularity patterns in data plots. The first attempt to build a bridge between the mathematical construct of a simple statistical model and certain chance regularity patterns was made in chapter 5 where a number of important theoretical concepts were related to observed data via the graphical display of a *t*-plot and related plots. This tentative bridge was reinforced in chapters 6–7 with some additional links established between theoretical concepts, such as dependence, and real data using the graphical display of a scatterplot and related plots. In both cases, however, we used intuitive arguments and no attempt was made to provide a more formal link between the observed data and the theoretical concepts.

10.4.1 What do we mean by chance regularity?

As argued in chapter 2, the essence of *chance regularity* comes in the form of two entwined characteristics of stochastic observable phenomena:

> chance: an inherent uncertainty relating to the occurence of particular out-
> comes,
>
> regularity: an abiding regularity of occurence associated with the several out-
> comes.

As suggested in chapter 5, the empirical characterization of chance can be viewed as the unpredictability of any one observation given the other observations. This can be seen in figure 10.1 (reproduced from chapter 5) as the observer moves from the first to the last observation and attempts to predict the next observation given the past; the direction of time can be easily reversed without changing anything. The empirical characterization of regularity comes in the form of the relative frequencies shown in figure 10.1 as the pile created when rotating the t-plot and letting the points drop vertically.

10.4.2 Formalizing chance?

Giving a precise definition to the notion of *chance* (randomness) has proved even more elusive than the definition of another fundamental feature of nature: beauty. Like beauty, chance cannot be defined but we think we can recognize it when we see it. Unlike beauty, however, recognizing chance in science should not be left to the eye of the beholder. With that in mind, let us consider a number of sequences and try to recognize the chance component of chance regularity.

Let us begin the discussion with the following two sequences of integers 0–9:

$s_1 = \{4,1,4,2,1,3,5,6,2,3,7,3,0,9,5,0,4,8,8,0,1,6,8,8,7,2,4,2,0,9,6,9,8,$
$\quad 0,7,8,5,6,9,6,7,1,8,7,5,3,7,6,9,4,8,0,7,3,1,7,6,6,7,9,7,3,7,9,9,0,7,$
$\quad 3,2,4,7,8,4,6,2,1,0,7,0,3,8,8,5,0,3,8,7,5,3,4,3,2,7,6,4,1,5,7,2,7,\dots\}$,

$s_2 = \{1,4,1,5,9,2,6,5,3,5,8,9,7,9,3,2,3,8,4,6,2,6,4,3,3,8,3,2,7,9,5,0,2,$
$\quad 8,8,4,1,9,7,1,6,9,3,9,9,3,7,5,1,0,5,8,2,0,9,7,4,9,4,4,5,9,2,3,0,7,8,$
$\quad 1,6,4,0,6,2,8,6,2,0,8,9,9,8,6,2,8,0,3,4,8,2,5,3,4,2,1,1,7,0,6,7,9,\dots\}$.

A close look at these sequences reveals that at first sight they appear to exhibit no recognizable patterns and intuition suggests that they seem to constitute chance sequences. In contrast, the sequence:

$s_3 = \{8,8,8,8,8,8,8,8,8,8,8,8,8,8,8,8,8,8,8,8,8,8,8,8,8,8,8,8,8,8,8,$
$\quad 8,8,8,8,8,8,8,8,8,8,8,8,8,8,8,8,8,8,8,8,8,8,8,8,8,8,8,8,8,8,8,8,8,8,$
$\quad 8,8,8,8,8,8,8,8,8,8,8,8,8,8,8,8,8,8,8,8,8,8,8,8,8,8,8,8,8,8,8,8,\dots\}$,

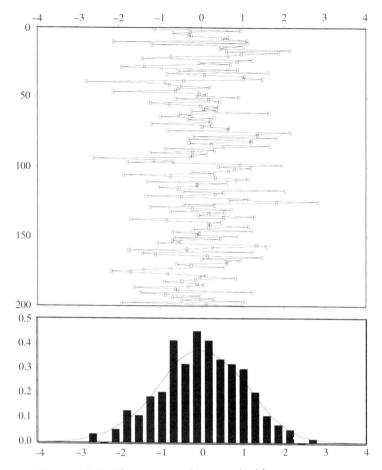

Figure 10.1 A histogram and its smoothed form

is clearly not a chance sequence because we can easily recognize the simple pattern of a repeated digit. Deciding on whether the next sequence is a chance sequence is slightly less obvious:

$s_4 = \{5,4,8,3,8,7,0,9,6,7,7,4,1,9,3,5,4,8,3,8,7,0,9,6,7,7,4,1,9,3,$
$5,4,8,3,8,7,0,9,6,7,7,4,1,9,3,5,4,8,3,8,7,0,9,6,7,7,4,1,9,3,$
$5,4,8,3,8,7,0,9,6,7,7,4,1,9,3,5,4,8,3,8,7,0,9,6,7,7,4,1,9,3,$
$5,4,8,3,8,7,0,9,6,8,\ldots\}.$

Sequence s_4 is not a chance sequence because after 15 integers the same pattern of integers is repeated. This particular sequence raises the crucial issue of having a large enough realization of a sequence in order to notice the repeated pattern. For example the sequence s_5 shown below appears to be a chance sequence.

$s_5 = \{3,1,9,5,8,7,6,2,8,8,6,5,9,7,9,3,8,1,4,4,3,2,9,8,9,6,9,0,7,2,1,6,4,$
$9,4,8,4,5,3,6,0,8,2,4,7,4,2,2,6,8,0,4,1,2,3,7,1,1,3,4,0,2,0,6,1,8,$
$5,6,7,0,1,0,3,0,9,2,7,8,3,5,0,5,1,5,4,6,3,9,1,7,5,2,5,7,7,3,1,9,5,\ldots\}.$

However, this is misleading because, as shown below, if we add another 30 terms in the sequence it is apparent that after 96 terms the sequence repeats itself!

$s_5 = \{$3,1,9,5,8,7,6,2,8,8,6,5,9,7,9,3,8,1,4,4,3,2,9,8,9,6,9,0,7,2,1,6,4,
9,4,8,4,5,3,6,0,8,2,4,7,4,2,2,6,8,0,4,1,2,3,7,1,1,3,4,0,2,0,6,1,8,
5,6,7,0,1,0,3,0,9,2,7,8,3,5,0,5,1,5,4,6,3,9,1,7,5,2,5,7,7,
3,1,9,5,8,7,6,2,8,8,6,5,9,7,9,3,8,1,4,4,3,2,9,8,9,6,9,0,7,2,1,6,4,9,...$\}$.

With the above examples in mind we can say that the essence of chance is the apparent lack of recognizable patterns or irregularity which renders the prediction of the next integer at any point of the sequence with any certainty impossible. What the sequences s_3, s_4 and s_5 have in common is that, in view of what is observed, one can easily guess the rest of the integers with certainty. These should be contrasted with sequences s_1 and s_2 which do not exhibit any discernible patterns to help us guess the next few digits with any certainty. How do we operationalize this notion of chance? Intuitively, we follow Von Mises and think of a gambling machine that fabricates (somehow) such sequences of integers and we are asked to place bets on the next number to be produced with the odds chosen by the machine. If there is no winning strategy, i.e. over the long run, the machine cannot be beaten by some strategy, the sequence exhibits chance regularity behavior. This involves not just the unpredictability of the next integer in the sequence but also the fact that the odds reflect the long-run relative frequencies of the various integers. Whatever the odds, no machine can make money using sequences such as s_3 or s_4!

The above intuitive explanation of chance, however, is not enough to provide a formalization of the concept. Several important recent developments have shed some additional light on the notion of chance regularity by quantifying the notion of lack of patterns. The most promising of these developments is based on the idea of Kolmogorov Complexity (see Kolmogorov (1965,1969)) which quantifies the notion of lack of patterns in terms of whether the sequence can be compressed (algorithmically). For instance, the sequence s_3 can be easily generated by a very simple algorithm in contrast to s_1 and s_2 where the only way to generate them is apparently to list their elements; see Solomonoff (1964), Chaitin (1966), Martin-Lof (1966a,b), Li and Vitanyi (1997) for further discussion. In this chapter we will adopt a more pragmatic attitude toward chance sequences. We consider a sequence as a chance sequence if when the probabilistic assumptions underlying the sequence are tested using a finite realization they are not rejected. It goes without saying that testing involves more formal ways to assess the chance attributes of sequences such as s_1 and s_2 than just eye-balling them (see chapter 15).

10.4.3 Formalizing regularity?

Before we can decide whether sequences s_1 and s_2 are amenable to modeling using some statistical model, we need to establish the regularity attribute at the aggregate level. As mentioned above, this regularity has to do with the odds offered by the gambling machine generating these sequences. For example, in the case of the data shown in figure 10.1 if the odds offered for values around zero (0) are the same as those around four (4) then somebody will make money in the long run by betting on the former values simply because the values around 0 come up much more often than those around 4. As mentioned above, the odds $(\ddot{o}_\ell, \ell=1,2,\ldots,m)$ reflect the probabilities $(p_\ell, \ell=1,2,\ldots,m)$ only in the case where:

$$\ddot{o}_\ell = \left(\frac{p_\ell}{1-p_\ell}\right), \ell=1,2,\ldots,m.$$

Hence, when these odds are offered no one can make money in the long run. Needless to say that we abstract from any personal attitudes toward risk on behalf of the gamblers.

The question that arises at this stage is whether in addition to the apparent chance attribute the sequences s_1 and s_2 also enjoy a regularity attribute. Clearly, any decision with regard to that should be made on the basis of whether the observed part of the sequence suggests a possible abiding regularity concerning occurrence of different outcomes. For large enough sequences we can consider the relative frequencies of the various integers involved and establish whether, as we increase the number of terms, the relative frequencies involved stabilize at certain constant values.

Consider the sequence s_1 first. The relative frequencies of the integers 0–9 for s_1, using the first 100 terms, yielded:

Integer value	0	1	2	3	4	5	6	7	8	9
Rel. frequency (s_1)	0.100	0.070	0.080	0.110	0.090	0.070	0.100	0.180	0.120	0.080

The general picture leaves some doubts with regard to the conjecture of a uniform distribution; the relative frequency of 7 is more than twice that of 5. However, increasing the number of terms to 1,000 it appears as though the conjecture has some basis:

Integer value	0	1	2	3	4	5	6	7	8	9
Rel. frequency (s_1)	0.108	0.098	0.108	0.083	0.100	0.104	0.091	0.103	0.113	0.092

This becomes more apparent as we increase the number of terms to 10,000:

Integer value	0	1	2	3	4	5	6	7	8	9
Rel. frequency (s_1)	0.095	0.100	0.100	0.098	0.102	0.100	0.103	0.096	0.103	0.102

The sequence s_1 after 50,000 terms yields relative frequencies which appear to converge toward $\frac{1}{10}$, indicating a (possibly) uniform distribution:

Integer value	0	1	2	3	4	5	6	7	8	9
Rel. frequency (s_1)	0.099	0.101	0.100	0.100	0.101	0.103	0.099	0.099	0.099	0.100

Let us consider the sequence s_2. Using the first 100 terms the relative frequencies for the same integers are:

Integer value	0	1	2	3	4	5	6	7	8	9
Rel. frequency (s_2)	0.080	0.080	0.120	0.110	0.100	0.080	0.090	0.070	0.130	0.130

As we can see, the relative frequency of 8 is almost twice as much as that of 7. On the other hand, the relative frequencies using the first 1,000 terms yielded:

Integer value	0	1	2	3	4	5	6	7	8	9
Rel. frequency (s_2)	0.093	0.116	0.103	0.102	0.094	0.095	0.094	0.095	0.101	0.105

The possible convergence is more apparent in the case of the first 10,000 terms of the sequence whose relative frequencies are:

Integer value	0	1	2	3	4	5	6	7	8	9
Rel. frequency (s_2)	0.097	0.102	0.102	0.975	0.101	0.105	0.102	0.969	0.949	0.101

Again, the sequence s_2 after 50,000 terms yields relative frequencies which appear to converge towards a uniform distribution:

Integer value	0	1	2	3	4	5	6	7	8	9
Rel. frequency (s_2)	0.101	0.101	0.097	0.099	0.100	0.101	0.100	0.100	0.101	0.100

On this evidence one might proceed to conjecture that for both sequences the regularity attribute can be modeled using a (discrete) uniform distribution:

$$f(x) = \frac{1}{10}, \text{ and } F(x) = \frac{x+1}{10}, \quad x = 0, 1, \ldots, 9.$$

In a certain sense this is the most *basic* form of chance regularity, with the gambling machine offering the same odds for all 10 integers.

It must be obvious to the reader that the sequences s_1 and s_2 were not generated by a regular icosahedron (symmetric die with twenty faces) with the same digit on opposite faces. Instead, they were generated using the sequence of digits from the decimal expansions of two *irrational numbers:*

$$s_1 = \text{decimal expansion} (\sqrt{2}), \quad s_2 = \text{decimal expansion} (\pi).$$

By the same token the sequences s_4 and s_5 represents the first 100 digits of the decimal expansion of the *rational numbers* $\frac{17}{31}$ and $\frac{31}{97}$, respectively. It is well-known from elementary number theory that the decimal expansions of all rational numbers is either finite or periodic but that of irrational numbers is non-periodic (see Courant and Robbins (1941)).

The conjecture that the regularity associated with the sequences s_1 and s_2 comes in the form of the Uniform distribution is of considerable interest in mathematics (number theory) because it concerns the decimal expansions of *irrational numbers.* For some additional evidence in relation to the regularity of the decimal expansions of irrational numbers consider yet another sequence of integers which represent the decimal expansion of the irrational number e:

$s_6 = \{7,1,8,2,8,1,8,2,8,4,5,9,0,4,5,2,3,5,3,6,0,2,8,7,4,7,1,3,5,2,6,6,2,4,$
$9,7,7,5,7,2,4,7,0,9,3,6,9,9,9,5,9,5,7,4,9,6,6,6,9,6,7,6,2,7,7,2,4,0,7,$
$6,6,3,0,3,5,3,5,4,7,5,9,4,5,7,1,3,8,2,1,7,8,5,2,5,1,6,6,4,2,7,4,\ldots\}.$

The relative frequencies of the integers 0–9 using the first 100 terms is:

Integer value	0	1	2	3	4	5	6	7	8	9
Rel. frequency (s_6)	0.050	0.060	0.120	0.080	0.110	0.130	0.120	0.160	0.070	0.100

The frequencies using the first 1000 terms are:

Integer value	0	1	2	3	4	5	6	7	8	9
Rel. frequency (s_6)	0.100	0.096	0.097	0.109	0.099	0.086	0.099	0.099	0.103	0.112

For the first 10,000 elements of the sequence s_6 the relative frequencies become:

Integer value	0	1	2	3	4	5	6	7	8	9
Rel. frequency (s_6)	0.097	0.099	0.100	0.101	0.098	0.099	0.108	0.101	0.099	0.097

Increasing the terms to the first 50,000, the relative frequencies appear to converge to 0.1:

Integer value	0	1	2	3	4	5	6	7	8	9
Rel. frequency (s_6)	0.099	0.101	0.099	0.101	0.099	0.101	0.103	0.099	0.099	0.099

Having let the rabbit out of the hat, several important questions arise naturally.

The *first* question concerns our conjecture that the relative frequencies of the digits 0–9 in the decimal expansions of irrational numbers converge to the uniform distribution. This is an educated conjecture with numerous precedents in the history of mathematics. The most famous precedent is arguably *Gauss's law of the distribution of prime numbers*; a prime number is an integer greater than 1 which has no divisors (among integers) other than itself and one. Gauss conjectured in 1849 that the number of prime numbers not exceeding x for very large values of x is approximately equal to:

$$F(x) \simeq \int_2^x \frac{1}{\ln u} \, du, \text{ for integer } x > 10^6.$$

Additional evidence for the conjecture was given by Chebyshev in 1854 who provided bounds for the approximation:

$$F(x) \simeq \frac{x}{\ln x}, \text{ for integer } x > 10^6.$$

The conjecture was proved fifty years later by Hadamard and Poussin in 1896; see Klein (1972) for a brief history of this result. The major difficulty of the proof is the *existence* of a smooth function $f(x)$ such that $F(x) \simeq \int_2^x f(u)du$. This is indeed the essence of the problem in proving the conjecture hazarded above.

The *second* question concerns the use of deterministic mathematical formulae (algorithms) to generate chance sequences! In a certain sense there is no uncertainty with regard to the next digit in the decimal expansion of $\sqrt{2}$ because the algorithm can produce it with certainty! Does this mean that all the discussion relating to these sequences and chance regularity is nonsense? The answer is clearly not because the chance attribute of sequences can only be assessed in terms of the initial finite realization of the sequence. If the information that this is the decimal expansion of a specific irrational number is not available, there is no way one can guess the generating rule by looking at these sequences. To put it differently if we were to leave out the first several dozen digits of the decimal expansion of a particular irrational number no one will be able to guess the irrational number and hence the generating algorithm. This is similar to the situation the modeler finds herself in when faced with observational data from an ongoing data generating process that started some time ago and will continue into the future. The assessment on whether a certain sequence is a chance sequence or not has to be made on pragmatic grounds by testing the probabilistic assumptions defining its chance regularity features. In the above cases we need to test three basic assumptions: uniformly distributed, independent and identically distributed. As shown in chapters 5–9 there are numerous forms of chance regularity sequences based on different probabilistic assumptions.

The above discussion suggests that both chance and regularity are features which come up not just in nature (games of chance, counts of emitted particles, etc.) but also in man-made notions such as the decimal expansions of irrational numbers or the distribution of prime numbers. The connection between the basic form of chance regularity and irrational numbers was first discovered by Weyl (1916) who proposed sequences obtained by considering the fractional part of multiples of an irrational number a:

$$\{u_k := \text{fractional part of } [ak], k = 1,2,\dots\}.$$

In other words, one multiplies the irrational number a by $1,2,3,4,\dots$ and retains only the decimal part of the multiplication. The result will be a sequence of real numbers between 0 and 1 which will be Uniformly distributed over this interval. Using the terminology introduced in chapter 5, this can be expressed in the language of mathematical connoisseurs:

$$\{u_k := [ak] \text{ modulo } 1, k = 1,2,\dots,T\}.$$

This suggestion has eventually led to numerous algorithms of the form:

(i) $\{u_{k+1} := [au_k] \text{ modulo } 1, k = 1,2,\dots\}$,
(ii) $\{u_{k+1} := [a + u_k]^m \text{ modulo } 1, m > 0, k = 1,2,\dots\}$,
(iii) $\{u_{k+1} := [bu_k + c] \text{ modulo } m, m > 0, k = 1,2,\dots\}$,

for generating what we called in chapter 5 **pseudo-random numbers**: numbers which behave as if they were a realization of an IID sample from a Uniform distribution.

As mentioned above, such pseudo-random sequences constitute the quintessential form of a random sequence because they can be transformed into many other forms of chance regularity. As argued in chapter 5, the probability integral transform and its inverse provide the modeler with a way to transform Uniform IID processes into (continuous or discrete) IID processes with arbitrary distributions. For convenience we repeat these results below.

Probability integral and its inverse transformations For any continuous random variable X, with a cdf $F_X(x)$ such that $y = F_X(x)$ is invertible and $x = F_X^{-1}(y)$.

(a)   For the random variable $Y = F_X(X)$,

$$Y = F_X(X) \sim U(0,1). \tag{10.9}$$

(b)   Let $Y \sim U(0,1)$ and define $X = F_X^{-1}(Y)$. Then X has a distribution with cdf $F_X(.)$.

Formally we should call the sequences s_1 and s_2 pseudo-random sequences because they are special cases of such deterministic algorithms whose fabrication of numbers appears to exhibit chance regularity and the algorithm cannot be deduced from the sequences themselves. As such the sequences s_1 and s_2 are not very good because their regularity attribute is not apparent in relatively small runs of 100 terms; typical sample sizes for real observations. A lot of effort has gone into algorithms designed to give rise to sequences of pseudo-random numbers which exhibit both chance and regularity in small runs; for further discussion of such algorithms see Niederreiter (1992). Part of the effort has been channeled into *testing* the IID attributes of such sequences. Several tests have been developed including the Kolmogorov distance test for the *distributional* attribute, the gap and run tests for *Independence* and the Kiefer test for *homogeneity* (see Knuth (1981), Niederreiter (1992) for the details). Some of these tests will be discussed in chapter 15.

The *final* question concerns the question posed at the beginning of this subsection. If the conjecture relating to the relative frequencies of the integers, hazarded above, turns out to be unprovable. How do we formalize the regularity noticed in all of the sequences we rendered chance sequences? The notable efforts by Von Mises and De Finetti focused primarily on formalizing the notion of probability. The *modus operandi* for Von Mises was the concept of a *collective* and for De Finetti it was the concept of *exchangeability*. In what follows we use the concept of an *empirical cumulative distribution function* (ecdf) instead of *relative frequencies* as the *modus operandi*. Instead of seeking the convergence of the relative frequencies at different points in an attempt to define the notion of probability at a point, we proceed to consider the convergence of cumulative frequencies over the whole of the real line. As noted above, De Finetti's representation theorem is implicitly based on the convergence of the ecdf. With that in mind we proceed to discuss the empirical distribution function in some detail.

The empirical cumulative distribution function

Let $h(z)$ be the *heaviside function* defined by: $h(z) = \begin{cases} 0, & \text{if } z < 0, \\ 1, & \text{if } z \geq 0. \end{cases}$

Define the *empirical stochastic process* $\{F_n(x,s)\}_{n=1}^{\infty}$ (see chapter 8) by:

$$F_n(x,s) = \frac{1}{n}\sum_{k=1}^{n} h(x - X_k(s)), \ x \in \mathbb{R}, \ s \in S, \tag{10.10}$$

or equivalently in terms of the indicator function $\mathbb{I}_A(x)$ defined above:

$$F_n(x,s) = \frac{1}{n}\sum_{k=1}^{n} \mathbb{I}_{(-\infty,x]}(X_k(s)), \ x \in \mathbb{R}, \ s \in S. \tag{10.11}$$

As a stochastic process (see chapter 8) this can be thought of as a mapping:

$$F_n(.,.): S \times \mathbb{R} \to U_n,$$

$$U_n := \left\{ 0, \frac{1}{n}, \frac{2}{n}, \ldots, \frac{(n-1)}{n}, 1 \right\}.$$

Viewing (10.11) $F_n(x,s)$ as the average of a set of random variables $\mathbb{1}_{(-\infty,x]}(X_i(s))$, $i = 1,2,\ldots,n$, we note that these are IID Bernoulli distributed random variables with:

$$\mathbb{P}(\mathbb{1}_{(-\infty,x]}(X_i) = 1) = F(x), \ \mathbb{P}(\mathbb{1}_{(-\infty,x]}(X_i) = 0) = [1 - F(x)].$$

Since, $nF_n(x,s) = \sum_{k=1}^{n} \mathbb{1}_{(-\infty,x]}(X_i(s))$, we show in chapter 11 (lemma 1) that its distribution is Binomial, i.e.

$$nF_n(x,s) \sim \mathrm{Bi}(n,F(x)), \ x \in \mathbb{R}.$$

Hence, the first two moments of this process take the form:

$$E(F_n(x,s)) = F(x), \ Var(F_n(x,s)) = \frac{1}{n} F(x)[1 - F(x)], \ x \in \mathbb{R}.$$

As argued in chapter 8, in order to understand the structure of a stochastic process we should look at it from the two different viewing angles: the random variable and the sample paths viewpoints. In the case of the above empirical stochastic process the functional viewpoint is particularly important. For a given realization of the sample $\mathbf{X} := (X_1, X_2, \ldots, X_n)$, say $\mathbf{x} := (x_1, x_2, \ldots, x_n)$, (given $s \in S$, say $\bar{s}$), the above empirical stochastic process reduces to the *empirical cumulative distribution function* (ecdf):

$$\hat{F}_n(x) = \frac{\text{[no. of } (X_1, X_2, \ldots, X_n) \text{ whose realization do not exceed } x]}{n} = \frac{1}{n} \sum_{k=1}^{n} \mathbb{1}_{(-\infty,x]}(X_k),$$

where the general form of this function is: $\hat{F}_n(.,\bar{s}): \mathbb{R} \to U_n$.

For a fixed $x \in \mathbb{R}$, say $\bar{x}$, the ecdf is:

$$\hat{F}_n(\bar{x},.): S \to U_n,$$

and is just a random variable defined on the probability space $(S, \Im, \mathbb{P}(.))$.

As mentioned above, in the present context given $s \in S$ refers to a sample realization and thus $\hat{F}_n(.,\bar{s})$ refers to the *relative frequency* of the observations not exceeding the value x. When viewed as a function of the observations $(x_1, x_2, \ldots, x_n)$, $\hat{F}_n(x)$ has the following properties:

(a) uniquely defined,
(b) its range is [0,1],
(c) non-decreasing and continuous on the right, and
(d) it is piecewise constant with jumps $\left(\text{multiples of } \frac{1}{n}\right)$ at the observed points,

i.e., it enjoys all the properties of its theoretical counterpart, the cdf. In terms of the *ordered sample* $(X_{[1]} \leq X_{[2]} \leq \ldots \leq X_{[n]})$ (see chapter 4) and its realization:

$$x_{[1]} \leq x_{[2]} \leq \ldots \leq x_{[n]}, \tag{10.12}$$

the ecdf function $\hat{F}_n(x)$ is defined by:

$$\hat{F}_n(x) := \begin{cases} 0 & \text{for } x < x_{[1]}, \\ \frac{k}{n} & \text{for } x_{[k]} \le x < x_{[k+1]}, \ k = 1, 2, \ldots, n-1, \\ 1 & \text{for } x \ge x_{[n]}. \end{cases}$$

In the case where all the values in (10.12) are distinct, strict inequalities hold, and at each point $x_{[k]}$ the function $\hat{F}_n(x)$ has a jump equal to $\frac{1}{n}$. In the case where some of the values are the same, say m of them have the same value, then at that point the function $\hat{F}_n(x)$ has a jump equal to $\frac{m}{n}$. That is, the ecdf assigns to each set $A_k := x_{k-1} < X_i \le x_k$, on the real line the proportion of the sample observations that lie in that set.

Kolmogorov (1933b), taking a break after founding the mathematical theory of probability with his monograph (published the same year), posed and answered the crucial question regarding whether the ecdf $\hat{F}_n(x)$ is a good approximation for the cdf $F(x)$.

Kolmogorov's distance theorem Let $X_1, X_2, \ldots, X_n, \ldots$ be IID random variables with cdf $F(x)$. Choosing the distance:

$$\Delta_n := \sup_{x \in \mathbb{R}} \left| \hat{F}_n(x) - F(x) \right|,$$

Kolmogorov went on to prove that in the case where $F(x)$ is *continuous*:

$$\lim_{n \to \infty} \mathbb{P}\left(\sqrt{n}\Delta_n \le z\right) = 1 - 2 \sum_{i=1}^{\infty} (-1)^{k+1} e^{-2k^2 z^2}, \text{ for } z > 0, \text{ uniformly in } z. \quad (10.13)$$

There are several things to NOTE about this result.

(i)   The usefulness of this result stems primarily from the fact that the asymptotic approximation in the case of a continuous $F(x)$ does not depend on the nature of the latter. It is crucial to NOTE that in the case of a discrete $F(x)$ the asymptotic approximation does depend on the nature of $F(x)$.

(ii)   The asymptotic approximation based on (10.13) is excellent for even small values such as $n > 20$.

(iii)   In view of the fact that the range of values of the ecdf is $U_n := \left\{0, \frac{1}{n}, \frac{2}{n}, \ldots, \frac{(n-1)}{n}, 1\right\}$, taking the limit as $n \to \infty$ amounts to filling up the interval $[0,1]$.

(iv)   The asymptotic behavior of $\hat{F}_n(x)$ is relatively easy to trace because the stochastic process defined by:

$$\left\{Z_n(t) = \sqrt{n}\left[\hat{F}_n(y_t) - F(y_t)\right], \ y_t = F^{-1}(t), \ t \in [0,1]\right\},$$

converges to a *Brownian Bridge process* (see chapter 8).

A moment's reflection suggests that the above result can be used as the bridge between the *regularity* component of stochastic phenomena, because the result in (10.13) renders testable and thus bestows empirical content to the cdf. The convergence in (10.13) involves probabilities (implicitly) but the convergence itself is convergence of ordinary functions. This is in contrast to convergence in probability and almost sure convergence underlying the LLN. Moreover, if we accept Renyi's viewpoint, the various limit theorems hold for the ecdf and can be used to corroborate the empirical content of the result in (10.13).

Glivenko-Canteli theorem Let $X_1, X_2, \ldots, X_n, \ldots$ be a sequence of IID random variables with cdf $F(x)$. Then:

$$\mathbb{P}\left(\lim_{n \to \infty} \Delta_n = 0\right) = 1.$$

It should come as no surprise to learn that Renyi (1970), who will be quite happy to use this theorem as the bridge between regularity in observations and a probability model (see the quotation above), calls this *the fundamental theorem of mathematical statistics*.

Using the Law of Iterated Logarithm (see chapter 9) we can measure the speed of convergence (or the extreme fluctuations) for the almost sure convergence of the Glivenko-Canteli theorem.

Law of Iterated Logarithm (LIL) Let $X_1, X_2, \ldots, X_n, \ldots$ be a sequence of IID random variables with cdf $F(x)$. Then:

$$\mathbb{P}\left(\limsup_{n \to \infty} \left[\frac{\sqrt{n}\,\Delta_n}{\sqrt{2 \ln \ln n}}\right] = \sup_{x \in \mathbb{R}} \sqrt{F(x)[1 - F(x)]}\right) = 1.$$

NOTE that the LIL brings out the dependence of the convergence on the nature of $F(x)$ in the case where the latter is discrete, since in the case of a continuous cdf:

$$\sup_{x \in \mathbb{R}} \sqrt{F(x)[1 - F(x)]} = \frac{1}{2}.$$

In this case the LIL can be expressed in the form:

$$\mathbb{P}\left(\limsup_{n \to \infty} \left[\frac{\sqrt{2n}\,\Delta_n}{\sqrt{2 \ln \ln n}}\right] = 1\right) = 1.$$

Central Limit Theorem (CLT) Let $X_1, X_2, \ldots, X_n, \ldots$ be a sequence of IID random variables with cdf $F(x)$. Then:

$$\sqrt{n}\left(\hat{F}_n(x) - F(x)\right) \underset{a}{\sim} N(0, F(x)[1 - F(x)]).$$

At this stage the discerning reader might be wondering why the emphasis on the ecdf $\hat{F}_n(x)$ even though the discussion in chapter 5 emphasized the smoothed histogram or what we might call the *empirical density function* $\hat{f}_n(x)$. It turns out that there is a direct link between the ecdf to the empirical density function in the sense that:

$$\hat{f}_n(x) = \frac{1}{2c_n}[\hat{F}_n(x + c_n) - \hat{F}_n(x - c_n)], \text{ as } c_n \underset{n \to \infty}{\to} 0 \text{ and } nc_n \underset{n \to \infty}{\to} \infty,$$

where $\{c_n\}_{n=1}^{\infty}$ is an appropriately chosen sequence of constants that goes to zero at a suitable rate.

For reference purposes we also note the relationship between the ecdf and certain other forms of the empirical density function used in chapter 5.

(i)   The *rolling histogram* takes the form:

$$\tilde{f}_n(x) = \frac{1}{2c_n}[\hat{F}_n(x_0 + (k+1)c_n) - \hat{F}_n(x_0 + kc_n)], \ x \in [x_0 + kc_n, x_0 + (k+1)c_n],$$

(ii)   The *kernel smoother* takes the form:

$$\hat{f}_n(x) = \frac{1}{nc_n} \sum_{k=1}^{n} \mathbb{K}\left(\frac{x - X_k}{c_n}\right).$$

The above limit theorems refer to the asymptotic behavior of $\hat{F}_n(x)$ at a particular point $X = x$, but implicitly cover the interval $(-\infty, x]$. From this we can proceed to the probabilities themselves by considering the behavior of $\hat{F}_n(x)$ over an arbitrary set of points:

$$\{x_0 < x_1 < x_2 < \cdots < x_{N-1} < x_N\}, \text{ where } x_0 = -\infty \text{ and } x_N = \infty,$$

$$\{0 = \hat{F}_n(x_0) < \hat{F}_n(x_1) < \cdots < \hat{F}_n(x_{N-1}) < \hat{F}_n(x_N) = 1\}.$$

The empirical distribution function (ecdf) at a particular point x_k is viewed as an accumulation of random variables:

$$\hat{F}_n(x_k) = \frac{1}{n} \sum_{j=1}^{k} \nu_j, \text{ where } \nu_k := \sum_{i=1}^{n} \mathbb{1}_{(xk-1, xk]}(X_i(s)), \; k = 1, 2, \ldots, N.$$

The random variable $\mathbb{1}_{(xk-1, xk]}(X_i(s))$, denotes the number of realizations of the event $A_k := \{x_{k-1} < X_i \leqslant x_k\}$ in n independent trials. Moreover:

$$E[\mathbb{1}_{(xk-1, xk]}(X_i(s))] = \mathbb{P}(A_k) = p_k, \; k = 1, 2, \ldots, N,$$

where the probabilities are defined via the cdf:

$$p_k := F(x_{k-1}) - F(x_k), \; k = 1, 2, \ldots, N.$$

It is also important to NOTE that the concept of an ecdf can be easily extended to higher dimensions. For example in the case of the cdf for the vector (X, Y) the ecdf takes the form:

$$\hat{F}_n(x, y) = \frac{[\text{no. of vectors } (X_k Y_k) \text{ such that } X_k \leq x \text{ and } Y_k \leq y]}{n}, \; (x, y) \in \mathbb{R}_X \times \mathbb{R}_Y.$$

Taken together, the above results provide a bridge between the theoretical concept of a cumulative distribution function (cdf) $F(x)$ and its empirical counterpart the ecdf $\hat{F}_n(x)$. This is also the backdrop for De Finetti's representation theorem which says that specifying the joint distribution of an exchangeable sequence of random variables $\{X_k\}_{k=1}^{\infty}$ can be done by utilizing the nature of the distribution that arises as the limit of the empirical distribution function (ecdf).

In concluding this subsection we note that the intended scope of the above limit theorems extends to the case of non-continuous $F(x)$ because the dependence on the nature of the unknown cdf presents no insurmountable difficulties in the context of *parametric* statistical inference; the form of $F(x)$ is always postulated a priori. The crucial feature of the *regularity* component in chance regularity is the convergence of the cumulative relative frequencies to a stable law.

10.4.4 Chance regularity and statistical models

The above results can be used to establish a direct link between the ecdf $\hat{F}_n(x)$ and the cdf $F(x)$ and thus bestow empirical content on the latter. Using the parametric form of the cdf $F(x;\theta)$ we can proceed to define a Probability model of the form:

$$\Phi_F = \{F(x;\theta),\ \theta \in \Theta,\ x \in \mathbb{R}_X\}. \tag{10.14}$$

The unknown parameters θ are viewed as a finite parameterization of $F(x)$, in the sense explained in the context of the parametric De Finetti representation theorem: restrict the set of all possible models $\mathcal{P}$ (whose elements are infinite dimensional) to a subset $\mathcal{P}_0$. In addition, as argued below the De Finetti representation theorem (reinterpreted) can be used to operationalize the specification problem of statistical inference: the choice of the appropriate Statistical model in view of the observations.

The Probability model defined in terms of the parametric family of densities:

$$\Phi = \{f(x;\theta),\ \theta \in \Theta,\ x \in \mathbb{R}_X\}, \tag{10.15}$$

is clearly a special case of (10.14) which is particularly useful because it is easier to assess utilizing graphical techniques such as the smoothed histogram (see chapter 5). Its empirical content emanates from the fact that the distribution assumption involved when postulating a Probability model of the form (10.15) is testable. In addition to the Kolmogorov distance test there are several additional tests which utilize difference distances between theoretical concepts such as the ecdf and their empirical counterparts. NOTE that the P-P and Q-Q plots discussed in chapter 5 are based on such comparisons.

In order to complete the bridge between chance regularity and the concept of a simple statistical model we need to consider the other pillar relating to the chance component and the concept of a random sample:

$$\mathbf{X}:=(X_1,X_2,...,X_n) \text{ a set of IID random variables with cdf } F(x;\theta).$$

In the above discussion of *chance* we mentioned the availability of tests which are designed to assess this attribute in either pseudo-random numbers or in real observations. Some of these tests will be discussed in chapter 15 after we introduce hypothesis testing.

We conclude this section by emphasizing that the concept of a statistical model derives its empirical content from the fact that the probabilistic assumptions making up the model are testable. This brings out the importance of several neglected aspects of empirical modeling, such as misspecification testing and respecification, to be discussed in the next chapter.

10.5 The probabilistic reduction approach to specification

According to the De Finetti representation theorem the sequence of arbitrarily distributed random variables $\{X_k\}_{k=1}^{\infty}$ is exchangeable if and only if for any $n>0$:

$$\mathbb{P}(X_1 \leq x_1, X_2 \leq x_2, ..., X_n \leq x_n) = \int_{\theta \in \Theta} \prod_{k=1}^{n} F(x_k;\theta) d\mathbb{Q}(\theta).$$

That is, conditional on $\mathbb{Q}(F)$, where:

$$\mathbb{Q}(F) = \lim_{n\to\infty} \mathbb{P}(\hat{F}_n), \; \mathbb{Q}(F): \mathcal{P}\to\Theta\subset\mathbb{R}^m, \; 0<m<n,$$

the sequence $\{X_k\}_{k=1}^{\infty}$ is IID. This result has been extended in a number of directions. For instance by imposing restrictions such as spherical symmetry and invariance the above representation gives rise to more specific distributional reductions which involve distributions such as the Normal and the Exponential. Moreover, when the exchangeability assumption is weakened to that of partial exchangeability the above reduction gives rise to products of conditional distributions, relaxing the Identically Distributed assumption, and thus extending the notion of a random sample to just an independent sample. In addition, by extending these results to vectors of random variables the above representation can accommodate various forms of dependence (see Bernardo and Smith (1994) for a detailed discussion).

Reinterpretation In the present context we interpret the De Finetti representation theorem as a formal way to reduce the joint distribution of the observable random variables $(X_1, X_2, \ldots, X_n)$ into a simplified product of distributions by imposing certain probabilistic assumptions. To be more specific, the reduction of the joint distribution of the observable random variables is achieved by imposing assumptions from the three broad categories used throughout chapters 4–9:

$$(D)\, \text{Distribution}, \quad (M)\, \text{Dependence}, \quad (H)\, \text{Heterogeneity}. \tag{10.16}$$

It should come as no surprise to the reader to discover that ever since chapter 4 we have been viewing statistical modeling in terms of reductions of joint distributions. In chapter 4 we argued that under the assumptions of a random sample the joint distribution of $(X_1, X_2, \ldots, X_n)$, known as the **Haavelmo distribution** (see Spanos (1989b)), can be reduced into a (simplified) product of univariate (identical) marginal distributions:

$$f(x_1, x_2, \ldots, x_n; \boldsymbol{\phi}) \overset{\mathrm{I}}{=} \prod_{k=1}^{n} f_k(x_k; \boldsymbol{\theta}_k) \overset{\mathrm{IID}}{=} \prod_{k=1}^{n} f(x_k; \boldsymbol{\theta}), \text{ for all } \mathbf{x} := (x_1, x_2, \ldots, x_n) \in \mathbb{R}^n. \tag{10.17}$$

Moreover, in the case of a non-random sample the corresponding reduction based on *sequential conditioning* takes the form:

$$f(x_1, x_2, \ldots, x_n; \boldsymbol{\phi}) \overset{\text{non-IID}}{=} f_1(x_1; \boldsymbol{\psi}_1) \prod_{k=2}^{n} f_k(x_k \mid x_{k-1}, \ldots, x_1; \boldsymbol{\psi}_k), \text{ for all } \mathbf{x} \in \mathbb{R}_X^n, \tag{10.18}$$

which is non-operational without restrictions on the dependence and heterogeneity of the sample. In chapter 8 we showed that restricting the dependence to Markov dependence and the heterogeneity to stationarity, the joint distribution $f(x_1, x_2, \ldots, x_T; \boldsymbol{\phi})$ is simplified to:

$$f(x_1, x_2, \ldots, x_T; \boldsymbol{\phi}) \overset{\text{Markov}}{=} f1(x_1; \boldsymbol{\psi}_1) \prod_{t=2}^{T} f_t(x_t \mid x_{t-1}; \boldsymbol{\psi}_t) =$$

$$\overset{\text{Stationary}}{=} f(x_1; \boldsymbol{\psi}_1) \prod_{t=2}^{T} f(x_t \mid x_{t-1}; \boldsymbol{\psi}). \tag{10.19}$$

This reduction can give rise to numerous operational models the most well-known being the **Normal Autoregressive** (AR(1)) **model**:

[1]   Statistical GM: $X_t = \alpha_0 + \alpha_1 X_{t-1} + u_t$, $t \in \mathbb{T}$,
[2]   Probability model:

$$\Phi = \left\{ f(x_1, x_2, \ldots, x_T : \boldsymbol{\theta}) = \prod_{t=2}^{T} \frac{(\sigma_0)^{-1}}{\sqrt{2\pi}} \exp\left\{ -\frac{1}{2} \frac{(x_t - \alpha_0 - \alpha_1 x_{t-1})^2}{\sigma_0^2} \right\}, \boldsymbol{\theta} \in \Theta, \mathbf{x} \in \mathbb{R}^T \right\},$$

where $\boldsymbol{\theta} := (\alpha_0, \alpha_1, \sigma_0^2) \in \Theta := \mathbb{R}^2 \times \mathbb{R}_+$.

[3]   Sampling model: $(X_1, X_2, \ldots, X_T)$ is a stationary and Markov dependent sample, sequentially drawn from $f(x_t | x_{t-1}; \boldsymbol{\theta})$, $t \in \mathbb{T}$.

We remind the reader that the *reduction assumptions* for this model were:

(D)   Distribution: Normal,
(M)   Dependence: Markov,
(H)   Heterogeneity: Stationarity.

Under the Normality assumption the conditional density $f(x_t | x_{t-1}; \psi)$ is Normal and takes the form:

$$(X_t | X_{t-1}) \sim N(\alpha_0 + \alpha_1 X_{t-1}, \sigma_0^2), \ t = 2, 3, \ldots$$

$$E(X_t) = \mu, \ Var(X_t) = \sigma(0), \ Cov(X_t, X_{t-1}) = \sigma(1), \ t \in \mathbb{T},$$

$$\alpha_0 := (1 - \alpha_1)\mu, \ \alpha_1 := \frac{\sigma(1)}{\sigma(0)}, \ \sigma_0^2 := \sigma(0) - \frac{\sigma(1)^2}{\sigma(0)}.$$

It turns out that most statistical models can be viewed as reductions of the Haavelmo distribution derived by imposing assumptions from these three broad categories (10.16). As exemplified in the next several chapters, this reduction enhances our understanding of the probabilistic structure of the statistical models and provides a framework which enables the modeler to consider the modeling procedure in a coherent way. In the next chapter it is argued that this framework is much broader than just postulating a statistical model and enables the modeler to consider a number of neglected facets of statistical modeling, such as specification, misspecification and respecification, in a coherent and internally consistent way.

10.5.1 The nature of statistical models

In chapter 1 we gave a tentative answer to the question: what is a statistical model and how does it differ from other types of models? The answer concentrated on how statistical models differ from theory models. A statistical model differs from other types of models in so far as it specifies a situation, a mechanism, or a process exclusively in terms of a **probabilistic structure**. In chapters 2–8 we elaborated on what constitutes probabilistic structure and specified general forms of statistical models beyond the simple. In this section we return to the original question in an attempt to elaborate on the nature of statistical models as they compare with theory models.

Statistical models are viewed as *first stage models* in the sense that their primary goal is to provide *statistically adequate descriptions* of observable stochastic phenomena; statistical models do not pretend to offer explanation. In this sense there are several things worth noting about the nature and structure of statistical models. *First,* statistical models are specified exclusively in terms of the *observable* random variables that presumably have given rise to the observed data. This should be contrasted with theory models (see chapters 1 and 7) which are defined in terms of theoretical concepts that might or might not have a direct connection with observational data. Even though the choice of the observed data is theory dependent, once chosen the observed data as such are no longer theory laden (see Van Fraassen (1980)). *Second,* as argued above, statistical models purport to provide probabilistic descriptions in the form of stochastic mechanisms. Probability theory furnishes a purely descriptive language which can be used to summarize (parsimoniously) the systematic information in the observed data in a *theory-neutral* way. As argued in chapter 1, the theory neutrality of the description is imperative if the data are to be used as an unprejudiced witness in the assessment of the theory's validity. It is claimed that this observational language, which is free of theory concepts, provides the appropriate framework for an adequate description and discovery of empirical (or stylized) facts.

Taken together, the above comments on the nature and structure of a statistical model suggest that a statistical model is viewed in a **descriptivist/semantic/relativist/ empiricist/anti-realist** light (see *inter alia* Caldwell (1982), Mäki (1989), Van Fraassen (1980), Boylan and O'Gorman (1995)). The *descriptive nature* of statistical models requires no further explanation because the primary objective of a statistical model is stated to be descriptive not explanative. The *semantic* and *relativist nature* of a statistical model, however, need to be discussed further. As shown throughout chapters 2–8, a statistical model is not a linguistic entity but it is defined in terms of a set-theoretic language (outcomes set, event space, probability set functions, etc.), leading to a *semantic conception* of a statistical model; see Suppe (1989) for the details. A statistical model describes the set of all possible stochastic mechanisms within the boundaries demarcated by its probability and sampling models. Moreover, a statistical model is defined relative to the probabilistic structure demarcated by the theory of probability as formulated at the time. As shown in chapter 8 the notion of probabilistic structure has changed considerably over the last century or so. As we come to recognize additional forms of chance regularity patterns, the probabilistic structure is enriched with additional concepts purporting to model the newly discovered systematic information; a primary example of this is the notion of dependence in the early 20th century. Moreover, the description as well as statistical adequacy are substantiated relative to the probabilistic structure available to the modeler. A statistical model is nothing more than a chance mechanism defined in terms of a set of probabilistic assumptions. When these assumptions are tested against the observable data in question and not rejected, we call the chosen model *statistically (or empirically) adequate.* In a nutshell, the adequacy of a statistical model is judged by the appropriateness of the assumptions (making up the model) in capturing the systematic information in the observed data. That is, the issue of whether a statistical model is truly independent of the conceptual framework in terms of which these facts are expressible, does not arise; *truth* is only relative to an overarching conceptual framework we call probability theory. This framework, however, changes over time (hopefully progressively) and there is no reason to believe that what we consider true in the present framework will be an absolute truth (whatever that means). For this reason we avoid the term truth and we use *validity* instead. For example, in the 1920s we had no idea of how to assess the validity of temporal dependence and until the 1970s temporal dependence was often assumed to coincide with temporal correlation. In the 1980s we learned to recognize and model second order temporal dependence (see chapter 8) but we have no idea what third-order dependence (see chapter 6) looks like as a chance regularity pattern. Moreover, there is no reason to believe that the distributions which are currently known exhaust all possible distributions necessary for empirical modeling. If the history of probability and statistics so far is any guide, we expect several new distributions, as well as additional forms of dependence and heterogeneity, to be uncovered (invented) in the future, enriching the overarching conceptual framework.

The *empiricist dimension* of a statistical model, as used in this book, comes very close to that of *constructive empiricism* as proposed by Van Fraassen without subscribing to the latter's denial of "any objective modality in nature" (Van Fraassen (1980), p. 202). Following Van Fraassen, the primary assessment criterion for a statistical model is its *empirical adequacy.* This empirical adequacy is assessed within the boundaries demarcated by the observed data in question, but in contrast to constructive empiricism, it is viewed relative to the overaching conceptual framework of probability theory. In this sense statistical models can be used for both descriptive and predictive purposes but they lack real explanatory power.

In contrast to a statistical model, a *theory model* (as well as an estimable model; see Spanos (1986)) is viewed in a more **realistic** light (see Devitt (1997), Caldwell (1982), Mäki (1989) and Poirier (1995)). Realism in current philosophy of science, however, has lost its precise meaning because, by some calculations, there are more sects of realism (see Leplin (1984)) than Bayesianism (see chapter 11). In the present context we use the term realism to include the following two conditions:

(i) the existence of an objective reality which is independent of the conceptual framework in terms of which this reality is expressible and

(ii) the main objective of a theory model is to uncover this objective reality, always within the human cognitive limitations. That is, the primary objective of a theory model is to *explain* this objective reality.

Given the difference in the nature and structure of a statistical and a theoretical model, the question that naturally arises at this stage is: How are the two models related? In terms of figure 1.2 in Spanos (1986), p. 21, a statistical model and a theory model are fused at the stage we call *identification* to give rise to what we called an *econometric model.* In the context of this model the statistical and theoretical information is synthesized by reparameterizing/restricting an empirically adequate estimated statistical model. In this sense a statistical model acquires explanatory power after it transmigrates into an econometric model. Hence, an econometric model is *a second stage model* whose primary objectives include description, explanation, and prediction.

The above discussion on the nature and structure of models (statistical and theoretical) touches upon several issues which are currently debated in the philosophy of science
literature; for further discussion of some of these issues see Boylan and O'Gorman
(1995). The thing that stands out from the above discussion is the possibility of enter-
taining different types of models whose nature and structure differ substantially without
giving rise to any contradictions in the context of empirical modeling; a modeler can be
an anti-realist, a quasi-realist, and a realist, at different stages of empirical modeling.

10.6 Parametric versus non-parametric models

10.6.1 The terminology

The notion of a statistical model as formulated in chapters 3 and 4 has its roots in Fisher
(1922a). This was in fact one of the decisive departures from the Pearson paradigm
where no such model was postulated a priori. In Pearson's approach, modeling commenced with the observed data and the modeler would proceed to choose a *descriptive
model* in terms of the Pearson family frequency curves using the observed data as the
only guide (see chapter 13). In contrast, statistical inference proper commences with the
modeler postulating a priori a statistical model purporting to describe the stochastic
mechanism underlying the observed data; not the observed data themselves. **Parametric
inference** refers to the statistical inference (Fisher's approach) based on statistical models
specified in terms of a parametric probability and a sampling model. The term *parametric* stems from the fact that the probability model is specified in terms of a family of densities (or distribution functions) indexed by some unknown *parameters* $\boldsymbol{\theta}$:

$$\Phi = \{f(x;\boldsymbol{\theta}), \boldsymbol{\theta} \in \Theta, x \in \mathbb{R}_X\}.$$

In contrast, the term *non-parametric* has been used to denote a variety of notions in
different contexts and thus one has to be careful when using the term. In the discussion
that follows we use the term *non-parametric* (or distribution free) to denote a simple statistical model whose probability model component is specified by:

$$F(x) \in \mathcal{P}_F \subset \mathcal{P}, \tag{10.20}$$

where $\mathcal{P}$, denotes the set of all possible distributions and $\mathcal{P}_F$ denotes a proper subset of
it. The latter is not defined directly in terms of a specific family of densities but indirectly
using assumptions relating to features of the distribution such as:

(a) the support set of the distribution,
(b) the existence of moments, and
(c) the smoothness of the distribution (discrete, continuous, differentiable, etc.).

These indirect distribution assumptions purport to narrow down the set of all possible
distributions $\mathcal{P}$ to a feasible subset. Note that in parametric statistical inference $\mathcal{P}_F = \Phi$.
For other interpretations of the term non-parametric see Stuart and Ord (1991).
    The term non-parametric model often creates the erroneous impression that the asso-

ciated statistical inference does not involve the use of a statistical model. The fact is that the non-parametric approach is statistical inference proper (within the Fisher paradigm), based on statistical models whose only difference from parametric inference is the use of implicit (instead of explicit) distribution assumptions. That is, in the context of the non-parametric approach there is an explicit sampling model which very rarely goes beyond the *random sample* assumption.

10.6.2 What difference does it make?

At first sight it seems as though the non-parametric approach has certain distinct advantages over the parametric in so far as the modeler does not commit herself to as many assumptions and thus the postulated model is less susceptible to the problem of statistical inadequacy. It turns out that this is more apparent than real in the sense that non-parametric models are often specified in terms of assumptions which are not even testable. What is real is the attempt to sidestep the problem of assessing the adequacy of the postulated model. The result of a vague and non-testable specification is at best the *precision* of the statistical inference results and at worst their *validity*.

The question of comparing parametric and non-parametric inference boils down to how effective the narrowing down of the set of all possible distributions can be in the two approaches, so as to ensure that the chosen subset $\mathcal{P}_F \subset \mathcal{P}$ includes the appropriate distribution. Once this is assured, the problem becomes one of using the data to reduce this subset to a singleton:

$$\mathcal{P}_F \overset{\text{data}}{\leadsto} F_0(x).$$

In parametric statistical inference the last step takes the form of a good estimator $\hat{\boldsymbol{\theta}}$ of $\boldsymbol{\theta}$. On the other hand, in non-parametric inference $\mathcal{P}_F$ is rarely reduced to a singleton, unless a non-parametric estimator of $F(x)$, such as the empirical cumulative distribution $\hat{F}_n(x)$, is used (see above).

The use of an implicitly defined broad subset $\mathcal{P}_F$ is often viewed as an important safeguard against misspecification; choosing an inappropriate statistical model. Common sense suggests that the broader the subset the higher the likelihood of containing the appropriate distribution. By the same token, the parametric approach is more susceptible to misspecification because it narrows down the set of all possible distributions considerably when a particular parametric family of densities is postulated. The problem is that this common sense reasoning is flawed. Firstly, the problem of misspecification has many other dimensions in addition to the distribution assumption. For simple statistical models, the validity of the independent and identically distributed assumptions is often more serious than the distribution assumption. Guarding against misspecification with regard to the distribution assumption, regardless of the other possible misspecifications, is a recipe for disaster as demonstrated by graphical techniques in chapter 5. Secondly, there is no reason to believe that a broader subset chosen on the basis of indirect assumptions is more reliable than a narrower subset chosen felicitously. It all depends on the nature of the appropriate distribution and on how the choice was made.

Example

Consider the case where the non-parametric modeler narrows down the possible distributions by postulating the indirect distribution assumption of the existence of the first four moments (a very broad subset indeed!) and the parametric modeler postulated the parametric family of the Student's t distribution. If the appropriate distribution is the Cauchy it is clear that the non-parametric modeler has no advantage over the parametric modeler. Indeed, as shown in chapter 5 the judicious use of Q-Q plots for checking the Student's t assumption will lead to the Cauchy distribution. Moreover, there are much more reliable ways to guard against misspecification than just being vague about the appropriate distribution.

Statistical adequacy In this book we pay particular attention to the problem of misspecification and guard against this potential problem in two ways. First, at the specification stage we propose several graphical techniques which, when utilized properly, can narrow down the set of all possible distributions drastically, to just a few parametric families. Second, at the misspecification testing stage the adequacy of the assumptions of the postulated statistical model is tested against the observed data before any statistical inference conclusions are drawn; see chapter 15.

Making minimal assumptions with regard to the distribution underlying the observed data, by implicitly defining a broad subset $\mathcal{P}_F$ at the specification stage, very often gives rise to vague statistical inference conclusions. As a general rule, the more specific the probabilistic assumptions making up the statistical model are, the more precise our statistical inference procedures will be: more accurate estimators (smaller variance), more powerful tests and shorter confidence and prediction intervals. Let us see how these indirect distribution assumptions contribute to the vagueness of the conclusions.

10.6.3 The effectiveness of indirect distribution assumptions

As argued in chapter 4, the basic components of a probability model (10.15) from the modeling viewpoint, are:

(i) the particular form of the density function $f(x;\theta)$, with the associated *unknown parameters* θ and their domain Θ, and

(ii) the *support* of the density $\mathbb{R}_X^* := \{x \in \mathbb{R} : f(x;\theta) > 0\}$.

Regardless of the narrowing down of the set of possible distributions using the existence of moments or smoothness restrictions, the modeler is required to decide on the support set of the appropriate distribution. This choice also contributes in the narrowing down. The fact that the two decisions are separated might lead to some potential problems in modeling. For example, returning to the marks data in chapter 1 (see table 1.6), the modeler can easily commit one of two obvious errors. He can either ignore the observed data and proceed to leave the support unrestricted (i.e., $\mathbb{R}_X^* = \mathbb{R}$) or he can decide on the support by just looking at the numbers in hand, say [40,100]. The range of values of the observed data is clearly relevant but not at the expense of ignoring the fact that the postulated model purports to model the phenomenon underlying the data, not the data themselves. At the same time leaving the support unrestricted will add to the vagueness of the specification. The observed data in question have a finite range of values but we need to keep in mind that some values that are possible might not have occurred in the specific data set. Hence, the random variable underlying the data has the support set $[0,100]$; or expressed in terms of *proportions* the support set is: $[0,1]$. In this case allowing for distributions with support $(-\infty,\infty)$ is clearly inappropriate. As remarked in chapter 4, in parametric inference the Beta probability model appears to be more appropriate because it utilizes all the information available.

Existence of moments and precision of inference

We consider the *existence* (or otherwise) of any **moments** as an indirect *distribution assumption* in the sense that the existence of the moments (boundedness of the integrals):

$$\mu_r' = \int_{x \in \mathbb{R}_X} x^r f(x) dx < \infty, \ r = 1,2,\dots$$

depends exclusively on the nature of the density function $f(x)$ and its *support*. In particular, the existence of certain moments depends crucially on the thickness of the tails of the density function, as indicated by the following result.

Moments and tails lemma For a random variable X and a positive real number p, $(p \in \mathbb{R}_+)$

$$\lim_{x \to \infty} x^p \mathbb{P}(|X| > x) = 0 \Rightarrow E(|X|^r) < \infty \text{ for } 0 \leq r < p.$$

For example the Normal distribution has slimmer tails than the Student's t and all its moments exist; for the latter distribution the moments after a certain p do not exist.

   In relation to the *support set* we NOTE that *all* moments exist when:

$$\mathbb{R}_X = [a,b], \ a < b < \infty, \ a \text{ and } b \text{ being real numbers,}$$

irrespective of the nature of $f(x)$. In this bounded support category we include distributions such as the Uniform and the Beta. At the other extreme we encountered the case of the Cauchy distribution, with support $\mathbb{R}_X = (-\infty,\infty)$, that has *no* moments! Between these two extremes we have numerous distributions, such as the Normal, the Student's t, the Chi-square, the Exponential, the Extreme value, the Gamma, the Logistic, and the Weibull (see appendix A), whose support set is infinite but some moments do exist. In this category we have distributions for which all moments exist (e.g., the Normal) and distributions for which only the first few moments exist. For example the Student's t distribution with $\nu = 5$, has moments up to order 4, but no higher moments exist. Another example is the Pareto distribution whose moments exist only up to a certain order less than its shape parameter.

The problem of moments The discussion of the problem of moments in chapter 4, suggests that, in general, moments do not determine distributions uniquely even if we use an *infinite* number of them. In addition, in general, no distribution is determined by a *finite* number of moments. In view of the fact that for modeling and statistical inference purposes we can only deal with a small number of moments (and certainly finite), using a few moments to narrow down the set of all possible distributions to a manageable subset is certainly the wrong approach. In chapter 4 it was also argued that the moments become effective in narrowing down the set of all possible distributions. However, if we are prepared to limit ourselves to a specific class of distributions the problem becomes tractable. As mentioned in chapter 4, if we limit the set of all possible distributions to that of the Pearson family, the modeler requires at most four moments to determine the particular distribution (see also chapter 12). Another example of a multivariate parametric family of distributions is the elliptically symmetric family where the first two moments characterize the particular members of the family (see Fang, Kotz and Ng (1990).

The question which arises at this stage is why don't we use existence of moments assumptions in modeling, given that they are more general than specific distribution assumptions? The answer in a nutshell is that distribution assumptions give rise to more accurate and sharp probabilistic results in statistical inference. Existence of moments restrictions compel the modeler to use **inequalities**, such as those mentioned in chapter 3, which are often *very crude* compared with what one can get when postulating a distribution assumption. The following examples attempt to give some idea of the crudeness of such inequalities when compared with direct distribution assumptions.

Examples

(i) Consider the distribution of the number of dots on the uppermost face of a fair die when cast, as shown below, and consider evaluating the probability associated with the event $\{|X - E(X)| > 2.5\}$, when (a) the exact distribution is used and (b) using some inequality.

outcomes	1	2	3	4	5	6
probabilities	$\frac{1}{6}$	$\frac{1}{6}$	$\frac{1}{6}$	$\frac{1}{6}$	$\frac{1}{6}$	$\frac{1}{6}$

$$E(X) = 1\left(\tfrac{1}{6}\right) + 2\left(\tfrac{1}{6}\right) + 3\left(\tfrac{1}{6}\right) + 4\left(\tfrac{1}{6}\right) + 5\left(\tfrac{1}{6}\right) + 6\left(\tfrac{1}{6}\right) = 3.5,$$

$$Var(X) = (1 - 3.5)^2\left(\tfrac{1}{6}\right) + (2 - 3.5)^2\left(\tfrac{1}{6}\right) + (3 - 3.5)^2\left(\tfrac{1}{6}\right) +$$
$$(4 - 3.5)^2\left(\tfrac{1}{6}\right) + (5 - 3.5)^2\left(\tfrac{1}{6}\right) + (6 - 3.5)^2\left(\tfrac{1}{6}\right) = 2.9166$$

(a)   Using the above probability distribution we can deduce that:

$$\mathbb{P}(|X - E(X)| > 2.5) = \mathbb{P}(|X - 3.5| > 2.5) = \mathbb{P}(1 > X > 6) = 0.$$

(b)   In contrast, Chebyshev's inequality yields:

$$\mathbb{P}(|X - 3.5| > 2.5) < \frac{2.9166}{(2.5)^2} = 0.467.$$

(ii) Consider the case where X is uniformly distributed with parameter θ:

$$X \sim U(-\theta, \theta), \text{ i.e., } f(x; \theta) = \tfrac{1}{2\theta}, \ E(X) = 0, \ Var(X) = \tfrac{\theta^2}{3}.$$

We can evaluate the actual probability to be:

$$\mathbb{P}(|X| \geq 1.5\sqrt{Var(X)}) = \mathbb{P}\left(|X| \geq 1.5\sqrt{\tfrac{\theta^2}{3}}\right) = 2\mathbb{P}(|X| \geq 0.866\theta)) = 2(0.067) = 0.134.$$

On the other hand, the upper bound given by the Chebyshev inequality is:

$$\mathbb{P}(|X| \geq (1.5)\sqrt{Var(X)}) = \mathbb{P}\left(|X| \geq (1.5)\sqrt{\left(\tfrac{\theta^2}{3}\right)}\right) \leq \tfrac{1}{(1.5)^2} = 0.444.$$

(iii) Consider the case where X has a geometric distribution, i.e.

$$f(x; \theta) = \theta(1 - \theta)^{x-1}, \ 0 \leq \theta \leq 1, \ x = 1,2,3,\ldots, \ E(X) = \tfrac{1}{\theta}, \ Var(X) = \tfrac{(1-\theta)}{\theta^2}.$$

Let us assume that $\theta = \tfrac{1}{2}$ (i.e., $E(X) = 2$, $Var(X) = 2$) and $\varepsilon = 2$. Evaluation of the true probability utilizing the nature of the distribution yields:

$$\mathbb{P}(|X - E(X)| > (\sqrt{2})\sqrt{Var(X)}) = \textstyle\sum_{x=5}^{\infty} \theta(1-\theta)^{x-1} = \tfrac{1}{16} = 0.0625.$$

On the other hand, the upper bound given by the Chebyshev inequality is:

$$\mathbb{P}(|X - E(X)| > (\sqrt{2})\sqrt{Var(X)}) = \mathbb{P}(|X - E(X)| > (\sqrt{2})\sqrt{2}) \leq \tfrac{1}{(\sqrt{2})^2} = 0.5.$$

As one can see from the above three examples, the estimate of the probability given by Chebyshev type bounds is very crude compared with the actual probability. The reader should be warned that these examples are typical and not extreme cases; when highly skewed distributions are used the results are much cruder!

We will see in chapters 12–15 that the results on estimation and testing are in effect probabilistic statements which without distribution assumptions will often be rather crude because they depend on inequalities such as those given in chapter 3. What is very important for our purposes here is that the more we are prepared to postulate in terms of additional assumptions (thus narrowing down the set of possible distributions even further), the sharper the results we can get from inequalities. Consider the example where we are prepared to postulate the existence of additional higher moments.

Example
Let $\{X_n\}_{n=1}^{\infty} := \{X_1, X_2, \ldots, X_n \ldots\}$ be a sequence of Independent and Identically Bernoulli Distributed (IID) random variables. It can be shown that:

$$S_n := \textstyle\sum_{k=1}^{n} X_k \sim \mathsf{Bi}(n\theta, n\theta(1 - \theta)).$$

Using Chebyshev's inequality (which assumes the existence of the moments up to the 2nd order) yields:

$$\mathbb{P}(|n^{-1}S_n - \theta| > \varepsilon) \leq \tfrac{\theta(1-\theta)}{n\varepsilon^2}.$$

On the other hand, if we assume the existence of the moments up to order 4, we can use Markov's inequality (see chapter 3) which yields:

$$\mathbb{P}(|Y - E(Y)|^4 > \varepsilon) \leq \tfrac{E(|Y - E(Y)|^4)}{\varepsilon^4}.$$

Noting that $E(|n^{-1}S_n - \theta|^4) = n\theta[1 + 3\theta(1 - \theta)(n - 2)]$ this yields:

$$\mathbb{P}(|n^{-1}S_n - \theta| > \varepsilon) \leq \frac{3}{(16)n^2\varepsilon^4}.$$

As can be seen, the estimate of the upper bound given by Markov's inequality converges much faster because it utilizes more information in relation to the existence of moments.

Finally, let us consider the case where we are prepared to make additional smoothness assumptions.

Example

Let X be a random variable with $E(X) = \mu$ and $Var(X) = \sigma^2$. If in addition we are prepared to assume that X is:

(i) continuous, and   (ii) unimodal with median m_0,

then, we can get the sharper Chebyshev-type inequality (see Biswas (1991)):

$$\mathbb{P}(|X - m_0| \geq \varepsilon) \leq \left(\frac{4}{9\varepsilon^2}\right) E(X - m_0)^2.$$

This upper bound is less than half of the ordinary (ignoring (i)–(ii)) Chebyshev upper bound:

$$\mathbb{P}(|X - m_0| \geq \varepsilon) \leq \left(\frac{1}{\varepsilon^2}\right) E(X - m_0)^2.$$

The ordered sample

In addition to the extensive use of inequalities in non-parametric statistical inference there is a pervasive use of *ordered samples* and their properties. The cornerstone of these results is the *probability integral transformation*, first encountered in chapter 4. This result says that in the case of a *continuous* cdf $F(x)$, irrespective of its nature, the random variable defined by $Y: = F(X)$ is Uniformly distributed:

$$Y: = F(X) \sim U(0,1).$$

NOTE that the continuity of $F(x)$ is indeed an indirect distribution assumption. This result enables the modeler to transform the original sample to a Uniformly distributed sample by applying the above transformation. This transformation, however, requires the modeler to know the exact form of the cdf function $F(x)$. Without this information, the modeler is forced to resort to asymptotic results.

Of particular interest is the ordered sample $(Y_{[1]}, Y_{[2]}, \ldots, Y_{[n]})$ (which contains all the relevant data information), the associated distribution results mentioned in chapter 4 and the empirical cumulative distribution (see chapter 10). These results enable the modeler to have an asymptotic distribution for the ordered sample, irrespective of the nature of the probability model and thus the modeler can proceed to derive a number of statistical inference results on estimation, testing, and prediction (see Dudewicz and Mishra (1988), Bickel and Doksum (1977)). However, these statistical inference results are in general less reliable and precise than the corresponding results based on parametric models.

Within the same class of techniques we include a number of methods based on the empirical cumulative distribution function (see above) including the various smoothing techniques designed to approximate certain features of an unknown Probability model (see Silverman (1986), Hardle (1990)).

10.6.4 Non-parametric models and statistical adequacy

Having called into question the conventional wisdom that the broader the postulated subset $\mathcal{P}_* \subset \mathcal{P}$ the lower the likelihood of misspecification, we proceed to consider the nature of the assumptions underlying the non-parametric models as they relate to assessing statistical adequacy. In view of the current popularity of kernel smoothing techniques it is interesting to discuss the assumptions underlying such statistical models. More often than not, the statistical model underlying the kernel smoothing results postulates a random sample and a probability model of the form (see Thompson and Tapia (1990), p. 46):

$\mathcal{P}_F := \{f(x) : f(x) \text{ has properties (a)–(c)}\}.$

(a) $f(x)$ has support $[a,b]$, $a < b < \infty$, $a \in \mathbb{R}$, $b \in \mathbb{R}$,
(b) $f(x)$ is bounded on $[a,b]$,
(c) $f(x)$ has continuous derivatives of up to order three except at the end points.

It is apparent that assumptions (b)–(c) are unverifiable and there is no way to assess their adequacy using the observed data. This constitutes a typical example of non-parametric statistical models whose stated purpose is to:

sacrifice a small percentage of parametric optimality in order to achieve greater insensitivity to misspecification...   (Scott (1992), p. 33)

The fact of the matter is that the recent trend in the derivation of techniques using non-parametric models leads statistical modeling toward models based on unverifiable assumptions. As for the *insensitivity to misspecification* it is apparent from the above discussion that the inference based on non-parametric models is likely to be insensitive to *information* not just misspecification. When the modeler assumes Normality but the data in question reject it as inappropriate, the modeler has learned something which can be exploited by respecifying the statistical model. Being oblivious to such non-Normality amounts to ignoring systematic information.

The first to be critical of non-parametric inference was Fisher, in relation to testing with experimental data:

They [the tests] assume less knowledge, or more ignorance, of the experimental material than do the standard tests, and this has been an attraction to some mathematicians who often discuss experimentation without personal knowledge of the material. In inductive logic, however, an erroneous assumption of ignorance is not innocuous; it often leads to manifest absurdities...   (Fisher (1935), p. 49)

Non-parametric models and robustness

It is well-known that the early literature on robustness was motivated by the undue reliance of the statistical inference literature on the assumption of Normality. In this sense most of the early results on robustness have been derived having the Normal distribution in mind and the meaning of the concept was colored by this motivation. A prime example of this attitude is the case of the robustness of estimators and test statistics to outliers. Ignoring the case where a data point has been typed incorrectly, an outlier is an unusual observation considered to be unlikely given the support of a certain implicit distribution. This, however, begs the question because a certain observation might be viewed as an outlier when the underlying distribution is Normal but perfectly acceptable if the underlying distribution is the Student's t! If, indeed, the appropriate distribution is the Student's t and the modeler chooses an estimator which is robust to observations in the extreme tails, the modeler ignores the most crucial observations in his sample; the chosen estimator is insensitive to information, not to misspecification. Oversimplifying the argument for the sake of the discussion, if we push the notion of robustness to its extreme, the best robust estimator will be the one which is completely oblivious to all systematic information in the data!

The more recent literature on robust statistics is at great pains to distinguish itself from non-parametric models. Hampel *et al.* (1986, p. 9) argue:

> Robust statistics is often confused with, or at least located close to nonparametric statistics, although it has nothing to do with it directly. The theories of robustness consider neighborhoods of parametric models and thus clearly belong to parametric statistics. Even if the term is used in a very vague sense, robust statistics considers the effects of only approximate fulfillment of assumptions, while nonparametric statistics makes rather weak but nevertheless strict assumptions (such as continuity of distribution or independence)...

10.6.5 Is there a role for non-parametric procedures?

Non-parametric techniques are very useful and have an important role to play in empirical modeling. This role, however, does not include using exclusively non-parametric models for empirical modeling. The above discussion brings out several limitations of these models when used as the exclusive vehicles of empirical modeling. In summary, non-parametric models usually:

(i)   depend on (implicit) probabilistic assumptions which are often non-testable,
(ii)   often require a large number of observations,
(iii) are not parsimonious,
(iv)   provide no bridge to relate them with the theory models,
(iv)   give rise to imprecise inference results.

The examples of indirect distribution assumptions forcing the modeler to use inequalities as an integral part of non-parametric inference, show most clearly that if the modeler wants precise and decisive inference (estimators and tests) in *modeling*, she should go the extra mile and postulate a specific parametric family of distributions. This, of course should be done in conjunction with assessing the credibility of the postulated statistical model, i.e., test the adequacy of the distribution assumption postulated. Hence, if the primary objective of the modeler is precise and reliable statistical inference, the combination of *specification* (postulating parametric statistical models), careful *misspecification testing* (testing the assumptions underlying the postulated model) and *respecification* (choosing a different model if the original is misspecified) is the procedure recommended in this book; see chapter 11 for more details.

The justification for using non-parametric inference based on the likely avoidance of potential misspecifications is not convincing for three reasons. First, the problem of departures from the assumptions of the postulated model, as argued above, can be dealt with more effectively in the context of specification, misspecification testing, and respecification of parametric models. Second, there is a price to be paid when the modeler chooses to be vague with the assumptions of the postulated model:

vague assumptions lead to nebulous inference conclusions!

Third, non-parametric models are often justified in cases where the modeler senses that the Normality assumption is inappropriate in an attempt to protect the validity of the results at the expense of some imprecision. This is a lame excuse because there are numerous distributions to postulate when the Normality assumption is invalid. As argued above, in such cases the modeler should respecify not indulge in damage control with doubtful benefits.

The question that naturally arises at this stage is whether there is a role for non-parametric inference in empirical modeling. The answer is unquestionably **yes**, but not for inference modeling as such. Indeed, it will be difficult to overestimate the usefulness of non-parametric techniques for both stages of modeling referred to above: specification and misspecification testing. At the **specification stage** non-parametric techniques, such as kernel smoothing, can be invaluable as an integral part of the *preliminary (exploratory) data analysis*. As argued in chapters 5–6, raw data plots, such as *t*-plots and scatterplots can, sometimes, be misleading because they are by definition data specific. The postulated statistical model, however, aspires to describe the stochastic mechanism that underlies the observed data, not just the observed numbers in hand. Smoothing techniques can reduce the data-specificity of such plots and provide the modeler with heedful ideas about appropriate parametric models. At the **misspecification stage** the aim is to assess the empirical adequacy of the postulated parametric model by testing the validity of the underlying assumptions. The modeler has to assess null hypotheses whose negation (the implicit alternative) is by its very nature non-parametric (cannot be specified in terms of the parameters of the postulated model). In this context non-parametric techniques are again invaluable because no parametric alternative hypotheses against which the null could be assessed are readily available; this is discussed further in chapter 15. It goes without saying that what the modeler learns during the misspecification testing against non-parametric implicit alternative hypotheses will be of paramount importance for the respecification stage of modeling (assuming that the original model turns out to be misspecified).

We conclude this section by reiterating once more that in this book we view non-parametric procedures, such as smoothing techniques, as complements, not substitutes, of parametric modeling procedures.

10.7 Summary and conclusions

It is interesting to note that between the 17th and early 20th centuries the distinction between observed relative frequencies and probabilities was commonly blurred. This was to be expected given the fact that the theory of probability as a mathematical discipline was formalized in the 20th century. During this early period there was no need for building a bridge between chance regularity patterns and probability concepts because it was implicitly assumed given. This is most apparent in the following often-quoted passage from Galton extolling the virtues of the Normal distribution (it should be read with figure 10.1 in mind):

I know of scarcely anything so apt to impress the imagination as the wonderful form of cosmic order expressed by the "Law of Frequency of Error." The law would have been personified by the Greeks and deified, if they had known of it. It reigns with serenity and in complete self-effacement amidst the wildest confusion. The huger the mob and the greater the apparent anarchy, the more perfect is its sway. It is the supreme law of Unreason. Whenever a large sample of chaotic elements are taken in hand and marshalled in the order of their magnitude, an unsuspected and most beautiful form of regularity proves to have been latent all along...   (Galton (1889), p. 86)

  The bridge between empirical regularities and probability proposed in this chapter comes in the form of the empirical cumulative distribution function (ecdf) and its relationship to its theoretical counterpart: the concept of a cumulative distribution function. The limit theorems that connect ecdf and cdf utilize only mathematical concepts of convergence and there is no circularity in the argument. As shown in the next four chapters the various facets of statistical inference, such as estimation (see chapter 13) and testing (see chapters 14–15), can be viewed directly or indirectly in terms of this relationship between the ecdf and the cdf.

10.8 Exercises

1 Explain briefly the following interpretations of probability:
   (i)   the lottery-based,
   (ii)   the frequency, and
   (iii) the degrees of belief.

2 "The lottery (classical) interpretation of probability is now considered to be a relic of a bygone age." Discuss.

3 Explain briefly the difference between the *frequency* and *degrees of belief* interpretations of probability. Why do we care?

4 Compare and contrast the two alternative flavors of the degrees of belief interpretation of probability.

5 Explain why the frequency interpretation of probability might be more appropriate for the empirical modeling of observational data but by the same token the degrees

of belief interpretation might be more germane to the analysis of experimental data.

6 Discuss Von Mises' attempt to build a bridge between chance regularity and the notion of probability.

7 Discuss De Finetti's representation theorem and compare its non-parametric and parametric forms.

8 How does De Finetti's representation theorem provides a bridge between chance regularity and the notion of a simple statistical model? How does the distribution of θ come into the picture?

9 Explain the notion of chance discussed in relation to the decimal expansions of irrational numbers in relation to predictability and lack of patterns.

10 Explain the notion of regularity discussed in relation to the decimal expansions of irrational numbers in relation to the existence of stable laws.

11 "Weyl's result shows that uniformly distributed chance sequences arise naturally in the theory of numbers. Starting with such sequences one can generate most other forms of chance regularity patterns." Discuss.

12 "The various limit theorems relating to the asymptotic behavior of the empirical cumulative distribution function bestow empirical content to the mathematical concept of a cdf $F(x)$." Explain and discuss.

13 Discuss Reyni's view that the Law of Large Numbers bestows empirical content to the concept of probability because there is no circularity problem in the argument.

14 "Misspecification testing bestows empirical content to the notion of a statistical model." Explain.

15 Compare and contrast parametric and non-parametric statistical inference.

16 "Non-parametric statistical models give rise to imprecise statistical inference results." Discuss.

17 "Non-parametric inference is proper statistical inference within the Fisher paradigm." Discuss.

18 "Robustness is part of parametric statistical inference and is often believed part of non-parametric inference." Discuss.

19 Discuss the use of non-parametric techniques in preliminary data analysis.

20 Discuss the possible role of non-parametric inference in misspecification testing.

21 "Non-parametric inference can be viewed as an inappropriate attempt to deal with the problem of misspecification." Discuss.

11 An introduction to statistical inference

11.1 Introduction

In the previous chapter a bridge was proposed between the mathematical concept of a *statistical model* and the empirical notion of *chance regularity* in an attempt to confer empirical content on the former. The central pillar supporting the bridge is the concept of the *empirical cumulative distribution function* (ecdf) $\hat{F}_n(x)$ which was shown to be the empirical counterpart to the cumulative distribution function $F(x)$. It must be noted, however, that the proposed bridge, as well as the discussion leading to it, predisposes the reader towards a particular approach to statistical inference known as the *classical (or frequentist) approach*, associated with the *frequency interpretation* of probability. To be more precise, the discussion that follows is partially in favour of what is known as *parametric statistical inference*. Moreover, the discussion of statistical inference in the next few chapters focuses attention on methods of the classical approach which are appropriate for the analysis of *non-experimental* (observational) as opposed to experimental data. These choices are not as arbitrary as they might seem at first sight, but they need to be justified. One of the aims of the present chapter is to justify these choices in order to place the discussion which follows in a less prejudiced perspective.

The main issues discussed in this chapter include:

(a) classical versus Bayesian statistical inference,
(b) experimental versus non-experimental data analysis, and
(c) sampling distributions.

11.1.1 A bird's eye view of the chapter

In section 2 we present a bird's eye view of the traditional facets of the classical approach to statistical inference: estimation, testing and prediction, as a prelude to the discussion which follows. In section 3 we discuss briefly the differences between the classical and Bayesian approaches in an attempt to provide additional insight into the classical approach. In section 4 we compare and contrast non-experimental and observational data as they relate to empirical modeling in an attempt to bring out certain neglected facets of empirical modeling: specification, misspecification and respecification; these facets are of secondary importance when modeling with experimental data. These neglected facets are discussed in section 5 where we propose a more coherent modeling procedure for modeling non-experimental data. In section 6 we provide a preliminary discussion of the notion around which the classical approach to inference revolves: the notion of a *sampling distribution*. Estimators, test statistics and predictors constitute functions $h(X_1, X_2, \ldots, X_n)$ of the postulated sample $(X_1, X_2, \ldots, X_n)$ and thus they are random variables themselves with distributions we call sampling distributions. All inference results depend crucially on such sampling distributions. In section 7 we consider the general problem of determining the distribution of $h(X_1, X_2, \ldots, X_n)$, assuming the joint distribution of $(X_1, X_2, \ldots, X_n)$ is known. Because of the inherent difficulties associated with this problem we often resort to approximations of such sampling distributions using hypothetical sampling procedures which are discussed in section 8.

It is of paramount importance to emphasize at the outset that in empirical modeling, the joint distribution of $(X_1, X_2, \ldots, X_n)$ is not actually known but assumed by the modeler in the form of the postulated statistical model. Hence, the validity of the sampling distribution results depend crucially on the validity of the postulated model. The neglected facets of modeling hold the key to ensuring that the modeler does not proceed mindlessly to use invalid inference results!

11.2 An introduction to the classical approach

The classical (frequency) approach to statistical inference was formulated by R. A. Fisher (1890–1962) by recasting the *biometric tradition* founded by Francis Galton and formulated by Karl Pearson and his co-workers. The first signs of Fisher's recasting of the inherited paradigm are discernible in his first statistics paper (see Fisher (1912)) written when he was a first year graduate student; immediately afterwards he abandoned his graduate studies at the University of Cambridge (England), where he also studied for his first degree; for what it is worth both Galton and Pearson also studied at Cambridge. Fisher (1922b) is arguably the paper that founded modern statistical inference and constitutes both a continuation and a break away from the inherited paradigm formulated by Pearson; see Fienberg and Hinkley (1980) for a commentary on this and other papers by Fisher. It took a very long time for the statistics profession to realize the shift of paradigms (see Spanos (1995b)). Indeed, Karl Pearson died in 1936 but even in his last paper (see Pearson (1936)) he does not seem to be fully aware of the fact that Fisher had turned the tables on him and that was the main reason he lost the argument to the superiority of maximum likelihood over his method of moments method of estimation; even though the method of maximum likelihood is completely hopeless in the context of the Pearson paradigm (see Fisher (1937) and chapter 13 for the details).

HISTORICAL GOSSIP. It is interesting to note that there was no love lost between Karl Pearson and R. A. Fisher, with the animosity between them going back to the mid 1910s when Pearson rejected two papers by Fisher when the latter submitted them for publication in *Biometrika*, the house journal of the biometric tradition which was under the complete control of Pearson. The extent of this animosity between these two giants of modern statistics is easily discernible in the following passage written by Fisher, 20 years(!) after Pearson's death:

The terrible weakness of his (Pearson's) mathematical and scientific work flowed from his incapacity in self-criticism, and his unwillingness to admit the possibility that he had anything to learn from others, even in biology, of which he knew very little. His mathematics, consequently, though always vigorous, were usually clumsy, and often misleading. In controversy, to which he was much addicted, he constantly showed himself to be without a sense of justice. In his dispute with Bateson on the validity of Mendelian inheritance he was the bull to a skillful matador…   (Fisher (1956), p. 3)

For more on the controversies between Pearson and Fisher see chapter 13.

11.2.1 The Fisher paradigm

Statistical inference, as formulated by Fisher, commences by postulating a priori a statistical model that purports to provide an adequate (probabilistic) description of the stochastic mechanism that presumably gave rise to the observed data in question. The simplest **generic** form of a **statistical model** is:

[i]   Probability model: $\Phi = \{f(x;\boldsymbol{\theta}), \boldsymbol{\theta} \in \Theta, x \in \mathbb{R}_X\}$,
[ii]   Sampling model: $\mathbf{X}_{(n)} := (X_1, X_2, \ldots, X_n)$ is a random sample.

The modeler views the observed data $\mathbf{x} := (x_1, x_2, \ldots, x_n)$ as a particular *realization* of the stochastic mechanism represented by the specified statistical model. In particular the observations are viewed as specific values taken by the random variables making up the sample in question. The sample, as a set of random variables can be thought of as:

$$\mathbf{X}_{(n)}(.): S \to X,$$

where X denotes the set of all possible values (often $\mathbb{R}^n$), known as the *sample space*. The observed data $\mathbf{x} := (x_1, x_2, \ldots, x_n)$, viewed as a *sample realization*, are interpreted as a point belonging to this space; one of many possible points. This, in effect, provides the basis for the **inductive argument** with respect to which statistical inference differs from descriptive statistics. This inductive argument, however, is embedded in a **deductive argument** which in a nutshell says:

if the premises are valid certain inference results necessarily follow.

The premises is nothing more than the postulated statistical model. Hence, the most crucial problem of *parametric* statistical inference is to ensure that the premises are valid (statistical adequacy) because otherwise the inference conclusions do not necessarily follow. Despite its impertinent nature, the common saying:

garbage in, garbage out,

describes the situation aptly. That is, the inference results depend crucially on the validity of the assumptions making up the model; assumptions such as independence and identical distribution in the case of a simple statistical model. Once, the parameter(s) $\boldsymbol{\theta}$ are determined by the data, the stochastic mechanism that underlies the observations, a specific form of the postulated statistical model, is completely specified and can be used to draw a number of conclusions relating to the stochastic phenomenon in question.

It is important to mention at this stage that Fisher did not just recast the Pearson paradigm but introduced most of the concepts, ideas and inference procedures in modern statistics. The overwhelming majority of the concepts and ideas in estimation, including properties of estimators and methods of estimation (maximum likelihood) can be traced back to Fisher (1912, 1922a, 1922b, 1925a, 1925b, 1935); see chapters 12–13. As far as testing is concerned we argue that Fisher's procedure has not been superseded by that of Neyman and Pearson as the traditional treatment would have us believe. Fisher testing is revisited in chapter 14 and a case is made in chapter 15 that it is tailor made for misspecification testing purposes. We mention in passing that Fisher (1935b) established the *experimental design tradition* as a legitimate paradigm in statistics; it has been the dominating paradigm in statistics for the last 50 years or so.

11.2.2 Basic concepts

Before we proceed to discuss the various facets of statistical inference in the context of the classical approach, it is imperative to take stock as well as emphasize some of the important notions mentioned in passing in the above introduction. To help us along we use the **simple Bernoulli model**:

[i]   Statistical GM: $X_i = E(X_i) + u_i, \ i \in \mathbb{N}$,
[ii]   Probability model: $\Phi = \{f(x;\theta) = \theta^x(1-\theta)^{1-x}, \ 0 \le \theta \le 1, \ x = 0,1\}$,
[iii] Sampling model: $\mathbf{X} := (X_1, X_2, \ldots, X_n)$ is a random sample.   (11.1)

The probability model comes in the form of the family of Bernoulli densities, one density for each value of θ as it varies in the parameter space $\Theta := [0,1]$; and thus the probability model represents an infinite set of such densities. The sampling model comes in the form of the random sample; a set of independent and identically distributed random variables (a random vector) $\mathbf{X}_{(n)}$ defined by:

$$\mathbf{X}_{(n)}(.): S \rightarrow \{0,1\}^n := \underbrace{\{0,1\} \times \{0,1\} \times \cdots \times \{0,1\}}_{n \text{ times}},$$

where $\mathcal{X} := \{0,1\}^n$ is the *sample space*.

The first important distinction is that between a *sample* and a *sample realization*.

   Sample A set of random variables $\mathbf{X}_{(n)} := (X_1, X_2, \ldots, X_n)$ with a specified probabilistic structure is referred to as the *sample*. As such a sample represents a random vector of the form: $\mathbf{X}_{(n)}(.): S \rightarrow \mathcal{X}$.

   Sample realization On the other hand a *sample realization* $\mathbf{x} := (x_1, x_2, \ldots x_n)$ is just one point belonging to the sample space $\mathcal{X}$.

In the case of the Bernoulli model the *sample realization* $\mathbf{x}$, say $n = 30$:

$$\mathbf{x} := (0,0,1,0,1,1,0,0,1,0,0,0,1,1,0,1,0,1,0,0,1,0,1,0,0,0,1,1,0,0),$$

is viewed as one point of the sample space $\mathcal{X} := \{0,1\}^n$. In other words, each random variable making up the sample takes one of two values as shown below.

Sample:	$\mathbf{X}_{(n)} := (X_1,$	$X_2,$	$X_3,$	$X_4,$	$X_5,$	$X_6,$	$\cdots$	$X_{30})$
	$\downarrow$	$\downarrow$	$\downarrow$	$\downarrow$	$\downarrow$	$\downarrow$		$\downarrow$
Sample realization: $\mathbf{x} :=$	(0)	0	1	0	1	1		$0)$

The random variables $X_1, X_2, \ldots, X_{30}$, however, could have taken different values in another sequence of 30 trials, say:

$$\mathbf{x}^{(1)} = (1,0,1,0,1,0,1,0,1,0,1,1,0,1,0,1,0,1,0,0,0,1,0,1,1,1,0,1),$$

or

$$\mathbf{x}^{(2)} = (1,0,0,1,0,0,1,1,1,0,1,0,1,0,0,1,0,1,0,0,0,1,0,1,1,1,0,0,1,0).$$

These sample realizations are all elements of the sample space $\mathcal{X} := \{0,1\}^n$, which represents all the possible sequences of zeros and ones, of size 30.

The second important issue raised above is that of *statistical inference* versus *descriptive statistics*. Postulating a statistical model a priori is the primary feature that renders *statistical inference* different from *descriptive statistics*. In descriptive statistics the modeler begins with a set of data in search of a model that conveniently summarizes the information in these data. In the context of *descriptive statistics* we can summarize this information in the form of a histogram or a pie chart but we cannot use such summaries to draw conclusions about the chance mechanism underlying the observed data. Statistical inference reverses the order by postulating a statistical model *a priori* and interpreting the data in its context. This will then enable us to use the one realization of the sample to draw conclusions about θ and thus about the chance mechanism described by the statistical model in question. In this sense the approach to statistics as formalized by Karl Pearson is clearly within the realm of descriptive statistics and does not constitute statistical inference in the modern sense of the term (see chapter 13).

After this short digression on the above two important issues we return to the question of coalescing the postulated statistical model with the observations. The *first* stage of this fusing of information comes in the form of amalgamating the probability and sampling models to define what we call the *distribution of the sample.*

Distribution of the sample   The joint distribution of the random variables $(X_1, X_2, \ldots, X_n)$ making up the sample, defined by:

$$D(X_1, X_2, \ldots, X_n; \boldsymbol{\theta}),$$

is referred to as the *distribution of the sample* (see figure 11.1).

The second stage combines the a priori information fused in the context of the distribution of the sample with the observed data to define the likelihood function:

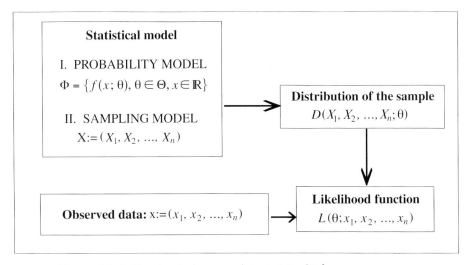

Figure 11.1 The classical approach to statistical inference

$$L(\boldsymbol{\theta};x_1,x_2, \ldots, x_n) \propto D(X_1,X_2, \ldots, X_n;\boldsymbol{\theta}),$$

where $\propto$ reads proportional to; see chapter 13 for further details.

The statistical inference procedures such as estimation, testing, and prediction are based on the information summarized by $D(X_1,X_2, \ldots, X_n;\boldsymbol{\theta})$. In this sense the appropriateness of these procedures depends crucially on the *validity of the assumptions* underlying the statistical model postulated. In cases where the underlying assumptions are not valid for the data in question, the inference results built on invalid assumptions will be very misleading.

Statistical inference constitutes a set of procedures for drawing valid conclusions about the stochastic mechanism underlying the observed data using (a) the a priori information, in the form of the postulated statistical model, in conjunction with (b) the sample realization $\mathbf{x} := (x_1,x_2,\ldots,x_n)$ as shown in figure 11.1.

Having introduced the basic concepts of the classical approach, we proceed to provide a bird's eye view of the main practical facets of statistical inference, traditionally known as estimation, testing, and prediction. It is noted at the outset that these facets do not provide a complete picture of what the classical approach to statistical modeling entails. Indeed, as argued in section 4 these three facets of inference provide a misleading picture of statistical modeling, especially in the case of non-experimental data.

11.2.3 Estimation

> How would we go about estimating an unknown parameter θ?

In the context of a postulated statistical model the data information comes in the form of a particular value of $\mathbf{X} := (X_1,X_2, \ldots, X_n)$ in $X \subset \mathbb{R}^n$ and we seek a value of θ in Θ which is

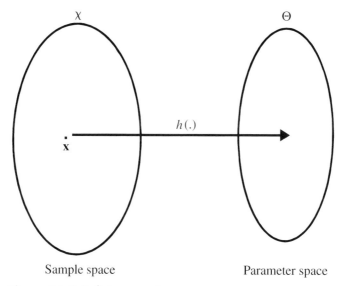

Sample space   Parameter space

Figure 11.2 Defining an estimator

(somehow) best supported by the sample realization **x**. In order to take into account the fact that **x** represents just one point in X, we define a rule which (hopefully) chooses the most representative value of θ in Θ as a mapping from X to Θ:

$$h(.): X \rightarrow \Theta.$$

This mapping, denoted by $\hat{\theta} = h(X_1, X_2, \ldots, X_n)$, is referred to as an **estimator** of θ; see figure 11.2. The particular value taken by this estimator based on the sample realization $\mathbf{X} = \mathbf{x}$ is referred to as an **estimate**:

$$\hat{\theta} = h(\mathbf{x}).$$

NOTE that we use the same symbol $\hat{\theta}$ to denote both the estimator, which is a function, and its value, which is just a number. When $\hat{\theta}$ is used without the right hand side, the meaning should be obvious from the context.

Example

It was shown above that in the Bernoulli model:

$$\theta = E(X).$$

This suggests that an obvious choice of an estimator of θ is the sample mean:

$$\hat{\theta} = \frac{1}{n} \Sigma_{i=1}^{n} X_i.$$

In chapter 13 we argue that this intuition can be used in a more general context in order to define estimators.

The estimator $\hat{\theta} = \frac{1}{n}\sum_{i=1}^{n} X_i$, being a function of the random variables $\mathbf{X} := (X_1, X_2, \ldots, X_n)$, **is a random variable itself**, and the estimate is just one of the many values $\hat{\theta}$ could have taken. In the case of the above Bernoulli example for each sample realization, say $\mathbf{x}^{(i)}$, $i = 1, 2, \ldots$ there is a different estimate, say:

$$\hat{\theta}^{(1)} = 0.40, \ \hat{\theta}^{(2)} = 0.55, \ \hat{\theta}^{(3)} = 0.45, \ \hat{\theta}^{(4)} = 0.50, \ \hat{\theta}^{(5)} = 0.35,$$

but all these are values of the same estimator $\hat{\theta} = h(\mathbf{X})$. That is, these are values taken by the random variable $\hat{\theta} = h(\mathbf{X})$ as specified by its sampling distribution, say $f(\hat{\theta})$. The latter gives all the possible values of $\hat{\theta} = h(\mathbf{X})$ along with the corresponding probabilities; see chapter 3 for the case of continuous random variables and the density function. The empirical counterpart to $f(\hat{\theta})$ can be fabricated by continuing the above process of getting additional sample realizations of $\mathbf{X}$ of size 30. Let us consider the (hypothetical) situation where the modeler can get N such size n sample realizations, say:

$$[\mathbf{x}^{(1)}, \mathbf{x}^{(2)}, \ldots, \mathbf{x}^{(N)}],$$

where N is large enough. These sample realizations would give rise to the corresponding estimates:

$$\hat{\theta}(k) = h(\mathbf{x}^{(k)}), \ k = 1, 2, \ldots, N,$$

whose histogram constitutes an empirical counterpart to $f(\hat{\theta})$; actually the smoothed histogram (see chapter 5) might provide a better approximation to $f(\hat{\theta})$. This simple idea has several ramifications which enables us to derive approximations for $f(\hat{\theta})$; two such approximating methods, the naive Monte Carlo and the Bootstrap, will be discussed in section 8.

This sampling distribution can be derived theoretically from the assumptions of the statistical model (assuming they are valid); see sections 6–7. The sampling distribution of $\hat{\theta}$ represents the different possible values of θ and the probabilities associated with these values. Hopefully, the true value θ_0 has a better chance of occurring on average, in the long-run as represented by the sampling distribution. In chapter 12 this notion of optimality will be formalized.

As we can see, interpreting the observed data as *one* of *many* different realizations of the sample, which is assumed to be *representative* of the chance mechanism from where the sample emanates, enables us to go beyond the data in hand and draw conclusions about the chance mechanism itself. This is so because once θ is given a numerical value (estimated), the chance mechanism as specified by the statistical model chosen a priori, becomes its idealized description of the phenomenon in question.

Defining a *single valued function* $h(.): \mathcal{X} \rightarrow \Theta$ of the form:

$$\hat{\theta} = h(X_1, X_2, \ldots, X_n),$$

is said to be the **point estimation**. Another form of estimation is **region estimation** which amounts to specifying a multi-valued function which defines a region in Θ (see figure 11.3).

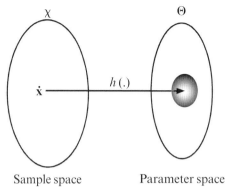

Sample space   Parameter space

Figure 11.3 Defining a region estimator

Example
In the case of the Bernoulli model we might be interested in specifying an *interval estima-tor* of θ which hopefully includes the true value of θ, say θ_0. This amounts to specifying an interval:

$$(\hat{\theta}_l, \hat{\theta}_u),$$

where $\hat{\theta}_l = h_1(\mathbf{X})$ and $\hat{\theta}_u = h_2(\mathbf{X})$ are two mappings from X to Θ, such that θ_0 is captured within this interval with a high probability, say 95 percent, i.e.

$$\mathbb{P}(\hat{\theta}_l \leq \theta_0 \leq \hat{\theta}_u) = 0.95.$$

Given that the two bounds $\hat{\theta}_l$ and $\hat{\theta}_u$ are mappings from X to Θ, they represent random variables (being functions of the sample $\mathbf{X}$). The above probabilistic statement says that in a long-run sequence of sample realizations, the intervals defined by $(\hat{\theta}_l, \hat{\theta}_u)$ are likely to include the true value of θ, 95 percent of the time. In any one sample realization, however, it is not known whether the interval includes θ_0 or not.

11.2.4 Hypothesis testing

Another form of statistical inference relates to testing hypotheses of interest about θ such as:

(a) $\theta = 0.5$,   (b) $\theta \geq 0.8$,   (c) $\theta \leq 0.7$.

As we can see, all these hypotheses define subsets of the parameter space $\Theta := [0,1]$ and our task is to construct a test which enables us to decide whether the hypothesis that the true θ belongs to this subset, say $\Theta_0 \subset \Theta$, is supported by the data.

A Neyman–Pearson test   A Neyman–Pearson test constitutes a *decision rule* which enables one to decide whether the observed sample realization $(x_1, x_2, \ldots, x_n)$ leads to the decision that $\theta \in \Theta_0$ or $\theta \in \Theta_1 := \Theta - \Theta_0$.
   In terms of the observation and parameter spaces this amounts to specifying a

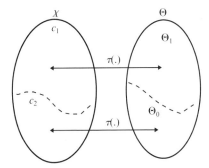

Figure 11.4 Defining a Neyman–Pearson test

mapping $\tau(.)$ which divides the observation space X into two sub-sets C_0 and C_1 which correspond to Θ_0 and Θ_1, respectively (see figure 11.4).

The mapping $\tau(.)$ is also a function of the sample **X** and thus any probabilistic statements relating to the hypothesis in question will be based on its *sampling distribution*. Given that we can never be sure that the decision taken on the basis of a particular sample is correct or not, we would like to make probabilistic statements about whether in a long-run sequence of trials we are likely to make the correct decision to accept or reject the hypothesis in question with high probability or not.

11.2.5 Prediction (or forecasting)

Prediction (or forecasting) is concerned with specifying appropriate functions of the sample $X_1, X_2, \ldots, X_n$ which enable us to predict beyond the data in hand such as the observation of X at $n+1$, denoted by X_{n+1}. That is, define an optimal function $q(.)$ such that:

$$\hat{X}_{n+1} = q(X_1, X_2, \ldots, X_n).$$

A natural choice of the function $q(.)$, which is optimal in a mean square sense is the conditional expectation of X_{n+1} given $X_1, X_2, \ldots, X_n$. As shown in chapter 7 the only function $q(X)$ which minimizes the mean of the squared error:

$$E\{X_{n+1} - q(X)\}^2,$$

is none other than the conditional expectation:

$$q(\mathbf{X}) = E(X_{n+1} | X_1, X_2, \ldots, X_n).$$

Example
In the case of the Bernoulli model the obvious way to derive the predictor of X_{n+1} is to utilize the statistical GM (see chapter 7) which is indeed based on such a conditional expectation. From the statistical GM we can see that the best way to predict X_{n+1} is to extend it beyond the sample period, i.e., postulate:

$$X_{n+1} = \theta + u_{n+1}.$$

Given that θ is unknown and $E(u_{n+1}) = 0$ the natural predictor is $\hat{X}_{n+1} = \hat{\theta}$. In this sense the mapping $q(.)$ is a composite mapping from X to Θ and then from Θ to the prediction space by X_p:

$$q(h(.)): X \to \Theta \to X_p.$$

From this we can see that $q(\mathbf{X})$ is also a random variable whose sampling distribution depends on that of $\hat{\theta}$. Hence, any probabilistic statements about the accuracy of $\hat{X}_{n+1}$ will be based on the sampling distribution of $\hat{\theta}$.

We conclude this section by reiterating that classical procedures of statistical inference are constructed and assessed through the idea of a sampling distribution.

11.3 The classical versus the Bayesian approach

The purpose of this section is to present very briefly the *Bayesian approach*, and contrast it to the classical approach to statistical inference; for a more detailed and (possibly) more balanced comparison between these two approaches see Poirier (1995). For completeness we also mention the approach which straddles these two approaches and is known as the *decision theoretic approach*.

As argued by Barnett (1982) the various approaches to statistical inference can be usefully classified using three primary issues:

(a)   the interpretation of *probability*,
(b)   what constitutes *relevant information* for statistical inference purposes, and
(c)   whether the role of statistics is *inferential* or/and *prescriptive* (decision-making).

11.3.1 The classical (frequency) approach

The classical approach is the approach adopted in this book and it will be discussed extensively in the next several chapters. For comparison with other approaches, however, we will discuss the classical approach very briefly with regard to the above primary issues.

(a)   The interpretation of probability underlying this approach to statistical inference is the *frequency interpretation* discussed extensively in the previous chapter.
(b)   In the context of the frequency interpretation of probability the observed data constitute the *only relevant information.*
(c)   The classical approach as shaped by Fisher is primarily inferential in nature but the dimension added by Neyman and Pearson is prescriptive.

Classical statistical inference begins with the modeler postulating a *statistical model*:

$$S: = (\Phi, \mathbf{X}_{(n)}),$$

where $\Phi = \{f(x;\theta), \theta \in \Theta, x \in \mathbb{R}_X\}$ denotes the *probability model* and $\mathbf{X}_{(n)}: = (X_1, X_2, \ldots, X_n)$ the *sampling model*, as defined in the previous chapters.

In the context of the classical approach the modeler interprets the observed data $\mathbf{x}: = (x_1, x_2, \ldots, x_n)$ as a particular *realization* of the stochastic mechanism represented by the specified statistical model. In particular the observations are viewed as specific values taken by the random variables making up the sample in question. This, in effect, provides the basis for the inductive argument with respect to which statistical inference differs from descriptive statistics. This interpretation leads naturally to statistical inference procedures which emphasize, *long-run behavior* under essentially similar circumstances.

11.3.2 The Bayesian approach

In order to avoid any misleading impressions we note at the outset that there are more versions of Bayesianism than ice-cream flavors! In this section we discuss some of the elements of the Bayesian approach which are shared by most versions of Bayesianism.

(a) The Bayesian approach to statistical inference adopts the degrees of belief interpretation of probability. The dominating version adopts the degrees of subjective (or personal) beliefs interpretation (see Bernado and Smith (1994)).

(b) In the context of the Bayesian approach, relevant information includes:
  (i)   the observed data and
  (ii) the prior beliefs relating to the distribution of $\boldsymbol{\theta}$.
  Moreover, the observed data constitute a unique outcome of a unique experiment, not one of many possible realizations.

(c) The Bayesian approach is primarily inferential in nature.

In view of the above degrees of subjective beliefs interpretation, it should come as no surprise to learn that the statistical inference procedures suggested by this interpretation emphasize *the revision of prior beliefs in view of the observed data*. That is, the primary role of the data is to revise the personal prior beliefs related to the values of θ in the parameter space Θ.

The prior beliefs are initially represented by the prior density (weighting) function:

$$\pi(.): \Theta \rightarrow [0,1],$$

which represents the modeler's assessment of how likely the various values of θ in Θ are a priori. For example if the modeler believes that $\theta = 0.1$ is less likely than $\theta = 0.5$ she should attach a higher density (weight) to the latter.

Using the information in the sample as summarized by the joint distribution of the sample $\mathbf{X}_{(n)} := (X_1, X_2, \ldots, X_n)$, denoted by $f(\mathbf{x}; \boldsymbol{\theta})$, the prior is revised to derive the *posterior*, denoted by $\varpi(\theta | \mathbf{x})$, via **Bayes' formula**:

$$\varpi(\theta | \mathbf{x}) = \frac{\pi(\boldsymbol{\theta}) \cdot f(\mathbf{x}; \boldsymbol{\theta})}{\int f(\mathbf{x}; \boldsymbol{\theta}) d\boldsymbol{\theta}}$$

Since the denominator does not depend on $\boldsymbol{\theta}$ we can consider it as a constant and express the above as a proportionality relationship of the form:

$$\varpi(\theta | \mathbf{x}) \propto \pi(\boldsymbol{\theta}) \cdot f(\mathbf{x}; \boldsymbol{\theta}),$$

where $\propto$ denotes proportionality. This procedure is summarized in figure 11.5.

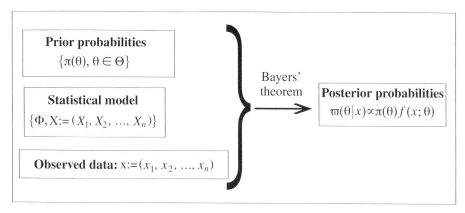

Figure 11.5 The Bayesian approach

11.3.3 The decision theoretic approach in a nutshell

The purpose of statistical inference as formalized by R. A. Fisher has always been inferential. Beginning with Neyman and Pearson (1928a,b,1933a,b), however, another dimension had been added: the decision theoretic dimension. As argued in chapter 14, the purpose of a Neyman–Pearson test is to decide whether to accept or reject a hypothesis concerning θ. This dimension was later extended and formalized by Wald (1950) by adding:

(i)   a set of possible actions and
(ii) a weighting (utility) function which assesses the gains and losses which would arise from different actions in different circumstances.

(a)   The interpretation of probability underlying this approach to statistical inference can be either the *frequency interpretation* or the *degrees of belief* interpretation of probability. The latter is used especially when a priori information relating to θ is utilized.
(b)   The relevant information in the context of the decision theoretical approach includes not only the sample information and any a priori information on θ, but also includes all consequential losses or gains that relate to the decision under consideration.
(c)   The decision theoretic approach as shaped by Wald, as the name suggests, is primarily decision oriented.

11.4 Experimental versus observational data

As argued in chapter 1, an important consideration in the statistical analysis of observed data is whether the modeler has an active role in the determination of the numerical values of some of the variables being measured. At one extreme we have the case where the modeler, working in the controlled environment of a laboratory, controls the environment and some of the factors (we call the inputs) and traces their effects on the other factors (we call outputs), establishing a causal relationship between inputs and outputs. At the other extreme we have the observational data where the modeler has no influence whatsoever, on the determination of the values of any of the variables involved (input and output). These often come in the form of historical data gathered by some agency which usually has nothing to do with the modeler.

11.4.1 Experimental data

Since the early 17th century, after Galileo's experiment of rolling balls down inclined planes of various heights (to confirm the law of falling bodies), the *experimental method* in conjunction with *causal explanation*, had been gaining ground to become almost synonymous to the method of science by the early twentieth century. The data from experiments which are performed on ideal substances and where the modeler has total control over all possible influences, do not usually require statistical analysis. More often than not, they reveal *the causal relationship* in question by mathematical approximation techniques. The majority of experiments in modern physics and chemistry, which take place in laboratories, belong to this category. The aim of such experiments is to isolate some aspects of a certain phenomenon of interest and by manipulating some of the factors, we call *inputs*, trace their effects on other magnitudes we call *outputs*, establishing a causal relationship between inputs and outputs. The key to a valid experiment is the *isolation* of the phenomenon of interest from any other (uncontrolled) influences. Such uncontrolled factors can influence the inputs, the outputs, as well as the environment in the context of which the experiment takes place. If this isolation cannot be achieved, the experiment is badly designed and the conclusions based on the resulting data can be very misleading. In order to minimize the possibility of uncontrolled influences, most experiments in physics, chemistry, and biomedical sciences take place in the controlled environment of a laboratory.

In a number of fields, such as biology and agriculture, it is not always possible to perform experiments in such a completely controlled environment. Consider the example of assessing the effect of a new fertilizer on yield; by controlling the input (amount of fertilizer applied) the modeler wants to establish a causal relationship between this input and the output: the crop yield. The experiment is likely to take place in a field where a number of factors that might influence the crop yield, such as rainfall, sunshine, quality of soil, cannot be completely controlled. As the modeler moves away from purified substances and cases where complete control is possible, a number of techniques, such as *randomization*, have been designed to neutralize the effects outside the modeler's control. In other words, the modeler purports to achieve *isolation* not by direct control but by other means. Techniques such as *randomization*, *blocking* and *replication* constitute powerful tools for the statistical analysis of data from such experiments developed in the first half of the 20th century. The father of modern experimental design techniques is R. A. Fisher whose monograph in 1935, entitled *The Design of Experiments*, established the field as a legitimate branch of statistics; the efforts to analyze data from such experiments go back to the German tradition in agricultural experiments in the early 19th century (see Gigerenzer *et al.* (1989)). To this early German tradition we can trace the crucial insight that the experimental design and the proper method for analyzing the resulting data are inextricably bound up. This insight is best encapsulated in Fisher's view that:

> To understand one aspect of the problem is to understand the other. Statistical procedure and experimental design are only two different aspects of the same whole, and that whole comprises all the logical requirements of the complete process of adding to natural knowledge by experimentation...
>
> (Fisher (1935), p. 3)

This suggests that the statistical model specification and the design of the experiment are the two sides of the same coin. The design purports to isolate the causal relationship between inputs and outputs and what is beyond the control of the experimenter should be non-systematic; often a white-noise error. In cases where the residuals from the estimated statistical model exhibit systematic information, chances are that the design has ignored certain influences which cannot be assumed away. The next step is to redesign the experiment in order to account for or at least neutralize these systematic effects.

The idea of experiments where the modeler does not have complete control over the environment, such as the one above, led eventually to experimental designs where the *environment* in the context of which the study takes place is not under the direct control of the modeler.

11.4.2 Sample survey data

In some fields where the design of controlled experiments is not possible, but the modeler is facing a fixed population of study units, several techniques of **survey sampling** have been developed. The design of laboratory experiments purports to isolate the phenomenon of interest by controlling or neutralizing all the factors involved. The design of surveys purports to isolate the phenomenon of interest by accounting for all influencing factors using a carefully designed sample survey. This entails the careful selection of the units to be sampled as well as the information to be collected.

The most widely used sample surveys are those relating to the voting intentions of a certain cohort of voters. The ideal experiment in this case is to have the voters vote twice, once for the pollsters and one for real. Of course one cannot ask the whole population of voters to register their intentions before the polling day and instead a sample survey is designed to cover only a small proportion of the voting population. For this sample survey to be reliable, however, the modeler has to choose the subset of the voting population carefully so as to be representative of the population. The survey designer will account for the different factors which influence voting intentions by carefully selecting the subset of voters to be asked and designing the questionnaire appropriately. The discussion of how one can design an effective questionnaire will take us well beyond the scope of this book but it is instructive to mention briefly some of the methods used to select the subset of voters in the context of sample survey data.

Stratified sampling This method of sampling is useful in cases where there is a priori information relating to the heterogeneity of the target population from one group to another; the elements of each group are roughly homogeneous. In order to utilize this heterogeneity information to improve the accuracy of the results, the modeler divides the population into these heterogeneous groups (strata) and proceeds to collect data from each stratum using random sampling; hence the name stratified sampling. It can be shown that the accuracy of the estimated mean for the population, as estimated by its variance, increases with the difference in the means between strata.

Cluster sampling This method of sampling is useful in cases where the target population is naturally divided into clusters and we need to economize on the cost of sampling. A way to do that is to draw a random sample of clusters first and then proceed to collect the data using random samples whose size reflects the proportion of the population represented by the cluster in question. For example, for a household consumption survey of the USA instead of drawing a random sample of, say, 5000 households from the whole of the USA by random sampling, one might draw a random sample of 100 counties first and then proceed to sample these proportionately to their population using random sampling.

Quota sampling This is a popular method for public-opinion polls in which the interviewer is instructed to poll a pre-specified quota of people with certain specific characteristics such as sex, age, income, etc. The aim in this case is to try to account for the factors influencing the decision, ignoring the randomness of the sample. This method can introduce all kind of unknown biases into the analysis of the data.

From the point of view of the statistical analysis of these data it is important to emphasize that the statistical model to be used for the analysis of the sample survey data is decided at the time of the survey design. In this sense, survey data are similar to experimental data where the statistical model specification and the design of the experiment are the two sides of the same coin. As mentioned above, the modeler aims at isolating the relationship between inputs and outputs by accounting for all influencing factors using a carefully designed sample survey. If the isolation is effective, what is not accounted for by the survey should be non-systematic. The relationship purports to be causal but establishing causality with sample survey data is considerably more difficult than in the context of a laboratory controlled environment. In cases where the residuals from the estimated statistical model exhibit systematic information the chances are that not all influencing factors have been accounted for.

The terminology developed for sample survey data analysis in the 1930s and 1940s was bequeathed to statistical inference in general. The term *population* was first introduced in the context of sample surveys to mean "a set of units such as people, states, households, and government agencies, about which the modeler wants some information." The term *sampling* was first introduced in this context to mean selecting a subset of the target population. The term *random sample*, discussed extensively in chapters 4–10, was first developed in the context of survey sample data to mean selecting a subset of the target population in such a way so that every unit in the population has the same probability of being selected. Unfortunately, as argued in the next subsection, this terminology can be very misleading in the context of observational data and their analysis.

11.4.3 Observational data

By observational data we mean data whose collection does not interfere with the phenomenon being measured. The observer is passive in the sense that she cannot influence (in any way) the numerical values of the variables being observed. This is in contrast to experimental and sample survey data where the modeler has an active role to play in the determination of the numerical values involved.

The question that naturally arises at this stage is whether the above experimental design framework can be used in the case of observational data. Historically, one of the strengths of statistics has been the ease by which a technique developed in the context of one discipline could be transferred to other disciplines. However, as argued by Gigerenzer *et al.* (1989, p. 273):

The techniques could be compared to the Trojan horse, packed with assumptions about content and interpretation that may or may not be made explicit, and that may or may not fit the new context of application. But these assumptions and their consequences come to light only once they are already within the gates of the discipline...

As argued in Spanos (1995b) (see also chapter 1), a case can be made that the experimental design paradigm has influenced unduly the statistical analysis of observational data. Traditional econometrics can be viewed as a hybrid of the experimental design and the *theory of errors* tradition going back to Gauss. The problem with this hybrid is that both of these traditions are appropriate for modeling observed data emanating from *nearly isolated systems* by courtesy of the experimenter or nature. The theory of errors tradition was developed in the context of astronomy and geodesy (see Stigler (1986)) where nature often plays the role of the experimenter, such as the example of estimating Kepler's second law. It is worth emphasizing that in this case, if the observations on:

r – the distance of the planet from the sun and
ϑ – the angle between the line joining the sun and the planet and the principal axis of the ellipse

refer to a planet such as Venus, it will be very difficult to discern the elliptical motion because of the third body problem; Venus is close to the earth. On the other hand, for planets such as Jupiter or even Mars, whose distance from the next planet is substantial, discerning the elliptical motion will be much easier. In the former case nature is not as generous in isolating the phenomenon of interest: the planets' motion around the sun. In the latter case the isolation is almost as good as the one in a laboratory. Hence, for such data there is no problem utilizing methods developed in the context of experimental design. However, in the case of observational data, which cannot be viewed as emanating from a nearly isolated system, such methods of data analysis are often inappropriate.

Viewing observational data **as if** they represent measurements in the context of a controlled experiment can be very misleading indeed. First, the terminology *population* versus *sample* is inept. Calling a hypothetical population the underlying stochastic mechanism, does not change the fact that for observational data this terminology is inappropriate because it carries connotations of observing an isolated system. What is the hypothetical population when observing the gyrations of exchange rates? What we usually observe is some on-going process which cannot be isolated from the rest of the economic system, not a population from which we select a representative sample. Unfortunately, the term *sample* has been ingrained in the statistical literature and thus we retain it but redefine it to mean *a set of random variables with a specified probabilistic structure*. Second, specifying an appropriate statistical model by attaching white-noise error terms to a theoretical model is well-suited for experimental data but inappropriate for most forms of observational data. As argued above (see also Spanos (1995b)), in modeling *experimental data* the problem of choosing a statistical model is relatively simple and thus no explicit discussion of it is often encountered in statistics textbooks. In the next section, we argue that for observational data the process of statistical inference in traditional textbooks, including the problem of specification, needs to be modified.

11.5 Neglected facets of statistical inference

In section 2 we argued that the traditional facets of statistical inference, estimation, testing, and prediction, do not provide a complete picture of the classical approach to statistical modeling. In what follows we argue that these three facets of inference provide a misleading picture of statistical modeling in the case of observational data.

The father of modern statistics, R. A. Fisher, in his classic 1922a paper "On the mathematical foundations of theoretical statistics," defined the main purpose of statistics to be the *reduction* of a large quantity of data to a few numerical values (parameters); a reduction which adequately summarizes all the *relevant information* in the original data (ibid., p. 311, see also Fisher (1925a), pp. 5–6). He went on to classify the problems of statistics into three broad headings:

(i)   Specification – the choice of an appropriate statistical model,
(ii)   Estimation – the choice of statistics for estimating the unknown parameters, and
(iii)   Distributions – the derivation of the sampling distributions of the statistics in (ii).

REMARK: Fisher classified hypothesis testing under estimation.

Of the three headings, the one which received the least attention since then is that of specification. Statistical inference (and modeling) pays little attention to the question of how a statistical model should be chosen. This attitude is aptly caricatured by Dawid (1982) as quoted by Lehmann (1990):

Where do probability models come from? To judge by the resounding silence over this question on the part of most statisticians, it seems highly embarrassing. In general, the theoretician is happy to accept that his abstract probability triple $(S, \Im, \mathbb{P}(.))$ was found under a gooseberry bush, while the applied statistician's model "just growed"…

On the issue of specification Fisher (1925a, p. 8) explained that:

This is not arbitrary, but requires an understanding of the way in which the data are supposed to, or did in fact, originate. Its further discussion depends on such fields as the theory of Sample Survey, or that of Experimental Design.

The main reason why the problem of specification received little attention is that the theory of modeling confined itself to sample survey and experimental design data. The purpose of this section is to provide an introduction to statistical model specification in the case of *observational data*, retaining the spirit of Fisher's view that the principal task of statistics is *the reduction of data*.

Another aspect of modeling that received relatively little attention is that of statistical adequacy. Under the heading problems of distribution, Fisher raises the problem of testing the *adequacy* of the specification (the postulated statistical model):

(iii) Problems of Distribution include the mathematical deduction of the exact nature of the distribution in random samples of our estimates of the parameters and other statistics designed to test the validity of our specification (test of Goodness of Fit)...

(Fisher (1925a), p. 8)

In this book we consider the issue of statistical adequacy of paramount importance and consider this aspect of modeling as a crucial component of specification.

Collecting the above arguments together we argue that the classical approach to statistical inference comprises the following stages:

(1) Specification, ⎫
(2) Estimation, ⎪
(3) Misspecification, ⎬ Statistically adequate model
(4) Respecification, ⎭
(5) Testing, confidence regions,
(6) Prediction.

11.5.1 Specification

The first stage in classical statistical inference is referred to as **specification**:

> postulating an appropriate statistical model for the data in question.

That is, in view of the observed data and the theoretical question of interest we proceed to choose what we consider the appropriate statistical model. This facet of modeling is crucial not only for observational data but for any type of data because an inappropriate choice at this stage will undermine the rest of the statistical inference results.

To see this consider the simplest case of sample survey data where the data refer to voting intentions, i.e., answers to the question:

> Will you vote for the Republican (R) or the Democratic (D) candidate in the next election?

Given that there are only two answers, R and D, we can define the random variable $X(R) = 0$ and $X(D) = 1$ which suggests that the Bernoulli model, as specified in section 2, might be an appropriate statistical model. For reference purposes it is instructive to note the assumptions underlying **the Bernoulli model**:

(D)   Distribution: Bernoulli,
(M)   Dependence: Independent,
(H)   Heterogeneity: Identical Distribution.

11.5.2 Misspecification

Given the importance of ensuring that the statistical model postulated is adequate for the data in question, it is only natural that we should test the assumptions underlying the model to ensure that our choice is indeed appropriate. **Misspecification testing** is concerned with testing the validity of the underlying assumptions of the postulated statistical model. If any of the assumptions underlying the statistical model of our choice are invalid for the data in question, the statistical inference results derived on the assumption that the model is adequate will be, in general, invalid. How to test the adequacy of the various probabilistic assumptions underlying the statistical model will be discussed in chapter 15.

Let us return to the Bernoulli model postulated above to discuss the question of statistical adequacy at an informal and intuitive level. *Under what circumstances would this model be an appropriate choice?* Given that by definition the random variable takes only two values the assumption of the Bernoulli distribution needs no justification but the other two assumptions of *Independence* and *Identical Distribution* need to be assessed and their validity established. As mentioned above a random sample in sample survey data corresponds to a case where the sample of people asked was selected from the population of potential voters in a way which *gives every voter the same chance of being asked*. For example, in the case where the election is for the next president of the USA but the people asked came from the same town it cannot be called a random sample. Similarly, if people were asked by dialing telephone numbers generated by a random number generator, it cannot be a random sample because this excludes people without phones. In the same way if we ask more than one person in each family we might introduce dependence because it is likely that people in the same family might influence each other's voting intentions.

Taking the argument a bit further, it might be reasonable to assume that different states often have different voting patterns (heterogeneity). In the case where there exists heterogeneity of voting intentions among states, the above statistical model is likely to be inappropriate because it does not utilize the systematic information that voting intentions are different among States.

11.5.3 Respecification

What does the modeler do in the case where the postulated model turns out to be statistically inadequate? The modeler has to **respecify**: choose another (hopefully) more appropriate statistical model. For instance, in the case of the above example, we need to respecify in order to allow for the heterogeneity of the sample in the sense that different States have different voting patterns (θ is different from state to state). As argued in the previous section, this entails two things. First, the modeler has to change the original Bernoulli model to a **non-homogeneous Bernoulli model**:

[i] Statistical GM: $X_{ik} = \theta_k + u_{ik}$, $k = 1,2,\ldots,N$, $i \in \mathbb{N}$,

[ii] Probability model
$$\Phi_k = \{f(x_k;\theta_k) = \theta_k^{x_k}(1-\theta_k)^{1-x_k},\ 0 \le \theta \le 1,\ x_k = 0,1,\ k = 1,2,\ldots,N\},$$

[iii] Sampling model: $\mathbf{X}_{(n)} := (X_1,X_2,\ldots,X_n)$, $n = \sum_{k=1}^{N} n_k$, an independent sample.   (11.2)

Second, the *random sampling* technique has to be replaced by *stratified sampling*: divide the voting population into strata and use random sampling within each stratum (State) (see above). For accurate results the modeler has to ensure that each sample size n_k is large enough and it contains a reasonable number of observations from each State so we can estimate each θ_k adequately.

The above discussion pinpoints potential problems when modelers go ahead and postulate statistical models without worrying about their validity. Choosing an **adequate statistical model** (appropriate *specification*) is the most important stage in statistical inference and often the most difficult. This is because such decisions cannot be based on prescribed recipes but have to be decided by the modeler on the basis of the question of interest and the particular data set in question.

11.6 Sampling distributions

The problem of establishing the sampling distributions of estimators and tests was considered by Fisher as one of the three basic facets of statistical inference, the other two being *specification* and *estimation*, as follows:

(iii) Problems of Distribution include the mathematical deduction of the exact nature of the distributions in random samples of our estimates of the parameters...

(Fisher (1925b), p. 8)

By definition, an estimator $\hat{\theta} = h(X_1,X_2,\ldots,X_n) := h(\mathbf{X})$ is just a function:
$$Y = h(X_1,X_2,\ldots,X_n),$$

of the random variables making up the sample. In theory its distribution can be derived, using the (joint) **distribution of the sample** $D(x_1,\ldots,x_n;\theta)$, by way of the following relationship:

$$F(\hat{\theta};\mathbf{x}) = \mathbb{P}(h(X_1,\ldots,X_n) \le \theta) = \overbrace{\int\int\cdots\int}^{n\ times}_{\{(x_1,\ldots,x_n):h(x_1,\ldots,x_n)\le\theta\}} D(x_1,\ldots,x_n;\theta)dx_1\ldots dx_n.$$
(11.3)

NOTE that the range of values over which the integration takes place is defined by:

$$\Theta(\mathbf{X}) := \{(x_1, \ldots, x_n) : h(x_1, \ldots, x_n) \leq \theta,\ \theta \in \Theta\}.$$

The distribution of a statistic $h(\mathbf{X})$ is called a **sampling distribution**, with its cdf and density functions denoted by $F(\hat{\theta}; \mathbf{x})$, $f(\hat{\theta}; \mathbf{x})$ to emphasize its dependence on the sample.

The relationship (11.3) suggests that to derive $F(\hat{\theta}; \mathbf{x})$ we need first to determine the distribution of the sample. The latter is determined by the form of the postulated probability and sampling models.

Example 1 Bernoulli
In the case of the simple Bernoulli model, we assume that the sample $(X_1, X_2, \ldots, X_n)$ constitutes a set of Independent and Identically Distributed (IID) Bernoulli random variables. This information implies that:

$$D(x_1, x_2, \ldots, x_n; \theta) = \prod_{i=1}^{n} f(x_i; \theta) = \prod_{i=1}^{n} \theta^{x_i}(1-\theta)^{1-x_i},$$

where the first equality follows from the IID (random sample) assumptions and the second utilizes the information specified by the probability model. Hence, the form of the distribution of the sample is:

$$D(x_1, x_2, \ldots, x_n; \theta) = \theta^{\sum_{i=1}^{n} x_i}(1-\theta)^{\sum_{i=1}^{n}(1-x_i)}.$$

Example 2 Normal
Similarly, the distribution of the sample for the Normal (one parameter) model is:

$$D(x_1, x_2, \ldots, x_n; \theta) = \prod_{i=1}^{n} f(x_i; \mu) = \prod_{i=1}^{n} \frac{1}{\sqrt{2\pi}} \exp\left\{-\tfrac{1}{2}(x_i - \mu)^2\right\} =$$

$$= \left(\frac{1}{\sqrt{2\pi}}\right)^n \exp\left\{-\tfrac{1}{2}\sum_{i=1}^{n}(x_i - \mu)^2\right\}.$$

Having specified the distribution of the sample utilizing the assumptions of the postulated statistical model, we can proceed to derive the distribution of the function $\hat{\theta} = h(X_1, X_2, \ldots, X_n)$ using (11.3). It is well known in mathematics that multiple integrals (or summations) are difficult to handle at the best of times. In order to get some idea about the difficulties involved, let us consider the derivation of sampling distributions in the case of two simple models, the Bernoulli and Normal models.

11.6.1 The Bernoulli model and related sampling distributions

In this subsection we assume that the underlying model is the **Bernoulli**, as specified above. Let us consider derivation of the distribution of the function:

$$\hat{\theta} := h(\mathbf{X}) = \sum_{i=1}^{n} X_i,$$

First, we need to determine the range of values of this function. Given that the random variables $(X_1, X_2, \ldots, X_n)$ take only two values 0 and 1, the range $h(\mathbf{X}) = \sum_{i=1}^{n} X_i$

is $\Theta(\mathbf{X}) := \{0,1,2,\ldots,n\}$ (ensure you understand why). The formula in (11.3) suggests summing the joint density:

$$D(x_1,x_2,\ldots,x_n;\theta) = \theta^{\sum_{i=1}^{n} x_i}(1-\theta)^{\sum_{i=1}^{n}(1-x_i)},$$

for all the values of $h(\mathbf{X})$ in $\Theta(\mathbf{X})$. To understand what this entails let us consider a heuristic derivation of the distribution for a particular value of $h(\mathbf{X})$, say $h(\mathbf{x}) = 3$ and $n = 4$. One way to get $h(\mathbf{x}) = 3$ in 4 trials is to get one zero first and then three ones, i.e.

$$\mathbf{x} := (x_1,x_2,x_3,x_4) = (0,1,1,1).$$

the probability of this event is:

$$f(x_1,x_2,x_3,x_4;\theta) = \theta^3(1-\theta),$$

because:

$$\mathbb{P}(X_i=1) = \theta, \ \mathbb{P}(X_i=0) = 1-\theta \text{ for } i = 1,2,3,4,$$

and the random variables X_1, X_2, X_3, X_4 are independent, implying that:

$$f(x_1,x_2,x_3,x_4;\theta) = \mathbb{P}(X_1=0) \cdot P(X_2=1) \cdot \mathbb{P}(X_3=1) \cdot \mathbb{P}(X_4=1).$$

The value $h(\mathbf{x}) = 3$, however, arises in three other orderings of zeros and ones:

$$(x_1,x_2,x_3,x_4) = (1,0,1,1), \ (x_1,x_2,x_3,x_4) = (1,1,0,1), \ (x_1,x_2,x_3,x_4) = (1,1,1,0).$$

In view of (11.3), we need to add all the probabilities associated with the value $h(\mathbf{x}) = 3$. Hence, the probability of the random variable $h(\mathbf{X})$ taking the value 3 is:

$$f(h(\mathbf{x}) = 3) = 4\theta^3(1-\theta).$$

In general, the probability of $h(\mathbf{X})$ taking the value k, in n trials takes the form:

$$f(h(\mathbf{x}) = k) = \binom{n}{k}\theta^k(1-\theta)^{n-k}, \ k = 0,1,2,\ldots,n,$$

where $\binom{n}{k} = \frac{n!}{k!(n-k)!}$ (NOTE: $4! = 4\cdot 3\cdot 2\cdot 1$) denotes the number of different orderings of k ones and $n-k$ zeros (see Feller (1968) for a discussion of combinatorics). This suggests that the sampling distribution of $h(\mathbf{X}) = \sum_{i=1}^{n} X_i$ is an (n-trial) Binomial with mean $n\theta$ and variance $n\theta(1-\theta)$:

$$\sum_{i=1}^{n} X_i \sim \mathsf{Bi}(n\theta,n\theta(1-\theta);n).$$

This result is particularly important in statistical inference and for reference purposes we state it as a lemma. We will collect the most important results in connection with this and other simple statistical models, such as the Normal, in a collection of lemmas.

Lemma 1
If $X_1,X_2,\ldots,X_n$ are Independent and Identically Distributed (IID) Bernoulli distributed random variables with parameter θ, i.e.:

$$X_k \sim \mathsf{Bi}(\theta,\theta(1-\theta);1), \ k = 1,2,\ldots,n,$$

then the function $Y_n = \Sigma_{k=1}^n X_k$ is Binomially distributed with parameter θ:

$$\sum_{k=1}^n X_k \sim \mathrm{Bi}(n\theta, n\theta(1-\theta); n).$$

11.6.2 The Normal model and related sampling distributions

A very important statistical model is the simple Normal model. Initially we will consider the simplest form of this model, the **Normal** (one parameter) **statistical model**:

[i] Statistical GM: $X_i = \mu + \varepsilon_i$, $i \in \mathbb{N}$,
[ii] Probability model:

$$\Phi = \left\{ f(x;\theta) = \tfrac{1}{\sqrt{2\pi}} \exp\left\{-\tfrac{1}{2}(x-\mu)^2\right\}, \theta := \mu \in \mathbb{R}, x \in \mathbb{R} \right\},$$

[iii] Sampling model: $\mathbf{X} := (X_1, X_2, \ldots X_n)$ is a random sample. (11.4)

In the case of the Normal (one-parameter) model, deriving the distribution of

$$h(\mathbf{X}) = \Sigma_{i=1}^n X_i,$$

via (11.3) turns out to be considerably more involved than that of the Bernoulli model.

To give the reader a taste of what such derivations entail, let us consider the simplest case where $n = 2$, i.e., derive the distribution of $Z = X_1 + X_2$. From the results in the next section we know that the density function of Z takes the general form:

$$f(z;\mu) = \int_{-\infty}^{\infty} f(z - x_2, x_2; \mu) dx_2, \quad -\infty < z < \infty.$$

In the present case X_1 and X_2 are independent, and thus:

$$f(z;\mu) = \int_{-\infty}^{\infty} f_1(z - x_2; \mu) \cdot f_2(x_2; \mu) dx_2, \quad -\infty < z < \infty,$$

where $f_1(.)$ and $f_2(.)$ denote the marginal distributions of X_1 and X_2, respectively. Using the normality of these densities we can deduce that:

$$f(z;\mu) = \int_{-\infty}^{\infty} \left[\tfrac{1}{\sqrt{2\pi}} \exp\left\{-\tfrac{1}{2}(z - x_2 - \mu)^2\right\} \right] \left[\tfrac{1}{\sqrt{2\pi}} \exp\left\{-\tfrac{1}{2}(x_2 - \mu)^2\right\} \right] dx_2,$$

$$f(z;\mu) = \int_{-\infty}^{\infty} \tfrac{1}{2\pi} \exp\left\{-\tfrac{1}{2}[(z - x_2 - \mu)^2 + (x_2 - \mu)^2]\right\} dx_2 \quad -\infty < z < \infty.$$

After some algebraic manipulations we can express this in the form:

$$f(z;\mu) = \left(\tfrac{(\sqrt{2})^{-1}}{\sqrt{2\pi}} \exp\left\{-\tfrac{1}{4}(z - \mu)^2\right\} \right) \int_{-\infty}^{\infty} \tfrac{\sqrt{2}}{\sqrt{2\pi}} \exp\left\{-\tfrac{1}{2}\left[\sqrt{2}\left(x_2 - \tfrac{1}{2}z\right)\right]^2\right\} dx_2,$$

which reduces to: $f(z;\mu) = \left(\tfrac{1}{\sqrt{2}}\right) \tfrac{1}{\sqrt{2\pi}} \exp\left\{-\tfrac{1}{2}\left(\tfrac{(z - 2\mu)}{\sqrt{2}}\right)^2\right\}$, $-\infty < z < \infty$,

because $\int_{-\infty}^{\infty} \left(\tfrac{1}{\sqrt{2\pi}} \sqrt{2} \exp\left\{-\tfrac{1}{2}\left[\sqrt{2}\left(x_2 - \tfrac{1}{2}z\right)\right]^2\right\} \right) dx_2 = 1$, being an integral of the form $\int_{-\infty}^{\infty} f(v) dv$, where $f(v)$ is the density of $N\left(\tfrac{1}{2}v, \tfrac{1}{2}\right)$. Looking at the formula for $f(z;\mu)$, we recognize the density function of $Z = X_1 + X_2$, to be:

$$(X_1 + X_2) \sim N(2\mu, 2).$$

This result can be extended to the case of any n, but the derivation of the distribution of $\sum_{i=1}^{n} X_i$ is much more complicated. We state the result, however, that for IID normal random variables:

$$X_i \sim N(\mu, 1), \; i = 1, 2, \ldots, n,$$

$$\sum_{i=1}^{n} X_i \sim N(n\mu, n).$$

This is a special case of a more general result given in the following lemma.

Lemma 2
If $X_1, X_2, \ldots, X_n$ are Independent, Normally distributed random variables with parameters $\theta_k := (\mu_k, \sigma_k^2)$, i.e. non-identically distributed random variables:

$$X_k \sim N(\mu_k, \sigma_k^2), \; k = 1, 2, \ldots, n,$$

then the function $Y_n = \sum_{k=1}^{n} X_k$ is also Normally distributed:

$$\sum_{i=1}^{n} X_k \sim N(\sum_{k=1}^{n} \mu_k, \sum_{k=1}^{n} \sigma_k^2).$$

As mentioned above, distributional results for functions of the sample (such as estimators and test statistics) are at a premium. In practice, determining the sampling distribution of $\hat{\theta}$, when the distribution of the sample $(X_1, X_2, \ldots, X_n)$ is assumed known, can be a very difficult mathematical problem (see next section). Indeed, the distributional results known in this area are few and often relate to simple functions of distributions such as the Normal, the Binomial, and the Exponential. Because of this we summarize some of these results in the following lemmas.

Lemma 3
Let Z be a *Normally* distributed random variable:

$$Z \sim N(\mu, \sigma^2),$$

the function $Y = \exp(Z)$ is **log-Normally** distributed with mean $m = \exp\left\{\mu + \frac{1}{2}\sigma^2\right\}$ and variance $\tau^2 = \exp\{(2\mu + \sigma^2)(e^{\sigma^2} - 1)\}$:

$$\exp(Z) \sim \ln N(m, \tau^2).$$

Lemma 4
If $Z_1, Z_2, \ldots, Z_n$ are IID *Standard Normal* random variables:

$$Z_k \sim N(0, 1), \; k = 1, 2, \ldots, n,$$

then the function $V_n = \sum_{k=1}^{n} Z_k^2$ is **Chi-square** distributed with n degrees of freedom:

$$\sum_{k=1}^{n} Z_k^2 \sim \chi^2(n).$$

Lemma 5

If Z_1 and Z_2 are IID *Standard Normal* random variables:

$$Z_k \sim N(0,1), \ k = 1,2,$$

then the function $U = \frac{Z_1}{Z_2}$ is **Cauchy** distributed:

$$\frac{Z_1}{Z_2} \sim C(0,1).$$

Lemma 6

Let $X_k \sim N(\mu_k, \sigma_k^2)$, $k = 1,2,\ldots,n$, be independently distributed, then the function:

$$Y_n = \sum_{k=1}^{n} \left(\frac{X_k}{\sigma_k}\right)^2,$$

is distributed as **non-central Chi-square** with n degrees of freedom and non-centrality parameter $\delta = \sum_{k=1}^{n}(\mu_k/\sigma_k)^2$ (see Spanos (1986)):

$$\sum_{k=1}^{n}\left(\frac{X_k}{\sigma_k}\right)^2 \sim \chi^2(n;\delta).$$

Lemma 7

Let Z and V be two independent random variables of the form:

$$Z \sim N(0,1), \ V \sim \chi^2(m).$$

Then the ratio $\left(\frac{Z}{(V/m)}\right)$ is **Student's t** distributed with m degrees of freedom:

$$\frac{Z}{\sqrt{\left(\frac{V}{m}\right)}} \sim St(m).$$

Lemma 8

Let V_1 and V_2 be two independent *Chi-square* random variables with m_1 and m_2 degrees of freedom:

$$V_1 \sim \chi^2(m_1), \ V_2 \sim \chi^2(m_2).$$

(a) The ratio $U = \left(\frac{V_1/m_1}{V_2/m_2}\right)$ is **(Fisher's) F** distributed with m_1 and m_2 degrees of freedom:

$$\left(\frac{\frac{V_1}{m_1}}{\frac{V_2}{m_2}}\right) \sim F(m_1,m_2).$$

(b) The sum $V = V_1 + V_2$ is also chi-square distributed with $m = m_1 + m_2$ degrees of freedom:

$$(V_1 + V_2) \sim \chi^2(m_1 + m_2).$$

Lemma 9

Let X_1 and X_2 be two independent *Exponential* random variables with the same parameter θ:

$$X_1 \sim \text{Ex}(\theta), \ X_2 \sim \text{Ex}(\theta).$$

(a) The difference $Y = X_1 - X_2$ is **Laplace** distributed with parameters $(0,\theta)$:

$$(X_1 - X_2) \sim \text{Lp}(0,\theta).$$

(b) The sum $W = X_1 + X_2$ is **Gamma** distributed with parameters $(\theta,2)$:

$$(X_1 + X_2) \sim \text{Gamma}(\theta,2).$$

Lemma 10

If $Z_1, Z_2, \ldots, Z_n$ are Independent, *Binomially* distributed random variables:

$$Z_k \sim \text{Bi}(\theta, n_k), \ k = 1,2,\ldots,n,$$

then the function $Y_n = \sum_{k=1}^{n} Z_k$ is **Binomially** distributed:

$$\sum_{i=1}^{n} Z_k \sim \text{Bi}(\theta, \sum_{k=1}^{n} n_k).$$

As we can see, the above results are of limited value because they cover only simple functions of very few variables. The question which naturally arises at this stage is:

What do we do in cases where the distribution of $h(X_1, X_2, \ldots, X_n)$ is unknowable?

In such cases we have to rely on *approximate results*, as n goes to infinity, which we need to derive using limit theorems (see chapter 9).

11.6.3 Is there a systematic way to derive sampling distributions?

The brief answer to the question posed above is: No! However, the discussion relating to the derivation of sampling distributions in the previous two subsections might give a misleading impression of what is involved. The truth of the matter is that such results are difficult to derive but in some cases there are certain methods which can be utilized effectively. In the next section we provide an overview of a number of useful techniques.

11.7 Functions of random variables

This is a very important issue for both probability theory and statistical inference because we often find ourselves faced with functions of random variables whose distribution we need but we only know the distribution of the original variables. The thing to note at the outset is that *a Borel function of other random variables (random variables) is a random variable itself.*

REMARK: we remind the reader that a Borel function is one which is a random variable relative to the Borel-field $\mathcal{B}(\mathbb{R})$, i.e., a function of a random variable X, say $Y = h(X)$ is a Borel function if:

$$(h(X) \leq y) \in \mathcal{B}(\mathbb{R}) \text{ for all } y \in \mathbb{R};$$

see chapter 3 for more details.

11.7.1 Functions of one random variable

Consider the case where the distribution of the random variable X is known and we want to derive the distribution of the random variable Y:

$$Y = h(X), \text{ where } h(.): \mathbb{R}_X \rightarrow \mathbb{R}_Y \text{ is a Borel function.}$$

Discrete random variables.

In the case of discrete random variables, as shown in chapter 3, we can go directly to the density function and argue from first principles as follows:

$$f_y(y) = \mathbb{P}(Y = y) = \mathbb{P}(h(X) = y) = \sum_{\{x:h(x)=y\}} f_x(x), \, y \in \mathbb{R}_Y. \tag{11.5}$$

We first identify the range of values of the random variable Y; via $\mathbb{R}_Y = \{y:y=h(x), x \in \mathbb{R}_X\}$, and then proceed to evaluate the probabilities associated with each value y by adding together the probabilities of X associated with that value, i.e., $\{x:h(x)=y\}$.

Example

Consider the random variable X with a density function as given below and let $Y = X^2$. Let us derive the density function of Y.

x	-2	-1	0	1	2
$f_x(x)$	0.2	0.1	0.2	0.3	0.2

Since $\mathbb{R}_X := \{-2, -1, 0, 1, 2\}$ we can deduce that $\mathbb{R}_Y = \{0, 1, 4\}$. Using (11.5):

$$\mathbb{P}(Y=0) = \mathbb{P}(X=0) = 0.2,$$
$$\mathbb{P}(Y=1) = \mathbb{P}(X=-1) + \mathbb{P}(X=1) = 0.4,$$
$$\mathbb{P}(Y=4) = \mathbb{P}(X=-2) + \mathbb{P}(X=2) = 0.4$$

y	0	1	4
$f_Y(y)$	0.2	0.4	0.4

Continuous random variables

As shown in chapter 3, in the case of continuous random variables we cannot define the density function directly from first principles and instead we proceed using the *cumulative distribution function* (cdf). Thus, the cdf of Y takes the form:

$$F_Y(y) = \mathbb{P}(Y \leq y) = \mathbb{P}(h(X) \leq y), \, y \in \mathbb{R}_Y. \tag{11.6}$$

The problem, however, is how to determine the probability of events of the form:

$$(h(X) \le y), \ y \in \mathbb{R}_Y, \tag{11.7}$$

since they involve both random variables. The obvious solution is to transform the inequality $(h(X) \le y)$ into an inequality which involves the random variable X only.

Invertible $h(.)$ Intuitively, we can think of a way to solve this problem in the case where $h(.)$ has an *inverse* by transforming (11.7) into:

$$(X \le h^{-1}(y)), \ y \in \mathbb{R}_Y, \tag{11.8}$$

and then proceed to derive the distribution of Y by evaluating the probabilities of the events (11.8). These probabilities can be evaluated using $F_X(.)$:

$$F_Y(y) = F_X(h^{-1}(y)) = \mathbb{P}(X \le h^{-1}(y)), \ y \in \mathbb{R}_Y. \tag{11.9}$$

Although this intuitive argument is basically correct, this case is of limited value because for $h(.)$ to have an inverse it has to be a *bijection*: one-to-one and onto; the onto part amounts to $h(\mathbb{R}_X) = \mathbb{R}_Y$. That is, the equation:

$$y = h(x), \text{ has a unique solution } x \in \mathbb{R}_X \text{ for each } y \in \mathbb{R}_Y.$$

From chapter 3 we have the following results which can be utilized.

Probability integral and its inverse transformations For any continuous random variable X, with a cdf $F_X(x)$ such that $y = F_X(x)$ is invertible and $x = F_X^{-1}(y)$.

(a)   For the random variable $Y = F_X(X)$:

$$Y = F_X(X) \sim U(0,1). \tag{11.10}$$

(b)   Let $Y \sim U(0,1)$ and define $X = F_X^{-1}(Y)$. Then X has a distribution with cdf $F_X(.)$.

These results depend crucially on the fact that both $F_X(x)$ and $F_X^{-1}(y)$ are increasing functions. Part (a) follows from (11.9) directly:

$$F_Y(y) = \mathbb{P}(F_X(X) \le y) = \mathbb{P}(X \le F_X^{-1}(y)) = F_X(F_X^{-1}(y)) = y, \ 0 \le y \le 1.$$

NOTE that $F_Y(y) = y, \ 0 \le y \le 1$ defines the cdf of the Uniform distribution over $[0,1]$.

Part (b) amounts to showing that $F_X(x) = F(x)$:

$$F_X(x) = \mathbb{P}(X \le x) = \mathbb{P}(F_X^{-1}(Y) \le x) = \mathbb{P}(Y \le F(x)) = F(x).$$

This is a remarkable result because it holds whatever the distribution of the continuous random variable X. Moreover, in cases where $F(x)$ is invertible this result can be used to transform a Uniformly distributed random variable into another random variable with a specific distribution. Part (b) can be extended to cases where $F(x)$ is not invertible by using the quantile transformation (see chapter 3). This enables us to use random numbers generated from a Uniform distribution to generate random numbers for several other distributions (see chapter 5).

The result in (11.9) can be specialized even further in terms of density functions as the following lemma demonstrates.

The change-of-variable lemma for densities Consider the function $Y = h(X)$, where X is a random variable and $h(.)$ satisfies the properties:

(a) $h(.)$ is strictly monotone (increasing or decreasing),
(b) $h(.)$ has a continuous non-vanishing derivative over the support set:

$$\mathbb{R}_X^* := \{x : f_x(x) > 0, x \in \mathbb{R}_X\}.$$

Then, Y is also continuous with density function satisfying the properties:

$$f_y(y) = f_x(h^{-1}(y)) \left| \frac{dh^{-1}(y)}{dy} \right|, \; y \in \mathbb{R}_Y^* := h^{-1}(\mathbb{R}_X^*). \tag{11.11}$$

There are several things to NOTE in relation to this result.

(1) A function $h(.) : A \to B$ is strictly monotone if for any $x_1 \in A$, $x_2 \in A$:

$$\text{if } x_1 > x_2 \Rightarrow h(x_1) > h(x_2) \text{ (increasing)},$$

$$\text{if } x_1 > x_2 \Rightarrow h(x_1) < h(x_2) \text{ (decreasing)}.$$

(2) If $h(.)$ is a strictly monotone function then it is one-to-one and onto.
(3) The assumption (b) is equivalent to assuming that $h(.)$ has a differentiable inverse; hence the use of $\frac{dh^{-1}(y)}{dy}$ in the above lemma. It is also equivalent to assuming that $h(.)$ is differentiable and its derivative is either positive or negative for all $x \in \mathbb{R}_X^*$.
(4) The result follows from (11.9) by differentiation using the chain rule:

$$\frac{dF_Y(y)}{dy} = \left(\frac{dF_X(h^{-1}(y))}{dx} \right) \cdot \left| \frac{dh^{-1}(y)}{dy} \right|.$$

Examples
(i) Consider the case where the density function of X takes the form:

$$f_x(x) = e^{-x}, \; x > 0,$$

and define the increasing function $Y := h(X) = \sqrt{X}$. The inverse function and its derivative are $x = h^{-1}(y) = y^2$, $y > 0$ and $\frac{dx}{dy} = 2y$. Hence:

$$f_y(y) = f_x(h^{-1}(y)) \left| \frac{dx}{dy} \right| = (e^{-y^2})(2y) = 2ye^{-y^2}, \; y > 0.$$

(ii) Consider the case where the density function of X takes the form:

$$f_x(x) = e^{-x}, \; x > 0,$$

and define the decreasing function $Y := h(X) = e^{-X}$. The inverse function and its derivative are $x = h^{-1}(y) = -\ln y$, $0 \leq y \leq 1$ and $\frac{dx}{dy} = -\frac{1}{y}$. Hence:

$$f_y(y) = f_x(h^{-1}(y)) \left| \frac{dx}{dy} \right| = (e^{\ln y}) \left(\left| \frac{-1}{y} \right| \right) = y\left(\frac{1}{y}\right) = 1, \; 0 \leq y \leq 1.$$

Hence, the distribution of $Y = e^{-X}$ is in fact uniform over $[0,1]$.

(iii)   Consider the case where the density function of X takes the form:

$$f_x(x) = 2x, \ 0 < x < 1,$$

and define the increasing function $Y := h(X) = 3X - 1$. The inverse function and its derivative are: $x = h^{-1}(y) = \frac{y+1}{3}, \ -1 < y < 2$ and $\frac{dx}{dy} = \frac{1}{3}$. Hence:

$$f_y(y) = f_x(h^{-1}(y)) \left| \frac{dx}{dy} \right| = 2\left(\frac{y+1}{3}\right)\left(\frac{1}{3}\right) = \left(\frac{2(y+1)}{9}\right), \ -1 < y < 2.$$

It is interesting to NOTE that in the case of *discrete* random variables the above lemma requires only the existence of the inverse of $h(.)$ and because of its one-to-one property (11.5) reduces to:

$$f_y(y) = f_x(h^{-1}(y)), \ y \in \mathbb{R}_Y := h^{-1}(\mathbb{R}_X).$$

After this short digression using monotonic functions $h(.)$ and densities for both random variables, let us return to the general result given by (11.6) to consider the question of transforming $(h(X) \le y)$ into an inequality which involves the random variable X only. To get some idea of the difficulties involved let us consider a simple example.

Example
Consider the case where $h(X) = X^2$, $x \in \mathbb{R}_X$. In view of the fact that:

$$(X^2 \le y) \Rightarrow \left(-\sqrt{y} \le X \le \sqrt{y}\right),$$

we deduce: $F_Y(y) := \mathbb{P}(X^2 \le y) = \mathbb{P}\left(-\sqrt{y} \le X \le \sqrt{y}\right) = F_X(\sqrt{y}) - F_X(-\sqrt{y})$.

Using this example we can systematize the general approach into the following steps:

step 1:   using $y = h(x)$, identify $\mathbb{R}_Y := \{y : y = h(x), x \in \mathbb{R}_X\}$; use the graph of $h(x)$,

step 2:   using a typical value y, identify the intervals $B_y = (Y \le y)$ and $A_x = (h(X) \le y)$,

step 3:   identify in terms of y the endpoints of the interval A_x,

step 4:   equate $F_Y(y)$ with the probability that X belongs to the set A_x.

The general procedure amounts to mapping the event $B_y = (Y \le y)$ into a statement about X via $X \in A_x$ where $A_x = (h(X) \le y)$ and then specifying the probability of B_y using the distribution of X via:

$$F_Y(y) = \mathbb{P}(X \in A_x) = \int_{B_y} f_x(x)dx.$$

NOTE that $B_y \subset \mathbb{R}_Y$ and $A_x \subset \mathbb{R}_X$. It is interesting to emphasize that the result of the above procedure depends crucially not only on $h(.)$ but also on $\mathbb{R}_X$.

Example
Consider the case where $Y = X^2$, where $X \sim U(0,1)$. In view of the fact that:

$$B_Y := \{y : y = h(x), x \in (0,1)\} = (0,1),$$

for $B_y = (X^2 \le y)$, $A_x = (0 \le X \le \sqrt{y})$, since $x \in (0,1)$,

we deduce: $F_Y(y) := \mathbb{P}(X^2 \le y) = \mathbb{P}(0 \le X \le \sqrt{y}) = F_X(\sqrt{y}) = \sqrt{y}$.
The last equality follows from the fact that the cdf of the Uniform distribution over $[0,1]$ takes the form $F_X(x) = x$.

11.7.2 Functions of several random variables

The problem we are facing in this section is the following. We know the joint distribution of the random variables $(X_1, X_2, \ldots, X_n)$ and we want to find the distribution of a function of these random variables:

$$Y = h(X_1, X_2, \ldots, X_n).$$

Discrete random variables.
In the case of two discrete random variables (X_1, X_2), we can define directly the density function and argue from first principles as follows:

$$f_y(y) = \mathbb{P}(Y = y) = \mathbb{P}(h(X_1, X_2) = y) = \sum_{\{(x_1,x_2):\, h(x_1,x_2)=y\}} f(x_1,x_2), \; y \in \mathbb{R}_Y. \qquad (11.12)$$

We first identify the range of values of Y via: $\mathbb{R}_Y = \{y : y = h(x_1,x_2), \, x_1 \in \mathbb{R}_{X_1}, \, x_2 \in \mathbb{R}_{X_2}\}$, and then proceed to evaluate the probabilities associated with each value y by adding together the probabilities of X associated with that value, i.e., $\{(x_1,x_2): h(X_1,X_2) = y\}$.

Example
Let $Y = 2X_1 + X_2$, where the joint distribution of X_1 and X_2 is:

$x_2 \backslash x_1$	0	1	2
0	0.2	0.2	0.2
2	0.1	0.1	0.2

The range of values of Y takes the form $\mathbb{R}_Y = \{0,2,4,6\}$ and thus:

$$\mathbb{P}(Y = 0) = 0.2, \; \mathbb{P}(Y = 2) = (0.1 + 0.2) = 0.3,$$
$$\mathbb{P}(Y = 6) = 0.2, \; \mathbb{P}(Y = 4) = (0.1 + 0.2) = 0.3.$$

y	0	2	4	6
$f(y)$	0.2	0.3	0.3	0.2

Continuous random variables
In the case of continuous random variables we cannot define the density function directly but indirectly via the cdf. In the case where Y is a function of two continuous random variables, say $Y = h(X_1, X_2)$, its cdf can be derived via:

$$F_Y(y) = \mathbb{P}(Y \le y) = \mathbb{P}(h(X_1, X_2) \le y) = \iint\limits_{\{(x_1,x_2):\, h(x_1,x_2)\le y\}} f(x_1,x_2)\, dx_1 dx_2. \qquad (11.13)$$

As in the univariate case the problem with this derivation is to transform the event:

$$(h(X_1,X_2) \leq y),$$

into an event in terms of X_1 and X_2 whose probability we can evaluate in terms of y.

Example

Consider the case where $Y = X_1 + X_2$ and the density functions of two independent random variables X_1 and X_2 take the form:

$$f_1(x_1) = e^{-x_1}, x_1 > 0, f_2(x_2) = e^{-x_2}, x_2 > 0.$$

note that $\mathbb{R}_Y = (0,\infty)$. Using the general result in (11.13) as follows:

$$F_Y(y) = \mathbb{P}(Y \leq y) = \mathbb{P}(X_1 + X_2 \leq y) = \int_0^y \int_0^{y-x_1} e^{-x_1-x_2} dx_1 dx_2 =$$

$$= \int_0^y e^{-x_1} e^{-x_2} \Big|_{x_2=0}^{x_2=y-x_1} dx_1 = \int_0^y e^{-x_1}(1 - e^{-y+x_1}) dx_1 =$$

$$= \int_0^y (e^{-x_1} - e^{-y}) dx_1 = e^{-x_1} - x_1 e^{-y} \Big|_{x_1=0}^{x_1=y} 1 - e^{-y} - ye^{-y}.$$

Hence, the density function of Y takes the form:

$$f_y(y) = ye^{-y}, y > 0. \tag{11.14}$$

It is interesting to note that in the above example we considered a very simple case of two independent random variables because in more general cases the manipulations involved are quite complicated. In the n-variable case the theoretical result is straightforward since:

$$F_Y(y) = \mathbb{P}(h(X_1, \ldots, X_n) \leq y) = \overbrace{\int\int\cdots\int}^{n \text{ times}}_{\{(x_1, \ldots, x_n) : h(x_1, \ldots, x_n) \leq y\}} f(x_1, \ldots, x_n) dx_1 \ldots dx_n. \tag{11.15}$$

However, this is of theoretical importance because only rarely can the modeler use (11.15) to derive the distribution of $Y = h(X_1, X_2, \ldots, X_n)$.

We conclude this section by mentioning the multivariate extension of the change-of-variable lemma for density functions. It turns out that it can be generalized directly with suitable notation. Suppose that $\mathbf{X} := (X_1, X_2, \ldots, X_n)$ are random variables with known joint density $f(x_1, x_2, \ldots, x_n)$, and define the n random variables $\mathbf{Y} := (Y_1, Y_2, \ldots, Y_n)$ via the one-to-one transformation and its inverse:

$$Y_1 = h_1(X_1, X_2, \ldots, X_n), \quad X_1 = h_1^{-1}(Y_1, Y_2, \ldots, Y_n),$$
$$Y_2 = h_2(X_1, X_2, \ldots, X_n), \quad X_2 = h_2^{-1}(Y_1, Y_2, \ldots, Y_n),$$
$$\vdots \quad \vdots \qquad\qquad\qquad \vdots \quad \vdots$$
$$Y_n = h_n(X_1, X_2, \ldots, X_n). \quad X_n = h_n^{-1}(Y_1, Y_2, \ldots, Y_n).$$

In matrix notation this transformation can be written in the form:

$$\mathbf{Y} = \mathbf{H}(\mathbf{X}), \mathbf{X} \in \mathbb{R}_X^n, \mathbf{Y} \in \mathbb{R}_Y^n, \text{ where } \mathbf{H}(.): \mathbb{R}_X^n \to \mathbb{R}_Y^n.$$

As in the univariate case, when this transformation is both differentiable and invertible we can proceed to derive the joint density of **Y**:

$$f_y(y_1,\ldots,y_n)=f_x(h_1^{-1}(y_1,\ldots,y_n),h_2^{-1}(y_1,\ldots,y_n),\ldots,h_n^{-1}(y_1,\ldots,y_n))|J(y_1,\ldots,y_n)|,$$

(11.16)

where $J(y_1,y_2,\ldots,y_n)$ denotes the Jacobian determinant of the inverse transformation:

$$J(y_1,y_2,\ldots,y_n)=\det\left(\left[\frac{\partial h_i^{-1}(y_1,\ y_2,\ \ldots,\ y_n)}{\partial y_j}\right]_{i,j=1}^n\right),$$

which is assumed to be non-zero. As we can see, the Jacobian determinant replaces $\left(\frac{dh^{-1}(y)}{dy}\right)$ in (11.11). It is important to note that this result provides us with the joint distribution of $Y:=(Y_1,Y_2,\ldots,Y_n)$ and thus if we require any of the marginal distributions we need to use the integrating out method discussed above.

Examples
Consider the case where the independent random variables (X_1,X_2) have density functions:

$$f_1(x_1)=e^{-x_1},\ x_1>0,\ f_2(x_2)=e^{-x_2},\ x_2>0.$$

(i)   Let the functions of interest be: $Y_1=X_1+X_2$ and $Y_2=X_1$. The first thing we need to establish is the range of values of the vector (X_1,X_2):

$$\{(y_1,y_2):y_1>0,0<y_2<y_1\}.$$

The inverse functions take the form $X_1=Y_2,\ X_2=Y_1-Y_2$.
Jacobian of the transformation:

$$J(y_1,y_2)=\det\begin{pmatrix}\frac{\partial x_1}{\partial y_1}&\frac{\partial x_1}{\partial y_2}\\\frac{\partial x_2}{\partial y_1}&\frac{\partial x_2}{\partial y_2}\end{pmatrix}=\det\begin{pmatrix}0&1\\1&-1\end{pmatrix}=-1.$$

Hence, the joint density of (Y_1,Y_2) takes the form:

$$f_y(y_1,y_2)=e^{-y_2-(y_1-y_2)}(1)=e^{-y_1},\ y_1>0,0<y_2<y_1.$$

The marginal density of Y_1 is derived by integrating out Y_2:

$$f_1(y_1)=\int_0^{y_1}e^{-y_1}dy_2=y_1e^{-y_1},\ y_1>0\},$$

which coincides with the answer derived directly in (11.14) above.

(ii)   Let the functions of interest be:

$$Y_1=\frac{X_2}{X_1}\text{ and }Y_2=X_1.$$

The first thing we need to establish is the range of values of the vector (X_1, X_2):

$$\{(y_1, y_2): y_1 > 0, y_2 > 0\}.$$

The inverse functions take the form: $X_1 = Y_2$, $X_2 = Y_1 \cdot Y_2$.

Jacobian of the transformation:

$$\mathbf{J}(y_1, y_2) = \det \begin{vmatrix} \frac{\partial x_1}{\partial y_1} & \frac{\partial x_1}{\partial y_2} \\ \frac{\partial x_2}{\partial y_1} & \frac{\partial x_2}{\partial y_2} \end{vmatrix} = \det \begin{pmatrix} 0 & 1 \\ y_2 & y_1 \end{pmatrix} = -y_2.$$

Hence, the joint density of (Y_1, Y_2) takes the form:

$$f_y(y_1, y_2) = e^{-y_2 - (y_1 \cdot y_2)}(y_2) = y_2 e^{-y_2(1+y_1)}, \ y_1 > 0, y_2 > 0.$$

Distributions of the basic arithmetic functions The result in (11.16) can be used to derive general results for the basic arithmetic functions of random variables. In order to avoid problems of discontinuities we assume at the outset that we are dealing with two random variables X_1 and X_2 which take only positive values and have an unknown joint density:

$$f_x(x_1, x_2), \ x_1 > 0, x_2 > 0.$$

(i) **Distribution of the sum** Let the functions of interest be: $Y_1 = X_1 + X_2$ and $Y_2 = X_1$. The range of values of the vector (X_1, X_2) takes the form:

$$\{(y_1, y_2): y_1 > 0, 0 < y_2 < y_1\}.$$

The inverse functions take the form: $X_1 = Y_2$, $X_2 = Y_1 - Y_2$. As shown the previous example the Jacobian is $\mathbf{J}(y_1, y_2) = -1$. The joint density of (Y_1, Y_2) takes the form:

$$f_y(y_1, y_2) = f_x(x_1, y_1 - x_1), \ y_1 > 0, 0 < y_2 < y_1.$$

The density function of Y_1 is derived by integrating out X_1:

$$f_1(y_1) = \int_0^\infty f_x(x_1, y_1 - x_1) dx_1, \ y_1 > 0.$$

In the general case where:

$$f_x(x_1, x_2), \ x_1 \in \mathbb{R}, x_2 \in \mathbb{R},$$

this result does not change in any appreciable way:

$$f_{x_1 + x_2}(y_1) = \int_{-\infty}^\infty f_x(x_1, y_1 - x_1) dx_1, \ y_1 > 0. \tag{11.17}$$

(ii) **Distribution of the product** Let the functions of interest be: $Y_1 = X_1 X_2$ and $Y_2 = X_1$. The range of values of the vector (X_1, X_2) takes the form:

$$\{(y_1, y_2): y_1 > 0, y_2 > 0\}.$$

The inverse functions take the form: $X_1 = Y_2$, $X_2 = \frac{Y_1}{Y_2}$.

Jacobian of the transformation:

$$J(y_1,y_2)=\det\begin{pmatrix}\frac{\partial x_1}{\partial y_1}&\frac{\partial x_1}{\partial y_2}\\\frac{\partial x_2}{\partial y_1}&\frac{\partial x_2}{\partial y_2}\end{pmatrix}=\det\begin{pmatrix}0&1\\\frac{1}{y_2}&-\frac{y_1}{y_2^2}\end{pmatrix}=-\frac{1}{y_2}.$$

The joint density of (Y_1,Y_2) takes the form:

$$f_y(y_1,y_2)=\frac{1}{x_1}f_x\left(x_1,\frac{y_1}{x_1}\right),y_1>0,y_2>0.$$

The density function of Y_1 is derived by integrating out X_1:

$$f_1(y_1)=\int_0^\infty\frac{1}{x_1}f_x\left(x_1,\frac{y_1}{x_1}\right)dx_1,\ y_1>0.$$

In the general case where:

$$f_x(x_1,x_2),\ x_1\in\mathbb{R},x_2\in\mathbb{R},$$

this result does not change in any appreciable way:

$$f_{x_1\cdot x_2}(y_1)=\int_{-\infty}^\infty\frac{1}{|x_1|}f_x\left(x_1,\frac{y_1}{x_1}\right)dx_1,\ y_1>0.\qquad(11.18)$$

(iii) **Distribution of the quotient** Let the functions of interest be: $Y_1=\frac{X_2}{X_1}$ and $Y_2=X_1$. The range of values of the vector (X_1,X_2) takes the form:

$$\{(y_1,y_2):y_1>0,y_2>0\}.$$

The inverse functions take the form: $X_1=Y_2$, $X_2=Y_1\cdot Y_2$. As shown above, the Jacobian of the transformation is $J(y_1,y_2)=-y_2$. The joint density of (Y_1,Y_2) takes the form:

$$f_y(y_1,y_2)=x_1f_x(x_1,y_1x_1),\ y_1>0,y_2>0.$$

The density function of Y_1 is derived by integrating out X_1:

$$f_1(y_1)=\int_0^\infty x_1f_x(x_1,y_1x_1)dx_1,\ y_1>0.$$

In the general case where:

$$f_x(x_1,x_2),\ x_1\in\mathbb{R},x_2\in\mathbb{R},$$

this result does not change in any appreciable way:

$$f_{\frac{x_1}{x_2}}(y_1)=\int_{-\infty}^\infty|x_1|f_x(x_1,y_1x_1)dx_1,\ y_1>0.\qquad(11.19)$$

We conclude this section by noting that the above result depends on the restriction that the transformation $H(.)$ is assumed to be one-to-one and onto. In view of this we extend this result in two directions. The first is to allow for transformations which are not onto:

$$Y=H(X),\ X\in\mathbb{R}_X^n,Y\in\mathbb{R}_Y^m,\text{ where }H(.):\mathbb{R}_X^n\to\mathbb{R}_Y^m,\ m<n.$$

The second is to relax the onto restriction and allow for transformations which are not one-to-one. For the details of these extensions which are rather involved, see Hoffmann-Jorgensen (1994).

11.8 Computer intensive techniques for approximating sampling distributions*

In the previous section we discussed the mathematical problem of deriving sampling distributions and the first impression is that these results are difficult to come by. Given that without them no statistical inference is possible we need to tackle the problem of sampling distributions somehow. One approximate solution to the problem is provided by the limit theorems discussed in chapter 9. Another way is to derive computer intensive approximations to sampling distributions by resampling. These techniques will be discussed in this section.

11.8.1 The multi-sample method

In section 2 above we discussed the (hypothetical) scenario where the modeler is in a position to get not just one sample realization $\mathbf{X} = \mathbf{x}$, where $\mathbf{X} := (X_1, X_2, \ldots, X_n)$, but N such realizations:

$$(\mathbf{x}^{(1)}, \mathbf{x}^{(2)}, \ldots, \mathbf{x}^{(N)}). \tag{11.20}$$

The idea is that under this scenario the modeler could view the estimates:

$$\hat{\theta}(k) = h(\mathbf{x}^{(k)}), \ k = 1, 2, \ldots, N,$$

as observations from the sampling distribution $f(\hat{\theta})$ of the estimator $\hat{\theta}$ of θ, and for large enough N evaluate the (smoothed) histogram of $\hat{\theta}(1), \hat{\theta}(2), \ldots, \hat{\theta}(N))$ to provide an approximation to $f(\hat{\theta})$.

The problem with this scenario is that in practice the modeler rarely has more than one sample realization and when he/she does, the number of realizations N is often not large enough to proceed along the lines of the above scenario. This practical difficulty, however, does not render this scenario of no interest. As the number crunching capacity of personal computers becomes generally available, the modeler could very easily replace the actual sample realizations (11.20) with hypothetical ones. In this section we consider two such methods which enable the modeler to derive approximations to the sampling distribution $f(\hat{\theta})$ or some of its numerical characteristics such as its moments and its quantiles.

11.8.2 The naive Monte Carlo method

Monte Carlo is a computer intensive method concerned with providing approximate solutions to mathematical problems by utilizing basic convergence results between probabilistic concepts and their sample counterparts (see Fishman (1996)). The most general way to describe the Monte Carlo method is as controlled statistical experiments designed and executed on the computer using pseudo-random numbers. Hence, several techniques developed in the context of the experimental design approach to statistical inference become relevant. In the present context we will focus mainly on the problem of using the Monte Carlo method to provide an approximation to the sampling distribution $f(\hat{\theta})$, where $\hat{\theta}$ is an estimator of an unknown parameter θ.

The idea underlying the Monte Carlo method is to replace the N sample realizations (11.20) (which are usually unavailable) with pseudo-random number realizations:

$$(\tilde{\mathbf{x}}^{(1)}, \tilde{\mathbf{x}}^{(2)}, \dots, \tilde{\mathbf{x}}^{(N)}), \tag{11.21}$$

which satisfy the properties of the postulated sample. In chapter 5 we discussed the question of generating such pseudo-random numbers using the probability integral transformation in conjunction with Uniform pseudo-random numbers. Armed with a large number of designed realizations generated by a computer the modeler can proceed to derive the estimates:

$$\tilde{\theta}(k) = h(\tilde{\mathbf{x}}^{(k)}), \ k = 1, 2, \dots, N,$$

and view them as observations from the sampling distribution $f(\hat{\theta})$. The intuitive way to proceed is to approximate $f(\hat{\theta})$ using the histogram (or the smoothed histogram) of the estimates $(\tilde{\theta}(1), \tilde{\theta}(2), \dots, \tilde{\theta}(N))$. It turns out that our intuition is correct for good theoretical reasons.

In chapter 10 we discussed the issue of using the *empirical cumulative distribution function* (ecdf) defined by:

$$\hat{F}_n(x) = \frac{[\text{no. of } (X_1, X_2, \dots, X_n) \text{ whose realization do not exceed } x]}{n}, \tag{11.22}$$

in order to approximate the true cdf $F(x)$. The *Glivenko–Canteli* result shows that the ecdf $\hat{F}_n(x)$ converges to the true cdf $F(x)$ almost surely (or with probability one), i.e.

$$\hat{F}_n(x) \overset{a.s.}{\to} F(x). \tag{11.23}$$

Given the direct relationship between the ecdf and the various empirical forms of density function, say $\hat{f}_n(x)$, such as the histogram, the rolling histogram, and the smoothed histogram (see chapter 10), we can consider them as good approximations of underlying density function $f(x)$. Indeed, under certain regularity restrictions:

$$\hat{f}_n(x) \overset{a.s.}{\to} f(x). \tag{11.24}$$

In order to illustrate the generality of the Monte Carlo method we note that utilizing other convergence results for sample statistics the modeler can use the simulated pseudo-random sample estimates $(\tilde{\theta}(1), \tilde{\theta}(2), \dots, \tilde{\theta}(N))$ to approximate other numerical characteristics of the underlying sampling distribution. The quintessential result in this context is the convergence of the sample raw moments to the distribution moments. As shown in chapter 12, in the context of a simple statistical model, we have almost sure (a.s.) convergence (see chapter 9) results of the form:

$$\hat{\mu}_r := \left[\frac{1}{n} \sum_{k=1}^{n} X_k^r \right] \overset{a.s.}{\to} \mu_r := \int_{x \in \mathbb{R}_X} x^r f(x) dx, \ r = 1, 2, \dots,$$

where μ_r denote the distribution raw moments (see chapter 3) and $\hat{\mu}_r$ the corresponding sample moments. The idea underlying the Monte Carlo method is that any mathematical problem which can be expressed in the form of the right-hand side integral can be solved approximately (to any desired degree of approximation) by utilizing left-hand side averaging. It is surprising to realize that numerous problems in mathematics, which often have nothing to do with probability, can be reduced to this form. For example, the problem of evaluating a multiple integral of the form:

$$\underset{\mathbf{x}\in\mathbb{R}^m}{\int\cdots\int} h(\mathbf{x})d\mathbf{x},$$

can be tackled using a Monte Carlo procedure which views this as $E(h(\mathbf{x}))$ with the underlying distribution being Uniform.

Full information Monte Carlo designs

The above procedure is called **naive Monte Carlo** because it makes no attempt to exploit some of the finer results of probability theory associated by introducing additional information into the structure of the problem in order to increase the efficiency of this method. This additional information includes the nature of the distribution $f(x)$, controlled dependence and designing more sophisticated forms of sampling models (see section 4 above); see Hendry (1984), Fishman (1996). It is interesting to note that in the context of the Monte Carlo method the design of experiments for exploiting the structure of different sampling models plays a very important role.

One of the strengths of the Monte Carlo procedure is that it can be easily adapted to provide approximate distributional results in the context of statistical models beyond the random sample case. The real difficulty in the case of non-random samples is to be able to simulate pseudo-random sample realizations which reflect the structure of the postulated statistical model. A particularly important concept in ensuring this is that of the appropriate *statistical generating mechanism* (GM) introduced in chapter 7. To illustrate the issues involved let us consider the **normal autoregressive model** (see chapter 8):

[1]   Statistical GM: $X_t = \alpha_0 + \alpha_1 X_{t-1} + u_t,\ t\in\mathbb{T}$,

[2]   Probability model:

$$\Phi = \left\{ f(x_1,x_2,\ldots,x_T: \boldsymbol{\theta}) = \prod_{t=2}^{T} \frac{(\sigma_0)^{-1}}{\sqrt{2\pi}} \exp\left\{ -\frac{1}{2}\frac{(x_t - \alpha_0 - \alpha_1 x_{t-1})^2}{\sigma_0^2} \right\}, \boldsymbol{\theta}\in\Theta, \mathbf{x}\in\mathbb{R}^T \right\},$$

where $\boldsymbol{\theta} := (\alpha_0, \alpha_1, \sigma_0^2)\in\Theta := \mathbb{R}^2\times\mathbb{R}_+$.

[3]   Sampling model: $(X_1, X_2, \ldots, X_T)$ is a stationary and Markov dependent sample, sequentially drawn from $f(x_t|x_{t-1}; \boldsymbol{\theta}),\ t\in\mathbb{T}$. $\qquad(11.25)$

As we can see from this, the underlying sample is Normal, stationary, and Markov dependent. The most widely used method to simulate pseudo-random sample realizations for this model is to use the statistical GM written in the form:

$$X_t = \alpha_0 + \alpha_1 X_{t-1} + \sigma_0 \varepsilon_t,\ \varepsilon_t \sim \mathsf{NIID}(0,1),\ t\in\mathbb{T}, \qquad\qquad(11.26)$$

where $\varepsilon_t \sim \text{NIID}(0,1)$ stands for standard Normal, Independent, and Identically Distributed random variables; the pseudo-random numbers required for the simulation. Armed with these pseudo-random numbers the modeler can generate the pseudo-random realizations via (11.26). For the generated sample realizations to reflect the structure of the postulated model, the specified parameters need to be related to the underlying probabilistic structure of the process $\{X_t\}_{t \in \mathbb{T}}$ in the sense that (see chapter 7):

$$\alpha_0 = (1 - \alpha_1)E(X_t), \ \alpha_1 = \tfrac{Cov(X_t, X_{t-1})}{Var(X_t)}, \ \sigma_0^2 = Var(X_t) - \alpha_1 Cov(X_t, X_{t-1}).$$

The problem of ensuring that these constraints are built into the simulation system is not as trivial as it might seem at first sight. In the traditional approach the modeler often focuses almost exclusively on the system properties of the generation mechanism to the demise of the statistical properties of the process as defined by the joint distribution. As a result, the implied parameterization sometimes differs from the one which apparently generates the pseudo-random numbers and the whole analysis can be very misleading.

In order to avoid some of these difficulties it is often preferable to generate the sample realizations for such models directly in terms of the joint distribution. In the case of the AR(1) model this entails simulating pseudo-random numbers from the bivariate Normal distribution:

$$\begin{pmatrix} X_t \\ X_{t-1} \end{pmatrix} \sim N\left(\begin{bmatrix} \mu \\ \mu \end{bmatrix}, \begin{bmatrix} \sigma(0) & \sigma(1) \\ \sigma(1) & \sigma(0) \end{bmatrix} \right), \ t \in \mathbb{T}, \tag{11.27}$$

where $\mu = E(X_t)$, $\sigma(0) = Var(X_t)$, $\sigma(1) = Cov(X_t, X_{t-1})$. NOTE that the Markov dependence enables us to specify the structure of the process using a bivariate distribution (see chapter 8). Given that there exists a one-to-one mapping between the parameters $(\alpha_0, \alpha_1, \sigma_0^2)$ and the distribution moments $(\mu, \sigma(0), \sigma(1))$, we can ensure the design values of the parameters without any difficulty. The above observations are particularly relevant to situations where the AR(1) model is sensitive to the initial conditions such as the case of a unit root (see Spanos (1990), Spanos and McCuirk (1998)).

11.8.3 The Bootstrap method

In an attempt to motivate the Bootstrap method let us consider the scenario where instead of replacing the actual sample realizations (11.20) with the pseudo-random number realizations (11.21), the modeler generates *pseudo-realizations* by sampling with replacement from the one actual realization $\mathbf{X} = \mathbf{x}$. That is, using the observed data $\mathbf{x} := (x_1, x_2, \ldots, x_n)$ generate the pseudo-realizations:

$$(\breve{\mathbf{x}}^{(1)}, \breve{\mathbf{x}}^{(2)}, \ldots, \breve{\mathbf{x}}^{(N)}), \tag{11.28}$$

where each $\breve{\mathbf{x}}^{(k)} := (\breve{\mathbf{x}}_1^{(k)}, \breve{\mathbf{x}}_2^{(k)}, \ldots, \breve{\mathbf{x}}_n^{(k)})$, $k = 1, 2, \ldots, N$, constitute pseudo-realizations created by selecting n numbers from $(x_1, x_2, \ldots, x_n)$ using *simple random sampling with replacement*; NOTE that if we sample without replacement there is only one such pseudo-realization possible, the original sample realization, but with replacement we can generate numerous pseudo-realizations. The question which arises at this stage is:

What are the properties of the pseudo-realizations (11.28)?

The fact that we generated (11.28) by *simple random sampling with replacement* amounts to giving each observation the same probability $\left(\frac{1}{n}\right)$ of being picked at each selection. This is reminiscent of the way we defined the ecdf (11.22) above. This means that if the original sample realization includes more values from a certain interval this should be reflected in the pseudo-samples (11.28). Hence, these samples can be viewed as samples from the ecdf. Given the relationship between the ecdf $\hat{F}_n(x)$ and the true cdf $F(x)$, we can think of these pseudo-realizations as indirectly relating to $F(x)$.

The idea underlying the **Bootstrap method** (proposed by Efron (1979)) is that, in cases where the number of observations n is large enough to render the approximation of $F(x)$ by $\hat{F}_n(x)$ reasonable, the pseudo-samples (11.28), called *Bootstrap sample realizations*, should reflect the properties of the underlying distribution $F(x)$. The Bootstrap samples constitute random sample realizations from the ecdf $\hat{F}_n(x)$ and thus indirectly from the underlying distribution $F(x)$. Moreover, as argued in chapter 3, the unknown parameters are related in some way to $F(x)$. For example in the case where the parameters are related to the moments we know that:

$$\mu'_r(\theta) = \int_{x \in \mathbb{R}_X} x^r dF(x; \theta) = \int_{x \in \mathbb{R}_X} x^r f(x; \theta) dx,$$

where the last equality holds when the density function exists. In this sense the unknown parameter(s) θ can be viewed as a functions of $F(x)$:

$$\theta = g(F),$$

and thus the estimator $\hat{\theta} = h(\mathbf{X})$ can be viewed as a function of the ecdf:

$$\hat{\theta} = g(\hat{F}_n),$$

assuming that the function $g(.)$ is continuous or at least well behaved in the sense that a small distance in the domain is mapped into a small distance in the range. Hence, the Bootstrap sample realizations (11.28) can be used in the same way as the real (11.20) and the pseudo-random number (11.21) realizations in order to derive approximations to the sampling distribution $f(\hat{\theta})$. Armed with a large number of pseudo-realizations (usually generated by a computer) the modeler can proceed to derive the estimates $(\check{\theta}(1), \hat{\theta}(2), \dots, \hat{\theta}(N))$:

$$\hat{\theta}(k) = h(\check{\mathbf{x}}^{(k)}), \ k = 1, 2, \dots, N,$$

and proceed is to approximate $f(\hat{\theta})$ using the histogram (or the smoothed histogram) of the estimates. Often, the estimates are used to approximate the first few moments of the sampling distribution. The Bootstrap procedure to approximate the mean of the sampling distribution $f(\hat{\theta})$ follows the same steps as the Monte Carlo method described above.

Viewed in the above light, the Bootstrap method differs from both the multisample and Monte Carlo in one important respect: the distribution underlying the postulated model is replaced with the ecdf of the observed sample. That is, by taking $N \to \infty$ the ecdf of the pseudo-realizations $[\breve{\mathbf{x}}^{(1)},\breve{\mathbf{x}}^{(2)},...,\breve{\mathbf{x}}^{(N)}]$ will converge to $\hat{F}_n(x)$ and not to $F(x)$. This renders the Bootstrap method vulnerable to two modeling problems. The first is the *data specificity* of the ecdf which will be reflected in the approximation results. This problem can be alleviated somewhat by reducing the data specificity of the ecdf by employing smoothing techniques (see chapter 5) associated with the empirical density function. This entails generating the pseudo-realizations (11.28) not from the ecdf but, say, the smoothed histogram which is less data specific. The second modeling problem with Bootstrap approximations is that they are vulnerable to *misspecifications* in the sense that if the postulated model is misspecified the Bootstrap approximation to any sampling distribution $f(\hat{\theta})$ will be misleading. For example, if the modeler has postulated a random sample but the observed realization exhibits dependence and/or heterogeneity, then $\hat{F}_n(x)$ will not, in general, be a good approximation of the postulated $F(x)$. This can play havoc with the Bootstrap approximations based on such an ecdf. Judicious empirical modeling, however, could turn this weakness into a strength by utilizing Bootstrap approximations as part of assessing the statistical adequacy of the postulated model.

In view of the data specificity problem, the Bootstrap method is rarely used to derive approximations to the sampling distribution $f(\hat{\theta})$, but it is often utilized to derive approximations to the moments of this distribution.

Approximating the standard deviation of an estimator

To illustrate the Bootstrap procedure let us consider the case where the problem is to approximate the standard deviation of the estimator $\hat{\theta} = h(\mathbf{X})$.

Step 1 Generate N pseudo-realizations $[\breve{\mathbf{x}}^{(1)},\breve{\mathbf{x}}^{(2)},...,\breve{\mathbf{x}}^{(N)}]$ by simple random sampling from the sample realization $\mathbf{x} = (x_1, x_2, ..., x_n)$.

Step 2 For each evaluate the function $h(.)$:

$$[h(\breve{\mathbf{x}}^{(1)}), h(\breve{\mathbf{x}}^{(2)}), ..., h(\breve{\mathbf{x}}^{(N)})] \tag{11.29}$$

these constitute the Bootstrap estimates $\breve{\theta}_k = h(\breve{\mathbf{x}}^{(k)})$, $k = 1, 2, ..., N$.

Step 3 Form the sample mean of the Bootstrap estimates:

$$\breve{\theta} = \tfrac{1}{N}\sum_{k=1}^{n} h(\breve{\mathbf{x}}^{(k)}).$$

Step 4 Evaluate the standard error of $\breve{\theta}$:

$$SE(\breve{\theta}) := \sqrt{Var(\breve{\theta})} = \tfrac{1}{N}\sum_{k=1}^{N}\left\{\tfrac{(h(\breve{\mathbf{x}}^{(k)}) - \breve{\theta})^2}{(N-1)}\right\} \tag{11.30}$$

This provides a measure of precision for $\breve{\theta}$ which can be utilized to control the accuracy of the approximation. We remind the reader that for any random variable Z with bounded variance *Chebyshev's inequality* (see chapter 3):

$$\mathbb{P}\left(\tfrac{|Z - E(Z)|}{\sqrt{Var(Z)}} > \varepsilon\right) \le \tfrac{1}{\varepsilon^2}, \text{ for any } \varepsilon > 0,$$

provides an upper bound on the accuracy of the difference $|Z - E(Z)|$. Hence, from (11.30) we can deduce that the precision of the approximation can be increased by increasing the number of pseudo-random number sample real-izations N.

The basic convergence result underlying the above procedure is that, in the case of a random sample, the sample mean $\overline{X}_n := \left[\frac{1}{n}\sum_{k=1}^n X_k\right]$ converges to the distribution mean $\mu := E(X)$, i.e.

$$\left[\frac{1}{n}\sum_{k=1}^n X_k\right] \overset{a.s.}{\to} \int_{x \in \mathbb{R}_X} xf(x)dx.$$

At a more mundane level, the sample mean $\overline{X}_n := \left[\frac{1}{n}\sum_{k=1}^n X_k\right]$ has the properties:

$$E(\overline{X}_n) = \mu, \ Var(\overline{X}_n) = \frac{\sigma^2}{n},$$

irrespective of the nature of the underlying distribution $D(\mu, \sigma^2)$; see chapter 12. For a thorough discussion of the Bootstrap method see Efron (1982), and Efron and Tibshirani (1993).

11.9 Exercises

1 Explain briefly the difference between *descriptive statistics* and *statistical inference* when faced with the problem of analyzing a set of observed data.

2 Define the concept of a *sample* and contrast it to that of a *sample realization*.

3 Explain briefly the difference between the *frequency* and *subjective* interpretations of probability. Why do we care?

4 How do we interpret the *observed data* in the classical (frequency) approach to statistical inference.

5 Explain the concept of the distribution of the sample.

6 Explain why estimation testing and prediction amounts to defining mappings between the sample and parameter spaces.

7 Compare briefly the frequency and Bayesian approaches to statistical inference.

8 Explain the main differences between experimental and observational data with regard to statistical inference.

9 Explain the following methods of sampling:
(i) simple random sampling, (ii) stratified sampling, (iii) cluster sampling, and (iv) quota sampling.

10 Explain briefly the notions of specification, misspecification, and respecification.

11 Explain why the concept of a sampling distribution is crucial for statistical inference.

12 "Defining the sampling distribution of a statistic is theoretically trivial but practically very difficult to derive." Discuss.

13 Explain the relationship between the Bernoulli and Binomial distributions.

14 "Linear functions of normally distributed random variables are normally distributed." Explain.

15 Explain the relationship between the Normal and the following distributions:
(i) Log-Normal, (ii) Chi-square, (iii) Student's t, and (iv) Cauchy distributions.

16 Derive the distribution of $Y=|X|$ assuming that the distribution of X is given below:

x	-2	-1	0	1	2
$f_x(x)$	0.3	0.1	0.1	0.2	0.3

17 Explain how the naive Monte Carlo method can be used to derive an approximation to the sampling distribution of an estimator.

18 Explain how the Bootstrap method can be used to derive an approximation to the sampling distribution of an estimator.

19 Compare and contrast the Monte Carlo and Bootstrap methods for deriving approximations to the sampling distribution of an estimator.

20 Explain how one can use the Bootstrap method to derive an approximate variance for an estimator.

12 Estimation I: Properties of estimators

12.1 Introduction

For any form of (parametric) statistical inference, as described in the previous chapter, the modeler needs two basic components:

(a) statistical model: $S := (\Phi, \mathbf{X})$, Φ – probability model, $\mathbf{X}$ – sampling model,
(b) set of data: $\mathbf{x} := (x_1, x_2, \ldots, x_n)$.

The data are then interpreted as a realization of the chance mechanism specified by the statistical model. The primary objective of statistical inference is to utilize the information in the data to draw conclusions relating to the chance mechanism in question. *Estimation* amounts to utilizing the information in the data to choose a particular value of θ from Θ. Once the parameter is estimated by some estimator $\hat{\theta}$, we have a *probabilistic description* of the chance mechanism in question $\hat{S} := (\hat{\Phi}, \mathbf{X})$. In the case of a simple statistical model, this stochastic mechanism can be described using the estimated probability model:

$$\hat{\Phi} = \{f(x;\hat{\theta}), x \in \mathbb{R}_X\}. \tag{12.1}$$

It is important to emphasize at the outset that estimation of θ is not the ultimate objective of modeling; estimating θ is a means to an end. The ultimate objective is to obtain an empirically adequate statistical description of the stochastic mechanism that gave rise to the data which, in the above case, is the estimated statistical model (12.1).

The theory of estimation in its modern form begins with Fisher's 1922 seminal paper "On the mathematical foundations of theoretical statistics" where some of the fundamental concepts of estimation, such as likelihood, information, efficiency, and consistency, were first proposed.

12.1.1 Bird's eye view of the chapter

In section 2 we discuss the notion of an estimator and related concepts and illustrate them using two basic examples which form the backbone of the discussion in this chapter. A crucial concept is that of a sampling distribution which forms the basis of the discussion of what constitutes a good estimator. The notion of a good estimator is formalized in terms of several properties defined in terms of the sampling distribution of the estimator. The properties of estimators are separated into finite sample properties (unbiasedness and efficiency) discussed in section 3 and asymptotic properties (consistency, asymptotic Normality, and asymptotic efficiency) discussed in section 4. Throughout the discussion we use two very simple statistical models, the Bernoulli and the Normal (one-parameter) in order to illustrate the various ideas and concepts. These examples are chosen to keep the mathematical manipulations to an absolute minimum. In section 5 we discuss the most widely used simple statistical model, the simple Normal model, in an attempt to bring out some of the more subtle features of optimal estimation. In section 6 we discuss a property of a statistic (a function of the sample) which can be used to devise optimal estimators: the property of sufficiency.

12.2 Defining an estimator

Estimating the unknown parameter θ, amounts to defining a function of the form:

$$h(.): X \rightarrow \Theta,$$

where X is the *sample space* (the set of all possible sample realizations), and Θ denotes the *parameter space* (the set of all possible values of θ). The function, denoted by:

$$\hat{\theta} = h(X_1, X_2, \ldots, X_n),$$

is referred to as an **estimator** of θ. An estimator, (being a function of the random variables $(X_1, X_2, \ldots, X_n)$), is itself a random variable which takes different values depending on the sample realization. A particular value of this estimator, based on a particular sample realization $(\check{x}_1, \check{x}_2, \ldots, \check{x}_n)$, is called an **estimate** of θ, and denoted by:

$$\hat{\theta} = h(\check{x}_1, \check{x}_2, \ldots, \check{x}_n).$$

The meaning of $\hat{\theta}$ is always clear from the context, depending on whether it denotes a random variable or a value of a random variable (a number).

Example 1
Consider the **simple Bernoulli model**:

[i]   Statistical GM: $X_i = \theta + \varepsilon_i, \ i \in \mathbb{N}$,
[ii] Probability model: $\Phi = \{f(x;\theta) = \theta^x(1-\theta)^{1-x}, 0 \le \theta \le 1, x = 0,1\}$,
[iii] Sampling model: $\mathbf{X} := (X_1, X_2, \ldots, X_n)$ is a random sample.

The following functions constitute likely estimators of θ:

(a) $\hat{\theta}_1 = X_1$,   (b) $\hat{\theta}_2 = \frac{1}{2}(X_1 + X_2)$,

(c) $\hat{\theta}_3 = \frac{1}{3}(X_1 + X_2 + X_n)$,   (d) $\hat{\theta}_n = \frac{1}{N}\sum_{i=1}^{n} X_i$,

(e) $\hat{\theta}_{n+1} = \left(\frac{1}{n+1}\right)\sum_{i=1}^{n} X_i$,   (f) $\hat{\theta}_{n+2} = \left(\frac{1}{n+2}\right)\sum_{i=1}^{n} X_i$,

Counter-examples

The following functions $h(X_1, X_2, \ldots, X_n)$ do *not* constitute estimators of θ:

(g) $\hat{\theta}_4 = (X_1 - X_n)$. The range of this function is not $\Theta := [0,1]$; it can take values outside it when $X_1 = 0$ and $X_n = 1$.

(h) $\hat{\theta}_5 = \left(\frac{1}{n}\right) \sum_{i=1}^{n} X_i^{\alpha}$. The domain of the function is not the sample space; it depends on some unknown scalar α.

(i) $\hat{\theta}_6 = 0.8$. Its domain is not the sample space.

Example 2

Consider the **simple** (one parameter) **Normal model**:

[i]   Statistical GM: $X_i = \mu + \varepsilon_i, \; i \in \mathbb{N}$,

[ii]   Probability model:

$$\Phi = \left\{ f(x;\theta) = \frac{1}{\sqrt{2\pi}} \exp\left\{ -\frac{1}{2}(x-\mu)^2 \right\}, \; \theta := \mu \in \mathbb{R}, \, x \in \mathbb{R} \right\},$$

[iii] Sampling model: $\mathbf{X} := (X_1, X_2, \ldots, X_n)$ is a random sample.

NOTE that the probability model is defined in terms of: $X \sim N(\mu, 1)$.
The following functions constitute possible estimators of μ:

(i) $\hat{\mu}_1 = X_1$,   (iii) $\hat{\mu}_3 = (X_1 - X_n)$,   (v) $\hat{\mu}_{n+1} = \left(\frac{1}{n+1}\right) \sum_{i=1}^{n} X_i$,

(ii) $\hat{\mu}_2 = \frac{1}{2}(X_1 + X_2)$,   (iv) $\hat{\mu}_n = \frac{1}{n} \sum_{i=1}^{n} X_i$,   (vi) $\hat{\mu}_{n+2} = \left(\frac{1}{n+2}\right) \sum_{i=1}^{n} X_i$.

Given that the parameter μ takes values over the whole of the real line ($\mathbb{R}$), it will be impossible to define a function of the sample $(X_1, X_2, \ldots, X_n)$ which is not an estimator of μ. In view of the fact that it is very easy to define numerous possible estimators, the question which naturally arises is: How does one choose among such estimators? Intuitively, the answer to this question is obvious: we choose the estimator which approximates the true unknown parameter θ_0 as accurately as possible. Formalizing the notion accurate approximation turns out to be rather involved because we cannot define it in the usual mathematical form $|\hat{\theta} - \theta_0| \simeq 0$, This is because such a distance:

(a) depends on the unknown parameter θ_0, and
(b) $\hat{\theta} = h(X_1, X_2, \ldots, X_n)$ is a random variable which can take many different values.

However, the fact that an estimator $\hat{\theta} = h(X_1, X_2, \ldots, X_n)$ is a random variable, suggests that any formalization of accurate approximation will involve its distribution, which we call the *sampling distribution* of $\hat{\theta}$.

12.2.1 Sampling distributions of estimators

The **sampling distribution** of an estimator $\hat{\theta} = h(X_1, X_2, \ldots, X_n) := h(\mathbf{X})$ is defined as the distribution of the function $h(X_1, X_2, \ldots, X_n)$. Its density function is denoted by:

$$f(\hat{\theta}; x_1, x_2, \ldots, x_n) := f(\hat{\theta}; \mathbf{x}),$$

in order to emphasize its dependence on the sample $(X_1, X_2, \ldots, X_n)$. As argued in chapter 11, the problem of establishing such sampling distributions was considered by Fisher as one of the three basic facets of statistical inference, the other two being *specification* and *estimation*:

(iii) Problems of Distribution include the mathematical deduction of the exact nature of the distributions in random samples of our estimates of the parameters ...

(Fisher (1925b), p. 8)

From the discussion in chapters 4 and 11 we know that mathematically we can define the cumulative distribution function (cdf) of any function $\hat{\theta} = h(X_1, X_2, \ldots, X_n)$ via:

$$\mathbb{P}(\hat{\theta} \leq y) = \underbrace{\int \int \cdots \int}_{\{h(X_1, X_2, \ldots, X_n) \leq \theta\}} f(x_1, x_2, \ldots, x_n; \theta) dx_1 dx_2 \cdots dx_n, \tag{12.2}$$

where

(a) $\Theta(\mathbf{X}) := \{h(X_1, X_2, \ldots, X_n) \leq y\}$ denotes the range of values of $Y = h(X_1, X_2, \ldots, X_n)$ for all $(x_1, x_2, \ldots, x_n) \in X$.

(b) $f(x_1, x_2, \ldots, x_n; \theta)$ denotes the **distribution of the sample**: the joint distribution of the random variables $\mathbf{X} := (X_1, X_2, \ldots, X_n)$.

Example 1 Bernoulli (continued)

Armed with lemma 1 of chapter 11, which says that *a summation of IID Bernoulli distributed random variables is Binomially distributed*, we can proceed to derive the sampling distributions of estimators (a)–(e). In view of the fact that all these estimators are linear functions of the sample, we can deduce that their sampling distributions are all Binomial. All that remains is to derive their mean and variance utilizing the properties of $E(.)$ (see chapter 3). For example the sampling distribution of $\hat{\theta}_n = \frac{1}{n}\sum_{i=1}^n X_i$ is Binomial with mean and variance:

$$E(\hat{\theta}_n) = \left(\frac{1}{n}\right) E(\sum_{i=1}^n X_i) = \left(\frac{1}{n}\right) \cdot n\theta = \theta,$$

$$Var(\hat{\theta}_n) = \left(\frac{1}{n}\right)^2 \sum_{i=1}^n Var(X_i) = \left(\frac{1}{n}\right)^2 (n\theta(1-\theta)) = \left(\frac{1}{n}\right)\theta(1-\theta).$$

These results are derived using the independence of the sample and the properties of the mean and the variance (see chapter 3). Hence, the sampling distributions are as follows:

(a) $\hat{\theta}_1 \sim \mathrm{Bi}(\theta, \theta(1-\theta);1)$,

(b) $\hat{\theta}_2 \sim \mathrm{Bi}\left(\theta, \frac{1}{2}\theta(1-\theta);2\right)$,

(c) $\hat{\theta}_3 \sim \mathrm{Bi}\left(\theta, \frac{1}{3}\theta(1-\theta);3\right)$,

(d) $\hat{\theta}_n \sim \mathrm{Bi}\left(\theta, \frac{\theta(1-\theta)}{n};n\right)$,

(e) $\hat{\theta}_{n+1} \sim \mathrm{Bi}\left(\left(\frac{n}{n+1}\right)\theta, \frac{n\theta(1-\theta)}{(n+1)^2};n\right)$,

(f) $\hat{\theta}_{n+2} \sim \mathrm{Bi}\left(\left(\frac{n}{n+2}\right)\theta, \frac{n\theta(1-\theta)}{(n+2)^2};n\right)$.

These distributional results suggest that the estimators (a)–(d) have sampling distributions with the same mean θ (equal to the parameter it purports to estimate) but different variances. The variance of $\hat{\theta}_n$ is smaller than any of the others, for any sample size $n > 3$. Indeed, the variance of $\hat{\theta}_n$ is n times smaller than the variance of the random variables in

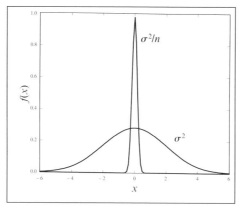

Figure 12.1 $X_i \sim N(0,\sigma^2)$ versus $\hat{\mu}_n \sim N(0,\sigma_n^2)$ for $\sigma^2 = 4$, $n = 12$

the sample! The sampling distribution of $\hat{\theta}_{n+1}$ is not centered at θ but its variance is smaller than the others. On the basis of its sampling distribution $\hat{\theta}_n$ seems to be the best estimator of θ in this group. This intuitive argument of best estimator will be formalized in the next section.

Example 2 Normal (continued)
Using lemma 2 of chapter 11, which says that the sum of Independent Normally distributed random variables is Normally distributed, we can deduce that for the Normal model the sampling distributions of estimators (i)–(vi) are:

(i) $\hat{\mu}_1 \sim N(\mu,1)$,   (iii) $\hat{\mu}_3 \sim N(0,2)$,   (v) $\hat{\mu}_{n+1} \sim N\left(\left(\frac{n}{n+1}\right)\mu, \frac{n}{(n+1)^2}\right)$,

(ii) $\hat{\mu}_2 \sim N(\mu,\frac{1}{2})$,   (iv) $\hat{\mu}_n \sim N\left(\mu, \frac{1}{n}\right)$,   (vi) $\hat{\mu}_{n+2} \sim N\left(\left(\frac{n}{n+2}\right)\mu, \frac{n}{(n+2)^2}\right)$.

On intuitive grounds $\hat{\mu}_n$ appears to be the best estimator in this group because its sampling distribution has mean equal to μ (the parameter it purports to estimate) and its variance $Var(\hat{\mu}_n) = \frac{\sigma^2}{n}$ is n times smaller than the variance of the individual random variables $Var(X_i)$, $i = 1,2,\ldots,n$. In figure 12.1 we can see how much the variance is reduced by as small a sample size as $n = 12$. This is an important result which is often exploited by various resampling techniques such as the Monte Carlo and the bootstrap methods (see chapter 11.8).

NOTE: the discerning reader will have noticed that the best estimators in both the Bernoulli and Normal models coincide. The question that naturally arises is:

> Is it a coincidence that for the parameters θ and μ of the Bernoulli and Normal models, respectively, the best estimator seems to be $\frac{1}{n}\sum_{i=1}^{n} X_i$?

The fact of the matter is that there is a good reason for this result. In both cases the parameter we want to estimate is the *distribution mean* $E(X)$ and the best estimator $\frac{1}{n}\sum_{i=1}^{n} X_i$ is the *sample mean*. The idea of estimating a distribution moment using the corresponding

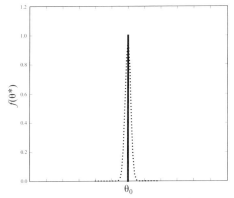

Figure 12.2 The distribution of the ideal estimator θ^* and a feasible "good" approximation

sample moment has a long history in statistics going back to the nineteenth century (see chapter 13, section 2).

12.3 Finite sample properties

12.3.1 Motivation: the ideal estimator

As shown in the previous section, it is very easy to define estimators. This raises the problem of choosing the best among these estimators. Given that estimators are *functions of the sample (random variables) they are random variables themselves*. Hence, any discussion of best would be related to their distribution.

The problem of defining a good estimator resembles a situation where an archer is standing at the foot of a hill with the target on the other side of the hill beyond his vision. What he has to do is devise a strategy (rule) relating to factors within his control, such as the shooting angle and the pulling power, which will ensure that the arrow will land as close to the target as possible. The modeler has to choose a rule (an estimator) in a way that ensures proximity to the unknown value of the parameter θ.

In order to motivate some of the optimal properties of estimators, let us consider first the notion of the **ideal estimator**. Ideally, we want to have an estimator, say:

$$\theta^* = h(\mathbf{X}),$$

which takes only one value (θ_0 the true value of θ), with probability one, irrespective of the sample realization. That is, the sampling distribution of θ^* takes the form:

$$\mathbb{P}(\theta^* = \theta_0) = 1,$$

i.e., θ^* equals θ_0 with probability one; it has a degenerate distribution. In figure 12.2 we can see the ideal estimator and what appears to be a good approximation of its sampling distribution.

In terms of the archer analogy, the ideal estimator amounts to a procedure that ensures that the archer hits the bull's eye every time. Unfortunately, for a given sample size n, no such estimator exists. Feasible estimators usually yield different estimates for different sample realizations. Thus, we need to consider optimality criteria which are based on a non-degenerate sampling distribution of the estimator in question. The best among such estimators will be the one which comes closest to the ideal estimator. How do we formalize the notion closest to the ideal estimator?

In view of the fact that no feasible estimator could approximate the sampling distribution of the ideal estimator (being degenerate), let us consider approximations based on the first two moments. Heuristically, we can view the *ideal estimator* in terms of its first two moments:

(i) $E(\theta^*) = \theta_0,$ (ii) $Var(\theta^*) = 0.$

This suggests that an optimal estimator will be one whose mean is located at the true value of the parameter it purports to estimate and its variance is zero. For a finite sample size n, the second property cannot be emulated by feasible estimators, but as n goes to infinity some estimators can indeed emulate it. Because of this we distinguish between **finite sample properties** (valid for any n) and **asymptotic properties** (valid as n goes to infinity).

12.3.2 Unbiasedness

We formalize the location property in the form of unbiasedness.

An estimator $\hat{\theta}$ is said to be an **unbiased estimator** of θ if its sampling distribution has a mean equal to the parameter θ_0 it purports to estimate, i.e.

$$E(\hat{\theta}) = \theta_0.$$

Otherwise $\hat{\theta}$ is said to be *biased*, the **bias** defined by: $b(\hat{\theta}; \theta_0) = E(\hat{\theta}) - \theta_0.$

REMARK: In order to avoid cumbersome notation, the subscript of θ_0 will be omitted when it does not seem necessary.

Example 1 (continued)
In the case of the estimators (a)–(f) above, we can see that $\hat{\theta}_1, \hat{\theta}_2, \hat{\theta}_3$ and $\hat{\theta}_n$ are unbiased estimators of θ but $\hat{\theta}_{n+1}$ and $\hat{\theta}_{n+2}$ are not. The bias of these estimators is:

(e) $b(\hat{\theta}_{n+1}) = -\left(\frac{1}{n+1}\right)\theta,$ (f) $b(\hat{\theta}_{n+2}) = -\left(\frac{1}{n+2}\right)\theta.$

Does this mean that the estimators $\hat{\theta}_{n+1}$ and $\hat{\theta}_{n+2}$ are inferior to the other estimators? As shown below, the answer is not as obvious as it appears at first sight, because unbiasedness is not the only property, or even the most desirable property for good estimators. Other properties related to higher moments are often more important.

The notion of unbiasedness is intuitively appealing but is not without its problems.

1 Unbiased estimators do not always exist.

Example 2

Consider the **simple Exponential model**:

[i]   Statistical GM: $X_k = (1/\theta) + u_k$, $k \in \mathbb{N}$,
[ii]   Probability model: $\Phi = \{ f(x;\theta) = \theta \exp\{ -\theta x \}, \theta > 0, x > 0 \}$,
[iii] Sampling model: $\mathbf{X} := (X_1, X_2, \dots X_n)$ is a random sample.

It can be shown (see Schervish (1995), p. 297) that no unbiased estimator of θ exists!

2 Unbiased estimators are not invariant to transformations of the unknown parameters.
That is, if $\hat{\theta}_n := h(\mathbf{X})$ is an unbiased estimator of θ, i.e.

$$E(\hat{\theta}_n) = \theta,$$

then, in general, for $\vartheta = g(\theta)$, where $g(.): \Theta \to \Theta$, and $\hat{\vartheta}_n = g(\hat{\theta}_n)$:

$$E(\hat{\vartheta}_n) \neq \vartheta.$$

Example 3 Exponential (continued)

Consider the simple Exponential model as specified above. We have seen that no unbiased estimator of θ exists, but we can show that for $\vartheta = \frac{1}{\theta}$, the estimator $\hat{\vartheta}_n = \frac{1}{n}(\sum_{i=1}^{n} X_i)$ is unbiased. This follows from the fact that:

$$E(\hat{\vartheta}_n) = \frac{1}{n} \sum_{i=1}^{n} E(X_i) = \left(\frac{1}{n}\right) \sum_{i=1}^{n} \vartheta = \frac{1}{n} n \vartheta = \vartheta.$$

12.3.3 Efficiency

The notion that the sampling distribution should be as concentrated around the true value of θ as possible can be formalized in terms of the variance of the sampling distribution of an estimator. This property is referred to as **efficiency**: how dispersed the estimator is around the true value of θ. We consider two forms of efficiency: relative and full efficiency.

Relative efficiency For two unbiased estimators $\hat{\theta}$ and $\hat{\vartheta}$ of θ, $\hat{\theta}$ is said to be *relatively more efficient* than $\hat{\vartheta}$ if:

$$Var(\hat{\theta}) \le Var(\hat{\vartheta}).$$

Example 1 Bernoulli (continued)

In the case of the unbiased estimators $\hat{\theta}_1, \hat{\theta}_2, \hat{\theta}_3$ and $\hat{\theta}_n$, $\hat{\theta}_2$ is relatively more efficient than $\hat{\theta}_1, \hat{\theta}_3$ is relatively more efficient than $\hat{\theta}_2$, and $\hat{\theta}_n$ is relatively more efficient than $\hat{\theta}_3$, i.e.

$$Var(\hat{\theta}_n) \le Var(\hat{\theta}_3) \le Var(\hat{\theta}_2) \le Var(\hat{\theta}_1).$$

Relative efficiency is not such a hot property because the comparison is always relative to some specific alternative estimators. This, however, suggests that an estimator which is better than some terrible estimators is not necessarily a good estimator. Hence, the question which immediately comes to mind is whether there is an ultimate low beyond which the variance of no estimator can go. This raises the issue of absolute or full efficiency.

The challenge of devising an absolute lower bound was met successfully in 1945–6 by two pioneers of modern statistics H. Cramer (1946a) and C. R. Rao (1945). Using different approaches they both reached the same conclusion. The absolute lower bound for unbiased estimators is related to a concept introduced by Fisher (1922a) and subsequently coined the Fisher information.

Fisher information for the sample

In the context of Probability theory we defined *information* in the context of a our universe of discourse, the probability space $(S, \Im, \mathbb{P}(.))$, in a very simple way. Any form of knowledge that reduces $\Im$ to some subset of it, is viewed as information. That is, knowing that our event space has been reduced from $\Im$ to $\Im_1$ where:

$$\Im_1 \subset \Im,$$

is viewed as information.

In statistical inference, information has to do with how the modeler utilizes the information to draw conclusions relating to the stochastic mechanism that gave rise to the data. Intuitively, information has to do with how well the modeler can filter the systematic information out of the observed data. The degree of our utilization of the systematic information in the data will be reflected by the precision of our estimates and test statistics relating to the unknown parameters $\boldsymbol{\theta}$. One such information measure is the Fisher information for the sample for regular probability models.

Regular probability models A probability model Φ is said to be regular if the distribution of the sample $f(\mathbf{x};\theta):=f(x_1,x_2,\ldots,x_n;\theta)$ satisfies the following regularity conditions:

(**Rf1**) the parameter space Θ is an open subset of $\mathbb{R}^m$, $m < n$,

(**Rf2**) the *support* of the distribution $X_0:=\{\mathbf{x}:f(\mathbf{x};\boldsymbol{\theta})>0\}$ is the same for all $\boldsymbol{\theta}\in\Theta$,

(**Rf3**) $\left(\frac{\partial \ln f(\mathbf{x};\boldsymbol{\theta})}{\partial \boldsymbol{\theta}}\right)$ exists and is finite for all $\boldsymbol{\theta}\in\Theta$, $\mathbf{x}\in X_0$,

(**Rf4**) for $h(\mathbf{X})$ we can interchange differentiation and integration, i.e.

$$\frac{\partial}{\partial\boldsymbol{\theta}}\left(\int\ldots\int h(\mathbf{x})\cdot f(\mathbf{x};\boldsymbol{\theta})dx_1\ldots dx_n\right)=\int\ldots\int h(\mathbf{x})\left[\frac{\partial}{\partial\boldsymbol{\theta}}f(\mathbf{x};\boldsymbol{\theta})\right]dx_1\ldots dx_n<\infty.$$

The first condition excludes boundary points to ensure that derivatives (from both sides of a point) exist. For such regular probability models we can proceed to define the Fisher information for the sample which is designed to provide a measure of the information rendered by the sample for a parameter $\theta\in\Theta$.

The **Fisher information** for the sample $(X_1,X_2,\ldots,X_n)$ is defined by:

$$I_n(\theta):=E\left\{\left(\frac{d\ln f(\mathbf{x};\theta)}{d\theta}\right)^2\right\}. \tag{12.3}$$

There are several things to NOTE about this concept.

(1)   Difficulties arise when the range of X depends on θ; see example 4 below.
(2)   Under the *regularity conditions* (I)–(III) it can be shown that:

$$I_n(\theta):=E\left\{\left(\tfrac{d \ln f(\mathbf{x};\theta)}{d\theta}\right)^2\right\}=E\left(-\tfrac{d^2 \ln f(\mathbf{x};\theta)}{d\theta^2}\right).$$

This often provides a more convenient way to derive Fisher's information and thus the Cramer–Rao lower bound.

(3)   The form of the Fisher information depends crucially on the postulated statistical model and it has nothing to do with estimators or test statistics. For example, in the case of an independent sample:

$$E\left(\tfrac{d \ln f(\mathbf{x};\theta)}{d\theta}\right)=\sum_{i=1}^{n}E\left(\tfrac{d \ln f(x_i;\theta)}{d\theta}\right),$$

and in the random sample case Fisher's information takes the even simpler form:

$$I_n(\theta)=n I(\theta):=nE\left\{\left(\tfrac{d \ln f(x;\theta)}{d\theta}\right)^2\right\},$$

where $f(x;\theta)$ denotes the density function of any one IID random variable X_k, $k=1,2,\ldots,n$ and:

$$I(\theta):=E\left\{\left(\tfrac{d \ln f(x;\theta)}{d\theta}\right)^2\right\},$$

represents the Fisher information for *a single observation*. Its dependence on the form of the probability model can be illustrated in the case of a random sample from a Normal (one parameter) distribution: $X_k \sim N(\theta,1)$, $k=1,2,\ldots,n$, i.e.

$$f(x;\theta)=\tfrac{1}{\sqrt{2\pi}}e^{-\frac{1}{2}(x-\theta)^2},\ \tfrac{d}{d\theta}\ln f(x;\theta)=(x-\theta),\ I(\theta)=1,\ I_n(\theta)=n.$$

NOTE: the term *information of the sample* stems from the fact that the variance of the best unbiased estimator equals the inverse of this. As the information increases this variance decreases and thus more information about θ is gained.

The Cramer–Rao inequality Using Fisher's information for the sample Cramer (1946a) and Rao (1945) proposed an absolute lower bound for unbiased estimators.

Cramer–Rao lower bound Assuming that the Fisher information for the sample exists and $I_n(\theta)>0$ for all $\theta\in\Theta$, the variance of any unbiased estimator of a parameter θ, say $\hat{\theta}$, cannot be smaller than the inverse of $I_n(\theta)$, i.e.

$$Var(\hat{\theta})\geq CR(\theta):=I_n^{-1}(\theta):=\left\{E\left(\tfrac{d \ln f(x;\theta)}{d\theta}\right)^2\right\}^{-1}. \tag{12.4}$$

In the case where the modeler is interested in some differentiable function of θ, say $q(\theta)$, and $\hat{q}(\theta)$ is an estimator of $q(\theta)$, the Cramer–Rao lower bound takes the form:

$$Var(\hat{q}(\theta))\geq CR(q(\theta)):=\left(\tfrac{d}{d\theta}E(q(\theta))\right)^2 I_n^{-1}(\theta). \tag{12.5}$$

Using (12.5) we can extend the Cramer–Rao lower bound to the case of any estimator, say $\tilde{\theta}$, (not necessarily unbiased):

$$Var(\tilde{\theta})\geq\left(\tfrac{dE(\hat{\theta})}{d\theta}\right)^2\left\{E\left(\tfrac{d \ln f(\mathbf{x};\theta)}{d\theta}\right)^2\right\}^{-1}, \tag{12.6}$$

for any estimator $\tilde{\theta}$ of θ.

The following example illustrates the usefulness of condition **Rf2** for the derivation of the Cramer–Rao lower bound.

Example 4
Consider the **simple Uniform model**:

[i]   Statistical GM: $X_k = E(X_k) + \epsilon_k,\ k \in \mathbb{N},$
[ii]   Probability model: $\Phi = \{f(x;\theta) = (1/\theta),\ \theta \in (0,\infty),\ 0 < x < \theta\},$
[iii] Sampling model: $\mathbf{X} := (X_1, X_2, \dots X_n)$ is a random sample.

In this case, the range of X depends on θ, and the regularity condition **Rf2** is not satisfied. If we use the Cramer–Rao (C–R) lower bound in this case we will get very misleading results because what appears to be a C–R lower bound:

$$\frac{d\ln f(x;\theta)}{d\theta} = \frac{d\ln}{d\theta}\left(\frac{1}{\theta^n}\right) = \frac{d}{d\theta}(-n\ln\theta) = -\frac{n}{\theta} \Rightarrow I_n(\theta) = \left(\frac{n}{\theta}\right)^2,$$

is not in fact applicable.

Full efficiency An *unbiased* estimator $\hat\theta$ is said to be a *fully efficient* estimator of θ if its variance achieves the *C–R lower bound*:

$$Var(\hat\theta) = CR(\theta) := I_n^{-1}(\theta).$$

A necessary and sufficient condition for an unbiased estimator $\hat\theta$ of θ to achieve this bound is that $(\hat\theta - \theta)$ can be expressed in the form:

$$(\hat\theta - \theta) = h(\theta)\left[\frac{d\ln f(x;\theta)}{d\theta}\right], \tag{12.7}$$

for some function $h(\theta)$.

Example 2 Normal (continued)
In the case of the Normal (one parameter) model, the distribution of the sample takes the form:

$$f(\mathbf{x};\theta) = \left(\frac{1}{\sqrt{2\pi}}\right)^n \exp\left\{-\frac{1}{2}\sum_{i=1}^n (x_i - \theta)^2\right\},\ \ln f(\mathbf{x};\theta) = -\frac{n}{2}\ln(2\pi) - \frac{1}{2}\sum_{i=1}^n (x_i - \theta)^2.$$

The first and second derivatives take the form:

$$\frac{d\ln f(\mathbf{x};\theta)}{d\theta} = \sum_{i=1}^n (x_i - \theta),\ \frac{d^2\ln f(\mathbf{x};\theta)}{d\theta^2} = -n.$$

Hence, $I_n(\theta) = n$, and the C–R lower bound is $CR(\theta) = \frac{1}{n}$, confirming that the estimator $\hat\mu_n = \frac{1}{n}\sum_{i=1}^n X_i$ is a fully efficient estimator. Equality (12.7) holds in this case since:

$$(\hat\mu_n - \mu) = \frac{1}{n}\left[\frac{d\ln f(\mathbf{x};\mu)}{d\mu}\right] = \frac{1}{n}\sum_{i=1}^n (X_i - \mu).$$

Example 1 Bernoulli (continued)
As shown above, the distribution of the sample for the Bernoulli model is:

$$f(\mathbf{x};\theta) = \theta^{\sum_{i=1}^n x_i}(1 - \theta)^{\sum_{i=1}^n (1-x_i)}.$$

Hence:

$$\ln f(\mathbf{x};\theta) = (\textstyle\sum_{i=1}^{n} X_i)\ln\theta + (\textstyle\sum_{i=1}^{n}[1 - X_i])\ln(1 - \theta),$$

$$\frac{d\ln f(\mathbf{x};\theta)}{d\theta} = (\textstyle\sum_{i=1}^{n} X_i)\left(\tfrac{1}{\theta}\right) - (\textstyle\sum_{i=1}^{n}[1 - X_i])\left(\tfrac{1}{1-\theta}\right),$$

$$\frac{d^2\ln f(\mathbf{x};\theta)}{d\theta^2} = -(\textstyle\sum_{i=1}^{n} X_i)\left(\tfrac{1}{\theta^2}\right) - (\textstyle\sum_{i=1}^{n}[1 - X_i])\left(\tfrac{1}{1-\theta}\right)^2.$$

$$E\!\left(-\frac{d^2\ln f(\mathbf{x};\theta)}{d\theta^2}\right) = \frac{n}{\theta(1 - \theta)}.$$

This follows from the fact that:

$$E(\textstyle\sum_{i=1}^{n} X_i) = n\theta,\; E(\textstyle\sum_{i=1}^{n}(1 - X_i)) = n - \textstyle\sum_{i=1}^{n} E(X_i) = n(1 - \theta),$$

and thus:

$$CR(\theta) = \frac{\theta(1 - \theta)}{n}.$$

If we return to the estimators (a)–(d) for θ, we can see that the only unbiased estimator of θ, which is fully efficient is $\hat{\theta}_n$, since:

$$Var(\hat{\theta}_n) = \frac{\theta(1 - \theta)}{n} = CR(\theta).$$

Example 4* Uniform (continued)

Consider the unbiased estimator $\hat{\theta}_n = \left(\frac{n+1}{n}\right)\max(X_1,X_2,\ldots,X_n)$ of θ. It can be shown that the sampling distribution of the largest order statistic $Y := \max(X_1,X_2,\ldots,X_n)$ is $f(y;\theta) = \frac{ny^{n-1}}{\theta^n},\; 0<y<\theta$ (see chapter 10). Using this, we will be led to the misleading conclusion that $\hat{\theta}_n$ is a super fully efficient estimator since:

$$E(\hat{\theta}_n) := \left(\frac{n+1}{n}\right)\int_0^\theta y\,\frac{ny^{n-1}}{\theta^n} = \theta,\; Var(\hat{\theta}_n) = \left(\frac{\theta^2}{n(n+2)}\right) < \left(\frac{\theta^2}{n^2}\right),$$

assuming that $I_n^{-1}(\theta) := \left(\frac{\theta^2}{n^2}\right)$ is the lower bound. Of course this argument is erroneous because the Fisher information is not definable in the case of the Uniform distribution because the regularity conditions do not hold.

12.3.4 Minimum MSE estimators

The above measures of efficiency enable us to choose between unbiased estimators but they offer no guidance on the question of choosing between a biased and an unbiased estimator such as $(\hat{\theta}_{n+1},\hat{\theta}_{n+2})$ and $(\hat{\theta}_1,\hat{\theta}_2,\hat{\theta}_3)$, respectively, in the context of the Bernoulli model. This is interesting because fully efficient and unbiased estimators do not always exist and unbiased estimators are not always good estimators. There are cases where we might chose a biased estimator in preference to an unbiased one, because the former has smaller variance. In the case of $\hat{\theta}_1$, $\hat{\theta}_2$ and $\hat{\theta}_3$ above, we can see that their variance can be considerably larger than those of $(\hat{\theta}_{n+1},\hat{\theta}_{n+2})$ for any reasonable value of n.

How do we compare biased and unbiased estimators?

If we want to penalize for the bias of an estimator $\hat{\vartheta}$, we should not use its variance as a measure of its dispersion, because this ignores the fact that $E(\hat{\vartheta}) \neq \theta_0$. Instead, we should use a measure of variation around θ_0. The most widely used such measure is the **Mean Square Error** defined at $\theta = \theta_0$ to be:

$$MSE(\hat{\vartheta};\theta_0):=E\{(\hat{\vartheta}-\theta_0)^2\}.$$

NOTE that in the case of an unbiased estimator $\hat{\theta}$, $MSE(\hat{\theta};\theta_0)=Var(\hat{\theta})$, but in the case of a biased estimator:

$$MSE(\hat{\vartheta};\theta_0):=E\{(\hat{\vartheta}-E(\hat{\vartheta})+E(\hat{\vartheta})-\theta_0)^2\}=Var(\hat{\vartheta})+[b(\hat{\vartheta};\theta_0)]^2,$$

where the *bias* was defined above to be:

$$b(\hat{\vartheta};\theta_0)=E(\hat{\vartheta})-\theta_0.$$

This can be derived directly from the definition of the *MSE* (verify!).

An estimator $\hat{\theta}$ is said to be a **minimum MSE estimator** of θ if:

$$MSE(\hat{\theta};\theta) \leq MSE(\hat{\vartheta};\theta),$$

for any other estimator $\hat{\vartheta}$ and all values of θ.

Example 1 Bernoulli (continued)

In terms of MSE, $(\hat{\theta}_{n+1}, \hat{\theta}_{n+2})$ are better estimators than $\hat{\theta}_1, \hat{\theta}_2$ and $\hat{\theta}_3$ since for $n > 3$:

$$MSE(\hat{\theta}_{n+1})=\left(\tfrac{n}{(n+1)^2}\right)\theta(1-\theta)+\left(\tfrac{-\theta}{(n+1)}\right)^2=\tfrac{n\theta(1-\theta)+\theta^2}{(n+1)^2}\leq MSE(\hat{\theta}_i),\ i=1,2,3,$$

$$MSE(\hat{\theta}_{n+2})=\left(\tfrac{n}{(n+2)^2}\right)\theta(1-\theta)+\left(\tfrac{-\theta}{(n+2)}\right)^2=\tfrac{n\theta(1-\theta)+\theta^2}{(n+2)^2}\leq MSE(\hat{\theta}_i),\ i=1,2,3,$$

and *most* values of θ. Moreover, $MSE(\hat{\theta}_{n+1}) > MSE(\hat{\theta}_{n+2})$.

Inadmissibility of estimators The above minimum MSE property can be utilized as an extension of both forms of efficiency defined above. In the case of any two estimators $\hat{\vartheta}_2$ and $\hat{\vartheta}_1$, if:

$$MSE(\hat{\vartheta}_2) \leq MSE(\hat{\vartheta}_1) \text{ for all } \theta \in \Theta,$$

we say that $\hat{\vartheta}_2$ *dominates* $\hat{\vartheta}_1$ in the MSE sense and $\hat{\vartheta}_1$ is said to be *inadmissible*.

Example 1 Bernoulli (continued)

In the case of $(\hat{\theta}_{n+1}, \hat{\theta}_{n+2})$:

$$MSE(\hat{\theta}_{n+2}) \leq MSE(\hat{\theta}_{n+1}) \text{ for all } \theta \in [0,1],$$

and thus $\hat{\theta}_{n+1}$ is inadmissible. However, both estimators achieve their respective Cramer–Rao lower bounds:

$$E(\hat{\theta}_{n+1})=\left(\tfrac{n}{n+1}\right)\theta,\ \tfrac{dE(\hat{\theta})}{d\theta}=\left(\tfrac{n}{n+1}\right),\ E(\hat{\theta}_{n+2})=\left(\tfrac{n}{n+2}\right)\theta,\ \tfrac{dE(\hat{\theta})}{d\theta}=\left(\tfrac{n}{n+2}\right).$$

Hence, from (12.6) the Cramer–Rao lower bounds for these biased estimators are:

$$CR(\hat{\theta}_{n+1}) = \left(\frac{n}{n+1}\right)^2 \left(\frac{\theta(1-\theta)}{n}\right) = \frac{n\theta(1-\theta)}{(n+1)^2}, \quad CR(\hat{\theta}_{n+1}) = \left(\frac{n}{n+2}\right)^2 \left(\frac{\theta(1-\theta)}{n}\right) = \frac{n\theta(1-\theta)}{(n+2)^2},$$

which equal their respective variances.

There is another sense in which $(\hat{\theta}_{n+1}, \hat{\theta}_{n+2})$ are much better estimators than the unbiased estimators $\hat{\theta}_1$, $\hat{\theta}_2$ and $\hat{\theta}_3$. This arises from the fact that the variances of $\hat{\theta}_1$, $\hat{\theta}_2$ and $\hat{\theta}_3$ are not only bigger than those of $(\hat{\theta}_{n+1}, \hat{\theta}_{n+2})$, but they do not decrease as additional observations are added to the sample.

This brings us conveniently to the asymptotic properties of estimators. We call such properties *asymptotic* because, in contrast to the above finite sample properties which relate to the finite sampling distribution $f(\hat{\theta};\mathbf{x})$, they relate to the sequence of sampling distributions $\{f(\hat{\theta}_n;\mathbf{x})\}_{n=1}^{\infty}$. In a nutshell, the asymptotic properties amount to extending the limit theorems discussed in chapter 9 (for the function $\sum_{k=1}^{n} X_k$), to the case of arbitrary functions $\hat{\theta}_n := h(X_1, X_2, \ldots, X_n)$.

12.4 Asymptotic properties

Since the ideal estimator θ^* defined by $\mathbb{P}(\theta^* = \theta) = 1$, is not possible for a fixed sample size n, the modeler would like to have estimators that achieve this ideal form as the sample size increases to infinity. That is, estimators whose sampling distribution approaches the ideal sampling distribution $\mathbb{P}(\theta^* = \theta) = 1$, in some probabilistic sense as $n \to \infty$.

The probabilistic sense in terms of which this can be achieved asymptotically comes in two versions: *convergence in probability* and *almost sure convergence* encountered in relation to the *Law of Large Numbers* (LLN) discussed in chapter 9. Convergence in probability, associated with the Weak LLN gives rise to the property known as consistency, while almost sure convergence gives rise to the property known as strong consistency. Moreover, the *Central Limit Theorem* can often be used to derive the distribution of $\hat{\theta}_n$: $= h(X_1, X_2, \ldots, X_n)$ as $n \to \infty$. The latter can be used as an approximation of the finite sample distribution of the estimator in question. It is noted again that without a sampling distribution no statistical inference is possible.

12.4.1 Consistency

An estimator $\hat{\theta}_n$ is said to be a **consistent** estimator of θ, if for any $\varepsilon > 0$:

$$\lim_{n \to \infty} \mathbb{P}(|\hat{\theta}_n - \theta| < \varepsilon) = 1, \text{ denoted by: } \hat{\theta}_n \overset{\mathbb{P}}{\to} \theta. \tag{12.8}$$

This reads "the limit of the probability of the event that $\hat{\theta}_n$ differs from the true θ by less than some positive constant $\varepsilon > 0$, goes to one as n goes to infinity"; see chapter 9.

REMARKS:
(i) $\hat{\theta}_n$ in this definition stands for a generic estimator and not the particular estimator used in example 1; the sub-script n is used to emphasize the role of the sample size.

(ii)   In a certain sense, consistency is an extension of the LLN for functions of the sample, say $h(X_1, X_2, \dots, X_n)$, other than the sum.

(iii)   In the case where $\hat{\theta}_n$ has a bounded variance, we can verify its consistency using **Chebyshev's inequality** (see chapter 3):

$$\mathbb{P}(|\hat{\theta}_n - \theta| \le \varepsilon) \ge 1 - \frac{E(\hat{\theta}_n - \theta)^2}{\varepsilon^2}.$$

This is because $E(\hat{\theta}_n - \theta)^2$ is just the mean square error of $\hat{\theta}_n$. Hence, if $MSE(\hat{\theta}_n) \to 0$ as $T \to \infty$ then $\frac{E(\hat{\theta}_n - \theta)^2}{\varepsilon^2} \to 0$ and (12.8) holds.

Using the definition $MSE(\hat{\theta}_n; \theta) = Var(\hat{\theta}_n) + [b(\hat{\theta}_n; \theta)]^2$ we can see that:

$$MSE(\hat{\theta}_n) \to 0 \text{ if } Var(\hat{\theta}_n) \to 0 \text{ and } b(\hat{\theta}_n; \theta) \to 0.$$

This suggests two easily verifiable conditions for $\hat{\theta}_n$ to be a *consistent* estimator of θ when the required moments of its sampling distribution exist:

(a) $\lim_{n \to \infty} E(\hat{\theta}_n) = \theta$,   (b) $\lim_{n \to \infty} Var(\hat{\theta}_n) = 0$.

This suggests that in the case where $\hat{\theta}_n$ has bounded variance, we can verify its consistency by checking the above (sufficient) conditions; they are only sufficient conditions because $\hat{\theta}_n$ could be consistent even though its variance might not exist. The notion of consistency based on (a)–(b) is sometimes called **mean-square consistency**.

Example 1 Bernoulli (continued)

In the case of the estimators $\hat{\theta}_1$, $\hat{\theta}_2$ and $\hat{\theta}_3$ we know that they are unbiased so that (i) is satisfied automatically. However, given that:

(a) $Var(\hat{\theta}_1) = \theta(1 - \theta)$,   (b) $Var(\hat{\theta}_2) = \frac{1}{2}\theta(1 - \theta)$ (c) $Var(\hat{\theta}_3) = \frac{1}{3}\theta(1 - \theta)$,

we can deduce that none of these estimators satisfies the second condition, and thus they are all **inconsistent**. Another way of looking at this is that the second moment of the sampling distributions of these estimators do not change as n changes. In other words for the *precision* of these estimators it does not matter whether one has $n = 5$ or $n = 10^5$. In contrast, the estimators $(\hat{\theta}_{n+1}, \hat{\theta}_{n+2})$, are consistent because:

(e) $\lim_{n \to \infty} E(\hat{\theta}_{n+1}) = \lim_{n \to \infty}\left(\frac{n\theta}{(n+1)}\right) = \theta,$ $\lim_{n \to \infty} Var(\hat{\theta}_{n+1}) = \lim_{n \to \infty}\left(\frac{n\theta(1 - \theta)}{(n+1)^2}\right) = 0,$

(f) $\lim_{n \to \infty} E(\hat{\theta}_{n+2}) = \lim_{n \to \infty}\left(\frac{n\theta}{(n+2)}\right) = \theta,$ $\lim_{n \to \infty} Var(\hat{\theta}_{n+2}) = \lim_{n \to \infty}\left(\frac{n\theta(1 - \theta)}{(n+2)^2}\right) = 0.$

It is important to emphasize the fact that consistency is a *minimal* property. That is, when an estimator is inconsistent it is not worth serious consideration, but the fact that it is consistent does not render it a good estimator. There are numerous examples of consistent estimators, however, which are practically useless (see Rao (1973), p. 344). The estimators $\hat{\theta}_1$, $\hat{\theta}_2$, and $\hat{\theta}_3$, being inconsistent, can be eliminated from the list of good estimators of θ and the choice is now between $\hat{\theta}_n$ and $\hat{\theta}_{n+1}$. Given that $\hat{\theta}_n$ is both unbiased and fully efficient and $\hat{\theta}_{n+1}$ is biased, we prefer $\hat{\theta}_n$ to $\hat{\theta}_{n+1}$.

Example 2 (continued)

Using the sampling distributions of the estimators (i)–(vi), derived above, we can see that:

(i) $E(\hat{\mu}_1) = \mu,$ $Var(\hat{\mu}_1) = 1,$ i.e., unbiased but inconsistent,

(ii) $E(\hat{\mu}_2) = \mu,$ $Var(\hat{\mu}_2) = \frac{1}{2},$ i.e., unbiased but inconsistent,

(iii) $E(\hat{\mu}_3) = 0,$ $Var(\hat{\mu}_3) = 2,$ i.e., biased and inconsistent,

(iv) $E(\hat{\mu}_n) = \mu,$ $Var(\hat{\mu}_n) = \frac{1}{n},$ i.e., unbiased, fully efficient,

(v) $E(\hat{\mu}_{n+1}) = \left(\frac{n\mu}{n+1}\right),$ $Var(\hat{\mu}_{n+1}) = \frac{n}{(n+1)^2},$ i.e., biased but consistent,

(vi) $E(\hat{\mu}_{n+2}) = \left(\frac{n\mu}{n+2}\right),$ $Var(\hat{\mu}_{n+1}) = \frac{n}{(n+2)^2},$ i.e., biased but consistent.

From the above comparison we can conclude that $\hat{\mu}_n = \frac{1}{n}\sum_{i=1}^{n} X_i$ is the best estimator of θ.

It is important to note that in the case of the above examples (and in most cases in practice), we utilize only their first two moments when deciding the optimality of the various estimators; the sampling distribution is not explicitly utilized. For statistical inference purposes in general, however, we often require the sample distribution itself, not just its first two moments.

12.4.2 Strong consistency

An estimator $\hat{\theta}_n$ is said to be a **strongly consistent** estimator of θ, if:

$$\mathbb{P}\left(\lim_{n\to\infty} \hat{\theta}_n = \theta\right) = 1, \text{ denoted by: } \hat{\theta}_n \overset{a.s.}{\to} \theta.$$

This is exactly the asymptotic version of the *ideal estimator* property defined above. The notion of convergence underlying strong consistency is known as **almost sure** (*a.s.*) **convergence**. In chapter 9 it is shown that almost sure convergence is stronger than convergence in probability and not surprisingly, the former implies the latter.

Example 1   Bernoulli (continued)

In the case of the estimator $\hat{\theta}_n$ of θ discussed above, we can use Borel's Strong LLN (see chapter 9) directly to deduce that: $\hat{\theta}_n \overset{a.s.}{\to} \theta.$

Example 2   Normal (continued)

In the case of the estimator $\hat{\mu}_n$ of μ discussed above, we can use Kolmogorov's second Strong LLN (see chapter 9) to deduce that: $\hat{\mu}_n \overset{a.s.}{\to} \mu.$

As mentioned above, consistency (weak and strong) is an extension of the Law of Large Numbers to functions of the sample, say $h(X_1, X_2, \ldots, X_n)$, beyond the sum $\sum_{i=1}^{n} X_i$. In the same way the next asymptotic property, known as asymptotic Normality, is an extension of the **Central Limit Theorem** (CLT), discussed in chapter 9.

12.4.3 Asymptotic Normality

An estimator $\hat{\theta}_n$ of θ is said to be **asymptotically Normal** if we can find a normalizing sequence $\{c_n\}_{n=1}^{\infty}$ such that:

$$c_n(\hat{\theta}_n - \theta) \underset{a}{\sim} N(0, V_{\infty}(\theta)), \text{ for } V_{\infty}(\theta) \neq 0.$$

REMARKS:
(a)   "$\underset{a}{\sim}$" reads "asymptotically distributed".
(b) $V_{\infty}(\theta)$ denotes the asymptotic variance of $\hat{\theta}_n$.
(c)   The sequence $\{c_n\}_{n=1}^{\infty}$ is a function of n. For example, in the case of a random sample the normalizing sequence is defined by $c_n = \sqrt{n}$.

Example 1 Bernoulli (continued)
In the case of the estimators $\hat{\theta}_n$ and $\hat{\theta}_{n+1}$ of θ discussed above, we can show that they have the same asymptotically Normal distribution:

$$\sqrt{n}(\hat{\theta}_n - \theta) \underset{a}{\sim} N(0, \theta(1 - \theta)), \ \sqrt{n}(\hat{\theta}_{n+1} - \theta) \underset{a}{\sim} N(0, \theta(1 - \theta)). \tag{12.9}$$

Example 2 Normal (continued)
In the case of the estimators $\hat{\mu}_n$ and $\hat{\mu}_{n+1}$ of μ discussed above, we can show that they have the same asymptotically Normal distribution:

$$\sqrt{n}(\hat{\mu}_n - \mu) \underset{a}{\sim} N(0,1), \ \ \sqrt{n}(\hat{\mu}_{n+1} - \mu) \underset{a}{\sim} N(0,1). \tag{12.10}$$

For **consistent and asymptotically Normal (CAN) estimators** of θ, we use the asymptotic variance in order to choose between them. The smallest possible asymptotic variance, in the case where the Cramer–Rao regularity conditions are satisfied is given by the **asymptotic Fisher information** defined in terms of:

$$I_{\infty}(\theta) = \lim_{n \to \infty}\left(\left(\tfrac{1}{c_n}\right)^2 \cdot I_n(\theta)\right), \ \ CR_{\infty}(\theta) = [I_{\infty}(\theta)]^{-1},$$

where $CR_{\infty}(\theta)$ stands for *Asymptotic Cramer–Rao lower bound*.

Example 1 Bernoulli (continued)
In the case of the Bernoulli model we showed above that $E\left(-\frac{d^2 \ln f(x;\theta)}{d\theta^2}\right) = \frac{n}{\theta(1 - \theta)}$.
Hence:

$$I_{\infty}(\theta) = \lim_{n \to \infty}\left(\left(\tfrac{1}{n}\right)\frac{n}{\theta(1 - \theta)}\right) = \frac{1}{\theta(1 - \theta)} \Rightarrow CR_{\infty}(\theta) = \theta(1 - \theta).$$

Example 2 Normal (continued)
In the case of the Normal model discussed above, we showed that $E\left(-\frac{d^2 \ln f(x;\theta)}{d\theta^2}\right) = n$.
Hence:

$$I_{\infty}(\theta) = \lim_{n \to \infty}\left(\left(\tfrac{1}{n}\right)n\right) = 1 \Rightarrow CR_{\infty}(\theta) = 1.$$

12.4.4 Asymptotic efficiency

A CAN estimator $\hat{\theta}_n$ of θ is said to be **asymptotically efficient** if:

$$c_n(\hat{\theta}_n - \theta) \underset{a}{\sim} N(0,[I_\infty(\theta)]^{-1}), \text{ assuming } I_\infty(\theta) \neq 0.$$

That is, the asymptotic variance equals *the asymptotic Cramer–Rao lower bound.*

Example 1 Bernoulli (continued)
In the case of the Bernoulli model we have shown above that the estimators in (12.9) are indeed asymptotically efficient.

Example 2 Normal (continued)
In the case of the Normal model we have shown above that the estimators in (12.10) are indeed asymptotically efficient.

This suggests that the CAN estimators $\hat{\theta}_n$ and $\hat{\theta}_{n+1}$ are both asymptotically efficient because they achieve the asymptotic Cramer–Rao lower bound. As we can see the estimator $\hat{\theta}_n$ stands out because it satisfies all the desirable properties, finite sample and asymptotic.

12.4.5 Sampling distributions and properties of estimators

The discussion in this and the previous section revolved mostly around the first two moments of the sampling distributions of the estimators. This might give the erroneous impression that the sampling distribution itself is not needed and only the first two moments are required. We defined unbiasedness and efficiency in terms of the mean and variance of the sampling distribution of an estimator, respectively. Although the definition of consistency:

$$\lim_{n\to\infty} \mathbb{P}(|\hat{\theta}_n - \theta| < \varepsilon) = 1,$$

brings forth the role of the sampling distribution in evaluating the sequence of probabilities:

$$\{p_n\}_{n=1}^{\infty}, \text{ where } p_n := \mathbb{P}(|\hat{\theta}_n - \theta| < \varepsilon),$$

the most convenient way to prove consistency is often asymptotic behavior of the MSE; the latter involves only the first two moments. Similarly, the other asymptotic properties involve the sampling distribution but often this is not explicitly obvious. The fact of the matter is that in statistical inference what is often needed is the sampling distribution of the estimator itself, not just the first few moments. Our focus on the first two moments is primarily based on convenience. There are several other properties which are not defined in terms of the moments of the sampling distribution but some other numerical characteristic.

Mode unbiasedness An estimator $\hat{\theta}_n$ of θ is said to be *mode unbiased* if the sampling distribution of $\hat{\theta}_n$ has a mode which coincides with the unknown parameter θ:

$$Mode(\hat{\theta}_n) = \theta, \text{ for all } \theta \in \Theta.$$

Example 4* Uniform (continued)
Consider the estimator of θ defined by:

$$\hat{\theta}_{[n]} = \max(X_1, X_2, \ldots, X_n).$$

It can be shown (see chapter 11) that the sampling distribution of $\hat{\theta}_{[n]}$ is:

$$f(x;\theta) = \frac{nx^{n-1}}{\theta^n}, \ 0 < x < \theta.$$

In view of the fact that for any $\theta > 0$ the density function $f(x;\theta)$ has a unique maximum at the point $h(\theta) = \theta$, the estimator $\hat{\theta}_{[n]}$ is a mode unbiased estimator of θ:

$$Mode(\hat{\theta}_{[n]}) = \theta, \text{ for all } \theta \in (0, \infty).$$

Median unbiasedness An estimator $\hat{\theta}_n$ of θ is said to be *median unbiased* if the sampling distribution of $\hat{\theta}_n$ has a median which coincides with the unknown parameter θ:

$$Median(\hat{\theta}_n) = \theta, \text{ for all } \theta \in \Theta.$$

Example 2 Normal (continued)
In the case of the Normal model we have shown above that the estimator $\hat{\mu}_n = \frac{1}{n}\sum_{k=1}^{n} X_k$ is mean unbiased with a Normal sampling distribution. The latter implies that $\hat{\mu}_n$ is also a *mode* and *median* unbiased estimator.

In addition to using numerical characteristics of the sampling distribution, there are other ways to define *closeness* of an estimator to the true value of the parameter which bring out the role of the sampling distribution more clearly. For example we can define the notion of closeness of two estimators $\hat{\theta}$ and $\tilde{\theta}$ of the unknown parameter θ to the true value θ_0 using the following *concentration* measure:

$$\mathbb{P}(|\hat{\theta} - \theta_0| \le c) \ge \mathbb{P}(|\tilde{\theta} - \theta_0| \le c), \text{ for all } c > 0.$$

In the case where the above condition is valid and strict inequality holds for some values of $c > 0$, then $\hat{\theta}$ is said to be more *concentrated* around θ_0 than $\tilde{\theta}$. As we can see, the above comparison involves the sampling distributions of the two estimators directly. A measure of closeness along these lines is **Pitman's closer** measure (see Pitman (1937)):

$$\mathbb{P}(|\hat{\theta} - \theta_0| < |\tilde{\theta} - \theta_0|) \ge \frac{1}{2}, \text{ for all } \theta \in \Theta.$$

Such measures will not be pursued any further in this book but they are noted to emphasize the role of the sampling distribution in assessing the optimality of estimators.

12.5 The simple Normal model

In the previous section we use two very simple examples in an attempt to keep the technical difficulties at a minimum and concentrate on the ideas and concepts. In this section
we utilize (arguably) the most widely discussed model in statistics in an effort to illustrate
some of the finer points of good estimators.

12.5.1 The sampling distribution of the sample mean

Example 5
Consider the **simple Normal** (two parameter) **model**:

[i] Statistical GM: $X_k = \mu + \varepsilon_k$, $k \in \mathbb{N}$,
[ii] Probability model:

$$\Phi = \left\{ f(x;\theta) = \tfrac{1}{\sigma\sqrt{2\pi}} \exp\left\{ -\tfrac{1}{2\sigma^2}(x-\mu)^2 \right\}, \; \theta := (\mu,\sigma^2) \in \mathbb{R} \times \mathbb{R}_+, \; x \in \mathbb{R} \right\},$$

[iii] Sampling model: $\mathbf{X} := (X_1, X_2, \ldots X_n)$ is a random sample

We have already decided that the best estimator of μ, in the case of a one-parameter
Normal model is:

$$\hat{\mu}_n = \tfrac{1}{n}\sum_{i=1}^n X_i. \tag{12.11}$$

The intuitive argument why this estimator turns out to be a good estimator was given
above as the matching of the distribution and the sample moments, what we call the
moment matching principle in the next chapter. That is, it seems as though $\hat{\mu}_n$ turned out
to be an optimal estimator because the unknown parameter μ is the mean of the Normal
distribution $(E(X) = \mu)$ and the above estimator is just the mean of the sample $(X_1, X_2, \ldots,$
$X_n)$. Using the same intuitive argument for σ^2, where we know that $Var(X) = \sigma^2$, we
should consider the *sample variance* as a possible estimator of σ^2:

$$\hat{\sigma}_n^2 = \tfrac{1}{n}\sum_{i=1}^n (X_i - \hat{\mu}_n)^2. \tag{12.12}$$

Using lemma 2 of chapter 11 we can deduce that the sampling distribution of $\hat{\mu}_n$ takes
the form:

$$\hat{\mu}_n \sim N\!\left(\mu, \tfrac{\sigma^2}{n}\right).$$

This sampling distribution can then be used to establish the properties of this estimator.
In the case of the one-parameter Normal model ($\sigma^2 = 1$), we have seen above that $\hat{\mu}_n$ is an
unbiased, fully efficient and strongly consistent estimator of μ. The only thing that
changes is the Cramer–Rao lower bound but as shown below $\hat{\mu}_n$ is fully efficient because
it achieves the new lower bound.
  Consider the new distribution of the sample:

$$f(\mathbf{x};\mu,\sigma^2) = \left(\tfrac{1}{\sigma\sqrt{2\pi}}\right)^n \exp\left\{ -\tfrac{1}{2\sigma^2}\sum_{i=1}^n (x_i - \mu)^2 \right\},$$

$$\ln f(\mathbf{x};\mu,\sigma^2) = -\tfrac{n}{2}\ln(2\pi) - \tfrac{n}{2}\ln(\sigma^2) - \tfrac{1}{2\sigma^2}\sum_{i=1}^n (x_i - \mu)^2,$$

$$\frac{\partial \ln f(x;\mu,\sigma^2)}{\partial\mu} = \frac{1}{\sigma^2}\sum_{i=1}^{n}(x_i-\mu), \quad \frac{\partial \ln f(x;\mu,\sigma^2)}{\partial\sigma^2} = -\frac{n}{2\sigma^2}+\frac{1}{2(\sigma^2)^2}\sum_{i=1}^{n}(x_i-\mu)^2,$$

$$\frac{\partial^2 \ln f(x;\mu,\sigma^2)}{\partial\mu^2} = \frac{1}{\sigma^2}\sum_{i=1}^{n}(-1), \quad \frac{\partial^2 \ln f(x;\mu,\sigma^2)}{\partial(\sigma^2)^2} = \frac{n}{2\sigma^4}-\frac{1}{\sigma^6}\sum_{i=1}^{n}(x_i-\mu)^2,$$

$$\frac{\partial^2 \ln f(x;\mu,\sigma^2)}{\partial\sigma^2\partial\mu} = -\frac{1}{\sigma^4}\sum_{i=1}^{n}(x_i-\mu).$$

In this case the *Fisher information matrix* for the sample takes the form:

$$I_n(\mu,\sigma^2):=\begin{pmatrix} E\left(-\frac{\partial^2 \ln f(x;\mu,\sigma^2)}{\partial\mu^2}\right) & E\left(-\frac{\partial^2 \ln f(x;\mu,\sigma^2)}{\partial\sigma^2\partial\mu}\right) \\ E\left(-\frac{\partial^2 \ln f(x;\mu,\sigma^2)}{\partial\sigma^2\partial\mu}\right) & E\left(-\frac{\partial^2 \ln f(x;\mu,\sigma^2)}{\partial(\sigma^2)^2}\right) \end{pmatrix}$$

and the Cramer–Rao lower bound for any unbiased estimators of (μ,σ^2) is:

$$CR(\mu,\sigma^2):=[I_n(\mu,\sigma^2)]^{-1}.$$

Since $E\left(-\frac{\partial^2 \ln f(x;\mu,\sigma^2)}{\partial\sigma^2\partial\mu}\right)=0$, the Fisher information matrix takes the form:

$$I_n(\mu,\sigma^2):=\begin{pmatrix} \frac{n}{\sigma^2} & 0 \\ 0 & \frac{n}{2\sigma^4} \end{pmatrix},$$

and thus the Cramer–Rao lower bound for any unbiased estimators of the two parameters is:

$$CR(\mu)=\frac{\sigma^2}{n}, \quad CR(\sigma^2)=\frac{2\sigma^4}{n}. \tag{12.13}$$

As we can see, $\hat\mu_n$ achieves this bound. Moreover, we can easily show that $\hat\mu_n$ enjoys all the optimal asymptotic properties: *consistency, asymptotic Normality, and efficiency*:

$$\sqrt{n}(\hat\mu_n-\mu)\underset{a}{\sim}N(0,\sigma^2).$$

12.5.2 The sampling distribution of the sample variance

In order to derive the *sampling distribution* of $\hat\sigma_n^2$ we note that it is a quadratic function of Normally distributed random variables; $(X_1,X_2,\dots,X_n)$ are NIID by assumption and $\hat\mu_n$ is Normal as a linear combination of these random variables. Using lemma 4 (the sum of squares of n independent standard Normal random variables is chi-square with n degrees of freedom), we can deduce that:

given that $Z_i=\left(\frac{x_i-\mu}{\sigma}\right)\sim N(0,1)\Rightarrow\sum_{i=1}^{n}Z_i^2=\sum_{i=1}^{n}\left(\frac{x_i-\mu}{\sigma}\right)^2\sim\chi^2(n).$

Our estimator, however, is not exactly in this form because it involves $\hat\mu_n$ instead of μ and the two are quite different; the former is a random variable, the latter is a constant. But we can show that:

$$\sum_{i=1}^{n}\left(\frac{X_i-\mu}{\sigma}\right)^2=\sum_{i=1}^{n}\left(\frac{X_i-\hat\mu_n}{\sigma}\right)^2+n\left(\frac{\hat\mu_n-\mu}{\sigma}\right)^2, \tag{12.14}$$

(see Spanos (1986), p. 240). Given (12.11) we can deduce that:

$$n\left(\frac{\hat{\mu}_n - \mu}{\sigma}\right)^2 \sim \chi^2(1).$$

In addition, we can show that $n\left(\frac{\hat{\mu}_n - \mu}{\sigma}\right)^2$ and $\sum_{i=1}^n \left(\frac{X_i - \hat{\mu}_n}{\sigma}\right)^2$ are independent since the latter can be written as a function only of $(X_2 - \hat{\mu}_n, X_3 - \hat{\mu}_n, ..., X_n - \hat{\mu}_n)$ and these quantities are independent of $\hat{\mu}_n$. Firstly, we note that:

$$\sum_{i=1}^n (X_i - \hat{\mu}_n)^2 = (X_1 - \hat{\mu}_n)^2 + \sum_{i=2}^n (X_i - \hat{\mu}_n)^2 = [\sum_{i=2}^n (X_i - \hat{\mu}_n)]^2 + \sum_{i=2}^n (X_i - \hat{\mu}_n)^2,$$

because of the fact that $\sum_{i=1}^n (X_i - \hat{\mu}_n) = 0$ and thus $(X_1 - \hat{\mu}_n) = \sum_{i=2}^n (X_i - \hat{\mu}_n)$, i.e.

$$\hat{\sigma}_n^2 = g(X_2 - \hat{\mu}_n, X_3 - \hat{\mu}_n, ..., X_n - \hat{\mu}_n).$$

The independence of $\hat{\sigma}_n^2$ and $\hat{\mu}_n$ follows from the fact that when any random variables are independent so are any functions of them (see chapter 4).

In view of the fact that the left-hand side of (12.14) is distributed as $\chi^2(n)$ and the right-hand side is composed of two independent random variables and one has a $\chi^2(1)$ distribution, it follows from lemma 8(b) (see chapter 11) that:

$$\left(\frac{n \cdot \hat{\sigma}_n^2}{\sigma^2}\right) = \sum_{i=1}^n \left(\frac{X_i - \hat{\mu}_n}{\sigma}\right)^2 \sim \chi^2(n-1). \tag{12.15}$$

Using the fact that the mean of a chi-square distributed random variable equals the degrees of freedom (see appendix A), we can deduce that $E\left(\frac{n \cdot \hat{\sigma}_n^2}{\sigma^2}\right) = (n-1)$, which implies that $\hat{\sigma}_n^2$ is a biased estimator of σ^2 since:

$$E(\hat{\sigma}_n^2) = \frac{(n-1)}{n} \sigma^2 \neq \sigma^2.$$

Because of this bias, the alternative, unbiased estimator:

$$s_n^2 := \left(\frac{n}{n-1} \hat{\sigma}_n^2\right) = \frac{n}{n-1} \sum_{i=1}^n (X_i - \hat{\mu}_n)^2, \; E(s_n^2) := \sigma^2.$$

is often preferred in practice.

The question which arises is whether s_n^2, in addition to unbiasedness, has any further advantages over $\hat{\sigma}_n^2$. To derive the variance of the unbiased estimator s_n^2 we use the result that the variance of a chi-square distributed random variable is equal to twice its degrees of freedom (see appendix A), to deduce that:

$$Var\left(\frac{(n-1)s_n^2}{\sigma^2}\right) = 2(n-1) \Rightarrow Var(s_n^2) = \frac{2\sigma^4}{n-1} > CR(\sigma^2) = \frac{2\sigma^4}{n}.$$

That is, the estimator s_n^2 does not achieve the Cramer–Rao lower bound.

Searching for fully efficient estimators using the Cramer–Rao lower bound has left two important questions unanswered. First: What do we do when the regularity conditions are not met? A partial answer to this is provided by the Chapman–Robbins inequality (see Stuart and Ord (1991)). Second: How do we judge estimators, like s_n^2, which do not achieve the lower bound?

The answer is provided by (12.7) above, since $\frac{d \ln f(x;\mu,\sigma^2)}{d\sigma^2} = \left(\frac{n}{2\sigma^4}\right)\left(\left[\frac{1}{n}\sum_{i=1}^n (x_i - \mu)^2\right] - \sigma^2\right)$, which implies that:

$$\left(\left[\frac{1}{n}\sum_{i=1}^n (x_i - \mu)^2\right] - \sigma^2\right) = \left(\frac{2\sigma^4}{n}\right)\left[\frac{d \ln f(x;\mu,\sigma^2)}{d\sigma^2}\right]. \tag{12.16}$$

Hence, the only unbiased estimator of σ^2 that will achieve the $CR(\sigma^2)$ is $\left[\frac{1}{n}\sum_{i=1}^{n}(x_i-\mu)^2\right]$ which constitutes an estimator, however, only if μ is known. In other words we know that there is no unbiased estimator that achieves this bound unless μ is known. In view of this information: How do we judge the optimality of s_n^2?

Let us compare s_n^2 to $\hat{\sigma}_n^2 = \left(\frac{n-1}{n}\right)s_n^2$:

(i) $Var(\hat{\sigma}_n^2) = \left(\frac{n-1}{n}\right)^2 \frac{2\sigma^4}{n-1} = \left(\frac{2(n-1)}{n^2}\right)\sigma^4,$

(ii) $MSE(\hat{\sigma}_n^2) = \left(\frac{2(n-1)}{n^2}\right)\sigma^4 + \left(\left[\frac{n-1}{n}\right]\sigma^2 - \sigma^2\right)^2 = \left(\frac{2(n-1)}{n^2}\right)\sigma^4.$

This enables us to argue that in terms of Mean Square Error $\hat{\sigma}_n^2$ has smaller concentration around the true value of σ^2 than s_n^2:

$$MSE(\hat{\sigma}_n^2) = \left(\frac{2(n-1)}{n^2}\right)\sigma^4 < MSE(s_n^2) = \left(\frac{2}{n-1}\right)\sigma^4.$$

In turn, $\hat{\sigma}_n^2$ does not achieve the Cramer–Rao lower bound for biased estimators given that:

$$CRB(\sigma^2) = \left(\frac{dE(\hat{\sigma}_n^2)}{d\sigma^2}\right)^2 \left\{E\left(\frac{d\ln f(\mathbf{x};\mu,\sigma^2)}{d\sigma^2}\right)^2\right\}^{-1} = \left(\frac{n-1}{n}\right)^2\left(\frac{2\sigma^4}{n}\right) = \left(\frac{2(n-1)^2}{n^3}\right)\sigma^4.$$

After all the above comparisons between the estimators $\hat{\sigma}_n^2$ and s_n^2 we are no wiser as to which one is optimal in terms of their concentration around the true value of σ^2 mainly because the Cramer–Rao lower bound cannot be achieved by either of these estimators. We know from (12.16) that no unbiased estimator of σ^2 that achieves the $CR(\sigma^2)$ bound exists. The question that naturally arises at this stage is: Is there another estimator that comes closer to this bound? The answer is provided by another lower bound which is more achievable.

Bhattacharyya (1946), viewing the Cramer–Rao inequality as based on the correlation between an estimator $h(\mathbf{X})$ and $\left(\frac{d\ln f(\mathbf{x};\theta)}{d\theta}\right) = \frac{1}{f(\mathbf{x};\theta)}\frac{df(\mathbf{x};\theta)}{d\theta}$, proposed a sharper inequality based on the multiple correlation between $h(\mathbf{X})$ and:

$$\left(\frac{1}{f(\mathbf{x};\theta)}\frac{df(\mathbf{x};\theta)}{d\theta}\right), \left(\frac{1}{f(\mathbf{x};\theta)}\frac{d^2f(\mathbf{x};\theta)}{d\theta^2}\right), \left(\frac{1}{f(\mathbf{x};\theta)}\frac{d^3f(\mathbf{x};\theta)}{d\theta^3}\right), \cdots, \left(\frac{1}{f(\mathbf{x};\theta)}\frac{d^m f(\mathbf{x};\theta)}{d\theta^m}\right), m \geq 1.$$

Instead of being able to express the difference $(\hat{\theta}_n - \theta)$ as a linear function of the first derivative (see (12.7)), it is extended to include higher derivatives in the sense that:

$$(\hat{\theta} - \theta) = h(\theta)\left[\frac{1}{f(\mathbf{x};\theta)}\right]\sum_{k=1}^{m}a_k\left[\frac{d^k f(\mathbf{x};\theta)}{d\theta^k}\right], \quad m \geq 1, \tag{12.17}$$

for a function $h(\theta)$ and constants $k = 1,2,\ldots,m$. In the case where (12.7) holds, we can use the **Bhattacharyya lower bound**:

$$Var(\hat{\theta}) \geq \sum_{i,j=1}^{m}c_{ij}(\theta)\cdot a_i a_j, \text{ for some } m \geq 1, \tag{12.18}$$

where $c_{ij} := E\left(\left(\frac{1}{f(\mathbf{x};\theta)}\frac{d^i f(\mathbf{x};\theta)}{d\theta^i}\right)\left(\frac{1}{f(\mathbf{x};\theta)}\frac{d^j f(\mathbf{x};\theta)}{d\theta^j}\right)\right)$, and the coefficients are defined by the system of equations:

$$\sum_{j=1}^{m}c_{ij}(\theta)\cdot a_j = 1, \quad i = 1,2,\ldots,m.$$

In the case where $[c_{ij}(\theta)]_{i,j=1}^m$ is positive definite with an inverse of the form $[c^{ij}(\theta)]_{i,j=1}^m$, the Bhattacharyya lower bound is:

$$Var(\hat{\theta}) \geq \sum_{i,j=1}^m c^{ij}(\theta), \text{ for some } m \geq 1.$$

In our case we have two unknown parameters and we cannot use (12.17) directly; it should be extended to include the cross-product terms. To show that the unbiased estimator s_n^2 achieves this bound we observe that:

$$\left(\frac{1}{f(\mathbf{x};\theta)}\frac{\partial f(\mathbf{x};\mu,\sigma^2)}{\partial \sigma^2}\right) := \frac{\partial \ln f(\mathbf{x};\mu,\sigma^2)}{\partial \sigma^2} = \frac{-n}{2\sigma^2} + \frac{1}{2\sigma^4}\sum_{i=1}^n (x_i - \hat{\mu}_n)^2 + \frac{n}{2\sigma^4}(\hat{\mu}_n - \mu)^2,$$

$$\left(\frac{1}{f(\mathbf{x};\theta)}\frac{\partial^2 f(\mathbf{x};\mu,\sigma^2)}{\partial \mu^2}\right) := \frac{\partial \ln f(\mathbf{x};\mu,\sigma^2)}{\partial \mu^2} + \left(\frac{\partial \ln f(\mathbf{x};\mu,\sigma^2)}{\partial \mu}\right)^2 = \frac{-n}{\sigma^2} + \frac{n^2}{\sigma^4}(\hat{\mu}_n - \mu)^2.$$

Taking the following linear combination of these two derivatives we can show that:

$$[s_n^2 - \sigma^2] = \left(\frac{2\sigma^4}{n}\right)\left\{\left(\frac{n}{n-1}\right)\left[\frac{\partial \ln f(\mathbf{x};\mu,\sigma^2)}{\partial \sigma^2}\right] - \left(\frac{1}{2(n-1)}\right)\left(\frac{1}{f(\mathbf{x};\theta)}\frac{\partial^2 f(\mathbf{x};\mu,\sigma^2)}{\partial \mu^2}\right)\right\},$$

which confirms that the unbiased estimator s_n^2 is the better in the sense that it achieves the Bhattacharyya lower bound.

In terms of their asymptotic properties both estimators $\hat{\sigma}_n^2$ and s_n^2 of σ^2 enjoy all the optimal asymptotic properties: consistency, asymptotic Normality and asymptotic efficiency:

$$\sqrt{n}(\hat{\sigma}_n^2 - \sigma^2) \underset{a}{\sim} N(0,2\sigma^4), \quad \sqrt{n}(s_n^2 - \sigma^2) \underset{a}{\sim} N(0,2\sigma^4),$$

in view of the fact that the asymptotic Fisher's information matrix is:

$$I_\infty(\mu,\sigma^2) = \lim_{n\to\infty}\left(\frac{1}{n}I_n(\mu,\sigma^2)\right) := \begin{pmatrix} \frac{1}{\sigma^2} & 0 \\ 0 & \frac{1}{2\sigma^4} \end{pmatrix}.$$

12.5.3 Reducing the bias: jackknife estimators

There are occasions in practice where we need to reduce the bias of a certain estimator. Let $\hat{\theta}_n(\mathbf{X})$ be a biased estimator of the unknown parameter θ and the **bias** expressed in the following convenient form:

$$E(\hat{\theta}_n(\mathbf{X})) - \theta = \frac{a_1(\theta)}{n} + \frac{a_2(\theta)}{n^2} + \cdots \frac{a_k(\theta)}{n^k} + \cdots \quad (12.19)$$

NOTE that in most cases encountered so far the bias is of the first-order form, i.e.

$$E(\hat{\theta}_n(\mathbf{X})) - \theta = \frac{a_1(\theta)}{n}.$$

Jackknifing Consider the sequence of estimators of θ specified with $n-1$ observations:

$$\tilde{\theta}_{n-1}(\mathbf{X}_{(k)}), \ k = 1,2,\ldots,n, \quad (12.20)$$

where $\mathbf{X}_{(k)} := (X_1,X_2,\ldots X_{k-1},X_{k+1},\ldots,X_n)$. That is, we use the same formula as that of $\hat{\theta}_n(\mathbf{X})$ but we leave the kth observation out every time. We proceed to define the average (the arithmetic mean) of these estimators:

$$\tilde{\theta}_n(\mathbf{X}) := \frac{1}{n}\sum_{k=1}^n \tilde{\theta}_{n-1}(\mathbf{X}_{(k)}), \quad (12.21)$$

and then take a convex combination of this and the original estimator to define the *jack-knife estimator*:

$$\bar{\theta}_n(\mathbf{X}) = n\hat{\theta}_n(\mathbf{X}) - (n-1)\tilde{\theta}_n(\mathbf{X}).$$ (12.22)

Quenouille (1956) showed that for the new estimator $\bar{\theta}_n(\mathbf{X})$ the first-order bias disappears, i.e.

$$E(\bar{\theta}_n(\mathbf{X})) - \theta = \frac{a_2(\theta)}{n^2} + \cdots \frac{a_k(\theta)}{n^k} + \cdots$$ (12.23)

In the case where the bias was first order the jackknife estimator is now unbiased. Moreover, the first-order bias can be estimated using:

$$\text{Bias}(\hat{\theta}_n(\mathbf{X})) = (n-1)[\tilde{\theta}_n(\mathbf{X}) - \hat{\theta}_n(\mathbf{X})].$$ (12.24)

Example
Consider the Normal model as specified above and the estimation of the parameter σ^2. Let us apply the jackknife estimator in the case of the biased estimator:

$$\sigma_n^2 := \frac{1}{n}\sum_{k=1}^{n}(X_k - \bar{X})^2.$$

As shown above, the bias of this estimator is of first order and takes the form:

$$E(\hat{\sigma}_n^2) - \sigma^2 = -\frac{\sigma^2}{n}.$$

$$\hat{\theta}_n(\mathbf{X}) = \frac{1}{n}\sum_{i=1}^{n}(X_i - \bar{X})^2 = \frac{1}{n}\sum_{i=1}^{n}X_i^2 - \frac{1}{n^2}(\sum_{i=1}^{n}X_i)^2,$$

$$\tilde{\theta}_{n-1}(\mathbf{X}_{(k)}) = \frac{1}{(n-1)}\sum_{\substack{i=1\\i\neq k}}^{n}X_i^2 + \frac{1}{(n-1)^2}\left(\sum_{\substack{i=1\\i\neq k}}^{n}X_i\right)^2$$

$$\tilde{\theta}_n(\mathbf{X}) = \frac{1}{n}\sum_{i=1}^{n}\tilde{\theta}_{n-1}(\mathbf{X}_{(i)}) = \frac{1}{n}\sum_{i=1}^{n}X_i^2 - \frac{1}{n(n-1)^2}[\sum_{i=1}^{n}X_i^2) + (n-2)(\sum_{i=1}^{n}X_i^2].$$

After substituting these into the jackknife estimator we get:

$$\bar{\theta}_n(\mathbf{X}) = \sum_{i=1}^{n}X_i^2 - \frac{1}{n}\left(\sum_{i=1}^{n}X_i\right)^2 - \frac{(n-1)}{n}\sum_{i=1}^{n}X_i^2 + \frac{1}{n(n-1)}\sum_{i=1}^{n}X_i^2 + \frac{(n-2)}{n(n-1)}\left(\sum_{i=1}^{n}X_i\right)^2 =$$

$$= \frac{1}{(n-1)}\sum_{i=1}^{n}X_i^2 - \frac{1}{n(n-1)}\left(\sum_{i=1}^{n}X_i\right)^2 = \frac{1}{(n-1)}\sum_{i=1}^{n}(X_i - \bar{X})^2.$$

As we can see the jackknife estimator coincides with the unbiased estimator s^2 discussed in the previous subsection.

The common sense idea underlying the notion of jackknifing is almost trivial but its intrinsic intuition is far reaching. Let us see how jackknifing works to eliminate the first-order bias of an estimator. Beginning with the general form of the bias as given in (12.19) one can argue that the estimator $\tilde{\theta}_{n-1}(\mathbf{X}_{(k)})$ satisfies the similar relationship but based on $(n-1)$ observations:

$$E(\tilde{\theta}_n(\mathbf{X})) - \theta = \frac{a_1(\theta)}{n-1} + \frac{a_2(\theta)}{(n-1)^2} + \cdots \frac{a_k(\theta)}{(n-1)^k} + \cdots$$

$$E(n\hat{\theta}_n(\mathbf{X}) - (n-1)\tilde{\theta}_n(\mathbf{X})) - \theta = -\frac{a_2(\theta)}{n(n-1)} + \cdots$$

What makes jackknifing a very interesting idea, however, is the fact that it involves the *smoothing* operation in the form of averaging as shown in (12.21). This is best seen in the context of the example where the smoothing amounts to averaging of the averages:

$$\bar{\theta}_n(\mathbf{X}) := \frac{1}{n}\sum_{k=1}^{n} \tilde{\theta}_{n-1}(\mathbf{X}_{(k)}) = \frac{1}{n}\sum_{i=1}^{n}\left[\frac{1}{(n-1)}\sum_{\substack{i=1\\i\neq k}}^{n} X_i^2 + \frac{1}{(n-1)^2}\left(\sum_{\substack{i=1\\i\neq k}}^{n} X_i\right)^2\right].$$

This idea has its roots in the mathematical theory of Cesaro summability of divergent series going back to the late 19th early 20th centuries. There are cases where the series $\left\{s_n = \sum_{k=1}^{n} a_k\right\}_{n=1}^{\infty}$ diverges but its smoother version $\left\{\tau_n = \frac{1}{n}\sum_{k=1}^{n} s_k\right\}_{n=1}^{\infty}$ converges (see Knopp (1947)). Moreover, when the series $\left\{s_n = \sum_{k=1}^{n} a_k\right\}_{n=1}^{\infty}$ converges then $\left\{\tau_n = \frac{1}{n}\sum_{k=1}^{n} s_k\right\}_{n=1}^{\infty}$ also converges to the same limit, i.e.

if $\lim_{n\to\infty} s_n = s \Rightarrow \lim_{n\to\infty} \tau_n = s.$

We conclude this section by noting that the idea of jackknifing can be easily extended to higher-order bias reduction.

12.6 Sufficient statistics and optimal estimators*

The discussion of optimal estimators so far has not shed any light on the circumstances under which best estimators may be obtained. Returning to the analogy of an archer standing at the foot of a hill with the target on the other side beyond his vision, we have discussed only the question of assessing the closeness once the arrow has landed. The question of devising a strategy relating to factors within his control, such as the shooting angle and the pulling power so as to ensure that the arrow will land as close to the target as possible, has not been discussed. The property of estimators known as sufficiency addresses this very question and in terms of this analogy it proposes attaching a kind of net to the arrow designed in a way that ensures optimal coverage.

12.6.1 Sufficiency

The idea of sufficiency goes back to Fisher (1922b) but the concept was formalized in the early 1930s. The notion of *sufficiency* raises the possibility of reducing the dimensionality of the observed data without any loss of information. The original sample information comes in the form of a set of data $\mathbf{x} := (x_1, x_2, \ldots, x_n)$, viewed as a realization of a particular sample $\mathbf{X} := (X_1, X_2, \ldots, X_n)$ as specified a priori by the statistical model $S := (\Phi, \mathbf{X})$. A statistic $h(\mathbf{X})$, a function defined on the sample space X (not necessarily an estimator), is *sufficient* if it summarizes the whole of the relevant information for the postulated statistical model S. It is often called a sufficient statistic for θ because the statistical model is determined once θ is determined. Intuitively, sufficiency refers to how well an estimator (a function of a statistic) utilizes the information in the sample as it relates to the postulated statistical model Φ. The usefulness of the notion of sufficiency arises from the fact that the statistic $h(\mathbf{X})$ is often of much lower dimension than the n-dimensional sample. Before embarking on definitions it is important to explain the intuition underlying the property using an example.

Example 1 Bernoulli (continued)
In the case of the Bernoulli model we know that the sample $\mathbf{X} := (X_1, X_2, \ldots, X_n)$ is made up of IID Bernoulli distributed random variables with $\mathbb{P}(X_k = 1) = \theta$ and $\mathbb{P}(X_k = 0) = (1 - \theta)$. A sample realization will involve a sequence of zeros and ones, e.g.

$$\mathbf{x} := (0, 1, 0, 0, 1, \ldots, 1).$$

In view of the fact that the exact location of ones in this realization is irrelevant because of the IID assumptions, it is intuitively obvious that knowing the sum is equivalent to knowing the exact realization. In this case it looks as though the statistic $h(\mathbf{X}) = \sum_{k=1}^{n} X_k$ contains all the relevant information as it relates to the Bernoulli statistical model Φ. That is, knowing the whole realization $\mathbf{x}$ is equivalent to knowing just the sum $h(\mathbf{x}) = \sum_{k=1}^{n} x_k$. The bottom line is that instead of carrying the n numbers of the sample realization we carry just one, their sum; a significant reduction in dimension. Hence, intuitively it seems that this statistic is sufficient for Φ (or θ).

This example brings out the desirability of a sufficient statistic by showing that the statistic itself contains the same information about θ as the original sample but it has a much lower dimensionality. The attraction of a sufficient statistic arises from the fact that if there exists a best estimator then it is necessarily a function of the sufficient statistic. Moreover, finding a sufficient statistic can be used as the first step to defining an optimal estimator. Let us discuss all these results beginning with the definition of sufficiency.

Intuitively, sufficiency of a statistic $Y = h(\mathbf{X})$ for a parameter θ means that when the value of the statistic is given, every other form of information is irrelevant for θ. This suggests that knowing the realization of whole sample $\mathbf{X}$, when the value of $Y = h(\mathbf{X})$ is known, adds no information relevant for θ (or Φ). Formalizing this intuitive idea gives rise to the following definition of sufficiency.

Sufficiency A statistic $h(\mathbf{X})$ is said to be a *sufficient statistic* for θ if and only if the conditional distribution of the sample $\mathbf{X}$ given $h(\mathbf{X}) = y$ does not depend on θ:

$$f(\mathbf{x} \mid h(\mathbf{x}) = y; \theta) = q(\mathbf{x}), \text{ for all } \mathbf{x} \in X, \ \theta \in \Theta. \tag{12.25}$$

This definition, although intuitive, does not provide the modeler with a direct way to find sufficient statistics. The modeler has to guess $h(\mathbf{X})$ first and then proceed to verify (12.25), which does not look trivial. The next theorem, due to Halmos and Savage (1949), simplifies the task of the modeler considerably.

Factorization theorem A statistic $h(\mathbf{X})$ is said to be a *sufficient statistic* for θ if and only if there exist functions $g(h(\mathbf{X}); \theta)$ and $v(\mathbf{X})$, where the former depends on $\mathbf{X}$ only through

$h(\mathbf{X})$ while the latter is free of θ, such that the distribution of the sample factors into the product:

$$f(\mathbf{x};\theta) = g(h(\mathbf{x});\theta) \cdot v(\mathbf{x}), \text{ for all } \mathbf{x} \in X, \, \theta \in \Theta. \tag{12.26}$$

Finding a sufficient statistic using this theorem entails inspection of the distribution of the sample and some imagination to be able to notice the factorization.

Example 2 Normal (continued)
Consider the Normal (one-parameter) model (σ^2 assumed known):

$$f(\mathbf{x};\mu) = \prod_{k=1}^{n} \frac{1}{\sigma\sqrt{2\pi}} = e^{-\left\{\frac{1}{2\sigma^2}(x_k - \mu)^2\right\}} = \left(\frac{1}{2\pi\sigma^2}\right)^{-\frac{n}{2}} \exp\left\{-\frac{1}{2\sigma^2}\sum_{k=1}^{n}(x_k - \mu)^2\right\} =$$

$$= \left(\frac{1}{2\pi\sigma^2}\right)^{-\frac{n}{2}} \exp\left\{-\frac{1}{2\sigma^2}\sum_{k=1}^{n}(x_k - \bar{x} + \bar{x} - \mu)^2\right\} =$$

$$= \left(\frac{1}{2\pi\sigma^2}\right)^{-\frac{n}{2}} \exp\left\{-\frac{1}{2\sigma^2}\sum_{k=1}^{n}(x_k - \bar{x})^2 + n(\bar{x} - \mu)^2\right\}.$$

This result can be used to factor the distribution of the sample into (12.26):

$$f(\mathbf{x};\mu) = \left[\exp\left\{-\frac{n}{2\sigma^2}(\bar{x} - \mu)^2\right\}\right] \cdot \left[\left(\frac{1}{2\pi\sigma^2}\right)^{-\frac{n}{2}} \exp\left\{-\frac{1}{2\sigma^2}\sum_{k=1}^{n}(x_k - \bar{x})^2\right\}\right],$$

where the first factor in square brackets depends on μ only through the statistic $\overline{X} = \frac{1}{n}\sum_{k=1}^{n} X_k$, and the second is free of μ. In view of the above theorem, the statistic $\overline{X}$ is sufficient for μ.

It is important to NOTE that the factorization theorem is directly related to the necessary and sufficient condition for the *full efficiency* of an estimator $\hat{\theta}$ of θ in the sense that the condition:

$$(\hat{\theta} - \theta) = h(\theta)\left[\frac{d\ln f(\mathbf{x};\theta)}{d\theta}\right],$$

implies that the distribution of the sample has the form (12.26). This suggests that an efficient estimator exists if and only if a sufficient statistic exists; the converse, however, is not necessarily true.

Example 5 Normal (continued)
Consider the Normal (two-parameter) model (σ^2 assumed unknown). Using the equality:

$$\sum_{k=1}^{n}(X_k - \mu)^2 = \left[\sum_{k=1}^{n}X_k^2\right] - 2\mu\left[\sum_{k=1}^{n}X_k\right] + n\mu^2 = h_2(\mathbf{X}) - 2\mu\left[h_1(\mathbf{X})\right] + n\mu^2,$$

we can proceed to factor the distribution of the sample into:

$$f(\mathbf{x};\mu,\sigma^2) = \left(\frac{1}{2\pi\sigma^2}\right)^{-\frac{n}{2}} \exp\left\{-\frac{1}{2\sigma^2}\sum_{k=1}^{n}(x_k - \mu)^2\right\} = g(h(\mathbf{x});\mu,\sigma^2) \cdot v(\mathbf{x}) =$$

$$= \left[\left(\frac{1}{2\pi\sigma^2}\right)^{-\frac{n}{2}} \exp\left\{-\frac{1}{2\sigma^2}h_2(\mathbf{X}) - 2\mu\left[h_1(\mathbf{X})\right] + n\mu^2\right\}\right] \cdot [1].$$

Hence, the statistics $(h_1(\mathbf{X}) := \sum_{k=1}^n X_k, \; h_2(\mathbf{X}) := \sum_{k=1}^n X_k^2$ are sufficient for the unknown parameters (μ, σ^2). Using these statistics we can define the estimators:

$$\hat{\mu}_n = \left(\tfrac{1}{n}\right) h_1(\mathbf{X}) = \left(\tfrac{1}{n}\right) \sum_{k=1}^n X_k,$$

$$s_n^2 := \left(\tfrac{1}{n-1}\right)[h_2(\mathbf{X}) - (h_1(\mathbf{X}))^2] = \left(\tfrac{1}{n-1}\right)\sum_{k=1}^n (X_k - \hat{\mu}_n)^2,$$

for the parameters (μ, σ^2), respectively. In the previous section it was demonstrated that these two estimators are indeed optimal.

Example 4 Uniform (continued)
The distribution of the sample in this case takes the form:

$$f(\mathbf{x};\theta) = \prod_{k=1}^n \left(\tfrac{1}{\theta}\right) = \left(\tfrac{1}{\theta^n}\right), \text{ for } 0 \le x_{[1]} \le x_{[n]} \le \theta,$$

where $X_{[1]} = \min(X_1, X_2, ..., X_n)$ and $X_{[n]} = \max(X_1, X_2, ..., X_n)$ are the two extreme order statistics. Using the heaviside function:

$$\mathfrak{h}(x) = \begin{cases} 0, \text{ for } x < 0, \\ 1, \text{ for } x \ge 1, \end{cases}$$

we can express $f(\mathbf{x};\theta)$ as: $f(\mathbf{x};\theta) = \left[\tfrac{1}{\theta^n}(\mathfrak{h}(\theta - x_{[n]}))\right] \cdot [\mathfrak{h}(x_{[1]})]$. This suggests that $X_{[n]}$ is a sufficient statistic for θ and when looking for optimal estimators we should consider functions of $X_{[n]}$. We remind the reader that we used the estimator $\hat{\theta}_n = \left(\tfrac{n}{n+1}\right) X_{[n]}$, in one of the illustrations relating to the Cramer–Rao lower bound.

12.6.2 Sufficiency and unbiasedness

Let us return to our primary goal which is to devise a strategy for defining optimal estimators. We will see in this section that there exists a direct relationship between sufficient statistics and unbiased estimators. Intuitively, the relationship between sufficiency and unbiasedness is that if the modeler begins with some arbitrary unbiased estimator and then defines another estimator by conditioning on a sufficient statistic, the resulting estimator will often have a smaller variance than the original unbiased estimator.

In order to derive this relationship we recall two important properties of conditional expectations for any two random variables X and Y such that $Var(X) < \infty$, $Var(Y) < \infty$:

(a) $E(E(Y|X)) = E(Y)$,
(b) $Var(Y) = E(Var(Y|X)) + Var(E(Y|X))$; see chapter 7, section 3.

Rao–Blackwell theorem (see Blackwell (1947), Rao (1949)) Let $\hat{\theta}$ be an unbiased estimator of θ $(E(\hat{\theta}) = \theta)$, and let $h(\mathbf{X})$ be a sufficient statistic for θ. The statistic defined by:

$$\tilde{\theta} = E(\hat{\theta}|h(\mathbf{X})),$$

satisfies the following properties:

(i) $\tilde{\theta}$ is an *estimator* of θ,
(ii)   unbiased: $E(\tilde{\theta}) = \theta$,
(iii)   relatively more efficient than $\hat{\theta}$: $Var(\tilde{\theta}) \le Var(\hat{\theta})$.

Property (ii) follows from the fact that:

$$E(\hat{\theta}) = E[E(\hat{\theta}|h(\mathbf{X}))] = E(\tilde{\theta}) = \theta,$$

and property (iii) from:

$$Var(\hat{\theta}) = Var(E(\hat{\theta}|h(\mathbf{X}))) + E[Var(\hat{\theta}|h(\mathbf{X}))] =$$
$$= Var(\tilde{\theta}) + E[Var(\hat{\theta}|h(\mathbf{X}))] \ge Var(\tilde{\theta}).$$

The discerning reader might be wondering if sufficiency is required for the above results to hold since no use of sufficiency is made in deriving (ii)–(iii). The truth of the matter is that $\tilde{\theta}$ is an estimator (it does not depend on unknown parameters) exactly because $h(\mathbf{X})$ is a sufficient statistic.

The Rao–Blackwell theorem provides a way to improve upon an unbiased estimator by offering a relatively more efficient estimator than the original but it does not tell us anything about the full efficiency of the resulting estimator. The modeler can proceed to check the Cramer–Rao lower bound but if the resulting estimator does not attain it, she is no wiser.

12.6.3 Minimal sufficiency

The above results suggest that when seeking best unbiased estimators the best strategy for the modeler is to check for the presence of sufficient statistics and then proceed to define optimal estimators in terms of these sufficient statistics using the Rao–Blackwell theorem or just inspiration. However, the sample itself $\mathbf{X}$ (and any one-to-one function of it) is a sufficient statistic (the trivial sufficient statistic) and this strategy will be fruitful only if it can be based on a sufficient statistic which economizes on the dimensions. This leads to the notion of a minimal sufficient statistic which achieves the maximum possible data reduction without any loss of information. In view of the fact that when seeking optimal estimators of θ we should consider functions of a sufficient statistic $h(\mathbf{X})$, say $g(h(\mathbf{X}))$, we call the latter a *necessary* statistic. The necessary statistic does not necessarily contain all the relevant information in the data. But when a statistic is both necessary and sufficient it must be a minimal sufficient statistic.

Minimal sufficient statistic A sufficient statistic $h(\mathbf{X})$ is *minimal* if every other sufficient statistic $g(\mathbf{X})$ is a function of it, i.e. for every sufficient statistic $g(\mathbf{X})$:

$$g(\mathbf{X}) = q(h(\mathbf{X})) \text{ for some function } q(.).$$

It is important to note that for any statistical model, as defined in this book, there always exists a minimal sufficient statistic; not excluding the sample itself in dimension.

Neither the definition of a sufficient statistic nor the factorization theorem provides an easy way to devise sufficient statistics. The following result, however, provides a relatively easy way to derive minimal sufficient statistics. The idea is due to Lehmann and Scheffe (1950).

Lehmann–Scheffe theorem 1 Suppose that there exists a statistic $h(\mathbf{X})$ such that for two different sample realizations $\mathbf{x}$ and $\mathbf{z}$ ($\mathbf{x} \in X$, $\mathbf{z} \in X$), the ratio:

$\frac{f(\mathbf{x};\theta)}{f(\mathbf{z};\theta)}$ is free of θ, if and only if $h(\mathbf{X}) = h(\mathbf{Z})$,

then $h(\mathbf{X})$ is a minimal sufficient statistic for θ.

Example 1 Bernoulli (continued)
In the case of the Bernoulli model the ratio:

$$\frac{f(\mathbf{x};\theta)}{f(\mathbf{z};\theta)} = \frac{\theta^{\sum_{k=1}^{n} x_k} (1-\theta)^{\sum_{k=1}^{n}(1-x_k)}}{\theta^{\sum_{k=1}^{n} z_k}(1-\theta)^{\sum_{k=1}^{n}(1-z_k)}} = \left(\frac{\theta}{1-\theta}\right)^{\sum_{k=1}^{n}(x_k - z_k)},$$

is free of θ if and only if: $\sum_{k=1}^{n} X_k = \sum_{k=1}^{n} Z_k$. Hence, the statistic $\left(\sum_{k=1}^{n} X_k\right)$ is not just sufficient but minimal sufficient.

Example 5 Normal (continued)
Consider the Normal (two-parameter) model (σ^2 unknown). The ratio:

$$\frac{f(\mathbf{x};\mu,\sigma^2)}{f(\mathbf{z};\mu,\sigma^2)} = \frac{\left(\frac{1}{2\pi\sigma^2}\right)^{-\frac{n}{2}} \exp\left\{-\frac{1}{2\sigma^2}\sum_{k=1}^{n}(x_k - \mu)^2\right\}}{\left(\frac{1}{2\pi\sigma^2}\right)^{-\frac{n}{2}} \exp\left\{-\frac{1}{2\sigma^2}\sum_{k=1}^{n}(z_k - \mu)^2\right\}} =$$

$$= \exp\left\{-\frac{1}{2\sigma^2}\left[\sum_{k=1}^{n} x_k^2 - \sum_{k=1}^{n} z_k^2\right] + \frac{n}{\sigma^2}\left[\sum_{k=1}^{n} x_k - \sum_{k=1}^{n} z_k\right]\right\},$$

is free of (μ,σ^2) if and only if:

$$\sum_{k=1}^{n} X_k^2 = \sum_{k=1}^{n} Z_k^2, \quad \sum_{k=1}^{n} X_k = \sum_{k=1}^{n} Z_k.$$

Hence, the statistics $\left(\sum_{k=1}^{n} X_k^2, \sum_{k=1}^{n} X_k\right)$ are not just sufficient but minimal sufficient.

12.6.4 Completeness

Returning to our primary goal which is to find optimal estimators using sufficient statistics, we observe that the notion of the minimal sufficient statistic cannot guarantee the uniqueness of this estimator because any one-to-one function of a minimal sufficient statistic is also minimal sufficient. To ensure the uniqueness of optimal estimators we need another property of sufficient statistics called completeness.

Completeness is a property of a family of densities and intuitively means that the only unbiased estimator of zero is zero itself. The family of densities $\Phi = \{f_x(x;\theta),\ \theta \in \Theta\}$ is said to be *complete* if, for every function $\tau(X)$, the following relationship holds:

$$E(\tau(X)) = 0 \Rightarrow \tau(X) = 0 \ (a.s) \text{ for all } x \in \{x : f_x(x;\theta) > 0\}.$$

This notion can be transplanted unchanged to the case of the distribution of the sample $f(\mathbf{x};\theta)$ by replacing X by the sample $\mathbf{X}$ in the above relationship. In the case of a sufficient statistic we need to define completeness in terms of the distribution of this statistic.

Completeness A sufficient statistic $Y = h(\mathbf{X})$ is said to be *complete* if the family of densities $G := \{f_y(y;\theta),\ \theta \in \Theta\}$ is complete.

NOTE: the usefulness of the property of completeness stems from the fact that if $h(\mathbf{X})$ is a complete sufficient statistic and $\hat{\theta} = g(h(\mathbf{X}))$ an unbiased estimator of θ, i.e.

$$E(g(h(\mathbf{X}))) = \theta,$$

then this estimator is unique.

The relationship between a complete sufficient statistic and a minimal sufficient statistic is that *a complete sufficient statistic is minimal sufficient* (see Lehmann and Scheffe (1950)). This brings us to the end of our search for best unbiased estimators by utilizing sufficient statistics. The main result is given by the following theorem (see Lehmann and Scheffe (1955)).

Lehmann–Scheffe theorem 2 Let $h(\mathbf{X})$ be a complete sufficient statistic for θ (or better, for a statistical model S). If there exists an unbiased estimator $\hat{\theta}$ of θ, which is a function of $h(\mathbf{X})$ (i.e. $\hat{\theta} = g(h(\mathbf{X}))$), then this estimator is both *best* and *unique*.

Example 4 Uniform (continued)
In an attempt to illustrate some of the above results let us return to the problematical Uniform model discussed above. In view of the fact that:

$$E(X) = \frac{\theta}{2},$$

it might be tempting to use the correspondence between the distribution and sample moments to derive the estimator $\hat{\theta} = 2\left(\frac{1}{n}\sum_{k=1}^{n} X_k\right)$. This is certainly not a bad estimator because it is both unbiased:

$$E(\hat{\theta}) = 2\left(\frac{1}{n}\sum_{k=1}^{n}(X_k)\right) = \left(\frac{2}{n}\right)\left(\frac{n\theta}{2}\right) = \theta.$$

and consistent:

$$Var(\hat{\theta}) = \frac{\theta^2}{3n} \to 0 \text{ as } n \to \infty.$$

However, it is not the best estimator. We know from the above discussion that:

$$X_{[n]} = \max\,(X_1, X_2, \ldots, X_n),$$

is a sufficient statistic for θ. Using the Rao–Blackwell theorem we proceed to define the estimator:

$$\tilde{\theta} = E(\hat{\theta}\,|\,X_{[n]}) = E\left(2\left(\frac{1}{n}\sum_{k=1}^{n} X_k\right)\,|\,X_{[n]}\right) = \left(\frac{n}{n+1}\right)X_{[n]}.$$

It turns out that the family of densities under consideration is complete and thus this estimator is the best unbiased estimator of θ; it is also unique.

The main drawback of the above mentioned strategy lies with ensuring that a certain minimal sufficient statistic is also complete. To get a taste of the difficulties consider the relatively simple case in the following example.

Example 1 Bernoulli (continued)
In the case of the Bernoulli model the statistic $S_n := \sum_{k=1}^{n} X_k$ is minimal sufficient with a sampling distribution (see lemma 1) of the form:

$$f(s_n;\theta) = \binom{n}{s} \theta^s (1 - \theta)^{n-s}, \; \theta \in [0,1].$$

Consider an estimator $l(\mathbf{X})$ such that $E(l(\mathbf{X})) = 0$ for all $\theta \in [0,1]$:

$$\sum_{s=0}^{n} l(\mathbf{X}) \binom{n}{s} \theta^s (1 - \theta)^{n-s} = 0, \text{ for all } \theta \in [0,1].$$

In view of the fact that the function $g(\theta) = \sum_{s=0}^{n} l(\mathbf{X}) \binom{n}{s} \theta^s (1 - \theta)^{n-s}$ is a polynomial in $\left(\frac{\theta}{1-\theta}\right)$ with roots at most n, it is equal to zero if and only if: $l(\mathbf{X}) = 0$, for all $s = 0,1,2,...,n$. This suggests that $S_n := \sum_{k=1}^{n} X_k$ is also a complete sufficient statistic.

Combining the above theorem with that of Rao–Blackwell, the modeler can form the following strategy: in the case where a complete sufficient statistic exists, she should begin with an arbitrary unbiased estimator and then proceed to derive the conditional expectation given the sufficient statistic; see Casela and Berger (1990).
     Returning to the analogy of an archer standing at the foot of a hill with the target on the other side beyond his vision, the question of devising a strategy relating to factors within his control, can now be answered: attach a net we call a complete sufficient statistic on the arrow in an attempt to specify an unbiased estimator.

12.6.5 Exponential family of distributions

There is an important family of densities for which the problem of finding a minimal sufficient statistic, that is also complete, is relatively easy. This is the exponential family (not the exponential model).

Exponential family of densities A probability model $\Phi = \{f(x;\theta), \theta \in \Theta\}$ is said to belong to the exponential family if the density function can be expressed in the form:

$$f(x;\theta) = c(\theta) \cdot h(x) \exp\left(\sum_{i=1}^{k} g_i(\theta) \cdot \tau_i(x)\right),$$

(a) $c(\theta) \geq 0,$
(b) $h(x) \geq 0,$
(c) $g_i(\theta), i = 1,2,...,k$: real-valued functions (free of x),
(d) $\tau_i(x), i = 1,2,...,k$: real-valued functions (free of θ).

Many well-known distributions such as the Normal, Gamma, Beta, Binomial, Poisson, and Negative Binomial belong to this family. For this family, the statistics:

$$\left(\sum_{j=1}^{n} \tau_i(x_j)\right), i = 1, 2, \ldots, k),$$

are minimal sufficient statistics for $(g_i(\theta), i = 1, 2, \ldots, k)$, and in the case where the number of unknown parameters in θ is k, these statistics are also complete.

12.7 What comes next?

The aim of this chapter has been to formalize the notion of an *optimal* estimator. Using the intuitive notion of an *ideal* estimator we motivated the finite sample properties of unbiasedness and efficiency and the asymptotic properties of consistency, asymptotic Normality and asymptotic efficiency. Using the notion of optimal reduction of the relevant information in the data we motivated the property of sufficiency. In the next chapter we proceed to discuss *methods of estimation* which often give rise to optimal estimators.

12.8 Exercises

1 Explain briefly what we do when we construct an *estimator*. Why is an estimator a random variable?

2 "Defining the sampling distribution of an estimator is theoretically trivial but deriving it is very difficult." Discuss.

3 For the Bernoulli statistical model:
  (i) Discuss whether the following functions constitute possible estimators of θ:

  (a) $\hat{\theta}_1 = X_n,$ (b) $\hat{\theta}_2 = \frac{1}{2}(X_1 - X_2),$ (c) $\hat{\theta}_3 = \frac{1}{3}(X_1 - X_2 + X_n),$

  (d) $\hat{\theta}_n = \frac{1}{n}\sum_{i=1}^{n} X_i,$ (e) $\hat{\theta}_n + 1 = \frac{1}{n+1}\sum_{i=1}^{n} X_i,$

  (ii) For those that constitute estimators derive their sampling distributions.

4 Explain briefly the properties of *unbiasedness* and *efficiency of* estimators.

5 "In assessing the optimality of an estimator we need to look at the first two moments of its sampling distribution only." Discuss.

6 Explain briefly what a *consistent* estimator is. What is the easiest way to prove consistency for estimators with bounded second moments?

7 Explain briefly the difference between *weak* and *strong consistency* of estimators.

8 "*Asymptotic Normality* of an estimator is an extension of the Central Limit Theorem for functions of the sample beyond the sample mean." Discuss.

9 Explain the difference between *full efficiency* and *asymptotic efficiency*.

10 Explain the notion of the *ideal* estimator and explain intuitively how its definition relates to the properties of unbiasedness, efficiency, and consistency.

11 Explain the difference between the Cramer–Rao and Bhattacharyya lower bounds.

12 Explain the notion of *sufficiency.*

13 Explain the notion of a *minimal sufficient statistic* and how it relates to best unbiased estimator.

14 Explain the Rao–Blackwell theorem and how it can be used to derive best, unbiased estimators.

15 Consider the **Normal** (two parameter) **statistical model.**

(a) Derive (not guess!) the sampling distributions of the following estimators:

(i) $\hat{\mu}_1 = X_n,$ (ii) $\hat{\mu}_2 = \frac{1}{3}(X_1 + X_2 + X_3),$

(iii) $\hat{\mu}_3 = (X_1 - X_n),$ (iv) $\hat{\mu}_n = \frac{1}{n}\sum_{i=1}^{n} X_i,$

(HINT: State explicitly any properties of $E(.)$ or any lemmas you use).

(b) Compare these estimators in terms of the optimal properties, unbiasedness, efficiency, and consistency.

(c) Compare and contrast the estimators $\hat{\sigma}_n^2 = \frac{1}{n}\sum_{i=1}^{n}(X_i - \hat{\mu}_n)^2$, and $s_n^2 = \frac{1}{n+1}\sum_{i=1}^{n}(X_i - \hat{\mu}_n)^2$, in terms of their properties.

13 Estimation II: Methods of estimation

13.1 Introduction

In the previous chapter we discussed estimators and their properties. The main desirable finite sample properties discussed in chapter 12 were:

Unbiasedness,   Efficiency,

with *Sufficiency* being a property relating to specific probability models. The desirable asymptotic properties discussed in the previous chapter were:

Consistency,   Asymptotic Normality,   Asymptotic efficiency.

The notion of the *ideal estimator* was used as a comparison rod in order to enhance the intuitive understanding of these properties. The question of how one can construct good estimators was sidestepped in the previous chapter. The primary objective of this chapter is to consider this question in some detail by discussing four estimation methods:

1   **The moment matching principle,**
2   **The least-squares method,**
3   **The method of moments,** and
4   **The maximum likelihood method.**

13.1.1 A bird's eye view of the chapter

In section 2 we discuss an approach to estimation that has intuitive appeal but lacks generality. We call this procedure the moment matching principle because we estimate unknown parameters by matching distribution and sample moments. The relationship between the distribution and the sample moments is also of interest in the context of the other methods. Section 3 introduces the least-squares method, first as a mathematical approximation method and then as a proper estimation method in modern statistical inference. In section 4 we discuss Pearson's method of moments and then compare it with the *parametric method of moments*, an adaptation of the original method for the current paradigm of statistical inference. The maximum likelihood method is discussed in section 5.

13.1.2 Methods of estimation: a preliminary view

The discussion that follows differs from the traditional textbook discussion in a number of ways which we summarize at the outset. It is argued that the *moment matching principle* arose during the 19th and early 20th century as part of the broader confusion between relative frequencies and probabilities. The same confusion permeates the method of moments as proposed by Pearson in 1895, designed to use the data in order to choose an adequate description in the form of a frequency curve from the Pearson family. Both of these procedures were developed in the context of what we nowadays call *descriptive statistics.* Pearson's method, however, was later adapted to suit the modern approach to statistical inference. In order to distinguish between Pearson's method and the adapted method we refer to the latter as the *parametric method of moments*. A particular thesis taken in the discussion that follows is that all estimation methods are better understood in the context of the statistical framework (paradigms) in which they were first developed. In this sense the only estimation method specifically developed for the modern approach to statistical inference, which entails postulating a statistical model a priori and interpreting the data as a realization of the stochastic mechanism described by this model, is that of *maximum likelihood*, proposed by Fisher in the 1920s; its roots can be traced back to Fisher (1912). The other three methods were developed in the context of different paradigms and it is important to keep that in mind when we discuss these methods. The least-squares method, as a *mathematical approximation technique* (approximating an unknown function over an interval), was developed in the early 1800s in the context of a statistical paradigm known as *the theory of errors.* In section 3 we propose an alternative interpretation of least squares as the sample equivalent to the orthogonal decomposition used to define the concept of a statistical generating mechanism (GM) in chapter 7.

The maximum likelihood (ML) method was specifically developed to utilize all the information available at the specification stage of modeling: the statistical model and the observed data. Because of that, the ML method has certain obvious advantages over the other methods. For example, the moment matching principle and the method of moments often yield less efficient estimators, because they do not utilize all the available information in the statistical model; they ignore part of the information relating to the probability model. This can be explained by the fact that the paradigm in the context of which these methods were developed, did not involve postulating a statistical model a priori. Instead, the modeling proceeded *from the data to the best descriptive model* in the form of a frequency curve. Similarly, least squares was originally developed as a *curve fitting* technique for functions defined over a certain domain. The probabilistic structure was later introduced into the formulation via the error of approximation in a non-essential way. In contrast, the method of maximum likelihood was designed for an approach where the modeler postulates a statistical model a priori and the observed data are viewed as a realization of the chance mechanism as specified by the postulated statistical model.

13.2 Moment matching principle

The **moment matching principle** cannot be credited to any one famous statistician because a case can be made that it essentially arose out of a fundamental confusion between distribution and sample moments. In his classic paper, that provided the foundations of modern statistical inference, Fisher attributed the neglect of the theoretical basis of statistical methods to two reasons:

(i)   *A philosophical reason*: since statistics is "a subject in which all results are liable to greater or smaller errors, precise definition of ideas or concepts is, if not impossible, at least not a practical necessity" (Fisher (1922b), p. 311).

(ii) *A methodological reason*: "it has happened that in statistics a purely verbal confusion has hindered the distinct formulation of statistical problems; for it is customary to apply the same name, *mean*, *standard deviation*, *correlation coefficient*, etc. both to the true value which we should like to know, but can only estimate, and the particular value at which we happen to arrive by our methods of estimation" (Fisher (1922b), p. 311).

Fisher pointed to a confusion between three different concepts: the moment of a probability distribution, its estimator and the corresponding estimate based on a specific sample realization. A confusion brought about owing to the use of the same term for all three different notions. Unfortunately for statistics this choice of inappropriate terminology still permeates the subject. The price of this inappropriate and often confused terminology is paid by the students and teachers of statistics who need to waste a lot of valuable time trying to distinguish between different concepts that carry the same terminology.

Table 13.1 presents three very different groups of moments carrying the same names. The first column presents these moments in the context of descriptive statistics where they represent ways to summarize the observed data using measures of location, dispersion, etc. As such these moments refer to the moments of what we call the relative frequencies of the observed data and they denote just summarizing numbers. These numbers should be contrasted with the sample moments in the third column where the formulae look identical apart from the fact that we use capital instead of small letters for X. Despite the appearance the sample moments are qualitatively very different from the descriptive statistics moments. The sample moments are functions of a sample $(X_1, X_2, \ldots, X_n)$ whose probabilistic structure is determined a priori by the statistical model chosen. As such the sample moments represent random variables as opposed to just numbers as in the case of the descriptive statistics moments. The latter, as pointed out by Fisher, also differ qualitatively from the particular values taken by the sample moments based on the particular sample realization, even though we often use identical notation; they represent a particular value of a random variable not just summarizing numbers. Finally, the moments of a probability distribution differ from all these other moments in so far as they represent unknown constants which are defined in terms of particular density functions. We chose to define these moments for continuous random variables in terms of integrals in order to make the contrast more apparent. For discrete random variables the raw moments are defined via:

Table 13.1. *Moments*

	Frequency	Probability	Sample
mean	$\frac{1}{n}\sum_{i=1}^{n} x_i := \bar{x},$	$\mu_1' := \int_{x\in\mathbb{R}_X} xf(x)dx,$	$\hat{\mu}_1'(\mathbf{X}) = \frac{1}{n}\sum_{i=1}^{n} X_i := \bar{X},$
variance	$\frac{1}{n}\sum_{i=1}^{n} (x_i-\bar{x})^2,$	$\mu_2 := \int_{x\in\mathbb{R}_X} (x-\bar{x})^2 f(x)dx,$	$\hat{\mu}_2(\mathbf{X}) = \frac{1}{n}\sum_{i=1}^{n} \left(X_i - \bar{X}\right)^2,$
raw moments	$\frac{1}{n}\sum_{i=1}^{n} x_i^r,$	$\mu_r' := \int_{x\in\mathbb{R}_X} x^r f(x)dx,$	$\hat{\mu}_r'(\mathbf{X}) = \frac{1}{n}\sum_{i=1}^{n} X_i^r,$
central moments	$\frac{1}{n}\sum_{i=1}^{n} (x_i-\bar{x})^r,$	$\mu_r := \int_{x\in\mathbb{R}_X} (x-E(x))^r f(x)dx,$	$\hat{\mu}_r(\mathbf{X}) = \frac{1}{n}\sum_{i=1}^{n} \left(X_i - \bar{X}\right)^r,$

where $r = 2,3,\ldots$

$$\mu_r' := E(X^r) = \sum_{x\in\mathbb{R}_X} x^r f(x), \; r = 1,2,\ldots$$

What distinguishes these moments from all the other ones is the presence of a particular density function in the definition. As argued in chapter 3, the probability distribution moments are often the best way to handle the unknown parameters $\boldsymbol{\theta}$. This follows from the fact that these moments depend crucially on the nature of the density function, which in turn is a function of $\boldsymbol{\theta}$, and thus the moments are functions of $\boldsymbol{\theta}$. This relationship is exemplified by the raw moments below:

$$\mu_r' := E(X^r) = \int_{x\in\mathbb{R}_X} x^r f(x;\boldsymbol{\theta})dx = \mu_r'(\boldsymbol{\theta}), \; r = 1,2,\ldots$$

The confusion between the various uses of the term moments is compounded by the fact that in statistical inference we often talk about the moments of the sample moments. In an attempt to deal with that difficulty we utilize the notation $(\mu_r'(.),\mu_r(.))$ which enables us to be specific on which moments we are referring to when it is not obvious from the context. Hence, the notation $\mu_r'(\bar{X})$, $r=1,2,3,\ldots$, denotes the raw moments of the sampling distribution of the sample mean.

During the 18th and 19th centuries the distinction between probabilities and relative frequencies did not exist; in the mind of the mathematicians of that time the two coincided. In view of this, it should come as no surprise to anyone to learn that the transition from descriptive statistics to statistical inference during the first part of the 20th century went largely unnoticed even by pioneers such as Karl Pearson (see below). Hence, the endemic practice of conflating distribution and sample (descriptive statistics) moments during this transition period became much later the *moment matching principle*:

defining estimators by matching distribution moments with sample moments.

The **moment matching principle** is implemented in two steps:

Step 1   Relate the unknown parameter θ to the moments of the distribution in terms of which the probability model is specified, say,

$$\theta = g(\mu_1', \mu_2').$$

Step 2   Substitute the sample moments in the place of the distribution moments:

$$\hat{\mu}_1' = \frac{1}{n}\sum_{i=1}^{n} X_i, \quad \hat{\mu}_2' = \frac{1}{n}\sum_{i=1}^{n} X_i^2,$$

i.e., construct an estimator of θ, via: $\hat{\theta} = g(\hat{\mu}_1', \hat{\mu}_2')$.

NOTE: it is worth noting at this stage that this procedure is the reverse of the one used for the Method of Moments (see below), where we have the relationship specified in terms of the moments, say $\mu_1' = h_1(\theta_1, \theta_2)$, $\mu_2' = h_2(\theta_1, \theta_2)$, substitute the sample moments in place of (μ_1', μ_2') and then solve for (θ_1, θ_2) to define their estimators.

Example 1   Consider the simple Bernoulli model:

[i]   Statistical GM: $X_k = \theta + \varepsilon_k,\ k \in \mathbb{N},$
[ii]   Probability model: $\Phi = \{f(x;\theta) = \theta^x(1-\theta)^{1-x},\ \theta \in [0,1],\ x = 0,1\},$
[iii] Sampling model: $\mathbf{X} := (X_1, X_2, \ldots X_n)$ is a random sample.

In view of the fact that for the **Bernoulli model** the unknown parameter θ coincides with the **mean** of X:

$$E(X) = \theta,$$

the moment matching principle suggests that a natural estimator for θ is the *sample mean*:

$$\hat{\theta} = \frac{1}{n}\sum_{i=1}^{n} X_i.$$

Example 2
Consider the **simple Normal model**:

[i]   Statistical GM: $X_k = \mu + u_k,\ k \in \mathbb{N},$
[ii]   Probability model:

$$\Phi = \left\{ f(x;\boldsymbol{\theta}) = \frac{1}{\sigma\sqrt{2\pi}}\exp\left\{ -\frac{1}{2\sigma^2}(x-\mu)^2 \right\},\ \boldsymbol{\theta} := (\mu,\sigma^2) \in \mathbb{R} \times \mathbb{R}_+,\ x \in \mathbb{R} \right\},$$

[iii] Sampling model: $\mathbf{X} := (X_1, X_2, \ldots X_n)$ is a random sample.

For the *Normal model* specified above the unknown parameters $\boldsymbol{\theta} := (\mu, \sigma^2)$ are related to the distribution moments via:

$$E(X) = \mu,\ Var(X) = \sigma^2.$$

The moment matching principle proposes the sample mean and the sample variance, respectively, as the obvious estimators of these parameters, i.e.

$$\hat{\mu} = \frac{1}{n}\sum_{i=1}^{n} X_i,\ \hat{\sigma}^2 = \frac{1}{n}\sum_{i=1}^{n}(X_i - \hat{\mu})^2.$$

Example 3

Consider the **Normal linear regression model**:

[i]   Statistical GM: $Y_t = \beta_0 + \beta_1 x_t + u_t,\ t \in \mathbb{N}$

[ii] Probability model:

$$\Phi = \left\{ f(y_t \mid x_t; \boldsymbol{\theta}) = \frac{\sigma^{-1}}{\sqrt{2\pi}} exp\left\{ -\frac{1}{2\sigma^2}(Y_t - \beta_0 - \beta_1 x_t)^2 \right\},\ \boldsymbol{\theta} := (\mu, \sigma^2) \in \mathbb{R}^2 \times \mathbb{R}_+,\ y_t \in \mathbb{R} \right\},$$

[iii] Sampling model: $\mathbf{Y} := (Y_1, Y_2, ..., Y_T)$ is an independent sample.
      sequentially drawn from $f(y_t \mid x_t; \boldsymbol{\theta}),\ t = 1, 2, ..., T$.

In this case the unknown parameters are related to the moments of the random variables y and X via:

$$\beta_0 = E(Y_t) - \beta_1 E(X_t),\ \beta_1 = \frac{Cov(Y_t, X_t)}{Var(X_t)},\ \sigma^2 = Var(Y_t) - \frac{(Cov(Y_t, X_t))^2}{Var(X_t)}.$$

By substituting the sample moments, in place of the distribution moments, we get the following *moment matching principle estimators*:

$$\hat{\beta}_0 = \overline{Y} - \hat{\beta}_1 \overline{x},\ \hat{\beta}_1 = \frac{\frac{1}{T}\sum_{t=1}^{T}(Y_t - \overline{Y})(x_t - \overline{x})}{\frac{1}{T}\sum_{t=1}^{T}(x_t - \overline{x})^2},\ \hat{\sigma}^2 = \frac{1}{T}\sum_{t=1}^{T}(Y_t - \overline{Y})^2 - \frac{\left(\frac{1}{T}\sum_{t=1}^{T}(Y_t - \overline{Y})(x_t - \overline{x})\right)^2}{\frac{1}{T}\sum_{t=1}^{T}(x_t - \overline{x})^2}.$$

In all the above cases the estimators suggested by the moment matching principle turn out to enjoy several optimal properties. For example, as shown in the previous chapter, $\hat{\theta}$ is an unbiased, efficient, and consistent estimator of θ, and $\hat{\mu}$ is an unbiased, efficient, and consistent estimator of μ. The question which naturally arises is whether the estimators suggested by the moment matching principle *always* enjoy such optimal properties. The answer is that such estimators tend to have good properties but often not as good as these examples suggest. Let us consider this statement in some more detail.

13.2.1 Sample moments and their properties

As argued above, the *raw* and *central moments* of a univariate random variable X:

$$\mu_r'(\theta) := \int_{x \in \mathbb{R}_X} x^r f(x; \theta) dx,\ r = 1, 2, ...\quad \mu_r(\theta) := \int_{x \in \mathbb{R}_X} (x - \mu)^r f(x; \theta) dx,\ r = 2, 3 ...$$

correspond to the *sample moments*:

$$\hat{\mu}_r' = \frac{1}{n}\sum_{i=1}^{n} X_i^r,\ r = 1, 2, 3 ...\quad \hat{\mu}_r = \frac{1}{n}\sum_{i=1}^{n}(X_i - \hat{\mu})^r,\ r = 2, 3 ...$$

Similarly, in chapter 4 we defined the *joint distribution raw and central moments*:

$$\hat{\mu}_{r,s}'(\theta) = \int_{x \in \mathbb{R}_X}\int_{y \in \mathbb{R}_Y} x^r y^s f(x, y; \theta) dxdy,\ r, s = 1, 2, 3 ...$$

$$\hat{\mu}_{r,s}(\theta) = \int_{x \in \mathbb{R}_X}\int_{y \in \mathbb{R}_Y} (x - \mu_x)^r(y - \mu_y)^s f(x, y; \theta) dxdy,\ r, s = 1, 2, 3 ...$$

Table 13.2. *Moments*

Distribution	Sample
$E(X) := \mu$	$\hat{\mu} = \frac{1}{n} \sum_{i=1}^{n} X_i,$
$Var(X) := \sigma^2$	$\hat{\sigma}^2 = \frac{1}{n} \sum_{i=1}^{n} (X_i - \hat{\mu})^2,$
$SD(X) := \sigma$	$\hat{\sigma} = \left(\frac{1}{n} \sum_{i=1}^{n} (X_i - \hat{\mu})^2 \right)^{\frac{1}{2}},$
$\alpha_3 := \frac{\mu_3}{\sigma^3}$	$\hat{\alpha}_3 = \left(\frac{1}{n} \sum_{i=1}^{n} (X_i - \hat{\mu})^3 \right) / \hat{\sigma}^3,$
$\alpha_4 := \frac{\mu_4}{\sigma^4}$	$\hat{\alpha}_4 = \left(\frac{1}{n} \sum_{i=1}^{n} (X_i - \hat{\mu})^4 \right) / \hat{\sigma}^4,$
$Cov(X, Y) := \sigma_{xy}$	$\hat{\sigma}_{xy} = \frac{1}{n} \sum_{i=1}^{n} (X_i - \hat{\mu}_x)(Y_i - \hat{\mu}_y).$

The corresponding *sample joint raw* and *central moments* are:

$$\hat{\mu}'_{r,s} = \frac{1}{n} \sum_{i=1}^{n} X_i^r Y_i^s, \quad \hat{\mu}_{r,s} = \frac{1}{n} \sum_{i=1}^{n} (X_i - \hat{\mu}_x)^r (Y_i - \hat{\mu}_y)^s, \quad r,s = 1,2,3 \dots$$

For implementing the moment matching principle, table 13.2 summarizes the first few distributions and the corresponding sample moments.

Of interest in the present context are the sampling distributions of the above sample moments and their properties. In general the distribution of any sample moment depends crucially on the probability and sampling models postulated. As we saw in the previous chapter, in the case of a random sample from the Bernoulli distribution, the estimator $\hat{\theta} = \frac{1}{n} \sum_{i=1}^{n} X_i$ (the sample mean) is Binomially distributed and turns out to be an unbiased, fully efficient, and consistent estimator of θ. Moreover, in the case of the simple Normal model, the estimator $\hat{\mu} = \frac{1}{n} \sum_{i=1}^{n} X_i$ is normally distributed and turns out to be an unbiased, fully efficient, and consistent estimator of μ.

In practice the moment matching principle estimators are often used in cases of incomplete *simple statistical models* where no explicit probability model is postulated a priori. In such cases, of course, we cannot determine the sampling distribution of an estimator (unless we resort to asymptotic theory) and the available results often relate to the first few moments of this unknown distribution. In the case of an *incomplete* simple statistical model (i.e., irrespective of the explicit nature of Φ, but assuming that the required moments exist) we can derive the results in table 13.3 for the *sample raw moments*.

These results suggest that, in the case of a random sample, irrespective of the underlying distribution (assuming the required moments exist), the sample raw moments provide **unbiased** and **consistent** *estimators* for the distribution raw moments.

Table 13.3. *Sample raw moments*

$$E(\hat{\mu}_r') = \mu_r', \; r = 1,2,3, \; \ldots,$$

$$Var(\hat{\mu}_r') = \frac{1}{n}(\mu_{2r}' - [\mu_r']^2), \;\; r = 1,2,3, \; \ldots,$$

$$Cov(\hat{\mu}_r', \hat{\mu}_s') = \frac{1}{n}(\mu_{r+s}' - \mu_r'[\mu_s']^2) \; r = 1,2,3, \ldots$$

Table 13.4. *Sample mean* $\hat{\mu} = \frac{1}{n}\sum_{i=1}^{n} X_i$

$$E(\hat{\mu}) = \mu,$$

$$Var(\hat{\mu}) = \frac{1}{n}\sigma^2,$$

$$\mu_3(\hat{\mu}) := E(\hat{\mu} - \mu)^3 = \frac{1}{n^3} E(X - \mu)^3,$$

$$\mu_4(\hat{\mu}) := E(\hat{\mu} - \mu)^4 = \frac{1}{n^3} E(X - \mu)^4 + \frac{3(n-1)}{n^3} [E(\hat{\mu} - \mu)^2]^2.$$

Table 13.5. *Sample central moments*

$$E(\hat{\mu}_r) = \left(1 - \frac{r}{n}\right)\mu_r + \frac{r(r-1)}{2n}\mu_{r-2}\mu_2 + o(n^{-1}) = \mu_r + O(n^{-1}),$$

$$Var(\hat{\mu}_r) = \frac{1}{n}(\mu_{2r} - \mu_r^2 + r^2\mu_2\mu_{r-1}^2 - 2r\mu_{r-1}\mu_{r+1}) + o(n^{-1})$$

$$Cov(\hat{\mu}_r, \hat{\mu}_s) = \frac{1}{n}(\mu_{r+s} - \mu_r\mu_s + rs\mu_2\mu_{s-1}\mu_{r-1} - r\mu_{r-1}\mu_{s+1} - s\mu_{r+1}\mu_{s-1}) + o(n^{-1})$$

Consistency follows from the fact that the variance of the sample raw moments $Var(\mu_r')$ goes to zero as $n \to \infty$.

A particularly important example of such moments is the sample mean whose first few moments are shown in table 13.4.

The formulae for the **sample central moments** are not as simple as those of the sample raw moments because they involve the sampling variation of the sample mean. Table 13.5 shows the approximation of the first two moments of the *sample central moments* (see Stuart and Ord (1994)) where the notation $o(n^k)$ and $O(n^k)$ denotes the order of approximation.

The NOTATION $a_n = o(n^k)$, for some $k \neq 0$, denotes a sequence $\{a_n\}_{n=1}^{\infty}$ *of order smaller than n^k*, i.e.

$$\lim_{n \to \infty} \left(\frac{a_n}{n^k}\right) = 0,$$

and the notation $a_n = O(n^k)$ denotes a sequence $\{a_n\}_{n=1}^{\infty}$ *at most of order n^k*, i.e.

$$\lim_{n \to \infty} \left(\frac{|a_n|}{n^k}\right) \leq K \text{ where } 0 < K < \infty,$$

(see Spanos (1986)). NOTE that for $k > 0$: $a_n = O(n^k) \Rightarrow a_n = o(n^{k+1})$.

Table 13.6. *Sample variance*

$$E(\hat{\sigma}^2) \quad = \left(\frac{n-1}{n}\right)\sigma^2,$$

$$Var(\hat{\sigma}^2) \quad = \frac{\mu_4 - \mu_2^2}{n} - \frac{2(\mu_4 - 2\mu_2^2)}{n^2} + \frac{\mu_4 - 3\mu_2^2}{n^3},$$

$$Cov(\hat{\mu},\hat{\sigma}^2) = \left(\frac{n-1}{n}\right)\mu_3,$$

Table 13.7. *Sample joint moments*

$$E(\hat{\mu}'_{r,s}) = \mu_{r,s}, \ r,s = 1,2,3,\ldots,$$

$$Var(\hat{\mu}'_{r,s}) = \frac{1}{n}(\mu'_{2r,2s} - [\hat{\mu}'_{r,s}]^2) \ r,s = 1,2,3,\ldots$$

To get some idea on what these approximations refer to, let us consider the moments of the sample variance, shown in table 13.6. The covariance of $\hat{\sigma}^2$ and $\hat{\mu}$ suggests that in the case where the random sample comes from a symmetric distribution ($\mu_3 = 0$), $\hat{\mu}$ and $\hat{\sigma}^2$ are uncorrelated i.e. $Cov(\hat{\mu},\hat{\sigma}^2) = 0$.

NOTE that μ_r, $r = 2,3,4$ denote the distribution moments of the underlying probability model. In the case of higher sample central moments, the results in table 13.5 are only approximate results in the sense that in the case where r is even:

$$Cov(\hat{\mu},\hat{\mu}_r) = \frac{1}{n}(\mu_{r+1} - r\mu_2\mu_{r-1}) + o(n^{-1}),$$

and thus for a symmetrical distribution μ_{r+1},μ_{r-1} will be zero because they are odd moments and thus uncorrelated to order n^{-1}:

$$Cov(\hat{\mu},\hat{\mu}_r) = 0 + o(n^{-1}).$$

The results on the sample central moments suggest that since:

(a) $\lim_{n\to\infty} E(\hat{\mu}_r) = \mu_r,$ (b) $\lim_{n\to\infty} Var(\hat{\mu}_r) = 0$, for $r = 2,3,\ldots \Rightarrow \hat{\mu}_r \xrightarrow{\mathbb{P}} \mu_r,$

i.e., $\hat{\mu}_r$ is a *consistent estimator* of μ_r, for $r = 2,3,\ldots$

In the case of the joint raw sample moments we can show (see table 13.7) that the results are very similar to the ordinary sample raw moments (see Stuart and Ord (1994)).

The most widely used statistic based on the second sample joint moment is the correlation coefficient:

$$\hat{\rho} = \frac{\sum_{i=1}^{n} (X_i - \hat{\mu}_x)(Y_i - \hat{\mu}_y)}{\sqrt{[\sum_{i=1}^{n}(X_i - \hat{\mu}_x)^2][\sum_{i=1}^{n}(Y_i - \hat{\mu}_y)^2]}}.$$

As we can see, the variance of the sample correlation coefficient is a highly complicated function of several joint moments of the distribution underlying the postulated

Table 13.8. *Sample correlation coefficient*

$$E(\hat{\rho}) = \rho + o(n^{-1}),$$

$$Var(\hat{\rho}) = \frac{\rho^2}{n} \left\{ \frac{\mu_{22}}{\mu_{11}^2} + \frac{1}{4} \left(\frac{\mu_{40}}{\mu_{20}^2} + \frac{\mu_{04}}{\mu_{02}^2} + \frac{2\mu_{22}}{\mu_{20}\mu_{02}} \right) - \left(\frac{\mu_{31}}{\mu_{11}\mu_{20}} + \frac{\mu_{13}}{\mu_{11}\mu_{02}} \right) \right\} + o(n^{-1}).$$

probability model. In the case of the bivariate Normal model with unit variances (see chapter 6) this expression reduces to:

$$Var(\hat{\rho}) = \frac{1}{n}(1 - \rho^2)^2 + o(n^{-1}).$$

It turns out that the above results for the sample moments simplify appreciably in the case of the simple Normal model; in table 13.9 we summarize these simplifications (see Stuart and Ord (1994)).

The results in relation to the first few moments of the sample moments show most clearly the difficulty in both deriving and operationalizing such results. To derive even approximate results for sample moments higher than the fourth turns out to be very messy and complicated. Fisher (1929), however, showed us that this is not the best way to proceed. Instead, he demonstrated that the so-called k-statistics related to the sample cumulants are much easier to handle because their sampling cumulants can be derived using combinatorial methods (see McCullagh (1987)).

So far we found that in the case of a random sample, estimators suggested by the moment matching principle are in general consistent and sometimes unbiased; the primary example of this procedure's success is the case of the raw moments.

What about efficiency and asymptotic normality?

Estimators suggested by the moment matching principle are often *inefficient* because the estimators ignore important information relating to the probability model: the nature of the underlying distribution. They are, however, asymptotically Normal. This result follows from the fact that a standardized form of the sample raw moments is normal with mean zero and variance $[\mu'_{2r} - (\mu'_r)^2]$ i.e.

$$\sqrt{n}(\hat{\mu}'_r - \mu'_r) \underset{\alpha}{\sim} N(0, [\mu'_{2r} - (\mu'_r)^2]),$$

where $\underset{\alpha}{\sim}$ reads asymptotically distributed as. Similarly:

$$\sqrt{n}(\hat{\mu}_r - \mu_r) \underset{\alpha}{\sim} N(0, V_\infty(\mu_r)), \text{ where } V_\infty(\mu_r) = (\mu_{2r} - 2r\mu_{r-1}\mu_{r+1} - \mu_r^2 + r^2\mu_2\mu_{r-1}^2).$$

13.2.2 Functions of the sample moments

As argued above, the estimation of a parameter θ using the moment matching principle involves relating it to certain distribution moments and then replacing the latter with the corresponding sample moments. Hence, often the above results cannot be used directly unless θ coincides with a certain distribution moment. In this sense it is of interest to consider the sampling distribution of function, say $g(.)$, of the sample moments. The

Table 13.9. *Variances of common statistics*

model	Simple generic statistical model	Normal
$\hat{\mu}_1'$:	$\frac{1}{n}(\mu_2),$	$\frac{1}{n}(\mu_2)$
$\hat{\mu}_2$:	$\frac{1}{n}(\mu_4 - \mu_2^2) + o(n^{-1}),$	$\frac{1}{n}(2\mu_2^2)$
$\sqrt{\hat{\mu}_2}$:	$\frac{1}{n4\mu_2}(\mu_6 - \mu_3^2) + o(n^{-1}),$	$\frac{1}{2n}(\mu_2)$
$\hat{\mu}_3$:	$\frac{1}{n}(\mu_4 - \mu_2^2 - 6\mu_4\mu_2 + 9\mu_2^3) + o(n^{-1}),$	$\frac{1}{n}(6\mu_2^3)$
$\hat{\mu}_4$:	$\frac{1}{n}(\mu_8 - \mu_4^2 - 8\mu_5\mu_3 + 16\mu_3^2\mu_2) + o(n^{-1}),$	$\frac{1}{n}(96\mu_2^4)$
$\hat{\alpha}_3$:	$\frac{1}{n}\left(\frac{\mu_6}{\mu_2^3} - 6\alpha_4 + 9 + \frac{\alpha_3^2}{4}(9\alpha_4 + 35) - \frac{3\mu_3\mu_5}{\mu_2^4}\right) + o(n^{-1}),$	$\frac{6n(n-1)}{(n-2)(n+1)(n+3)}$
$\hat{\alpha}_4$:	$\frac{1}{n}\left(\frac{\mu_8}{\mu_2^4} - \frac{4\mu_6\mu_4}{\mu_2^5} + 4\alpha_4^2 - \alpha_4^2 + 16\alpha_4\alpha_3^2 - \frac{8\mu_3\mu_5}{\mu_2^4} - 16\alpha_3^2\right) + o(n^{-1}),$	$\frac{24n(n-1)^2(n+5)^{-1}}{(n-3)(n-2)(n+3)}$

easiest way to deal with this problem is to derive approximate results based on a Taylor's series expansion of the function of the sample moment (see Serfling (1980)):

$$g(\hat{\mu}_r') = g(\mu_r') + \frac{\partial g(\mu_r')}{\partial \mu_r'}(\hat{\mu}_r' - \mu_r') + \frac{1}{2}\frac{\partial^2 g(\mu_r')}{\partial(\mu_r')^2}(\hat{\mu}_r' - \mu_r')^2 + \dots$$

In view of the fact that $E(\hat{\mu}_r' - \mu_r') = 0$, this expansion can be utilized to derive approximate results for the first few moments of this function (see Sargan (1974)):

$$E(g(\hat{\mu}_r')) \simeq g(\mu_r') + \frac{1}{2}\frac{\partial^2 g(\mu_r')}{\partial^2 \mu_r'}E(\hat{\mu}_r' - \mu_r')^2,$$

$$Var(g(\hat{\mu}_r')) \simeq \left[\frac{\partial^2 g(\mu_r')}{\partial(\mu_r')^2}\right]^2 E(\hat{\mu}_r' - \mu_r')^2,$$

where $\simeq$ denotes the asymptotic approximation. Using these results we can deduce that in the case of a differentiable function $g(.)$ of the sample moments whose derivative at μ_r' (the true value) is non-zero, i.e., $\frac{\partial g(\mu_r')}{\partial \mu_r'} \neq 0$:

$$\sqrt{n}(g(\hat{\mu}_r') - g(\mu_r')) \underset{\alpha}{\sim} N\left(0, \left[\frac{\partial g(\mu_r')}{\partial \mu_r'}\right]^2[\mu_{2r}' - (\mu_r')^2]\right).$$

The derivations get a bit more complicated when the function $g(.)$ involves more than one sample moment. Consider the case where $g(\hat{\mu}_1', \hat{\mu}_2', \dots, \hat{\mu}_m')$, $m < n$:

$$g(\hat{\mu}_1', \hat{\mu}_2', \dots, \hat{\mu}_m') = g(\mu_1', \mu_2', \dots, \mu_m') + \sum_{k=1}^m \frac{\partial g(\mu')}{\partial \mu_k'}(\hat{\mu}_k' - \mu_k')O(n^{-1}),$$

where $\mu = (\hat{\mu}_1', \hat{\mu}_2', \dots, \hat{\mu}_m')$. From this we can deduce that:

$$E(g(\hat{\mu}_1', \hat{\mu}_2', \dots, \hat{\mu}_m')) \simeq g(\mu_1', \mu_2', \dots, \mu_m')$$

$$Var(g(\hat{\mu}_1', \hat{\mu}_2', \dots, \hat{\mu}_m')) \simeq E\left\{\sum_{k=1}^m \frac{\partial g(\mu')}{\partial \mu_k'}(\hat{\mu}_k' - \mu_k')\right\}^2 =$$

$$= \sum_{k=1}^m \left[\frac{\partial g(\mu')}{\partial \mu_k'}\right]^2 Var(\hat{\mu}_k') + \sum_{k=1}^m \sum_{\substack{\ell=1 \\ k \neq \ell}}^m \left(\frac{\partial g(\mu')}{\partial \mu_k'}\right)\left(\frac{\partial g(\mu')}{\partial \mu_\ell'}\right)Cov(\hat{\mu}_k', \hat{\mu}_\ell').$$

We remind the reader once more that these results are based on the restrictive assumption of a random sample.

13.3 The least-squares method

13.3.1 The principle of least squares

The principle of least squares was originally proposed as a mathematical approximation procedure by Legendre in 1805; see Harter (1974–76). The principle provided a way to *approximate*:

an *unknown* function $y = g(x)$, by a *half-known* function $h(x) = \sum_{i=0}^{k} a_i \phi_i(x)$

where $\phi_0(x), \phi_1(x), \phi_2(x), ..., \phi_k(x)$ are appropriately chosen *known* functions of x:

(e.g., $\phi_0(x) = 1, \ \phi_1(x) = x, \ \phi_2(x) = x^2, ..., \phi_k(x) = x^k$),

in a way which ensures that the $g(x)$ and $h(x)$ agree as well as possible over a certain domain D; often a set of T discrete points ($T > k$). The notion of optimal approximation, in the least-squares sense is defined in terms of minimizing the sum of squared errors, where the **error** is defined by:

$$\epsilon_t = \left(y_t - \sum_{i=0}^{k} a_i \phi_i(x_t) \right),$$

over the domain $D = \{(y_t, x_t), \ t = 1, 2, ..., T\}$ That is, the parameters $a_0, a_1, a_2, ..., a_k$ are chosen in order to minimize the objective function:

$$\ell(a_0, a_1, a_2, ..., a_k) = \sum_{t=1}^{T} \left(y_t - \sum_{i=0}^{k} a_i \phi_i(x_t) \right)^2.$$

NOTE:
(i)   For the least-squares method the linearity that matters is the linearity in the parameters $a_0, a_1, ..., a_k$; not the linearity in x as in the case of the Normal/linear regression model (see Spanos (1986, forthcoming)),
(ii) No probabilistic assumptions are involved in the above problem.

Example
In the simple case where $k = 1$ and $\phi_0 = 1$, $\phi_1 = x$, the objective function takes the form:

$$\ell(a_0, a_1) = \sum_{t=1}^{T} (y_t - a_0 - a_1 x_t)^2.$$

In view of the fact that the function is infinitely differentiable we can find the minimum using calculus. The first-order conditions give rise to the so-called *normal equations*:

$$\frac{\partial \ell}{\partial a_0} = (-2) \sum_{t=1}^{T} (y_t - a_0 - a_1 x_t) = 0, \ \frac{\partial \ell}{\partial a_1} = (-2) \sum_{t=1}^{T} (y_t - a_0 - a_1 x_t) x_t = 0,$$

whose solution yields:

$$\hat{\alpha}_0 = \bar{y} - \hat{\alpha}_1 \bar{x}, \ \hat{\alpha}_1 = \frac{\sum_{t=1}^{T} (y_t - \bar{y})(x_t - \bar{x})}{\sum_{t=1}^{T} (x_t - \bar{x})^2}, \ \text{for} \sum_{t=1}^{T} (x_t - \bar{x})^2 \neq 0,$$

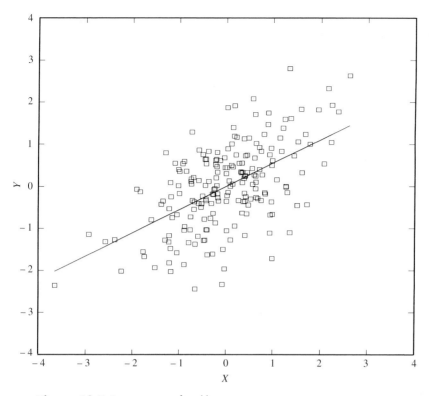

Figure 13.1 Least-squares fitted line

where $\bar{y} = \frac{1}{T}\sum_{t=1}^{T} y_t$ and $\bar{x} = \frac{1}{T}\sum_{t=1}^{T} x_t$. This can be viewed geometrically as fitting a line to a scatter plot of $\{(x_t, y_t), t = 1, 2, \ldots, T\}$ as shown in figure 13.1.

Legendre's main justification for the least-squares method was that in the case where the approximating function is a constant, i.e., $h(x) = a_0$, the value of a_0 which minimizes the function:

$$\ell(a_0) = \sum_{t=1}^{T}(y_t - a_0)^2,$$

coincides with the *arithmetic mean*:

$$\hat{\alpha}_0 = \frac{1}{T}\sum_{t=1}^{T} y_t.$$

This follows from the first-order condition:

$$\frac{d\ell}{da_0} = (-2)\sum_{t=1}^{T}(y_t - a_0) = 0.$$

At that time, the arithmetic mean was considered to be the best way to summarize the information contained in the T data points $y_1, y_2, \ldots, y_T$.

The first probabilistic interpretation of least squares was proposed by Gauss in 1809. He argued that for a sequence of T independent random variables $y_1, y_2, \ldots, y_T$, whose density functions $f(y_t)$ satisfy certain regularity conditions, if the arithmetic mean $\bar{y}$ is the most probable combination for all values of the random variables and each $T \geq 1$, then for some $\sigma^2 > 0$ (see Heyde and Seneta (1977)) their density function is Normal:

$$f(y_t) = [2\pi\sigma^2]^{-\frac{1}{2}} \exp\left\{-\frac{1}{2\sigma^2} y_t^2\right\}.$$

Using this argument, Gauss went on to recast the least-squares approximation argument in the following probabilistic form:

$$y_t = \sum_{i=0}^{k} a_i \phi_i(x_t) + \epsilon_t, \quad \epsilon_t \sim \text{NIID}(0, \sigma^2), \quad t = 1, 2, \ldots, T,$$

and $\phi_0(x), \phi_1(x), \ldots, \phi_k(x)$ are known functions of x; NIID stands for Normal, Independent and Identically Distributed.

A more convincing argument for the use of the Normal distribution for the errors was provided by Laplace in 1812 in the form of the law of the errors; known as the *Central Limit Theorem* (see chapter 9). The idea was that in cases where the errors represent the sum of several influencing factors, which individually do not dominate the summation, the distribution of the sum approaches the normal as the number of influencing factors increases to infinity. Laplace also noted that the *minimization* of:

$$\sum_{t=1}^{T} (y_t - h(x_t))^2,$$

is equivalent to the *maximization* of the logarithm of the joint distribution of the errors:

$$\ln f(\epsilon_1, \epsilon_2, \ldots, \epsilon_T) = -\frac{T}{2} \ln(2\pi\sigma^2) - \frac{1}{2\sigma^2} \sum_{t=1}^{T} (y_t - h(x_t))^2.$$

This idea can be viewed as a predecessor of the method known today as the maximum likelihood method (see below).

In terms of **finite sample** properties of least-squares estimators, the most celebrated result is the Gauss–Markov theorem discussed next.

13.3.2 Gauss–Markov theorem

Let the statistical relationship between y_t and the x_{it}s be:

$$y_t = \sum_{i=0}^{k} a_i \phi_i(x_t) + \epsilon_t, \quad t = 1, 2, \ldots, T,$$

where $\phi_0(x), \phi_1(x), \ldots, \phi_k(x)$ are known functions of x. Under the assumptions:

(i) $E(\epsilon_t) = 0$, $t = 1, 2, \ldots, T$,

(ii) $Cov(\epsilon_t, \epsilon_s) = \begin{cases} \sigma^2, & t = s, \\ 0, & t \neq s, \end{cases} \quad t, s = 1, 2, \ldots, T,$

(iii) $\phi_0(x), \phi_1(x), \ldots, \phi_k(x)$ are linearly independent (in the mathematical sense) functions of x,

we can deduce that the least-squares estimators:

$$\hat{\alpha}_i = \sum_{t=1}^{T} \gamma_t(i) y_t, \quad i = 0,1,2,\ldots,k, \tag{13.1}$$

(where $\gamma_t(i)$ are functions of $\phi_0(x), \phi_1(x), \ldots, \phi_k(x)$), are:

(a) **Best** (relatively efficient): $Var(\hat{a}_i) \leq Var(\check{a}_i)$, $i=0,1,2,\ldots,k$, for every other *linear* estimator $\check{a}_i$ which is also *unbiased*,
(b) **Linear** functions of $(y_1, y_2, \ldots, y_T)$,
(c) **Unbiased** estimators of a_i: $E(\hat{a}_i) = a_i$, $i = 0,1,2,\ldots,k$.

That is, the least-squares estimators (13.1) are best, within the class of linear (in terms of y_t) and unbiased estimators (BLUE).

NOTES:

(a) There is no distributional assumption involved in the above specification and thus we cannot consider the question of full efficiency.
(b) The Gauss–Markov theorem depends crucially on the linearity of the statistical GM in terms of the unknown parameters $(a_0, a_1, \ldots, a_k)$. On the other hand, the linearity of the Normal/linear regression, discussed in chapter 7, is with respect to the conditioning variables.
(c) The Gauss–Markov theorem is useful in cases where we only want to consider estimators which are linear in y_t. If we allow estimators which are non-linear in y_t we can do much better than the least-squares estimators (see Judge *et al.* (1988)).

Asymptotic properties
$\hat{a}_1$ can be shown to be both consistent and asymptotically normal under certain restrictions on the behavior of $\sum_{t=1}^{T} x_t^2$ as $T \to \infty$. In particular:

(i) $\sum_{t=1}^{T} x_t^2 \to \infty$, as $T \to \infty$, implies $\hat{a}_1 \xrightarrow{\mathbb{P}} a_1$.

(ii) $\lim_{T \to \infty} \left(\frac{1}{T} \sum_{t=1}^{T} x_t^2 \right) = q_x$, implies $\sqrt{T}(\hat{a}_1 - a_1) \underset{a}{\sim} N(0, \sigma^2[1/q_x])$.

Before we proceed to a more statistical interpretation of the method of least squares, it is important to emphasize that despite the introduction of the probabilistic terminology, such as distributions and means, the method, as described above, is essentially one of mathematical approximation. Moreover, its probabilistic interpretation is not as robust to changes in the distributional assumption of Normality as often assumed (see Pearson (1920)).

13.3.3 The statistical least-squares method

The purpose of this section is to reinterpret the least-squares method as a general estimation method in the context of the statistical model specification given in chapter 7. In particular, to relate the least-squares method with the specification of the statistical Generating Mechanism (GM).

As argued in chapter 7, the statistical GM for the statistical models in this book are based on the following decomposition scheme:

$$y_t = E(y_t | \mathcal{D}_t) + u_t, \quad t \in \mathbb{T}. \tag{13.2}$$

where y_t is a random variable such that $Var(y_t)<\infty$. The primary aim for the modeler is to choose $\mathcal{D}_t$ so as to ensure that no *systematic information* in the data is left in the non-systematic component (error) u_t. The idea is to choose $\mathcal{D}_t$ in order to *minimize* the non-systematic component u_t, defined as the *unmodeled* part of y_t:

$$u_t = y_t - E(y_t|\mathcal{D}_t), \quad t \in \mathbb{T},$$

or equivalently to choose $\mathcal{D}_t$ in order to maximize the systematic component:

$$\mu_t = E(y_t|\mathcal{D}_t), \quad t \in \mathbb{T}.$$

By construction the error is non-systematic relative to the information set $\mathcal{D}_t$, i.e.

$$\left. \begin{array}{ll} \text{(i)} & E(u_t|\mathcal{D}_t)=0, \\[2mm] \text{(ii)} & E(\mu_t \cdot u_t|\mathcal{D}_t)=0, \end{array} \right\} \quad t \in \mathbb{T} \qquad (13.3)$$

(see chapter 7). On the basis of the probabilistic assumptions, the systematic component will take a parametric form, say:

$$E(y_t|\mathcal{D}_t)=g(x_t;\theta), \quad t \in \mathbb{T}. \qquad (13.4)$$

The least-squares method ensures that the properties (13.3) are satisfied by the estimated systematic and non-systematic components. This is ensured by choosing the value of the unknown parameter θ, say $\hat{\theta}_{LS}$, that minimizes the sum of squares of the errors $\{u_t, t=1,2,\ldots,T\}$. That is, least-squares suggests minimizing the loss function:

$$\ell(\theta) = \textstyle\sum_{t=1}^{T}(y_t - g(x_t;\theta))^2,$$

with respect to θ. For the value $\hat{\theta}_{LS}$ the loss function takes its minimum at the point:

$$\ell(\hat{\theta}_{LS}) = \textstyle\sum_{t=1}^{T}(y_t - g(x_t;\hat{\theta}_{LS}))^2,$$

and the estimated systematic and non-systematic components are:

$$\hat{\mu}_t = g(x_t;\hat{\theta}_{LS}) \text{ and } \hat{u}_t = y_t - g(x_t;\hat{\theta}_{LS}).$$

The optimality of the least-squares estimators stems from the fact that the conditions (13.3) are valid for the estimated components in the sense that:

$$\tfrac{1}{T}\textstyle\sum_{t=1}^{T}\hat{u}_t = 0, \text{ and } \tfrac{1}{T}\textstyle\sum_{t=1}^{T}(g(x_t;\hat{\theta}_{LS}) \cdot \hat{u}_t) = 0.$$

Example 1 Bernoulli (continued)
The statistical GM of the Bernoulli model takes the form:

$$X_i = E(X_i|\mathcal{D}_i) + u_i, \quad i \in \mathbb{N} \equiv \{1,2,3,\ldots\},$$

where $\mathcal{D}_i = \{S,\theta\}$ (the non-informative set) and thus $E(X_i|\mathcal{D}_i)=E(X_i)=\theta$. The least-squares method for estimating θ based on the sample $(X_1,X_2,\ldots,X_n)$ amounts to minimizing:

$$\ell(\theta) = \textstyle\sum_{k=1}^{n}(X_k - \theta)^2.$$

From elementary calculus we know that the easiest way to locate the minimum of a differentiable function is to solve the first-order condition:

$\frac{d\ell}{d\theta} = (-2)\sum_{k=1}^{n}(X_k - \theta) = 0$ for θ, which yields: $\hat{\theta}_{LS} = \frac{1}{n}\sum_{k=1}^{n}X_k$.

We know that $\ell(\hat{\theta}_{LS}) = \sum_{k=1}^{n}(X_k - \hat{\theta}_{LS})^2$ is a minimum of $\ell(\theta)$ since: $\left(\frac{d^2\ell}{d\theta^2}\right)\Big|_{\theta=\hat{\theta}_{LS}} = 2n > 0$. $\hat{\theta}_{LS}$

and $\hat{u}_k = (X_k - \hat{\theta}_{LS})$ satisfy the properties:

(a) $\frac{1}{n}\sum_{k=1}^{n}\hat{u}_k = 0$,   (b) $\frac{1}{n}\sum_{k=1}^{n}\hat{\theta}_{LS}\hat{u}_k = 0$,

since $\sum_{k=1}^{n}(X_k - \hat{\theta}_{LS}) = \sum_{k=1}^{n}X_k - n\hat{\theta}_{LS} = \sum_{k=1}^{n}X_k - \sum_{k=1}^{n}X_k = 0$,

$\sum_{k=1}^{n}(\hat{\theta}_{LS}[X_k - \hat{\theta}_{LS}]) = \hat{\theta}_{LS}\sum_{k=1}^{n}(X_k - \hat{\theta}_{LS}) = 0$.

NOTICE that the least-squares estimator of θ coincides with the estimator suggested by the moment matching principle and shares the same optimal properties: unbiased, fully efficient, consistent, and asymptotically normal.

Example 2 Normal (continued)

The statistical GM of the Normal model takes the same form:

$X_t = \mu + u_t$, $t \in \mathbb{N}$,

and thus the least-squares method for estimating μ based on the sample $(X_1, X_2, \ldots, X_T)$ amounts to minimizing:

$\ell(\mu) = \sum_{t=1}^{T}(X_t - \mu)^2$.

Solving the first-order condition $\frac{d\ell}{d\mu} = (-2)\sum_{t=1}^{T}(X_t - \mu) = 0$ for μ, yields:

$\hat{\mu}_{LS} = \frac{1}{T}\sum_{t=1}^{T}X_t$.

As in the Bernoulli case $\hat{\mu}_{LS}$ and $\hat{u}_t = (X_t - \hat{\mu}_{LS})$ satisfy the sample equivalents to the conditions (13.3). Again, the least-squares estimator of μ coincides with the estimator suggested by the moment matching principle, and it enjoys the same optimal properties such as unbiasedness, full efficiency, consistency, and asymptotic Normality (see chapter 12). The least-squares method does not suggest an estimator for σ^2, but intuition suggests that we can use the minimum of the objective function $\ell(\theta)$ to define the following estimator of σ^2:

$\hat{\sigma}^2 = \frac{1}{T}\sum_{t=1}^{T}(X_t - \hat{\mu}_{LS})^2$.

This is also the estimator suggested by the moment matching principle. As shown in the previous chapter the sampling distribution of $\hat{\sigma}^2$ takes the form:

$\left(\frac{T\hat{\sigma}^2}{\sigma^2}\right) = \sum_{t=1}^{T}\left(\frac{X_t - \hat{\mu}}{\sigma}\right)^2 \sim \chi^2(n-1)$,

and thus $\hat{\sigma}^2$ is a biased estimator of σ^2 since $E(\hat{\sigma}^2) = \frac{(T-1)}{T}\sigma^2 \neq \sigma^2$. Because of this bias, the alternative estimator:

$$s^2 = \frac{1}{T-1}\Sigma_{t=1}^T(X_t - \hat{\mu}_{LS})^2,$$

is often used in practice (see the discussion in chapter 12).

13.3.4 Properties of least-squares estimators

In the above statistical interpretation of least squares it is clear that the finite sample properties of least-squares estimators depend crucially on the probabilistic assumptions relating to the random variable y_t and the conditioning information set $\mathcal{D}_t$. In view of this, the only general optimality results for least-squares estimators are asymptotic. Under certain regularity conditions and in view of the fact that the estimated systematic and non-systematic component:

$$\hat{\mu}_t = g(x_t;\hat{\theta}_{LS}), \;\; \hat{u}_t = y_t - g(x_t;\hat{\theta}_{LS}),$$

respectively, satisfy the orthogonality conditions:

$$\text{(a)} \;\; \frac{1}{T}\Sigma_{t=1}^T \hat{u}_t = 0, \qquad \text{(b)} \;\; \frac{1}{T}\Sigma_{t=1}^T[g(x_t;\hat{\theta}_{LS})\hat{u}_t] = 0,$$

we can show that the least-squares estimator $\hat{\theta}_{LS}$ of θ, is both consistent and asymptotically normal. The regularity conditions relate to the function $g(x_t;\theta)$, ensuring the existence and uniqueness of the least-squares estimator $\hat{\theta}_{LS}$ as a solution to the minimization of the loss function:

$$\ell(\theta) = \Sigma_{t=1}^T(y_t - g(x_t;\theta))^2.$$

In particular, in the case of an independent sample:

$$\hat{\theta}_{LS} \overset{\mathbb{P}}{\to} \theta,$$

and:

$$\sqrt{T}(\hat{\theta}_{LS} - \theta) \underset{\alpha}{\sim} \mathsf{N}(0, V_\infty(\theta)),$$

but $\hat{\theta}_{LS}$ is *not* necessarily asymptotically efficient.

13.4   The method of moments

The method of moments was originally proposed in 1895 by Karl Pearson in the context of what we nowadays call (sophisticated) *descriptive statistics*. The original method was proposed as both a specification and an estimation method but was later (in the 1920s) adapted as just an estimation method in the context of modern statistical inference. In order to understand the limitations of the method in the latter context, it is advisable to consider the method in the context originally intended. The current approach to statistical inference replaced descriptive statistics only gradually and to some extent, this change went largely unnoticed. The change of paradigms from descriptive statistics to statistical inference proper was under way in the 1910s but it was not completed until the mid 1930s. The confusion between the distribution and sample moments in the statistical literature of the first quarter of the 20th century attests to the

Figure 13.2 The Pearson method of moments

fact that the switch of paradigms was neither obvious nor clear to many participants. Karl Pearson died in 1936 without realizing that his method was inferior to the maximum likelihood method mainly because it was developed for a very different approach to statistics; an approach for which the maximum likelihood method was useless.

13.4.1 Pearson's method of moments

Descriptive statistics, as an approach to data modeling, proceeds *from the data* and using techniques such as the histogram seeks a parsimonious summary of the data in terms of a frequency curve: *a descriptive model*. When Pearson proposed his method of moments the idea was that the modeler would use the data raw moments in order to choose the most appropriate frequency curve from a specific family, the Pearson family. This is very different from the classical approach to statistics where a *statistical model* (a chance mechanism) is postulated *a priori* and the observed data are interpreted as a realization of the postulated chance mechanism.

The Pearson approach to statistics can be summarized as shown in figure 13.2.

The Pearson family of frequency curves can be expressed in terms of the following differential equation in four unknown parameters:

$$\frac{df(x)}{dx} = f(x)\left[\frac{(x-a)}{b_0 + b_1 x + b_2 x^2}\right]. \tag{13.5}$$

Depending on the values taken by the parameters (a,b_0,b_1,b_2), this equation can generate numerous frequency curves such as the normal, the Student's t, the Beta, the Gamma, the Laplace, and the Pareto; in the context of modern probability they are known as density functions. Pearson invented this family of frequency curves by noticing that the normal density function $\phi(x)$ satisfies the following differential equation:

$$\frac{d\phi(x)}{dx} = \phi(x)\left[\frac{(x-a)}{b_0}\right], \text{ where } \mu = a \text{ and } \sigma^2 = -b_0.$$

Using the corresponding difference equations associated with the Binomial and Hypergeometric distributions, he went on to extend this to the differential equation (13.5).

In the context of probability theory we have seen that we can relate the unknown parameters, say $(\theta_1,\theta_2,\theta_3,\theta_4)$, to the moments of a given density function $f(x;\theta_1,\theta_2,\theta_3,\theta_4)$ (see chapter 3) via:

$$\mu'_r(\theta_1,\theta_2,\theta_3,\theta_4) = \int_{x\in\mathbb{R}_X} x^r f(x;\theta_1,\theta_2,\theta_3,\theta_4)dx, \text{ for } r = 1,2,\dots$$

By interpreting frequency curves as density functions, one can adapt the above relationship in conjunction with the differential equation (13.5) to relate the Pearson family to the raw moments by integrating both sides:

$$\int_{x\in\mathbb{R}_X} x^r(b_0 + b_1x + b_2x^2)df = \int_{x\in\mathbb{R}_X} x^r(x-a)f(x)dx, \text{ for } r = 1,2,\dots$$

Collecting terms of the same power in x, we get the following recursive relationship among the moments and the parameters (see Stuart and Ord (1991)):

$$kb_0\mu'_{k-1} + \{(k+1)b_1 - a\}\mu'_k + \{(k+2)b_2 + 1\}\mu'_{k+1} = 0, \ k = 1,2,\dots$$

From this we can see that the first four moments μ'_1, μ'_2, μ'_3, and μ'_4 are sufficient to select the particular $f(x)$ from the Pearson family via the first four equations:

$$(b_1 - a) + (2b_2 + 1)\mu'_1 = 0$$
$$b_0 + (2b_1 - a)\mu'_1 + (3b_2 + 1)\mu'_2 = 0$$
$$2b_0\mu'_1 + (3b_1 - a)\mu'_2 + (4b_2 + 1)\mu'_3 = 0$$
$$3b_0\mu'_2 + (4b_1 - a)\mu'_3 + (5b_2 + 1)\mu'_4 = 0.$$

Pearson proposed substituting the first four raw data moments $\hat{\mu}'_1$, $\hat{\mu}'_2$, $\hat{\mu}'_3$, and $\hat{\mu}'_4$, in the above system and solving it for the parameters (a,b_0,b_1,b_2). The solution to these equations would deal with two different problems simultaneously:

(a) **specification**: the choice of a descriptive model (a frequency curve) on the basis of the particular values of $\hat{\mu}'_1$, $\hat{\mu}'_2$, $\hat{\mu}'_3$, and $\hat{\mu}'_4$, and

(b) **estimation**: attribution of numerical values to the unknown parameters (a,b_0,b_1,b_2). For example, in the case where the derived numerical values of the parameters were: $b_0 < 0$, $b_1 \approx 0$, and $b_2 \approx 0$, the data suggest that the most appropriate descriptive model, among those of the Pearson family, is the Normal frequency curve.

It is instructive to view the above procedure in the context of classical statistical inference where the statistical model is chosen a priori and the data are viewed as a realization of the chance mechanism described by the postulated model. The *first* important difference between the two approaches is that there is no built-in *inductive* argument in the Pearson approach which is essentially one of descriptive statistics. *Second*, the Pearson approach seems to ignore the notion of a sampling model. In effect the approach involves the implicit assumption that the data constitute a realization of a *random sample*. In other words, it only considers simple statistical models. The *third* important limitation of the Pearson approach is that the family of descriptive models is restricted to the ones in the *Pearson family*.

In addition to being important from a historical viewpoint, the Pearson method of selecting a density function using the estimated moments is also of some interest in the context of statistical inference, in cases where the finite sample distribution of a statistic is unknown and the asymptotically normal distribution is suspected to be misleading. In such cases it might be of interest to consider fitting the Pearson family in order to get some idea as to the nature of the non-normality.

13.4.2 The parametric method of moments

The parametric method of moments (PMM) is an adaptation of the above method for application to statistical inference proper. In the latter case the appropriate probability model is chosen a priori and thus the only role left for the method of moments is to estimate its parameters using the sample moments. As argued in chapter 3 the best way to handle unknown parameters is to relate them to the moments of the density function in question via:

$$\mu'_r(\theta_1,\theta_2,\ldots,\theta_k)=\int_{x\in\mathbb{R}_X} x^r f(x;\theta_1,\theta_2,\ldots,\theta_k)dx, \ r=1,2,\ldots$$

The idea behind the PMM is to match the required population raw moments to their corresponding sample moments:

$$\hat{\mu}'_r=\tfrac{1}{T}\textstyle\sum_{t=1}^T X^r_t, r=1,2,3,$$

and solve the resulting system of equations for the unknown parameters $(\theta_1,\theta_2,\ldots,\theta_k)$.

Example 2 (continued)
In the case of the *Normal model* we have two unknown parameters $\boldsymbol{\theta}:=(\mu,\sigma^2)$ and thus we need at least two raw moments. The *first step* is to derive the relationship between these parameters and the population moments:

$$\mu'_r(\mu,\sigma^2)=\int_{x\in\mathbb{R}_X} x^r f(x;\mu,\sigma^2)dx, \ r=1,2.$$

In view of the fact that the moment generating function (mgf) is: $m_x(t)=e^{\mu t+\frac{1}{2}\sigma^2 t^2}$ (see chapter 3), we can deduce that:

$$\mu'_1=\tfrac{dm_x(t)}{dt}\Big|_{t=0}=e^{\mu t+\frac{1}{2}\sigma^2 t^2}\Big(\mu+\tfrac{1}{2}\sigma^2 t\Big)\Big|_{t=0}=\mu,$$

$$\mu'_2=\tfrac{d^2m_x(t)}{dt^2}\Big|_{t=0}=e^{\mu t+\frac{1}{2}\sigma^2 t^2}\Big(\mu+\tfrac{1}{2}\sigma^2 t\Big)^2+\Big(e^{\mu t+\frac{1}{2}\sigma^2 t^2}\Big)\sigma^2\Big|_{t=0}=\mu^2+\sigma^2.$$

The *second step* is to equate the population and sample moments and solve for the unknown parameters, i.e.

$$\hat{\mu}'_1:=\tfrac{1}{T}\textstyle\sum_{t=1}^T X_t=\mu, \ \hat{\mu}'_2:=\tfrac{1}{T}\textstyle\sum_{t=1}^T X^2_t=\sigma^2+\mu^2.$$

Solving these for μ and σ^2 we deduce that the PMM estimators are:

$$\hat{\mu}=\tfrac{1}{T}\textstyle\sum_{t=1}^T X_t, \ \hat{\sigma}^2=\tfrac{1}{T}\textstyle\sum_{t=1}^T(X_t-\hat{\mu})^2.$$

From our previous discussion we know that these estimators coincide with the estimators suggested by the moment matching principle and the least-squares method and they enjoy several optimal properties. In particular, $\hat{\mu}$ is an unbiased, fully efficient, and consistent estimator of μ. $\hat{\sigma}^2$ is not unbiased, but it can be transformed into an unbiased estimator using $s^2=\left(\tfrac{T}{T-1}\right)\hat{\sigma}^2$. s^2 is not just unbiased, it is also relatively efficient, consistent, and an asymptotically normal estimator of σ^2.

Example 4 Consider the **simple Gamma model:**

[i]   Statistical GM: $X_t=\alpha\beta+u_t, \ t\in\mathbb{N},$
[ii]   Probability model:

$$\Phi = \left\{ f(x;\boldsymbol{\theta}) = \frac{1}{\beta\Gamma[\alpha]}\left(\frac{x}{\beta}\right)^{\alpha-1}\exp\left\{-\left(\frac{x}{\beta}\right)\right\}, \boldsymbol{\theta}:=(\alpha,\beta)\in\mathbb{R}_+^2, x>0\right\},$$

[iii]   Sampling model: $\mathbf{X}:=(X_1,X_2,\ldots,X_T)$ is a random sample.

In view of the fact that the mgf is: $m_x(t)=(1-\alpha t)^{-\beta}$, we can deduce that (see chapter 3):

$$\mu_1 = \frac{dm_x(t)}{dt}\Big|_{t=0} = -\beta(-\alpha)(1-\alpha t)^{-\beta-1}\Big|_{t=0} = \alpha\beta,$$

$$\mu_2 = \frac{d^2m_x(t)}{dt^2}\Big|_{t=0} = \beta\alpha^2(\beta+1)(1-\alpha t)^{-\beta-2}\Big|_{t=0} = \beta(\beta+1)\alpha^2,$$

or equivalently $E(X)=\alpha\beta$, $Var(X)=\alpha\beta^2$. Hence, the PMM estimators are derived by solving the system of equations: $\hat{\mu}_1'=\alpha\beta$, $\hat{\mu}_2'=\beta(\beta+1)\alpha^2$, yielding:

$$\hat{\beta} = (\bar{X}^2/\hat{\sigma}^2), \quad \hat{\alpha} = (\hat{\sigma}^2/\bar{X}),$$

where $\bar{X}=\frac{1}{T}\sum_{t=1}^{T}X_t$ and $\hat{\sigma}^2=\frac{1}{T}\sum_{t=1}^{T}(X_t-\bar{X})^2$.

Example 5   Consider the **simple log-Normal model:**

[i]   Statistical GM: $X_t=\theta+u_t,\ t\in\mathbb{N},$
[ii]   Probability model:

$$\Phi = \left\{ f(x;\boldsymbol{\theta}) = \left(\frac{1}{x\sigma\sqrt{2\pi}}\right)\exp\left\{-\left(\frac{\ln x-\mu}{2\sigma^2}\right)^2\right\}, \boldsymbol{\theta}:=(\mu,\sigma^2), x>0\right\},$$

[iii]   Sampling model: $\mathbf{X}:=(X_1,X_2,\ldots X_T)$ is a random sample.

This example will bring out the non-invariance of the PMM estimator to transformations. In view of the following relationships:

$$\mu_1' = e^{\mu+\frac{1}{2}\sigma^2}, \quad \mu_2' = \left(e^{\mu+\frac{1}{2}\sigma^2}\right)e^{\sigma^2},$$

the most direct way to derive PMM estimators of $\boldsymbol{\theta}:=(\mu,\sigma^2)$ is to solve the following equations for the unknown parameters:

$$\frac{1}{n}\sum_{k=1}^{n}X_k = e^{\mu+\frac{1}{2}\sigma^2}, \quad \frac{1}{n}\sum_{k=1}^{n}X_k^2 = \left(e^{\mu+\frac{1}{2}\sigma^2}\right)e^{\sigma^2}.$$

This yields the following estimators:

$$\hat{\mu} = \ln\left\{\frac{\sqrt{T}\left[\frac{1}{T}\sum_{t=1}^{T}X_t\right]^2}{\sqrt{\sum_{t=1}^{T}X_t^2}}\right\}, \quad \hat{\sigma}^2 = \ln\left\{\frac{\frac{1}{T}\sum_{t=1}^{T}X_t^2}{\left[\frac{1}{T}\sum_{t=1}^{T}X_t\right]^2}\right\}.$$

Another way to derive PMM estimators of $\boldsymbol{\theta}:=(\mu,\sigma^2)$ in this case is to utilize the information that: $E(\ln X)=\mu$, $Var(\ln X)=\sigma^2$, to derive the alternative PMM estimators:

$$\hat{\mu}=\frac{1}{T}\sum_{t=1}^{T}X_t, \quad \hat{\sigma}^2=\frac{1}{T}\sum_{t=1}^{T}(\ln X_t-\hat{\mu})^2,$$

which are indeed very different from those above.

Finally, it is important to note that PMM estimators do not coincide with the estimators suggested by the *moment matching principle*. The obvious counter example is provided by the linear regression model, discussed above, where the method of moments cannot be applied directly because we are dealing with conditional moments.

13.4.3 Properties of PMM estimators

In general, the only optimal properties that PMM estimators enjoy are asymptotic. As shown above, in the case of a random sample $(X_1, X_2, \ldots, X_T)$, the sample raw moments:

$$\hat{\mu}'_r = \frac{1}{T} \sum_{t=1}^{T} X_t^r, r = 1,2,\ldots$$

are consistent estimators of the population raw moments (assuming they exist), i.e.

$$\hat{\mu}'_r \overset{\mathbb{P}}{\Rightarrow} \mu'_r.$$

In the case where $\mu'_r(\theta_1, \theta_2, \ldots, \theta_k)$ is a well-behaved function of the θs we can deduce that for the PMM estimators $\hat{\theta} := (\hat{\theta}_1, \hat{\theta}_2, \ldots, \hat{\theta}_k)$, where $\hat{\theta}_i := \hat{\theta}_i(\hat{\mu}'_1, \hat{\mu}'_2, \ldots, \hat{\mu}'_k)$, $i = 1,2,\ldots,k$:

$$\hat{\theta}_{PMM} \overset{\mathbb{P}}{\Rightarrow} \theta, \text{ and } \sqrt{T}(\hat{\theta}_{PMM} - \theta) \underset{\alpha}{\sim} N(0, V_\infty(\theta)),$$

but these estimators are not necessarily asymptotically efficient.

The question of the optimal properties of PMM estimators as opposed to those of maximum likelihood estimators, discussed next, goes back to the 1930s. Fisher (1937) argued that the method of moments gave rise to *inefficient* estimators except in cases where the distribution in question was close to the normal. Karl Pearson mounted a spirited reply but lost the argument because he did not realize that Fisher had changed the rules of the game from those of descriptive statistics (use the data to choose a descriptive model) to those of statistical inference (postulate a statistical model a priori and use the data to estimate the parameters of this model). As argued below the method of maximum likelihood is tailor-made for statistical inference but it is completely useless in the context of the Pearson approach. The fact that the PMM method often gives rise to less-efficient estimators should not come as a surprise because a glance at the above discussion reveals that the method does not utilize all the information contained in the postulated model. From the probability model it utilizes only the part of the information referring to some of the moments of the postulated density, and it is well known that, more often than not, knowing a finite number of moments is not equivalent to knowing the distribution itself (see chapter 3).

13.5 The maximum likelihood method

13.5.1 The likelihood function

As mentioned in the introduction, the maximum likelihood (ML) method was specifically developed for the modern approach to statistical inference proposed by Fisher (1912,1922b,1925a). This approach postulates a statistical model $S := (\Phi, \mathbf{X})$ purporting to describe (probabilistically) the stochastic mechanism that gave rise to the observed data $\mathbf{x} := (x_1, x_2, \ldots, x_n)$. As shown in figure 13.3, the a priori information in the form of the statistical model is encapsulated by the **distribution of the sample** $\mathbf{X} := (X_1, X_2, \ldots, X_n)$:

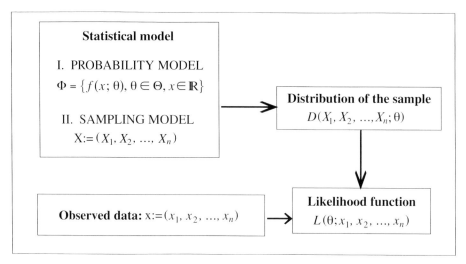

Figure 13.3 The classical approach to statistical inference

$$D(X_1, X_2, \ldots, X_n; \boldsymbol{\theta}),$$

the joint distribution of the random variables making up the sample.

NOTATION: in order to emphasize the difference between the sample and a sample realization, we use the notation $D(X_1, X_2, \ldots, X_n; \boldsymbol{\theta})$ and not the notation $f(x_1, x_2, \ldots, x_n; \boldsymbol{\theta})$ used in the previous chapters.

The *likelihood method,* viewing the observed data $\mathbf{x}$ as a realization of the sample, defines the **likelihood function** to be proportional to the distribution of the sample, but interpreted as a function of $\boldsymbol{\theta}$:

$$L(\boldsymbol{\theta}; x_1, x_2, \ldots, x_n) \propto D(X_1, X_2, \ldots, X_n; \boldsymbol{\theta})$$

In this sense the likelihood function appraises the *likelihood,* associated with the different values of $\boldsymbol{\theta}$, to have been the true parameters of the stochastic mechanism that gave rise to the particular sample realization $\mathbf{x}$. NOTE that the proportionality is important for mathematical purposes because $L(\boldsymbol{\theta}; x_1, x_2, \ldots, x_n)$ is interpreted as a function of $\boldsymbol{\theta}$ but $D(X_1, X_2, \ldots, X_n; \boldsymbol{\theta})$ is a function of $\mathbf{X}$ and they usually have very different dimensions. An equivalent way to define the likelihood function is:

$$L(\boldsymbol{\theta}; x_1, x_2, \ldots, x_n) := k(\mathbf{x}) \cdot D(X_1, X_2, \ldots, X_n; \boldsymbol{\theta}),$$

where $k(\mathbf{x})$ depends only on the sample realization $\mathbf{x}$ and not on $\boldsymbol{\theta}$. Formally, the likelihood function is defined by:

$$L(.; \mathbf{x}): \Theta \rightarrow [0, \infty),$$

and thus likelihood could not be interpreted as attaching probabilities to $\boldsymbol{\theta}$.

The fact that the maximum likelihood method is tailor-made for the modern approach

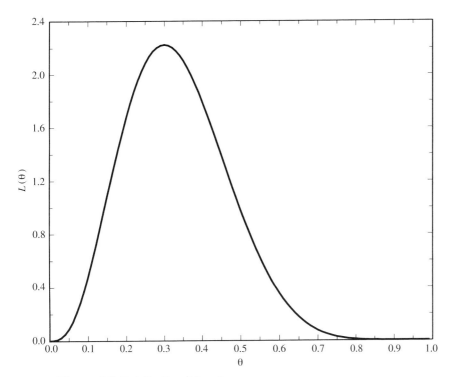

Figure 13.4 A likelihood function

to statistical inference can be seen from diagram. 13.3, where the distribution of the sample is defined so as to incorporate all relevant information contained in the statistical model postulated. This is in contrast to the parametric method of moments where only the information relating θ the moments of $f(x;\theta)$ is utilized.

In an attempt to provide some intuitive understanding for the notion of the likelihood function let us consider the following example.

Example 1 (continued)
In the case of the *Bernoulli model* the distribution of the sample takes the form:

$$D(X_1,X_2,\ldots,X_n;\theta) = \prod_{k=1}^{n} f(x_k;\theta) = \prod_{k=1}^{n} \theta^{x_k}(1-\theta)^{1-x_k} = \theta^{\sum_{k=1}^{n} x_k}(1-\theta)^{\sum_{k=1}^{n}(1-x_k)}.$$

The first equality follows from the sampling assumption of a random sample (IID random variables) and the second from the probability assumption that the X_ks are Bernoulli distributed. The likelihood function is defined by:

$$L(\theta;\mathbf{x}) \propto \theta^{\sum_{k=1}^{n} x_k}(1-\theta)^{\sum_{k=1}^{n}(1-x_k)}.$$

In figure 13.4 the likelihood function $L(\theta;\mathbf{x})$ is shown in the case where $k(\mathbf{x}) = 1000$ (chosen to avoid very small numbers) and the sample realization is:

$$\mathbf{x} := (0,0,0,1,0,0,1,0,0,1).$$

As we can see, $L(\theta;\mathbf{x})$ is a continuous function of θ, in contrast to $D(\mathbf{x};\theta)$ which is a discrete function of $\mathbf{x}$ or equivalently $y_n = \sum_{k=1}^{n} x_k$.

13.5.2 Maximum likelihood estimators

In order to be able to derive results of some generality we confine the discussion to *regular statistical models* which satisfy the restrictions **Rf1–Rf4** which ensure the existence of the Fisher information (see chapter 12). The extent to which these regularity conditions restrict the probability models has been discussed in the previous chapter; see Gourieroux and Monfort (1995) for more details.

For simplicity of exposition and notational convenience, let us consider the case where θ is a scalar. Estimating by maximum likelihood amounts to finding that particular value $\hat{\theta} = h(\mathbf{x})$ which maximizes the likelihood function, i.e.

$$L(\hat{\theta};\mathbf{x}) = \max_{\theta \in \Theta} L(\theta;\mathbf{x}).$$

$\hat{\theta} = h(\mathbf{X})$ is referred to as the **maximum likelihood estimator** (MLE) of θ and $\hat{\theta} = h(\mathbf{x})$ as the maximum likelihood **estimate**. There are several things to note about this definition:

(a)   the MLE $\hat{\theta}_{ML}$ may not exist,
(b)   the MLE $\hat{\theta}_{ML}$ may not be unique,
(c)   the MLE may not have a closed-form expression $\hat{\theta} = h(\mathbf{X})$.

Despite the pathological cases for which existence and uniqueness of the MLE $\hat{\theta}$ is not guaranteed (Gourieroux and Monfort (1995)), in the overwhelming number of cases in practice $\hat{\theta}$ exists and is unique.

In order to reduce the pathological cases for which $\hat{\theta}$ may not exist we often restrict our discussion to cases where:

Rf5 $L(.;\mathbf{x}):\Theta \to [0,\infty)$, is **continuous** at all points $\theta \in \Theta$.

Moreover, in an attempt to reduce the pathological cases for which $\hat{\theta}$ may not be unique we restrict our discussion to cases where θ is **identifiable**:

Rf6.   For all $\theta_1 \neq \theta_2$ where $\theta_1 \in \Theta$, $\theta_2 \in \Theta$, $f(\mathbf{x};\theta_1) \neq f(\mathbf{x};\theta_2)$, $\mathbf{x} \in \mathbb{R}_X^n$.

In the case where the likelihood function is differentiable one can locate the maximum by differentiating $L(\theta;\mathbf{x})$. The MLE is derived by solving the first-order conditions:

$$\frac{dL(\theta;\mathbf{x})}{d\theta} = g(\hat{\theta}_{ML}) = 0, \text{ given that } \frac{d^2 L(\theta;\mathbf{x})}{d\theta^2}\Big|_{\theta = \hat{\theta}_{MLE}} < 0.$$

Often, it is preferable to maximize the log likelihood function instead, because they have the same maximum (the logarithm being a monotonic transformation):

$$\frac{d \ln L(\theta;\mathbf{x})}{d\theta} = \ell(\hat{\theta}_{ML}) = \left(\frac{1}{L}\right)\frac{dL(\theta;\mathbf{x})}{d\theta} = \left(\frac{1}{L}\right)g(\hat{\theta}_{ML}) = 0, \text{ given } L \neq 0.$$

Example 1 (continued)
In the case of the *Bernoulli model* the log likelihood function is:

$$\ln L(\theta;\mathbf{x}) = \text{const} + (\Sigma_{k=1}^{n} x_k)\ln\theta + (\Sigma_{k=1}^{n}[1 - x_k])\ln(1-\theta),$$

where const stands for the constant of proportionality. Differentiating the log likelihood with respect to θ yields:

$$\tfrac{d}{d\theta}\ln L(\theta;\mathbf{x}) = \tfrac{1}{\theta}(\Sigma_{k=1}^{n} x_k) - \left(\tfrac{1}{1-\theta}\right)(\Sigma_{k=1}^{n}[1-x_k]) = 0,$$

or

$$(\Sigma_{k=1}^{n} x_k)(1 - \hat{\theta}) = \hat{\theta}(n - \Sigma_{i=1}^{n} x_k) \Rightarrow \hat{\theta}_{ML} = \tfrac{1}{n}\Sigma_{i=1}^{n} X_i.$$

As we can see, the maximum likelihood Estimator (MLE) coincides with the estimator suggested by all three previous methods, the moment matching principle, the least-squares and parametric method of moments (PMM). We can ensure that this is indeed a maximum by considering the second derivative evaluated at $\theta = \hat{\theta}_{ML}$. Since, $\hat{\theta}_{ML} > 0$ and $n > (\Sigma_{i=1}^{n} x_n)$ we can deduce that $\hat{\theta}_{ML}$ defines a maximum since the second-order condition evaluated at $\hat{\theta}_{ML}$ is negative:

$$\tfrac{d^2}{d\theta^2}\ln L(\theta;\mathbf{x}) = -\tfrac{1}{\theta^2}\Sigma_{k=1}^{n} x_k - \left(\tfrac{1}{1-\theta}\right)^2 \cdot (\Sigma_{k=1}^{n}[1 - x_k])|_{\theta = \hat{\theta}_{MLE}} < 0.$$

The score function

The quantity $\tfrac{d}{d\theta}\ln L(\theta;\mathbf{x})$ was encountered in chapter 12 in relation to full efficiency, but at that point we used the log of the distribution of the sample, $\ln f(\mathbf{x};\theta)$, instead of $\ln L(\theta;\mathbf{x})$ to define the **Fisher information**:

$$I_n(\boldsymbol{\theta}) := E\left\{\left(\tfrac{\partial \ln f(\mathbf{x};\boldsymbol{\theta})}{\partial \boldsymbol{\theta}}\right)^2\right\} \qquad (13.6)$$

In terms of the log-likelihood function the **Cramer–Rao inequality** takes the form:

$$Var(\hat{\theta}) \geq \left[E\left\{\left(\tfrac{\partial \ln L(\theta;\mathbf{x})}{\partial \theta}\right)^2\right\}\right]^{-1}, \qquad (13.7)$$

for *any unbiased estimator* $\hat{\theta}$ of θ.

The function $s(\theta;\mathbf{X}) := \tfrac{d}{d\theta}\ln L(\theta;\mathbf{X})$, when viewed as a function of $\mathbf{X}$, is called the **score function** and enjoys the following properties:

(sc1) $E[s(\theta;\mathbf{X})] = 0$,
(sc2) $Var[s(\theta;\mathbf{X})] = E[s(\theta;\mathbf{X})]^2 = E\left(-\tfrac{d^2}{d\theta^2}\ln L(\theta;\mathbf{X})\right) := I_n(\theta).$

As shown in the previous chapter, an unbiased estimator $\hat{\theta}$ of θ achieves the Cramer–Rao lower bound if and only if $(\hat{\theta} - \theta)$ can be expressed in the form:

$$(\hat{\theta} - \theta) = h(\theta) \cdot s(\theta;\mathbf{X}),$$

for some function $h(\theta)$.

Example 1 (continued)
In the case of the *Bernoulli model* the score function takes the form:

$$s(\theta;\mathbf{X}) := \tfrac{d}{d\theta}\ln L(\theta;\mathbf{X}) = \tfrac{1}{\theta}(\Sigma_{k=1}^{n} X_k) - \left(\tfrac{1}{1-\theta}\right)(\Sigma_{k=1}^{n}[1 - X_k]).$$

In view of the fact that:

$$(\hat{\theta}_{ML} - \theta) = \left[\frac{\theta(1-\theta)}{n}\right] s(\theta;\mathbf{X}),$$

we can deduce that $\hat{\theta}_{ML} = \frac{1}{n}\sum_{i=1}^{n} X_i$ is indeed fully efficient. This is confirmed using the Fisher information:

$$\frac{d^2 \ln L(\theta;\mathbf{x})}{d\theta^2} = -\left(\sum_{i=1}^{n} X_i\right)\left(\frac{1}{\theta^2}\right) - \left(\sum_{i=1}^{n}[1-X_i]\right)\left(\frac{1}{1-\theta}\right)^2.$$

$$E\left(-\frac{d^2 \ln f(\mathbf{x};\theta)}{d\theta^2}\right) = \frac{n}{\theta(1-\theta)} \Rightarrow CR(\theta) = \frac{\theta(1-\theta)}{n}.$$

Single-parameter case

Example 6 Consider the simple exponential model:

[i]   Statistical GM: $X_t = \theta + u_k, \, k \in \mathbb{N}$

[ii] Probability model: $\Phi = \{ f(x;\theta) = \frac{1}{\theta} \exp\{-\left(\frac{x}{\theta}\right)\}, \, \theta > 0, x > 0 \}.$

[iii] Sampling model: $\mathbf{X} := (X_1, X_2, \dots X_n)$ is a random sample.

The distribution of the sample takes the form:

$$D(X_1, X_2, \dots, X_n; \theta) = \prod_{k=1}^{n} f(x_k; \theta) = \prod_{k=1}^{n} \frac{1}{\theta} \exp\{-\left(\frac{1}{\theta}\right)x_k\} = \left(\frac{1}{\theta}\right)^n \exp\left\{-\frac{1}{\theta}\sum_{k=1}^{n} x_k\right\},$$

and thus the log-likelihood function is:

$$\ln L(\theta;\mathbf{x}) = \text{const} - n\ln(\theta) - \frac{1}{\theta}\sum_{k=1}^{n} x_k.$$

$$\frac{d}{d\theta}\ln L(\theta;\mathbf{x}) = -\frac{n}{\theta} + \frac{1}{\theta^2}\sum_{k=1}^{n} x_k = 0, \Rightarrow \hat{\theta}_{ML} = \frac{1}{n}\sum_{k=1}^{n} X_k.$$

In view of the fact that $E(X_t) = \theta$, this estimator coincides with the estimators suggested by the moment matching principle, the parametric method of moments as well as the least-squares method. The second-order condition:

$$\frac{d^2}{d\theta^2}\ln L(\theta;\mathbf{x}) = \frac{n}{\theta^2} - \frac{2}{\theta^3}\sum_{k=1}^{n} x_t\Big|_{\theta = \hat{\theta}ML} = -\frac{n}{\hat{\theta}_{ML}^2} < 0,$$

ensures that $\ln L(\hat{\theta};\mathbf{x})$ is a maximum and not a minimum or a point of inflection. Using the second derivative of the log-likelihood function we can derive the Fisher information:

$$I_n(\theta) := E\left(-\frac{d^2}{d\theta^2}\ln L(\theta;\mathbf{x})\right) = \frac{n}{\theta^2}.$$

13.5.3 Multi-parameter case

In the case where $\boldsymbol{\theta}$ contains more than one parameter, say $\boldsymbol{\theta} := (\theta_1, \theta_2)$, the first-order conditions for the MLEs take the form of a system of equations:

$$\left(\frac{\partial \ln L(\boldsymbol{\theta};\mathbf{x})}{\partial \theta_1}\right) = 0, \quad \left(\frac{\partial \ln L(\boldsymbol{\theta};\mathbf{x})}{\partial \theta_2}\right) = 0,$$

which need to be solved simultaneously in order to derive the MLEs.

Example 2 (continued)

In the case of the **Normal model,** the random sample assumption implies that the likelihood function takes the form:

$$L(\mu,\sigma^2;\mathbf{x}) \propto \prod_{k=1}^{n}\left(\tfrac{1}{\sigma\sqrt{2\pi}}\exp\left(-\tfrac{1}{2\sigma^2}(x_k-\mu)^2\right)\right) = \left(\tfrac{1}{\sigma\sqrt{2\pi}}\right)^n \exp\left\{-\tfrac{1}{2\sigma^2}\sum_{k=1}^{n}(x_k-\mu)^2\right\}.$$

The log-likelihood function is:

$$\ln L(\mu,\sigma^2;\mathbf{x}) = \text{const} - \tfrac{n}{2}\ln\sigma^2 - \tfrac{1}{2\sigma^2}\sum_{k=1}^{n}(x_k-\mu)^2.$$

Hence, we can derive the MLEs of μ and σ^2 via the first-order conditions:

$$\left(\tfrac{\partial \ln L(\boldsymbol{\theta};\mathbf{x})}{\partial\mu}\right) = -\tfrac{1}{2\sigma^2}(-2)\sum_{k=1}^{n}(x_k-\mu)=0, \quad \left(\tfrac{\partial \ln L(\boldsymbol{\theta};\mathbf{x})}{\partial\sigma^2}\right) = -\tfrac{n}{2\sigma^2}+\tfrac{1}{2\sigma^4}\sum_{k=1}^{n}(x_k-\mu)^2=0.$$

Solving these for μ and σ^2 yields:

$$\hat{\mu}_{ML} = \tfrac{1}{n}\sum_{k=1}^{n}X_k \text{ and } \hat{\sigma}^2_{ML} = \tfrac{1}{n}\sum_{k=1}^{n}(X_k-\hat{\mu}_{ML})^2.$$

Again, the MLEs coincide with the estimators suggested by the other three methods. In $L(\hat{\boldsymbol{\theta}};\mathbf{x})$ for $\hat{\boldsymbol{\theta}}:=(\hat{\mu},\hat{\sigma}^2)$ is indeed a maximum since the second derivatives at $\boldsymbol{\theta}=\hat{\boldsymbol{\theta}}$ take the following signs:

$$\left(\tfrac{\partial^2 \ln L(\boldsymbol{\theta};\mathbf{x})}{\partial\mu^2}\right)\Big|_{\theta=\hat{\theta}_{MLE}} = -\left(\tfrac{n}{\sigma^2}\right)\Big|_{\theta=\hat{\theta}_{MLE}} = -\tfrac{n}{\hat{\sigma}^2}<0,$$

$$\left(\tfrac{\partial^2 \ln L(\boldsymbol{\theta};\mathbf{x})}{\partial\sigma^2\partial\mu}\right)\Big|_{\theta=\hat{\theta}_{MLE}} = -\tfrac{1}{\sigma^4}\sum_{k=1}^{n}(x_k-\mu)\Big|_{\theta=\hat{\theta}_{MLE}}=0$$

$$\left(\tfrac{\partial^2 \ln L(\boldsymbol{\theta};\mathbf{x})}{\partial\sigma^4}\right)\Big|_{\theta=\hat{\theta}_{MLE}} = \tfrac{n}{2\sigma^4}-\tfrac{1}{\sigma^6}\sum_{k=1}^{n}(x_k-\mu)^2\Big|_{\theta=\hat{\theta}_{MLE}}=-\tfrac{n^2}{\hat{\sigma}^6}<0,$$

and thus $\left(\tfrac{\partial^2 \ln L(\boldsymbol{\theta};\mathbf{x})}{\partial\mu^2}\right)\left(\tfrac{\partial^2 \ln L(\boldsymbol{\theta};\mathbf{x})}{\partial\sigma^4}\right) - \left(\tfrac{\partial^2 \ln L(\boldsymbol{\theta};\mathbf{x})}{\partial\sigma^2\partial\mu}\right)\Big|_{\theta=\hat{\theta}_{MLE}}>0.$

For the simple Normal model the second derivatives of the log-likelihood and their expected values are:

$$\left(\tfrac{\partial^2 \ln L(\boldsymbol{\theta};\mathbf{x})}{\partial\mu^2}\right) = -\tfrac{n}{\sigma^2}, \qquad\qquad E\left(-\tfrac{\partial^2 \ln L(\boldsymbol{\theta};\mathbf{x})}{\partial\mu^2}\right) = \tfrac{n}{\sigma^2},$$

$$\left(\tfrac{\partial^2 \ln L(\boldsymbol{\theta};\mathbf{x})}{\partial\sigma^2\partial\mu}\right) = -\tfrac{1}{\sigma^4}\sum_{k=1}^{n}(x_k-\mu), \qquad E\left(-\tfrac{\partial^2 \ln L(\boldsymbol{\theta};\mathbf{x})}{\partial\sigma^2\partial\mu}\right)=0, \qquad\qquad (13.8)$$

$$\left(\tfrac{\partial^2 \ln L(\boldsymbol{\theta};\mathbf{x})}{\partial\sigma^4}\right) = \tfrac{n}{2\sigma^4}-\tfrac{1}{\sigma^6}\sum_{k=1}^{n}(x_k-\mu)^2, \qquad E\left(-\tfrac{\partial^2 \ln L(\boldsymbol{\theta};\mathbf{x})}{\partial\sigma^4}\right)=\tfrac{n}{2\sigma^4}.$$

These results suggest that the Fisher information matrix takes the form:

$$I_n(\boldsymbol{\theta}) = \begin{pmatrix} \tfrac{n}{\sigma^2}, & 0 \\ 0, & \tfrac{n}{2\sigma^4} \end{pmatrix}.$$

Hence, Cramer–Rao lower bounds for any unbiased estimators of μ and σ^2 are (see chapter 12):

(a) $CR(\mu)=\tfrac{\sigma^2}{n}$ (b) $CR(\sigma^2)=\tfrac{2\sigma^4}{n}$.

In view of the fact that (see chapter 12):

(i) $\hat{\mu}_{ML}\sim N\left(\mu,\tfrac{\sigma^2}{n}\right)$,   (ii) $\left(\tfrac{n\,\hat{\sigma}^2_{ML}}{\sigma^2}\right)\sim\chi^2(n-1)$.

$\hat{\mu}_{ML}$ is an unbiased, efficient, and consistent estimator of μ but $\hat{\sigma}^2_{ML}$ is not unbiased, it is, however, consistent and asymptotically Normal and asymptotically efficient (see chapter 12 for the details).

At this point it is important to digress for a few seconds in order to introduce a concept sometimes used in place of the Fisher information matrix. The concept is called the **observed information matrix** and it is defined by:

$$J_n(\boldsymbol{\theta}) = -\left(\frac{\partial^2 \ln L(\boldsymbol{\theta;x})}{\partial \boldsymbol{\theta} \partial \boldsymbol{\theta'}}\right).$$

In the case of the simple Normal model this matrix takes the form:

$$J_n(\boldsymbol{\theta}) = \begin{pmatrix} \frac{n}{\sigma^2}, & \frac{1}{\sigma^4}\sum_{k=1}^{n}(x_k - \mu) \\ \frac{1}{\sigma^4}\sum_{k=1}^{n}(x_k - \mu), & -\frac{n}{2\sigma^4}+\frac{1}{\sigma^6}\sum_{k=1}^{n}(x_k - \mu)^2 \end{pmatrix}$$

As we can see this is much easier to evaluate because there are no expectations to be taken.

Before the reader jumps to the erroneous conclusion that all three methods of estimation yield identical estimators, let us consider the following example where the MLE and the PMM estimators are different.

Example 4 (continued)
In the case of the *Gamma model*, the distribution of the sample takes the form:

$$D(X_1, X_2, \ldots, X_n; \alpha, \beta) = \prod_{k=1}^{n} f(x_k; \alpha, \beta) = \prod_{k=1}^{n}\left(\frac{\beta^{-\alpha}x_k^{\alpha-1}}{\Gamma[\alpha]}\right)\exp\left\{-\left(\frac{x_k}{\beta}\right)\right\}.$$

The log-likelihood function, with $\boldsymbol{\theta} := (\alpha, \beta)$ takes the form:

$$\ln L(\boldsymbol{\theta;x}) = \text{const} - n\ln\Gamma[\alpha] - n\alpha\ln\beta + (\alpha-1)\sum_{k=1}^{n}\ln x_k - \sum_{k=1}^{n}\left(\frac{x_k}{\beta}\right),$$

where $\Gamma[\beta]$ is the Gamma function (see appendix A).

$$\left(\frac{\partial \ln L(\boldsymbol{\theta;x})}{\partial \beta}\right) = -\frac{n\alpha}{\beta}+\frac{1}{\beta^2}\sum_{k=1}^{n}x_k = 0, \quad \left(\frac{\partial \ln L(\boldsymbol{\theta;x})}{\partial \alpha}\right) = -n\psi'[\alpha] - n\ln\beta + \sum_{k=1}^{n}\ln x_k = 0,$$

where $\psi'[z] := \frac{d}{dz}\ln\Gamma[z]$, is known as the di-gamma function (see Abramowitz and Stegum (1970)). Solving the first equation yields: $\hat{\beta}_{ML} = \frac{\bar{X}_n}{\hat{\alpha}}$, where $\bar{X}_n = \frac{1}{n}\sum_{k=1}^{n}X_k$. Substituting this into the second equation yields:

$$\ell(\alpha) = -n\psi'[\alpha] - n\ln\left(\frac{\bar{X}_n}{\hat{\alpha}}\right) + \sum_{k=1}^{n}\ln X_k = 0, \tag{13.9}$$

which cannot be solved explicitly for $\hat{\alpha}$; it can be solved numerically. Before we consider the question of numerical evaluation it is worth noting that these MLEs are different from the PMM estimators of α and β:

$$\hat{\beta}_{PMM} = \frac{\bar{X}_n^2}{\hat{\sigma}^2}, \quad \hat{\alpha}_{PMM} = \frac{\hat{\sigma}^2}{\bar{X}_n}, \tag{13.10}$$

derived in the previous section.

Numerical evaluation

As in the case of the simple Gamma model discussed above, when solving the first-order conditions for MLEs the modeler will often have to use numerical methods because no closed form expression $\hat{\theta} = h(\mathbf{X})$ can be derived. The problem is then to solve numerically the score function equation:

$$\ell(\theta) = 0,$$

which is a non-linear function of θ. There are several numerical algorithms which can be used to solve this problem which are appropriate for different circumstances. One of the simplest and most widely used algorithms is the **Newton–Raphson** which we can describe briefly as follows.

Step 1 Choose an initial (tentative) solution: θ_0.
Step 2 The Newton–Raphson algorithm improves this solution by choosing:

$$\theta_1 = \theta_0 - [\ell'(\theta_0)]^{-1}\ell(\theta_0), \text{ where } \ell'(\theta_0) = \tfrac{d\ell(\theta_0)}{d\theta}.$$

This is based on taking a first-order Taylor approximation:

$$\ell(\theta_1) \simeq \ell(\theta_0) + (\theta_1 - \theta_0)\ell'(\theta_0),$$

setting it equal to zero: $\ell(\theta_1) = 0$, and solving it for θ_1. This provides a quadratic approximation of the function $\ell(\theta)$.

Step 3 Continue iterating using the algorithm:

$$\hat{\theta}_{k+1} = \hat{\theta}_k - [\ell'(\hat{\theta}_k)]^{-1}\ell(\hat{\theta}_k), \ k = 1,2,\dots,N+1,$$

until the difference between $\hat{\theta}_{k+1}$ and $\hat{\theta}_k$ is less than a pre-assigned small value ϵ, say $\epsilon = 0.00001$, i.e.

$$|\hat{\theta}_{N+1} - \hat{\theta}_N| < \epsilon.$$

NOTE that $[-\ell'(\hat{\theta}_k)]$ is the observed information (matrix) encountered above.

Step 4 The MLE is chosen to be the value $\hat{\theta}_{N+1}$ for which: $\ell'(\hat{\theta}_{N+1}) \simeq 0$.

As can be seen, this algorithm requires the choice of an initial guess for the estimator which often is chosen to be the PMM estimator.

A related numerical algorithm, known as the **method of scoring**, replaces $\ell'(\hat{\theta}_k)$ with the Fisher information $I_n(\theta)$, the justification being the convergence result:

$$\tfrac{1}{n}\ell'(\hat{\theta}_k) \overset{a.s.}{\to} I_n(\theta),$$

yielding the iteration scheme:

$$\hat{\theta}_{k+1} = \hat{\theta}_k - \tfrac{1}{n}[I_n(\hat{\theta}_k)]^{-1}\ell(\hat{\theta}_k), \ k = 1,2,\dots,N+1.$$

IMPORTANT: It turns out that all the modeler needs to do in order to achieve asymptotically efficient estimators is to use any one of the above iteration schemes for one iteration! One iteration is sufficient for asymptotic efficiency.

For an extensive discussion of such numerical algorithms used in econometrics, see

Gourieroux and Monfort (1995), Hendry (1995), and Davidson and McKinnon (1993).

Example 7
Consider the **simple Logistic (one parameter) model**:

[i]   Statistical GM: $X_k = E(X_k) + \epsilon_k$, $k \in \mathbb{N}$,

[ii]   Probability model: $\Phi = \left\{ f(x;\theta) = \frac{\exp(-(x - \theta))}{[1 + \exp(-(x - \theta))]^2}, \ \theta \in \mathbb{R}, x \in \mathbb{R} \right\}$,

[iii] Sampling model: $\mathbf{X} := (X_1, X_2, \dots X_n)$ is a random sample.

The log-likelihood function and the first-order conditions are:

$$\ln L(\theta; \mathbf{x}) = -\sum_{k=1}^{n} (x_k - \theta) - 2 \sum_{k=1}^{n} \ln[1 + \exp(-(x_k - \theta))],$$

$$\frac{d \ln L(\theta; \mathbf{x})}{d\theta} = n - 2 \sum_{k=1}^{n} \frac{\exp(-(x_k - \theta))}{[1 + \exp(-(x_k - \theta))]} = 0.$$

The MLEs of θ can be derived using the Newton–Raphson algorithm with:

$$\ell'(\theta) = -2 \sum_{k=1}^{n} \frac{\exp(x_k - \theta)}{[1 + \exp(x_k - \theta)]^2},$$

and $\overline{X}_n$ as an initial value for θ. For comparison purposes we NOTE that:

$$\sqrt{n}(\overline{X}_n - \theta) \underset{\alpha}{\sim} \mathsf{N}\left(0, \frac{\pi^2}{3}\right), \text{ where } \frac{\pi^2}{3} = 3.2899, \text{ and } \sqrt{n}(\hat{\theta}_{MLE} - \theta) \underset{\alpha}{\sim} \mathsf{N}(0, 3).$$

Example 4 (continued).
In the case of the **Gamma model**, the MLEs of $\boldsymbol{\theta} := (\alpha, \beta)$ can be derived using the Newton–Raphson algorithm with:

$$\ell'(\boldsymbol{\theta}) = n \begin{pmatrix} \psi''[\alpha], & \frac{1}{\beta} \\ \frac{1}{\beta}, & \frac{2\overline{X}_n - \alpha\beta}{\beta^3} \end{pmatrix},$$

where $\psi''[z] := \frac{d^2}{dz^2} \ln \Gamma[z]$, is known as the tri-gamma function (see Abramowitz and Stegum (1970)). The scoring method simplifies this to:

$$\mathcal{I}_n(\boldsymbol{\theta}) = \begin{pmatrix} \psi''[\alpha], & \frac{1}{\beta} \\ \frac{1}{\beta}, & \frac{\alpha}{\beta^2} \end{pmatrix}.$$

Both numerical algorithms require some initial estimates for (α, β) for which the modeler can use the PMM estimates (13.10). Using the Newton–Raphson algorithm to evaluate (13.9) yields the iteration scheme:

$$\hat{\alpha}_{k+1} = \hat{\alpha}_k + \frac{\frac{1}{n}\sum_{k=1}^{n} \ln X_k - \ln(\overline{X}_n) - \psi'[\hat{\alpha}_k] + \ln(\hat{\alpha}_k)}{\psi'[\hat{\alpha}_k] - \frac{1}{\hat{\alpha}_k}}, \ k = 1, 2, \dots$$

Likelihood and the Kullback–Leibler distance*
Some intuition on what MLEs are all about can be gained by considering the relationship between the log-likelihood function and the Kullback–Leibler distance (see

Kullback (1959)). Consider the simple statistical model whose probability model takes the form:

$$\Phi = \{f(x;\theta) := [p_1(\theta), p_2(\theta), \ldots, p_m(\theta)], \text{ corresponding to } [x_1, x_2, \ldots, x_m], \ \theta \in \Theta\}.$$

Assuming that n_k represents the number of X_is taking the value x_k, the average log-likelihood function in this case takes the form:

$$\frac{1}{n} \ln L(\theta; \mathbf{x}) = \sum_{k=1}^{n} \ln f(x_k; \theta) = \sum_{k=1}^{m} \left(\frac{n_k}{n}\right) \ln p_k(\theta).$$

The last expression can be related to the **Kullback–Leibler information distance** between two densities:

$$\mathcal{K}(f_0, f_1) := E\left(\ln \frac{f_0(x)}{f_1(x)}\right) = \int_{x \in \mathbb{R}_X} \ln\left(\frac{f_0(x)}{f_1(x)}\right) f_0(x) dx,$$

first encountered in chapter 6 in relation to measuring dependence. This measure in the case where the two distributions involved are:

$$\hat{f}(\mathbf{x}) := \left(\frac{n_1}{n}, \frac{n_2}{n}, \ldots, \frac{n_m}{n}\right) \text{ and } f(x; \theta) := [p_1(\theta), p_2(\theta), \ldots, p_m(\theta)],$$

takes the form:

$$\mathcal{K}(\hat{f}, f) = \sum_{k=1}^{m} \left(\frac{n_k}{n}\right) \ln\left[\frac{\left(\frac{n_k}{n}\right)}{p_k(\theta)}\right] = -\sum_{k=1}^{m} \left(\frac{n_k}{n}\right) \ln p_k(\theta) + \sum_{k=1}^{m} \left(\frac{n_k}{n}\right) \ln\left(\frac{n_k}{n}\right).$$

In view of the fact that the last term is a constant, this suggests that an equivalent way to view the derivation of the MLE $\hat{\theta}_{ML}$ is by minimizing the Kullback–Leibler distance. Intuitively, this implies that the MLE is derived by minimizing the distance between the postulated probability model and the empirical frequencies. For the mathematical connoisseurs this can be written more formally in terms of the distance between the empirical cdf and the postulated cdf using the Riemann–Stieltjes integral (see Stuart and Ord (1994)):

$$\mathcal{K}(\hat{F}, F) = \int_{x \in \mathbb{N}} \ln\left(\frac{d\hat{F}(x)}{dF(x;\theta)}\right) d\hat{F}(\mathbf{x}).$$

This observation strengthens the case argued in chapter 10 that the estimated cdf provides the bridge between probability theory and statistical inference.

Example

For argument's sake let us assume that in the case of the *Bernoulli model*, Θ takes only two values, say $\Theta = \{0.2\} \cup \{0.8\}$; instead of the usual $[0,1]$. Remembering that $\theta = \mathbb{P}(X = 1)$: What is the likeliest value of θ to have given rise to the sample realization

$$\mathbf{x} := (0,0,0,1,0,0,1,0,0,1)?$$

In view of the fact that the event $X = 1$, has occurred only in three out of the ten cases, intuition suggests that the true value of θ is more likely to be $\theta = 0.2$ instead of $\theta = 0.8$. In terms of the Kullback–Leibler distance the empirical frequency $\frac{3}{10}$ is much closer to $\theta = 0.2$ than $\theta = 0.8$.

13.5.4 Properties of MLEs

Finite sample properties
Maximum likelihood estimators are not unbiased in general but enjoy a very useful property instead: they are invariant with respect to well-behaved functional parameterizations.

[1] Parameterization invariance
For $\phi = g(\theta)$ a well-behaved (Borel) function of θ, the MLE of ϕ is given by:

$$\hat{\phi}_{ML} = g(\hat{\theta}_{ML}).$$

Example 6 (continued)
In the case of the **Exponential model** specified above, we are often interested in $\phi = \frac{1}{\theta}$. From this property of MLEs we can deduce that the MLE of ϕ is:

$$\hat{\phi}_{ML} = \frac{1}{\hat{\theta}_{ML}} = \frac{n}{\sum_{k=1}^{n} x_k}. \tag{13.11}$$

In order to confirm this let us express the density function in terms of ϕ, i.e.:

$$f(x;\theta) = \phi \exp\{-\phi x\},$$

and derive the MLE of ϕ by maximizing the log-likelihood function:

$$\ln L(\phi;\mathbf{x}) = \text{const} + n \ln(\phi) - \phi \sum_{k=1}^{n} x_k,$$

Given that $\frac{\partial}{\partial \phi} \ln L(\phi;x) = \frac{n}{\phi} - \sum_{k=1}^{n} x_k = 0$, the result is (13.11).

This property is particularly useful in the context of the approach advocated in this book because the theoretical parameters of interest rarely coincide with the statistical parameters and this property enables us to derive the MLEs of the former. In view of the fact that in general:

$$E(\hat{\phi}_{ML}) \neq g(E(\hat{\theta}_{ML})),$$

we can think of the bias in some MLEs as the price we have to pay for the invariance property. Thus, if $\hat{\theta}_{ML}$ is an unbiased estimator of θ, i.e. $E(\hat{\theta}_{ML}) = \theta$, there is no reason to believe that $\hat{\phi}_{ML}$ is going to be an unbiased estimator of ϕ; in general $E(\hat{\phi}_{ML}) \neq \phi$.

[2] Unbiasedness – full efficiency
In a regular statistical model (see chapter 12), if an unbiased estimator, which also attains the Cramer–Rao lower bound, exists, say $\hat{\theta}_U$, then it coincides with the maximum likelihood estimator $\hat{\theta}_{ML}$, i.e., $\hat{\theta}_U = \hat{\theta}_{ML}$.

Example 8
Consider the **simple Poisson model**:

[i]   Statistical GM: $X_k = E(X_k) + \epsilon_k$, $k \in \mathbb{N}$,

[ii]   Probability model: $\Phi = \left\{ f(x;\theta) = \left(\frac{e^{-\theta} \theta^x}{x!} \right), \theta > 0, x \in \mathbb{N}_0 = \{0,1,2,\ldots\} \right\}$,

[iii]   Sampling model: $\mathbf{X}:=(X_1, X_2, \ldots, X_n)$ is a random sample.

In view of the fact that $E(X_t) = \theta$, we can deduce that the estimator suggested by the previous three estimation methods would be: $\hat{\theta}_U = \frac{1}{n} \sum_{k=1}^n X_k$. Using the linearity of $E(.)$ (see chapter 3) we can show that:

$$E(\hat{\theta}_U) = \theta \text{ and } Var(\hat{\theta}_U) = \frac{\theta}{n}.$$

From the distribution of the sample:

$$D(X_1, X_2, \ldots, X_n; \theta) = \prod_{k=1}^n f(x_k; \theta) = \prod_{k=1}^n \theta^{x_k} e^{-\theta} (1/(x_k)!) = \theta^{\sum_{k=1}^n x_k} e^{-n\theta} \prod_{k=1}^n (1/(x_k)!),$$

we can derive the Cramer–Rao lower bound. In view of:

$$\frac{d^2}{d\theta^2} \ln L(\mathbf{x}; \theta) = \frac{d}{d\theta} \left(-n + \frac{1}{\theta} \sum_{k=1}^n X_k \right) = -\left(\frac{1}{\theta^2} \sum_{k=1}^n X_k \right).$$

$$I_n(\theta) = E \left(-\frac{d^2}{d\theta^2} \ln L(\mathbf{x}; \theta) \right) = \frac{n}{\theta}, \Rightarrow CR(\theta) = \frac{\theta}{n}.$$

This suggests that $\hat{\theta}_U$ is both unbiased and fully efficient. In view of the above property of MLEs, $\hat{\theta}_U$ must coincide with the MLE of θ. In order to verify this result, let us derive the MLE of θ. The first-order condition:

$$\frac{d}{d\theta} \ln L(\mathbf{x}; \theta) = -n + \frac{1}{\theta} \sum_{k=1}^n X_k = 0, \Rightarrow \hat{\theta}_{ML} = \frac{1}{n} \sum_{k=1}^n X_k.$$

This, indeed, coincides with the unbiased, fully efficient estimator $\hat{\theta}_U$.

[3] Sufficiency

As argued in chapter 12, the notion of a sufficient statistic is best operationalized using the *Factorization theorem*.

A statistic $h(\mathbf{X})$ is said to be a *sufficient statistic* for θ if and only if there exist functions $g(h(\mathbf{X}); \theta)$ and $v(\mathbf{X})$, where the former depends on $\mathbf{X}$ only through $h(\mathbf{X})$ while the latter is free of θ, such that the distribution of the sample factors into the product:

$$f(\mathbf{x}; \theta) = g(h(\mathbf{x}); \theta) \cdot v(\mathbf{x}), \text{ for all } \mathbf{x} \in \mathbf{X}, \ \theta \in \Theta. \tag{13.12}$$

This suggests that if there exists a sufficient statistic $h(\mathbf{X})$ then the MLE is a function of it because:

$$L(\mathbf{x}; \theta) = [k(\mathbf{x}) \cdot v(\mathbf{x})] g(h(\mathbf{x}); \theta),$$

and maximizing the likelihood function is equivalent to maximizing $g(h(\mathbf{x}); \theta)$, which depends on the sample only through the sufficient statistic.

Asymptotic properties (random sample)

Let us consider the asymptotic properties of MLEs in the simple random sample case where:

$$I_n(\theta) = nI(\theta). \tag{13.13}$$

In order to be able to derive general results we need to impose some regularity conditions in addition to **Rf1–Rf6** used so far:

Rf7. $E(\ln f(x;\theta))$ exists,

Rf8. $\frac{1}{n}\ln L(\theta;\mathbf{x}) \overset{a.s.}{\to} E(\ln f(x;\theta))$ for all $\theta \in \Theta$.

[4] Consistency

(a)   **Weak consistency** Under these regularity conditions, MLEs are weakly consistent, i.e., for some $\varepsilon > 0$,

$$\lim_{n\to\infty} \mathbb{P}(|\hat{\theta}_{ML} - \theta| < \varepsilon) = 1, \text{ denoted by: } \hat{\theta}_{ML} \overset{\mathbb{P}}{\to} \theta.$$

(b)   **Strong consistency** Under these regularity conditions, MLEs are strongly consistent, i.e.

$$\mathbb{P}(\lim_{n\to\infty} \hat{\theta}_{ML} = \theta) = 1, \text{ denoted by: } \hat{\theta}_{ML} \overset{a.s.}{\to} \theta.$$

See chapter 9 for a discussion regarding these two different modes of convergence.

[5] Asymptotic Normality

For asymptotic Normality of MLEs we need to ensure that in addition to the regularity conditions **Rf1–Rf6**, mentioned above, the following conditions hold (Gourieroux and Monfort (1995)):

Rf9   The Fisher information for one observation: $0 < I(\theta) < \infty$,

where $I(\theta) := E\left(\left[\frac{d \ln f(x;\theta)}{d\theta}\right]^2\right) = E\left(\left[\frac{d^2 \ln f(x;\theta)}{d\theta^2}\right]\right)$,

Rf10 $\ln L(\theta;\mathbf{x})$ is twice differentiable in an open interval around θ.

Under the regularity conditions **Rf1–Rf10**, MLEs are asymptotically Normal, i.e.

$$\sqrt{n}(\hat{\theta}_{ML} - \theta) \underset{\alpha}{\sim} N(0, V_\infty(\theta)),$$

where $V_\infty(\theta)$ denotes the asymptotic variance of $\hat{\theta}_{ML}$.

[6] Asymptotic Efficiency

Under the same regularity conditions the asymptotic variance of maximum likelihood estimators achieves the asymptotic Cramer–Rao lower bound, which in view of (13.13) takes the form:

$$V_\infty(\hat{\theta}_{ML}) = I^{-1}(\theta).$$

Examples

(1) *The Bernoulli model.* The above results in relation to this model suggest that:

$$\sqrt{n}(\hat{\theta}_{ML} - \theta) \underset{\alpha}{\sim} N(0, \theta(1-\theta)).$$

(2) *The Exponential model.* The above results in relation to this model suggest that:

$$\sqrt{n}(\hat{\theta}_{ML} - \theta) \underset{\alpha}{\sim} N(0, \theta^2).$$

(3) *The Normal model.* In view of the results in (13.8) we can deduce that:

$$\sqrt{n}(\hat{\mu}_{ML} - \mu) \underset{\alpha}{\sim} N(0,\sigma^2), \ \sqrt{n}(\hat{\sigma}^2_{ML} - \sigma^2) \underset{\alpha}{\sim} N(0,2\sigma^4).$$

Asymptotic properties (non-ID but independent sample)

The above asymptotic properties need to be modified somewhat in the case where the sample is independent but non-identically distributed. In this case, the relationship between the individual observation Fisher information $I(\theta)$ and the sample Fisher information $I_n(\theta)$ are not related as in (13.13). Instead, the two are related via:

$$I_n(\theta) = \sum_{k=1}^{n} I_k(\theta), \text{ where } I_k(\theta) = E\left(\left|\frac{d\ln f(x_k;\theta)}{d\theta}\right|^2\right), \tag{13.14}$$

because of independence. For the above properties to hold we need to impose certain restrictions on $I_n(\theta)$. These restrictions will be related to its asymptotic behavior and in particular its *order of magnitude* (see Spanos (1986), ch. 10). In crude terms these conditions amount to:

(1) $\lim_{n\to\infty} I_n(\theta) = \infty$.

(2)   There exists a sequence $\{c_n\}_{n=1}^{\infty}$ such that

$$\lim_{n\to\infty}\left(\frac{1}{c_n^2} I_n(\theta)\right) = I_\infty(\theta), \text{ where } 0 < I_\infty^{-1}(\theta) < \infty.$$

The first condition ensures consistency and the second ensures asymptotic Normality.

   Asymptotic Normality under these conditions takes the form:

$$c_n(\hat{\theta}_{ML} - \theta) \underset{\alpha}{\sim} N(0, I_\infty^{-1}(\theta)).$$

Example 3 (continued)

Consider the simple Normal linear regression model. It turns out that the MLEs of $\theta := (\beta_0, \beta_1, \sigma^2)$ coincide with the *moment matching principle estimators*:

$$\hat{\beta}_0 = \bar{y} - \hat{\beta}_1\bar{x}, \ \hat{\beta}_1 = \frac{\sum_{k=1}^{n}(y_k - \bar{y})(x_k - \bar{x})}{\sum_{k=1}^{n}(x_k - \bar{x})^2}, \ \hat{\sigma}^2 = \frac{1}{n}\sum_{k=1}^{n}(y_t - \bar{y})^2 - \frac{\left(\frac{1}{n}\sum_{k=1}^{n}(y_k - \bar{y})(x_k - \bar{x})\right)^2}{\frac{1}{n}\sum_{k=1}^{n}(x_k - \bar{x})^2}. \tag{13.15}$$

To see this let us define the likelihood function:

$$L(\beta_0,\beta_1,\sigma^2;\mathbf{y}) \propto \prod_{k=1}^{n} \frac{1}{\sigma\sqrt{2\pi}}\exp\left\{-\frac{1}{2\sigma^2}(y_k - \beta_0 - \beta_1 x_k)^2\right\} =$$

$$= (\sigma^{-2})^n (2\pi)^{-\frac{n}{2}}\exp\left\{-\frac{1}{2\sigma^2}\sum_{k=1}^{n}(y_k - \beta_0 - \beta_1 x_k)^2\right\}.$$

As is often the case, for locating the MLEs we use the log likelihood function, which in the present case is:

$$\ln L(\theta;\mathbf{y}) = \text{const} - \frac{n}{2}\ln\sigma^2 - \frac{1}{2\sigma^2}\sum_{k=1}^{n}(y_k - \beta_0 - \beta_1 x_k)^2.$$

Hence, by solving the first-order conditions:

$$\frac{\partial \ln L(\theta;\mathbf{y})}{\partial\beta_0} = -\frac{1}{2\sigma^2}(-2)\sum_{k=1}^{n}(y_k - \beta_0 - \beta_1 x_k) = 0,$$

$$\frac{\partial \ln L(\theta;\mathbf{y})}{\partial\beta_1} = -\frac{1}{2\sigma^2}(-2)\sum_{k=1}^{n}(y_k - \beta_0 - \beta_1 x_k)x_k = 0,$$

$$\frac{\partial \ln L(\theta;\mathbf{y})}{\partial\sigma^2} = -\frac{n}{2\sigma^2} + \frac{1}{2\sigma^4}\sum_{k=1}^{n}(y_k - \beta_0 - \beta_1 x_k)^2 = 0,$$

we get the MLEs (13.15). In order to see the difficulties in relation to the order of magnitude of the Fisher information matrix let us derive it. The second derivatives and their expected values yield:

$$\left(\frac{\partial^2 \ln L(\boldsymbol{\theta};\mathbf{y})}{\partial \beta_0^2}\right) = -\frac{n}{\sigma^2}, \qquad \Rightarrow E\left(-\frac{\partial^2 \ln L(\boldsymbol{\theta};\mathbf{y})}{\partial \beta_0^2}\right) = \frac{T}{\sigma^2},$$

$$\left(\frac{\partial^2 \ln L(\boldsymbol{\theta};\mathbf{y})}{\partial \beta_1^2}\right) = -\frac{1}{\sigma^2}\sum_{k=1}^{n} x_k^2 \qquad \Rightarrow E\left(-\frac{\partial^2 \ln L(\boldsymbol{\theta};\mathbf{y})}{\partial \beta_1^2}\right) = \frac{1}{\sigma^2}\sum_{k=1}^{n} x_k^2,$$

$$\left(\frac{\partial^2 \ln L(\boldsymbol{\theta};\mathbf{y})}{\partial \beta_1 \partial \beta_0}\right) = -\frac{1}{\sigma^2}\sum_{k=1}^{n} x_k \qquad \Rightarrow E\left(-\frac{\partial^2 \ln L(\boldsymbol{\theta};\mathbf{y})}{\partial \beta_1 \partial \beta_0}\right) = \frac{1}{\sigma^2}\sum_{k=1}^{n} x_k,$$

$$\left(\frac{\partial^2 \ln L(\boldsymbol{\theta};\mathbf{y})}{\partial \sigma^2 \partial \beta_0}\right) = -\frac{1}{\sigma^4}\sum_{k=1}^{n} u_k \qquad \Rightarrow E\left(-\frac{\partial^2 \ln L(\boldsymbol{\theta};\mathbf{y})}{\partial \sigma^2 \partial \beta_0}\right) = 0,$$

$$\left(\frac{\partial^2 \ln L(\boldsymbol{\theta};\mathbf{y})}{\partial \sigma^2 \partial \beta_1}\right) = -\frac{1}{\sigma^4}\sum_{k=1}^{n} u_k x_k \qquad \Rightarrow E\left(-\frac{\partial^2 \ln L(\boldsymbol{\theta};\mathbf{y})}{\partial \sigma^2 \partial \beta_1}\right) = 0,$$

$$\left(\frac{\partial^2 \ln L(\boldsymbol{\theta};\mathbf{y})}{\partial \sigma^4}\right) = -\frac{n}{2\sigma^4} - \frac{1}{\sigma^6}\sum_{k=1}^{n} u_k^2 \qquad \Rightarrow E\left(-\frac{\partial^2 \ln L(\boldsymbol{\theta};\mathbf{y})}{\partial \sigma^4}\right) = \frac{n}{2\sigma^4},$$

where $u_t = y_t - \beta_0 - \beta_1 x_t$. Hence, the information matrix takes the form:

$$I_n(\beta_0, \beta_1, \sigma^2) = \begin{pmatrix} \frac{n}{\sigma^2} & \frac{1}{\sigma^2}\sum_{k=1}^{n} x_k & 0 \\ \frac{1}{\sigma^2}\sum_{k=1}^{n} x_k & \frac{1}{\sigma^2}\sum_{k=1}^{n} x_k^2 & 0 \\ 0 & 0 & \frac{n}{2\sigma^4} \end{pmatrix}. \qquad (13.16)$$

For consistency we require this information matrix to converge to infinity as in **(1)**. This is achieved if:

$$\sum_{k=1}^{n} x_k^2 \underset{n\to\infty}{\to} \infty.$$

However, for the asymptotic Normality of the estimator $\hat{\beta}_1$ the modeler is also required to know the rate of convergence of $\left(\sum_{k=1}^{n} x_k^2\right)$ in order to define the normalizing sequence $\{c_n\}_{n=1}^{\infty}$. In the absence of any such information he/she can always use:

$$c_n = \left(\sum_{k=1}^{n} x_k^2\right)^{\frac{1}{2}} \Rightarrow \left(\sum_{k=1}^{n} x_k^2\right)^{\frac{1}{2}} (\hat{\beta}_1 - \beta_1) \underset{\alpha}{\sim} N(0, \sigma^2).$$

Asymptotic properties (non-random sample)*

In the case of a non-random sample $\mathbf{X}_n := (X_1, X_2, \dots, X_n)$ the Fisher information does not satisfy either (13.13) or (13.14). The easiest way to derive a comparable form is via the sequential conditioning employed in chapters 6–8 for non-random samples. In view of the fact that:

$$D(X_1, X_2, \dots X_n; \boldsymbol{\psi}) = D(X_1; \boldsymbol{\theta}_1) \cdot \prod_{k=2}^{n} D_k(X_k | X_{k-1}, \dots X_1; \boldsymbol{\theta}_k), \mathbf{X} \in \aleph.$$

In cases where the parameter index-dependence can be restricted by imposing a certain heterogeneity restriction, the weaker form of which is: $\lim_{n\to\infty} \boldsymbol{\theta}_n = \boldsymbol{\theta}$, the log-likelihood function can be expressed in the form:

$$\ln L_n(\boldsymbol{\theta};\mathbf{x}) \propto \sum_{k=1}^{n} \ln D_k(X_k | X_{k-1}, \dots X_1; \boldsymbol{\theta}), \boldsymbol{\theta} \in \Theta,$$

where for $k=1$ the distribution is the initial marginal $D(X_1;\boldsymbol{\theta})$. The score function takes the form:

$$s_n(\boldsymbol{\theta};\mathbf{x}) := \frac{\partial}{\partial\boldsymbol{\theta}}\ln L_n(\boldsymbol{\theta};\mathbf{x}) = \sum_{k=1}^{n}\frac{\partial}{\partial\boldsymbol{\theta}}\ln D_k(X_k|X_{k-1},\ldots,X_1;\boldsymbol{\theta}) := \sum_{k=1}^{n}u_k(\boldsymbol{\theta};x),\ \boldsymbol{\theta}\in\Theta.$$

Hence, viewing $s_k(\boldsymbol{\theta};.)$ and $u_k(\boldsymbol{\theta};.)$ as functions of the past history of X_{k+1}:

$$\mathbf{X}_k := (X_1,X_2,\ldots,X_k),$$

we can deduce that for $s_0(\boldsymbol{\theta})=0$:

(i) $u_k(\boldsymbol{\theta};\mathbf{X}_k) = s_k(\boldsymbol{\theta};\mathbf{X}_k) - s_{k-1}(\boldsymbol{\theta};\mathbf{X}_{k-1}),\ k=1,2,\ldots,n,$
(ii) $s_n(\boldsymbol{\theta};\mathbf{X}) = \sum_{k=1}^{n}[s_k(\boldsymbol{\theta};\mathbf{X}_k) - s_{k-1}(\boldsymbol{\theta};\mathbf{X}_{k-1})],$

or equivalently:

$$s_k(\boldsymbol{\theta};\mathbf{X}_k) = s_{k-1}(\boldsymbol{\theta};\mathbf{X}_{k-1}) + u_k(\boldsymbol{\theta};\mathbf{X}_k),\ k=1,2,\ldots,n.$$

These results suggest that the processes $\{s_k(\boldsymbol{\theta};\mathbf{X}_k)\}_{k=1}^{\infty}$ and $\{u_k(\boldsymbol{\theta};\mathbf{X}_k)\}_{k=1}^{\infty}$ are a martingale and a martingale difference process relative to $\sigma(\mathbf{X}_{k-1})$, respectively, since:

(iii) $E(u_k(\boldsymbol{\theta};\mathbf{X}_k)|\sigma(\mathbf{X}_{k-1}))=0,$
(iv) $E(s_k(\boldsymbol{\theta};\mathbf{X}_k)|\sigma(\mathbf{X}_{k-1}))=s_{k-1}(\boldsymbol{\theta};\mathbf{X}_{k-1}),$ $k=1,2,\ldots,n;$

see chapter 8. Moreover, $\{s_k(\boldsymbol{\theta};\mathbf{X}_k)\}_{k=1}^{\infty}$ is a zero mean martingale because:

$$E(s_k(\boldsymbol{\theta};\mathbf{X}_k)) = E\{E(s_k(\boldsymbol{\theta};\mathbf{X}_k)|\sigma(\mathbf{X}_{k-1}))\} = 0,\ k=1,2,\ldots,n,$$

confirming property **sc1** of the score function mentioned above.

Given that the MLE $\hat{\theta}_{ML}$ is a root of the score function equation $s_n(\theta;\mathbf{X})=0$, and $\{s_k(\boldsymbol{\theta};\mathbf{X}_k),\ \sigma(\mathbf{X}_{k-1})\}_{k=1}^{\infty}$ is zero mean martingale which can be written as a summation:

$$s_n(\theta;\mathbf{X}) = \sum_{k=1}^{n}u_k(\theta;\mathbf{X}_k),$$

we can use the limit theorems of chapter 9 to prove both consistency and asymptotic Normality. The easiest way to see this is to define the *conditional information* (second-order) process:

$$\xi_n(\theta;\mathbf{X}) = \sum_{k=1}^{n}E(u_k^2(\theta;\mathbf{X}_k)|\sigma(\mathbf{X}_{k-1})),$$

which is also a martingale, because the martingale difference process $\{u_k(\boldsymbol{\theta};\mathbf{X}_k)\}_{k=1}^{\infty}$ behaves like an uncorrelated process (see chapter 8). NOTE that the Fisher information is just the mean of this process, i.e.

$$I_n(\theta) = E(s_n^2(\theta;\mathbf{X})) = E(\xi_n(\theta;\mathbf{X})).$$

Under certain regularity conditions analogous to the conditions on the information matrix in the non-ID case, it can be shown that:

(a) $[I_n(\theta)]^{-1}\sum_{k=1}^{n}u_k(\theta;\mathbf{X}_k) \xrightarrow[n\to\infty]{a.s.} 0,$
(b) $[I_n(\theta)]^{-\frac{1}{2}}\sum_{k=1}^{n}u_k(\theta;\mathbf{X}_k) \xrightarrow[n\to\infty]{\mathbb{D}} N(0,1),$

Example 9

Consider **the Normal autoregressive model**:

[1] Statistical GM: $X_k = \alpha X_{k-1} + u_k, \ k \in \mathbb{N}$,
[2] Probability model:

$$\Phi = \left\{ f(x_1,\ldots,x_n;\boldsymbol{\theta}) = f(x_1;\boldsymbol{\theta}) \prod_{t=2}^{n} f(x_k|x_{k-1};\boldsymbol{\theta}), \ \boldsymbol{\theta} \in (-1,1) \times \mathbb{R}_{+}, \ \mathbf{x} \in \mathbb{R}^n \right\},$$

$$f(x_1;\boldsymbol{\theta}) = \frac{\sqrt{1-\alpha^2}}{\sigma_0\sqrt{2\pi}} \exp\left\{ -\frac{(1-\alpha^2)}{2}\frac{x_k^2}{\sigma_0^2} \right\}, f(x_k|x_{k-1};\boldsymbol{\theta}) = \frac{1}{\sigma_0\sqrt{2\pi}} \exp\left\{ -\frac{1}{2}\frac{(x_k-\alpha x_{k-1})^2}{\sigma_0^2} \right\}$$

$$\boldsymbol{\theta} := (\alpha,\sigma_0^2), \ \alpha = \frac{E(X_{k-1}X_k)}{E(X_{k-1}^2)}, \ \sigma_0^2 = E(X_{k-1}^2) - \frac{[E(X_{k-1}X_k)]^2}{E(X_{k-1}^2)},$$

[3] Sampling model: $(X_1, X_2, \ldots, X_n)$ is a stationary and Markov dependent sample, sequentially drawn from $f(x_k|x_{k-1};\boldsymbol{\theta}), k \in \mathbb{N}$.

The distribution of the sample $\mathbf{X} := (X_1, X_2, \ldots, X_n)$ is determined via:

$$X_1 \sim N\left(0, \frac{\sigma_0^2}{1-\alpha^2}\right).$$

$$\begin{pmatrix} X_k \\ X_{k-\tau} \end{pmatrix} \sim N\left(\begin{bmatrix} 0 \\ 0 \end{bmatrix}, \begin{bmatrix} \left(\frac{\sigma_0^2}{1-\alpha^2}\right) & \left(\frac{\sigma_0^2}{1-\alpha^2}\right)\alpha^{|\tau|} \\ \left(\frac{\sigma_0^2}{1-\alpha^2}\right)\alpha^{|\tau|} & \left(\frac{\sigma_0^2}{1-\alpha^2}\right) \end{bmatrix} \right), \ k,\tau = 1,2,\ldots,n.$$

The log-likelihood function takes the form:

$$\ln L(\boldsymbol{\theta};\mathbf{x}) = \frac{1}{2}\ln(1-\alpha^2) - \frac{n}{2}\ln\sigma_0^2 - \frac{1}{2\sigma_0^2}\{d_{00} - 2\alpha d_{01} + \alpha^2 d_{11}\},$$

$$d_{ij} = \sum_{k=j+1}^{n-i} x_k x_{k+i-j}, \ i,j=0,1.$$

The first-order conditions are:

$$\left. \begin{array}{l} \frac{\partial \ln L(\boldsymbol{\theta};\mathbf{x})}{\partial \sigma_0^2} = -\frac{n}{2\sigma_0^2} + \frac{1}{2\sigma_0^4}\{d_{00} - 2\alpha d_{01} + \alpha^2 d_{11}\} = 0, \\ \frac{\partial \ln L(\boldsymbol{\theta};\mathbf{x})}{\partial \alpha} = -\frac{\alpha}{(1-\alpha^2)} - \frac{\alpha d_{11} - 2d_{01}}{2\sigma_0^2} = 0, \end{array} \right\} \Rightarrow$$

$$\hat{\sigma}_0^2 = \frac{1}{n}\{d_{00} - 2\hat{\alpha}d_{01} + \hat{\alpha}^2 d_{11}\},$$

$$\left[\left(\frac{n-1}{n}\right)d_{11}\right]\hat{\alpha}^3 + \left[\left(\frac{n-2}{n}\right)d_{01}\right]\hat{\alpha}^2 - \left[d_{11} + \left(\frac{d_{00}}{n}\right)\right]\hat{\alpha} + d_{01} = 0.$$

The first equation gives the MLE of σ^2 but the second is a cubic equation with three roots but the only relevant one is the root related to the interval $(-1,1)$. Although there is a closed-form solution to this equation it is highly complicated and often α is estimated using a numerical approximation algorithm such as the Newton–Raphson described above.

The derivation can be simplified significantly by leaving the distribution of the first observation out and obtain the approximate MLE based on:

$$\ln L(\boldsymbol{\theta};\mathbf{x}) = -\frac{n-1}{2}\ln\sigma_0^2 - \frac{1}{2\sigma_0^2}\sum_{k=2}^{n}(x_k - \alpha x_{k-1})^2.$$

Hence, we get the approximate MLEs by solving the first-order conditions:

$$\frac{\partial \ln L(\boldsymbol{\theta};\mathbf{x})}{\partial \alpha} = \frac{1}{\sigma_0^2}\Sigma_{k=1}^n (x_k - \alpha x_{k-1})x_{k-1} = 0, \Rightarrow \hat{\alpha} = \frac{\Sigma_{k=2}^n x_k x_{k-1}}{\Sigma_{k=2}^n x_{k-1}^2},$$

$$\frac{\partial \ln L(\boldsymbol{\theta};\mathbf{x})}{\partial \sigma_0^2} = -\frac{n-1}{2\sigma_0^2} + \frac{1}{2\sigma_0^4}\sum_{k=2}^n (x_k - \alpha x_{k-1})^2 = 0, \Rightarrow \hat{\sigma}_0^2 = \frac{1}{n-1}\sum_{k=2}^n (x_k - \hat{\alpha} x_{k-1})^2.$$

$$\left(\frac{\partial^2 \ln L(\boldsymbol{\theta};\mathbf{x})}{\partial \alpha^2}\right) = -\frac{1}{\sigma_0^2}\Sigma_{k=2}^n x_{k-1}^2 \Rightarrow E\left(-\frac{\partial^2 \ln L(\boldsymbol{\theta};\mathbf{x})}{\partial \alpha^2}\Big|\sigma(\mathbf{X}_{k-1})\right) = \frac{1}{\sigma_0^2}\Sigma_{k=2}^n x_{k-1}^2,$$

$$\left(\frac{\partial^2 \ln L(\boldsymbol{\theta};\mathbf{x})}{\partial \sigma_0^2 \partial \alpha}\right) = -\frac{1}{\sigma_0^4}\Sigma_{k=2}^n (x_k - \alpha x_{k-1})x_{k-1} \Rightarrow E\left(-\frac{\partial^2 \ln L(\boldsymbol{\theta};\mathbf{x})}{\partial \sigma_0^2 \partial \alpha}\Big|\sigma(\mathbf{X}_{k-1})\right) = 0,$$

$$\left(\frac{\partial^2 \ln L(\boldsymbol{\theta};\mathbf{x})}{\partial \sigma_0^4}\right) = \frac{n-1}{2\sigma_0^4} - \frac{1}{\sigma_0^6}\Sigma_{k=2}^n (x_k - \alpha x_{k-1})^2 \Rightarrow E\left(-\frac{\partial^2 \ln L(\boldsymbol{\theta};\mathbf{x})}{\partial \sigma_0^4}\Big|\sigma(\mathbf{X}_{k-1})\right) = \frac{n-1}{2\sigma_0^4}.$$

The *conditional information matrix* takes the form:

$$\boldsymbol{\xi}_n(\alpha,\sigma_0^2;\mathbf{X}) = \begin{pmatrix} \frac{1}{\sigma_0^2}\Sigma_{k=2}^n x_{k-1}^2 & 0 \\ & \\ 0 & \frac{n-1}{2\sigma_0^4} \end{pmatrix}$$

which reminds one of the linear regression discussed above. Given that:

$$I_n(\alpha) = E\left\{E\left(-\frac{\partial^2 \ln L(\boldsymbol{\theta};\mathbf{x})}{\partial \alpha^2}\Big|\sigma(\mathbf{X}_{k-1})\right)\right\} = \frac{1}{\sigma_0^2}E(\Sigma_{k=2}^n x_{k-1}^2) = \frac{1}{\sigma_0^2}\left(\frac{\sigma_0^2}{1-\alpha^2}\right) = \frac{1}{1-\alpha^2}.$$

Hence, we can conclude that:

$$\sqrt{n}(\hat{\alpha} - \alpha) \underset{\alpha}{\sim} N(0, (1-\alpha^2)), \quad \sqrt{n}(\hat{\sigma}_0^2 - \sigma_0^2) \underset{\alpha}{\sim} N(0, 2\sigma_0^4).$$

Heyde (1975) suggests using the conditional information for normalization:

$$\sqrt{\Sigma_{k=2}^n x_{k-1}^2}(\hat{\alpha} - \alpha) \underset{\alpha}{\sim} N(0, \sigma_0^2).$$

13.5.5 The maximum likelihood method and its critics

The results relating to MLEs discussed above justify the wide acceptance of the maximum likelihood (ML) as the method of choice for estimation purposes. It turns out that there are good reasons for the ML method to be preferred for testing purposes as well (see chapter 14). Despite the wide acceptance of the ML method there are also critics who point to several examples where the method does not yield satisfactory results. Such examples include cases where (a) the sample size is inappropriately small, (b) the regularity conditions do not hold, and (c) the postulated model is ill-specified. As far as the first category of examples is concerned, searching for a good estimator in cases where the sample size is inappropriately small, the criticism is completely misplaced because the modeler is looking for the famous free lunch. The criticism of the ML method based on examples which do not satisfy the regularity conditions is also some-what misplaced because if the modeler seeks methods with any generality the regularity conditions are inevitable. Without regularity conditions each estimation problem will be viewed as unique; no unifying principles are possible. The third category deserves more discussion because it brings out an important problem in empirical modeling. In this cat-egory we classify all statistical models which specify unknown parameters which either increase with the sample size or are related to some extraneously imposed operation such as truncation or censoring of the sample (see Cohen (1991)). From the latter category let us consider the quintessential example.

Example 10

Consider **the Neyman and Scott (1948) model**:

[i] $X_{ij} = E(X_{ij}) + \epsilon_{ij}$, $i \in \mathbb{N}, j \in \mathbb{N}$,

where $E(X_{ij}) = \mu_i$,

[ii] $\Phi = \left\{ f(\mathbf{x}; \boldsymbol{\theta}) = \prod_{i=1}^{n} \prod_{j=1}^{N} \frac{1}{\sigma\sqrt{2\pi}} e^{\{-\frac{1}{2\sigma^2}(x_{ij} - \mu_i)^2\}}, \boldsymbol{\theta} \in \mathbb{R}^n \times \mathbb{R}_+, x_{ij} \in \mathbb{R} \right\}$,

[iii] $\mathbf{X} := (\mathbf{X}_1, \mathbf{X}_2, \ldots, \mathbf{X}_n)$, $\mathbf{X}_k := (X_{k1}, X_{k2}, \ldots, X_{kN})$ an independent sample.

The "MLEs" are derived by solving the first-order conditions:

$$\frac{\partial \ln L(\boldsymbol{\theta};\mathbf{x})}{\partial \mu_i} = \frac{1}{\sigma^2}\sum_{j=1}^{N}(X_{ij} - \mu_i) = 0,$$

$$\left. \frac{\partial \ln L(\boldsymbol{\theta};\mathbf{x})}{\partial \sigma^2} = -\frac{nN}{2\sigma^2} + \frac{1}{2\sigma^4}\sum_{i=1}^{n}\sum_{j=1}^{N}(X_{ij} - \mu_i)^2 = 0, \right\} \Rightarrow$$

$$\hat{\mu}_i = \frac{1}{N}\sum_{j=1}^{N}X_{ij}, \quad \hat{\sigma}^2 = \frac{1}{nN}\sum_{i=1}^{n}\sum_{j=1}^{N}(X_{ij} - \hat{\mu}_i)^2 = \frac{1}{n}\sum_{i=1}^{n}s_i^2,$$

where $s_i^2 := \frac{1}{N}\sum_{j=1}^{N}(X_{ij} - \hat{\mu}_i)^2$. The commonly used argument against the ML method is based on the result that:

$$E(s_i^2) = \frac{(N-1)}{N}\sigma^2 \Rightarrow \hat{\sigma}^2 \overset{a.s.}{\to} \frac{(N-1)}{N}\sigma^2,$$

and thus $\hat{\sigma}^2$ is an inconsistent estimator of σ^2.

A moment's reflection, however, reveals that the inconsistency argument based on $n \to \infty$, is ill thought out because at the same time the number of unknown parameters $(\mu_1, \mu_2, \ldots, \mu_n)$ increases to infinity! The modeler should be skeptical of any method of estimation which yields a consistent estimator of σ^2 without imposing some additional restrictions relating to what happens to μ_n as $n \to \infty$. We consider the fact that the ML method does not yield optimal estimators in cases where the statistical model is ill-specified as an argument in its favor, not against it!

13.6 Exercises

1   Compare the first two moments of the sample raw and sample central moments as they relate to the parameters they purport to estimate.

2   Compare least squares as a mathematical approximation method and the statistical least-squares method.

3   Compare and contrast Pearson's method of moments with the parametric method of moments.

4   Explain why it constitutes an anachronism to compare the maximum likelihood method to the parametric method of moments.

5   "Comparing maximum likelihood and parametric method of moments estimators on efficiency grounds is not a very interesting exercise." Discuss.

6   Describe the main drawbacks of Pearson's approach to deriving a descriptive model.

7   Explain the moment matching principle and compare it with the parametric method of moments.

8   For the Bernoulli statistical model derive the least-squares estimator of θ, its sampling distribution and its properties.

9   Consider the simple Normal statistical model.

     (a)   Derive the MLEs of (μ, σ^2) and their sampling distributions.
     (b)   Derive the least-squares estimators of (μ, σ^2) and their sampling distributions.
     (c)   Compare these estimators in terms of the optimal properties, unbiasedness, full efficiency and consistency.

10   Consider the simple Normal statistical model with $\mu = 0$, i.e. the probability model is:

$$\Phi = \left\{ f(x;\theta) = \tfrac{1}{\sigma\sqrt{2\pi}} \exp\left\{ -\tfrac{1}{2\sigma^2} x^2 \right\}, \ \theta := \sigma^2 > 0, \ x \in \mathbb{R} \right\}.$$

Derive the MLE of θ and compare it with the estimator:

$$\tilde{\sigma}^2 = \tfrac{1}{n+2} \sum_{k=1}^{n} X_k,$$

in terms of their MSE.

11   Consider the simple Laplace statistical model based on the probability model:

$$\Phi = \left\{ f(x;\theta) = \frac{1}{2\theta} e^{-\frac{1}{\theta}|x|}, \ \theta > 0, \ x \in \mathbb{R} \right\}.$$

Derive the MLE of θ and compare it with the PMM estimator.

12   Consider the simple Pareto statistical model based on the probability model:

$$\Phi = \{ f(x;\theta) = \theta x_0^{\theta} x^{-(\theta+1)}, \ \theta > 0, \ x > x_0 > 0, \ x \in \mathbb{R} \}.$$

Derive the MLE of θ and compare it with the PMM and least-squares estimators.

13   State the optimal properties of maximum likelihood estimators (finite sample and asymptotic).

14   Explain the difference between:

     (a)   Fisher's sample and individual observation information,
     (b)   Fisher's information and observational information matrix,
     (c)   Fisher's information and conditional information matrix.

15   "The maximum likelihood method minimizes the distance between the theoretical

probabilities and their empirical counterparts as defined by the empirical cumulative distribution function (ecdf)." Discuss.

16* Derive the iterative scheme for the score method in evaluating the MLE first-order conditions in the case of the simple Logistic model.

17* Derive the iterative scheme for the score method in evaluating the MLE of α in the case of the simple Gamma model.

18* Explain why the processes $\{s_k(\boldsymbol{\theta};\mathbf{X}_k)\}_{k=1}^{\infty}$ and $\{u_k(\boldsymbol{\theta};\mathbf{X}_k)\}_{k=1}^{\infty}$, defined in section 5.4, constitute a martingale and a martingale difference process relative to $\sigma(\mathbf{X}_{k-1})$, respectively.

14 Hypothesis testing

14.1 Introduction

14.1.1 The inherent difficulties in mastering hypothesis testing

Hypothesis testing is one of the most important but also one of the most confusing parts of statistical inference for several reasons, including the following:

(i)   the need to introduce numerous new concepts before one is able to define the problem adequately,

(ii) the fact that the current textbook discussion of the problem constitutes an inept hybrid of two fundamentally different approaches to testing (what Gigerenzer (1987) called the "hybrid theory"), and

(iii) the fact that there is no single method for constructing "good" tests under most circumstances, comparable to the method of maximum likelihood in estimation.

An attempt is made to alleviate these problems by utilizing a number of teaching techniques, the most important of which is the historical development of testing since the late 19th century. It must be said that this is used as a teaching device and no attempt is made to provide a complete account of the historical development of testing; a major task which is yet to be undertaken. The historical dimension of testing is used primarily to ease the problem of introducing too many concepts too quickly and to bring out the differences between the Fisher and the Neyman–Pearson approaches to testing.

As a prelude to the discussion we summarize a number of crucial differences between the traditional account of testing and the interpretations proposed in the discussion that follows:

(a)   the testing hybrid "forged" by the statistical textbooks in the 1960s is deficient,

(b)   the Neyman–Pearson formulation has not superseded that of Fisher,

(c)   the two formulations are fundamentally different but complementary,

(d)   the Neyman–Pearson approach is better suited to *testing within* the boundaries demarcated by the postulated model, and

(e)   the Fisher approach is better suited to *testing outside* the same boundaries.

The discussion throughout this chapter is interspersed with examples and some of the most difficult concepts are often introduced via such examples.

14.1.2 A bird's eye view of the chapter

In section 2 we discuss the Fisher approach (often called *pure significance testing*), considered as a natural extension of the testing procedures inherited from Edgeworth and Pearson. In section 3 the Neyman–Pearson approach is examined, paying particular attention to its relationship with the Fisher approach. Section 4 discusses briefly the three asymptotic test procedures: likelihood ratio, efficient score and Wald test procedures. In section 5 the two approaches are compared and contrasted. It is argued that the Fisher approach is better suited to testing hypotheses which go beyond the boundaries demarcated by the postulated statistical model. On the other hand, the Neyman–Pearson approach is essentially testing within the boundaries of the postulated statistical model. In this sense the two approaches, although fundamentally different, are considered as complementary.

IMPORTANT: like every other form of statistical inference, hypothesis testing commences with the modeler postulating a statistical model which purports to describe the stochastic mechanism that gave rise to the observed data in question and thus the inference results depend crucially on the adequacy of the postulated statistical model.

14.2 Leading up to the Fisher approach

Hypothesis testing during the early 19th century amounted to nothing more than an informal comparison between the values of the parameters specified by the hypothesis in question and the corresponding estimates. That is, the test of a hypothesis of the form:

$$\theta = \theta_0, \tag{14.1}$$

took the form of checking whether the discrepancy between an estimate $\hat{\theta}$ of θ and the specified value θ_0 was "close to zero" or not, i.e.

$$|\hat{\theta} - \theta_0| \approx 0. \tag{14.2}$$

How large should the discrepancy be to be considered "large enough" was never formalized adequately.

   At this early stage we can discern several features which will be retained in the subsequent development of hypothesis testing. These features include:

(i)   a primitive notion of a hypothesis of interest: $\theta = \theta_0$, and
(ii) a distance function: $|\hat{\theta} - \theta_0|$.

This is clearly the prehistory of testing. The actual history of testing begins with Edgeworth.

14.2.1 Edgeworth

A typical example of a testing procedure at the end of the 19th century is provided by Edgeworth (1885) in comparing the difference between two means. The idea was to compare two different samples (or sub-samples) in order to assess whether they have the same mean or not. One way to view this problem is to begin with a sample $\mathbf{X} := (X_1, X_2, \ldots, X_n)$ and divide it into two subsamples of size $n_1 > 2$ and $n_2 > 2$ observations $(n = n_1 + n_2)$, respectively:

$$\mathbf{X} := (X_1, X_2, \ldots, X_{n_1}, X_{n_1+1}, \ldots, X_n).$$

Common sense and statistical knowledge at the time suggested looking at the first two subsample moments (retrospectively interpreted as moment matching principle estimators):

$$\hat{\mu}_1 = \frac{1}{n_1}\sum_{i=1}^{n_1} X_i, \ \hat{\sigma}_1^2 = \frac{1}{n_1}\sum_{i=1}^{n_1}(X_i - \hat{\mu}_1)^2, \ \hat{\mu}_2 = \frac{1}{n_2}\sum_{i=n_1+1}^{n} X_i, \ \hat{\sigma}_2^2 = \frac{1}{n_2}\sum_{i=n_1+1}^{n}(X_i - \hat{\mu}_2)^2,$$

Edgeworth argued that if the standardized distance between the two subsample means is greater than some pre-specified constant:

$$\xi(\mathbf{X}) = \frac{|\hat{\mu}_1 - \hat{\mu}_2|}{\sqrt{(\hat{\sigma}_1^2 + \hat{\sigma}_1^2)}} > 2\sqrt{2}, \tag{14.3}$$

the difference between the two means could *not* be justified as "accidental" and it would appear to be *significant*. Where did the constant come from? At the time the only distribution available for this kind of statistical analysis was the Normal and inevitably the constant $2\sqrt{2}$ was related to it. It turns out that the probability of the Normal distribution beyond the value $\pm 2\sqrt{2}$ is equal to 0.005; the value of accidental occurrence.

Retrospectively, Edgeworth's test could be interpreted as a test of the hypothesis:

$$\mu_1 = \mu_2 = \mu,$$

allowing for the possibility that the variances are different, i.e.

$$X_k \sim N(\mu_1, \sigma_1^2), \ k = 1, 2, \ldots, n_1, \ X_k \sim N(\mu_2, \sigma_2^2), \ k = n_1 + 1, \ldots, n,$$

in the context of a **simple Normal model:**

[i] Statistical GM: $X_k = E(X_k) + u_k$, $k \in \mathbb{N}$,
[ii] Probability model: $\qquad\qquad\qquad\qquad\qquad\qquad\qquad\qquad$ (14.4)

$$\Phi = \left\{ f(x;\boldsymbol{\theta}) = \frac{1}{\sigma\sqrt{2\pi}}\exp\left\{-\frac{1}{2\sigma^2}(x-\mu)^2\right\}, \ \boldsymbol{\theta} := (\mu,\sigma^2) \in \mathbb{R} \times \mathbb{R}_+, x \in \mathbb{R} \right\},$$

[iii] Sampling model: $\mathbf{X} := (X_1, X_2, \ldots, X_n)$ is a random sample.

Comparing this result with the primitive notion of testing before Edgeworth's time we can see that he added two features:

(iii) the notion of a (standardized) distance: $\xi(\mathbf{X})$,
(iv) a rejection rule: $\xi(\mathbf{X}) > 2\sqrt{2}$.

All four features were developed further by Pearson and later formalized by Fisher in the early 20th century.

14.2.2 Pearson

The first important test which straddles both the Pearson and Fisher statistical traditions (see chapter 13), is the so-called Pearson's chi-square test. Pearson (1900) proposed this test as a way to measure the "goodness of fit" in the case of choosing a descriptive model for a particular data set from within the Pearson family (**Pearson** (a,b_0,b_1,b_2)), as described in chapter 13.

Using the first four raw moments of the "sample" $\mathbf{X} := (X_1, X_2, \ldots, X_n)$, Pearson's procedure would estimate the four parameters that define the Pearson family. In turn these estimates $\hat{\boldsymbol{\theta}} := (\hat{a}, \hat{b}_0, \hat{b}_1, \hat{b}_2)$ would select a member of the Pearson family, say $f_0(x)$, that best describes the data with $f_0(x; \hat{\boldsymbol{\theta}})$ its empirical counterpart. The hypothesis of interest for Pearson was whether the choice of $f_0(x)$ is a valid one, i.e.

$$f(x) = f_0(x), \text{ where } f(x) \in \textbf{Pearson } (a,b_0,b_1,b_2). \tag{14.5}$$

Given that the Pearson procedure amounted to fitting a curve over the histogram it is not surprising to discover that Pearson derived the test by comparing the empirical frequencies (not *relative* frequencies) $(\hat{f}_i, i = 1, 2, \ldots, m)$ to the corresponding theoretical frequencies $(f_i, i = 1, 2, \ldots, m)$ (as specified by $f_0(x)$), where the intervals $(i = 1, 2, \ldots, m)$ are mutually exclusive and cover the range of values of the random variable in question. The standardized *distance* function took the sum of standardized squares form:

$$\eta(\mathbf{X}) = \sum_{i=1}^{m} \frac{(\hat{f}_i - f_i)^2}{f_i}. \tag{14.6}$$

It was shown that, *assuming* that the theoretical frequency curve $f_0(x)$ is appropriate, $\eta(\mathbf{X})$ has asymptotically a chi-square distribution with $m - 1$ degrees of freedom, i.e.

$$\eta(\mathbf{X}) \underset{\alpha}{\sim} \chi^2(m-1). \tag{14.7}$$

NOTES:

(i)   The use of asymptotic distributions was used routinely during the 19th and early 20th centuries. What eventually changed this practice was the seminal result by Gosset (1908).

(ii)   The important thing about this result is that the (asymptotic) distribution does not depend on either the nature of the frequency curve chosen by the data or the number of data points; it is very sensitive, however, to the number of intervals m.

(iii) The distributional result in (14.7) is derived on the implicit assumption that the hypothesis of interest is valid; this is an assumption which was made explicitly by Fisher.

Intuition suggests that the larger the value of η the worse the fit. Hence, for a given value of $\eta(\mathbf{X})$, say $\eta(\mathbf{x})$ (based on the observed data $\mathbf{x}$), the modeler would decide whether the distance was large enough to indicate a "bad fit" using the tail probability of $\chi^2(m-1)$:

$$\mathbb{P}(\eta(\mathbf{X}) > \eta(\mathbf{x})) = p. \tag{14.8}$$

A small value of p corresponds to a large value of η, and thus the smaller the value of p the worse the fit.

Karl Pearson's contributions to testing can be summarized as follows:

(a) the broadening of the specification of the hypothesis of interest,
(b) the derivation of a distance function whose distribution is free of $f_0(x)$, and
(c) the use of the tail probability for assessing the validity of the hypothesis of interest.

The use of the tail probability is implicit in Edgeworth but Pearson formalized that by bringing out explicitly the (asymptotic) distribution of the distance function. Thus, Pearson, in addition to improving some of the inherited features, added some more:

(v) the distribution (14.7) of a distance function and
(vi) the tail probability (14.8).

The *common sense logic* of the tail probability was that if the value of $\eta(\mathbf{X})$ happened to belong to a high probability area of the chi-square distribution then the observed data apparently lend support to the hypothesis of interest, but if it falls into a very low probability area (in the remote right tail of the distribution) it does not.

Although the above goodness of fit test was developed by Pearson for testing within the Pearson family, when viewed in the context of statistical inference, its applicability is broader than its original intended scope, as the following example illustrates.

Example
Consider one of the most important historical examples using Mendel's data based on his classic breeding pea-plants experiment as it relates to the shape and color of peas. Mendel's theory of heredity with regard to the random variables X – shape, Y – color, defined as follows:

$$X(\text{round}) = 0, \ X(\text{wrinkled}) = 1, \ Y(\text{yellow}) = 0, \ Y(\text{green}) = 1,$$

gave rise to a bivariate distribution of the form:

Table 14.1. *The bivariate distribution* f(x,y)

$y\backslash x$	0	1	$f_y(y)$
0	0.5625	0.1875	0.750
1	0.1875	0.0625	0.250
$f_x(x)$	0.750	0.250	1.000

In a random sample of size 556, Mendel's data gave rise to the observed relative frequencies as given in table 14.2.

Table 14.2. *Observed relative frequencies*

y\x	0	1	$\hat{f}_y(y)$
0	$\left(\frac{315}{556}\right)=0.566$	$\left(\frac{101}{556}\right)=0.182$	0.748
1	$\left(\frac{108}{556}\right)=0.194$	$\left(\frac{32}{556}\right)=0.058$	0.252
$\hat{f}_x(x)$	0.760	0.240	1.000

Applying Pearson's chi-square test using the expected frequencies:

$$(0.5625)(556)=312.75,\ (0.1875)(556)=104.25,\ (0.0625)(556)=34.75,$$

$$\eta(\mathbf{X})=\left(\frac{(315-312.75)^2}{312.75}\right)+\left(\frac{(108-104.25)^2}{104.25}\right)+\left(\frac{(101-104.25)^2}{104.25}\right)+\left(\frac{(32-34.75)^2}{34.75}\right)=0.470.$$

Using the tail probability of $\chi^2(3)$ yields: $\mathbb{P}(\eta(\mathbf{X})>0.470)=0.925.$

In view of this value, the data provide excellent support for Mendel's theory. It should be noted that a lot of statisticians, including Fisher, consider these data suspiciously "accurate."

In concluding this subsection we note that when one views Pearson's contribution retrospectively (from the point of view of modern statistical inference, and not in the context of Pearson's descriptive statistics (see chapter 13)), two important issues are apparent:

(i)   hypotheses are ultimately statements about distributions and not about parameters as such,

(ii) *testing* can be *within* or *without* the boundaries of the postulated statistical model.

In the case of the chi-square test given above the testing is without because the hypothesis goes beyond the boundaries of the postulated model; it tests its validity.

14.2.3 Gosset

Gosset's 1908 seminal paper provided the cornerstone upon which Fisher founded modern statistical inference. At that time it was known that in the case of the simple Normal model (see (14.4)), the estimator $\hat{\mu}_n=\frac{1}{n}\sum_{i=1}^n X_i$ had the following "sampling" distribution:

$$\hat{\mu}_n\sim N\left(\mu,\frac{\sigma^2}{n}\right)\Rightarrow\tau(\mathbf{X};\mu,\sigma^2):=\left(\frac{\sigma^2}{n}\right)^{-\frac{1}{2}}(\hat{\mu}_n-\mu)=\frac{\sqrt{n}(\hat{\mu}_n-\mu)}{\sigma}\sim N(0,1).$$

It was also known that in the case where σ^2 is replaced by the estimator $s=\frac{1}{n-1}\sum_{i=1}^n(X_i-\hat{\mu}_n)^2$, the distribution of the function:

$$\tau(\mathbf{X};\mu)=\frac{\sqrt{n}(\hat{\mu}_n-\mu)}{s}\nsim N(0,1),\tag{14.9}$$

where $\not\sim$ reads "is not distributed as." It was well-known that it was Normal only asymptotically:

$$\tau(\mathbf{X};\mu) = \frac{\sqrt{n}(\hat{\mu}_n - \mu)}{s} \underset{\alpha}{\not\sim} \mathsf{N}(0,1). \tag{14.10}$$

This is because $\tau(\mathbf{X};\mu) = \frac{\sqrt{n}(\hat{\mu}_n - \mu)}{s}$ is a ratio of a Normally distributed random variable $\hat{\mu}_n$ and the square root of the random variable s^2, whose distribution was not known. Gosset went on to "guess" the distribution of s^2 by deriving its first four raw moments and substituting them into the four equations of the Pearson family (see chapter 13). This exercise led him to conclude that s^2 *most probably* had a chi-square distribution. After establishing that $\hat{\mu}_n$ and s^2 were uncorrelated (and erroneously thinking that this was the same as being independent), he went on to derive the distribution of the ratio (14.9) using an almost heuristic argument by today's standards. In today's terminology, using lemma 7 of chapter 11, $\tau(\mathbf{X};\mu)$ is the ratio of two independent random variables, the numerator $U = \frac{\sqrt{n}(\hat{\mu}_n - \mu)}{\sigma}$ is Normally distributed and the denominator $V = \frac{(n-1)s^2}{\sigma^2}$, is chi-square distributed, hence:

$$\tau(\mathbf{X};\mu) = \left(\frac{\sqrt{n}(\hat{\mu}_n - \mu)}{s} \right) \sim \mathsf{St}(n-1), \tag{14.11}$$

where $\mathsf{St}(n-1)$ denotes a Student's t distribution with $(n-1)$ degrees of freedom. The most remarkable thing about this result is that, in contrast to (14.10), it was the *first finite sample result*; a distributional result that was valid for any sample size, not just for large n.

Gosset's result (14.11) is important for hypothesis testing because it represents the first pivotal quantity, the quintessence of many *test statistics*.

A pivotal function for θ is a monotonic function of θ of the form $q(\mathbf{X},\theta)$:

$$q(.,.):\mathbf{X} \times \Theta \to \mathbb{R},$$

whose "sampling" distribution is free of the unknown parameters ($\boldsymbol{\theta}$). That is, given the distribution of the sample $D(\mathbf{X};\theta)$, the distribution of $q(\mathbf{X},\theta)$ is the same for all $\boldsymbol{\theta} \in \Theta$.

The function (14.11) is a pivot because its distribution is known and free from the unknown parameters (μ,σ^2) of the underlying statistical model because $\mathsf{St}(n-1)$ does not involve these parameters. Another important pivotal quantity has already been encountered above:

$$\nu(\mathbf{X},\sigma^2) = \frac{(n-1)s^2}{\sigma^2} \sim \chi^2(n-1).$$

Again its distribution is free of any unknown parameters.

A statistic $h(\mathbf{X})$, in contrast to the notion of a pivotal function, is a function of the form:

$$h(.):\mathbf{X} \to \mathbb{R}.$$

That is, it does not involve any unknown parameters (see chapter 11).

14.2.4 Fisher's formulation

The result (14.11) was formally proved and extended by Fisher (1915) and used subsequently as a basis for several tests of hypotheses associated with a number of different statistical models in a series of papers, culminating with his 1925 book.

Fisher used the result (14.11) to derive a test for what he called:

Null hypothesis: $H_0 : \mu = \mu_0$.

In terms of the modern statistical inference framework, Fisher considered the question of deriving a test for the above null hypothesis in the context of **the simple Normal model** (see (14.4)). His reasoning was based on defining a standardized distance such that the further away the "true" value of μ is from the value specified by H_0, the larger the distance, leading to:

$$\frac{(\hat{\mu}_n - \mu_0)}{\sqrt{s^2/n}} = \frac{\sqrt{n}(\hat{\mu}_n - \mu_0)}{s}.$$

Fisher went on to derive a test statistic arguing that even though (14.11) holds for the "true" value of μ, under the assumption that H_0 is valid, the true value is μ_0 and one can infer:

$$\tau(\mathbf{X}) = \left(\frac{\sqrt{n}(\hat{\mu}_n - \mu_0)}{s} \right) \overset{H_0}{\sim} \mathsf{St}(n-1), \tag{14.12}$$

where "$\overset{H_0}{\sim}$" reads "under H_0 is distributed as".

A test statistic The essence of Fisher's result (14.12) is that he transformed Gosset's pivotal function $\tau(\mathbf{X}, \boldsymbol{\theta})$ into a *test statistic* $\tau(\mathbf{X})$: distance function of the sample (a statistic) whose distribution is known and does not depend on any unknown parameters $\boldsymbol{\theta}$. This was achieved by deriving the distribution of the statistic $\tau(\mathbf{X}, \boldsymbol{\theta}_0)$, which does not involve any unknown parameters under $H_0 : \boldsymbol{\theta} = \boldsymbol{\theta}_0$; that is, derive the sampling distribution of $\tau(\mathbf{X}, \boldsymbol{\theta})$ assuming that the null hypothesis is valid.

Using this result, Fisher proceeded to derive a measure of "how much a particular sample realization deviates from H_0," based on the probability of the tail area of the distribution (14.12) beyond the observed value $\tau(\mathbf{x})$ of the statistic $\tau(\mathbf{X})$. This measure, known as the probability value or *p*-**value** for short, takes the form:

$$\mathbb{P}(\tau(\mathbf{X}) \geq \tau(\mathbf{x}); H_0 \text{ is valid}) = p. \tag{14.13}$$

By definition the *p*-value evaluates the worst-case scenario for the null hypothesis in the sense that it involves the observed value of the statistic and realizations more damning for the null. It measures the probability of observing a sample realization that would produce a statistic value equal to or worse than the one already observed. Fisher's interpretation of the *p*-value can be considered as a formalization of the inherited view:

if the *p*-value is small this implies that either the observed realization of the test statistic constitutes a very rare event or the postulated null hypothesis is invalid.

In cases where the *p*-value is small the first choice is considered practically impossible and the modeler adopts the view that the postulated hypothesis is invalid. In view of the fact that the greater the value of $\tau(\mathbf{x})$ the smaller the p-value, the modeler can interpret small values of p as evidence against H_0; the smaller the value of p the less plausible is H_0. In a certain sense the p-value might be interpreted as *a measure of how appropriately the null hypothesis describes the mechanism giving rise to the observed data.* In the early stages of his work Fisher suggested p-values of 0.05 and 0.01 to be used as intuitive thresholds. Later on, however, he insisted that one should separate the p-value from the decision to accept or reject H_0 (see Fisher (1935a, 1956)).

In summary, Fisher built on the previous work of Edgeworth and Pearson but provided more structure to the hypothesis testing procedure by:

(a) introducing explicitly the notion of a null hypothesis,
(b) utilizing the notion of a pivotal function,
(c) introducing the notion of the finite sample distribution of the pivot under H_0,
(d) formalizing the notion of a p-value,
(e) introducing the inferential nature of hypothesis testing.

In the context of the Fisher approach, to define a test one requires a "distance function" which utilizes a "good" estimator of the parameter in question. This is, then, transformed into a *pivotal function*, such as (14.11). This pivotal function, under H_0, involves no unknown parameters and thus it becomes a *test statistic*. To make a decision on the validity of H_0, one uses a measure of how much a particular realization deviates from H_0. For Fisher the decision to be made is whether the evidence suggests that the null hypothesis is plausible or not.

Examples

1   In the case of **the simple Normal model** (see (14.4)), using the marks data in table 1.6 (see chapter 1), consider testing the null hypothesis:

$$H_0: \mu = 70.$$

For the scores data (see table 1.6): $\hat{\mu}_n = 71.686$, $s^2 = 13.606$ and $n = 70$. Substituting these into the pivotal function (14.12) yields:

$$\tau(\mathbf{x}) = \frac{\sqrt{70}(71.686 - 70)}{\sqrt{13.606}} = 3.824, \; \mathbb{P}(|\tau(\mathbf{X})| \geq 3.824; \mu_0 = 70) = 0.00014,$$

where the value 0.00014 is found from the St(69) tables. The relatively low p-value indicates that the data do not support the validity of H_0.

2   **Arbuthnot's conjecture.** The most widely discussed hypothesis during the 18th century was the famous hypothesis of Arbuthnot (1710) based on the observation that in the city of London, for a period of 82 consecutive years, there were systematically more male than female births in any one year; Arbuthnot's conjecture was that the odds of males to females in newborns is not "fair." The "fair game" hypothesis can be formulated in the context of **the simple Bernoulli model**:

[i]   Statistical GM: $X_i = E(X_i) + \epsilon_i$, $i \in \mathbb{N}$,
[ii]   Probability model: $\Phi = \{f(x;\theta) = \theta^x (1 - \theta)^{1-x}, \theta \in [0,1], x = 0,1\}$,   (14.14)
[iii]   Sampling model: $\mathbf{X} := (X_1, X_2, \ldots, X_n)$ is a random sample.

The random variable is defined by: {female} = {$X = 1$}, {male} = {$X = 0$}, and the null hypothesis is specified as follows:

$$H_0: \theta = 0.5.$$

3   **N. Bernoulli's conjecture** N. Bernoulli took the conjecture one step further and proposed the odds 18:17 for males (see Hacking (1965)). The Bernoulli conjecture can be formulated in the form of the null hypothesis:

$$H_0: \theta = 0.4857.$$

Both of the above hypotheses take the general form: $H_0: \theta = \theta_0$, $\theta_0 \in (0,1)$. The distance function which suggests itself in this case is: $|\hat{\theta}_n - \theta_0|$, where $\hat{\theta}_n = \frac{1}{n} \sum_{k=1}^{n} X_i$; shown in chapter 12 to be the "best" estimator of θ. Given that $\hat{\theta}_n$ is a random variable, $|\hat{\theta}_n - \theta_0|$ is an event whose probability of occurrence can be appraised using the sampling distribution of $\hat{\theta}_n$. In chapter 12, it was also shown that $\hat{\theta}_n$ is *Binomially distributed* with mean θ and variance $[\theta(1 - \theta)/n]$, denoted by:

$$\hat{\theta}_n \sim \text{Bi}\left(\theta, \frac{\theta(1-\theta)}{n}; n\right).$$

This suggests that: $\tau(\mathbf{X};\theta) := \frac{\sqrt{n}(\hat{\theta}_n - \theta_0)}{\sqrt{\theta_0(1 - \theta_0)}} \sim \text{Bi}((\theta - \theta_0), 1; n)$. Hence, we can proceed to derive the *test statistic*:

$$\tau(\mathbf{X}) := \frac{\sqrt{n}(\hat{\theta}_n - \theta_0)}{\sqrt{\theta_0(1 - \theta_0)}} \overset{H_0}{\sim} \text{Bi}(0,1; n). \tag{14.15}$$

Testing Bernoulli's conjecture The observed data refer to the number of births (male, female) during the period 1974–6 in Cyprus: $n = 25928$, 13375 males and 12553 females.

$$\hat{\theta}_n = \frac{12553}{25928} = 0.48415, \quad \tau(\mathbf{x}) = \frac{\sqrt{25928}(0.48415 - 0.4857)}{\sqrt{0.4857(0.5143)}} = -0.49988.$$

$$\mathbb{P}(|\tau(\mathbf{X})| > -0.49988; \theta = 0.4857) = 0.617.$$

The high p-value suggests that the evidence is strongly in favor of H_0; Bernoulli's conjecture is supported by the data in the case of Cyprus!

Although Fisher initially offered some rules of thumb in relation to p-values and the strength of evidence for or against the null hypothesis, he was later at great pains to explain that they were just crude guidelines. In the following table we offer similar "rules of thumb" guidelines to help the uninitiated, knowing that they can be easily criticized as *ad hoc* and unwarranted.

p-value	**Interpretation**
$p > 0.10$:	data indicating strong support for H_0,
$0.05 < p < 0.10$:	data indicating some support for H_0,
$0.02 < p < 0.05$:	data indicate lack of support for H_0,
$p < 0.01$:	data indicate strong lack of support for H_0.

14.2.5 Summary

Testing in the context of the Fisher approach commences with the specification of a null hypothesis, whose simplest form is:

$$H_0 : \theta = \theta_0.$$

Despite appearances, a *null hypothesis* is not just a statement about a parameter, it is ultimately *a statement about the underlying statistical model* and as such it can take a number of different forms. For simplicity we restrict ourselves to this simple form in this section.

The construction of a test can be summarized in the following steps.

Step 1 Specify a "distance" which intuitively makes sense to consider H_0 as valid when this distance is "small." Typically this entails choosing a good estimator, say $\hat{\theta}$ of the unknown parameter θ and taking a function of the difference between this estimator and the value specified by the Null hypothesis such as $|\hat{\theta} - \theta_0|$ or $(\hat{\theta} - \theta_0)^2$.

Step 2 Transform the distance function into a pivotal function. This often entails standardizing the distance $(\hat{\theta} - \theta_0)$ using the distribution of $\hat{\theta}$ under H_0 (assuming H_0 is valid):

$$\tau(\mathbf{X}) = \frac{|\hat{\theta} - \theta_0|}{[Var(\hat{\theta})]^{\frac{1}{2}}} \text{ or } \tau(\mathbf{X}) = \frac{(\hat{\theta} - \theta_0)^2}{Var(\hat{\theta})},$$

and determining the distribution of $\tau(\mathbf{X})$. This sometimes involves substituting out any unknown parameters and then deriving the distribution of $\tau(\mathbf{X})$ assuming H_0 is valid. In cases where the exact distribution of $\tau(\mathbf{X})$ under H_0 is unknown, we approximate it using the asymptotic distribution of $\tau(\mathbf{X})$ under H_0, instead.

Step 3 Using the distribution of $\tau(\mathbf{X})$ under H_0, specify the p-value as follows:

$$\mathbb{P}(\tau(\mathbf{X}) \geq \tau(\mathbf{x}); H_0 \text{ is valid}) = p. \tag{14.16}$$

Hence, the **main elements of a Fisher test** $\{\tau(\mathbf{X}), p\}$ are:

(i)   a null hypothesis H_0,
(ii)   a test statistic $\tau(\mathbf{X})$,
(iii) the distribution of $\tau(\mathbf{X})$ under H_0,
(iv)   the p-value $\mathbb{P}(\tau(\mathbf{X}) \geq \tau(\mathbf{x}); H_0 \text{ is valid}) = p$,

where $\tau(\mathbf{x})$ denotes the value of the test statistic $\tau(\mathbf{X})$, given the particular sample realization $\mathbf{X} = \mathbf{x}$. The p-value may be seen as indicating how satisfactory H_0 is, given the observed data. In a certain sense the p-value represents the worst-case scenario for the null hypothesis, taking into account not just the observed sample realization but also more unfavorable realizations. The question of accepting or rejecting H_0 is a separate issue and the p-value should not be confused with the *significance level* of the Neyman–Pearson testing framework discussed next.

14.3 The Neyman–Pearson framework

The above summary brings out an important limitation of the Fisher approach:

How does the modeler choose the test statistic $\tau(\mathbf{X})$?

The common sense arguments used by Fisher do not amount to an optimal procedure for deriving the "best" possible test, analogous to that of a "best" estimator. This provided the motivation for Neyman and Pearson (1928a) whose stated purpose was to deal with this limitation of the Fisher approach; something that Fisher never accepted and that led to numerous heated exchanges between Neyman and Fisher (see, e.g., Fisher (1956)). Neyman and Pearson (1928a,b,1933a,b) motivated their own approach to testing by arguing that Fisher had no logical basis for:

(a) his choice of test statistics such as (14.12) and
(b) his use of the p-value as a measure of credence bestowed upon H_0 by the sample realization.

It was clear that for each null hypothesis one could construct several test statistics and the Fisher approach did not provide a way to decide which one is the most appropriate among these functions. Their solution to this problem was to view hypothesis testing as a *choice between rival hypotheses* and thus change the focus of hypothesis testing from providing a measure of how much credence the observed data lend to the null, to deciding whether to accept or reject the null hypothesis on the basis of the observed data. The key to their approach was the introduction of the notion of an **alternative hypothesis** to supplement the notion of the null hypothesis and thus transform testing into a choice among different hypotheses.

In an attempt to keep our eyes on the forest we will consider the unfolding of the Neyman–Pearson argument in stages. Before we set out to consider the Neyman–Pearson procedure it is worth repeating again that underlying every form of statistical inference there exists (a) a statistical model $(\Phi,\mathbf{X})$ postulated a priori and (b) a set of observed data $\mathbf{x}:=(x_1,x_2, \ldots, x_n)$ viewed as a *realization* of the *sample* $\mathbf{X}:=(X_1,X_2, \ldots, X_n)$; $\mathbf{x}$ constitutes a point in the n-dimensional **sample space** $\aleph\subset\mathbb{R}^n_x$ (see chapters 10–11).

14.3.1 Stage I – The notion of an alternative hypothesis

The hypothesis of interest in connection with the simple Normal and Bernoulli models was of the simple form:

$$H_0:\theta=\theta_0.$$

The Neyman–Pearson specification of the null and alternative hypotheses often takes the form:

$$H_0:\theta=\theta_0 \text{ against } H_1:\theta\neq\theta_0, \text{ but } \theta\in\Theta-\{\theta_0\}. \tag{14.17}$$

This specification divides the parameter space Θ of the statistical model in question, into two mutually exclusive subsets:

$\Theta_0 := \{\theta_0\}$ and $\Theta_1 := \Theta - \{\theta_0\}$, where $\Theta_0 \cap \Theta_1 = \emptyset$, $\Theta_0 \cup \Theta_1 = \Theta$.

Examples

(a) In the case of the simple Normal model the null hypothesis $H_0: \mu = 10$, can now be reconsidered in the Neyman–Pearson formulation in conjunction with an alternative hypothesis, taking the form: $H_0: \mu = 10$ against $H_1: \mu \in \mathbb{R} - \{10\}$, where $\Theta_0 := \{10\}$ is a single number and $\Theta_1 := \mathbb{R} - \{10\}$; $\mathbb{R}$ excluding the number 10.

(b) In the case of the simple Bernoulli model the null hypothesis $H_0: \theta = 0.5$, can now be reconsidered in the Neyman–Pearson formulation in conjunction with an alternative hypothesis, taking the form: $H_0: \theta = 0.5$ against $H_1: \theta \in [0,1] - \{0.5\}$, where $\Theta_0 := \{0.5\}$ and $\Theta_1 := [0,1] - \{0.5\}$ is the interval $[0,1]$ excluding the number 0.5.

A more general formulation of the Neyman–Pearson specification of the null and the alternative hypotheses takes the form:

$$H_0: \theta \in \Theta_0 \text{ against } H_1: \theta \in \Theta_1 := \Theta - \Theta_0. \tag{14.18}$$

Examples

(i) In the case of the **simple Normal model** (see (14.4)) the null and alternative hypotheses can be of the form: $H_0: \mu \in [40,100]$ against $H_1: \mu \in \mathbb{R} - [40,100]$, where $\Theta_0 = [40,100]$ and $\Theta_1 = \mathbb{R} - [40,100]$.

(ii) In the case of the simple Bernoulli model the null and alternative hypotheses can be of the form: $H_0: \theta \in [0,0.5]$ against $H_1: \theta \in (0.5,1]$.

The Neyman–Pearson specification of the null and alternative hypotheses given in (14.18) in effect divides the postulated (original) probability model:

$$\Phi = \{ f(x;\theta), \theta \in \Theta, x \in \mathbb{R}_X \},$$

into mutually exclusive subsets using the partition of the parameter space $\Theta = \Theta_0 \cup \Theta_1$:

$$\Phi_0 = \{ f(x;\theta), \theta \in \Theta_0, x \in \mathbb{R}_X \}, \ \Phi_1 = \{ f(x;\theta), \theta \in \Theta_1, x \in \mathbb{R}_X \}.$$

This formulation brings out the fact that the null and alternatives hypotheses are ultimately about *distributions* and not parameters as it appears at first sight. Hence, assuming that the "true" probability distribution for the data in question is $f(x)$, a more heedful way to specify these hypotheses is in terms of their Probability models implicit in each case:

$$H_0: f(x) \in \Phi_0 \text{ against } H_1: f(x) \in \Phi_1. \tag{14.19}$$

Simple versus composite hypotheses

In the case where Φ_0 or Φ_1 include only one element (distribution), we say that the null or the alternative is *simple*, respectively; otherwise we call it *composite*. In the examples (a) and (b) above the null hypothesis is simple but the alternative is composite. In the examples (i) and (ii) both the null and alternative hypotheses are composite.

Example

Consider **the simple Normal model** (see (14.4)) and the hypothesis:

$$H_0: \mu = \mu_0, \text{ against } H_0: \mu = \mu_1, (\mu_1 > \mu_0).$$

Case A: σ^2 *is known.* The null and the alternative hypotheses H_0 and H_1 are simple because the probability models under H_0 and H_1, are respectively:

$$\Phi_0 = \{f(x; \mu_0), x \in \mathbb{R}_X\} \text{ and } \Phi_1 = \{f(x; \mu_1), x \in \mathbb{R}_X\}.$$

That is, H_0 and H_1 are simple because Φ_0 and Φ_1 contain just one element.

Case B: σ^2 *is unknown.* In this case the null hypothesis: $H_0: \mu = \mu_0$ is composite because $\Phi_0 = \{f(x; \mu_0, \sigma^2), \sigma^2 \in \mathbb{R}_+, x \in \mathbb{R}_X\}$, represents a whole family of such density functions, one for each value of $\sigma^2 > 0$. By the same token, the specification:

$$H_0: \mu = \mu_0, \sigma^2 = \sigma_0^2 \text{ against } H_1: \mu = \mu_1, \sigma^2 = \sigma_1^2,$$

has a simple H_0 and a simple H_1, because both Φ_0 and Φ_1 are singletons:

$$\Phi_0 = \{f(x; \mu_0, \sigma_0^2), x \in \mathbb{R}_X\} \text{ and } \Phi_1 = \{f(x; \mu_1, \sigma_1^2), x \in \mathbb{R}_X\}.$$

An even more flexible form of the Neyman–Pearson specification of the null and alternative hypotheses is:

$$H_0: \theta \in \Theta_0 \text{ against } H_1: \theta \in \Theta_1 \subset \Theta, \Theta_1 \cap \Theta_0 = \emptyset. \tag{14.20}$$

Examples

(i) In the case of the simple Normal model the null and alternative hypotheses can be of the form: $H_0: \mu = \mu_0$ against $H_1: \mu > \mu_0$.

(ii) In the case of N. Bernoulli's conjecture, the specification of the null and the alternative hypotheses would take the form: $H_0: \theta = 0.4857$ against $H_1: \theta > 0.4857$. This is because we are only interested in alternatives in the direction of a "fair game."

In these cases the alternative hypothesis is not defined in terms of the complement of Θ_0 with respect to Θ, but as a subset of it. This is designed to provide the modeler with the flexibility to ignore certain parts of the parameter space of no interest in order to improve the properties of the test (in terms of power; see below).

14.3.2 Stage II – The rejection region

The main aim of testing becomes the *formulation of a decision rule* which for any realization $\mathbf{x}$ of the postulated sample $\mathbf{X}$ enables the modeler to decide whether to accept or reject H_0. In the case of a null hypothesis as specified in (14.17), the decision to accept or reject H_0 will be based on a test statistic $\tau(\mathbf{X})$. In effect the test statistic implies a partition

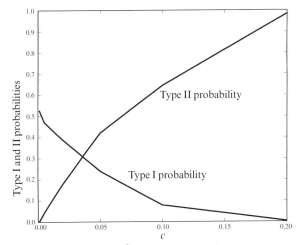

Figure 14.1 Defining a Neyman–Pearson test

of the sample space $\aleph$ into two complementary sets C_0 and C_1, known as the acceptance and rejection regions, respectively:

$$C_0 \cup C_1 = \aleph \text{ and } C_0 \cap C_1 = \varnothing.$$

The decisions to accept or reject H_0 can be specified in terms of these two regions (see figure 14.4):

(i) if $\mathbf{x} \in C_0$: accept H_0,   (ii) if $\mathbf{x} \in C_1$: reject H_0.

Examples

(i)   In the case of the simple Normal model, testing the hypotheses: $H_0: \mu = 70$ against $H_1: \mu \neq 70$, could be based on the test statistic:

$$\tau(\mathbf{X}) = \left(\frac{\sqrt{n}(\hat{\mu}_n - 70)}{s} \right) \overset{H_0}{\sim} \mathrm{St}(n-1),$$

and intuition suggests that the likely rejection region will be of the form:

$$C_1 = \{\mathbf{x}: |\tau(\mathbf{X})| > c\},$$

for some $c > 0$ chosen appropriately.

(ii)   In the case of the simple Bernoulli model, testing Bernoulli's conjecture:

$$H_0: \theta = 0.48 \text{ against } H_1: \theta > 0.48, \tag{14.21}$$

$$\tau(\mathbf{X}) := \frac{\sqrt{n}(\hat{\theta}_n - 0.48)}{\sqrt{0.48(0.52)}} \overset{H_0}{\sim} \mathrm{Bi}(0,1;n),$$

and again intuition suggests that the likely rejection region will be of the form:

$$C_1 = \{\mathbf{x}: \tau(\mathbf{X}) > c\},$$

for some $c > 0$ chosen appropriately.

14.3.3 Stage III – The two types of errors

In the case of both hypotheses as specified above the decision to accept or reject H_0 is accompanied by the possiblity of committing one of two types of errors:

(i)   **type I error:** reject the null hypothesis when in fact it is valid,
(ii) **type II error:** accept the null hypothesis when in fact it is invalid.

It is interesting to note that Neyman and Pearson (1928a) criticized Fisher for recognizing only the type I error and ignoring the type II error. This criticism, however, was rather misplaced because Fisher did not see hypothesis testing as a decision to accept or reject H_0. He viewed hypothesis testing as an inferential procedure which enabled the modeler to assess the support bestowed by the data on the hypothesis in question.

	H_0 VALID	H_0 INVALID
Accept H_0	correct decision	type II error
Reject H_0	type I error	correct decision

(a) The probability of type I error

The probability of type I error at a point $\theta = \theta_0$, in its general form can be expressed by:

$$\mathbb{P}(\mathbf{x} \in C_1; \theta = \theta_0) = \alpha.$$

Consider the simple Bernoulli model (see (14.14)) and the hypothesis as specified by:

$$H_0 : \theta = 0.5 \text{ against } H_1 : \theta \neq 0.5.$$

Intuition suggests that the rejection region for H_0 will take the form $|\theta_n - 0.5| > c$, where c is some constant and the statement "when in fact H_0 is valid" suggests that the relevant distribution for evaluating the probability of type I error is (14.15). That is, we need to evaluate:

$$\mathbb{P}(|\hat{\theta}_n - 0.5| > c; H_0 \text{ is valid}) = \alpha,$$

for different values of $c = 0.005, 0.01, 0.02, 0.05, 0.1, 0.2$, using the Binomial probabilities tables:[1]

$$\mathbb{P}(|\hat{\theta}_n - 0.5| > 0.005) \approx 0.472, \quad \mathbb{P}(|\hat{\theta}_n - 0.5| > 0.050) \approx 0.239,$$
$$\mathbb{P}(|\hat{\theta}_n - 0.5| > 0.010) \approx 0.444, \quad \mathbb{P}(|\hat{\theta}_n - 0.5| > 0.100) \approx 0.078,$$
$$\mathbb{P}(|\hat{\theta}_n - 0.5| > 0.020) \approx 0.388, \quad \mathbb{P}(|\hat{\theta}_n - 0.5| > 0.200) \approx 0.0024.$$

NOTE that $n = 50$. As we can see, by making the interval around $\hat{\theta}_n$ smaller the probability of type I error increases (see figure 14.1). The question which naturally arises at this stage is:

---

[1] How to get these probabilities is not important at this stage.

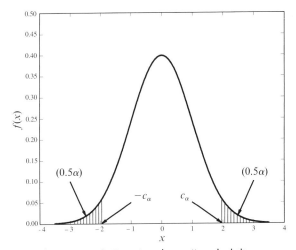

Figure 14.2 Type I and type II probability

Why don't we just make this interval very large?

In the case where the interval is rather large, say $0.1 < \hat{\theta}_n < 0.9$, i.e., $c = 0.4$, the probability of making the wrong decision is very close to zero. In particular:

$$\mathbb{P}(|\hat{\theta}_n - 0.5| > 0.4) \approx 0.000.$$

The problem with this suggestion is that as we enlarge this interval we increase the probability of making another incorrect decision: accept the null when it is invalid (*type II error*).

(b) The probability of type II error
The probability of type II error at a point $\theta = \theta_1$, in its general form, can be expressed by:

$$\mathbb{P}(\mathbf{x} \in C_0;\ \theta = \theta_1) = \beta(\theta_1).$$

In the case of **the simple Bernoulli model**, to be able to evaluate the probability of type II error we need the distribution of the test statistic (14.15):

$$\tau(\mathbf{X}) := \frac{\sqrt{n}(\hat{\theta}_n - 0.5)}{\sqrt{\theta(1-\theta)}}, \text{ under } H_1 : \theta \neq 0.5.$$

This raises the problem: Which values in $\Theta_1 := [0,1] - \{0.5\}$ do we choose? For the sake of the argument let us choose the value $\theta = 0.55$. This implies that the relevant distribution for the test statistic is:

$$\tau(\mathbf{X};\theta) := \frac{\sqrt{n}(\hat{\theta}_n - 0.5)}{\sqrt{\theta(1-\theta)}} \overset{H_1}{\sim} \mathrm{Bi}\left(\frac{\sqrt{n}(0.55 - 0.5)}{\sqrt{0.55(1-0.55)}}, 1; n\right). \tag{14.22}$$

In the case of type II error, making the wrong decision amounts to deciding to accept H_0; deciding that the difference $|\hat{\theta}_n - 0.5|$ is not "significantly different from zero". Using the distribution (14.22) we can evaluate the probability of type II error using the same values of c as for the type I probability $c = 0.005, 0.01, 0.02, 0.05, 0.1, 0.2$, $\mathbb{P}(|\hat{\theta}_n - 0.5| \leq c;\ \theta = 0.55) = \beta(0.55)$, as follows:

$$\mathbb{P}(|\hat{\theta}_n - 0.5| > 0.005) \simeq 0.043, \quad \mathbb{P}(|\hat{\theta}_n - 0.5| > 0.050) \simeq 0.422,$$
$$\mathbb{P}(|\hat{\theta}_n - 0.5| > 0.010) \simeq 0.089, \quad \mathbb{P}(|\hat{\theta}_n - 0.5| > 0.100) \simeq 0.645,$$
$$\mathbb{P}(|\hat{\theta}_n - 0.5| > 0.020) \simeq 0.178, \quad \mathbb{P}(|\hat{\theta}_n - 0.5| > 0.200) \simeq 0.984.$$

From these probabilities we can see that in contrast to the type I error, the probability of type II error decreases as the interval around the null hypothesis becomes smaller.

How do we interpret the two types of errors? The interpretation of Neyman and Pearson is in terms of repeating the experiment a very large number of times (the long run). That is, a 0.05 type I probability means that in repeated trials of the same experiment (statistical model) 5 percent of these cases will be erroneously rejected (see Neyman and Pearson (1933a)). This interpretation was the focus of disagreement between Neyman and Fisher for several decades. Fisher kept insisting that even if this procedure is appropriate for long sequences of trials in quality control, it is completely inappropriate for scientific inference (see Fisher (1956)).

Rejection Region	$\mathbb{P}$(type I error; $\theta = 0.5$)	$\mathbb{P}$(type II error; $\theta = 0.55$)
$(\mathbf{x}:|\hat{\theta}_n - 0.5| \leq 0.005)$	0.472,	0.043,
$(\mathbf{x}:|\hat{\theta}_n - 0.5| \leq 0.010)$	0.444,	0.089,
$(\mathbf{x}:|\hat{\theta}_n - 0.5| \leq 0.020)$	0.388,	0.178,
$(\mathbf{x}:|\hat{\theta}_n - 0.5| \leq 0.050)$	0.239,	0.422,
$(\mathbf{x}:|\hat{\theta}_n - 0.5| \leq 0.100)$	0.078,	0.645,
$(\mathbf{x}:|\hat{\theta}_n - 0.5| \leq 0.200)$	0.002,	0.984.

The above table and figure 14.1 suggest that there is a trade-off between the probabilities of type I and type II errors: as we decrease the probability of type I error the probability of type II error increases and vice versa.

How do we solve this trade-off problem?

14.3.4 Stage IV – Constructing optimal tests

The Neyman–Pearson (1928a,b,1933a,b) solution is to treat the null hypothesis as more important than the alternative. This means that we would rather ensure that the probability of rejecting the null when valid (type I error) is small, and then choose a test which minimizes the probability of type II error. In the above context, this amounts to deciding that the type I error probability is small, say $\alpha = 0.05$ or $\alpha = 0.01$, and choose a test which minimizes the type II error. That is, assuming that we reject the null when $|\tau(\mathbf{X})| > c_\alpha$, for some constant c_α, we choose the test statistic $\tau(\mathbf{X})$ in such a way that:

(a) $\mathbb{P}(|\tau(\mathbf{X})| > c_\alpha; H_0 \text{ valid}) = \alpha$,

(b) $\mathbb{P}(|\tau(\mathbf{X})| \leq c_\alpha; H_1(\theta) \text{ valid}) = \beta(\theta)$ for $\theta \in \Theta_1$ is minimized.

NOTE: the notation $H_1(\theta)$ is used to emphasize the dependence of H_1 on θ as the latter varies over the parameter space Θ_1.

The above solution amounts to a convention which views the type I error as much more serious and thus the null and alternative hypotheses are treated asymmetrically. By fixing the type I error to be a small number, say 0.01, we view it as much more important than the type II error. Hence, we consider the mistake to reject the null when valid to be much more serious than accepting the null when false. An emotionally charged way to rationalize this conventional choice is in terms of the analogy with a criminal offense trial. The jury in a criminal offense trial are instructed by the judge to find the defendant not guilty unless they have been convinced "beyond any reasonable doubt" by the evidence presented in court during the deliberations. That is, they are instructed to choose between:

H_0: **not guilty**, against H_1: **guilty**.

The clause beyond any reasonable doubt amounts to fixing the type I error to a very small value. This is designed to protect innocent people from being found guilty (see Neyman–Pearson (1928a,b,1933a,b)). This strategy, however, increases the risk of "letting a lot of crooks off the hook." The reader should be CAUTIONED that the use of the above analogy is designed to make the Neyman–Pearson convention easier to accept. In particular, to make the asymmetric treatment of the null and the alternative seem natural.

The above optimization problem is rather involved and we are going to avoid the details until the next subsection. Once the test statistic $\tau(\mathbf{X})$ is chosen, we can use its distribution under H_0 in order to derive the value c_α, beyond which $|\tau(\mathbf{X})|$ is considered to be "significantly different from zero." Because of this, α is sometimes called the **significance level**. This amounts to solving for the unknown c_α in the probabilistic equation:

$$\mathbb{P}(|\tau(\mathbf{X})| > c_\alpha; H_0 \text{ valid}) = \alpha. \tag{14.23}$$

REMARK: It is important to note that this probabilistic equation does not always have a unique solution c_α, especially in the case where the distribution of $\tau(\mathbf{X})$ is discrete. In such cases we use approximate values as in the Bernoulli example.

Formally c_α is defined as the point beyond which the probability, as determined by the distribution of the test statistic, is equal to α. This, however, depends on whether the test in question is one-sided or two-sided as in the above case.

One-sided versus two-sided tests

In the case of the simple Normal model discussed above we concentrated almost exclusively on the hypothesis:

$$H_0: \mu = \mu_0 \text{ against } H_1: \mu \neq \mu_0, \tag{14.24}$$

which is a **two-sided** hypothesis. The fact that the alternative hypothesis is of the form $H_1: \mu \neq \mu_0$ means that H_0 can be invalid for values of $\hat{\mu}$ smaller or larger than μ_0. On the other hand, the hypothesis:

$$H_0: \mu = \mu_0 \text{ against } H_1: \mu > \mu_0, \tag{14.25}$$

is **one-sided** because H_0 can be invalid only for values of $\hat{\mu}$ larger than μ_0. The one-sided and two-sided features of the hypotheses are crucial because they affect both the form of the rejection region as well as the value c_α.

Example 1

Let us return to the **simple Normal model** (see (14.4)).

Case A: σ^2 is known. For testing (14.24) and (14.25) it turns out that the test statistic coincides:

$$\kappa(\mathbf{X}) := \tfrac{\sqrt{n}(\hat{\mu}_n - \mu_0)}{\sigma} \overset{H_0}{\sim} N(0,1). \tag{14.26}$$

However, the rejction regions for (14.24) and (14.25) are, respectively:

$$C_1 = \{\mathbf{x} : |\kappa(\mathbf{x})| > c_\alpha\} \text{ and } C_1 = \{\mathbf{x} : \kappa(\mathbf{x}) > c_\alpha\}.$$

This, in turn, effects the value of c_α in the sense that for the two tests:

$$\int_{c_\alpha}^{\infty} \phi(z)\,dz = \tfrac{1}{2}\alpha \text{ and } \int_{c_\alpha}^{\infty} \phi(z)\,dz = \alpha,$$

where $\phi(z)$ is the standard normal density (see figures 14.3 and 14.4), respectively.

Standard Normal tables

One-sided values	Two-sided values
$\alpha = 0.100$: $c_\alpha = 1.28$,	$\alpha = 0.100$: $c_\alpha = 1.65$,
$\alpha = 0.050$: $c_\alpha = 1.65$,	$\alpha = 0.050$: $c_\alpha = 1.96$,
$\alpha = 0.025$: $c_\alpha = 1.96$,	$\alpha = 0.025$: $c_\alpha = 2.00$,
$\alpha = 0.010$: $c_\alpha = 2.33$,	$\alpha = 0.010$: $c_\alpha = 2.58$,
$\alpha = 0.001$: $c_\alpha = 3.10$.	$\alpha = 0.001$: $c_\alpha = 3.30$.

Case B: σ^2 is unknown. As in case A, for testing (14.24) and (14.25) it turns out that the test statistic is the same:

$$\tau(\mathbf{X}) := \tfrac{\sqrt{n}(\hat{\mu}_n - \mu_0)}{s} \overset{H_0}{\sim} St(n - 1). \tag{14.27}$$

In addition to (14.24) and (14.25) we can consider the one-sided hypothesis:

$$H_0 : \mu = \mu_0 \text{ against } H_1 : \mu < \mu_0, \tag{14.28}$$

The rejction regions for (14.24), (14.25) and (14.28) are, respectively:

$$C_1 = \{\mathbf{x} : |\tau(\mathbf{x})| > c_\alpha\},\ C_1 = \{\mathbf{x} : \tau(\mathbf{x}) > c_\alpha\} \text{ and } C_1 = \{\mathbf{x} : \tau(\mathbf{x}) < c_\alpha\}.$$

The value of c_α for the three tests are, respectively:

$$\int_{c_\alpha}^{\infty} \varphi(z)\,dz = \tfrac{1}{2}\alpha,\ \int_{c_\alpha}^{\infty} \varphi(z)\,dz = \alpha \text{ and } \int_{c_\alpha}^{\infty} \varphi(z)\,dz = 1 - \alpha,$$

where $\varphi(z)$ is the Student's t density. The test defined by $\{\tau(\mathbf{X}), C_1, \alpha\}$ above is known as the **t-test**.

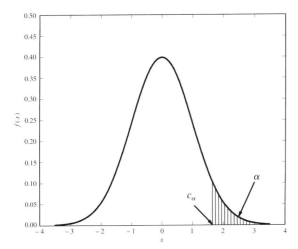

Figure 14.3 c_α for a two-sided test

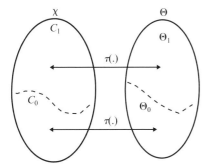

Figure 14.4 c_α for a one-sided test

Student's t tables ($n = 60$)

One-sided values	Two-sided values
$\alpha = 0.100$: $c_\alpha = 1.296$,	$\alpha = 0.100$: $c_\alpha = 1.671$,
$\alpha = 0.050$: $c_\alpha = 1.671$,	$\alpha = 0.050$: $c_\alpha = 2.000$,
$\alpha = 0.025$: $c_\alpha = 2.000$,	$\alpha = 0.025$: $c_\alpha = 2.300$,
$\alpha = 0.010$: $c_\alpha = 2.390$,	$\alpha = 0.010$: $c_\alpha = 2.660$,
$\alpha = 0.001$: $c_\alpha = 3.232$.	$\alpha = 0.001$: $c_\alpha = 3.460$.

In order to avoid misleading the reader into thinking that for two-sided tests c_a is always determined via $\int_{c_\alpha}^{\infty} f(z)dz = \frac{1}{2}\alpha$, we NOTE that this is the case only when dealing with symmetric distributions.

Example 2

Let us return to the **simple Bernoulli model** (see (14.14)) to reconsider Arbuthnot's and N. Bernoulli's conjectures in the context of the Neyman–Pearson approach. The observed data refer to the number of births (male, female) during the period 1993–5 in Cyprus: $n = 30862$, 16029 males and 14833 females. It should come as no surprise to discover that the pivotal function and the test statistic remain the same as those derived in the Fisher approach:

$$\tau(\mathbf{X};\theta) := \frac{\sqrt{n}(\hat{\theta}_n - \theta_0)}{\sqrt{\theta_0(1-\theta_0)}}, \quad \tau(\mathbf{X}) := \frac{\sqrt{n}(\hat{\theta}_n - \theta_0)}{\sqrt{\theta_0(1-\theta_0)}} \overset{H_0}{\sim} \mathrm{Bi}(0,1;n).$$

(i)   *Arbuthnot's conjecture* might be expressed in the following form:

$$H_0: \theta = 0.5 \text{ against } H_1: \theta < 0.5. \tag{14.29}$$

$$\hat{\theta}_n = \frac{14833}{30862} = 0.48062, \ \tau(\mathbf{x}) = \frac{\sqrt{30862}(0.48062 - 0.5)}{\sqrt{0.5(0.5)}} = -6.8092.$$

In view of the fact that the alternative is one-sided the rejection region is:

$$C_1 = \{\mathbf{x} : \tau(\mathbf{x}) < c_\alpha\},$$

where c_α can be evaluated using the Normal tables because the sample size is large enough for the Normal approximation to the Binomial to be reliable. For a significance level $\alpha = 0.01$, $c_\alpha = -2.33$ thus we reject H_0.

(ii)   *N. Bernoulli's conjecture* can be expressed in the following form:

$$H_0: \theta = 0.4857 \text{ against } H_1: \theta > 0.4857. \tag{14.30}$$

$$\hat{\theta}_n = \frac{14833}{30862} = 0.48062, \ \tau(\mathbf{x}) = \frac{\sqrt{30862}(0.48062 - 0.4857)}{\sqrt{0.4857(0.5143)}} = -1.7856.$$

In view of the fact that the alternative is one-sided the rejection region is:

$$C_1 = \{\mathbf{x} : \tau(\mathbf{x}) > c_\alpha\},$$

where c_α can again be evaluated using the Normal tables. For a significance level $\alpha = 0.01$, $c_\alpha = 2.33$ and since the value of the statistic is considerably smaller, we accept H_0.

14.3.5 A general formulation: summary

The general formulation of a hypothesis in the Neyman–Pearson approach is:

$$H_0: \theta \in \Theta_0 \text{ against } H_1: \theta \in \Theta_1 := \Theta - \Theta_0. \tag{14.31}$$

(i) $H_0: \theta \in \Theta_0$ is referred to as the **null hypothesis**, where $\Theta_0 \subset \Theta$.

(ii) $H_1: \theta \in \Theta_1 := \Theta - \Theta_0$ is referred to as the **alternative hypothesis**.

As argued above, the principal element of a test is the test statistic $\tau(\mathbf{X})$ which provides the basis for accepting or rejecting H_0. This amounts to separating the sample space $\aleph$ into two mutually exclusive regions, C_0 and $C_1: \mathbf{X} = C_0 \cup C_1$ and $C_0 \cap C_1 = \emptyset$:

$C_0 := \{\mathbf{x} : \tau(\mathbf{x}) \leq c_\alpha\}$ – *the acceptance region*, and

$C_1 := \{\mathbf{x} : \tau(\mathbf{x}) > c_\alpha\}$ – *the rejection region* (see figure 14.4).

The decision rule takes the form:

(i)   if $\mathbf{x} \in C_0$, **accept** H_0,   (ii)   if $\mathbf{x} \in C_1$, **reject** H_0.

The choice of the test statistic $\tau(\mathbf{X})$ is made so as to ensure that:

(a) $\mathbb{P}(\mathbf{x} \in C_1; H_0 \text{ valid}) = \alpha$,
(b) $\mathbb{P}(\mathbf{x} \in C_0; H_1(\theta) \text{ valid}) = \beta(\theta)$ for $\theta \in \Theta_1$ is minimized.

The **main components of a Neyman–Pearson (N–P) test** $\{\tau(\mathbf{X}), C_1, \alpha\}$ are:

(i)   a null (H_0) and an alternative (H_1) hypothesis,
(ii)   a test statistic $\tau(\mathbf{X})$,
(iii) the distribution of $\tau(\mathbf{X})$ under H_0,
(iv)   the significance level (or size) α, and
(v)   the rejection region C_1.

NOTES:

(i)   **Significance level and *p*-value.** It is very important to distinguish between the notion of a *p*-value in the context of a Fisher test and that of a significance level in the context of the Neyman–Pearson approach. Even though the two can be related mathematically, they constitute very different notions in different contexts. The role of the *p*-value is inferential and that of the significance level is decision making. This is why the use of *p*-values in the context of the Neyman–Pearson approach was considered to be a sacrilege by Fisher (1956).

(ii)   **Accept and fail to reject.** Because of the asymmetric treatment of the type I and type II errors, when we reject H_0 we consider it invalid because the probability of making a mistake is set to a small number α. On the other hand, when the modeler accepts H_0 he/she has no idea of the magnitude of the type II error; he/she has no control over it; just the comforting thought that for a good test it must be reasonably high. For this reason some books use the terminology "fail to reject" H_0 instead of "accept".

(iii) **Where is the type II error?** It is important to emphasize that even though the type II error does not seem to play any role in the above definition of a test, the fact of the matter is that the test statistic $\tau(\mathbf{X})$ and the rejection region are chosen by minimizing the probability of type II error.

14.3.6 Optimality of tests

The N–P test components (i)–(v) specify a test, but to determine how good the test is we need to consider the question of minimizing the probability of type II error. An equivalent way to consider the optimality of a test is to consider the power of the test.

Power of a test The probability of rejecting the null hypothesis when it is invalid (taking the correct decision when rejecting H_0) is called **the power of the test** at *some value* $\theta_1 \in \Theta_1$, and denoted by:

$$\mathcal{P}(\theta_1) = \mathbb{P}(\mathbf{x} \in C_1; H_1 \text{ valid}).$$

That is, the power of a test refers to the probability of rejecting H_0 when H_1 is valid, i.e. the true distribution belongs to the family $\Phi_1 = \{f(x;\theta), \theta \in \Theta_1, x \in \mathbb{R}_X\}$.

Given that under the alternative $H_1: \theta \in \Theta_1$, Φ_1 often includes more than one element, we need to consider the power of a test over the whole of the parameter space specified by the alternative hypothesis. With this in mind we define the **power function** as follows:

$$\mathcal{P}_n(\theta) = \mathbb{P}(\mathbf{x} \in C_1) \text{ for } \theta \in \Theta, \tag{14.32}$$

viewed as a function of $\theta \in \Theta$. NOTE that this function is defined over the whole of the parameter space of the postulated statistical model. In view of this, we can use the power function to define the probability of type I error as well. The subscript is used to emphasize the dependence of the power function on the sample size.

In the case of a simple null hypothesis $H_0: \theta = \theta_0$, the **significance level** can be defined via the power function as:

$$\mathcal{P}_n(\theta_0) = \alpha,$$

but in the case where under the null θ takes more than one value, say $\theta \in \Theta_0$, and Θ_0 has more than one point, we define the **size of the test** to be:

$$\alpha = \max_{\theta \in \Theta_0} \mathcal{P}_n(\theta),$$

where $\max_{\theta \in \Theta_0}$ denotes the maximum for all values of $\theta \in \Theta_0$. That is, the size of the test is the maximum probability, over all possible values of θ in Θ_0, of making the wrong decision to reject the null hypothesis.

Example
t-test In the case of **the simple Normal model** (see (14.4)) with the hypothesis:

$$H_0: \mu = \mu_0 \text{ against } H_1: \mu \neq \mu_0, \tag{14.33}$$

and σ^2 unknown, to derive the power function (14.32) we need to know its distribution under H_1. However, it is clear that under H_1, the test statistic (14.27) can no longer have mean zero because $E(\hat{\mu}_n) \neq \mu_0$. In view of this, its distribution, under the assumptions of the statistical model, is non-central Student's t (see Spanos (1986), p. 112), with **noncentrality parameter** $\delta = \left(\frac{\sqrt{n}(\mu - \mu_0)}{\sigma}\right)$, denoted by:

$$\tau(\mathbf{X}) = \left(\frac{\sqrt{n}(\hat{\mu}_n - \mu_0)}{s}\right) \overset{H_1}{\sim} \mathsf{St}(\delta; n - 1). \tag{14.34}$$

Let us see how this distribution arises. Under H_1 (say $\mu = \mu_1$) the test statistic that has a Student's t distribution is:

$$\tau_1(\mathbf{X}) = \left(\frac{\sqrt{n}(\hat{\mu}_n - \mu_1)}{s}\right) \overset{H_1}{\sim} \mathsf{St}(n - 1). \tag{14.35}$$

The problem is to relate the two quantities: $\tau(\mathbf{X})$ and $\tau_1(\mathbf{X})$. After some obvious manipulations one can show that:

$$\tau(\mathbf{X}) = \left[\tau_1(\mathbf{X}) + \frac{\sqrt{n}(\mu_1 - \mu_0)}{s} \right] \sim St(\delta; n-1),$$

where the non-centrality parameter is nothing more than the non-zero mean of the distribution, i.e. $\delta = E\left(\frac{\sqrt{n}(\mu_1 - \mu_0)}{s}\right)$. The power function for $\mu \in \mathbb{R} - \{\mu_0\}$ is:

$$\mathcal{P}_n(\mu) = \mathbb{P}(\mathbf{x} : |\tau(\mathbf{X})| \geq c_\alpha) =$$

$$= \mathbb{P}\left(\tau_1(\mathbf{X}) \geq c_\alpha - \frac{\sqrt{n}(\mu_1 - \mu_0)}{s}\right) + \mathbb{P}\left(\tau_1(\mathbf{X}) \leq -c_\alpha - \frac{\sqrt{n}(\mu_1 - \mu_0)}{s}\right).$$

As we can see from the above formula, given s^2, the power of the t-test increases as n and $(\mu_1 - \mu_0)$ increase and thus the more available the observations and the further away θ_1 is from the null (θ_0), the more the power (a very desirable property).

Using the power function we can define the notion of *an optimal test*. In a nutshell the best test is the one with maximum power for all values of $\theta \in \Theta_1$ (when it exists!).

Uniformly most powerful tests (UMP) We say that a N–P test $\{\tau^*(\mathbf{X}), C_1, \alpha\}$ is optimal if it has greater power than *any other* test $\{\tau(\mathbf{X}), C_1, \alpha\}$:

$$\mathcal{P}_n(\theta; \{\tau^*(\mathbf{X}), C_1, \alpha\}) \geq \mathcal{P}_n(\theta; \{\tau(\mathbf{X}), C_1, \alpha\}), \text{ for all } \theta \in \Theta_1.$$

The test $\{\tau^*(\mathbf{X}), C_1, \alpha\}$ is called *uniformly most powerful*.

The ideal test The notion of the *ideal test* is analogous to that of the ideal estimator and is defined as the test $\{\tau^*(\mathbf{X}), C_1\}$ with the following properties:

(1) $\mathcal{P}_n(\theta; \{\tau^*(\mathbf{X}), C_1\}) = 0$, for all $\theta \in \Theta_0$,
(2) $\mathcal{P}_n(\theta; \{\tau^*(\mathbf{X}), C_1\}) = 1$, for all $\theta \in \Theta_1$.

That is, its probability of rejecting H_0 when valid is zero and the probability of rejecting H_0 when invalid is one; its power takes the shape of the letter **T** at the point $\theta = \theta_0$, as illustrated by the solid line in figure 14.5.

Unfortunately, no such tests exist for a given sample size n, and thus we look for tests that come as close to the ideal case as possible (see the dotted line in figure 14.5). The dotted line suggests that a feasible but good test will be one that might tolerate low power for values of θ very close to θ_0, since the error in accepting $H_0 : \theta = \theta_0$ is not that serious. On the other hand, as the distance $|\theta - \theta_0|$ increases the power should increase with it because accepting the null will be a more serious error.

Existence of UMP tests As we will see in the next subsection, UMP tests do often exist. For cases beyond the simple case where we have only two distributions to compare, we need to impose further restrictions on either the statistical model or the class of tests considered in order to be able to find a best test. One such restriction on the class of tests considered, which can help us decide among the above tests, is that of *unbiased-ness*.

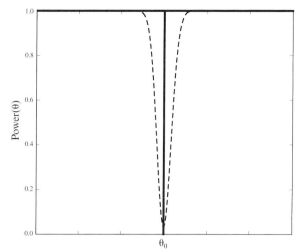

Figure 14.5 Power function of the ideal test and a "good" approximation

Unbiased test A test for the null hypothesis H_0 against H_1 is said to be *unbiased* of size α, if the probability of rejecting H_0 when invalid is greater than the probability of rejecting H_0 when valid, i.e.

$$\sup_{\theta \in \Theta_0} \mathcal{P}_n(\theta) \leq \alpha < \inf_{\theta \in \Theta_1} \mathcal{P}_n(\theta).$$

Although in the case of the statistical hypothesis (14.24) there is no UMP test, the t-test $\{\tau(\mathbf{X}), C_1, \alpha\}$ constitutes a UMP test within the class of unbiased tests.

Another desirable property for a test is that of consistency. Analogous to the case of estimation, a *consistent test* is one which achieves the ideal test status asymptotically (as the sample size $n \to \infty$).

Consistent test A test $\{\tau_n(\mathbf{X}), C_1, \alpha\}$ is said to be consistent if:

$$\lim_{n \to \infty} \mathcal{P}_n(\theta) = 1 \text{ for all } \theta \in \Theta_1.$$

Example

The t-test, as defined by $\{\tau(\mathbf{X}), C_1, \alpha\}$ where:

$$\tau(\mathbf{X}) = \left(\frac{\sqrt{n}(\hat{\mu}_n - \mu_0)}{s} \right), \quad C_1 = \{\mathbf{x} : |\tau(\mathbf{x})| > c_\alpha\},$$

in testing the hypothesis $H_0 : \mu = \mu_0$ against $H_1 : \mu \neq \mu_0$, in the context of the simple Normal model, enjoys the following properties:

(i)   unbiased,
(ii)   UMP within the class of unbiased tests (see Lehmann (1986)), and
(iii)   Consistent:

$$\lim_{n \to \infty} \mathcal{P}_n(\theta) = \lim_{n \to \infty} \mathbb{P}\left(\tau_1(\mathbf{X}) \geq c_\alpha - \frac{\sqrt{n}(\mu_1 - \mu_0)}{s} \right) + \lim_{n \to \infty} \mathbb{P}\left(\tau_1(\mathbf{X}) \leq -c_\alpha - \frac{\sqrt{n}(\mu_1 - \mu_0)}{s} \right) = 1.$$

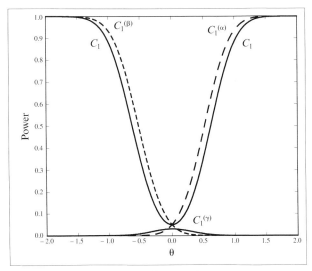

Figure 14.6 Comparison of power function

It is also interesting to note that the test statistic $\tau(\mathbf{X})$ defines the optimal tests for the one-sided alternatives:

$$(\alpha)\ H_0:\mu=\mu_0,\text{ against }H_1:\mu>\mu_0,\quad(\beta)\ H_0:\mu=\mu_0,\text{ against }H_1:\mu<\mu_0.$$

The tests defined by the rejection regions:

$$C_1^{(\alpha)}=\{\mathbf{x}:\tau(\mathbf{x})>c_\alpha\}\text{ and }C_1^{(\beta)}=\{\mathbf{x}:\tau(\mathbf{x})<c_\alpha\},$$

are UMP for the hypotheses (α) and (β), respectively. In terms of power, the one-sided test based on $C_1^{(\alpha)}$ has more power than the two-sided test for values of $\mu>\mu_0$ but less power for $\mu<\mu_0$. Similarly, the one-sided test based on $C_1^{(\beta)}$ has more power than the two-sided test for values of $\mu<\mu_0$ but less power for $\mu>\mu_0$ (see figure 14.6). Hence, for $\mu\neq\mu_0$ there is no UMP test, but the test based on C_1 above is UMP unbiased, because the other two are clearly biased; their power functions fall below the size α of the test.

It is very important to emphasize that a Neyman–Pearson test is $\{\tau(\mathbf{X}),C_1,\alpha\}$, not just a test statistic, and the definition of the rejection region plays a crucial role for the optimality of a test. For instance, using the same test statistic $\tau(\mathbf{X})=\left(\frac{\sqrt{n}(\hat{\mu}_n-\mu_0)}{s}\right)$ we can define the tests $\{\tau(\mathbf{X}),C_1,\alpha\}$ and $\{\tau(\mathbf{X}),C_1,\alpha\}$ for the hypotheses:

$$(\gamma)\ H_0:\mu=\mu_0,\text{ against }H_1:\mu\neq\mu_0,$$

based on: $C_1=\{\mathbf{x}:|\tau(\mathbf{x})|\geq c_\alpha\},\quad C_1^{(\alpha)}=\{\mathbf{x}:|\tau(\mathbf{x})|\leq c_\alpha\}$. The power of the test based on C_1 is reasonable (a UMP unbiased test) but that of the test based on $C_1^{(\beta)}$ is terrible; as shown in figure 14.6, this test is *uniformly biased*: its power is uniformly lower than the size of the test!

The one question we have not addressed so far is how we decide what is an appropriate *distance* to be used as a basis for a test statistic. In the next subsection we will consider two of the most important methods of finding optimal tests, the Neyman–Pearson lemma and the likelihood ratio procedure.

14.3.7 Methods for finding optimal tests

In the context of the Neyman–Pearson (N–P) formulation, we can define an optimal α-size test as $\{\tau(\mathbf{X}), C_1, \alpha\}$ derived by way of the following optimization:

$$\max_{\theta \in \Theta_1} \mathcal{P}_n(\theta) \text{ such that } \max_{\theta \in \Theta_0} \mathcal{P}_n(\theta) \leq \alpha.$$

An optimal N–P test is a UMP test. Neyman and Pearson (1933a,1936b) were able to solve the problem of deriving optimal tests only in the simplest of cases: when both H_0 and H_1 are simple. They showed that in this simple case a UMP test exists and they provided a procedure to derive it.

The Neyman–Pearson lemma

The Neyman–Pearson lemma provides the cornerstone upon which the whole procedure is built. Its limitation, however, is that it provides optimal tests only in one simple case.

Consider the case where the statistical hypothesis is specified in terms of a *simple H_0* and a *simple H_1* as follows:

$$H_0: \theta = \theta_0 \text{ against } H_1: \theta = \theta_1. \tag{14.36}$$

NOTE that in this case: $\Phi_0 = \{f(x; \theta_0), x \in \mathbb{R}_X\}$ and $\Phi_1 = \{f(x; \theta_1), x \in \mathbb{R}_X\}$. In view of the fact that the decision to accept or reject will be based on a comparison between these two densities, intuition suggests that their ratio will provide a basis for such a comparison. It turns out that our intuition is perfectly correct. A size α test can be defined by:

$$C_1 = \left\{\mathbf{x}: \frac{f(x; \theta_1)}{f(x; \theta_0)} > k\right\}, k \geq 0, \text{ such that } \mathbb{P}\left(\left|\frac{f(x; \theta_1)}{f(x; \theta_0)}\right| > k; H_0 \text{ valid}\right) = \alpha. \tag{14.37}$$

(a) Any test defined by (14.37) constitutes a UMP test of size α for (14.36).

(b) If there exists a test satisfying (14.37) for $k > 0$, then every UMP size α test coincides with (14.37).

It is important to emphasize that this lemma does not provide the modeler with a complete answer to the question of deriving an optimal test, even in the case of a simple H_0 and a simple H_1. What it does is to guarantee the existence of an optimal test (in this simple case) and provide us with the procedure to derive it. That is, it states that the test statistic must be a function of the ratio $\frac{f(\mathbf{x}; \theta_1)}{f(\mathbf{x}; \theta_0)}$, where $f(\mathbf{x}; \theta)$ denotes the distribution of the sample, i.e.

$$\tau(\mathbf{X}) = h\left(\frac{f(\mathbf{x}; \theta_1)}{f(\mathbf{x}; \theta_0)}\right).$$

The form of he function $h(.)$ is determined by the modeler on a case by case basis.

Example

In the context of the simple Normal model (see (14.4)), assuming σ^2 is known, consider the simple hypothesis:

$$H_0 : \mu = \mu_0 \text{ against } H_1 : \mu = \mu_1 \ (\mu_1 > \mu_0). \tag{14.38}$$

Note that the unknown parameter μ in this case can only take one of two values, i.e. $\mu \in \{\mu_0, \mu_1\}$. In view of the random sample assumption:

$$f(\mathbf{x}; \mu_1) = \prod_{i=1}^{n} f(x_i; \mu_1) = \prod_{i=1}^{n} \frac{1}{\sigma \sqrt{2\pi}} \exp\left\{ -\frac{1}{2\sigma^2} [x_i - \mu_1]^2 \right\},$$

$$f(\mathbf{x}; \mu_0) = \prod_{i=1}^{n} f(x_i; \mu_0) = \prod_{i=1}^{n} \frac{1}{\sigma \sqrt{2\pi}} \exp\left\{ -\frac{1}{2\sigma^2} [x_i - \mu_0]^2 \right\}.$$

$$\frac{f(\mathbf{x}; \mu_1)}{f(\mathbf{x}; \mu_0)} = \exp\left\{ -\frac{1}{2\sigma^2} \sum_{i=1}^{n} [(x_i - \mu_1)^2 - (x_i - \mu_0)^2] \right\} = e^{-\{\frac{n}{\sigma^2}(\mu_1 - \mu_0)\hat{\mu}_n - \frac{n}{2\sigma^2}(\mu_1^2 - \mu_0^2)\}}.$$

As it stands the ratio does not constitute a test statistic, but after some manipulation we can define the well-known statistic (see Spanos (1986), p. 297):

$$\tau(\mathbf{X}) = h\left(\frac{f(\mathbf{x}; \theta_1)}{f(\mathbf{x}; \theta_0)} \right) = \frac{\sqrt{n}(\hat{\mu}_n - \mu_0)}{\sigma}.$$

The optimal test is defined by the rejection region $C_1 = \{\mathbf{x} : \tau(\mathbf{x}) > c_\alpha\}$.

In practice, UMP tests constitute the exception rather than the rule. Beyond the simple hypotheses case, there is no single method which will yield an optimal test. A method which often yields good tests is the so-called likelihood ratio procedure.

Likelihood ratio test

The likelihood ratio test procedure can be viewed as a generalization of the Neyman–Pearson lemma in the sense that its form is similar and the test can be applied to cases where the null and/or the alternative are composite hypotheses.
For the **likelihood ratio** test:

(a)   The hypothesis of interest can be of the general form:

$$H_0 : \boldsymbol{\theta} \in \Theta_0 \text{ against } H_1 : \boldsymbol{\theta} \in \Theta_1.$$

(b)   The test statistic is related to the ratio: $\Lambda_n(\mathbf{X}) := \left(\frac{\max\limits_{\theta \in \Theta} L(\boldsymbol{\theta}; \mathbf{X})}{\max\limits_{\theta \in \Theta_0} L(\boldsymbol{\theta}; \mathbf{X})} \right). \tag{14.39}$

(c)   The rejection region is: $C_1 = \{\mathbf{x} : \tau(\mathbf{X}) = h(\Lambda_n(\mathbf{X})) > k\}, \tag{14.40}$

where $L(\boldsymbol{\theta}; \mathbf{x})$ denotes the likelihood function (see chapter 12).
In figure 14.7 we can see the case where the maximum over $\theta \in \Theta$ coincides with the left boundary point θ_0 of Θ_0 with $\hat{\theta}$ the overall MLE; the likelihood ratio is $\Lambda_n(\mathbf{X}) = \frac{OB}{OA}$.
NOTE: instead of the ratio $\Lambda_n(\mathbf{X})$ most textbooks use its inverse:

$$\lambda_n(\mathbf{X}) = \frac{\max\limits_{\theta \in \Theta_0} L(\boldsymbol{\theta}; \mathbf{X})}{\max\limits_{\theta \in \Theta} L(\boldsymbol{\theta}; \mathbf{X})} = \frac{OA}{OB},$$

with the rejection region modified accordingly to: $C_1 = \{\mathbf{x} : \lambda_n(\mathbf{X}) \leq k^*\}$.

Examples
1 Consider the simple Normal model (see (14.4)) and the hypothesis:

$$H_0 : \mu = \mu_0 \text{ against } H_1 : \mu \neq \mu_0.$$

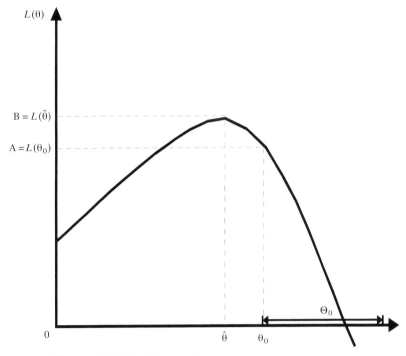

Figure 14.7 Likelihood ratio test

From chapter 13 we know that the maximum likelihood estimators in the two cases are:

$$\max_{\theta \in \Theta} L(\boldsymbol{\theta};\mathbf{x}) \Rightarrow \hat{\mu}_n = \frac{1}{n}\Sigma_{i=1}^n X_i \text{ and } \hat{\sigma}^2 = \frac{1}{n}\Sigma_{i=1}^n (X_i - \hat{\mu}_n)^2,$$

$$\max_{\theta \in \Theta_0} L(\boldsymbol{\theta};\mathbf{x}) \Rightarrow \tilde{\sigma}^2 = \frac{1}{n}\Sigma_{i=1}^n (X_i - \mu_0)^2.$$

$$\max_{\theta \in \Theta} L(\boldsymbol{\theta};\mathbf{x}) = L(\hat{\boldsymbol{\theta}};\mathbf{x}) = \left(\left[\frac{1}{n}\Sigma_{i=1}^n (x_i - \hat{\mu}_n)^2\right](2\pi e)\right)^{-\frac{n}{2}},$$

$$\max_{\theta \in \Theta_0} L(\boldsymbol{\theta};\mathbf{x}) = L(\tilde{\boldsymbol{\theta}};\mathbf{x}) = \left(\left[\frac{1}{n}\Sigma_{i=1}^n (x_i - \mu_0)^2\right](2\pi e)\right)^{-\frac{n}{2}}.$$

Hence, the likelihood ratio is: $\frac{L(\hat{\boldsymbol{\theta}};\mathbf{x})}{L(\tilde{\boldsymbol{\theta}};\mathbf{x})} = \left(\frac{\Sigma_{i=1}^n (x_i - \mu_0)^2}{\Sigma_{i=1}^n (x_i - \hat{\mu}_n)^2}\right)^{\frac{n}{2}} = \left(1 + \frac{\tau(\mathbf{x})^2}{n-1}\right)^{\frac{n}{2}}.$

NOTICE that: $\tau(\mathbf{X}) := h\left(\frac{L(\hat{\boldsymbol{\theta}};\mathbf{X})}{L(\tilde{\boldsymbol{\theta}};\mathbf{X})}\right) = \frac{\sqrt{n}(\hat{\mu}_n - \mu_0)}{s}$, is the test statistic for the t-test, which defines a Neyman–Pearson test in conjunction with the *rejection region:*

$$C_1 = \{\mathbf{x}: |\tau(\mathbf{x})| > c_\alpha\}.$$

2 Consider the simple Normal model (see (14.4)) and the hypothesis:

$$H_0: \sigma^2 = \sigma_0^2 \text{ against } H_1: \sigma^2 \neq \sigma_0^2.$$

From the previous chapter we know that the maximum likelihood estimators in the two cases are as follows:

$$\max_{\theta\in\Theta} L(\boldsymbol{\theta};\mathbf{x}) = L(\hat{\boldsymbol{\theta}};\mathbf{x}) \Rightarrow \hat{\mu}_n = \frac{1}{n}\Sigma_{i=1}^n X_i \text{ and } \hat{\sigma}^2 = \frac{1}{n}\Sigma_{i=1}^n (X_i - \hat{\mu}_n)^2,$$

$$\max_{\theta\in\Theta_0} L(\boldsymbol{\theta};\mathbf{x}) = L(\tilde{\boldsymbol{\theta}};\mathbf{x}) \Rightarrow \hat{\mu}_n = \frac{1}{n}\Sigma_{i=1}^n X_i.$$

$$\max_{\theta\in\Theta} L(\boldsymbol{\theta};\mathbf{x}) = (2\pi e\hat{\sigma}^2)^{-\frac{n}{2}}, \ \max_{\theta\in\Theta_0} L(\boldsymbol{\theta};\mathbf{x}) = (2\pi\sigma_0^2)^{-\frac{n}{2}}\exp\left\{-\frac{n\hat{\sigma}^2}{2\sigma_0^2}\right\}.$$

Hence, the likelihood ratio is $\frac{L(\tilde{\boldsymbol{\theta}};\mathbf{x})}{L(\hat{\boldsymbol{\theta}};\mathbf{x})} = (v(\mathbf{x})e^{-v(\mathbf{x})+1})^{-\frac{n}{2}}$, where $v(\mathbf{x}) = (\hat{\sigma}^2/\sigma_0^2)$. In view of the pivotal quantity:

$$v(\mathbf{X},\sigma^2) = \frac{(n-1)s^2}{\sigma^2} \sim \chi^2(n-1), \tag{14.41}$$

we can define the test statistic: $v(\mathbf{X}) = \frac{n\hat{\sigma}^2}{\sigma_0^2} \overset{H_0}{\sim} \chi(n-1)$, and thus the rejection region (14.40) is transformed into:

$$C_1 = \{\mathbf{x}: v(\mathbf{X}) > c_2 \text{ or } v(\mathbf{X}) < c_1\},$$

where for a size α test; the constants $c_1 < c_2$ are chosen such that:

$$\int_0^{c_1}\psi(x)dx = \int_{c_2}^\infty\psi(x)dx = \frac{\alpha}{2},$$

where $\psi(x)$ denotes the chi-square density function. The test defined by $\{v(\mathbf{X}), C_1, \alpha\}$ turns out to be UMP unbiased (see Lehmann (1986)).

Whither UMP tests?
Good tests in the sense of uniformly most powerful (UMP) do not exist in general. In order to be able to derive such tests we need to restrict both the family of statistical models and the form of the hypotheses. In particular, restricting ourselves to **simple statistical models**, UMP tests exist in cases where:

(1) $\Phi = \{f(x;\theta), \theta\in\Theta, x\in\mathbb{R}_X\}$ has a *monotone likelihood ratio*, and
(2) the hypotheses of interest are *one-sided*, i.e., any one of the form:
    (a) $H_0: \theta = \theta_0$ against $H_1: \theta > \theta_0$,
    (b) $H_0: \theta = \theta_0$ against $H_1: \theta < \theta_0$,
    (c) $H_0: \theta \leq \theta_0$ against $H_1: \theta > \theta_0$,
    (d) $H_0: \theta \geq \theta_0$ against $H_1: \theta < \theta_0$.

Monotone likelihood ratio
A probability model $\Phi = \{f(x;\theta), \theta\in\Theta, x\in\mathbb{R}_X\}$ has a monotone likelihood ratio if there exists a statistic $\tau(\mathbf{x})$ such that for all $\theta_0 < \theta_1$:

$$\frac{L(\theta_1;\mathbf{x})}{L(\theta_0;\mathbf{x})} = h(\tau(\mathbf{x});\theta_0,\theta_1), \text{ where } h(.) \text{ is an increasing or decreasing fuction of } \tau(\mathbf{x}).$$

Example
The well-known one-parameter exponential family of distributions (see chapter 12), defines probability models with monotone likelihood ratios (see Lehmann (1986)).

Lemma 1 Let $\Phi = \{f(x;\theta),\ \theta\in\Theta,\ x\in\mathbb{R}_X\}$ have an increasing likelihood ratio. Then for any significance level α, there exists a UMP test for testing:

$$H_0: \theta = \theta_0 \text{ against } H_1: \theta > \theta_0,$$

defined by the rejection region: $C_1 = \{\mathbf{x}:\tau(\mathbf{X})>c_\alpha\}$.
   The same test is UMP for the hypothesis:

$$H_0: \theta \leq \theta_0 \text{ against } H_1: \theta > \theta_0,$$

For testing:

$$H_0: \theta \geq \theta_0 \text{ against } H_1: \theta < \theta_0,$$

the rejection region of an α significance level UMP test is: $C_1 = \{\mathbf{x}:\tau(\mathbf{X})<c_\alpha\}$.

Lemma 2 Let $\Phi = \{f(x;\theta),\ \theta\in\Theta,\ x\in\mathbb{R}_X\}$ have a decreasing likelihood ratio. Then for any significance level α, there exists a UMP test for testing:

$$H_0: \theta = \theta_0 \text{ against } H_1: \theta > \theta_0,$$

defined by the rejection region: $C_1 = \{\mathbf{x}:\tau(\mathbf{X})<c_\alpha\}$.
   The same test is UMP for the hypothesis:

$$H_0: \theta \geq \theta_0 \text{ against } H_1: \theta > \theta_0,$$

For testing the hypothesis:

$$H_0: \theta \geq \theta_0 \text{ against } H_1: \theta < \theta_0,$$

the rejection region of an α significance level UMP test is: $C_1 = \{\mathbf{x}:\tau(\mathbf{X})>c_\alpha\}$.

Example
Consider the **simple Exponential model:**

[i]   Statistical GM: $X_i = E(X_i) + \epsilon_i,\ i\in\mathbb{N}$,
[ii]   Probability model: $\Phi = \{f(x;\theta)=\frac{1}{\theta}e^{-\frac{x}{\theta}},\ \theta\in(0,\infty),\ x\in\mathbb{R}_+\}$,
[iii] Sampling model: $\mathbf{X}:=(X_1,X_2,\ldots,X_n)$ is a random sample.

Consider deriving an α-size test for the hypothesis:

$$H_0: \theta = \theta_0 \text{ against } H_1: \theta > \theta_0,$$

at significance level $\alpha=0.05$. The denominator of the ratio refers to the estimated likelihood function. The likelihood and likelihood ratio for $\theta_1 > \theta_0$ are:

$$L(\theta;\mathbf{x}) = \left(\frac{1}{\theta}\right)^n e^{-\frac{1}{\theta}\Sigma_k x_k} \text{ and } \frac{L(\theta_0;\mathbf{x})}{L(\theta_1;\mathbf{x})} = \frac{\left(\frac{1}{\theta_0}\right)^n e^{-\frac{1}{\theta_0}\Sigma_k x_k}}{\left(\frac{1}{\theta_1}\right)^n e^{-\frac{1}{\theta_1}\Sigma_k x_k}} = \left(\frac{\theta_1}{\theta_0}\right)^n e^{-\left(\frac{\theta_1-\theta_0}{\theta_1\theta_0}\right)\Sigma_k x_k}.$$

Hence, the likelihood ratio is an increasing function of the statistic $\sum_{k=1}^{n} x_k$. In view of the pivotal function:

$$\xi(\mathbf{X};\theta) = \frac{2\sum_{k=1}^{n} x_k}{\theta} \sim \chi^2(2n),$$

we can use the test statistic: $\xi(\mathbf{X}) = \frac{2\sum_{k=1}^{n} x_k}{\theta} \overset{H_0}{\sim} \chi^2(2n)$, to define a UMP test based on the rejection region: $C_1 = \{\mathbf{x}:\xi(\mathbf{X})>c_\alpha\}$.

Where does this leave the Neyman–Pearson approach?

Neyman and Pearson (1928a) set out to improve upon Fisher's approach to testing by making the choice of a test statistic less ad hoc and arbitrary and replacing the questionable p-value with a more formal decision rule. The success of their research program should be assessed in terms of their stated objectives. In so far as the choice of a test statistic is concerned, it is generally accepted that they have improved upon Fisher's legacy but their success is not an unqualified triumph. Having defined what an optimal test is, *uniformly most powerful*, it turns out that such optimal tests are the exception and not the rule. The introduction of additional properties such as unbiasedness and consistency can be interpreted by a cynic as a way to shrink the set of optimal tests so we can prove existence in the context of the smaller set. In relation to methods of deriving optimal tests the same cynic might argue that the only clear cut result in the Neyman–Pearson approach is their namesake lemma which is just an existence result of very limited scope. Constructing an optimal test using this lemma is not straightforward.

As far as the replacement of the p-value with a more *formal decision rule* is concerned, we argued above that this has been achieved on the basis of a convention; we agreed to treat the null and the alternative hypotheses asymmetrically. The same cynic who objected to the choice of a test statistic will also object to this decision rule as arbitrary! Indeed, as argued in the next section, the textbook hybrid on testing considers p-values much less arbitrary than the choice of a significance level.

14.4 Asymptotic test procedures*

It is often the case in practice that sensible distance functions, such as the likelihood ratio, do not often yield test statistics in the sense that their sampling distribution is either unknown or it depends on unknown parameters. In such cases we often need to resort to asymptotic theory; allow the sample size n to increase and consider the asymptotic behavior of functions of the likelihood ratio. Asymptotic theory, however, raises certain difficulties in relation to the power, size and optimality of a test.

14.4.1 Asymptotic power and size

As argued above, one of the asymptotic properties good tests should enjoy is that of consistency. If tests are not consistent we do not consider them as serious contenders when comparisons of power are discussed. This, however, raises an important difficulty when comparing the asymptotic properties of the various tests because all consistent tests are asymptotically indistinguishable in terms of power; they all have power one! There are several useful ways to deal with this difficulty but no one offers the answer we seek: which test is asymptotically best in a way comparable to maximum likelihood in estimation? The basic difficulty arises because any asymptotic measure should take account of three different dimensions:

(i)   the size of the test: $\alpha \in [0,1]$,
(ii)   the power of the test: $\beta \in [0,1]$,
(iii) the parameter: $\theta \in \Theta$.

A particularly useful way to combine all three dimensions comes in the form of the following concept:

> $N_\tau(\alpha,\beta,\theta)$: the number of observations a particular test (actually a sequence of test statistics $\{\tau_n\}_{n=1}^\infty$) of size α required in order to achieve a certain power level β given an alternative value of the parameter θ.

More formally, $N_\tau(\alpha,\beta,\theta)$ can be defined in terms of the minimal size of the test for which the power is not less than β, for $0 < \alpha < \beta$:

$$\alpha_n(\beta,\theta) := \sup_{\theta \in \Theta_0} \{\mathbb{P}(\mathbf{x} : \tau_n(\mathbf{X}) \geq c_n)\},$$

$$N_\tau(\alpha,\beta,\theta) = \min_{m \geq n} \{n : \alpha_m(\beta,\theta) \geq \alpha\}.$$

Using this concept we can compare two tests $\{\tau_n\}_{n=1}^\infty$ and $\{\tau_n'\}_{n=1}^\infty$ by defining the efficiency of the former relative to the latter as:

$$RE(\alpha,\beta,\theta) = \frac{N_{\tau'}(\alpha,\beta,\theta)}{N_\tau(\alpha,\beta,\theta)}.$$

When this ratio is greater than unity the test defined by $\{\tau_n\}_{n=1}^\infty$ is relatively more efficient than the one defined by $\{\tau_n'\}_{n=1}^\infty$ because, given the size α, the latter requires more observations to achieve the same power. Although this concept of relative efficiency has an obvious intuitive appeal, it turns out that, more often than not, it is very difficult, and often impossible, to evaluate even for some values of θ, let alone having to evaluate it for all values $\theta \in \Theta_1 := \Theta - \Theta_0$.

The obvious answer is to find a way to render this measure free of some of the three dimension parameters (α,β,θ); asymptotic arguments then enter the picture. The problem of dealing with the three dimensions (i)–(iii) still remains and our only option is to keep two of the dimensions fixed and let the other converge to some limiting value of interest. This strategy gives rise to three different asymptotic relative efficiency (ARE) measures:

Bahadur	$ARE(\beta,\theta) := \lim_{\alpha \to 0} ARE(\alpha,\beta,\theta),$	for $\beta \in (0,1),\ \theta \in \Theta_1,$
Hodges-Lehmann	$ARE(\alpha,\theta) := \lim_{\beta \to 1} ARE(\alpha,\beta,\theta),$	for $\alpha \in (0,1),\ \theta \in \Theta_1,$
Pitman	$ARE(\alpha,\beta,\theta_0) := \lim_{\theta \to \theta_0} ARE(\alpha,\beta,\theta),$	for $0 < \alpha < \beta \leq 1.$

In all three cases the hope is that at the limit the ARE measure will not depend on the values of the two dimensions left free. This, however, is not always the case leading to additional difficulties.

In econometrics the most widely used measure of ARE is Pitman's, often called the *local Pitman drift*. This specification of the null and the alternative often takes the form:

$$H_0: \theta = \theta_0 \text{ against } H_1: \theta_n = \theta_0 + \frac{\delta}{\sqrt{n}}, \ \delta > 0.$$

This is called local Pitman drift because the alternative hypotheses are defined around the null and as $n \to \infty$ they converge to the null hypothesis. The asymptotic power fuction is defined by:

$$\mathcal{P}_\infty(\theta) = \lim_{n \to \infty} \mathcal{P}_n(\theta_n) \text{ for } \theta_n = \theta_0 + \frac{\delta}{\sqrt{n}},$$

where the limit depends crucially on the chosen level α, the asymptotic size:

$$\sup_{n \to \infty} (\mathcal{P}_\infty(\theta_0)) = \alpha.$$

In cases where the distribution under the null and the alternative are asymptotically Normal, the Pitman ARE is the easiest to apply (see Gourieroux and Monfort (1995), vol. II).

14.4.2 Asymptotic likelihood ratio test

In section 3 we interpreted the **likelihood ratio** (LR) **test** as a direct generalization of the Neyman–Pearson ratio and defined by:

$$\lambda_n(\mathbf{X}) = \frac{\max_{\theta \in \Theta_0} L(\theta; \mathbf{X})}{\max_{\theta \in \Theta} L(\theta; \mathbf{X})}. \tag{14.42}$$

More often than not, however, this ratio does not yield a test statistic even after it has been transformed. In such cases, we resort to asymptotic distribution theory which states that *under certain restrictions* (see Wilks (1938)):

$$-2 \ln \lambda_n(\mathbf{X}) = -2\left(\ln L(\tilde{\boldsymbol{\theta}}; \mathbf{X}) - \ln L(\hat{\boldsymbol{\theta}}; \mathbf{X})\right) \overset{H_0}{\underset{\alpha}{\sim}} \chi^2(r),$$

where $\overset{H_0}{\underset{\alpha}{\sim}}$ reads "under H_0 is asymptotically distributed as" and r denotes *the number of restrictions* involved in restricting Θ to Θ_0.

The rejection region of the asymptotic likelihood ratio test is defined by:

$$C_1 = \{\mathbf{x}: -2 \ln \lambda_n(\mathbf{x}) \geq c_\alpha\}. \tag{14.43}$$

The asymptotic likelihood ratio test defined by (14.43), under the same regularity conditions required for maximum likelihood estimators, can be shown to be consistent and have size α (see Wilks (1962)). In addition, the asymptotic likelihood ratio test is optimal in the sense of asymptotic relative efficiency as defined above (see Brown (1971), Kourouklis (1988)).

Example
Consider the **simple Poisson model**:

[i]   Statistical GM: $X_i = E(X_i) + \epsilon_i,\ i \in \mathbb{N}$,

[ii]   Probability model: $\Phi = \left\{ f(x;\theta) = \frac{e^{-\theta}\theta^x}{x!},\ \theta \in (0,\infty),\ x = 0,1,2,3, \dots \right\}$,

[iii] Sampling model: $\mathbf{X} := (X_1, X_2, \dots X_n)$ is a random sample.

Consider a test for the hypothesis:

$$H_0: \theta = \theta_0 \text{ against } H_1: \theta \neq \theta_0,$$

at significance level α. In view of the fact that H_0 is simple the likelihood ratio (14.12) takes the simpler form:

$$\lambda_n(\mathbf{X}) = \frac{L(\theta_0;\mathbf{X})}{\max_{\theta \in \Theta} L(\theta;\mathbf{X})}. \tag{14.44}$$

The denominator of the ratio refers to the estimated likelihood function $L(\hat{\theta}_n;\mathbf{X})$, where $\hat{\theta}_n$ is the MLE of θ. The likelihood and log-likelihood functions are:

$$L(\theta;\mathbf{x}) = \frac{e^{-n\theta}\theta^{\Sigma_k x_k}}{\prod_{k=1}^n x_k!} \text{ and } \ln L(\theta;\mathbf{x}) = -n\theta + \ln \theta \left(\Sigma_{k=1}^n x_k \right) - \ln \prod_{k=1}^n x_k!,$$

$$\frac{d}{d\theta} \ln L(\theta;\mathbf{x}) = 0 \Rightarrow \hat{\theta}_n = \left(\frac{1}{n} \Sigma_{k=1}^n x_k \right).$$

Hence, $\lambda_n(\mathbf{X}) = \dfrac{\max_{\theta \in \Theta_0} L(\theta;\mathbf{X})}{\max_{\theta \in \Theta} L(\theta;\mathbf{X})} = \dfrac{[e^{-n\theta_0}][\theta_0^{\Sigma_k x_k}][\prod_{k=1}^n x_k!]^{-1}}{(e^{-\Sigma_k x_k})(\hat{\theta}_n^{\Sigma_k x_k})[\prod_{k=1}^n x_k!]^{-1}} = e^{-n(\theta_0 - \hat{\theta}_n)} \left(\frac{\theta_0}{\hat{\theta}_n} \right)^{\Sigma_k x_k},$

$$-2 \ln \lambda_n(\mathbf{X}) = 2n \left[\theta_0 - \hat{\theta}_n + \hat{\theta}_n \ln \left(\frac{\hat{\theta}_n}{\theta_0} \right) \right].$$

The Bartlett correction
In an attempt to improve the finite sample approximation of the asymptotic likelihood ratio statistic:

$$\kappa_n(\mathbf{X}) := -2 \ln \lambda_n(\mathbf{X}) \overset{H_0}{\underset{\alpha}{\sim}} \chi^2(r),$$

Bartlett (1937) put forward a common sense argument to adjust this statistic. This argument proposes the choice of a sequence $\{c_n\}_{n=1}^{\infty}$ such that:

(i) $c_n \underset{n \to \infty}{\to} 1$,   (ii) $E(c_n \kappa_n(\mathbf{X})) = r$.

The first condition is to ensure no changes in the asymptotic distribution and the second to adjust the statistic to have a mean which coincides with the mean of the distribution for each n; NOTE that if $v \sim \chi^2(m)$, then $E(v) = m$.

More formally, if the expected value of the statistic $\kappa_n(\mathbf{X})$ can be expressed in the form of a Taylor's series expansion (see chapter 12):

$$E(\kappa_n(\mathbf{X})) = r \left[1 + \frac{b(\mathbf{X})}{n} + O(n^{-2}) \right],$$

where $O(n^{-2})$ denotes the residual term of smaller order than the retained part (see Spanos (1986)) and $b(\mathbf{X})$ is some known or estimable function, then:

$$c_n = \left[1 + \frac{b(\mathbf{X})}{n}\right]^{-1}.$$

The Bartlett adjusted test statistic takes the form:

$$\kappa_n^B(\mathbf{X}) = \left(\frac{\kappa_n(\mathbf{X})}{1 + \frac{b(\mathbf{X})}{n}}\right), \text{ with } E(\kappa_n^B(\mathbf{X})) = r + O(n^{-2}).$$

The Bartlett adjustment often leads to better approximations even in cases where the equality in (ii) is only approximately valid.

14.4.3 Asymptotically equivalent tests

The above asymptotic likelihood ratio test gave rise to two other, asymptotically equivalent tests.

For exposition purposes let us consider the simple form (14.44) of the likelihood ratio. Taking a second-order Taylor's approximation of the numerator

$$\ell(\theta_0) := \ln L(\theta_0; \mathbf{x}),$$

about $\hat{\theta}_n$ yields:

$$-2\ln \lambda_n(\mathbf{X}) = -2[\ell(\theta_0) - \ell(\hat{\theta}_n)] = -2\left\{(\theta_0 - \hat{\theta}_n)\ell'(\hat{\theta}_n) + \tfrac{1}{2}(\theta_0 - \hat{\theta}_n)^2\ell''(\bar{\theta})\right\},$$

where $\bar{\theta} \in (\theta_0, \hat{\theta}_n)$, $\ell'(.)$ and $\ell''(.)$ denote the first and second derivatives of the log-likelihood function, respectively (see Gourieroux and Monfort (1995), vol. II). In view of the fact that $\ell'(\hat{\theta}_n) = 0$ (this is the first order condition for the derivation of the MLE of θ), we can conclude that:

$$-2\ln \lambda_n(\mathbf{X}) = -(\theta_0 - \hat{\theta}_n)^2\ell''(\bar{\theta}) = -n(\theta_0 - \hat{\theta}_n)^2\left(\frac{\ell''(\theta_0)}{n}\right) + o_p(1),$$

where $o_p(1)$ denotes the asymptotically negligible terms (see Spanos (1986)).
From chapter 13 we know that:

$$E(-\ell''(\theta_0)) = I_n(\theta_0), \quad \lim_{n\to\infty}\left(\frac{I_n(\theta_0)}{n}\right) = I_\infty(\theta_0),$$

where $I_n(\theta_0)$ and $I_\infty(\theta_0)$ are Fisher's information and asymptotic information, respectively. Hence, the above approximation can be written in the form:

$$-2\ln \lambda_n(\mathbf{X}) = n(\theta_0 - \hat{\theta}_n)^2 I_\infty(\theta_0) + o_p(1).$$

Using these results, Wald (1943) proposed the statistic:

$$w(\mathbf{X}) = n(\theta_0 - \hat{\theta}_n)^2 I_\infty(\hat{\theta}_n).$$

In the case where $I_\infty(\theta)$ is a continuous function of θ: $I_\infty(\hat{\theta}_n) = I_\infty(\theta_0) + o_p(1)$, under H_0, and thus the two statistics are asymptotically equivalent, i.e.

$$-2\ln \lambda_n(\mathbf{X}) \underset{a}{\approx} w(\mathbf{X}),$$

where $\underset{\alpha}{\approx}$ reads asymptotically equal; $w(\mathbf{X})$ is known as the **Wald test statistic**. This means that for testing the simple hypothesis:

$$H_0 : \theta = \theta_0 \text{ against } H_1 : \theta \neq \theta_0,$$

the Wald test statistic gives rise to the same test (asymptotically) as $-2\ln \lambda_n(\mathbf{X})$, i.e.

$$w(\mathbf{X}) = n(\theta_0 - \hat{\theta}_n)^2 I_\infty(\hat{\theta}_n) \overset{H_0}{\underset{\alpha}{\approx}} \chi^2(1).$$

Another asymptotically equivalent test can be derived using another approximate equality derived in chapter 13:

$$\sqrt{n}(\theta_0 - \hat{\theta}_n) \underset{\alpha}{\approx} \frac{1}{\sqrt{n}} \ell'(\theta_0) I_\infty^{-1}(\theta_0),$$

where $\ell'(\theta_0)$ is the *score function* evaluated at $\theta = \theta_0$, i.e.

$$\ell'(\theta_0) := \frac{d}{d\theta} \ln L(\theta_0; \mathbf{x}) \bigg|_{\theta = \theta_0} = s(\mathbf{x}; \theta_0). \tag{14.45}$$

We remind ourselves that the *score function* (viewed as a function of $\mathbf{X} \in X$ given θ) satisfies the following properties:

[i] $E[s(\mathbf{X}; \theta)] \overset{\circledcirc}{=} 0,$

[ii] $Var[s(\mathbf{X}; \theta)] \overset{\circledcirc}{=} E\left(-\frac{d^2}{d\theta^2}\ln L(\theta; \mathbf{X})\right) := I_n(\theta),$ (14.46)

[iii] $\frac{1}{\sqrt{n}} s(\mathbf{X}; \theta) \overset{\circledcirc}{\underset{\alpha}{\approx}} \mathsf{N}(0, I_\infty(\theta)),$

where $\circledcirc$ reads under the correct specfication. The properties [i]–[iii] can be used to derive natural pivotal functions in testing hypotheses. For example, in the case of the simple hypothesis:

$$H_0 : \theta = \theta_0, \text{ against } H_1 : \theta \neq \theta_0$$

we can replace the true but unknown θ by its value under H_0 and define the asymptotic test statistic:

$$s(\mathbf{X}) = \frac{1}{n}[\ell'(\theta_0)]^2 (I_\infty(\theta_0))^{-1} \overset{H_0}{\underset{\alpha}{\approx}} \chi^2(1). \tag{14.47}$$

Hence, all three test statistics $2\ln \lambda_n(\mathbf{X})$, $w(\mathbf{X})$ and $s(\mathbf{X})$ have the same asymptotic distribution under H_0 (see Serfling (1980)). The test (14.47) was proposed by Rao (1947) and is known as the (efficient) **score test**. This test statistic can be formally derived using optimization subject to restrictions (see Silvey (1959)) and thus it is also known as a **Lagrange multiplier test**, especially in econometrics.

The relationship between these three test statistics can be seen in figure 14.8 where $\ell(\theta) := \ln L(\theta; \mathbf{X})$ is plotted against θ (see Buse (1982)). As we can see, the score test statistic is based on the slope of the tangent line at $\theta = \theta_0$ and the likelihood ratio is based on the distance $[\ell(\theta_0) - \ell(\hat{\theta})]$.

In the general case where the hypothesis of interest is composite and comes in the form of r (possibly) non-linear restrictions:

$$H_0 : \mathbf{h}(\boldsymbol{\theta}) = 0, \text{ against } H_1 : \mathbf{h}(\boldsymbol{\theta}) \neq 0,$$

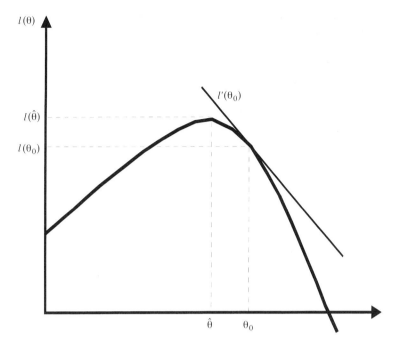

Figure 14.8 LR, ES, and W tests

the asymptotic test takes the form:

$$\xi(\mathbf{X}) \overset{H_0}{\underset{\alpha}{\approx}} \chi^2(r), \ C_1 = \{\mathbf{x} : \xi(\mathbf{X}) \ge c_\alpha\},$$

where $\xi(\mathbf{X})$ is any one of the three (asymptotically equivalent) test statistics (see Spanos (1986)):

(a) $-2\ln \lambda_n(\mathbf{X}) \underset{\alpha}{\approx} n(\hat{\boldsymbol{\theta}} - \tilde{\boldsymbol{\theta}})' \mathcal{I}_\infty(\boldsymbol{\theta}_0)(\hat{\boldsymbol{\theta}} - \tilde{\boldsymbol{\theta}})$,

(b) $w(\mathbf{X}) = (\mathbf{h}(\hat{\boldsymbol{\theta}})' \ (Cov[\mathbf{h}(\hat{\boldsymbol{\theta}})])^{-1}(\mathbf{h}(\hat{\boldsymbol{\theta}}))$,

(c) $s(\mathbf{X}) = \frac{1}{n}(s(\tilde{\boldsymbol{\theta}};\mathbf{X}))' \ (\mathcal{I}_\infty(\tilde{\boldsymbol{\theta}}))^{-1}(s(\tilde{\boldsymbol{\theta}};\mathbf{X}))$.

NOTE that $\ell(\hat{\boldsymbol{\theta}}) := \sup_{\boldsymbol{\theta} \in \Theta} \ln L(\boldsymbol{\theta};\mathbf{x})$ and $\ell(\tilde{\boldsymbol{\theta}}) := \sup_{\mathbf{h}(\boldsymbol{\theta})=0} (\ln L(\boldsymbol{\theta};\mathbf{x}))$, i.e. $\hat{\boldsymbol{\theta}}$ and $\tilde{\boldsymbol{\theta}}$ denote the *unrestricted* and *restricted* MLE estimators of $\boldsymbol{\theta}$, respectively. By comparing the above three test statistics, the differences that stand out are:

(i) $-2\ln \lambda_n(\mathbf{X})$ is defined in terms of both the restricted and unrestricted MLEs,

(ii) $w(\mathbf{X})$ is defined in terms of the unrestricted MLE only, and

(iii) $s(\hat{\boldsymbol{\theta}};\mathbf{X})$ is defined in terms of the restricted MLE only.

The choice of the distance underlying each of the above test statistics:

$$\text{(a)} \ \|\tilde{\boldsymbol{\theta}} - \hat{\boldsymbol{\theta}}\|, \quad \text{(b)} \ \|\mathbf{h}(\hat{\boldsymbol{\theta}})\|, \quad \text{(c)} \ \|s(\tilde{\boldsymbol{\theta}};\mathbf{X}\|,$$

can be easily rationalized on intuitive grounds. NOTE that $\mathbf{h}(\tilde{\boldsymbol{\theta}})$ or $s(\hat{\boldsymbol{\theta}};\mathbf{X})$ could not be utilized to define test distances because by definition they are both equal to zero! It turns out that the distance $\|\mathbf{h}(\hat{\boldsymbol{\theta}})\|$ is not invariant to reparameterizations as are the distances $\|\tilde{\boldsymbol{\theta}} - \hat{\boldsymbol{\theta}}\|$ and $\|\mathbf{s}(\tilde{\boldsymbol{\theta}};\mathbf{X})\|$. For this reason the Wald test should be used with caution.

14.5 Fisher versus Neyman–Pearson

During the period when the statistical textbook hybrid approach was forged (more than 25 years after the controversy between Fisher and Neyman–Pearson began), Fisher (1956) reiterated his disagreement in no uncertain terms:

It is to be feared, therefore, that the principles of Neyman and Pearson's "Theory of Testing Hypotheses" are liable to mislead those who follow them into much wasted effort and disappointment, and that its authors are not inclined to warn students of these dangers.

(Fisher (1956), p. 92)

Is this just the rear guard action of a disillusioned scientist who lost the argument? Not quite.

A hasty comparison between the Fisher and Neyman–Pearson approaches is likely to reveal that the main difference between the two approaches is the fact that the null hypothesis ($H_0: \theta \in \Theta_0$) in the former approach is supplemented with an alternative hypothesis ($H_1: \theta \in \Theta_1 = \Theta - \Theta_0$) in the latter approach. After all, this alternative hypothesis gives rise to the two types of errors in the Neyman–Pearson context and the choice of an optimal test statistic arises as a result of maximizing the power function over the parameter space Θ_1. All these concepts are inextricably bound up with the notion of an alternative hypothesis. In addition to deriving (at least theoretically) the test statistic as part of an optimization problem, the Neyman–Pearson approach replaces the p-value with a decision rule based on the notion of the significance level (or size) α of a test. Hence, in cases where the null and the alternative hypothesis of interest can be specified in terms of the parameter space Θ of the statistical model $\{\Phi,\mathbf{X}\}$ postulated a priori by the modeler, the Neyman–Pearson approach provides a more satisfactory solution to the problem of choosing a test $\{\tau(\mathbf{X}),C_1,\alpha\}$, a test statistic, and the associated rejection region, which are optimal in a sense defined in terms of the power function. The *modus operandi* of the Neyman–Pearson approach is the *power function* which ensures that the test chosen has maximum power in the direction of the specified alternative. Moreover, the key to defining the power function is the *alternative hypothesis* which takes an *explicit parametric form*.

In view of such a comparison, it is generally accepted that the Neyman–Pearson formulation has added some rigor and coherence to the Fisher formulation and in some ways it has superseded the latter. The Fisher approach is rarely mentioned in statistics textbooks (a notable exception is Cox and Hinkley (1974)). However, a closer look at the argument that the main difference between the Fisher and the Neyman–Pearson approaches is the presence of an *alternative hypothesis* in the latter, suggests that this is rather misleading.

The line of argument adopted in this book is that the Neyman–Pearson method constitutes a different approach to hypothesis testing which can be utilized to improve upon *some aspects* of the Fisher approach. However, the intended scope of the Fisher approach is much broader than that of the Neyman–Pearson approach. Indeed, as argued in the next chapter, the Fisher approach is more germane to misspecification testing.

14.5.1 The basic objective of testing

The first important difference between the Fisher and Neyman–Pearson approaches to testing is clearly their basic objective. The main objective of the Fisher approach is to use the data as evidence to bear upon the validity of the null hypothesis. That is, the focus is **inferential:**

to what extent does the sample realization *lend credence* to the null hypothesis.

On the other hand, the main purpose of the Neyman–Pearson approach is **behavioral:**

make a decision to accept or reject the null hypothesis by comparing its data based support to that of the alternative hypothesis.

The differences, however, do not stop at the basic objective.

14.5.2 Testing within versus testing without

The key to the real difference between the Fisher and Neyman–Pearson approaches is the fact that a null hypothesis is essentially a hypothesis concerning the "true" stochastic mechanism that gave rise to the observed data as it relates to the postulated statistical model. The fact that the hypothesis is often specified via the parameter space is of secondary importance. In order to trace the implications of this let us consider a hypothesis in the context of a simple statistical model.

As argued above, the Neyman–Pearson specification of a hypothesis takes the form:

$$H_0: \boldsymbol{\theta} \in \Theta_0 \text{ against } H_1: \boldsymbol{\theta} \in \Theta_1 := \Theta - \Theta_0. \tag{14.48}$$

In the case of a simple statistical model, this specification constitutes in effect a partition of the postulated (original) probability model:

$$\Phi = \{f(x;\boldsymbol{\theta}), \boldsymbol{\theta} \in \Theta, x \in \mathbb{R}_X\},$$

into two mutually exclusive subsets corresponding to the partition of the parameter space $\Theta = \Theta_0 \cup \Theta_1$:

$$\Phi_0 = \{f(x;\boldsymbol{\theta}), \boldsymbol{\theta} \in \Theta_0, x \in \mathbb{R}_X\}, \ \Phi_1 = \{f(x;\boldsymbol{\theta}), \boldsymbol{\theta} \in \Theta_1, x \in \mathbb{R}_X\}.$$

In a sense, the null hypothesis is posing the question whether the "true" probability distribution, say $f(x)$, belongs to a proper subset Φ_0 of the originally postulated family of distributions Φ:

$$\text{does } f(x) \in \Phi_0 \subset \Phi? \tag{14.49}$$

It turns out that a most useful way to bring out the difference between the two approaches to testing is to view them in relation to how they complete this question.

(a)   The Neyman–Pearson approach transforms this question into:

$$H_0: f(x) \in \Phi_0 \text{ against } H_1: f(x) \in \Phi_1, \ \Phi_0 \cup \Phi_1 = \Phi. \tag{14.50}$$

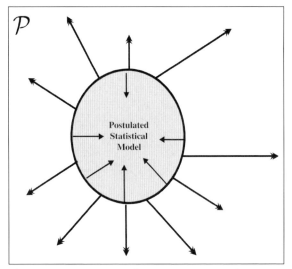

Figure 14.9 Testing within versus testing without

(b)   The Fisher approach transforms (14.49) into:

$$H_0 : f(x) \in \Phi_0 \text{ against } H_1 : f(x) \in [\mathcal{P} - \Phi_0], \qquad (14.51)$$

   $\mathcal{P}$ is *the set of all possible statistical models* (parametric or otherwise)!

NOTE that we can view $\mathcal{P}$ as the set of all possible families of distributions without any loss of generality given that, as shown in chapters 4–8, all dependence and heterogeneity assumptions can be expressed in terms of distributions.

   The notions of testing within and testing without can be visualized in terms of figure 14.9 where the arrows pointing inwards denote testing within the boundaries of the postulated statistical model and those pointing outwards denote testing beyond these boundaries.

   As argued above, in the context of the Neyman–Pearson approach the optimality of a test depends crucially on the particular Φ ; the power function is defined in terms of $\theta \in \Theta$. The search for answering question (14.49) begins and ends within the boundaries of the postulated statistical model. In contrast, a Fisher search begins with Φ_0 but allows for a much broader scouring.

   At this stage the reader might object to the presence of an alternative hypothesis in the context of the Fisher specification. After all, Fisher himself denied the existence of the concept, as defined by Neyman and Pearson, in the context of his approach. However, even Fisher could not deny the fact that for every null hypothesis in his approach there is the *implicit alternative* hypothesis: the *null is not valid*. The latter notion is discernible in all of Fisher's discussions on testing (see in particular Fisher (1925a,1956)). We can interpret Fisher's objections as being directed toward the nature of the Neyman–Pearson alternative, and in particular the restriction that the alternative should lie within the boundaries of the postulated model. Hence, *the crucial difference between the two approaches is not the presence or absence of an alternative hypothesis but its nature.*

   In the case of a Fisher test the implicit alternative is much broader than that of a N–P test. This constitutes simultaneously a strength and a weakness of a Fisher test. It is a strength because the modeler is assured that the "true" statistical model lies within the union of the null and alternative hypotheses, i.e.

$$f(x) \in \mathcal{P} = \Phi_0 \cup [\mathcal{P} - \Phi_0].$$

No such assurance exists in the case of a N–P test; the possibility that $f(x) \in [\mathcal{P} - \Phi]$ is a real one. The Neyman–Pearson approach leaves the possibility open that both the null and the alternative hypotheses are invalid, which will invalidate the N–P test. As argued above, this approach pre-supposes statistical adequacy: the validity of the postulated statistical model. This suggests that the crucial difference between the two approaches can be best defined in terms of the concept of the *implicit maintained hypothesis:*

(a) **Neyman–Pearson**: $\Phi = \Phi_0 \cup \Phi_1$, where $\Phi = \{f(x;\boldsymbol{\theta}), \boldsymbol{\theta} \in \Theta, x \in \mathbb{R}_X\}$
(b) **Fisher**: $\mathcal{P} = \Phi_0 \cup [\mathcal{P} - \Phi_0], \Phi_0 = \{f(x;\boldsymbol{\theta}), \boldsymbol{\theta} \in \Theta_0, x \in \mathbb{R}_X\},$

which is nothing more than the union of the null and alternative hypotheses. This shows that the implicit maintained hypothesis for a Fisher test is much broader since:

$$\Phi_1 \subset [\mathcal{P} - \Phi_0], \text{ and } [\mathcal{P} - \Phi_0] \text{ is not necessarily parametric.}$$

An alternative but equivalent way to view the crucial difference between the Fisher and Neyman–Pearson approaches is in terms of the domain of search for the "true" statistical model in the two cases. The Neyman–Pearson approach can be viewed as **testing within** the boundaries demarcated by the postulated statistical model.

Example
Consider the case where the postulated statistical model is the simple Normal model (see (14.4)). Testing the hypotheses:

(i) $H_0 : \mu = \mu_0$ against $H_1 : \mu \neq \mu_0$,
(ii) $H_0 : \sigma^2 = \sigma_0^2$ against $H_1 : \sigma^2 \neq \sigma_0^2$, $(\mu,\sigma^2) \in \mathbb{R} \times \mathbb{R}_+,$ (14.52)

constitutes testing within because in all cases the null *and* the alternative hypotheses specify subsets of the postulated probability model:

$$\Phi = \{f(x;\boldsymbol{\theta}) = \tfrac{1}{\sigma\sqrt{2\pi}} \exp\{-\tfrac{1}{2\sigma^2}(x - \mu)^2\}, \boldsymbol{\theta} := (\mu,\sigma^2) \in \mathbb{R} \times \mathbb{R}_+\}.$$

In contrast, the Fisher approach can be viewed as **testing without** (outside) the boundaries demarcated by the postulated statistical model.

The vast domain of the implicit alternative is also the main weakness of the Fisher approach because of the difficulties in operationalizing the notion of searching through the set $[\mathcal{P} - \Phi_0]$. In contrast, in the context of the Neyman–Pearson approach the search through the set Φ_1 is easily operationalized in terms of the power function, defined for all $\theta \in \Theta$. In the context of the Fisher approach this is clearly an open question which needs to be explored further. However, it is worth mentioning certain obvious directions of departure for such research.

(i) Fisher's own results point toward a direction of *local departures*, in the sense that a Fisher test statistic is evaluated at the null hypothesis and no attempt is made to define tests with power in particular directions of departures; both the estimators and test statistics are evaluated under the null in order to determine the p-value. Naturally, any departures from the null that such a test statistic can be sensitive toward could only be of a local nature, in general.

(ii)   Another suggestion which arises by reading Fisher's own testing is that opearationalizing the search beyond the boundaries of the null hypothesis can be based on features of the postulated distribution (moments, quantiles, ordered sample, etc.) beyond the pre-specified parameters of the statistical model $\theta \in \Theta$. This is often referred to as a *non-parametric* specification of the implicit alternative hypothesis. A cursory glance at Fisher's three books (see Fisher (1925a,1935a,1956)) reveals that a number of tests favored by Fisher, such as goodness of fit, independence and homogeneity tests, belong to this category. Within the same category one can classify the modern *smoothing techniques* (such as kernel smoothing) which attempt to approximate theoretical concepts such as the density function and conditional moments without postulating specific parametric forms a priori. The primary danger with this procedure is to end up with data-specific summaries.

In connection with both of the above suggestions a modeler trained in the Neyman–Pearson tradition is likely to question the appropriateness of such tests on the ground that "they are likely to have low power with respect to certain directions of departures from the null." This of course begs the question: Why should these tests have power against departures in specific directions, unless there is information that such departures are likely? Moreover, one can go one step further and pose the question whether "power" is indeed the relevant concept in the context of searching beyond the boundaries of the null hypothesis?

Starting with the latter question first, even Fisher could not exorcize the notion of "power" from his approach to testing. In an unguarded moment he conceded the relevance of the power function "for comparing the sensitiveness, in some chosen respect, of different possible tests of significance" (see Fisher (1925a), p. 11). This is hardly surprising given that the presence of an implicit alternative hypothesis (the invalidity of the null) in the Fisher approach cannot be denied. As a result, a more general notion, which measures the *sensitivity* of a test statistic in detecting departures from the null, is both relevant and desirable. However, there is no reason why this sensitivity should be considered only in relation to the pre-specified parameters of the statistical model $\theta \in \Theta$. This suggests that the concept of sensitivity (power) should be extended to include such non-parametric alternatives. Returning to the first question on power with respect to specific directions of departures from the null hypothesis, it is clear that this question arises when there is information for possible departures in these directions. As argued in chapters 11 and 15, in the context of the probabilistic reduction approach to statistical model specification, such information is often readily available and the issue of testing with respect to specific directions of departures from the null could be addressed in that framework. If this information is not available local searching is indeed the natural way to proceed.

14.5.3 Fisher testing revisited

With the hindsight of the developments in testing since the 1930s and the above discussion of the Fisher and the Neyman–Pearson approaches in mind, let us re-evaluate the initial criticisms of a Fisher test voiced by Neyman and Pearson (1928a) in relation to the arbitrariness of the choice of the test statistic and the inappropriateness of the p-value.

The use of the p-value

The question which naturally arises at this stage is: What happened to the original Neyman–Pearson criticism of the inappropriateness of the p-value? It is ironic that in most modern textbooks on statistical inference the p-value is considered as part and parcel of the Neyman–Pearson approach to testing! The commonly used justification for using the p-value, often called the *observed significance level*, in the context of a N–P test, is that:

the critical value c_α depends on the significance level α, which is often arbitrary, except for the requirement of being "small"…   (Azzalini (1996))

Both Fisher and Neyman would turn in their graves if they were to find out how the modern textbook hybrid on hypothesis testing managed to reconcile what they considered irreconcilable differences! As argued by Gigerenzer (1987) the current textbook version of hypothesis testing constitutes a monstrous hybrid of these two fundamentally different approaches to testing. After all, the significance level is a property of the test itself, irrespective of any observed data, but the p-value is a measure which is inextricably bound up with the specific data under consideration.

The choice of a test statistic

There is no doubt that initially the choice of pivotal functions and the resulting test statistics seemed *ad hoc* and arbitrary. It is also generally accepted that the Neyman–Pearson formulation has provided a more formal framework in the context of which such choices could be made. However, the truth of the matter is that the only formal result in this context remains the Neyman–Pearson lemma which is of very limited practical value. Of more practical value is the likelihood ratio test, but again its value in relation to the Neyman–Pearson stated objective is limited because it yields UMP tests only in a few cases where the ratio is a monotone function of a certain statistic. In all other cases the modeler finds himself scrambling to transform the likelihood ratio in ways that enable him to *recognize* known pivotal quantities; the same thing Neyman and Pearson criticized Fisher for! This was the case in testing the hypotheses (14.52). This solution, however, takes us all the way back to Fisher's view that there are certain natural "test distances" based on pivotal functions whose form depends on the particular statistical model postulated.

By the 1940s it was known that there are certain natural pivotal functions associated with the location/scale families of distributions (see Casella and Berger (1990)):

Type of density	Form of density	Pivotal functions
Location	$f(x-\mu)$	$(\hat{\mu}_n - \mu)$
Scale	$\frac{1}{\sigma}f(\frac{x}{\sigma})$	$\left(\frac{\hat{\mu}_n}{\sigma}\right)$
Location-scale	$\frac{1}{\sigma}f(\frac{x-\mu}{\sigma})$	$\left(\frac{\hat{\mu}_n - \mu}{s}\right)$

In addition, these pivotal functions can be used in conjuction with the following lemma to derive more general results.

Pivotal quantities lemma

Let $q(\mathbf{X}, \ell(\boldsymbol{\theta}))$ be a pivotal quantity for $\ell(\boldsymbol{\theta})$ and consider the hypotheses:

(a) $H_0: \ell(\boldsymbol{\theta}) = a_0$ against $H_1: \ell(\boldsymbol{\theta}) \neq a_0$,
(b) $H_0: \ell(\boldsymbol{\theta}) = a_0$ against $H_1: \ell(\boldsymbol{\theta}) > a_0$,
(c) $H_0: \ell(\boldsymbol{\theta}) = a_0$ against $H_1: \ell(\boldsymbol{\theta}) < a_0$,

where a_0 is a known constant. In the case where:

$$\tau(\mathbf{X}) = q(\mathbf{X}, a_0),$$

$\tau(\mathbf{X})$ is a test statistic for testing all the above (a)–(c) hypotheses.

Example

The t-test discussed above is a particular case of this result with $\ell(\mu) = \mu$ and the pivotal quantity as given by Gosset (see (14.11)); see Barndorff-Nielsen and Cox (1994) for further discussion on pivots.

Returning to the likelihood ratio method, the only general procedure for deriving "optimal" (close to UMP) tests in the Neyman–Pearson approach, we note that in cases where the modeler cannot recognize a known pivotal function (the rule rather than the exception in econometric modeling), the only way to define a test is to use the asymptotic form of the ratio. A glance at the likelihood ratio test statistic $\lambda_n(\mathbf{X}) = \frac{\max_{\theta \in \Theta_0} L(\theta; \mathbf{X})}{\max_{\theta \in \Theta} L(\theta; \mathbf{X})}$ reveals that it could not be used within the context of the Fisher approach because it confines the testing to be within the boundaries of the postulated model; we include only models parametrized by $\theta \in \Theta$. As mentioned above, however, this test is asymptotically equivalent to the score test which can be interpreted as a Fisher test because it only involves the evaluation of the likelihood function under the null hypothesis! As shown above, for the simple hypothesis $H_0: \theta = \theta_0$:

$$\frac{1}{\sqrt{n}} s(\mathbf{X}; \theta_0) \overset{H_0}{\underset{\alpha}{\sim}} N(0, \mathcal{I}_\infty(\theta_0)),$$

can be used as the natural distance function to define an asymptotic test statistic of the form:

$$s(\mathbf{X}) = \frac{1}{n} [s(\theta_0; \mathbf{X})]^2 (\mathcal{I}_\infty(\theta_0))^{-1} \overset{H_0}{\underset{\alpha}{\sim}} \chi^2(1).$$

Moreover, this result can be easily extended to the case of a vector of parameters as well the case where the null hypothesis involves only a subset of the unknown parameters. The crucial feature of the score test that in certain cases it enables us to view it as a Fisher test is that the alternative hypothesis does not enter the derivation! By the same token, the Wald test cannot be viewed as a Fisher test.

It is interesting to NOTE that when the "heated" exchanges between Fisher and Neyman–Pearson took place (see Hacking (1965)), between the late 1920s and the mid 1940s, the above asymptotic test procedures were yet to be developed. In a certain sense the above result "takes the sting out of" the Neyman–Pearson argument that the distance functions for the Fisher tests are *ad hoc* and arbitrary. The fact of the matter is that the score function often provides a natural distance for testing purposes because it constitutes a kind of natural "metric" for the particular family of distributions postulated (see Rachev (1992) on probability metrics). There is a touch of irony in this result because the leading proponent of finite sample statistical inference (Fisher) is vindicated (at least partially) by asymptotic theory!

14.6 Conclusion

In the introduction to this chapter we refer to the thesis by Gigerenzer (1987) in relation to the "hybrid theory of testing". Gigerenzer *et al.* (1989, p. 106) described the situation as follows:

Although the debate [Fisher versus Neyman–Pearson] continues among statisticians, it was silently resolved in the "cookbooks" written in the 1940s to the 1960s, largely by non-statisticians, to teach students in the social sciences "the rules of statistics". Fisher's theory of significance testing, which was historically first, was merged with concepts from the Neyman–Pearson theory and taught as "statistics" per se. We call this compromise the "hybrid theory" of statistical inference, and it goes without saying that neither Fisher nor Neyman and Pearson would have looked with favor on this offspring of their forced marriage ...

The above discussion proposes a reinterpretation of both the Fisher and the Neyman–Pearson approaches to testing, viewing them as complementary not as substitutes. Their two main differences come in the form of their:

(i) basic objective,   and   (ii) implicit maintained hypothesis.

This renders the Neyman–Pearson better suited for testing within and the Fisher approach better suited for testing without the boundaries of the postulated model. As argued in the next chapter, misspecification testing constitutes the quintessential form of testing without and thus the Fisher approach, as formalized above, is tailor made for such a purpose; the Neyman–Pearson approach needs to be modified in order to be used for misspecification testing purposes.

14.7 Exercises

1   Compare a test as viewed by Edgeworth and Pearson. What has Pearson added to testing a hypothesis of interest?

2   Describe the Fisher procedure for testing a hypothesis of the form:
$$H_0 : \theta \in \Theta_0.$$

3   Explain the concept of a p-value as used by Fisher.

4   "A hypothesis of interest in a Neyman–Pearson test specified by:
$$H_0 : \theta \in \Theta_0, \text{ against } H_1 : \theta \in \Theta_1,$$
is ultimately a hypothesis about distributions and not parameters." Explain.

5   Explain the notions of a simple and a composite hypothesis.

6   Explain the notions of a type I and type II error. Why does one increase when the other decreases?

7 How does the Neyman–Pearson procedure solve the problem of a trade-off between the type I and type II errors?

8 Explain why we care about one-sided tests.

9 "A Neyman–Pearson test is not just a test statistic." Explain.

10 How do we define an optimal test? How is that related to the notion of an optimal estimator? (hint: think of the ideal in each case).

11 Explain the notions of (a) the power of a test at a point and (b) the power function.

12 What do we mean by a uniformly most powerful test? "UMP tests are scarce." Explain.

13 Explain the notions of (a) unbiased test and (b) Consistent test.

14 Explain the Neyman–Pearson lemma and comment on its limitations.

15 Explain the likelihood ratio test procedure and comment on its relationship to the Neyman–Pearson lemma.

16 Explain why when the postulated model is misspecified all Neyman–Pearson type tests will be invalid.

17 In the context of the simple Normal model derive tests for the following hypotheses:

$$H_0:\mu>_0, \quad H_1:\mu\leq\mu_0,$$
$$H_0:\mu<\mu_0, \quad H_1:\mu\geq\mu_0,$$
$$H_0:\sigma^2>\sigma_0^2, \quad H_1:\sigma^2\leq\sigma_0^2,$$
$$H_0:\sigma^2<\sigma_0^2, \quad H_1:\sigma^2\geq\sigma_0^2.$$

18 Compare and contrast the Fisher and Neyman–Pearson approaches to hypothesis testing.

19 "The main difference between the Fisher and Neyman–Pearson approaches to testing is that the latter involves an alternative hypothesis." Explain why this is a red herring.

20 Explain the notions testing within and testing without.

21 Using the following data on the number of births in Cyprus:

year	males	females	total
1993	5442	5072	10514
1994	5335	5044	10379
1995	5152	4717	9869

test, in the Neyman–Pearson framework, the following hypotheses at $\alpha=0.01$:

(a) Arbuthnot's conjecture for each year separately:

$H_0:\theta=0.5$ against $H_1:\theta<0.5$.

(b) N. Bernoulli's conjecture for each year separately:

$H_0:\theta=0.4857$ against $H_1:\theta>0.4857$.

(c) Repeat (a)–(b) as Fisher tests.

22 Explain how the power of the t-test increases with the sample size. State any desirable properties of the t-test.

15 Misspecification testing

15.1 Introduction

Misspecification testing is concerned with testing the adequacy of the probabilistic assumptions comprising the postulated statistical model, in the light of the observed data. In the present book a statistical model is defined as a set of compatible probabilistic assumptions from the three basic categories:

(D) Distribution, (M) Dependence and (H) Heterogeneity, (15.1)

(see chapters 4–14). A statistical model purports to provide an adequate description of the stochastic mechanism that gave rise to the observed data in question; adequate in the sense that it captures all the systematic (statistical) information in the data.

In order to make the discussion more specific, let us consider the **simple Normal model**:

[i]   Statistical GM: $X_k = E(X_k) + \varepsilon_k$, $k \in \mathbb{N}$,

[ii] Probability model:

$$\Phi = \left\{ f(x; \boldsymbol{\theta}) = \frac{1}{\sigma\sqrt{2\pi}} \exp\left\{ -\frac{1}{2\sigma^2}(x - \mu)^2 \right\}, \ \boldsymbol{\theta} \in \mathbb{R} \times \mathbb{R}_+, x \in \mathbb{R} \right\},$$

$$\boldsymbol{\theta} := (\mu, \sigma^2), \text{ where } \mu = E(X_k), \ \sigma^2 = Var(X_k), k \in \mathbb{N}, \tag{15.2}$$

[iii] Sampling model: $\mathbf{X} := (X_1, X_2, \ldots, X_n)$ is a random sample.

This model comprises three probabilistic assumptions:

[1]: $X_k \sim N_k(.)$, for all $k = 1, 2, \ldots, n$,
[2]: $(X_1, X_2, \ldots, X_n)$ are Independent,
[3]: $(X_1, X_2, \ldots, X_n)$ are Identically Distributed.

Misspecification testing amounts to assessing the validity of the assumptions [1]–[3], given a particular data set $\mathbf{x} := (x_1, x_2, \ldots, x_n)$. It is important to emphasize once more the requirement for internal consistency of the model assumptions with regard to the coherence of any form of statistical inference based on such models. For instance, in the above case the distribution could not have been the Cauchy (see appendix A) because the decomposition in [i] does not exist in the latter case since $E(X_k) = \infty$.

15.1.1 A bird's eye view of the chapter

After some introductory remarks tracing the roots of misspecification testing, the problem of testing the assumptions underlying the postulated statistical model is formulated in section 2. We proceed to discuss the appropriateness of the two procedures to testing discussed in chapter 14, the Fisher and Neyman–Pearson approaches. It is argued that the Fisher approach is better suited for misspecification testing purposes. In section 3 we discuss an assortment of misspecification tests proposed in the literature as a prelude to a more systematic approach to the problem of deriving such tests in the context of the probabilistic reduction (PR) approach discussed in section 4. It is argued that the PR approach provides certain distinct advantages in misspecification testing. In section 5 we consider several empirical examples in order to illustrate both misspecification testing (testing without) and hypothesis testing (testing within).

15.1.2 Tracing the roots of misspecification testing

Historically we can trace the problem of misspecification testing back to the early 20th century in connection with Pearson's *goodness of fit* chi-square test (see chapter 14). This was the first misspecification test whose primary objective was to assess the validity of the modeler's choice of a frequency curve to describe the data in question.

As argued in chapter 13, Pearson's approach to statistics revolved around choosing a frequency curve from the Pearson family which was supposed to describe the observed data best. This choice was made on the basis of the first four sample raw moments. Pearson's chi-square test in this context amounted to assessing whether some distance between the observed frequencies and the theoretical frequencies (the chosen frequency curve) is significantly different from zero. This is a misspecification test for the adequacy of a distributional assumption. As argued in chapter 13, Pearson's approach to statistics was essentially within the descriptive statistics framework, but a number of his results can be re-interpreted in the context of modern statistical inference.

A statistical model, as defined in this book, also involves certain dependence and heterogeneity assumptions. These assumptions, however, were not explicitly specified in the early 20th century. Indeed, at that time the independence assumption was implicit in almost all modeling with the exception of certain discussions on temporal correlation (see Hooker (1905)) in the emerging time series literature (see Morgan (1990) for further details). Moreover, heterogeneity was viewed as a distribution problem in the sense that the early view of bimodality was interpreted as being caused by the superposition of different Normal densities (see Pearson (1895,1896)). As mentioned below, it was not until the 1920s that the possibility of handling observed data exhibiting non-IID features was raised.

The problem of misspecification testing itself is clearly stated for the first time in Fisher's classic[1] *Statistical Methods for Research Workers*, first published in 1925:

---

[1] 'Classic' is used in the sense that everybody quotes but nobody reads.

(iii) Problems of Distribution include the mathematical deduction of the exact nature of the distribution in random samples of our estimates of the parameters and other statistics designed **to test the validity of our specification**[2] (test of Goodness of Fit).   (p. 8)

In chapter 4 of the same book, Fisher discussed Pearson's chi-square test and how it can be applied to test not only the distribution assumption but also the independence and homogeneity assumptions. It is true that the tests of the latter two assumptions are limited to simple discrete random variables taking a small number of values, but the fact of the matter is that, viewed retrospectively, they constitute the first simple misspecification tests. Hence, when Fisher refers to goodness of fit in the above quotation he had more in mind the testing the validity of the distribution assumption. Fisher's utilization of Pearson's chi-square test in the context of experimental design modeling, and his popularization of the t-test and *F*-tests, gave rise to numerous attempts to extend and robustify them; render them less sensitive to departures from the Normality assumption. Early attempts to test the randomness of the sample were based on the so-called *runs* (see Gibbons (1985)). These results are known today as *non-parametric tests* which utilize ordered samples (see chapters 4, 11) and ranks (see below). Naturally, these tests ignore some aspects of the data such as the nature of the measurement scale and support set. By the late 1930s, however, the result proved by Kolmogorov (1933b) provided the foundation for a new class of misspecification tests for distribution assumptions based on the empirical cumulative distribution function (see chapter 10).

The problem of testing the more general temporal independence and homogeneity assumptions had to wait for a few more years. The necessity for testing the validity of the temporal independence and homogeneity assumptions was noted by Yule (1921) but was stated for the first time most clearly by Yule (1926), in his classic paper on *non-sense correlations*. Referring to the formula of correlation he argued that:

it is generally as well to examine the particular assumptions from which it [a theoretical formula] was deduced and see which of them are inapplicable to the case in point...(pp. 328–9)

Yule went on to refer explicitly to the notions of Independence and Identical distribution at an informal level and proceeded to call their validity into question in the case of his data on marriage and mortality:

Neither series, obviously, in the least resembles a random series as required by assumption (3) [temporal independence]...   (p. 329)

After this classic paper by Yule, modelers dealing with time series data in the context of the **Normal/Linear regression:**

[i]   Statistical GM: $Y_t = \beta_0 + \beta_1 x_t + u_t, \ t \in \mathbb{T}$,

[ii]   Probability model:

$$\Phi = \left\{ f(y_t | x_t; \theta) = \frac{1}{\sigma\sqrt{2\pi}} \exp\left\{ -\frac{(y_t - \beta_0 - \beta_1 x_t)^2}{2\sigma^2} \right\}, \ \theta \in \mathbb{R}^2 \times \mathbb{R}_+, \ y_t \in \mathbb{R} \right\},$$

$$\theta := (\beta_0, \beta_1, \sigma^2), \ \beta_0 = E(Y_t) - \beta_1 E(X_t), \ \beta_1 = \frac{Cov(Y_t, X_t)}{Var(X_t)},$$

---

[2] Emphasis added.

$$\sigma^2 = Var(Y_t) - \frac{[Cov(Y_t, X_t)]^2}{Var(X_t)}, \tag{15.3}$$

[iii]   Sampling model: $(Y_1, Y_2, ..., Y_T)$ is an independent sample,

were painfully aware of the dangers of deriving nonsensical conclusions. Indeed, one can make a case that econometric modeling moved away from time series data until the early 1950s in an attempt to avoid invalid conclusions.

The first result in relation to deriving a misspecification test for temporal correlation in the context of the simple Normal model (15.2) was given by Von Neumann (1941). He proposed what is known nowadays as the Von Neumann ratio:

$$v(\mathbf{X}) = \frac{\sum_{k=2}^{n}(\hat{\varepsilon}_k - \hat{\varepsilon}_{k-1})^2}{\sum_{k=1}^{n}\hat{\varepsilon}_k^2}, \text{ where } \hat{\varepsilon}_k = X_k - \hat{\mu}, \ \hat{\mu} = \frac{1}{n}\sum_{k=1}^{n}X_k.$$

It can be shown that this statistic can be approximated by:

$$v(\mathbf{X}) \approx 2(1 - \hat{\rho}), \text{ where } \hat{\rho} = \frac{\sum_{k=2}^{n}(X_k - \hat{\mu})(X_{k-1} - \hat{\mu})}{\sum_{k=2}^{n}(X_{k-1} - \hat{\mu})^2},$$

showing most clearly that it is based on the first-order sample autocorrelation coefficient of the process $\{X_k\}_{k=1}^{\infty}$. Von Neumann (1941) and Anderson (1942) gave the exact distribution of this coefficient (see Anderson (1948)):

$$\hat{\rho} = \frac{1}{2}(v(\mathbf{X}) - 2) \sim D(.);$$

see Anderson (1971), p. 345, for the table of percentage points of this distribution. This test can be viewed as one of the earliest misspecification tests for temporal first-order dependence. Indeed, even in the 1950s informal tests of temporal independence were primarily based on the significance of the first few estimated sample autocorrelation coefficients:

$$\hat{\rho}(\tau) = \frac{\sum_{k=\tau+1}^{n}(X_k - \hat{\mu})(X_{k-1} - \hat{\mu})}{\sum_{k=2}^{n}(X_{k-1} - \hat{\mu})^2}, \ \tau = 1, 2, ...$$

The Durbin–Watson test statistic extends the Von Neumann result to testing first-order temporal dependence in the context of the Normal/Linear regression model (15.3) and takes the form:

$$DW(\mathbf{X}) = \frac{\sum_{k=2}^{n}(\hat{u}_k - \hat{u}_{k-1})^2}{\sum_{k=1}^{n}\hat{u}_k^2}, \text{ where } \hat{u}_k = Y_k - \hat{\beta}_0 - \hat{\beta}_1 x_k, \ k = 1, 2, ..., n.$$

The distribution of this test statistic was tabulated by Durbin and Watson (1950,1951).

Despite this early recognition, the importance of misspecification testing was not fully appreciated by the statistical and econometric literatures until the 1970s. Indicative of this situation is the fact that until the early 1970s the only misspecification test (although not explicitly recognized as such) printed out by most computer packages on linear regression models was the Durbin–Watson test. The reason for this apparent neglect of misspecification testing is twofold. Firstly, the distinction between testing within and testing without has been blurred to this day and thus misspecification testing was not separated from hypothesis testing. To the best of this author's knowledge, the first attempt to systematize misspecification testing and separate the two types of testing in a textbook, was made in Spanos (1986); this attempt, however, was incomplete because at the time the difference between the Fisher and Neyman–Pearson approaches was not very clear to the author. Secondly, the fact that the mainstream statistical literature has concentrated almost exclusively on statistical techniques for analyzing experimental type data, where the problem of misspecification is less crucial, contributed to this neglect.

15.2   Misspecification testing: formulating the problem

In order to motivate some of the concepts needed to formulate the problem of misspecification testing let us consider the *simple Normal model* as specified in (15.2). The probabilistic assumptions specifying the model can be tested by the hypotheses:

(a) $H_0: X_k \sim N_k(.), k = 1, \ldots, n,$ $H_1: X_k \sim D_k(.) \neq N_k(.),$
(b) $H_0: (X_1, X_2, \ldots, X_n)$ are (I), $H_1: (X_1, X_2, \ldots, X_n)$ are non-(I),
(c) $H_0: (X_1, X_2, \ldots, X_n)$ are (ID), $H_1: (X_1, X_2, \ldots, X_n)$ are non-(ID).

As we can see, these hypotheses lie outside the boundaries of the postulated model $(\Phi, \mathbf{X})$ with the implicit maintained hypothesis being $\mathcal{P}$, the set *of all possible probability models*.

How do we specify the set of all possible models?

When postulating a statistical model $(\Phi, \mathbf{X})$, as an adequate description of the stochastic mechanism that gave rise to the observed data $\mathbf{x} := (x_1, x_2, \ldots, x_n)$, we view the latter as a realization of the postulated sample $\mathbf{X} := (X_1, X_2, \ldots, X_n)$. The key to the inductive argument of modern statistical inference is held by the assumption that the observed data constitute one observation in *the set of all possible sample realizations X*, we called the *sample space* (see chapter 11). In the above example of the simple Normal model, the sample space takes the form $X = \mathbb{R}^n$.

In general, the **sample space** is defined as the product of the support of the random variables $(X_1, \ldots, X_n)$ (see chapter 3), i.e.

$$X = \mathbb{R}_{X_1} \times \mathbb{R}_{X_2} \times \ldots \times \mathbb{R}_{X_n}.$$

$\mathcal{P}$ can now be defined as *the family of all joint distributions* $f(x_1, x_2, \ldots, x_n)$ *over X*. For example, in the case where the support of the random variables making up the sample is the real line, $\mathcal{P}$ includes all continuous joint distributions over $\mathbb{R}^n$. Hence, the pair $(\mathcal{P}, X)$ constitutes the modeler's universe of discourse.

Postulating a statistical model amounts to choosing a subset $\mathcal{P}_\theta \subset \mathcal{P}$ whose most general form is:

$$\mathcal{P}_\theta := \{f(x_1, x_2, \ldots, x_n; \boldsymbol{\theta}), \boldsymbol{\theta} \in \Theta, (x_1, x_2, \ldots, x_n) \in X\}, \text{ where } X = \mathbb{R}_{X_1} \times \mathbb{R}_{X_2} \times \ldots \times \mathbb{R}_{X_n}.$$

For example, in the simple Normal model case this subset takes the form:

$$\mathcal{P}_\theta := \left\{ f(x_1, x_2, \ldots, x_n; \boldsymbol{\theta}) = \prod_{k=1}^{n} \frac{1}{\sigma\sqrt{2\pi}} e^{\{-\frac{1}{2\sigma^2}(x_k - \mu)^2\}}, \boldsymbol{\theta} := (\mu, \sigma^2) \in \mathbb{R} \times \mathbb{R}_+, \mathbf{x} \in \mathbb{R}^n \right\}.$$

Given that there is a one-to-one relationship between $\Theta := \mathbb{R} \times \mathbb{R}_+$ and $\mathcal{P}_\theta$, for simplicity we often identify the latter with the parametric probability model Φ defined in terms of the marginal distribution (see (15.2)).

REMARK: it must be stressed that so far we assumed that $\mathcal{P}_\theta$ coincides with Φ only for notational convenience; it should have been $\mathcal{P}_\theta$ all along but in the simple statistical model case it is notationally so much more convenient to use marginal instead of joint distributions.

Using these concepts we can formalize *misspecification testing* in the form of the general hypothesis:

$$H_0: f_0(\mathbf{x}) \in \mathbb{P}_\theta, \text{ against } H_1: f_0(\mathbf{x}) \in [\mathcal{P} - \mathbb{P}_\theta], \tag{15.4}$$

where $f_0(\mathbf{x})$ denotes the true (joint) distribution of the sample. This shows most clearly that, by definition, misspecification testing constitutes a particular form of *testing without*, where:

(i)   the null (H_0) is the postulated statistical model,
(ii)   the implicit alternative (H_1) is its complement with respect to the set of all possible statistical models, and
(iii)   the primary objective is to assess the validity of the postulated model in the light of the observed data.

The main difficulty with the misspecification testing problem is:

How does one operationalize $H_1: f_0(\mathbf{x}) \in [\mathcal{P} - \mathbb{P}_\theta]$?

As shown in the next two subsections, this is still an open question, but a number of suggestions have been made in the literature. Most of these suggestions amount to confining H_1 to the "neighborhood" of the postulated model. We discuss this question in relation to the two alternative approaches to testing discussed in chapter 14.

15.2.1 The Fisher approach and misspecification testing

In view of the discussion in chapter 14 and the above arguments, it must be obvious to the reader that the view adopted in this book is that the Fisher approach is the preferred approach to misspecification testing for three reasons.

(i)   The basic objective of misspecification testing coincides with that of Fisher testing: to utilize the observed data information to bear upon the validity of the hypothesis in question.
(ii)   The hypothesis (15.4) defines a Fisher test with the implicit alternative being the complement for the null hypothesis with respect to the set of all possible statistical models.
(iii)   The null and alternative hypotheses do not have to be defined in terms of the parameter space of the postulated model.

Indeed, one can go as far as pronounce the Fisher approach as tailor made for misspecification testing purposes for an additional reason. A Fisher test, even in the case of a parametric null hypothesis:

$$H_0: \theta = \theta_0,$$

is implicitly about the validity of $f(\mathbf{x}; \theta)$ and less about $\theta = \theta_0$ as such. Let us look at a Fisher test more closely. The *p*-value:

$$\mathbb{P}(\tau(\mathbf{X}) > \tau(\mathbf{x}); H_0 \text{ valid}) = p,$$

on the basis of which the data induced support for the null hypothesis is assessed, depends crucially on the distribution of $\tau(\mathbf{X})$ under the *broader implicit null*:

$$f_0(\mathbf{x}) \in \mathfrak{P}_{\theta_0} \subset \mathfrak{P}_{\theta},$$

which includes H_0 as part of the postulated statistical model. This implies that, when the data do not seem to lend any credence to H_0 it might be because the postulated model (which includes the null as a subset) is invalid! For example, in the case of the null hypothesis $H_0: \mu = 70$, in the context of a simple Normal model, the null might get no support from the observed data because the Normality, or/and the Independence or/and the Identical Distribution assumptions are invalid. Hence, a Fisher test for a parametric null hypothesis is indirectly a test for the validity of the postulated model.

In summary, the main advantages of the Fisher approach for misspecification testing purposes are its generality and its basic objective. The null hypothesis (H_0) might take a parametric form but the alternative (H_1) will be non-parametric in the sense that it cannot be defined in terms of the parameterization $\theta \in \Theta$ of the postulated model. In contrast, the Neyman–Pearson approach requires both to be specified in terms of the parameter space of a postulated model and its basic objective is to choose between the null and the alternative hypotheses.

Fisher parametric (local) misspecification tests*

The question that arises at this stage is whether the Fisher approach can be used to derive misspecification tests based on a parametric specification of the null hypothesis. Returning to misspecification testing as defined in (15.4), this amounts to deriving general misspecification tests based on the hypotheses:

$$H_0: \boldsymbol{\theta} = \boldsymbol{\theta}_0, \ (\boldsymbol{\theta}_0 \in \Theta_0), \text{ against } H_0: f_0(\mathbf{x}) \in [\mathcal{P} - \mathfrak{P}_{\theta_0}]. \tag{15.5}$$

As mentioned above, apart from the various pivotal functions for specific families of distributions, another promising approach seems to be the score function suggesting natural *distances* as the basis of such tests. Let us consider that possibility in some more detail. For simplicity we consider the question where θ is a scalar.

In the previous section we argued that the score function enjoyed three useful properties (see chapters 13–14) whose validity depends crucially on the assumption of *correct specification*. Let us return to those properties in order to explore that connection in more detail. Assuming that $f_0(\mathbf{x})$ denotes the true distribution of the sample:

[i] $E[s(\mathbf{X}; \theta)] \overset{©}{=} 0,$

where $\overset{©}{=}$ reads equal under the assumption of correct specification, can be proved as follows.

Step 1 Using the definition of the score function as a function of $\mathbf{X}$, $s(\mathbf{X}; \theta) = \frac{d}{d\theta} \ln f(\mathbf{x}; \theta)$:

$$E\left(\frac{d}{d\theta} \ln f(\mathbf{x}; \theta)\right) = \int_{x \in X} \left(\frac{d}{d\theta} \ln f(\mathbf{x}; \theta)\right) f_0(\mathbf{x}) d\mathbf{x} = \int_{x \in X} \frac{1}{f(\mathbf{x};\theta)} \left(\frac{df(\mathbf{x};\theta)}{d\theta}\right) f_0(\mathbf{x}) d\mathbf{x}.$$

Step 2 Assuming correct specification: $f(\mathbf{x}; \theta) = f_0(\mathbf{x}),$

$$\int_{x \in X} \frac{1}{f(x;\theta)} \left(\frac{df(x;\theta)}{d\theta} \right) f_0(\mathbf{x}) d\mathbf{x} = \int_{x \in X} \left(\frac{df(x;\theta)}{d\theta} \right) d\mathbf{x} = \frac{d}{d\theta} \int_{x \in X} f_0(\mathbf{x}) d\mathbf{x} = 0,$$

where the second equality follows from the assumption that we can interchange integration and differentiation. It is clear from the above derivation that in the case where the assumption of correct specification does not hold, the score function does not have mean zero. Intuition suggests that even though the estimated score function $s(\mathbf{X}; \hat{\theta}_{MLE})$ cannot be used as a test distance because it is zero by definition, as argued in the previous section, there is no reason not to use $s(\mathbf{X}; \theta_0)$.

Example

Consider the simple Normal model (15.2) with one unknown parameter $\theta = \mu$, (σ^2 is assumed known for simplicity). The log-likelihood and the derivatives take the form:

$$\ell(\mu_0) := \ln f(\mathbf{x};\theta) = -\frac{n}{2} \ln (2\pi) - \frac{n}{2} \ln (\sigma^2) - \frac{1}{2\sigma^2} \sum_{k=1}^{n} (X_k - \mu_0)^2.$$

$$\ell'(\mu_0) := \frac{d \ln f(x;\theta)}{d\theta} = \frac{1}{\sigma^2} \sum_{k=1}^{n} (X - \mu_0), \quad \frac{d^2 \ln f(x;\theta)}{d\theta^2} = -\frac{n}{\sigma^2}.$$

As shown in the previous section, the distance that suggests itself is:

$$s(\mathbf{X}) = \frac{1}{n} [\ell'(\mu_0)]^2 (I_\infty(\mu_0))^{-1} = \frac{\sigma^2}{n} \left[\frac{1}{\sigma^2} \sum_{k=1}^{n} (X - \mu_0) \right]^2 = \left(\frac{n(\bar{X} - \mu_0)^2}{\sigma^2} \right) \overset{H_0}{\underset{\alpha}{\sim}} \chi^2(1).$$

This example brings out several interesting issues which deserve some further discussion.

The **first** is that the above test is asymptotically equivalent to the well known t-test discussed above. This confirms our conjecture above that, even in cases where a test in connection with a parameter value is considered, the Fisher test will be implicitly a test of misspecification. The lesson to be learned from this is that the score function will bring out *natural distance functions* relating to a parameter(s) $\boldsymbol{\theta}$, but the modeler should not rely on the asymptotic distribution; he/she should look for finite sample results when available or improve upon the asymptotic approximation. The **second** issue worth elaborating on is that the above example brings out a weakness of the score test when used for misspecification testing purposes. The weakness is that the resulting test will inevitably revolve around the particular parameterization of the postulated model. This restricts the scope of the misspecification test considerably.

Let us turn to the second property showing that the variance of the score function coincides with the Fisher Information:

$$[ii] \quad Var[s(\mathbf{X};\theta)] \overset{\copyright}{=} E(s^2(\mathbf{X};\theta)) := I_n(\theta).$$

Step 1 By definition: $E(s^2(\mathbf{X};\theta)) = \int_{x \in X} \left(\frac{1}{f(x;\theta)} \left(\frac{df(x;\theta)}{d\theta} \right) \right)^2 f_0(\mathbf{x}) d\mathbf{x}.$
In view of the fact that:

$$\frac{d^2}{d\theta^2} \ln f(\mathbf{x};\theta) = \frac{d}{d\theta} \left(\frac{1}{f(x;\theta)} \frac{df(x;\theta)}{d\theta} \right) = \frac{1}{f(x;\theta)} \frac{d^2 f(x;\theta)}{d\theta^2} - \left(\frac{1}{f(x;\theta)} \frac{df(x;\theta)}{d\theta} \right)^2,$$

$$\left(\frac{1}{f(x;\theta)} \frac{df(x;\theta)}{d\theta} \right)^2 = \frac{1}{f(x;\theta)} \frac{d^2 f(x;\theta)}{d\theta^2} - \frac{d^2}{d\theta^2} \ln f(\mathbf{x};\theta).$$

Substituting this into the above definition:

$$\int_{x \in X} \left(\frac{1}{f(x;\theta)} \left(\frac{df(x;\theta)}{d\theta} \right) \right)^2 f_0(\mathbf{x}) d\mathbf{x} = \int_{x \in X} \left(\frac{1}{f(x;\theta)} \frac{d^2 f(x;\theta)}{d\theta^2} - \frac{d^2}{d\theta^2} \ln f(\mathbf{x};\theta) \right) f_0(\mathbf{x}) d\mathbf{x}.$$

Step 2 Under the assumption of correct specification:

$$\int_{x\in X}\left(\frac{1}{f(x;\theta)}\frac{d^2 f(x;\theta)}{d\theta^2}\right)f_0(x)dx = \int_{x\in X}\left(\frac{d^2 f(x;\theta)}{d\theta^2}\right)dx = \frac{d}{d\theta}\int_{x\in X}\left(\frac{df(x;\theta)}{d\theta}\right)dx = 0,$$

where the last equality depends on property [i], and thus:

$$E(s^2(X;\theta)) = \int_{x\in X}\left(\frac{d^2}{d\theta^2}\ln f(x;\theta)\right)f_0(x)dx := J_n(\theta).$$

The above derivation makes it clear that the equality:

$$I_n(\theta) := E\left(\left(\frac{d\ln f(x;\theta)}{d\theta}\right)^2\right) = -E\left(\frac{d^2\ln f(x;\theta)}{d\theta^2}\right) := J_n(\theta),$$

holds only under the assumption of correct specification. Hence, intuition suggests that an obvious distance to be used for testing the assumption of correct specification is:

$$|I_n(\theta_0) - J_n(\theta_0)| \approx 0.$$

White (1982) proposed **the Information matrix test** in the general case where θ involves k unknown parameters based on the sample analogues of these quantities. In such a case these two matrices, because of symmetry, have at most $r = \frac{1}{2}k(k+1)$ different elements. Hence, the best way to set up a test is to consider the elements defined in terms of the derivatives of the log-density function:

$$\delta_\ell(X;\boldsymbol{\theta}) = \left(\frac{\partial\ln f(x;\theta)}{\partial\theta_i}\right)\left(\frac{\partial\ln f(x;\theta)}{\partial\theta_j}\right) + \frac{\partial^2\ln f(x;\theta)}{\partial\theta_i\theta_j}, \ \ell = 1,2,\ldots,m, \ (m\le r).$$

The sample equivalent of this quantity is:

$$\hat{\delta}_\ell(X) = \frac{1}{n}\sum_{k=1}^{n}\delta_\ell(X_k;\hat{\boldsymbol{\theta}}), \ \ell = 1,2,\ldots,m,$$

and the test is defined in terms of the quadratic form of $\hat{\boldsymbol{\delta}}(X) := (\hat{\delta}_1(X),\hat{\delta}_2(X),\ldots,\hat{\delta}_m(X))^\top$:

$$n(\hat{\boldsymbol{\delta}}(X))^\top \left(\widehat{Cov}\left(\hat{\boldsymbol{\delta}}(X)\right)\right)^{-1}\hat{\boldsymbol{\delta}}(X) \overset{H0}{\underset{\alpha}{\sim}} \chi^2(m).$$

Example
Consider the simple Normal model with two unknown parameter $\boldsymbol{\theta} := (\mu,\sigma^2)$. The log-likelihood and the derivatives takes the form:

$$\ln f(x;\boldsymbol{\theta}) = -\frac{1}{2}\ln(2\pi) - \frac{1}{2}\ln\sigma^2 - \frac{1}{2\sigma^2}(X-\mu)^2,$$

$$\frac{\partial\ln f(x;\boldsymbol{\theta})}{\partial\mu} = \frac{1}{\sigma^2}(X-\mu), \ \frac{\partial^2\ln f(x;\boldsymbol{\theta})}{\partial\mu^2} = -\frac{1}{\sigma^2},$$

$$\frac{\partial\ln f(x;\boldsymbol{\theta})}{\partial\sigma^2} = -\frac{1}{2\sigma^2} + \frac{1}{2\sigma^4}(X-\mu)^2, \ \frac{\partial^2\ln f(x;\boldsymbol{\theta})}{\partial\sigma^4} = \frac{1}{2\sigma^4} - \frac{1}{\sigma^6}(X-\mu)^2,$$

$$\frac{\partial^2\ln f(x;\boldsymbol{\theta})}{\partial\mu\partial\sigma^2} = -\frac{1}{\sigma^4}(X-\mu),$$

$$\left(\frac{\partial\ln f(x;\boldsymbol{\theta})}{\partial\mu}\right)^2 + \frac{\partial^2\ln f(x;\boldsymbol{\theta})}{\partial\mu^2} = \frac{(X-\mu)^2}{\sigma^4} = \frac{1}{\sigma^2},$$

$$\left(\frac{\partial\ln f(x;\boldsymbol{\theta})}{\partial\sigma^2}\right)^2 + \frac{\partial^2\ln f(x;\boldsymbol{\theta})}{\partial\sigma^4} = \frac{1}{4\sigma^4} + \frac{(X-\mu)^4}{4\sigma^8} - \frac{3(X-\mu)^2}{2\sigma^6} + \frac{1}{2\sigma^4},$$

$$\left(\frac{\partial \ln f(x;\boldsymbol{\theta})}{\partial \mu}\right)\left(\frac{\partial \ln f(x;\boldsymbol{\theta})}{\partial \sigma^2}\right) + \frac{\partial^2 \ln f(x;\boldsymbol{\theta})}{\partial \mu \partial \sigma^2} = -\frac{(X-\mu)}{2\sigma^4} + \frac{(X-\mu)^3}{2\sigma^6} - \frac{(X-\mu)}{\sigma^4},$$

$$\hat{\delta}_1(\mathbf{X}) = \frac{1}{\hat{\sigma}^2}\left(\frac{\sum_{k=1}^n (X-\hat{\mu})^2}{\hat{\sigma}^2} - \frac{n}{\hat{\sigma}^2}\right) = 0,$$

$$\hat{\delta}_2(\mathbf{X}) = \frac{1}{4(\hat{\sigma}^2)^2}\left(\frac{\sum_{k=1}^n (X-\hat{\mu})^4}{(\hat{\sigma}^2)^2} - 3\right),$$

$$\hat{\delta}_3(\mathbf{X}) = \left(\frac{1}{2\hat{\sigma}^2}\right)\frac{\sum_{k=1}^n (X-\hat{\mu})^3}{(\hat{\sigma}^2)^{\frac{3}{2}}}.$$

These statistics show most clearly that the Information matrix test for the simple Normal model yields the skewness-kurtosis test (15.22) discussed in the next section.

This example brings out the main weakness of the Information matrix test. As in the case of the *score test* (see chapter 14), it cannot be a general test of misspecification because it depends crucially on the parameterization of the postulated model. In this case the Information matrix test provides a test for Normality but ignores the Independence and Identical Distribution assumptions. To construct a more general test, we need to take expectations of the score and the information matrix with respect to more general (encompassing) models of the type proposed in section 4 below, in the context of the Probabilistic Reduction approach to misspecification testing. Moreover, in view of the fact that these tests depend exclusively on evaluating the postulated model under the null, these tests can only have local power properties.

In concluding this section we note that Chesher (1984) has shown that the Information matrix misspecification test can be re-interpreted as a score test for the heterogeneity of the parameters $\boldsymbol{\theta}$. The parameterization of the heterogeneity was chosen to be:

$$\boldsymbol{\theta} \sim \mathsf{ID}(\boldsymbol{\theta}_0, \Omega), \text{ with } H_0 : \Omega = \mathbf{0}.$$

In view of the above discussion of the Fisher parametric misspecification tests, this should come as no surprise. The local nature of these tests suggests that there will be several alternative re-interpretations of the Information matrix test based on parametrizations relating to $\boldsymbol{\theta}$.

15.2.2 The Neyman–Pearson approach and misspecification testing

As argued in the previous chapter, the Neyman–Pearson approach to hypothesis testing constitutes *testing within* the boundaries demarcated by the postulated statistical model:

$$\mathfrak{P}_\theta := \{f(x_1, x_2, \ldots, x_n; \boldsymbol{\theta}), \ \boldsymbol{\theta} \in \Theta, \ (x_1, x_2, \ldots, x_n) \in X\}.$$

Hence, as it stands the approach cannot be used to test the model assumptions for three interrelated reasons:

(i) H_1 by its very nature, lies outside the boundaries of the postulated model $\mathfrak{P}_\theta$,
(ii) H_0 cannot not be specified in the form $\theta \in \Theta_0 \subset \Theta$, and
(iii) a N–P test implicitly assumes that the postulated model $\mathfrak{P}_\theta$ is valid.

As argued in chapter 14, the Neyman–Pearson approach reduces the testing problem to a choice between two mutually exclusive subsets $\mathfrak{P}_{\theta_0}$ and $\mathfrak{P}_{\theta_1}$ of $\mathfrak{P}_\theta$ where $\Theta = \Theta_0 \cup \Theta_1$:

$$\mathfrak{P}_{\theta_0} := \{f(x_1,x_2,\ldots,x_n;\boldsymbol{\theta}),\ \boldsymbol{\theta}\in\Theta_0,\ (x_1,x_2,\ldots,x_n)\in X\},$$
$$\mathfrak{P}_{\theta_1} := \{f(x_1,x_2,\ldots,x_n;\boldsymbol{\theta}),\ \boldsymbol{\theta}\in\Theta_1,\ (x_1,x_2,\ldots,x_n)\in X\}.$$

For this procedure to be logically coherent we require that the true distribution $f_0(x)$ belongs to the postulated model $\mathfrak{P}_{\theta_0}$. If this assumption is invalid then the modeler commits:

an **error** of the **quintessential type.**

The type I and II errors pale in comparison with the seriousness of this error: the test will force the modeler to choose between two inappropriate models! Note also that any decision based on optimality considerations is likely to be erroneous in general. As argued in chapter 14, in order to ensure logical coherence, the modeler is advised to use a N–P test (for testing within) after the statistical adequacy of the postulated statistical model has been established.

The question of modifying the Neyman–Pearson in order to be usable in the context of misspecification testing will be discussed in some detail in section 4 below.

15.3 A smorgasbord of misspecification tests

In this section we consider an assortment of misspecification tests that have been discussed in the literature. These tests are grouped in terms of the fundamental taxonomy (15.1). The procedure underlying the derivation of these tests is often *ad hoc* and relies primarily on the imagination of the author to formulate the null hypothesis in an interesting way. These misspecification tests are viewed as Fisher type tests whose formulation is necessarily beyond the boundaries of the postulated model. In the next section we propose a more systematic procedure to derive such tests in the context of the probabilistic reduction framework.

15.3.1 Testing distribution assumptions

Pearson's chi-square test

The first misspecification test for distributional assumptions was the chi-square test proposed by Pearson (1900); see chapter 14. Over the last century this test has proved to be one of the most general and flexible tests in the modeler's armory. Its great virtue is that it can be applied to both continuous and discrete as well as multivariate distributions.

A particularly insightful way to derive this test from first principles is in the context of a multinomial distribution:

$$f(x_1,x_2,\ldots,x_n;\boldsymbol{\theta}) = \frac{n!}{x_0!x_1!x_2!\ldots x_n!}\prod_{k=0}^{n}\theta_0^{x_0}\theta_1^{x_1}\cdots\theta_n^{x_n},\ x_k=0,1,2,\ldots,n,\ k\leq n,$$

$$\boldsymbol{\theta}:=(\theta_1,\theta_2,\ldots,\theta_n),\ x_0=n-\sum_{k=1}^{n}x_k,\ \theta_0=1-\sum_{k=1}^{n}\theta_k.$$

Let us consider the (theoretical) hypothesis:

$$H_0:\theta_1=\theta_1^*,\ \theta_2=\theta_2^*,\ldots,\theta_n=\theta_n^*\ \text{against}\ H_1:\theta_1\neq\theta_1^*\ \text{or}\ \theta_2\neq\theta_2^*\ \text{or}\cdots\text{or}\ \theta_n\neq\theta_n^*.$$

The log-likelihood function is:

$$\ell(\boldsymbol{\theta}) = \ln(n!) - \sum_{k=0}^{n} \ln(x_k!) + \sum_{k=1}^{n} x_k \ln(\theta_k) + x_0(1 - \sum_{k=1}^{n} \ln(\theta_k)).$$

The derivation of the MLEs takes the form:

$$\frac{\partial \ell(\boldsymbol{\theta})}{\partial \theta_k} = \frac{x_k}{\theta_k} - \frac{x_0}{\theta_0} = 0, \Rightarrow \hat{\theta}_k = \frac{x_k}{n}, \; k = 1, 2, \ldots, n.$$

This leads to the asymptotic likelihood ratio test statistic:

$$-2 \ln \lambda_n(\mathbf{X}) = 2 \sum_{k=0}^{n} x_k \ln(\hat{\theta}_k / \theta_k^*) \overset{H_0}{\underset{\alpha}{\sim}} \chi^2(n).$$

This is clearly of theoretical interest only because if we view $(X_1, X_2, \ldots, X_n)$ as the relevant random sample then the heterogeneity of the postulated model implies that in effect we have one observation x_k for each unknown parameter θ_k! However, as Fisher (1924) showed, if the sample represents grouped random variables, (i.e. our random sample is $(\mathbf{X}_1, \mathbf{X}_2, \ldots, \mathbf{X}_m)$ where each $\mathbf{X}_k$, represents a group of $n_k > 1$ random variables taking the value k, where $k = 0, 1, 2, \ldots, m$, and $\sum_{k=0}^{n} n_k = n$), then the MLE becomes $\hat{\theta}_k = \frac{n_k}{n}$ and the asymptotic likelihood ratio statistic takes the operational form:

$$G^2(\mathbf{X}) = 2 \sum_{k=0}^{m} n_k \ln\left(\frac{n_k}{n\theta_k}\right) \overset{H_0}{\underset{\alpha}{\sim}} \chi^2(m). \tag{15.6}$$

Fisher derived this as an asymptotically equivalent test statistic to Pearson's chi-square which takes the form:

$$\eta(\mathbf{X}) = \sum_{k=0}^{m} \frac{(n_k - n\theta_k)^2}{n\theta_k} \overset{H_0}{\underset{\alpha}{\sim}} \chi^2(m). \tag{15.7}$$

NOTE that n_k is the observed frequency of the random variables taking the value k and $n\theta_k$ the expected frequency. Interestingly enough Pearson's test can be viewed as a score test (see Azzalini (1996), pp. 136–7).

It turns out that the test statistics (15.6)–(15.7) are applicable to more general situations than just the multinomial distribution. They apply to any random variable X whose distribution can be reduced to a finite set of probabilities: $(p_1, p_2, \ldots, p_m)$, associated with non-overlapping intervals which constitute a partition of $\mathbb{R}_X$, i.e.

$$(B_1, B_2, \ldots, B_m), \text{ where } B_i \cap B_j = \emptyset, \; i \neq j, i, j = 1, 2, \ldots, m, \text{ and } \bigcup_{k=1}^{m} B_k = \mathbb{R}_X.$$

Theoretically these probabilities can be defined by:

(a) continuous: $p_k = \int_{B_k} f(x)dx,$
(b) discrete: $p_k = \sum_{x_i \in B_k} f(x_i),$ $\Big\} k = 1, 2, \ldots, m$

The applicability of the tests based on (15.6)–(15.7) derives from the fact that in a random sample $(X_1, X_2, \ldots, X_n)$ if we assume that N_k is the observed number of X_is in the interval B_k, then N_k has a Binomial distribution with parameters (p_k, n), $k = 1, 2, \ldots, m$; assuming that the assumption relating to the form of the original distribution $f(x)$ is valid! Hence, $E(N_k) = np_k$, giving rise to the statistic:

$$\eta(\mathbf{X}) = \sum_{k=1}^{m} \frac{(N_k - np_k)^2}{np_k} \overset{H_0}{\underset{\alpha}{\sim}} \chi^2(m-1). \tag{15.8}$$

It is clear from this argument that in the case where the random variable X is discrete and takes only a finite number of values the above test statistic takes all the information into consideration. However, when X is a continuous random variable it is obvious that certain relevant information is ignored by the test statistic (15.8). Moreover, care should be taken when the intervals $(B_1, B_2, \ldots, B_m)$ are chosen because the test statistic depends crucially on this choice. Empirical studies suggest that the best choice is the case where the associated probabilities under the postulated $f(x)$ are the same, giving rise to an unbiased chi-square test (see Mann and Wald (1942)).

Example

Let us return to chapter 10 where we conjectured that the probability of occurrence of the integers 0–9 in the decimal expansion of irrational numbers is Uniform. It turns out that the worst in terms of the chi-square test is that for the decimal expansion of e. The relative frequencies of the decimal expansion of e form the 5000 term expansion:

Integer value	0	1	2	3	4	5	6	7	8	9
Frequency	4947	5056	4969	5026	4966	5046	5132	4959	4972	4925

Applying the chi-square test to the frequencies yields:

$$\eta(\mathbf{x}) = \frac{(4947-5000)^2}{5000} + \frac{(5056-5000)^2}{5000} + \frac{(4969-5000)^2}{5000} + \frac{(5026-5000)^2}{5000} + \frac{(4966-5000)^2}{5000} +$$

$$+ \frac{(5046-5000)^2}{5000} + \frac{(5132-5000)^2}{5000} + \frac{(4959-5000)^2}{5000} + \frac{(4972-5000)^2}{5000} + \frac{(4925-5000)^2}{5000} = 7.274.$$

In view of the fact that $\mathbb{P}(\eta(\mathbf{X}) > \eta(\mathbf{x}); H_0 \text{ is valid}) = 0.609$, the hypothesis appears to be supported by the observations.

The main purpose of Fisher (1924) was to show that in cases where the evaluation of the probabilities $(p_1, p_2, \ldots, p_m)$, depends on q unknown parameters $\boldsymbol{\theta}$:

$$(p_1(\boldsymbol{\theta}), p_2(\boldsymbol{\theta}), \ldots, p_m(\boldsymbol{\theta})),$$

and thus the modeler has to estimate $(\boldsymbol{\theta})$ before evaluating these probabilities, the statistic becomes:

$$\eta(\mathbf{X}) = \sum_{k=1}^{m} \frac{(N_k - np_k(\hat{\boldsymbol{\theta}}))^2}{np_k(\hat{\boldsymbol{\theta}})} \overset{H_0}{\underset{\alpha}{\sim}} \chi^2(m - q - 1). \tag{15.9}$$

There followed a heated exchange between Fisher and Pearson with the latter maintaining that estimating $\boldsymbol{\theta}$ does not affect the asymptotic distribution; Pearson was wrong in his disagreements with Fisher!

Tests based on the ECDF

In chapter 5 we discussed several graphical techniques, such as the P-P and Q-Q plots, which are related to the Empirical Cumulative Distribution Function (ecdf):

$$\hat{F}_n(x) = \frac{[\text{no. of } (X_1, X_2, \ldots, X_n) \text{ whose realization do not exceed } x]}{n},$$

but no attempt was made to measure its difference from the postulated cdf $F_0(x)$.

Kolmogorov's test In chapter 10 we discussed Kolmogorov's distance theorem which quantifies this difference in the case of a random sample $X_1, X_2, \ldots, X_n$ using the distance:

$$\Delta_n := \sup_{x \in \mathbb{R}} |\hat{F}_n(x) - F_0(x)|.$$

Kolmogorov (1933b) proved that in the case where $F_0(x)$ is *continuous*:

$$\lim_{n \to \infty} \mathbb{P}(\sqrt{n}\,\Delta_n \leq z) = 1 - 2\sum_{k=1}^{\infty}(-1)^{k+1}e^{-2k^2z^2}, \text{ for } z > 0, \text{ uniformly in } z. \quad (15.10)$$

In view of the fact that the right-hand side involves no unknown parameters, this result can be used to derive a Fisher misspecification test for the hypothesis:

$$H_0: F(x) = F_0(x), \, x \in \mathbb{R}. \quad (15.11)$$

The *p*-value is defined by: $\mathbb{P}(\sqrt{n}\,\Delta_n(\mathbf{X}) \geq \bar{d}; H_0 \text{ valid}) = p$.

Approximations to such probabilities exist in the literature (see Stephens (1970)).

The implementation of this test can be made even easier using the *probability integral transformation* (see chapter 3) which says that $F_0(x)$ viewed as a transformation of the random variable X reduces the latter to a Uniformly distributed random variable:

$$Z = F_0(X) \sim \mathsf{U}(0,1). \quad (15.12)$$

Using this result the distance simplifies to:

$$\Delta_n := \sup_{z \in [0,1]} |\hat{F}_n(z) - z|.$$

This test can be extended to the more realistic case where $F_0(x; \boldsymbol{\theta})$ includes some unknown parameters ($\boldsymbol{\theta}$):

$$H_0: F(x) \in \Phi_0(x; \boldsymbol{\theta}), \, \boldsymbol{\theta} \in \Theta, \, x \in \mathbb{R}_x.$$

The distance takes the form:

$$\hat{\Delta}_n(\mathbf{X}) = \sup_{-\infty < x < \infty} |F_n(x) - \Phi_0(x; \hat{\boldsymbol{\theta}})|, \, x \in \mathbb{R}_x,$$

where $\hat{\boldsymbol{\theta}}$ is the MLE estimator of the parameter(s) $\boldsymbol{\theta}$. In general, the asymptotic distribution of this statistic will depend on the nature of the underlying distribution (see Stephens (1986)).

Using the division points for the range of the sample $\mathbf{x} := (x_1, x_2, \ldots, x_1)$, say $t_0 < t_1 < \cdots < t_m$, one can show that the ecdf and the Pearson chi-square test are related via:

$$\eta(\mathbf{X}) = n\sum_{k=1}^{m} \frac{[\Delta\hat{F}_n(t_k) - \Delta F_0(t_k)]^2}{\Delta F_0(t_k)}, \text{ where } \Delta F(t_k) := F(t_{k+1}) - F(t_k). \quad (15.13)$$

It turns out that Pearson (1900) chose the weights $(1/\Delta F_0(t_k))$ for the sums of squares of the distance between the observed frequencies and postulated probabilities because the asymptotic distribution of $\eta(\mathbf{X})$ is free of the true distribution $F_0(x)$. The next several statistics can be viewed in the context of such weighted averages.

Quadratic statistics An alternative way to quantify the difference between the ecdf $\hat{F}_n(x)$ and the postulated cdf $F_0(x)$ is in the form of the **Cramer–Von Mises statistic**:

$$\omega^2 = n \int_{-\infty}^{\infty} (\hat{F}_n(x) - F_0(x))^2 \, dF_0(x), \tag{15.14}$$

where $dF_0(x)$ can be thought of as $f_0(x)dx$. This can be viewed as a weighted average of the form:

$$\omega^2 = \int_{-\infty}^{\infty} (\hat{F}_n(x) - F_0(x))^2 \, w(x) d(x), \tag{15.15}$$

which is a continuous index analogue of (15.3) with weights $w(x) := nf_0(x)$. It turned out that this was an inappropriate choice of weight because the integral often diverges. Using the transformed random variable Z (see (15.12)) this can be written in the form:

$$\omega^2 = \int_0^1 \hat{v}_n^2(z) dz, \text{ where } \hat{v}_n(z) := \sqrt{n} \left(\hat{F}_n(z) - z \right). \tag{15.16}$$

As argued in chapter 8, $\hat{v}_n(z)$ converges to a *Brownian bridge*. In terms of the ordered (Uniform) sample this simplifies to:

$$\omega^2 = \frac{1}{12n} + \sum_{k=1}^{n} \left(Z_{[k]} - \left(\frac{2k-1}{2n} \right) \right)^2.$$

Watson (1961,1962) proposed a centered form of the Cramer–Von Mises:

$$U^2 = n \int_{-\infty}^{\infty} [(\hat{F}_n(x) - F_0(x)) - \int_{-\infty}^{\infty} (\hat{F}_n(u) - F_0(u)) \, dF_0(u)]^2 \, dF_0(x), \tag{15.17}$$

which, in terms of the ordered sample, simplifies to:

$$U^2 = \frac{1}{12n} + \sum_{k=1}^{n} \left[Z_{[k]} - \left(\frac{2k-1}{2n} \right) \right]^2 - n(\bar{x} - 0.5)^2.$$

Another variant of the Cramer–Von Mises statistic is the distance:

$$A^2 = n \int_{-\infty}^{\infty} \left[\frac{(\hat{F}_n(x) - F_0(x))^2}{F_0(x)(1 - F_0(x))} \right] dF_0(x), \tag{15.18}$$

proposed by Anderson and Darling (1952,1954), which simplifies to:

$$A^2 = -n - \frac{1}{n} \sum_{k=1}^{n} \{(2k-1)[\ln Z_{[k]} - \ln (1 - \ln Z_{[n+1-k]})]\}.$$

The asymptotic distributions and the power of these statistics have been studied extensively in the literature (see D'Agostino and Stephens (1986), Durbin (1973)).

We conclude this subsection by noting that the above test statistics (15.10), (15.17), (15.14), and (15.18) can be used to quantify the distances discussed in relation to P-P and Q-Q plots discussed in chapter 5.

Tests based on the ordered sample

Another family of misspecification tests for distributional assumptions related to P-P and Q-Q plots (see chapter 5) is the one based on the **ordered sample**:

$$(X_{[1]}, X_{[2]}, \dots, X_{[n]}) \text{ where } X_{[1]} < X_{[2]} < \cdots < X_{[n]}.$$

As argued in chapter 5, the basic idea underlying these plots is that in the case where the random variable X can be standardized by a location (a) and a scale parameter (b), say $Y = \left[\frac{X-a}{b} \right]$, we could use the ordered sample to derive the relationship:

$$E(X_{[k]}) = a + bE(Y_{[k]}), \ k = 1, 2, \dots, n. \tag{15.19}$$

By choosing $E(X_{[k]})$ and $E(Y_{[k]})$ judiciously we could formulate a variety of graphical techniques based on their cross-plot which, under the distributional assumption in question, is expected to give rise to a straight line. For example, a P-P plot utilizes the cross-plot:

$$\left\{\left(\frac{k}{n+1}, F_X(X_{[k]})\right), k = 1,2,\ldots,n\right\}, \text{ where } \frac{k}{n+1} = E[F_X(X_{[k]})].$$

On the other hand, a Q-Q plot utilizes the cross-plot:

$$\{(F_X^{-1}(q_k), X_{[k]})), k = 1,2,\ldots,n\}, \text{ where } F_X^{-1}(q_k) \simeq E(X_{[k]});$$

see chapter 5 for the details regarding the transformation $F_X(X_{[k]})$ and its inverse.

In empirical modeling the relationship (15.19) is expected to be only approximate and thus it can be profitably viewed in the context of an *auxiliary regression* of the form:

$$X_{[k]} = a + bE(Y_{[k]}) + v_k, k = 1,2,\ldots,n,$$

where $v_k = X_{[k]} - a - bE(Y_{[k]})$, $k = 1,2,\ldots,n$. In this sense, the graphical techniques based on closeness to a straight line can be also quantified in terms of goodness of fit measures for this auxiliary regression; how close the observed points are to the hypothetical line.

Testing Normality In the case of a random sample $(X_1, X_2, \ldots, X_n)$ from the Normal distribution:

$$X_k \sim \mathsf{N}(\mu, \sigma^2), k = 1,2,\ldots,n,$$

and $f(y) = \frac{\exp(-y^2)}{\sqrt{2\pi}}$. Hence, the auxiliary regression takes the form:

$$X_{[k]} = \mu + \sigma m_k + v_k, k = 1,2,\ldots,n,$$

where $m_k := E(Y_{[k]}) \simeq F_X^{-1}\left(\frac{k - 0.375}{n + 0.125}\right)$, F_X^{-1} being the inverse of the standard Normal cdf. The estimated σ and the square correlation coefficients take the form:

$$\hat{\sigma} = \frac{\sum_{k=1}^n (X_{[k]} - \bar{X})(m_k - \bar{m})}{\sum_{k=1}^n (m_k - \bar{m})^2}, \quad \hat{\rho}^2 = \frac{[\sum_{k=1}^n (X_{[k]} - \bar{X})(m_k - \bar{m})]^2}{[\sum_{k=1}^n (X_{[k]} - \bar{X})^2] \cdot [\sum_{k=1}^n (m_k - \bar{m})^2]} = \frac{\hat{\sigma}^2 \sum_{k=1}^n (m_k - \bar{m})^2}{[\sum_{k=1}^n (X_k - \bar{X})^2]}.$$

Shapiro and Francia (1972) proposed a test for Normality based on the hypothesis:

$$H_0 : \rho^2 = 0,$$

and derived the empirical distribution of $\hat{\rho}^2$ using Monte Carlo simulations (see chapter 11). This test was proposed as an alternative (for sample sizes $n > 50$) to the test put forward earlier by Shapiro and Wilk (1965). The latter test is of a similar form to that of $\hat{\rho}^2$ but based on the statistic:

$$W(\mathbf{X}) = \frac{[\sum_{k=1}^n \alpha_k X_{[k]}]^2}{[\sum_{k=1}^n (X_k - \bar{X})^2]}, \quad 0 \le W \le 1,$$

where the weights $(\alpha_k, k = 1,2,\ldots,n)$ were tabulated originally by the authors for $n = 3$ to $n = 50$. Tables of the distribution of W have been derived by Monte Carlo simulation (see chapter 11) and reported in Shapiro and Wilk (1965) for sample sizes up to $n = 50$; see D'Agostino and Stephens (1986) for further details. The p-value is defined by:

$$\mathbb{P}(W(\mathbf{X}) < W(\mathbf{x}); H_0 \text{ valid}) = p.$$

Tests based on moments

As argued in chapter 3, assessing distributional assumptions using moments is not a good idea in general, because the latter do not characterize the former. Moreover, when the moments do characterize the distribution, more often than not, an infinite number of moments is needed. On the other hand, when we confine ourselves within a certain family of distributions, only a small number of moments are required to characterize individual members of the family. The classic example is the Pearson family which is defined in terms of the first four moments. Within this family we can characterize several distributions using these moments. For example, the Normal distribution is characterized by:

$$\alpha_3 := \frac{E(X - E(X))^3}{(\sqrt{Var(X)})^3} = 0, \quad \alpha_4 := \frac{E(X - E(X))^4}{(\sqrt{Var(X)})^4} = 3,$$

where (α_3, α_4) denote the skewness and kurtosis coefficients, respectively (see chapter 3). This was recognized by Pearson (1895) in the paper that introduced the Pearson family. He proceeded to estimate these coefficients using their sample analogues:

$$\hat{\alpha}_3 := \frac{\frac{1}{n}\sum_{k=1}^{n}(X_k - \bar{X})^3}{\left(\sqrt{\frac{1}{n}\sum_{k=1}^{n}(X_k - \bar{X})^2}\right)^3}, \quad \hat{\alpha}_4 := \frac{\frac{1}{n}\sum_{k=1}^{n}(X_k - \bar{X})^4}{\left(\sqrt{\frac{1}{n}\sum_{k=1}^{n}(X_k - \bar{X})^2}\right)^4},$$

and derived their asymptotic distribution under the assumption:

$$H_0 : X_k \sim \text{NIID}(0, \sigma^2), \ k = 1, 2, \ldots, n, \tag{15.20}$$

$$\begin{pmatrix} \sqrt{n}\hat{\alpha}_3 \\ \sqrt{n}\hat{\alpha}_4 \end{pmatrix} \underset{\alpha}{\sim} \text{N}\left(\begin{bmatrix} 0 \\ 3 \end{bmatrix}, \begin{bmatrix} 6 & 0 \\ 0 & 24 \end{bmatrix}\right). \tag{15.21}$$

Using this result, he derived the implied equal probability ellipses (see chapter 6). Using the graphs of these ellipses, Pearson argued that the Normality of any random sample could be assessed and recommended the use of the Pearson family when the departures from Normality appear to be serious enough.

These results were first utilized by Fisher (1929) who suggested the asymptotic **skewness kurtosis test** given by:

$$sk(\mathbf{X}) = \frac{n}{6}\hat{\alpha}_3^2 + \frac{n}{24}(\hat{\alpha}_4 - 3)^2 \overset{H0}{\underset{\alpha}{\sim}} \chi^2(2), \ \mathbb{P}(sk(\mathbf{X}) > sk(\mathbf{x}); H_0 \text{ is valid}) = p. \tag{15.22}$$

The next important development was made by E. Pearson (1930) who was able to derive the third and fourth moments of $(\hat{\alpha}_3, \hat{\alpha}_4)$ under the Normality of the sample assumption. Fisher (1930a) and Hsu and Lawley (1939) derived the exact moments up to the sixth, showing that these higher moments were important enough to call into question the use of asymptotic results based on the first two moments. Using these results several attempts were made to approximate the sampling distribution of $(\hat{\alpha}_3, \hat{\alpha}_4)$ under the Normality of the sample assumption. A good approximation to the sampling distribution of $\hat{\alpha}_3$ was suggested by D'Agostino (1970) using the Johnson's S_U distribution (see chapter 4). It was later found that the same distribution can be used to approximate the sampling distribution of $\hat{\alpha}_4$. In view of the fact that for testing Normality we need to combine $(\hat{\alpha}_3, \hat{\alpha}_4)$, the basic difficulty proved to be their dependence. It turns out that even under the Normality of the sample assumption, $\hat{\alpha}_3$ and $\hat{\alpha}_4$ are uncorrelated but not independent:

$$E(\hat{\alpha}_3 \cdot \hat{\alpha}_4) = 0 \text{ but } E(\hat{\alpha}_3^2 \cdot \hat{\alpha}_4) \neq E(\hat{\alpha}_3^2) \cdot E(\hat{\alpha}_4)$$

(see Bowman and Shenton (1975)). In the light of this, the skewness-kurtosis test (15.22) should be used with caution because it ignores not just the dependence between $\hat{\alpha}_3$ and $\hat{\alpha}_4$ but also the higher-order moments! In an attempt to take these factors into consideration D'Agostino and Pearson (1973) proposed a test which is based on the approximation of the distribution of $(\hat{\alpha}_3, \hat{\alpha}_4)$ under the Normality of the sample assumption:

$$D'AP(\mathbf{X}) = h_1^2(\hat{\alpha}_3) + h_2^2(\hat{\alpha}_4) \overset{H_0}{\underset{\alpha}{\sim}} \chi^2(2), \tag{15.23}$$

where $h_1(.)$ and $h_2(.)$ represent their Normalizing transformations:

$$h_1(\hat{\alpha}_3(\mathbf{X})) = \delta \ln\left[(Y/a) + \sqrt{\{(Y/a)^2 + 1\}}\right],$$

$$h_2(\hat{\alpha}_4(\mathbf{X})) = \frac{1}{\sqrt{(2/9V)}}\left(\left(1 - \frac{2}{9V}\right) - \left[\frac{1 - (2/V)}{1 + Z\sqrt{2/(V-4)}}\right]^{\frac{1}{3}}\right),$$

$$Y = \hat{\alpha}_3\left(\frac{(n+1)(n+3)}{6(n-2)}\right)^{\frac{1}{2}}, \ \delta = (\ln w)^{-\frac{1}{2}}, \ \alpha = \left(\frac{2}{w^2-1}\right)^{\frac{1}{2}}, \ w^2 = \sqrt{2\left(\frac{3(n^2+27n-70)(n+1)(n+3)}{(n-2)(n+5)(n+7)(n+9)}\right)} - 1.$$

$$Z = \frac{\hat{\alpha}_4 - \frac{3(n-1)}{n+1}}{\sqrt{\frac{24n(n-2)(n-3)}{(n+1)^2(n+3)(n+5)}}}, \ V = 6 + \frac{8}{U}\left[\frac{2}{U} + \left\{1 + \frac{4}{U^2}\right\}^{\frac{1}{2}}\right], \ U = \frac{6(n^2-5n+2)}{(n+7)(n+9)}\left(\frac{6(n+3)(n+5)}{n(n-2)(n-3)}\right)^{\frac{1}{2}}$$

(see D'Agostino and Stephens (1986)).

The same Normalizing transformations have been used by D'Agostino (1970) to propose a **skewness test** for Normality based on the test statistic:

$$h_1(\hat{\alpha}_3(\mathbf{X})) \overset{H_0}{\underset{\alpha}{\sim}} \mathsf{N}(0,1).$$

Similarly, a **kurtosis test** for Normality based on the following test statistic:

$$h_2(\hat{\alpha}_4(\mathbf{X})) \overset{H_0}{\underset{\alpha}{\sim}} \mathsf{N}(0,1).$$

Both of these tests can be used as one sided or two sided, depending on the situation. They can be best used to shed some light on the source of the evidence against Normality when the omnibus test (15.23) is used.

Tests based on the skewness and kurtosis coefficients can be used to assess other distributional assumptions, especially within the Pearson family. This line of research has not been explored extensively beyond the Normal distribution mainly because of the inherent difficulties of characterizing distributions using moments.

15.3.2 Testing dependence assumptions

Assessing the appropriateness of the **independence** assumption using graphical techniques, such as the t-plot and the scatterplot, has been discussed in chapters 5–6.

Non-parametric tests of independence

In its most general form *independence* of a sample $(X_1, X_2, \ldots, X_n)$ is defined in terms of joint and marginal distributions by:

$$F(x_1, x_2, \ldots, x_n; \boldsymbol{\phi}) \overset{1}{=} \prod_{k=1}^{n} F_k(x_k; \boldsymbol{\theta}_k), \text{ for all } \mathbf{x} := (x_1, x_2, \ldots, x_n) \in \mathbb{R}^n. \tag{15.24}$$

As shown in chapter 6, in the case of dependence the corresponding reduction based on *sequential conditioning* takes the form:

$$F(x_1, x_2, \ldots, x_n; \boldsymbol{\phi}) \overset{\text{non-I}}{=} F_1(x_1; \boldsymbol{\psi}_1) \prod_{k=2}^{n} F_k(x_k | x_{k-1}, \ldots, x_1; \boldsymbol{\psi}_k), \text{ for all } \mathbf{x} \in \mathbb{R}_X^n. \tag{15.25}$$

The simplest form of testing contemporaneous independence comes in the case of the two random variables where:

Independence: $H_0: f(x,y) = f_x(x) \cdot f_y(y)$ for all $(x,y) \in \mathbb{R}_X \times \mathbb{R}_Y$.

Spearman's test This test is based on the following distance:

$$S(X,Y) = 3 \int_{-\infty}^{\infty} \int_{-\infty}^{\infty} [2F_x(x) - 1][2F_y(y) - 1] f(x,y) dx dy,$$

as a measure of dependence (see chapter 4). This test was proposed by Spearman in 1904 and the idea behind it is to measure the way the grades of X and Y co-vary.

First we arrange the values of X and Y in an ascending order, i.e., $(x_{[1]}, x_{[2]}, \ldots, x_{[n]})$ and $(y_{[1]}, y_{[2]}, \ldots, y_{[n]})$, where $x_{[1]}$ is the smallest value taken by $X, x_{[2]}$ is the second smallest, and $x_{[n]}$ the largest value. Next, we define

rank(x_i) = the number of values x_j less than or equal to x_i.

Numerical illustration Consider the following sample realization:

$$(x_1, x_2, x_3, x_4, x_5, x_6) = (2, 8, 1, 6, 4, 9),$$
$$(x_{[1]}, x_{[2]}, x_{[3]}, x_{[4]}, x_{[5]}, x_{[6]}) = (1, 2, 4, 6, 8, 9),$$
$$(r_1, r_2, r_3, r_4, r_5, r_6) = (2, 5, 1, 4, 3, 6).$$

NOTE that for the test to be used the random variables X and Y must be measured on the ordinal scale or higher (see chapter 1). In the case of random variables measured on the interval or ratio scales there is some loss of information when replacing the original observations with their ranks.

Let the ranks of X and Y be denoted by r_i and s_i, $i = 1, 2, \ldots, n$, respectively. *Spearman's rank correlation coefficient* is defined by:

$$r_s(\mathbf{X}, \mathbf{Y}) = -\frac{\sum_{i=1}^{n}(r_i - \bar{r})(s_i - \bar{s})}{\sqrt{\sum_{i=1}^{n}(r_i - \bar{r})^2 \sum_{i=1}^{n}(s_i - \bar{s})^2}}.$$

In view of the fact that:

(i) $\quad \bar{r} := \frac{1}{n}\sum_{i=1}^{n} r_i = \bar{s} := \frac{1}{n}\sum_{i=1}^{n} s_i = \frac{1}{2}(n+1),$

(ii) $\quad \frac{1}{n}\sum_{i=1}^{n}(r_i - \bar{r})^2 = \frac{1}{n}\sum_{i=1}^{n}(s_i - \bar{s})^2 = \frac{(n^2 - 1)}{12},$

we can deduce that:

$$r_s(\mathbf{X}, \mathbf{Y}) = \frac{12}{n(n^2 - 1)}\sum_{i=1}^{n}\left(r_i - \frac{1}{2}(n+1)\right)\left(s_i - \frac{1}{2}(n+1)\right) = 1 - \frac{6}{n(n^2 - 1)}\sum_{i=1}^{n}(r_i - s_i)^2.$$

For small values of n, $(n \leq 10)$ the distribution of $r_s(\mathbf{X}, \mathbf{Y})$ has been tabulated (see Kanji (1993)). For large values of n we use the asymptotic distribution:

$$\left(\sqrt{n-1}\right)r_s(\mathbf{X},\mathbf{Y}) \overset{H_0}{\underset{\alpha}{\sim}} N(0,1).$$

The p-value for this test is defined by: $\mathbb{P}(|r_s(\mathbf{X},\mathbf{Y})| > r_s(\mathbf{x},\mathbf{y}); H_0$ is valid$)=p$.

Kendall's tau test This test is based on the following measure of dependence between two random variables (X, Y):

$$\tau = 2\mathbb{P}((X_1 - X_2)(Y_1 - Y_2) > 0) - 1,$$

where τ can be viewed as the correlation coefficient of the indicator functions of $(X_1 - X_2) > 0$ and $(Y_1 - Y_2) > 0$. As such it can be viewed as the product moment correlation of signs of concordance (see chapter 6). Kendall's test statistic is defined by:

$$\hat{\tau}(\mathbf{X},\mathbf{Y}) = \frac{1}{n(n-1)} \sum_{i=1}^{n} \sum_{\substack{j=1 \\ i \neq j}}^{n} \text{sign}(X_i - X_j) \cdot \text{sign}(Y_i - Y_j),$$

and purports to measure "the extent to which the two samples follow a monotone order." In this sense Kendall's test can be applied to random variables whose measurement scale is the Nominal scale (see chapter 1); this is in contrast to Spearman's where the random variables must be of ordinal scale or higher.

For small values of n, $(n \leq 10)$ the distribution of r_s has been tabulated (see Kanji (1993)). For large values of n we use the asymptotic distribution:

$$\left[\frac{3\sqrt{n(n-1)}}{\sqrt{2(2n+5)}} \right] \hat{\tau}(\mathbf{X},\mathbf{Y}) \overset{H_0}{\underset{\alpha}{\sim}} N(0,1).$$

The p-value for this test is defined by: $\mathbb{P}(|\hat{\tau}(\mathbf{X},\mathbf{Y})| > \hat{\tau}(\mathbf{x},\mathbf{y}); H_0$ is valid$)=p$.

In concluding this subsection we NOTE that the above misspecification tests for testing contemporaneous independence between the pairs (X_k, Y_k), $k = 1, 2, \ldots, n$, can be easily modified for testing temporal independence using the pairs (k, X_k), $k = 1, 2, \ldots, n$.

Moment-based tests of independence

The discussion of dependence in chapters 6–7 suggested that the easiest way to operationalize dependence was in terms of the moments and in particular the relationship between joint, marginal and conditional moments. In this section we will concentrate on deriving a test for linear dependence using the second moments over time.

Assuming that $\{X_k\}_{k=1}^{\infty}$ is a second-order stationary stochastic process we can proceed to measure the first-order dependence using the autocorrelation coefficients:

$$\rho(\tau) = \frac{Cov(X_t, X_{t-\tau})}{Var(X_t)}, \quad \tau = 1, 2, \ldots, n-1.$$

$$\hat{\rho}_n(\tau) = \frac{\left[\frac{1}{n} \sum_{k=\tau}^{n} X_k X_{k-\tau} \right] - \left[\frac{1}{n} \sum_{k=1}^{n} X_k^2 \right]}{\left[\frac{1}{n} \sum_{k=1}^{n} X_k^2 \right] - \left[\frac{1}{n} \sum_{k=1}^{n} X_k \right]^2}, \quad \tau = 1, 2, \ldots, n-1.$$

An obvious way to specify the null hypothesis of no linear dependence is:

$$H_0 : \rho(1) = \rho(2) = \cdots = \rho(m) = 0, \text{ for } m < (n-1).$$

Box and Pierce (1970) proposed the test statistic:

$$q(\mathbf{X}) = n \sum_{\tau=1}^{m} \hat{\rho}_n^2(\tau) \overset{H_0}{\underset{\alpha}{\sim}} \chi^2(m).$$

Ljung and Box (1978) proposed a better finite sample approximation:

$$LB(\mathbf{X}) = \sum_{\tau=1}^{m} \left[\frac{n(n+2)}{(n+\tau)} \right] \hat{\rho}_n^2(\tau) \overset{H_0}{\underset{\alpha}{\sim}} \chi^2(m).$$

McLeod and Li (1983) have extended the above test to the case of *second-order depen-*
dence as measured by the correlation between the squares of the random variables
involved:

$$\gamma(\tau) = \frac{Cov(X_t^2 X_{t-\tau}^2)}{Var(X_t^2)}, \ \tau = 1,2,\ldots,m < (n-1).$$

$\gamma(\tau)$ can be estimated by: $\hat{\gamma}_n(\tau) = \frac{\sum_{k=\tau}^{n}(\hat{u}_k^2 - \hat{\sigma}^2)(\hat{u}_{k-\tau}^2 - \hat{\sigma}_n^2)}{\sum_{k=1}^{n}(\hat{u}_k^2 - \hat{\sigma}_n^2)^2}, \ \tau = 1,2,\ldots,m < (n-1),$ where

$\hat{u}_k := X_k - \hat{\mu}_n, \ \hat{\mu}_n := \frac{1}{n}\sum_{k=1}^{n} X_k, \ \hat{\sigma}_n^2 = \frac{1}{n}\sum_{k=1}^{n} \hat{u}_k^2.$ The McLeod–Li test statistic takes the form:

$$ML(\mathbf{X}) = \sum_{\tau=1}^{m} \left[\frac{n(n+2)}{(n+\tau)} \right] \hat{\gamma}_n^2(\tau) \overset{H_0}{\underset{\alpha}{\sim}} \chi^2(m).$$

15.3.3 Testing heterogeneity assumptions

In the context of a sequence of Independent random variables $\{X_k\}_{k=1}^{\infty}$ the **Identical
Distribution** (ID) assumption amounts to:

$$H_0: F_k(x_k) = F(x_k), \ k = 1,2,\ldots$$

This, however, is not directly testable when we only have a finite sample $(X_1, X_2, \ldots, X_n)$
because we have only one observation for each $F_k(x_k)$. In order to derive operational tests
we need to make certain assumptions in relation to the type of heterogeneity the modeler
has in mind.

This can be illustrated in the case where the heterogeneity is related to the mean of the
postulated distribution. In this case the null hypothesis can be operationalized using the
specification:

$$H_0: F_k(x_k - \mu_k) = F(x_k), \text{ where } \mu_k = \delta_0 + \delta_1 k, \text{ for } k = 1,2,\ldots$$

Parametric In the case of a parametric statistical model (say the simple Normal model)
this can be embedded within the postulated model by extending its mean to be heterogeneous and then testing the hypothesis:

$$H_0: \delta_1 = 0.$$

Non-parametric One of the earliest non-parametric tests for heterogeneity was based on
the signs of the differences:

$$(X_i - X_j), \text{ for all } i \neq j, \ i,j = 1,2,\ldots,n.$$

By defining the sign function:

$$S_{ij} = \begin{cases} 1 & \text{if } (X_i - X_j) < 0, \\ 0 & \text{if } (X_i - X_j) > 0, \end{cases}$$

we can define several test statistics of the form:

$$\sum_{1\leq i\leq j\leq n} c_{ij}S_{ij},$$ where c_{ij} denotes non-negative weights.

Two such test statistics are the Mann (1945) and Daniels (1950), defined by:

$$M = \sum_{1\leq i\leq j\leq n} S_{ij}, \quad D = \sum_{1\leq i\leq j\leq n} (j-i)S_{ij},$$

respectively. Using the assumption that under the random sample assumption all $n!$ orderings of the sample $(X_1, X_2, \ldots, X_n)$ are equally likely, we can deduce that:

$$E(M) = \tfrac{1}{4}n(n-1), \quad Var(M) = \tfrac{1}{72}n(n-1)(2n+5),$$

$$E(D) = \tfrac{1}{12}n(n^2-1), \quad Var(D) = \tfrac{1}{144}n^2(n-1)(n+1)^2.$$

For large enough samples we can use their asymptotic distributions for specifying misspecification tests. For small samples, it interesting to note the relationship between these test statistics and Spearman's test statistic in the case where the pairs are (k, X_k), $k = 1, 2, \ldots, n$; e.g.

$$D = \tfrac{1}{12}(n^3 - n)(1 + \mathfrak{r}_s).$$

This relationship can be utilized to derive trend tests using the tables for Spearman's coefficient. As shown by Cox and Stuart (1955) (see also Bhattacharyya (1984)) these tests have reasonably good *asymptotic relative efficiency* (see chapter 14).

In relation to all the above non-parametric tests it is important to note that they ignore important systematic information which can be crucial in practice. For instance, whatever the nature of the stochastic process $\{X_k\}_{k=1}^{\infty}$ we reduce it to a binary process with considerable loss of information relating to the support of the original process as well as to its measurement scale, i.e. we reduce the original measurement scale to the ordinal scale (see chapter 1).

Kiefer's test Under the IID assumption, the empirical counterpart to $F(x_k)$ is the ecdf $\hat{F}_n(x)$, as defined above, which uses all n observations. Common sense suggests that one way to test homogeneity is to use overlapping subsets of the sample $(X_1, X_2, \ldots, X_n)$ to evaluate different ecdfs and then compare them. With this in mind consider the following procedure.

Chose $m < n$ and define the random vectors:

$$\mathbf{Y}_k := (x_k, x_{k+1}, \ldots, x_{k+m-1}), \ k = 1, 2, \ldots, N.$$

We can proceed to define the ecdf for these vectors using:

$$\hat{F}_N(\mathbf{y}) := \frac{1}{N} \sum_{i=1}^{N} \mathbb{I}_{(-\infty, \mathbf{y}]}(\mathbf{Y}_i),$$

and the distance function:

$$\Delta_N := \sup_{\mathbf{y} \in \mathbb{R}^m} | \hat{F}_N(\mathbf{y}) - F(\mathbf{y}) |.$$

Kiefer (1961) proved that in the case of continuous distributions, for any $\varepsilon > 0$ and some constant $c > 0$:

$$\mathbb{P}\big(\sqrt{N}\Delta_N\le z\big)\ge 1-ce^{-(2-\varepsilon)z^2},\ \text{for } z>0. \tag{15.26}$$

This can be used in conjunction with the LIL:

$$\mathbb{P}\Big(\lim_{N\to\infty}\sup\Big[\tfrac{\sqrt{2N}\,\Delta_N}{\sqrt{2\ln\ln N}}\Big]=1\Big)=1,$$

to set up a test for the ID assumption similar to the Kolmogorov distance test discussed above.

15.3.4 Testing randomness

In chapter 5 we used the notion of runs (up or down) in order to provide an intuitive way to assess the absence of predictability. The notion of runs ignores the numerical values of the data series and concentrates just on the sign of the differences between successive observations, i.e. replace the original observations $(x_1,x_2,...,x_n)$ with the signs of the sequence:

$$(d_1,d_2,...,d_{n-1}),\ \text{where } d_k=x_{k+1}-x_k,\ k=1,2,...,n.$$

For instance, the observations 65–105 in figure 5.4 give rise to the following pattern of ups and downs:

$$+--+-+--+++-++--+-+--+-++-+-+++-++-++-+-.$$

From this sequence of pluses and minuses we discern no regular pattern to be utilized to guess the next up or down. The patterns we have in mind come in the form of **runs**: a sub-sequence of one type (pluses only or minuses only) immediately preceded and succeeded by an element of the other type. In the above case, the runs do not exhibit any regularity because the number of runs up and down are, respectively:

$$\{1,1,1,3,2,1,1,1,2,1,3,2,2,1\}^+,\ \{2,1,2,1,2,1,2,1,1,1,1,1,1,1\}^-.$$

In chapter 5 we considered informally the random variables (see Levene (1952)):

$R-$ number of runs of any size, $\qquad E(R)=\big(\tfrac{2n-1}{3}\big),$

R_k- number of runs of size k, $\qquad E(R_k)=2n\big(\tfrac{k^2+3k-1}{(k+3)!}\big)-2\big(\tfrac{k^3+3k^2-k-4}{(k+3)!}\big),$

R'_k- number of runs of size k or greater, $\quad E(R'_k)=2n\big(\tfrac{k+1}{(k+2)!}\big)-2\big(\tfrac{k^2+k-1}{(k+2)!}\big).$

For large enough sample size (we strongly advise the reader to avoid these tests for small n), the standardized forms of these random variables can be shown to be approximately Normally distributed. The test based on R takes the form:

$$\mathbb{P}(|Z_R|>z_R;\ H_0\ \text{is valid})=p,$$

$$Z_R=\frac{R-E(R)}{\sqrt{Var(R)}}=\frac{R-\big(\tfrac{2n-1}{3}\big)}{\sqrt{\tfrac{16n-29}{90}}}\overset{\text{random sample}}{\underset{\alpha}{\sim}}N(0,1).$$

The tests based on the other random variables are formulated similarly; for the variances see chapter 5.

It is important to note that these tests will be sensitive to departures from both the independence and the identical distribution assumptions; hence the label tests for randomness.

Examples
(i) In the case of the above data:

$$n = 40, \ R = 28, \ E(R) = 26.3, \ SD(R) = 2.606,$$

hence the null hypothesis of randomness is not rejected since:

$$\mathbb{P}(|Z_R| > 0.652; \ H_0 \text{ is valid}) = 0.514.$$

(ii) In the case of the observed data shown in figure 5.24 (argued in chapter 5 that they exhibit positive dependence) the observations 65–105 give rise to the following sequences of runs up and down:

$$\{5,4,2,1,1,2,1,2,3,3\}^+, \ \{1,1,3,3,1,2,2,1,2\}^-.$$

For these data the null hypothesis of randomness is strongly rejected since:

$$\mathbb{P}(|Z_R| > -4.604; \ H_0 \text{ is valid}) = 0.000.$$

(iii) In the case of the observed data shown in figure 5.25 (argued in chapter 5 that they exhibit negative dependence) the observations 65–105 give rise to the following sequences of runs up and down:

$$\{1,1,1,1,1,1,1,4,1,1,1,1,1,1,1,1,1\}^+, \ \{1,1,1,1,1,1,1,1,1,1,1,2,1,1,1,1,1,1\}^-.$$

For these data the null hypothesis of randomness is also strongly rejected since:

$$\mathbb{P}(|Z_R| > 4.490; \ H_0 \text{ is valid}) = 0.000.$$

(iv) In the case of the exam scores data shown in figure 1.1 and figure 1.2, under two different orderings, alphabetical and sitting order, we conjectured in chapters 1 and 5 that the latter exhibits positive dependence but the former exhibits randomness. Let us consider these conjectures more formally.

(a) In the case of the scores data arranged in an alphabetical order we observe the following runs:

$$\{1,1,4,1,1,3,1,1,1,1,2,1,1,1,1,1,1,2,2,1,1,2,3,1,1\}^+,$$

$$\{1,1,3,1,1,2,2,1,2,1,2,2,3,1,2,1,2,1,2,1,2,1,1,1,1\}^-.$$

For these data the null hypothesis of randomness is accepted since:

$$\mathbb{P}(|Z_R| > 1.063; \ H_0 \text{ is valid}) = 0.288.$$

(b) In the case of the scores data arranged in sitting order we observe the following runs:

$$\{3,2,4,4,1,4,3,6,1,4\}^+, \ \{2,2,2,4,3,3,7,4,6,1,3\}^-,$$

For these data the null hypothesis of randomness is strongly rejected since:

$$\mathbb{P}(|Z_R|> -7.267; H_0 \text{ is valid}) = 0.000.$$

These results confirm the conjectures made in chapters 1 and 5.

An alternative asymptotic test can be derived using the result by Wolfowitz (1944) that assuming k changes with the sample size n in such a way so as $\frac{(k+1)}{n} = \frac{1}{k}$, $K > 0$:

$$\lim_{n\to\infty} \mathbb{P}(R_k = j) = \frac{(2K)^j e^{-2K}}{j!}, j = 0,1,2,\ldots$$

That is, the asymptotic distribution is Poisson distributed.

Levene test The results in Levene (1952) can be used to derive a *portmanteau test* which utilizes both the runs up and down of size up to some m: $1 \leq m < n$. Using the notation:

$\hat{r}_k$ – number of runs up of size k, $\check{r}_k$ – number of runs down of size k, $k = 1, \ldots, m < n$

we can construct an asymptotic *runs up and down chi-square test* by noting that for $\mathbf{r} := (\hat{r}_1, \hat{r}_2, \ldots, \hat{r}_m, \check{r}_1, \check{r}_2, \check{r}_m)'$:

$$RD(\mathbf{X}) := (\mathbf{r} - E(\mathbf{r}))^\top (Cov(\mathbf{r}))^{-1}(\mathbf{r} - E(\mathbf{r})) \overset{H_0}{\underset{\alpha}{\sim}} \chi^2(2m).$$

This test is likely to be sensitive to departures from the IID assumptions when they give rise to systematic runs. For further details see Spanos (1996a).

15.4 The probabilistic reduction approach and misspecification

It should come as no surprise to the reader that the thesis adopted in this book is that the Probabilistic Reduction (PR) approach discussed in chapters 1, 7, 10, provides a framework in the context of which misspecification testing can be systematically operationalized. The primary reason for this is that the PR approach provides a broader than the traditional view of the statistical model which enables the modeler to visualize what lies beyond the postulated statistical model. This broad view of the postulated statistical model can be utilized for misspecification testing purposes:

(a) to provide guidance for a judicious choice of appropriate misspecification tests in the light of the information provided by the observed data patterns, and

(b) to specify broader *parametrically encompassing models* in the context of which the postulated model can be tested.

In an attempt to make the discussion more specific, we consider the question of deriving misspecification tests in the context of the simple Normal model (see (15.2)). As argued in chapter 10, the PR approach views the specification of a statistical model as the narrowing down of the set of all possible statistical models using judiciously chosen reduction assumptions. The choice of these assumptions is made on the basis of preliminary data analysis using (mostly) graphical techniques. This reduction is operationalized by viewing a statistical model as a reduction (simplification) of the joint distribution of all the observable r.v.(s), say X_t, for the whole of the sample period, $t = 1, 2, \ldots, T$:

$$D(X_1, X_2, \ldots, X_T; \psi);$$

the latter is referred to as the *Haavelmo distribution*.

REMARK: it is important to NOTE that concentrating on the joint distribution for $t = 1, 2, \ldots, T$, entails no loss of generality; Kolmogorov's extension theorem ensures that the structure of any stochastic processes $\{Z_t\}_{t=1}^{\infty}$ satisfying the consistency condition (see chapter 8) can be specified in terms of finite joint distributions. In order to avoid unnecessary additional notation we take this joint distribution to coincide with the sample size even though the postulated statistical model holds beyond the observation period.

The simplification of the Haavelmo distribution takes the form of reducing the joint distribution using probabilistic assumptions from all three basic categories (15.1) utilized throughout chapters 2–14. In the case of the simple Normal model, the reduction assumptions regarding the process $\{X_t, t \in \mathbb{T}\}$ are:

(D) Distribution: (N) Normal,
(M) Dependence: (I) Independent,
(H) Homogeneity: (ID) Identical Distribution.

The details of the Reduction as a narrowing down of the specification are given below:

$$D(X_1, X_2, \ldots, X_T; \psi) \overset{\text{I}}{=} \prod_{t=1}^{T} f_t(x_t; \theta_t) \overset{\text{IID}}{=} \prod_{t=1}^{T} f(x_t; \theta), \ (x_1, x_2, \ldots, x_T) \in \mathbb{R}^T. \tag{15.27}$$

The first equality follows after the imposition of independence and the second by supplementing independence with the identical distribution assumption. The Normality assumption ensures that the marginal distributions $f(x_t; \theta)$, $t = 1, 2, \ldots, T$, are Normal. In an important sense the PR approach constitutes an attempt to operationalize the reduction of $\mathcal{P}$ to the subset we call the postulated model, as symbolically shown in figure 15.1.

It is interesting to note that in the case of this simple model there is a one-to-one correspondence between the reduction and model assumptions (see (15.2)) in the sense that the former imply and are implied by the latter:

Reduction assumptions		**Model assumptions**
[D] $D(X_1, X_2, \ldots, X_T; \psi)$ is N,		[1] $X_k \sim \mathrm{N}_k(.), k = 1, \ldots, n,$
[M] $(X_1, X_2, \ldots, X_T)$ are I,	$\Leftrightarrow$	[2] $(X_1, X_2, \ldots, X_n)$ are I,
[H] $(X_1, X_2, \ldots, X_T)$ are ID,		[3] $(X_1, X_2, \ldots, X_n)$ are ID.

NOTES:
(i) This result follows from the fact that under the assumptions of IID, the assumption

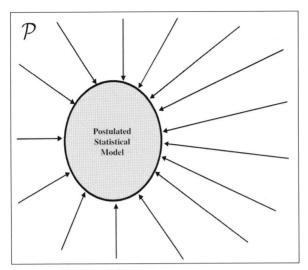

$\mathcal{P}$

Postulated
Statistical
Model

Figure 15.1 Formalizing the reduction process

of Normality of the marginal distributions implies joint Normality; without the IID assumptions this does not follow.

(ii) It is important to NOTE that in the case of more complicated statistical models, such as the Normal/Linear regression model, the reduction assumptions imply the model assumptions but not vice versa.

From the point of view of misspecification testing the above PR approach offers several advantages. First, the Haavelmo distribution defines the relevant *informational universe of discourse*. This is of fundamental importance when modeling observational data because the Haavelmo distribution provides the most general (non-operational) description of the relevant information and thus all misspecification tests should pose the question of unaccounted systematic information relative to the information contained in this distribution. In the case of the simple Normal model, the relevant information for misspecification testing purposes can be formalized in the context of the most general form of reduction which imposes no reduction assumptions beyond the existence of the relevant distributions. As shown in chapter 7, this takes the form of sequential conditioning:

$$D(X_1,X_2,\ldots,X_T;\psi) = \prod_{t=1}^{T} f_t(x_t|x_{t-1},x_{t-2},\ldots,x_1;\theta_t), (x_1,x_2,\ldots,x_T) \in \mathbb{R}^T. \quad (15.28)$$

As shown below, a number of misspecification tests can be developed by making this reduction operational via the imposition of reduction assumptions weaker than those imposed by the ones giving rise to the postulated model. This raises the question of: How are these weaker assumptions chosen? The answer to this leads naturally to the second advantage of the PR approach.

The broader framework provided by the PR approach enables the modeler to make educated guesses with regard to the direction of likely departures from the postulated statistical model. We remind the reader that in chapters 5–6 we discussed the question of assessing probabilistic assumptions using t-plots, scatterplots, and other related graphs; directions of possible departures can be detected at the initial specification stage.

Third, the PR approach brings out the collective nature of misspecification testing in the sense that the model assumptions should not be considered in isolation but as part of a broader (and internally consistent) set of probabilistic assumptions. This is apparent when the model assumptions are viewed in relation to the reduction assumptions. Hence, when testing any one of the model assumptions assuming that the others are valid can lead to misleading conclusions. As shown in chapter 5, assessing the Normality assumption when the temporal independence assumption is invalid can be very misleading; see figure 5.39 where data from a Normal distribution give rise to a bimodal smoothed density because of the presence of temporal dependence. Related to this is the (internal) consistency of the operational forms of the alternative hypotheses. In some sense these alternative hypotheses should not be mutually inconsistent; ideally these hypotheses should form an internally consistent set of probabilistic assumptions, i.e., an alternative encompassing model (not necessarily parametric). The way the PR approach circumvents these problems is to derive misspecification tests by weakening the reduction (as opposed to the model) assumptions in the context of the general reduction (15.28). The more general reduction will lead naturally to a consistent set of probabilistic assumptions which specify a statistical model which encompasses the postulated model parametrically.

In order to be more specific, let us return to the simple Normal model where, in view of the random sample assumption, the information set presumed appropriate a priori is the non-informative event space:

$$\mathcal{D}_0 = (S,\emptyset).$$

In the context of the PR approach this choice yields the statistical Generating Mechanism (GM):

$$X_t = E(X_t | \mathcal{D}_0) + u_t, \ t \in \mathbb{T},$$

with the corresponding orthogonal decomposition of higher conditional moments being:

$$u_t^r = E(u_t^r | \mathcal{D}_0) + \varepsilon_{rt}, \ r = 2,3,\dots,t \in \mathbb{T}.$$

By combining the IID assumptions with some distributional assumption, Normality, in the present case, leads to the postulated statistical model.

A more heedful way to view the above orthogonal decompositions is in relation to the most general form of the conditioning information set in the context of the Haavelmo distribution $D(X_1,X_2,\dots,X_T;\psi)$. This comes in the form of the past history of X_t, say $(X_{t-1},X_{t-2},\dots,X_1)$, defining the information set:

$$\mathcal{D}_{t-1}^0 = \sigma(X_{t-1},X_{t-2},\dots,X_1).$$

Within this context the first two conditional moments under the reduction assumptions of NIID take the form:

$$
\left.
\begin{aligned}
E(X_t|\sigma(X_{t-1},X_{t-2},\dots,X_1)) &= E(X_t) = \mu, \\
Var(X_t|\sigma(X_{t-1},X_{t-2},\dots,X_1)) &= Var(X_t) = \sigma^2,
\end{aligned}
\right\} t \in \mathbb{T}.
$$

Common sense suggests that an obvious way to proceed in the direction of misspecification testing is to modify judiciously the reduction assumptions, individually or in combination, and via the reduction procedure give rise to alternative statistical models. Any departures from the reduction assumptions evident in the data in question can be utilized to determine the direction of possible departures. Misspecification tests which are known to have power (sensitivity) in these directions can then be chosen.

An interesting example of such a process is to modify the Normal in favor of, say, the Student's-t distribution, maintaining the IID assumptions. This will give rise to the simple Student's-t model with the same first moment as the Normal but variance:

$$
Var(X_t) = \left(\frac{\nu}{\nu-2}\right)\sigma^2, \ t \in \mathbb{T},
$$

where ν denotes the degrees of freedom. A moment's reflection suggests that for the modeler to entertain such a change in the reduction assumptions there must be some a priori information indicating that departures from Normality in the direction of the Student's-t distribution are more likely than departures in the direction of the Gamma or some other distribution. In the context of the PR approach this is often the case because part of the specification process is a preliminary data analysis using a variety of graphical techniques. This procedure will give rise to misspecification tests which search beyond the boundaries of the postulated model in specific directions. However, this does not seem to be the best way to proceed in cases where the a priori information is not very specific. A safer alternative is to weaken (instead of modify) the reduction assumptions and entertain scenarios where the reduction assumptions are more general than the ones giving rise to the postulated model. Let us explain this in the context of the simple Normal model.

15.4.1 Testing Independence

Consider the scenario where the *Independence assumption* is weakened to that of *Markovness*, leaving the other assumptions the same. The presence of dependence abrogates the initial choice of the information set $\mathcal{D}_0$, rendering $(X_{t-1},X_{t-2},\dots,X_1)$, the past history' of X_t, relevant. In view of Markovness the relevant the information set is:

$$
\mathcal{D}_{t-1} = \sigma(X_{t-1}).
$$

In turn this will give rise to different conditional moment functions:

$$
E(X_t|\mathcal{D}_{t-1}) = \alpha_0 + \alpha_1 X_{t-1} + u_t, \ E(u_t^2|\mathcal{D}_{t-1}) = \sigma_0^2, \ t \in \mathbb{T}.
$$

To see how the reduction procedure will lead to a different but encompassing model, let us replace the above the reduction assumptions with:

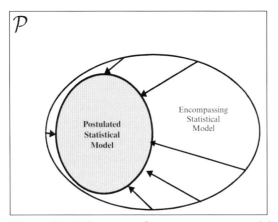

Figure 15.2 The notion of an encompassing model and misspecification testing

(D)   Distribution: **(N)** Normal,
(M)   Dependence: **(M)** Markov dependent,
(H)   Homogeneity: **(S)**   second-order stationary.

These reduction assumptions give rise to the simplification:

$$D(X_1,X_2,\ldots,X_T;\psi) \overset{M}{=} f_1(x_1;\varphi_1)\prod_{t=2}^{T} f_t(x_t|x_{t-1};\varphi_t) \overset{S\&M}{=} f(x_1;\varphi_1)\prod_{t=2}^{T} f(x_t|x_{t-1};\varphi), \quad (15.29)$$

for all $(x_1,x_2,\ldots,x_T)\in\mathbb{R}_X^T$, where $f(x_t|x_{t-1};\varphi)$ is the conditional Normal distribution. As shown in chapter 8, this reduction gives rise to the **Normal autoregressive model:**

[1]   Statistical GM: $X_t = \alpha_0 + \alpha_1 X_{t-1} + u_t$, $t\in\mathbb{T}$,

[2]   Probability model:

$$\Phi = \left\{ f(x_1,x_2,\ldots,x_T;\varphi) = f(x_1;\varphi_1)\prod_{t=2}^{T} \frac{(\sigma_0)^{-1}}{\sqrt{2\pi}} \exp\left\{ -\frac{1}{2}\frac{(x_t - \alpha_0 - \alpha_1 x_{t-1})^2}{\sigma_0^2} \right\}, \varphi\in\Psi, \mathbf{x}\in\mathbb{R}^T \right\},$$

$$\varphi := (\alpha_0,\alpha_1,\sigma_0^2)\in\Psi := \mathbb{R}^2\times\mathbb{R}_+, \mathbf{x} = (x_1,x_2,\ldots,x_T),$$

[3]   Sampling model: $(X_1,X_2,\ldots,X_T)$ is a stationary and Markov dependent sample, sequentially drawn from $f(x_t|\mathbf{x}_{t-1};\varphi)$, $t\in\mathbb{T}$.   (15.30)

This relation between the simple Normal and the Normal autoregressive models, respectively, can be visualized in terms of figure 15.2 where the former is the postulated statistical model and the latter is the encompassing model.

The t-test
Within the Normal autoregressive model the modeler can proceed to test the independence assumption, which is now specified in the form:

$$H_0:(X_1,X_2,\ldots,X_T) \text{ are Independent}, H_1:(X_1,X_2,\ldots,X_T) \text{ are Markov dependent}.$$

This test in the context of the encompassing model takes the parametric form:

$$H_0: \alpha_1 = 0, \text{ against } H_1: \alpha_1 \neq 0. \tag{15.31}$$

The optimal test for (15.31) is the well known t-test discussed extensively in chapter 14 based on the test statistic:

$$\tau(\mathbf{X}) = \frac{\sqrt{T}(\hat{\alpha}_1)}{s} \overset{H_0}{\underset{\alpha}{\simeq}} St(n-2).$$

(i) $\overset{H_0}{\underset{\alpha}{\simeq}}$ reads asymptotically approximated under the null by,

(ii) $\hat{\alpha}_1 = \frac{\sum_{t=1}^{T}(X_t - \bar{X})(X_{t-1} - \bar{X})}{\sum_{t=1}^{T}(X_{t-1} - \bar{X})^2}$, $s^2 = \frac{1}{T-2}\sum_{t=1}^{T}(X_t - \hat{\alpha}_0 - \hat{\alpha}_1 X_{t-1})^2$, $\hat{\alpha}_0 = \bar{X} - \hat{\alpha}_1 \bar{X}_{-1}$,

$$\bar{X} = \frac{1}{T}\sum_{t=1}^{T} X_t, \quad \bar{X}_{-1} = \frac{1}{T-1}\sum_{t=1}^{T-1} X_t.$$

At this stage it is imperative to NOTE that the problem of misspecification testing, which is by its very nature testing without (the boundaries of) the postulated model, has been transformed into testing within a parametrically encompassing model. This can be seen by comparing the parameterization of the postulated model (*simple Normal*):

$$\boldsymbol{\theta} := (\mu, \sigma^2) \in \Theta := \mathbb{R} \times \mathbb{R}_+,$$

with that of the encompassing model (*Normal autoregressive*):

$$\boldsymbol{\varphi} := (\alpha_0, \alpha_1, \sigma_0^2) \in \Psi := \mathbb{R}^2 \times \mathbb{R}_+.$$

The restriction, as specified by H_0 in (15.31), reduces the Normal autoregressive model to the simple Normal model. This can be easily seen via the parameterizations of these models:

$$\alpha_1 = \frac{Cov(X_t, X_{t-1})}{Var(X_t)}, \quad \alpha_0 = E(X_t) - \alpha_1 E(X_{t-1}), \quad \sigma_0^2 = Var(X_t) - \alpha_1 Cov(X_t, X_{t-1}),$$

and thus: $\boldsymbol{\varphi}|_{\alpha_1=0} \Rightarrow \boldsymbol{\theta}: \alpha_1 = 0 \Rightarrow \alpha_0 = E(X_t) = \mu$ and $\sigma_0^2 = Var(X_t) = \sigma^2$, which coincide with the parameters of the *simple Normal model*. Hence, the testing without the postulated model with parameter space Θ has been transformed into testing within the parameterization Ψ. The role of the encompassing model in misspecification testing for the postulated model can be visualized in figure 15.2.

When one compares the parameterization of α_1 with the correlation coefficient with one lag:

$$\rho(1) = \frac{Cov(X_t, X_{t-1})}{Var(X_t)},$$

it is apparent that the two coincide. Hence, the above t-test coincides with the test for the hypothesis:

$$H_0: \rho(1) = 0, \text{ against } H_1: \rho(1) \neq 0.$$

In some sense the above encompassing model provides a coherent way to operationalize the test based on the correlation coefficient using the auxiliary regression:

$$X_t = \alpha_0 + \alpha_1 X_{t-1} + u_t, \quad t \in \mathbb{T}.$$

As shown below, the PR approach operationalizes several tests (known and new) based on auxiliary regressions.

The *F*-test

The Normal AR(1), viewed as an encompassing model for the simple Normal model, can be easily extended to the AR(*m*) with statistical GM:

$$X_t = \alpha_0 + \sum_{k=1}^{m} \alpha_k X_{t-k} + u_t, \ T > m \geq 1, t \in \mathbb{T}, \tag{15.32}$$

in order to give rise to a more general misspecification test. The hypothesis of interest:

$H_0 : (X_1, X_2, \ldots, X_T)$ are Independent, $H_1 : (X_1, X_2, \ldots, X_T)$ are Markov (*m*) dependent,

takes the parametric form:

$$H_0 : \alpha_1 = 0, \ \alpha_2 = 0, \cdots, \alpha_m = 0, \text{ against } H_1 : \alpha_1 \neq 0, \text{ or } \alpha_2 \neq 0, \cdots, \text{ or } \alpha_m \neq 0.$$

This hypothesis can be tested using the *F*-test statistic:

$$F(\mathbf{X}) := \frac{\sum_{t=1}^{T} \hat{\varepsilon}_t^2 \sum_{t=1}^{T} \hat{u}_t^2}{\sum_{t=1}^{T} \hat{u}_t^2} \left(\frac{T - m - 1}{m} \right) \overset{H_0}{\underset{\alpha}{\simeq}} \mathsf{F}(m, T - m - 1), \tag{15.33}$$

(i) $\mathsf{F}(m,n)$ denotes the *F*-distribution with *m* and *n* degrees of freedom,

(ii) $\sum_{t=1}^{T} \hat{\varepsilon}_t^2, \ \hat{\varepsilon}_t := (X_t - \hat{\mu}), \ \hat{\mu} = \frac{1}{T} \sum_{t=1}^{T} X_t$, denotes the residual sum of squares from the statistical GM:

$$X_t = \mu + \varepsilon_k, t \in \mathbb{T},$$

(iii) $\sum_{t=1}^{T} \hat{u}_t^2, \ \hat{u}_t := X_t - \hat{\alpha}_0 - \sum_{k=1}^{m} \hat{\alpha}_k X_{t-k}$, denotes the Residual Sum of Squares from the statistical GM (15.32); see Spanos (forthcoming) for the details with regard to the estimation of the parameters.

As shown above, in the case where $m = 1$ discussed above, the *F*-test reduces to the t-test. This *F*-test for independence was first proposed in Spanos (1986).

The above *F*-test can be seen as an alternative way to operationalize the hypothesis specified in terms of the correlation coefficients:

$$H_0 : \rho(1) = \rho(2) = \cdots = \rho(m) = 0, \text{ for } m < (n - 1).$$

The main difference between the *F*-test as specified above and the Box–Pierce (1970) or the Ljung and Box (1978) tests discussed in the previous section, is that the former utilizes the *partial correlation coefficients* (see chapter 6) instead of the ordinary correlation coefficients for lags up to *m*. We recommend the *F*-test because of its superior power properties (see Spanos (1986), p. 401).

Testing second-order dependence

The t- and *F*-test proposed above in relation to testing independence in the context of the simple Normal model are clearly misspecification tests designed to detect first-order dependence (see chapters 4, 6). This is because they are based on correlation and partial correlation coefficients which measure first-order dependence.

As mentioned in the previous section, a natural way to measure second-order dependence is via:

$$\gamma(\tau) = \frac{Cov(X_t^2 X_{t-\tau}^2)}{Var(X_t^2)}, \ \tau = 1, 2, \ldots, m < (n - 1).$$

Using the analogy with the correlation coefficient, an obvious way to embed $\gamma(1)$ in an auxiliary regression is:

$$X_t^2 = \gamma_0 + \gamma_1 X_{t-1}^2 + \omega_t, \ t \in \mathbb{T}, \tag{15.34}$$

where $\gamma_1 := \frac{Cov(X_t^2 X_{t-1}^2)}{Var(X_t^2)}$. This gives rise to the hypothesis:

$$H_0: \gamma_1 = 0, \text{ against } H_1: \gamma_1 \neq 0,$$

which can be tested using a t-test as discussed above. Similarly, the testing of the extended hypothesis:

$$H_0: \gamma_1 = \gamma_2 = \cdots = \gamma_m = 0, \text{ against } H_1: \gamma_1 \neq 0 \text{ or } \gamma_2 \neq 0 \text{ or } \cdots \text{ or } \gamma_m \neq 0, \tag{15.35}$$

in the context of the auxiliary regression:

$$X_t^2 = \gamma_0 + \sum_{k=1}^m \gamma_k X_{t-k}^2 + \sum_{i=1}^m \sum_{\substack{i=1 \\ i>j}}^m \delta_{ij} X_{t-i} X_{t-j} + \omega_t, \ t \in \mathbb{T}, \tag{15.36}$$

leads to the *F*-test discussed above.

REMARK: it is important to note that in the context of the simple Normal model there is no need to use the error in order to define the auxiliary regressions since $\varepsilon_t = X_t - \mu$.

The *F*-test for the hypothesis (15.35) can be interpreted as a substitute of the McLeod–Li test discussed in the previous section, in the same sense that the *F*-test for first-order dependence is a substitute for the Ljung–Box test.

We conclude this section by noting that this type of auxiliary regressions can be extended to higher moments, not just the first two, but this will be considered in some detail in Spanos (forthcoming), in the context of the Normal/linear model.

15.4.2 Testing Independence/homogeneity

Consider the scenario where in addition to the weakening of the *Independence assumption* to that of *Markovness*, the modeler allows for some heterogeneity in the form of trending means. For illustration purposes, let us assume that the trending means take the form:

$$E(X_t) = \delta_0 + \delta_1 t, \ t \in \mathbb{T}.$$

Using the reduction assumptions:

(D)   Distribution: (N)   Normality,
(M)   Dependence: (M)   Markov dependence,
(H)   Homogeneity: (S)   first-order linear trend, covariance stationarity,

in the context of the reduction in (15.29), enables us to concentrate only on the bivariate joint distribution, i.e.

$$\begin{pmatrix} X_t \\ X_{t-1} \end{pmatrix} \sim N\left(\begin{bmatrix} (\delta_0 + \delta_1 t) \\ (\delta_0 + \delta_1 (t-1)) \end{bmatrix}, \begin{bmatrix} \sigma_{11} & \sigma_{12} \\ \sigma_{12} & \sigma_{22} \end{bmatrix} \right).$$

The conditional density $f(x_t|x_{t-1};\phi)$ takes the form:

$$(X_t|X_{t-1}) \sim N(a_0 + \gamma t + a_1 X_{t-1}, \sigma_0^2),$$

$$a_0 := (\delta_0(1-a_1) + a_1\delta_1), \ \gamma = \delta_1(1-a_1), \ a_1 := \frac{\sigma_{12}}{\sigma_{22}}, \ \sigma_0^2 := \sigma_{11} - \frac{\sigma_{12}^2}{\sigma_{22}}.$$

This gives rise to the **Normal autoregressive model with a trend**:

[1] Statistical GM: $X_t = a_0 + \gamma t + a_1 X_{t-1} + u_t, \ t \in \mathbb{T},$

[2] Probability model:

$$\Phi = \left\{ f(x_1, x_2, \ldots, x_T; \phi) = f(x_1; \phi_1) \prod_{t=2}^{T} \frac{(\sigma_0)^{-1}}{\sqrt{2\pi}} \exp\left\{ -\frac{1}{2} \frac{(x_t - a_0 - \gamma t - a_1 x_{t-1})^2}{\sigma_0^2} \right\} \right\},$$

$$\phi \in \Psi^*, \ \mathbf{x} \in \mathbb{R}^T, \ \phi := (a_0, \gamma, a_1, \sigma_0^2) \in \Psi^* := \mathbb{R}^3 \times \mathbb{R}_+,$$

[3] Sampling model: $(X_1, X_2, \ldots, X_T)$ is a stationary and Markov dependent and mean-heterogeneous sample, sequentially drawn from $f(x_t|x_{t-1};\phi), \ t \in \mathbb{T}.$ (15.37)

In the context of the new encompassing model the null hypothesis for testing both Independence and Identical distribution takes the parametric form:

$$H_0: \gamma = 0 \text{ and } a_1 = 0, \text{ against } H_1: \gamma \neq 0 \text{ or } a_1 \neq 0.$$ (15.38)

The optimal test in this case is also the F-test as specified in (15.33) with $\hat{u}_t := X_t - \hat{a}_0 - \hat{\gamma}t - \hat{a}_1 X_{t-1}.$

15.4.3 Testing Normality/Independence

The encompassing model can be extended further by also weakening the distributional assumption of Normality. The idea is to postulate a family of distributions which includes Normality as a special case. In cases where the IID assumptions are maintained this family can be a univariate family such as the Pearson family. In cases where the modeler wants to weaken the IID assumptions, as well, this family has to be multivariate. In both cases the choice has to be guided by the observed data patterns revealed by a preliminary data analysis. For example, in the case where there is information to suggest that although bell shape symmetry is satisfied by the data, the Normality assumption is suspect, the elliptical symmetric family might be an appropriate choice. Using the reduction assumptions:

(D) Distribution: (ε) Elliptically symmetric,
(M) Dependence: (M) Markov dependence,
(H) Homogeneity: (S) second-order stationarity,

the simplification in (15.29) gives rise to the **elliptical autoregressive model:**

[i] Statistical GM: $X_t = \alpha_0 + \alpha_1 X_{t-1} + \epsilon_k, \ t \in \mathbb{T},$

[ii] Probability model:

$$\Phi = \left\{ f(x_1, x_2, \ldots, x_T; \boldsymbol{\theta}) = f(x_1; \boldsymbol{\theta}_1) \prod_{t=2}^{T} f(x_t|x_{t-1};\boldsymbol{\psi}) \in E - \text{elliptically symmetric} \right\},$$

$$\boldsymbol{\psi} := (\alpha_0, \alpha_1, \sigma_0^2, \gamma) \in \Omega := \mathbb{R}^2 \times \mathbb{R}_+ \times \mathbb{R}^m, \ \mathbf{x} \in \mathbb{R}^T,$$

[iii] Sampling model: $\mathbf{X} := (X_1, X_2, \ldots, X_T)$ is a Markov/stationary sample.

As it stands this does not constitute an operational model. To give rise to an operational parametric model we need to choose a particular member of the elliptically symmetric family (see Fang *et al.* (1990)); the subset of parameters γ vary with the particular distribution. These parameters are related to the skedastic function which takes the general form:

$$E(u_t^2 | \sigma(X_{t-1})) = h(X_{t-1}), \; t \in \mathbb{T}. \tag{15.39}$$

As shown in Spanos (1995a), there is a general form for the function $h(.)$ which applies to the whole elliptically symmetric family which can be estimated non-parametrically. Such non-parametrically estimated forms can be utilized to derive tests of dynamic hetero-skedasticity, which in the context of the elliptically symmetric family constitute tests of Normality. This is because within this family the Normal is the only distribution for which:

$$E(u_t^2 | \sigma(X_{t-1})) = \sigma^2, \; t \in \mathbb{T}.$$

It is interesting to NOTE that the misspecification test based on the auxiliary regression (15.34) can be placed within the context of (15.39) when the underlying distribution is assumed to be Student's t.

In concluding this subsection we reiterate again that in the context of the PR approach the relevant information is often available by looking at a number of data plots (see chapters 5–6), regarding specific directions of possible departures from the assumptions of the postulated model. This information can be utilized to choose the encompassing models and the resulting misspecification tests. In addition, this information can be utilized to shed some light on the question of respecification (see chapter 10).

At this stage it is imperative to discuss the nature of the misspecification tests (t-tests and F-tests) as presented above.

15.4.4 Are these Neyman–Pearson tests?

The question which naturally arises at this stage is whether the above parametric hypotheses lead naturally to a parametric test in the Neyman–Pearson tradition of testing within. After all both the t-test and F-test are well known Neyman–Pearson tests. In relation to the parametric set up it looks as though this is indeed testing within the encompassing model with the postulated model denoting the null hypothesis. Indeed, the testing without (the boundaries of) the postulated model has been transformed into testing within a parametrically encompassing model.

In the general case the **parametrically encompassing model** takes the form:

$$\mathfrak{P}_\psi := \{f(x_1, x_2, \ldots, x_n; \psi), \; \psi \in \Psi, \; (x_1, x_2, \ldots, x_n) \in \mathcal{X}\}.$$

and the **postulated model**:

$$\mathfrak{P}_\theta := \{f(x_1, x_2, \ldots, x_n; \theta), \; \theta \in \Theta, \; (x_1, x_2, \ldots, x_n) \in \mathcal{X}\}.$$

where $\Theta \subset \Psi$.

In view of the above discussion, the first modification required for the Neyman–Pearson approach to be used for misspecification testing purposes is to construct an encompassing model in the context of which certain parametric restrictions ensure that this model subsumes to the postulated statistical model. These restrictions constitute a way to parameterize of the misspecification test in the context of the encompassing model.

Does this imply that the tests themselves are Neyman–Pearson tests?

The short answer is No, for several reasons.

First, in view of the fact that the Neyman–Pearson approach implicitly assumes that:

the encompassing model $\mathfrak{P}_{\psi}$ is statistically adequate,

(see chapter 14), the possibility exists that neither model is appropriate. In view of the fact that the implicit maintained model is Ψ, the possibility that the true model lies in $[\mathcal{P} - \mathfrak{P}_{\psi}]$ should be explicitly acknowledged. This possibility raises several issues the most important of which is that the modeler should not adopt the alternative (encompassing model) when the data indicate no support for the null (the postulated model). This is in contrast to the Neyman–Pearson framework, with a decision rule defined as a choice between H_0 and H_1, and the modeler is supposed to adopt the alternative model. In the terminology of chapters 1 and 10, the issue of misspecification testing should be separated from that of respecification (choosing an alternative statistical model).

Second, despite the testing within (the encompassing model) and the parameterization of the hypothesis of interest in terms of Ψ, the above misspecification tests are in essence Fisher tests, where the set of all possible models $\mathcal{P}$ is restricted to the encompassing model. The primary objective of these tests coincides with that of a Fisher test: to determine the extent to which the observed data lend credence to the null hypothesis. Hence, when a Neyman–Pearson test is used for misspecification testing purposes the modeler needs to replace its basic objective with that of the Fisher test. The significance level α, interpreted in terms of what happens in the long run when the experiment is repeated a large number of times, is irrelevant because the question the modeler poses concerns the particular sample realization.

In terms of figure 14.9 (modified opposite as figure 15.3), used to visualize the difference between testing without and testing within in chapter 14, we can view the encompassing model as a way to systematize the searching beyond the boundaries of the postulated model. This should be contrasted with the *ad hoc* searching for possible departures which relax one assumption at a time retaining the rest of the structure of the postulated model (see figure 15.4). A number of misspecification tests in the traditional textbook approach constitute examples of such *ad hoc* searches which often give rise to self-contradictory assumptions; a set of assumptions without internal consistency. For example, the traditional literature proceeds to test for dynamic heteroskedasticity and/or non-linearity in the context of an autoregressive model and at the same time maintain the Normality assumption (see Spanos (1995a) for the implicit inconsistency). This, in effect reduces the set of specified statistical models down to the empty set!

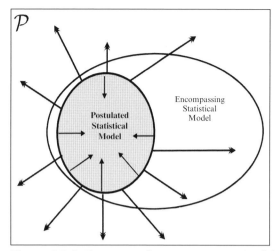

Figure 15.3 The notion of an encompassing model and testing without

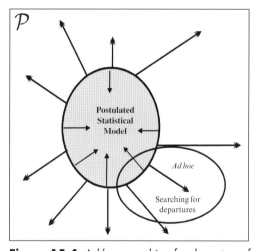

Figure 15.4 *Ad hoc* searching for departures from the postulated model

15.5 Empirical examples

We conclude this chapter with empirical examples designed to emphasize some of the important points relating to testing (both within and without) using observed data.

15.5.1 Econometrics exam scores

Consider the data given in table 15.1 which represent the exam scores in an Econometrics exam in 1994, arranged in alphabetical order.

A cursory look at the t-plot shown in figure 15.5 suggests that the data do not exhibit any dependence or/and heterogeneity (see chapter 5 on reading t-plots). Moreover, the

Table 15.1. *Data on econometrics exam scores*

69.0	77.0	96.0	93.0	51.0	85.0	71.0	62.0	56.0	69.0	70.0	46.0
78.0	92.0	41.0	65.0	80.0	44.0	51.0	64.0	91.0	61.0	80.0	76.0
56.0	43.0	53.0	80.0	67.0	64.0	99.0	45.0	70.0	78.0	88.0	68.0
91.0	55.0	58.0	82.0	58.0	65.0	50.0	60.0	85.0	61.0	57.0	51.0
74.0	58.0	73.0	98.0	70.0	86.0	80.0	42.0	70.0	72.0	79.0	94.0
62.0	47.0	74.0	69.0	83.0	84.0	91.0	69.0	74.0	56.0	81.0	72.0

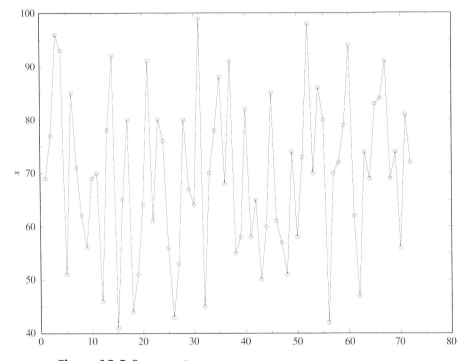

Figure 15.5 Econometrics exam scores

smoothed histogram (see chapter 5) of the (standardized) data (compare the solid line in figure 15.6 with the standard normal density in dotted line) suggests that the Normality assumption does not seem unreasonable.

REMARK: the apparent discrepancy between the smoothed histogram and the Normal density does not seem at first sight serious enough to render the Normality assumption inappropriate.

On the above evidence furnished by the simple graphical techniques, the modeler might proceed by adopting the simple Normal model as appropriate to describe the stochastic mechanism that has given rise to the above data. As part of the department's policy for the comparability of examination grading the professor is asked to provide evidence that:

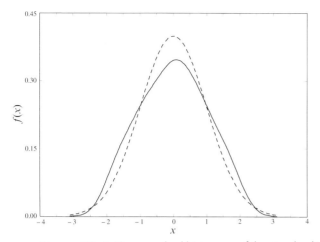

Figure 15.6 The smoothed histogram of the standardized scores data

$$H_0: \mu = 70 \text{ against } H_1: \mu \neq 70. \tag{15.40}$$

Estimating the simple Normal model yielded:

$$X_t = 69.583 + \underset{(15.056)}{\hat{\varepsilon}_t}, T = 72, \tag{15.41}$$
$$\underset{(1.774)}{}$$

where the numbers in parentheses refers to the estimated standard errors.

Before we proceed to test the hypothesis (15.40) in the context of the estimated model we need to assess its statistical adequacy. This is because as argued in chapter 14 a N–P test depends crucially on the validity of the postulated statistical model. The Neyman–Pearson theory is appropriate for testing *within the boundaries* demarcated by the postulated model. In general, when any of the assumptions underlying the model in question are invalid, the estimators involved are no longer optimal and they do not have the distributions the modeler assumes they have. As a result the test statistics do not follow the assumed distributions and in a sense the modeler is looking up the wrong tables to calculate the size or/and the power of the test.

In the case of the simple Normal model (see (15.2) the underlying assumptions are:

(i)   Normality: $X_k \sim N_k(.)$, for all $k = 1,2,\ldots,n$,
(ii) Independence of the sample $(X_1, X_2, \ldots, X_n)$, and
(iii) Identical distribution for the sample $(X_1, X_2 \ldots, X_n)$.

Let us discuss the validity of these assumptions for the econometric exam scores in reverse order.

Misspecification testing

It is important to emphasize at the outset that it is always advisable to apply the various misspecification tests in conjunction with the corresponding graphical techniques discussed in chapters 5–6. As part of the preliminary data analysis we report the following summary statistics:

Sample mean: $\bar{x} = \frac{1}{T}\sum_{k=1}^{T} x_k = 69.583$,

Sample variance: $\frac{1}{T-1}\sum_{k=1}^{T}(x_k - \bar{x})^2 = 226.68$,

Sample skewness: 0.009,

Sample kurtosis: 2.185,

Sample median: 70,

min$(x_1, x_2, ..., x_T)$:   41,   max$(x_1, x_2, ..., x_T)$:   99,
1st quartile: 58,   3rd quartile: 80.

NOTE that these sample summary statistics can be very misleading in cases where the IID assumptions are not valid!

Testing homogeneity (ID)

Let us consider testing the ID assumption using the auxiliary regression with a first-order trend polynomial:

$$X_t = \underset{(3.602)}{67.642} + \underset{(0.086)}{0.053} \cdot t + \underset{(15.122)}{\hat{\varepsilon}_t}, \quad T = 72. \tag{15.42}$$

The misspecification test amounts to testing the significance of the coefficient of t, which is the familiar t-test:

$$\tau(\mathbf{x}) = \left(\frac{0.053}{0.086}\right) = 0.620[0.537].$$

This test indicates no departures from the ID assumption. This can be easily seen in figure 15.5 where no apparent departures from homogeneity are discernible. The same t-plot suggests that there is no need for other misspecification tests based on alternative forms of heterogeneity.

A general graphical technique that can be used to assess the presence of heterogeneity is the t-plot of the *recursive estimates* of the first two moments. In an attempt to allow the data to indicate any departures from the Identical Distribution (ID) assumption, we estimate the mean and the variance using an initial small sub-sample, say $T_1 < T$:

$$\hat{\mu}(T_1) = \frac{1}{T_1}\sum_{k=1}^{T_1} X_k, \quad \hat{\sigma}^2(T_1) = \frac{1}{T_1 - 1}\sum_{k=1}^{T_1}(X_k - \hat{\mu}(T_1))^2,$$

and then update these estimates recursively by increasing the sample size by one observation at a time, i.e.

$$\left. \begin{array}{l} \hat{\mu}(t) = \frac{1}{t}\sum_{k=1}^{t} X_k, \\ \hat{\sigma}^2(t) = \frac{1}{t-1}\sum_{k=1}^{t}(X_k - \hat{\mu}(t))^2, \end{array} \right\} \quad t = T_1 + 1, T_1 + 2, ..., T.$$

This will give rise to two sequences of estimates:

$$\{(\hat{\mu}(T_1), \hat{\mu}(T_1 + 1), ..., \hat{\mu}(T)), (\hat{\sigma}^2(T_1), \hat{\sigma}^2(T_1 + 1), ..., \hat{\sigma}^2(T))\},$$

which can be plotted over the index. The idea is that if the observed data exhibit heterogeneity over the index set $t = 1, 2, ..., T$, this will show as systematic departures from the

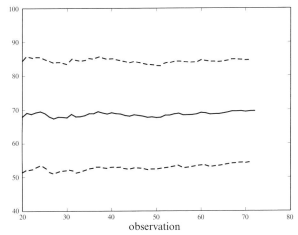

Figure 15.7 Recursive estimates of $E(X)$ for the Econometrics exam scores

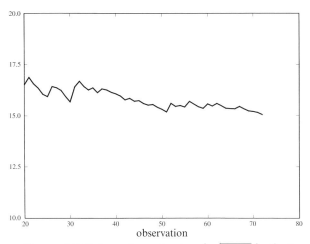

Figure 15.8 Recursive estimates of $\sqrt{Var(X)}$ for the Econometrics exam scores

constant value assumed by the ID assumption. In figure 15.7 we can see the t-plot of the recursive estimates for the mean using $T_1 = 20$ together with the dotted lines representing one standard deviation on either side of the mean. Under normal circumstances we would expect the recursive mean estimates to be relatively constant and the dotted lines to exhibit a narrowing of the gap between them and $\hat{\mu}(t)$ as $t \rightarrow T$ (information increases). The recursive mean estimates appear to hover just below the value 70 with the one standard dotted lines exhibiting mild convergence. In figure 15.8 we can see the recursive estimates of the standard deviation $\left(\sqrt{Var(X)}\right)$ which appears to be hovering just above the value 15, exhibiting signs of convergence.

Testing Independence

(i)   The first misspecification test for temporal non-correlation to be applied is the Ljung–Box test for $m = 4$:

$$LB(\mathbf{X}) = \sum_{\tau=1}^{4} \left(\frac{72(74)}{(68)}\right) \hat{\rho}_n^2(\tau) = 3.259[0.515],$$

where the number in square brackets refers to the p-value. This test does not indicate departures from first-order Independence. Applying this test using several other values of m confirms this conclusion.

(ii)   The second misspecification test to be applied is the N–P type encompassing test which compares the estimated simple Normal model (15.41) with the AR(2) model:

$$X_t = \underset{(12.211)}{81.175} - \underset{(0.121)}{0.032} X_{t-1} - \underset{(0.121)}{0.137} X_{t-2} + \underset{(15.322)}{\hat{u}_t}, \; T = 70. \tag{15.43}$$

The misspecification test is just the F-test for the joint significance of the coefficients of X_{t-1} and X_{t-2}:

$$F(\mathbf{x}) = 0.662[0.519],$$

where $F(\mathbf{x})$ denotes the value of the F-statistic with 2 and 67 degrees of freedom. This result confirms the conclusion of the previous test.

As argued above, both of the above temporal dependence misspecification tests restrict the form of possible dependence to first-order. It is often advisable to test for higher-order dependence as well.

(iii) The McLeod–Li test for second-order temporal dependence which for $m = 4$ yields:

$$ML(\mathbf{X}) = \sum_{\tau=1}^{4} \left(\frac{72(74)}{(68)}\right) \hat{\gamma}_n^2(\tau) = 4.150[0.386],$$

which indicates no departures from the assumption of Independence. Applying this test for several other values of m confirms this conclusion.

(iv)   The F-test for second-order dependence based on the auxiliary regression:

$$\hat{X}_t^2 = \underset{(937.384)}{5883.648} - \underset{(0.545)}{0.283} X_{t-1}^2 - \underset{(0.474)}{0.327} X_{t-2}^2 + \underset{(1.005)}{0.468} X_{t-1}X_{t-2}, \; T = 70, \tag{15.44}$$

which tests the joint significance of the coefficients of $(X_{t-1}^2, X_{t-2}^2, X_{t-1}X_{t-2})$, yields:

$$F(\mathbf{x}) = 0.385[0.765],$$

confirming the conclusion of the previous test.

Testing Independence/homogeneity

The assumptions of IID define what we called throughout this book randomness. A first stage misspecification test for randomness has been proposed above using the results in Levene (1952). This is a first stage test because it can be used for any data set irrespective of the nature of the measurement scale (see chapter 1) because it abstracts from the numerical values of the data and considers only the so-called runs up and down (see also chapter 5). The Levene test for randomness is based on the joint contribution of runs (up and down) up to a certain length m; often m is just the maximum length of the observed runs. In the case of the econometrics exam scores data, the *Levene randomness test* for $m = 1, \ldots, 4$ yields:

$$RD(\mathbf{x};2) = 3.290[0.193], \quad RD(\mathbf{x};4) = 3.998[0.408],$$

$$RD(\mathbf{x};6) = 4.983[0.546], \quad RD(\mathbf{x};8) = 5.863[0.193],$$

which indicate no departures from the IID assumptions.

(i)   Another misspecification test for randomness can be devised by combining the F-tests for Independence and Identically Distributed assumptions. That is, the auxiliary regression (15.42) can be combined with (15.43) and (15.44) in order to test Independence and homogeneity jointly by assessing the joint significance of the coefficients of (t, X_{t-1}, X_{t-2}) based on the auxiliary regression:

$$X_t = \underset{(12.459)}{79.289} + \underset{(0.091)}{0.074} \cdot t - \underset{(0.121)}{0.032}\, X_{t-1} - \underset{(0.122)}{0.142}\, X_{t-2} + \underset{(15.361)}{\hat{u}_t}, \; T = 70,$$

$$F(\mathbf{x}) = 0.659[0.580],$$

where $F(\mathbf{x})$ denotes the value of the F-statistic with 3 and 66 degrees of freedom.

(ii)   The F-test for second-order dependence and trend heterogeneity, based on the auxiliary regression:

$$\hat{X}_t^2 = \underset{(1044.297)}{5639.490} + \underset{(13.057)}{7.087} \cdot t - \underset{(0.553)}{0.242}\, X_{t-1}^2 - \underset{(0.481)}{0.292}\, X_{t-2}^2 + \underset{(1.023)}{0.384}\, X_{t-1}X_{t-2}, \; T = 70,$$

$$(15.45)$$

which tests the joint significance of the coefficients of $(t, X_{t-1}^2, X_{t-2}^2, X_{t-1}X_{t-2})$, yields:

$$F(\mathbf{x}) = 0.385[0.765],$$

where $F(\mathbf{x})$ denotes the value of the F-statistic with 4 and 65 degrees of freedom.

Both of the above tests indicate no departures from the Independence/homogeneity assumptions.

Testing Normality

As discussed above, testing Normality can take a number of different forms.

(i)   The first family of tests for the Normality assumption to be utilized is the D'Agostino–Pearson which is based on the skewness and kurtosis coefficients. For the above data:

$$\hat{\alpha}_3 = -0.009, \; \hat{\alpha}_4 = 2.185.$$

The skewness-kurtosis and the D'Agostino–Pearson misspecification tests for Normality yields:

$$sk(\mathbf{x}) = 1.996[0.367], \; D'AP(\mathbf{x}) = 4.025[0.134],$$

indicating no departures from the Normality assumption.

(ii)   Another group of tests for Normality, widely used in the literature, is the one utilizing the Empirical Cumulative Distribution Function (see section 3):

Kolmogorov: $\Delta_n = 0.043[0.150]$,
Anderson–Darling: $A_2 = 0.271[0.664]$.

(iii)   A third group of tests is based on the *ordered sample*. The initial test in this category is:

Shapiro–Wilk: $W = 0.964[0.110]$.

As we can see, none of these tests indicates apparent departures from Normality.

Testing within: Neyman–Pearson tests

Taken together the above misspecification tests suggest that the simple Normal model appears to provide a statistically adequate description of the mechanism that gave rise to the above data. This enables the modeler to proceed to test within the boundaries of the postulated model the hypothesis (15.40). The appropriate statistic is the well known t-test statistic:

$$\tau(\mathbf{X}) = \left(\frac{\sqrt{n}(\hat{\mu}_n - \mu_0)}{s}\right) \overset{H_0}{\sim} \mathrm{St}(n-1), \tag{15.46}$$

where $\overset{H_0}{\sim}$ reads under H_0 is distributed as (see chapter 14).

For the above data: $\hat{\mu}_n = 72.15$, $s = 13.335$ and the sample size $n = 72$:

$$\tau(\mathbf{x}) = \left(\frac{\sqrt{n}(\hat{\mu}_n - 70)}{s}\right) = \left(\frac{(6.32)(2.15)}{13.335}\right) = 1.019.$$

In view of the fact that for $\alpha = 0.05$, $c_\alpha = 2.021$, we can see that H_0 is accepted in this case because the value of the test statistic is within the acceptance region.

Another feature of the distribution which is of interest is the hypothesis:

$$H_0: \sigma^2 = 144 \text{ against } H_1: \sigma^2 \neq 144. \tag{15.47}$$

The appropriate test statistic is given by (see chapter 14):

$$\nu(\mathbf{X}) = \frac{(n-1)s^2}{\sigma_0^2} \overset{H_0}{\sim} \chi^2(n-1).$$

Substituting the estimates into the test statistic yields:

$$\nu(\mathbf{x}) = \frac{(39)(13.335)^2}{(12)^2} = 48.160.$$

From the chi-square tables we can determine the values $c_1 < c_2$ for the two-sided test for $\alpha = 0.05$ and d.f. $= 39: c_1 = 24.433$ and $c_2 = 59.342$. In view of the fact that the value of the test statistic lies between these two critical values we accept H_0. This decision does not change even if we use a one-sided alternative $H_1: \sigma^2 > 144$, since the critical value for $\alpha = 0.05$ is $c = 55.759$.

A cautionary note

We conclude this subsection with a cautionary note. The fact that the various misspecification tests applied to the Econometrics exam scores data indicate no departures from the assumptions of the postulated model, does not mean that the modeler can be sure that the postulated model is valid! For example, a closer scrutiny of the Normality assumption using separate D'Agostino skewness and kurtosis tests reveals a somewhat different story:

$$D' AS(\mathbf{x}) = -0.034[0.486], \; D' AK(\mathbf{x}) = -2.006[0.022].$$

These results indicate that, although the data do lend support to the symmetry assumption, they call into question the mesokurticity of the underlying distribution. Indeed, they suggest that the underlying distribution is symmetric but platykurtic; the platykurticity is indicated by a negative sign. In the next subsection we pursue the potency of the misspecification tests based on the skewness and kurtosis coefficients further using the dice data. In the last subsection we return to the Econometrics exam scores data in an attempt to reconsider the distribution assumption by respecifying the simple Normal to the simple Beta model.

15.5.2 The dice data

A data set used in chapter 1 refers to 100 replications of casting two dice and adding the number of dots appearing on the uppermost faces, shown in table 1.2 (see chapter 1). We conjectured then that the observed data exhibit the random sample features (IID) and the distribution is triangular as shown in figure 1.2. The discussion that follows constitutes an attempt to warn the modeler of the dangers in choosing a statistical model without putting much thought into it and then applying some of these misspecification tests uncritically.

Let us assume that the modeler proceeds to choose the simple Normal because it is very convenient in the sense that several statistical inference results relating to estimation, testing and prediction are available. Moreover, these results are easily applied using any statistical computer package. In contrast, if the modeler proceeds to choose a simple statistical model such as the Beta, very few inference results are available and rarely implementable using well known statistical computer packages.

Estimation of the simple Normal model using the dice data yielded:

$$X_t = 7.080 + \hat{\varepsilon}_t \; , \; T = 100. \tag{15.48}$$
$$\begin{smallmatrix}(0.245)&(2.448)\end{smallmatrix}$$

Assuming that this estimated model is statistically adequate, the estimate of the mean seems very close to the true value known to be $\mu = 7.0$. Before we make any pronouncements to that effect, let us proceed to consider the statistical adequacy of this estimated model.

Misspecification testing

Testing homogeneity (ID)
In addition to the runs test applied in section 3 above let us consider testing the ID assumption using the auxiliary regression with a first-order trend polynomial:

$$X_t = 7.193 - 0.002 \cdot t + \hat{\varepsilon}_t \; , \; T = 100.$$
$$\begin{smallmatrix}(0.496)&(0.009)&(0.793)\end{smallmatrix}$$

The misspecification test amounts to testing the significance of the coefficient of t, which is the familiar t-test:

$$\tau(\mathbf{x}) = \left(\frac{0.002}{0.009}\right) = 0.263[0.793].$$

This test indicates no departures from the assumption of ID.

Testing Independence

Consider testing Independence using the same misspecification tests used above.

(i)   The Ljung–Box misspecification test for $m = 4$:

$$LB(\mathbf{X}) = \sum_{\tau=1}^{4} \left(\frac{100(102)}{(96)}\right) \hat{\rho}_n^2(\tau) = 3.667[0.453].$$

The p-value in square brackets suggests the data lend credence to the hypothesis of Independence for these data.

(ii)   The second misspecification test to be applied is the N–P type encompassing test which compares the AR(1) model:

$$X_t = 7.856 - 0.103\, X_{t-1} + \hat{u}_t , \quad T = 99,$$
$$\quad\;\; {\scriptstyle(0.759)} \quad {\scriptstyle(0.101)} \quad\quad {\scriptstyle(2.425)}$$

with the estimated model (15.48). This is just the t-test for the significance of the coefficient of X_{t-1} in the AR(1) model, which yields:

$$\left(\frac{-0.103}{0.101}\right) = -1.021[0.310],$$

confirming that the data do lend credence to the independence assumption.

(iii)   The third misspecification test to be applied is the McLeod–Li test for second-order dependence with $m = 4$:

$$ML(\mathbf{X}) = \sum_{\tau=1}^{4} \left(\frac{100(102)}{(96)}\right) \hat{\gamma}_n^2(\tau) = 3.469[0.483].$$

None of the above tests indicates departures from the Independence assumption.

Testing Independence/homogeneity

The *Levene randomness test* for $m = 1,2,3$ yields:

$$RD(\mathbf{x};2) = 1.906[0.386], \quad RD(\mathbf{x};4) = 4.448[0.349], \quad RD(\mathbf{x};6) = 5.651[0.463],$$

which indicates no departures from the IID assumptions.

Testing Normality

In an attempt to illustrate some of the dangers of using misspecification tests thoughtlessly, let us ignore (for a few minutes) that the underlying distribution for the dice data is triangular (known to the modeler) and proceed to test whether the distribution is Normal! The sample skewness and kurtosis coefficients are:

$$(\hat{\alpha}_3 = -0.035, \hat{\alpha}_4 = 2.3362).$$

(i)   The skewness-kurtosis (asymptotic) test yielded:

$$sk(\mathbf{x}) = \frac{100}{6}(-0.035)^2 + \frac{100}{24}(2.362 - 3)^2 = 1.716[0.424].$$

The *p*-value suggests that the data do lend credence to the Normality assumption, if we take this result at face value.

(ii)   The D'Agostino–Pearson skewness-kurtosis test yielded:

$$D' AP(\mathbf{x}) = 2.677[0.262],$$

which also suggests (not as strongly) that the data do lend credence to the Normality assumption!

A moment's reflection suggest that these results are misleading because we know that the distribution is (a) discrete and (b) triangular. Ignoring the discrete nature of the random variable in question for a moment, the question that arises is: Why do we get the above results? The simple answer is that the above tests involve the joint hypothesis:

$$H_0: \alpha_3 = 0 \text{ and } \alpha_4 = 3,$$

which assess both the symmetry and the mesokurtosis of the underlying distribution. As with all joint hypotheses one component can be valid and the other invalid but the overall result might go either way. In the present case, symmetry is not at issue but mesokurtosis is. Hence, a more appropriate test for departures from Normality should be based on the single hypothesis:

$$H_0: \alpha_4 = 3.$$

The D'Agostino kurtosis test yielded:

$$D' AK(\mathbf{x}) = -1.629[0.051],$$

which gives some indication that the underlying distribution is more likely to be platykurtic rather than mesokurtic (Normal)! The indication, however, is not clear cut. NOTE that the kurtosis coefficient of the distribution in table 1.3 is: $\alpha_4 = 2.3657$.

   The above discussion brings out an important **cautionary note** in relation to misspecification testing:

   Do not rely exclusively on pre-packaged misspecification tests!

The idea of using a set of misspecification tests, as pre-packaged by the author of the computer program, for all data sets, runs contrary to the spirit of the above discussion of misspecification testing. As shown below, if the modeler were to use other misspecification tests, some of them would indicate departures from Normality.

(iii)   The Anderson–Darling test yields:

$$A^2 = 0.772[0.044],$$

which indicates departures from Normality; ignoring again the discreteness of the random variable

(iv)   The Shapiro–Wilk test yields:

$$W = 0.958[0.015],$$

which indicates apparent departures from Normality.

Testing the underlying distributional assumption

Returning to the distribution in figure 1.5, we can see that the above misspecification tests are completely inappropriate because the underlying random variable is clearly discrete! In the scores data, discussed above, the underlying variable can be viewed as continuous (even though its observed values are all integers) because theoretically all values between 0 and 100 are possible and the integers represent rounded off real numbers.

In view of the discrete nature of the underlying random variable, the modeler should proceed to assess whether the underlying distribution that gave rise to the observed data is indeed the one specified in table 1.3 (see chapter 1). A natural misspecification test for this assessment is Pearson's chi-square test, which yields:

$$\eta(\mathbf{X}) = \frac{(3-2.7778)^2}{2.7778} + \frac{(5-5.5556)^2}{5.5556} + \frac{(8-8.3333)^2}{8.3333} + \frac{(11-11.111)^2}{11.111} + \frac{(13-13.889)^2}{13.889} + \frac{(17-16.667)^2}{16.667} +$$

$$+ \frac{(14-13.889)^2}{13.889} + \frac{(11-11.111)^2}{11.111} + \frac{(9-8.3333)^2}{8.3333} + \frac{(6-5.5556)^2}{5.5556} + \frac{(3-2.7778)^2}{2.7778} = 0.2591.$$

In view of the fact that $\mathbb{P}(\eta(\mathbf{X}) > \eta(\mathbf{x}); H_0 \text{ is valid}) = 0.999$, the observed data lend (strong) credence to the hypothesis that the underlying distribution is the one defined in table 1.3.

15.5.3 Macro-Economic Principles exam scores: sitting arrangement

Let us return to the macro-principles exam scores, first encountered in chapter 1, which was informally discussed using graphical techniques in chapter 5. In both chapters we speculated that the exam scores, when ordered according to the sitting arrangement during the exam, exhibited positive dependence; cheating had taken place. Let us consider testing this conjecture formally in the context of the simple Normal model.

Estimating the simple Normal model using these data yielded:

$$X_t = \underset{(1.6264)}{71.686} + \underset{(13.606)}{\hat{\varepsilon}_t}, \ T = 70.$$

Misspecification testing

Testing homogeneity (ID)

Let us consider testing the ID assumption using the auxiliary regression with a first-order trend polynomial:

$$X_t = \underset{(3.303)}{69.986} + \underset{(0.081)}{0.048 \cdot t} + \underset{(13.670)}{\hat{\varepsilon}_t}, \ T = 70.$$

The misspecification test amounts to testing the significance of the coefficient of t, which is the familiar t-test:

$$\tau(\mathbf{x}) = \left(\frac{0.048}{0.081}\right) = 0.570[0.556].$$

This test indicates no departures from the assumption of ID.

Testing Independence

(i)   Consider first the Ljung–Box misspecification test for $m = 4$:

$$LB(\mathbf{X}) = \sum_{\tau=1}^{4} \left(\tfrac{70(72)}{(66)}\right) \hat{\rho}_n^2(\tau) = 22.600[0.015].$$

The p-value in square brackets suggests the data lend no credence to the hypothesis of Independence for these data.

(ii)   The second misspecification test to be applied is the N–P type encompassing test which compares the AR(3) model:

$$X_t = \underset{(10.290)}{57.015} + \underset{(0.117)}{0.486}\, X_{t-1} - \underset{(0.131)}{0.036}\, X_{t-2} - \underset{(0.114)}{0.243}\, X_{t-3} + \underset{(11.097)}{\hat{u}_t}\,, \ T = 67, \qquad (15.49)$$

with the simple Normal model:

$$X_t = \underset{(1.594)}{71.642} + \underset{(13.044)}{\hat{\varepsilon}_t}\,, \ T = 67.$$

The N–P test is just the F-test for the joint significance of the coefficients of $(X_{t-1}, X_{t-2}, X_{t-3})$ in the AR(3) model which yields the F-statistic (with 3 and 63 degrees of freedom):

$$F(\mathbf{x}) = \frac{\sum_{t=1}^{T}\hat{\varepsilon}_t^2 - \sum_{t=1}^{T}\hat{u}_t^2}{\sum_{t=1}^{T}\hat{u}_t^2}\left(\frac{T-m-1}{m}\right) = \frac{11229.403 - 7758.486}{7758.486}\left(\frac{63}{3}\right) = 9.395[0.000],$$

confirming the result of the previous test.

The question that naturally arises in the mind of a discerning reader at this stage is: Why use three lags in the encompassing AR model and does it make much difference if the modeler uses just one lag? The answer in a nutshell is that the primary objective of the auxiliary regression (15.49) is to achieve a statistically adequate specification of the conditional mean; a more satisfactory answer will take us well beyond the confines of the present discussion (see the discussion in the context of the Normal/linear regression model in Spanos (1986, forthcoming)) but we can reassure the reader that even if one chooses the AR(1) as the encompassing model:

$$X_t = \underset{(7.660)}{38.175} + \underset{(0.105)}{0.468}\, X_{t-1} + \underset{(11.511)}{\hat{\varepsilon}_t}\,, \ T = 67.$$

the answer would be no different. The N–P t-test for the significance of the coefficient of X_{t-1} in the AR(1) model:

$$\left(\tfrac{0.468}{0.105}\right) = 4.457[0.000],$$

confirms the result of the above F-test.

REMARK: the details about the choice between the t-test and the F-test in the AR model are discussed further in the context of the Normal/linear regression model in Spanos (forthcoming).

It is interesting to note that the McLeod–Li test for second-order spatial dependence for $m = 4$ yields:

$$ML(\mathbf{X}) = \sum_{\tau=1}^{4} \left(\tfrac{70(72)}{(66)}\right) \hat{\gamma}_n^2(\tau) = 1.904[0.753],$$

which indicates that no second-order dependence seems to be present.

Testing Independence/homogeneity

The *Levene randomness test* for $m = 2, \ldots, 7$ yields:

$RD(\mathbf{x};4) = 56.712[0.000],$ $RD(\mathbf{x};6) = 109.488[0.000],$ $RD(\mathbf{x};8) = 142.295[0.000],$

$RD(\mathbf{x};10) = 485.951[0.000],$ $RD(\mathbf{x};12) = 609.560[0.000],$ $RD(\mathbf{x};14) = 1065.441[0.000].$

The p-values are zero to at least 14 decimal places in all the above cases, indicating very significant departures from the IID assumptions.

15.5.4 Macro-Economic Principles exam scores: alphabetical ordering

In contrast to the sitting arrangement of the exam scores in Macro-Principles, we conjectured in chapter 1 that the data in alphabetical order exhibited no dependence. Let us test this conjecture using proper misspecification tests.

Estimating the simple Normal model using these data yielded:

$$X_t = 71.686 + \underset{(13.606)}{\hat{\varepsilon}_t}, \; T = 70.$$
$$_{(1.6264)}$$

It is interesting to NOTE that the estimated unknown parameters are identical to those of the sitting arrangement data. In a certain sense, the alphabetic ordering of the same data disregards useful dependence information. As in the case above, before any hypotheses within the boundaries of this model can be reliably tested, we need to consider its statistical adequacy.

Misspecification testing

Testing homogeneity (ID)

Let us consider testing the ID assumption using the auxiliary regression with a first-order trend polynomial:

$$X_t = \underset{(3.310)}{70.952} + \underset{(0.081)}{0.021 \cdot t} + \underset{(13.699)}{(13.699)} \, \hat{\varepsilon}_t, \; T = 70.$$

The misspecification test amounts to testing the significance of the coefficient of t, which is the familiar t-test:

$$\tau(\mathbf{x}) = \left(\frac{0.021}{0.081} \right) = 0.255[0.799].$$

This test indicates no departures from the assumption of ID.

In an attempt to confirm this result we present the *recursive estimates* for the mean and standard deviation for the Macro-Principles exam scores in figures 15.9–15.10. In figure 15.9 we can see the t-plot of the recursive estimates for the mean using $T_1 = 20$ together with the dotted lines representing one standard deviation on either side of the mean. The recursive mean estimates appear to hover just above the value 70 with the one-standard dotted lines exhibiting mild convergence. In figure 15.10 we can see the recursive estimates of the standard deviation $\left(\sqrt{Var(x)} \right)$ which appear to be hovering around the value 13. The plot also exhibits signs of convergence.

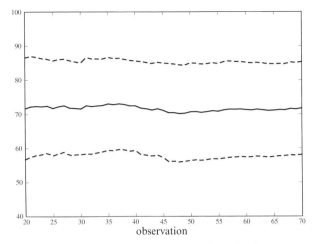

Figure 15.9 Recursive estimates of E(X) for the Macro exam scores

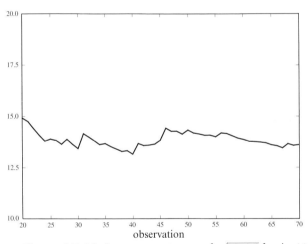

Figure 15.10 Recursive estimates of $\sqrt{Var(X)}$ for the Macro exam scores

Testing Independence
As in the case of the previous empirical examples we test Independence using a variety of
first- and second-order dependence tests.

(i)   The Ljung–Box misspecification test for $m=4$ yields:

$$LB(\mathbf{X}) = \sum_{\tau=1}^{4} \left(\tfrac{70(72)}{(66)} \right) \hat{\rho}_n^2(\tau) = 3.234[0.518].$$

In contrast to the data ordered by sitting arrangement, the p-value in square
brackets suggests the data in alphabetical order lend strong credence to the
hypothesis of Independence for these data.

(ii)   The N–P type encompassing test which compares the AR(3) model:

$$X_t = 72.294 \underset{(16.176)}{} - 0.091 \underset{(0.127)}{} X_{t-1} + 0.108 \underset{(0.123)}{} X_{t-2} - 0.026 \underset{(0.123)}{} X_{t-3} + \hat{u}_t \underset{(13.184)}{} , T = 67,$$

with the simple Normal model:

$$X_t = 71.641 + \underset{(1.594)}{} \hat{\varepsilon}_t \underset{(13.044)}{} , T = 67.$$

The N–P type encompassing test is simply the *F*-test for the joint significance of the coefficients of $(X_{t-1}, X_{t-2}, X_{t-3})$ in the AR(3) model, which yields:

$$F(\mathbf{x}) = \frac{11229.403 - 10951.312}{10951.312} \left(\frac{63}{3}\right) = 0.533[0.661],$$

confirming the result of the previous test. NOTE that the conclusion does not change when we use the AR(1) or AR(2) models.

(iii)   The McLeod–Li test for second-order spatial dependence for $m = 4$ yields:

$$ML(\mathbf{X}) = \sum_{\tau=1}^{4} \left(\frac{70(72)}{(66)}\right) \hat{\gamma}_n^2(\tau) = 1.831[0.767],$$

which indicates that no second-order dependence appears to be present in the observed data.

(iv)   The N–P type encompassing test for second-order dependence based on the auxiliary regression:

$$\hat{X}_t^2 = 5487.187 \underset{(1009.719)}{} - 0.295 \underset{(0.458)}{} X_{t-1}^2 - 0.078 \underset{(0.436)}{} X_{t-2}^2 - 0.352 \underset{(0.887)}{} X_{t-1}X_{t-2}, T = 68,$$

which tests the joint significance of the coefficients of $(X_{t-1}^2, X_{t-2}^2, X_{t-1}X_{t-2})$, yields:

$$F(\mathbf{x}) = 0.656[0.582].$$

This test reinforces the results of the previous tests, indicating no departures from the Independence/homogeneity assumptions.

Testing Independence/homogeneity
(i)   The *Levene randomness test* for $m = 1, \ldots, 4$ yields:

$$RD(\mathbf{x};2) = 1.961[0.375], \quad RD(\mathbf{x};4) = 3.982[0.408],$$

$$RD(\mathbf{x};6) = 4.219[0.647], \quad RD(\mathbf{x};8) = 5.032[0.754],$$

which indicate no departures from the IID assumptions.

(ii)   The *F*-test for the joint significance of the coefficients of $(t, X_{t-1}, X_{t-2}, X_{t-3})$ based on the auxiliary regression yielded:

$$X_t = 71.561 \underset{(16.511)}{} + 0.107 \underset{(0.092)}{} \cdot t - 0.091 \underset{(0.128)}{} X_{t-1} + 0.106 \underset{(0.125)}{} X_{t-2} + 0.025 \underset{(0.124)}{} X_{t-3} + \hat{u}_t \underset{(13.282)}{} , T = 67,$$

$$F(\mathbf{x}) = 0.413[0.799],$$

where $F(\mathbf{x})$ denotes the value of the *F*-statistic with 4 and 62 degrees of freedom.

(iii)   The *F*-test for second-order dependence and trend heterogeneity is based on the auxiliary regression:

$$\hat{X}_t^2 = \underset{(1095.475)}{5389.490} + \underset{(11.986)}{2.892 \cdot t} - \underset{(0.469)}{0.275 \ X_{t-1}^2} - \underset{(0.447)}{0.058 \ X_{t-2}^2} + \underset{(0.911)}{0.308 \ X_{t-1} X_{t-2}}, \ T = 68,$$
$$(15.50)$$

and tests the joint significance of the coefficients of $(t, X_{t-1}^2, X_{t-2}^2, X_{t-1} X_{t-2})$. This test yields:

$$F(\mathbf{x}) = 0.499[0.737],$$

where $F(\mathbf{x})$ denotes the value of the F-statistic with 4 and 63 degrees of freedom.

No indications of departures from independence/homogeneity are apparent on the basis of all the above tests.

Testing Normality

In view of the discussion in connection with the Econometrics exam scores and the dice data, we use a variety of tests in testing the Normality assumption.

(i)   The D'Agostino–Pearson family of tests which are based on the skewness and kurtosis coefficients:

$$\hat{\alpha}_3 = -0.024, \ \hat{\alpha}_4 = 2.565.$$

The D'Agostino–Pearson test which combines the skewness and kurtosis coefficients yields:

$$D' AP(\mathbf{x}) = 0.559[0.756].$$

The D'Agostino skewness and kurtosis separate tests yield, respectively:

$$D' AS(\mathbf{x}) = -0.091[0.464], \ D' AK(\mathbf{x}) = -0.628[0.265].$$

(ii)   The ecdf based tests yield:

Kolmogorov: $\Delta_n^2 = 0.033[0.974],$ Anderson–Darling: $A^2 = 0.139[0.150].$

(iii)   The ordered sample based test yields:

Shapiro–Wilk: $W = 0.980[0.646].$

As we can see, none of the above misspecification tests indicates departures from the Normality assumption.

Testing within: Neyman–Pearson test

Having established the statistical adequacy of the scores data when arranged in alphabetical order, we can proceed to consider the hypothesis of interest:

$$H_0: \mu = 70 \text{ against } H_1: \mu \neq 70.$$

For the above data: $\hat{\mu}_T = 71.686$, $s = 13.606$ and the sample size $T = 70$:

$$\tau(\mathbf{x}) = \left(\frac{\sqrt{T}(\hat{\mu}_n - 70)}{s} \right) = \left(\frac{\sqrt{70}(71.686 - 70))}{13.606} \right) = 1.037.$$

In view of the fact that for $\alpha = 0.05$, $c_\alpha = 1.990$, we can see that H_0 is accepted in this case because the value of the test statistic is within the acceptance region.

15.5.5 Revisiting the scores data: the simple Beta model

In modelling the scores data, on both the Econometrics and Macro-Principles exams, we assumed that the simple Normal model is appropriate. The estimated statistical model in the case of the Econometrics exam scores data took the form:

$$\hat{\Phi} = \left\{ f(x;\hat{\boldsymbol{\theta}}) = \frac{1}{15.056\sqrt{2\pi}}\exp\left\{ -\frac{1}{2(15.056)^2}(x - 69.583)^2 \right\}, \ x \in \mathbb{R} \right\}. \tag{15.51}$$

The misspecification testing results confirmed that the initial choice appeared to be statistically adequate. The dice data discussed above, however, should serve as a warning that sometimes the misspecification tests we use in particular cases might not be powerful enough to discriminate between distributions which are close in terms of the distance employed by the test statistic in question. Indeed, the D'Agostino test for excess kurtosis provides a hint that the underlying distribution might be platykurtic.

As argued in chapter 10, the choice of the Normal distribution ignores the fact that the range of values of the scores data is actually restricted within well defined upper and lower bounds. That is, the support of the Normal distribution is the real line $\mathbb{R}$, but the range of values for the exam scores is confined within the range $[0,100]$. In view of this, the question which naturally arises at this stage is:

How does a modeler justify the choice of the simple Normal model?

The answer is often phrased in terms of convenience and simplicity. The simple Normal model ignores the information about the range of values for the exam score data but in exchange enables the modeler to stay within very familiar grounds where there exist numerous (well tried) inference results relating to estimation and testing. This answer has some merits but is not entirely convincing.

An alternative distribution which can account for the bounded range of the exam scores data is the Beta distribution. In appendix A we specified the *standard Beta distribution* with density:

$$f(y;\boldsymbol{\theta}) = \frac{1}{B[\alpha,\beta]} y^{\alpha-1}(1 - y)^{\beta-1}, \ \boldsymbol{\theta} := (\alpha,\beta) \in \mathbb{R}_+^2, \ y \in [0,1],$$

whose support is the interval $[0,1]$. The exam scores data can be easily accommodated within this range by dividing them by 100. The modeling of the scores data using the **simple Beta model** where the support is specified as the interval $[a,b]$, $b > a$:

[i]   Statistical GM: $X_k = a + \frac{\alpha}{\alpha+\beta}(b - a) + \varepsilon_k$, $k \in \mathbb{N}$,

[ii] Probability model:

$$\Phi = \left\{ f(x;\boldsymbol{\theta}) = \frac{1}{B[\alpha,\beta]} \frac{(x - a)^{\alpha-1}(b - x)^{\beta-1}}{(b - a)^{\alpha+\beta-1}}, \ \boldsymbol{\theta} := (\alpha,\beta) \in \mathbb{R}_+^2, \ x \in [a,b] \right\},$$

$$E(X) = a + \frac{\alpha}{\alpha+\beta}(b - a), \ Var(X) = \frac{\alpha\beta}{(\alpha + \beta)^2(\alpha + \beta - 1)}(b - a)^2,$$

[iii] Sampling model: $\mathbf{X} := (X_1, X_2, \ldots, X_n)$ is a random sample,

is pursued further in Spanos (1998). It is shown that the latter model has certain distinct advantages over the Normal model.

15.6   Conclusion

Misspecification testing constitutes one of the most crucial facets of empirical modeling because it provides the means to assess the empirical validity of a statistical model, which in turn offers the foundation for valid statistical inference. The primary aim of the modeler is to utilize misspecification testing to detect departures from the underlying assumptions of the postulated model. Such departures are viewed as a *blessing* (not a nuisance) because they provide the modeler with an opportunity to take account of additional systematic information in the data. By its very nature misspecification testing is *testing without* (outside the boundaries of the postulated model), and as argued above, the Fisher approach, as formalized in chapter 14, is the approach of choice. The Neyman–Pearson approach can be applied to misspecification testing only after it is reformulated to take account of the nature of misspecification testing; this is because, as argued in chapter 14, the Neyman–Pearson approach is essentially *testing within* (the boundaries of the postulated statistical model). The notion of a parametrically encompassing model, as defined above, plays an important role in this reformulation, by transforming the testing without to testing within.

As the above empirical examples exemplify, misspecification testing will often tax the imagination and knowledge of the modeler and should be applied with thoughtfulness. Empirical modeling should not rely exclusively on pre-packaged misspecification tests viewed as a universally applicable battery. Computer software developers should allow for a lot of flexibility in designing one's own misspecification tests. As shown above, in the context of the probabilistic reduction (PR) approach there are systematic ways to design such tests with the only constraint being the imagination of the modeler. Moreover, the graphical techniques discussed in chapters 5–6 constitute an indispensable component of misspecification testing. The modeler is advised to utilize a variety of misspecification tests, always in conjunction with the appropriate graphical techniques.

We conclude this chapter by admonishing the traditional attitude that the modeler should be economical with the number of misspecification tests because otherwise (a) the modeler abuses the data (somehow) and (b) the modeler cannot keep track of the overall significance level. The first charge is often related to some metaphysical notion that the modeler loses certain degrees of freedom every time a misspecification test is applied; some traditional critics are often being sarcastic about applied papers, which, according to them contain more misspecification tests than observations. The fact of the matter is that the probabilistic structure of the data, the assessment of which constitutes the primary objective, remains unchanged however many misspecification tests are applied. For instance, if the observed data exhibit, say, temporal dependence, they will continue to exhibit such a feature after as many misspecification tests as the modeler cares to apply! The second charge relating to the overall significance level has already been answered above, since the notion of a significance level has no place in misspecification testing. What the modeler should be careful about is the traditional way to derive misspecification tests by relaxing the model assumptions one at a time, assuming that the rest are valid; this often leads to contradicting assumptions. The PR approach guards against such a possibility by placing the emphasis of the derivation of such tests on the reduction, not the model assumptions. Moreover, the PR approach naturally gives rise to joint as opposed to individual assumption misspecification tests (see the discussion on misspecification tests for the Normal/linear regression in Spanos (forthcoming).

15.7 Exercises

1   Discuss the notion of statistical adequacy and explain the role of misspecification testing in establishing it.

2   "Goodness of fit tests are by definition misspecification tests." Explain.

3   Specify the general form of misspecification testing for a statistical model $\mathfrak{P}_\theta$.

4   For the simple Normal model $\mathfrak{P}_\theta$ state the underlying probabilistic assumptions and the general form of the misspecification test for this model.

5   Explain why the Neyman–Pearson approach cannot be used in the context of the postulated model $\mathfrak{P}_\theta$.

6   "In the context of misspecification testing using the Neyman–Pearson approach, rejecting the null should never interpreted as accepting the alternative." Explain this statement and comment whether you agree or disagree and why.

7   Explain why the reduction approach offers certain advantages in dealing with the misspecification testing problem.

8   Explain why a misspecification test in terms of its basic objective is a Fisher test.

9   "In the context of a parametric model $\mathfrak{P}_\theta$, a Fisher test for a hypothesis of the form:

$$H_0 : \theta = \theta_0,$$

is indirectly a test for the adequacy of the postulated model." Explain; take a particular example such as the t-test if it helps.

10   Discuss the advantages and disadvantages of Pearson's goodness of fit test.

11   The first 500 terms of the decimal expansion of the irrational number $\sqrt{2}$ yields the following relative frequencies for the integers (0,1,2,3,4,5,6,7,8,9):

Integer value	0	1	2	3	4	5	6	7	8	9
Frequency	4931	5064	4976	4977	5143	4969	4973	4990	4971	5006

Use the Pearson chi-square test to test the hypothesis that the distribution underlying this is discrete Uniform.

12   Explain why applying the Kolmogorov distance test to the data given in question 11 is not a good idea.

13   Explain the asymptotic skewness-kurtosis test for Normality and its D'Agostino–Pearson formulation.

14   Discuss the conditional mean lemma and how it can be extended in order to provide the basis on which misspecification tests based on the conditional moments can be derived.

15   Explain why Spearman's test statistic is essentially the sample correlation coefficient between the ranks of two random variables.

16   Explain under what circumstances a modeler would naturally use Kendall's tau and not Spearman's rank correlation test.

17   Explain the Daniels test for the presence of mean heterogeneity. What is its main disadvantage when applied to data which exhibit Normality?

18   Discuss the Information matrix test and explain why it can only be a local misspecification test.

19   Explain the idea that by postulating encompassing statistical models we transform misspecification tests which are naturally testing without to testing within. Under what conditions are these tests valid?

20*   Using the encompassing elliptical autoregressive model, explain why under the Student's t distributional assumption the test $H_0: \alpha_1 = 0$, based on:

$$X_k = \alpha_0 + \alpha_1 X_k - 1 + \epsilon_k, \ k \in \mathbb{N},$$

is no longer a test for temporal independence.

21   Using the observations 65–105 in figure 5.4 derive misspecification tests for randomness based on the number of runs (up or down) of:
(a)   order 1,
(b)   order 2, and
(c)   order 2 or more.

22   Using the observations 65–105 in figure 5.5 derive misspecification tests for randomness based on the number of runs (up or down) of:
(a)   order 1,
(b)   order 2, and
(c)   order 2 or more.

23   Using the observations exhibited in figures 1.1 and 1.2 (see table 1.2) derive misspecification tests for randomness based on the number of runs (up or down) of:
(a) order 1,
(b) order 2, and
(c) order 2 or more.

24 Confirm that the distribution shown in figure 1.5 is platykurtic with kurtosis coefficient: $\alpha_4 = 2.3657$.

25 Assess the identical distribution assumption for the dice data shown in table 1.2, using the plot of the recursive estimates for the mean and variance. Explain the common sense logic underlying these plots.

26 Compare the estimated simple Normal (see section 15.5.4) and Beta (see section 15.5.5) models for the econometrics exam scores and discuss the problem of choosing between them.

27 Compare and contrast the Ljung–Box test and the F-test based on the auxiliary regression (15.32).

28. Compare and contrast the McLeod–Li test and the F-test based on the auxiliary regression (15.36).

29 Discuss the advantages of the probabilistic reduction approach for misspecification testing purposes. Are there any disadvantages?

30 The probabilistic reduction approach can be utilized to specify parametrically encompassing models which in conjunction with a modified Neyman–Pearson procedure can be used for misspecification testing purposes. What modifications are necessary for the Neyman–Pearson procedure to be used for misspecification testing purposes?

References

Abramowitz, M. and I. A. Stegum (eds.) (1970) *Handbook of Mathematical Functions with Formulas, Graphs, and Mathematical Tables*, Dover, New York.

Agresti, A. (1990) *Categorical Data Analysis*, Wiley, New York.

Ali, M. M., N. N. Mikhail, and M. S. Haq (1978) "A class of bivariate distributions including the bivariate logistic," *Journal of Multivariate Analysis*, **8**, 405–412.

Amemiya, T. (1994) *Introduction to Statistics and Econometrics*, Harvard University Press, Cambridge, MA.

Anscombe, F. J. (1973) "Graphs in statistical analysis," *The American Statistician*, **27**, 17–22.

Anderson, R. L. (1942) "Distribution of the serial correlation coefficient," *Annals of Mathematical Statistics*, **13**, 1–13.

Anderson, T. W. (1948) "On the theory of testing serial correlation," *Skandinavisk Aktuarietidskrift*, **31**, 88–116.

(1971) *The Statistical Analysis of Time Series*, Wiley, New York.

Anderson, T. W. and D. A. Darling (1952) "Asymptotic theory of certain goodness-of-fit criteria based on stochastic processes," *Annals of Mathematical Statistics*, **23**, 193–212.

(1954) "A test of goodness-of-fit," *Journal of the American Statistical Association*, **49**, 765–769.

Andreou, E., N. Pittis, and A. Spanos (1996) "On modeling speculative prices: a review of the empirical literature," Working Paper, University of Cyprus.

Andreou, E. and A. Spanos (1997) "Testing trend versus difference stationarity and statistical adequacy," Working Paper, University of Cyprus.

Arbuthnot, J. (1710) "An argument for Divine Providence, taken from the constant regularity observ'd in the birth of both sexes," *Philosophical Transactions*, **27**, 186–190. Reprinted in M.G. Kendall, and R. I. Plackett (eds.) (1977) *Studies in the History of Statistics and Probability, vol. II*, Charles Griffin, London.

Arnold, B. C., E. Castillio, and J.-M. Sarabia (1992) *Conditionally Specified Distributions*, Lecture Notes in Statistics 73, Springer-Verlag, New York.

Ash, R. B. (1972) *Real Analysis and Probability*, Academic Press, London.

Azzalini, A. (1996) *Statistical Inference: Based on the Likelihood*, Chapman and Hall, London.

Bachelier, L. (1900) "Théorie de la spéculation," *Annales Scientifiques de l'Ecole Normale Supérieure*, **17**, 21–86.

(1912) *Calcul des probabilites*, Gauthier-Villars, Paris.

Bahadur, R. R. (1960) "On the asymptotic efficiency of tests and estimates," *Sankhya*, **22**, 229–252.

Balanda, K. P. and H. L. MacGillivray (1988) "Kurtosis: a critical review," *The American Statistician*, **42**, 111–119.

Banerjee, A., J. Dolado, J. W. Galbraith, and D. F. Hendry (1993) *Co-integration, Error-correction, and the Econometric Analysis of Non-stationary Data*, Oxford University Press, Oxford.

Barndorff-Nielsen, O. and D. R. Cox (1989) *Asymptotic Techniques for Use in Statistics*, Chapman and Hall, London.

  (1994) *Inference and Asymptotics*, Chapman and Hall, London.

Barnett, V. (1982) *Comparative Statistical Inference* (2nd edn.), Wiley, New York.

Bartlett, M. S. (1937) "Properties of sufficiency and statistical tests," *Proceedings of the Royal Society*, A, **160**, 268–282.

Bayes, T. (1763) "An essay towards solving a problem in the doctrine of chances," *Philosophical Transactions of the Royal Society of London*, **53**, 370–418. Reprinted in E. S. Pearson and M.G. Kendall (eds.) (1970) *Studies in the History of Statistics and Probability*, Charles Griffin, London.

Beeck, P. V. (1972) "An application of the Fourier method to the problem of sharpening the Berry-Esseen inequality," *Zeitschrift fur Wahrscheinlichkeitstheorie und Vernwadte Gebiete*, **23**, 187–197.

Bernardo, J. M. and A. F. M. Smith (1994) *Bayesian Theory*, Wiley and Sons, New York.

Bernoulli, J. (1713) *Ars Conjectandi*, Thurnisiorum, Basel.

Berry, A. C. (1941) "The accuracy of the Gaussian approximation to the sum of independent random variables," *Transactions of the American Mathematical Society*, **49**, 122–136.

Bhat, B. R. (1985) *Modern Probability Theory: An Introductory Textbook*, Wiley, New York.

Bhattacharya, A. (1946) "On some analogues of the amount of information and their uses in statistical estimation," *Sankhya*, **8**, 1–14, 201–218, 315–328.

Bhattacharya, R. N. (1977) "Refinements of the multidimensional central limit theorem and applications," *Annals of Probability*, **5**, 1–27.

Bhattacharya, R. N. and E. C. Waymire (1990) *Stochastic Processes with Applications*, Wiley, New York.

Bhattacharyya, G. K. (1984) "Tests of randomness against trend or serial correlation," in P. R. Krishnaiah, and P. K. Sen (eds.), *Handbook of Statistics, vol. IV*, North-Holland, Amsterdam, chapter 5.

Bickel, P. J. and K. A. Doksum (1977) *Mathematical Statistics*, Holden-Day, San Francisco.

Bierens, H. J. (1994) *Topics in Advanced Econometrics*, Cambridge University Press, Cambridge.

Billingsley, P. (1968) *Convergence of Probability Measures*, Wiley, New York.

  (1986) *Probability and Measure* (2nd edn.), Wiley, New York.

Binmore, K. G. (1980) *Foundations of Analysis: A Straightforward Introduction*, Book 1, *Logic, Sets and Numbers*, Cambridge University Press, Cambridge.

  (1981) *Foundations of Analysis: A Straightforward Introduction*, Book 2, *Topological Ideas*, Cambridge University Press, Cambridge.

  (1992) *Fun and Games: A Text on Game Theory*, D. C. Heath and Co., MA.

  (1993) *Mathematical Analysis: A Straightforward Approach* (2nd edn.), Cambridge University Press, Cambridge.

Bishop, Y. V., S. E. Fienberg, and P. W. Holland (1975) *Discrete Multivariate Analysis*, MIT Press, Cambridge, MA.

Biswas, S. (1991) *Topics in Statistical Methodology*, Wiley, New Delhi.

Blackwell, D. (1947) "Conditional expectation and unbiased sequential estimation," *Annals of Mathematical Statistics*, **18**, 105–110.

Boole, G. (1854) *An Investigation of the Laws of Thought on which are Founded the Mathematical Theories of Logic and Probabilities*, London; Dover edition 1954.

Borel, E. (1909) "Les probabilitiés dénombrables et leurs applications arithmétiques" *Rend. Circ. Mat Palermo*, **27**, 247–271.

Bowman, K. O. and B. R. Shenton (1975) "Omnibus test contours for departures from normality based on $\sqrt{b_1}$ and b_2," *Biometrika*, **62**, 243–250.

Box, G. E. P. and G. M. Jenkins (1976) *Time Series Analysis: Forecasting and Control* (revised edn.) Holden-Day, San Francisco.

Box, G. E. P. and M. E. Muller (1958) "A note on the generation of normal deviates," *Annals of Mathematical Statistics*, **29**, 610–611.

Box, G. E. P. and D. A. Pierce (1970) "Distribution of residual autocorrelations in autoregressive-integrated moving average time series models," *Journal of the American Statistical Association*, **65**, 1509–1526.

Boylan, T. A. and P. F. O'Gorman (1995) *Beyond Rhetoric and Realism in Economics: Towards a Reformulation of Economic Methodology*, Routledge, London.

Breiman, L. (1968) *Probability*, Addison-Wesley, London.

Brown, L. D. (1971) "Nonlocal asymptotic optimality of appropriate likelihood ratio tests," *Annals of Mathematical Statistics*, **42**, 1206–1240.

Buse, A. (1982) "The likelihood ratio, Wald and Lagrange multiplier tests: an expository note," *The American Statistician*, **36**, 153–157.

Cacoullos, T. (1966) "Estimation of a multivariate density," *Annals of the Institute of Statistical Mathematics*, **18**, 179–189.

Caldwell, B. (1982) *Beyond Positivism: Economic Methodology in the Twentieth Century*, George Allen & Unwin, London.

Campbell, J. Y., A. W. Lo, and A. C. MacKinlay (1997) *The Econometrics of Financial Markets*, Princeton University Press, Princeton.

Carnap, R. (1950) *Logical Foundations of Probability*, University of Chicago Press, Chicago. (1951) *The Nature and Application of Inductive Logic*, University of Chicago Press, Chicago.

Casella, G. and R. L. Berger (1990) *Statistical Inference*, Wadsworth, CA.

Castillo, E. (1988) *Extreme Value Theory in Engineering*, Academic Press, London.

Chaitin, G. (1966) "On the length of the programs for computing finite binary sequences," *J. ACM*, **13**, 547–569.

Chambers, J. W. Cleveland, B. Kleiner, and P. Tukey (1983) *Graphical Methods for Data Analysis*, Duxbury, Boston.

Chapman, D. G. and H. E. Robbins (1951) "Minimum variance estimation without regularity conditions," *Annals of Mathematical Statistics*, **22**, 581–586.

Cherian, K. C. (1941) "A bivariate correlated gamma-type distribution function," *Journal of the Indian Mathematical Society*, **5**, 133–144.

Chester, A. (1984) "Testing for neglected heterogeneity," *Econometrica*, **52**, 153–173.

Chow, Y. S. and H. Teicher (1978) *Probability Theory: Independence, Interchangeability, Martingales*, Springer-Verlag, New York.

Christ, C. F. (1985) "The early progress in estimating quantitative economic relationships in America," *American Economic Review*, **75**, 36–52.

Chung, K. L. (1974) *A Course in Probability Theory* (2nd edn.), Academic Press, New York. (1982) *Lectures from Markov Processes to Brownian Motion*, Springer-Verlag, New York.

Church, A. (1940) "On the concept of a random sequence," *Bulletin of the American Mathematical Society*, **46**, 130–135.

Cleveland, W. S. (1985) *The Elements of Graphing Data*, Hobart Press, New Jersey.

Cohen, A. C. (1991) *Truncated and Censored Samples*, Marcel Dekker, New York.

Courant, R. and H. Robbins (1941) *What is Mathematics? An Elementary Approach to Ideas and Methods*, Oxford University Press, New York.

Cox, D. R. (1977) "The role of significance testing," *Scandinavian Journal of Statistics*, **4**, 49–70.

Cox, D. R. and D. V. Hinkley (1974) *Theoretical Statistics*, Chapman and Hall, London.

Cox, D. R. and A. Stuart (1955) "Some quick sign tests for trend in location and dispersion," *Biometrika*, **42**, 80–95.

Cramer, H. (1928) "On the composition of elementary errors. Second paper: statistical applications," *Skand. Aktuarietidsk.*, **1/2**, 141–180.

  (1946a) *Mathematical Methods of Statistics*, Princeton University Press, Princeton.

  (1946b) "A contribution to the theory of statistical estimation," *Skand. Aktuarietidsk.* **29**, 85–96.

  (1972) "On the history of certain expansions used in mathematical statistics," *Biometrika*, **59**, 205–207.

  (1976) "Half a century with probability theory: some personal recollections," *Annals of Probability*, **4**, 509–546.

Cuthbertson, K., S. G. Hall, and M. P. Taylor (1992) *Applied Econometric Techniques*, Philip Allan, New York.

D'Agostino, R. B. (1970) "Transformation to Normality of the null distribution of g_1," *Biometrika*, **57**, 679–681.

  (1986) "Graphical Analysis," in D'Agostino and Stephens (1986), chapter 2.

D'Agostino, R. B. and E. S. Pearson (1973) "Tests for departure from normality. Empirical results for the distributions of b_2 and $\sqrt{b_1}$," *Biometrika*, **60**, 613–622.

D'Agostino, R. B. and M. A. Stephens (eds.) (1986) *Goodness-Of-Fit Techniques*, Marcel Dekker, New York.

Daniels, H. E. (1950) "Rank correlation and population models," *Journal of the Royal Statistical Society*, B, **12**, 171–181.

David, H. A. (1981) *Order Statistics* (2nd edn.), Wiley, New York.

Davidson, J. (1994) *Stochastic Limit Theory*, Oxford University Press, Oxford.

Davidson, R. and J. G. McKinnon (1993) *Estimation and Inference in Econometrics*, Oxford University Press, Oxford.

Davis, J. B., D. W. Hands, and U. Maki (1997) *Handbook of Economic Methodology*, Edward Elgar, Cheltenham.

De Finetti, B. (1937) *Foresight: Its Logical Laws, Its Subjective Sources*, reprinted in H. E. Kyburg and H. E. Smokler (1964).

  (1974) *Theory of Probability 1*, Wiley, New York.

De Moivre, A. (1718) *The Doctrine of Chances: Or a Method of Calculating the Probability of Events in Play*, W. Pearson, London.

Devitt, M. (1997) *Realism and Truth* (2nd edn.), Princeton University Press, Princeton.

Devroye, L. (1986) *Non-Uniform Random Variate Generation*, Springer-Verlag, New York.

Dhrymes, P. J. (1970) *Econometrics: Statistical Foundations and Applications*, Harper and Row, London.

  (1971) *Distributed Lags: Problems of Estimation and Formulation*, Oliver and Boyd, Edinburgh.

  (1989) *Topics in Advanced Econometrics: Probability Foundations*, Springer-Verlag, New York.

  (1998) *Time Series, Unit Roots, and Cointegration*, Academic Press, New York.

Diaconis, P. and D. Freedman (1984) "Partial exchangeability and sufficiency," in J. K. Ghosh and J. Roy (eds.) *Statistics: Applications and New Directions*, Indian Statistical Institute, Calcutta.

Diaconis, P. and D. Freedman (1990) "Cauchy's equation and de Finetti's theorem," *Scandinavian Journal of Statistics*, **17**, 235–274.

Donsker, M. (1951) "An invariance principle for certain probability limit theorems," *Memoirs of the American Mathematical Society*, **6**, 1–12.

Doob, J. L. (1953) *Stochastic Processes*, Wiley, New York.

Doornik, J. A. and D. F. Hendry (1997) *PcGive Professional 9.0 for Windows*, International Thomson Business Press, London.

Dudewicz, E. J. and S. N. Mishra (1988) *Modern Mathematical Statistics*, Wiley, New York.

Durbin, J. (1973) *Distribution Theory for Tests Based on the Sample Distribution Function*, SIAM, Philadelphia.

Durbin, J. and G. S. Watson (1950) "Testing for serial correlation in least squares regression I," *Biometrika*, **37**, 409–428.

(1951) "Testing for serial correlation in least squares regression II," *Biometrika*, **38**, 159–178.

Dudewicz, E. J. and S. N. Mishra (1988) *Modern Mathematical Statistics*, Wiley, New York.

Edgeworth, F. Y. (1885) "Observations and statistics: an essay on the theory of errors of observation and the first principles of statistics," *Transactions of the Cambridge Philosophical Society*, **14**, 138–169.

Edwards, D. (1995) *Introduction to Graphical Modelling*, Springer-Verlag, New York.

Efron, B. (1979) "Bootstrap methods: Another look at the jackknife," *Annals of Statistics*, **7**, 1–26.

(1982) *The Jackknife, the Bootstrap and Other Resampling Plans*, Society of Industrial and Applied Mathematics, Philadelphia.

Efron, B. and R. J. Tibshirani (1993) *An Introduction to the Bootstrap*, Chapman and Hall, London.

Eichhorn, W. (1978) *Functional Equations in Economics*, Addison-Wesley, London.

Einstein, A. (1905) "Ueber die von der molikularkinetischen Theorie der Warme geforderte Bewegung von in Flussigkeiten suspendierten Teilchen," *Annualen der Physik*, **17**, 132–148.

Engle, R. F. (1984) "Wald, Likelihood ratio and Lagrange multiplier tests in econometrics," in Z. Griliches and M. D. Intriligator (eds.), *Handbook of Econometrics*, vol. II, North-Holland, Amsterdam.

Engle, R. F., D. F. Hendry and J.-F. Richard (1983) "Exogeneity," *Econometrica*, **51**, 277–304.

Erdos, P. and M. Kac (1946) "On certain limit theorems in the theory of probability," *Bulletin of the American Mathematical Society*, **52**, 292–302.

Esseen, C. G. (1945) "Fourier analysis of distribution functions. A mathematical study of the Laplace-Gaussian law," *Acta Mathematica*, **77**, 1–125.

Evans, M., N. Hastings, and B. Peacock (1993) *Statistical Distributions* (2nd edn.), Wiley, New York.

Fang, K.-T., S. Kotz, and K.-W. Ng (1990) *Symmetric Multivariate and Related Distributions*, Chapman and Hall, London.

Feller, W. (1968) *An Introduction to Probability Theory and Its Applications 1* (3rd edn.), Wiley, New York.

(1971) *An Introduction to Probability Theory and Its Applications 2* (2nd edn.), Wiley, New York.

Fienberg, S. E. and D. V. Hinkley (eds.) (1980) *R. A. Fisher: An Appreciation*, Lecture Notes in Statistics 1, Springer-Verlag, New York.

Fine, T. L. (1973) *Theories of Probability: An Examination of Foundations*, Academic Press, London.

Fisher, R. A. (1912) "On the absolute criterion for fitting frequency curves," *Messenger of Mathematics*, **41**, 155–160.

(1915) "Frequency distribution of the values of the correlation coefficient in samples from an indefinitely large population," *Biometrika*, **10**, 507–521.

(1922a) "On the mathematical foundations of theoretical statistics," *Philosophical Transactions of the Royal Society* A, **222**, 309–368.

(1922b) "On the interpretation of χ^2 from contingency tables, and the calculation of p," *Journal of the Royal Statistical Society*, **85**, 87–94.

(1924) "The conditions under which χ^2 measures the discrepancy between observation and hypothesis," *Journal of the Royal Statistical Society*, **87**, 442–450.

(1925a) *Statistical Methods for Research Workers*, Oliver and Boyd, Edinburgh.

(1925b) "Theory of statistical estimation," *Proceedings of the Cambridge Philosophical Society*, **22**, 700–725.

(1928a) "The general sampling distribution of the multiple correlation coefficient," *Proceedings of the Royal Statistical Society*, A, **121**, 654–673.

(1928b) "On a property connecting the χ^2 measure of discrepancy with the method of maximum likelihood," *Atti. Cong. Int. Mat. Bologna*, **6**, 95–100.

(1929) "Moments and product moments of sampling distributions," *Proceedings of the London Mathematical Society*, **30**(2), 199–205.

(1930a) *The Genetical Theory of Natural Selection*, Clarendon Press, Oxford.

(1930b) "The moments of the distribution for normal samples of measures of depareture from normality," *Proceedings of the Royal Statistical Society*, A, **130**, 16–28. Reprinted in Fisher (1950) pp. 198–238.

(1934a) "Two new properties of the mathematical likelihood," *Proceedings of the Royal Statistical Society*, A, **144**, 285–307.

(1934b) "Probability, likelihood and quantity of information in the logic of uncertain inference," *Proceedings of the Royal Statistical Society*, A, **146**, 1–8.

(1935a) *The Design of Experiments*, Oliver and Boyd, Edinburgh.

(1935b) "The logic of inductive inference," *Journal of the Royal Statistical Society*, **98**, 39–54.

(1935c) "The mathematical distributions used in the common test of significance," *Econometrica*, **3**, 353–365.

(1937) "Professor Karl Pearson and the method of moments," *Annals of Eugenics*, **7**, 303–318. Reprinted in Fisher (1950), pp. 302–318.

(1950) (ed.) *Contributions to Mathematical Statistics*, Wiley, New York.

(1956) *Statistical Methods and Scientific Inference*, Oliver and Boyd, Edinburgh.

Fisher, R. A. and E. A. Cornish (1937) "Moments and cumulants in the specification of distributions," *Review of the Institute of Mathematical Statistics*, **5**, 307–322.

Fishman, G. S. (1996) *Monte Carlo: Concepts, Algorithms, and Applications*, Springer, New York.

Frechet, M. (1951) "Sur les tableaux de correlation dont les marges sont données," *Ann. Univ. Lyon*, section A, series 3, **14**, 53–57.

Frisch, R. (1929) "Correlation and scatter in statistical variables," *Nordic Statistical Journal*, **8**, 36–102.

(1934) *Statistical Confluence Analysis by Means of Complete Regression Schemes*, Universitetets Okonomiske Institutt, Oslo.

Galambos, J. (1995) *Advanced Probability Theory* (2nd edn.), Marcel Dekker, New York.

Galton, F. (1869) *Hereditary Genius: An Inquiry Into its Laws and Consequences*, Macmillan, London.

(1875a) "Statistics by intercomparison, with remarks on the Law of Frequency Error," *Philosophical Magazin*, series 4, **49**, 33–46.

(1875b) "A Theory of Heredity," *Contemporary Review*, **27**, 80–95.

(1877) "Typical laws of Heredity," *Proceedings of the Royal Institution of Great Britain*, **8**, 282–301.

(1883) *Inquiries into Human Faculty and Its Development*, London.

(1885) "Regression towards Mediocrity in Hereditary Stature," *Journal of the Anthropological Institute*, **14**, 246–263.

(1886) "Family likeness in stature," *Proceedings of the Royal Society*, **40**, 42–72; with an appendix by J. D. H. Dickson, pp. 63–66.

(1888) "Co-relations and their measurement, chiefly from anthropometric data," *Proceedings of the Royal Society*, **35**, 135–145.

(1889) *Natural Inheritance*, Macmillan, London.

(1908) *Memoirs of My Life* (2nd edn.), Methuen, London.

Gan, F. F., K. J. Koehler, and J. C. Thomson (1991) "Probability plots and distribution curves for assessing the fit of probability models," *The American Statistician*, **45**, 14–21.

Gauss, C. F. (1809) *Theoria motus corporum celestium*, Perthes et Besser (1827), Hamburg.

Gibbons, J. D. (1985) *Nonparametric Statistical Inference* (2nd edn.), Marcel Dekker, New York.

Gigerenzer, G. (1987) "Probabilistic thinking and the flight against subjectivity," in L. Kruger, G. Gigerenzer, and M. S. Morgan (eds.) (1987), chapter 1.

Gigerenzer, G., Z. Swijtink, T. Porter, L. Daston, J. Beatty, and L. Kruger (1989) *The Empire of Chance: How Probability Changed Science and Everyday Life*, Cambridge University Press, Cambridge.

Glymour, C. (1980) *Theory and Evidence*, Princeton University Press, Princeton.

Gnedenko, B. V. (1943) "Sur la distribution limité de terme maximum d'une série aleatoire," *Annals of Mathematics*, **44**, 423–453.

(1969) *The Theory of Probability*, MIR Publishers, Moscow.

Gnedenko, B. V. and A. N. Kolmogorov (1954) *Limit Distributions for Sums of Independent Random Variables*, Addison-Wesley, Cambridge, MA.

Godfey, L. G. (1988) *Misspecification Tests in Econometrics*, Cambridge University Press, Cambridge.

Goldberger, A. S. (1968) *Topics in Regression Analysis*, Macmillan, New York.

(1991) *A Course in Econometrics*, Harvard University Press, Cambridge, MA.

Goodman, L. and W. H. Kruskal (1954) "Measures of association for cross classifications," *Journal of the American Statistical Association*, **49**, 732–764.

Gossett, W. (1908) ("Student") "The probable error of the mean," *Biometrika*, **6**, 1–25.

Gourieroux, C. and A. Monfort (1995) *Statistical Analysis and Econometric Models* (2 volumes), Cambridge University Press, Cambridge.

Granger, C. W. J. (1982) "Generating mechanisms, models and causality," in W. Hildebrand (ed.), *Advances in Econometrics*, Cambridge University Press, Cambridge, chapter 8.

(1990) (ed.) *Modelling Economic Series*, Clarendon Press, Oxford.

Granger, C. W. J. and T. Terasvirta (1993) *Modelling Nonlinear Economic Relationships*, Oxford University Press, Oxford.

Graunt, J. (1662) *Natural and Political Observations Mentioned in a Following Index and Made Upon the Bills of Mortality*, Arno Press, New York (1975).

Griliches, Z. (1984) "Economic data issues," in Z. Griliches and M. D. Intriligator (eds.), *Handbook of Econometrics*, vol III, North-Holland, Amsterdam, chapter 25.

Grimmett, G. R. and D. R. Stirzaker (1982) *Probability and Random Processes*, Clarendon Press, Oxford.

Gumbel, E. J. (1960) "Bivariate exponential distributions," *Journal of the American Statistical Association*, **55**, 698–707.

(1961) "Bivariate logistic distributions," *Journal of the American Statistical Association*, **56**, 335–349.

Gujarati, D. N. (1995) *Basic Econometrics* (3rd edn.), McGraw-Hill, New York.

Haavelmo, T. (1944) "The probability approach to econometrics," *Econometrica*, **12**, suppl., 1–115.

Hacking, I. (1965) *Logic of Statistical Inference*, Cambridge University Press, Cambridge.

(1975) *The Emergence of Probability*, Cambridge University Press, Cambridge.

(1990) *The Taming of Chance*, Cambridge University Press, Cambridge.

Hald, A. (1990) *A History of Probability and Statistics and Their Applications before 1750*, Wiley, New York.

Hall, P. and C. C. Heyde (1980) *Martingale Limit Theory and Its Application*, Academic Press, New York.

Halmos, P. R. and L. J. Savage (1949) "Application of the Radon–Nikodym theorem to the theory of sufficient statistics," *Annals of Mathematical Statistics*, **36**, 225–241.

Härdle, W. (1990) *Applied Nonparametric Regression*, Cambridge University Press, Cambridge.

Harter, H. L. (1974–6) "The methods of least-squares and some alternatives, parts I-VI," *International Statistical Review*, **42–44**.

Hartman, P. and A. Wintner (1941) "On the law of iterated logarithm," *American Journal of Mathematics*, **63**, 169–176.

Harvey, A. (1990) *The Econometric Analysis of Time Series* (2nd edn.), MIT Press, Cambridge, MA.

Hampel, F. R., E. M. Ronchetti, P. J. Rousseeuw, and W. A. Stahel (1986) *Robust Statistics: The Approach Based on Influence Functions*, Wiley, New York.

Hardy, G. H., J. E. Littlewood, and G. Polya (1952), *Inequalities* (2nd edn.), Cambridge University Press, Cambridge.

Hausdorff, F. (1914) *Grundzuge der Mengenlehre*, De Gruyter, Leipzig.

Hendry, D. F. (1984) "Monte Carlo Experimentation in Econometrics," in Z. Griliches and M. D. Intriligator (eds.), *Handbook of Econometrics*, vol. II, North-Holland, Amsterdam.

(1993) *Econometrics: Alchemy or Science?*, Blackwell, Oxford.

(1995) *Dynamic Econometrics*, Oxford University Press, Oxford.

Hendry, D. F. and A. Spanos (1980) "Disequilibrium and latent variables," London School of Economics, mimeo.

Hendry, D. F. and M. S. Morgan (eds.) (1995) *The Foundations of Econometric Analysis*, Cambridge University Press, Cambridge.

Hendry, D. F., A. Spanos, and N. Ericsson (1989) "Trygve Haavelmo's contributions to econometrics," *Socialokonomen*, **11**, pp. 12–17.

Herrndorf, N. (1984) "A functional limit theorem for weakly dependent sequences of random variables," *Annals of Probability*, **12**, 141–153.

Heron, D. (1911) "The danger of certain formulae suggested as substitutes for the correlation coefficient," *Biometrika*, **8**, 109–122.

Heyde, C. C. (1963) "On a property of the Lognormal distribution," *Journal of the Royal Statistical Society*, B, **25**, 392–393.

(1975) "Remarks on efficiency in estimation for Branching processes," *Biometrika*, **62**, 49–55.

Heyde, C. C. and E. Seneta (1977) *I. J. Bieyname: Statistical Theory Anticipated*, Springer-Verlag, New York.

Hodges, J. and E. L. Lehmann (1956) "The efficiency of some nonparametric competitors of the t-test," *Annals of Mathematical Statistics*, **26**, 324–335.

Hoeffding, W. (1948) "A class of statistics with asymptotically normal distribution," *Annals of Mathematical Statistics*, **19**, 293–325.

Hoffmann-Jorgensen, J. (1994) *Probability with a View Toward Statistics*, Chapman and Hall, London.

Hooker, R. H. (1905) "On the correlation of successive observations illustrated by corn prices," *Journal of the Royal Statistical Society*, **68**, 696–703.

Hsu, C. T. and D. N. Lawley (1939) "The derivation of the fifth and sixth moments of b_2 on samples from a normal population," *Biometrika*, 31, 238–252.

Hume, D. (1739) *A Treatise of Human Nature*, London.

Intriligator, M. D. (1978) *Econometric Models, Techniques and Applications*, North-Holland, Amsterdam.

Isserlis, L. (1916) "On certain probable errors and correlation coefficients of multiple frequency distributions with skew regression," *Biometrika*, **11**, 185–190.

Jarque, C. M. and A. K. Bera (1980) "Efficient tests for normality, homoskedasticity and serial independence of regression residuals," *Economic Letters*, **6**, 255–259.

Jeffreys, H. (1939) *Theory of Probability*, Oxford University Press, Oxford (3rd edn., 1961).

Johnson, M. E. (1987) *Multivariate Statistical Simulation*, Wiley, New York.

Johnson, N. L. (1949) "Systems of frequency curves generated by methods of translation," *Biometrika*, **36**, 149–176.

Johnson, N. L., S. Kotz, and N. Balakrishnan (1994) *Continuous Univariate Distributions*, vol. I (2nd edn.), Wiley, New York.

(1995) *Continuous Univariate Distributions*, vol. II (2nd edn.), Wiley, New York.

Johnson, N. L., S. Kotz, and A. W. Kemp (1992) *Univariate Discrete Distributions* (2nd edn.), Wiley, New York.

Johnston, J. (1963) *Econometric Methods*, McGraw-Hill, New York (2nd edn., 1972, 3rd edn., 1989).

Judge, G. G., C. R. Hill, W. E. Griffiths, H. Lutkepohl, and T-C. Lee (1988) *Introduction to the Theory and Practice of Econometrics*, Wiley, New York.

Kanji, G. K. (1993) *100 Statistical Tests*, Sage, London.

Karr, A. F. (1993) *Probability*, Springer-Verlag, New York.

Kelker, D. (1970) "Distribution theory of spherical distributions and a location-scale parameter generalization," *Sankhya*, series A, **32**, 419–430.

Kendall, M.G. (1938) "A new measure of rank correlation," *Biometrika*, **30**, 81–93.

Kendall, M.G. and R. I. Plackett (eds.) (1977) *Studies in the History of Statistics and Probability, vol. II*, Charles Griffin, London.

Keuzenkamp, H. A. (1994) Probability, econometrics and truth: a treatise on the foundations of econometric inference, Ph. D. thesis, University of Amsterdam.

Kevles, D. J. (1985) *In the Name of Eugenics: Genetics and the Uses of Human Heredity*, Harvard University Press, Cambridge, MA.

Keynes, J. M. (1921) *A Treatise on Probability*, Macmillan, London.

Khazanie, R. (1976) *Basic Probability Theory and Applications*, Goodyear Publishing Co., City CA.

Khintchine, A. Y. (1924) "Uber einen Satz der Wahrscheinlichkeitsrechnung," *Mathematicheske Sbornik*, **2**, 79–119.

(1934) "Korrelationstheorie der stationaren zufalligen Prozesse," *Mathematische Annuale*, **109**, 604–615.

(1937) "A new derivation of a formula of P. Levy," *Byull. Moskov Gos. Univ.*, **1**.

Kiefer, J. (1961) "On large deviations of the empiric D.F. of vector chance variables and the law of iterated logarithm," *Pacific Journal of Mathematics*, **11**, 649–660.

Kibble, W. F. (1941) "A two-variate gamma type distribution," *Sankhya*, **5**, 137–150.

Klein, M. (1972) *Mathematical Thought from Ancient to Modern Times*, Oxford University Press, New York.

Kmenta, J. (1971) *Elements of Econometrics*, Macmillan, New York.

Knopp, K. (1947) *Theory and Application of Infinite Series*, Dover edition (1990), New York.

Knuth, D. E. (1981) *The Art of Computer Programming*, vol. II: *Seminumerical Algorithms* (2nd edn.), Addison-Welsley, MA.

Kolmogorov, A. N. (1927) "Sur la loi des grands nombres," *C. R. Acad. Sci. Paris*, **185**, 917–919. English translation "On the Law of Large Numbers," reprinted in Shiryayev (1992), pp. 11–12.

   (1928a) "Sur une formule limité de M. A. Khintchine," *C. R. Acad. Sci. Paris*, **186**, 824–825. English translation "On a limit formula of A. Khintchine," reprinted in Shiryayev (1992), pp. 13–14.

   (1928b) "Uber die Summen durch den Zufall bestimmter unabhangiger Grossen," *Mathematische Annuale*, **99**, 309–319. English translation "On Sums of Independent Random Variables," reprinted in Shiryayev (1992), pp. 15–31.

   (1929a) "Uber das Gesetz des iterierten Logarithmus," *Mathematische Annuale*, **101**, 126–135. English translation "On the Law of the Iterated Logarithm," reprinted in Shiryayev (1992), pp. 32–42.

   (1929b) "General measure theory and probability calculus," *Trudy Kommunist. Akad. Razd. Mat.*, **1**, 8–21. English translation reprinted in Shiryayev (1992), pp. 48–59.

   (1930) "Sur la loi forte des grands nombres," *C. R. Acad. Sci. Paris*, **191**, 910–912. English translation "On the Strong Law of Large Numbers," reprinted in Shiryayev (1992), pp. 60–61.

   (1931) "Uber die analytischen Methoden in der *Wahrscheinlichkeitrechnung*," *Mathematische Annuale*, **104**, 415–458. English translation "On Analytical Methods in Probability Theory," reprinted in Shiryayev (1992), pp. 62–108.

   (1933a) *Grundbegriffe der Wahrscheinlichkeitrechnung*, Berlin. *Foundations of the Theory of Probability* (2nd English edn.), Chelsea Publishing Co. New York.

   (1933b) "Sulla determinazione empirica di una legge di distribuzune," *Giorna. Inst. Ital. Attuari*, **4**, 83–91. English translation "On the empirical determination of a distribution law," reprinted in Shiryayev (1992), pp. 139–146.

   (1941a) "Stationary sequences in Hilbert space," *Byull. Moskov. Gos. Univ. Mat.*, **2**, 1–40. English translation reprinted in Shiryayev (1992), pp. 228–271.

   (1941b) "Interpolation and extrapolation of stationary random sequences," *Izv. Akad. Nauk. SSSR Ser. Mat.*, **5**, 3–14. English translation reprinted in Shiryayev (1992), pp. 272–284.

   (1963) "On tables of random numbers," *Sankhya*, series A, **25**, 369–376.

   (1965) "Three approaches to the quantitative definition of information," *Problems Inform. Transmission*, **1**, 1–7.

   (1969) "The logical foundations of information theory and probability theory," *Problemy Peredachi Informatsii*, **5**, 3–7.

Kolmogorov, A. N. and S. V. Fomin (1970) *Introductory Real Analysis*, Dover, New York.

Koopmans, T. C. (1937) *Linear Regression Analysis of Economic Time Series*, Netherlands Economic Institute, Publication no. 20, F. Bahn, Haarlem.

   (1950) (ed.) *Statistical Inference in Dynamic Econometric Models*, Cowles Commission Monograph 10, New York.

Kourouklis, S. (1988) "Hodges-Lehmann efficacies of certain tests in multivariate analysis and regression analysis," *Canadian Journal of Statistics*, **16**, 87–95.

Krishnaiah, P. R. and P. K. Sen (1984) *Handbook of Statistics 4: Nonparametric Statistics*, North-Holland, Amsterdam.

Kruger, L., L. J. Daston, and M. Heidelberger (1987) *The Probabilistic Revolution, vol. I: Ideas in History*, MIT Press, Cambridge, MA.

Kruger, L., G. Gigerenzer, and M. S. Morgan (1987) *The Probabilistic Revolution, vol. II: Ideas in the Sciences*, MIT Press, Cambridge, MA.

Kullback, S. (1959) *Information Theory and Statistics*, Wiley, New York.

Kyburg, H. E. and H. E. Smokler (eds.) (1964) *Studies in Subjective Probability*, Wiley, New York.

Laplace, P. S. (1774) "Memoire sur la probabilité des causes par les événements," *Mémoires de l'Academie royale des sciences présentes par divers savants*, **6**, 621–656. Translated by Stephen M. Stigler, *Statistical Science*, 1986, **1**, 359–78.

(1812) *Théorie analytique des probabilités* (3rd edn, 1820 with supplements).Courceir, Paris.

(1814) *Essai Philosophique sur les probabilités*, Courceir, Paris: English translation *A Philosophical Essay on Probabilities*, reprinted (1951) by Dover, New York.

Lauritzen, S. L. and N. Wermuth (1989) "Graphical models for associations between variables, some which are qualitative and some quantintative," *Annals of Statistics*, **17**, 31–54.

Lauritzen, S. L. (1996) *Graphical Models*, Clarendon Press, Oxford.

Le Cam, L. (1953) "On some asymptotic properties of maximum likelihood estimates and related Bayes estimates," *University of California Publications in Statistics*, **1**, 277–330.

(1956) "On the asymptotic theory of estimation and testing hypotheses," *Proceedings of the Third Berkeley Symposium on Mathematical Statistics and Probability*, 129–156.

Lehmann, E. L. (1975) *Nonparametrics: Statistical Methods Based on Ranks*, Holden-Day, San Francisco.

(1986) *Testing Statistical Hypotheses* (2nd edn.), Wiley, New York.

(1990) "Model specification: the views of Fisher and Neyman, and later developments," *Statistical Science*, **5**, 160–168.

Lehmann, E. L. and H. Scheffé (1950) "Completeness, similar regions and unbiased estimation I," *Sankhya*, **10**, 305–340.

(1955) "Completeness, similar regions and unbiased estimation II," *Sankhya*, **15**, 219–236.

Leibniz, G. W. (1705) *Nouveaux essais sur l'entendement hemain*; in *Samtliche Schriften und Briefe*, Sechste Reuhe: Philosophische Schriften, vol. VI, Academie Verlag, Berlin.

Lenoir, M. (1913) *Variation of Supply and Demand Curves: Influence on Prices*, M. Giard et E. Briere, Paris; 56–62 translated in Hendry and Morgan (1995).

Leplin, J. (1984) (ed.) *Scientific Realism*, University of California Press, Berkeley.

Levene, H. (1952) "On the power function of tests of randomness based on runs up and down," *Annals of Mathematical Statistics*, **23**, 34–56.

Levene, H. and J. Wolfowitz (1944) "The covariance matrix of runs up and down," *Annals of Mathematical Statistics*, **15**, 58–69.

Levy, P. (1934) "Sur les integrales dont les éléments sont des variables aleatoires indépendantes," *Ann. Scuola Norm. Super. Pisa*, series 23, 337–366.

(1937) *Théorie de l'addition des variables aleatoires*, Gauthier-Villars, Paris.

Lewis, P. A. W. and E. J. Orav (1989) *Simulation Methodology for Statisticians, Operations Analysts, and Engineers*, vol. I, Wadsworth, CA.

Li, M. and P. M. B. Vitanyi (1997) *An Introduction of Kolmogorov Complexity and Its Applications* (2nd edn.), Springer-Verlag, New York.

Lindeberg, J. W. (1922) "Eine neue Herleitung des Exponentialgesetzes in der Wahrscheinlichkeitsrechnung," *Math. Z.*, **15**, 211–225.

Ljung, G. M, and G. E. P. Box (1978) "On a measure of lack of fit in time series models," *Biometrika*, **65**, 297–303.

Loeve, M. (1963) *Probability Theory* (3rd edn.), Van Nostrand, New York.

Luenberger, D. G. (1969) *Optimization by Vector Space Methods*, Wiley, New York.

MacKenzie, D. A. (1981) *Statistics in Britain 1865–1930*, Edinburgh University Press, Edinburgh.

Maddala, G. S. (1977) *Econometrics*, McGraw-Hill, New York.

Maistrov, L. E. (1974) *Probability Theory: a Historical Sketch*, Academic Press, London.

Mäki, U. (1989) "On the problem of Realism in Economics," *Reicerche Economiche*, **43**, 176–198.

Mann, H. B. (1945) "Nonparametric tests against trend," *Econometrica*, **13**, 245–259.

Mann, H. B. and A. Wald (1942) "On the choice of the number of class intervals in the application of the chi-square test," *Annals of Mathematical Statistics*, **13**, 306–317.

(1943) "On stochastic limit and order relationships," *Annals of Mathematical Statistics*, **14**, 390–402.

Manski, C. F. (1988) *Analog Estimation Methods in Econometrics*, Chapman and Hall, London.

Mardia, K. V. (1962) "Multivariate Pareto distributions," *Annals of Mathematical Statistics*, **33**, 1008–1015.

(1970) *Families of Bivariate Distributions*, Charles Griffin, London.

Markov, A. A. (1951) *A. A. Markov's Selected Works*, Academy of Sciences, USSR, Moscow.

Marshall, A. W. and I. Olkin (1967a) "A multivariate exponential distributions," *Journal of the American Statistical Association*, **62**, 30–44.

(1967b) "A generalized bivariate exponential distribution," *Journal of Applied Probability*, **4**, 291–302.

Martin-Löf, P. (1966a) "The definition of a random sequence," *Information and Control*, **9**, 602–619.

(1966b) "On the concept of a random sequence," *Theory of Probability and Applications*, **11**, 177–179.

(1969) "The literature on von Mises' collectives revisited," *Theoria*, **35**, 12–37.

McAlister, D. (1879) "On the law of the geometric mean," *Proceedings of the Royal Society*, **34**, 367–376.

McCullagh, P. (1987), *Tensor Methods in Statistics*, Chapman and Hall, London.

McGabe, B. and A. Tremayne (1993) *Elements of Modern Asymptotic Theory with Statistical Applications*, Manchester University Press, Manchester.

McGuirk, A., P. Driscoll, and J. Alwang (1993) "Misspecification testing: a comprehensive approach," *American Journal of Agricultural Economics*, **75**, 1044–1055.

McGuirk, A., J. Robertson, and A. Spanos (1993) "Modeling exchange-rate dynamics: thick tails and non-linear dependence," *Econometric Reviews*, **12**(1), 33–63.

McKay, A. T. (1934) "Sampling from batches," *Journal of the Royal Statistical Society*, Series B, **1**, 207–216.

McLeish, D. L. (1975) "A maximal inequality and dependent strong laws," *Annals of Probability*, **3**, 829–839.

McLeod, A. I., and W. K. Li (1983) "Diagnostic Checking ARMA time series models using squared-residual autocorrelations," *Journal of Time Series Analysis*, **4**, 269–273.

Mills, T. C. (1993) *The Econometric Modelling of Financial Time Series*, Cambridge University Press, Cambridge.

Mizon, G. E. (1977) "Model selection procedures," in M. J. Artis and A. R. Nobay (eds.), *Studies in Modern Economic Analysis*, Basil Blackwell, Oxford, chapter 4.

  (1984) "The encompassing approach to econometrics," in D. F. Hendry and K. F. Wallis (eds.), *Econometrics and Quantitative Economics,* Basil Blackwell, Oxford.

Mizon, G. E. and J.-F. Richard (1986) "The encompassing principle and its application to testing non-nested hypotheses," *Econometrica*, **54**, 657–678.

Mood, A. M., F. A. Graybill, and D. C. Boes (1974) *Introduction to the Theory of Statistics*, McGraw-Hill, New York.

Moore, H. L. (1911) *Law of Wages*, Macmillan, New York.

Moran, P. A. P. (1968) *An Introduction to Probability Theory*, Oxford University Press, Oxford.

  (1971) "Maximum-likelihood estimation in non-standard conditions," *Proceedings of the Cambridge Philosophical Society*, **70**, 441–459.

Morgan, M. S. (1990) *The History of Econometric Ideas*, Cambridge University Press, Cambridge.

Morgenstern, D. (1956) "Einfache Beispiele zweidimensionaler Verteilungen," *Mitt. Math. Statist.*, **8**, 234–235.

Morgenstern, O. (1963) *On the Accuracy of Economic Observations* (2nd edn.), Princeton University Press, Princeton.

Muirhead, R. J. (1982) *Aspects of Multivariate Statistical Theory*, Wiley, New York.

Narumi, S. (1923a) "On the general forms of bivariate frequency distributions which are mathematically possible when regression and variation are subjected to limiting conditions I," *Biometrika*, **15**, 77–88.

  (1923b) "On the general forms of bivariate frequency distributions which are mathematically possible when regression and variation are subjected to limiting conditions II," *Biometrika*, **15**, 209–221.

Neveu, J. (1975) *Discrete Parameter Martingale*, North-Holland, Amsterdam.

Neyman, J. and E. S. Pearson (1928a) "On the use and interpretation of certain test criteria for purposes of statistical inference, part I," *Biometrika*, **20**, 175–240.

  (1928b) "On the use and interpretation of certain test criteria for purposes of statistical inference, part II," *Biometrika*, **20**, 263–294.

  (1933a) "On the problem of the most efficient tests of statistical hypotheses," *Philosophical Transactions of the Royal Society*, A, **231**, 289–337.

  (1933b) "The testing of statistical hypotheses in relation to probabilities a priori," *Proceedings of the Cambridge Philosophical Society*, **24**, 492–510.

  (1936a) "Contributions to the theory of testing statistical hypotheses," *Statistical Research Memoirs*, **1**, 1–37.

  (1936b) "Sufficient statistics and uniformly most powerful test of statistical hypotheses," *Statistical Research Memoirs*, **2**, 113–137.

  (1938) "Contributions to the theory of testing statistical hypotheses," *Statistical Research Memoirs*, **1**, 25–57.

Neyman, J. and E. L. Scott (1948) "Consistent estimates based on partially consistent observations," *Econometrica*, **16**, 1–32.

Niederreiter, H. (1992) *Random Number Generation and Quasi-Monte Carlo Methods*, Society for Industrial and Applied Mathematics, Philadelphia.

Ord, J. K. (1972) *Families of Frequency Distributions*, Charles Griffin, London.

Pagan, A. R. (1984) "Model evaluation by variable addition," in D. F. Hendry and K. F. Wallis (eds.), *Econometrics and Quantitative Economics*, Blackwell, Oxford, chapter 1.

(1987) "Three econometric methodologies: a critical appraisal," *Journal of Economic Surveys*, **1**, 3–24. Reprinted in Granger (1990).

Parthasarathy, K. R. (1977) *Introduction to Probability and Measure*, Macmillan Press, Delhi.

Parzen, E. (1962) *Stochastic Processes*, Holden-Day, San Francisco.

Pearl, J. (1988) *Probabilistic Reasoning in Intelligent Systems: Networks of Plausible Inference*, Morgan Kaufman, San Mateo, CA.

Pearson, E. S. (1930) "A futher development of tests for normality," *Biometrika*, **22**, 239.

Pearson E. S. and Kendall, M.G. (eds.) (1970) *Studies in the History of Statistics and Probability*, Charles Griffin, London.

Pearson, K. (1892) *The Grammar of Science*, Scott, London.

(1894) "Contributions to the mathematical theory of evolution I. On the dissection of asymmetrical frequency curves," *Philosophical Transactions of the Royal Society of London*, series A, **185**, 71–110.

(1895) "Contributions to the mathematical theory of evolution II. Skew variation in homogeneous material," *Philosophical Transactions of the Royal Society of London*, series A, **186**, 343–414.

(1896) "Contributions to the mathematical theory of evolution III. Regression, heredity and panmixia," *Philosophical Transactions of the Royal Society of London*, series A, **187**, 253–318.

(1897) "On a form of spurious correlation which may arise when indices are used in the measurement of organs," *Proceedings of the Royal Society of London*, **60**, 489–498.

(1900) "On a criterion that a given system of deviations from the probable in the case of correlated system of variables is such that it can be reasonably supposed to have arisen in random sampling," *Philosophical Magazine*, **50**(5), 157–175.

(1901) "Contributions to the mathematical theory of evolution VII. On the correlation of characters not quantitatively measurable," *Philosophical Transactions of the Royal Society of London*, series A, **195**, 1–47.

(1902) "On the systematic fitting of curves to observations and measurement," *Biometrika*, **1**, 265–303.

(1903) "Contributions to the mathematical theory of evolution. On homotyposis in homologous but differentiated organs," *Proceedings of the Royal Society of London*, **71**, 288–313.

(1904) "Contributions to the mathematical theory of evolution XIII. On contingency and its relation to association and normal correlation," *Drapers' Company Research Memoirs, Biometric series*, I.

(1905) "Contributions to the mathematical theory of evolution XIV. On the general theory of skew correlation and non-linear regression," *Drapers' Company Research Memoirs, Biometric series*, II.

(1906) "Skew frequency curves, a rejoinder to Professor Kapteyn," *Biometrika*, **5**, 168–171.

(1910) "On a new method of determining correlation when one variable is given by alternative and the other by multiple categories," *Biometrika*, **7**, 248–257.

(1913a) "On the measurement of the influence of 'broad categories' on correlation," *Biometrika*, **9**, 116–139.

(1913b) "Note on the surface of constant association," *Biometrika*, **9**, 534–537.

(1920) "Notes on the history of correlation," *Biometrika*, **13**, 25–45.

(1923a) "Notes on skew frequency surfaces," *Biometrika*, **15**, 222–230.

(1923b) "Notes on non-skew frequency surfaces," *Biometrika*, **15**, 231–244.

(1924) "On a certain double hypergeometric series and its representation by continuous frequency surfaces," *Biometrika*, **16**, 172–188.

(1925) "The fifteen constant bivariate frequency surface," *Biometrika*, **17**, 268–313.

(1936) "Method of moments and maximum likelihood," *Biometrika*, **28**, 34–59.

Pearson, K. and L. N. G. Filon (1898) "Contributions to the mathematical theory of evolution IV. On the probable errors of frequency constants and on the influence of random selection on variation and correlation," *Philosophical Transactions of the Royal Society of London*, series A, **189**, 229–311.

Pearson, K. and D. Heron (1913) "On theories of association," *Biometrika*, **9**, 159–315.

Petrov, V. V. (1995) *Limit Theorems of Probability Theory: Sequences of Independent Random Variables*, Clarendon Press, Oxford.

Petty, W. (1690) *Political Arithmetick*, Edward Arber, Birmingham.

Pfeiffer, P. E. (1978) *Concepts of Probability Theory* (2nd edn.), Dover, New York.

Phillips, P. C. B. (1987) "Time series regression with a unit root," *Econometrica,* **55**, 277–301.

Pindyck, R. and D. Rubinfeld (1976) *Econometric Models and Economic Forecasts*, McGraw-Hill, New York (2nd edn., 1981).

Pitman, E. J. G. (1937) "The 'closest' estimates of statistical parameters," *Proceedings of the Cambridge Philosophical Society*, **33**, 212–222.

(1979) *Some Basic Theory for Statistical Inference*, Chapman and Hall, London.

Placket, R. L. (1965) "A class of bivariate distributions," *Journal of the American Statistical Association*, **60**, 512–522.

Playfair, W. (1786) *The Commercial and Political Atlas*, Corry, London.

(1801) *Statistical Breviary*, Wallis, London.

Poirier, D. J. (1995) *Intermediate Statistics and Econometrics: A Comparative Approach*, MIT Press, Cambridge, MA.

Poisson, S. D. (1837) *Recherchés sur la probabilitè des jugements en matière criminelle et en matière civile, précédes des règles générales du calcul des probabilités,* Bachelier, Paris.

Porter, T. M. (1986) *The Rise of Statistical Thinking 1820–1900*, Princeton University Press, Princeton.

(1995) *Trust in Numbers: The Pursuit of Objectivity in Science and Public life*, Princeton University Press, Princeton.

Pretorius, S. J. (1930) "Skew bivariate frequency surfaces, examined in the light of numerical illustrations," *Biometrika*, **22**, 109–223.

Prokhorov, Y. V. (1956) "Convergence of random processes and limit theorems in probability theory," *Theory of Probability and Applications*, **1**, 157–214.

Quenouille, M. H. (1956) "Notes on bias in estimation," *Biometrika*, **43**, 353–360.

Quetelet, L. A. J. (1849) *Letters on the Theory of Probability*, Layton, London.

Rachev, initial (1992), *Probability Metrics and the Stability of Stochastic Models*, Wiley, New York.

Ramanathan, R. (1993) *Statistical Methods in Econometrics*, Academic Press, London.

Ramsey, F. P. (1926) "Truth and Probability," reprinted in Kyburg and Smokler (1964).

Ramsey, J. B. (1969) "Tests for specification errors in Classical Linear Least-Squares Regression Analysis," *Journal of the Royal Statistical Society*, series B, **31**, 350–371.

Rao, C. R. (1945) "Information and accuracy attainable in estimation of statistical parameters," *Bulletin of Calcutta Mathematical Society*, **37**, 81–91.

(1947) "Large sample tests of statistical hypotheses concerning several parameters with applications to problems of estimation," *Proceedings of the Cambridge Philosophical Society*, **43**, 40–57.

(1949) "Sufficient statistics and minimum variance estimates," *Proceedings of the Cambridge Philosophical Society*, **45**, 218–231.

(1973) *Linear Statistical Inference and Its Applications* (2nd edn.), Wiley, New York.

Renyi, A. (1970) *Probability Theory*, North-Holland, Amsterdam.

Revesz, P. (1967) *The Laws of Large Numbers*, Academic Press, New York.

Rice, J. A. (1995) *Mathematical Statistics and Data Analysis* (2nd edn.), Duxbury Press, City CA.

Richard, J.-F. (1980) "Models with several regimes and changes in exogeneity," *The Review of Economic Studies*, **47**, 1–20.

Ripley, B. D. (1988) *Statistical Inference for Spatial Processes*, Cambridge University Press, Cambridge.

Rohatgi, V. K. (1976) *An Introduction to Probability Theory and Mathematical Statistics*, Wiley, New York.

Romano, J. P. and A. F. Siegel (1986) *Counterexamples in Probability and Statistics*, Wadsworth & Brooks, Monterey, CA.

Rosenblatt, M. (1952) "Remarks on a multivariate transformation," *Annals of Mathematical Statistics*, **23**, 470–472.

   (1956) "Remarks on some nonparametric estimates of a density function," *Annals of Mathematical Statistics*, **27**, 832–35.

Sargan, J. D. (1974) "On the validity of Nagar's expansion for the moments of econometrics estimators," *Econometrica*, **42**, 169–176.

Savage, L. J. (1954) *The Foundations of Statistics*, Wiley, New York.

Schervish, M. J. (1995) *Theory of Statistics*, Springer-Verlag, New York.

Schlesinger, G. (1974) *Confirmation and Confirmability*, Clarendon Press, Oxford.

Scott, D. W. (1992) *Multivariate Density Estimation*, Wiley, New York.

Seal, H. L. (1967) "The historical development of the Gauss linear model," *Biometrika*, **54**, 1–24.

Sen, P. K. and J. M. Singer (1993) *Large Sample Methods in Statistics: An Introduction with Applications*, Chapman and Hall, London.

Serfling, R. J. (1980) *Approximation Theorems of Mathematical Statistics*, Wiley, New York.

Shapiro, S. S. and M. B. Wilk (1965) "An analysis of variance test for Normality (complete samples)," *Biometrika*, **52**, 591–611.

Shiryayev, A. N. (1984) *Probability*, Springer-Verlag, New York.

   (1992) (ed.) *Selected Works of A. N. Kolmogorov*, vol. II: *Probability Theory and Mathematical Statistics*, Kluwer, Dordrecht.

Silverman, B. W. (1986) *Density Estimation for Statistics and Data Analysis*, Chapman and Hall, London.

Silvey, S. D. (1959) "The Lagrange Multiplier test," *Annals of Mathematical Statistics*, **30**, 389–407.

Slutsky, E. (1927) "The summation of random causes as the source of cyclic processes" (in Russian); English translation in *Econometrica*, **5** (1937).

Smirnov, N. V. (1948) "Tables for estimating the goodness of fit of empirical distributions," *Annals of Mathematical Statistics*, **19**, 279–281.

Solomonoff, R. J. (1964) "A formal theory of inductive inference", *Information and Control*, **7**, 1–22.

Spanos, A. (1986) *Statistical Foundations of Econometric Modelling*, Cambridge University Press, Cambridge.

   (1987) "Error autocorrelation revisited: the AR(1) case," *Econometric Reviews*, **6**, 285–94.

   (1989a) "Early empirical findings on the consumption function, stylized facts or fiction: a retrospective view," *Oxford Economic Papers*, **41**, 150–169.

   (1989b) "On re-reading Haavelmo: a retrospective view of econometric modeling," *Econometric Theory*, **5**, 405–429.

   (1990) "The Simultaneous Equations Model revisited: statistical adequacy and identification," *Journal of Econometrics*, **44**, 87–108.

(1992a) "The Student's t autoregressive model with dynamic heteroskedasticity," Virginia Polytechnic Institute and State University, mimeo.

(1992b) "Joint misspecification tests in linear regression," Virginia Polytechnic Institute and State University, mimeo.

(1994) "On modeling heteroskedasticity: the Student's t and elliptical regression models," *Econometric Theory*, **10**, 286–315.

(1995a) "On Normality and the Linear Regression model," *Econometric Reviews*, **14**(2), 195–203.

(1995b) "On theory testing in econometrics: modeling with nonexperimental data," *Journal of Econometrics*, **67**, 189–226.

(1996a) "A non-parametric test for randomness based on the runs up and down," Working Paper, University of Cyprus.

(1996b) "Parametric versus non-parametric modeling," Working Paper, University of Cyprus.

(1996c) "Testing the Student's t assumption: a standardized P-P plot," Working Paper, University of Cyprus.

(1997a) "Statistical versus theoretical information: complementary viewing angles in empirical modeling," Working Paper, University of Cyprus.

(1997b) "Econometric testing," in J. B. Davis, D. W. Hands, and U. Maki (eds.) *Handbook of Economic Methodology*, Publisher, City.

(1998) "On modeling exam scores data: the Beta versus the Normal model," Working Paper, University of Cyprus.

(forthcoming) *An Introduction to Modern Econometrics: Empirical Modelling Using Regression and Related Statistical Models*, forthcoming in 2001, Cambridge University Press, Cambridge.

Spanos, A. and A. McGuirk (1998) "Testing for unit roots revisited: statistical parameterization and encompassing models," Virginia Polytechnic Institute and State University, mimeo.

Spearman, C. (1904) "The proof and measurement of association between two things," *American Journal of Psychology*, **15**, 72–101.

Spielman, S. (1976) "Exchangeability and the certainty of objective randomness," *Journal of Philosophical Logic*, **5**, 399–406.

Srinivasan, S. K. and K. M. Mehata (1988) *Stochastic Processes* (2nd edn.), McGraw-Hill, New York.

Steffensen, J. F. (1922) "A correlation-formula," *Skand. Aktuarietidsk*, **5**, 73–91.

Stephens, M. A. (1970) "Use of the Kolmogorov–Smirnov, Cramer–von Mises and related statistics without extensive tables," *Journal of the Royal Statistical Society*, series B, **32**, 115–128.

(1986) "Tests based on EDF statistics," in D'Agostino and Stephens (1986), chapter 4.

Stigler, G. J. (1954) "The early history of the empirical studies of consumer behavior," *The Journal of Political Economy*, **62**, 95–113. Reprinted in Stigler (1964),

(1962) "Henry L. Moore and Statistical Economics," *Econometrica*, **30**, 1–21.

(1964) *Essays in the History of Economics*, University of Chicago Press, Chicago.

Stigler, S. M. (1986) *The History of Statistics: The Measurement of Uncertainty Before 1900*, Harvard University Press, Cambridge, MA.

Stigum, B. P. (1990) *Toward a Formal Science of Economics*, MIT Press, Cambridge, MA.

Stock, J. H. and M. W. Watson (1988) "Testing for common trends," *Journal of the American Statistical Association*, **83**, 1097–1107.

Stoyanov, J. M. (1987) *Counterexamples in Probability*, Wiley, New York.

Strang, G. (1991) *Calculus*, Wellesley-Cambridge Press, Wellesley, MA.

Stuart, A. and M. G. Kendall (1971) *Statistical Papers of George Udny Yule*, Griffin, London.

Stuart, A. and J. K. Ord (1991) *Kendall's Advanced Theory of Statistics*, vol. II: *Classical Inference and Relationships* (5th edn.), Oxford University Press, New York.

(1994) *Kendall's Advanced Theory of Statistics*, vol. I: *Distribution Theory* (6th edn.), Arnold, London

Suppe, F. (1989) *The Semantic Conception of Theories and Scientific Realism*, University of Illinois Press, Urbana.

Theil, H. (1950) "A rank-invariant method of linear and polynomial regression analysis," *Nederl. Akad. Wetensch. Proc.*, Series. A, **53**, 386–392.

Thompson, J. R. and R. A. Tapia (1990) *Nonparametric Function Estimation, Modeling, and Simulation*, Society of Industrial and Applied Mathematics, Philadelphia.

Tong, H. (1990) *Non-linear Time Series*, Clarendon Press, Oxford.

Tukey, J. W. (1962) "The future of data analysis," *Annals of Mathematical Statistics*, **3**, 1–67.

(1977) *Exploratory Data Analysis*, Addison-Wesley, Cambridge, MA.

Van Fraassen, B. C. (1980) *The Scientific Image*, Clarendon Press, Oxford.

Vanmarcke, E. (1983) *Random Fields: Analysis and Synthesis*, MIT Press, Cambridge, MA.

Van Uven, M. J. (1925a,b; 1926; 1929) "On treating skew correlation," *Ned. Akad. Wetensch. Proc.*, **28**, 797–811, 919–1035; **29**, 580–590; **32**, 408–413.

(1947a,b; 1948a,b) "Extensions of Pearson's probability distributions to two variables, I, II, II, IV," *Ned. Akad. Wetensch. Proc.*, **50**, 1063–1070, 1252–1264; **51**, 41–51, 191–196.

Venn, J. (1866) *The Logic of Chance*, Macmillan, London.

Ville, J. (1939) *Etude critique de la notion de collectif*, Gauthier-Villars, Paris.

Von Mises, R. (1931) *Warscheinlichkeitsrechnung und ihre Anwendungen in der Statistik und theoretischen Physik*, Franz Deuticke, Leipzig/Vienna.

(1981) *Probability, Statistics and Truth* (2nd edn.), Dover, New York (original German edition (1928) *Wahrscheinlichkeit, Statistik und Wahrheit*).

Von Neumann, J. (1941) "Distribution of ratio of the mean square successive difference to variance," *Annals of Mathematical Statistics*, **12**, 367–395.

Von Plato, J. (1994), *Creating Modern Probability: Its Mathematics, Physics and Philosophy in Historical Perspective*, Cambridge University Press, Cambridge.

Wald, A. (1943) "Tests of statistical hypotheses concerning several parameters when the number of observations is large," *Transactions of the American Mathematical Society*, **54**, 426–482.

(1950) *Statistical Decision Functions*, Wiley, New York.

Watson, G. S. (1961) "Goodness-of-fit tests on a circle, part I," *Biometrika*, **48**, 109–114.

(1962) "Goodness-of-fit tests on a circle, part II," *Biometrika*, **49**, 57–63.

Weyl, H. (1916) "Ueber die Gleichverteilung von Zahlen mod. Eins," *Mathematische Annuale*, **77**, 313–352.

White, H. (1982) "Maximum likelihood estimation of misspecified models," *Econometrica*, **50**, 1–26.

Wilk, M. B. and R. Gnadadesikan (1968) "Probability plotting methods for the analysis of data," *Biometrika*, **55**, 1–19.

Wilks, S. S. (1938) "The large-sample distribution of the likelihood ratio for testing composite hypotheses," *Annals of Mathematical Statistics*, **9**, 60–62.

(1962) *Mathematical Statistics*, Wiley, New York.

Williams, D. (1991) *Probability with Martingales*, Cambridge University Press, Cambridge.

Wittaker, J. (1990) *Graphical Models in Applied Multivariate Statistics*, Wiley, New York.

Wold, H. O. (1938) *A Study in the Analysis of Stationary Time Series*, Almquist and Wicksell, Uppsala.

Wolfowitz, J. (1944) "Asymptotic distribution of runs up and down," *Annals of Mathematical Statistics*, **15**, 163–172.

Working, E. J. (1927) "What do statistical demand curves show?" *Quartely Journal of Economics*, **39**, 503–543.

Yule, G. U. (1895–6) "On the correlation of total Pauperism with proportion of out-relief," *Economic Journal*, **5**, 603–611, **6**, 613–623.

(1896) "Notes on the history of Pauperism in England and Wales from 1850, treated by the Method of Frequency Curves, with an introduction on the method," *Journal of the Royal Statistical Society*, **59**, 318–349.

(1897) "On the theory of correlation," *Journal of the Royal Statistical Society*, **60**, 812–54.

(1900) "On the association of attributes in statistics: with illustrations from the material of the Childhood Society &c," *Philosophical Transactions*, series A, **194**, 257–319; reprinted in Stuart and Kendall (1971), pp. 7–69.

(1911) *An Introduction to the Theory of Statistics*, Griffin, London; 14th edn., with M. G. Kendall (1950), Edward Arnold, London.

(1912) "On the methods of measuring association between two attributes," *Journal of the Royal Statistical Society*, **75**; reprinted in Stuart and Kendall (1971), pp. 107–170.

(1921) "On the time-correlation problem," *Journal of the Royal Statistical Society*, **84**, 497–526; reprinted in Stuart and Kendall (1971).

(1926) "Why do we sometimes get nonsense correlations between time series – a study in sampling and the nature of time series," *Journal of the Royal Statistical Society*, **89**, 1–64; reprinted in Stuart and Kendall (1971).

(1927) "On a method of investigating periodicities in disturbed series, with special reference to Wolfer's sunspot numbers," *Philosophical Transactions of the Royal Society*, series A, **226**, 267–298.

Zaman, A. (1996) *Statistical Foundations for Econometric Techniques*, Academic Press, London.

Zellner, A. (1971) *An Introduction to Bayesian Inference in Econometrics*, Wiley, New York.

Index